STATE PROFILES

STATE PROFILES

THE POPULATION AND ECONOMY OF EACH U.S. STATE

Fourth Edition
2009

Edited by Mary Meghan Ryan

Bernan Press

Lanham, Maryland

Published in the United States of America
Published in the United States of America
by Bernan Press, a wholly owned subsidiary of
The Rowman & Littlefield Publishing Group, Inc.
4501 Forbes Boulevard, Suite 200
Lanham, Maryland 20706

Bernan Press
800-865-3457
info@bernan.com
www.bernan.com

ISBN 13: 978-1-59888-368-8
E-ISBN: 978-1-59888-403-6

∞™ The paper used in this publication meets the minimum requirements of American National Standard
for Information Sciences—Permanence of Paper for Printed Library Materials, ANSI/NISO Z39.48-1992.
Manufactured in the United States of America.

CONTENTS

LIST OF TABLES

The following tables are included for each state. Select tables are included for the District of Columbia.

Table 1. Population by Sex, Age, Race, and Hispanic Origin
Table 2. Marital Status
Table 3. Households and Housing Characteristics
Table 4. Median Income and Poverty Status, 2007
Table 5. Health Insurance Coverage Status for All Persons and Children Under 18 Years of Age
Table 6. Employment Status by Demographic Group, Preliminary 2008
Table 7. Employment Status of the Civilian Noninstitutional Population Age 16 Years and Over
Table 8. Employment and Average Wages by Industry
Table 9. Employment Characteristics by Family Type
Table 10. School Enrollment and Educational Attainment, 2007
Table 11. Educational Indicators
Table 12. Reported Voting and Registration of the Voting-Age Population, November 2008
Table 13. Crime
Table 14. State Government Finances, 2007
Table 15. State Government Tax Collections, 2008
Table 16. Agriculture

Bernan Press is pleased to present the fourth edition of *State Profiles*, a publication that provides a state-by-state view of the United States, including population composition by age, sex, race, and ethnicity; marital status; households and housing; income and poverty; health insurance; employment; educational indicators; voting; crime; agriculture and other important aspects of the economy.

This publication focuses on the 50 states and the District of Columbia, each of which possesses considerable differences in economic structure and demographics and has experienced various changes over time. Changes at the national level, including the diminished importance of agriculture and manufacturing and the growing influence of global trade, have resulted in today's information-based, service-providing economy. While national trends have laid the broad framework for change, each state has been affected differently. Cyclical fluctuations have also affected states in various ways during the nationwide recessions and the subsequent recovery periods. Recessions and recoveries spread unevenly among regions and states. Migration patterns have also reflected these changes, as states have inexperienced different influxes of workers from within the country and new residents from abroad.

Beyond the market forces, economic circumstances have been influenced by local and national government policies and expenditures on items such as education, health care, energy production and conservation, national defense, and homeland security.

The information provided in *State Profiles* aims to illuminate these trends. As such, the information is of interest not only to researchers and policy analysts but also to businesses seeking a broad basis for investments and expansion or relocation plans. The volume also profiles recent voting patterns, which will be of interest to political scientists.

DATA SELECTION

The fourth edition of *State Profiles* generally continues the broad selection of information from the three previous editions. Most of the data have been updated through 2007 or 2008, as demographic estimates from the U.S. Census Bureau became available. More recent data are also included on employment, unemployment, earnings, income, and other economic data from various government sources.

As in the past, space constraints have influenced the amount of data presented for each state. The editor has focused on selecting and highlighting the most meaningful and relevant data. Nonetheless, this fourth edition expands upon the available information to include more detailed data on the demographics of each state, as well as voting and crime data. For most of the subjects addressed in this edition, further data are generally available from the source government agencies. Locations of source information are listed in notes and definitions at the end of the volume.

Although the editor has taken care to present accurate data, all statistical data are subject to a degree of error, resulting from sampling variability, erroneous reporting, and other causes. Many of the data are subject to subsequent revision.

The data in this book meet the publication standards of the federal agencies from which they were obtained. The responsibilities of the editor and publisher of this volume are limited to reasonable care in the reproduction and presentation of the data from the established sources.

USING THIS BOOK: ORGANIZATION AND CONTENTS

STATE PROFILES 2009 PROVIDES:

- An overview of the United States
- Rankings of states for key demographic and economic indicators
- An 8-page chapter on each state of tables and figures to summarize and illustrate demographic and economic characteristics
- Notes and definitions to guide users through information used in this volume

THE STATE RANKINGS. The ranking tables shown in the pages following the U.S. overview give state rankings by 30 characteristics, including population, land area, demographic and age composition, place of birth, employment, income, per capita state taxes, housing values, poverty, health indicators, education, and voter participation. These rankings provide the user with a quick analysis of the performance of each state in relation to the other states.

References to rankings in the text only include the fifty states; the District of Columbia is excluded.

THE STATE CHAPTERS. Each chapter follows a standard format and contains text highlighting the key features shown in the tables and figures. The text on the introductory page for each state is derived from many of the same data sources as the tables. In some instances, alternate government sources were used. Therefore, some data in the text may not match the data in the tables. Many of these tables and figures contain references to the U.S. averages for the same characteristics. The emphasis of the text varies from state to state, reflecting their diversity.

Each of the state chapters is organized as follows:

Population: This table provides data on the state's total population and average annual population growth in comparison with the national average. It also shows the major population groups by sex, age, race, and ethnicity.

Marital status: The table shows the marital status for all men and women age 15 years and over.

Households: Data on household types, size, units (whether owner- or renter-occupied), median gross rent, and median value of owner-occupied housing are included.

Income and poverty: Median household and family income and poverty rates by sex and age are contained in this table.

Health insurance coverage: This table provides information on health insurance, by type and coverage.

Employment: This section presents various tables that illustrate each state's particular economic configuration. Employment status by detailed demographic group, labor force, participation rates, employment, unemployment, average wages and salaries by industry, and employment by family type.

Education: This section provides the user with details on educational attainment, elementary and secondary school enrollment, student/teacher ratios, per student expenditures, and higher education enrollments.

Voter participation: Information is given on voter registration and voter participation in the 2008 presidential election, categorized by sex and race and ethnicity.

Crime: This table include the number and rates of violent and property crime.

Government finance: This section provides data on revenues and expenditures by source. In addition, state government tax information is included.

Agriculture: In this table, data are provided on the number of farms, acreage, and land value.

Exports: This figure provides detailed information on each state's leading exports.

NOTES AND DEFINITIONS. Each chapter relies on the same standard set of federal data sources. Since the basic data sources are common to all chapters, the main body of the volume contains few footnotes. All the basic data and their definitions and sources are identified in the notes and definition section at the end of the volume. It provides brief descriptions, methodologies, data availability, information on calculations made by the editor, and references to additional sources of information. The notes are organized by topic, paralleling the structure of the state chapters.

INTRODUCTION

From 2000 through 2008, the United States experienced several fluctuations in its economy. In March 2001 a recession began, however, eight months later in November 2001, it was over. While the recovery from that recession was not equally felt in all states, for the next several years, the economy expanded. In December 2007 another recession, which has lasted much longer, began. *State Profiles: The Population and Economy of Each U.S. State* creates a snapshot of each state's economy by presenting data on key economic indicators. In addition to economic data, *State Profiles* provides demographic and social characteristics for each state and the District of Columbia. Each state's chapter includes information on topics such as population, health, marital status, crime, government finance, housing, agriculture, education, and citizen participation in the 2008 election.

SUMMARY

The U.S. population grew 8.0 percent between 2000 and 2008. The West experienced the fastest growth during this period, growing at a rate of 12.1 percent followed by the South at 11.5 percent, and the Midwest at 3.4 percent. The Northeast was the slowest growing region of the country, growing at a rate of only 2.5 percent. Louisiana and North Dakota were the only two states that experienced a decline in their population from 2000 to 2008, while Michigan, Rhode Island, and West Virginia all grew by less than 1 percent.

In 2008, Michigan had the highest unemployment rate in the country at 8.4 percent, followed by Rhode Island at 7.8 percent. The national unemployment rate climbed to 5.8 percent in 2008 after remaining steady at 4.6 percent from 2006 to 2007. From 2007 to 2008, the unemployment rate declined in one state, remained the same in three states, and increased in all the others.

There were nearly 112.4 million households in 2007, defined as one or more persons occupying a single housing unit, such as a house, apartment, or room. The average household size was 2.6 and families made up 67 percent of all households. By 2008, the number of households increased to 113.1 million, the average size did not change and the percentage of households that were families declined slightly to 66 percent.

The median housing value in the United States was $197,600 in 2008—only 1.7 percent higher than the median value of $194,300 in 2007. Median values have been increasing at a declining rate in recent years. Between 2005 and 2006 median values increased 10.6 percent and between 2006 and 2007 values increased by 4.9 percent. Housing prices have typically been the highest in the Northeast and the West and lowest in the South and Midwest.

Fastest-Growing States, Percent Population Change, 2000–2008

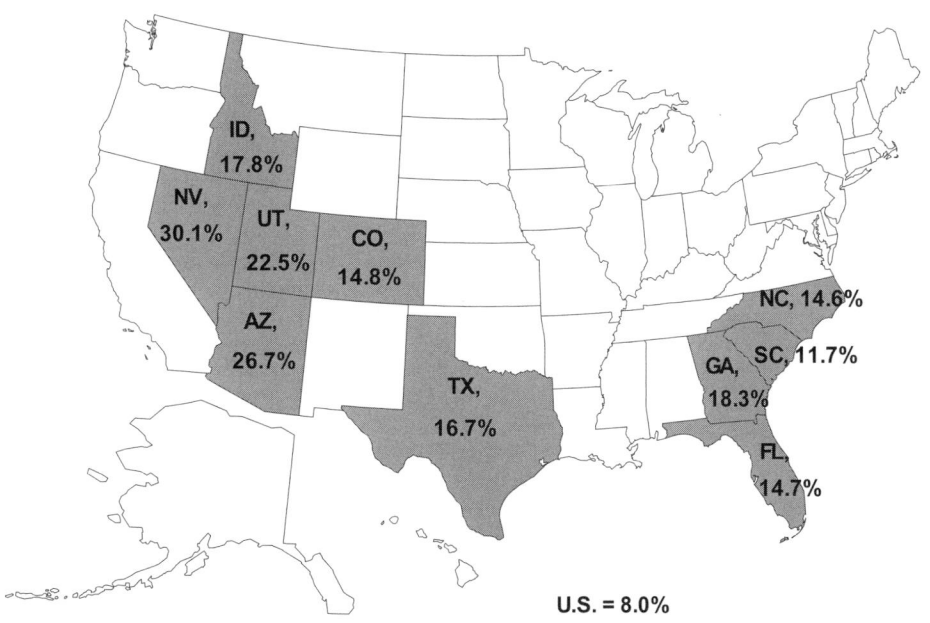

U.S. = 8.0%

UNITED STATES RANKINGS

Population, 2008			Land area, 2000			Population density, 2008		
Popu-lation rank	State	Population	Land area rank	State	Land area (square kilometers)	Density rank	State	Density (per square kilometer)
	United States	304 059 724		United States..........................	9 161 924		United States..........................	33.2
1	California..............................	36 756 666	1	Alaska	1 481 347	1	District of Columbia	3 722.2
2	Texas....................................	24 326 974	2	Texas	678 051	2	New Jersey	452.0
3	New York	19 490 297	3	California	403 933	3	Rhode Island	388.3
4	Florida	18 328 340	4	Montana	376 979	4	Massachusetts.......................	320.0
5	Illinois	12 901 563	5	New Mexico	314 309	5	Connecticut	279.0
6	Pennsylvania	12 448 279	6	Arizona	294 312	6	Maryland...............................	222.5
7	Ohio	11 485 910	7	Nevada	284 448	7	Delaware...............................	172.5
8	Michigan	10 003 422	8	Colorado	268 627	8	New York	159.4
9	Georgia	9 685 744	9	Wyoming	251 489	9	Florida...................................	131.2
10	North Carolina	9 222 414	10	Oregon..................................	248 631	10	Ohio......................................	108.3
11	New Jersey	8 682 661	11	Idaho	214 314	11	Pennsylvania..........................	107.2
12	Virginia.................................	7 769 089	12	Utah	212 751	12	California	91.0
13	Washington	6 549 224	13	Kansas	211 900	13	Illinois...................................	89.6
14	Arizona	6 500 180	14	Minnesota	206 189	14	Hawaii...................................	77.4
15	Massachusetts	6 497 967	15	Nebraska	199 099	15	Virginia	75.8
16	Indiana	6 376 792	16	South Carolina	196 540	16	North Carolina	73.1
17	Tennessee	6 214 888	17	North Dakota	178 647	17	Indiana	68.6
18	Missouri................................	5 911 605	18	Missouri	178 414	18	Michigan...............................	68.0
19	Maryland...............................	5 633 597	19	Oklahoma	177 847	19	Georgia.................................	64.6
20	Wisconsin..............................	5 627 967	20	Washington	172 348	20	Tennessee..............................	58.2
21	Minnesota	5 220 393	21	Georgia..................................	149 976	21	South Carolina	57.4
22	Colorado	4 939 456	22	Michigan	147 121	22	New Hampshire	56.6
23	Alabama	4 661 900	23	Iowa	144 701	23	Kentucky...............................	41.5
24	South Carolina	4 479 800	24	Illinois...................................	143 961	24	Wisconsin..............................	40.0
25	Louisiana	4 410 796	25	Wisconsin..............................	140 663	25	Louisiana	39.1
26	Kentucky...............................	4 269 245	26	Florida	139 670	26	Washington	38.0
27	Oregon..................................	3 790 060	27	Arkansas	134 856	27	Texas	35.9
28	Oklahoma	3 642 361	28	Alabama	131 426	28	Alabama	35.5
29	Connecticut	3 501 252	29	North Carolina.......................	126 161	29	Missouri................................	33.1
30	Iowa	3 002 555	30	New York	122 283	30	West Virginia..........................	29.1
31	Mississippi	2 938 618	31	Mississippi	121 488	31	Vermont................................	25.9
32	Arkansas	2 855 390	32	Pennsylvania	116 074	32	Minnesota	25.3
33	Kansas	2 802 134	33	Louisiana	112 825	33	Mississippi	24.2
34	Utah	2 736 424	34	Tennessee	106 752	34	Arizona	22.1
35	Nevada	2 600 167	35	Ohio	106 056	35	Arkansas	21.2
36	New Mexico...........................	1 984 356	36	Kentucky...............................	102 896	36	Iowa	20.8
37	West Virginia	1 814 468	37	Virginia.................................	102 548	37	Oklahoma	20.5
38	Nebraska	1 783 432	38	Indiana	92 895	38	Colorado	18.4
39	Idaho	1 523 816	39	Maine	79 931	39	Maine	16.5
40	Maine	1 316 456	40	South Carolina	77 983	40	Oregon..................................	15.2
41	New Hampshire	1 315 809	41	West Virginia	62 361	41	Kansas	13.2
42	Hawaii	1 288 198	42	Maryland...............................	25 314	42	Utah	12.9
43	Rhode Island	1 050 788	43	Vermont................................	23 956	43	Nevada	9.1
44	Montana	967 440	44	New Hampshire	23 227	44	Nebraska	9.0
45	Delaware	873 092	45	Massachusetts.......................	20 306	45	Idaho	7.1
46	South Dakota	804 194	46	New Jersey	19 211	46	New Mexico...........................	6.3
47	Alaska	686 293	47	Hawaii	16 635	47	South Dakota	4.1
48	North Dakota	641 481	48	Connecticut	12 548	48	North Dakota	3.6
49	Vermont................................	621 270	49	Delaware	5 060	49	Montana	2.6
50	District Of Columbia..............	591 833	50	Rhode Island	2 706	50	Wyoming	2.1
51	Wyoming...............................	532 668	51	District of Columbia..............	159	51	Alaska	0.5

Percent population change, 2000–2008			Percent under 20 years old, 2008			Percent 65 years old and over, 2008		
Percent change rank	State	Percent change	Under 20 years old rank	State	Percent under 20 years old	65 years old and over rank	State	Percent 65 years old and over
	United States	8.0		United States	27.2		United States	12.8
1	Nevada	30.1	1	Utah	34.2	1	Florida	17.4
2	Arizona	26.7	2	Texas	30.5	2	West Virginia	15.7
3	Utah	22.5	3	Idaho	29.9	3	Pennsylvania	15.3
4	Georgia	18.3	4	Mississippi	29.2	4	Maine	15.1
5	Idaho	17.8	5	Georgia	29.1	5	Hawaii	14.8
6	Texas	16.7	6	Alaska	29.0	5	Iowa	14.8
7	Colorado	14.8	7	Arizona	28.9	7	North Dakota	14.7
8	Florida	14.7	8	California	28.6	8	South Dakota	14.4
9	North Carolina	14.6	9	New Mexico	28.3	9	Arkansas	14.3
10	South Carolina	11.7	10	Louisiana	28.2	10	Montana	14.2
11	Delaware	11.4	11	Nebraska	28.1	11	Rhode Island	14.1
12	Washington	11.1	12	Kansas	27.9	12	Delaware	13.9
13	Oregon	10.8	12	Nevada	27.9	12	Vermont	13.9
14	Virginia	9.8	14	Illinois	27.7	14	Alabama	13.8
15	Alaska	9.5	14	Indiana	27.7	15	Connecticut	13.7
16	Tennessee	9.2	16	Oklahoma	27.6	15	Ohio	13.7
17	New Mexico	9.1	17	South Dakota	27.5	17	Missouri	13.6
18	California	8.5	18	Arkansas	27.3	18	Nebraska	13.5
19	Wyoming	7.9	19	North Carolina	27.1	18	Oklahoma	13.5
20	Montana	7.2	20	Colorado	27.0	20	Massachusetts	13.4
21	Arkansas	6.8	20	Wyoming	27.0	20	New York	13.4
23	New Hampshire	6.5	22	Alabama	26.9	22	Arizona	13.3
22	South Dakota	6.5	22	Minnesota	26.9	22	Kentucky	13.3
24	Maryland	6.4	24	Iowa	26.8	22	New Jersey	13.3
25	Hawaii	6.3	24	Michigan	26.8	22	Oregon	13.3
26	Minnesota	6.1	24	Missouri	26.8	22	South Carolina	13.3
27	Missouri	5.7	24	South Carolina	26.8	22	Wisconsin	13.3
28	Kentucky	5.6	28	Maryland	26.7	28	Tennessee	13.2
29	Oklahoma	5.6	29	Delaware	26.6	29	Kansas	13.1
31	Indiana	4.9	29	Ohio	26.6	29	New Mexico	13.1
30	Wisconsin	4.9	31	Tennessee	26.3	31	Michigan	13.0
32	Alabama	4.8	31	Virginia	26.3	32	New Hampshire	12.9
33	Kansas	4.2	33	Kentucky	26.2	33	Indiana	12.8
34	Nebraska	4.2	33	New Jersey	26.2	34	Mississippi	12.6
35	Illinois	3.9	33	Wisconsin	26.2	35	Minnesota	12.5
36	District of Columbia	3.5	36	Connecticut	26.1	36	North Carolina	12.4
38	Maine	3.3	36	Washington	26.1	37	Wyoming	12.3
37	Mississippi	3.3	38	North Dakota	25.8	38	Illinois	12.2
39	New Jersey	3.2	39	New York	25.7	38	Louisiana	12.2
40	Connecticut	2.8	40	Montana	25.5	40	Maryland	12.1
41	New York	2.7	41	Oregon	25.4	40	Virginia	12.1
42	Iowa	2.6	42	Rhode Island	25.3	42	Idaho	12.0
43	Massachusetts	2.3	43	Pennsylvania	25.2	42	Washington	12.0
44	Vermont	2.0	44	Massachusetts	25.1	44	District of Columbia	11.9
45	Pennsylvania	1.4	44	New Hampshire	25.1	45	Nevada	11.4
46	Ohio	1.2	46	Hawaii	24.7	46	California	11.2
47	Michigan	0.7	47	Florida	24.3	47	Colorado	10.3
48	West Virginia	0.3	48	Vermont	23.9	48	Texas	10.2
49	Rhode Island	0.2	48	West Virginia	23.9	49	Georgia	10.1
50	North Dakota	-0.1	50	Maine	23.5	50	Utah	9.0
51	Louisiana	-1.3	51	District of Columbia	22.6	51	Alaska	7.3

Percent White rank	State	Percent White	Percent Black rank	State	Percent Black	Hispanic or Latino rank	State	Percent Hispanic or Latino
	United States	79.8		United States......................	12.8		United States.........................	15.4
1	Maine	96.4	1	District of Columbia..............	54.4	1	New Mexico	44.9
1	Vermont...............................	96.4	2	Mississippi	37.2	2	California	36.6
3	New Hampshire.....................	95.5	3	Louisiana	32.0	3	Texas	36.5
4	Idaho	94.6	4	Georgia	30.0	4	Arizona	30.1
5	West Virginia........................	94.5	5	Maryland	29.4	5	Nevada..................................	25.7
6	Iowa	94.2	6	South Carolina	28.5	6	Florida...................................	21.0
7	Wyoming	93.9	7	Alabama	26.4	7	Colorado................................	20.2
8	Utah	92.9	8	North Carolina......................	21.6	8	New York	16.7
9	Nebraska..............................	91.4	9	Delaware	20.9	9	New Jersey	16.3
9	North Dakota	91.4	10	Virginia	19.9	10	Illinois...................................	15.2
11	Montana	90.5	11	New York	17.3	11	Connecticut	12.0
12	Oregon	90.1	12	Tennessee.............................	16.8	11	Utah	12.0
13	Kentucky..............................	89.9	13	Florida..................................	15.9	13	Rhode Island	11.6
14	Colorado..............................	89.7	14	Arkansas	15.8	14	Oregon	11.0
14	Wisconsin	89.7	15	Illinois..................................	14.9	15	Idaho	10.2
16	Minnesota............................	89.0	16	New Jersey	14.5	16	Washington............................	9.8
17	Kansas	88.7	17	Michigan	14.2	17	Kansas	9.1
18	Rhode Island	88.5	18	Ohio	12.0	18	Hawaii	8.7
19	South Dakota	88.2	19	Texas	11.9	19	District of Columbia	8.6
20	Indiana	88.0	20	Missouri	11.5	19	Massachusetts........................	8.6
21	Arizona	86.5	21	Pennsylvania..........................	10.8	21	Georgia.................................	8.0
22	Massachusetts......................	86.2	22	Connecticut	10.3	22	Nebraska................................	7.9
23	Pennsylvania	85.4	23	Indiana	9.1	23	Wyoming	7.7
24	Missouri	85.0	24	Nevada.................................	8.1	24	Oklahoma	7.6
25	Ohio	84.8	25	Oklahoma	8.0	25	North Carolina	7.4
26	Connecticut	84.3	26	Kentucky..............................	7.7	26	Delaware................................	6.8
26	Washington	84.3	27	Massachusetts.......................	7.0	26	Virginia	6.8
28	New Mexico	84.0	28	California	6.7	28	Maryland	6.7
29	Texas	82.4	29	Rhode Island	6.4	29	Alaska	6.1
30	Michigan..............................	81.2	30	Kansas	6.2	30	Arkansas	5.6
31	Nevada................................	80.9	31	Wisconsin	6.1	31	Indiana	5.2
32	Arkansas	80.8	32	Minnesota............................	4.6	32	Wisconsin	5.1
33	Tennessee	80.4	33	Nebraska..............................	4.5	33	Pennsylvania...........................	4.8
34	Florida.................................	79.8	34	Alaska	4.3	34	Iowa.....................................	4.2
35	Illinois.................................	79.1	34	Colorado	4.3	35	Michigan	4.1
36	Oklahoma	78.1	36	Arizona	4.2	35	Minnesota..............................	4.1
37	California	76.6	37	Washington...........................	3.7	35	South Carolina	4.1
38	New Jersey	76.0	38	West Virginia.........................	3.6	38	Tennessee..............................	3.7
39	Delaware..............................	74.3	39	Hawaii	3.1	39	Louisiana...............................	3.4
40	North Carolina	73.9	40	New Mexico	3.0	40	Missouri	3.2
41	New York	73.4	41	Iowa	2.7	41	Montana	3.0
42	Virginia	73.0	42	Oregon.................................	2.0	42	Alabama	2.9
43	Alabama	71.0	43	Utah	1.3	43	New Hampshire.......................	2.6
44	Alaska	70.6	43	Wyoming..............................	1.3	43	Ohio	2.6
45	South Carolina	68.7	45	New Hampshire......................	1.2	43	South Dakota	2.6
46	Georgia................................	65.4	46	North Carolina	1.1	46	Kentucky................................	2.4
47	Louisiana..............................	64.8	46	South Dakota	1.1	47	Mississippi	2.2
48	Maryland	63.4	48	Maine	1.0	48	North Dakota	2.1
49	Mississippi	60.6	49	Idaho	0.9	49	Vermont................................	1.4
50	District of Columbia	40.1	49	Vermont...............................	0.9	50	Maine	1.3
51	Hawaii	29.7	51	Montana	0.7	51	West Virginia..........................	1.1

[1] May be of any race.

Percent born in state of residence, 2007			Percent foreign-born population, 2007			Birth rate, 2006		
Born in state of residence rank	State	Percent born in state of residence	Foreign born rank	State	Percent foreign born	Birth rate rank	State	Birth rate (per 1,000 population)
	United States	58.9		United States........................	12.6		United States........................	14.2
1	Louisiana	79.5	1	California	27.4	1	Utah.......................................	21.0
2	Michigan	76.0	2	New York	21.8	2	Texas	17.0
3	Pennsylvania	75.2	3	New Jersey	19.9	3	Arizona	16.6
4	Ohio	74.9	4	Nevada..................................	19.4	4	Idaho	16.5
5	Iowa	72.3	5	Florida...................................	18.9	5	Alaska	16.4
6	Mississippi	72.1	6	Hawaii	17.3	6	Nevada...................................	16.0
7	Wisconsin	71.9	7	Texas	16.0	7	Georgia..................................	15.9
8	West Virginia	71.7	8	Arizona	15.6	8	Mississippi	15.8
9	Kentucky	71.4	9	Massachusetts.......................	14.2	9	California	15.4
10	Alabama	71.3	10	Illinois	13.8	10	New Mexico	15.3
11	North Dakota.........................	69.6	11	Connecticut	12.8	11	South Dakota	15.2
12	Minnesota	68.9	12	Rhode Island	12.7	12	Nebraska................................	15.1
13	Indiana	68.5	13	District of Columbia..............	12.6	12	Oklahoma	15.1
14	Illinois	66.8	14	Maryland................................	12.4	14	Colorado................................	14.9
15	Missouri	66.7	15	Washington............................	12.3	14	Wyoming	14.9
16	South Dakota.........................	66.6	16	Virginia	10.3	16	Hawaii	14.8
17	Nebraska................................	65.8	17	Colorado................................	10.0	16	Kansas	14.8
18	New York	64.2	18	Oregon...................................	9.8	16	Louisiana	14.8
19	Massachusetts	63.9	19	New Mexico	9.3	19	District of Columbia	14.7
20	Maine	63.5	20	Georgia..................................	9.1	20	Arkansas................................	14.6
21	Utah.......................................	63.1	21	Utah.......................................	8.2	21	North Carolina	14.4
22	Tennessee..............................	62.3	22	Delaware................................	7.6	21	South Carolina	14.4
23	Oklahoma..............................	61.4	23	Alaska	7.2	23	Minnesota	14.2
24	Arkansas................................	61.1	24	North Carolina.......................	7.0	24	Illinois	14.1
25	Texas.....................................	60.7	25	Minnesota	6.6	24	Virginia	14.1
26	South Carolina	60.1	26	Michigan	6.1	26	Delaware................................	14.0
27	North Carolina	59.1	27	Kansas	6.0	26	Indiana	14.0
28	Kansas	58.9	28	Idaho	5.6	26	Tennessee..............................	14.0
29	Rhode Island	58.7	28	Nebraska................................	5.6	29	Missouri	13.9
30	Georgia..................................	55.8	30	Pennsylvania	5.4	30	Kentucky	13.8
31	Connecticut	55.5	31	New Hampshire......................	5.1	30	Maryland................................	13.8
32	Hawaii	54.6	32	Oklahoma..............................	5.0	32	Alabama	13.7
33	Montana	54.5	33	Wisconsin	4.5	33	Iowa......................................	13.6
34	Vermont	52.7	34	South Carolina	4.3	33	North Dakota.........................	13.6
35	California	52.6	35	Arkansas................................	4.2	33	Washington............................	13.6
36	New Jersey	52.4	35	Indiana	4.2	36	Montana	13.2
37	New Mexico...........................	51.3	37	Tennessee..............................	4.1	36	New Jersey	13.2
38	Virginia	50.5	38	Iowa	3.9	36	Oregon...................................	13.2
39	Maryland................................	48.1	39	Ohio......................................	3.7	39	Florida...................................	13.1
40	Washington	47.0	40	Missouri	3.5	39	Ohio......................................	13.1
41	Idaho	46.5	41	Vermont	3.4	41	New York	13.0
42	Delaware................................	45.5	41	Maine	3.4	41	Wisconsin	13.0
43	Oregon...................................	45.4	43	Louisiana	3.3	43	Michigan	12.6
44	Colorado................................	42.5	44	Wyoming	3.1	44	Massachusetts.......................	12.1
44	New Hampshire	42.5	45	Alabama	3.0	45	Pennsylvania	12.0
46	Wyoming	42.1	46	Kentucky	2.5	46	Connecticut	11.9
47	District of Columbia	39.7	47	North Dakota.........................	2.4	47	Rhode Island	11.6
48	Alaska....................................	38.7	48	South Dakota.........................	1.8	48	West Virginia	11.5
49	Arizona..................................	35.6	49	Mississippi	1.7	49	New Hampshire......................	10.9
50	Florida	34.0	49	Montana	1.7	50	Maine	10.7
51	Nevada..................................	23.0	51	West Virginia.........................	1.3	51	Vermont.................................	10.4

Percent high school graduates,[1] 2007			Percent college graduates (bachelor's degree or more),[1] 2007			Median household income, 2007		
Percent high school rank	State	Percent high school graduates	Percent college graduates rank	State	Percent college graduates	Median income rank	State	Median income (dollars)
	United States	84.5		United States	27.5		United States	50 740
1	Wyoming	91.2	1	District of Columbia	47.5	1	Maryland	68 080
2	Minnesota	91.0	2	Massachusetts	37.9	2	New Jersey	67 035
3	New Hampshire	90.5	3	Maryland	35.2	3	Connecticut	65 967
4	Alaska	90.5	4	Colorado	35.0	4	Alaska	64 333
5	Vermont	90.3	5	Connecticut	34.7	5	Hawaii	63 746
6	Utah	90.2	6	New Jersey	33.9	6	New Hampshire	62 369
7	Montana	90.0	7	Vermont	33.6	7	Massachusetts	62 365
8	Iowa	89.6	8	Virginia	33.6	8	California	59 948
9	Nebraska	89.6	9	New Hampshire	32.5	9	Virginia	59 562
10	Maine	89.4	10	New York	31.7	10	Minnesota	55 802
11	Hawaii	89.4	11	Minnesota	31.0	11	Washington	55 591
12	Washington	89.3	12	Washington	30.3	12	Colorado	55 212
13	Kansas	89.1	13	Rhode Island	29.8	13	Utah	55 109
14	Wisconsin	89.0	14	California	29.5	14	Nevada	55 062
15	North Dakota	89.0	15	Illinois	29.5	15	Delaware	54 610
16	Colorado	88.9	16	Hawaii	29.2	16	District of Columbia	54 317
17	Massachusetts	88.4	17	Kansas	28.8	17	Illinois	54 124
18	Idaho	88.4	18	Utah	28.7	18	Rhode Island	53 568
19	South Dakota	88.2	19	Oregon	28.3	19	New York	53 514
20	Oregon	88.0	20	Nebraska	27.5	20	Wyoming	51 731
21	Connecticut	88.0	21	Georgia	27.1	21	Wisconsin	50 578
22	Michigan	87.4	22	Montana	27.0	22	Vermont	49 907
23	Maryland	87.4	23	Maine	26.7	23	Arizona	49 889
24	Delaware	87.4	24	Delaware	26.1	24	Georgia	49 136
25	Ohio	87.1	25	Alaska	26.0	25	Oregon	48 730
26	New Jersey	87.0	26	Pennsylvania	25.8	26	Pennsylvania	48 576
27	Pennsylvania	86.8	27	Florida	25.8	27	Michigan	47 950
28	Virginia	85.9	28	North Dakota	25.7	28	Florida	47 804
29	Indiana	85.8	29	North Carolina	25.6	29	Texas	47 548
30	District of Columbia	85.7	30	Wisconsin	25.4	30	Kansas	47 451
31	Illinois	85.7	31	Arizona	25.3	31	Indiana	47 448
32	Missouri	85.6	32	Texas	25.2	32	Iowa	47 292
33	Florida	84.9	33	South Dakota	25.0	33	Nebraska	47 085
34	Oklahoma	84.8	34	New Mexico	24.8	34	Ohio	46 597
35	New York	84.1	35	Michigan	24.7	35	Idaho	46 253
36	Nevada	83.7	36	Missouri	24.5	36	Maine	45 888
37	Arizona	83.5	37	Idaho	24.5	37	Missouri	45 114
38	North Carolina	83.0	38	Iowa	24.3	38	North Carolina	44 670
39	Rhode Island	83.0	39	Ohio	24.1	39	North Dakota	43 753
40	Georgia	82.9	40	South Carolina	23.5	40	Montana	43 531
41	New Mexico	82.3	41	Wyoming	23.4	41	South Dakota	43 424
42	South Carolina	82.1	42	Oklahoma	22.8	42	South Carolina	43 329
43	Tennessee	81.4	43	Indiana	22.1	43	Tennessee	42 367
44	West Virginia	81.2	44	Tennessee	21.8	44	Oklahoma	41 567
45	Arkansas	81.1	45	Nevada	21.8	45	New Mexico	41 452
46	Alabama	80.4	46	Alabama	21.4	46	Louisiana	40 926
47	California	80.2	47	Louisiana	20.4	47	Alabama	40 554
48	Kentucky	80.1	48	Kentucky	20.0	48	Kentucky	40 267
49	Louisiana	79.9	49	Arkansas	19.3	49	Arkansas	38 134
50	Texas	79.1	50	Mississippi	18.9	50	West Virginia	37 060
51	Mississippi	78.5	51	West Virginia	17.3	51	Mississippi	36 338

[1] 25 years old or over.

Percent owner-occupied housing units, 2007			Median value of owner-occupied housing units, 2007			Percent of mortgaged owners paying 30 percent or more of income for housing expenses, 2007		
Owner-occupied housing units rank	State	Percent owner-occupied housing units	Median value rank	State	Median value (dollars)	Percent of income for housing rank	State	Percent owner-occupied
	United States	67.2		United States........................	194 300		United States....................	37.5
1	Minnesota	75.2	1	Hawaii................................	555 400	1	California	53.0
2	West Virginia	74.9	2	California	532 300	2	Nevada.............................	49.0
3	Michigan	74.8	3	District of Columbia..............	450 900	3	Florida	48.9
4	New Hampshire	74.1	4	New Jersey	372 300	4	New Jersey	46.1
5	Maine	74.0	5	Massachusetts.....................	366 400	5	Hawaii	45.8
6	Iowa	73.7	6	Maryland............................	347 000	6	Rhode Island......................	42.3
7	Vermont	72.8	7	Nevada..............................	311 300	7	New York	41.5
8	Delaware	72.5	8	New York	311 000	8	Massachusetts	41.3
9	Idaho	72.1	9	Connecticut	309 200	9	Oregon..............................	40.8
10	Utah	71.7	10	Washington	300 800	10	Washington........................	40.6
11	Indiana	71.6	11	Rhode Island	292 800	11	New Hampshire	40.5
11	Pennsylvania	71.6	12	Virginia	262 100	12	Connecticut........................	40.3
13	Mississippi.....................	71.3	13	New Hampshire	261 800	13	Arizona	39.5
14	Alabama	70.9	14	Oregon..............................	257 300	13	Vermont............................	39.5
15	Kentucky	70.7	15	Delaware	239 700	15	District of Columbia..........	38.7
15	Missouri........................	70.7	16	Arizona	237 700	15	Illinois...............................	38.7
17	Florida	70.6	17	Colorado............................	233 900	17	Colorado............................	37.9
18	Kansas	70.2	18	Alaska	231 300	17	Maryland...........................	37.9
19	Illinois	70.1	19	Florida	230 400	19	Michigan...........................	36.3
19	Wisconsin	70.1	20	Utah.................................	218 700	20	Delaware...........................	35.9
21	Connecticut	70.0	21	Minnesota..........................	213 600	21	Virginia	35.5
21	New Mexico	70.0	22	Illinois...............................	208 800	22	Maine	35.4
21	South Carolina................	70.0	23	Vermont............................	205 400	23	Alaska	34.9
24	Maryland........................	69.9	24	Idaho	178 100	24	Georgia	34.6
24	Tennessee	69.9	25	Maine	176 000	24	Minnesota..........................	34.6
26	Ohio	69.7	26	Wyoming	172 300	26	New Mexico	34.0
27	Montana	69.6	27	Montana	170 000	27	Montana	33.6
28	Virginia	69.5	28	Wisconsin...........................	168 800	28	Utah.................................	33.5
29	Wyoming........................	69.3	29	Georgia	164 500	28	Wisconsin...........................	33.5
30	Colorado	68.8	30	New Mexico	155 400	30	Idaho	33.1
30	Nebraska	68.8	31	Pennsylvania	155 000	31	Pennsylvania	32.9
32	Georgia	68.5	32	Michigan	153 100	32	Mississippi.........................	32.6
33	North Carolina	68.3	33	North Carolina	145 700	33	Texas................................	31.9
34	Oklahoma	68.2	34	Missouri............................	138 600	34	Tennessee..........................	31.5
35	Arizona..........................	68.1	35	Ohio	137 800	35	South Carolina	31.3
35	South Dakota..................	68.1	36	South Carolina	133 900	36	North Carolina	30.7
37	Louisiana	67.9	37	Tennessee..........................	130 800	36	Ohio	30.7
38	Arkansas........................	67.7	38	Louisiana	126 800	38	Louisiana	29.6
39	New Jersey	67.3	39	Indiana	122 900	39	Alabama............................	29.1
40	Washington	66.1	40	Nebraska	122 200	39	Missouri............................	29.1
41	North Dakota..................	65.7	41	Kansas	121 200	41	Kentucky	27.0
42	Texas............................	65.2	42	Texas................................	120 900	42	Indiana	26.9
43	Massachusetts	65.1	43	South Dakota	118 700	42	Nebraska	26.9
44	Oregon	64.6	44	Iowa.................................	117 900	44	Arkansas...........................	26.5
45	Rhode Island	63.6	45	Alabama	115 600	45	Oklahoma	26.2
46	Alaska	63.0	46	Kentucky	114 300	46	South Dakota	25.8
47	Nevada..........................	60.4	47	North Dakota	106 800	47	Kansas..............................	25.7
48	Hawaii...........................	59.6	48	Oklahoma	103 000	48	West Virginia......................	25.5
49	California.......................	58.0	49	Arkansas	101 000	49	Iowa.................................	25.3
50	New York	55.5	50	Mississippi.........................	96 000	50	Wyoming	24.4
51	District of Columbia	44.5	50	West Virginia......................	96 000	51	North Dakota	21.4

Median gross rent of renter-occupied housing units, 2007			Unemployment rate, 2008			Per capita state taxes, 2006–2007		
Median rent rank	State	Median rent (dollars)	Unemployment rate rank	State	Unemployment rate	State taxes rank	State	State taxes per capita (dollars)
	United States	789		United States........................	5.8		United States........................	X
1	Hawaii	1 194	1	Michigan..............................	8.4	1	Alaska..................................	5 037
2	California	1 078	2	Rhode Island	7.8	2	Vermont...............................	4 119
3	New Jersey...........................	1 026	3	California	7.2	3	Hawaii..................................	3 969
4	Maryland	1 000	4	District of Columbia..............	7.0	4	Wyoming..............................	3 873
5	Nevada	980	5	Mississippi	6.9	5	Connecticut	3 668
6	Massachusetts......................	946	5	South Carolina	6.9	6	Minnesota............................	3 421
7	District of Columbia	934	7	Alaska	6.7	7	Delaware..............................	3 360
8	Connecticut	931	7	Nevada................................	6.7	8	New Jersey...........................	3 351
9	Florida	925	9	Illinois..................................	6.5	9	New York..............................	3 273
10	Alaska	918	9	Ohio....................................	6.5	10	Massachusetts......................	3 204
11	Delaware..............................	910	11	Kentucky..............................	6.4	11	California	3 139
12	New York	907	11	Oregon................................	6.4	12	North Dakota	2 787
13	New Hampshire	892	11	Tennessee............................	6.4	13	Washington..........................	2 735
13	Virginia	892	14	North Carolina......................	6.3	14	Maine	2 719
15	Rhode Island	830	15	Florida	6.2	15	Maryland..............................	2 687
16	Arizona	819	15	Georgia................................	6.2	16	New Mexico..........................	2 642
17	Washington	816	17	Missouri...............................	6.1	17	Rhode Island	2 615
18	Colorado..............................	788	18	Indiana................................	5.9	18	Arkansas	2 608
19	Illinois.................................	783	19	Connecticut	5.7	19	Wisconsin.............................	2 585
20	Georgia................................	768	20	Arizona	5.5	20	West Virginia........................	2 569
21	Vermont...............................	756	20	New Jersey...........................	5.5	21	Louisiana..............................	2 530
22	Oregon	743	22	Maine	5.4	22	North Carolina	2 496
23	Texas...................................	734	22	Minnesota............................	5.4	23	Kansas	2 483
24	Utah....................................	733	22	New York..............................	5.4	24	Pennsylvania.........................	2 480
25	Minnesota............................	711	22	Pennsylvania.........................	5.4	25	Nevada	2 458
26	Pennsylvania	685	26	Massachusetts......................	5.3	26	Montana	2 422
27	Michigan..............................	683	26	Washington..........................	5.3	27	Virginia	2 408
28	North Carolina	678	28	Arkansas	5.1	28	Illinois..................................	2 379
29	Wisconsin	673	29	Alabama	5.0	29	Michigan..............................	2 368
30	Idaho	654	30	Colorado..............................	4.9	30	Idaho	2 359
31	Louisiana..............................	651	30	Idaho	4.9	31	Kentucky..............................	2 333
32	Maine	650	30	Texas...................................	4.9	32	Nebraska..............................	2 294
33	South Carolina	645	33	Delaware..............................	4.8	33	Oklahoma	2 286
34	Ohio....................................	643	33	Vermont...............................	4.8	34	Utah....................................	2 226
35	Indiana................................	638	35	Wisconsin.............................	4.7	35	Indiana................................	2 208
36	New Mexico..........................	637	36	Louisiana..............................	4.6	36	Mississippi	2 191
37	Wyoming..............................	636	37	Montana	4.5	37	Iowa....................................	2 165
38	Tennessee	634	38	Kansas	4.4	38	Ohio....................................	2 164
39	Kansas	623	38	Maryland..............................	4.4	39	Oregon................................	2 066
40	Missouri...............................	618	40	West Virginia........................	4.3	40	South Carolina	1 971
41	Nebraska..............................	614	41	New Mexico..........................	4.2	41	Florida.................................	1 958
42	Mississippi	609	42	Iowa....................................	4.1	42	Arizona	1 956
43	Alabama	601	43	Virginia	4.0	43	Alabama	1 916
44	Oklahoma	588	44	Hawaii.................................	3.9	44	Georgia................................	1 904
45	Montana	579	45	New Hampshire.....................	3.8	45	Colorado..............................	1 894
46	Arkansas	573	45	Oklahoma	3.8	46	Tennessee............................	1 847
47	Iowa	567	47	Utah....................................	3.4	47	Missouri...............................	1 821
48	Kentucky..............................	563	48	Nebraska..............................	3.3	48	Texas...................................	1 686
49	South Dakota	526	49	North Dakota	3.2	49	New Hampshire.....................	1 653
50	West Virginia........................	525	50	Wyoming.............................	3.1	50	South Dakota	1 579
51	North Dakota	516	51	South Dakota	3.0	X	District of Columbia	X

	Exports of goods by state of origin, 2008		Percent of children under 18 years old below the poverty level, 2007			Percent of persons below the poverty level, 2007		
Exports rank	State	Exports (milions of dollars)	Poverty rate rank	State	Poverty rate	Poverty rate rank	State	Poverty rate
	United States	1 287 442		United States........................	13.0		United States..........................	18.0
1	Texas....................................	192 222	1	Mississippi	20.6	1	Mississippi	29.3
2	California	144 806	2	Louisiana...............................	18.6	2	Louisiana...............................	26.8
3	New York	81 386	3	New Mexico	18.1	3	Arkansas	25.8
4	Washington	54 498	4	Arkansas	17.9	4	New Mexico	25.5
5	Florida..................................	54 238	5	Kentucky...............................	17.3	5	Alabama	24.3
6	Illinois	53 677	6	Alabama	16.9	6	Kentucky...............................	23.9
7	Ohio	45 628	6	West Virginia	16.9	7	Texas	23.2
8	Michigan...............................	45 136	8	District of Columbia..............	16.4	8	Tennessee..............................	23.0
9	Louisiana...............................	41 908	9	Texas	16.3	9	West Virginia	22.8
10	New Jersey	35 643	10	Oklahoma	15.9	10	District of Columbia	22.7
11	Pennsylvania	34 649	10	Tennessee..............................	15.9	11	Oklahoma	22.5
12	Massachusetts.......................	28 369	12	South Carolina	15.0	12	South Carolina	20.9
13	Georgia.................................	27 514	13	Georgia.................................	14.3	13	Arizona	20.2
14	Indiana.................................	26 502	13	North Carolina	14.3	14	Georgia.................................	19.7
15	North Carolina	25 091	15	Arizona	14.2	15	North Carolina	19.5
16	Tennessee	23 238	16	Montana	14.1	16	Michigan...............................	19.4
17	Wisconsin	20 570	17	Michigan...............................	14.0	17	New York	19.4
18	South Carolina	19 853	18	New York	13.7	18	Ohio.....................................	18.5
19	Arizona	19 784	19	Ohio.....................................	13.1	19	Montana	18.3
20	Oregon	19 352	19	South Dakota	13.1	20	Missouri	17.7
21	Minnesota............................	19 186	21	Missouri	13.0	21	Rhode Island	17.5
22	Kentucky..............................	19 121	22	Oregon	12.9	22	Indiana.................................	17.3
23	Virginia................................	18 942	23	California	12.4	23	California	17.3
24	Alabama	15 879	24	Indiana.................................	12.3	24	Florida..................................	17.1
25	Connecticut	15 384	25	Florida..................................	12.1	25	Oregon	16.9
26	Missouri	12 852	25	Idaho	12.1	26	South Dakota	16.8
27	Kansas	12 514	25	North Dakota	12.1	27	Illinois	16.6
28	Iowa	12 125	28	Colorado	12.0	28	Colorado	16.3
29	Maryland	11 383	28	Maine	12.0	29	Pennsylvania..........................	16.3
30	Utah	10 306	28	Rhode Island	12.0	30	Idaho	15.9
31	Colorado	7 713	31	Illinois	11.9	31	Maine	15.4
32	Mississippi............................	7 323	32	Pennsylvania..........................	11.6	32	Nevada	15.3
33	Nevada	6 121	33	Washington...........................	11.4	33	Washington...........................	15.0
34	Arkansas	5 776	34	Kansas	11.2	34	Nebraska...............................	14.9
35	West Virginia........................	5 643	34	Nebraska...............................	11.2	35	Delaware...............................	14.7
36	Nebraska...............................	5 412	36	Iowa	11.0	36	Kansas	14.6
37	Oklahoma	5 077	37	Wisconsin..............................	10.8	37	Wisconsin..............................	14.4
38	Idaho	5 005	38	Nevada	10.7	38	Iowa	13.6
39	Delaware...............................	4 898	39	Delaware...............................	10.5	39	North Dakota	13.4
40	New Hampshire.....................	3 752	40	Vermont................................	10.1	40	Virginia	13.0
41	Vermont...............................	3 697	41	Massachusetts.......................	9.9	41	Massachusetts.......................	12.9
42	Alaska	3 542	41	Virginia	9.9	42	Vermont................................	12.4
43	Maine	3 016	43	Utah	9.7	43	Minnesota.............................	12.0
44	New Mexico..........................	2 783	44	Minnesota.............................	9.5	44	Wyoming	11.6
45	North Dakota	2 772	45	Alaska	8.9	45	New Jersey	11.6
46	Rhode Island	1 974	46	Wyoming	8.7	46	Alaska	11.5
47	South Dakota	1 654	47	New Jersey	8.6	47	Connecticut	11.1
48	Montana...............................	1 395	48	Maryland	8.3	48	Utah.....................................	11.0
49	District of Columbia	1 196	49	Hawaii	8.0	49	Maryland	10.5
50	Wyoming	1 081	50	Connecticut	7.9	50	Hawaii..................................	9.8
51	Hawaii	960	51	New Hampshire.....................	7.1	51	New Hampshire.....................	8.8

Energy consumption per person, 2008			Defense contracts, 2007			Value of agricultural products sold, 2007		
Consumption rank	State	Per capita consumption (million Btu)	Defense contracts rank	State	Defense contracts (millions of dollars)	Agricultural sales rank	State	Value of sales (millions of dollars)
	United States	333.1		United States	294 025		United States	297 220
1	Alaska	1 112.2	1	Virginia	33 481	1	California	33 885
2	Wyoming	937.9	2	California	33 384	2	Texas	21 001
3	Louisiana	896.1	3	Texas	30 012	3	Iowa	20 418
4	North Dakota	644.1	4	Florida	11 926	4	Nebraska	15 506
5	Texas	501.7	5	Pennsylvania	11 253	5	Kansas	14 413
6	Kentucky	468.7	6	Maryland	10 478	6	Illinois	13 329
7	Alabama	466.3	7	Missouri	10 141	7	Minnesota	13 180
8	West Virginia	458.5	8	Massachusetts	10 138	8	North Carolina	10 314
9	Indiana	454.1	9	Arizona	9 120	9	Wisconsin	8 967
10	Montana	453.2	10	Alabama	8 735	10	Indiana	8 271
11	Oklahoma	448.1	11	Georgia	8 668	11	Florida	7 785
12	Mississippi	419.3	12	Connecticut	8 559	12	Missouri	7 513
13	Arkansas	407.4	13	New York	7 603	13	Arkansas	7 509
14	Iowa	406.2	14	New Jersey	6 854	14	Georgia	7 113
15	South Carolina	394.4	15	Ohio	6 277	15	Ohio	7 070
16	Kansas	381.3	16	Indiana	5 816	16	Washington	6 793
17	Tennessee	380.8	17	Washington	5 304	17	South Dakota	6 570
18	Nebraska	373.8	18	Michigan	5 249	18	North Dakota	6 084
19	Minnesota	353.5	19	Illinois	5 058	19	Colorado	6 061
20	Delaware	352.5	20	Mississippi	4 821	20	Pennsylvania	5 809
21	New Mexico	351.8	21	Colorado	4 321	21	Oklahoma	5 806
22	Idaho	351.6	22	District of Columbia	4 085	22	Michigan	5 753
23	Maine	348.2	23	South Carolina	3 864	23	Idaho	5 689
24	South Dakota	344.9	24	Wisconsin	3 461	24	Mississippi	4 877
25	Ohio	339.6	25	Tennessee	3 240	25	Kentucky	4 825
26	Georgia	336.8	26	North Carolina	2 951	26	New York	4 419
27	Virginia	333.1	27	Utah	2 881	27	Alabama	4 416
28	Missouri	327.7	28	Louisiana	2 827	28	Oregon	4 386
29	Wisconsin	326.3	29	Kentucky	2 712	29	Arizona	3 235
30	Washington	322.2	30	Oklahoma	2 097	30	Virginia	2 906
31	Pennsylvania	317.1	31	Hawaii	2 096	31	Montana	2 803
32	Illinois	308.8	32	Kansas	2 013	32	Louisiana	2 618
33	Nevada	307.6	33	Minnesota	1 873	33	Tennessee	2 617
34	Utah	304.7	34	Alaska	1 851	34	South Carolina	2 353
35	Oregon	301.2	35	Maine	1 459	35	New Mexico	2 175
36	New Jersey	300.6	36	New Hampshire	1 385	36	Maryland	1 835
37	District of Columbia	299.9	37	New Mexico	1 246	37	Utah	1 416
38	North Carolina	299.8	38	Iowa	1 149	38	Wyoming	1 158
39	Colorado	299.6	39	Oregon	1 128	39	Delaware	1 083
40	Michigan	296.8	40	Nevada	861	40	New Jersey	987
41	Vermont	263.7	41	Vermont	805	41	Vermont	674
42	Hawaii	259.8	42	Arkansas	691	42	Maine	617
43	Maryland	259.3	43	Nebraska	676	43	West Virginia	592
44	Florida	255.3	44	Rhode Island	498	44	Connecticut	552
45	Arizona	248.3	45	North Dakota	412	45	Hawaii	514
46	Connecticut	242.8	46	South Dakota	345	46	Nevada	513
47	New Hampshire	238.7	47	West Virginia	298	47	Massachusetts	490
48	California	232.3	48	Delaware	268	48	New Hampshire	199
49	Massachusetts	229.9	49	Wyoming	209	49	Rhode Island	66
50	New York	204.3	50	Montana	202	50	Alaska	57
51	Rhode Island	203.7	51	Idaho	180	51	District of Columbia	X

Violent crime rate rank	State	Violent crime rate (per 100,000 population)	Voting rank	State	Percent voting	Percent lacking health insurance rank	State	Percent lacking health insurance
	Violent crime rate, 2008 (violent crimes known to police)			**Voter turnout for the presidential election, 2008**			**Percent of persons lacking health insurance, 2007**	
	United States	467		United States	63.6		United States	15.3
1	District of Columbia	1 414	1	Minnesota	75.0	1	Texas	25.2
2	South Carolina	788	2	District of Columbia..............	74.1	2	New Mexico	22.5
3	Tennessee	753	3	Maine	71.2	3	Florida	20.2
4	Nevada	751	3	New Hampshire	71.2	4	Mississippi	18.8
5	Louisiana	730	3	Wisconsin	71.2	5	Louisiana	18.5
6	Florida	723	6	Louisiana	70.3	6	Arizona	18.3
7	Delaware	689	7	Iowa	70.2	7	Alaska	18.2
8	New Mexico	664	8	Mississippi	69.7	7	California	18.2
9	Alaska	661	9	Virginia	68.7	9	Oklahoma	17.8
10	Maryland	642	10	Colorado	68.4	10	Georgia	17.5
11	Michigan	536	11	Maryland	68.3	11	Nevada	17.2
12	Illinois	533	12	Michigan	67.8	12	Oregon	16.8
13	Arkansas	529	12	South Dakota	67.8	13	Colorado	16.4
14	California	523	14	Oregon	67.6	13	North Carolina	16.4
15	Texas	511	15	North Carolina.......................	67.5	13	South Carolina	16.4
16	Missouri	505	15	North Dakota	67.5	16	Arkansas	16.1
17	Oklahoma	500	17	Rhode Island	67.4	17	New Jersey	15.8
18	Georgia	493	18	Delaware	67.3	18	Montana	15.6
19	Arizona	483	18	Nebraska	67.3	19	Virginia	14.8
20	North Carolina	466	20	Connecticut	67.2	20	Tennessee	14.4
21	Kansas	453	21	Massachusetts	67.1	21	West Virginia	14.1
22	Alabama	448	22	Washington	66.8	22	Idaho	13.9
23	Massachusetts	432	23	Missouri	65.8	23	Maryland	13.7
24	Pennsylvania	417	24	South Carolina	65.6	24	Kentucky	13.6
25	New York	414	25	Ohio	65.5	25	Illinois	13.4
26	Colorado	348	26	Montana	65.4	26	Nebraska	13.2
27	Ohio	343	27	Alaska	65.0	26	New York	13.2
28	Indiana	334	28	Vermont	64.7	28	Utah	12.8
29	Washington	333	29	Wyoming	64.3	29	Kansas	12.7
30	New Jersey	329	30	Georgia	64.2	30	Missouri	12.6
31	Nebraska	302	31	New Jersey	64.1	31	Alabama	12.0
32	Kentucky	295	32	Florida	63.8	32	Ohio	11.7
33	Iowa	295	33	California	63.4	33	Michigan	11.6
34	Mississippi	291	34	Kansas	63.3	34	Indiana	11.4
35	Wisconsin	291	35	Kentucky	63.1	35	Washington	11.3
36	Minnesota............................	289	36	Illinois	62.6	36	Delaware	11.2
37	Oregon	288	36	New Mexico	62.6	37	Rhode Island	10.8
38	Montana	288	38	Alabama	62.4	38	New Hampshire	10.5
39	West Virginia........................	275	38	Pennsylvania.........................	62.4	39	South Dakota	10.1
40	Hawaii	273	40	Idaho	61.4	40	Pennsylvania.........................	9.5
41	Virginia	270	41	Indiana	60.5	41	Connecticut	9.4
42	Connecticut	256	42	Arizona	59.9	42	Iowa.....................................	9.3
43	Idaho	239	42	Nevada	59.9	43	Maine	8.8
44	Wyoming	239	44	New York	58.8	44	Minnesota............................	8.3
45	Utah	235	45	Oklahoma	58.7	45	Wisconsin.............................	8.2
46	Rhode Island	227	46	Texas	56.1	46	Hawaii	7.5
47	South Dakota	169	47	Tennessee	55.5	47	Massachusetts	5.4
48	North Dakota	142	48	Arkansas	53.8	X	District of Columbia	...
49	New Hampshire....................	137	49	West Virginia	53.4	X	North Dakota	...
50	Vermont	124	50	Utah	53.1	X	Vermont	...
51	Maine	118	51	Hawaii...................................	51.8	X	Wyoming	...

ALABAMA

Facts and Figures

Location: Southeastern United States; bordered on the N by Tennessee, on the E by Georgia, on the S by Florida and the Gulf of Mexico, and on the W by Mississippi

Area: 52,419 sq. mi. (135,765 sq. km.); rank—30th

Population: 4,661,900 (2008 est.); rank—23rd

Principal Cities: capital—Montgomery; largest—Birmingham

Statehood: December 14, 1819; 22nd state

U.S. Congress: 2 senators, 7 representatives

State Motto: *Audemus jura nostra defendere* ("We dare defend our rights")

State Song: "Alabama"

State Nicknames: The Yellowhammer State; The Heart of Dixie; The Cotton State

Abbreviations: AL; Ala.

State Symbols: flower—camellia; tree—Southern longleaf pine; bird—yellowhammer

At a Glance

- With an increase in population of 4.8 percent, Alabama ranked 32nd among the states in growth from 2000 to 2008.
- An estimated 39,035 marriages took place in Alabama in 2008, compared to 19,509 divorces.
- The 2007 home ownership rate in Alabama was 73.3 percent, giving it a ranking of 14th among the states.
- Alabama's median household income in 2007 was $40,554, 46th among the states.
- In Alabama, 16.9 percent of the population lived below the poverty level in 2007, ranking it 6th along with West Virginia.
- In 2006-07, 13.6 percent of Alabamans did not have health insurance, compared to 15.5 percent of the total U.S. population.
- In 2007, 4 percent of Alabamans were unemployed, compared to 4.6 percent nationwide.
- Alabama ranked 45th in the nation with 21.4 percent of its population 25 years old and over having a bachelor's degree in 2007.
- Alabama's violent crime rate in 2007 was 448 per 100,000 population, compared to 466.9 for the entire nation.
- Alabama had one physician for every 412 people in 2007, compared to one physician for every 325 people nationwide.
- In the 2008 election, 61.8 percent of Alabama's eligible voters voted, compared to 61.7 percent of eligible voters nationwide.
- Alabama ranked 20th among the states receiving federal aid in 2007, with $1,485 per capita.
- Alabama's gross domestic product was $166 billion in 2007; it ranked 25th among the states.
- With $14.4 billion in exports in 2007, Alabama ranked 24th in exports.
- Alabamans consumed 2.14 trillion Btu's of energy in 2006; the state ranked 16th in total consumption.
- In 2007, Alabama exported $616 million worth of agricultural products, less than 1 percent of the U.S. total.

Table AL-1. Population by Sex, Age, Race, and Hispanic Origin

(Number, percent.)

Sex, age, race, and Hispanic origin	1990	2000	2008	Average annual percent change, 2000–2008
Total Population	4 040 587	4 447 100	4 661 900	0.6
Percent of total U.S. population	1.6	1.6	1.5	X
Sex				
Male	1 936 162	2 146 504	2 258 087	0.6
Female	2 104 425	2 300 596	2 403 813	0.6
Age				
Under 5 years	283 295	295 992	310 504	0.6
5 to 19 years	913 426	960 177	943 644	-0.2
20 to 64 years	2 320 877	2 611 133	2 766 085	0.7
65 years and over	522 989	579 798	641 667	1.3
Median age (years)	32.9	35.8	37.5	X
Race and Hispanic Origin[1]				
One race				
White	2 975 797	3 162 808	3 311 216	0.6
Black	1 020 705	1 155 930	1 229 787	0.8
American Indian and Alaskan Native	16 506	22 430	24 825	1.3
Asian[2]	21 797	31 346	44 541	4.5
Native Hawaiian and Other Pacific Islander	X	1 409	1 945	4.1
Two or more races	X	44 179	49 586	1.5
Hispanic (of any race)	24 629	75 830	134 810	7.5

[1]Data on race in 2000 and 2008 are not comparable to 1990. Individuals could only report one race in the 1990 census but could report one or more races on the 2000 census.
[2]Data in 1990 refer to Asian and Pacific Islanders.

Table AL-2. Marital Status

(Number, percent distribution.)

Sex and marital status	1990	2000	2007
Males, 15 Years and Over	1 488 017	1 666 798	1 768 636
Never married	27.3	26.7	29.9
Now married, except separated	60.4	59.0	54.1
Separated	1.8	1.8	2.0
Widowed	2.7	2.8	3.0
Divorced	7.8	9.8	11.0
Females, 15 Years and Over	1 676 275	1 847 401	1 934 049
Never married	20.8	21.4	24.5
Now married, except separated	53.3	52.5	48.4
Separated	2.5	2.5	2.8
Widowed	14.1	12.4	11.7
Divorced	9.4	11.2	12.5

Table AL-3. Households and Housing Characteristics

(Number, percent, and dollars.)

Item	1990	2000	2007	Average annual percent change, 2000–2007
Total Households	1 506 790	1 737 080	1 816 313	0.6
Family households	1 103 835	1 215 968	1 245 126	0.3
Married-couple family	858 327	906 916	891 473	-0.2
Other family	245 508	309 052	353 653	1.9
Male householder, no wife present	44 288	62 586	83 526	4.2
Female householder, no husband present	201 220	246 466	270 127	1.3
Nonfamily households	402 955	521 112	571 187	1.3
Householder living alone	358 078	453 898	497 840	1.3
Householder not living alone	44 877	67 214	73 347	1.3
Housing Characteristics				
Total housing units	1 670 379	1 963 711	2 137 012	1.2
Occupied housing units	1 506 790	1 737 080	1 816 313	0.6
Owner-occupied	1 061 897	1 258 705	1 287 825	0.3
Renter-occupied	444 893	478 375	528 488	1.4
Average size	2.62	2.49	2.48	X
Financial Characteristics				
Median gross rent of renter-occupied housing units (dollars)	325	447	601	4.3
Median monthly owner costs for housing units with a mortgage (dollars)	555	816	1 049	3.7
Median value of owner-occupied housing units (dollars)	53 200	85 100	115 600	4.5

Table AL-4. Median Income and Poverty Status, 2007

(Number, percent.)

Characteristic	State		U.S.	
	Number	Percent	Number	Percent
Median Income				
Households (dollars)	40 554	X	50 740	X
Families (dollars)	50 770	X	61 173	X
Below Poverty Level				
Sex				
Male	319 787	14.8	16 576 071	11.5
Female	440 048	18.8	21 476 176	14.3
Age				
Under 18 years	269 086	24.3	13 097 100	18.0
Related children under 18 years	264 227	24.0	12 728 964	17.6
18 to 64 years	419 146	15.0	21 495 507	11.6
65 years and over	71 603	11.9	3 459 640	9.5

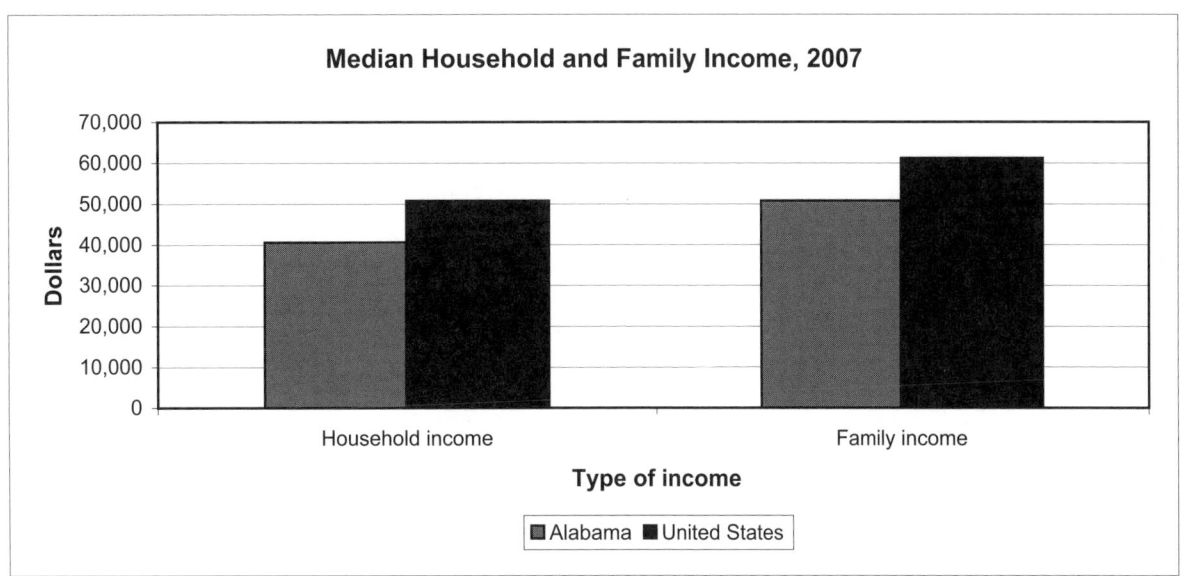

Table AL-5. Health Insurance Coverage Status for All Persons and Children Under 18 Years of Age

(Number, percent.)

Item	2000	2001	2002	2003	2004	2005	2006	2007
ALL PERSONS	4 380	4 388	4 440	4 427	4 512	4 524	4 532	4 570
Covered by Private or Government Health Insurance								
Number	3 823	3 841	3 900	3 841	3 950	3 867	3 843	4 021
Percent	87.3	87.5	87.8	86.8	87.5	85.5	84.8	88.0
Not Covered								
Number	557	548	539	586	562	657	689	549
Percent	12.7	12.5	12.2	13.2	12.5	14.5	15.2	12.0
Percent in the U.S. not covered	13.7	14.1	14.7	15.1	14.9	15.3	15.8	15.3
CHILDREN UNDER 18 YEARS OF AGE	1 131	1 143	1 128	1 101	1 096	1 083	1 114	1 123
Covered by Private or Government Health Insurance								
Number	1 027	1 044	1 012	1 014	1 027	1 034	1 032	1 041
Percent	90.8	91.4	89.7	92.1	93.7	95.5	92.6	92.7
Not Covered								
Number	104	99	116	87	69	49	82	82
Percent	9.2	8.6	10.3	7.9	6.3	4.5	7.4	7.3
Percent in the U.S. not covered	11.6	11.3	11.2	11.0	10.5	10.9	11.7	11.0

Table AL-6. Employment Status by Demographic Group, Preliminary 2008

(Number, percent.)

Characteristic	Civilian noninstitutional population	Civilian labor force		Employment		Unemployed	
		Number	Percent of population	Number	Percent of population	Number	Unemployment rate
TOTAL	3 592	2 185	60.8	2 062	57.4	123	5.6
Sex							
Men	1 700	1 158	68.0	1 083	63.7	75	6.5
Women	1 892	1 027	54.0	979	51.7	48	4.7
Race, Sex, and Hispanic Origin							
White	2 616	1 590	60.8	1 525	58.3	64	4.1
Men	1 261	875	69.4	832	66.0	43	4.9
Women	1 355	715	52.7	693	51.1	22	3.1
Black or African American	882	531	60.1	477	54.1	53	10.0
Men	389	242	62.2	214	54.9	29	11.8
Women	493	288	58.4	264	53.5	24	8.5
Hispanic	105	87	82.8	83	79.2	4	4.3
Men	66	64	97.0	61	92.8	3	4.4
Women	39	. . .	. . .	. . .	. . .	. . .	. . .
Age							
16 to 19 years	254	93	36.4	74	29.1	19	20.1
20 to 24 years	341	241	70.7	213	62.5	28	11.5
25 to 34 years	582	471	80.8	442	75.9	29	6.1
35 to 44 years	597	488	81.7	466	78.1	22	4.5
45 to 54 years	642	479	74.6	463	72.1	16	3.3
55 to 64 years	562	311	55.3	303	53.9	8	2.6
65 years and over	613	103	16.8	100	16.4	2	2.2

Note: Data in Table 6 are from the Current Population Survey (CPS) and do not match the estimates in Table 7. See notes and definitions for more details.

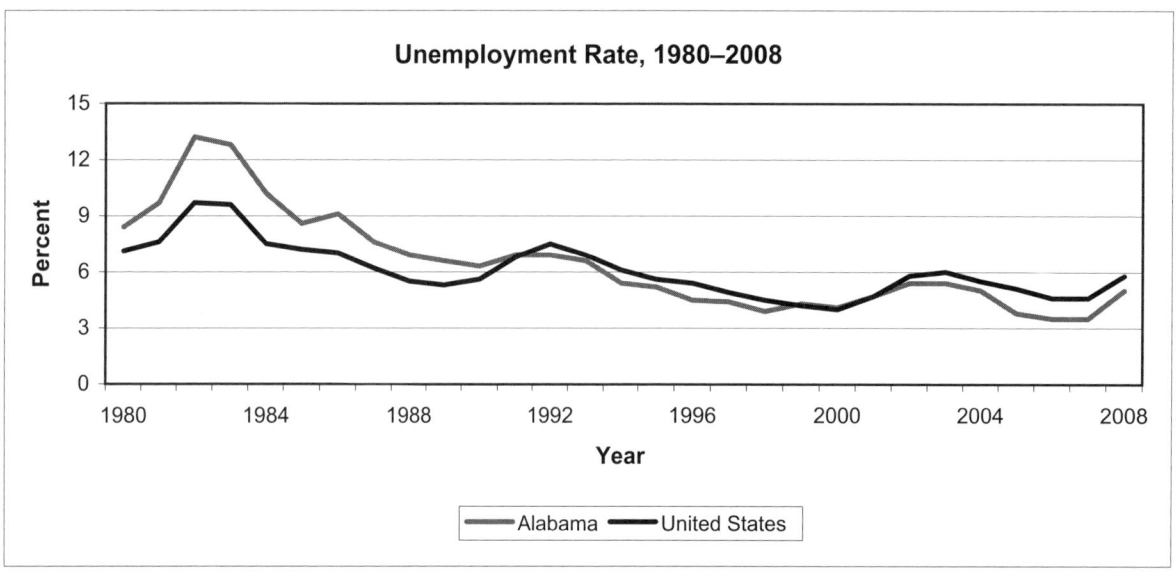

Table AL-7. Employment Status of the Civilian Noninstitutional Population Age 16 Years and Over

(Number, percent.)

Year	Civilian labor force	Civilian participation rate	Employed	Unemployed	Unemployment rate
1998	2 142 512	64.1	2 059 310	83 202	3.9
1999	2 162 603	64.3	2 070 210	92 393	4.3
2000	2 154 545	63.8	2 067 147	87 398	4.1
2001	2 134 845	62.9	2 034 909	99 936	4.7
2002	2 107 858	61.9	1 994 748	113 110	5.4
2003	2 104 209	61.5	1 989 784	114 425	5.4
2004	2 113 781	61.4	2 007 153	106 628	5.0
2005	2 124 149	61.1	2 042 925	81 224	3.8
2006	2 166 071	61.5	2 090 387	75 684	3.5
2007	2 175 716	61.1	2 099 615	76 101	3.5
2008	2 162 479	60.2	2 053 502	108 977	5.0

Table AL-8. Employment and Average Wages by Industry

(Estimates for 2001–2006 are based on the 2002 North American Industry Classification System [NAICS]. Estimates for 2007 are based on the 2007 NAICS.)

Industry	2001	2002	2003	2004	2005	2006	2007
	Number of jobs						
WAGE AND SALARY EMPLOYMENT BY INDUSTRY	2 007 366	1 990 053	1 986 705	2 020 854	2 059 706	2 097 044	2 119 276
Farm Wage and Salary Employment	7 910	8 645	7 977	9 041	7 714	8 340	7 329
Nonfarm Wage and Salary Employment	1 999 456	1 981 408	1 978 728	2 011 813	2 051 992	2 088 704	2 111 947
Private wage and salary employment	1 614 334	1 592 317	1 584 982	1 612 372	1 651 678	1 683 831	1 702 005
Forestry, fishing, hunting, and other	D	13 363	12 884	12 851	12 617	12 123	11 867
Mining	8 012	7 938	7 430	7 456	8 122	8 383	8 241
Utilities	14 448	14 095	13 618	13 524	12 713	12 992	13 388
Construction	109 436	104 751	103 789	106 505	109 723	113 911	116 675
Manufacturing	330 741	310 064	295 100	293 570	301 308	304 907	298 464
Durable goods manufacturing	179 392	173 371	166 012	169 364	179 429	188 390	187 659
Nondurable goods manufacturing	151 349	136 693	129 088	124 206	121 879	116 517	110 805
Wholesale trade	81 158	79 147	77 900	79 065	80 405	82 471	83 040
Retail trade	236 408	235 125	236 315	239 653	243 243	243 061	248 810
Transportation and warehousing	55 577	52 536	52 029	53 215	55 571	57 832	58 499
Information	35 908	34 288	31 832	31 391	30 979	30 253	28 058
Finance and insurance	70 800	70 250	72 611	72 861	73 678	74 051	73 733
Real estate and rental and leasing	24 818	24 956	25 106	25 453	25 445	25 560	26 512
Professional and technical services	85 626	87 464	91 218	94 222	95 786	99 725	101 990
Management of companies and enterprises	8 951	9 532	10 852	11 906	12 316	13 332	14 714
Administrative and waste services	94 147	94 099	91 633	97 708	104 756	106 623	109 477
Educational services	22 006	22 364	23 107	24 099	24 621	25 976	26 046
Health care and social assistance	165 025	171 754	176 410	179 564	185 857	192 298	197 357
Arts, entertainment, and recreation	15 985	15 618	15 713	16 603	17 452	18 006	18 491
Accommodation and food services	D	138 543	141 639	145 617	149 896	154 461	158 173
Other services, except public administration	104 017	106 430	105 796	107 109	107 190	107 866	108 470
Government and government enterprises	385 122	389 091	393 746	399 441	400 314	404 873	409 942
	Dollars						
AVERAGE WAGES AND SALARIES BY INDUSTRY	29 436	30 480	31 566	32 723	33 967	35 473	36 748
Average Farm Wages and Salaries	18 154	17 724	14 704	17 931	18 326	17 867	21 205
Average Nonfarm Wages and Salaries	29 480	30 536	31 634	32 789	34 026	35 543	36 802
Average private wages and salaries	29 155	30 105	31 139	32 373	33 565	35 072	36 153
Forestry, fishing, hunting, and other	D	25 031	26 083	26 977	27 735	28 645	29 817
Mining	51 092	52 433	53 451	54 564	59 029	58 772	62 149
Utilities	67 094	67 473	74 175	77 140	80 560	80 463	83 876
Construction	30 816	31 475	32 176	33 018	34 961	36 924	39 258
Manufacturing	34 695	36 149	37 577	39 447	40 455	42 194	43 562
Durable goods manufacturing	36 565	38 171	39 936	42 010	43 116	44 862	45 849
Nondurable goods manufacturing	32 478	33 584	34 544	35 953	36 538	37 880	39 688
Wholesale trade	39 928	40 947	42 506	45 209	47 622	49 934	51 792
Retail trade	19 887	20 589	21 120	21 735	22 523	23 307	23 708
Transportation and warehousing	31 883	33 518	34 618	36 238	37 601	38 715	39 864
Information	42 099	43 330	42 907	44 896	45 916	47 141	47 970
Finance and insurance	41 073	43 736	46 272	48 904	52 171	57 318	58 487
Real estate and rental and leasing	24 367	26 092	27 559	29 024	30 212	31 771	33 173
Professional and technical services	47 528	48 336	50 946	52 301	53 606	56 257	58 527
Management of companies and enterprises	51 257	51 303	55 386	60 545	65 346	67 227	69 994
Administrative and waste services	18 105	19 387	20 921	21 303	22 045	22 742	23 344
Educational services	19 976	21 063	21 338	22 423	22 502	22 634	24 409
Health care and social assistance	31 888	32 932	33 013	34 728	36 080	37 448	38 389
Arts, entertainment, and recreation	15 449	16 121	16 712	17 020	17 325	17 957	18 124
Accommodation and food services	D	11 712	12 034	12 286	12 699	13 162	13 522
Other services, except public administration	19 243	20 063	20 913	21 491	22 511	23 338	24 448
Government and government enterprises	30 844	32 297	33 627	34 470	35 929	37 500	39 493

Table AL-9. Employment Characteristics by Family Type

(Number, percent.)

Family type and labor force status	2005		2006		2007	
	Total	Families with own children under 18 years	Total	Families with own children under 18 years	Total	Families with own children under 18 years
TOTAL FAMILIES	1 223 725	543 566	1 222 858	531 453	1 245 126	545 788
FAMILY TYPE AND LABOR FORCE STATUS						
Married Coupled Families	891 157	356 092	888 609	348 704	891 473	349 424
Both husband and wife in labor force	47.7	61.9	48.9	63.7	49.1	62.9
Husband in labor force, wife not in labor force	24.6	30.0	23.8	28.8	24.1	29.8
Wife in labor force, husband not in labor force	8.0	4.8	8.1	4.6	7.7	4.1
Both husband and wife not in labor force	19.7	3.3	19.2	2.9	19.1	3.2
Other Families	332 568	187 474	334 249	182 749	353 653	196 364
Female householder, no husband present	78.6	82.0	77.6	81.7	76.4	80.2
In labor force	51.0	63.5	50.0	63.2	49.4	62.3
Not in labor force	27.6	18.5	27.7	18.5	27.0	17.8
Male householder, no wife present	21.4	18.0	22.4	18.3	23.6	19.8
In labor force	15.9	15.6	16.7	16.6	17.0	17.3
Not in labor force	5.5	2.3	5.7	1.6	6.6	2.5

Table AL-10. School Enrollment and Educational Attainment, 2007

(Number, percent.)

Item	State	U.S.
Enrollment		
Total population 3 years and over	4 447 376	289 295 761
Enrolled in school	1 162 213	79 329 527
Enrolled in preschool (percent)	5.9	6.2
Enrolled in grades K-12 (percent)	69.8	67.6
Enrolled in college or graduate school (percent)	24.3	26.2
Attainment		
Total population 25 years and over	3 045 893	197 892 369
Less than a high school diploma (percent)	19.6	15.5
High school diploma or more (percent)	80.4	84.5
Bachelor's degree or more (percent)	21.4	27.5
Graduate degree or more (percent)	8.0	10.1

Table AL-11. Educational Indicators

(Number, percent.)

Item	State	U.S.
Public Schools, 2006–2007 (except where noted)		
Number of school districts	163	17 742
Number of schools	1 587	99 639
Number of students	743 632	49 315 842
Student-teacher ratio	13.2	15.5
Expenditures per student (dollars)	$8 398	. . .
Averaged freshman graduation rate, 2005–2006	66.2	. . .
Dropout rate, grades 9–12, 2005–2006	2.5	3.7
Students eligible for free or reduced-price lunch (percent)	51.0	41.2
English-language learners (percent)	2.5	5.1
Students with IEP (percent)	11.9	12.7
Private Schools, 2007–2008 (except where noted)		
Number of schools	423	33 740
Number of students	72 037	5 072 451
High school graduates, 2006–2007	4 576	306 605
Student-teacher ratio	11.2	11.1

Table AL-12. Reported Voting and Registration of the Voting-Age Population, November 2008

(Number in thousands, percent.)

Item	Total population	Total citizen population	Registered			Voted		
			Total registered	Percent registered (total population)	Percent registered (total citizen population)	Total voted	Percent voted (total population)	Percent voted (total citizen population)
U.S. total	225 499	206 072	146 311	64.9	71.0	131 144	58.2	63.6
State total	3 497	3 404	2 438	69.7	71.6	2 126	60.8	62.4
Sex								
Male	1 654	1 593	1 092	66.0	68.5	927	56.1	58.2
Female	1 843	1 811	1 346	73.0	74.3	1 199	65.0	66.2
Race								
White alone	2 541	2 473	1 791	70.5	72.4	1 543	60.7	62.4
White non-Hispanic alone	2 474	2 470	1 791	72.4	72.5	1 543	62.4	62.5
Black alone	875	875	611	69.9	69.9	547	62.5	62.5
Asian alone	32	8	. . .	. . .	. . .	. . .	. . .	. . .
Hispanic (of any race)	71	7	4	. . .	. . .	4	. . .	. . .
White alone or in combination	2 579	2 511	1 824	70.7	72.6	1 576	61.1	62.8
Black alone or in combination	892	892	626	70.1	70.1	561	62.9	62.9
Asian alone or in combination	32	8	. . .	. . .	. . .	. . .	. . .	. . .

Table AL-13. Crime

(Number, rate per 100,000.)

Item	State			U.S.		
	2007	2008	Percent change	2007	2008	Percent change
Population	4 627 851	4 661 900	0.7	301 621 157	304 059 724	0.8
VIOLENT CRIME						
Number	20 732	21 111	1.8	1 408 337	1 382 012	-1.9
Rate	448.0	452.8	1.1	466.9	454.5	-2.7
Murder and Nonnegligent Manslaughter						
Number	412	353	-14.3	16 929	16 272	-3.9
Rate	8.9	7.6	-14.9	5.6	5.4	-4.7
Forcible Rape						
Number	1 545	1 617	4.7	90 427	89 000	-1.6
Rate	33.4	34.7	3.9	30.0	29.3	-2.4
Robbery						
Number	7 398	7 346	-0.7	445 125	441 855	-0.7
Rate	159.9	157.6	-1.4	147.6	145.3	-1.5
Aggravated Assault						
Number	11 377	11 795	3.7	855 856	834 885	-2.5
Rate	245.8	253.0	2.9	283.8	274.6	-3.2
PROPERTY CRIME						
Number	183 798	190 343	3.6	9 843 481	9 767 915	-0.8
Rate	3 971.6	4 082.9	2.8	3 263.5	3 212.5	-1.6
Burglary						
Number	45 331	50 408	11.2	2 179 140	2 222 196	2.0
Rate	979.5	1 081.3	10.4	722.5	730.8	1.2
Larceny-Theft						
Number	124 237	126 477	1.8	6 568 572	6 588 873	0.3
Rate	2 684.6	2 713.0	1.1	2 177.8	2 167.0	-0.5
Motor Vehicle Theft						
Number	14 230	13 458	-5.4	1 095 769	956 846	-12.7
Rate	307.5	288.7	-6.1	363.3	314.7	-13.4

Table AL-14. State Government Finances, 2007

(Dollars, percent distribution.)

Item	Thousands of dollars	Percent distribution
Total Revenue	27 536 360	X
General revenue	21 287 228	77.3
Intergovernmental revenue	7 732 269	28.1
Taxes	8 868 314	32.2
General sales	2 278 027	8.3
Selective sales	2 112 359	7.7
License taxes	477 462	1.7
Individual income tax	3 019 510	11.0
Corporate income tax	505 886	1.8
Other taxes	475 070	1.7
Current charges	2 976 073	10.8
Miscellaneous general revenue	1 710 572	6.2
Utility revenue	0	0.0
Liquor store revenue	236 032	0.9
Insurance trust revenue	6 013 100	21.8
Total Expenditure	23 192 507	100.0
Intergovernmental expenditure	6 088 940	26.3
Direct expenditure	17 103 567	73.7
Current operation	12 220 463	52.7
Capital outlay	1 871 280	8.1
Insurance benefits and repayments	2 319 053	10.0
Assistance and subsidies	409 178	1.8
Interest on debt	283 593	1.2
Exhibit: Salaries and wages	3 795 023	16.4
Total Expenditure	23 192 507	100.0
General expenditure	20 674 219	89.1
Intergovernmental expenditure	6 088 940	26.3
Direct expenditure	14 585 279	62.9
Education	9 350 536	40.3
Public welfare	4 768 598	20.6
Hospitals	1 622 375	7.0
Health	643 313	2.8
Highways	1 358 627	5.9
Police protection	167 962	0.7
Correction	514 385	2.2
Natural resources	277 607	1.2
Parks and recreation	29 410	0.1
Government administration	551 538	2.4
Interest on general debt	283 593	1.2
Other and unallocable	1 106 275	4.8
Utility expenditure	0	0.0
Liquor store expenditure	199 235	0.9
Insurance trust expenditure	2 319 053	10.0
Debt at End of Fiscal Year	7 059 343	X
Cash and Security Holdings	43 865 486	X

Table AL-15. State Government Tax Collections, 2008

(Dollars, percent distribution.)

Item	Thousands of dollars	Percent distribution
Total Taxes	9 070 530	X
Property taxes	301 034	3.3
Sales and gross receipts	4 433 108	48.9
General sales and gross receipts	2 287 288	25.2
Selective sales taxes	2 145 820	23.7
Alcoholic beverages	164 827	1.8
Amusements	86	0.0
Insurance premiums	293 955	3.2
Motor fuels	545 726	6.0
Pari-mutuels	2 668	0.0
Public utilities	782 444	8.6
Tobacco products	145 020	1.6
Other selective sales	211 094	2.3
Licenses	487 934	5.4
Alcoholic beverages	3 431	0.0
Corporation	103 042	1.1
Hunting and fishing	15 835	0.2
Motor vehicle	212 687	2.3
Motor vehicle operators	17 762	0.2
Public utility	13 051	0.1
Occupation and business, NEC	122 125	1.3
Other licenses	1	0.0
Income taxes	3 602 361	39.7
Individual income	3 077 553	33.9
Corporation net income	524 808	5.8
Other taxes	246 093	2.7
Documentary and stock transfer	48 512	0.5
Severance	197 581	2.2

Table AL-16. Agriculture

(Number, acres, and dollars.)

Item	2002 Number	2002 Percent of total	2007 Number	2007 Percent of total	Percent change, 2002–2007
Number of farms	45 126		48 753		8.0
Farm Size					
Average size of farm (acres)	197		185		-6.1
Farms by size (number of farms)					
Fewer than 50 acres	16 746	37.1	19 589	40.2	17.0
50 to 499 acres	24 642	54.6	25 420	52.1	3.2
500 acres or more	3 738	8.3	3 744	7.7	0.2
Land (Acres)					
Total land in farms	8 904 387		9 033 537		1.5
Total cropland	3 732 751	41.9	3 142 958	34.8	-15.8
Total harvested cropland	1 995 139	22.4	1 994 743	22.1	0.0
Irrigated land	108 783	1.2	112 819	1.2	3.7
Value of Sales (Dollars)					
Agricultural products sold ($1,000)	3 264 949		4 415 550		35.2
Average sales per farm	72 352		90 570		25.2
Sales of crops	590 268	18.1	676 987	15.3	14.7
Sales of livestock, poultry, and their products	2 674 681	81.9	3 738 563	84.7	39.8
Value of Sales (Number of Farms)					
Less than $10,000	32 069	71.1	33 742	69.2	5.2
$10,000 to $99,999	8 386	18.6	10 282	21.1	22.6
$100,000 to $999,999	4 036	8.9	3 437	7.0	-14.8
$1,000,000 or more	635	1.4	1 292	2.7	103.5
Farms by Type of Organization (Number of Farms)					
Family	42 359	93.9	45 014	92.3	6.3
Partnership	1 882	4.2	2 377	4.9	26.3
Corporation	658	1.5	1 017	2.1	54.6
Other: cooperative, estate or trust, institutional, etc	227	0.5	345	0.7	52.0
Value of Land and Buildings (Dollars)					
Estimated market value of land and buildings ($1,000)	20 704 133		15 126 339		-26.9
Land and buildings average value per farm	424 674		335 217		-21.1
Average value per acre	2 292		1 698		-25.9
Government Payments					
Number of farms receiving government payments	12 863	28.5	14 428	29.6	12.2
Payments (thousands of dollars)	77 930		124 692		60.0
Average payment per farm	6 058		8 642		42.7
Farm Operator Characteristics					
Farm operators whose principal occupation is farming	23 950	53.1	19 416	39.8	-18.9
Farm operators whose principal occupation is other	21 176	46.9	29 337	60.2	38.5
Average age principal operator (years)	56.6		57.6		1.8

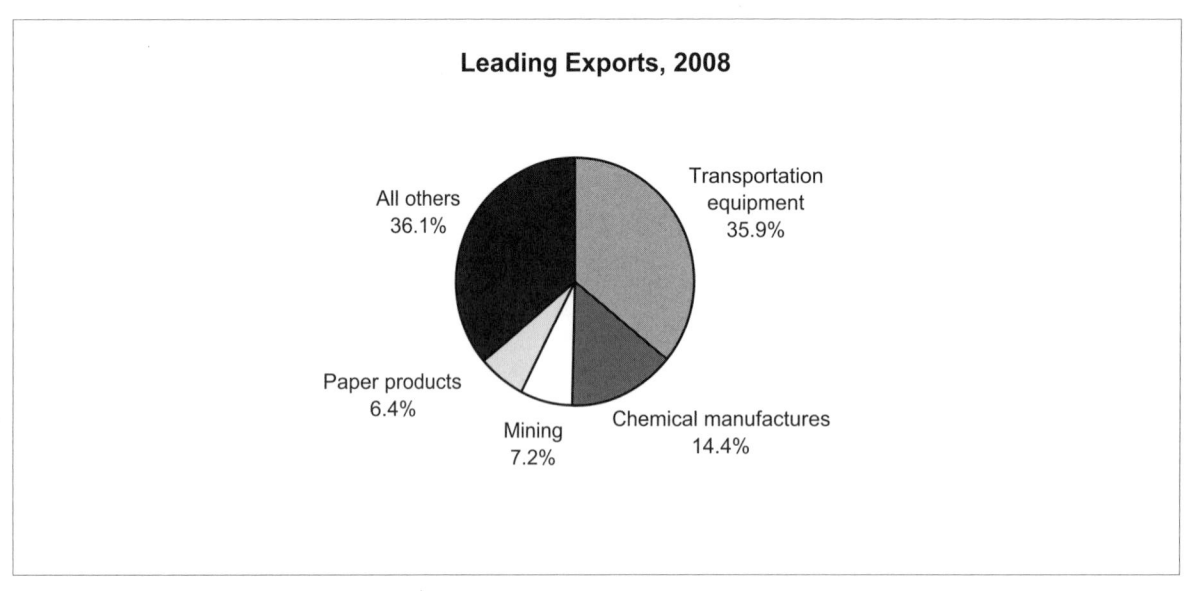

Leading Exports, 2008

All others 36.1%
Transportation equipment 35.9%
Paper products 6.4%
Mining 7.2%
Chemical manufactures 14.4%

ALASKA

Facts and Figures

Location: Northwestern North America; bordered on the N by the Arctic Ocean, on the E by Canada, on the S by the Pacific Ocean and the Gulf of Alaska, and on the W by the Bering Sea

Area: 663,267 sq. mi. (1,717,854 sq. sq. km.); rank—1st

Population: 686,293 (2008 est.); rank—47th

Principal Cities: capital—Juneau; largest—Anchorage

Statehood: January 3, 1959; 49th state

U.S. Congress: 2 senators, 1 representative

State Motto: North to the Future

State Song: "Alaska's Flag"

State Nicknames: The Last Frontier; The Land of the Midnight Sun

Abbreviations: AK

State Symbols: flower—forget-me-not; tree—Sitka spruce; bird—willow ptarmigan

At a Glance

- With an increase in population of 9.5 percent, Alaska ranked 15th among the states in growth from 2000 to 2008.
- An estimated 5,847 marriages took place in Alaska in 2008, compared to 2,921 divorces.
- The 2007 home ownership rate in Alaska was 66.6 percent, giving it a ranking of 41st among the states.
- Alaska's median household income in 2007 was $64,333, 4th among the states.
- In Alaska, 8.9 percent of the population lived below the poverty level in 2007, ranking it 44th.
- In 2006-07, 17.4 percent of Alaskans did not have health insurance, compared to 15.5 percent of the total U.S. population.
- In 2007, 6.2 percent of Alaskans were unemployed, compared to 4.6 percent nationwide.
- Alaska ranked 24th in the nation with 26 percent of its population 25 years old and over having a bachelor's degree in 2007.
- Alaska's violent crime rate in 2007 was 661.2 per 100,000 population, compared to 466.9 for the entire nation.
- Alaska had one physician for every 398 people in 2007, compared to one physician for every 325 people nationwide.
- In the 2008 election, 68.3 percent of Alaska's eligible voters voted, compared to 61.7 percent of eligible voters nationwide.
- Alaska ranked 2nd among the states receiving federal aid in 2007, with $3,568 per capita.
- Alaska's gross domestic product was $45 billion in 2007; it ranked 45th among the states.
- With $4 billion in exports in 2007, Alaska ranked 39th in exports.
- Alaskans consumed 753.5 billion Btu's of energy in 2006; the state ranked 37th in total consumption.
- In 2007, Alaska exported $4 million worth of agricultural products, less than 1 percent of the U.S. total.

Table AK-1. Population by Sex, Age, Race, and Hispanic Origin

(Number, percent.)

Sex, age, race, and Hispanic origin	1990	2000	2008	Average annual percent change, 2000–2008
Total Population	550 043	626 932	686 293	1.1
Percent of total U.S. population	0.2	0.2	0.2	X
Sex				
Male	289 867	324 112	357 607	1.2
Female	260 176	302 820	328 686	1.0
Age				
Under 5 years	54 897	47 591	52 083	1.1
5 to 19 years	132 066	160 526	147 060	-1.1
20 to 64 years	340 711	383 116	436 873	1.7
65 years and over	22 369	35 699	50 277	4.4
Median age (years)	29.3	32.4	33.3	X
Race and Hispanic Origin[1]				
One race				
White	415 492	434 534	484 682	1.4
Black	22 451	21 787	29 274	3.8
American Indian and Alaskan Native	85 698	98 043	104 990	0.9
Asian[2]	19 728	25 116	31 043	2.7
Native Hawaiian and Other Pacific Islander	X	3 309	4 499	3.9
Two or more races	X	34 146	31 805	-0.9
Hispanic (of any race)	17 803	25 852	41 853	6.2

[1]Data on race in 2000 and 2008 are not comparable to 1990. Individuals could only report one race in the 1990 census but could report one or more races on the 2000 census.
[2]Data in 1990 refer to Asian and Pacific Islanders.

Table AK-2. Marital Status

(Number, percent distribution.)

Sex and marital status	1990	2000	2007
Males, 15 Years and Over	212 540	243 024	281 531
Never married	31.9	32.5	36.8
Now married, except separated	54.5	53.6	49.4
Separated	2.0	1.7	1.8
Widowed	1.2	1.4	1.5
Divorced	10.4	10.8	10.5
Females, 15 Years and Over	187 691	225 837	256 048
Never married	21.8	24.1	27.7
Now married, except separated	59.1	55.6	52.0
Separated	2.4	2.3	2.4
Widowed	4.8	5.6	5.3
Divorced	11.9	12.5	12.7

Table AK-3. Households and Housing Characteristics

(Number, percent, and dollars.)

Item	1990	2000	2007	Average annual percent change, 2000–2007
Total Households	188 915	221 600	236 421	0.9
Family households	132 837	152 337	162 345	0.9
Married-couple family	106 079	116 318	122 261	0.7
Other family	26 758	36 019	40 084	1.5
Male householder, no wife present	8 529	12 082	13 439	1.5
Female householder, no husband present	18 229	23 937	26 645	1.5
Nonfamily households	56 078	69 263	74 076	1.0
Householder living alone	41 826	52 060	57 090	1.3
Householder not living alone	14 252	17 203	16 986	-0.2
Housing Characteristics				
Total housing units	232 608	260 978	282 271	1.1
Occupied housing units	188 915	221 600	236 421	0.9
Owner-occupied	105 989	138 509	149 018	1.1
Renter-occupied	82 926	83 091	87 403	0.7
Average size	2.80	2.74	2.80	X
Financial Characteristics				
Median gross rent of renter-occupied housing units (dollars)	559	720	918	3.5
Median monthly owner costs for housing units with a mortgage (dollars)	1 059	1 315	1 711	-3.2
Median value of owner-occupied housing units (dollars)	94 400	144 200	231 300	-3.1

Table AK-4. Median Income and Poverty Status, 2007

(Number, percent.)

Characteristic	State		U.S.	
	Number	Percent	Number	Percent
Median Income				
Households (dollars)	64 333	X	50 740	X
Families (dollars)	72 865	X	61 173	X
Below Poverty Level				
Sex				
Male	30 474	8.8	16 576 071	11.5
Female	29 151	9.1	21 476 176	14.3
Age				
Under 18 years	20 439	11.5	13 097 100	18.0
Related children under 18 years	18 910	10.7	12 728 964	17.6
18 to 64 years	36 707	8.3	21 495 507	11.6
65 years and over	2 479	5.4	3 459 640	9.5

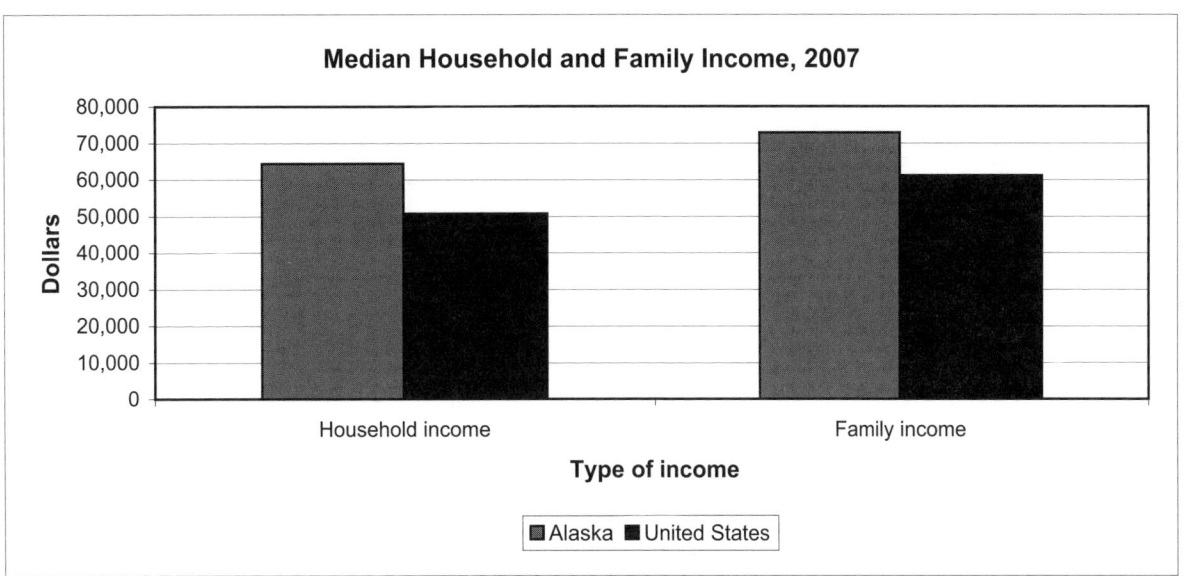

Median Household and Family Income, 2007

Table AK-5. Health Insurance Coverage Status for All Persons and Children Under 18 Years of Age

(Number, percent.)

Item	2000	2001	2002	2003	2004	2005	2006	2007
ALL PERSONS	624	634	635	645	649	659	659	675
Covered by Private or Government Health Insurance								
Number	510	536	518	525	542	545	550	552
Percent	81.7	84.5	81.5	81.3	83.5	82.8	83.5	81.8
Not Covered								
Number	114	98	117	121	107	113	109	123
Percent	18.3	15.5	18.5	18.7	16.5	17.2	16.5	18.2
Percent in the U.S. not covered	13.7	14.1	14.7	15.1	14.9	15.3	15.8	15.3
CHILDREN UNDER 18 YEARS OF AGE	189	193	195	194	185	187	181	185
Covered by Private or Government Health Insurance								
Number	161	174	169	170	167	171	163	164
Percent	84.9	89.7	86.7	87.8	90.3	91.6	89.7	88.6
Not Covered								
Number	29	20	26	24	18	16	19	21
Percent	15.1	10.3	13.3	12.2	9.7	8.4	10.3	11.4
Percent in the U.S. not covered	11.6	11.3	11.2	11.0	10.5	10.9	11.7	11.0

Table AK-6. Employment Status by Demographic Group, Preliminary 2008

(Number, percent.)

Characteristic	Civilian noninstitutional population	Civilian labor force		Employment		Unemployed	
		Number	Percent of population	Number	Percent of population	Number	Unemployment rate
TOTAL	506	360	71.1	335	66.3	24	6.8
Sex							
Men	255	195	76.0	181	70.8	14	7.1
Women	251	165	66.0	155	61.7	11	6.4
Race, Sex, and Hispanic Origin							
White	386	279	72.5	265	68.6	15	5.3
Men	198	154	77.6	145	73.3	9	5.5
Women	188	126	67.1	120	63.7	6	5.1
Black or African American	18	13	71.9	12	63.2	2	12.1
Men	9	7	75.5	6	67.3	1	10.9
Women	9	6	68.1	5	58.8	1	13.6
Hispanic	20	15	74.6	13	67.6	1	9.3
Men	9	7	81.0	7	73.2	1	9.7
Women	11	8	69.7	7	63.4	1	9.0
Age							
16 to 19 years	45	21	46.6	17	38.6	4	17.3
20 to 24 years	51	38	74.1	34	66.9	4	9.8
25 to 34 years	88	72	82.5	67	76.1	6	7.8
35 to 44 years	89	75	84.0	71	79.6	4	5.2
45 to 54 years	112	95	85.2	91	81.2	5	4.8
55 to 64 years	73	48	66.6	46	63.2	2	5.1
65 years and over	49	10	20.7	10	19.7	1	4.9

Note: Data in Table 6 are from the Current Population Survey (CPS) and do not match the estimates in Table 7. See notes and definitions for more details.

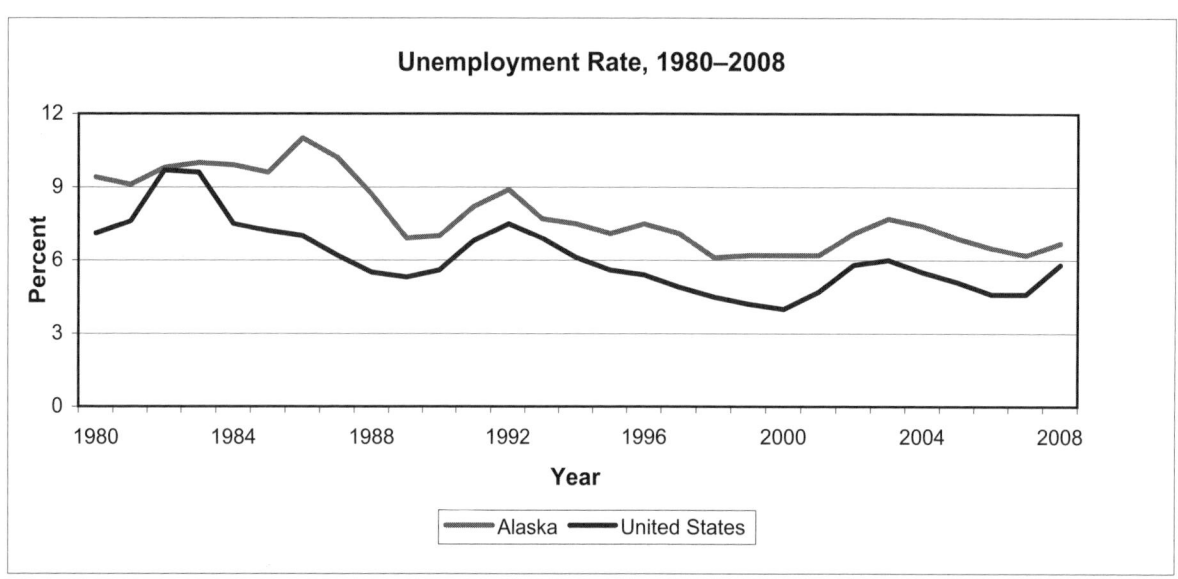

Table AK-7. Employment Status of the Civilian Noninstitutional Population Age 16 Years and Over

(Number, percent.)

Year	Civilian labor force	Civilian participation rate	Employed	Unemployed	Unemployment rate
1998	313 079	73.4	293 939	19 140	6.1
1999	316 507	73.2	297 019	19 488	6.2
2000	319 002	73.1	299 324	19 678	6.2
2001	321 484	72.5	301 694	19 790	6.2
2002	328 385	72.6	305 112	23 273	7.1
2003	336 549	72.9	310 762	25 787	7.7
2004	339 859	72.0	314 753	25 106	7.4
2005	344 379	71.6	320 644	23 735	6.9
2006	349 733	71.3	326 852	22 881	6.5
2007	351 701	70.8	330 065	21 636	6.2
2008	357 136	71.2	333 376	23 760	6.7

Table AK-8. Employment and Average Wages by Industry

(Estimates for 2001–2006 are based on the 2002 North American Industry Classification System [NAICS]. Estimates for 2007 are based on the 2007 NAICS.)

Industry	2001	2002	2003	2004	2005	2006	2007
				Number of jobs			
WAGE AND SALARY EMPLOYMENT BY INDUSTRY	316 753	322 021	326 945	333 110	339 155	346 493	349 589
Farm Wage and Salary Employment	289	360	359	364	356	353	348
Nonfarm Wage and Salary Employment	316 464	321 661	326 586	332 746	338 799	346 140	349 241
Private wage and salary employment	218 549	221 428	225 689	232 090	237 428	241 802	244 417
Forestry, fishing, hunting, and other	D	893	917	831	869	694	583
Mining	D	10 314	9 583	9 728	10 451	12 195	13 751
Utilities	1 612	1 792	1 812	1 822	1 851	1 847	1 849
Construction	15 576	16 612	17 641	18 457	19 178	18 682	18 128
Manufacturing	12 595	11 199	11 660	12 375	12 663	13 385	13 296
Durable goods manufacturing	D	D	1 757	1 859	1 981	1 980	2 138
Nondurable goods manufacturing	D	D	9 903	10 516	10 682	11 405	11 158
Wholesale trade	6 330	6 318	6 256	6 440	6 516	6 672	6 704
Retail trade	34 318	35 044	35 036	36 049	36 943	36 940	37 190
Transportation and warehousing	19 401	19 265	19 226	19 408	19 477	19 905	20 041
Information	7 272	7 057	7 032	6 882	6 929	6 975	6 938
Finance and insurance	8 548	8 334	8 720	8 814	8 913	9 034	9 176
Real estate and rental and leasing	4 505	4 553	4 888	4 989	5 161	5 118	5 075
Professional and technical services	11 429	11 488	11 794	11 987	12 394	12 746	13 211
Management of companies and enterprises	1 809	1 915	1 093	1 111	1 136	1 216	1 187
Administrative and waste services	11 033	10 849	10 873	10 905	11 132	11 190	11 513
Educational services	3 006	3 077	3 065	2 995	2 952	3 030	3 080
Health care and social assistance	27 539	29 646	32 968	35 648	36 572	37 452	37 185
Arts, entertainment, and recreation	4 144	4 213	4 174	4 210	4 491	4 528	4 633
Accommodation and food services	24 554	25 352	26 026	26 606	27 051	27 486	28 031
Other services, except public administration	D	13 507	12 925	12 833	12 749	12 707	12 846
Government and government enterprises	97 915	100 233	100 897	100 656	101 371	104 338	104 824
				Dollars			
AVERAGE WAGES AND SALARIES BY INDUSTRY	35 744	37 001	37 846	39 135	40 472	42 139	44 222
Average Farm Wages and Salaries	24 346	24 161	24 359	28 610	28 784	28 870	32 023
Average Nonfarm Wages and Salaries	35 755	37 015	37 860	39 146	40 484	42 152	44 234
Average private wages and salaries	34 853	35 774	36 348	37 535	38 615	40 376	42 772
Forestry, fishing, hunting, and other	D	50 636	49 344	49 043	48 269	46 042	48 600
Mining	D	90 905	87 398	91 961	94 643	98 583	103 796
Utilities	57 119	58 103	59 036	60 291	61 304	61 597	64 430
Construction	49 038	50 714	52 450	52 862	55 712	58 294	62 528
Manufacturing	30 103	32 732	34 463	33 585	35 741	35 458	37 515
Durable goods manufacturing	D	D	38 930	38 902	40 730	42 793	44 647
Nondurable goods manufacturing	D	D	33 671	32 645	34 816	34 185	36 148
Wholesale trade	39 625	40 558	41 515	43 073	44 910	46 016	48 197
Retail trade	23 679	24 509	25 423	25 763	25 813	26 497	27 216
Transportation and warehousing	42 733	44 103	45 298	47 688	47 779	48 623	52 389
Information	42 910	44 408	44 854	47 936	48 369	49 840	51 545
Finance and insurance	41 134	42 909	45 393	46 247	48 306	51 473	53 723
Real estate and rental and leasing	26 277	27 497	27 898	29 355	30 156	30 997	32 088
Professional and technical services	44 556	45 623	46 204	48 552	51 575	53 993	58 332
Management of companies and enterprises	49 609	46 793	59 914	63 151	64 488	72 548	74 328
Administrative and waste services	28 364	29 858	29 586	31 275	33 079	35 123	37 145
Educational services	22 644	25 276	25 465	26 010	26 605	27 015	27 354
Health care and social assistance	32 552	33 529	34 237	35 249	35 400	36 699	38 314
Arts, entertainment, and recreation	14 451	15 129	16 296	17 666	17 617	18 053	18 634
Accommodation and food services	16 823	17 363	18 061	18 935	19 193	20 063	20 726
Other services, except public administration	D	25 990	26 343	27 549	27 627	28 917	30 037
Government and government enterprises	37 768	39 758	41 244	42 861	44 864	46 270	47 641

Table AK-9. Employment Characteristics by Family Type

(Number, percent.)

Family type and labor force status	2005		2006		2007	
	Total	Families with own children under 18 years	Total	Families with own children under 18 years	Total	Families with own children under 18 years
TOTAL FAMILIES	157 187	83 842	157 939	82 894	162 345	82 969
FAMILY TYPE AND LABOR FORCE STATUS						
Married Coupled Families	116 353	57 334	117 329	55 831	122 261	57 499
Both husband and wife in labor force	57.4	63.4	59.0	64.0	59.4	63.1
Husband in labor force, wife not in labor force	24.2	30.4	22.5	28.5	23.2	30.4
Wife in labor force, husband not in labor force	6.8	3.7	7.6	5.1	6.3	4.0
Both husband and wife not in labor force	11.5	2.6	10.9	2.5	11.1	2.5
Other Families	40 834	26 508	40 610	27 063	40 084	25 470
Female householder, no husband present	67.7	67.8	69.1	72.5	66.5	70.7
In labor force	51.3	57.0	52.2	58.9	50.9	60.2
Not in labor force	16.4	10.8	16.9	13.6	15.6	10.5
Male householder, no wife present	32.3	32.2	30.9	27.5	33.5	29.3
In labor force	27.2	27.9	26.9	26.1	29.3	26.9
Not in labor force	5.1	4.2	4.0	1.4	4.2	2.4

Table AK-10. School Enrollment and Educational Attainment, 2007

(Number, percent.)

Item	State	U.S.
Enrollment		
Total population 3 years and over	651 727	289 295 761
Enrolled in school	185 067	79 329 527
Enrolled in preschool (percent)	5.7	6.2
Enrolled in grades K-12 (percent)	69.9	67.6
Enrolled in college or graduate school (percent)	24.4	26.2
Attainment		
Total population 25 years and over	421 818	197 892 369
Less than a high school diploma (percent)	9.5	15.5
High school diploma or more (percent)	90.5	84.5
Bachelor's degree or more (percent)	26.0	27.5
Graduate degree or more (percent)	9.9	10.1

Table AK-11. Educational Indicators

(Number, percent.)

Item	State	U.S.
Public Schools, 2006–2007 (except where noted)		
Number of school districts	54	17 742
Number of schools	509	99 639
Number of students	132 608	49 315 842
Student-teacher ratio	16.8	15.5
Expenditures per student (dollars)	$12 324	...
Averaged freshman graduation rate, 2005–2006	66.5	...
Dropout rate, grades 9–12, 2005–2006	8.0	3.7
Students eligible for free or reduced-price lunch (percent)	34.0	41.2
English-language learners (percent)	15.7	5.1
Students with IEP (percent)	13.4	12.7
Private Schools, 2007–2008 (except where noted)		
Number of schools	63	33 740
Number of students	4 173	5 072 451
High school graduates, 2006–2007	198	306 605
Student-teacher ratio	9.0	11.1

Table AK-12. Reported Voting and Registration of the Voting-Age Population, November 2008

(Number in thousands, percent.)

Item	Total population	Total citizen population	Registered — Total registered	Registered — Percent registered (total population)	Registered — Percent registered (total citizen population)	Voted — Total voted	Voted — Percent voted (total population)	Voted — Percent voted (total citizen population)
U.S. total	225 499	206 072	146 311	64.9	71.0	131 144	58.2	63.6
State total	488	468	345	70.8	73.7	304	62.4	65.0
Sex								
Male	246	241	171	69.6	71.1	152	61.8	63.2
Female	242	228	174	72.0	76.5	152	62.9	66.8
Race								
White alone	364	355	278	76.4	78.4	251	69.0	70.8
White non-Hispanic alone	351	344	271	77.1	78.7	245	69.8	71.2
Black alone	17	15	10	...	...	7	...	...
Asian alone	23	17	9	...	...	7	...	...
Hispanic (of any race)	15	13	9	...	...	8	...	...
White alone or in combination	390	380	294	75.5	77.3	266	68.3	69.9
Black alone or in combination	20	18	10	...	...	8	...	...
Asian alone or in combination	25	19	11	...	...	9	...	...

Table AK-13. Crime

(Number, rate per 100,000.)

Item	State 2007	State 2008	State Percent change	U.S. 2007	U.S. 2008	U.S. Percent change
Population	683 478	686 293	0.4	301 621 157	304 059 724	0.8
VIOLENT CRIME						
Number	4 519	4 474	-1.0	1 408 337	1 382 012	-1.9
Rate	661.2	651.9	-1.4	466.9	454.5	-2.7
Murder and Nonnegligent Manslaughter						
Number	44	28	-36.4	16 929	16 272	-3.9
Rate	6.4	4.1	-36.6	5.6	5.4	-4.7
Forcible Rape						
Number	529	441	-16.6	90 427	89 000	-1.6
Rate	77.4	64.3	-17.0	30.0	29.3	-2.4
Robbery						
Number	583	645	10.6	445 125	441 855	-0.7
Rate	85.3	94.0	10.2	147.6	145.3	-1.5
Aggravated Assault						
Number	3 363	3 360	-0.1	855 856	834 885	-2.5
Rate	492.0	489.6	-0.5	283.8	274.6	-3.2
PROPERTY CRIME						
Number	23 098	20 124	-12.9	9 843 481	9 767 915	-0.8
Rate	3 379.5	2 932.3	-13.2	3 263.5	3 212.5	-1.6
Burglary						
Number	3 682	3 240	-12.0	2 179 140	2 222 196	2.0
Rate	538.7	472.1	-12.4	722.5	730.8	1.2
Larceny-Theft						
Number	16 998	15 246	-10.3	6 568 572	6 588 873	0.3
Rate	2 487.0	2 221.5	-10.7	2 177.8	2 167.0	-0.5
Motor Vehicle Theft						
Number	2 418	1 638	-32.3	1 095 769	956 846	-12.7
Rate	353.8	238.7	-32.5	363.3	314.7	-13.4

Table AK-14. State Government Finances, 2007

(Dollars, percent distribution.)

Item	Thousands of dollars	Percent distribution
Total Revenue	12 477 998	X
General revenue	10 336 331	82.8
Intergovernmental revenue	2 288 253	18.3
Taxes	3 442 930	27.6
General sales	0	0.0
Selective sales	219 776	1.8
License taxes	127 226	1.0
Individual income tax	0	0.0
Corporate income tax	813 762	6.5
Other taxes	2 282 166	18.3
Current charges	540 355	4.3
Miscellaneous general revenue	4 064 793	32.6
Utility revenue	17 192	0.1
Liquor store revenue	0	0.0
Insurance trust revenue	2 124 475	17.0
Total Expenditure	9 191 744	100.0
Intergovernmental expenditure	1 365 793	14.9
Direct expenditure	7 825 951	85.1
Current operation	5 530 107	60.2
Capital outlay	959 289	10.4
Insurance benefits and repayments	825 260	9.0
Assistance and subsidies	182 754	2.0
Interest on debt	328 541	3.6
Exhibit: Salaries and wages	1 449 862	15.8
Total Expenditure	9 191 744	100.0
General expenditure	8 290 628	90.2
Intergovernmental expenditure	1 365 793	14.9
Direct expenditure	6 924 835	75.3
Education	1 985 407	21.6
Public welfare	1 478 593	16.1
Hospitals	31 850	0.3
Health	242 726	2.6
Highways	1 203 249	13.1
Police protection	78 978	0.9
Correction	237 144	2.6
Natural resources	273 914	3.0
Parks and recreation	14 224	0.2
Government administration	529 109	5.8
Interest on general debt	320 603	3.5
Other and unallocable	1 894 831	20.6
Utility expenditure	75 856	0.8
Liquor store expenditure	0	0.0
Insurance trust expenditure	825 260	9.0
Debt at End of Fiscal Year	6 553 080	X
Cash and Security Holdings	59 081 173	X

Table AK-15. State Government Tax Collections, 2008

(Dollars, percent distribution.)

Item	Thousands of dollars	Percent distribution
Total Taxes	8 424 714	X
Property taxes	81 518	1.0
Sales and gross receipts	279 569	3.3
Selective sales taxes	279 569	3.3
Alcoholic beverages	39 103	0.5
Amusements	9 456	0.1
Insurance premiums	54 698	0.6
Motor fuels	41 985	0.5
Public utilities	4 091	0.0
Tobacco products	73 451	0.9
Other selective sales	56 785	0.7
Licenses	142 914	1.7
Alcoholic beverages	1 924	0.0
Amusements	1	0.0
Corporation	878	0.0
Hunting and fishing	33 280	0.4
Motor vehicle	53 453	0.6
Public utility	354	0.0
Occupation and business, NEC	42 209	0.5
Other licenses	10 815	0.1
Income taxes	981 673	11.7
Corporation net income	981 673	11.7
Other taxes	6 939 040	82.4
Severance	6 939 040	82.4

Table AK-16. Agriculture
(Number, acres, and dollars.)

Item	2002		2007		Percent change, 2002–2007
	Number	Percent of total	Number	Percent of total	
Number of farms	609		686		12.6
Farm Size					
Average size of farm (acres)	1 479		1 285		-13.1
Farms by size (number of farms)					
Fewer than 50 acres	256	42.0	329	48.0	28.5
50 to 499 acres	255	41.9	267	38.9	4.7
500 acres or more	98	16.1	90	13.1	-8.2
Land (Acres)					
Total land in farms	900 715		881 585		-2.1
Total cropland	98 131	10.9	86 238	9.8	-12.1
Total harvested cropland	31 824	3.5	30 772	3.5	-3.3
Irrigated land	2 742	0.3	3 730	0.4	36.0
Value of Sales (Dollars)					
Agricultural products sold ($1,000)	46 143		57 019		23.6
Average sales per farm	75 768		83 119		9.7
Sales of crops	20 543	44.5	24 749	43.4	20.5
Sales of livestock, poultry, and their products	25 600	55.5	32 271	56.6	26.1
Value of Sales (Number of Farms)					
Less than $10,000	362	59.4	403	58.7	11.3
$10,000 to $99,999	176	28.9	206	30.0	17.0
$100,000 to $999,999	64	10.5	66	9.6	3.1
$1,000,000 or more	7	1.1	11	1.6	57.1
Farms by Type of Organization (Number of Farms)					
Family	497	81.6	550	80.2	10.7
Partnership	30	4.9	42	6.1	40.0
Corporation	36	5.9	52	7.6	44.4
Other: cooperative, estate or trust, institutional, etc	46	7.6	42	6.1	-8.7
Value of Land and Buildings (Dollars)					
Estimated market value of land and buildings ($1,000)	344 607		330 816		-4.0
Land and buildings average value per farm	502 342		543 213		8.1
Average value per acre	391		367		-6.1
Government Payments					
Number of farms receiving government payments	72	11.8	78	11.4	8.3
Payments (thousands of dollars)	1 765		1 645		-6.8
Average payment per farm	24 516		21 086		-14.0
Farm Operator Characteristics					
Farm operators whose principal occupation is farming	370	60.8	365	53.2	-1.4
Farm operators whose principal occupation is other	239	39.2	321	46.8	34.3
Average age principal operator (years)	55.2		56.2		1.8

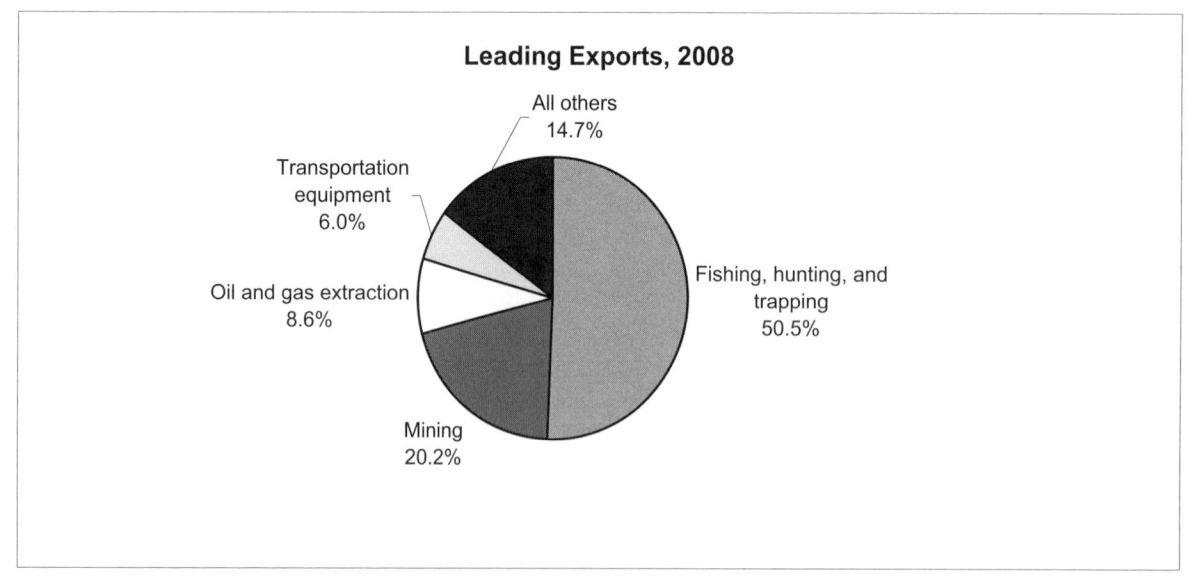

Leading Exports, 2008

All others 14.7%

Transportation equipment 6.0%

Oil and gas extraction 8.6%

Mining 20.2%

Fishing, hunting, and trapping 50.5%

Facts and Figures

Location: Southwestern United States; bordered on the North by Utah, on the East by New Mexico, on the South by Mexico, and on the West by Nevada and California; Arizona is one of the Four Corner states—at its NE corner it touches Colorado, New Mexico, and Utah

Area: 113,998 sq. mi. (295,254 sq. km.); rank—6th

Population: 6,500,180 (2008 est.); rank—16th

Principal Cities: capital—Phoenix; largest—Phoenix

Statehood: February 14, 1912; 48th state

U.S. Congress: 2 senators, 8 representatives

State Motto: *Ditat Deus* ("God enriches")

State Song: "Arizona"

State Nickname: The Grand Canyon State

Abbreviations: AZ; Ariz.

State Symbols: flower—saguaro cactus blossom; tree—paloverde; bird—cactus wren

At a Glance

- With an increase in population of 26.7 percent, Arizona ranked 2nd among the states in growth from 2000 to 2008.
- An estimated 37,772 marriages took place in Arizona in 2008, compared to 23,985 divorces.
- The 2007 home ownership rate in Arizona was 70.4 percent; its ranking of 25th among the states was tied with that of Missouri and South Dakota.
- Arizona's median household income in 2007 was $49,889, 22nd among the states.
- In Arizona, 14.2 percent of the population lived below the poverty level in 2007, ranking it 14th.
- In 2006-07, 19.6 percent of Arizonans did not have health insurance, compared to 15.5 percent of the total U.S. population.
- In 2007, 3.9 percent of Arizonans were unemployed, compared to 4.6 percent nationwide.
- Arizona ranked 30th in the nation with 25.3 percent of its population 25 years old and over having at least a bachelor's degree in 2007.
- Arizona's violent crime rate in 2007 was 482.7 per 100,000 population, compared to 466.9 for the entire nation.
- Arizona had one physician for every 403 people in 2007, compared to one physician for every 325 people nationwide.
- In the 2008 election, 56 percent of Arizona's eligible voters voted, compared to 61.7 percent of eligible voters nationwide.
- Arizona ranked 28th among the states receiving federal aid in 2007, with $1,365 per capita.
- Arizona's gross domestic product was $247 billion in 2007; it ranked 17th among the states.
- With $19.2 billion in exports in 2007, Arizona ranked 18th in exports.
- Arizonans consumed 1.5 trillion Btu's of energy in 2006; the state ranked 24th in total consumption.
- In 2007, Arizona exported $506 million worth of agricultural products, less than 1 percent of the U.S. total.

Table AZ-1. Population by Sex, Age, Race, and Hispanic Origin

(Number, percent.)

Sex, age, race, and Hispanic origin	1990	2000	2008	Average annual percent change, 2000–2008
Total Population	3 665 228	5 130 632	6 500 180	3.0
Percent of total U.S. population	1.5	1.8	2.1	X
Sex				
Male	1 810 691	2 561 057	3 256 691	3.0
Female	1 854 537	2 569 575	3 243 489	3.0
Age				
Under 5 years	292 859	382 386	515 910	3.8
5 to 19 years	801 019	1 135 802	1 361 967	2.3
20 to 64 years	2 092 576	2 944 605	3 759 730	3.1
65 years and over	478 774	667 839	862 573	3.3
Median age (years)	32.0	34.2	35.1	X
Race and Hispanic Origin[1]				
One race				
White	2 963 186	3 873 611	5 623 026	4.8
Black	110 524	158 873	270 159	6.9
American Indian and Alaskan Native	203 527	255 879	315 727	2.7
Asian[2]	55 206	92 236	162 014	7.3
Native Hawaiian and Other Pacific Islander	X	6 733	13 259	8.8
Two or more races	X	146 526	115 995	-2.9
Hispanic (of any race)	688 338	1 295 617	1 955 630	5.3

[1]Data on race in 2000 and 2008 are not comparable to 1990. Individuals could only report one race in the 1990 census but could report one or more races on the 2000 census.
[2]Data in 1990 refer to Asian and Pacific Islanders.

Table AZ-2. Marital Status

(Number, percent distribution.)

Sex and marital status	1990	2000	2007
Males, 15 Years and Over	1 384 911	1 966 032	2 457 859
Never married	29.6	29.6	34.6
Now married, except separated	57.3	56.4	50.4
Separated	1.8	1.6	1.5
Widowed	2.3	2.6	2.5
Divorced	9.0	9.8	10.9
Females, 15 Years and Over	1 447 361	2 013 304	2 479 898
Never married	21.7	22.6	26.7
Now married, except separated	54.1	53.6	48.1
Separated	2.2	2.1	2.3
Widowed	10.4	9.4	9.2
Divorced	11.6	12.3	13.8

Table AZ-3. Households and Housing Characteristics

(Number, percent, and dollars.)

Item	1990	2000	2007	Average annual percent change, 2000–2007
Total Households	1 368 843	1 901 327	2 251 546	2.4
Family households	940 106	1 287 367	1 491 772	2.1
Married-couple family	747 806	986 303	1 114 544	1.8
Other family	192 300	301 064	377 228	3.3
Male householder, no wife present	49 980	90 283	112 701	3.2
Female householder, no husband present	142 320	210 781	264 527	3.3
Nonfamily households	428 737	613 960	759 774	3.1
Householder living alone	337 681	472 006	606 611	3.6
Householder not living alone	91 056	141 954	153 163	1.1
Housing Characteristics				
Total housing units	1 659 430	2 189 189	2 667 550	2.9
Occupied housing units	1 368 843	1 901 327	2 251 546	2.4
Owner-occupied	878 561	1 293 556	1 533 145	2.5
Renter-occupied	490 282	607 771	718 401	2.4
Average size	2.62	2.64	2.77	X
Financial Characteristics				
Median gross rent of renter-occupied housing units (dollars)	438	619	819	4.1
Median monthly owner costs for housing units with a mortgage (dollars)	769	1 039	1 711	7.4
Median value of owner-occupied housing units (dollars)	79 700	121 300	231 300	9.7

Table AZ-4. Median Income and Poverty Status, 2007

(Number, percent.)

Characteristic	State		U.S.	
	Number	Percent	Number	Percent
Median Income				
Households (dollars)	49 889	X	50 740	X
Families (dollars)	58 627	X	61 173	X
Below Poverty Level				
Sex				
Male	404 883	13.1	16 576 071	11.5
Female	476 374	15.2	21 476 176	14.3
Age				
Under 18 years	330 910	20.2	13 097 100	18.0
Related children under 18 years	322 332	19.8	12 728 964	17.6
18 to 64 years	481 357	12.7	21 495 507	11.6
65 years and over	68 990	8.6	3 459 640	9.5

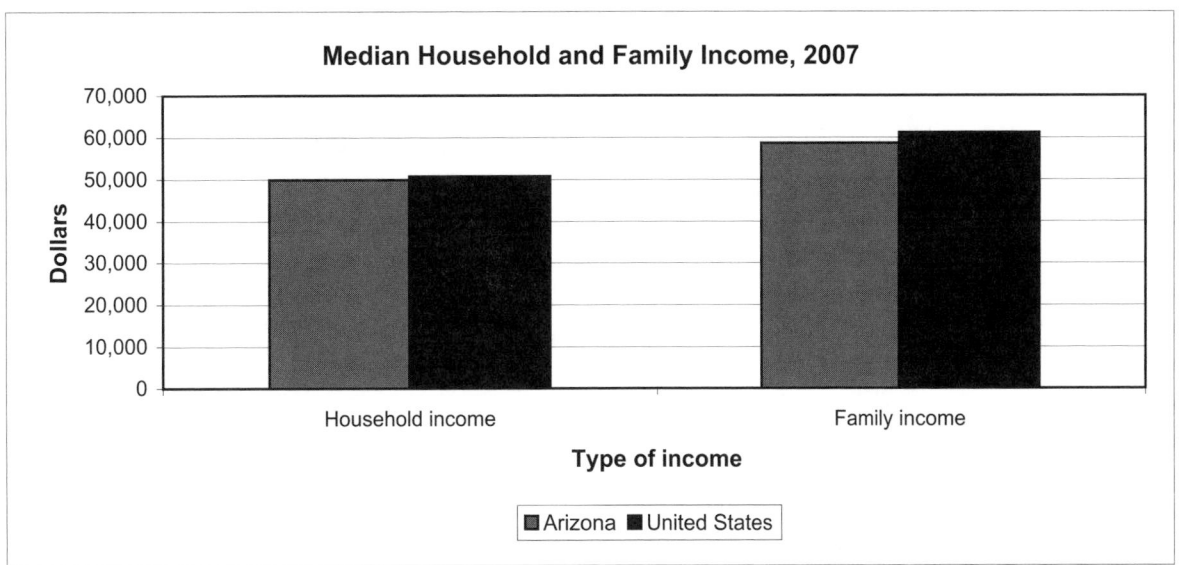

Table AZ-5. Health Insurance Coverage Status for All Persons and Children Under 18 Years of Age

(Number, percent.)

Item	2000	2001	2002	2003	2004	2005	2006	2007
ALL PERSONS	5 199	5 316	5 442	5 576	5 768	6 047	6 269	6 368
Covered by Private or Government Health Insurance								
Number	4 365	4 383	4 555	4 648	4 807	4 864	4 958	5 204
Percent	84.0	82.5	83.7	83.3	83.3	80.4	79.1	81.7
Not Covered								
Number	834	933	887	929	961	1 183	1 311	1 164
Percent	16.0	17.5	16.3	16.7	16.7	19.6	20.9	18.3
Percent in the U.S. not covered	13.7	14.1	14.7	15.1	14.9	15.3	15.8	15.3
CHILDREN UNDER 18 YEARS OF AGE	1 435	1 532	1 478	1 529	1 567	1 627	1 662	1 697
Covered by Private or Government Health Insurance								
Number	1 247	1 262	1 264	1 307	1 350	1 359	1 379	1 463
Percent	86.9	82.4	85.5	85.5	86.2	83.6	83.0	86.2
Not Covered								
Number	188	270	214	222	217	267	283	234
Percent	13.1	17.6	14.5	14.5	13.8	16.4	17.0	13.8
Percent in the U.S. not covered	11.6	11.3	11.2	11.0	10.5	10.9	11.7	11.0

Table AZ-6. Employment Status by Demographic Group, Preliminary 2008

(Number, percent.)

Characteristic	Civilian noninstitutional population	Civilian labor force		Employment		Unemployed	
		Number	Percent of population	Number	Percent of population	Number	Unemployment rate
TOTAL	4 868	3 133	64.4	2 948	60.6	185	5.9
Sex							
Men	2 400	1 723	72.0	1 613	67.2	110	6.4
Women	2 468	1 410	57.0	1 336	54.1	75	5.3
Race, Sex, and Hispanic Origin							
White	4 281	2 769	64.7	2 611	61.0	158	5.7
Men	2 113	1 531	72.5	1 434	67.9	97	6.3
Women	2 168	1 238	57.1	1 176	54.2	62	5.0
Black or African American	200	130	65.0	118	58.9	12	9.3
Men	98	67	68.5	62	62.8	6	8.3
Women	102	63	61.6	56	55.2	7	10.4
Hispanic	1 309	863	65.9	790	60.3	73	8.4
Men	666	530	79.7	478	71.8	52	9.8
Women	644	332	51.6	312	48.4	21	6.3
Age							
16 to 19 years	348	136	39.0	109	31.2	27	20.0
20 to 24 years	402	299	74.3	263	65.5	35	11.9
25 to 34 years	926	753	81.3	712	76.9	41	5.4
35 to 44 years	855	688	80.5	659	77.1	29	4.2
45 to 54 years	840	676	80.5	648	77.2	28	4.1
55 to 64 years	727	454	62.4	437	60.2	16	3.6
65 years and over	771	128	16.7	120	15.6	9	6.6

Note: Data in Table 6 are from the Current Population Survey (CPS) and do not match the estimates in Table 7. See notes and definitions for more details.

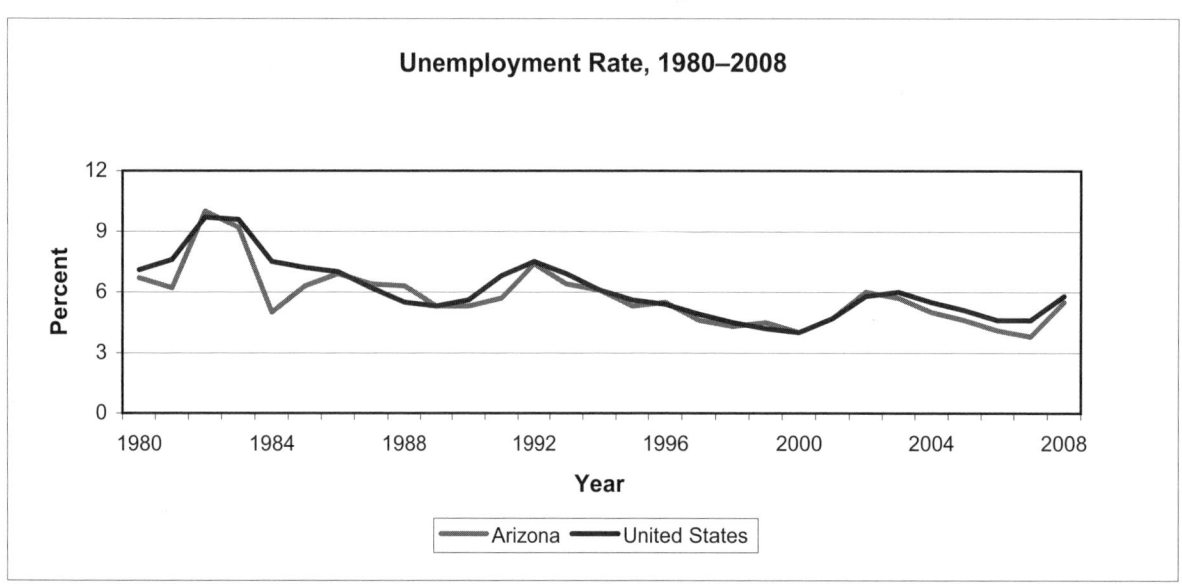

Table AZ-7. Employment Status of the Civilian Noninstitutional Population Age 16 Years and Over

(Number, percent.)

Year	Civilian labor force	Civilian participation rate	Employed	Unemployed	Unemployment rate
1998	2 382 361	64.7	2 278 864	103 497	4.3
1999	2 466 281	65.5	2 355 357	110 924	4.5
2000	2 505 306	65.1	2 404 916	100 390	4.0
2001	2 574 976	65.1	2 453 453	121 523	4.7
2002	2 674 357	65.8	2 512 714	161 643	6.0
2003	2 728 952	65.4	2 573 137	155 815	5.7
2004	2 788 964	64.8	2 650 277	138 687	5.0
2005	2 866 720	64.3	2 733 551	133 169	4.6
2006	2 971 211	64.2	2 849 057	122 154	4.1
2007	3 036 011	63.8	2 920 242	115 769	3.8
2008	3 132 667	64.2	2 960 199	172 468	5.5

Table AZ-8. Employment and Average Wages by Industry

(Estimates for 2001–2006 are based on the 2002 North American Industry Classification System [NAICS]. Estimates for 2007 are based on the 2007 NAICS.)

Industry	2001	2002	2003	2004	2005	2006	2007
	Number of jobs						
WAGE AND SALARY EMPLOYMENT BY INDUSTRY	2 377 452	2 377 704	2 417 608	2 503 649	2 637 603	2 766 672	2 800 193
Farm Wage and Salary Employment	12 097	11 816	12 774	13 222	14 098	13 774	14 000
Nonfarm Wage and Salary Employment	2 365 355	2 365 888	2 404 834	2 490 427	2 623 505	2 752 898	2 786 193
Private wage and salary employment	1 966 914	1 955 932	1 984 378	2 064 867	2 191 230	2 315 466	2 337 626
Forestry, fishing, hunting, and other	21 185	20 648	19 153	18 908	17 557	17 846	16 573
Mining	9 546	8 750	8 016	8 310	8 619	9 904	11 586
Utilities	11 026	11 183	11 423	11 475	11 861	12 444	12 782
Construction	180 387	179 557	183 814	199 684	228 025	248 912	232 405
Manufacturing	202 636	184 941	177 488	178 122	181 376	186 541	183 073
Durable goods manufacturing	164 676	149 025	141 694	142 994	146 113	150 636	147 627
Nondurable goods manufacturing	37 960	35 916	35 794	35 128	35 263	35 905	35 446
Wholesale trade	97 415	95 704	94 790	97 390	102 050	107 730	110 960
Retail trade	277 134	279 730	285 604	298 974	318 245	333 749	342 831
Transportation and warehousing	66 009	65 905	66 278	68 389	70 773	75 184	75 771
Information	53 860	52 114	49 741	48 060	45 143	44 635	43 052
Finance and insurance	111 601	113 279	118 576	122 018	128 218	134 617	134 777
Real estate and rental and leasing	45 822	45 828	44 906	47 351	50 904	53 560	54 278
Professional and technical services	111 188	108 745	110 731	116 823	125 544	136 772	140 614
Management of companies and enterprises	20 883	20 488	20 788	22 483	23 342	25 290	26 999
Administrative and waste services	198 778	193 157	197 562	206 551	228 176	243 074	243 521
Educational services	24 791	28 670	31 624	34 783	38 569	41 112	43 374
Health care and social assistance	200 607	209 249	222 470	232 739	244 914	258 749	271 524
Arts, entertainment, and recreation	30 761	30 778	30 887	32 063	33 280	35 425	37 376
Accommodation and food services	203 836	203 983	206 615	214 918	227 138	237 427	241 080
Other services, except public administration	99 449	103 223	103 912	105 826	107 496	112 495	115 050
Government and government enterprises	398 441	409 956	420 456	425 560	432 275	437 432	448 567
	Dollars						
AVERAGE WAGES AND SALARIES BY INDUSTRY	33 023	33 706	34 697	36 302	37 871	39 711	41 223
Average Farm Wages and Salaries	26 582	31 843	25 924	27 164	29 019	30 061	31 948
Average Nonfarm Wages and Salaries	33 056	33 716	34 744	36 350	37 919	39 759	41 269
Average private wages and salaries	33 037	33 500	34 479	36 108	37 636	39 440	40 934
Forestry, fishing, hunting, and other	15 000	15 545	16 695	17 783	19 391	20 452	22 106
Mining	47 327	46 858	50 101	53 604	56 876	59 332	62 586
Utilities	64 513	66 922	66 084	66 409	72 169	74 739	80 834
Construction	34 024	34 449	34 948	36 078	38 074	40 917	42 534
Manufacturing	47 966	48 852	50 493	52 611	53 625	56 636	58 385
Durable goods manufacturing	51 398	52 686	54 476	56 703	57 774	61 133	62 803
Nondurable goods manufacturing	33 080	32 943	34 727	35 953	36 432	37 771	39 983
Wholesale trade	48 679	48 724	50 011	53 767	55 626	57 770	61 370
Retail trade	24 426	24 793	25 601	26 430	27 490	28 377	28 500
Transportation and warehousing	37 053	37 481	38 670	41 067	42 134	43 454	45 357
Information	43 469	42 746	43 646	45 719	47 926	51 187	53 269
Finance and insurance	46 449	47 387	50 437	52 241	57 277	58 946	59 585
Real estate and rental and leasing	30 662	31 981	33 447	35 971	40 036	43 089	42 353
Professional and technical services	49 127	49 724	49 939	52 428	56 346	58 703	62 108
Management of companies and enterprises	53 305	54 001	59 269	68 808	63 437	65 703	74 253
Administrative and waste services	23 489	24 275	25 003	26 408	27 613	28 811	30 084
Educational services	27 301	28 842	29 397	32 537	32 468	32 360	33 348
Health care and social assistance	34 204	35 753	37 047	38 938	40 260	42 454	44 359
Arts, entertainment, and recreation	29 143	30 035	29 705	29 828	30 015	32 399	31 854
Accommodation and food services	14 474	14 858	15 424	16 272	16 987	17 673	18 908
Other services, except public administration	21 371	21 595	22 236	23 085	24 151	25 311	26 488
Government and government enterprises	33 154	34 743	35 996	37 526	39 353	41 449	43 013

Table AZ-9. Employment Characteristics by Family Type

(Number, percent.)

Family type and labor force status	2005		2006		2007	
	Total	Families with own children under 18 years	Total	Families with own children under 18 years	Total	Families with own children under 18 years
TOTAL FAMILIES	1 459 460	689 999	1 476 269	684 125	1 491 772	691 171
FAMILY TYPE AND LABOR FORCE STATUS						
Married Coupled Families	1 078 453	462 206	1 104 808	466 953	1 114 544	466 642
Both husband and wife in labor force	45.4	55.9	46.5	57.6	46.1	56.7
Husband in labor force, wife not in labor force	25.3	36.6	25.6	35.7	25.9	37.0
Wife in labor force, husband not in labor force	7.0	4.0	6.5	3.9	6.7	3.8
Both husband and wife not in labor force	22.2	3.4	21.4	2.8	21.3	2.5
Other Families	381 007	227 793	371 461	217 172	377 228	224 529
Female householder, no husband present	71.1	72.8	69.0	73.3	70.1	72.4
In labor force	50.7	58.7	49.3	59.4	50.4	58.0
Not in labor force	20.4	14.1	19.7	13.9	19.7	14.4
Male householder, no wife present	28.9	27.2	31.0	26.7	29.9	27.6
In labor force	24.1	24.4	25.7	24.7	24.3	25.1
Not in labor force	4.8	2.8	5.3	2.0	5.5	2.5

Table AZ-10. School Enrollment and Educational Attainment, 2007

(Number, percent.)

Item	State	U.S.
Enrollment		
Total population 3 years and over	6 045 187	289 295 761
Enrolled in school	1 650 562	79 329 527
Enrolled in preschool (percent)	5.4	6.2
Enrolled in grades K-12 (percent)	70.7	67.6
Enrolled in college or graduate school (percent)	23.9	26.2
Attainment		
Total population 25 years and over	4 075 825	197 892 369
Less than a high school diploma (percent)	16.5	15.5
High school diploma or more (percent)	83.5	84.5
Bachelor's degree or more (percent)	25.3	27.5
Graduate degree or more (percent)	9.2	10.1

Table AZ-11. Educational Indicators

(Number, percent.)

Item	State	U.S.
Public Schools, 2006–2007 (except where noted)		
Number of school districts	610	17 742
Number of schools	2 077	99 639
Number of students	1 068 249	49 315 842
Student-teacher ratio	20.3	15.5
Expenditures per student (dollars)	$7 338	. . .
Averaged freshman graduation rate, 2005–2006	70.5	. . .
Dropout rate, grades 9–12, 2005–2006	6.4	3.7
Students eligible for free or reduced-price lunch (percent)	40.7	41.2
English-language learners (percent)	12.1	5.1
Students with IEP (percent)	11.6	12.7
Private Schools, 2007–2008 (except where noted)		
Number of schools	361	33 740
Number of students	51 590	5 072 451
High school graduates, 2006–2007	2 593	306 605
Student-teacher ratio	12.2	11.1

Table AZ-12. Reported Voting and Registration of the Voting-Age Population, November 2008

(Number in thousands, percent.)

Item	Total population	Total citizen population	Registered			Voted		
			Total registered	Percent registered (total population)	Percent registered (total citizen population)	Total voted	Percent voted (total population)	Percent voted (total citizen population)
U.S. total	225 499	206 072	146 311	64.9	71.0	131 144	58.2	63.6
State total	4 688	4 169	2 874	61.3	68.9	2 497	53.3	59.9
Sex								
Male	2 326	2 067	1 382	59.4	66.9	1 191	51.2	57.6
Female	2 362	2 102	1 492	63.2	71.0	1 306	55.3	62.1
Race								
White alone	4 163	3 678	2 539	61.0	69.0	2 226	53.5	60.5
White non-Hispanic alone	2 970	2 916	2 150	72.4	73.7	1 952	65.7	67.0
Black alone	185	182	121	65.2	66.4	95	51.5	52.4
Asian alone	105	80	52	49.7	65.1	48	45.7	59.9
Hispanic (of any race)	1 227	796	410	33.4	51.5	291	23.7	36.6
White alone or in combination	4 225	3 740	2 580	61.1	69.0	2 264	53.6	60.5
Black alone or in combination	206	198	131	63.6	66.4	106	51.2	53.5
Asian alone or in combination	113	88	57	50.0	64.0	52	46.3	59.3

Table AZ-13. Crime

(Number, rate per 100,000.)

Item	State			U.S.		
	2007	2008	Percent change	2007	2008	Percent change
Population	6 338 755	6 500 180	2.5	301 621 157	304 059 724	0.8
VIOLENT CRIME						
Number	30 600	29 059	-5.0	1 408 337	1 382 012	-1.9
Rate	482.7	447.0	-7.4	466.9	454.5	-2.7
Murder and Nonnegligent Manslaughter						
Number	468	407	-13.0	16 929	16 272	-3.9
Rate	7.4	6.3	-15.2	5.6	5.4	-4.7
Forcible Rape						
Number	1 856	1 673	-9.9	90 427	89 000	-1.6
Rate	29.3	25.7	-12.1	30.0	29.3	-2.4
Robbery						
Number	9 618	9 697	0.8	445 125	441 855	-0.7
Rate	151.7	149.2	-1.7	147.6	145.3	-1.5
Aggravated Assault						
Number	18 658	17 282	-7.4	855 856	834 885	-2.5
Rate	294.3	265.9	-9.7	283.8	274.6	-3.2
PROPERTY CRIME						
Number	279 794	278 920	-0.3	9 843 481	9 767 915	-0.8
Rate	4 414.0	4 291.0	-2.8	3 263.5	3 212.5	-1.6
Burglary						
Number	57 825	56 481	-2.3	2 179 140	2 222 196	2.0
Rate	912.2	868.9	-4.7	722.5	730.8	1.2
Larceny-Theft						
Number	173 580	185 221	6.7	6 568 572	6 588 873	0.3
Rate	2 738.4	2 849.5	4.1	2 177.8	2 167.0	-0.5
Motor Vehicle Theft						
Number	48 389	37 218	-23.1	1 095 769	956 846	-12.7
Rate	763.4	572.6	-25.0	363.3	314.7	-13.4

Table AZ-14. State Government Finances, 2007

(Dollars, percent distribution.)

Item	Thousands of dollars	Percent distribution
Total Revenue	29 875 612	X
General revenue	24 181 785	80.9
Intergovernmental revenue	8 122 068	27.2
Taxes	12 396 587	41.5
General sales	5 683 866	19.0
Selective sales	1 655 038	5.5
License taxes	402 597	1.3
Individual income tax	3 196 156	10.7
Corporate income tax	986 170	3.3
Other taxes	472 760	1.6
Current charges	1 598 695	5.4
Miscellaneous general revenue	2 064 435	6.9
Utility revenue	28 301	0.1
Liquor store revenue	0	0.0
Insurance trust revenue	5 665 526	19.0
Total Expenditure	28 332 841	100.0
Intergovernmental expenditure	9 860 543	34.8
Direct expenditure	18 472 298	65.2
Current operation	13 380 387	47.2
Capital outlay	1 313 852	4.6
Insurance benefits and repayments	2 828 181	10.0
Assistance and subsidies	480 745	1.7
Interest on debt	469 133	1.7
Exhibit: Salaries and wages	3 152 977	11.1
Total Expenditure	28 332 841	100.0
General expenditure	25 473 702	89.9
Intergovernmental expenditure	9 860 543	34.8
Direct expenditure	15 613 159	55.1
Education	9 160 086	32.3
Public welfare	7 249 710	25.6
Hospitals	70 490	0.2
Health	1 450 493	5.1
Highways	1 968 139	6.9
Police protection	252 728	0.9
Correction	946 922	3.3
Natural resources	336 109	1.2
Parks and recreation	204 024	0.7
Government administration	706 242	2.5
Interest on general debt	466 409	1.6
Other and unallocable	2 662 350	9.4
Utility expenditure	30 958	0.1
Liquor store expenditure	0	0.0
Insurance trust expenditure	2 828 181	10.0
Debt at End of Fiscal Year	9 546 428	X
Cash and Security Holdings	51 214 388	X

Table AZ-15. State Government Tax Collections, 2008

(Dollars, percent distribution.)

Item	Thousands of dollars	Percent distribution
Total Taxes	13 705 901	X
Property taxes	901 872	6.6
Sales and gross receipts	8 146 095	59.4
General sales and gross receipts	6 433 468	46.9
Selective sales taxes	1 712 627	12.5
Alcoholic beverages	64 556	0.5
Amusements	569	0.0
Insurance premiums	470 297	3.4
Motor fuels	731 345	5.3
Pari-mutuels	430	0.0
Public utilities	38 010	0.3
Tobacco products	407 420	3.0
Licenses	420 770	3.1
Alcoholic beverages	11 994	0.1
Amusements	37	0.0
Corporation	23 226	0.2
Hunting and fishing	29 232	0.2
Motor vehicle	218 763	1.6
Motor vehicle operators	27 082	0.2
Occupation and business, NEC	98 925	0.7
Other licenses	11 511	0.1
Income taxes	4 193 087	30.6
Individual income	3 408 576	24.9
Corporation net income	784 511	5.7
Other taxes	44 077	0.3
Death and gift	320	0.0
Severance	43 757	0.3

Table AZ-16. Agriculture

(Number, acres, and dollars.)

Item	2002		2007		Percent change, 2002–2007
	Number	Percent of total	Number	Percent of total	
Number of farms	7 294		15 637		114.4
Farm Size					
Average size of farm (acres)	3 645		1 670		-54.2
Farms by size (number of farms)					
Fewer than 50 acres	4 231	58.0	12 530	80.1	196.1
50 to 499 acres	1 778	24.4	1 847	11.8	3.9
500 acres or more	1 285	17.6	1 260	8.1	-1.9
Land (Acres)					
Total land in farms	26 586 577		26 117 899		-1.8
Total cropland	1 261 894	4.7	1 205 425	4.6	-4.5
Total harvested cropland	887 966	3.3	832 406	3.2	-6.3
Irrigated land	931 735	3.5	876 158	3.4	-6.0
Value of Sales (Dollars)					
Agricultural products sold ($1,000)	2 395 447		3 234 552		35.0
Average sales per farm	328 413		206 852		-37.0
Sales of crops	1 587 775	66.3	1 913 014	59.1	20.5
Sales of livestock, poultry, and their products	807 672	33.7	1 321 538	40.9	63.6
Value of Sales (Number of Farms)					
Less than $10,000	4 690	64.3	12 730	81.4	171.4
$10,000 to $99,999	1 412	19.4	1 854	11.9	31.3
$100,000 to $999,999	796	10.9	663	4.2	-16.7
$1,000,000 or more	396	5.4	390	2.5	-1.5
Farms by Type of Organization (Number of Farms)					
Family	5 695	78.1	13 721	87.7	140.9
Partnership	841	11.5	962	6.2	14.4
Corporation	593	8.1	729	4.7	22.9
Other: cooperative, estate or trust, institutional, etc	165	2.3	225	1.4	36.4
Value of Land and Buildings (Dollars)					
Estimated market value of land and buildings ($1,000)	19 545 145		10 625 602		-45.6
Land and buildings average value per farm	1 249 929		1 456 759		16.5
Average value per acre	748		398		-46.8
Government Payments					
Number of farms receiving government payments	833	11.4	1 140	7.3	36.9
Payments (thousands of dollars)	31 760		55 947		76.2
Average payment per farm	38 127		49 077		28.7
Farm Operator Characteristics					
Farm operators whose principal occupation is farming	4 296	58.9	9 553	61.1	122.4
Farm operators whose principal occupation is other	2 998	41.1	6 084	38.9	102.9
Average age principal operator (years)	54.9		58.5		6.6

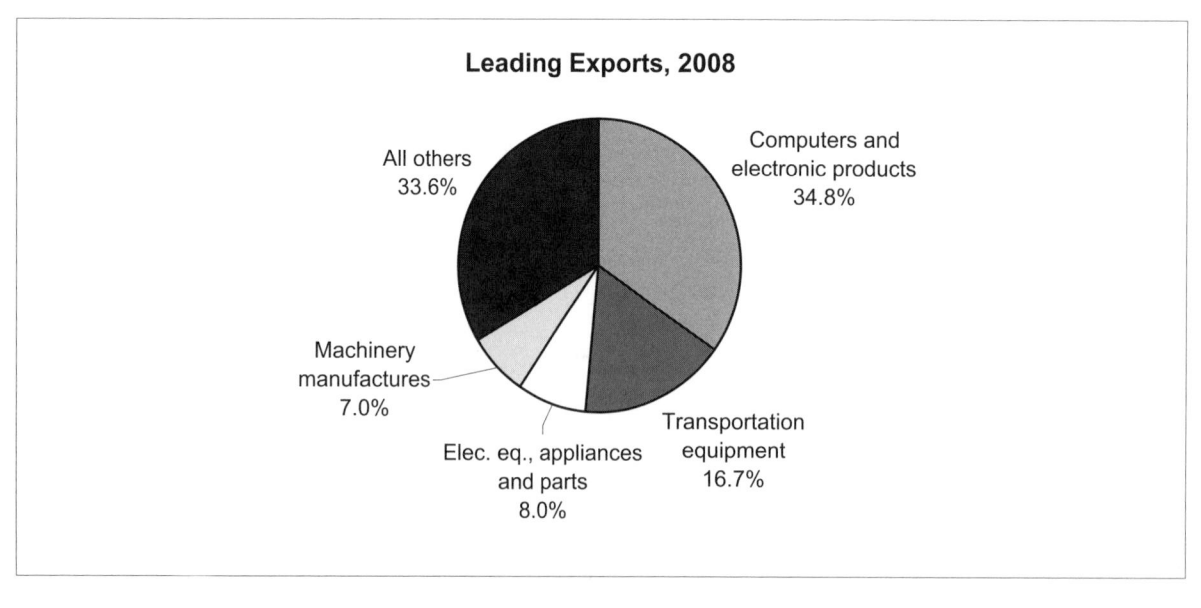

Leading Exports, 2008

All others 33.6%

Computers and electronic products 34.8%

Machinery manufactures 7.0%

Elec. eq., appliances and parts 8.0%

Transportation equipment 16.7%

ARKANSAS

Facts and Figures

Location: South central United States; bordered on the N by Missouri, on the E by Tennessee and Mississippi, on the S by Louisiana, and on the W by Oklahoma and Texas

Area: 53,179 sq. mi. (137,733 sq. km.); rank—29th

Population: 2,855,390 (2008 est.); rank—32nd

Principal Cities: capital—Little Rock; largest—Little Rock

Statehood: June 15, 1836; 25th state

U.S. Congress: 2 senators, 4 representatives

State Motto: *Regnat populus* ("The people rule")

State Song: "Arkansas"

State Nicknames: The Natural State; The Land of Opportunity

Abbreviations: AR; Ark.

State Symbols: flower—apple blossom; tree—pine; bird—mockingbird

At a Glance

- With an increase in population of 6.8 percent, Arkansas ranked 21st among the states in growth from 2000 to 2008.
- An estimated 30,961 marriages took place in Arkansas in 2008, compared to 15,908 divorces.
- The 2007 home ownership rate in Arkansas was 69.5 percent, giving it a ranking of 33rd among the states.
- Arkansas's median household income in 2007 was $38,134, 48th among the states.
- In Arkansas, 17.9 percent of the population lived below the poverty level in 2007, ranking it 4th.
- In 2006-07, 17.5 percent of Arkansans did not have health insurance, compared to 15.5 percent of the total U.S. population.
- In 2007, 5.6 percent of Arkansans were unemployed, compared to 4.6 percent nationwide.
- Arkansas ranked 48th in the nation with 19.3 percent of its population 25 years old and over having a bachelor's degree in 2007.
- Arkansas's violent crime rate in 2007 was 529.4 per 100,000 population, compared to 466.9 for the entire nation.
- Arkansas had one physician for every 433 people in 2007, compared to one physician for every 325 people nationwide.
- In the 2008 election, 53.4 percent of Arkansas's eligible voters voted, compared to 61.7 percent of eligible voters nationwide.
- Arkansas ranked 15th among the states receiving federal aid in 2007, with $1,581 per capita.
- Arkansas's gross domestic product was $95 billion in 2007; it ranked 34th among the states.
- With $4.9 billion in exports in 2007, Arkansas ranked 34th in exports.
- Arkansans consumed 1.14 trillion Btu's of energy in 2006; the state ranked 30th in total consumption.
- In 2007, Arkansas exported $2.1 billion worth of agricultural products, about 2.6 percent of the U.S. total.

Table AR-1. Population by Sex, Age, Race, and Hispanic Origin

(Number, percent.)

Sex, age, race, and Hispanic origin	1990	2000	2008	Average annual percent change, 2000–2008
Total Population	2 350 725	2 673 400	2 855 390	0.8
Percent of total U.S. population	0.9	0.9	0.9	X
Sex				
Male	1 133 076	1 304 693	1 398 635	0.9
Female	1 217 649	1 368 707	1 456 755	0.8
Age				
Under 5 years	164 667	181 585	202 070	1.3
5 to 19 years	530 770	578 924	578 232	0.0
20 to 64 years	1 305 230	1 538 872	1 667 883	1.0
65 years and over	350 058	374 019	407 205	1.1
Median age (years)	33.7	36.0	37.2	X
Race and Hispanic Origin[1]				
One race				
White	1 944 744	2 138 598	2 306 697	1.0
Black	373 912	418 950	450 037	0.9
American Indian and Alaskan Native	12 773	17 808	24 302	4.0
Asian[2]	12 530	20 220	30 654	5.3
Native Hawaiian and Other Pacific Islander	X	1 668	2 883	7.1
Two or more races	X	35 744	40 817	1.7
Hispanic (of any race)	19 876	86 866	159 525	7.9

[1]Data on race in 2000 and 2008 are not comparable to 1990. Individuals could only report one race in the 1990 census but could report one or more races on the 2000 census.
[2]Data in 1990 refer to Asian and Pacific Islanders.

Table AR-2. Marital Status

(Number, percent distribution.)

Sex and marital status	1990	2000	2007
Males, 15 Years and Over	868 546	1 015 594	1 091 269
Never married	24.2	24.2	27.7
Now married, except separated	63.2	61.0	56.1
Separated	1.7	1.6	2.0
Widowed	2.9	2.7	2.9
Divorced	8.1	10.4	11.3
Females, 15 Years and Over	966 364	1 096 069	1 160 527
Never married	17.5	18.4	21.6
Now married, except separated	56.5	55.7	51.3
Separated	2.1	2.2	2.7
Widowed	14.4	12.2	12.0
Divorced	9.4	11.6	12.3

Table AR-3. Households and Housing Characteristics

(Number, percent, and dollars.)

Item	1990	2000	2007	Average annual percent change, 2000–2007
Total Households	891 179	1 042 696	1 102 734	0.8
Family households	651 555	732 261	756 113	0.5
Married-couple family	527 358	566 401	570 075	0.1
Other family	124 197	165 860	186 038	1.7
Male householder, no wife present	25 273	39 299	44 877	1.9
Female householder, no husband present	98 924	126 561	141 161	1.6
Nonfamily households	239 624	310 435	346 621	1.6
Householder living alone	213 778	266 585	297 996	1.6
Householder not living alone	25 846	43 850	48 625	1.5
Housing Characteristics				
Total housing units	1 000 667	1 173 043	1 287 472	1.3
Occupied housing units	891 179	1 042 696	1 102 734	0.8
Owner-occupied	619 938	723 535	746 839	0.5
Renter-occupied	271 241	319 161	355 895	1.6
Average size	2.57	2.49	2.50	X
Financial Characteristics				
Median gross rent of renter-occupied housing units (dollars)	328	453	573	3.4
Median monthly owner costs for housing units with a mortgage (dollars)	514	737	920	3.2
Median value of owner-occupied housing units (dollars)	46 000	72 800	101 000	4.8

Table AR-4. Median Income and Poverty Status, 2007

(Number, percent.)

Characteristic	State		U.S.	
	Number	Percent	Number	Percent
Median Income				
Households (dollars)	38 134	X	50 740	X
Families (dollars)	47 021	X	61 173	X
Below Poverty Level				
Sex				
Male	218 249	16.2	16 576 071	11.5
Female	273 803	19.4	21 476 176	14.3
Age				
Under 18 years	177 805	25.8	13 097 100	18.0
Related children under 18 years	174 108	25.4	12 728 964	17.6
18 to 64 years	268 396	15.9	21 495 507	11.6
65 years and over	45 851	12.1	3 459 640	9.5

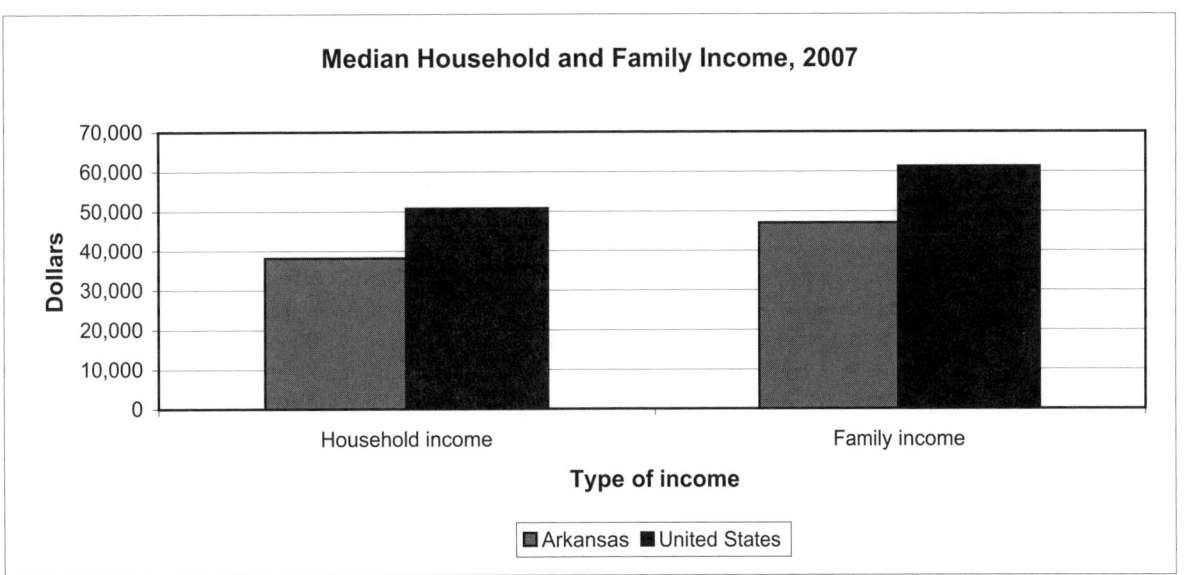

Table AR-5. Health Insurance Coverage Status for All Persons and Children Under 18 Years of Age

(Number, percent.)

Item	2000	2001	2002	2003	2004	2005	2006	2007
ALL PERSONS	2 651	2 657	2 692	2 671	2 731	2 760	2 758	2 805
Covered by Private or Government Health Insurance								
Number	2 284	2 238	2 262	2 214	2 290	2 277	2 237	2 354
Percent	86.2	84.2	84.0	82.9	83.8	82.5	81.1	83.9
Not Covered								
Number	367	419	431	457	441	482	521	451
Percent	13.8	15.8	16.0	17.1	16.2	17.5	18.9	16.1
Percent in the U.S. not covered	13.7	14.1	14.7	15.1	14.9	15.3	15.8	15.3
CHILDREN UNDER 18 YEARS OF AGE	694	692	671	675	692	673	699	720
Covered by Private or Government Health Insurance								
Number	615	613	605	606	649	600	634	675
Percent	88.7	88.5	90.2	89.9	93.8	89.3	90.7	93.8
Not Covered								
Number	78	79	66	68	43	72	65	44
Percent	11.3	11.5	9.8	10.1	6.2	10.7	9.3	6.2
Percent in the U.S. not covered	11.6	11.3	11.2	11.0	10.5	10.9	11.7	11.0

Table AR-6. Employment Status by Demographic Group, Preliminary 2008

(Number, percent.)

Characteristic	Civilian noninstitutional population	Civilian labor force		Employment		Unemployed	
		Number	Percent of population	Number	Percent of population	Number	Unemployment rate
TOTAL	2 183	1 374	62.9	1 303	59.7	71	5.2
Sex							
Men	1 050	724	69.0	682	65.0	42	5.8
Women	1 133	650	57.0	621	54.8	29	4.5
Race, Sex, and Hispanic Origin							
White	1 790	1 132	63.2	1 082	60.4	50	4.4
Men	868	603	69.5	575	66.2	29	4.7
Women	921	528	57.3	507	55.0	21	4.0
Black or African American	313	194	62.1	176	56.2	19	9.5
Men	140	92	65.7	81	57.9	11	11.8
Women	173	102	59.2	95	54.7	8	7.5
Hispanic	84	66	78.1	62	74.2	3	5.0
Men	48	43	89.1	41	84.6	2	5.0
Women	36	...	...	...	...	...	...
Age							
16 to 19 years	152	54	35.7	44	29.0	10	18.8
20 to 24 years	182	141	77.4	127	69.9	14	9.7
25 to 34 years	404	337	83.6	319	79.1	18	5.3
35 to 44 years	338	287	84.9	275	81.2	13	4.4
45 to 54 years	400	307	76.7	297	74.0	11	3.5
55 to 64 years	343	197	57.4	193	56.1	5	2.3
65 years and over	363	50	13.7	49	13.4	1	2.8

Note: Data in Table 6 are from the Current Population Survey (CPS) and do not match the estimates in Table 7. See notes and definitions for more details.

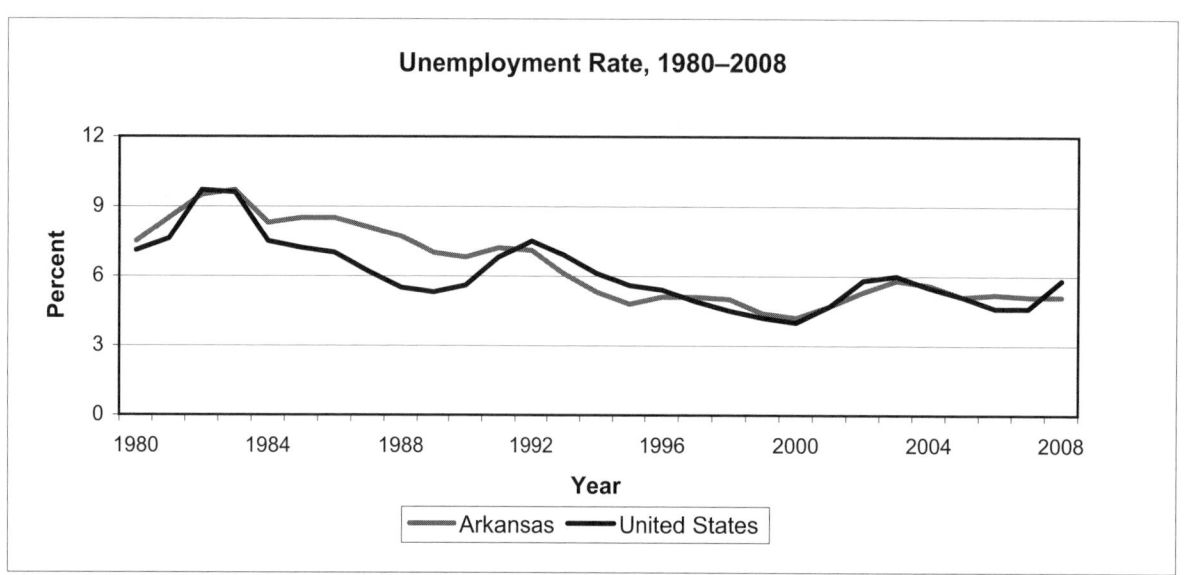

Table AR-7. Employment Status of the Civilian Noninstitutional Population Age 16 Years and Over

(Number, percent.)

Year	Civilian labor force	Civilian participation rate	Employed	Unemployed	Unemployment rate
1998	1 241 706	62.7	1 179 338	62 368	5.0
1999	1 253 739	62.6	1 198 016	55 723	4.4
2000	1 260 256	62.2	1 207 352	52 904	4.2
2001	1 252 680	61.4	1 194 024	58 656	4.7
2002	1 272 357	62.0	1 204 467	67 890	5.3
2003	1 269 842	61.4	1 195 942	73 900	5.8
2004	1 294 274	62.1	1 221 553	72 721	5.6
2005	1 335 550	63.3	1 267 655	67 895	5.1
2006	1 354 156	63.4	1 284 177	69 979	5.2
2007	1 361 176	63.0	1 291 981	69 195	5.1
2008	1 370 259	62.9	1 300 542	69 717	5.1

Table AR-8. Employment and Average Wages by Industry

(Estimates for 2001–2006 are based on the 2002 North American Industry Classification System [NAICS]. Estimates for 2007 are based on the 2007 NAICS.)

Industry	2001	2002	2003	2004	2005	2006	2007
	Number of jobs						
WAGE AND SALARY EMPLOYMENT BY INDUSTRY	1 222 541	1 216 792	1 216 658	1 230 524	1 249 007	1 274 179	1 278 626
Farm Wage and Salary Employment	13 576	13 141	13 575	12 288	11 371	12 867	11 634
Nonfarm Wage and Salary Employment	1 208 965	1 203 651	1 203 083	1 218 236	1 237 636	1 261 312	1 266 992
Private wage and salary employment	999 347	993 101	988 501	1 000 550	1 014 657	1 032 543	1 035 127
Forestry, fishing, hunting, and other	14 191	14 032	12 979	13 083	12 627	12 027	11 516
Mining	3 884	3 649	3 691	3 959	4 138	5 038	6 828
Utilities	6 872	6 861	6 729	6 548	6 633	6 853	6 838
Construction	55 712	56 672	53 060	53 952	56 691	58 948	58 450
Manufacturing	228 835	215 649	207 456	205 316	202 795	200 555	191 016
Durable goods manufacturing	125 144	115 976	110 261	108 719	107 688	106 905	100 738
Nondurable goods manufacturing	103 691	99 673	97 195	96 597	95 107	93 650	90 278
Wholesale trade	46 265	45 500	45 319	46 664	48 256	48 600	48 784
Retail trade	135 480	133 922	132 918	134 697	135 900	137 281	138 289
Transportation and warehousing	58 137	59 722	59 695	58 969	59 969	61 271	61 610
Information	21 011	20 416	20 389	20 223	20 108	19 963	19 867
Finance and insurance	36 091	36 597	37 288	37 285	37 259	38 451	38 706
Real estate and rental and leasing	13 351	13 243	13 219	13 667	14 133	14 674	14 917
Professional and technical services	31 661	32 825	34 387	35 961	37 808	39 363	40 748
Management of companies and enterprises	21 995	21 482	21 438	22 714	23 579	24 096	24 782
Administrative and waste services	50 025	48 849	49 933	51 242	52 558	53 122	53 843
Educational services	11 192	12 417	12 798	12 663	12 935	13 104	13 734
Health care and social assistance	124 120	128 189	132 270	135 281	139 119	144 403	148 375
Arts, entertainment, and recreation	9 463	9 429	9 650	9 665	9 808	9 972	10 290
Accommodation and food services	78 803	79 444	80 042	82 805	85 832	89 040	90 814
Other services, except public administration	52 259	54 203	55 240	55 856	54 509	55 782	55 720
Government and government enterprises	209 618	210 550	214 582	217 686	222 979	228 769	231 865
	Dollars						
AVERAGE WAGES AND SALARIES BY INDUSTRY	26 632	27 461	28 268	29 622	30 659	31 652	33 328
Average Farm Wages and Salaries	19 434	19 617	18 436	22 269	19 781	17 193	19 751
Average Nonfarm Wages and Salaries	26 713	27 546	28 379	29 697	30 759	31 799	33 453
Average private wages and salaries	26 684	27 419	28 189	29 494	30 482	31 548	33 389
Forestry, fishing, hunting, and other	21 667	22 115	22 853	23 802	24 888	26 777	27 899
Mining	37 878	38 124	39 546	41 746	45 813	51 938	54 130
Utilities	53 091	54 312	56 471	60 986	62 894	61 893	65 655
Construction	28 987	30 165	29 720	30 937	32 585	33 918	36 108
Manufacturing	29 815	30 727	31 845	33 211	34 168	35 017	36 655
Durable goods manufacturing	30 104	31 225	32 436	33 845	35 051	36 077	37 844
Nondurable goods manufacturing	29 467	30 148	31 175	32 497	33 170	33 807	35 328
Wholesale trade	37 207	38 886	40 346	43 440	45 437	48 348	50 934
Retail trade	17 676	18 282	19 003	19 518	20 085	20 746	21 512
Transportation and warehousing	32 963	33 787	33 924	35 610	37 148	38 010	38 652
Information	35 042	35 497	36 513	38 728	40 583	43 127	75 869
Finance and insurance	37 218	37 849	39 970	41 718	42 906	44 412	46 814
Real estate and rental and leasing	21 676	22 759	23 293	24 681	26 082	27 136	28 274
Professional and technical services	39 724	40 455	41 676	43 508	44 302	45 615	47 646
Management of companies and enterprises	58 864	59 156	60 155	65 313	66 529	70 922	70 607
Administrative and waste services	16 399	17 205	18 223	18 464	19 568	20 307	21 117
Educational services	17 909	18 657	19 244	19 852	20 396	21 393	22 556
Health care and social assistance	28 158	28 932	29 651	31 037	31 849	32 466	33 340
Arts, entertainment, and recreation	14 016	14 287	14 574	15 211	15 790	16 892	17 474
Accommodation and food services	10 555	10 858	11 173	11 537	11 791	12 259	12 837
Other services, except public administration	18 661	19 341	19 919	20 899	21 358	22 215	23 284
Government and government enterprises	26 853	28 148	29 255	30 630	32 019	32 934	33 739

Table AR-9. Employment Characteristics by Family Type

(Number, percent.)

Family type and labor force status	2005		2006		2007	
	Total	Families with own children under 18 years	Total	Families with own children under 18 years	Total	Families with own children under 18 years
TOTAL FAMILIES	742 444	332 323	758 195	333 447	756 113	335 310
FAMILY TYPE AND LABOR FORCE STATUS						
Married Coupled Families	555 545	220 408	567 229	224 782	570 075	224 674
Both husband and wife in labor force	50.5	66.7	51.0	66.2	49.9	64.2
Husband in labor force, wife not in labor force	21.2	25.5	21.6	26.6	22.1	27.2
Wife in labor force, husband not in labor force	8.6	4.2	7.9	4.5	8.5	5.1
Both husband and wife not in labor force	19.8	3.6	19.5	2.7	19.4	3.4
Other Families	186 899	111 915	190 966	108 665	186 038	110 636
Female householder, no husband present	75.2	77.7	74.4	77.2	75.9	79.7
In labor force	50.9	59.5	51.6	62.5	51.3	63.9
Not in labor force	24.4	18.3	22.8	14.6	24.6	15.9
Male householder, no wife present	24.8	22.3	25.6	22.8	24.1	20.3
In labor force	18.4	19.3	20.1	20.3	18.0	17.4
Not in labor force	6.4	3.0	5.5	2.5	6.1	2.8

Table AR-10. School Enrollment and Educational Attainment, 2007

(Number, percent.)

Item	State	U.S.
Enrollment		
Total population 3 years and over	2 717 853	289 295 761
Enrolled in school	709 261	79 329 527
Enrolled in preschool (percent)	6.5	6.2
Enrolled in grades K-12 (percent)	70.7	67.6
Enrolled in college or graduate school (percent)	22.8	26.2
Attainment		
Total population 25 years and over	1 861 810	197 892 369
Less than a high school diploma (percent)	18.9	15.5
High school diploma or more (percent)	81.1	84.5
Bachelor's degree or more (percent)	19.3	27.5
Graduate degree or more (percent)	6.5	10.1

Table AR-11. Educational Indicators

(Number, percent.)

Item	State	U.S.
Public Schools, 2006–2007 (except where noted)		
Number of school districts	292	17 742
Number of schools	1 114	99 639
Number of students	476 409	49 315 842
Student-teacher ratio	13.6	15.5
Expenditures per student (dollars)	$8 391	. . .
Averaged freshman graduation rate, 2005–2006	80.4	. . .
Dropout rate, grades 9–12, 2005–2006	3.1	3.7
Students eligible for free or reduced-price lunch (percent)	58.6	41.2
English-language learners (percent)	. . .	5.1
Students with IEP (percent)	13.7	12.7
Private Schools, 2007–2008 (except where noted)		
Number of schools	305	33 740
Number of students	34 850	5 072 451
High school graduates, 2006–2007	1 379	306 605
Student-teacher ratio	11.1	11.1

Table AR-12. Reported Voting and Registration of the Voting-Age Population, November 2008

(Number in thousands, percent.)

Item	Total population	Total citizen population	Registered			Voted		
			Total registered	Percent registered (total population)	Percent registered (total citizen population)	Total voted	Percent voted (total population)	Percent voted (total citizen population)
U.S. total	225 499	206 072	146 311	64.9	71.0	131 144	58.2	63.6
State total	2 108	2 030	1 317	62.5	64.9	1 092	51.8	53.8
Sex								
Male	1 002	952	584	58.2	61.3	477	47.6	50.1
Female	1 106	1 078	734	66.3	68.1	615	55.6	57.1
Race								
White alone	1 733	1 679	1 125	64.9	67.0	931	53.7	55.5
White non-Hispanic alone	1 658	1 658	1 117	67.4	67.4	928	55.9	55.9
Black alone	308	301	160	52.0	53.2	133	43.1	44.1
Asian alone	23	6	. . .	. . .	. . .	. . .	. . .	. . .
Hispanic (of any race)	74	20	8	. . .	. . .	3	. . .	. . .
White alone or in combination	1 768	1 714	1 152	65.1	67.2	954	53.9	55.6
Black alone or in combination	313	306	164	52.2	53.4	136	43.5	44.5
Asian alone or in combination	23	6	. . .	. . .	. . .	. . .	. . .	. . .

Table AR-13. Crime

(Number, rate per 100,000.)

Item	State			U.S.		
	2007	2008	Percent change	2007	2008	Percent change
Population	2 834 797	2 855 390	0.7	301 621 157	304 059 724	0.8
VIOLENT CRIME						
Number	15 007	14 374	-4.2	1 408 337	1 382 012	-1.9
Rate	529.4	503.4	-4.9	466.9	454.5	-2.7
Murder and Nonnegligent Manslaughter						
Number	191	162	-15.2	16 929	16 272	-3.9
Rate	6.7	5.7	-15.8	5.6	5.4	-4.7
Forcible Rape						
Number	1 268	1 395	10.0	90 427	89 000	-1.6
Rate	44.7	48.9	9.2	30.0	29.3	-2.4
Robbery						
Number	3 024	2 735	-9.6	445 125	441 855	-0.7
Rate	106.7	95.8	-10.2	147.6	145.3	-1.5
Aggravated Assault						
Number	10 524	10 082	-4.2	855 856	834 885	-2.5
Rate	371.2	353.1	-4.9	283.8	274.6	-3.2
PROPERTY CRIME						
Number	112 061	109 508	-2.3	9 843 481	9 767 915	-0.8
Rate	3 953.1	3 835.1	-3.0	3 263.5	3 212.5	-1.6
Burglary						
Number	32 072	33 694	5.1	2 179 140	2 222 196	2.0
Rate	1 131.4	1 180.0	4.3	722.5	730.8	1.2
Larceny-Theft						
Number	72 979	69 303	-5.0	6 568 572	6 588 873	0.3
Rate	2 574.4	2 427.1	-5.7	2 177.8	2 167.0	-0.5
Motor Vehicle Theft						
Number	7 010	6 511	-7.1	1 095 769	956 846	-12.7
Rate	247.3	228.0	-7.8	363.3	314.7	-13.4

Table AR-14. State Government Finances, 2007

(Dollars, percent distribution.)

Item	Thousands of dollars	Percent distribution
Total Revenue	18 175 873	X
General revenue	14 161 006	77.9
Intergovernmental revenue	4 286 094	23.6
Taxes	7 391 778	40.7
General sales	2 904 401	16.0
Selective sales	950 307	5.2
License taxes	298 309	1.6
Individual income tax	2 168 441	11.9
Corporate income tax	362 983	2.0
Other taxes	707 337	3.9
Current charges	1 752 177	9.6
Miscellaneous general revenue	730 957	4.0
Utility revenue	0	0.0
Liquor store revenue	0	0.0
Insurance trust revenue	4 014 867	22.1
Total Expenditure	14 948 566	100.0
Intergovernmental expenditure	4 300 048	28.8
Direct expenditure	10 648 518	71.2
Current operation	8 128 452	54.4
Capital outlay	919 377	6.2
Insurance benefits and repayments	1 186 604	7.9
Assistance and subsidies	239 278	1.6
Interest on debt	174 807	1.2
Exhibit: Salaries and wages	1 749 690	11.7
Total Expenditure	14 948 566	100.0
General expenditure	13 761 962	92.1
Intergovernmental expenditure	4 300 048	28.8
Direct expenditure	9 461 914	63.3
Education	6 023 402	40.3
Public welfare	3 624 917	24.2
Hospitals	742 881	5.0
Health	238 276	1.6
Highways	897 313	6.0
Police protection	70 632	0.5
Correction	331 717	2.2
Natural resources	221 573	1.5
Parks and recreation	44 290	0.3
Government administration	526 971	3.5
Interest on general debt	174 807	1.2
Other and unallocable	865 183	5.8
Utility expenditure	0	0.0
Liquor store expenditure	0	0.0
Insurance trust expenditure	1 186 604	7.9
Debt at End of Fiscal Year	4 508 511	X
Cash and Security Holdings	27 389 883	X

Table AR-15. State Government Tax Collections, 2008

(Dollars, percent distribution.)

Item	Thousands of dollars	Percent distribution
Total Taxes	7 530 504	X
Property taxes	682 174	9.1
Sales and gross receipts	3 778 217	50.2
General sales and gross receipts	2 807 943	37.3
Selective sales taxes	970 274	12.9
Alcoholic beverages	42 843	0.6
Amusements	6 681	0.1
Insurance premiums	147 434	2.0
Motor fuels	471 214	6.3
Pari-mutuels	5 282	0.1
Tobacco products	147 482	2.0
Other selective sales	149 338	2.0
Licenses	307 342	4.1
Alcoholic beverages	1 959	0.0
Amusements	308	0.0
Corporation	22 835	0.3
Hunting and fishing	20 167	0.3
Motor vehicle	140 112	1.9
Motor vehicle operators	14 816	0.2
Public utility	9 200	0.1
Occupation and business, NEC	96 901	1.3
Other licenses	1 044	0.0
Income taxes	2 687 405	35.7
Individual income	2 344 876	31.1
Corporation net income	342 529	4.5
Other taxes	75 366	1.0
Documentary and stock transfer	35 219	0.5
Severance	27 820	0.4
Other	12 327	0.2

Table AR-16. Agriculture

(Number, acres, and dollars.)

Item	2002		2007		Percent change, 2002–2007
	Number	Percent of total	Number	Percent of total	
Number of farms	47 483		49 346		3.9
Farm Size					
Average size of farm (acres)	305		281		-7.9
Farms by size (number of farms)					
Fewer than 50 acres	12 950	27.3	17 700	35.9	36.7
50 to 499 acres	27 666	58.3	25 506	51.7	-7.8
500 acres or more	6 867	14.5	6 140	12.4	-10.6
Land (Acres)					
Total land in farms	14 502 793		13 872 862		-4.3
Total cropland	9 576 047	66.0	8 432 221	60.8	-11.9
Total harvested cropland	7 457 599	51.4	7 367 068	53.1	-1.2
Irrigated land	4 149 766	28.6	4 460 682	32.2	7.5
Value of Sales (Dollars)					
Agricultural products sold ($1,000)	4 950 397		7 508 806		51.7
Average sales per farm	104 256		152 166		46.0
Sales of crops	1 620 384	32.7	2 900 973	38.6	79.0
Sales of livestock, poultry, and their products	3 330 014	67.3	4 607 833	61.4	38.4
Value of Sales (Number of Farms)					
Less than $10,000	28 620	60.3	29 426	59.6	2.8
$10,000 to $99,999	10 349	21.8	11 850	24.0	14.5
$100,000 to $999,999	7 673	16.2	5 816	11.8	-24.2
$1,000,000 or more	841	1.8	2 254	4.6	168.0
Farms by Type of Organization (Number of Farms)					
Family	43 458	91.5	42 470	86.1	-2.3
Partnership	2 626	5.5	4 667	9.5	77.7
Corporation	1 182	2.5	1 854	3.8	56.9
Other: cooperative, estate or trust, institutional, etc	217	0.5	355	0.7	63.6
Value of Land and Buildings (Dollars)					
Estimated market value of land and buildings ($1,000)	32 505 792		21 225 836		-34.7
Land and buildings average value per farm	658 732		447 104		-32.1
Average value per acre	2 343		1 469		-37.3
Government Payments					
Number of farms receiving government payments	7 811	16.5	11 461	23.2	46.7
Payments (thousands of dollars)	238 577		269 448		12.9
Average payment per farm	30 544		23 510		-23.0
Farm Operator Characteristics					
Farm operators whose principal occupation is farming	27 411	57.7	21 960	44.5	-19.9
Farm operators whose principal occupation is other	20 072	42.3	27 386	55.5	36.4
Average age principal operator (years)	54.9		56.5		2.9

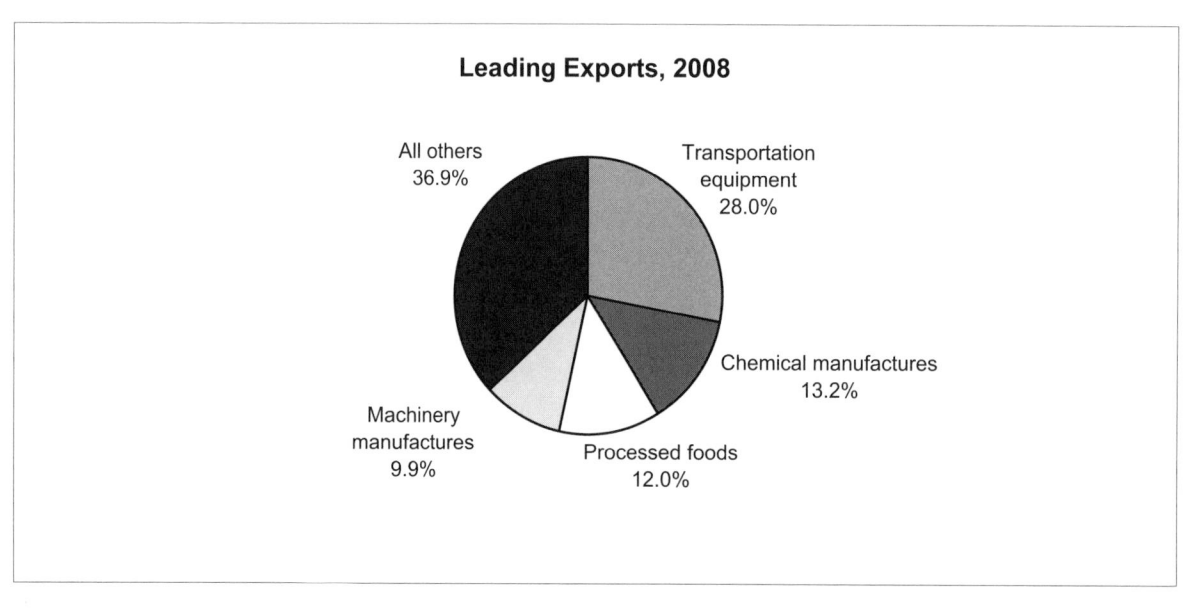

Leading Exports, 2008

All others 36.9%

Transportation equipment 28.0%

Chemical manufactures 13.2%

Processed foods 12.0%

Machinery manufactures 9.9%

Facts and Figures

Location: Western United States; bordered on the N by Oregon, on the E by Nevada and Arizona, on the S by Mexico, and on the W by the Pacific Ocean

Area: 163,696 sq. mi. (423,970 sq. km.); rank—3rd

Population: 36,756,666 (2008 est.); rank—1st

Principal Cities: capital—Sacramento; largest—Los Angeles

Statehood: September 9, 1850; 31st state

U.S. Congress: 2 senators, 53 representatives

State Motto: *Eureka* ("I have found it")

State Song: "I Love You, California"

State Nickname: The Golden State

Abbreviations: CA; Cal; Calif.

State Symbols: flower—California poppy; tree—redwood; bird—California valley quail

At a Glance

- With an increase in population of 8.5 percent, California ranked 18th among the states in growth from 2000 to 2008.
- An estimated 246,802 marriages took place in California in 2008; California does not report its number of divorces.
- The 2007 home ownership rate in California was 58.3 percent, giving it a ranking of 49th among the states.
- California's median household income in 2007 was $59,948, 8th among the states.
- In California, 12.4 percent of the population lived below the poverty level in 2007, ranking it 22nd.
- In 2006-07, 18.5 percent of Californians did not have health insurance, compared to 15.5 percent of the total U.S. population.
- In 2007, 5.3 percent of Californians were unemployed, compared to 4.6 percent nationwide.
- California ranked 13th in the nation with 29.5 percent of its population 25 years old and over having a bachelor's degree in 2007; its ranking was the same as that of Illinois.
- California's violent crime rate in 2007 was 522.6 per 100,000 population, compared to 466.9 for the entire nation.
- California had one physician for every 324 people in 2007, compared to one physician for every 325 people nationwide.
- In the 2008 election, 61.7 percent of California's eligible voters voted, the same percentage as eligible voters nationwide.
- California ranked 26th among the states receiving federal aid in 2007, with $1,374 per capita.
- California's gross domestic product was $1.8 trillion in 2007; it ranked 1st among the states.
- With $134.3 billion in exports in 2007, California ranked 2nd in exports.
- Californians consumed 8.42 trillion Btu's of energy in 2006; the state ranked 2nd in total consumption.
- In 2007, California exported $1.3 billion worth of agricultural products, 14 percent of the U.S. total.

Table CA-1. Population by Sex, Age, Race, and Hispanic Origin

(Number, percent.)

Sex, age, race, and Hispanic origin	1990	2000	2008	Average annual percent change, 2000–2008
Total Population	29 760 021	33 871 648	36 756 666	1.0
Percent of total U.S. population	12.0	12.0	12.1	X
Sex				
Male	14 897 627	16 874 892	18 388 022	1.1
Female	14 862 394	16 996 756	18 368 644	1.0
Age				
Under 5 years	2 397 715	2 486 981	2 704 659	1.1
5 to 19 years	6 254 473	7 747 590	7 795 549	0.1
20 to 64 years	17 972 281	20 041 419	22 141 962	1.3
65 years and over	3 135 552	3 595 658	4 114 496	1.7
Median age (years)	31.3	33.3	34.8	X
Race and Hispanic Origin[1]				
One race				
White	20 524 327	20 170 059	28 170 328	4.3
Black	2 208 801	2 263 882	2 451 453	1.0
American Indian and Alaskan Native	242 164	333 346	443 719	3.6
Asian[2]	2 845 659	3 697 513	4 581 890	2.7
Native Hawaiian and Other Pacific Islander	X	116 961	157 112	3.8
Two or more races	X	1 607 646	952 164	-6.3
Hispanic (of any race)	7 687 938	10 966 556	13 457 397	2.6

[1]Data on race in 2000 and 2008 are not comparable to 1990. Individuals could only report one race in the 1990 census but could report one or more races on the 2000 census.
[2]Data in 1990 refer to Asian and Pacific Islanders.

Table CA-2. Marital Status

(Number, percent distribution.)

Sex and marital status	1990	2000	2007
Males, 15 Years and Over	11 518 004	12 844 669	14 327 899
Never married	35.0	33.8	38.2
Now married, except separated	52.9	54.1	49.8
Separated	2.2	2.0	2.0
Widowed	2.1	2.2	2.1
Divorced	7.8	7.9	7.9
Females, 15 Years and Over	11 642 977	13 231 494	14 503 263
Never married	25.2	26.5	30.9
Now married, except separated	50.8	50.7	46.5
Separated	3.1	2.9	2.9
Widowed	9.9	8.9	8.5
Divorced	11.0	11.0	11.0

Table CA-3. Households and Housing Characteristics

(Number, percent, and dollars.)

Item	1990	2000	2007	Average annual percent change, 2000–2007
Total Households	10 381 206	11 502 870	12 200 672	0.8
Family households	7 139 394	7 920 049	8 330 684	0.7
Married-couple family	5 469 522	5 877 084	6 065 746	0.5
Other family	1 669 872	2 042 965	2 264 938	1.5
Male householder, no wife present	477 692	594 455	701 452	2.4
Female householder, no husband present	1 192 180	1 448 510	1 563 486	1.1
Nonfamily households	3 241 812	3 582 821	3 869 988	1.1
Householder living alone	2 429 867	2 708 308	3 030 693	1.6
Householder not living alone	811 945	874 513	839 295	-0.6
Housing Characteristics				
Total housing units	11 182 882	12 214 549	13 308 705	1.2
Occupied housing units	10 381 206	11 502 870	12 200 672	0.8
Owner-occupied	5 773 943	6 546 334	7 076 972	1.1
Renter-occupied	4 607 263	4 956 536	5 123 700	0.5
Average size	2.79	2.87	2.93	X
Financial Characteristics				
Median gross rent of renter-occupied housing units (dollars)	620	747	1 078	5.4
Median monthly owner costs for housing units with a mortgage (dollars)	1 077	1 478	2 314	6.6
Median value of owner-occupied housing units (dollars)	194 300	211 500	532 300	14.1

Table CA-4. Median Income and Poverty Status, 2007

(Number, percent.)

Characteristic	State		U.S.	
	Number	Percent	Number	Percent
Median Income				
Households (dollars)	59 948	X	50 740	X
Families (dollars)	67 484	X	61 173	X
Below Poverty Level				
Sex				
Male	2 007 341	11.3	16 576 071	11.5
Female	2 425 673	13.5	21 476 176	14.3
Age				
Under 18 years	1 591 295	17.3	13 097 100	18.0
Related children under 18 years	1 546 064	16.9	12 728 964	17.6
18 to 64 years	2 522 872	11.1	21 495 507	11.6
65 years and over	318 847	8.2	3 459 640	9.5

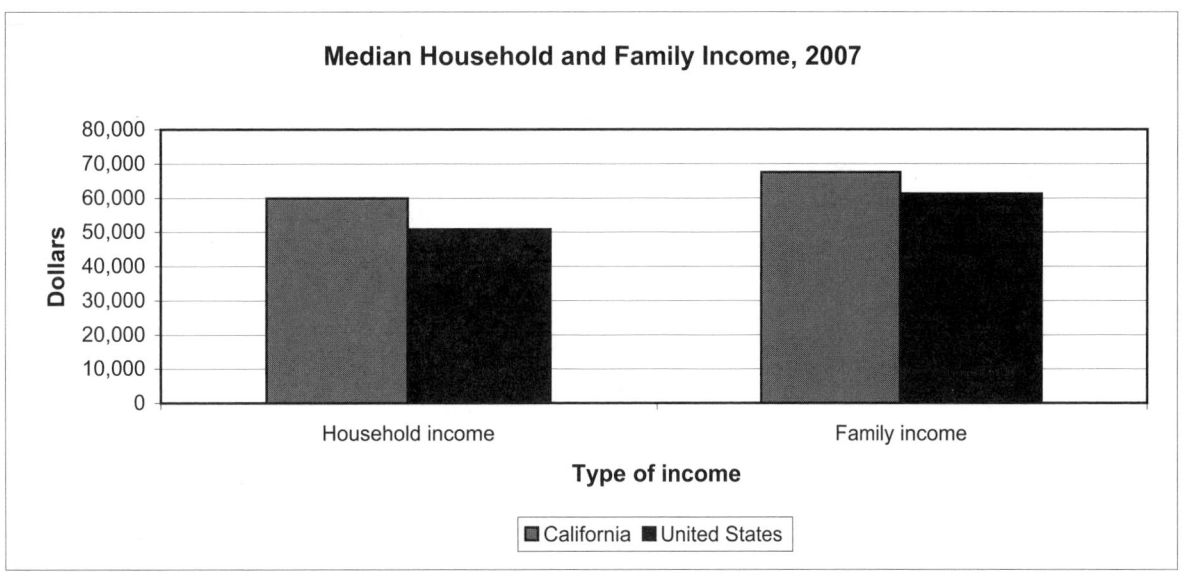

Table CA-5. Health Insurance Coverage Status for All Persons and Children Under 18 Years of Age

(Number, percent.)

Item	2000	2001	2002	2003	2004	2005	2006	2007
ALL PERSONS	34 004	34 488	35 159	35 394	35 854	35 940	36 208	36 295
Covered by Private or Government Health Insurance								
Number	27 850	27 915	28 928	29 072	29 413	29 182	29 417	29 682
Percent	81.9	80.9	82.3	82.1	82.0	81.2	81.2	81.8
Not Covered								
Number	6 154	6 573	6 231	6 322	6 441	6 757	6 791	6 613
Percent	18.1	19.1	17.7	17.9	18.0	18.8	18.8	18.2
Percent in the U.S. not covered	13.7	14.1	14.7	15.1	14.9	15.3	15.8	15.3
CHILDREN UNDER 18 YEARS OF AGE	9 549	9 875	9 629	9 563	9 590	9 738	9 571	9 423
Covered by Private or Government Health Insurance								
Number	8 135	8 414	8 313	8 398	8 462	8 429	8 346	8 410
Percent	85.2	85.2	86.3	87.8	88.2	86.6	87.2	89.3
Not Covered								
Number	1 414	1 461	1 316	1 165	1 128	1 309	1 225	1 013
Percent	14.8	14.8	13.7	12.2	11.8	13.4	12.8	10.7
Percent in the U.S. not covered	11.6	11.3	11.2	11.0	10.5	10.9	11.7	11.0

Table CA-6. Employment Status by Demographic Group, Preliminary 2008

(Number, percent.)

Characteristic	Civilian noninstitutional population	Civilian labor force		Employment		Unemployed	
		Number	Percent of population	Number	Percent of population	Number	Unemployment rate
TOTAL	28 021	18 431	65.8	17 113	61.1	1 318	7.1
Sex							
Men	13 767	10 209	74.0	9 456	68.7	753	7.4
Women	14 253	8 222	58.0	7 657	53.7	565	6.9
Race, Sex, and Hispanic Origin							
White	21 768	14 406	66.2	13 391	61.5	1 015	7.0
Men	10 832	8 166	75.4	7 584	70.0	582	7.1
Women	10 936	6 240	57.1	5 807	53.1	433	6.9
Black or African American	1 788	1 117	62.5	989	55.3	129	11.5
Men	831	542	65.2	474	57.0	68	12.6
Women	957	576	60.2	515	53.8	61	10.5
Hispanic	9 261	6 318	68.2	5 725	61.8	592	9.4
Men	4 747	3 801	80.1	3 450	72.7	351	9.2
Women	4 514	2 517	55.8	2 276	50.4	241	9.6
Age							
16 to 19 years	2 159	737	34.1	558	25.8	179	24.3
20 to 24 years	2 627	1 885	71.7	1 654	62.9	232	12.3
25 to 34 years	5 176	4 231	81.7	3 931	75.9	301	7.1
35 to 44 years	5 300	4 373	82.5	4 127	77.9	246	5.6
45 to 54 years	5 100	4 111	80.6	3 894	76.4	217	5.3
55 to 64 years	3 685	2 429	65.9	2 322	63.0	107	4.4
65 years and over	3 973	664	16.7	628	15.8	36	5.5

Note: Data in Table 6 are from the Current Population Survey (CPS) and do not match the estimates in Table 7. See notes and definitions for more details.

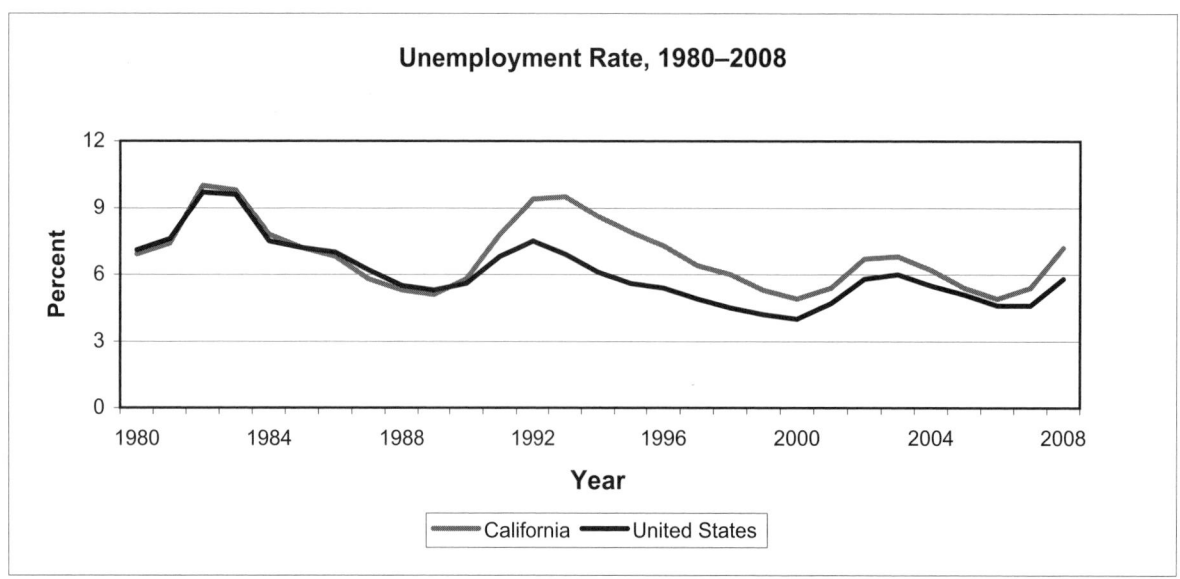

Table CA-7. Employment Status of the Civilian Noninstitutional Population Age 16 Years and Over

(Number, percent.)

Year	Civilian labor force	Civilian participation rate	Employed	Unemployed	Unemployment rate
1998	16 166 912	66.6	15 203 693	963 219	6.0
1999	16 430 580	66.5	15 566 900	863 680	5.3
2000	16 857 578	67.1	16 024 341	833 237	4.9
2001	17 152 106	67.1	16 220 033	932 073	5.4
2002	17 343 579	66.8	16 180 799	1 162 780	6.7
2003	17 390 668	66.1	16 200 064	1 190 604	6.8
2004	17 444 436	65.5	16 354 779	1 089 657	6.2
2005	17 629 159	65.5	16 671 914	957 245	5.4
2006	17 821 106	65.4	16 948 374	872 732	4.9
2007	18 077 963	65.6	17 108 702	969 261	5.4
2008	18 391 844	65.9	17 059 574	1 332 270	7.2

Table CA-8. Employment and Average Wages by Industry

(Estimates for 2001–2006 are based on the 2002 North American Industry Classification System [NAICS]. Estimates for 2007 are based on the 2007 NAICS.)

Industry	2001	2002	2003	2004	2005	2006	2007
	Number of jobs						
WAGE AND SALARY EMPLOYMENT BY INDUSTRY	15 894 113	15 808 474	15 773 528	15 866 949	16 072 270	16 332 688	16 456 083
Farm Wage and Salary Employment	208 090	240 108	240 951	210 576	178 408	158 978	161 750
Nonfarm Wage and Salary Employment	15 686 023	15 568 366	15 532 577	15 656 373	15 893 862	16 173 710	16 294 333
Private wage and salary employment	13 067 448	12 886 860	12 853 996	13 004 433	13 243 176	13 501 703	13 575 948
Forestry, fishing, hunting, and other	214 636	208 481	211 397	211 264	216 898	220 192	225 631
Mining	23 922	21 211	20 646	21 482	22 249	23 967	25 049
Utilities	54 924	55 555	55 636	56 353	56 244	56 749	58 321
Construction	807 774	802 440	819 891	882 999	939 273	965 127	921 752
Manufacturing	1 800 460	1 651 508	1 550 904	1 535 244	1 516 641	1 509 058	1 469 904
Durable goods manufacturing	1 174 793	1 060 493	983 786	972 617	967 978	960 490	928 545
Nondurable goods manufacturing	625 667	591 015	567 118	562 627	548 663	548 568	541 359
Wholesale trade	665 123	657 828	657 386	662 971	685 135	711 048	728 591
Retail trade	1 625 535	1 634 826	1 643 816	1 669 528	1 710 070	1 732 725	1 741 873
Transportation and warehousing	458 486	438 046	427 213	430 363	435 901	441 108	450 511
Information	565 544	507 131	481 422	489 782	476 941	474 709	475 707
Finance and insurance	595 490	606 352	634 460	642 017	662 220	667 893	640 078
Real estate and rental and leasing	278 365	280 207	285 311	288 319	295 860	301 263	293 641
Professional and technical services	995 598	962 563	963 535	968 431	1 017 139	1 073 778	1 115 583
Management of companies and enterprises	287 081	270 777	256 101	234 456	223 891	212 828	207 452
Administrative and waste services	960 551	944 853	937 813	943 919	967 863	996 780	999 705
Educational services	269 034	286 297	293 525	299 320	303 981	313 995	325 111
Health care and social assistance	1 256 631	1 302 544	1 335 194	1 350 318	1 363 168	1 392 511	1 439 641
Arts, entertainment, and recreation	241 395	244 143	248 890	250 360	251 355	257 582	264 520
Accommodation and food services	1 154 197	1 164 042	1 180 198	1 212 513	1 247 677	1 287 295	1 321 682
Other services, except public administration	812 702	848 056	850 658	854 794	850 670	863 095	871 196
Government and government enterprises	2 618 575	2 681 506	2 678 581	2 651 940	2 650 686	2 672 007	2 718 385
	Dollars						
AVERAGE WAGES AND SALARIES BY INDUSTRY	40 619	40 610	41 830	44 052	45 831	48 021	50 182
Average Farm Wages and Salaries	21 420	17 138	16 562	21 106	26 926	29 840	27 559
Average Nonfarm Wages and Salaries	40 874	40 972	42 222	44 361	46 043	48 200	50 407
Average private wages and salaries	40 875	40 691	41 867	44 107	45 825	47 978	50 103
Forestry, fishing, hunting, and other	18 415	19 460	19 865	20 919	21 377	22 308	23 312
Mining	70 141	73 083	76 978	88 253	88 830	97 369	106 671
Utilities	68 744	69 193	73 695	82 103	85 588	91 852	92 649
Construction	41 892	42 427	42 504	43 763	45 644	48 337	51 640
Manufacturing	51 058	50 754	53 528	56 259	59 569	62 877	65 910
Durable goods manufacturing	58 315	57 526	60 565	63 601	66 756	71 683	75 201
Nondurable goods manufacturing	37 432	38 603	41 321	43 566	46 890	47 458	49 974
Wholesale trade	50 194	50 429	51 968	54 210	56 531	59 436	62 298
Retail trade	27 634	27 838	28 255	28 925	29 408	29 942	30 892
Transportation and warehousing	38 297	39 457	40 169	41 885	42 435	44 621	45 536
Information	70 993	70 434	73 300	80 170	84 090	87 793	90 907
Finance and insurance	72 398	71 971	73 860	80 267	84 315	87 214	92 135
Real estate and rental and leasing	36 967	37 929	40 063	42 850	45 186	48 240	49 881
Professional and technical services	67 856	66 325	67 521	70 447	73 399	77 431	81 857
Management of companies and enterprises	65 534	62 289	65 002	75 392	77 531	83 988	89 968
Administrative and waste services	26 909	27 253	27 871	29 596	30 439	31 983	34 055
Educational services	27 244	28 342	29 800	31 087	32 277	33 811	35 015
Health care and social assistance	35 544	37 548	39 111	41 181	43 189	45 465	47 291
Arts, entertainment, and recreation	37 079	38 871	42 230	44 549	44 913	46 807	47 632
Accommodation and food services	15 946	16 468	16 931	17 823	18 282	19 052	19 899
Other services, except public administration	22 117	22 360	23 220	24 222	24 850	25 597	26 862
Government and government enterprises	40 868	42 325	43 922	45 606	47 131	49 324	51 925

Table CA-9. Employment Characteristics by Family Type

(Number, percent.)

Family type and labor force status	2005		2006		2007	
	Total	Families with own children under 18 years	Total	Families with own children under 18 years	Total	Families with own children under 18 years
TOTAL FAMILIES	8 281 119	4 204 800	8 303 793	4 239 440	8 330 684	4 209 889
FAMILY TYPE AND LABOR FORCE STATUS						
Married Coupled Families	6 011 121	2 969 746	6 051 701	3 010 321	6 065 746	2 989 583
Both husband and wife in labor force	48.9	55.3	50.9	57.6	51.1	58.2
Husband in labor force, wife not in labor force	27.8	36.1	27.5	35.4	26.9	34.9
Wife in labor force, husband not in labor force	6.8	4.3	6.7	3.9	6.6	3.9
Both husband and wife not in labor force	16.5	4.3	15.0	3.1	15.4	3.0
Other Families	2 269 998	1 235 054	2 252 092	1 229 119	2 264 938	1 220 306
Female householder, no husband present	68.6	72.2	69.0	72.5	69.0	72.9
In labor force	47.1	55.7	48.4	56.8	48.2	56.9
Not in labor force	21.5	16.5	20.6	15.7	20.8	16.0
Male householder, no wife present	31.4	27.8	31.0	27.5	31.0	27.1
In labor force	25.5	24.8	25.7	24.9	25.2	24.3
Not in labor force	5.9	2.9	5.3	2.7	5.8	2.8

Table CA-10. School Enrollment and Educational Attainment, 2007

(Number, percent.)

Item	State	U.S.
Enrollment		
Total population 3 years and over	34 952 975	289 295 761
Enrolled in school	10 328 045	79 329 527
Enrolled in preschool (percent)	5.7	6.2
Enrolled in grades K-12 (percent)	66.7	67.6
Enrolled in college or graduate school (percent)	27.6	26.2
Attainment		
Total population 25 years and over	23 331 762	197 892 369
Less than a high school diploma (percent)	19.8	15.5
High school diploma or more (percent)	80.2	84.5
Bachelor's degree or more (percent)	29.5	27.5
Graduate degree or more (percent)	10.5	10.1

Table CA-11. Educational Indicators

(Number, percent.)

Item	State	U.S.
Public Schools, 2006–2007 (except where noted)		
Number of school districts	1 130	17 742
Number of schools	10 063	99 639
Number of students	6 406 750	49 315 842
Student-teacher ratio	20.8	15.5
Expenditures per student (dollars)	$8 952	. . .
Averaged freshman graduation rate, 2005–2006	69.2	. . .
Dropout rate, grades 9–12, 2005–2006	3.7	3.7
Students eligible for free or reduced-price lunch (percent)	48.7	41.2
English-language learners (percent)	. . .	5.1
Students with IEP (percent)	10.5	12.7
Private Schools, 2007–2008 (except where noted)		
Number of schools	4 013	33 740
Number of students	607 141	5 072 451
High school graduates, 2006–2007	34 878	306 605
Student-teacher ratio	12.1	11.1

Table CA-12. Reported Voting and Registration of the Voting-Age Population, November 2008

(Number in thousands, percent.)

Item	Total population	Total citizen population	Registered			Voted		
			Total registered	Percent registered (total population)	Percent registered (total citizen population)	Total voted	Percent voted (total population)	Percent voted (total citizen population)
U.S. total	225 499	206 072	146 311	64.9	71.0	131 144	58.2	63.6
State total	26 993	21 816	14 885	55.1	68.2	13 828	51.2	63.4
Sex								
Male	13 259	10 554	6 948	52.4	65.8	6 429	48.5	60.9
Female	13 734	11 262	7 937	57.8	70.5	7 398	53.9	65.7
Race								
White alone	20 823	16 837	11 775	56.5	69.9	10 982	52.7	65.2
White non-Hispanic alone	12 581	12 048	8 783	69.8	72.9	8 255	65.6	68.5
Black alone	1 682	1 646	1 105	65.7	67.2	1 073	63.8	65.2
Asian alone	3 473	2 562	1 522	43.8	59.4	1 343	38.7	52.4
Hispanic (of any race)	8 859	5 193	3 263	36.8	62.8	2 961	33.4	57.0
White alone or in combination	21 259	17 191	12 004	56.5	69.8	11 197	52.7	65.1
Black alone or in combination	1 860	1 769	1 187	63.8	67.1	1 151	61.9	65.1
Asian alone or in combination	3 626	2 688	1 599	44.1	59.5	1 410	38.9	52.5

Table CA-13. Crime

(Number, rate per 100,000.)

Item	State			U.S.		
	2007	2008	Percent change	2007	2008	Percent change
Population	36 553 215	36 756 666	0.6	301 621 157	304 059 724	0.8
VIOLENT CRIME						
Number	191 025	185 173	-3.1	1 408 337	1 382 012	-1.9
Rate	522.6	503.8	-3.6	466.9	454.5	-2.7
Murder and Nonnegligent Manslaughter						
Number	2 260	2 142	-5.2	16 929	16 272	-3.9
Rate	6.2	5.8	-5.7	5.6	5.4	-4.7
Forcible Rape						
Number	9 013	8 903	-1.2	90 427	89 000	-1.6
Rate	24.7	24.2	-1.8	30.0	29.3	-2.4
Robbery						
Number	70 542	69 385	-1.6	445 125	441 855	-0.7
Rate	193.0	188.8	-2.2	147.6	145.3	-1.5
Aggravated Assault						
Number	109 210	104 743	-4.1	855 856	834 885	-2.5
Rate	298.8	285.0	-4.6	283.8	274.6	-3.2
PROPERTY CRIME						
Number	1 108 660	1 080 747	-2.5	9 843 481	9 767 915	-0.8
Rate	3 033.0	2 940.3	-3.1	3 263.5	3 212.5	-1.6
Burglary						
Number	237 025	237 835	0.3	2 179 140	2 222 196	2.0
Rate	648.4	647.1	-0.2	722.5	730.8	1.2
Larceny-Theft						
Number	652 243	650 385	-0.3	6 568 572	6 588 873	0.3
Rate	1 784.4	1 769.4	-0.8	2 177.8	2 167.0	-0.5
Motor Vehicle Theft						
Number	219 392	192 527	-12.2	1 095 769	956 846	-12.7
Rate	600.2	523.8	-12.7	363.3	314.7	-13.4

Table CA-14. State Government Finances, 2007

(Dollars, percent distribution.)

Item	Thousands of dollars	Percent distribution
Total Revenue	299 948 562	X
General revenue	189 543 916	63.2
Intergovernmental revenue	49 889 749	16.6
Taxes	114 736 981	38.3
General sales	32 669 175	10.9
Selective sales	7 764 358	2.6
License taxes	7 501 648	2.5
Individual income tax	53 318 287	17.8
Corporate income tax	11 157 898	3.7
Other taxes	2 325 615	0.8
Current charges	13 878 295	4.6
Miscellaneous general revenue	11 038 891	3.7
Utility revenue	5 920 206	2.0
Liquor store revenue	0	0.0
Insurance trust revenue	104 484 440	34.8
Total Expenditure	233 578 021	100.0
Intergovernmental expenditure	92 415 603	39.6
Direct expenditure	141 162 418	60.4
Current operation	94 215 741	40.3
Capital outlay	8 857 338	3.8
Insurance benefits and repayments	29 397 246	12.6
Assistance and subsidies	2 907 776	1.2
Interest on debt	5 784 317	2.5
Exhibit: Salaries and wages	25 414 823	10.9
Total Expenditure	233 578 021	100.0
General expenditure	198 541 221	85.0
Intergovernmental expenditure	92 415 603	39.6
Direct expenditure	106 125 618	45.4
Education	72 804 824	31.2
Public welfare	56 306 480	24.1
Hospitals	6 245 491	2.7
Health	11 494 714	4.9
Highways	9 122 677	3.9
Police protection	1 450 630	0.6
Correction	8 093 209	3.5
Natural resources	4 864 214	2.1
Parks and recreation	461 605	0.2
Government administration	8 415 688	3.6
Interest on general debt	5 360 317	2.3
Other and unallocable	13 921 372	6.0
Utility expenditure	5 639 554	2.4
Liquor store expenditure	0	0.0
Insurance trust expenditure	29 397 246	12.6
Debt at End of Fiscal Year	114 701 797	X
Cash and Security Holdings	579 171 352	X

Table CA-15. State Government Tax Collections, 2008

(Dollars, percent distribution.)

Item	Thousands of dollars	Percent distribution
Total Taxes	117 361 976	X
Property taxes	2 279 103	1.9
Sales and gross receipts	39 825 808	33.9
General sales and gross receipts	31 972 874	27.2
Selective sales taxes	7 852 934	6.7
Alcoholic beverages	327 260	0.3
Insurance premiums	2 172 936	1.9
Motor fuels	3 421 457	2.9
Pari-mutuels	34 949	0.0
Public utilities	754 799	0.6
Tobacco products	1 037 457	0.9
Other selective sales	104 076	0.1
Licenses	7 642 180	6.5
Alcoholic beverages	47 839	0.0
Amusements	12 555	0.0
Corporation	61 467	0.1
Hunting and fishing	95 460	0.1
Motor vehicle	2 704 632	2.3
Motor vehicle operators	235 185	0.2
Public utility	669 928	0.6
Occupation and business, NEC	3 795 476	3.2
Other licenses	19 638	0.0
Income taxes	67 595 067	57.6
Individual income	55 745 970	47.5
Corporation net income	11 849 097	10.1
Other taxes	19 818	0.0
Death and gift	6 303	0.0
Severance	13 515	0.0

Table CA-16. Agriculture

(Number, acres, and dollars.)

Item	2002		2007		Percent change, 2002–2007
	Number	Percent of total	Number	Percent of total	
Number of farms	79 631		81 033		1.8
Farm Size					
Average size of farm (acres)	346		313		-9.5
Farms by size (number of farms)					
Fewer than 50 acres	49 134	61.7	53 358	65.8	8.6
50 to 499 acres	22 097	27.7	19 953	24.6	-9.7
500 acres or more	8 400	10.5	7 722	9.5	-8.1
Land (Acres)					
Total land in farms	27 589 027		25 364 695		-8.1
Total cropland	10 994 161	39.8	9 464 647	37.3	-13.9
Total harvested cropland	8 466 321	30.7	7 633 173	30.1	-9.8
Irrigated land	8 709 353	31.6	8 016 159	31.6	-8.0
Value of Sales (Dollars)					
Agricultural products sold ($1,000)	25 737 173		33 885 064		31.7
Average sales per farm	323 205		418 164		29.4
Sales of crops	19 152 722	74.4	22 903 021	67.6	19.6
Sales of livestock, poultry, and their products	6 584 451	25.6	10 982 043	32.4	66.8
Value of Sales (Number of Farms)					
Less than $10,000	36 662	46.0	37 721	46.6	2.9
$10,000 to $99,999	23 384	29.4	24 271	30.0	3.8
$100,000 to $999,999	14 546	18.3	13 399	16.5	-7.9
$1,000,000 or more	5 039	6.3	5 642	7.0	12.0
Farms by Type of Organization (Number of Farms)					
Family	64 442	80.9	64 001	79.0	-0.7
Partnership	8 953	11.2	9 552	11.8	6.7
Corporation	5 070	6.4	5 750	7.1	13.4
Other: cooperative, estate or trust, institutional, etc	1 166	1.5	1 730	2.1	48.4
Value of Land and Buildings (Dollars)					
Estimated market value of land and buildings ($1,000)	162 533 390		96 129 402		-40.9
Land and buildings average value per farm	2 005 768		1 206 822		-39.8
Average value per acre	6 408		3 526		-45.0
Government Payments					
Number of farms receiving government payments	7 228	9.1	7 444	9.2	3.0
Payments (thousands of dollars)	168 698		240 242		42.4
Average payment per farm	23 340		32 273		38.3
Farm Operator Characteristics					
Farm operators whose principal occupation is farming	49 132	61.7	40 910	50.5	-16.7
Farm operators whose principal occupation is other	30 499	38.3	40 123	49.5	31.6
Average age principal operator (years)	56.8		58.4		2.8

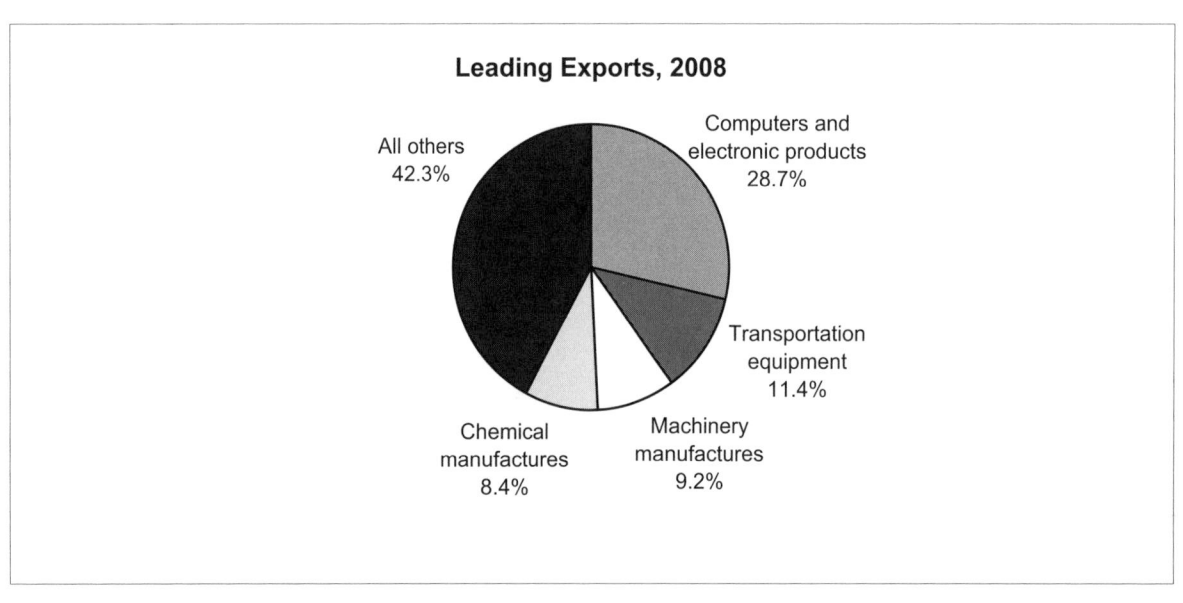

Leading Exports, 2008

All others 42.3%

Computers and electronic products 28.7%

Transportation equipment 11.4%

Machinery manufactures 9.2%

Chemical manufactures 8.4%

COLORADO

Facts and Figures

Location: Western United States; bordered on the N by Wyoming and Nebraska, on the E by Nebraska and Kansas, on the S by Oklahoma and New Mexico, and on the W by Utah; Colorado is one of the Four Corner states—at its SW corner it touches Arizona, New Mexico, and Utah

Area: 104,094 sq. mi. (269,601 sq. km.); rank—8th

Population: 4,939,456 (2008 est.); rank—22nd

Principal Cities: capital—Denver; largest—Denver

Statehood: August 1, 1876; 38th state

U.S. Congress: 2 senators, 7 representatives

State Motto: *Nil sine numine* ("Nothing without providence")

State Songs: "Where the Columbines Grow"; "Rocky Mountain High"

State Nicknames: The Centennial State; Colorful Colorado

Abbreviations: CO; Colo.

State Symbols: flower—Rocky Mountain columbine; tree—Colorado blue spruce; bird—lark bunting

At a Glance

- With an increase in population of 14.8 percent, Colorado ranked 7th among the states in growth from 2000 to 2008.
- An estimated 37,876 marriages took place in Colorado in 2008, compared to 20,992 divorces.
- The 2007 home ownership rate in Colorado was 70.2 percent, giving it a ranking of 31st along with Tennessee.
- Colorado's median household income in 2007 was $55,212, 12th among the states.
- In Colorado, 12 percent of the population lived below the poverty level in 2007, ranking it 27th along with Maine and Rhode Island.
- In 2006-07, 16.8 percent of Coloradans did not have health insurance, compared to 15.5 percent of the total U.S. population.
- In 2007, 3.7 percent of Coloradans were unemployed, compared to 4.6 percent nationwide.
- Colorado ranked 3rd in the nation with 35 percent of its population 25 years old and over having a bachelor's degree in 2007.
- Colorado's violent crime rate in 2007 was 347.8 per 100,000 population, compared to 466.9 for the entire nation.
- Colorado had one physician for every 335 people in 2007, compared to one physician for every 325 people nationwide.
- In the 2008 election, 69.8 percent of Colorado's eligible voters voted, compared to 61.7 percent of eligible voters nationwide.
- Colorado ranked 48th among the states receiving federal aid in 2007, with $1,012 per capita.
- Colorado's gross domestic product was $236 billion in 2007; it ranked 20th among the states.
- With $7.4 billion in exports in 2007, Colorado ranked 31st in exports.
- Coloradans consumed 1.43 trillion Btu's of energy in 2006; the state ranked 27th in total consumption.
- In 2007, Colorado exported $1.1 billion worth of agricultural products, 1.4 percent of the U.S. total.

Table CO-1. Population by Sex, Age, Race, and Hispanic Origin

(Number, percent.)

Sex, age, race, and Hispanic origin	1990	2000	2008	Average annual percent change, 2000–2008
Total Population	3 294 394	4 301 261	4 939 456	1.7
Percent of total U.S. population	1.3	1.5	1.6	X
Sex				
Male	1 631 295	2 165 983	2 491 041	1.8
Female	1 663 099	2 135 278	2 448 415	1.7
Age				
Under 5 years	252 893	297 505	358 280	2.4
5 to 19 years	705 448	927 163	974 401	0.6
20 to 64 years	2 006 610	2 660 520	3 095 681	1.9
65 years and over	329 443	416 073	511 094	2.6
Median age (years)	32.4	34.3	35.7	X
Race and Hispanic Origin[1]				
One race				
White	2 905 474	3 560 005	4 432 376	2.8
Black	133 146	165 063	211 249	3.1
American Indian and Alaskan Native	27 776	44 241	60 375	4.0
Asian[2]	59 862	95 213	131 084	4.1
Native Hawaiian and Other Pacific Islander	X	4 621	7 469	6.2
Two or more races	X	122 187	96 903	-2.9
Hispanic (of any race)	424 302	735 601	997 062	3.9

[1]Data on race in 2000 and 2008 are not comparable to 1990. Individuals could only report one race in the 1990 census but could report one or more races on the 2000 census.
[2]Data in 1990 refer to Asian and Pacific Islanders.

Table CO-2. Marital Status

(Number, percent distribution.)

Sex and marital status	1990	2000	2007
Males, 15 Years and Over	1 255 439	1 694 635	1 942 484
Never married	29.7	30.5	33.1
Now married, except separated	57.3	56.6	52.8
Separated	1.8	1.4	1.5
Widowed	1.9	1.9	1.9
Divorced	9.3	9.6	10.8
Females, 15 Years and Over	1 305 576	1 690 734	1 925 233
Never married	22.0	23.4	25.6
Now married, except separated	54.7	54.7	51.3
Separated	2.3	1.8	2.0
Widowed	9.1	7.6	7.4
Divorced	12.0	12.5	13.7

Table CO-3. Households and Housing Characteristics

(Number, percent, and dollars.)

Item	1990	2000	2007	Average annual percent change, 2000–2007
Total Households	1 282 489	1 658 238	1 859 965	1.7
Family households	854 214	1 084 461	1 202 485	1.5
Married-couple family	690 292	858 671	934 426	1.2
Other family	163 922	225 790	268 059	2.5
Male householder, no wife present	39 353	66 811	87 801	4.0
Female householder, no husband present	124 569	158 979	180 258	1.8
Nonfamily households	428 275	573 777	657 480	2.0
Householder living alone	340 962	435 778	527 167	2.8
Householder not living alone	87 313	137 999	130 313	-0.8
Housing Characteristics				
Total housing units	1 477 349	1 808 037	2 127 358	2.4
Occupied housing units	1 282 489	1 658 238	1 859 965	1.7
Owner-occupied	798 277	1 116 137	1 280 207	2.0
Renter-occupied	484 212	542 101	579 758	1.0
Average size	2.51	2.53	2.56	X
Financial Characteristics				
Median gross rent of renter-occupied housing units (dollars)	418	671	788	2.3
Median monthly owner costs for housing units with a mortgage (dollars)	800	1 197	1 569	3.9
Median value of owner-occupied housing units (dollars)	82 400	166 600	233 900	5.0

Table CO-4. Median Income and Poverty Status, 2007

(Number, percent.)

Characteristic	State		U.S.	
	Number	Percent	Number	Percent
Median Income				
Households (dollars)	55 212	X	50 740	X
Families (dollars)	67 491	X	61 173	X
Below Poverty Level				
Sex				
Male	253 817	10.6	16 576 071	11.5
Female	315 569	13.3	21 476 176	14.3
Age				
Under 18 years	191 725	16.3	13 097 100	18.0
Related children under 18 years	185 240	15.9	12 728 964	17.6
18 to 64 years	337 279	10.9	21 495 507	11.6
65 years and over	40 382	8.5	3 459 640	9.5

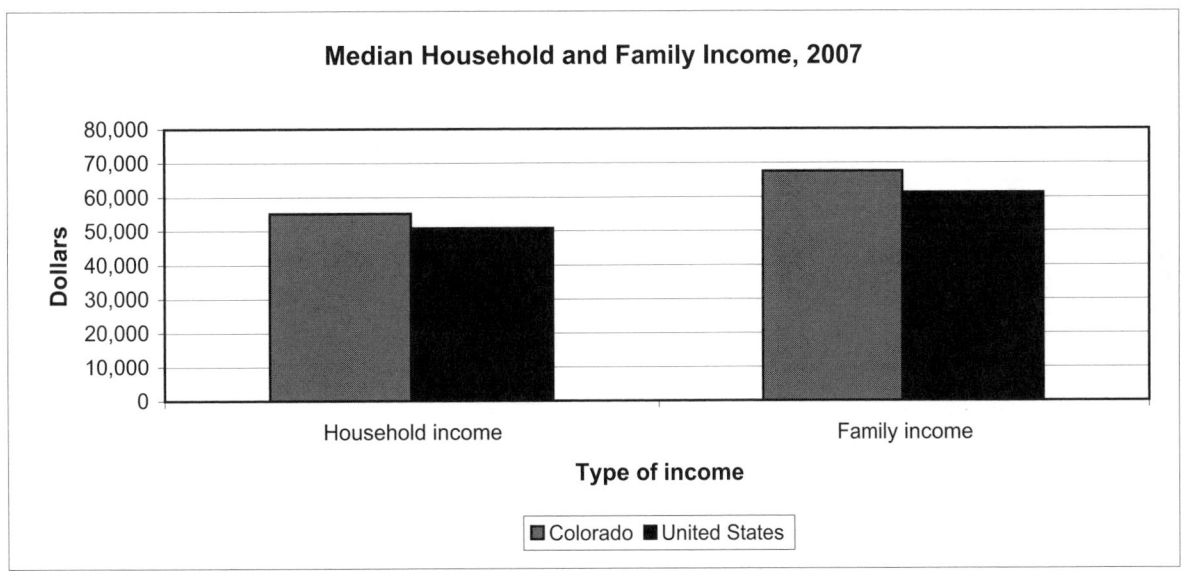

Table CO-5. Health Insurance Coverage Status for All Persons and Children Under 18 Years of Age

(Number, percent.)

Item	2000	2001	2002	2003	2004	2005	2006	2007
ALL PERSONS	4 341	4 410	4 477	4 480	4 524	4 641	4 803	4 877
Covered by Private or Government Health Insurance								
Number	3 743	3 752	3 801	3 735	3 806	3 869	3 977	4 077
Percent	86.2	85.1	84.9	83.4	84.1	83.4	82.8	83.6
Not Covered								
Number	598	659	676	745	719	772	826	801
Percent	13.8	14.9	15.1	16.6	15.9	16.6	17.2	16.4
Percent in the U.S. not covered	13.7	14.1	14.7	15.1	14.9	15.3	15.8	15.3
CHILDREN UNDER 18 YEARS OF AGE	1 129	1 189	1 141	1 163	1 169	1 187	1 209	1 208
Covered by Private or Government Health Insurance								
Number	968	1 036	986	1 009	998	1 024	1 033	1 051
Percent	85.8	87.1	86.4	86.7	85.4	86.3	85.4	87.0
Not Covered								
Number	160	154	155	155	170	163	176	157
Percent	14.2	12.9	13.6	13.3	14.6	13.7	14.6	13.0
Percent in the U.S. not covered	11.6	11.3	11.2	11.0	10.5	10.9	11.7	11.0

Table CO-6. Employment Status by Demographic Group, Preliminary 2008

(Number, percent.)

Characteristic	Civilian noninstitutional population	Civilian labor force		Employment		Unemployed	
		Number	Percent of population	Number	Percent of population	Number	Unemployment rate
TOTAL	3 792	2 735	72.1	2 603	68.6	132	4.8
Sex							
Men	1 886	1 513	80.0	1 434	76.0	79	5.2
Women	1 906	1 222	64.0	1 169	61.3	53	4.3
Race, Sex, and Hispanic Origin							
White	3 446	2 495	72.4	2 381	69.1	114	4.6
Men	1 722	1 386	80.5	1 318	76.5	68	4.9
Women	1 724	1 109	64.3	1 063	61.7	46	4.1
Black or African American	147	103	70.4	91	61.9	12	12.0
Men	76	57	74.9	50	65.6	7	12.4
Women	71	47	65.6	41	58.0	5	11.6
Hispanic	662	476	71.9	444	67.0	32	6.8
Men	346	290	83.8	267	77.3	23	7.8
Women	316	186	58.9	176	55.8	10	5.2
Age							
16 to 19 years	247	111	44.8	87	35.4	23	21.1
20 to 24 years	323	258	79.8	237	73.5	20	7.9
25 to 34 years	716	619	86.4	591	82.6	27	4.4
35 to 44 years	731	628	85.9	609	83.4	18	2.9
45 to 54 years	762	660	86.6	637	83.6	23	3.5
55 to 64 years	543	377	69.4	362	66.7	15	3.9
65 years and over	471	83	17.7	79	16.7	5	5.6

Note: Data in Table 6 are from the Current Population Survey (CPS) and do not match the estimates in Table 7. See notes and definitions for more details.

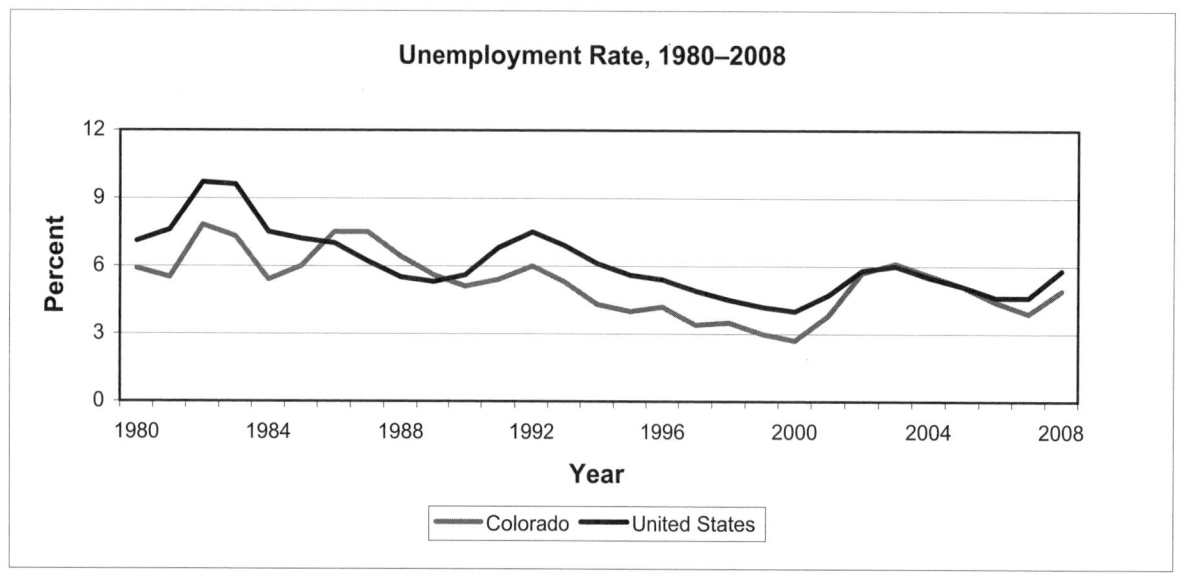

Table CO-7. Employment Status of the Civilian Noninstitutional Population Age 16 Years and Over

(Number, percent.)

Year	Civilian labor force	Civilian participation rate	Employed	Unemployed	Unemployment rate
1998	2 307 907	74.2	2 226 296	81 611	3.5
1999	2 340 938	73.3	2 269 668	71 270	3.0
2000	2 364 990	72.4	2 300 192	64 798	2.7
2001	2 395 264	71.6	2 303 494	91 770	3.8
2002	2 442 734	71.7	2 304 109	138 625	5.7
2003	2 492 340	72.1	2 339 532	152 808	6.1
2004	2 535 421	72.5	2 392 952	142 469	5.6
2005	2 580 752	72.6	2 448 150	132 602	5.1
2006	2 642 744	72.8	2 526 986	115 758	4.4
2007	2 686 427	72.6	2 582 486	103 941	3.9
2008	2 730 447	72.3	2 596 309	134 138	4.9

Table CO-8. Employment and Average Wages by Industry

(Estimates for 2001–2006 are based on the 2002 North American Industry Classification System [NAICS]. Estimates for 2007 are based on the 2007 NAICS.)

Industry	2001	2002	2003	2004	2005	2006	2007
	Number of jobs						
WAGE AND SALARY EMPLOYMENT BY INDUSTRY	2 370 244	2 325 508	2 297 975	2 320 783	2 372 923	2 425 681	2 475 048
Farm Wage and Salary Employment	15 603	12 905	15 537	14 451	14 549	14 554	12 659
Nonfarm Wage and Salary Employment	2 354 641	2 312 603	2 282 438	2 306 332	2 358 374	2 411 127	2 462 389
Private wage and salary employment	1 963 110	1 909 806	1 876 437	1 900 586	1 945 549	1 994 432	2 038 676
Forestry, fishing, hunting, and other	6 235	6 322	6 605	6 542	6 958	6 995	6 806
Mining	12 974	13 018	13 224	14 475	16 986	20 637	25 009
Utilities	8 055	8 184	7 890	7 949	7 978	8 138	7 981
Construction	174 020	166 734	156 009	157 373	166 020	173 505	173 462
Manufacturing	183 268	167 739	154 930	152 748	151 844	150 807	148 008
Durable goods manufacturing	125 672	113 240	102 346	101 871	101 625	100 719	98 408
Nondurable goods manufacturing	57 596	54 499	52 584	50 877	50 219	50 088	49 600
Wholesale trade	101 140	96 572	93 851	93 292	94 898	97 773	100 785
Retail trade	253 463	249 936	246 961	248 818	253 552	256 076	261 424
Transportation and warehousing	68 991	65 646	64 418	65 273	65 244	65 847	67 731
Information	107 550	93 622	84 995	81 020	77 543	76 142	76 945
Finance and insurance	105 434	105 227	106 500	107 340	110 083	112 615	111 193
Real estate and rental and leasing	47 958	47 363	47 366	47 520	48 450	49 169	49 540
Professional and technical services	159 970	150 056	149 322	154 860	163 675	170 456	178 547
Management of companies and enterprises	17 861	18 912	20 746	23 418	25 033	27 148	28 263
Administrative and waste services	139 151	130 617	128 327	132 655	135 808	142 387	149 559
Educational services	29 552	31 342	31 857	33 740	36 006	36 808	38 230
Health care and social assistance	186 638	193 592	197 740	202 253	207 091	212 890	221 229
Arts, entertainment, and recreation	44 758	45 347	43 949	45 265	46 239	46 718	47 355
Accommodation and food services	207 642	207 802	207 188	211 748	217 133	223 702	228 360
Other services, except public administration	108 450	111 775	114 559	114 297	115 008	116 619	118 249
Government and government enterprises	391 531	402 797	406 001	405 746	412 825	416 695	423 713
	Dollars						
AVERAGE WAGES AND SALARIES BY INDUSTRY	37 252	37 384	38 298	39 683	41 046	42 909	44 790
Average Farm Wages and Salaries	21 521	30 832	22 541	25 938	29 432	28 826	35 607
Average Nonfarm Wages and Salaries	37 357	37 421	38 405	39 769	41 118	42 994	44 837
Average private wages and salaries	37 918	37 658	38 580	39 908	41 258	43 306	45 249
Forestry, fishing, hunting, and other	17 034	17 325	17 871	17 848	18 303	19 000	21 273
Mining	74 907	64 501	66 387	83 497	82 872	83 742	86 673
Utilities	65 121	64 215	64 333	71 659	71 800	92 419	77 455
Construction	38 947	39 235	39 330	40 288	41 499	43 227	45 558
Manufacturing	47 446	48 578	49 890	51 625	53 721	54 954	56 831
Durable goods manufacturing	51 257	52 672	54 085	55 807	58 090	59 670	61 233
Nondurable goods manufacturing	39 131	40 071	41 724	43 253	44 878	45 470	48 098
Wholesale trade	52 415	52 178	53 751	56 160	58 023	61 586	65 980
Retail trade	23 848	24 158	24 537	25 069	25 400	25 850	26 588
Transportation and warehousing	38 901	39 769	39 300	40 261	40 457	43 590	43 264
Information	65 784	63 162	66 508	65 644	68 410	76 176	77 062
Finance and insurance	55 683	55 101	58 147	59 064	62 234	65 095	68 829
Real estate and rental and leasing	33 443	34 128	35 420	36 807	38 850	41 088	43 247
Professional and technical services	60 982	60 484	61 952	64 901	67 173	70 790	75 157
Management of companies and enterprises	76 804	70 529	75 821	88 027	99 506	103 610	111 032
Administrative and waste services	26 624	27 640	28 495	29 246	29 833	30 576	31 638
Educational services	25 620	25 243	26 530	26 993	27 712	28 843	30 298
Health care and social assistance	33 566	35 062	36 037	37 454	38 293	39 572	41 156
Arts, entertainment, and recreation	28 252	28 078	29 294	28 226	28 777	31 226	32 203
Accommodation and food services	14 668	14 873	15 297	15 968	16 372	17 050	18 156
Other services, except public administration	24 152	24 836	25 801	26 932	27 299	28 426	29 802
Government and government enterprises	34 540	36 298	37 600	39 120	40 457	41 503	42 856

Table CO-9. Employment Characteristics by Family Type

(Number, percent.)

Family type and labor force status	2005		2006		2007	
	Total	Families with own children under 18 years	Total	Families with own children under 18 years	Total	Families with own children under 18 years
TOTAL FAMILIES	1 164 221	574 525	1 196 223	581 273	1 202 485	583 318
FAMILY TYPE AND LABOR FORCE STATUS						
Married Coupled Families	907 833	413 056	934 148	419 803	934 426	416 956
Both husband and wife in labor force	57.3	64.0	57.1	63.5	57.2	64.8
Husband in labor force, wife not in labor force	22.6	29.3	23.6	30.8	23.5	29.8
Wife in labor force, husband not in labor force	6.3	4.0	6.0	3.4	5.8	3.2
Both husband and wife not in labor force	13.9	2.7	13.3	2.2	13.5	2.1
Other Families	256 388	161 469	262 075	161 470	268 059	166 362
Female householder, no husband present	68.8	72.8	69.3	73.5	67.2	69.7
In labor force	51.8	59.5	52.7	60.2	52.0	58.5
Not in labor force	17.1	13.3	16.7	13.3	15.2	11.1
Male householder, no wife present	31.2	27.2	30.7	26.5	32.8	30.3
In labor force	26.6	25.1	25.4	24.7	28.0	28.8
Not in labor force	4.6	2.1	5.3	1.9	4.7	1.5

Table CO-10. School Enrollment and Educational Attainment, 2007

(Number, percent.)

Item	State	U.S.
Enrollment		
Total population 3 years and over	4 651 132	289 295 761
Enrolled in school	1 247 277	79 329 527
Enrolled in preschool (percent)	6.3	6.2
Enrolled in grades K-12 (percent)	66.9	67.6
Enrolled in college or graduate school (percent)	26.8	26.2
Attainment		
Total population 25 years and over	3 203 704	197 892 369
Less than a high school diploma (percent)	11.1	15.5
High school diploma or more (percent)	88.9	84.5
Bachelor's degree or more (percent)	35.0	27.5
Graduate degree or more (percent)	12.5	10.1

Table CO-11. Educational Indicators

(Number, percent.)

Item	State	U.S.
Public Schools, 2006–2007 (except where noted)		
Number of school districts	201	17 742
Number of schools	1 736	99 639
Number of students	794 026	49 315 842
Student-teacher ratio	16.9	15.5
Expenditures per student (dollars)	$8 286	...
Averaged freshman graduation rate, 2005–2006	75.5	...
Dropout rate, grades 9–12, 2005–2006	7.8	3.7
Students eligible for free or reduced-price lunch (percent)	34.0	41.2
English-language learners (percent)	...	5.1
Students with IEP (percent)	...	12.7
Private Schools, 2007–2008 (except where noted)		
Number of schools	415	33 740
Number of students	48 945	5 072 451
High school graduates, 2006–2007	2 524	306 605
Student-teacher ratio	10.1	11.1

Table CO-12. Reported Voting and Registration of the Voting-Age Population, November 2008

(Number in thousands, percent.)

Item	Total population	Total citizen population	Registered			Voted		
			Total registered	Percent registered (total population)	Percent registered (total citizen population)	Total voted	Percent voted (total population)	Percent voted (total citizen population)
U.S. total	225 499	206 072	146 311	64.9	71.0	131 144	58.2	63.6
State total	3 694	3 374	2 437	66.0	72.2	2 308	62.5	68.4
Sex								
Male	1 840	1 665	1 190	64.7	71.5	1 123	61.0	67.5
Female	1 854	1 710	1 247	67.2	72.9	1 185	63.9	69.3
Race								
White alone	3 344	3 097	2 262	67.6	73.0	2 137	63.9	69.0
White non-Hispanic alone	2 771	2 731	2 049	73.9	75.0	1 954	70.5	71.5
Black alone	150	138	85	56.9	61.6	81	54.4	58.9
Asian alone	131	70	48	36.7	...	48	36.7	...
Hispanic (of any race)	590	380	225	38.1	59.1	195	33.1	51.4
White alone or in combination	3 378	3 131	2 284	67.6	73.0	2 160	63.9	69.0
Black alone or in combination	160	149	89	55.8	60.1	86	53.4	57.6
Asian alone or in combination	143	82	55	38.8	67.6	55	38.8	67.6

Table CO-13. Crime

(Number, rate per 100,000.)

Item	State			U.S.		
	2007	2008	Percent change	2007	2008	Percent change
Population	4 861 515	4 939 456	1.6	301 621 157	304 059 724	0.8
VIOLENT CRIME						
Number	16 906	16 946	0.2	1 408 337	1 382 012	-1.9
Rate	347.8	343.1	-1.3	466.9	454.5	-2.7
Murder and Nonnegligent Manslaughter						
Number	153	157	2.6	16 929	16 272	-3.9
Rate	3.1	3.2	1.0	5.6	5.4	-4.7
Forcible Rape						
Number	1 998	2 098	5.0	90 427	89 000	-1.6
Rate	41.1	42.5	3.3	30.0	29.3	-2.4
Robbery						
Number	3 453	3 365	-2.5	445 125	441 855	-0.7
Rate	71.0	68.1	-4.1	147.6	145.3	-1.5
Aggravated Assault						
Number	11 302	11 326	0.2	855 856	834 885	-2.5
Rate	232.5	229.3	-1.4	283.8	274.6	-3.2
PROPERTY CRIME						
Number	146 141	140 725	-3.7	9 843 481	9 767 915	-0.8
Rate	3 006.1	2 849.0	-5.2	3 263.5	3 212.5	-1.6
Burglary						
Number	28 751	28 256	-1.7	2 179 140	2 222 196	2.0
Rate	591.4	572.0	-3.3	722.5	730.8	1.2
Larceny-Theft						
Number	100 598	98 950	-1.6	6 568 572	6 588 873	0.3
Rate	2 069.3	2 003.3	-3.2	2 177.8	2 167.0	-0.5
Motor Vehicle Theft						
Number	16 792	13 519	-19.5	1 095 769	956 846	-12.7
Rate	345.4	273.7	-20.8	363.3	314.7	-13.4

Table CO-14. State Government Finances, 2007

(Dollars, percent distribution.)

Item	Thousands of dollars	Percent distribution
Total Revenue	26 881 361	X
General revenue	18 481 180	68.8
Intergovernmental revenue	4 732 975	17.6
Taxes	9 205 912	34.2
General sales	2 218 951	8.3
Selective sales	1 231 257	4.6
License taxes	343 346	1.3
Individual income tax	4 795 423	17.8
Corporate income tax	479 445	1.8
Other taxes	137 490	0.5
Current charges	2 550 986	9.5
Miscellaneous general revenue	1 991 307	7.4
Utility revenue	0	0.0
Liquor store revenue	0	0.0
Insurance trust revenue	8 400 181	31.2
Total Expenditure	21 243 982	100.0
Intergovernmental expenditure	6 000 582	28.2
Direct expenditure	15 243 400	71.8
Current operation	10 005 070	47.1
Capital outlay	1 069 262	5.0
Insurance benefits and repayments	3 235 338	15.2
Assistance and subsidies	210 204	1.0
Interest on debt	723 526	3.4
Exhibit: Salaries and wages	3 255 396	15.3
Total Expenditure	21 243 982	100.0
General expenditure	17 980 929	84.6
Intergovernmental expenditure	6 000 582	28.2
Direct expenditure	11 980 347	56.4
Education	7 646 922	36.0
Public welfare	4 271 325	20.1
Hospitals	394 763	1.9
Health	758 113	3.6
Highways	1 085 183	5.1
Police protection	114 975	0.5
Correction	895 827	4.2
Natural resources	272 789	1.3
Parks and recreation	82 091	0.4
Government administration	812 908	3.8
Interest on general debt	701 400	3.3
Other and unallocable	944 633	4.4
Utility expenditure	27 715	0.1
Liquor store expenditure	0	0.0
Insurance trust expenditure	3 235 338	15.2
Debt at End of Fiscal Year	14 905 758	X
Cash and Security Holdings	64 491 284	X

Table CO-15. State Government Tax Collections, 2008

(Dollars, percent distribution.)

Item	Thousands of dollars	Percent distribution
Total Taxes	9 624 636	X
Sales and gross receipts	3 519 589	36.6
General sales and gross receipts	2 312 731	24.0
Selective sales taxes	1 206 858	12.5
Alcoholic beverages	35 472	0.4
Amusements	108 187	1.1
Insurance premiums	190 750	2.0
Motor fuels	637 193	6.6
Pari-mutuels	2 747	0.0
Public utilities	11 810	0.1
Tobacco products	220 699	2.3
Licenses	377 179	X
Alcoholic beverages	6 085	0.1
Amusements	714	X
Corporation	13 115	0.1
Hunting and fishing	75 023	X
Motor vehicle	219 590	2.3
Motor vehicle operators	13 587	X
Public utility	14 250	0.1
Occupation and business, NEC	33 717	X
Other licenses	1 098	0.0
Income taxes	5 575 967	57.9
Individual income	5 067 981	X
Corporation net income	507 986	5.3
Other taxes	151 901	1.6
Death and gift	427	X
Severance	151 474	X

Table CO-16.　Agriculture

(Number, acres, and dollars.)

Item	2002		2007		Percent change, 2002–2007
	Number	Percent of total	Number	Percent of total	
Number of farms	31 369		37 054		18.1
Farm Size					
Average size of farm (acres)	991		853		-13.9
Farms by size (number of farms)					
Fewer than 50 acres	10 288	32.8	13 635	36.8	32.5
50 to 499 acres	11 971	38.2	13 977	37.7	16.8
500 acres or more	9 110	29.0	9 442	25.5	3.6
Land (Acres)					
Total land in farms	31 093 336		31 604 911		1.6
Total cropland	11 530 700	37.1	11 483 936	36.3	-0.4
Total harvested cropland	4 346 955	14.0	5 888 926	18.6	35.5
Irrigated land	2 590 654	8.3	2 867 957	9.1	10.7
Value of Sales (Dollars)					
Agricultural products sold ($1,000)	4 525 196		6 061 134		33.9
Average sales per farm	144 257		163 576		13.4
Sales of crops	1 216 278	26.9	1 981 399	32.7	62.9
Sales of livestock, poultry, and their products	3 308 918	73.1	4 079 735	67.3	23.3
Value of Sales (Number of Farms)					
Less than $10,000	18 962	60.4	23 690	63.9	24.9
$10,000 to $99,999	8 477	27.0	8 266	22.3	-2.5
$100,000 to $999,999	3 403	10.8	4 368	11.8	28.4
$1,000,000 or more	527	1.7	730	2.0	38.5
Farms by Type of Organization (Number of Farms)					
Family	27 280	87.0	30 164	81.4	10.6
Partnership	2 109	6.7	3 762	10.2	78.4
Corporation	1 629	5.2	2 342	6.3	43.8
Other: cooperative, estate or trust, institutional, etc	351	1.1	786	2.1	123.9
Value of Land and Buildings (Dollars)					
Estimated market value of land and buildings ($1,000)	33 058 456		23 757 228		-28.1
Land and buildings average value per farm	892 170		757 613		-15.1
Average value per acre	1 046		756		-27.7
Government Payments					
Number of farms receiving government payments	10 163	32.4	11 572	31.2	13.9
Payments (thousands of dollars)	125 774		155 980		24.0
Average payment per farm	12 376		13 479		8.9
Farm Operator Characteristics					
Farm operators whose principal occupation is farming	18 331	58.4	14 958	40.4	-18.4
Farm operators whose principal occupation is other	13 038	41.6	22 096	59.6	69.5
Average age principal operator (years)	54.5		57.0		4.6

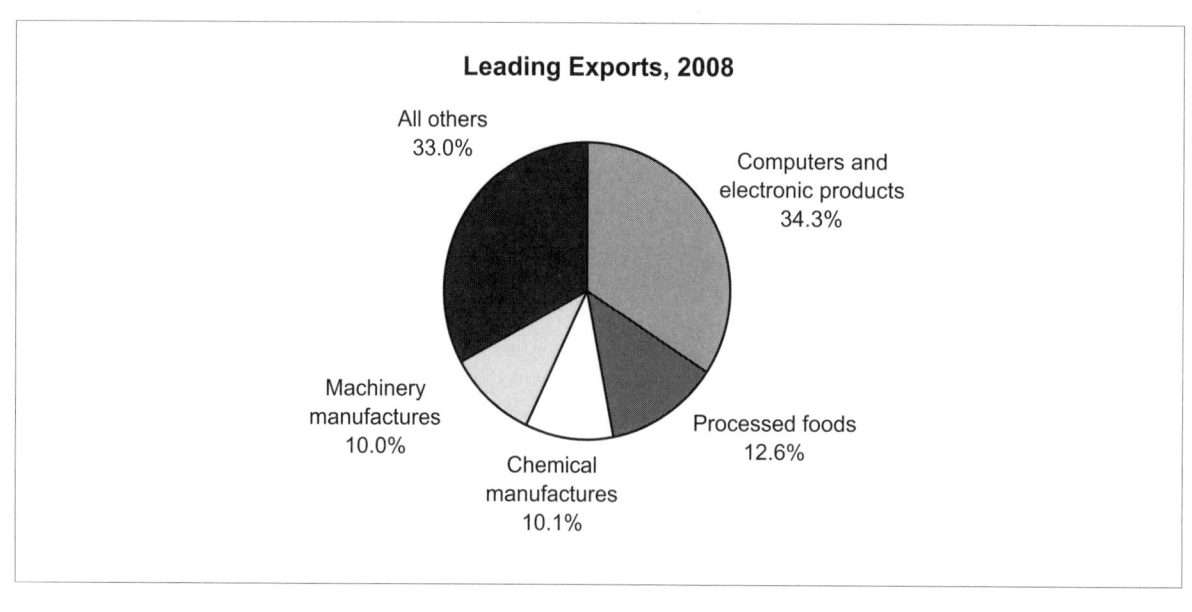

Leading Exports, 2008

All others 33.0%

Computers and electronic products 34.3%

Processed foods 12.6%

Chemical manufactures 10.1%

Machinery manufactures 10.0%

CONNECTICUT

Facts and Figures

Location: Northeastern United States; bordered on the N by Massachusetts, on the E by Rhode Island, on the S by Long Island Sound, and on the W by New York

Area: 5,543 sq. mi. (14,357); rank—48th

Population: 3,501,252 (2008 est.); rank—29th

Principal Cities: capital—Hartford; largest—Bridgeport

Statehood: January 9, 1788; 5th state

U.S. Congress: 2 senators, 5 representatives

State Motto: *Qui transtulit sustinet* ("He who transplanted still sustains")

State Song: "Yankee Doodle"

State Nicknames: The Constitution State; The Nutmeg State

Abbreviations: CT; Conn.

State Symbols: flower—mountain laurel; tree—white oak; bird—American robin

At a Glance

- With an increase in population of 2.8 percent, Connecticut ranked 39th among the states in growth from 2000 to 2008.
- An estimated 19,105 marriages took place in Connecticut in 2008, compared to 11,369 divorces.
- The 2007 home ownership rate in Connecticut was 70.3 percent, giving it a ranking of 28th along with North Carolina and Oklahoma.
- Connecticut's median household income in 2007 was $65,967, 3rd among the states.
- In Connecticut, 7.9 percent of the population lived below the poverty level in 2007, ranking it 49th.
- In 2006-07, 9.4 percent of Connecticuters did not have health insurance, compared to 15.5 percent of the total U.S. population.
- In 2007, 4.5 percent of Connecticuters were unemployed, compared to 4.6 percent nationwide.
- Connecticut ranked 4th in the nation with 34.7 percent of its population 25 years old and over having a bachelor's degree in 2007.
- Connecticut's violent crime rate in 2007 was 256 per 100,000 population, compared to 466.9 for the entire nation.
- Connecticut had one physician for every 237 people in 2007, compared to one physician for every 325 people nationwide.
- In the 2008 election, 67.2 percent of Connecticut's eligible voters voted, compared to 61.7 percent of eligible voters nationwide.
- Connecticut ranked 22nd among the states receiving federal aid in 2007, with $1,422 per capita.
- Connecticut's gross domestic product was $216 billion in 2007; it ranked 23rd among the states.
- With $13.8 billion in exports in 2007, Connecticut ranked 25th in exports.
- Connecticuters consumed 848.9 billion Btu's of energy in 2006; the state ranked 33rd in total consumption.
- In 2007, Connecticut exported $116 million worth of agricultural products, less than 1 percent of the U.S. total.

Table CT-1. Population by Sex, Age, Race, and Hispanic Origin

(Number, percent.)

Sex, age, race, and Hispanic origin	1990	2000	2008	Average annual percent change, 2000–2008
Total Population	3 287 116	3 405 565	3 501 252	0.3
Percent of total U.S. population	1.3	1.2	1.2	X
Sex				
Male	1 592 873	1 649 319	1 707 410	0.4
Female	1 694 243	1 756 246	1 793 842	0.3
Age				
Under 5 years	228 356	223 344	211 637	-0.7
5 to 19 years	614 957	702 358	701 992	0.0
20 to 64 years	1 997 896	2 009 680	2 109 616	0.6
65 years and over	445 907	470 183	478 007	0.2
Median age (years)	34.3	37.4	39.4	X
Race and Hispanic Origin[1]				
One race				
White	2 859 353	2 780 355	2 950 808	0.7
Black	274 269	309 843	361 879	2.0
American Indian and Alaskan Native	6 654	9 639	13 387	4.2
Asian[2]	50 698	82 313	121 248	5.0
Native Hawaiian and Other Pacific Islander	X	1 366	2 861	9.7
Two or more races	X	74 848	51 069	-4.7
Hispanic (of any race)	213 116	320 323	419 391	3.4

[1]Data on race in 2000 and 2008 are not comparable to 1990. Individuals could only report one race in the 1990 census but could report one or more races on the 2000 census.
[2]Data in 1990 refer to Asian and Pacific Islanders.

Table CT-2. Marital Status

(Number, percent distribution.)

Sex and marital status	1990	2000	2007
Males, 15 Years and Over	1 269 569	1 284 881	1 364 373
Never married	32.5	30.0	34.4
Now married, except separated	56.8	58.0	53.6
Separated	1.4	1.3	1.3
Widowed	2.7	2.7	2.7
Divorced	6.6	7.9	8.1
Females, 15 Years and Over	1 385 814	1 411 369	1 469 757
Never married	25.8	24.5	28.9
Now married, except separated	51.6	52.3	48.1
Separated	2.0	1.8	1.8
Widowed	11.8	10.8	10.2
Divorced	8.8	10.5	11.0

Table CT-3. Households and Housing Characteristics

(Number, percent, and dollars.)

Item	1990	2000	2007	Average annual percent change, 2000–2007
Total Households	1 230 479	1 301 670	1 320 714	0.2
Family households	864 493	881 170	885 471	0.1
Married-couple family	684 660	676 467	673 742	-0.1
Other family	179 833	204 703	211 729	0.5
Male householder, no wife present	39 448	47 292	51 621	1.3
Female householder, no husband present	140 385	157 411	160 108	0.2
Nonfamily households	365 986	420 500	435 243	0.5
Householder living alone	297 161	344 224	356 145	0.5
Householder not living alone	68 825	76 276	79 098	0.5
Housing Characteristics				
Total housing units	1 320 850	1 385 975	1 438 548	0.5
Occupied housing units	1 230 479	1 301 670	1 320 714	0.2
Owner-occupied	807 481	869 729	924 839	0.9
Renter-occupied	422 998	431 941	395 875	-1.2
Average size	2.59	2.53	2.56	X
Financial Characteristics				
Median gross rent of renter-occupied housing units (dollars)	598	681	931	4.6
Median monthly owner costs for housing units with a mortgage (dollars)	1 096	1 426	1 971	4.7
Median value of owner-occupied housing units (dollars)	176 700	166 900	309 200	9.2

Table CT-4. Median Income and Poverty Status, 2007

(Number, percent.)

Characteristic	State		U.S.	
	Number	Percent	Number	Percent
Median Income				
Households (dollars)	65 967	X	50 740	X
Families (dollars)	81 421	X	61 173	X
Below Poverty Level				
Sex				
Male	116 914	7.1	16 576 071	11.5
Female	151 966	8.7	21 476 176	14.3
Age				
Under 18 years	89 373	11.1	13 097 100	18.0
Related children under 18 years	85 530	10.6	12 728 964	17.6
18 to 64 years	151 365	7.1	21 495 507	11.6
65 years and over	28 142	6.4	3 459 640	9.5

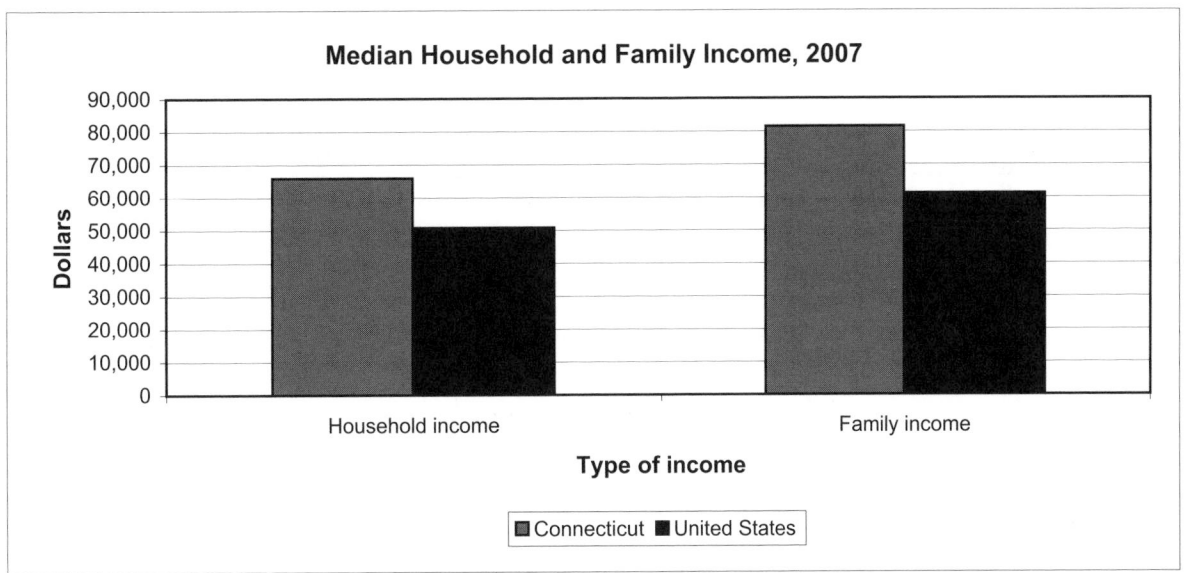

Table CT-5. Health Insurance Coverage Status for All Persons and Children Under 18 Years of Age

(Number, percent.)

Item	2000	2001	2002	2003	2004	2005	2006	2007
ALL PERSONS	3 370	3 392	3 382	3 421	3 492	3 487	3 462	3 476
Covered by Private or Government Health Insurance								
Number	3 057	3 071	3 051	3 076	3 112	3 106	3 137	3 150
Percent	90.7	90.5	90.2	89.9	89.1	89.1	90.6	90.6
Not Covered								
Number	313	321	331	346	381	381	325	326
Percent	9.3	9.5	9.8	10.1	10.9	10.9	9.4	9.4
Percent in the U.S. not covered	13.7	14.1	14.7	15.1	14.9	15.3	15.8	15.3
CHILDREN UNDER 18 YEARS OF AGE	831	815	884	853	840	832	820	819
Covered by Private or Government Health Insurance								
Number	776	758	817	785	780	768	771	776
Percent	93.3	93.1	92.4	92.1	92.9	92.3	94.0	94.8
Not Covered								
Number	55	57	67	68	60	64	49	43
Percent	6.7	6.9	7.6	7.9	7.1	7.7	6.0	5.2
Percent in the U.S. not covered	11.6	11.3	11.2	11.0	10.5	10.9	11.7	11.0

Table CT-6. Employment Status by Demographic Group, Preliminary 2008
(Number, percent.)

Characteristic	Civilian noninstitutional population	Civilian labor force		Employment		Unemployed	
		Number	Percent of population	Number	Percent of population	Number	Unemployment rate
TOTAL	2 739	1 891	69.0	1 782	65.1	109	5.7
Sex							
Men	1 314	984	75.0	925	70.4	59	6.0
Women	1 425	907	64.0	857	60.1	50	5.5
Race, Sex, and Hispanic Origin							
White	2 339	1 609	68.8	1 526	65.2	83	5.2
Men	1 125	842	74.9	798	70.9	44	5.2
Women	1 215	767	63.2	728	60.0	39	5.1
Black or African American	258	181	70.1	159	61.5	22	12.3
Men	116	83	71.9	70	60.7	13	15.6
Women	142	98	68.6	88	62.2	9	9.4
Hispanic	276	194	70.4	172	62.4	22	11.3
Men	133	102	76.7	91	68.0	12	11.4
Women	142	92	64.5	82	57.3	10	11.2
Age							
16 to 19 years	202	92	45.7	76	37.8	16	17.2
20 to 24 years	206	159	77.1	141	68.6	17	10.9
25 to 34 years	391	333	85.3	314	80.3	20	5.9
35 to 44 years	523	446	85.3	426	81.5	20	4.4
45 to 54 years	548	462	84.3	441	80.5	21	4.5
55 to 64 years	411	300	73.0	289	70.3	11	3.7
65 years and over	458	98	21.5	95	20.6	4	4.0

Note: Data in Table 6 are from the Current Population Survey (CPS) and do not match the estimates in Table 7. See notes and definitions for more details.

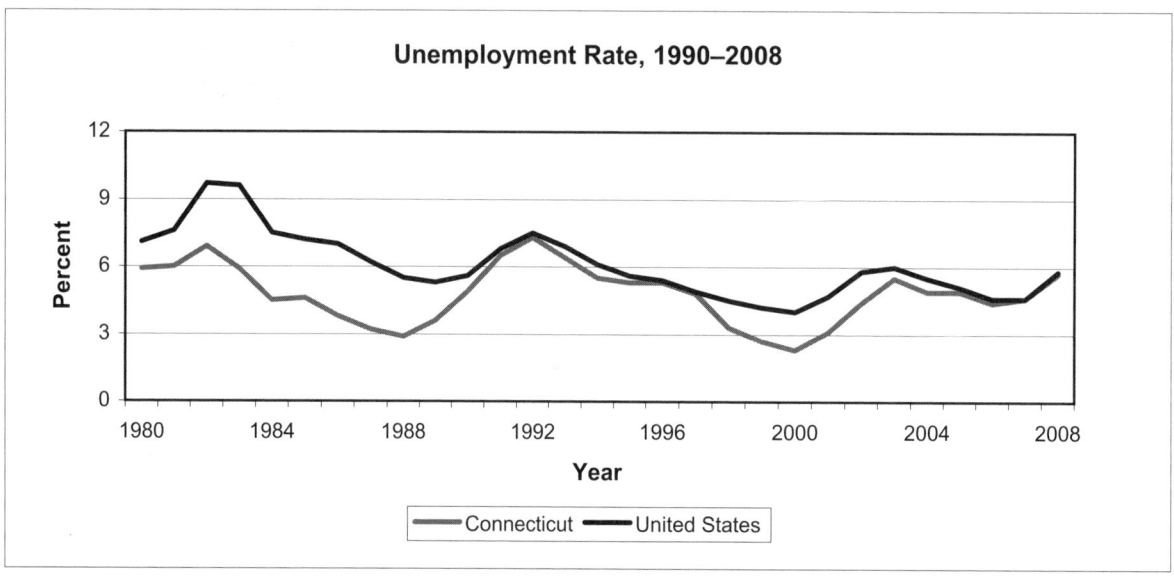

Table CT-7. Employment Status of the Civilian Noninstitutional Population Age 16 Years and Over
(Number, percent.)

Year	Civilian labor force	Civilian participation rate	Employed	Unemployed	Unemployment rate
1998	1 741 640	67.7	1 684 831	56 809	3.3
1999	1 742 217	67.5	1 696 007	46 210	2.7
2000	1 736 831	66.9	1 697 670	39 161	2.3
2001	1 754 839	67.1	1 700 046	54 793	3.1
2002	1 778 994	67.5	1 700 949	78 045	4.4
2003	1 795 000	67.6	1 696 857	98 143	5.5
2004	1 792 084	67.2	1 703 865	88 219	4.9
2005	1 808 762	67.4	1 720 346	88 416	4.9
2006	1 829 024	67.7	1 748 368	80 656	4.4
2007	1 850 345	68.2	1 765 835	84 510	4.6
2008	1 876 125	68.8	1 769 223	106 902	5.7

Table CT-8. Employment and Average Wages by Industry

(Estimates for 2001–2006 are based on the 2002 North American Industry Classification System [NAICS]. Estimates for 2007 are based on the 2007 NAICS.)

Industry	2001	2002	2003	2004	2005	2006	2007
	Number of jobs						
WAGE AND SALARY EMPLOYMENT BY INDUSTRY	1 765 799	1 751 155	1 729 813	1 739 721	1 750 876	1 767 713	1 781 976
Farm Wage and Salary Employment	6 228	6 262	6 481	5 406	5 280	4 853	4 758
Nonfarm Wage and Salary Employment	1 759 571	1 744 893	1 723 332	1 734 315	1 745 596	1 762 860	1 777 218
Private wage and salary employment	1 499 207	1 480 710	1 462 291	1 469 441	1 478 349	1 495 259	1 508 951
Forestry, fishing, hunting, and other	1 164	1 133	1 128	1 092	966	976	914
Mining	728	717	712	724	715	745	722
Utilities	9 301	9 082	8 840	8 684	8 605	6 698	6 676
Construction	67 986	65 881	64 322	68 178	68 402	69 487	70 900
Manufacturing	227 605	212 606	201 476	198 899	196 433	194 813	192 321
Durable goods manufacturing	169 387	157 477	148 557	147 526	146 400	145 952	145 132
Nondurable goods manufacturing	58 218	55 129	52 919	51 373	50 033	48 861	47 189
Wholesale trade	68 518	66 831	65 685	66 118	67 465	68 698	68 777
Retail trade	200 850	200 853	196 239	197 456	198 166	197 045	197 027
Transportation and warehousing	41 002	40 076	41 152	42 027	43 046	43 455	43 730
Information	44 816	41 269	39 743	39 054	38 247	37 857	38 379
Finance and insurance	125 652	125 777	126 141	123 990	124 929	127 042	126 870
Real estate and rental and leasing	22 000	21 417	21 012	20 908	21 465	21 756	21 839
Professional and technical services	99 859	96 813	93 585	92 782	93 392	96 296	96 899
Management of companies and enterprises	28 437	27 150	26 928	25 258	25 018	26 241	26 687
Administrative and waste services	86 868	83 327	81 663	84 302	86 657	88 426	89 200
Educational services	52 227	54 149	55 715	56 418	56 513	57 439	59 334
Health care and social assistance	216 775	223 072	225 282	227 983	231 157	236 216	242 887
Arts, entertainment, and recreation	24 420	24 865	25 332	25 926	25 475	25 191	25 652
Accommodation and food services	98 312	100 591	102 489	104 183	106 758	109 929	112 822
Other services, except public administration	82 687	85 101	84 847	85 459	84 940	86 949	87 315
Government and government enterprises	260 364	264 183	261 041	264 874	267 247	267 601	268 267
	Dollars						
AVERAGE WAGES AND SALARIES BY INDUSTRY	45 947	45 864	47 334	49 818	51 733	53 912	56 966
Average Farm Wages and Salaries	18 571	24 391	20 161	23 984	19 730	24 708	22 064
Average Nonfarm Wages and Salaries	46 044	45 942	47 436	49 898	51 830	53 992	57 060
Average private wages and salaries	47 026	46 649	48 193	50 856	52 926	55 208	58 323
Forestry, fishing, hunting, and other	18 652	19 019	18 830	19 282	20 821	22 029	23 548
Mining	50 853	52 958	55 930	55 131	57 547	61 467	61 288
Utilities	77 999	73 789	80 112	97 334	87 677	97 038	105 505
Construction	48 191	48 374	48 062	49 674	51 452	52 922	55 953
Manufacturing	55 710	55 909	58 445	61 348	62 996	65 676	69 322
Durable goods manufacturing	53 693	54 289	57 015	60 114	61 747	64 410	67 861
Nondurable goods manufacturing	61 578	60 535	62 460	64 893	66 650	69 459	73 814
Wholesale trade	65 570	64 536	65 072	67 887	72 718	77 550	79 794
Retail trade	27 023	27 145	27 757	28 414	28 762	29 504	30 159
Transportation and warehousing	35 234	36 235	37 538	39 423	40 988	42 824	47 104
Information	57 670	56 166	57 472	60 911	63 263	65 687	68 895
Finance and insurance	98 219	98 364	104 379	118 477	128 236	135 211	146 080
Real estate and rental and leasing	42 487	42 892	43 058	44 591	46 893	49 697	53 596
Professional and technical services	72 323	69 305	70 375	72 687	75 528	77 667	82 909
Management of companies and enterprises	104 817	97 212	107 332	122 802	130 152	137 181	157 687
Administrative and waste services	28 640	29 397	30 235	31 423	32 321	33 845	36 590
Educational services	33 919	35 348	36 660	37 682	38 738	40 592	42 474
Health care and social assistance	36 119	37 306	38 427	39 830	41 082	42 359	43 663
Arts, entertainment, and recreation	25 725	24 640	25 205	25 996	27 397	29 018	29 860
Accommodation and food services	16 493	16 856	17 178	17 918	18 175	18 822	19 328
Other services, except public administration	24 111	24 708	25 595	26 169	26 873	27 653	28 880
Government and government enterprises	40 389	41 974	43 193	44 583	45 765	47 201	49 953

Table CT-9. Employment Characteristics by Family Type

(Number, percent.)

Family type and labor force status	2005		2006		2007	
	Total	Families with own children under 18 years	Total	Families with own children under 18 years	Total	Families with own children under 18 years
TOTAL FAMILIES	893 288	416 870	894 348	430 067	885 471	419 896
FAMILY TYPE AND LABOR FORCE STATUS						
Married Coupled Families	675 144	295 307	680 656	310 225	673 742	301 659
Both husband and wife in labor force	57.0	66.0	58.2	67.2	58.0	68.4
Husband in labor force, wife not in labor force	20.7	27.5	21.2	27.4	21.2	26.8
Wife in labor force, husband not in labor force	7.1	3.9	6.8	3.7	6.8	3.4
Both husband and wife not in labor force	15.3	2.5	13.8	1.7	14.0	1.4
Other Families	218 144	121 563	213 692	119 842	211 729	118 237
Female householder, no husband present	74.1	79.7	75.1	79.1	75.6	79.6
In labor force	54.0	63.7	55.6	65.2	57.0	66.6
Not in labor force	20.2	16.1	19.5	13.9	18.7	12.9
Male householder, no wife present	25.9	20.3	24.9	20.9	24.4	20.4
In labor force	20.5	17.2	20.0	18.7	19.9	18.1
Not in labor force	5.4	3.0	4.9	2.2	4.5	2.3

Table CT-10. School Enrollment and Educational Attainment, 2007

(Number, percent.)

Item	State	U.S.
Enrollment		
Total population 3 years and over	3 375 713	289 295 761
Enrolled in school	940 370	79 329 527
Enrolled in preschool (percent)	6.6	6.2
Enrolled in grades K-12 (percent)	65.8	67.6
Enrolled in college or graduate school (percent)	27.6	26.2
Attainment		
Total population 25 years and over	2 359 568	197 892 369
Less than a high school diploma (percent)	12.0	15.5
High school diploma or more (percent)	88.0	84.5
Bachelor's degree or more (percent)	34.7	27.5
Graduate degree or more (percent)	15.4	10.1

Table CT-11. Educational Indicators

(Number, percent.)

Item	State	U.S.
Public Schools, 2006–2007 (except where noted)		
Number of school districts	198	17 742
Number of schools	1 115	99 639
Number of students	575 100	49 315 842
Student-teacher ratio	14.7	15.5
Expenditures per student (dollars)	$13 659	. . .
Averaged freshman graduation rate, 2005–2006	80.9	. . .
Dropout rate, grades 9–12, 2005–2006	1.8	3.7
Students eligible for free or reduced-price lunch (percent)	27.3	41.2
English-language learners (percent)	4.6	5.1
Students with IEP (percent)	11.2	12.7
Private Schools, 2007–2008 (except where noted)		
Number of schools	423	33 740
Number of students	76 520	5 072 451
High school graduates, 2006–2007	7 993	306 605
Student-teacher ratio	9.3	11.1

Table CT-12. Reported Voting and Registration of the Voting-Age Population, November 2008

(Number in thousands, percent.)

Item	Total population	Total citizen population	Registered			Voted		
			Total registered	Percent registered (total population)	Percent registered (total citizen population)	Total voted	Percent voted (total population)	Percent voted (total citizen population)
U.S. total	225 499	206 072	146 311	64.9	71.0	131 144	58.2	63.6
State total	2 651	2 396	1 761	66.4	73.5	1 610	60.8	67.2
Sex								
Male	1 270	1 146	830	65.4	72.5	760	59.8	66.3
Female	1 381	1 250	931	67.4	74.4	851	61.6	68.0
Race								
White alone	2 233	2 085	1 583	70.9	76.0	1 455	65.2	69.8
White non-Hispanic alone	2 013	1 926	1 492	74.1	77.5	1 379	68.5	71.6
Black alone	251	224	133	52.9	59.1	121	48.4	54.1
Asian alone	136	61	31	22.7	. . .	21	15.5	. . .
Hispanic (of any race)	253	191	104	40.8	54.3	89	35.2	46.8
White alone or in combination	2 247	2 098	1 592	70.9	75.9	1 464	65.2	69.8
Black alone or in combination	257	230	137	53.2	59.3	125	48.8	54.4
Asian alone or in combination	144	66	35	24.4	. . .	24	16.4	. . .

Table CT-13. Crime

(Number, rate per 100,000.)

Item	State			U.S.		
	2007	2008	Percent change	2007	2008	Percent change
Population	3 502 309	3 501 252	0.0	301 621 157	304 059 724	0.8
VIOLENT CRIME						
Number	8 965	10 427	16.3	1 408 337	1 382 012	-1.9
Rate	256.0	297.8	16.3	466.9	454.5	-2.7
Murder and Nonnegligent Manslaughter						
Number	106	123	16.0	16 929	16 272	-3.9
Rate	3.0	3.5	16.1	5.6	5.4	-4.7
Forcible Rape						
Number	658	674	2.4	90 427	89 000	-1.6
Rate	18.8	19.3	2.5	30.0	29.3	-2.4
Robbery						
Number	3 607	3 907	8.3	445 125	441 855	-0.7
Rate	103.0	111.6	8.3	147.6	145.3	-1.5
Aggravated Assault						
Number	4 594	5 723	24.6	855 856	834 885	-2.5
Rate	131.2	163.5	24.6	283.8	274.6	-3.2
PROPERTY CRIME						
Number	84 052	86 087	2.4	9 843 481	9 767 915	-0.8
Rate	2 399.9	2 458.7	2.5	3 263.5	3 212.5	-1.6
Burglary						
Number	15 162	15 011	-1.0	2 179 140	2 222 196	2.0
Rate	432.9	428.7	-1.0	722.5	730.8	1.2
Larceny-Theft						
Number	59 723	62 113	4.0	6 568 572	6 588 873	0.3
Rate	1 705.2	1 774.0	4.0	2 177.8	2 167.0	-0.5
Motor Vehicle Theft						
Number	9 167	8 963	-2.2	1 095 769	956 846	-12.7
Rate	261.7	256.0	-2.2	363.3	314.7	-13.4

Table CT-14. State Government Finances, 2007

(Dollars, percent distribution.)

Item	Thousands of dollars	Percent distribution
Total Revenue	25 492 170	X
General revenue	20 382 270	80.0
Intergovernmental revenue	4 167 175	16.3
Taxes	12 847 554	50.4
General sales	3 030 353	11.9
Selective sales	1 933 329	7.6
License taxes	362 255	1.4
Individual income tax	6 335 078	24.9
Corporate income tax	824 915	3.2
Other taxes	361 624	1.4
Current charges	1 614 442	6.3
Miscellaneous general revenue	1 753 099	6.9
Utility revenue	27 404	0.1
Liquor store revenue	0	0.0
Insurance trust revenue	5 082 496	19.9
Total Expenditure	22 115 190	100.0
Intergovernmental expenditure	3 831 974	17.3
Direct expenditure	18 283 216	82.7
Current operation	12 311 151	55.7
Capital outlay	1 653 862	7.5
Insurance benefits and repayments	2 787 177	12.6
Assistance and subsidies	388 033	1.8
Interest on debt	1 142 993	5.2
Exhibit: Salaries and wages	4 088 537	18.5
Total Expenditure	22 115 190	100.0
General expenditure	19 009 516	86.0
Intergovernmental expenditure	3 831 974	17.3
Direct expenditure	15 177 542	68.6
Education	5 339 202	24.1
Public welfare	5 136 934	23.2
Hospitals	1 297 077	5.9
Health	839 811	3.8
Highways	742 087	3.4
Police protection	205 351	0.9
Correction	668 179	3.0
Natural resources	103 206	0.5
Parks and recreation	46 518	0.2
Government administration	1 095 676	5.0
Interest on general debt	1 142 993	5.2
Other and unallocable	2 392 482	10.8
Utility expenditure	318 497	1.4
Liquor store expenditure	0	0.0
Insurance trust expenditure	2 787 177	12.6
Debt at End of Fiscal Year	23 836 187	X
Cash and Security Holdings	45 218 877	X

Table CT-15. State Government Tax Collections, 2008

(Dollars, percent distribution.)

Item	Thousands of dollars	Percent distribution
Total Taxes	13 367 631	X
Sales and gross receipts	5 177 376	38.7
General sales and gross receipts	3 178 903	23.8
Selective sales taxes	1 998 473	15.0
Alcoholic beverages	42 311	0.3
Amusements	451 789	3.4
Insurance premiums	199 297	1.5
Motor fuels	450 095	3.4
Pari-mutuels	8 308	0.1
Public utilities	173 058	1.3
Tobacco products	317 257	2.4
Other selective sales	356 358	2.7
Licenses	352 999	2.6
Alcoholic beverages	6 478	0.0
Amusements	35	0.0
Corporation	17 399	0.1
Hunting and fishing	3 485	0.0
Motor vehicle	201 364	1.5
Motor vehicle operators	39 202	0.3
Occupation and business, NEC	79 686	0.6
Other licenses	5 350	0.0
Income taxes	7 534 426	56.4
Individual income	7 000 225	52.4
Corporation net income	534 201	4.0
Other taxes	302 830	2.3
Death and gift	166 318	1.2
Documentary and stock transfer	136 512	1.0

Table CT-16. Agriculture

(Number, acres, and dollars.)

Item	2002		2007		Percent change, 2002–2007
	Number	Percent of total	Number	Percent of total	
Number of farms	4 191		4 916		17.3
Farm Size					
Average size of farm (acres)	85		83		-2.4
Farms by size (number of farms)					
Fewer than 50 acres	2 609	62.3	3 126	63.6	19.8
50 to 499 acres	1 464	34.9	1 687	34.3	15.2
500 acres or more	118	2.8	103	2.1	-12.7
Land (Acres)					
Total land in farms	357 154		405 616		13.6
Total cropland	170 673	47.8	163 686	40.4	-4.1
Total harvested cropland	131 248	36.7	136 833	33.7	4.3
Irrigated land	10 139	2.8	9 901	2.4	-2.3
Value of Sales (Dollars)					
Agricultural products sold ($1,000)	470 637		551 553		17.2
Average sales per farm	112 297		112 195		-0.1
Sales of crops	327 527	69.6	401 372	72.8	22.5
Sales of livestock, poultry, and their products	143 110	30.4	150 181	27.2	4.9
Value of Sales (Number of Farms)					
Less than $10,000	2 821	67.3	3 213	65.4	13.9
$10,000 to $99,999	931	22.2	1 212	24.7	30.2
$100,000 to $999,999	366	8.7	396	8.1	8.2
$1,000,000 or more	73	1.7	95	1.9	30.1
Farms by Type of Organization (Number of Farms)					
Family	3 436	82.0	3 967	80.7	15.5
Partnership	341	8.1	485	9.9	42.2
Corporation	338	8.1	389	7.9	15.1
Other: cooperative, estate or trust, institutional, etc	76	1.8	75	1.5	-1.3
Value of Land and Buildings (Dollars)					
Estimated market value of land and buildings ($1,000)	5 137 872		3 533 470		-31.2
Land and buildings average value per farm	1 045 133		840 302		-19.6
Average value per acre	12 667		9 491		-25.1
Government Payments					
Number of farms receiving government payments	254	6.1	352	7.2	38.6
Payments (thousands of dollars)	3 681		4 122		12.0
Average payment per farm	14 492		11 710		-19.2
Farm Operator Characteristics					
Farm operators whose principal occupation is farming	2 077	49.6	2 273	46.2	9.4
Farm operators whose principal occupation is other	2 114	50.4	2 643	53.8	25.0
Average age principal operator (years)	55.4		57.6		4.0

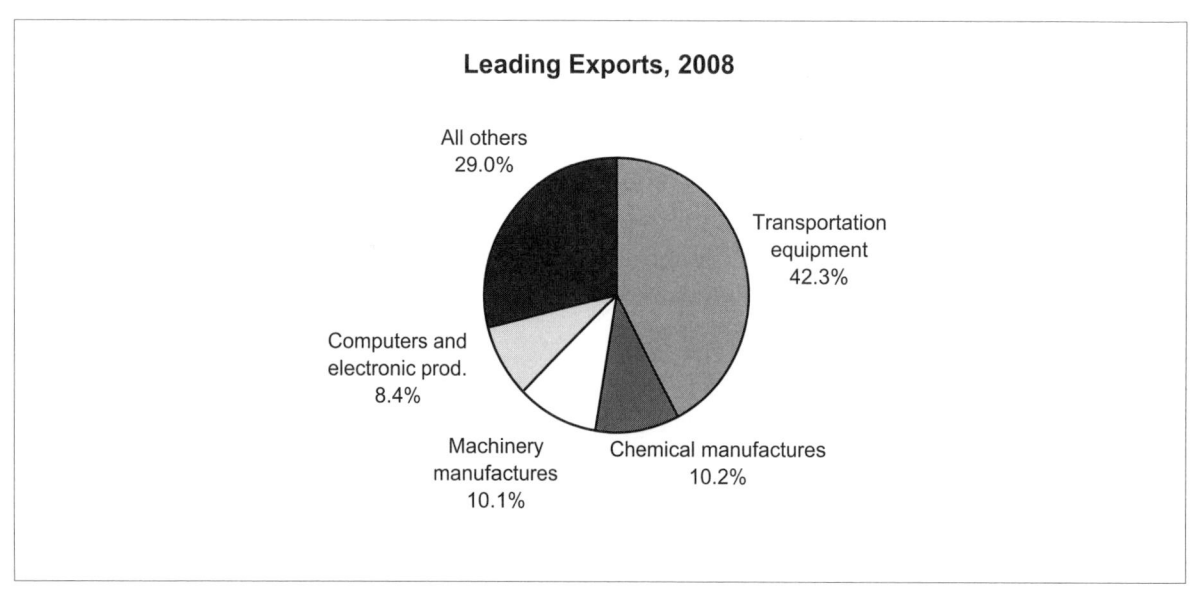

Leading Exports, 2008

All others 29.0%

Transportation equipment 42.3%

Computers and electronic prod. 8.4%

Machinery manufactures 10.1%

Chemical manufactures 10.2%

DELAWARE

Facts and Figures

Location: Northeastern United States; bordered on the N by Pennsylvania, on the E by New Jersey, and on the S and W by Maryland

Area: 2,489 sq. mi. (6,447 sq. km.); rank—49th

Population: 873,092 (2008 est.); rank—45th

Principal Cities: capital—Dover; largest—Wilmington

Statehood: December 7, 1787; 1st state

U.S. Congress: 2 senators, 1 representative

State Motto: Liberty and Independence

State Song: "Our Delaware"

State Nickname: The First State

Abbreviations: DE; Del.

State Symbols: flower—peach blossom; tree—American holly; bird—blue hen chicken

At a Glance

- With an increase in population of 11.4 percent, Delaware ranked 11th among the states in growth from 2000 to 2008.
- An estimated 5,391 marriages took place in Delaware in 2008, compared to 3,147 divorces.
- The 2007 home ownership rate in Delaware was 76.8 percent, giving it a ranking of 2nd among the states.
- Delaware's median household income in 2007 was $54,610, 15th among the states.
- In Delaware, 10.5 percent of the population lived below the poverty level in 2007, ranking it 38th.
- In 2006-07, 11.7 percent of Delawareans did not have health insurance, compared to 15.5 percent of the total U.S. population.
- In 2007, 3.5 percent of Delawareans were unemployed, compared to 4.6 percent nationwide.
- Delaware ranked 23rd in the nation with 26.1 percent of its population 25 years old and over having a bachelor's degree in 2007.
- Delaware's violent crime rate in 2007 was 689.2 per 100,000 population, compared to 466.9 for the entire nation.
- Delaware had one physician for every 352 people in 2007, compared to one physician for every 325 people nationwide.
- In the 2008 election, 66.2 percent of Delaware's eligible voters voted, compared to 61.7 percent of eligible voters nationwide.
- Delaware ranked 23rd among the states receiving federal aid in 2007, with $1,421 per capita.
- Delaware's gross domestic product was $60 billion in 2007; it ranked 39th among the states.
- With $4 billion in exports in 2007, Delaware ranked 38th in exports.
- Delawareans consumed 300.6 billion Btu's of energy in 2006; the state ranked 47th in total consumption.
- In 2007, Delaware exported $160 million worth of agricultural products, less than 1 percent of the U.S. total.

Table DE-1. Population by Sex, Age, Race, and Hispanic Origin

(Number, percent.)

Sex, age, race, and Hispanic origin	1990	2000	2008	Average annual percent change, 2000–2008
Total Population	666 168	783 600	873 092	1.4
Percent of total U.S. population	0.3	0.3	0.3	X
Sex				
Male	322 968	380 541	423 336	1.3
Female	343 200	403 059	449 756	1.4
Age				
Under 5 years	48 824	51 531	59 319	1.8
5 to 19 years	136 310	166 719	172 844	0.5
20 to 64 years	400 299	463 624	519 241	1.4
65 years and over	80 735	101 726	121 688	2.3
Median age (years)	32.7	36.0	38.2	X
Race and Hispanic Origin[1]				
One race				
White	535 094	584 773	648 411	1.3
Black	112 460	150 666	182 890	2.5
American Indian and Alaskan Native	2 019	2 731	3 691	3.8
Asian[2]	9 057	16 259	25 129	5.6
Native Hawaiian and Other Pacific Islander	X	283	593	9.7
Two or more races	X	13 033	12 378	-0.6
Hispanic (of any race)	15 820	37 277	59 093	5.9

[1]Data on race in 2000 and 2008 are not comparable to 1990. Individuals could only report one race in the 1990 census but could report one or more races on the 2000 census.
[2]Data in 1990 refer to Asian and Pacific Islanders.

Table DE-2. Marital Status

(Number, percent distribution.)

Sex and marital status	1990	2000	2007
Males, 15 Years and Over	251 905	296 619	331 964
Never married	30.6	29.4	33.6
Now married, except separated	57.4	57.4	52.9
Separated	2.1	1.8	1.4
Widowed	2.7	2.8	3.2
Divorced	7.2	8.7	9.0
Females, 15 Years and Over	275 435	324 042	362 904
Never married	24.9	25.3	28.2
Now married, except separated	52.0	50.9	48.0
Separated	2.6	2.2	1.9
Widowed	11.4	10.7	10.5
Divorced	9.2	10.9	11.4

Table DE-3. Households and Housing Characteristics

(Number, percent, and dollars.)

Item	1990	2000	2007	Average annual percent change, 2000–2007
Total Households	247 497	298 736	328 477	1.4
Family households	175 867	204 590	224 451	1.3
Married-couple family	137 983	153 136	162 982	0.9
Other family	37 884	51 454	61 469	2.6
Male householder, no wife present	8 565	12 468	16 208	3.8
Female householder, no husband present	29 319	38 986	45 261	2.2
Nonfamily households	71 630	94 146	104 026	1.4
Householder living alone	57 451	74 639	84 638	1.8
Householder not living alone	14 179	19 507	19 388	-0.1
Housing Characteristics				
Total housing units	289 919	343 072	388 619	1.8
Occupied housing units	247 497	298 736	328 477	1.4
Owner-occupied	173 813	216 038	238 141	1.4
Renter-occupied	73 684	82 698	90 336	1.3
Average size	2.61	2.54	2.56	X
Financial Characteristics				
Median gross rent of renter-occupied housing units (dollars)	495	639	910	5.2
Median monthly owner costs for housing units with a mortgage (dollars)	763	1 101	1 478	4.3
Median value of owner-occupied housing units (dollars)	99 700	130 400	239 700	9.1

Table DE-4. Median Income and Poverty Status, 2007

(Number, percent.)

Characteristic	State		U.S.	
	Number	Percent	Number	Percent
Median Income				
Households (dollars)	54 610	X	50 740	X
Families (dollars)	66 198	X	61 173	X
Below Poverty Level				
Sex				
Male	36 146	8.9	16 576 071	11.5
Female	51 810	12.0	21 476 176	14.3
Age				
Under 18 years	29 382	14.7	13 097 100	18.0
Related children under 18 years	28 525	14.3	12 728 964	17.6
18 to 64 years	49 839	9.5	21 495 507	11.6
65 years and over	8 735	7.8	3 459 640	9.5

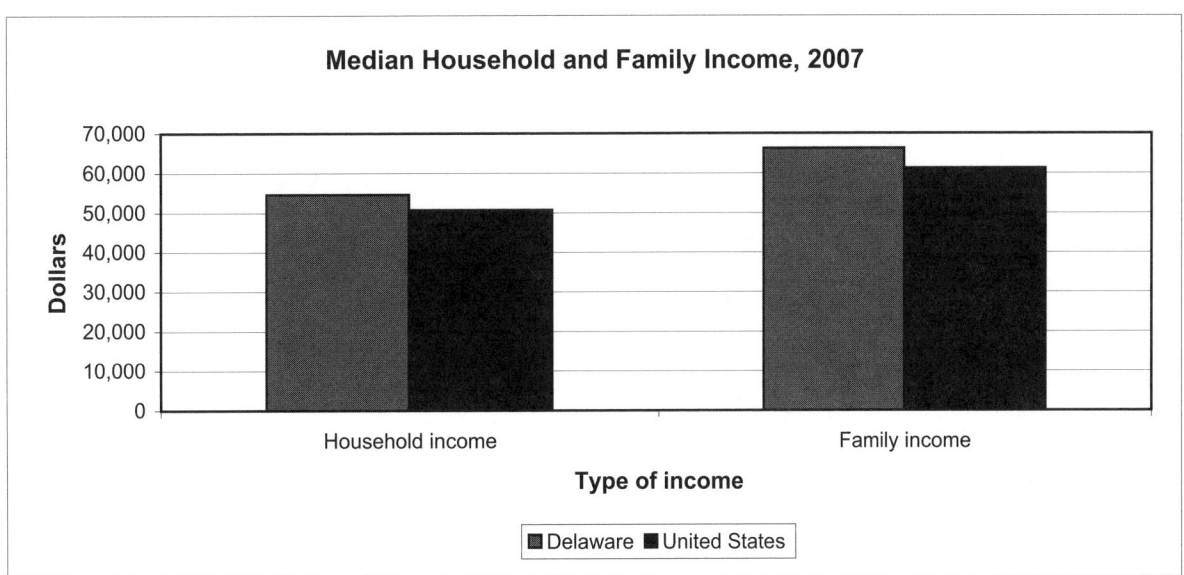

Table DE-5. Health Insurance Coverage Status for All Persons and Children Under 18 Years of Age

(Number, percent.)

Item	2000	2001	2002	2003	2004	2005	2006	2007
ALL PERSONS	779	791	798	820	826	844	862	863
Covered by Private or Government Health Insurance								
Number	709	720	724	734	717	742	757	766
Percent	91.1	91.1	90.6	89.6	86.7	87.8	87.9	88.8
Not Covered								
Number	69	71	75	86	110	103	105	96
Percent	8.9	8.9	9.4	10.4	13.3	12.2	12.1	11.2
Percent in the U.S. not covered	13.7	14.1	14.7	15.1	14.9	15.3	15.8	15.3
CHILDREN UNDER 18 YEARS OF AGE	199	199	195	199	195	197	206	209
Covered by Private or Government Health Insurance								
Number	186	182	178	185	172	173	182	194
Percent	93.5	91.6	91.3	92.8	88.5	88.1	88.3	92.5
Not Covered								
Number	13	17	17	14	22	23	24	16
Percent	6.5	8.4	8.7	7.2	11.5	11.9	11.7	7.5
Percent in the U.S. not covered	11.6	11.3	11.2	11.0	10.5	10.9	11.7	11.0

Table DE-6. Employment Status by Demographic Group, Preliminary 2008

(Number, percent.)

Characteristic	Civilian noninstitutional population	Civilian labor force		Employment		Unemployed	
		Number	Percent of population	Number	Percent of population	Number	Unemployment rate
TOTAL	678	447	66.0	425	62.7	22	5.0
Sex							
Men	321	234	73.0	221	68.8	13	5.5
Women	357	213	60.0	204	57.2	9	4.4
Race, Sex, and Hispanic Origin							
White	515	337	65.3	323	62.7	14	4.1
Men	247	180	72.9	172	69.6	8	4.4
Women	268	157	58.4	151	56.3	6	3.6
Black or African American	133	90	67.8	83	62.3	7	8.1
Men	59	41	70.1	37	62.9	4	10.1
Women	74	49	65.9	46	61.8	3	6.3
Hispanic	37	27	72.5	25	67.9	2	6.3
Men	21	19	88.6	17	82.0	1	7.5
Women	16	8	51.1	8	49.2	...	3.6
Age							
16 to 19 years	53	22	41.8	19	35.0	4	16.3
20 to 24 years	53	41	76.7	38	70.8	3	7.8
25 to 34 years	111	94	85.4	89	80.4	5	5.8
35 to 44 years	114	98	85.5	94	82.7	3	3.2
45 to 54 years	132	112	84.9	109	82.1	4	3.3
55 to 64 years	101	62	61.0	59	58.8	2	3.7
65 years and over	113	18	15.9	17	15.2	1	4.4

Note: Data in Table 6 are from the Current Population Survey (CPS) and do not match the estimates in Table 7. See notes and definitions for more details.

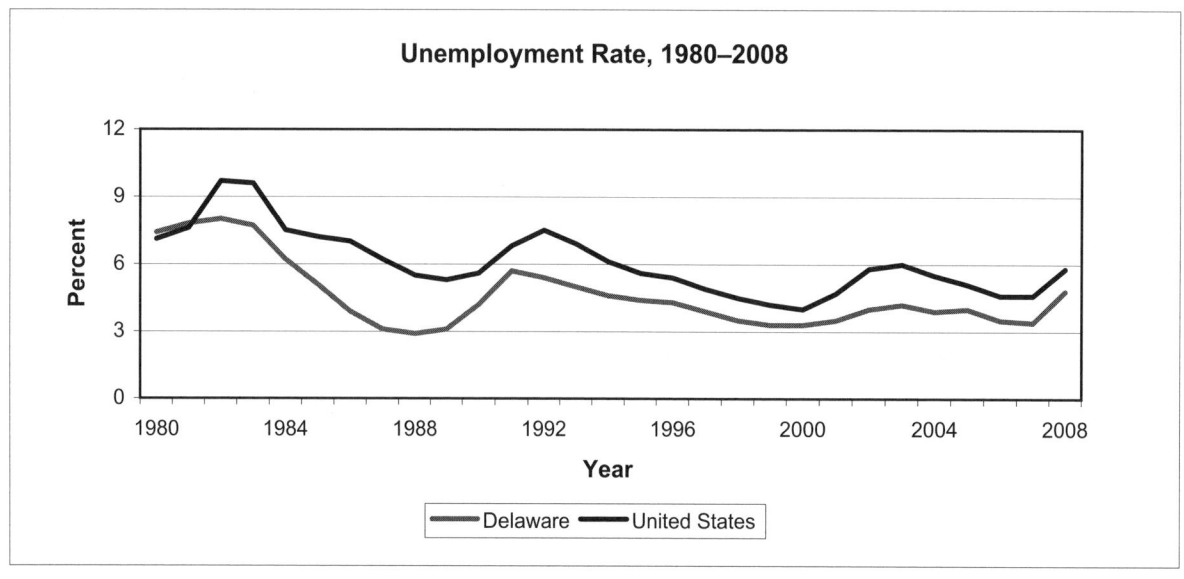

Table DE-7. Employment Status of the Civilian Noninstitutional Population Age 16 Years and Over

(Number, percent.)

Year	Civilian labor force	Civilian participation rate	Employed	Unemployed	Unemployment rate
1998	397 319	68.3	383 360	13 959	3.5
1999	401 139	68.0	387 808	13 331	3.3
2000	416 503	69.7	402 777	13 726	3.3
2001	418 714	69.2	404 135	14 579	3.5
2002	417 885	68.1	401 301	16 584	4.0
2003	421 061	67.6	403 504	17 557	4.2
2004	424 913	67.1	408 266	16 647	3.9
2005	432 701	67.1	415 491	17 210	4.0
2006	438 617	66.9	423 267	15 350	3.5
2007	440 912	66.2	425 707	15 205	3.4
2008	442 902	65.5	421 838	21 064	4.8

Table DE-8. Employment and Average Wages by Industry

(Estimates for 2001–2006 are based on the 2002 North American Industry Classification System [NAICS]. Estimates for 2007 are based on the 2007 NAICS.)

Industry	2001	2002	2003	2004	2005	2006	2007
	Number of jobs						
WAGE AND SALARY EMPLOYMENT BY INDUSTRY	440 205	435 681	436 010	445 101	451 148	455 636	457 322
Farm Wage and Salary Employment	1 878	1 803	1 575	1 544	1 537	1 588	1 554
Nonfarm Wage and Salary Employment	438 327	433 878	434 435	443 557	449 611	454 048	455 768
Private wage and salary employment	371 324	366 547	366 753	376 095	381 285	384 455	384 930
Forestry, fishing, hunting, and other	D	647	633	614	666	636	633
Mining	D	85	73	73	D	16	L
Utilities	2 244	2 222	2 194	2 191	2 185	2 184	2 133
Construction	25 327	25 071	25 234	27 396	D	30 294	28 461
Manufacturing	39 506	37 061	35 700	34 774	33 436	33 493	33 386
Durable goods manufacturing	17 312	16 253	14 641	14 555	13 777	14 160	13 979
Nondurable goods manufacturing	22 194	20 808	21 059	20 219	19 659	19 333	19 407
Wholesale trade	13 565	13 835	14 373	15 004	15 126	15 328	15 089
Retail trade	52 174	52 650	53 405	54 185	55 223	55 304	55 979
Transportation and warehousing	10 313	10 220	10 246	11 268	10 801	11 272	11 490
Information	8 090	7 277	6 917	6 607	6 712	6 730	6 942
Finance and insurance	42 293	42 269	40 324	39 343	41 307	40 005	39 341
Real estate and rental and leasing	6 526	6 351	6 443	6 692	6 800	6 702	6 889
Professional and technical services	28 798	26 855	27 363	28 526	26 614	26 353	26 767
Management of companies and enterprises	11 668	11 694	11 354	12 495	12 458	12 016	11 410
Administrative and waste services	25 814	22 503	21 842	22 631	23 241	23 969	23 800
Educational services	5 903	6 211	6 180	6 252	6 648	7 010	7 294
Health care and social assistance	42 856	44 059	45 661	47 017	48 938	50 284	52 287
Arts, entertainment, and recreation	7 740	8 669	9 055	9 303	9 380	9 298	8 865
Accommodation and food services	29 280	29 711	30 177	31 652	32 194	32 554	32 979
Other services, except public administration	18 431	19 157	19 579	20 072	20 600	21 007	21 176
Government and government enterprises	67 003	67 331	67 682	67 462	68 326	69 593	70 838
	Dollars						
AVERAGE WAGES AND SALARIES BY INDUSTRY	37 502	38 733	40 116	41 683	43 747	45 371	46 318
Average Farm Wages and Salaries	18 544	23 714	23 337	23 670	19 661	21 521	19 699
Average Nonfarm Wages and Salaries	37 583	38 796	40 176	41 746	43 830	45 454	46 408
Average private wages and salaries	38 371	39 125	40 573	42 022	44 176	45 882	46 780
Forestry, fishing, hunting, and other	D	15 692	16 839	17 425	17 111	18 594	19 425
Mining	D	38 588	43 260	43 781	D	37 500	L
Utilities	77 824	86 297	78 618	78 000	80 704	83 722	83 630
Construction	37 460	38 509	38 909	40 445	D	45 976	46 601
Manufacturing	43 864	44 548	50 049	50 424	52 083	53 958	59 607
Durable goods manufacturing	47 268	49 775	56 682	55 988	58 812	62 702	72 545
Nondurable goods manufacturing	41 209	40 464	45 437	46 418	47 368	47 554	50 288
Wholesale trade	52 302	53 168	58 324	62 056	63 546	71 993	70 349
Retail trade	21 694	22 390	23 063	23 963	24 378	25 017	25 456
Transportation and warehousing	34 217	33 525	33 848	36 076	37 975	38 190	38 863
Information	50 083	49 400	49 775	51 847	52 085	53 749	54 690
Finance and insurance	62 133	63 191	67 101	71 458	81 926	84 173	80 842
Real estate and rental and leasing	32 808	32 634	33 530	36 894	37 210	38 426	39 822
Professional and technical services	67 065	68 481	67 421	69 631	72 220	73 509	77 058
Management of companies and enterprises	64 471	67 131	68 256	66 131	67 408	77 465	80 401
Administrative and waste services	21 108	22 375	23 661	24 954	27 810	29 554	30 835
Educational services	25 790	26 617	28 448	30 515	30 552	31 841	32 386
Health care and social assistance	35 821	37 114	38 522	40 597	41 873	43 088	45 017
Arts, entertainment, and recreation	20 968	21 959	22 637	22 701	22 800	23 969	25 727
Accommodation and food services	14 803	15 181	15 424	16 135	16 656	17 641	18 264
Other services, except public administration	23 118	23 761	25 566	26 031	26 156	27 451	28 236
Government and government enterprises	33 218	37 004	38 029	40 205	41 895	43 095	44 390

Table DE-9. Employment Characteristics by Family Type

(Number, percent.)

Family type and labor force status	2005		2006		2007	
	Total	Families with own children under 18 years	Total	Families with own children under 18 years	Total	Families with own children under 18 years
TOTAL FAMILIES	216 182	100 262	213 565	96 199	224 451	98 097
FAMILY TYPE AND LABOR FORCE STATUS						
Married Coupled Families	159 638	65 537	157 209	65 144	162 982	63 420
Both husband and wife in labor force	53.9	68.9	52.5	67.8	53.9	67.3
Husband in labor force, wife not in labor force	20.4	23.6	20.6	26.0	20.8	27.4
Wife in labor force, husband not in labor force	7.7	4.6	7.6	4.7	7.2	3.1
Both husband and wife not in labor force	18.1	2.8	19.4	1.5	18.2	2.2
Other Families	56 544	34 725	56 356	31 055	61 469	34 677
Female householder, no husband present	75.2	80.3	73.0	76.8	73.6	79.1
In labor force	57.4	68.9	56.4	65.7	53.6	65.2
Not in labor force	17.8	11.3	16.7	11.1	20.0	13.9
Male householder, no wife present	24.8	19.7	27.0	23.2	26.4	20.9
In labor force	20.2	17.3	21.4	22.0	21.2	19.6
Not in labor force	4.6	2.4	5.6	1.2	5.2	1.2

Table DE-10. School Enrollment and Educational Attainment, 2007

(Number, percent.)

Item	State	U.S.
Enrollment		
Total population 3 years and over	829 418	289 295 761
Enrolled in school	221 134	79 329 527
Enrolled in preschool (percent)	6.0	6.2
Enrolled in grades K-12 (percent)	65.6	67.6
Enrolled in college or graduate school (percent)	28.4	26.2
Attainment		
Total population 25 years and over	573 935	197 892 369
Less than a high school diploma (percent)	12.6	15.5
High school diploma or more (percent)	87.4	84.5
Bachelor's degree or more (percent)	26.1	27.5
Graduate degree or more (percent)	10.4	10.1

Table DE-11. Educational Indicators

(Number, percent.)

Item	State	U.S.
Public Schools, 2006–2007 (except where noted)		
Number of school districts	39	17 742
Number of schools	241	99 639
Number of students	122 254	49 315 842
Student-teacher ratio	15.2	15.5
Expenditures per student (dollars)	$11 760	. . .
Averaged freshman graduation rate, 2005–2006	76.3	. . .
Dropout rate, grades 9–12, 2005–2006	5.5	3.7
Students eligible for free or reduced-price lunch (percent)	36.9	41.2
English-language learners (percent)	5.4	5.1
Students with IEP (percent)	15.8	12.7
Private Schools, 2007–2008 (except where noted)		
Number of schools	214	33 740
Number of students	26 403	5 072 451
High school graduates, 2006–2007	1 797	306 605
Student-teacher ratio	10.8	11.1

Table DE-12. Reported Voting and Registration of the Voting-Age Population, November 2008

(Number in thousands, percent.)

Item	Total population	Total citizen population	Registered			Voted		
			Total registered	Percent registered (total population)	Percent registered (total citizen population)	Total voted	Percent voted (total population)	Percent voted (total citizen population)
U.S. total	225 499	206 072	146 311	64.9	71.0	131 144	58.2	63.6
State total	648	606	447	69.1	73.8	408	63.0	67.3
Sex								
Male	308	283	204	66.2	72.0	184	59.6	64.7
Female	339	323	243	71.7	75.4	224	66.1	69.5
Race								
White alone	493	472	355	72.1	75.3	324	65.6	68.6
White non-Hispanic alone	460	456	348	75.6	76.3	318	69.2	69.8
Black alone	125	120	83	66.5	69.5	78	62.2	65.0
Asian alone	22	8	4	. . .	. . .	3	. . .	. . .
Hispanic (of any race)	38	19	9	. . .	. . .	7	. . .	. . .
White alone or in combination	496	475	357	72.0	75.2	325	65.6	68.5
Black alone or in combination	127	121	84	66.5	69.4	79	62.2	65.0
Asian alone or in combination	22	8	4	. . .	. . .	3	. . .	. . .

Table DE-13. Crime

(Number, rate per 100,000.)

Item	State			U.S.		
	2007	2008	Percent change	2007	2008	Percent change
Population	864 764	873 092	1.0	301 621 157	304 059 724	0.8
VIOLENT CRIME						
Number	5 960	6 141	3.0	1 408 337	1 382 012	-1.9
Rate	689.2	703.4	2.1	466.9	454.5	-2.7
Murder and Nonnegligent Manslaughter						
Number	37	57	54.1	16 929	16 272	-3.9
Rate	4.3	6.5	52.6	5.6	5.4	-4.7
Forcible Rape						
Number	336	366	8.9	90 427	89 000	-1.6
Rate	38.9	41.9	7.9	30.0	29.3	-2.4
Robbery						
Number	1 706	1 838	7.7	445 125	441 855	-0.7
Rate	197.3	210.5	6.7	147.6	145.3	-1.5
Aggravated Assault						
Number	3 881	3 880	*	855 856	834 885	-2.5
Rate	448.8	444.4	-1.0	283.8	274.6	-3.2
PROPERTY CRIME						
Number	29 143	31 303	7.4	9 843 481	9 767 915	-0.8
Rate	3 370.1	3 585.3	6.4	3 263.5	3 212.5	-1.6
Burglary						
Number	6 341	6 760	6.6	2 179 140	2 222 196	2.0
Rate	733.3	774.3	5.6	722.5	730.8	1.2
Larceny-Theft						
Number	20 486	22 002	7.4	6 568 572	6 588 873	0.3
Rate	2 369.0	2 520.0	6.4	2 177.8	2 167.0	-0.5
Motor Vehicle Theft						
Number	2 316	2 541	9.7	1 095 769	956 846	-12.7
Rate	267.8	291.0	8.7	363.3	314.7	-13.4

Table DE-14. State Government Finances, 2007

(Dollars, percent distribution.)

Item	Thousands of dollars	Percent distribution
Total Revenue	7 432 535	X
General revenue	6 312 846	84.9
Intergovernmental revenue	1 241 741	16.7
Taxes	2 905 905	39.1
General sales	0	0.0
Selective sales	459 209	6.2
License taxes	1 006 434	13.5
Individual income tax	1 025 416	13.8
Corporate income tax	302 222	4.1
Other taxes	112 624	1.5
Current charges	934 571	12.6
Miscellaneous general revenue	1 230 629	16.6
Utility revenue	11 919	0.2
Liquor store revenue	0	0.0
Insurance trust revenue	1 107 770	14.9
Total Expenditure	6 751 452	100.0
Intergovernmental expenditure	1 194 559	17.7
Direct expenditure	5 556 893	82.3
Current operation	4 184 189	62.0
Capital outlay	577 189	8.5
Insurance benefits and repayments	433 474	6.4
Assistance and subsidies	111 453	1.7
Interest on debt	250 588	3.7
Exhibit: Salaries and wages	2 162 325	32.0
Total Expenditure	6 751 452	100.0
General expenditure	6 229 345	92.3
Intergovernmental expenditure	1 194 559	17.7
Direct expenditure	5 034 786	74.6
Education	2 140 583	31.7
Public welfare	1 324 814	19.6
Hospitals	63 217	0.9
Health	374 705	5.5
Highways	408 068	6.0
Police protection	104 878	1.6
Correction	265 937	3.9
Natural resources	112 614	1.7
Parks and recreation	59 198	0.9
Government administration	486 071	7.2
Interest on general debt	250 588	3.7
Other and unallocable	638 672	9.5
Utility expenditure	88 633	1.3
Liquor store expenditure	0	0.0
Insurance trust expenditure	433 474	6.4
Debt at End of Fiscal Year	5 242 613	X
Cash and Security Holdings	13 994 315	X

Table DE-15. State Government Tax Collections, 2008

(Dollars, percent distribution.)

Item	Thousands of dollars	Percent distribution
Total Taxes	2 930 955	X
Sales and gross receipts	484 515	16.5
Selective sales taxes	484 515	16.5
Alcoholic beverages	14 735	0.5
Insurance premiums	93 974	3.2
Motor fuels	117 746	4.0
Pari-mutuels	143	0.0
Public utilities	49 805	1.7
Tobacco products	125 337	4.3
Other selective sales	82 775	2.8
Licenses	1 033 345	35.3
Alcoholic beverages	804	0.0
Amusements	434	0.0
Corporation	618 856	21.1
Hunting and fishing	1 995	0.1
Motor vehicle	46 413	1.6
Motor vehicle operators	2 814	0.1
Public utility	6 888	0.2
Occupation and business, NEC	244 748	8.4
Other licenses	110 393	3.8
Income taxes	1 315 535	44.9
Individual income	1 006 859	34.4
Corporation net income	308 676	10.5
Other taxes	97 560	3.3
Death and gift	460	0.0
Documentary and stock transfer	95 966	3.3
Other	1 134	0.0

Table DE-16. Agriculture

(Number, acres, and dollars.)

Item	2002 Number	2002 Percent of total	2007 Number	2007 Percent of total	Percent change, 2002–2007
Number of farms	2 391		2 546		6.5
Farm Size					
Average size of farm (acres)	226		200		-11.5
Farms by size (number of farms)					
Fewer than 50 acres	1 250	52.3	1 453	57.1	16.2
50 to 499 acres	878	36.7	848	33.3	-3.4
500 acres or more	263	11.0	245	9.6	-6.8
Land (Acres)					
Total land in farms	540 080		510 253		-5.5
Total cropland	457 201	84.7	432 773	84.8	-5.3
Total harvested cropland	433 105	80.2	409 468	80.2	-5.5
Irrigated land	97 167	18.0	104 562	20.5	7.6
Value of Sales (Dollars)					
Agricultural products sold ($1,000)	618 853		1 083 035		75.0
Average sales per farm	258 826		425 387		64.4
Sales of crops	150 404	24.3	210 635	19.4	40.0
Sales of livestock, poultry, and their products	468 449	75.7	872 400	80.6	86.2
Value of Sales (Number of Farms)					
Less than $10,000	881	36.8	1 043	41.0	18.4
$10,000 to $99,999	486	20.3	514	20.2	5.8
$100,000 to $999,999	922	38.6	582	22.9	-36.9
$1,000,000 or more	102	4.3	407	16.0	299.0
Farms by Type of Organization (Number of Farms)					
Family	2 015	84.3	2 006	78.8	-0.4
Partnership	136	5.7	210	8.2	54.4
Corporation	212	8.9	282	11.1	33.0
Other: cooperative, estate or trust, institutional, etc	28	1.2	48	1.9	71.4
Value of Land and Buildings (Dollars)					
Estimated market value of land and buildings ($1,000)	5 279 399		2 343 953		-55.6
Land and buildings average value per farm	2 073 605		980 323		-52.7
Average value per acre	10 347		4 054		-60.8
Government Payments					
Number of farms receiving government payments	617	25.8	950	37.3	54.0
Payments (thousands of dollars)	8 643		8 896		2.9
Average payment per farm	14 009		9 364		-33.2
Farm Operator Characteristics					
Farm operators whose principal occupation is farming	1 659	69.4	1 504	59.1	-9.3
Farm operators whose principal occupation is other	732	30.6	1 042	40.9	42.3
Average age principal operator (years)	54.8		55.4		1.1

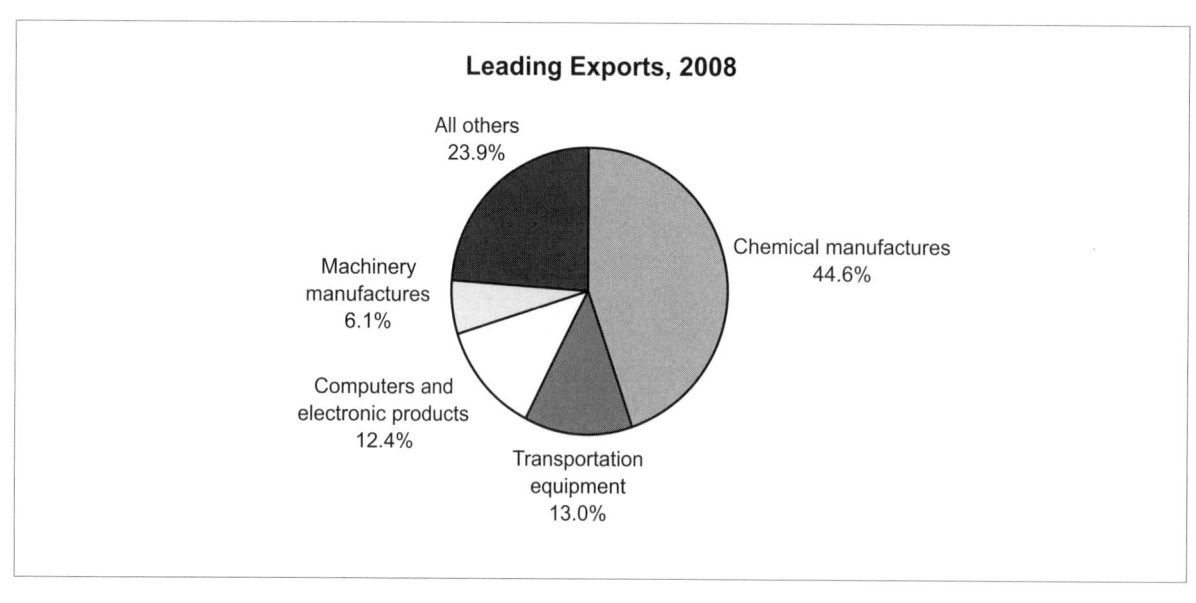

Leading Exports, 2008

All others 23.9%

Chemical manufactures 44.6%

Machinery manufactures 6.1%

Computers and electronic products 12.4%

Transportation equipment 13.0%

DISTRICT OF COLUMBIA

Facts and Figures:

Location: South Atlantic United States; bordered on the SE, NE, and NW by Maryland and on the SW by Virginia

Area: 61.4 sq. mi. (2000 est.)

Population: 591,833 (2008 est.)

Official Motto: Justitia omnibus ("Justice for All")

Abbreviation: D.C.

Symbols: flower—American beauty rose; tree—scarlet oak; bird—wood thrush

At a Glance

- From 2000 to 2008, the population of the District of Columbia increased by 3.5 percent.
- In 2008, 54.4 percent of the population was Black, 40.1 percent was White, 3.4 percent was Asian, 0.4 percent was American Indian and Alaskan Native, and 0.1 percent was Native Hawaiian and Other Pacific Islander.
- Median household income was $57,936 and median family income was $66,722 in 2008.
- In 2008, 85.8 percent of D.C. residents age 25 years and over were high school graduates. Furthermore, over 48 percent had a bachelor's degree or higher and 26.7 percent had a graduate or professional degree. Nationwide, only 10.2 percent of the population 25 years of age and over had a graduate or professional degree.
- The District of Columbia had one of the highest unemployment rates in the country in 2008 at 7.0 percent, up from 5.5 percent in 2007.
- The median value of a house was $474,100 in 2008.
- Median gross rent was $1,011 in 2008.
- Among all the states, voter turnout was among the highest in D.C in 2008 with nearly 75 percent of eligible voters voting.
- In 2008, 17.2 percent of people were in poverty. The poverty rate was higher for women (18.6 percent) than for men (15.7 percent).
- In 2006–07, 10.4 percent of people did not have health insurance in the District of Columbia.
- The violent crime rate was 1,437.7 per 100,000 population in 2008—an increase from 1,414.3 per 100,000 population in 2007.

Table DC-1. Population by Sex, Age, Race, and Hispanic Origin

(Number, percent.)

Sex, age, race, and Hispanic origin	1990	2000	2008	Average annual percent change, 2000–2008
Total Population	606 900	572 059	591 833	0.4
Percent of total U.S. population	0.2	0.2	0.2	X
Sex				
Male	282 970	269 366	279 880	0.5
Female	323 930	302 693	311 953	0.4
Age				
Under 5 years	37 351	32 536	36 352	1.4
5 to 19 years	102 592	103 270	97 319	-0.7
20 to 64 years	389 110	366 355	387 514	0.7
65 years and over	77 847	69 898	70 648	0.1
Median age (years)	33.2	34.6	34.9	X
Race and Hispanic Origin[1]				
One race				
White	179 667	176 101	237 092	3.8
Black	399 604	343 312	322 021	-0.8
American Indian and Alaskan Native	1 466	1 713	2 367	4.1
Asian[2]	11 214	15 189	20 120	3.6
Native Hawaiian and Other Pacific Islander	X	348	598	7.0
Two or more races	X	13 446	9 635	-4.1
Hispanic (of any race)	32 710	44 953	51 124	1.6

[1]Data on race in 2000 and 2008 are not comparable to 1990. Individuals could only report one race in the 1990 census but could report one or more races on the 2000 census.
[2]Data in 1990 refer to Asian and Pacific Islanders.

Table DC-2. Marital Status

(Number, percent distribution.)

Sex and marital status	1990	2000	2007
Males, 15 Years and Over	232 989	219 706	229 811
Never married	50.8	51.2	56.1
Now married, except separated	32.0	32.8	29.8
Separated	5.5	3.9	3.6
Widowed	3.6	3.4	2.1
Divorced	8.1	8.7	8.5
Females, 15 Years and Over	275 245	254 711	264 424
Never married	45.0	46.0	51.8
Now married, except separated	26.1	27.5	24.2
Separated	6.1	4.4	3.7
Widowed	12.8	11.6	9.5
Divorced	10.1	10.6	10.8

Table DC-3. Households and Housing Characteristics

(Number, percent, and dollars.)

Item	1990	2000	2007	Average annual percent change, 2000–2007
Total Households	249 634	248 338	251 039	0.2
Family households	122 087	114 166	108 181	-0.8
Married-couple family	63 110	56 631	55 790	-0.2
Other family	58 977	57 535	52 391	-1.3
Male householder, no wife present	10 402	10 503	9 434	-1.5
Female householder, no husband present	48 575	47 032	42 957	-1.3
Nonfamily households	127 547	134 172	142 858	0.9
Householder living alone	103 626	108 744	120 261	1.4
Householder not living alone	23 921	25 428	22 597	-1.7
Housing Characteristics				
Total housing units	278 489	274 845	284 235	0.5
Occupied housing units	249 634	248 338	251 039	0.2
Owner-occupied	97 108	101 214	111 813	1.4
Renter-occupied	152 526	147 124	139 226	-0.8
Average size	2.26	2.16	2.20	X
Financial Characteristics				
Median gross rent of renter-occupied housing units (dollars)	479	618	934	6.1
Median monthly owner costs for housing units with a mortgage (dollars)	950	1 291	2 094	7.2
Median value of owner-occupied housing units (dollars)	121 700	157 200	450 900	16.2

Table DC-4. Median Income and Poverty Status, 2007

(Number, percent.)

Characteristic	State		U.S.	
	Number	Percent	Number	Percent
Median Income				
Households (dollars)	54 317	X	50 740	X
Families (dollars)	66 672	X	61 173	X
Below Poverty Level				
Sex				
Male	38 519	14.7	16 576 071	11.5
Female	53 415	17.9	21 476 176	14.3
Age				
Under 18 years	25 597	22.7	13 097 100	18.0
Related children under 18 years	25 147	22.4	12 728 964	17.6
18 to 64 years	57 169	15.0	21 495 507	11.6
65 years and over	9 168	13.7	3 459 640	9.5

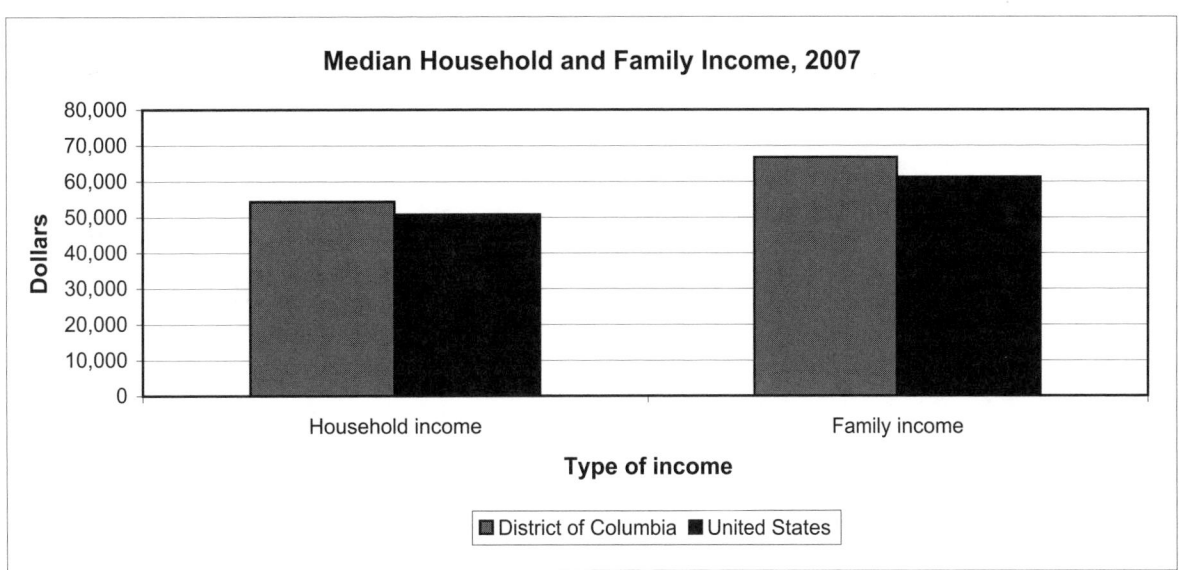

Table DC-5. Health Insurance Coverage Status for All Persons and Children Under 18 Years of Age

(Number, percent.)

Item	2000	2001	2002	2003	2004	2005	2006	2007
ALL PERSONS	553	554	572	554	547	540	569	582
Covered by Private or Government Health Insurance								
Number	478	487	500	478	479	468	503	526
Percent	86.4	87.9	87.5	86.3	87.7	86.8	88.4	90.5
Not Covered								
Number	75	67	72	76	67	71	66	55
Percent	13.6	12.1	12.5	13.7	12.3	13.2	11.6	9.5
Percent in the U.S. not covered	13.7	14.1	14.7	15.1	14.9	15.3	15.8	15.3
CHILDREN UNDER 18 YEARS OF AGE	111	111	118	109	113	112	115	112
Covered by Private or Government Health Insurance								
Number	100	102	109	97	105	105	105	105
Percent	90.5	92.1	92.3	89.2	92.6	93.7	91.3	93.8
Not Covered								
Number	11	9	9	12	8	7	10	7
Percent	9.5	7.9	7.7	10.8	7.4	6.3	8.7	6.2
Percent in the U.S. not covered	11.6	11.3	11.2	11.0	10.5	10.9	11.7	11.0

Table DC-6. Employment Status by Demographic Group, Preliminary 2008

(Number, percent.)

Characteristic	Civilian noninstitutional population	Civilian labor force		Employment		Unemployed	
		Number	Percent of population	Number	Percent of population	Number	Unemployment rate
TOTAL	480	332	69.2	310	64.7	22	6.6
Sex							
Men	221	165	75.0	155	70.1	10	6.2
Women	259	167	65.0	155	60.0	12	7.0
Race, Sex, and Hispanic Origin							
White	206	165	80.0	159	77.3	5	3.3
Men	103	88	85.8	85	82.9	3	3.5
Women	103	76	74.1	74	71.7	2	3.1
Black or African American	251	150	59.8	135	53.6	15	10.3
Men	108	69	63.5	62	57.3	7	9.8
Women	143	81	57.0	73	50.9	9	10.7
Hispanic	40	32	80.6	31	76.8	2	4.7
Men	22	19	87.3	18	83.8	1	4.0
Women	18	13	72.4	13	68.3	1	5.6
Age							
16 to 19 years	26	7	26.2	4	17.4	2	33.6
20 to 24 years	54	41	75.2	37	68.0	4	9.6
25 to 34 years	113	97	85.7	92	80.7	6	5.9
35 to 44 years	82	72	87.1	68	82.3	4	5.5
45 to 54 years	79	62	79.0	59	74.8	3	5.3
55 to 64 years	64	42	65.3	39	61.7	2	5.5
65 years and over	62	12	19.1	12	18.6	...	2.5

Note: Data in Table 6 are from the Current Population Survey (CPS) and do not match the estimates in Table 7. See notes and definitions for more details.

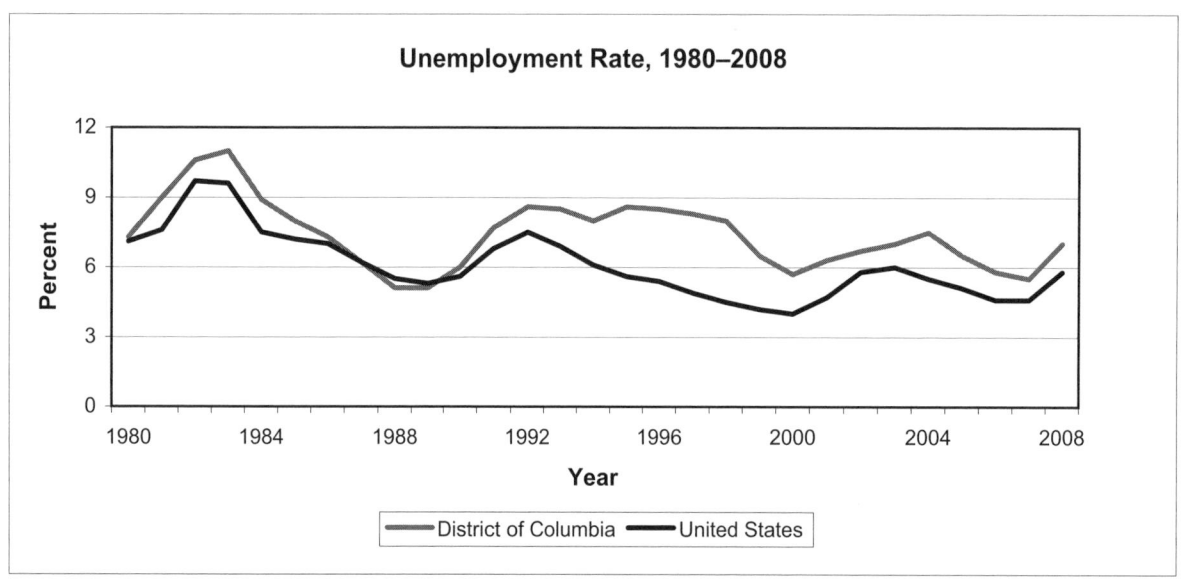

Unemployment Rate, 1980–2008

District of Columbia ——— United States

Table DC-7. Employment Status of the Civilian Noninstitutional Population Age 16 Years and Over

(Number, percent.)

Year	Civilian labor force	Civilian participation rate	Employed	Unemployed	Unemployment rate
1998	293 820	64.9	270 242	23 578	8.0
1999	308 085	67.4	288 016	20 069	6.5
2000	309 421	67.5	291 916	17 505	5.7
2001	305 817	66.2	286 649	19 168	6.3
2002	305 211	65.9	284 615	20 596	6.7
2003	306 907	66.3	285 361	21 546	7.0
2004	311 787	67.0	288 397	23 390	7.5
2005	318 472	67.9	297 710	20 762	6.5
2006	321 442	67.8	302 893	18 549	5.8
2007	327 218	68.5	309 116	18 102	5.5
2008	332 703	69.0	309 528	23 175	7.0

Table DC-8. Employment and Average Wages by Industry

(Estimates for 2001–2006 are based on the 2002 North American Industry Classification System [NAICS]. Estimates for 2007 are based on the 2007 NAICS.)

Industry	2001	2002	2003	2004	2005	2006	2007
	Number of jobs						
WAGE AND SALARY EMPLOYMENT BY INDUSTRY	705 176	716 363	718 814	725 451	730 801	736 284	741 459
Farm Wage and Salary Employment	0	0	0	0	0	0	0
Nonfarm Wage and Salary Employment	705 176	716 363	718 814	725 451	730 801	736 284	741 459
Private wage and salary employment	459 767	465 413	464 199	471 325	477 273	484 434	492 469
Forestry, fishing, hunting, and other	D	D	9 760	9 760	9 760	9 760	9 760
Mining	D	D	45	27	D	0	0
Utilities	D	D	2 597	2 530	2 609	2 469	2 405
Construction	12 133	12 978	13 650	13 018	D	13 268	13 257
Manufacturing	3 495	D	2 652	2 513	2 163	1 802	1 726
Durable goods manufacturing	1 360	D	971	886	712	627	568
Nondurable goods manufacturing	2 135	D	1 681	1 627	1 451	1 175	1 158
Wholesale trade	4 495	4 369	4 626	4 707	4 736	4 848	5 263
Retail trade	17 973	17 930	18 181	18 494	18 414	18 823	18 969
Transportation and warehousing	D	D	5 479	5 196	5 032	4 815	4 444
Information	D	25 957	25 094	24 347	23 044	22 716	22 291
Finance and insurance	17 681	17 658	17 552	17 176	16 852	16 825	16 686
Real estate and rental and leasing	10 429	10 141	10 148	10 315	10 340	10 466	10 658
Professional and technical services	97 932	99 176	99 611	102 111	105 782	108 288	109 140
Management of companies and enterprises	2 340	2 237	1 591	1 440	1 452	1 383	1 494
Administrative and waste services	42 617	42 185	42 971	42 532	43 724	44 181	45 031
Educational services	41 065	41 932	42 269	45 490	45 966	48 481	49 314
Health care and social assistance	52 948	56 657	54 707	54 535	54 253	54 414	57 234
Arts, entertainment, and recreation	5 504	5 727	6 067	5 859	6 354	6 157	6 314
Accommodation and food services	D	43 398	44 938	46 490	48 873	49 684	50 133
Other services, except public administration	61 361	64 052	62 261	64 785	64 589	66 054	68 350
Government and government enterprises	245 409	250 950	254 615	254 126	253 528	251 850	248 990
	Dollars						
AVERAGE WAGES AND SALARIES BY INDUSTRY	55 379	57 396	59 626	63 194	66 198	69 312	72 587
Average Farm Wages and Salaries	0	0	0	0	0	0	0
Average Nonfarm Wages and Salaries	55 379	57 396	59 626	63 194	66 198	69 312	72 587
Average private wages and salaries	53 257	54 340	56 407	59 558	61 848	65 259	68 796
Forestry, fishing, hunting, and other	D	D	100 805	99 356	99 706	96 857	98 207
Mining	D	D	158 822	142 556	D	0	0
Utilities	D	D	68 164	72 308	75 979	83 482	88 909
Construction	43 417	45 896	46 470	48 362	D	52 238	54 171
Manufacturing	63 161	D	64 942	73 343	75 410	78 213	75 932
Durable goods manufacturing	73 697	D	83 680	102 574	100 347	94 855	79 963
Nondurable goods manufacturing	56 450	D	54 118	57 425	63 173	69 332	73 955
Wholesale trade	63 317	64 646	72 012	75 538	81 123	84 051	90 433
Retail trade	25 659	26 252	26 721	27 761	28 517	29 154	29 290
Transportation and warehousing	D	D	47 331	49 870	50 613	53 873	56 896
Information	D	75 767	78 805	84 258	89 661	91 784	97 186
Finance and insurance	97 394	94 993	99 018	110 947	110 814	124 877	137 760
Real estate and rental and leasing	46 074	47 551	51 283	56 762	60 670	69 125	71 543
Professional and technical services	82 229	84 246	86 901	92 674	96 270	102 671	109 504
Management of companies and enterprises	131 568	129 442	130 053	144 231	167 168	208 095	270 091
Administrative and waste services	28 218	29 162	30 473	32 957	35 154	37 761	40 419
Educational services	33 034	35 449	38 831	38 214	38 666	38 661	40 001
Health care and social assistance	40 272	40 515	44 056	46 876	48 234	51 017	52 448
Arts, entertainment, and recreation	49 575	45 792	43 032	41 398	49 967	55 966	53 739
Accommodation and food services	D	24 427	25 389	26 891	27 828	28 912	30 045
Other services, except public administration	47 662	49 648	52 508	55 111	58 553	60 519	63 668
Government and government enterprises	59 357	63 062	65 494	69 937	74 385	77 109	80 083

Table DC-9. Employment Characteristics by Family Type

(Number, percent.)

Family type and labor force status	2005		2006		2007	
	Total	Families with own children under 18 years	Total	Families with own children under 18 years	Total	Families with own children under 18 years
TOTAL FAMILIES	108 483	46 920	108 759	42 232	108 181	45 089
FAMILY TYPE AND LABOR FORCE STATUS						
Married Coupled Families	54 212	18 943	55 871	18 333	55 790	18 752
Both husband and wife in labor force	56.1	64.4	60.1	70.1	58.3	65.7
Husband in labor force, wife not in labor force	19.7	23.7	18.9	25.2	19.8	27.0
Wife in labor force, husband not in labor force	8.3	7.0	6.7	3.6	6.9	4.0
Both husband and wife not in labor force	15.9	5.0	14.3	1.1	15.0	3.2
Other Families	54 271	27 977	52 888	23 899	52 391	26 337
Female householder, no husband present	81.4	84.2	82.2	88.2	82.0	87.0
In labor force	49.1	61.1	50.9	63.7	55.6	70.3
Not in labor force	32.3	23.1	31.3	24.5	26.4	16.8
Male householder, no wife present	18.6	15.8	17.8	11.8	18.0	13.0
In labor force	13.1	13.1	12.8	10.8	12.5	10.2
Not in labor force	5.5	2.7	5.0	1.0	5.5	2.8

Table DC-10. School Enrollment and Educational Attainment, 2007

(Number, percent.)

Item	State	U.S.
Enrollment		
Total population 3 years and over	564 337	289 295 761
Enrolled in school	148 734	79 329 527
Enrolled in preschool (percent)	6.3	6.2
Enrolled in grades K-12 (percent)	53.3	67.6
Enrolled in college or graduate school (percent)	40.4	26.2
Attainment		
Total population 25 years and over	401 018	197 892 369
Less than a high school diploma (percent)	14.3	15.5
High school diploma or more (percent)	85.7	84.5
Bachelor's degree or more (percent)	47.5	27.5
Graduate degree or more (percent)	26.0	10.1

Table DC-11. Educational Indicators

(Number, percent.)

Item	State	U.S.
Public Schools, 2006–2007 (except where noted)		
Number of school districts	56	17 742
Number of schools	235	99 639
Number of students	72 850	49 315 842
Student-teacher ratio	13.5	15.5
Expenditures per student (dollars)	$15 511	...
Averaged freshman graduation rate, 2005–2006	...	...
Dropout rate, grades 9–12, 2005–2006	...	3.7
Students eligible for free or reduced-price lunch (percent)	52.7	41.2
English-language learners (percent)	6.1	5.1
Students with IEP (percent)	12.1	12.7
Private Schools, 2007–2008 (except where noted)		
Number of schools	92	33 740
Number of students	17 985	5 072 451
High school graduates, 2006–2007	1 665	306 605
Student-teacher ratio	8.2	11.1

Table DC-12. Reported Voting and Registration of the Voting-Age Population, November 2008

(Number in thousands, percent.)

Item	Total population	Total citizen population	Registered			Voted		
			Total registered	Percent registered (total population)	Percent registered (total citizen population)	Total voted	Percent voted (total population)	Percent voted (total citizen population)
U.S. total	225 499	206 072	146 311	64.9	71.0	131 144	58.2	63.6
State total	469	413	324	69.0	78.3	306	65.3	74.1
Sex								
Male	216	186	140	65.1	75.6	132	61.3	71.2
Female	254	228	183	72.3	80.5	174	68.7	76.5
Race								
White alone	203	166	139	68.4	83.8	130	64.0	78.4
White non-Hispanic alone	161	151	130	80.7	86.1	121	75.3	80.4
Black alone	242	231	173	71.5	74.8	165	68.4	71.6
Asian alone	15	9	6	...	...	5	...	...
Hispanic (of any race)	50	18	11	...	...	11	...	...
White alone or in combination	208	170	142	68.4	83.8	134	64.1	78.5
Black alone or in combination	246	235	176	71.4	74.9	168	68.2	71.5
Asian alone or in combination	17	10	7	...	...	7	...	...

Table DC-13. Crime

(Number, rate per 100,000.)

Item	State			U.S.		
	2007	2008	Percent change	2007	2008	Percent change
Population	588 292	591 833	0.6	301 621 157	304 059 724	0.8
VIOLENT CRIME						
Number	8 320	8 509	2.3	1 408 337	1 382 012	-1.9
Rate	1 414.3	1 437.7	1.7	466.9	454.5	-2.7
Murder and Nonnegligent Manslaughter						
Number	181	186	2.8	16 929	16 272	-3.9
Rate	30.8	31.4	2.1	5.6	5.4	-4.7
Forcible Rape						
Number	192	186	-3.1	90 427	89 000	-1.6
Rate	32.6	31.4	-3.7	30.0	29.3	-2.4
Robbery						
Number	4 261	4 430	4.0	445 125	441 855	-0.7
Rate	724.3	748.5	3.3	147.6	145.3	-1.5
Aggravated Assault						
Number	3 686	3 707	0.6	855 856	834 885	-2.5
Rate	626.6	626.4	*	283.8	274.6	-3.2
PROPERTY CRIME						
Number	28 908	30 211	4.5	9 843 481	9 767 915	-0.8
Rate	4 913.9	5 104.6	3.9	3 263.5	3 212.5	-1.6
Burglary						
Number	3 926	3 788	-3.5	2 179 140	2 222 196	2.0
Rate	667.4	640.0	-4.1	722.5	730.8	1.2
Larceny-Theft						
Number	17 382	19 958	14.8	6 568 572	6 588 873	0.3
Rate	2 954.7	3 372.2	14.1	2 177.8	2 167.0	-0.5
Motor Vehicle Theft						
Number	7 600	6 465	-14.9	1 095 769	956 846	-12.7
Rate	1 291.9	1 092.4	-15.4	363.3	314.7	-13.4

Table DC-14. Government Finances, 2005–2006

(Dollars, percent distribution.)

Item	Thousands of dollars	Percent distribution
Total Revenue	11 074 878	X
General revenue	9 170 577	82.8
Intergovernmental revenue	3 060 038	27.6
Taxes	4 545 231	41.0
General sales	817 066	7.4
Selective sales	440 409	4.0
Individual income tax	1 232 384	11.1
Corporate income tax	219 801	2.0
Other taxes	594 926	5.4
Current charges	573 538	5.2
Miscellaneous general revenue	991 770	9.0
Utility revenue	792 500	7.2
Liquor store revenue	0	0.0
Insurance trust revenue	1 111 801	10.0
Total Expenditure	10 090 556	100.0
Intergovernmental expenditure	0	0.0
Direct expenditure	10 090 556	100.0
Current operation	7 606 593	75.4
Capital outlay	1 890 540	18.7
Insurance benefits and repayments	128 012	1.3
Assistance and subsidies	135 895	1.3
Interest on debt	329 516	3.3
Exhibit: Salaries and wages	2 442 612	24.2
Total Expenditure	10 090 556	100.0
General expenditure	8 003 672	79.3
Education	1 477 644	14.6
Public welfare	1 840 853	18.2
Hospitals	161 498	1.6
Health	507 701	5.0
Highways	95 730	0.9
Police protection	493 234	4.9
Correction	205 558	2.0
Natural resources	301	0.0
Parks and recreation	332 182	3.3
Government administration	X	4.5
Interest on general debt	319 538	3.2
Other and unallocable	745 344	7.4
Utility expenditure	1 958 872	19.4
Liquor store expenditure	0	0.0
Insurance trust expenditure	128 012	1.3
Debt at End of Fiscal Year	8 020 359	X
Cash and Security Holdings	11 513 333	X

Table DC-15. State Government Tax Collections, 2008

(Dollars, percent distribution.)

Item	Thousands of dollars	Percent distribution
Total Taxes	827 085	X
Property taxes	18 905	2.3
Sales and gross receipts	295 841	35.8
General sales and gross receipts	254 595	30.8
Selective sales taxes	41 246	5.0
Alcoholic beverages	1 332	0.2
Insurance premiums	159	0.0
Motor fuels	6 161	0.7
Tobacco products	9 368	1.1
Other selective sales	24 226	2.9
Licenses	57 420	6.9
Alcoholic beverages	X	0.0
Corporation	X	0.0
Motor vehicle	7 123	0.9
Motor vehicle operators	1 104	0.1
Public utility	34 378	4.2
Occupation and business, NEC	4 665	0.6
Other licenses	10 150	1.2
Income taxes	343 038	41.5
Individual income	257 693	31.2
Corporation net income	85 345	10.3
Other taxes	111 881	13.5
Death and gift	55 440	6.7
Documentary and stock transfer	56 441	6.8

There are no agricultural data for the District of Columbia.

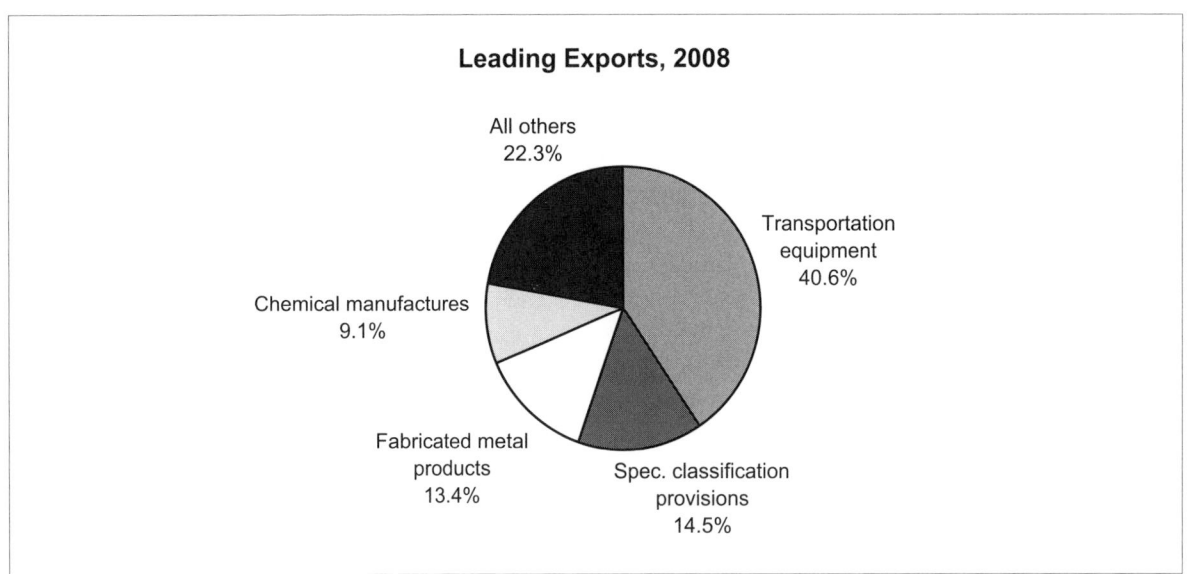

FLORIDA

Facts and Figures

Location: Southeastern United States; bordered on the N by Georgia and Alabama, on the E by the Atlantic Ocean, on the S by the Straits of Florida, and on the W by Alabama and the Gulf of Mexico

Area: 65,755 sq. mi. (170,304 sq. km.); rank—22nd

Population: 18,328,340 (2008 est.); rank—4th

Principal Cities: capital—Tallahassee; largest—Jacksonville

Statehood: March 3, 1845; 27th state

U.S. Congress: 2 senators, 25 representatives

State Motto: In God We Trust

State Song: "The Swanee River (Old Folks at Home)"

State Nickname: The Sunshine State

Abbreviations: FL; Fla.

State Symbols: flower—orange blossom; tree—Sabal palm (cabbage palm); bird—mockingbird

At a Glance

- With an increase in population of 14.7 percent, Florida ranked 8th among the states in growth from 2000 to 2008.
- An estimated 147,941 marriages took place in Florida in 2008, compared to 82,055 divorces.
- The 2007 home ownership rate in Florida was 71.8 percent, giving it a ranking of 18th among the states.
- Florida's median household income in 2007 was $47,804, 27th among the states.
- In Florida, 12.1 percent of the population lived below the poverty level in 2007, ranking it 24th along with Idaho and North Dakota.
- In 2006-07, 20.7 percent of Floridians did not have health insurance, compared to 15.5 percent of the total U.S. population.
- In 2007, 4.1 percent of Floridians were unemployed, compared to 4.6 percent nationwide.
- Florida ranked 25th in the nation with 25.8 percent of its population 25 years old and over having a bachelor's degree in 2007; its ranking was the same as Pennsylvania's.
- Florida's violent crime rate in 2007 was 722.6 per 100,000 population, compared to 466.9 for the entire nation.
- Florida had one physician for every 332 people in 2007, compared to one physician for every 325 people nationwide.
- In the 2008 election, 67.5 percent of Florida's eligible voters voted, compared to 61.7 percent of eligible voters nationwide.
- Florida ranked 45th among the states receiving federal aid in 2007, with $1,101 per capita.
- Florida's gross domestic product was $735 billion in 2007; it ranked 4th among the states.
- With $44.8 billion in exports in 2007, Florida ranked 6th in exports.
- Floridians consumed 4.6 trillion Btu's of energy in 2006; the state ranked 3rd in total consumption.
- In 2007, Florida exported $1.9 billion worth of agricultural products, 2.3 percent of the U.S. total.

Table FL-1. Population by Sex, Age, Race, and Hispanic Origin

(Number, percent.)

Sex, age, race, and Hispanic origin	1990	2000	2008	Average annual percent change, 2000–2008
Total Population	12 937 926	15 982 378	18 328 340	1.7
Percent of total U.S. population	5.2	5.7	6.0	X
Sex				
Male	6 261 719	7 797 715	9 005 282	1.8
Female	6 676 207	8 184 663	9 323 058	1.6
Age				
Under 5 years	849 596	945 823	1 140 516	2.4
5 to 19 years	2 361 752	3 102 809	3 322 417	0.9
20 to 64 years	7 357 147	9 126 149	10 677 610	2.0
65 years and over	2 369 431	2 807 597	3 187 797	1.6
Median age (years)	36.2	38.7	40.2	X
Race and Hispanic Origin[1]				
One race				
White	10 749 285	12 465 029	14 628 044	2.0
Black	1 759 534	2 335 505	2 916 174	2.8
American Indian and Alaskan Native	36 335	53 541	91 412	6.9
Asian[2]	154 302	266 256	416 318	5.7
Native Hawaiian and Other Pacific Islander	X	8 625	17 658	9.4
Two or more races	X	376 315	258 734	-4.6
Hispanic (of any race)	1 574 143	2 682 715	3 845 069	4.6

[1]Data on race in 2000 and 2008 are not comparable to 1990. Individuals could only report one race in the 1990 census but could report one or more races on the 2000 census.
[2]Data in 1990 refer to Asian and Pacific Islanders.

Table FL-2. Marital Status

(Number, percent distribution.)

Sex and marital status	1990	2000	2007
Males, 15 Years and Over	5 027 000	6 232 987	7 261 401
Never married	26.6	27.3	31.9
Now married, except separated	59.2	56.9	52.0
Separated	2.1	2.1	2.0
Widowed	3.1	3.2	3.2
Divorced	9.0	10.5	10.9
Females, 15 Years and Over	5 498 857	6 714 003	7 665 121
Never married	19.0	20.5	24.5
Now married, except separated	53.6	51.9	47.8
Separated	2.5	2.7	2.6
Widowed	13.8	12.3	11.6
Divorced	11.1	12.7	13.6

Table FL-3. Households and Housing Characteristics

(Number, percent, and dollars.)

Item	1990	2000	2007	Average annual percent change, 2000–2007
Total Households	5 134 869	6 337 929	7 088 960	1.6
Family households	3 511 825	4 210 760	4 626 215	1.4
Married-couple family	2 791 734	3 192 266	3 415 012	1.0
Other family	720 091	1 018 494	1 211 203	2.5
Male householder, no wife present	171 535	259 494	331 314	3.6
Female householder, no husband present	548 556	759 000	879 889	2.1
Nonfamily households	1 623 044	2 127 169	2 462 745	2.1
Householder living alone	1 309 954	1 687 303	1 981 833	2.3
Householder not living alone	313 090	439 866	480 912	1.3
Housing Characteristics				
Total housing units	6 100 262	7 302 947	8 716 601	2.6
Occupied housing units	5 134 869	6 337 929	7 088 960	1.6
Owner-occupied	3 452 160	4 441 799	5 005 708	1.7
Renter-occupied	1 682 709	1 896 130	2 083 252	1.4
Average size	2.46	2.46	2.52	X
Financial Characteristics				
Median gross rent of renter-occupied housing units (dollars)	481	641	925	5.4
Median monthly owner costs for housing units with a mortgage (dollars)	718	1 004	1 577	6.7
Median value of owner-occupied housing units (dollars)	76 500	105 500	230 400	11.8

Table FL-4. Median Income and Poverty Status, 2007

(Number, percent.)

Characteristic	State		U.S.	
	Number	Percent	Number	Percent
Median Income				
Households (dollars)	47 804	X	50 740	X
Families (dollars)	56 966	X	61 173	X
Below Poverty Level				
Sex				
Male	939 345	10.8	16 576 071	11.5
Female	1 219 487	13.3	21 476 176	14.3
Age				
Under 18 years	678 038	17.1	13 097 100	18.0
Related children under 18 years	654 826	16.6	12 728 964	17.6
18 to 64 years	1 197 804	11.0	21 495 507	11.6
65 years and over	282 990	9.4	3 459 640	9.5

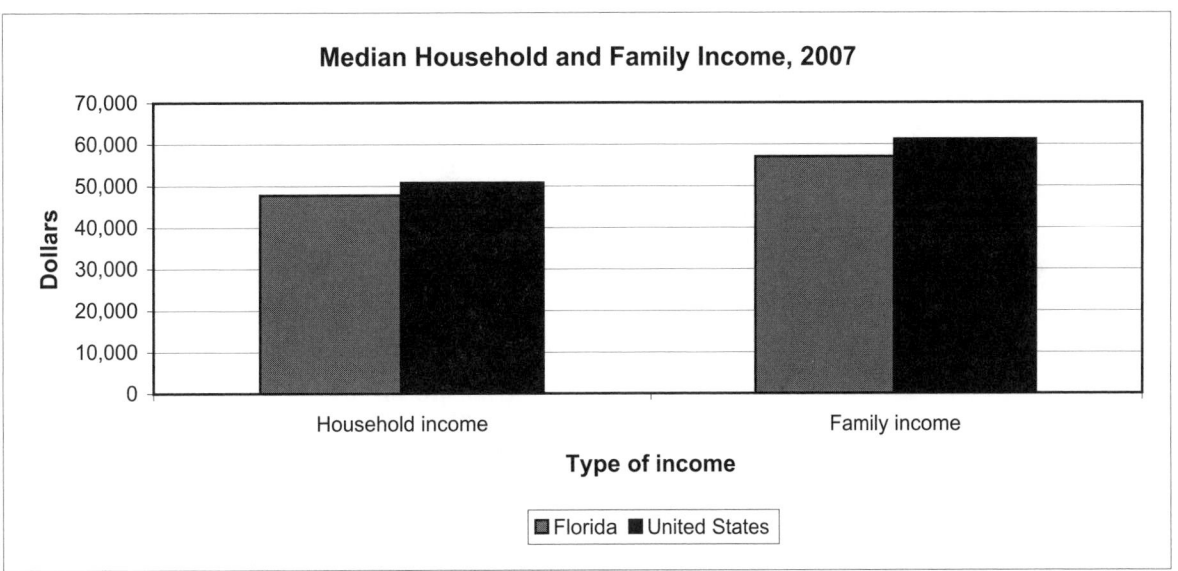

Table FL-5. Health Insurance Coverage Status for All Persons and Children Under 18 Years of Age

(Number, percent.)

Item	2000	2001	2002	2003	2004	2005	2006	2007
ALL PERSONS	16 017	16 348	16 429	16 921	17 468	17 886	18 062	18 074
Covered by Private or Government Health Insurance								
Number	13 290	13 563	13 689	13 952	14 086	14 270	14 233	14 426
Percent	83.0	83.0	83.3	82.5	80.6	79.8	78.8	79.8
Not Covered								
Number	2 727	2 785	2 740	2 969	3 382	3 616	3 828	3 648
Percent	17.0	17.0	16.7	17.5	19.4	20.2	21.2	20.2
Percent in the U.S. not covered	13.7	14.1	14.7	15.1	14.9	15.3	15.8	15.3
CHILDREN UNDER 18 YEARS OF AGE	3 754	3 926	3 872	3 977	4 060	4 038	4 076	4 084
Covered by Private or Government Health Insurance								
Number	3 112	3 323	3 331	3 375	3 477	3 307	3 305	3 298
Percent	82.9	84.7	86.0	84.9	85.6	81.9	81.1	80.8
Not Covered								
Number	642	603	541	602	583	731	771	785
Percent	17.1	15.3	14.0	15.1	14.4	18.1	18.9	19.2
Percent in the U.S. not covered	11.6	11.3	11.2	11.0	10.5	10.9	11.7	11.0

Table FL-6. Employment Status by Demographic Group, Preliminary 2008

(Number, percent.)

Characteristic	Civilian noninstitutional population	Civilian labor force		Employment		Unemployed	
		Number	Percent of population	Number	Percent of population	Number	Unemployment rate
TOTAL	14 515	9 214	63.5	8 654	59.6	560	6.1
Sex							
Men	6 994	4 895	70.0	4 575	65.4	321	6.6
Women	7 521	4 319	57.0	4 080	54.2	239	5.5
Race, Sex, and Hispanic Origin							
White	11 948	7 482	62.6	7 066	59.1	415	5.6
Men	5 820	4 052	69.6	3 815	65.6	237	5.8
Women	6 128	3 430	56.0	3 251	53.0	179	5.2
Black or African American	2 055	1 358	66.1	1 238	60.2	120	8.8
Men	936	657	70.2	586	62.5	71	10.9
Women	1 119	701	62.6	652	58.3	48	6.9
Hispanic	2 892	1 976	68.3	1 831	63.3	145	7.4
Men	1 432	1 113	77.7	1 023	71.5	90	8.1
Women	1 460	863	59.1	807	55.3	56	6.5
Age							
16 to 19 years	945	326	34.5	275	29.1	51	15.6
20 to 24 years	1 065	794	74.6	702	65.9	92	11.6
25 to 34 years	2 216	1 884	85.0	1 764	79.6	120	6.4
35 to 44 years	2 503	2 138	85.4	2 035	81.3	103	4.8
45 to 54 years	2 731	2 228	81.6	2 118	77.6	109	4.9
55 to 64 years	2 173	1 393	64.1	1 334	61.4	59	4.3
65 years and over	2 881	451	15.7	427	14.8	25	5.5

Note: Data in Table 6 are from the Current Population Survey (CPS) and do not match the estimates in Table 7. See notes and definitions for more details.

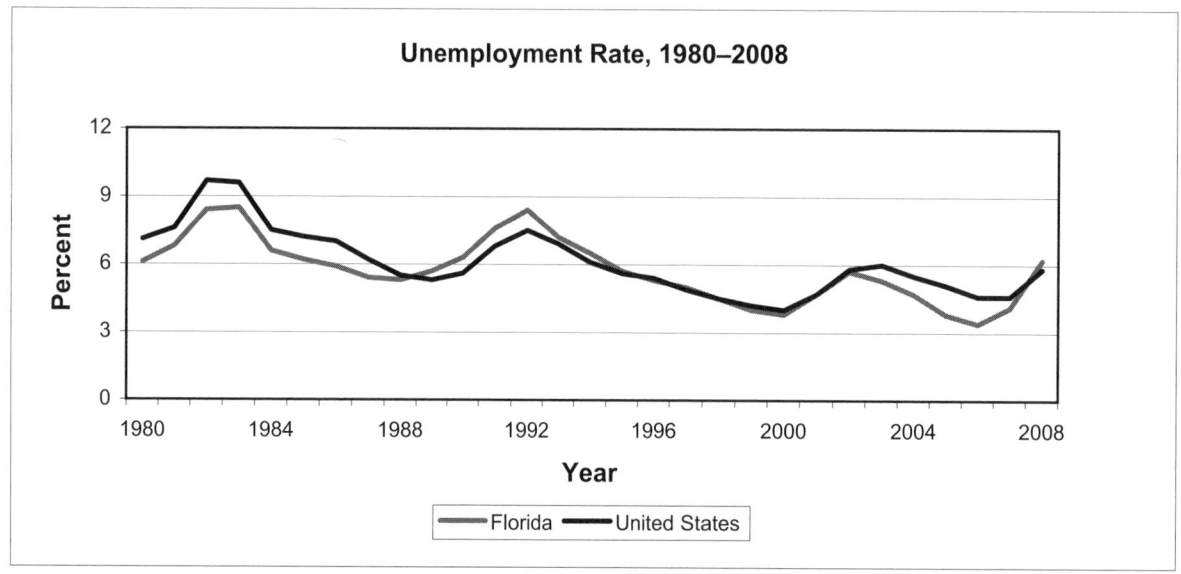

Table FL-7. Employment Status of the Civilian Noninstitutional Population Age 16 Years and Over

(Number, percent.)

Year	Civilian labor force	Civilian participation rate	Employed	Unemployed	Unemployment rate
1998	7 572 631	62.8	7 232 345	340 286	4.5
1999	7 710 988	62.8	7 401 659	309 329	4.0
2000	7 869 690	63.0	7 569 406	300 284	3.8
2001	7 998 062	62.8	7 624 718	373 344	4.7
2002	8 124 930	62.6	7 662 511	462 419	5.7
2003	8 218 800	62.1	7 785 547	433 253	5.3
2004	8 388 829	62.0	7 998 202	390 627	4.7
2005	8 630 977	62.3	8 300 224	330 753	3.8
2006	8 889 263	62.9	8 587 732	301 531	3.4
2007	9 088 439	63.5	8 716 798	371 641	4.1
2008	9 231 462	63.9	8 659 856	571 606	6.2

Table FL-8. Employment and Average Wages by Industry

(Estimates for 2001–2006 are based on the 2002 North American Industry Classification System [NAICS]. Estimates for 2007 are based on the 2007 NAICS.)

Industry	2001	2002	2003	2004	2005	2006	2007
	Number of jobs						
WAGE AND SALARY EMPLOYMENT BY INDUSTRY	7 643 817	7 658 977	7 755 184	7 990 878	8 279 765	8 500 760	8 489 432
Farm Wage and Salary Employment	54 064	52 647	57 404	52 218	44 977	46 993	47 223
Nonfarm Wage and Salary Employment	7 589 753	7 606 330	7 697 780	7 938 660	8 234 788	8 453 767	8 442 209
Private wage and salary employment	6 475 900	6 481 558	6 556 548	6 777 857	7 056 847	7 258 290	7 233 225
Forestry, fishing, hunting, and other	76 882	74 851	76 139	75 384	77 442	76 963	76 335
Mining	6 255	5 496	5 422	5 485	5 416	4 675	4 818
Utilities	28 126	25 421	24 532	24 168	24 357	24 796	24 034
Construction	440 724	446 301	487 203	545 791	627 401	686 218	626 432
Manufacturing	437 211	411 812	395 812	398 700	406 765	414 039	398 443
Durable goods manufacturing	291 881	272 438	259 897	265 276	274 538	282 869	269 183
Nondurable goods manufacturing	145 330	139 374	135 915	133 424	132 227	131 170	129 260
Wholesale trade	320 731	318 821	322 503	333 557	346 316	356 576	365 053
Retail trade	967 072	957 510	959 475	985 274	1 020 245	1 047 897	1 049 068
Transportation and warehousing	217 496	214 007	209 380	212 408	221 408	226 756	227 136
Information	189 687	179 298	173 372	168 972	170 080	168 802	162 875
Finance and insurance	330 999	335 355	344 757	353 494	366 517	381 262	378 573
Real estate and rental and leasing	153 246	157 527	162 409	170 841	179 206	189 050	183 643
Professional and technical services	399 484	398 637	414 106	437 561	463 095	485 418	486 260
Management of companies and enterprises	59 607	67 289	68 204	70 098	72 528	74 296	79 402
Administrative and waste services	776 989	764 977	731 845	732 477	762 799	724 776	718 016
Educational services	100 336	107 043	110 014	115 519	119 633	123 348	129 657
Health care and social assistance	761 241	779 016	805 842	827 899	844 977	883 983	910 642
Arts, entertainment, and recreation	173 166	169 965	170 293	178 167	183 150	188 351	194 403
Accommodation and food services	639 127	649 405	669 685	709 619	733 489	755 021	768 733
Other services, except public administration	397 521	418 827	425 555	432 443	432 023	446 063	449 702
Government and government enterprises	1 113 853	1 124 772	1 141 232	1 160 803	1 177 941	1 195 477	1 208 984
	Dollars						
AVERAGE WAGES AND SALARIES BY INDUSTRY	31 297	32 257	33 360	34 978	36 594	38 254	39 505
Average Farm Wages and Salaries	18 113	19 747	15 395	19 940	21 898	24 446	27 008
Average Nonfarm Wages and Salaries	31 391	32 344	33 494	35 077	36 675	38 331	39 575
Average private wages and salaries	30 929	31 718	32 792	34 313	35 967	37 681	38 827
Forestry, fishing, hunting, and other	14 954	15 616	15 956	16 630	17 007	17 949	18 682
Mining	44 615	45 786	45 739	46 754	49 197	53 560	56 765
Utilities	59 401	54 213	56 597	65 528	66 892	64 564	67 099
Construction	33 487	33 999	34 618	36 150	37 926	40 122	41 437
Manufacturing	37 877	39 275	40 690	42 228	43 273	45 477	47 230
Durable goods manufacturing	39 128	40 927	42 283	43 851	45 056	47 601	49 481
Nondurable goods manufacturing	35 366	36 047	37 644	39 000	39 571	40 898	42 542
Wholesale trade	45 368	45 900	47 695	50 120	52 581	55 690	57 256
Retail trade	22 662	23 250	23 960	24 851	25 841	26 584	26 559
Transportation and warehousing	34 671	35 476	36 536	37 941	39 178	40 954	42 316
Information	46 427	46 041	47 333	50 911	52 746	54 910	56 832
Finance and insurance	48 862	50 511	53 541	56 231	59 284	61 654	64 485
Real estate and rental and leasing	30 323	31 389	33 538	35 732	38 884	39 625	39 811
Professional and technical services	49 635	50 124	50 603	52 810	55 561	58 665	61 016
Management of companies and enterprises	60 907	63 929	68 109	71 048	80 393	83 362	88 858
Administrative and waste services	22 916	24 747	24 760	25 631	27 140	28 439	29 196
Educational services	25 769	26 446	27 545	28 588	29 652	31 108	32 476
Health care and social assistance	33 100	34 332	35 584	37 306	38 547	40 003	41 362
Arts, entertainment, and recreation	27 606	27 937	29 508	31 098	31 770	32 803	33 520
Accommodation and food services	15 546	15 742	16 396	17 271	18 334	19 193	19 851
Other services, except public administration	21 333	21 592	22 594	23 619	24 637	25 744	26 820
Government and government enterprises	34 074	35 953	37 528	39 542	40 911	42 276	44 051

Table FL-9. Employment Characteristics by Family Type

(Number, percent.)

Family type and labor force status	2005 Total	2005 Families with own children under 18 years	2006 Total	2006 Families with own children under 18 years	2007 Total	2007 Families with own children under 18 years
TOTAL FAMILIES	4 594 803	1 919 568	4 632 974	1 931 018	4 626 215	1 911 874
FAMILY TYPE AND LABOR FORCE STATUS						
Married Coupled Families	3 379 273	1 250 776	3 452 127	1 293 023	3 415 012	1 248 936
Both husband and wife in labor force	45.6	62.0	47.6	63.9	47.6	64.6
Husband in labor force, wife not in labor force	21.6	30.2	21.5	29.7	21.4	29.0
Wife in labor force, husband not in labor force	7.3	4.1	7.2	4.1	7.4	3.9
Both husband and wife not in labor force	25.5	3.7	23.7	2.3	23.6	2.4
Other Families	1 215 530	668 792	1 180 847	637 995	1 211 203	662 938
Female householder, no husband present	73.4	77.4	72.9	77.6	72.6	76.7
In labor force	52.0	63.3	52.5	64.0	53.2	64.7
Not in labor force	21.5	14.0	20.5	13.6	19.4	12.0
Male householder, no wife present	26.6	22.6	27.1	22.4	27.4	23.3
In labor force	21.3	20.4	21.7	20.1	22.2	21.0
Not in labor force	5.3	2.2	5.4	2.3	5.2	2.3

Table FL-10. School Enrollment and Educational Attainment, 2007

(Number, percent.)

Item	State	U.S.
Enrollment		
Total population 3 years and over	17 564 477	289 295 761
Enrolled in school	4 315 302	79 329 527
Enrolled in preschool (percent)	6.8	6.2
Enrolled in grades K-12 (percent)	67.5	67.6
Enrolled in college or graduate school (percent)	25.7	26.2
Attainment		
Total population 25 years and over	12 588 083	197 892 369
Less than a high school diploma (percent)	15.1	15.5
High school diploma or more (percent)	84.9	84.5
Bachelor's degree or more (percent)	25.8	27.5
Graduate degree or more (percent)	8.9	10.1

Table FL-11. Educational Indicators

(Number, percent.)

Item	State	U.S.
Public Schools, 2006–2007 (except where noted)		
Number of school districts	77	17 742
Number of schools	4 009	99 639
Number of students	2 671 513	49 315 842
Student-teacher ratio	16.4	15.5
Expenditures per student (dollars)	$8 567	. . .
Averaged freshman graduation rate, 2005–2006	63.6	. . .
Dropout rate, grades 9–12, 2005–2006	4.0	3.7
Students eligible for free or reduced-price lunch (percent)	45.2	41.2
English-language learners (percent)	8.8	5.1
Students with IEP (percent)	14.9	12.7
Private Schools, 2007–2008 (except where noted)		
Number of schools	1 938	33 740
Number of students	329 646	5 072 451
High school graduates, 2006–2007	18 583	306 605
Student-teacher ratio	11.1	11.1

Table FL-12. Reported Voting and Registration of the Voting-Age Population, November 2008

(Number in thousands, percent.)

Item	Total population	Total citizen population	Registered			Voted		
			Total registered	Percent registered (total population)	Percent registered (total citizen population)	Total voted	Percent voted (total population)	Percent voted (total citizen population)
U.S. total	225 499	206 072	146 311	64.9	71.0	131 144	58.2	63.6
State total	14 069	12 462	8 774	62.4	70.4	7 951	56.5	63.8
Sex								
Male	6 774	5 928	4 049	59.8	68.3	3 677	54.3	62.0
Female	7 294	6 534	4 725	64.8	72.3	4 274	58.6	65.4
Race								
White alone	11 674	10 505	7 533	64.5	71.7	6 806	58.3	64.8
White non-Hispanic alone	8 980	8 644	6 213	69.2	71.9	5 635	62.8	65.2
Black alone	1 968	1 685	1 069	54.3	63.5	985	50.1	58.5
Asian alone	267	157	96	35.9	61.0	84	31.3	53.1
Hispanic (of any race)	2 909	1 988	1 380	47.4	69.4	1 227	42.2	61.7
White alone or in combination	11 776	10 582	7 576	64.3	71.6	6 849	58.2	64.7
Black alone or in combination	2 073	1 753	1 110	53.6	63.3	1 026	49.5	58.5
Asian alone or in combination	283	161	100	35.3	61.9	88	30.9	54.3

Table FL-13. Crime

(Number, rate per 100,000.)

Item	State			U.S.		
	2007	2008	Percent change	2007	2008	Percent change
Population	18 251 243	18 328 340	0.4	301 621 157	304 059 724	0.8
VIOLENT CRIME						
Number	131 880	126 265	-4.3	1 408 337	1 382 012	-1.9
Rate	722.6	688.9	-4.7	466.9	454.5	-2.7
Murder and Nonnegligent Manslaughter						
Number	1 201	1 168	-2.7	16 929	16 272	-3.9
Rate	6.6	6.4	-3.2	5.6	5.4	-4.7
Forcible Rape						
Number	6 151	5 972	-2.9	90 427	89 000	-1.6
Rate	33.7	32.6	-3.3	30.0	29.3	-2.4
Robbery						
Number	38 162	36 273	-4.9	445 125	441 855	-0.7
Rate	209.1	197.9	-5.3	147.6	145.3	-1.5
Aggravated Assault						
Number	86 366	82 852	-4.1	855 856	834 885	-2.5
Rate	473.2	452.0	-4.5	283.8	274.6	-3.2
PROPERTY CRIME						
Number	746 347	758 934	1.7	9 843 481	9 767 915	-0.8
Rate	4 089.3	4 140.8	1.3	3 263.5	3 212.5	-1.6
Burglary						
Number	181 833	188 467	3.6	2 179 140	2 222 196	2.0
Rate	996.3	1 028.3	3.2	722.5	730.8	1.2
Larceny-Theft						
Number	490 858	506 958	3.3	6 568 572	6 588 873	0.3
Rate	2 689.4	2 766.0	2.8	2 177.8	2 167.0	-0.5
Motor Vehicle Theft						
Number	73 656	63 509	-13.8	1 095 769	956 846	-12.7
Rate	403.6	346.5	-14.1	363.3	314.7	-13.4

Table FL-14. State Government Finances, 2007

(Dollars, percent distribution.)

Item	Thousands of dollars	Percent distribution
Total Revenue	95 044 996	X
General revenue	66 005 588	69.4
Intergovernmental revenue	19 239 807	20.2
Taxes	35 738 291	37.6
General sales	21 748 908	22.9
Selective sales	5 786 459	6.1
License taxes	1 875 317	2.0
Individual income tax	0	0.0
Corporate income tax	2 442 516	2.6
Other taxes	3 885 091	4.1
Current charges	5 625 600	5.9
Miscellaneous general revenue	5 401 890	5.7
Utility revenue	17 864	0.0
Liquor store revenue	0	0.0
Insurance trust revenue	29 021 544	30.5
Total Expenditure	72 773 050	100.0
Intergovernmental expenditure	19 680 891	27.0
Direct expenditure	53 092 159	73.0
Current operation	36 361 614	50.0
Capital outlay	6 732 984	9.3
Insurance benefits and repayments	6 949 166	9.5
Assistance and subsidies	1 888 470	2.6
Interest on debt	1 159 925	1.6
Exhibit: Salaries and wages	8 268 077	11.4
Total Expenditure	72 773 050	100.0
General expenditure	65 738 088	90.3
Intergovernmental expenditure	19 680 891	27.0
Direct expenditure	46 057 197	63.3
Education	22 249 987	30.6
Public welfare	17 340 927	23.8
Hospitals	697 587	1.0
Health	3 305 874	4.5
Highways	6 855 857	9.4
Police protection	462 320	0.6
Correction	2 542 387	3.5
Natural resources	2 215 080	3.0
Parks and recreation	190 695	0.3
Government administration	2 899 987	4.0
Interest on general debt	1 159 925	1.6
Other and unallocable	5 817 462	8.0
Utility expenditure	85 796	0.1
Liquor store expenditure	0	0.0
Insurance trust expenditure	6 949 166	9.5
Debt at End of Fiscal Year	36 331 829	X
Cash and Security Holdings	202 273 752	X

Table FL-15. State Government Tax Collections, 2008

(Dollars, percent distribution.)

Item	Thousands of dollars	Percent distribution
Total Taxes	35 849 998	X
Property taxes	2 100	0.0
Sales and gross receipts	29 297 023	81.7
General sales and gross receipts	21 518 100	60.0
Selective sales taxes	7 778 923	21.7
Alcoholic beverages	609 185	1.7
Insurance premiums	714 400	2.0
Motor fuels	2 289 166	6.4
Pari-mutuels	28 108	0.1
Public utilities	3 159 400	8.8
Tobacco products	443 732	1.2
Other selective sales	534 932	1.5
Licenses	1 875 355	X
Alcoholic beverages	36 833	0.1
Amusements	5 040	0.0
Corporation	220 112	0.6
Hunting and fishing	15 501	0.0
Motor vehicle	1 153 139	3.2
Motor vehicle operators	161 590	0.5
Public utility	33 175	0.1
Occupation and business, NEC	246 783	X
Other licenses	3 182	0.0
Income taxes	2 208 600	6.2
Corporation net income	2 208 600	6.2
Other taxes	2 466 920	6.9
Death and gift	12 220	X
Documentary and stock transfer	2 398 700	6.7
Severance	56 000	0.2

Table FL-16. Agriculture

(Number, acres, and dollars.)

Item	2002		2007		Percent change, 2002–2007
	Number	Percent of total	Number	Percent of total	
Number of farms	44 081		47 463		7.7
Farm Size					
Average size of farm (acres)	236		195		-17.4
Farms by size (number of farms)					
Fewer than 50 acres	28 627	64.9	32 864	69.2	14.8
50 to 499 acres	12 460	28.3	12 004	25.3	-3.7
500 acres or more	2 994	6.8	2 595	5.5	-13.3
Land (Acres)					
Total land in farms	10 414 877		9 231 570		-11.4
Total cropland	3 715 257	35.7	2 953 340	32.0	-20.5
Total harvested cropland	2 313 537	22.2	2 112 129	22.9	-8.7
Irrigated land	1 815 174	17.4	1 552 118	16.8	-14.5
Value of Sales (Dollars)					
Agricultural products sold ($1,000)	6 242 272		7 785 228		24.7
Average sales per farm	141 609		164 027		15.8
Sales of crops	5 041 433	80.8	6 256 228	80.4	24.1
Sales of livestock, poultry, and their products	1 200 839	19.2	1 529 000	19.6	27.3
Value of Sales (Number of Farms)					
Less than $10,000	27 943	63.4	31 036	65.4	11.1
$10,000 to $99,999	11 031	25.0	11 194	23.6	1.5
$100,000 to $999,999	4 000	9.1	3 965	8.4	-0.9
$1,000,000 or more	1 107	2.5	1 268	2.7	14.5
Farms by Type of Organization (Number of Farms)					
Family	37 119	84.2	39 792	83.8	7.2
Partnership	2 429	5.5	2 417	5.1	-0.5
Corporation	4 076	9.2	4 693	9.9	15.1
Other: cooperative, estate or trust, institutional, etc	457	1.0	561	1.2	22.8
Value of Land and Buildings (Dollars)					
Estimated market value of land and buildings ($1,000)	52 053 543		29 330 433		-43.7
Land and buildings average value per farm	1 096 718		665 376		-39.3
Average value per acre	5 639		2 836		-49.7
Government Payments					
Number of farms receiving government payments	2 554	5.8	4 664	9.8	82.6
Payments (thousands of dollars)	21 818		45 343		107.8
Average payment per farm	8 543		9 722		13.8
Farm Operator Characteristics					
Farm operators whose principal occupation is farming	22 998	52.2	20 904	44.0	-9.1
Farm operators whose principal occupation is other	21 083	47.8	26 559	56.0	26.0
Average age principal operator (years)	57.0		58.4		2.5

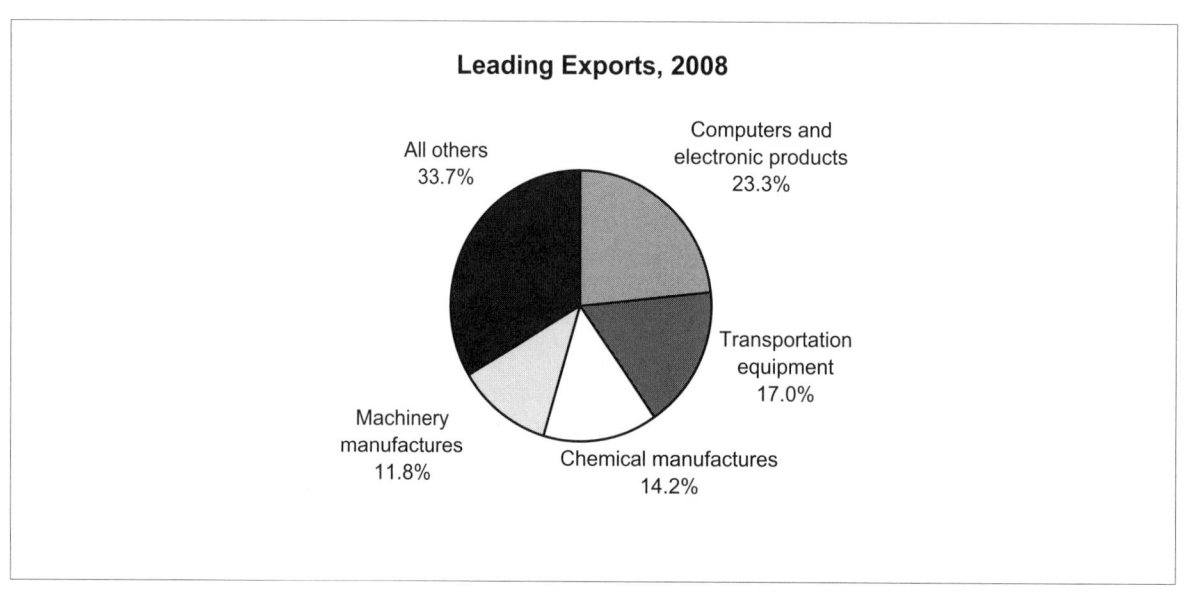

Leading Exports, 2008

All others 33.7%

Computers and electronic products 23.3%

Transportation equipment 17.0%

Chemical manufactures 14.2%

Machinery manufactures 11.8%

GEORGIA

Facts and Figures

Location: Southeastern United States; bordered on the N by Tennessee and North Carolina, on the E by South Carolina and the Atlantic Ocean, on the S by Florida, and on the W by Florida and Alabama

Area: 59,425 sq. mi. (153,909 sq. km.); rank—24th

Population: 9,685,744 (2008 est.); rank—9th

Principal Cities: capital—Atlanta; largest—Atlanta

Statehood: January 2, 1788; 4th state

U.S. Congress: 2 senators, 13 representatives

State Motto: Wisdom, Justice, and Moderation

State Song: "Georgia on My Mind"

State Nicknames: The Empire State of the South; The Peach State

Abbreviations: GA; Ga.

State Symbols: flower—Cherokee rose; tree—live oak; bird—brown thrasher

At a Glance

- With an increase in population of 18.3 percent, Georgia ranked 4th among the states in growth from 2000 to 2008.
- An estimated 57,361 marriages took place in Georgia in 2008; Georgia does not report its number of divorces.
- The 2007 home ownership rate in Georgia was 67.6 percent, giving it a ranking of 38th among the states.
- Georgia's median household income in 2007 was $49,136, 23rd among the states.
- In Georgia, 14.3 percent of the population lived below the poverty level in 2007, ranking it 12th along with North Carolina.
- In 2006-07, 17.6 percent of Georgians did not have health insurance, compared to 15.5 percent of the total U.S. population.
- In 2007, 4.3 percent of Georgians were unemployed, compared to 4.6 percent nationwide.
- Georgia ranked 20th in the nation with 27.1 percent of its population 25 years old and over having a bachelor's degree in 2007.
- Georgia's violent crime rate in 2007 was 493.2 per 100,000 population, compared to 466.9 for the entire nation.
- Georgia had one physician for every 411 people in 2007, compared to one physician for every 325 people nationwide.
- In the 2008 election, 61.4 percent of Georgia's eligible voters voted, compared to 61.7 percent of eligible voters nationwide.
- Georgia ranked 46th among the states receiving federal aid in 2007, with $1,099 per capita.
- Georgia's gross domestic product was $397 billion in 2007; it ranked 10th among the states.
- With $23.4 billion in exports in 2007, Georgia ranked 14th in exports.
- Georgians consumed 3.15 trillion Btu's of energy in 2006; the state ranked 9th in total consumption.
- In 2007, Georgia exported $1.5 billion worth of agricultural products, 1.8 percent of the U.S. total.

Table GA-1. Population by Sex, Age, Race, and Hispanic Origin

(Number, percent.)

Sex, age, race, and Hispanic origin	1990	2000	2008	Average annual percent change, 2000–2008
Total Population	6 478 216	8 186 453	9 685 744	2.1
Percent of total U.S. population	2.6	2.9	3.2	X
Sex				
Male	3 144 503	4 027 113	4 764 975	2.1
Female	3 333 713	4 159 340	4 920 769	2.1
Age				
Under 5 years	495 535	595 150	740 521	2.8
5 to 19 years	1 447 718	1 819 620	2 075 140	1.7
20 to 64 years	3 880 693	4 986 408	5 889 059	2.1
65 years and over	654 270	785 275	981 024	2.8
Median age (years)	31.4	33.4	34.9	X
Race and Hispanic Origin[1]				
One race				
White	4 600 148	5 327 281	6 333 287	2.2
Black	1 746 565	2 349 542	2 907 944	2.7
American Indian and Alaskan Native	13 348	21 737	35 528	6.3
Asian[2]	75 781	173 170	276 615	6.0
Native Hawaiian and Other Pacific Islander	X	4 246	8 315	8.8
Two or more races	X	114 188	124 055	1.0
Hispanic (of any race)	108 922	435 227	777 244	7.5

[1]Data on race in 2000 and 2008 are not comparable to 1990. Individuals could only report one race in the 1990 census but could report one or more races on the 2000 census.
[2]Data in 1990 refer to Asian and Pacific Islanders.

Table GA-2. Marital Status

(Number, percent distribution.)

Sex and marital status	1990	2000	2007
Males, 15 Years and Over	2 404 921	3 092 736	3 615 406
Never married	29.8	30.4	34.6
Now married, except separated	57.6	56.5	51.2
Separated	2.3	2.0	2.0
Widowed	2.2	2.1	2.2
Divorced	8.2	9.0	9.9
Females, 15 Years and Over	2 627 194	3 273 889	3 823 008
Never married	22.9	24.4	28.3
Now married, except separated	52.0	51.5	46.8
Separated	3.1	2.7	2.8
Widowed	11.7	9.8	9.4
Divorced	10.3	11.6	12.8

Table GA-3. Households and Housing Characteristics

(Number, percent, and dollars.)

Item	1990	2000	2007	Average annual percent change, 2000–2007
Total Households	2 366 615	3 006 369	3 417 115	1.8
Family households	1 713 072	2 111 647	2 328 569	1.4
Married-couple family	1 306 756	1 548 800	1 670 425	1.1
Other family	406 316	562 847	658 144	2.3
Male householder, no wife present	76 675	127 437	152 682	2.6
Female householder, no husband present	329 641	435 410	505 462	2.2
Nonfamily households	653 543	894 722	1 088 546	2.8
Householder living alone	537 702	710 523	907 193	3.6
Householder not living alone	115 841	184 199	181 353	-0.2
Housing Characteristics				
Total housing units	2 638 418	3 281 737	3 961 643	2.7
Occupied housing units	2 366 615	3 006 369	3 417 115	1.8
Owner-occupied	1 536 759	2 029 154	2 341 965	2.1
Renter-occupied	829 856	977 215	1 075 150	1.4
Average size	2.66	2.65	2.72	X
Financial Characteristics				
Median gross rent of renter-occupied housing units (dollars)	433	613	768	3.3
Median monthly owner costs for housing units with a mortgage (dollars)	737	1 039	1 343	3.7
Median value of owner-occupied housing units (dollars)	70 700	111 200	164 500	5.8

Table GA-4. Median Income and Poverty Status, 2007

(Number, percent.)

Characteristic	State		U.S.	
	Number	Percent	Number	Percent
Median Income				
Households (dollars)	49 136	X	50 740	X
Families (dollars)	58 403	X	61 173	X
Below Poverty Level				
Sex				
Male	582 301	12.9	16 576 071	11.5
Female	741 527	15.6	21 476 176	14.3
Age				
Under 18 years	490 381	19.7	13 097 100	18.0
Related children under 18 years	482 092	19.4	12 728 964	17.6
18 to 64 years	723 628	12.3	21 495 507	11.6
65 years and over	109 819	12.1	3 459 640	9.5

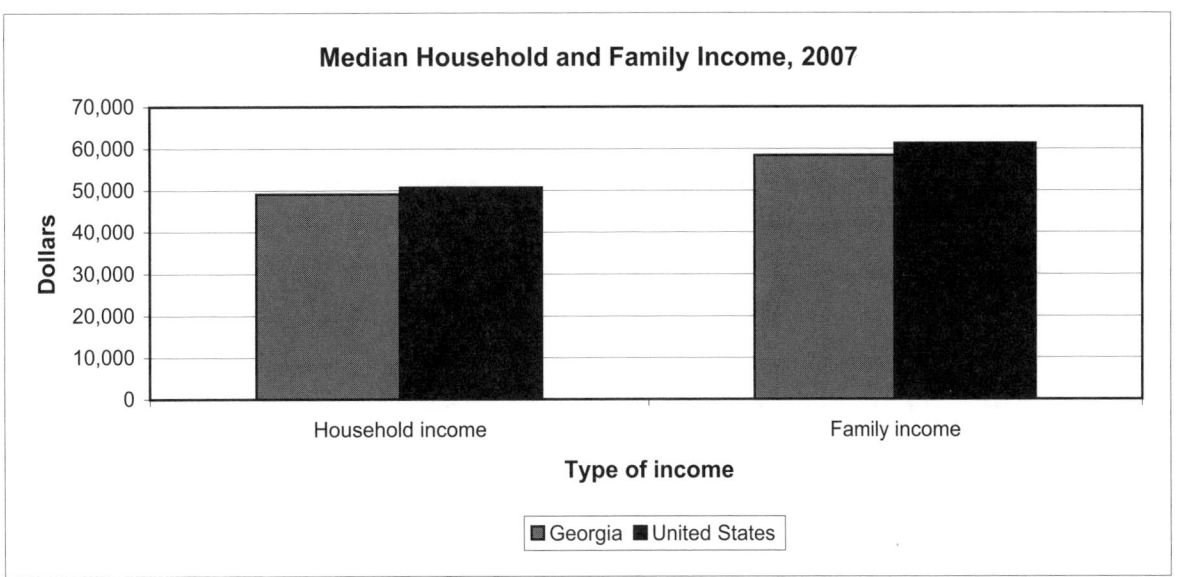

Table GA-5. Health Insurance Coverage Status for All Persons and Children Under 18 Years of Age

(Number, percent.)

Item	2000	2001	2002	2003	2004	2005	2006	2007
ALL PERSONS	8 124	8 289	8 426	8 571	8 706	9 045	9 347	9 493
Covered by Private or Government Health Insurance								
Number	6 979	6 976	7 105	7 199	7 237	7 391	7 688	7 831
Percent	85.9	84.2	84.3	84.0	83.1	81.7	82.3	82.5
Not Covered								
Number	1 145	1 312	1 321	1 372	1 469	1 654	1 659	1 662
Percent	14.1	15.8	15.7	16.0	16.9	18.3	17.7	17.5
Percent in the U.S. not covered	13.7	14.1	14.7	15.1	14.9	15.3	15.8	15.3
CHILDREN UNDER 18 YEARS OF AGE	2 229	2 326	2 270	2 298	2 340	2 371	2 455	2 517
Covered by Private or Government Health Insurance								
Number	2 005	2 003	2 001	1 994	2 073	2 110	2 141	2 228
Percent	90.0	86.1	88.2	86.8	88.6	89.0	87.2	88.5
Not Covered								
Number	223	323	269	303	267	260	314	289
Percent	10.0	13.9	11.8	13.2	11.4	11.0	12.8	11.5
Percent in the U.S. not covered	11.6	11.3	11.2	11.0	10.5	10.9	11.7	11.0

Table GA-6. Employment Status by Demographic Group, Preliminary 2008

(Number, percent.)

Characteristic	Civilian noninstitutional population	Civilian labor force		Employment		Unemployed	
		Number	Percent of population	Number	Percent of population	Number	Unemployment rate
TOTAL	7 234	4 904	67.8	4 588	63.4	316	6.4
Sex							
Men	3 457	2 623	76.0	2 465	71.3	158	6.0
Women	3 777	2 281	60.0	2 124	56.2	157	6.9
Race, Sex, and Hispanic Origin							
White	4 844	3 288	67.9	3 128	64.6	161	4.9
Men	2 385	1 839	77.1	1 755	73.6	83	4.5
Women	2 459	1 450	59.0	1 372	55.8	78	5.3
Black or African American	2 080	1 394	67.0	1 252	60.2	142	10.2
Men	917	663	72.2	595	64.9	68	10.2
Women	1 163	731	62.9	657	56.5	75	10.2
Hispanic	497	372	74.7	341	68.6	30	8.2
Men	293	263	89.9	245	83.5	19	7.0
Women	204	108	52.9	96	47.2	12	10.8
Age							
16 to 19 years	488	160	32.7	123	25.3	36	22.7
20 to 24 years	656	469	71.4	415	63.2	54	11.5
25 to 34 years	1 360	1 143	84.0	1 061	78.0	82	7.2
35 to 44 years	1 421	1 197	84.3	1 138	80.1	59	4.9
45 to 54 years	1 406	1 149	81.7	1 097	78.1	52	4.5
55 to 64 years	1 012	636	62.8	611	60.3	25	4.0
65 years and over	890	150	16.9	143	16.0	8	5.0

Note: Data in Table 6 are from the Current Population Survey (CPS) and do not match the estimates in Table 7. See notes and definitions for more details.

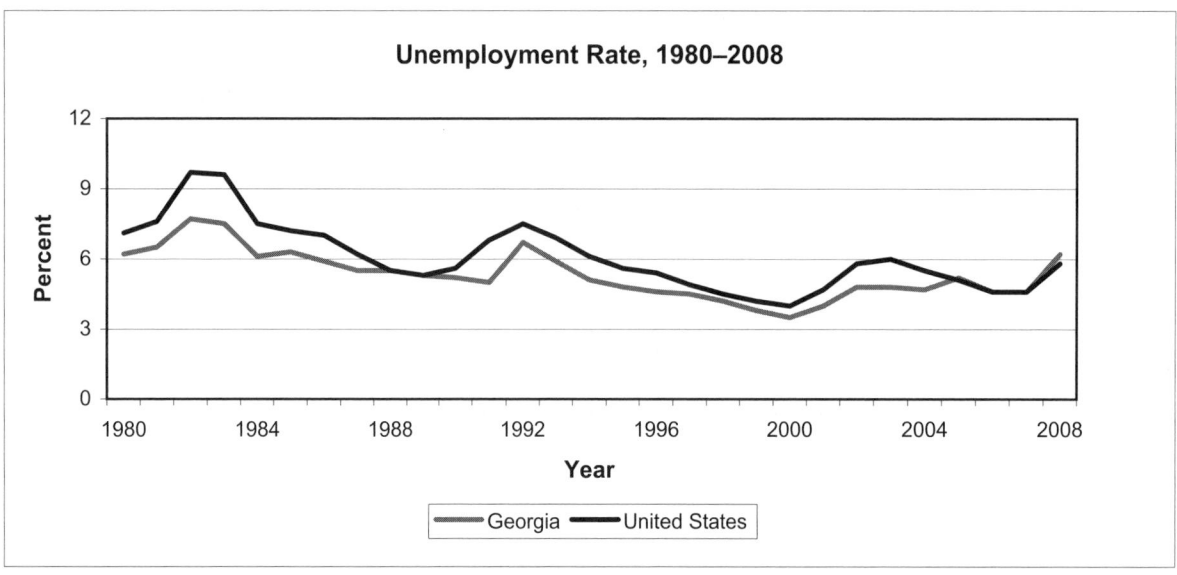

Unemployment Rate, 1980–2008

Table GA-7. Employment Status of the Civilian Noninstitutional Population Age 16 Years and Over

(Number, percent.)

Year	Civilian labor force	Civilian participation rate	Employed	Unemployed	Unemployment rate
1998	4 029 245	68.8	3 861 646	167 599	4.2
1999	4 106 678	68.7	3 951 684	154 994	3.8
2000	4 242 889	69.6	4 095 362	147 527	3.5
2001	4 283 156	68.8	4 112 868	170 288	4.0
2002	4 345 402	68.4	4 135 381	210 021	4.8
2003	4 382 182	67.7	4 173 787	208 395	4.8
2004	4 460 137	67.6	4 249 007	211 130	4.7
2005	4 613 585	68.3	4 373 348	240 237	5.2
2006	4 727 059	68.3	4 507 769	219 290	4.6
2007	4 798 003	67.8	4 578 828	219 175	4.6
2008	4 847 650	67.3	4 545 675	301 975	6.2

Table GA-8. Employment and Average Wages by Industry

(Estimates for 2001–2006 are based on the 2002 North American Industry Classification System [NAICS]. Estimates for 2007 are based on the 2007 NAICS.)

Industry	2001	2002	2003	2004	2005	2006	2007
	Number of jobs						
WAGE AND SALARY EMPLOYMENT BY INDUSTRY	4 162 240	4 110 267	4 094 472	4 153 844	4 253 306	4 346 002	4 398 956
Farm Wage and Salary Employment	16 023	16 851	17 413	17 347	20 419	16 283	15 581
Nonfarm Wage and Salary Employment	4 146 217	4 093 416	4 077 059	4 136 497	4 232 887	4 329 719	4 383 375
Private wage and salary employment	3 437 354	3 369 376	3 340 603	3 391 589	3 477 065	3 558 812	3 597 341
Forestry, fishing, hunting, and other	22 085	20 666	20 377	20 370	20 984	21 625	20 601
Mining	8 026	7 418	7 277	7 154	7 035	7 094	6 960
Utilities	20 739	20 760	20 484	20 292	20 009	20 266	20 741
Construction	213 813	205 125	204 640	208 829	217 503	227 220	229 737
Manufacturing	511 856	478 918	456 281	454 225	453 934	453 218	436 520
Durable goods manufacturing	231 388	214 561	203 664	205 120	209 974	211 886	205 419
Nondurable goods manufacturing	280 468	264 357	252 617	249 105	243 960	241 332	231 101
Wholesale trade	217 985	210 844	206 576	209 403	215 834	219 581	223 460
Retail trade	479 285	468 417	460 280	461 844	475 021	486 896	495 528
Transportation and warehousing	163 344	157 451	155 907	159 147	162 891	166 199	169 996
Information	143 557	132 775	123 141	120 217	114 235	114 068	112 664
Finance and insurance	157 669	157 453	160 337	162 055	165 330	170 165	170 207
Real estate and rental and leasing	60 645	59 750	60 661	61 799	64 594	66 728	67 066
Professional and technical services	210 280	204 466	205 731	205 440	215 248	225 553	233 401
Management of companies and enterprises	64 659	58 469	50 602	53 534	53 487	53 004	53 158
Administrative and waste services	253 717	252 091	247 668	264 217	283 215	288 743	290 162
Educational services	66 085	69 666	69 594	68 194	70 207	71 735	74 572
Health care and social assistance	318 817	330 501	342 969	354 513	365 289	377 377	389 684
Arts, entertainment, and recreation	41 185	39 004	38 505	39 354	40 662	42 449	44 042
Accommodation and food services	302 882	306 574	318 002	328 514	337 933	349 313	359 319
Other services, except public administration	180 725	189 028	191 571	192 488	193 654	197 578	199 523
Government and government enterprises	708 863	724 040	736 456	744 908	755 822	770 907	786 034
	Dollars						
AVERAGE WAGES AND SALARIES BY INDUSTRY	34 559	35 178	36 116	37 388	38 653	39 975	41 574
Average Farm Wages and Salaries	18 190	17 737	14 843	17 494	17 290	17 986	20 579
Average Nonfarm Wages and Salaries	34 623	35 250	36 206	37 471	38 756	40 058	41 649
Average private wages and salaries	35 201	35 598	36 467	37 851	39 096	40 412	42 067
Forestry, fishing, hunting, and other	22 184	21 835	22 425	23 763	24 714	25 994	27 319
Mining	45 474	47 410	49 295	51 673	53 478	54 546	57 847
Utilities	64 169	67 112	68 268	68 378	72 300	73 007	73 034
Construction	35 749	36 062	36 895	38 424	39 949	41 857	43 551
Manufacturing	37 394	38 300	39 539	41 418	42 235	44 106	45 499
Durable goods manufacturing	39 792	40 344	41 581	43 446	44 370	47 056	47 416
Nondurable goods manufacturing	35 415	36 641	37 892	39 749	40 398	41 517	43 795
Wholesale trade	52 838	52 772	53 795	56 345	58 651	61 544	63 660
Retail trade	22 518	22 877	23 587	24 137	24 602	25 254	25 565
Transportation and warehousing	42 938	43 753	44 575	46 104	43 664	43 266	48 586
Information	57 265	56 987	59 668	61 373	65 349	68 603	73 742
Finance and insurance	54 820	56 305	58 339	61 407	63 073	66 293	69 537
Real estate and rental and leasing	35 008	36 404	37 311	40 161	42 366	46 146	47 417
Professional and technical services	55 967	56 312	56 875	58 785	61 511	64 128	67 158
Management of companies and enterprises	58 141	60 217	65 499	72 531	89 625	82 085	88 421
Administrative and waste services	24 553	25 227	26 758	27 592	28 581	29 581	30 922
Educational services	26 829	27 427	28 388	30 184	31 284	34 761	36 037
Health care and social assistance	33 588	34 790	35 586	36 974	38 150	39 009	40 398
Arts, entertainment, and recreation	27 602	30 417	29 255	28 377	29 575	29 654	30 596
Accommodation and food services	14 262	14 321	14 644	15 164	15 695	16 367	16 711
Other services, except public administration	22 255	22 688	23 626	24 341	25 208	26 106	26 948
Government and government enterprises	31 819	33 629	35 026	35 745	37 193	38 422	39 735

Table GA-9. Employment Characteristics by Family Type

(Number, percent.)

Family type and labor force status	2005		2006		2007	
	Total	Families with own children under 18 years	Total	Families with own children under 18 years	Total	Families with own children under 18 years
TOTAL FAMILIES	2 285 356	1 139 649	2 296 694	1 118 172	2 328 569	1 139 646
FAMILY TYPE AND LABOR FORCE STATUS						
Married Coupled Families	1 643 907	764 519	1 639 379	739 242	1 670 425	767 813
Both husband and wife in labor force	53.5	62.1	54.0	63.4	54.7	65.2
Husband in labor force, wife not in labor force	25.2	30.7	25.3	31.4	24.4	29.6
Wife in labor force, husband not in labor force	7.2	4.2	6.6	3.1	6.5	3.0
Both husband and wife not in labor force	14.2	3.0	14.1	2.1	14.4	2.2
Other Families	641 449	375 130	657 315	378 930	658 144	371 833
Female householder, no husband present	75.6	79.8	74.9	80.0	76.8	81.4
In labor force	53.9	64.8	54.5	66.5	55.3	66.6
Not in labor force	21.7	14.9	20.4	13.4	21.5	14.8
Male householder, no wife present	24.4	20.2	25.1	20.0	23.2	18.6
In labor force	19.2	17.9	20.5	17.9	18.8	16.3
Not in labor force	5.2	2.3	4.6	2.2	4.4	2.2

Table GA-10. School Enrollment and Educational Attainment, 2007

(Number, percent.)

Item	State	U.S.
Enrollment		
Total population 3 years and over	9 110 544	289 295 761
Enrolled in school	2 611 111	79 329 527
Enrolled in preschool (percent)	7.2	6.2
Enrolled in grades K-12 (percent)	69.0	67.6
Enrolled in college or graduate school (percent)	23.9	26.2
Attainment		
Total population 25 years and over	6 074 860	197 892 369
Less than a high school diploma (percent)	17.1	15.5
High school diploma or more (percent)	82.9	84.5
Bachelor's degree or more (percent)	27.1	27.5
Graduate degree or more (percent)	9.5	10.1

Table GA-11. Educational Indicators

(Number, percent.)

Item	State	U.S.
Public Schools, 2006–2007 (except where noted)		
Number of school districts	204	17 742
Number of schools	2 506	99 639
Number of students	1 629 157	49 315 842
Student-teacher ratio	14.3	15.5
Expenditures per student (dollars)	$9 102	. . .
Averaged freshman graduation rate, 2005–2006	62.4	. . .
Dropout rate, grades 9–12, 2005–2006	5.2	3.7
Students eligible for free or reduced-price lunch (percent)	50.3	41.2
English-language learners (percent)	5.5	5.1
Students with IEP (percent)	12.1	12.7
Private Schools, 2007–2008 (except where noted)		
Number of schools	910	33 740
Number of students	136 987	5 072 451
High school graduates, 2006–2007	7 574	306 605
Student-teacher ratio	9.8	11.1

Table GA-12. Reported Voting and Registration of the Voting-Age Population, November 2008

(Number in thousands, percent.)

Item	Total population	Total citizen population	Registered			Voted		
			Total registered	Percent registered (total population)	Percent registered (total citizen population)	Total voted	Percent voted (total population)	Percent voted (total citizen population)
U.S. total	225 499	206 072	146 311	64.9	71.0	131 144	58.2	63.6
State total	7 018	6 515	4 624	65.9	71.0	4 183	59.6	64.2
Sex								
Male	3 323	3 038	2 105	63.3	69.3	1 883	56.7	62.0
Female	3 695	3 477	2 519	68.2	72.4	2 300	62.3	66.1
Race								
White alone	4 729	4 387	3 111	65.8	70.9	2 789	59.0	63.6
White non-Hispanic alone	4 235	4 183	2 983	70.5	71.3	2 683	63.4	64.1
Black alone	2 014	1 928	1 414	70.2	73.4	1 309	65.0	67.9
Asian alone	229	155	60	26.0	38.5	53	23.0	34.1
Hispanic (of any race)	541	234	150	27.7	63.9	128	23.6	54.5
White alone or in combination	4 754	4 413	3 134	65.9	71.0	2 809	59.1	63.6
Black alone or in combination	2 046	1 959	1 442	70.5	73.6	1 334	65.2	68.1
Asian alone or in combination	229	155	60	26.0	38.5	53	23.0	34.1

Table GA-13. Crime

(Number, rate per 100,000.)

Item	State			U.S.		
	2007	2008	Percent change	2007	2008	Percent change
Population	9 544 750	9 685 744	1.5	301 621 157	304 059 724	0.8
VIOLENT CRIME						
Number	47 075	46 384	-1.5	1 408 337	1 382 012	-1.9
Rate	493.2	478.9	-2.9	466.9	454.5	-2.7
Murder and Nonnegligent Manslaughter						
Number	718	636	-11.4	16 929	16 272	-3.9
Rate	7.5	6.6	-12.7	5.6	5.4	-4.7
Forcible Rape						
Number	2 178	2 195	0.8	90 427	89 000	-1.6
Rate	22.8	22.7	-0.7	30.0	29.3	-2.4
Robbery						
Number	17 340	17 357	0.1	445 125	441 855	-0.7
Rate	181.7	179.2	-1.4	147.6	145.3	-1.5
Aggravated Assault						
Number	26 839	26 196	-2.4	855 856	834 885	-2.5
Rate	281.2	270.5	-3.8	283.8	274.6	-3.2
PROPERTY CRIME						
Number	372 342	388 935	4.5	9 843 481	9 767 915	-0.8
Rate	3 901.0	4 015.5	2.9	3 263.5	3 212.5	-1.6
Burglary						
Number	90 690	100 629	11.0	2 179 140	2 222 196	2.0
Rate	950.2	1 038.9	9.3	722.5	730.8	1.2
Larceny-Theft						
Number	239 058	248 678	4.0	6 568 572	6 588 873	0.3
Rate	2 504.6	2 567.5	2.5	2 177.8	2 167.0	-0.5
Motor Vehicle Theft						
Number	42 594	39 628	-7.0	1 095 769	956 846	-12.7
Rate	446.3	409.1	-8.3	363.3	314.7	-13.4

Table GA-14. State Government Finances, 2007

(Dollars, percent distribution.)

Item	Thousands of dollars	Percent distribution
Total Revenue	45 067 031	X
General revenue	36 313 631	80.6
Intergovernmental revenue	13 005 370	28.9
Taxes	18 170 913	40.3
General sales	5 915 521	13.1
Selective sales	1 828 741	4.1
License taxes	497 388	1.1
Individual income tax	8 799 415	19.5
Corporate income tax	1 017 187	2.3
Other taxes	112 661	0.2
Current charges	2 990 763	6.6
Miscellaneous general revenue	2 146 585	4.8
Utility revenue	231	0.0
Liquor store revenue	0	0.0
Insurance trust revenue	8 753 169	19.4
Total Expenditure	41 843 352	100.0
Intergovernmental expenditure	10 515 856	25.1
Direct expenditure	31 327 496	74.9
Current operation	20 390 323	48.7
Capital outlay	5 501 850	13.1
Insurance benefits and repayments	4 052 613	9.7
Assistance and subsidies	830 496	2.0
Interest on debt	552 214	1.3
Exhibit: Salaries and wages	4 292 075	10.3
Total Expenditure	41 843 352	100.0
General expenditure	37 748 738	90.2
Intergovernmental expenditure	10 515 856	25.1
Direct expenditure	27 232 882	65.1
Education	15 580 870	37.2
Public welfare	9 685 127	23.1
Hospitals	730 547	1.7
Health	1 150 842	2.8
Highways	5 009 405	12.0
Police protection	267 801	0.6
Correction	1 465 496	3.5
Natural resources	463 217	1.1
Parks and recreation	187 393	0.4
Government administration	715 887	1.7
Interest on general debt	552 214	1.3
Other and unallocable	1 939 939	4.6
Utility expenditure	42 001	0.1
Liquor store expenditure	0	0.0
Insurance trust expenditure	4 052 613	9.7
Debt at End of Fiscal Year	11 370 040	X
Cash and Security Holdings	77 655 026	X

Table GA-15. State Government Tax Collections, 2008

(Dollars, percent distribution.)

Item	Thousands of dollars	Percent distribution
Total Taxes	18 183 117	X
Property taxes	81 928	0.5
Sales and gross receipts	7 688 845	42.3
General sales and gross receipts	5 796 653	31.9
Selective sales taxes	1 892 192	10.4
Alcoholic beverages	165 640	0.9
Insurance premiums	348 218	1.9
Motor fuels	1 011 202	5.6
Tobacco products	233 158	1.3
Other selective sales	133 974	0.7
Licenses	526 149	2.9
Alcoholic beverages	2 343	0.0
Amusements	136	0.0
Corporation	62 302	0.3
Hunting and fishing	20 907	0.1
Motor vehicle	296 648	1.6
Motor vehicle operators	64 896	0.4
Public utility	26	0.0
Occupation and business, NEC	70 090	0.4
Other licenses	8 801	0.0
Income taxes	9 788 518	53.8
Individual income	8 845 476	48.6
Corporation net income	943 042	5.2
Other taxes	97 677	0.5
Death and gift	50	0.0
Documentary and stock transfer	14 421	0.1
Other	83 206	0.5

Table GA-16. Agriculture

(Number, acres, and dollars.)

Item	2002		2007		Percent change, 2002–2007
	Number	Percent of total	Number	Percent of total	
Number of farms	49 311		47 846		-3.0
Farm Size					
Average size of farm (acres)	218		212		-2.8
Farms by size (number of farms)					
Fewer than 50 acres	19 328	39.2	19 747	41.3	2.2
50 to 499 acres	25 122	50.9	23 676	49.5	-5.8
500 acres or more	4 861	9.9	4 423	9.2	-9.0
Land (Acres)					
Total land in farms	10 744 239		10 150 539		-5.5
Total cropland	4 676 567	43.5	4 478 168	44.1	-4.2
Total harvested cropland	3 245 784	30.2	3 390 437	33.4	4.5
Irrigated land	870 810	8.1	1 017 773	10.0	16.9
Value of Sales (Dollars)					
Agricultural products sold ($1,000)	4 911 752		7 112 866		44.8
Average sales per farm	99 608		148 662		49.2
Sales of crops	1 579 596	32.2	2 142 270	30.1	35.6
Sales of livestock, poultry, and their products	3 332 156	67.8	4 970 596	69.9	49.2
Value of Sales (Number of Farms)					
Less than $10,000	34 163	69.3	32 368	67.7	-5.3
$10,000 to $99,999	8 876	18.0	8 705	18.2	-1.9
$100,000 to $999,999	5 151	10.4	4 685	9.8	-9.0
$1,000,000 or more	1 121	2.3	2 088	4.4	86.3
Farms by Type of Organization (Number of Farms)					
Family	45 050	91.4	41 703	87.2	-7.4
Partnership	2 490	5.0	3 850	8.0	54.6
Corporation	1 484	3.0	1 909	4.0	28.6
Other: cooperative, estate or trust, institutional, etc	287	0.6	384	0.8	33.8
Value of Land and Buildings (Dollars)					
Estimated market value of land and buildings ($1,000)	31 635 808		22 552 975		-28.7
Land and buildings average value per farm	661 201		457 427		-30.8
Average value per acre	3 117		2 112		-32.2
Government Payments					
Number of farms receiving government payments	15 510	31.5	14 546	30.4	-6.2
Payments (thousands of dollars)	118 535		224 523		89.4
Average payment per farm	7 642		15 435		102.0
Farm Operator Characteristics					
Farm operators whose principal occupation is farming	25 076	50.9	20 106	42.0	-19.8
Farm operators whose principal occupation is other	24 235	49.1	27 740	58.0	14.5
Average age principal operator (years)	56.5		57.8		2.3

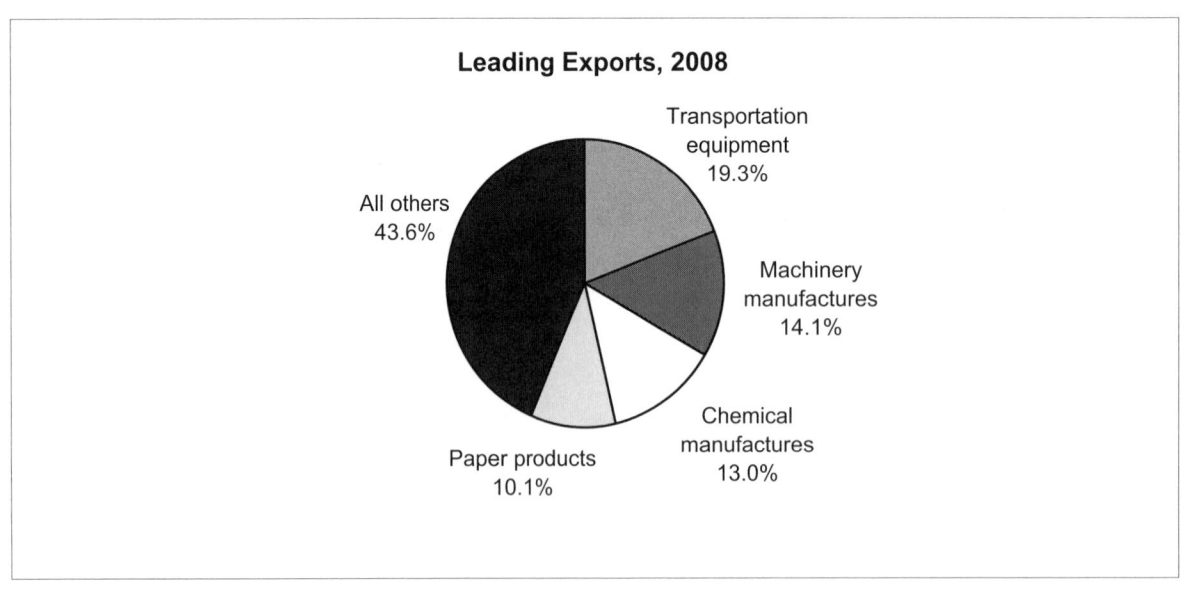

Leading Exports, 2008

Transportation equipment 19.3%

Machinery manufactures 14.1%

Chemical manufactures 13.0%

Paper products 10.1%

All others 43.6%

HAWAII

Facts and Figures

Location: North Pacific Ocean

Area: 10,931 sq. mi. (28,311 sq. km.); rank—43rd

Population: 1,288,198 (2008 est.); rank—42nd

Principal Cities: capital—Honolulu; largest—Honolulu

Statehood: August 21, 1959; 50th state

U.S. Congress: 2 senators, 2 representatives

State Motto: *Ua mau ke ea o ka'ina i ka pono* ("The life of the land is perpetuated in righteousness")

State Song: "Hawai'i Pono' (Hawaii's Own)"

State Nickname: The Aloha State

Abbreviations: HI

State Symbols: flower—native yellow hibiscus; tree—kukui (candlenut tree); bird—nene (Hawaiian goose)

At a Glance

- With an increase in population of 18.3 percent, Hawaii ranked 25th among the states in growth from 2000 to 2008.
- An estimated 25,068 marriages took place in Hawaii in 2008; Hawaii does not report divorces.
- The 2007 home ownership rate in Hawaii was 60.1 percent, giving it a ranking of 48th among the states.
- Hawaii's median household income in 2007 was $63,746, 5th among the states.
- In Hawaii, 8 percent of the population lived below the poverty level in 2007, ranking it 48th.
- In 2006-07, 8.2 percent of Hawaiians did not have health insurance, compared to 15.5 percent of the total U.S. population.
- In 2007, 2.9 percent of Hawaiians were unemployed, compared to 4.6 percent nationwide.
- Hawaii ranked 15th in the nation with 29.2 percent of its population 25 years old and over having a bachelor's degree in 2007.
- Hawaii's violent crime rate in 2007 was 272.8 per 100,000 population, compared to 466.9 for the entire nation.
- Hawaii had one physician for every 275 people in 2007, compared to one physician for every 325 people nationwide.
- In the 2008 election, 50.5 percent of Hawaii's eligible voters voted, compared to 61.7 percent of eligible voters nationwide.
- Hawaii ranked 16th among the states receiving federal aid in 2007, with $1,543 per capita.
- Hawaii's gross domestic product was $62 billion in 2007; it ranked 38th among the states.
- With $560 million in exports in 2007, Hawaii ranked 50th in exports.
- Hawaiians consumed 332.2 billion Btu's of energy in 2006; the state ranked 45th in total consumption.
- In 2007, Hawaii exported $88 million worth of agricultural products, less than 1 percent of the U.S. total.

Table HI-1. Population by Sex, Age, Race, and Hispanic Origin

(Number, percent.)

Sex, age, race, and Hispanic origin	1990	2000	2008	Average annual percent change, 2000–2008
Total Population	1 108 229	1 211 537	1 288 198	0.8
Percent of total U.S. population	0.4	0.4	0.4	X
Sex				
Male	563 891	608 671	649 519	0.8
Female	544 338	602 866	638 679	0.7
Age				
Under 5 years	83 223	78 163	87 207	1.4
5 to 19 years	227 294	249 088	231 083	-0.9
20 to 64 years	672 707	723 685	779 841	0.9
65 years and over	125 005	160 601	190 067	2.1
Median age (years)	32.5	36.2	38.0	X
Race and Hispanic Origin[1]				
One race				
White	369 616	294 102	382 174	3.3
Black	27 195	22 003	39 620	7.6
American Indian and Alaskan Native	5 099	3 535	7 569	10.0
Asian[2]	685 236	503 868	506 159	0.1
Native Hawaiian and Other Pacific Islander	X	113 539	117 004	0.4
Two or more races	X	259 343	235 672	-1.2
Hispanic (of any race)	81 390	87 699	112 320	3.1

[1]Data on race in 2000 and 2008 are not comparable to 1990. Individuals could only report one race in the 1990 census but could report one or more races on the 2000 census.
[2]Data in 1990 refer to Asian and Pacific Islanders.

Table HI-2. Marital Status

(Number, percent distribution.)

Sex and marital status	1990	2000	2007
Males, 15 Years and Over	441 420	481 768	522 244
Never married	34.5	34.6	35.0
Now married, except separated	54.8	53.7	52.6
Separated	1.5	1.4	1.5
Widowed	2.1	2.2	2.5
Divorced	7.2	8.1	8.4
Females, 15 Years and Over	428 783	484 107	524 756
Never married	24.9	25.9	27.5
Now married, except separated	55.3	52.5	50.0
Separated	1.8	1.7	1.7
Widowed	9.0	9.8	10.6
Divorced	9.0	10.0	10.2

Table HI-3. Households and Housing Characteristics

(Number, percent, and dollars.)

Item	1990	2000	2007	Average annual percent change, 2000–2007
Total Households	356 267	403 240	439 685	1.2
Family households	263 456	287 068	306 623	0.9
Married-couple family	210 468	216 077	227 109	0.7
Other family	52 988	70 991	79 514	1.6
Male householder, no wife present	15 579	21 068	22 665	1.0
Female householder, no husband present	37 409	49 923	56 849	1.9
Nonfamily households	92 811	116 172	133 062	2.0
Householder living alone	68 985	88 153	104 263	2.4
Householder not living alone	23 826	28 019	28 799	0.4
Housing Characteristics				
Total housing units	389 810	460 542	506 751	1.4
Occupied housing units	356 267	403 240	439 685	1.2
Owner-occupied	191 911	227 888	261 918	2.0
Renter-occupied	164 356	175 352	177 767	0.2
Average size	3.01	2.92	2.84	X
Financial Characteristics				
Median gross rent of renter-occupied housing units (dollars)	650	779	1 194	6.3
Median monthly owner costs for housing units with a mortgage (dollars)	1 008	1 636	2 099	3.6
Median value of owner-occupied housing units (dollars)	242 600	272 700	555 400	10.7

Table HI-4. Median Income and Poverty Status, 2007

(Number, percent.)

Characteristic	State		U.S.	
	Number	Percent	Number	Percent
Median Income				
Households (dollars)	63 746	X	50 740	X
Families (dollars)	73 879	X	61 173	X
Below Poverty Level				
Sex				
Male	46 544	7.4	16 576 071	11.5
Female	53 507	8.5	21 476 176	14.3
Age				
Under 18 years	27 608	9.8	13 097 100	18.0
Related children under 18 years	26 602	9.4	12 728 964	17.6
18 to 64 years	61 088	7.7	21 495 507	11.6
65 years and over	11 355	6.3	3 459 640	9.5

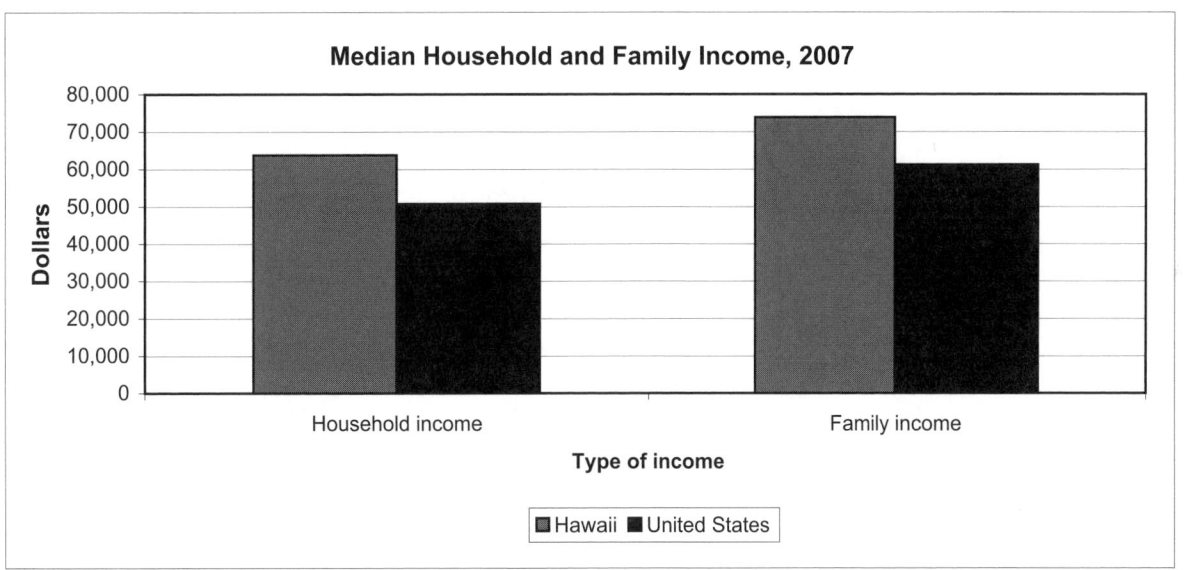

Median Household and Family Income, 2007

Table HI-5. Health Insurance Coverage Status for All Persons and Children Under 18 Years of Age

(Number, percent.)

Item	2000	2001	2002	2003	2004	2005	2006	2007
ALL PERSONS	1 203	1 213	1 224	1 253	1 249	1 279	1 255	1 267
Covered by Private or Government Health Insurance								
Number	1 093	1 102	1 104	1 134	1 145	1 169	1 144	1 172
Percent	90.9	90.8	90.2	90.5	91.7	91.4	91.2	92.5
Not Covered								
Number	110	111	120	119	104	110	110	96
Percent	9.1	9.2	9.8	9.5	8.3	8.6	8.8	7.5
Percent in the U.S. not covered	13.7	14.1	14.7	15.1	14.9	15.3	15.8	15.3
CHILDREN UNDER 18 YEARS OF AGE	299	311	327	313	286	306	298	291
Covered by Private or Government Health Insurance								
Number	278	285	304	292	275	290	279	277
Percent	93.0	91.8	92.9	93.1	96.1	94.7	93.7	95.2
Not Covered								
Number	21	26	23	22	11	16	19	14
Percent	7.0	8.2	7.1	6.9	3.9	5.3	6.3	4.8
Percent in the U.S. not covered	11.6	11.3	11.2	11.0	10.5	10.9	11.7	11.0

Table HI-6. Employment Status by Demographic Group, Preliminary 2008

(Number, percent.)

Characteristic	Civilian noninstitutional population	Civilian labor force		Employment		Unemployed	
		Number	Percent of population	Number	Percent of population	Number	Unemployment rate
TOTAL	1 000	660	66.0	633	63.3	28	4.2
Sex							
Men	487	353	73.0	337	69.1	17	4.7
Women	513	307	60.0	296	57.7	11	3.6
Race, Sex, and Hispanic Origin							
White	223	147	65.7	140	62.6	7	4.8
Men	110	80	73.1	77	70.0	3	4.2
Women	113	66	58.6	63	55.3	4	5.6
Black or African American	...	...	...	...	...	...	...
Men	...	...	...	...	...	...	...
Women	...	...	...	...	...	...	...
Hispanic	61	44	71.5	41	67.0	3	6.3
Men	31	23	74.5	21	69.4	2	6.8
Women	30	21	68.5	19	64.4	1	5.9
Age							
16 to 19 years	70	29	40.7	24	33.6	5	17.4
20 to 24 years	85	63	73.7	57	66.8	6	9.3
25 to 34 years	166	140	84.4	133	80.2	7	4.9
35 to 44 years	158	137	87.2	134	85.1	3	2.4
45 to 54 years	189	159	84.3	155	82.0	5	2.8
55 to 64 years	154	101	65.7	99	64.5	2	1.8
65 years and over	178	31	17.3	30	17.1	...	1.4

Note: Data in Table 6 are from the Current Population Survey (CPS) and do not match the estimates in Table 7. See notes and definitions for more details.

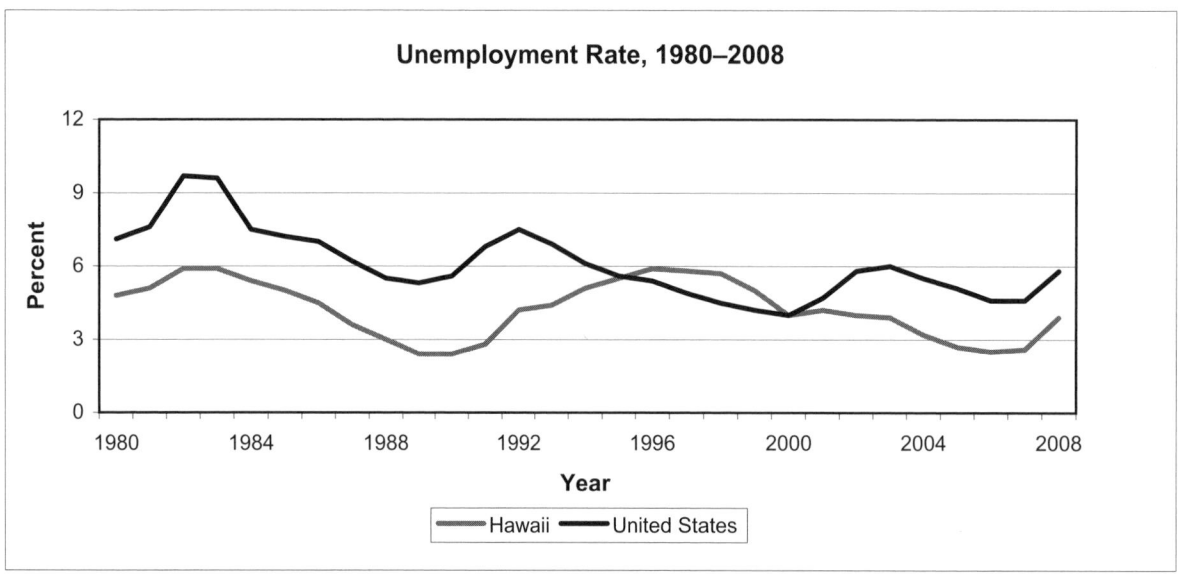

Unemployment Rate, 1980–2008

(Legend: Hawaii — United States)

Table HI-7. Employment Status of the Civilian Noninstitutional Population Age 16 Years and Over

(Number, percent.)

Year	Civilian labor force	Civilian participation rate	Employed	Unemployed	Unemployment rate
1998	604 302	67.5	570 152	34 150	5.7
1999	606 660	67.4	576 314	30 346	5.0
2000	609 018	67.6	584 858	24 160	4.0
2001	615 255	67.7	589 216	26 039	4.2
2002	608 937	66.3	584 354	24 583	4.0
2003	616 324	66.3	592 469	23 855	3.9
2004	618 149	65.2	598 175	19 974	3.2
2005	630 624	65.7	613 372	17 252	2.7
2006	642 891	66.2	627 058	15 833	2.5
2007	645 947	65.8	628 902	17 045	2.6
2008	654 261	66.0	628 429	25 832	3.9

Table HI-8. Employment and Average Wages by Industry

(Estimates for 2001–2006 are based on the 2002 North American Industry Classification System [NAICS]. Estimates for 2007 are based on the 2007 NAICS.)

Industry	2001	2002	2003	2004	2005	2006	2007
	Number of jobs						
WAGE AND SALARY EMPLOYMENT BY INDUSTRY	635 362	635 964	648 466	663 969	681 125	697 359	704 880
Farm Wage and Salary Employment	6 980	7 020	7 055	6 838	6 641	6 646	6 211
Nonfarm Wage and Salary Employment	628 382	628 944	641 411	657 131	674 484	690 713	698 669
Private wage and salary employment	459 829	459 101	469 735	483 667	501 975	515 826	522 425
Forestry, fishing, hunting, and other	2 131	2 103	2 081	1 872	1 641	1 552	1 169
Mining	249	225	266	282	292	289	307
Utilities	2 680	2 711	2 697	2 736	2 883	2 945	3 029
Construction	25 466	26 677	28 820	30 371	35 824	38 474	40 110
Manufacturing	16 622	15 403	15 107	15 666	15 772	15 697	15 449
Durable goods manufacturing	D	D	D	4 401	4 553	4 560	4 673
Nondurable goods manufacturing	D	D	D	11 265	11 219	11 137	10 776
Wholesale trade	16 687	16 571	17 035	17 315	17 953	18 269	18 682
Retail trade	68 488	66 302	66 538	69 187	71 851	72 594	72 498
Transportation and warehousing	25 913	23 991	24 514	25 876	28 778	30 630	30 571
Information	11 927	11 757	10 622	10 916	10 890	10 785	10 737
Finance and insurance	16 410	16 385	16 658	16 976	17 115	17 604	17 459
Real estate and rental and leasing	12 844	12 306	12 783	12 846	13 327	13 567	13 587
Professional and technical services	22 496	23 257	23 854	24 277	24 748	25 588	25 894
Management of companies and enterprises	5 964	6 519	6 730	6 858	7 348	7 523	7 624
Administrative and waste services	36 745	38 980	40 677	41 198	39 915	42 902	44 222
Educational services	12 844	13 259	14 077	13 880	14 400	14 303	14 637
Health care and social assistance	53 104	54 323	55 894	57 645	59 741	60 945	62 389
Arts, entertainment, and recreation	11 776	11 675	11 760	12 075	12 455	12 333	12 710
Accommodation and food services	88 997	87 484	89 576	93 391	96 356	97 887	99 052
Other services, except public administration	28 486	29 173	30 046	30 300	30 686	31 939	32 299
Government and government enterprises	168 553	169 843	171 676	173 464	172 509	174 887	176 244
	Dollars						
AVERAGE WAGES AND SALARIES BY INDUSTRY	31 304	32 898	34 107	35 832	37 221	38 789	40 519
Average Farm Wages and Salaries	24 330	24 480	23 413	27 454	27 380	26 962	30 231
Average Nonfarm Wages and Salaries	31 382	32 992	34 224	35 919	37 318	38 903	40 610
Average private wages and salaries	30 072	31 181	32 253	33 968	34 954	36 369	37 883
Forestry, fishing, hunting, and other	23 785	25 169	24 310	22 835	24 725	25 193	24 537
Mining	57 968	63 747	67 395	79 404	86 795	86 522	82 414
Utilities	65 795	66 306	70 742	73 464	72 268	75 117	75 769
Construction	47 082	49 098	49 531	50 936	53 863	55 863	59 345
Manufacturing	29 974	30 607	31 345	32 460	33 603	35 500	37 610
Durable goods manufacturing	D	D	D	38 757	40 623	43 316	45 539
Nondurable goods manufacturing	D	D	D	30 000	30 753	32 300	34 172
Wholesale trade	37 997	38 889	40 405	42 345	43 234	44 945	47 283
Retail trade	21 981	22 759	24 003	24 576	25 042	25 984	26 795
Transportation and warehousing	36 286	36 846	36 455	36 499	36 234	35 989	38 444
Information	43 225	43 088	45 362	48 391	47 817	52 983	53 460
Finance and insurance	46 723	50 767	51 067	54 326	55 300	56 398	56 687
Real estate and rental and leasing	30 650	32 351	34 595	37 186	39 132	40 397	41 674
Professional and technical services	45 512	47 418	49 475	51 158	55 203	57 466	60 268
Management of companies and enterprises	55 320	60 235	60 719	84 137	71 651	69 881	71 869
Administrative and waste services	21 945	22 995	24 102	25 584	25 737	26 642	28 142
Educational services	25 229	25 290	26 192	28 074	28 506	30 352	31 503
Health care and social assistance	34 346	34 831	35 934	37 340	38 326	39 666	40 782
Arts, entertainment, and recreation	20 626	21 228	22 253	23 325	24 220	25 403	26 185
Accommodation and food services	21 534	22 274	23 322	24 949	25 617	27 108	28 142
Other services, except public administration	23 394	23 902	24 599	25 564	26 564	27 827	28 983
Government and government enterprises	34 953	37 886	39 618	41 358	44 196	46 376	48 696

Table HI-9. Employment Characteristics by Family Type

(Number, percent.)

Family type and labor force status	2005		2006		2007	
	Total	Families with own children under 18 years	Total	Families with own children under 18 years	Total	Families with own children under 18 years
TOTAL FAMILIES	305 789	126 305	301 102	121 383	306 623	127 177
FAMILY TYPE AND LABOR FORCE STATUS						
Married Coupled Families	229 666	94 000	222 725	89 133	227 109	94 062
Both husband and wife in labor force	50.3	64.6	53.9	68.5	53.9	66.4
Husband in labor force, wife not in labor force	20.1	25.7	19.9	24.5	19.7	26.5
Wife in labor force, husband not in labor force	9.0	5.2	7.6	4.2	8.3	4.4
Both husband and wife not in labor force	20.5	4.4	18.6	2.8	18.1	2.7
Other Families	76 123	32 305	78 377	32 250	79 514	33 115
Female householder, no husband present	70.7	75.1	69.0	72.7	71.5	76.6
In labor force	44.7	61.1	42.8	58.1	44.3	59.0
Not in labor force	26.0	14.0	26.3	14.6	27.2	17.6
Male householder, no wife present	29.3	24.9	31.0	27.3	28.5	23.4
In labor force	21.8	22.7	23.6	25.1	21.2	21.3
Not in labor force	7.4	2.2	7.4	2.2	7.3	2.1

Table HI-10. School Enrollment and Educational Attainment, 2007

(Number, percent.)

Item	State	U.S.
Enrollment		
Total population 3 years and over	1 229 117	289 295 761
Enrolled in school	308 926	79 329 527
Enrolled in preschool (percent)	5.9	6.2
Enrolled in grades K-12 (percent)	66.2	67.6
Enrolled in college or graduate school (percent)	27.9	26.2
Attainment		
Total population 25 years and over	873 724	197 892 369
Less than a high school diploma (percent)	10.6	15.5
High school diploma or more (percent)	89.4	84.5
Bachelor's degree or more (percent)	29.2	27.5
Graduate degree or more (percent)	9.9	10.1

Table HI-11. Educational Indicators

(Number, percent.)

Item	State	U.S.
Public Schools, 2006–2007 (except where noted)		
Number of school districts	1	17 742
Number of schools	287	99 639
Number of students	180 728	49 315 842
Student-teacher ratio	16.0	15.5
Expenditures per student (dollars)	$11 060	. . .
Averaged freshman graduation rate, 2005–2006	75.5	. . .
Dropout rate, grades 9–12, 2005–2006	4.7	3.7
Students eligible for free or reduced-price lunch (percent)	40.8	41.2
English-language learners (percent)	8.7	5.1
Students with IEP (percent)	11.7	12.7
Private Schools, 2007–2008 (except where noted)		
Number of schools	136	33 740
Number of students	33 441	5 072 451
High school graduates, 2006–2007	2 386	306 605
Student-teacher ratio	11.6	11.1

Table HI-12. Reported Voting and Registration of the Voting-Age Population, November 2008

(Number in thousands, percent.)

Item	Total population	Total citizen population	Registered			Voted		
			Total registered	Percent registered (total population)	Percent registered (total citizen population)	Total voted	Percent voted (total population)	Percent voted (total citizen population)
U.S. total	225 499	206 072	146 311	64.9	71.0	131 144	58.2	63.6
State total	977	883	522	53.5	59.1	457	46.8	51.8
Sex								
Male	478	433	250	52.3	57.7	223	46.6	51.4
Female	499	450	272	54.6	60.5	235	47.1	52.2
Race								
White alone	239	226	149	62.1	65.7	136	57.0	60.3
White non-Hispanic alone	215	206	141	65.6	68.6	130	60.6	63.4
Black alone	18	16	2	. . .	. . .	2	. . .	. . .
Asian alone	403	359	220	54.6	61.5	199	49.2	55.4
Hispanic (of any race)	49	45	17	. . .	. . .	15	. . .	. . .
White alone or in combination	379	365	222	58.5	60.8	198	52.2	54.2
Black alone or in combination	23	21	5	. . .	. . .	4	. . .	. . .
Asian alone or in combination	548	502	290	52.9	57.7	252	46.0	50.1

Table HI-13. Crime

(Number, rate per 100,000.)

Item	State			U.S.		
	2007	2008	Percent change	2007	2008	Percent change
Population	1 283 388	1 288 198	0.4	301 621 157	304 059 724	0.8
VIOLENT CRIME						
Number	3 501	3 512	0.3	1 408 337	1 382 012	-1.9
Rate	272.8	272.6	-0.1	466.9	454.5	-2.7
Murder and Nonnegligent Manslaughter						
Number	22	25	13.6	16 929	16 272	-3.9
Rate	1.7	1.9	13.2	5.6	5.4	-4.7
Forcible Rape						
Number	326	365	12.0	90 427	89 000	-1.6
Rate	25.4	28.3	11.5	30.0	29.3	-2.4
Robbery						
Number	1 105	1 086	-1.7	445 125	441 855	-0.7
Rate	86.1	84.3	-2.1	147.6	145.3	-1.5
Aggravated Assault						
Number	2 048	2 036	-0.6	855 856	834 885	-2.5
Rate	159.6	158.1	-1.0	283.8	274.6	-3.2
PROPERTY CRIME						
Number	54 228	46 004	-15.2	9 843 481	9 767 915	-0.8
Rate	4 225.4	3 571.2	-15.5	3 263.5	3 212.5	-1.6
Burglary						
Number	9 097	9 379	3.1	2 179 140	2 222 196	2.0
Rate	708.8	728.1	2.7	722.5	730.8	1.2
Larceny-Theft						
Number	38 416	31 492	-18.0	6 568 572	6 588 873	0.3
Rate	2 993.3	2 444.7	-18.3	2 177.8	2 167.0	-0.5
Motor Vehicle Theft						
Number	6 715	5 133	-23.6	1 095 769	956 846	-12.7
Rate	523.2	398.5	-23.8	363.3	314.7	-13.4

Table HI-14. State Government Finances, 2007

(Dollars, percent distribution.)

Item	Thousands of dollars	Percent distribution
Total Revenue	11 176 293	X
General revenue	9 073 319	81.2
Intergovernmental revenue	2 063 945	18.5
Taxes	5 093 842	45.6
General sales	2 557 644	22.9
Selective sales	670 321	6.0
License taxes	156 238	1.4
Individual income tax	1 560 306	14.0
Corporate income tax	100 847	0.9
Other taxes	48 486	0.4
Current charges	1 158 402	10.4
Miscellaneous general revenue	757 130	6.8
Utility revenue	0	0.0
Liquor store revenue	0	0.0
Insurance trust revenue	2 102 974	18.8
Total Expenditure	9 848 210	100.0
Intergovernmental expenditure	138 054	1.4
Direct expenditure	9 710 156	98.6
Current operation	7 634 781	77.5
Capital outlay	639 902	6.5
Insurance benefits and repayments	878 141	8.9
Assistance and subsidies	98 982	1.0
Interest on debt	458 350	4.7
Exhibit: Salaries and wages	2 372 147	24.1
Total Expenditure	9 848 210	100.0
General expenditure	8 969 744	91.1
Intergovernmental expenditure	138 054	1.4
Direct expenditure	8 831 690	89.7
Education	3 239 562	32.9
Public welfare	1 494 003	15.2
Hospitals	454 936	4.6
Health	611 503	6.2
Highways	306 179	3.1
Police protection	15 661	0.2
Correction	197 273	2.0
Natural resources	142 296	1.4
Parks and recreation	78 091	0.8
Government administration	427 641	4.3
Interest on general debt	458 350	4.7
Other and unallocable	1 544 249	15.7
Utility expenditure	325	0.0
Liquor store expenditure	0	0.0
Insurance trust expenditure	878 141	8.9
Debt at End of Fiscal Year	5 959 064	X
Cash and Security Holdings	19 551 589	X

Table HI-15. State Government Tax Collections, 2008

(Dollars, percent distribution.)

Item	Thousands of dollars	Percent distribution
Total Taxes	5 147 480	X
Sales and gross receipts	3 302 090	64.1
General sales and gross receipts	2 619 595	50.9
Selective sales taxes	682 495	13.3
Alcoholic beverages	45 620	0.9
Insurance premiums	99 158	1.9
Motor fuels	93 991	1.8
Public utilities	127 481	2.5
Tobacco products	89 265	1.7
Other selective sales	226 980	4.4
Licenses	156 781	3.0
Corporation	1 575	0.0
Hunting and fishing	424	0.0
Motor vehicle	111 262	2.2
Motor vehicle operators	404	0.0
Public utility	15 819	0.3
Occupation and business, NEC	25 790	0.5
Other licenses	1 507	0.0
Income taxes	1 650 129	32.1
Individual income	1 544 835	30.0
Corporation net income	105 294	2.0
Other taxes	38 480	0.7
Death and gift	164	0.0
Documentary and stock transfer	38 316	0.7

Table HI-16. Agriculture

(Number, acres, and dollars.)

Item	2002		2007		Percent change, 2002–2007
	Number	Percent of total	Number	Percent of total	
Number of farms	5 398		7 521		39.3
Farm Size					
Average size of farm (acres)	241		149		-38.2
Farms by size (number of farms)					
Fewer than 50 acres	4 749	88.0	6 785	90.2	42.9
50 to 499 acres	481	8.9	577	7.7	20.0
500 acres or more	168	3.1	159	2.1	-5.4
Land (Acres)					
Total land in farms	1 300 499		1 121 329		-13.8
Total cropland	211 120	16.2	177 626	15.8	-15.9
Total harvested cropland	109 461	8.4	103 120	9.2	-5.8
Irrigated land	69 194	5.3	58 635	5.2	-15.3
Value of Sales (Dollars)					
Agricultural products sold ($1,000)	533 423		513 626		-3.7
Average sales per farm	98 819		68 292		-30.9
Sales of crops	445 356	83.5	429 916	83.7	-3.5
Sales of livestock, poultry, and their products	88 067	16.5	83 711	16.3	-4.9
Value of Sales (Number of Farms)					
Less than $10,000	3 037	56.3	4 940	65.7	62.7
$10,000 to $99,999	1 876	34.8	2 053	27.3	9.4
$100,000 to $999,999	414	7.7	453	6.0	9.4
$1,000,000 or more	71	1.3	75	1.0	5.6
Farms by Type of Organization (Number of Farms)					
Family	4 629	85.8	6 363	84.6	37.5
Partnership	225	4.2	437	5.8	94.2
Corporation	472	8.7	617	8.2	30.7
Other: cooperative, estate or trust, institutional, etc	72	1.3	104	1.4	44.4
Value of Land and Buildings (Dollars)					
Estimated market value of land and buildings ($1,000)	8 620 668		4 583 552		-46.8
Land and buildings average value per farm	842 875		1 146 213		36.0
Average value per acre	3 507		7 688		119.2
Government Payments					
Number of farms receiving government payments	113	2.1	218	2.9	92.9
Payments (thousands of dollars)	886		2 378		168.4
Average payment per farm	7 841		10 908		39.1
Farm Operator Characteristics					
Farm operators whose principal occupation is farming	3 125	57.9	3 861	51.3	23.6
Farm operators whose principal occupation is other	2 273	42.1	3 660	48.7	61.0
Average age principal operator (years)	56.5		58.6		3.7

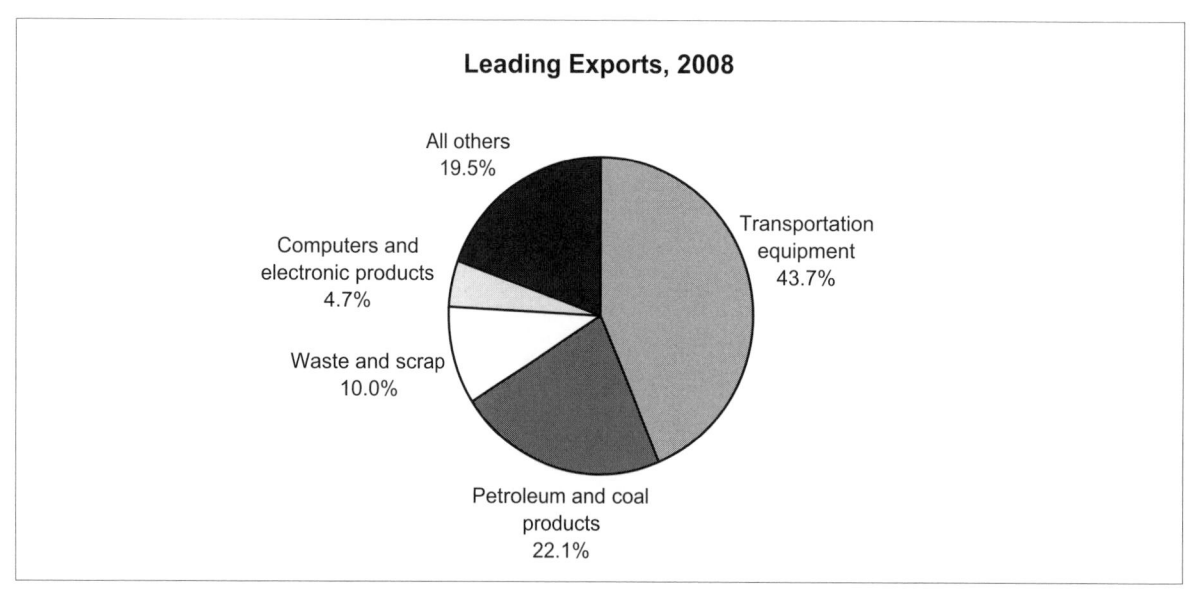

Leading Exports, 2008

All others 19.5%

Computers and electronic products 4.7%

Waste and scrap 10.0%

Petroleum and coal products 22.1%

Transportation equipment 43.7%

IDAHO

Facts and Figures

Location: Northwestern United States; bordered on the N by Canada, on the E by Montana and Wyoming, on the S by Nevada and Utah, and on the W by Washington and Oregon

Area: 83,570 sq. mi. (216,446 sq. km.); rank—14th

Population: 1,523,816 (2008 est.); rank—39th

Principal Cities: capital—Boise; largest—Boise

Statehood: July 3, 1890; 43rd state

U.S. Congress: 2 senators, 2 representatives

State Motto: *Esto perpetua* ("Let it be perpetual")

State Song: "Here We Have Idaho"

State Nickname: The Gem State

Abbreviations: ID; Ida.

State Symbols: flower—syringa (mock orange); tree—Western white pine; bird—mountain bluebird

At a Glance

- With an increase in population of 17.8 percent, Idaho ranked 5th among the states in growth from 2000 to 2008.
- An estimated 14,536 marriages took place in Idaho in 2008, compared to 7,182 divorces.
- The 2007 home ownership rate in Idaho was 74.5 percent, giving it a ranking of 5th among the states.
- Idaho's median household income in 2007 was $46,253, 34th among the states.
- In Idaho, 12.1 percent of the population lived below the poverty level in 2007, ranking it 24th along with Florida and North Dakota.
- In 2006-07, 14.6 percent of Idahoans did not have health insurance, compared to 15.5 percent of the total U.S. population.
- In 2007, 3 percent of Idahoans were unemployed, compared to 4.6 percent nationwide.
- Idaho ranked 35th in the nation with 24.5 percent of its population 25 years old and over having a bachelor's degree in 2007; its ranking was the same as Missouri's.
- Idaho's violent crime rate in 2007 was 239.4 per 100,000 population, compared to 466.9 for the entire nation.
- Idaho had one physician for every 501 people in 2007, compared to one physician for every 325 people nationwide.
- In the 2008 election, 63.3 percent of Idaho's eligible voters voted, compared to 61.7 percent of eligible voters nationwide.
- Idaho ranked 29th among the states receiving federal aid in 2007, with $1,358 per capita.
- Idaho's gross domestic product was $51 billion in 2007; it ranked 42nd among the states.
- With $4.7 billion in exports in 2007, Idaho ranked 35th in exports.
- Idahoans consumed 514 billion Btu's of energy in 2006; the state ranked 40th in total consumption.
- In 2007, Idaho exported $1.2 billion worth of agricultural products, about 1.4 percent of the U.S. total.

Table ID-1. Population by Sex, Age, Race, and Hispanic Origin

(Number, percent.)

Sex, age, race, and Hispanic origin	1990	2000	2008	Average annual percent change, 2000–2008
Total Population	1 006 749	1 293 953	1 523 816	2.1
Percent of total U.S. population	0.4	0.5	0.5	X
Sex				
Male	500 956	648 660	766 580	2.1
Female	505 793	645 293	757 236	2.0
Age				
Under 5 years	80 193	97 643	121 746	2.8
5 to 19 years	260 667	316 222	334 443	0.7
20 to 64 years	544 624	734 172	885 477	2.4
65 years and over	121 265	145 916	182 150	2.8
Median age (years)	31.5	33.2	34.4	X
Race and Hispanic Origin[1]				
One race				
White	950 451	1 177 304	1 441 540	2.6
Black	3 370	5 456	14 470	13.0
American Indian and Alaskan Native	13 780	17 645	23 209	3.5
Asian[2]	9 365	11 889	17 394	4.9
Native Hawaiian and Other Pacific Islander	X	1 308	2 044	5.7
Two or more races	X	25 609	25 159	-0.2
Hispanic (of any race)	52 927	101 690	155 827	5.5

[1]Data on race in 2000 and 2008 are not comparable to 1990. Individuals could only report one race in the 1990 census but could report one or more races on the 2000 census.
[2]Data in 1990 refer to Asian and Pacific Islanders.

Table ID-2. Marital Status

(Number, percent distribution.)

Sex and marital status	1990	2000	2007
Males, 15 Years and Over	367 363	493 045	577 712
Never married	24.9	26.1	26.8
Now married, except separated	63.5	61.0	59.5
Separated	1.2	1.0	1.2
Widowed	2.0	2.1	1.9
Divorced	8.5	9.9	10.7
Females, 15 Years and Over	378 964	498 579	582 213
Never married	17.7	19.6	21.0
Now married, except separated	60.9	59.0	57.2
Separated	1.4	1.3	1.2
Widowed	10.2	8.6	8.5
Divorced	9.7	11.4	12.1

Table ID-3. Households and Housing Characteristics

(Number, percent, and dollars.)

Item	1990	2000	2007	Average annual percent change, 2000–2007
Total Households	360 723	469 645	560 567	2.6
Family households	263 194	335 588	397 576	2.5
Married-couple family	224 198	276 511	323 424	2.3
Other family	38 996	59 077	74 152	3.3
Male householder, no wife present	10 113	18 228	24 717	4.4
Female householder, no husband present	28 883	40 849	49 435	2.8
Nonfamily households	97 529	134 057	162 991	2.8
Householder living alone	80 800	105 175	129 246	3.0
Householder not living alone	16 729	28 882	33 745	2.2
Housing Characteristics				
Total housing units	413 327	527 824	631 022	2.6
Occupied housing units	360 723	469 645	560 567	2.6
Owner-occupied	252 734	339 960	403 904	2.5
Renter-occupied	107 989	129 685	156 663	2.7
Average size	2.73	2.69	2.61	X
Financial Characteristics				
Median gross rent of renter-occupied housing units (dollars)	330	515	654	3.5
Median monthly owner costs for housing units with a mortgage (dollars)	561	887	1 162	3.9
Median value of owner-occupied housing units (dollars)	58 000	106 300	178 100	7.7

Table ID-4. Median Income and Poverty Status, 2007

(Number, percent.)

Characteristic	State		U.S.	
	Number	Percent	Number	Percent
Median Income				
Households (dollars)	46 253	X	50 740	X
Families (dollars)	54 342	X	61 173	X
Below Poverty Level				
Sex				
Male	76 300	10.4	16 576 071	11.5
Female	101 506	13.9	21 476 176	14.3
Age				
Under 18 years	63 591	15.9	13 097 100	18.0
Related children under 18 years	61 403	15.4	12 728 964	17.6
18 to 64 years	100 925	11.2	21 495 507	11.6
65 years and over	13 290	8.0	3 459 640	9.5

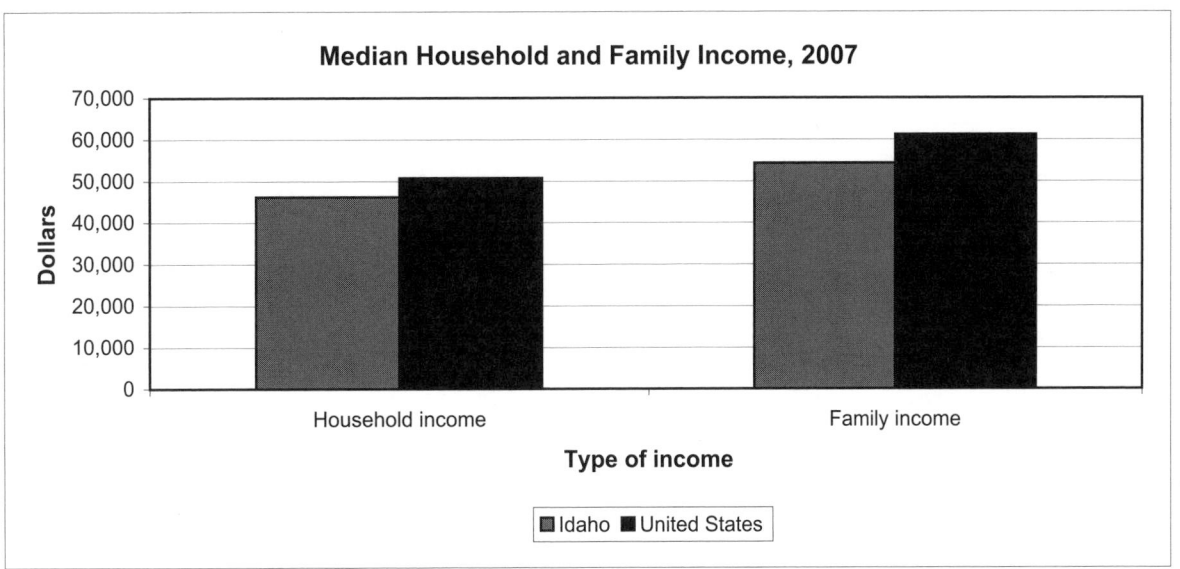

Table ID-5. Health Insurance Coverage Status for All Persons and Children Under 18 Years of Age

(Number, percent.)

Item	2000	2001	2002	2003	2004	2005	2006	2007
ALL PERSONS	1 290	1 315	1 300	1 360	1 375	1 442	1 475	1 501
Covered by Private or Government Health Insurance								
Number	1 096	1 110	1 075	1 113	1 175	1 229	1 248	1 292
Percent	85.0	84.4	82.7	81.9	85.5	85.2	84.6	86.1
Not Covered								
Number	194	205	225	247	200	213	227	209
Percent	15.0	15.6	17.3	18.1	14.5	14.8	15.4	13.9
Percent in the U.S. not covered	13.7	14.1	14.7	15.1	14.9	15.3	15.8	15.3
CHILDREN UNDER 18 YEARS OF AGE	379	380	368	374	384	394	402	415
Covered by Private or Government Health Insurance								
Number	323	335	320	325	352	349	350	369
Percent	85.3	88.2	86.7	86.8	91.5	88.6	87.0	89.0
Not Covered								
Number	56	45	49	49	33	45	52	46
Percent	14.7	11.8	13.3	13.2	8.5	11.4	13.0	11.0
Percent in the U.S. not covered	11.6	11.3	11.2	11.0	10.5	10.9	11.7	11.0

Table ID-6. Employment Status by Demographic Group, Preliminary 2008
(Number, percent.)

Characteristic	Civilian noninstitutional population	Civilian labor force		Employment		Unemployed	
		Number	Percent of population	Number	Percent of population	Number	Unemployment rate
TOTAL	1 138	756	66.5	715	62.9	41	5.4
Sex							
Men	564	414	73.0	390	69.1	25	5.9
Women	573	342	60.0	325	56.8	16	4.8
Race, Sex, and Hispanic Origin							
White	1 088	719	66.1	682	62.7	38	5.2
Men	538	394	73.2	371	69.1	22	5.7
Women	550	326	59.2	310	56.4	15	4.7
Black or African American	...	...	...	...	...	...	...
Men	...	...	...	...	...	...	...
Women	...	...	...	...	...	...	...
Hispanic	97	71	73.9	65	67.5	6	8.6
Men	52	42	80.6	38	72.3	4	10.4
Women	45	30	66.1	28	61.9	2	6.3
Age							
16 to 19 years	98	47	48.1	39	39.9	8	17.0
20 to 24 years	92	76	82.4	67	73.4	8	11.0
25 to 34 years	206	169	82.0	162	78.7	7	4.1
35 to 44 years	192	160	83.7	154	80.4	6	3.9
45 to 54 years	198	168	85.0	162	81.7	7	3.9
55 to 64 years	165	108	65.4	104	62.9	4	3.8
65 years and over	188	28	15.0	27	14.5	1	3.2

Note: Data in Table 6 are from the Current Population Survey (CPS) and do not match the estimates in Table 7. See notes and definitions for more details.

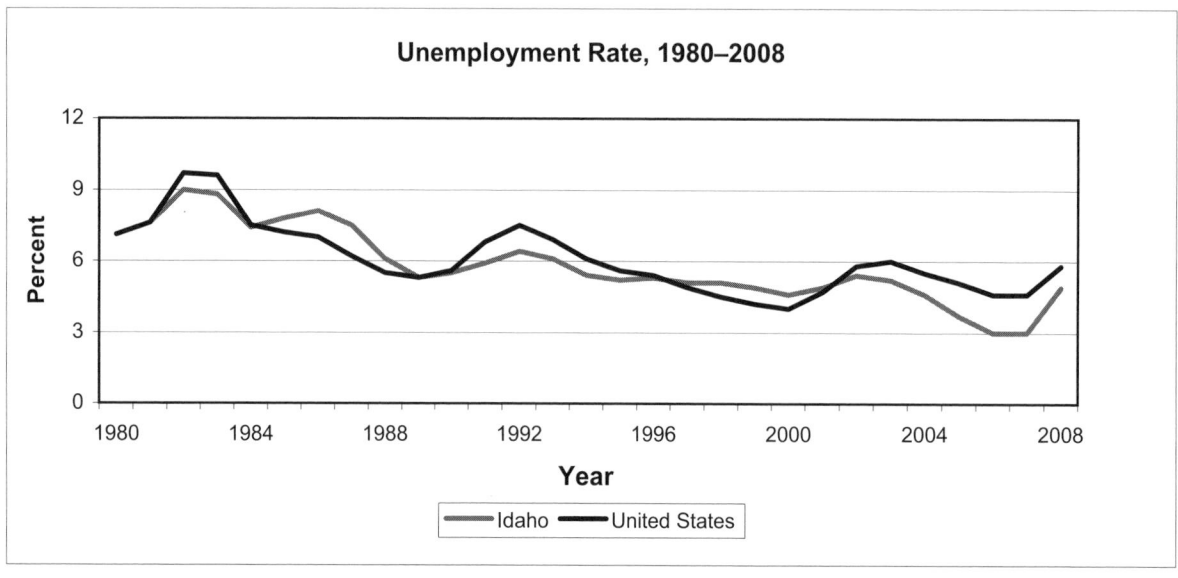

Table ID-7. Employment Status of the Civilian Noninstitutional Population Age 16 Years and Over
(Number, percent.)

Year	Civilian labor force	Civilian participation rate	Employed	Unemployed	Unemployment rate
1998	647 873	70.7	614 748	33 125	5.1
1999	652 884	69.9	620 962	31 922	4.9
2000	662 958	69.7	632 451	30 507	4.6
2001	677 855	69.9	644 816	33 039	4.9
2002	683 184	69.2	646 142	37 042	5.4
2003	688 291	68.4	652 161	36 130	5.2
2004	698 123	68.0	666 080	32 043	4.6
2005	720 673	68.4	693 851	26 822	3.7
2006	735 859	68.0	713 520	22 339	3.0
2007	748 709	67.5	726 091	22 618	3.0
2008	754 879	66.7	718 097	36 782	4.9

Table ID-8. Employment and Average Wages by Industry

(Estimates for 2001–2006 are based on the 2002 North American Industry Classification System [NAICS]. Estimates for 2007 are based on the 2007 NAICS.)

Industry	2001	2002	2003	2004	2005	2006	2007
			Number of jobs				
WAGE AND SALARY EMPLOYMENT BY INDUSTRY	620 855	622 469	627 298	642 788	665 866	693 843	709 165
Farm Wage and Salary Employment	15 914	16 220	15 291	15 286	14 584	14 591	13 785
Nonfarm Wage and Salary Employment	604 941	606 249	612 007	627 502	651 282	679 252	695 380
Private wage and salary employment	485 686	485 122	488 632	502 759	526 233	553 640	568 676
Forestry, fishing, hunting, and other	12 497	12 372	12 385	12 124	12 169	11 659	11 272
Mining	1 997	1 776	1 813	1 969	2 196	2 399	2 679
Utilities	1 795	1 932	1 880	1 880	1 955	2 025	2 075
Construction	39 363	37 950	38 216	41 421	46 826	53 942	54 181
Manufacturing	69 153	65 397	62 670	62 670	63 529	66 024	66 346
Durable goods manufacturing	43 387	40 660	38 510	39 309	40 981	43 166	42 815
Nondurable goods manufacturing	25 766	24 737	24 160	23 361	22 548	22 858	23 531
Wholesale trade	25 851	25 358	24 883	25 214	26 993	27 824	29 005
Retail trade	74 807	74 618	74 803	76 124	79 160	82 917	85 993
Transportation and warehousing	17 218	16 889	17 037	17 474	17 956	18 569	19 245
Information	9 666	9 237	9 210	9 745	10 354	10 630	10 926
Finance and insurance	17 275	18 092	18 856	19 258	20 335	21 946	22 338
Real estate and rental and leasing	6 822	6 774	7 190	7 713	8 317	8 978	9 135
Professional and technical services	30 761	30 427	30 946	30 994	32 731	34 795	35 927
Management of companies and enterprises	7 759	7 589	7 342	7 400	7 684	7 705	7 850
Administrative and waste services	31 168	33 050	33 605	36 853	39 455	41 085	41 094
Educational services	7 047	7 607	8 145	8 466	8 777	9 154	9 420
Health care and social assistance	53 836	56 608	58 689	61 104	63 412	65 976	69 372
Arts, entertainment, and recreation	7 428	7 722	8 079	8 136	8 231	8 983	9 682
Accommodation and food services	46 680	46 600	47 458	48 533	50 106	51 938	54 725
Other services, except public administration	24 563	25 124	25 425	25 681	26 047	27 091	27 411
Government and government enterprises	119 255	121 127	123 375	124 743	125 049	125 612	126 704
			Dollars				
AVERAGE WAGES AND SALARIES BY INDUSTRY	27 188	27 721	28 200	29 412	30 512	32 198	33 217
Average Farm Wages and Salaries	21 553	24 881	23 230	24 865	29 750	29 139	32 832
Average Nonfarm Wages and Salaries	27 336	27 797	28 325	29 523	30 529	32 263	33 225
Average private wages and salaries	27 281	27 577	28 088	29 256	30 330	32 220	33 196
Forestry, fishing, hunting, and other	19 106	20 186	20 857	22 392	23 451	25 055	25 939
Mining	38 731	40 102	43 331	44 086	45 749	50 707	55 755
Utilities	47 910	68 291	53 624	53 421	53 217	55 696	57 140
Construction	31 055	31 063	30 676	31 041	32 067	33 605	37 403
Manufacturing	37 580	38 168	39 476	41 324	42 585	45 198	46 238
Durable goods manufacturing	41 684	42 648	44 424	46 360	47 592	50 544	51 702
Nondurable goods manufacturing	30 670	30 805	31 589	32 850	33 485	35 102	36 296
Wholesale trade	34 408	34 527	35 445	37 348	39 236	41 900	44 208
Retail trade	20 224	20 571	21 377	22 293	23 959	25 227	24 851
Transportation and warehousing	29 778	30 168	30 458	32 040	33 341	34 531	34 996
Information	33 098	33 416	34 431	36 320	36 427	38 133	38 430
Finance and insurance	37 056	37 556	39 407	40 405	42 835	44 924	46 263
Real estate and rental and leasing	20 787	21 360	21 896	23 691	26 553	28 049	28 777
Professional and technical services	41 956	42 167	43 126	44 888	46 313	48 563	49 778
Management of companies and enterprises	63 690	60 778	61 080	68 324	66 799	85 416	81 357
Administrative and waste services	17 933	18 490	19 904	21 482	21 707	22 983	23 864
Educational services	19 699	20 927	21 672	22 023	22 520	22 379	23 573
Health care and social assistance	27 077	27 790	28 338	29 275	29 874	31 465	32 912
Arts, entertainment, and recreation	18 485	19 522	16 010	16 327	16 737	17 807	18 508
Accommodation and food services	10 697	10 983	11 325	11 851	12 252	13 100	13 448
Other services, except public administration	17 621	17 810	18 280	19 048	19 626	20 670	21 387
Government and government enterprises	27 561	28 678	29 263	30 600	31 367	32 453	33 353

Table ID-9. Employment Characteristics by Family Type

(Number, percent.)

Family type and labor force status	2005		2006		2007	
	Total	Families with own children under 18 years	Total	Families with own children under 18 years	Total	Families with own children under 18 years
TOTAL FAMILIES	372 230	184 204	382 686	183 989	397 576	193 523
FAMILY TYPE AND LABOR FORCE STATUS						
Married Coupled Families	299 467	137 219	313 995	139 789	323 424	145 816
Both husband and wife in labor force	53.0	61.0	52.4	60.6	52.8	62.1
Husband in labor force, wife not in labor force	23.5	31.6	24.8	33.7	25.4	33.9
Wife in labor force, husband not in labor force	6.8	4.5	6.3	4.3	6.3	2.5
Both husband and wife not in labor force	16.8	2.8	16.5	1.4	15.5	1.5
Other Families	72 763	46 985	68 691	44 200	74 152	47 707
Female householder, no husband present	70.9	71.7	68.6	70.9	66.7	68.9
In labor force	51.1	58.7	50.3	59.5	50.4	58.2
Not in labor force	19.8	13.0	18.3	11.4	16.3	10.7
Male householder, no wife present	29.1	28.3	31.4	29.1	33.3	31.1
In labor force	24.3	24.7	24.3	25.3	28.2	29.4
Not in labor force	4.8	3.5	7.1	3.8	5.2	1.7

Table ID-10. School Enrollment and Educational Attainment, 2007

(Number, percent.)

Item	State	U.S.
Enrollment		
Total population 3 years and over	1 428 493	289 295 761
Enrolled in school	393 854	79 329 527
Enrolled in preschool (percent)	5.5	6.2
Enrolled in grades K–12 (percent)	72.8	67.6
Enrolled in college or graduate school (percent)	21.7	26.2
Attainment		
Total population 25 years and over	946 131	197 892 369
Less than a high school diploma (percent)	11.6	15.5
High school diploma or more (percent)	88.4	84.5
Bachelor's degree or more (percent)	24.5	27.5
Graduate degree or more (percent)	7.6	10.1

Table ID-11. Educational Indicators

(Number, percent.)

Item	State	U.S.
Public Schools, 2006–2007 (except where noted)		
Number of school districts	129	17 742
Number of schools	732	99 639
Number of students	267 380	49 315 842
Student-teacher ratio	18.1	15.5
Expenditures per student (dollars)	$6 648	. . .
Averaged freshman graduation rate, 2005–2006	80.5	. . .
Dropout rate, grades 9–12, 2005–2006	2.7	3.7
Students eligible for free or reduced-price lunch (percent)	37.3	41.2
English-language learners (percent)	6.2	5.1
Students with IEP (percent)	10.6	12.7
Private Schools, 2007–2008 (except where noted)		
Number of schools	190	33 740
Number of students	20 878	5 072 451
High school graduates, 2006–2007	908	306 605
Student-teacher ratio	12.4	11.1

Table ID-12. Reported Voting and Registration of the Voting-Age Population, November 2008

(Number in thousands, percent.)

Item	Total population	Total citizen population	Registered			Voted		
			Total registered	Percent registered (total population)	Percent registered (total citizen population)	Total voted	Percent voted (total population)	Percent voted (total citizen population)
U.S. total	225 499	206 072	146 311	64.9	71.0	131 144	58.2	63.6
State total	1 095	1 049	723	66.0	68.9	644	58.8	61.4
Sex								
Male	538	516	352	65.3	68.1	313	58.2	60.7
Female	556	533	371	66.7	69.6	331	59.4	62.0
Race								
White alone	1 045	1 002	697	66.7	69.6	621	59.5	62.0
White non-Hispanic alone	925	918	662	71.6	72.1	592	64.0	64.5
Black alone	11	11	8	. . .	. . .	8	. . .	. . .
Asian alone	17	14	7	. . .	. . .	6	. . .	. . .
Hispanic (of any race)	122	86	37	29.9	42.4	30	24.9	35.3
White alone or in combination	1 050	1 007	700	66.7	69.5	624	59.4	61.9
Black alone or in combination	11	11	8	. . .	. . .	8	. . .	. . .
Asian alone or in combination	17	14	7	. . .	. . .	6	. . .	. . .

Table ID-13. Crime

(Number, rate per 100,000.)

Item	State			U.S.		
	2007	2008	Percent change	2007	2008	Percent change
Population	1 499 402	1 523 816	1.6	301 621 157	304 059 724	0.8
VIOLENT CRIME						
Number	3 589	3 483	-3.0	1 408 337	1 382 012	-1.9
Rate	239.4	228.6	-4.5	466.9	454.5	-2.7
Murder and Nonnegligent Manslaughter						
Number	49	23	-53.1	16 929	16 272	-3.9
Rate	3.3	1.5	-53.8	5.6	5.4	-4.7
Forcible Rape						
Number	578	551	-4.7	90 427	89 000	-1.6
Rate	38.5	36.2	-6.2	30.0	29.3	-2.4
Robbery						
Number	233	241	3.4	445 125	441 855	-0.7
Rate	15.5	15.8	1.8	147.6	145.3	-1.5
Aggravated Assault						
Number	2 729	2 668	-2.2	855 856	834 885	-2.5
Rate	182.0	175.1	-3.8	283.8	274.6	-3.2
PROPERTY CRIME						
Number	33 685	32 019	-4.9	9 843 481	9 767 915	-0.8
Rate	2 246.6	2 101.2	-6.5	3 263.5	3 212.5	-1.6
Burglary						
Number	6 977	6 701	-4.0	2 179 140	2 222 196	2.0
Rate	465.3	439.8	-5.5	722.5	730.8	1.2
Larceny-Theft						
Number	24 482	23 650	-3.4	6 568 572	6 588 873	0.3
Rate	1 632.8	1 552.0	-4.9	2 177.8	2 167.0	-0.5
Motor Vehicle Theft						
Number	2 226	1 668	-25.1	1 095 769	956 846	-12.7
Rate	148.5	109.5	-26.3	363.3	314.7	-13.4

Table ID-14. State Government Finances, 2007

(Dollars, percent distribution.)

Item	Thousands of dollars	Percent distribution
Total Revenue	9 095 154	X
General revenue	6 409 015	70.5
Intergovernmental revenue	1 842 758	20.3
Taxes	3 536 574	38.9
General sales	1 277 533	14.0
Selective sales	391 265	4.3
License taxes	264 108	2.9
Individual income tax	1 406 462	15.5
Corporate income tax	188 229	2.1
Other taxes	8 977	0.1
Current charges	562 478	6.2
Miscellaneous general revenue	467 205	5.1
Utility revenue	0	0.0
Liquor store revenue	105 964	1.2
Insurance trust revenue	2 580 175	28.4
Total Expenditure	6 895 319	100.0
Intergovernmental expenditure	1 931 829	28.0
Direct expenditure	4 963 490	72.0
Current operation	3 485 759	50.6
Capital outlay	561 201	8.1
Insurance benefits and repayments	669 893	9.7
Assistance and subsidies	116 064	1.7
Interest on debt	130 573	1.9
Exhibit: Salaries and wages	983 367	14.3
Total Expenditure	6 895 319	100.0
General expenditure	6 145 614	89.1
Intergovernmental expenditure	1 931 829	28.0
Direct expenditure	4 213 785	61.1
Education	2 506 932	36.4
Public welfare	1 485 151	21.5
Hospitals	43 860	0.6
Health	139 552	2.0
Highways	632 101	9.2
Police protection	47 038	0.7
Correction	210 533	3.1
Natural resources	189 751	2.8
Parks and recreation	43 694	0.6
Government administration	287 204	4.2
Interest on general debt	130 573	1.9
Other and unallocable	429 225	6.2
Utility expenditure	0	0.0
Liquor store expenditure	79 812	1.2
Insurance trust expenditure	669 893	9.7
Debt at End of Fiscal Year	2 812 655	X
Cash and Security Holdings	17 414 615	X

Table ID-15. State Government Tax Collections, 2008

(Dollars, percent distribution.)

Item	Thousands of dollars	Percent distribution
Total Taxes	3 651 917	X
Sales and gross receipts	1 743 294	47.7
General sales and gross receipts	1 347 327	36.9
Selective sales taxes	395 967	10.8
Alcoholic beverages	7 562	0.2
Insurance premiums	83 213	2.3
Motor fuels	239 881	6.6
Pari-mutuels	1 650	0.0
Public utilities	1 599	0.0
Tobacco products	54 781	1.5
Other selective sales	7 281	0.2
Licenses	270 270	7.4
Alcoholic beverages	1 655	0.0
Amusements	411	0.0
Corporation	2 279	0.1
Hunting and fishing	36 403	1.0
Motor vehicle	124 369	3.4
Motor vehicle operators	7 293	0.2
Public utility	33 655	0.9
Occupation and business, NEC	60 054	1.6
Other licenses	4 151	0.1
Income taxes	1 628 712	44.6
Individual income	1 438 518	39.4
Corporation net income	190 194	5.2
Other taxes	9 641	0.3
Death and gift	32	0.0
Severance	6 758	0.2
Other	2 851	0.1

Table ID-16. Agriculture

(Number, acres, and dollars.)

Item	2002 Number	2002 Percent of total	2007 Number	2007 Percent of total	Percent change, 2002–2007
Number of farms	25 017		25 349		1.3
Farm Size					
Average size of farm (acres)	470		454		-3.4
Farms by size (number of farms)					
Fewer than 50 acres	12 310	49.2	12 388	48.9	0.6
50 to 499 acres	8 196	32.8	8 670	34.2	5.8
500 acres or more	4 511	18.0	4 291	16.9	-4.9
Land (Acres)					
Total land in farms	11 767 294		11 497 383		-2.3
Total cropland	6 152 611	52.3	5 918 899	51.5	-3.8
Total harvested cropland	4 313 288	36.7	4 225 786	36.8	-2.0
Irrigated land	3 288 522	27.9	3 299 889	28.7	0.3
Value of Sales (Dollars)					
Agricultural products sold ($1,000)	3 908 262		5 688 765		45.6
Average sales per farm	156 224		224 418		43.7
Sales of crops	1 787 172	45.7	2 324 789	40.9	30.1
Sales of livestock, poultry, and their products	2 121 090	54.3	3 363 976	59.1	58.6
Value of Sales (Number of Farms)					
Less than $10,000	15 708	62.8	15 245	60.1	-2.9
$10,000 to $99,999	5 416	21.6	5 788	22.8	6.9
$100,000 to $999,999	3 204	12.8	3 330	13.1	3.9
$1,000,000 or more	689	2.8	986	3.9	43.1
Farms by Type of Organization (Number of Farms)					
Family	22 041	88.1	21 308	84.1	-3.3
Partnership	1 543	6.2	2 124	8.4	37.7
Corporation	1 218	4.9	1 533	6.0	25.9
Other: cooperative, estate or trust, institutional, etc	215	0.9	384	1.5	78.6
Value of Land and Buildings (Dollars)					
Estimated market value of land and buildings ($1,000)	22 674 602		15 342 391		-32.3
Land and buildings average value per farm	894 497		613 303		-31.4
Average value per acre	1 972		1 270		-35.6
Government Payments					
Number of farms receiving government payments	7 098	28.4	9 214	36.3	29.8
Payments (thousands of dollars)	93 934		99 494		5.9
Average payment per farm	13 234		10 798		-18.4
Farm Operator Characteristics					
Farm operators whose principal occupation is farming	13 857	55.4	11 579	45.7	-16.4
Farm operators whose principal occupation is other	11 160	44.6	13 770	54.3	23.4
Average age principal operator (years)	54.1		56.5		4.4

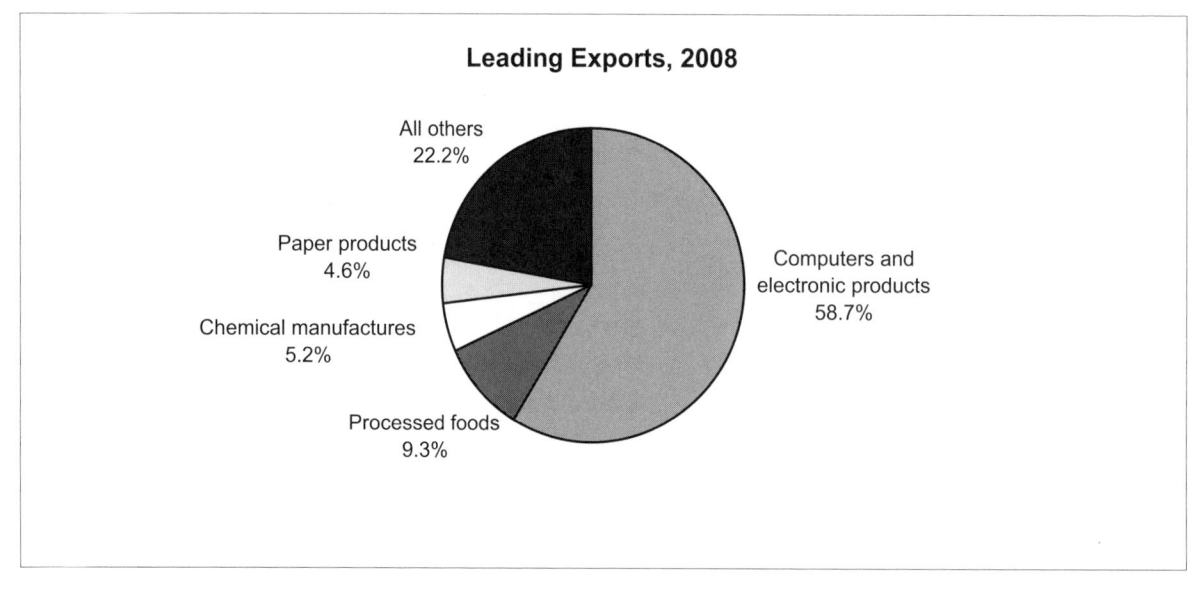

Leading Exports, 2008

All others 22.2%

Paper products 4.6%

Chemical manufactures 5.2%

Processed foods 9.3%

Computers and electronic products 58.7%

Facts and Figures

Location: North central United States; bordered on the N by Wisconsin, on the E by Lake Michigan and Indiana, on the S by Kentucky, and on the W by Iowa and Missouri

Area: 57,914 sq. mi. (149,998 sq. km.); rank—25th

Population: 12,901,563 (2008 est.); rank—5th

Principal Cities: capital—Springfield; largest—Chicago

Statehood: December 3, 1818; 21st state

U.S. Congress: 2 senators, 19 representatives

State Motto: State Sovereignty, National Union

State Song: "Illinois"

State Nicknames: The Prairie State; The Land of Lincoln

Abbreviations: IL; Ill.

State Symbols: flower—native violet; tree—white oak; bird—cardinal

At a Glance

- With an increase in population of 3.9 percent, Illinois ranked 35th among the states in growth from 2000 to 2008.
- An estimated 75,882 marriages took place in Illinois in 2008, compared to 32,237 divorces.
- The 2007 home ownership rate in Illinois was 69.4 percent, giving it a ranking of 34th along with Kansas.
- Illinois's median household income in 2007 was $54,124, 16th among the states.
- In Illinois, 11.9 percent of the population lived below the poverty level in 2007, ranking it 30th.
- In 2006-07, 13.7 percent of Illinoisans did not have health insurance, compared to 15.5 percent of the total U.S. population.
- In 2007, 5.1 percent of Illinoisans were unemployed, compared to 4.6 percent nationwide.
- Illinois ranked 13th in the nation with 29.5 percent of its population 25 years old and over having a bachelor's degree in 2007; its ranking was the same as California's.
- Illinois's violent crime rate in 2007 was 533.2 per 100,000 population, compared to 466.9 for the entire nation.
- Illinois had one physician for every 321 people in 2007, compared to one physician for every 325 people nationwide.
- In the 2008 election, 62.8 percent of Illinois's eligible voters voted, compared to 61.7 percent of eligible voters nationwide.
- Illinois ranked 37th among the states receiving federal aid in 2007, with $1,259 per capita.
- Illinois's gross domestic product was $610 billion in 2007; it ranked 5th among the states.
- With $48.9 billion in exports in 2007, Illinois ranked 5th in exports.
- Illinoisans consumed 3.9 trillion Btu's of energy in 2006; the state ranked 4th in total consumption.
- In 2007, Illinois exported $4.8 billion worth of agricultural products, 5.8 percent of the U.S. total.

Table IL-1. Population by Sex, Age, Race, and Hispanic Origin

(Number, percent.)

Sex, age, race, and Hispanic origin	1990	2000	2008	Average annual percent change, 2000–2008
Total Population	11 430 602	12 419 293	12 901 563	0.5
Percent of total U.S. population	4.6	4.4	4.2	X
Sex				
Male	5 552 233	6 080 336	6 359 906	0.6
Female	5 878 369	6 338 957	6 541 657	0.4
Age				
Under 5 years	848 141	876 549	894 368	0.3
5 to 19 years	2 451 088	2 728 957	2 677 612	-0.2
20 to 64 years	6 694 828	7 313 762	7 754 275	0.7
65 years and over	1 436 545	1 500 025	1 575 308	0.6
Median age (years)	32.7	34.7	36.0	X
Race and Hispanic Origin[1]				
One race				
White	8 952 978	9 125 471	10 209 408	1.4
Black	1 694 273	1 876 875	1 919 701	0.3
American Indian and Alaskan Native	21 836	31 006	45 128	4.8
Asian[2]	285 311	423 603	558 933	3.5
Native Hawaiian and Other Pacific Islander	X	4 610	9 353	9.2
Two or more races	X	235 016	159 040	-4.8
Hispanic (of any race)	904 446	1 530 262	1 967 121	3.2

[1]Data on race in 2000 and 2008 are not comparable to 1990. Individuals could only report one race in the 1990 census but could report one or more races on the 2000 census.
[2]Data in 1990 refer to Asian and Pacific Islanders.

Table IL-2. Marital Status

(Number, percent distribution.)

Sex and marital status	1990	2000	2007
Males, 15 Years and Over	4 282 894	4 685 982	4 977 517
Never married	32.6	31.9	35.8
Now married, except separated	56.1	56.1	52.0
Separated	1.7	1.6	1.5
Widowed	2.7	2.5	2.4
Divorced	7.0	7.9	8.3
Females, 15 Years and Over	4 666 480	5 021 855	5 231 077
Never married	25.4	26.1	29.8
Now married, except separated	50.8	51.3	47.7
Separated	2.3	2.0	2.0
Widowed	12.5	10.7	9.8
Divorced	9.1	9.9	10.6

Table IL-3. Households and Housing Characteristics

(Number, percent, and dollars.)

Item	1990	2000	2007	Average annual percent change, 2000–2007
Total Households	4 202 240	4 591 779	4 759 579	0.5
Family households	2 924 880	3 105 513	3 180 087	0.3
Married-couple family	2 271 962	2 353 892	2 358 203	0.0
Other family	652 918	751 621	821 884	1.3
Male householder, no wife present	147 173	187 903	218 173	2.2
Female householder, no husband present	505 745	563 718	603 711	1.0
Nonfamily households	1 277 360	1 486 266	1 579 492	0.9
Householder living alone	1 081 113	1 229 807	1 325 202	1.1
Householder not living alone	196 247	256 459	254 290	-0.1
Housing Characteristics				
Total housing units	4 506 275	4 885 615	5 246 116	1.0
Occupied housing units	4 202 240	4 591 779	4 759 579	0.5
Owner-occupied	2 699 182	3 088 884	3 334 539	1.1
Renter-occupied	1 503 058	1 502 895	1 425 040	-0.8
Average size	2.65	2.63	2.63	X
Financial Characteristics				
Median gross rent of renter-occupied housing units (dollars)	445	605	783	3.8
Median monthly owner costs for housing units with a mortgage (dollars)	767	1 198	1 625	4.5
Median value of owner-occupied housing units (dollars)	80 100	130 800	208 800	6.9

Table IL-4. Median Income and Poverty Status, 2007

(Number, percent.)

Characteristic	State		U.S.	
	Number	Percent	Number	Percent
Median Income				
Households (dollars)	54 124	X	50 740	X
Families (dollars)	65 761	X	61 173	X
Below Poverty Level				
Sex				
Male	662 587	10.7	16 576 071	11.5
Female	833 661	13.1	21 476 176	14.3
Age				
Under 18 years	525 294	16.6	13 097 100	18.0
Related children under 18 years	511 142	16.3	12 728 964	17.6
18 to 64 years	846 337	10.7	21 495 507	11.6
65 years and over	124 617	8.5	3 459 640	9.5

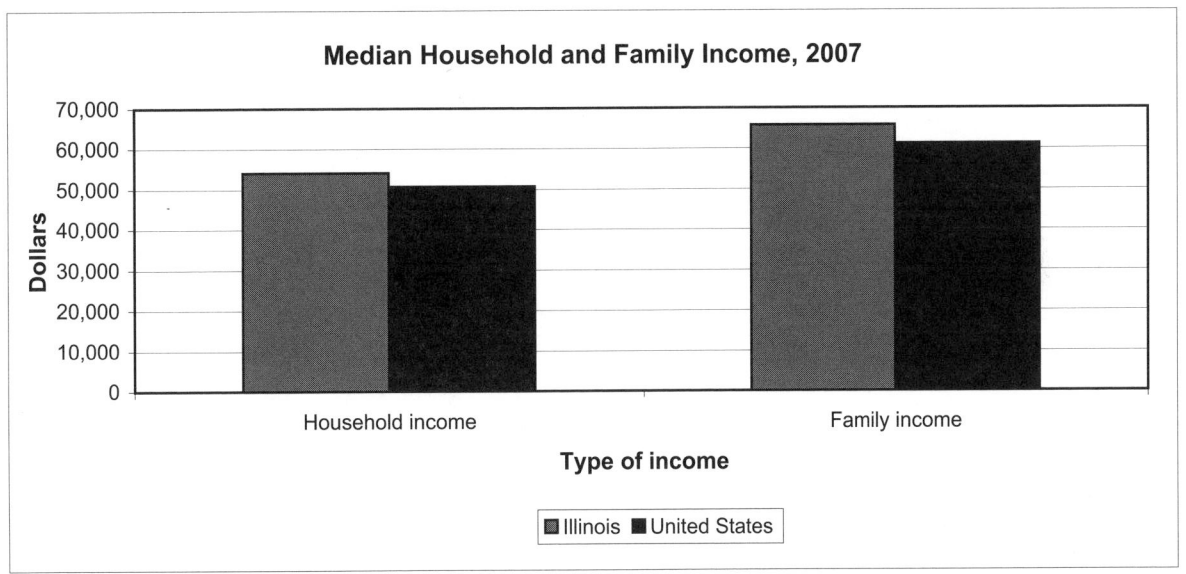

Table IL-5. Health Insurance Coverage Status for All Persons and Children Under 18 Years of Age

(Number, percent.)

Item	2000	2001	2002	2003	2004	2005	2006	2007
ALL PERSONS	12 301	12 331	12 504	12 628	12 592	12 608	12 644	12 688
Covered by Private or Government Health Insurance								
Number	10 669	10 716	10 810	10 867	10 952	10 878	10 867	10 988
Percent	86.7	86.9	86.5	86.1	87.0	86.3	86.0	86.6
Not Covered								
Number	1 632	1 616	1 694	1 761	1 640	1 730	1 776	1 700
Percent	13.3	13.1	13.5	13.9	13.0	13.7	14.0	13.4
Percent in the U.S. not covered	13.7	14.1	14.7	15.1	14.9	15.3	15.8	15.3
CHILDREN UNDER 18 YEARS OF AGE	3 139	3 092	3 312	3 210	3 242	3 276	3 188	3 180
Covered by Private or Government Health Insurance								
Number	2 821	2 781	2 954	2 903	2 900	2 947	2 886	2 970
Percent	89.9	89.9	89.2	90.4	89.4	89.9	90.5	93.4
Not Covered								
Number	318	311	358	307	342	329	302	210
Percent	10.1	10.1	10.8	9.6	10.6	10.1	9.5	6.6
Percent in the U.S. not covered	11.6	11.3	11.2	11.0	10.5	10.9	11.7	11.0

Table IL-6. Employment Status by Demographic Group, Preliminary 2008

(Number, percent.)

Characteristic	Civilian noninstitutional population	Civilian labor force		Employment		Unemployed	
		Number	Percent of population	Number	Percent of population	Number	Unemployment rate
TOTAL	9 912	6 704	67.6	6 263	63.2	440	6.6
Sex							
Men	4 814	3 591	75.0	3 345	69.5	246	6.9
Women	5 098	3 112	61.0	2 918	57.2	194	6.2
Race, Sex, and Hispanic Origin							
White	7 976	5 470	68.6	5 158	64.7	312	5.7
Men	3 930	3 003	76.4	2 824	71.9	179	6.0
Women	4 046	2 468	61.0	2 334	57.7	134	5.4
Black or African American	1 375	842	61.2	740	53.8	102	12.1
Men	605	363	60.0	313	51.6	51	14.0
Women	770	479	62.2	428	55.5	51	10.7
Hispanic	1 215	903	74.4	844	69.4	60	6.6
Men	650	564	86.8	530	81.7	33	5.9
Women	565	339	60.1	313	55.4	26	7.8
Age							
16 to 19 years	746	327	43.8	257	34.5	70	21.3
20 to 24 years	946	706	74.6	624	65.9	82	11.6
25 to 34 years	1 668	1 395	83.6	1 316	78.9	79	5.6
35 to 44 years	1 835	1 549	84.4	1 477	80.5	73	4.7
45 to 54 years	1 948	1 614	82.9	1 525	78.3	90	5.5
55 to 64 years	1 310	855	65.3	820	62.6	35	4.1
65 years and over	1 459	258	17.6	245	16.8	12	4.8

Note: Data in Table 6 are from the Current Population Survey (CPS) and do not match the estimates in Table 7. See notes and definitions for more details.

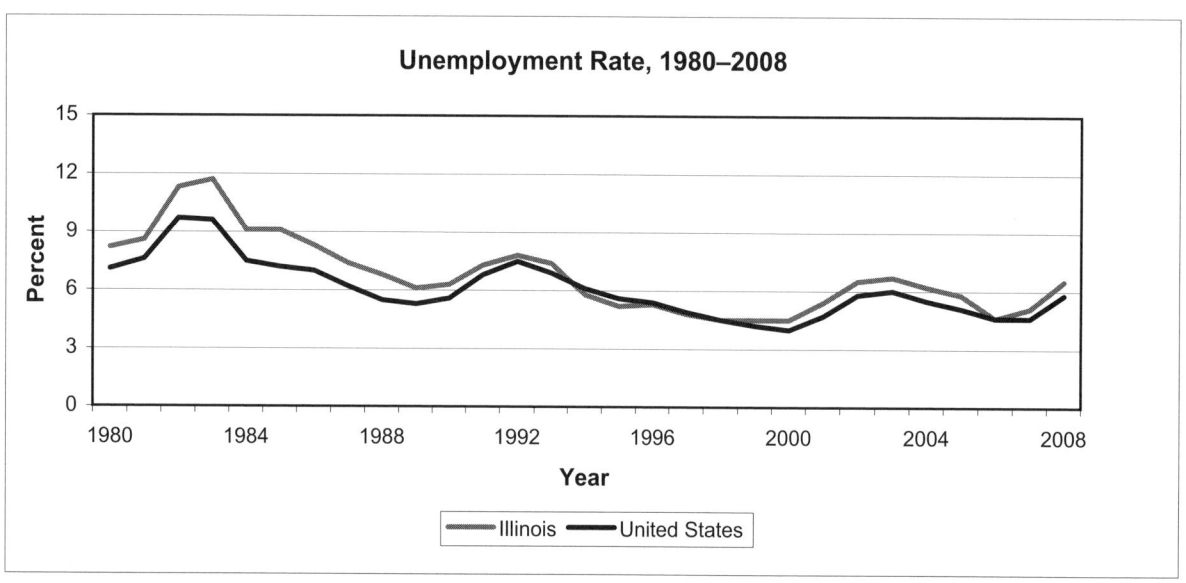

Unemployment Rate, 1980–2008

Table IL-7. Employment Status of the Civilian Noninstitutional Population Age 16 Years and Over

(Number, percent.)

Year	Civilian labor force	Civilian participation rate	Employed	Unemployed	Unemployment rate
1998	6 330 665	68.6	6 047 050	283 615	4.5
1999	6 429 466	69.1	6 143 130	286 336	4.5
2000	6 467 692	69.2	6 176 837	290 855	4.5
2001	6 464 511	68.7	6 113 536	350 975	5.4
2002	6 387 086	67.4	5 969 393	417 693	6.5
2003	6 343 273	66.5	5 916 830	426 443	6.7
2004	6 365 454	66.4	5 968 561	396 893	6.2
2005	6 433 119	66.6	6 061 314	371 805	5.8
2006	6 557 959	67.4	6 255 169	302 790	4.6
2007	6 689 636	68.2	6 348 650	340 986	5.1
2008	6 697 335	67.8	6 263 651	433 684	6.5

Table IL-8. Employment and Average Wages by Industry

(Estimates for 2001–2006 are based on the 2002 North American Industry Classification System [NAICS]. Estimates for 2007 are based on the 2007 NAICS.)

Industry	2001	2002	2003	2004	2005	2006	2007
	Number of jobs						
WAGE AND SALARY EMPLOYMENT BY INDUSTRY	6 246 520	6 133 893	6 066 766	6 064 355	6 107 600	6 188 057	6 234 950
Farm Wage and Salary Employment	20 084	15 938	17 576	15 240	17 105	17 797	17 792
Nonfarm Wage and Salary Employment	6 226 436	6 117 955	6 049 190	6 049 115	6 090 495	6 170 260	6 217 158
Private wage and salary employment	5 325 179	5 208 751	5 146 399	5 152 796	5 197 042	5 274 760	5 316 881
Forestry, fishing, hunting, and other	8 150	7 772	7 643	7 266	7 234	6 778	7 039
Mining	10 113	9 792	9 414	9 301	9 802	10 206	10 050
Utilities	29 686	28 395	24 781	24 158	23 500	23 190	23 128
Construction	287 465	285 580	284 001	278 309	278 727	285 135	279 954
Manufacturing	821 188	760 300	721 033	702 360	694 806	688 940	680 556
Durable goods manufacturing	509 005	460 211	432 469	423 611	421 446	423 006	417 999
Nondurable goods manufacturing	312 183	300 089	288 564	278 749	273 360	265 934	262 557
Wholesale trade	319 214	307 787	302 834	300 768	306 035	311 768	315 520
Retail trade	664 507	652 139	646 515	644 336	646 805	648 945	656 339
Transportation and warehousing	243 172	233 473	230 259	233 963	237 015	241 093	245 052
Information	154 471	138 690	127 961	121 620	119 217	117 401	117 077
Finance and insurance	323 081	320 444	323 093	320 642	321 790	325 765	322 809
Real estate and rental and leasing	89 181	88 120	87 251	86 340	86 966	87 691	87 384
Professional and technical services	385 902	366 795	353 091	352 415	365 710	379 789	383 792
Management of companies and enterprises	73 443	83 141	85 619	88 983	92 475	95 853	96 808
Administrative and waste services	375 129	362 581	361 716	384 626	391 233	402 753	412 513
Educational services	122 307	124 533	126 987	129 208	133 337	140 593	144 466
Health care and social assistance	614 732	625 747	632 767	640 239	651 034	664 497	679 473
Arts, entertainment, and recreation	83 549	85 129	86 085	85 105	84 826	84 906	85 034
Accommodation and food services	416 819	416 743	422 373	430 936	438 007	448 397	456 521
Other services, except public administration	303 070	311 590	312 976	312 221	308 523	311 060	313 366
Government and government enterprises	901 257	909 204	902 791	896 319	893 453	895 500	900 277
	Dollars						
AVERAGE WAGES AND SALARIES BY INDUSTRY	38 475	39 141	39 988	41 742	43 211	45 037	47 021
Average Farm Wages and Salaries	18 102	20 935	23 337	29 262	22 850	20 616	24 810
Average Nonfarm Wages and Salaries	38 541	39 188	40 036	41 773	43 268	45 107	47 085
Average private wages and salaries	38 951	39 439	40 275	42 010	43 541	45 514	47 604
Forestry, fishing, hunting, and other	24 058	24 207	24 195	25 183	26 988	28 754	30 515
Mining	50 122	51 319	51 158	53 191	55 672	57 120	60 161
Utilities	78 025	79 041	78 937	82 562	88 911	92 590	95 937
Construction	47 573	48 523	49 143	50 238	52 348	55 258	56 971
Manufacturing	43 715	44 831	46 214	48 573	50 344	52 503	54 905
Durable goods manufacturing	44 173	45 033	46 375	49 108	51 182	53 423	55 694
Nondurable goods manufacturing	42 969	44 522	45 973	47 760	49 053	51 040	53 651
Wholesale trade	52 960	53 494	54 578	57 436	59 220	62 110	65 712
Retail trade	22 844	23 461	23 779	24 385	24 730	25 371	26 291
Transportation and warehousing	40 017	40 742	40 858	42 351	43 556	46 204	46 089
Information	52 958	52 329	54 046	56 797	58 905	61 134	65 362
Finance and insurance	65 802	66 330	69 307	74 368	76 332	81 616	90 032
Real estate and rental and leasing	39 681	41 688	41 397	44 166	46 996	51 926	53 085
Professional and technical services	63 895	64 262	65 761	68 945	72 098	74 860	77 691
Management of companies and enterprises	87 690	82 185	85 752	94 296	98 966	101 090	108 973
Administrative and waste services	25 229	25 456	26 071	26 816	27 978	29 030	30 987
Educational services	29 194	30 162	31 725	32 942	33 521	34 720	36 154
Health care and social assistance	32 974	34 093	35 204	36 523	37 791	39 142	40 425
Arts, entertainment, and recreation	25 641	27 046	27 054	27 791	28 888	29 849	31 258
Accommodation and food services	14 473	14 478	14 858	15 530	16 289	17 115	17 722
Other services, except public administration	24 608	25 762	26 320	27 345	28 027	29 005	30 387
Government and government enterprises	36 115	37 753	38 678	40 411	41 677	42 714	44 021

Table IL-9. Employment Characteristics by Family Type

(Number, percent.)

Family type and labor force status	2005		2006		2007	
	Total	Families with own children under 18 years	Total	Families with own children under 18 years	Total	Families with own children under 18 years
TOTAL FAMILIES	3 126 131	1 508 676	3 146 342	1 517 075	3 180 087	1 529 536
FAMILY TYPE AND LABOR FORCE STATUS						
Married Coupled Families	2 330 118	1 073 018	2 355 451	1 075 079	2 358 203	1 078 491
Both husband and wife in labor force	54.5	63.7	55.6	64.8	55.3	64.3
Husband in labor force, wife not in labor force	23.0	29.5	23.1	30.1	23.5	30.3
Wife in labor force, husband not in labor force	6.9	3.7	6.6	3.2	6.5	3.4
Both husband and wife not in labor force	15.7	3.0	14.7	1.9	14.7	2.0
Other Families	796 013	435 658	790 891	441 996	821 884	451 045
Female householder, no husband present	74.5	79.1	74.3	78.9	73.5	77.5
In labor force	53.0	65.5	53.8	65.0	53.1	63.6
Not in labor force	21.5	13.6	20.5	13.9	20.4	13.8
Male householder, no wife present	25.5	20.9	25.7	21.1	26.5	22.5
In labor force	19.9	18.4	20.8	19.0	21.4	20.4
Not in labor force	5.6	2.5	5.0	2.1	5.1	2.2

Table IL-10. School Enrollment and Educational Attainment, 2007

(Number, percent.)

Item	State	U.S.
Enrollment		
Total population 3 years and over	12 328 102	289 295 761
Enrolled in school	3 533 208	79 329 527
Enrolled in preschool (percent)	7.2	6.2
Enrolled in grades K-12 (percent)	65.9	67.6
Enrolled in college or graduate school (percent)	26.9	26.2
Attainment		
Total population 25 years and over	8 354 987	197 892 369
Less than a high school diploma (percent)	14.3	15.5
High school diploma or more (percent)	85.7	84.5
Bachelor's degree or more (percent)	29.5	27.5
Graduate degree or more (percent)	11.0	10.1

Table IL-11. Educational Indicators

(Number, percent.)

Item	State	U.S.
Public Schools, 2006–2007 (except where noted)		
Number of school districts	1 082	17 742
Number of schools	4 395	99 639
Number of students	2 118 276	49 315 842
Student-teacher ratio	15.0	15.5
Expenditures per student (dollars)	$9 596	...
Averaged freshman graduation rate, 2005–2006	79.7	...
Dropout rate, grades 9–12, 2005–2006	3.9	3.7
Students eligible for free or reduced-price lunch (percent)	37.5	41.2
English-language learners (percent)	8.2	5.1
Students with IEP (percent)	15.4	12.7
Private Schools, 2007–2008 (except where noted)		
Number of schools	1 924	33 740
Number of students	264 012	5 072 451
High school graduates, 2006–2007	15 105	306 605
Student-teacher ratio	12.7	11.1

Table IL-12. Reported Voting and Registration of the Voting-Age Population, November 2008

(Number in thousands, percent.)

Item	Total population	Total citizen population	Registered			Voted		
			Total registered	Percent registered (total population)	Percent registered (total citizen population)	Total voted	Percent voted (total population)	Percent voted (total citizen population)
U.S. total	225 499	206 072	146 311	64.9	71.0	131 144	58.2	63.6
State total	9 521	8 681	6 151	64.6	70.9	5 436	57.1	62.6
Sex								
Male	4 623	4 204	2 900	62.7	69.0	2 521	54.5	60.0
Female	4 897	4 477	3 252	66.4	72.6	2 914	59.5	65.1
Race								
White alone	7 750	7 128	5 160	66.6	72.4	4 520	58.3	63.4
White non-Hispanic alone	6 700	6 468	4 783	71.4	73.9	4 214	62.9	65.2
Black alone	1 298	1 260	826	63.6	65.5	784	60.4	62.2
Asian alone	360	213	109	30.2	51.2	78	21.7	36.7
Hispanic (of any race)	1 081	671	385	35.6	57.4	314	29.0	46.8
White alone or in combination	7 805	7 178	5 190	66.5	72.3	4 547	58.3	63.3
Black alone or in combination	1 318	1 280	843	64.0	65.9	798	60.5	62.3
Asian alone or in combination	375	228	115	30.6	50.4	84	22.4	36.9

Table IL-13. Crime

(Number, rate per 100,000.)

Item	State			U.S.		
	2007	2008	Percent change	2007	2008	Percent change
Population	12 852 548	12 901 563	0.4	301 621 157	304 059 724	0.8
VIOLENT CRIME						
Number	68 528	67 780	-1.1	1 408 337	1 382 012	-1.9
Rate	533.2	525.4	-1.5	466.9	454.5	-2.7
Murder and Nonnegligent Manslaughter						
Number	752	790	5.1	16 929	16 272	-3.9
Rate	5.9	6.1	4.7	5.6	5.4	-4.7
Forcible Rape						
Number	4 103	4 118	0.4	90 427	89 000	-1.6
Rate	31.9	31.9	*	30.0	29.3	-2.4
Robbery						
Number	23 100	24 054	4.1	445 125	441 855	-0.7
Rate	179.7	186.4	3.7	147.6	145.3	-1.5
Aggravated Assault						
Number	40 573	38 818	-4.3	855 856	834 885	-2.5
Rate	315.7	300.9	-4.7	283.8	274.6	-3.2
PROPERTY CRIME						
Number	377 322	378 355	0.3	9 843 481	9 767 915	-0.8
Rate	2 935.8	2 932.6	-0.1	3 263.5	3 212.5	-1.6
Burglary						
Number	75 524	78 968	4.6	2 179 140	2 222 196	2.0
Rate	587.6	612.1	4.2	722.5	730.8	1.2
Larceny-Theft						
Number	267 911	266 815	-0.4	6 568 572	6 588 873	0.3
Rate	2 084.5	2 068.1	-0.8	2 177.8	2 167.0	-0.5
Motor Vehicle Theft						
Number	33 887	32 572	-3.9	1 095 769	956 846	-12.7
Rate	263.7	252.5	-4.2	363.3	314.7	-13.4

Table IL-14. State Government Finances, 2007

(Dollars, percent distribution.)

Item	Thousands of dollars	Percent distribution
Total Revenue	71 255 039	X
General revenue	52 377 362	73.5
Intergovernmental revenue	14 234 320	20.0
Taxes	30 578 017	42.9
General sales	7 817 291	11.0
Selective sales	6 493 099	9.1
License taxes	2 440 961	3.4
Individual income tax	10 469 797	14.7
Corporate income tax	2 936 360	4.1
Other taxes	420 509	0.6
Current charges	3 895 406	5.5
Miscellaneous general revenue	3 669 619	5.1
Utility revenue	0	0.0
Liquor store revenue	0	0.0
Insurance trust revenue	18 877 677	26.5
Total Expenditure	59 302 221	100.0
Intergovernmental expenditure	14 259 666	24.0
Direct expenditure	45 042 555	76.0
Current operation	29 686 739	50.1
Capital outlay	3 695 239	6.2
Insurance benefits and repayments	8 265 338	13.9
Assistance and subsidies	1 118 125	1.9
Interest on debt	2 277 114	3.8
Exhibit: Salaries and wages	8 099 483	13.7
Total Expenditure	59 302 221	100.0
General expenditure	51 036 882	86.1
Intergovernmental expenditure	14 259 666	24.0
Direct expenditure	36 777 216	62.0
Education	15 353 554	25.9
Public welfare	15 565 800	26.2
Hospitals	953 052	1.6
Health	2 255 034	3.8
Highways	4 695 631	7.9
Police protection	452 122	0.8
Correction	1 209 228	2.0
Natural resources	300 115	0.5
Parks and recreation	274 148	0.5
Government administration	1 242 406	2.1
Interest on general debt	2 277 114	3.8
Other and unallocable	6 458 678	10.9
Utility expenditure	1	0.0
Liquor store expenditure	0	0.0
Insurance trust expenditure	8 265 338	13.9
Debt at End of Fiscal Year	54 535 159	X
Cash and Security Holdings	136 239 934	X

Table IL-15. State Government Tax Collections, 2008

(Dollars, percent distribution.)

Item	Thousands of dollars	Percent distribution
Total Taxes	31 890 597	X
Property taxes	59 134	0.2
Sales and gross receipts	15 471 663	48.5
General sales and gross receipts	7 935 417	24.9
Selective sales taxes	7 536 246	23.6
Alcoholic beverages	158 067	0.5
Amusements	706 440	2.2
Insurance premiums	316 282	1.0
Motor fuels	1 334 664	4.2
Pari-mutuels	8 358	0.0
Public utilities	1 919 902	6.0
Tobacco products	613 651	1.9
Other selective sales	2 478 882	7.8
Licenses	2 474 318	7.8
Alcoholic beverages	11 488	0.0
Amusements	1 200	0.0
Corporation	234 492	0.7
Hunting and fishing	35 343	0.1
Motor vehicle	1 368 331	4.3
Motor vehicle operators	66 742	0.2
Occupation and business, NEC	751 114	2.4
Other licenses	5 608	0.0
Income taxes	13 435 843	42.1
Individual income	10 320 239	32.4
Corporation net income	3 115 604	9.8
Other taxes	449 639	1.4
Death and gift	372 798	1.2
Documentary and stock transfer	76 841	0.2

Table IL-16. Agriculture

(Number, acres, and dollars.)

Item	2002		2007		Percent change, 2002–2007
	Number	Percent of total	Number	Percent of total	
Number of farms	73 027		76 860		5.2
Farm Size					
Average size of farm (acres)	374		348		-7.0
Farms by size (number of farms)					
Fewer than 50 acres	19 672	26.9	29 195	38.0	48.4
50 to 499 acres	35 853	49.1	31 526	41.0	-12.1
500 acres or more	17 502	24.0	16 139	21.0	-7.8
Land (Acres)					
Total land in farms	27 310 833		26 775 100		-2.0
Total cropland	24 171 260	88.5	23 707 699	88.5	-1.9
Total harvested cropland	22 562 904	82.6	22 611 443	84.4	0.2
Irrigated land	390 843	1.4	474 454	1.8	21.4
Value of Sales (Dollars)					
Agricultural products sold ($1,000)	7 676 239		13 329 107		73.6
Average sales per farm	105 115		173 421		65.0
Sales of crops	5 871 542	76.5	10 876 415	81.6	85.2
Sales of livestock, poultry, and their products	1 804 697	23.5	2 452 692	18.4	35.9
Value of Sales (Number of Farms)					
Less than $10,000	30 263	41.4	36 034	46.9	19.1
$10,000 to $99,999	23 290	31.9	17 536	22.8	-24.7
$100,000 to $999,999	18 780	25.7	20 489	26.7	9.1
$1,000,000 or more	694	1.0	2 801	3.6	303.6
Farms by Type of Organization (Number of Farms)					
Family	64 468	88.3	65 748	85.5	2.0
Partnership	5 296	7.3	6 509	8.5	22.9
Corporation	2 584	3.5	3 433	4.5	32.9
Other: cooperative, estate or trust, institutional, etc	679	0.9	1 170	1.5	72.3
Value of Land and Buildings (Dollars)					
Estimated market value of land and buildings ($1,000)	101 538 246		66 667 341		-34.3
Land and buildings average value per farm	1 321 080		913 251		-30.9
Average value per acre	3 792		2 425		-36.0
Government Payments					
Number of farms receiving government payments	47 857	65.5	56 811	73.9	18.7
Payments (thousands of dollars)	412 636		487 293		18.1
Average payment per farm	8 622		8 577		-0.5
Farm Operator Characteristics					
Farm operators whose principal occupation is farming	46 822	64.1	37 223	48.4	-20.5
Farm operators whose principal occupation is other	26 205	35.9	39 637	51.6	51.3
Average age principal operator (years)	55.1		56.2		2.0

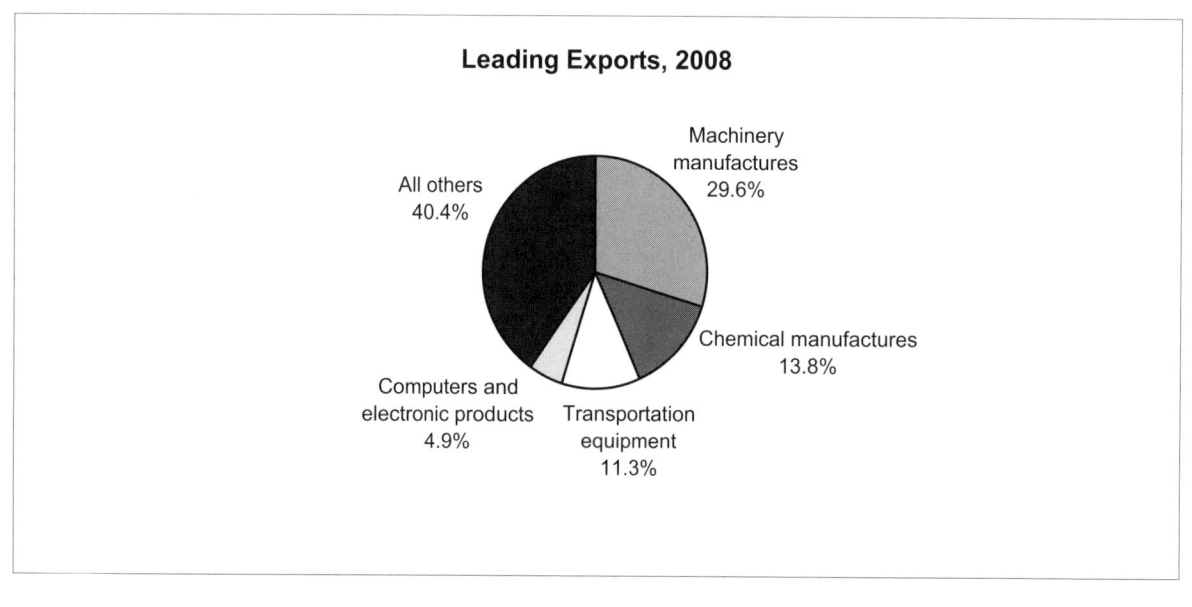

Leading Exports, 2008

Machinery manufactures 29.6%

All others 40.4%

Chemical manufactures 13.8%

Transportation equipment 11.3%

Computers and electronic products 4.9%

INDIANA

Facts and Figures

Location: East north central United States; bordered on the N by Michigan and Lake Michigan, on the E by Ohio, on the S by Kentucky, and on the W by Illinois

Area: 36,418 sq. mi. (94,321 sq. km.); rank—38th

Population: 6,376,792 (2008 est.); rank—15th

Principal Cities: capital—Indianapolis; largest—Indianapolis

Statehood: December 11, 1816; 19th state

U.S. Congress: 2 senators, 9 representatives

State Motto: The Crossroads of America

State Song: "On the Banks of the Wabash, Far Away"

State Nickname: The Hoosier State

Abbreviations: IN; Ind.

State Symbols: flower—peony; tree—tulip tree; bird—cardinal

At a Glance

- With an increase in population of 4.9 percent, Indiana ranked 31st among the states in growth from 2000 to 2008.
- An estimated 50,671 marriages took place in Indiana in 2008; Indiana does not report its number of divorces.
- The 2007 home ownership rate in Indiana was 73.8 percent; its ranking of 9th was tied with that of New Hampshire.
- Indiana's median household income in 2007 was $47,448, 30th among the states.
- In Indiana, 12.3 percent of the population lived below the poverty level in 2007, ranking it 23rd.
- In 2006-07, 11.6 percent of Indianans did not have health insurance, compared to 15.5 percent of the total U.S. population.
- In 2007, 4.6 percent of Indianans were unemployed, which was the same as the national average.
- Indiana ranked 42nd in the nation with 22.1 percent of its population 25 years old and over having a bachelor's degree in 2007.
- Indiana's violent crime rate in 2007 was 333.6 per 100,000 population, compared to 466.9 for the entire nation.
- Indiana had one physician for every 410 people in 2007, compared to one physician for every 325 people nationwide.
- In the 2008 election, 59.4 percent of Indiana's eligible voters voted, compared to 61.7 percent of eligible voters nationwide.
- Indiana ranked 44th among the states receiving federal aid in 2007, with $1,146 per capita.
- Indiana's gross domestic product was $246 billion in 2007; it ranked 18th among the states.
- With $26 billion in exports in 2007, Indiana ranked 12th in exports.
- Indianans consumed 2.86 trillion Btu's of energy in 2006; the state ranked 11th in total consumption.
- In 2007, Indiana exported $2.4 billion worth of agricultural products, about 2.9 percent of the U.S. total.

Table IN-1. Population by Sex, Age, Race, and Hispanic Origin

(Number, percent.)

Sex, age, race, and Hispanic origin	1990	2000	2008	Average annual percent change, 2000–2008
Total Population	5 544 159	6 080 485	6 376 792	X
Percent of total U.S. population	2.2	2.2	2.1	-0.6
Sex				
Male	2 688 281	2 982 474	3 142 510	0.7
Female	2 855 878	3 098 011	3 234 282	0.5
Age				
Under 5 years	398 656	423 215	443 089	0.6
5 to 19 years	1 244 555	1 340 171	1 320 534	-0.2
20 to 64 years	3 204 752	3 564 268	3 799 330	0.8
65 years and over	696 196	752 831	813 839	1.0
Median age (years)	32.7	35.2	36.7	X
Race and Hispanic Origin[1]				
One race				
White	5 020 700	5 320 022	5 611 577	0.7
Black	432 092	510 034	578 088	1.6
American Indian and Alaskan Native	12 720	15 815	20 390	3.2
Asian[2]	37 617	59 126	86 768	4.9
Native Hawaiian and Other Pacific Islander	X	2 005	3 136	5.8
Two or more races	X	75 672	76 833	0.2
Hispanic (of any race)	98 788	214 536	332 225	5.6

[1]Data on race in 2000 and 2008 are not comparable to 1990. Individuals could only report one race in the 1990 census but could report one or more races on the 2000 census.
[2]Data in 1990 refer to Asian and Pacific Islanders.

Table IN-2. Marital Status

(Number, percent distribution.)

Sex and marital status	1990	2000	2007
Males, 15 Years and Over	2 064 662	2 308 917	2 453 302
Never married	27.6	27.9	30.5
Now married, except separated	60.3	58.5	54.5
Separated	1.2	1.2	1.3
Widowed	2.4	2.4	2.5
Divorced	8.5	10.0	11.2
Females, 15 Years and Over	2 263 865	2 462 123	2 582 623
Never married	21.3	22.0	24.6
Now married, except separated	54.7	54.3	51.0
Separated	1.5	1.5	1.7
Widowed	12.1	10.6	9.8
Divorced	10.4	11.6	12.9

Table IN-3. Households and Housing Characteristics

(Number, percent, and dollars.)

Item	1990	2000	2007	Average annual percent change, 2000–2007
Total Households	2 065 355	2 336 306	2 462 278	0.8
Family households	1 480 351	1 602 501	1 662 403	0.5
Married-couple family	1 202 020	1 251 458	1 265 979	0.2
Other family	278 331	351 043	396 424	1.8
Male householder, no wife present	60 703	91 671	108 498	2.4
Female householder, no husband present	217 628	259 372	287 926	1.5
Nonfamily households	585 004	733 805	799 875	1.2
Householder living alone	496 841	605 428	666 234	1.4
Householder not living alone	88 163	128 377	133 641	0.6
Housing Characteristics				
Total housing units	2 246 046	2 532 319	2 777 953	1.3
Occupied housing units	2 065 355	2 336 306	2 462 278	0.8
Owner-occupied	1 450 898	1 669 162	1 763 734	0.8
Renter-occupied	614 457	667 144	698 544	0.7
Average size	2.61	2.53	2.50	X
Financial Characteristics				
Median gross rent of renter-occupied housing units (dollars)	374	521	638	2.9
Median monthly owner costs for housing units with a mortgage (dollars)	561	869	1 098	3.4
Median value of owner-occupied housing units (dollars)	53 500	94 300	122 900	3.9

Table IN-4. Median Income and Poverty Status, 2007

(Number, percent.)

Characteristic	State		U.S.	
	Number	Percent	Number	Percent
Median Income				
Households (dollars)	47 448	X	50 740	X
Families (dollars)	57 734	X	61 173	X
Below Poverty Level				
Sex				
Male	328 001	10.9	16 576 071	11.5
Female	429 812	13.8	21 476 176	14.3
Age				
Under 18 years	267 610	17.3	13 097 100	18.0
Related children under 18 years	257 850	16.7	12 728 964	17.6
18 to 64 years	431 479	11.2	21 495 507	11.6
65 years and over	58 724	7.8	3 459 640	9.5

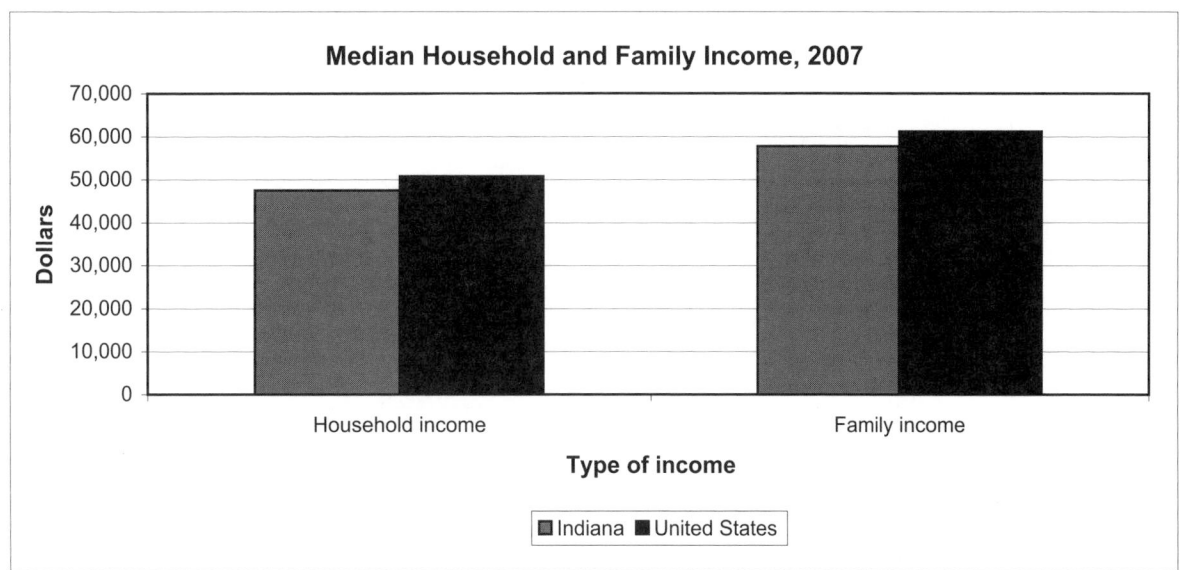

Median Household and Family Income, 2007

Indiana ■ United States

Table IN-5. Health Insurance Coverage Status for All Persons and Children Under 18 Years of Age

(Number, percent.)

Item	2000	2001	2002	2003	2004	2005	2006	2007
ALL PERSONS	6 016	6 036	6 100	6 149	6 136	6 141	6 337	6 263
Covered by Private or Government Health Insurance								
Number	5 365	5 361	5 351	5 356	5 289	5 308	5 590	5 546
Percent	89.2	88.8	87.7	87.1	86.2	86.4	88.2	88.6
Not Covered								
Number	650	674	750	792	847	832	748	717
Percent	10.8	11.2	12.3	12.9	13.8	13.6	11.8	11.4
Percent in the U.S. not covered	13.7	14.1	14.7	15.1	14.9	15.3	15.8	15.3
CHILDREN UNDER 18 YEARS OF AGE	1 505	1 467	1 607	1 585	1 605	1 614	1 582	1 593
Covered by Private or Government Health Insurance								
Number	1 337	1 311	1 463	1 454	1 469	1 457	1 459	1 511
Percent	88.8	89.3	91.1	91.7	91.5	90.2	92.2	94.8
Not Covered								
Number	169	156	143	131	137	158	123	83
Percent	11.2	10.7	8.9	8.3	8.5	9.8	7.8	5.2
Percent in the U.S. not covered	11.6	11.3	11.2	11.0	10.5	10.9	11.7	11.0

Table IN-6. Employment Status by Demographic Group, Preliminary 2008

(Number, percent.)

Characteristic	Civilian noninstitutional population	Civilian labor force		Employment		Unemployed	
		Number	Percent of population	Number	Percent of population	Number	Unemployment rate
TOTAL	4 887	3 251	66.5	3 056	62.5	194	6.0
Sex							
Men	2 375	1 730	73.0	1 617	68.1	113	6.5
Women	2 513	1 521	61.0	1 440	57.3	81	5.3
Race, Sex, and Hispanic Origin							
White	4 442	2 969	66.8	2 814	63.4	155	5.2
Men	2 174	1 593	73.3	1 501	69.0	92	5.8
Women	2 268	1 376	60.7	1 313	57.9	63	4.5
Black or African American	380	243	63.9	206	54.3	37	15.1
Men	167	114	68.0	95	57.0	18	16.2
Women	213	129	60.7	111	52.1	18	14.1
Hispanic	214	160	74.5	145	67.8	14	9.1
Men	122	109	89.3	98	80.2	11	10.2
Women	92	51	55.1	48	51.4	3	6.6
Age							
16 to 19 years	380	149	39.2	123	32.5	25	17.1
20 to 24 years	396	295	74.4	260	65.7	34	11.7
25 to 34 years	762	630	82.7	587	77.0	44	6.9
35 to 44 years	945	802	84.9	758	80.3	44	5.5
45 to 54 years	917	765	83.4	733	79.9	32	4.1
55 to 64 years	712	490	68.9	478	67.1	13	2.6
65 years and over	775	120	15.4	117	15.1	3	2.1

Note: Data in Table 6 are from the Current Population Survey (CPS) and do not match the estimates in Table 7. See notes and definitions for more details.

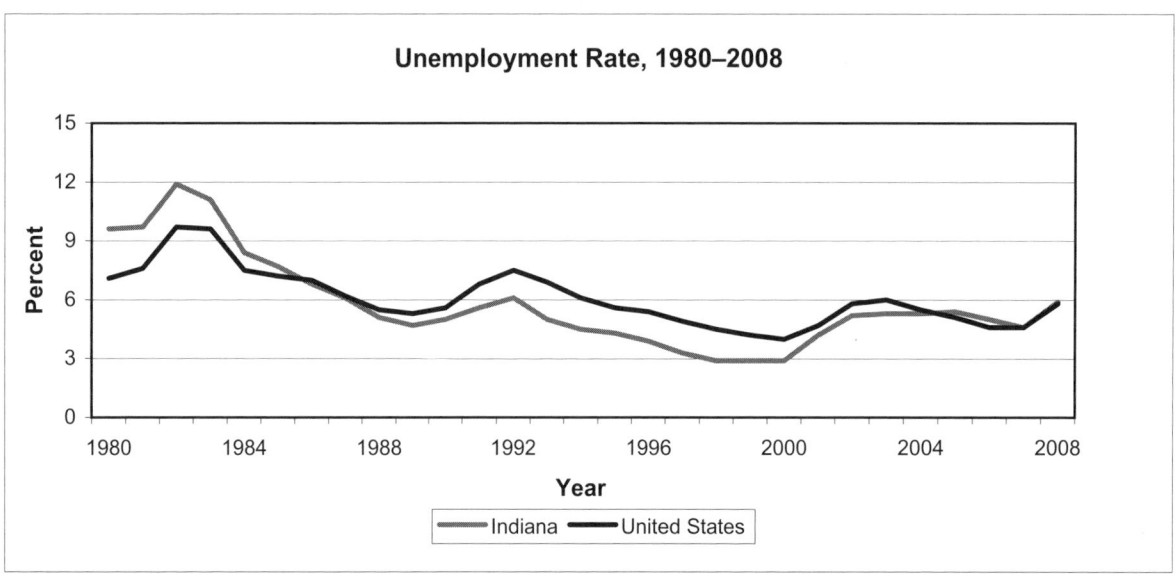

Table IN-7. Employment Status of the Civilian Noninstitutional Population Age 16 Years and Over

(Number, percent.)

Year	Civilian labor force	Civilian participation rate	Employed	Unemployed	Unemployment rate
1998	3 124 509	68.8	3 033 444	91 065	2.9
1999	3 136 581	68.6	3 046 922	89 659	2.9
2000	3 144 379	68.3	3 052 719	91 660	2.9
2001	3 152 135	68.1	3 020 985	131 150	4.2
2002	3 165 768	68.0	3 002 515	163 253	5.2
2003	3 165 978	67.6	2 997 847	168 131	5.3
2004	3 165 300	67.1	2 997 800	167 500	5.3
2005	3 200 103	67.3	3 028 470	171 633	5.4
2006	3 235 132	67.5	3 074 927	160 205	5.0
2007	3 221 054	66.6	3 074 079	146 975	4.6
2008	3 230 367	66.3	3 039 795	190 572	5.9

Table IN-8. Employment and Average Wages by Industry

(Estimates for 2001–2006 are based on the 2002 North American Industry Classification System [NAICS]. Estimates for 2007 are based on the 2007 NAICS.)

Industry	2001	2002	2003	2004	2005	2006	2007
	Number of jobs						
WAGE AND SALARY EMPLOYMENT BY INDUSTRY	3 053 716	3 018 088	3 012 117	3 035 272	3 057 781	3 081 875	3 093 243
Farm Wage and Salary Employment	14 424	11 418	11 900	11 003	11 753	13 437	11 942
Nonfarm Wage and Salary Employment	3 039 292	3 006 670	3 000 217	3 024 269	3 046 028	3 068 438	3 081 301
Private wage and salary employment	2 608 479	2 572 630	2 558 699	2 583 203	2 604 998	2 624 441	2 632 856
Forestry, fishing, hunting, and other	4 486	3 641	3 822	3 889	4 065	4 136	4 224
Mining	6 833	6 860	6 692	6 743	6 544	6 645	6 722
Utilities	15 079	14 849	14 445	14 547	14 762	14 848	14 790
Construction	153 886	151 754	150 730	153 769	153 850	155 970	156 452
Manufacturing	618 569	591 326	575 367	574 218	574 135	568 173	552 761
Durable goods manufacturing	458 517	435 335	421 200	420 391	421 197	416 089	403 257
Nondurable goods manufacturing	160 052	155 991	154 167	153 827	152 938	152 084	149 504
Wholesale trade	125 031	122 099	119 675	120 550	123 581	125 315	127 246
Retail trade	359 995	351 476	345 493	343 382	342 211	340 482	338 408
Transportation and warehousing	113 148	107 713	106 755	109 337	113 550	117 053	117 858
Information	44 995	42 683	40 980	41 064	40 476	40 025	40 270
Finance and insurance	108 894	106 213	107 182	104 977	103 190	103 979	103 268
Real estate and rental and leasing	37 763	36 579	36 443	37 169	37 820	37 833	36 955
Professional and technical services	92 954	91 985	92 231	94 526	96 579	99 221	102 550
Management of companies and enterprises	26 462	26 492	27 088	27 050	26 440	26 728	28 287
Administrative and waste services	135 137	140 766	141 064	151 021	157 802	160 211	164 848
Educational services	50 163	52 491	53 531	54 822	56 107	57 705	59 733
Health care and social assistance	296 908	303 743	311 610	316 360	323 365	330 853	339 689
Arts, entertainment, and recreation	46 707	46 441	47 287	47 070	46 370	45 834	45 642
Accommodation and food services	227 029	227 606	229 134	232 646	236 491	240 535	243 655
Other services, except public administration	144 440	147 913	149 170	150 063	147 660	148 895	149 498
Government and government enterprises	430 813	434 040	441 518	441 066	441 030	443 997	448 445
	Dollars						
AVERAGE WAGES AND SALARIES BY INDUSTRY	31 129	31 959	32 754	34 113	34 883	35 928	36 908
Average Farm Wages and Salaries	18 106	20 943	22 560	29 610	26 282	21 892	26 901
Average Nonfarm Wages and Salaries	31 191	32 001	32 794	34 129	34 916	35 989	36 947
Average private wages and salaries	31 481	32 276	33 083	34 419	35 168	36 329	37 312
Forestry, fishing, hunting, and other	15 927	17 687	18 239	20 015	19 627	21 081	22 232
Mining	45 874	46 635	47 938	49 777	51 721	55 382	57 439
Utilities	58 328	59 011	60 532	62 850	64 483	67 116	68 256
Construction	36 701	37 568	38 490	39 336	40 798	42 109	44 748
Manufacturing	42 033	43 898	45 395	47 585	48 149	49 887	51 081
Durable goods manufacturing	42 086	44 238	46 079	48 197	48 637	50 113	51 405
Nondurable goods manufacturing	41 881	42 949	43 527	45 913	46 804	49 268	50 210
Wholesale trade	41 447	42 527	44 085	46 138	47 445	49 676	51 431
Retail trade	19 705	20 390	20 929	21 542	21 799	22 156	22 575
Transportation and warehousing	33 134	34 772	35 456	36 562	37 247	38 414	39 483
Information	38 043	38 925	40 461	43 237	43 300	44 606	46 236
Finance and insurance	44 386	44 259	45 615	48 446	49 571	51 581	52 730
Real estate and rental and leasing	25 418	26 667	27 788	28 886	30 085	31 592	32 633
Professional and technical services	42 066	42 750	43 651	45 072	47 171	48 646	51 164
Management of companies and enterprises	65 325	61 704	61 264	65 965	71 926	73 736	72 660
Administrative and waste services	21 142	21 363	21 908	22 756	23 287	24 289	24 964
Educational services	21 493	22 128	22 149	22 795	24 191	25 383	26 025
Health care and social assistance	31 195	32 272	33 056	34 464	35 336	36 356	37 287
Arts, entertainment, and recreation	25 091	26 006	26 643	27 814	28 460	29 706	30 998
Accommodation and food services	11 634	11 865	12 059	12 477	12 728	13 188	13 485
Other services, except public administration	20 941	21 812	22 303	23 135	23 824	24 542	25 571
Government and government enterprises	29 434	30 373	31 121	32 432	33 430	33 983	34 800

Table IN-9. Employment Characteristics by Family Type

(Number, percent.)

Family type and labor force status	2005		2006		2007	
	Total	Families with own children under 18 years	Total	Families with own children under 18 years	Total	Families with own children under 18 years
TOTAL FAMILIES	1 639 949	764 563	1 645 031	763 834	1 662 403	765 595
FAMILY TYPE AND LABOR FORCE STATUS						
Married Coupled Families	1 261 777	528 393	1 248 625	518 041	1 265 979	522 254
Both husband and wife in labor force	54.5	66.0	56.3	68.6	55.8	68.6
Husband in labor force, wife not in labor force	21.6	27.0	21.1	26.2	21.6	25.9
Wife in labor force, husband not in labor force	7.1	3.7	6.8	3.6	7.0	3.6
Both husband and wife not in labor force	16.8	3.3	15.8	1.6	15.6	2.0
Other Families	378 172	236 170	396 406	245 793	396 424	243 341
Female householder, no husband present	73.4	75.2	71.6	73.8	72.6	74.8
In labor force	52.4	60.5	52.3	60.6	53.2	61.4
Not in labor force	21.0	14.7	19.4	13.2	19.5	13.5
Male householder, no wife present	26.6	24.8	28.4	26.2	27.4	25.2
In labor force	21.7	22.1	23.4	24.1	22.1	22.9
Not in labor force	4.9	2.7	5.0	2.1	5.3	2.2

Table IN-10. School Enrollment and Educational Attainment, 2007

(Number, percent.)

Item	State	U.S.
Enrollment		
Total population 3 years and over	6 084 869	289 295 761
Enrolled in school	1 669 122	79 329 527
Enrolled in preschool (percent)	6.0	6.2
Enrolled in grades K-12 (percent)	68.3	67.6
Enrolled in college or graduate school (percent)	25.7	26.2
Attainment		
Total population 25 years and over	4 143 519	197 892 369
Less than a high school diploma (percent)	14.2	15.5
High school diploma or more (percent)	85.8	84.5
Bachelor's degree or more (percent)	22.1	27.5
Graduate degree or more (percent)	7.9	10.1

Table IN-11. Educational Indicators

(Number, percent.)

Item	State	U.S.
Public Schools, 2006–2007 (except where noted)		
Number of school districts	367	17 742
Number of schools	1 969	99 639
Number of students	1 045 940	49 315 842
Student-teacher ratio	17.0	15.5
Expenditures per student (dollars)	$9 080	. . .
Averaged freshman graduation rate, 2005–2006	73.3	. . .
Dropout rate, grades 9–12, 2005–2006	2.9	3.7
Students eligible for free or reduced-price lunch (percent)	37.5	41.2
English-language learners (percent)	4.1	5.1
Students with IEP (percent)	17.1	12.7
Private Schools, 2007–2008 (except where noted)		
Number of schools	807	33 740
Number of students	104 062	5 072 451
High school graduates, 2006–2007	4 788	306 605
Student-teacher ratio	12.8	11.1

Table IN-12. Reported Voting and Registration of the Voting-Age Population, November 2008

(Number in thousands, percent.)

Item	Total population	Total citizen population	Registered			Voted		
			Total registered	Percent registered (total population)	Percent registered (total citizen population)	Total voted	Percent voted (total population)	Percent voted (total citizen population)
U.S. total	225 499	206 072	146 311	64.9	71.0	131 144	58.2	63.6
State total	4 686	4 562	3 105	66.3	68.1	2 758	58.8	60.5
Sex								
Male	2 280	2 207	1 465	64.3	66.4	1 290	56.6	58.4
Female	2 406	2 354	1 640	68.2	69.6	1 468	61.0	62.3
Race								
White alone	4 264	4 156	2 851	66.9	68.6	2 516	59.0	60.5
White non-Hispanic alone	4 080	4 067	2 811	68.9	69.1	2 485	60.9	61.1
Black alone	370	360	228	61.5	63.3	219	59.2	60.9
Asian alone	19	13	3	. . .	. . .	3	. . .	. . .
Hispanic (of any race)	196	102	45	23.0	44.5	36	18.3	35.3
White alone or in combination	4 285	4 176	2 866	66.9	68.6	2 527	59.0	60.5
Black alone or in combination	381	371	236	61.9	63.5	225	58.9	60.5
Asian alone or in combination	21	15	5	. . .	. . .	5	. . .	. . .

Table IN-13. Crime

(Number, rate per 100,000.)

Item	State			U.S.		
	2007	2008	Percent change	2007	2008	Percent change
Population	6 345 289	6 376 792	0.5	301 621 157	304 059 724	0.8
VIOLENT CRIME						
Number	21 165	21 283	0.6	1 408 337	1 382 012	-1.9
Rate	333.6	333.8	0.1	466.9	454.5	-2.7
Murder and Nonnegligent Manslaughter						
Number	356	327	-8.1	16 929	16 272	-3.9
Rate	5.6	5.1	-8.6	5.6	5.4	-4.7
Forcible Rape						
Number	1 742	1 720	-1.3	90 427	89 000	-1.6
Rate	27.5	27.0	-1.8	30.0	29.3	-2.4
Robbery						
Number	7 872	7 532	-4.3	445 125	441 855	-0.7
Rate	124.1	118.1	-4.8	147.6	145.3	-1.5
Aggravated Assault						
Number	11 195	11 704	4.5	855 856	834 885	-2.5
Rate	176.4	183.5	4.0	283.8	274.6	-3.2
PROPERTY CRIME						
Number	215 526	212 715	-1.3	9 843 481	9 767 915	-0.8
Rate	3 396.6	3 335.8	-1.8	3 263.5	3 212.5	-1.6
Burglary						
Number	46 919	48 645	3.7	2 179 140	2 222 196	2.0
Rate	739.4	762.8	3.2	722.5	730.8	1.2
Larceny-Theft						
Number	149 050	146 615	-1.6	6 568 572	6 588 873	0.3
Rate	2 349.0	2 299.2	-2.1	2 177.8	2 167.0	-0.5
Motor Vehicle Theft						
Number	19 557	17 455	-10.7	1 095 769	956 846	-12.7
Rate	308.2	273.7	-11.2	363.3	314.7	-13.4

Table IN-14. State Government Finances, 2007

(Dollars, percent distribution.)

Item	Thousands of dollars	Percent distribution
Total Revenue	32 429 387	X
General revenue	27 337 514	84.3
Intergovernmental revenue	7 941 998	24.5
Taxes	14 008 033	43.2
General sales	5 423 501	16.7
Selective sales	2 328 728	7.2
License taxes	496 368	1.5
Individual income tax	4 615 605	14.2
Corporate income tax	987 111	3.0
Other taxes	156 720	0.5
Current charges	3 136 281	9.7
Miscellaneous general revenue	2 251 202	6.9
Utility revenue	0	0.0
Liquor store revenue	0	0.0
Insurance trust revenue	5 091 873	15.7
Total Expenditure	28 809 586	100.0
Intergovernmental expenditure	8 178 674	28.4
Direct expenditure	20 630 912	71.6
Current operation	14 914 519	51.8
Capital outlay	1 906 332	6.6
Insurance benefits and repayments	2 249 832	7.8
Assistance and subsidies	694 551	2.4
Interest on debt	865 678	3.0
Exhibit: Salaries and wages	3 695 037	12.8
Total Expenditure	28 809 586	100.0
General expenditure	26 522 496	92.1
Intergovernmental expenditure	8 178 674	28.4
Direct expenditure	18 343 822	63.7
Education	10 317 966	35.8
Public welfare	6 823 359	23.7
Hospitals	247 022	0.9
Health	587 329	2.0
Highways	1 689 200	5.9
Police protection	229 609	0.8
Correction	632 737	2.2
Natural resources	288 238	1.0
Parks and recreation	73 251	0.3
Government administration	669 180	2.3
Interest on general debt	865 678	3.0
Other and unallocable	4 098 927	14.2
Utility expenditure	37 258	0.1
Liquor store expenditure	0	0.0
Insurance trust expenditure	2 249 832	7.8
Debt at End of Fiscal Year	19 180 194	X
Cash and Security Holdings	63 337 852	X

Table IN-15. State Government Tax Collections, 2008

(Dollars, percent distribution.)

Item	Thousands of dollars	Percent distribution
Total Taxes	14 916 295	X
Property taxes	7 170	0.0
Sales and gross receipts	8 196 096	54.9
General sales and gross receipts	5 738 829	38.5
Selective sales taxes	2 457 267	16.5
Alcoholic beverages	44 707	0.3
Amusements	817 631	5.5
Insurance premiums	188 794	1.3
Motor fuels	856 301	5.7
Pari-mutuels	4 226	0.0
Public utilities	14 842	0.1
Tobacco products	519 871	3.5
Other selective sales	10 895	0.1
Licenses	799 999	5.4
Alcoholic beverages	10 719	0.1
Amusements	304 930	2.0
Corporation	3 364	0.0
Hunting and fishing	16 709	0.1
Motor vehicle	190 165	1.3
Motor vehicle operators	226 096	1.5
Occupation and business, NEC	43 592	0.3
Other licenses	4 424	0.0
Income taxes	5 747 018	38.5
Individual income	4 837 524	32.4
Corporation net income	909 494	6.1
Other taxes	166 012	1.1
Death and gift	165 582	1.1
Severance	430	0.0

Table IN-16. Agriculture

(Number, acres, and dollars.)

Item	2002		2007		Percent change, 2002–2007
	Number	Percent of total	Number	Percent of total	
Number of farms	60 296		60 938		1.1
Farm Size					
Average size of farm (acres)	250		242		-3.2
Farms by size (number of farms)					
Fewer than 50 acres	24 031	39.9	29 253	48.0	21.7
50 to 499 acres	27 954	46.4	24 005	39.4	-14.1
500 acres or more	8 311	13.8	7 680	12.6	-7.6
Land (Acres)					
Total land in farms	15 058 670		14 773 184		-1.9
Total cropland	12 909 002	85.7	12 716 037	86.1	-1.5
Total harvested cropland	11 937 370	79.3	12 108 940	82.0	1.4
Irrigated land	313 130	2.1	397 113	2.7	26.8
Value of Sales (Dollars)					
Agricultural products sold ($1,000)	4 783 158		8 271 291		72.9
Average sales per farm	79 328		135 733		71.1
Sales of crops	2 992 747	62.6	5 319 019	64.3	77.7
Sales of livestock, poultry, and their products	1 790 411	37.4	2 952 272	35.7	64.9
Value of Sales (Number of Farms)					
Less than $10,000	32 549	54.0	33 127	54.4	1.8
$10,000 to $99,999	17 386	28.8	15 129	24.8	-13.0
$100,000 to $999,999	9 817	16.3	10 983	18.0	11.9
$1,000,000 or more	544	0.9	1 699	2.8	212.3
Farms by Type of Organization (Number of Farms)					
Family	53 864	89.3	52 553	86.2	-2.4
Partnership	3 463	5.7	4 614	7.6	33.2
Corporation	2 632	4.4	2 978	4.9	13.1
Other: cooperative, estate or trust, institutional, etc	337	0.6	793	1.3	135.3
Value of Land and Buildings (Dollars)					
Estimated market value of land and buildings ($1,000)	52 936 772		38 441 073		-27.4
Land and buildings average value per farm	868 699		637 645		-26.6
Average value per acre	3 583		2 567		-28.4
Government Payments					
Number of farms receiving government payments	26 841	44.5	35 864	58.9	33.6
Payments (thousands of dollars)	224 701		260 809		16.1
Average payment per farm	8 372		7 272		-13.1
Farm Operator Characteristics					
Farm operators whose principal occupation is farming	33 612	55.7	25 510	41.9	-24.1
Farm operators whose principal occupation is other	26 684	44.3	35 428	58.1	32.8
Average age principal operator (years)	53.7		55.0		2.4

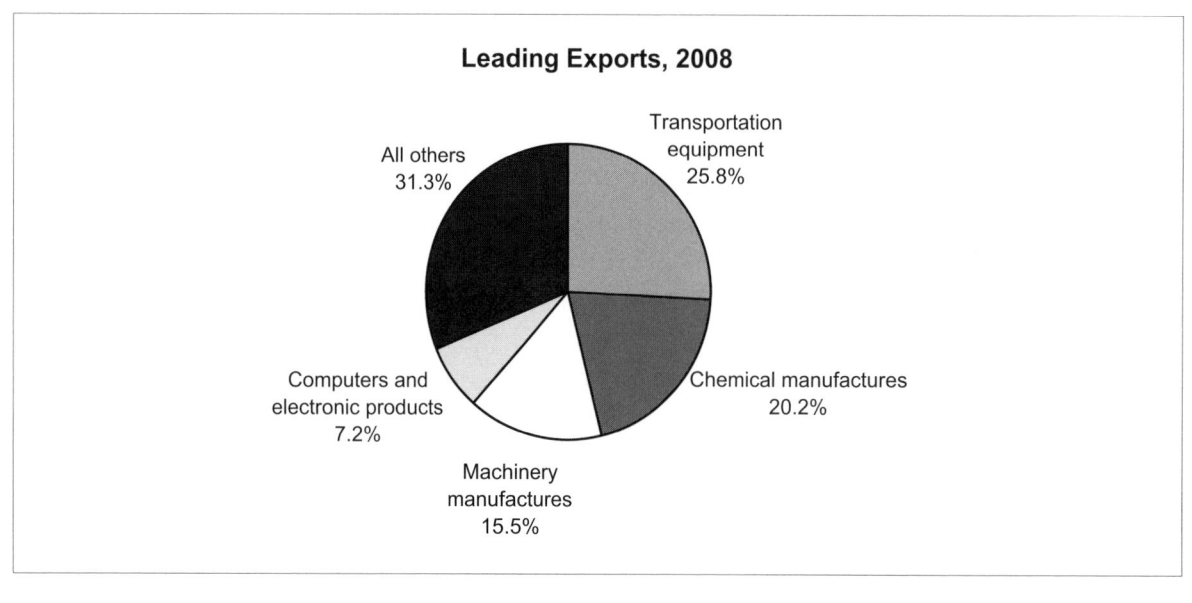

Leading Exports, 2008

All others 31.3%

Transportation equipment 25.8%

Chemical manufactures 20.2%

Machinery manufactures 15.5%

Computers and electronic products 7.2%

IOWA

Facts and Figures

Location: North central United States; bordered on the N by Minnesota, on the E by Wisconsin and Illinois, on the S by Missouri, and on the W by Nebraska and South Dakota

Area: 56,272 sq. mi. (145,743 sq. km.); rank—26th

Population: 3,002,555 (2008 est.); rank—30th

Principal Cities: capital—Des Moines; largest—Des Moines

Statehood: December 28, 1846; 29th state

U.S. Congress: 2 senators, 5 representatives

State Motto: Our Liberties We Prize and Our Rights We Will Maintain

State Song: "The Song of Iowa"

State Nickname: The Hawkeye State

Abbreviations: IA; Ia.

State Symbols: flower—wild prairie rose; tree—oak; bird—Eastern goldfinch

At a Glance

- An estimated 19,564 marriages took place in Iowa in 2008, compared to 7,269 divorces.
- The 2007 home ownership rate in Iowa was 73.7 percent, giving it a ranking of 11th along with Vermont.
- Iowa's median household income in 2007 was $47,292, 31st among the states.
- In Iowa, 11 percent of the population lived below the poverty level in 2007, ranking it 35th.
- In 2006-07, 9.9 percent of Iowans did not have health insurance, compared to 15.5 percent of the total U.S. population.
- In 2007, 3.7 percent of Iowans were unemployed, compared to 4.6 percent nationwide.
- Iowa ranked 37th in the nation with 24.3 percent of its population 25 years old and over having a bachelor's degree in 2007.
- Iowa's violent crime rate in 2007 was 294.7 per 100,000 population, compared to 466.9 for the entire nation.
- Iowa had one physician for every 457 people in 2007, compared to one physician for every 325 people nationwide.
- In the 2008 election, 69.9 percent of Iowa's eligible voters voted, compared to 61.7 percent of eligible voters nationwide.
- Iowa ranked 40th among the states receiving federal aid in 2007, with $1,236 per capita.
- Iowa's gross domestic product was $129 billion in 2007; it ranked 30th among the states.
- With $9.7 billion in exports in 2007, Iowa ranked 28th in exports.
- Iowans consumed 1.2 trillion Btu's of energy in 2006; the state ranked 29th in total consumption.
- In 2007, Iowa exported $5.2 billion worth of agricultural products, about 6.4 percent of the U.S. total.

Table IA-1. Population by Sex, Age, Race, and Hispanic Origin

(Number, percent.)

Sex, age, race, and Hispanic origin	1990	2000	2008	Average annual percent change, 2000–2008
Total Population	2 776 755	2 926 324	3 002 555	0.3
Percent of total U.S. population	1.1	1.0	1.0	X
Sex				
Male	1 344 802	1 435 515	1 482 872	0.4
Female	1 431 953	1 490 809	1 519 683	0.2
Age				
Under 5 years	193 203	188 413	201 321	0.8
5 to 19 years	612 971	639 570	602 223	-0.7
20 to 64 years	1 544 475	1 662 128	1 754 457	0.7
65 years and over	426 106	436 213	444 554	0.2
Median age (years)	34.0	36.6	38.1	X
Race and Hispanic Origin[1]				
One race				
White	2 683 090	2 748 640	2 827 520	0.4
Black	48 090	61 853	80 516	3.4
American Indian and Alaskan Native	7 349	8 989	12 644	4.4
Asian[2]	25 476	36 635	47 486	3.3
Native Hawaiian and Other Pacific Islander	X	1 009	1 523	5.3
Two or more races	X	31 778	32 866	0.4
Hispanic (of any race)	32 647	82 473	126 453	5.5

[1]Data on race in 2000 and 2008 are not comparable to 1990. Individuals could only report one race in the 1990 census but could report one or more races on the 2000 census.
[2]Data in 1990 refer to Asian and Pacific Islanders.

Table IA-2. Marital Status

(Number, percent distribution.)

Sex and marital status	1990	2000	2007
Males, 15 Years and Over	1 033 960	1 126 566	1 173 415
Never married	27.2	28.2	30.3
Now married, except separated	62.6	59.8	56.7
Separated	1.0	0.9	1.2
Widowed	2.6	2.5	2.5
Divorced	6.6	8.5	9.2
Females, 15 Years and Over	1 136 037	1 198 297	1 229 935
Never married	20.5	21.8	23.7
Now married, except separated	56.8	55.8	53.7
Separated	1.2	1.1	1.4
Widowed	13.6	11.6	10.7
Divorced	8.0	9.6	10.5

Table IA-3. Households and Housing Characteristics

(Number, percent, and dollars.)

Item	1990	2000	2007	Average annual percent change, 2000–2007
Total Households	1 064 325	1 149 276	1 214 353	0.8
Family households	740 819	769 684	794 320	0.5
Married-couple family	629 893	633 254	640 275	0.2
Other family	110 926	136 430	154 045	1.7
Male householder, no wife present	25 785	38 160	43 574	1.9
Female householder, no husband present	85 141	98 270	110 471	1.7
Nonfamily households	323 506	379 592	420 033	1.5
Householder living alone	275 466	313 083	345 655	1.4
Householder not living alone	48 040	66 509	74 378	1.6
Housing Characteristics				
Total housing units	1 143 669	1 232 511	1 329 388	1.1
Occupied housing units	1 064 325	1 149 276	1 214 353	0.8
Owner-occupied	745 377	831 419	894 841	1.1
Renter-occupied	318 948	317 857	319 512	0.1
Average size	2.52	2.46	2.37	X
Financial Characteristics				
Median gross rent of renter-occupied housing units (dollars)	336	470	567	2.7
Median monthly owner costs for housing units with a mortgage (dollars)	553	829	1 100	4.1
Median value of owner-occupied housing units (dollars)	45 500	82 500	117 900	5.2

Table IA-4. Median Income and Poverty Status, 2007

(Number, percent.)

Characteristic	State		U.S.	
	Number	Percent	Number	Percent
Median Income				
Households (dollars)	47 292	X	50 740	X
Families (dollars)	59 587	X	61 173	X
Below Poverty Level				
Sex				
Male	136 883	9.6	16 576 071	11.5
Female	181 063	12.4	21 476 176	14.3
Age				
Under 18 years	94 586	13.6	13 097 100	18.0
Related children under 18 years	90 865	13.1	12 728 964	17.6
18 to 64 years	191 737	10.8	21 495 507	11.6
65 years and over	31 623	7.7	3 459 640	9.5

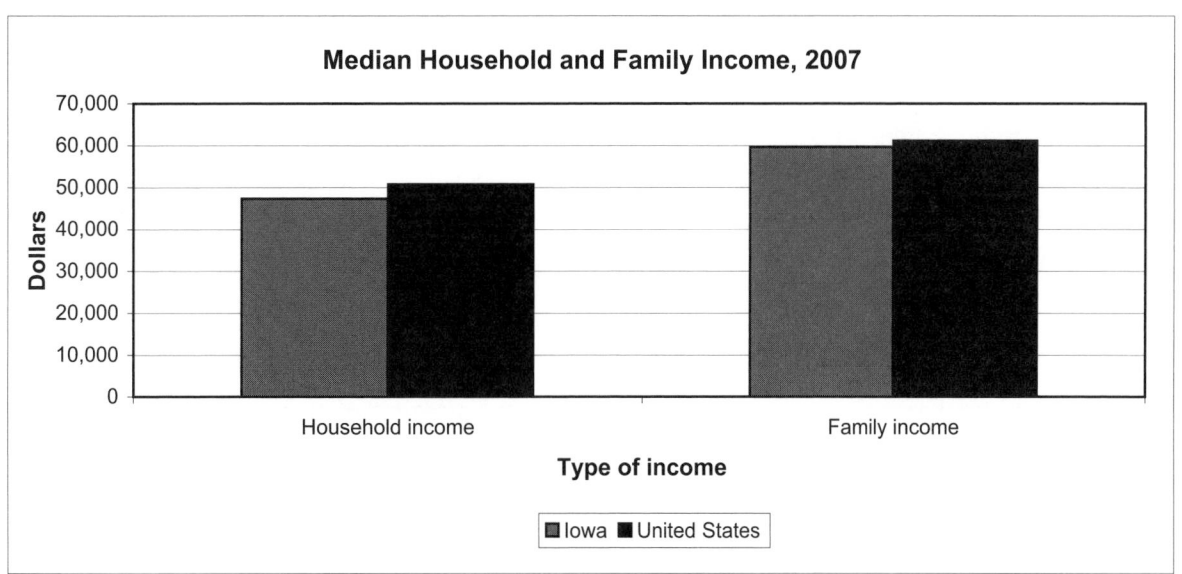

Table IA-5. Health Insurance Coverage Status for All Persons and Children Under 18 Years of Age

(Number, percent.)

Item	2000	2001	2002	2003	2004	2005	2006	2007
ALL PERSONS	2 861	2 861	2 903	2 921	2 906	2 909	2 919	2 970
Covered by Private or Government Health Insurance								
Number	2 622	2 649	2 641	2 604	2 639	2 668	2 612	2 695
Percent	91.6	92.6	91.0	89.1	90.8	91.7	89.5	90.7
Not Covered								
Number	239	211	262	318	266	241	307	275
Percent	8.4	7.4	9.0	10.9	9.2	8.3	10.5	9.3
Percent in the U.S. not covered	13.7	14.1	14.7	15.1	14.9	15.3	15.8	15.3
CHILDREN UNDER 18 YEARS OF AGE	729	717	712	698	683	683	708	709
Covered by Private or Government Health Insurance								
Number	678	684	671	640	642	649	664	675
Percent	93.0	95.4	94.3	91.6	94.1	95.0	93.7	95.2
Not Covered								
Number	51	33	41	59	40	34	44	34
Percent	7.0	4.6	5.7	8.4	5.9	5.0	6.3	4.8
Percent in the U.S. not covered	11.6	11.3	11.2	11.0	10.5	10.9	11.7	11.0

Table IA-6. Employment Status by Demographic Group, Preliminary 2008

(Number, percent.)

Characteristic	Civilian noninstitutional population	Civilian labor force		Employment		Unemployed	
		Number	Percent of population	Number	Percent of population	Number	Unemployment rate
TOTAL	2 329	1 691	72.6	1 623	69.7	68	4.0
Sex							
Men	1 139	887	78.0	849	74.5	39	4.3
Women	1 190	803	68.0	774	65.1	29	3.6
Race, Sex, and Hispanic Origin							
White	2 191	1 591	72.6	1 531	69.9	60	3.8
Men	1 065	830	77.9	796	74.7	34	4.1
Women	1 126	761	67.6	735	65.3	26	3.4
Black or African American	55	42	76.4	37	66.8	5	12.5
Men	32	26	79.4	23	70.0	3	11.9
Women	23	. . .	. . .	. . .	. . .	. . .	. . .
Hispanic	99	78	79.1	72	72.8	6	8.0
Men	53	46	87.3	43	81.7	3	6.4
Women	46	32	69.5	29	62.4	3	10.2
Age							
16 to 19 years	155	97	62.7	85	55.2	12	12.0
20 to 24 years	206	178	86.3	167	81.3	10	5.9
25 to 34 years	391	343	87.8	329	84.3	14	4.0
35 to 44 years	379	337	89.0	326	86.0	11	3.4
45 to 54 years	458	399	87.0	387	84.4	12	3.0
55 to 64 years	351	254	72.3	247	70.5	6	2.5
65 years and over	391	84	21.4	81	20.8	2	2.9

Note: Data in Table 6 are from the Current Population Survey (CPS) and do not match the estimates in Table 7. See notes and definitions for more details.

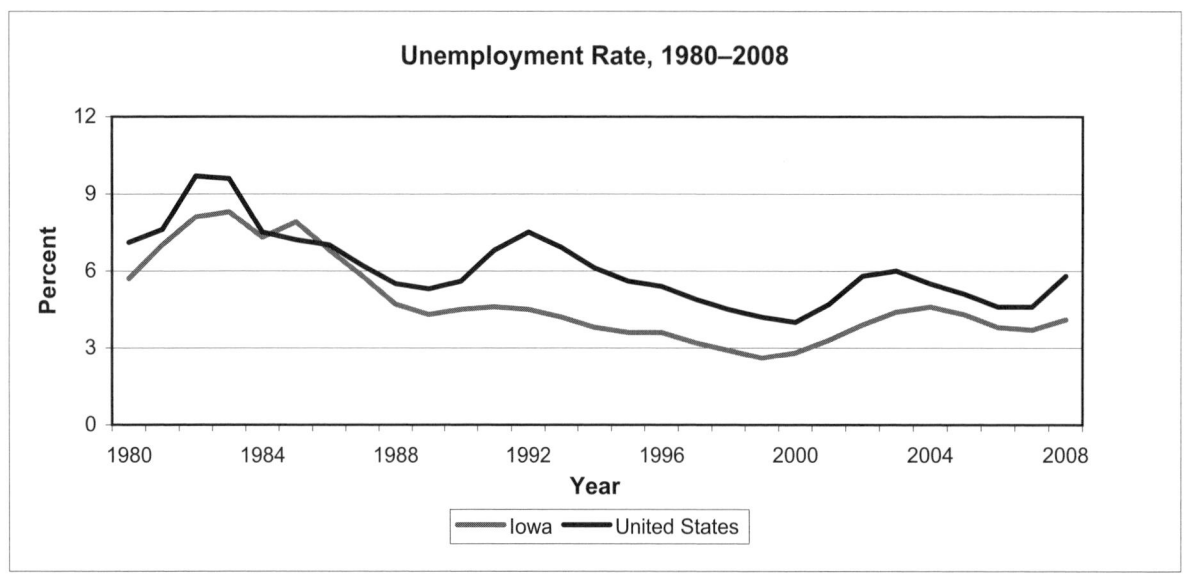

Table IA-7. Employment Status of the Civilian Noninstitutional Population Age 16 Years and Over

(Number, percent.)

Year	Civilian labor force	Civilian participation rate	Employed	Unemployed	Unemployment rate
1998	1 602 865	72.4	1 556 479	46 386	2.9
1999	1 602 634	72.1	1 560 848	41 786	2.6
2000	1 601 920	71.7	1 557 081	44 839	2.8
2001	1 622 012	72.4	1 568 638	53 374	3.3
2002	1 632 108	72.6	1 567 836	64 272	3.9
2003	1 608 241	71.4	1 537 341	70 900	4.4
2004	1 609 738	71.1	1 534 991	74 747	4.6
2005	1 630 003	71.6	1 559 555	70 448	4.3
2006	1 656 855	72.3	1 594 628	62 227	3.8
2007	1 664 431	72.1	1 602 147	62 284	3.7
2008	1 675 981	72.1	1 606 976	69 005	4.1

Table IA-8. Employment and Average Wages by Industry

(Estimates for 2001–2006 are based on the 2002 North American Industry Classification System [NAICS]. Estimates for 2007 are based on the 2007 NAICS.)

Industry	2001	2002	2003	2004	2005	2006	2007
	Number of jobs						
WAGE AND SALARY EMPLOYMENT BY INDUSTRY	1 535 305	1 519 251	1 512 922	1 534 845	1 561 097	1 584 862	1 597 762
Farm Wage and Salary Employment	14 760	14 843	14 474	14 938	17 743	16 276	15 248
Nonfarm Wage and Salary Employment	1 520 545	1 504 408	1 498 448	1 519 907	1 543 354	1 568 586	1 582 514
Private wage and salary employment	1 263 686	1 247 449	1 240 027	1 259 850	1 283 336	1 306 335	1 318 194
Forestry, fishing, hunting, and other	5 971	5 305	5 812	6 366	6 694	6 732	6 934
Mining	2 028	1 947	1 892	2 065	2 113	2 165	2 140
Utilities	8 374	8 803	7 673	7 531	6 963	6 919	7 017
Construction	66 645	66 888	67 507	71 035	74 090	77 022	75 311
Manufacturing	242 218	229 273	221 897	225 036	231 191	233 373	231 435
Durable goods manufacturing	147 575	137 319	132 191	136 822	141 666	143 955	142 521
Nondurable goods manufacturing	94 643	91 954	89 706	88 214	89 525	89 418	88 914
Wholesale trade	68 812	67 466	66 152	66 646	68 021	68 360	68 973
Retail trade	191 995	187 818	185 848	186 099	185 489	185 676	184 387
Transportation and warehousing	49 299	49 553	49 658	51 479	53 518	55 383	56 420
Information	37 963	35 319	33 708	33 698	33 396	33 090	33 728
Finance and insurance	79 866	81 746	83 823	85 314	86 152	89 349	91 717
Real estate and rental and leasing	15 108	15 211	15 160	15 096	15 216	15 025	14 401
Professional and technical services	40 193	39 662	39 321	40 211	41 041	42 812	44 153
Management of companies and enterprises	7 333	7 613	9 738	10 298	11 750	12 579	13 888
Administrative and waste services	61 795	60 591	59 643	60 857	62 760	64 221	66 017
Educational services	33 280	33 162	32 799	34 657	35 624	36 454	37 667
Health care and social assistance	160 222	161 543	162 877	164 513	167 615	171 271	174 002
Arts, entertainment, and recreation	21 487	21 620	20 757	20 749	20 853	21 961	22 164
Accommodation and food services	105 289	105 778	107 098	108 974	112 136	114 761	117 610
Other services, except public administration	65 808	68 151	68 664	69 226	68 714	69 182	70 230
Government and government enterprises	256 859	256 959	258 421	260 057	260 018	262 251	264 320
	Dollars						
AVERAGE WAGES AND SALARIES BY INDUSTRY	28 159	28 952	30 061	31 411	32 287	33 489	34 980
Average Farm Wages and Salaries	22 944	21 088	28 001	32 025	32 211	22 265	34 557
Average Nonfarm Wages and Salaries	28 210	29 030	30 081	31 405	32 403	33 605	34 984
Average private wages and salaries	28 070	28 865	29 924	31 335	32 295	33 521	34 864
Forestry, fishing, hunting, and other	14 156	16 013	18 583	21 834	21 883	22 665	24 898
Mining	36 711	39 069	39 186	40 511	42 624	42 358	44 067
Utilities	55 712	57 634	61 497	67 089	67 281	67 744	74 248
Construction	34 073	34 783	35 510	36 320	38 200	40 638	42 159
Manufacturing	37 114	38 188	39 832	42 142	43 036	44 302	45 990
Durable goods manufacturing	38 829	39 900	41 849	44 272	45 253	46 839	48 535
Nondurable goods manufacturing	34 439	35 630	36 860	38 838	39 528	40 217	41 910
Wholesale trade	36 845	38 256	39 291	41 536	43 447	45 087	47 319
Retail trade	18 871	19 487	19 879	20 359	20 470	20 839	21 392
Transportation and warehousing	33 067	33 597	34 662	36 374	37 203	38 173	39 698
Information	34 890	34 838	36 666	38 662	39 569	41 938	42 299
Finance and insurance	41 556	42 828	45 561	48 184	50 478	53 776	56 020
Real estate and rental and leasing	25 390	26 737	27 811	28 663	29 826	30 614	32 087
Professional and technical services	37 908	38 877	40 204	41 324	43 366	44 898	47 513
Management of companies and enterprises	46 935	50 061	52 842	55 813	60 690	62 937	66 314
Administrative and waste services	19 406	19 834	20 797	21 687	22 004	23 254	24 514
Educational services	18 471	19 518	20 330	20 288	20 466	21 040	21 861
Health care and social assistance	27 380	28 592	29 524	30 966	31 812	32 584	33 716
Arts, entertainment, and recreation	16 616	17 005	17 111	17 743	18 033	18 656	19 265
Accommodation and food services	10 426	10 645	10 961	11 359	11 632	12 034	12 493
Other services, except public administration	18 953	19 499	20 164	20 954	21 506	22 314	23 533
Government and government enterprises	28 895	29 830	30 836	31 742	32 935	34 026	35 582

Table IA-9. Employment Characteristics by Family Type

(Number, percent.)

Family type and labor force status	2005 Total	2005 Families with own children under 18 years	2006 Total	2006 Families with own children under 18 years	2007 Total	2007 Families with own children under 18 years
TOTAL FAMILIES	790 132	359 769	796 970	362 714	794 320	359 409
FAMILY TYPE AND LABOR FORCE STATUS						
Married Coupled Families	638 800	259 889	641 334	262 028	640 275	257 205
Both husband and wife in labor force	60.0	75.3	61.5	77.2	61.5	76.7
Husband in labor force, wife not in labor force	16.3	19.0	16.6	18.3	17.0	19.2
Wife in labor force, husband not in labor force	7.2	3.9	6.8	3.3	6.3	2.7
Both husband and wife not in labor force	16.5	1.8	15.2	1.1	15.2	1.4
Other Families	151 332	99 880	155 636	100 686	154 045	102 204
Female householder, no husband present	74.9	75.6	71.0	74.2	71.7	74.4
In labor force	56.9	62.4	53.1	60.8	54.9	63.2
Not in labor force	18.0	13.2	18.0	13.4	16.8	11.2
Male householder, no wife present	25.1	24.4	29.0	25.8	28.3	25.6
In labor force	20.3	21.5	24.4	23.9	23.2	23.5
Not in labor force	4.9	2.9	4.5	1.9	5.1	2.1

Table IA-10. School Enrollment and Educational Attainment, 2007

(Number, percent.)

Item	State	U.S.
Enrollment		
Total population 3 years and over	2 869 970	289 295 761
Enrolled in school	777 228	79 329 527
Enrolled in preschool (percent)	6.6	6.2
Enrolled in grades K-12 (percent)	66.0	67.6
Enrolled in college or graduate school (percent)	27.4	26.2
Attainment		
Total population 25 years and over	1 974 476	197 892 369
Less than a high school diploma (percent)	10.4	15.5
High school diploma or more (percent)	89.6	84.5
Bachelor's degree or more (percent)	24.3	27.5
Graduate degree or more (percent)	7.5	10.1

Table IA-11. Educational Indicators

(Number, percent.)

Item	State	U.S.
Public Schools, 2006–2007 (except where noted)		
Number of school districts	376	17 742
Number of schools	1 532	99 639
Number of students	483 122	49 315 842
Student-teacher ratio	13.6	15.5
Expenditures per student (dollars)	$8 791	. . .
Averaged freshman graduation rate, 2005–2006	86.9	. . .
Dropout rate, grades 9–12, 2005–2006	2.1	3.7
Students eligible for free or reduced-price lunch (percent)	32.1	41.2
English-language learners (percent)	3.8	5.1
Students with IEP (percent)	14.7	12.7
Private Schools, 2007–2008 (except where noted)		
Number of schools	242	33 740
Number of students	41 796	5 072 451
High school graduates, 2006–2007	2 261	306 605
Student-teacher ratio	12.3	11.1

Table IA-12. Reported Voting and Registration of the Voting-Age Population, November 2008

(Number in thousands, percent.)

Item	Total population	Total citizen population	Registered			Voted		
			Total registered	Percent registered (total population)	Percent registered (total citizen population)	Total voted	Percent voted (total population)	Percent voted (total citizen population)
U.S. total	225 499	206 072	146 311	64.9	71.0	131 144	58.2	63.6
State total	2 244	2 137	1 630	72.6	76.3	1 501	66.9	70.2
Sex								
Male	1 097	1 040	765	69.7	73.6	699	63.7	67.2
Female	1 147	1 096	865	75.4	78.9	801	69.9	73.1
Race								
White alone	2 084	2 005	1 550	74.4	77.3	1 422	68.2	70.9
White non-Hispanic alone	1 986	1 977	1 532	77.1	77.5	1 405	70.7	71.1
Black alone	71	68	42	. . .	. . .	42	. . .	. . .
Asian alone	58	32	11	. . .	. . .	11	. . .	. . .
Hispanic (of any race)	101	31	21	20.7	. . .	20	19.8	. . .
White alone or in combination	2 104	2 025	1 569	74.6	77.5	1 439	68.4	71.1
Black alone or in combination	74	71	45	. . .	. . .	45	. . .	. . .
Asian alone or in combination	61	35	15	. . .	. . .	15	. . .	. . .

Table IA-13. Crime

(Number, rate per 100,000.)

Item	State			U.S.		
	2007	2008	Percent change	2007	2008	Percent change
Population	2 988 046	3 002 555	0.5	301 621 157	304 059 724	0.8
VIOLENT CRIME						
Number	8 805	8 520	-3.2	1 408 337	1 382 012	-1.9
Rate	294.7	283.8	-3.7	466.9	454.5	-2.7
Murder and Nonnegligent Manslaughter						
Number	37	76	105.4	16 929	16 272	-3.9
Rate	1.2	2.5	104.4	5.6	5.4	-4.7
Forcible Rape						
Number	904	888	-1.8	90 427	89 000	-1.6
Rate	30.3	29.6	-2.2	30.0	29.3	-2.4
Robbery						
Number	1 313	1 248	-5.0	445 125	441 855	-0.7
Rate	43.9	41.6	-5.4	147.6	145.3	-1.5
Aggravated Assault						
Number	6 551	6 308	-3.7	855 856	834 885	-2.5
Rate	219.2	210.1	-4.2	283.8	274.6	-3.2
PROPERTY CRIME						
Number	78 154	72 689	-7.0	9 843 481	9 767 915	-0.8
Rate	2 615.6	2 420.9	-7.4	3 263.5	3 212.5	-1.6
Burglary						
Number	16 941	16 450	-2.9	2 179 140	2 222 196	2.0
Rate	567.0	547.9	-3.4	722.5	730.8	1.2
Larceny-Theft						
Number	56 328	51 907	-7.8	6 568 572	6 588 873	0.3
Rate	1 885.1	1 728.8	-8.3	2 177.8	2 167.0	-0.5
Motor Vehicle Theft						
Number	4 885	4 332	-11.3	1 095 769	956 846	-12.7
Rate	163.5	144.3	-11.7	363.3	314.7	-13.4

Table IA-14. State Government Finances, 2007

(Dollars, percent distribution.)

Item	Thousands of dollars	Percent distribution
Total Revenue	19 053 312	X
General revenue	14 119 773	74.1
Intergovernmental revenue	4 378 744	23.0
Taxes	6 469 752	34.0
General sales	1 786 668	9.4
Selective sales	980 958	5.1
License taxes	615 343	3.2
Individual income tax	2 666 601	14.0
Corporate income tax	325 077	1.7
Other taxes	95 105	0.5
Current charges	2 064 465	10.8
Miscellaneous general revenue	1 206 812	6.3
Utility revenue	0	0.0
Liquor store revenue	180 251	0.9
Insurance trust revenue	4 753 288	24.9
Total Expenditure	15 461 766	100.0
Intergovernmental expenditure	3 892 136	25.2
Direct expenditure	11 569 630	74.8
Current operation	7 977 492	51.6
Capital outlay	1 292 035	8.4
Insurance benefits and repayments	1 495 901	9.7
Assistance and subsidies	464 646	3.0
Interest on debt	339 556	2.2
Exhibit: Salaries and wages	2 137 369	13.8
Total Expenditure	15 461 766	100.0
General expenditure	13 842 578	89.5
Intergovernmental expenditure	3 892 136	25.2
Direct expenditure	9 950 442	64.4
Education	5 353 934	34.6
Public welfare	3 612 004	23.4
Hospitals	1 021 701	6.6
Health	229 321	1.5
Highways	1 445 447	9.3
Police protection	94 776	0.6
Correction	259 104	1.7
Natural resources	255 776	1.7
Parks and recreation	37 251	0.2
Government administration	513 798	3.3
Interest on general debt	339 556	2.2
Other and unallocable	679 910	4.4
Utility expenditure	0	0.0
Liquor store expenditure	123 287	0.8
Insurance trust expenditure	1 495 901	9.7
Debt at End of Fiscal Year	6 727 065	X
Cash and Security Holdings	35 280 203	X

Table IA-15. State Government Tax Collections, 2008

(Dollars, percent distribution.)

Item	Thousands of dollars	Percent distribution
Total Taxes	6 892 026	X
Sales and gross receipts	2 960 567	43.0
General sales and gross receipts	1 840 862	26.7
Selective sales taxes	1 119 705	16.2
Alcoholic beverages	14 449	0.2
Amusements	294 467	4.3
Insurance premiums	111 647	1.6
Motor fuels	442 183	6.4
Pari-mutuels	4 102	0.1
Tobacco products	252 857	3.7
Licenses	639 764	9.3
Alcoholic beverages	10 704	0.2
Amusements	22 917	0.3
Corporation	39 825	0.6
Hunting and fishing	26 549	0.4
Motor vehicle	404 006	5.9
Motor vehicle operators	15 000	0.2
Public utility	12 868	0.2
Occupation and business, NEC	105 979	1.5
Other licenses	1 916	0.0
Income taxes	3 195 641	46.4
Individual income	2 848 393	41.3
Corporation net income	347 248	5.0
Other taxes	96 054	1.4
Death and gift	79 783	1.2
Documentary and stock transfer	16 271	0.2

Table IA-16. Agriculture

(Number, acres, and dollars.)

Item	2002		2007		Percent change, 2002–2007
	Number	Percent of total	Number	Percent of total	
Number of farms	90 655		92 856		2.4
Farm Size					
Average size of farm (acres)	350		331		-5.4
Farms by size (number of farms)					
Fewer than 50 acres	21 089	23.3	26 533	28.6	25.8
50 to 499 acres	48 969	54.0	47 046	50.7	-3.9
500 acres or more	20 597	22.7	19 277	20.8	-6.4
Land (Acres)					
Total land in farms	31 729 490		30 747 550		-3.1
Total cropland	27 153 291	85.6	26 316 332	85.6	-3.1
Total harvested cropland	23 994 343	75.6	23 799 380	77.4	-0.8
Irrigated land	142 109	0.4	189 518	0.6	33.4
Value of Sales (Dollars)					
Agricultural products sold ($1,000)	12 273 634		20 418 096		66.4
Average sales per farm	135 388		219 890		62.4
Sales of crops	6 071 272	49.5	10 343 585	50.7	70.4
Sales of livestock, poultry, and their products	6 202 362	50.5	10 074 511	49.3	62.4
Value of Sales (Number of Farms)					
Less than $10,000	32 075	35.4	35 816	38.6	11.7
$10,000 to $99,999	31 165	34.4	23 982	25.8	-23.0
$100,000 to $999,999	25 897	28.6	28 845	31.1	11.4
$1,000,000 or more	1 518	1.7	4 213	4.5	177.5
Farms by Type of Organization (Number of Farms)					
Family	78 699	86.8	77 452	83.4	-1.6
Partnership	5 792	6.4	6 990	7.5	20.7
Corporation	5 279	5.8	6 509	7.0	23.3
Other: cooperative, estate or trust, institutional, etc	885	1.0	1 905	2.1	115.3
Value of Land and Buildings (Dollars)					
Estimated market value of land and buildings ($1,000)	104 186 583		64 154 298		-38.4
Land and buildings average value per farm	1 122 023		707 730		-36.9
Average value per acre	3 388		2 005		-40.8
Government Payments					
Number of farms receiving government payments	63 074	69.6	74 939	80.7	18.8
Payments (thousands of dollars)	538 896		706 286		31.1
Average payment per farm	8 544		9 425		10.3
Farm Operator Characteristics					
Farm operators whose principal occupation is farming	61 935	68.3	48 637	52.4	-21.5
Farm operators whose principal occupation is other	28 720	31.7	44 219	47.6	54.0
Average age principal operator (years)	54.3		56.1		3.3

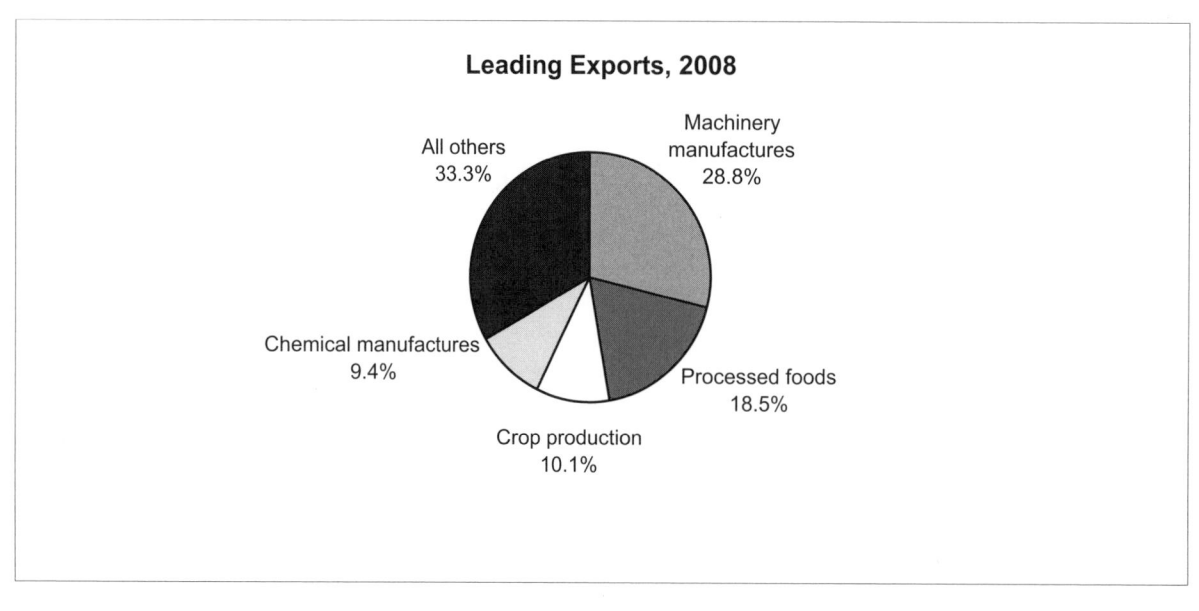

Leading Exports, 2008

All others 33.3%
Machinery manufactures 28.8%
Chemical manufactures 9.4%
Crop production 10.1%
Processed foods 18.5%

KANSAS

Facts and Figures

Location: Central United States; bordered on the N by Nebraska, on the E by Missouri, on the S by Oklahoma, and on the W by Colorado

Area: 82,277 sq. mi. (213,096 sq. km.); rank—15th

Population: 2,802,134 (2008 est.); rank—33rd

Principal Cities: capital—Topeka; largest—Wichita.

Statehood: January 29, 1861; 34th state

U.S. Congress: 2 senators, 4 representatives

State Motto: *Ad astra per aspera* ("To the stars through difficulties")

State Song: "Home on the Range"

State Nicknames: The Sunflower State; The Jayhawk State

Abbreviations: KS; Kan.; Kans.

State Symbols: flower—wild native sunflower; tree—cottonwood; bird—Western meadowlark

At a Glance

- With an increase in population of 4.2 percent, Kansas ranked 34th among the states in growth from 2000 to 2008.
- An estimated 18,693 marriages took place in Kansas in 2008, compared to 9,971 divorces.
- The 2007 home ownership rate in Kansas was 69.4 percent, giving it a ranking of 34th along with Illinois.
- Kansas's median household income in 2007 was $47,451, 29th among the states.
- In Kansas, 11.2 percent of the population lived below the poverty level in 2007, ranking it 33rd along with Nebraska.
- In 2006-07, 12.5 percent of Kansans did not have health insurance, compared to 15.5 percent of the total U.S. population.
- In 2007, 4.1 percent of Kansans were unemployed, compared to 4.6 percent nationwide.
- Kansas ranked 16th in the nation with 28.8 percent of its population 25 years old and over having a bachelor's degree in 2007.
- Kansas's violent crime rate in 2007 was 452.7 per 100,000 population, compared to 466.9 for the entire nation.
- Kansas had one physician for every 387 people in 2007, compared to one physician for every 325 people nationwide.
- In the 2008 election, 62.5 percent of Kansas's eligible voters voted, compared to 61.7 percent of eligible voters nationwide.
- Kansas ranked 41st among the states receiving federal aid in 2007, with $1,229 per capita.
- Kansas's gross domestic product was $117 billion in 2007; it ranked 32nd among the states.
- With $10.3 billion in exports in 2007, Kansas ranked 27th in exports.
- Kansans consumed 1.1 trillion Btu's of energy in 2006; the state ranked 32nd in total consumption.
- In 2007, Kansas exported $3.8 billion worth of agricultural products, about 4.7 percent of the U.S. total.

Table KS-1. Population by Sex, Age, Race, and Hispanic Origin

(Number, percent.)

Sex, age, race, and Hispanic origin	1990	2000	2008	Average annual percent change, 2000–2008
Total Population	2 477 574	2 688 418	2 802 134	0.5
Percent of total U.S. population	1.0	1.0	0.9	X
Sex				
Male	1 214 645	1 328 474	1 391 821	0.6
Female	1 262 929	1 359 944	1 410 313	0.5
Age				
Under 5 years	188 390	188 708	202 529	0.9
5 to 19 years	547 630	609 710	579 901	-0.6
20 to 64 years	1 398 983	1 533 771	1 652 998	0.9
65 years and over	342 571	356 229	366 706	0.4
Median age (years)	32.8	35.2	36.2	X
Race and Hispanic Origin[1]				
One race				
White	2 231 986	2 313 944	2 485 597	0.9
Black	143 076	154 198	172 342	1.4
American Indian and Alaskan Native	21 965	24 936	28 895	1.9
Asian[2]	31 750	46 806	62 468	3.7
Native Hawaiian and Other Pacific Islander	X	1 313	2 131	6.2
Two or more races	X	56 496	50 701	-1.3
Hispanic (of any race)	93 670	188 252	255 409	3.9

[1]Data on race in 2000 and 2008 are not comparable to 1990. Individuals could only report one race in the 1990 census but could report one or more races on the 2000 census.
[2]Data in 1990 refer to Asian and Pacific Islanders.

Table KS-2. Marital Status

(Number, percent distribution.)

Sex and marital status	1990	2000	2007
Males, 15 Years and Over	924 895	1 025 114	1 079 349
Never married	26.5	27.4	29.9
Now married, except separated	62.3	59.9	56.4
Separated	1.1	1.1	1.4
Widowed	2.4	2.3	2.7
Divorced	7.8	9.2	9.7
Females, 15 Years and Over	988 835	1 075 542	1 121 373
Never married	19.2	20.8	22.9
Now married, except separated	57.5	56.4	53.1
Separated	1.3	1.3	1.5
Widowed	12.4	10.6	10.0
Divorced	9.6	10.9	12.5

Table KS-3. Households and Housing Characteristics

(Number, percent, and dollars.)

Item	1990	2000	2007	Average annual percent change, 2000–2007
Total Households	944 726	1 037 891	1 088 835	0.7
Family households	658 600	701 547	728 136	0.5
Married-couple family	552 495	567 924	575 169	0.2
Other family	106 105	133 623	152 967	2.0
Male householder, no wife present	24 672	36 962	44 618	2.7
Female householder, no husband present	81 433	96 661	108 349	1.6
Nonfamily households	286 126	336 344	360 699	1.0
Householder living alone	245 156	280 387	302 756	1.1
Householder not living alone	40 970	55 957	57 943	0.5
Housing Characteristics				
Total housing units	1 044 112	1 131 200	1 219 100	1.1
Occupied housing units	944 726	1 037 891	1 088 835	0.7
Owner-occupied	641 762	718 703	763 887	0.9
Renter-occupied	302 964	319 188	324 948	0.3
Average size	2.53	2.51	2.47	X
Financial Characteristics				
Median gross rent of renter-occupied housing units (dollars)	372	498	623	3.3
Median monthly owner costs for housing units with a mortgage (dollars)	628	888	1 169	4.0
Median value of owner-occupied housing units (dollars)	51 800	83 500	121 200	5.5

Table KS-4. Median Income and Poverty Status, 2007

(Number, percent.)

Characteristic	State		U.S.	
	Number	Percent	Number	Percent
Median Income				
Households (dollars)	47 451	X	50 740	X
Families (dollars)	60 510	X	61 173	X
Below Poverty Level				
Sex				
Male	134 431	10.1	16 576 071	11.5
Female	165 779	12.2	21 476 176	14.3
Age				
Under 18 years	99 590	14.6	13 097 100	18.0
Related children under 18 years	94 540	13.9	12 728 964	17.6
18 to 64 years	173 576	10.4	21 495 507	11.6
65 years and over	27 044	8.1	3 459 640	9.5

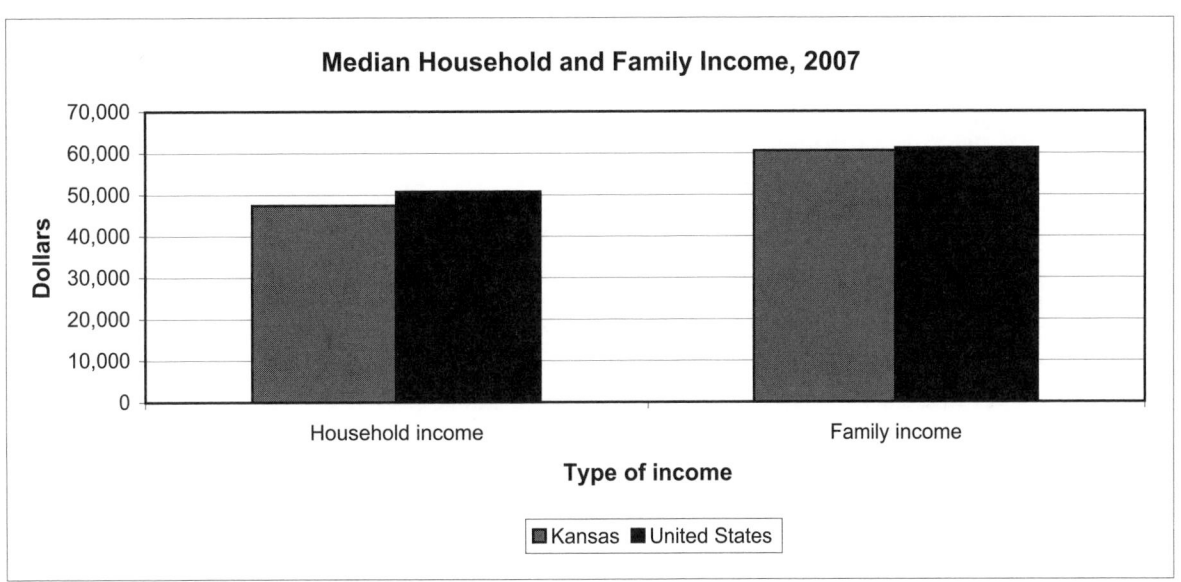

Table KS-5. Health Insurance Coverage Status for All Persons and Children Under 18 Years of Age

(Number, percent.)

Item	2000	2001	2002	2003	2004	2005	2006	2007
ALL PERSONS	2 653	2 642	2 685	2 683	2 674	2 695	2 723	2 722
Covered by Private or Government Health Insurance								
Number	2 379	2 354	2 419	2 408	2 388	2 417	2 387	2 376
Percent	89.7	89.1	90.1	89.7	89.3	89.7	87.7	87.3
Not Covered								
Number	274	288	266	275	286	278	335	345
Percent	10.3	10.9	9.9	10.3	10.7	10.3	12.3	12.7
Percent in the U.S. not covered	13.7	14.1	14.7	15.1	14.9	15.3	15.8	15.3
CHILDREN UNDER 18 YEARS OF AGE	676	638	711	704	687	692	697	710
Covered by Private or Government Health Insurance								
Number	605	590	654	661	644	648	646	655
Percent	89.6	92.5	92.0	94.0	93.7	93.8	92.7	92.3
Not Covered								
Number	71	48	57	42	44	43	51	54
Percent	10.4	7.5	8.0	6.0	6.3	6.2	7.3	7.7
Percent in the U.S. not covered	11.6	11.3	11.2	11.0	10.5	10.9	11.7	11.0

Table KS-6. Employment Status by Demographic Group, Preliminary 2008

(Number, percent.)

Characteristic	Civilian noninstitutional population	Civilian labor force		Employment		Unemployed	
		Number	Percent of population	Number	Percent of population	Number	Unemployment rate
TOTAL	2 120	1 509	71.2	1 442	68.0	67	4.5
Sex							
Men	1 034	802	78.0	767	74.2	35	4.3
Women	1 086	707	65.0	675	62.1	33	4.6
Race, Sex, and Hispanic Origin							
White	1 865	1 334	71.5	1 281	68.7	54	4.0
Men	910	712	78.2	683	75.1	28	4.0
Women	955	623	65.2	597	62.5	25	4.1
Black or African American	120	83	68.9	74	61.6	9	10.7
Men	58	42	72.1	38	65.6	4	9.0
Women	62	41	65.8	36	57.8	5	12.3
Hispanic	127	100	78.3	92	72.1	8	7.8
Men	65	57	87.9	53	81.8	4	6.9
Women	62	43	68.3	39	62.1	4	9.0
Age							
16 to 19 years	160	86	53.7	76	47.3	10	11.9
20 to 24 years	199	164	82.3	150	75.3	14	8.5
25 to 34 years	361	318	88.0	303	83.8	15	4.7
35 to 44 years	349	300	85.8	289	82.6	11	3.7
45 to 54 years	402	343	85.4	333	82.9	10	2.9
55 to 64 years	320	228	71.3	223	69.7	5	2.2
65 years and over	328	70	21.5	68	20.8	2	3.3

Note: Data in Table 6 are from the Current Population Survey (CPS) and do not match the estimates in Table 7. See notes and definitions for more details.

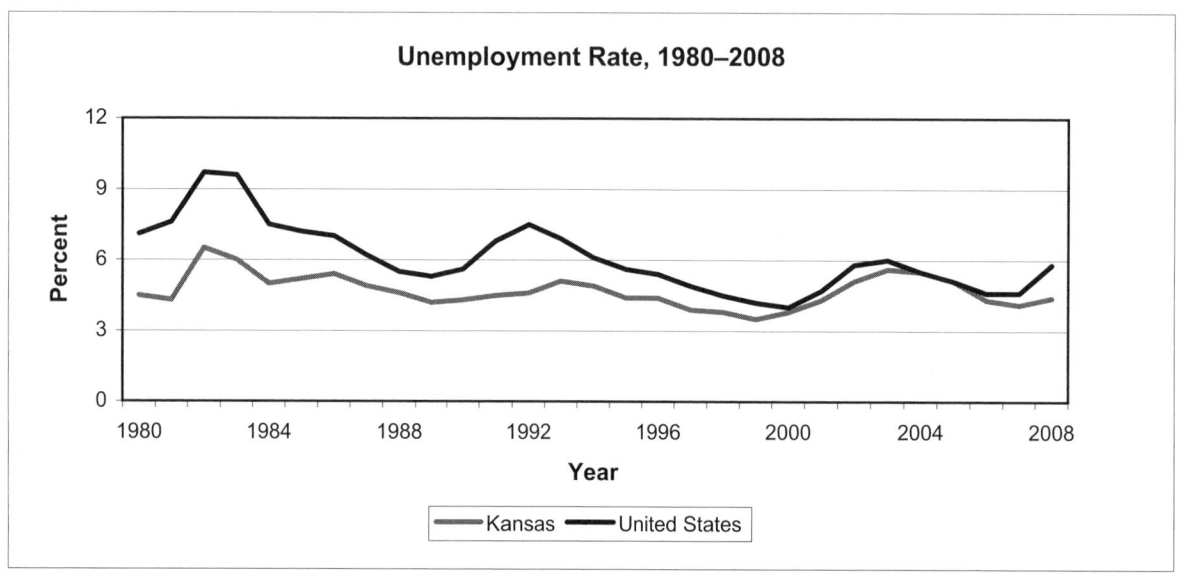

Table KS-7. Employment Status of the Civilian Noninstitutional Population Age 16 Years and Over

(Number, percent.)

Year	Civilian labor force	Civilian participation rate	Employed	Unemployed	Unemployment rate
1998	1 401 588	71.0	1 348 793	52 795	3.8
1999	1 409 556	70.8	1 359 908	49 648	3.5
2000	1 405 104	70.2	1 351 988	53 116	3.8
2001	1 408 103	69.9	1 347 715	60 388	4.3
2002	1 424 054	70.2	1 350 960	73 094	5.1
2003	1 445 385	70.8	1 364 787	80 598	5.6
2004	1 462 277	71.2	1 381 343	80 934	5.5
2005	1 468 018	70.9	1 393 319	74 699	5.1
2006	1 474 044	70.8	1 410 048	63 996	4.3
2007	1 485 237	70.7	1 425 049	60 188	4.1
2008	1 496 943	70.7	1 431 340	65 603	4.4

Table KS-8. Employment and Average Wages by Industry

(Estimates for 2001–2006 are based on the 2002 North American Industry Classification System [NAICS]. Estimates for 2007 are based on the 2007 NAICS.)

Industry	2001	2002	2003	2004	2005	2006	2007
	Number of jobs						
WAGE AND SALARY EMPLOYMENT BY INDUSTRY	1 441 132	1 426 161	1 408 988	1 417 943	1 423 860	1 447 606	1 479 021
Farm Wage and Salary Employment	13 188	11 974	12 504	12 715	11 411	11 290	11 811
Nonfarm Wage and Salary Employment	1 427 944	1 414 187	1 396 484	1 405 228	1 412 449	1 436 316	1 467 210
Private wage and salary employment	1 144 643	1 127 719	1 108 916	1 118 922	1 127 185	1 145 848	1 170 839
Forestry, fishing, hunting, and other	5 047	5 178	5 194	5 160	5 602	5 165	5 216
Mining	7 061	6 536	6 541	7 088	7 619	8 843	9 374
Utilities	7 499	7 028	7 137	7 226	7 298	7 313	7 361
Construction	67 007	65 479	65 272	65 496	65 137	66 999	68 078
Manufacturing	196 212	184 987	175 149	177 765	181 504	184 158	187 163
Durable goods manufacturing	125 217	113 628	105 798	108 093	112 494	115 452	118 403
Nondurable goods manufacturing	70 995	71 359	69 351	69 672	69 010	68 706	68 760
Wholesale trade	61 784	61 884	60 032	60 278	60 154	60 145	61 666
Retail trade	161 788	158 783	156 263	155 281	152 201	152 017	153 531
Transportation and warehousing	46 855	45 857	45 843	45 810	45 983	47 087	48 337
Information	51 077	47 427	44 683	41 740	39 720	39 892	41 015
Finance and insurance	54 311	55 876	56 785	56 725	56 860	59 001	60 394
Real estate and rental and leasing	15 952	15 459	15 516	15 734	15 888	15 873	15 916
Professional and technical services	56 823	55 563	54 526	57 937	58 167	60 204	62 507
Management of companies and enterprises	12 352	10 803	10 141	9 636	10 795	11 422	11 774
Administrative and waste services	64 103	64 069	61 867	65 002	69 830	72 346	76 212
Educational services	17 420	17 915	18 056	16 734	16 898	16 629	17 348
Health care and social assistance	142 950	146 111	147 523	151 051	153 035	155 199	159 499
Arts, entertainment, and recreation	14 900	14 734	13 080	14 167	14 324	14 594	14 607
Accommodation and food services	97 138	97 380	98 186	99 765	100 522	102 795	103 723
Other services, except public administration	64 364	66 650	67 122	66 327	65 648	66 166	67 118
Government and government enterprises	283 301	286 468	287 568	286 306	285 264	290 468	296 371
	Dollars						
AVERAGE WAGES AND SALARIES BY INDUSTRY	29 540	30 216	30 948	32 288	33 467	35 328	36 695
Average Farm Wages and Salaries	27 648	27 118	26 651	31 679	30 414	32 638	37 925
Average Nonfarm Wages and Salaries	29 558	30 242	30 987	32 293	33 491	35 349	36 685
Average private wages and salaries	30 174	30 736	31 472	32 688	33 949	35 907	37 228
Forestry, fishing, hunting, and other	17 557	17 952	18 278	18 633	18 102	19 629	21 291
Mining	38 347	36 519	39 569	42 102	44 145	47 255	48 605
Utilities	60 553	65 494	58 617	62 121	64 737	66 677	70 869
Construction	33 658	34 129	34 215	34 775	37 208	39 238	41 174
Manufacturing	39 232	40 530	41 230	42 952	43 737	47 109	48 077
Durable goods manufacturing	41 697	43 397	44 106	45 933	46 718	51 076	51 744
Nondurable goods manufacturing	34 885	35 966	36 842	38 327	38 876	40 443	41 762
Wholesale trade	41 443	42 593	43 650	45 923	48 454	50 913	53 104
Retail trade	19 598	19 961	20 410	20 805	21 325	22 388	22 972
Transportation and warehousing	35 014	35 396	36 552	37 700	38 929	39 828	40 655
Information	45 525	47 699	51 081	55 944	56 331	59 376	63 197
Finance and insurance	41 858	43 017	45 648	47 009	48 711	50 466	52 704
Real estate and rental and leasing	24 871	26 202	26 842	27 860	29 167	30 486	30 863
Professional and technical services	41 912	42 286	42 572	44 171	47 592	50 085	52 570
Management of companies and enterprises	50 430	50 147	52 333	57 143	66 879	77 389	79 557
Administrative and waste services	22 639	23 202	24 164	24 752	26 641	28 944	29 945
Educational services	20 225	20 421	20 971	21 580	22 176	23 740	24 678
Health care and social assistance	28 103	28 830	29 787	30 855	31 855	33 118	34 377
Arts, entertainment, and recreation	14 057	14 525	14 104	14 679	14 777	15 038	15 552
Accommodation and food services	11 442	11 498	12 026	12 648	12 755	13 288	13 253
Other services, except public administration	19 553	20 233	21 032	21 752	22 541	23 409	24 545
Government and government enterprises	27 067	28 295	29 114	30 750	31 683	33 146	34 539

Table KS-9. Employment Characteristics by Family Type

(Number, percent.)

Family type and labor force status	2005		2006		2007	
	Total	Families with own children under 18 years	Total	Families with own children under 18 years	Total	Families with own children under 18 years
TOTAL FAMILIES	715 841	340 729	724 553	343 678	728 136	347 509
FAMILY TYPE AND LABOR FORCE STATUS						
Married Coupled Families	564 704	241 504	571 689	245 631	575 169	252 179
Both husband and wife in labor force	57.7	68.9	59.6	70.2	59.8	70.9
Husband in labor force, wife not in labor force	21.3	25.5	21.0	25.2	20.5	24.3
Wife in labor force, husband not in labor force	6.5	3.6	6.0	3.0	6.3	2.9
Both husband and wife not in labor force	14.5	2.0	13.4	1.6	13.5	1.8
Female householder, no husband present	73.1	75.2	73.2	74.8	70.8	73.8
In labor force	54.8	63.3	56.5	64.3	54.4	63.5
Not in labor force	18.3	11.9	16.7	10.6	16.4	10.3
Male householder, no wife present	26.9	24.8	26.8	25.2	29.2	26.2
In labor force	21.9	22.5	23.0	23.6	24.7	23.8
Not in labor force	5.0	2.3	3.8	1.6	4.5	2.3

Table KS-10. School Enrollment and Educational Attainment, 2007

(Number, percent.)

Item	State	U.S.
Enrollment		
Total population 3 years and over	2 659 851	289 295 761
Enrolled in school	763 888	79 329 527
Enrolled in preschool (percent)	6.6	6.2
Enrolled in grades K-12 (percent)	66.2	67.6
Enrolled in college or graduate school (percent)	27.2	26.2
Attainment		
Total population 25 years and over	1 790 086	197 892 369
Less than a high school diploma (percent)	10.9	15.5
High school diploma or more (percent)	89.1	84.5
Bachelor's degree or more (percent)	28.8	27.5
Graduate degree or more (percent)	9.8	10.1

Table KS-11. Educational Indicators

(Number, percent.)

Item	State	U.S.
Public Schools, 2006–2007 (except where noted)		
Number of school districts	332	17 742
Number of schools	1 428	99 639
Number of students	469 506	49 315 842
Student-teacher ratio	13.3	15.5
Expenditures per student (dollars)	$9 243	. . .
Averaged freshman graduation rate, 2005–2006	77.6	. . .
Dropout rate, grades 9–12, 2005–2006	2.5	3.7
Students eligible for free or reduced-price lunch (percent) ...	38.9	41.2
English-language learners (percent)	6.2	5.1
Students with IEP (percent)	14.0	12.7
Private Schools, 2007–2008 (except where noted)		
Number of schools	246	33 740
Number of students	43 413	5 072 451
High school graduates, 2006–2007	2 378	306 605
Student-teacher ratio	12.4	11.1

Table KS-12. Reported Voting and Registration of the Voting-Age Population, November 2008

(Number in thousands, percent.)

Item	Total population	Total citizen population	Registered			Voted		
			Total registered	Percent registered (total population)	Percent registered (total citizen population)	Total voted	Percent voted (total population)	Percent voted (total citizen population)
U.S. total	225 499	206 072	146 311	64.9	71.0	131 144	58.2	63.6
State total	2 037	1 926	1 343	65.9	69.7	1 219	59.8	63.3
Sex								
Male	992	939	617	62.2	65.7	552	55.7	58.8
Female	1 045	987	726	69.5	73.5	667	63.8	67.5
Race								
White alone	1 762	1 700	1 213	68.8	71.3	1 105	62.7	65.0
White non-Hispanic alone	1 641	1 631	1 174	71.5	72.0	1 069	65.1	65.5
Black alone	120	114	68	56.5	59.6	62	51.3	54.0
Asian alone	70	37	19	. . .	. . .	19	. . .	. . .
Hispanic (of any race)	136	76	43	31.8	56.6	39	28.8	51.3
White alone or in combination	1 811	1 748	1 241	68.5	71.0	1 126	62.2	64.4
Black alone or in combination	131	125	73	55.5	58.2	66	50.7	53.1
Asian alone or in combination	76	43	25	32.4	. . .	23	30.4	. . .

Table KS-13. Crime

(Number, rate per 100,000.)

Item	State			U.S.		
	2007	2008	Percent change	2007	2008	Percent change
Population	2 775 997	2 802 134	0.9	301 621 157	304 059 724	0.8
VIOLENT CRIME						
Number	12 566	11 505	-8.4	1 408 337	1 382 012	-1.9
Rate	452.7	410.6	-9.3	466.9	454.5	-2.7
Murder and Nonnegligent Manslaughter						
Number	107	113	5.6	16 929	16 272	-3.9
Rate	3.9	4.0	4.6	5.6	5.4	-4.7
Forcible Rape						
Number	1 231	1 190	-3.3	90 427	89 000	-1.6
Rate	44.3	42.5	-4.2	30.0	29.3	-2.4
Robbery						
Number	2 016	1 684	-16.5	445 125	441 855	-0.7
Rate	72.6	60.1	-17.2	147.6	145.3	-1.5
Aggravated Assault						
Number	9 212	8 518	-7.5	855 856	834 885	-2.5
Rate	331.8	304.0	-8.4	283.8	274.6	-3.2
PROPERTY CRIME						
Number	102 120	94 635	-7.3	9 843 481	9 767 915	-0.8
Rate	3 678.7	3 377.2	-8.2	3 263.5	3 212.5	-1.6
Burglary						
Number	20 263	19 612	-3.2	2 179 140	2 222 196	2.0
Rate	729.9	699.9	-4.1	722.5	730.8	1.2
Larceny-Theft						
Number	73 293	67 628	-7.7	6 568 572	6 588 873	0.3
Rate	2 640.2	2 413.4	-8.6	2 177.8	2 167.0	-0.5
Motor Vehicle Theft						
Number	8 564	7 395	-13.7	1 095 769	956 846	-12.7
Rate	308.5	263.9	-14.5	363.3	314.7	-13.4

Table KS-14. State Government Finances, 2007

(Dollars, percent distribution.)

Item	Thousands of dollars	Percent distribution
Total Revenue	14 998 530	X
General revenue	12 003 844	80.0
Intergovernmental revenue	3 156 389	21.0
Taxes	6 893 359	46.0
General sales	2 242 025	14.9
Selective sales	815 004	5.4
License taxes	302 685	2.0
Individual income tax	2 744 934	18.3
Corporate income tax	527 427	3.5
Other taxes	261 284	1.7
Current charges	1 207 659	8.1
Miscellaneous general revenue	746 437	5.0
Utility revenue	0	0.0
Liquor store revenue	0	0.0
Insurance trust revenue	2 994 686	20.0
Total Expenditure	13 183 436	100.0
Intergovernmental expenditure	3 869 984	29.4
Direct expenditure	9 313 452	70.6
Current operation	6 582 271	49.9
Capital outlay	1 058 528	8.0
Insurance benefits and repayments	1 201 935	9.1
Assistance and subsidies	171 658	1.3
Interest on debt	299 060	2.3
Exhibit: Salaries and wages	2 965 227	22.5
Total Expenditure	13 183 436	100.0
General expenditure	11 981 501	90.9
Intergovernmental expenditure	3 869 984	29.4
Direct expenditure	8 111 517	61.5
Education	5 329 513	40.4
Public welfare	2 970 898	22.5
Hospitals	296 477	2.2
Health	179 841	1.4
Highways	1 240 990	9.4
Police protection	108 582	0.8
Correction	317 649	2.4
Natural resources	200 618	1.5
Parks and recreation	30 068	0.2
Government administration	429 297	3.3
Interest on general debt	299 060	2.3
Other and unallocable	578 508	4.4
Utility expenditure	0	0.0
Liquor store expenditure	0	0.0
Insurance trust expenditure	1 201 935	9.1
Debt at End of Fiscal Year	5 671 144	X
Cash and Security Holdings	22 063 928	X

Table KS-15. State Government Tax Collections, 2008

(Dollars, percent distribution.)

Item	Thousands of dollars	Percent distribution
Total Taxes	7 159 748	X
Property taxes	79 026	1.1
Sales and gross receipts	3 091 221	43.2
General sales and gross receipts	2 264 747	31.6
Selective sales taxes	826 474	11.5
Alcoholic beverages	106 299	1.5
Amusements	500	0.0
Insurance premiums	133 913	1.9
Motor fuels	431 755	6.0
Pari-mutuels	1 948	0.0
Public utilities	851	0.0
Tobacco products	118 253	1.7
Other selective sales	32 955	0.5
Licenses	303 696	4.2
Alcoholic beverages	2 653	0.0
Amusements	148	0.0
Corporation	54 786	0.8
Hunting and fishing	21 478	0.3
Motor vehicle	172 111	2.4
Motor vehicle operators	17 270	0.2
Public utility	5 373	0.1
Occupation and business, NEC	27 180	0.4
Other licenses	2 697	0.0
Income taxes	3 472 862	48.5
Individual income	2 944 851	41.1
Corporation net income	528 011	7.4
Other taxes	212 943	3.0
Death and gift	44 247	0.6
Severance	168 696	2.4

Table KS-16. Agriculture

(Number, acres, and dollars.)

Item	2002 Number	2002 Percent of total	2007 Number	2007 Percent of total	Percent change, 2002–2007
Number of farms	64 414		65 531		1.7
Farm Size					
Average size of farm (acres)	733		707		-3.5
Farms by size (number of farms)					
Fewer than 50 acres	11 189	17.4	12 164	18.6	8.7
50 to 499 acres	30 932	48.0	33 100	50.5	7.0
500 acres or more	22 293	34.6	20 267	30.9	-9.1
Land (Acres)					
Total land in farms	47 227 944		46 345 827		-1.9
Total cropland	29 542 022	62.6	28 216 064	60.9	-4.5
Total harvested cropland	18 976 719	40.2	19 886 655	42.9	4.8
Irrigated land	2 678 277	5.7	2 762 748	6.0	3.2
Value of Sales (Dollars)					
Agricultural products sold ($1,000)	8 746 244		14 413 182		64.8
Average sales per farm	135 782		219 944		62.0
Sales of crops	2 418 447	27.7	4 887 212	33.9	102.1
Sales of livestock, poultry, and their products	6 327 797	72.3	9 525 971	66.1	50.5
Value of Sales (Number of Farms)					
Less than $10,000	31 140	48.3	31 792	48.5	2.1
$10,000 to $99,999	22 255	34.5	19 550	29.8	-12.2
$100,000 to $999,999	10 317	16.0	12 435	19.0	20.5
$1,000,000 or more	702	1.1	1 754	2.7	149.9
Farms by Type of Organization (Number of Farms)					
Family	57 238	88.9	55 706	85.0	-2.7
Partnership	4 062	6.3	5 549	8.5	36.6
Corporation	2 242	3.5	2 774	4.2	23.7
Other: cooperative, estate or trust, institutional, etc	872	1.4	1 502	2.3	72.2
Value of Land and Buildings (Dollars)					
Estimated market value of land and buildings ($1,000)	42 204 526		32 581 256		-22.8
Land and buildings average value per farm	644 039		505 999		-21.4
Average value per acre	911		687		-24.6
Government Payments					
Number of farms receiving government payments	39 191	60.8	44 433	67.8	13.4
Payments (thousands of dollars)	328 244		427 144		30.1
Average payment per farm	8 375		9 613		14.8
Farm Operator Characteristics					
Farm operators whose principal occupation is farming	40 645	63.1	30 873	47.1	-24.0
Farm operators whose principal occupation is other	23 769	36.9	34 658	52.9	45.8
Average age principal operator (years)	56.0		57.7		3.0

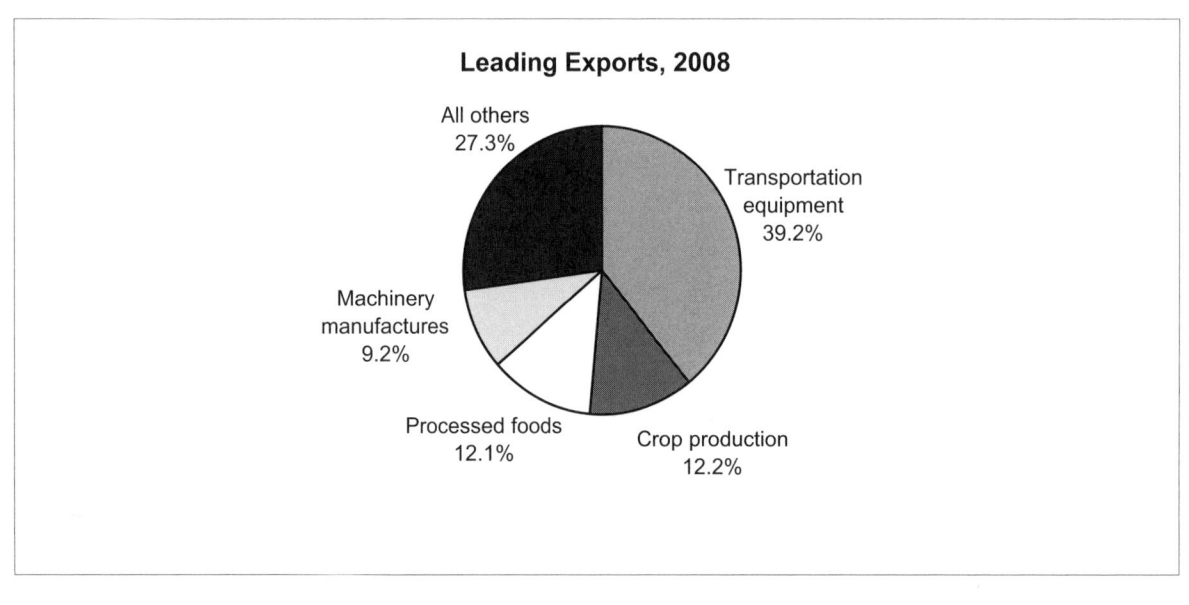

Leading Exports, 2008

All others 27.3%

Transportation equipment 39.2%

Machinery manufactures 9.2%

Processed foods 12.1%

Crop production 12.2%

KENTUCKY

Facts and Figures

Location: East central United States; bordered on the N by Illinois, Indiana, and Ohio, on the E by West Virginia and Virginia, on the S by Tennessee, and on the W by Missouri and Illinois

Area: 40,409 sq. mi. (104,659 sq. km.); rank—37th

Population: 4,269,245 (2008 est.); rank—26th

Principal Cities: capital—Frankfort; largest—Lexington

Statehood: June 1, 1792; 15th state

U.S. Congress: 2 senators, 6 representatives

State Motto: United We Stand, Divided We Fall

State Song: "My Old Kentucky Home"

State Nickname: The Bluegrass State

Abbreviations: KY; Ky.

State Symbols: flower—goldenrod; tree—tulip poplar; bird—cardinal

At a Glance

- With an increase in population of 5.6 percent, Kentucky ranked 28th among the states in growth from 2000 to 2008.
- An estimated 35,239 marriages took place in Kentucky in 2008, compared to 21,029 divorces.
- The 2007 home ownership rate in Kentucky was 72.9 percent, giving it a ranking of 16th along with Pennsylvania.
- Kentucky's median household income in 2007 was $40,267, 47th among the states.
- In Kentucky, 17.3 percent of the population lived below the poverty level in 2007, ranking it 5th.
- In 2006-07, 14.6 percent of Kentuckians did not have health insurance, compared to 15.5 percent of the total U.S. population.
- In 2007, 5.4 percent of Kentuckians were unemployed, compared to 4.6 percent nationwide.
- Kentucky ranked 47th in the nation with 20 percent of its population 25 years old and over having a bachelor's degree in 2007.
- Kentucky's violent crime rate in 2007 was 295 per 100,000 population, compared to 466.9 for the entire nation.
- Kentucky had one physician for every 385 people in 2007, compared to one physician for every 325 people nationwide.
- In the 2008 election, 57.9 percent of Kentucky's eligible voters voted, compared to 61.7 percent of eligible voters nationwide.
- Kentucky ranked 19th among the states receiving federal aid in 2007, with $1,504 per capita.
- Kentucky's gross domestic product was $154 billion in 2007; it ranked 27th among the states.
- With $19.7 billion in exports in 2007, Kentucky ranked 17th in exports.
- Kentuckians consumed 1.97 trillion Btu's of energy in 2006; the state ranked 18th in total consumption.
- In 2007, Kentucky exported $1.2 billion worth of agricultural products, about 1.5 percent of the U.S. total.

Table KY-1. Population by Sex, Age, Race, and Hispanic Origin

(Number, percent.)

Sex, age, race, and Hispanic origin	1990	2000	2008	Average annual percent change, 2000–2008
Total Population	3 685 296	4 041 769	4 269 245	0.7
Percent of total U.S. population	1.5	1.4	1.4	X
Sex				
Male	1 785 235	1 975 368	2 088 142	0.7
Female	1 900 061	2 066 401	2 181 103	0.7
Age				
Under 5 years	250 871	265 901	284 601	0.9
5 to 19 years	825 905	847 743	831 909	-0.2
20 to 64 years	2 141 675	2 423 332	2 586 868	0.8
65 years and over	466 845	504 793	565 867	1.4
Median age (years)	32.9	35.9	37.7	X
Race and Hispanic Origin[1]				
One race				
White	3 391 832	3 640 889	3 838 236	0.7
Black	262 907	295 994	329 225	1.3
American Indian and Alaskan Native	5 769	8 616	11 006	3.1
Asian[2]	17 812	29 744	42 335	4.5
Native Hawaiian and Other Pacific Islander	X	1 460	2 002	4.0
Two or more races	X	42 443	46 441	1.1
Hispanic (of any race)	21 984	59 939	101 981	6.9

[1]Data on race in 2000 and 2008 are not comparable to 1990. Individuals could only report one race in the 1990 census but could report one or more races on the 2000 census.
[2]Data in 1990 refer to Asian and Pacific Islanders.

Table KY-2. Marital Status

(Number, percent distribution.)

Sex and marital status	1990	2000	2007
Males, 15 Years and Over	1 378 871	1 551 174	1 651 196
Never married	26.2	25.9	30.0
Now married, except separated	61.8	59.9	53.5
Separated	1.4	1.5	2.0
Widowed	2.6	2.6	2.8
Divorced	7.9	10.2	11.7
Females, 15 Years and Over	1 514 810	1 665 993	1 762 852
Never married	19.4	19.7	23.1
Now married, except separated	55.8	55.0	49.7
Separated	1.9	2.1	2.4
Widowed	13.2	11.5	11.5
Divorced	9.7	11.8	13.2

Table KY-3. Households and Housing Characteristics

(Number, percent, and dollars.)

Item	1990	2000	2007	Average annual percent change, 2000–2007
Total Households	1 379 782	1 590 647	1 655 767	0.6
Family households	1 015 998	1 104 398	1 114 146	0.1
Married-couple family	816 732	857 944	833 000	-0.4
Other family	199 266	246 454	281 146	1.9
Male householder, no wife present	39 606	58 497	73 423	3.3
Female householder, no husband present	159 660	187 957	207 723	1.4
Nonfamily households	363 784	486 249	541 621	1.6
Householder living alone	321 247	414 095	463 141	1.6
Householder not living alone	42 537	72 154	78 480	1.2
Housing Characteristics				
Total housing units	1 506 845	1 750 927	1 906 198	1.2
Occupied housing units	1 379 782	1 590 647	1 655 767	0.6
Owner-occupied	960 469	1 125 397	1 170 947	0.6
Renter-occupied	419 313	465 250	484 820	0.6
Average size	2.60	2.47	2.49	X
Financial Characteristics				
Median gross rent of renter-occupied housing units (dollars)	319	445	563	3.4
Median monthly owner costs for housing units with a mortgage (dollars)	536	816	1 021	3.3
Median value of owner-occupied housing units (dollars)	50 100	86 700	114 300	4.0

Table KY-4. Median Income and Poverty Status, 2007

(Number, percent.)

Characteristic	State		U.S.	
	Number	Percent	Number	Percent
Median Income				
Households (dollars)	40 267	X	50 740	X
Families (dollars)	50 291	X	61 173	X
Below Poverty Level				
Sex				
Male	309 994	15.5	16 576 071	11.5
Female	404 086	19.1	21 476 176	14.3
Age				
Under 18 years	234 959	23.9	13 097 100	18.0
Related children under 18 years	228 300	23.4	12 728 964	17.6
18 to 64 years	411 912	15.7	21 495 507	11.6
65 years and over	67 209	12.9	3 459 640	9.5

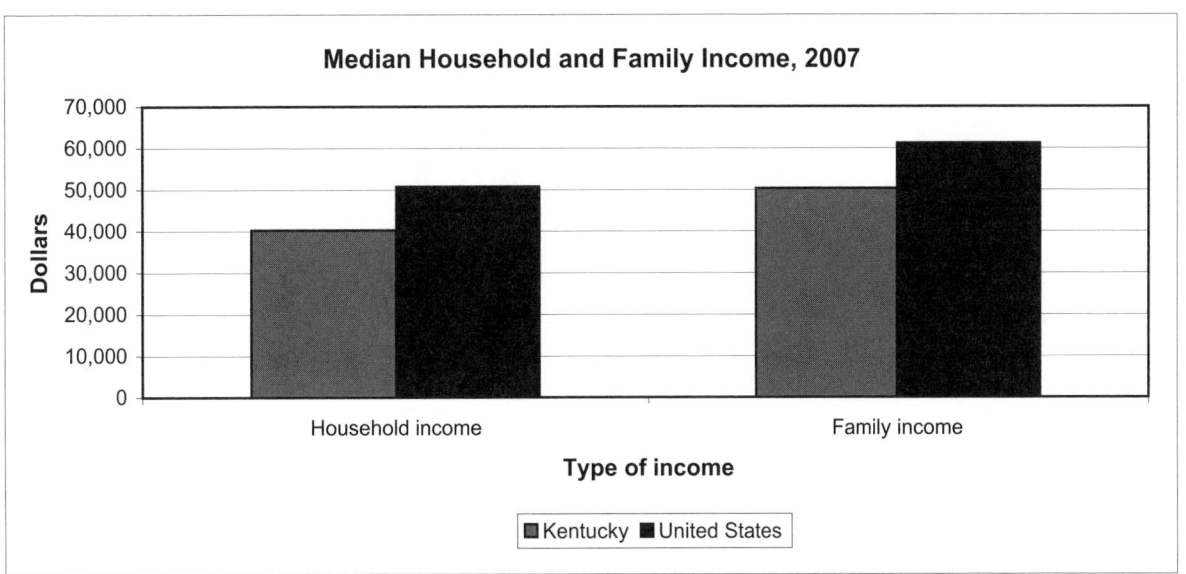

Table KY-5. Health Insurance Coverage Status for All Persons and Children Under 18 Years of Age

(Number, percent.)

Item	2000	2001	2002	2003	2004	2005	2006	2007
ALL PERSONS	4 003	3 996	4 046	4 110	4 074	4 052	4 106	4 207
Covered by Private or Government Health Insurance								
Number	3 482	3 538	3 518	3 570	3 518	3 554	3 467	3 637
Percent	87.0	88.5	86.9	86.9	86.4	87.7	84.4	86.4
Not Covered								
Number	521	459	528	540	556	498	639	570
Percent	13.0	11.5	13.1	13.1	13.6	12.3	15.6	13.6
Percent in the U.S. not covered	13.7	14.1	14.7	15.1	14.9	15.3	15.8	15.3
CHILDREN UNDER 18 YEARS OF AGE	1 006	993	969	1 016	981	991	1 006	1 026
Covered by Private or Government Health Insurance								
Number	918	901	847	912	901	924	908	944
Percent	91.2	90.7	87.4	89.8	91.8	93.3	90.3	92.0
Not Covered								
Number	88	92	122	104	81	67	98	82
Percent	8.8	9.3	12.6	10.2	8.2	6.7	9.7	8.0
Percent in the U.S. not covered	11.6	11.3	11.2	11.0	10.5	10.9	11.7	11.0

Table KY-6. Employment Status by Demographic Group, Preliminary 2008

(Number, percent.)

Characteristic	Civilian noninstitutional population	Civilian labor force		Employment		Unemployed	
		Number	Percent of population	Number	Percent of population	Number	Unemployment rate
TOTAL	3 300	2 022	61.3	1 895	57.4	127	6.3
Sex							
Men	1 584	1 086	69.0	1 015	64.1	70	6.5
Women	1 716	937	55.0	880	51.3	57	6.1
Race, Sex, and Hispanic Origin							
White	3 005	1 839	61.2	1 737	57.8	102	5.6
Men	1 445	992	68.6	932	64.5	60	6.0
Women	1 559	848	54.4	805	51.6	43	5.1
Black or African American	225	139	61.9	119	52.8	21	14.8
Men	105	71	67.3	62	59.1	9	12.2
Women	120	69	57.3	57	47.2	12	17.6
Hispanic	62	44	71.0	41	66.0	3	6.9
Men	36	31	87.5	29	82.0	2	6.3
Women	26	. . .	. . .	. . .	. . .	. . .	. . .
Age							
16 to 19 years	230	96	41.8	78	33.9	18	19.0
20 to 24 years	293	208	71.2	185	63.3	23	11.0
25 to 34 years	545	431	79.2	401	73.6	31	7.1
35 to 44 years	578	456	78.8	430	74.3	26	5.7
45 to 54 years	639	477	74.7	457	71.5	21	4.4
55 to 64 years	483	260	53.8	254	52.6	6	2.3
65 years and over	532	93	17.5	91	17.0	3	3.0

Note: Data in Table 6 are from the Current Population Survey (CPS) and do not match the estimates in Table 7. See notes and definitions for more details.

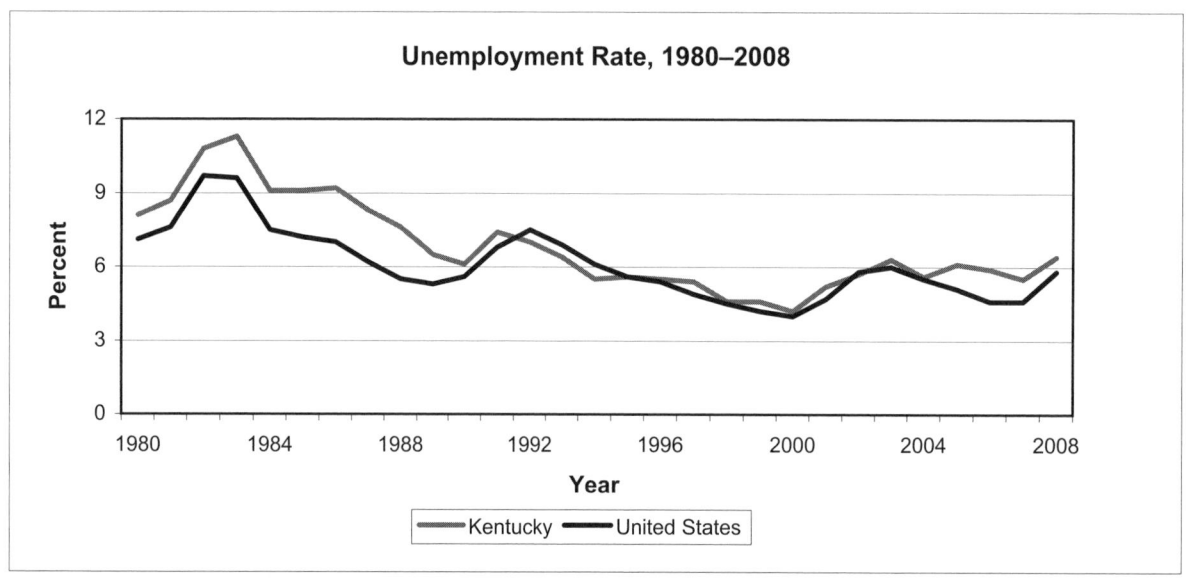

Table KY-7. Employment Status of the Civilian Noninstitutional Population Age 16 Years and Over

(Number, percent.)

Year	Civilian labor force	Civilian participation rate	Employed	Unemployed	Unemployment rate
1998	1 920 292	63.3	1 832 775	87 517	4.6
1999	1 944 384	63.5	1 854 270	90 114	4.6
2000	1 949 013	63.1	1 866 348	82 665	4.2
2001	1 954 142	62.9	1 852 056	102 086	5.2
2002	1 950 470	62.4	1 838 495	111 975	5.7
2003	1 971 751	62.5	1 848 059	123 692	6.3
2004	1 963 852	61.9	1 854 703	109 149	5.6
2005	1 992 625	62.2	1 871 981	120 644	6.1
2006	2 027 794	62.6	1 908 784	119 010	5.9
2007	2 036 459	62.3	1 923 471	112 988	5.5
2008	2 042 915	61.9	1 911 240	131 675	6.4

Table KY-8. Employment and Average Wages by Industry

(Estimates for 2001–2006 are based on the 2002 North American Industry Classification System [NAICS]. Estimates for 2007 are based on the 2007 NAICS.)

Industry	2001	2002	2003	2004	2005	2006	2007
	Number of jobs						
WAGE AND SALARY EMPLOYMENT BY INDUSTRY	1 902 744	1 881 235	1 884 459	1 900 073	1 926 757	1 952 204	1 972 308
Farm Wage and Salary Employment	16 721	16 183	20 265	19 584	15 200	15 180	14 657
Nonfarm Wage and Salary Employment	1 886 023	1 865 052	1 864 194	1 880 489	1 911 557	1 937 024	1 957 651
Private wage and salary employment	1 537 262	1 518 194	1 515 269	1 530 643	1 556 655	1 576 525	1 593 455
Forestry, fishing, hunting, and other	12 709	11 904	11 681	11 354	11 647	11 894	12 063
Mining	19 947	19 823	18 776	19 373	21 148	22 698	21 841
Utilities	7 147	6 743	6 461	6 392	6 478	6 510	6 609
Construction	91 206	86 733	86 738	86 647	87 534	86 263	88 230
Manufacturing	294 931	277 499	267 757	265 403	264 049	262 770	257 470
Durable goods manufacturing	187 580	174 537	167 019	166 604	167 872	167 536	162 898
Nondurable goods manufacturing	107 351	102 962	100 738	98 799	96 177	95 234	94 572
Wholesale trade	73 861	72 840	74 019	75 474	76 033	77 203	78 689
Retail trade	223 200	219 208	217 837	218 158	218 826	218 714	221 024
Transportation and warehousing	83 923	81 323	80 449	81 637	85 178	86 585	89 289
Information	33 495	31 900	30 499	28 539	28 556	28 961	30 196
Finance and insurance	63 651	65 440	66 743	69 216	70 313	73 617	74 943
Real estate and rental and leasing	20 813	20 377	20 338	20 160	20 449	20 561	20 529
Professional and technical services	61 177	60 874	61 106	61 373	64 172	66 191	68 791
Management of companies and enterprises	13 775	13 461	14 120	15 741	16 025	16 278	17 305
Administrative and waste services	84 935	85 346	85 258	90 373	96 565	101 171	100 662
Educational services	26 951	27 435	26 814	27 149	28 512	28 527	29 453
Health care and social assistance	189 928	197 517	202 977	205 221	210 119	213 440	216 737
Arts, entertainment, and recreation	18 424	18 648	18 658	19 089	19 326	19 765	20 106
Accommodation and food services	136 782	137 178	140 136	144 961	148 182	151 611	155 085
Other services, except public administration	80 407	83 945	84 902	84 383	83 543	83 766	84 433
Government and government enterprises	348 761	346 858	348 925	349 846	354 902	360 499	364 196
	Dollars						
AVERAGE WAGES AND SALARIES BY INDUSTRY	29 334	30 302	31 250	32 551	33 546	34 776	36 015
Average Farm Wages and Salaries	13 308	16 898	14 219	14 590	14 948	17 338	15 591
Average Nonfarm Wages and Salaries	29 476	30 419	31 435	32 739	33 694	34 913	36 168
Average private wages and salaries	29 526	30 278	31 239	32 505	33 327	34 484	35 751
Forestry, fishing, hunting, and other	20 201	20 175	21 438	22 287	22 881	24 951	24 997
Mining	45 204	45 742	46 241	48 529	52 281	55 759	57 055
Utilities	61 052	56 744	56 769	58 307	60 236	63 273	64 186
Construction	32 785	33 283	34 142	34 479	35 766	37 317	39 602
Manufacturing	38 009	39 601	41 089	42 912	43 885	45 291	46 811
Durable goods manufacturing	39 413	41 056	42 855	44 793	45 404	46 781	48 329
Nondurable goods manufacturing	35 555	37 133	38 161	39 740	41 232	42 669	44 196
Wholesale trade	40 192	41 295	42 375	44 989	46 517	48 205	50 780
Retail trade	19 030	19 722	20 339	20 895	21 279	21 965	22 447
Transportation and warehousing	39 212	39 666	41 681	43 733	43 302	43 468	46 040
Information	35 098	35 279	35 720	38 221	38 505	40 319	40 234
Finance and insurance	40 224	41 739	44 048	46 101	48 006	50 616	52 865
Real estate and rental and leasing	23 806	25 028	25 791	26 827	27 837	28 726	31 529
Professional and technical services	41 998	42 079	43 133	45 127	46 224	48 120	49 755
Management of companies and enterprises	64 192	68 686	73 800	77 257	81 665	86 094	85 333
Administrative and waste services	18 407	19 546	19 941	20 506	21 052	21 934	22 705
Educational services	17 816	18 292	19 380	20 179	21 026	21 066	22 019
Health care and social assistance	30 454	31 349	32 223	33 761	34 785	35 970	37 490
Arts, entertainment, and recreation	17 166	18 051	19 218	19 645	19 597	19 911	20 895
Accommodation and food services	12 200	12 696	12 803	13 101	13 300	13 676	13 766
Other services, except public administration	19 764	20 404	21 462	22 225	22 824	23 238	24 208
Government and government enterprises	29 260	31 033	32 284	33 760	35 304	36 787	37 991

Table KY-9. Employment Characteristics by Family Type

(Number, percent.)

Family type and labor force status	2005		2006		2007	
	Total	Families with own children under 18 years	Total	Families with own children under 18 years	Total	Families with own children under 18 years
TOTAL FAMILIES	1 119 243	505 479	1 106 404	493 913	1 114 146	497 136
FAMILY TYPE AND LABOR FORCE STATUS						
Married Coupled Families	851 851	348 859	832 504	336 756	833 000	335 498
Both husband and wife in labor force	48.4	61.2	49.9	64.8	50.4	64.8
Husband in labor force, wife not in labor force	22.5	28.2	22.5	27.1	21.5	26.5
Wife in labor force, husband not in labor force	9.0	5.9	8.3	4.7	8.6	4.7
Both husband and wife not in labor force	20.1	4.7	19.2	3.4	19.6	3.9
Other Families	267 392	156 620	273 900	157 157	281 146	161 638
Female householder, no husband present	75.6	79.5	75.0	78.4	73.9	76.6
In labor force	50.2	61.0	48.8	60.6	48.0	58.9
Not in labor force	25.4	18.6	26.2	17.8	25.9	17.8
Male householder, no wife present	24.4	20.5	25.0	21.6	26.1	23.4
In labor force	17.2	16.8	17.8	18.1	19.4	20.1
Not in labor force	7.2	3.7	7.1	3.5	6.8	3.3

Table KY-10. School Enrollment and Educational Attainment, 2007

(Number, percent.)

Item	State	U.S.
Enrollment		
Total population 3 years and over	4 073 946	289 295 761
Enrolled in school	1 048 177	79 329 527
Enrolled in preschool (percent)	5.9	6.2
Enrolled in grades K-12 (percent)	69.8	67.6
Enrolled in college or graduate school (percent)	24.3	26.2
Attainment		
Total population 25 years and over	2 840 026	197 892 369
Less than a high school diploma (percent)	19.9	15.5
High school diploma or more (percent)	80.1	84.5
Bachelor's degree or more (percent)	20.0	27.5
Graduate degree or more (percent)	8.0	10.1

Table KY-11. Educational Indicators

(Number, percent.)

Item	State	U.S.
Public Schools, 2006–2007 (except where noted)		
Number of school districts	195	17 742
Number of schools	1 538	99 639
Number of students	683 152	49 315 842
Student-teacher ratio	15.8	15.5
Expenditures per student (dollars)	$7 940	. . .
Averaged freshman graduation rate, 2005–2006	77.2	. . .
Dropout rate, grades 9–12, 2005–2006	3.3	3.7
Students eligible for free or reduced-price lunch (percent)	48.5	41.2
English-language learners (percent)	1.6	5.1
Students with IEP (percent)	16.0	12.7
Private Schools, 2007–2008 (except where noted)		
Number of schools	404	33 740
Number of students	67 376	5 072 451
High school graduates, 2006–2007	4 028	306 605
Student-teacher ratio	11.9	11.1

Table KY-12. Reported Voting and Registration of the Voting-Age Population, November 2008

(Number in thousands, percent.)

Item	Total population	Total citizen population	Registered Total registered	Registered Percent registered (total population)	Registered Percent registered (total citizen population)	Voted Total voted	Voted Percent voted (total population)	Voted Percent voted (total citizen population)
U.S. total	225 499	206 072	146 311	64.9	71.0	131 144	58.2	63.6
State total	3 179	3 094	2 259	71.1	73.0	1 952	61.4	63.1
Sex								
Male	1 525	1 474	1 044	68.4	70.8	892	58.5	60.5
Female	1 653	1 620	1 215	73.5	75.0	1 060	64.1	65.4
Race								
White alone	2 886	2 840	2 074	71.9	73.0	1 794	62.2	63.2
White non-Hispanic alone	2 837	2 826	2 064	72.8	73.0	1 785	62.9	63.2
Black alone	211	195	136	64.7	70.0	128	60.6	65.5
Asian alone	33	11	2	. . .	. . .	. . .	. . .	. . .
Hispanic (of any race)	52	17	13	. . .	. . .	13	. . .	. . .
White alone or in combination	2 917	2 871	2 102	72.1	73.2	1 818	62.3	63.3
Black alone or in combination	226	210	149	65.9	70.9	138	61.0	65.6
Asian alone or in combination	37	15	6	. . .	. . .	4	. . .	. . .

Table KY-13. Crime

(Number, rate per 100,000.)

Item	State 2007	State 2008	State Percent change	U.S. 2007	U.S. 2008	U.S. Percent change
Population	4 241 474	4 269 245	0.7	301 621 157	304 059 724	0.8
VIOLENT CRIME						
Number	12 513	12 646	1.1	1 408 337	1 382 012	-1.9
Rate	295.0	296.2	0.4	466.9	454.5	-2.7
Murder and Nonnegligent Manslaughter						
Number	204	198	-2.9	16 929	16 272	-3.9
Rate	4.8	4.6	-3.6	5.6	5.4	-4.7
Forcible Rape						
Number	1 381	1 408	2.0	90 427	89 000	-1.6
Rate	32.6	33.0	1.3	30.0	29.3	-2.4
Robbery						
Number	4 069	4 004	-1.6	445 125	441 855	-0.7
Rate	95.9	93.8	-2.2	147.6	145.3	-1.5
Aggravated Assault						
Number	6 859	7 036	2.6	855 856	834 885	-2.5
Rate	161.7	164.8	1.9	283.8	274.6	-3.2
PROPERTY CRIME						
Number	106 813	110 314	3.3	9 843 481	9 767 915	-0.8
Rate	2 518.3	2 583.9	2.6	3 263.5	3 212.5	-1.6
Burglary						
Number	27 683	28 839	4.2	2 179 140	2 222 196	2.0
Rate	652.7	675.5	3.5	722.5	730.8	1.2
Larceny-Theft						
Number	70 455	73 808	4.8	6 568 572	6 588 873	0.3
Rate	1 661.1	1 728.8	4.1	2 177.8	2 167.0	-0.5
Motor Vehicle Theft						
Number	8 675	7 667	-11.6	1 095 769	956 846	-12.7
Rate	204.5	179.6	-12.2	363.3	314.7	-13.4

Table KY-14. State Government Finances, 2007

(Dollars, percent distribution.)

Item	Thousands of dollars	Percent distribution
Total Revenue	25 425 381	X
General revenue	20 058 096	78.9
Intergovernmental revenue	6 338 156	24.9
Taxes	9 895 207	38.9
General sales	2 817 636	11.1
Selective sales	1 772 659	7.0
License taxes	459 329	1.8
Individual income tax	3 041 535	12.0
Corporate income tax	988 065	3.9
Other taxes	815 983	3.2
Current charges	2 513 432	9.9
Miscellaneous general revenue	1 311 301	5.2
Utility revenue	0	0.0
Liquor store revenue	0	0.0
Insurance trust revenue	5 367 285	21.1
Total Expenditure	23 680 419	100.0
Intergovernmental expenditure	4 469 153	18.9
Direct expenditure	19 211 266	81.1
Current operation	13 304 538	56.2
Capital outlay	1 916 163	8.1
Insurance benefits and repayments	2 817 162	11.9
Assistance and subsidies	698 908	3.0
Interest on debt	474 495	2.0
Exhibit: Salaries and wages	3 532 348	14.9
Total Expenditure	23 680 419	100.0
General expenditure	20 863 257	88.1
Intergovernmental expenditure	4 469 153	18.9
Direct expenditure	16 394 104	69.2
Education	7 963 410	33.6
Public welfare	5 827 463	24.6
Hospitals	1 007 977	4.3
Health	577 490	2.4
Highways	2 138 616	9.0
Police protection	191 395	0.8
Correction	471 523	2.0
Natural resources	361 199	1.5
Parks and recreation	106 225	0.4
Government administration	779 245	3.3
Interest on general debt	474 495	2.0
Other and unallocable	964 219	4.1
Utility expenditure	0	0.0
Liquor store expenditure	0	0.0
Insurance trust expenditure	2 817 162	11.9
Debt at End of Fiscal Year	10 857 128	X
Cash and Security Holdings	44 730 785	X

Table KY-15. State Government Tax Collections, 2008

(Dollars, percent distribution.)

Item	Thousands of dollars	Percent distribution
Total Taxes	10 056 293	X
Property taxes	503 105	5.0
Sales and gross receipts	4 718 517	46.9
General sales and gross receipts	2 875 836	28.6
Selective sales taxes	1 842 681	18.3
Alcoholic beverages	107 507	1.1
Amusements	220	0.0
Insurance premiums	151 809	1.5
Motor fuels	617 826	6.1
Pari-mutuels	5 670	0.1
Public utilities	56 906	0.6
Tobacco products	178 558	1.8
Other selective sales	724 185	7.2
Licenses	469 761	4.7
Alcoholic beverages	6 136	0.1
Amusements	245	0.0
Corporation	75 832	0.8
Hunting and fishing	25 520	0.3
Motor vehicle	212 037	2.1
Motor vehicle operators	19 945	0.2
Public utility	12 418	0.1
Occupation and business, NEC	113 539	1.1
Other licenses	4 089	0.0
Income taxes	4 016 768	39.9
Individual income	3 483 138	34.6
Corporation net income	533 630	5.3
Other taxes	348 142	3.5
Death and gift	51 001	0.5
Documentary and stock transfer	3 807	0.0
Severance	293 334	2.9

Table KY-16. Agriculture

(Number, acres, and dollars.)

Item	2002		2007		Percent change, 2002–2007
	Number	Percent of total	Number	Percent of total	
Number of farms	86 541		85 260		-1.5
Farm Size					
Average size of farm (acres)	160		164		2.5
Farms by size (number of farms)					
Fewer than 50 acres	30 100	34.8	29 814	35.0	-1.0
50 to 499 acres	51 578	59.6	50 459	59.2	-2.2
500 acres or more	4 863	5.6	4 987	5.8	2.5
Land (Acres)					
Total land in farms	13 843 706		13 993 121		1.1
Total cropland	8 412 354	60.8	7 278 098	52.0	-13.5
Total harvested cropland	4 978 994	36.0	5 057 883	36.1	1.6
Irrigated land	36 751	0.3	58 730	0.4	59.8
Value of Sales (Dollars)					
Agricultural products sold ($1,000)	3 080 080		4 824 561		56.6
Average sales per farm	35 591		56 586		59.0
Sales of crops	1 110 209	36.0	1 404 769	29.1	26.5
Sales of livestock, poultry, and their products	1 969 871	64.0	3 419 792	70.9	73.6
Value of Sales (Number of Farms)					
Less than $10,000	58 257	67.3	56 737	66.5	-2.6
$10,000 to $99,999	23 165	26.8	22 601	26.5	-2.4
$100,000 to $999,999	4 753	5.5	5 096	6.0	7.2
$1,000,000 or more	366	0.4	826	1.0	125.7
Farms by Type of Organization (Number of Farms)					
Family	79 297	91.6	76 140	89.3	-4.0
Partnership	5 764	6.7	7 334	8.6	27.2
Corporation	1 119	1.3	1 429	1.7	27.7
Other: cooperative, estate or trust, institutional, etc	361	0.4	357	0.4	-1.1
Value of Land and Buildings (Dollars)					
Estimated market value of land and buildings ($1,000)	37 532 557		25 462 631		-32.2
Land and buildings average value per farm	440 213		294 056		-33.2
Average value per acre	2 682		1 824		-32.0
Government Payments					
Number of farms receiving government payments	22 825	26.4	29 511	34.6	29.3
Payments (thousands of dollars)	94 053		103 104		9.6
Average payment per farm	4 121		3 494		-15.2
Farm Operator Characteristics					
Farm operators whose principal occupation is farming	46 939	54.2	33 935	39.8	-27.7
Farm operators whose principal occupation is other	39 602	45.8	51 325	60.2	29.6
Average age principal operator (years)	55.2		56.5		2.4

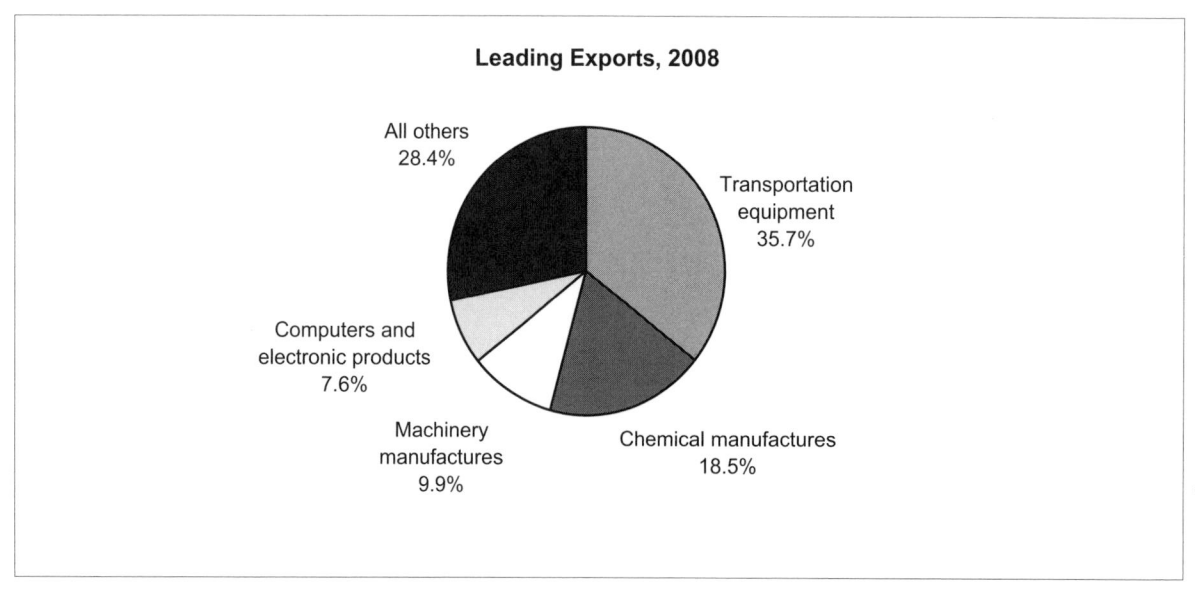

Leading Exports, 2008

All others 28.4%

Transportation equipment 35.7%

Computers and electronic products 7.6%

Machinery manufactures 9.9%

Chemical manufactures 18.5%

LOUISIANA

Facts and Figures

Location: South central United States; bordered on the N by Arkansas, on the E by Mississippi, on the S by the Gulf of Mexico, and on the W by Texas

Area: 51,840 sq. mi. (134,264 sq. km.); rank—31st

Population: 4,410,796 (2008 est.); rank—25th

Principal Cities: capital—Baton Rouge; largest—New Orleans

Statehood: April 30, 1812; 18th state

U.S. Congress: 2 senators, 7 representatives

State Motto: Union, Justice, Confidence

State Song: "Give Me Louisiana"

State Nicknames: The Pelican State; The Bayou State

Abbreviations: LA; La.

State Symbols: flower—magnolia; tree—bald cypress; bird—Eastern brown pelican

At a Glance

- With a decrease in population of 1.3 percent, Louisiana was one of only two states to lose population from 2000 to 2008; the other was North Dakota.
- An estimated 36,276 marriages took place in Louisiana in 2008; Louisiana does not report its number of divorces.
- The 2007 home ownership rate in Louisiana was 71.5 percent; its ranking of 20th was tied with that of New Mexico and Virginia.
- Louisiana's median household income in 2007 was $40,926, 45th among the states.
- In Louisiana, 18.6 percent of the population lived below the poverty level in 2007, ranking it 2nd.
- In 2006-07, 20.2 percent of Louisianans did not have health insurance, compared to 15.5 percent of the total U.S. population.
- In 2007, 4.3 percent of Louisianans were unemployed, compared to 4.6 percent nationwide.
- Louisiana ranked 46th in the nation with 20.4 percent of its population 25 years old and over having a bachelor's degree in 2007.
- Louisiana's violent crime rate in 2007 was 729.5 per 100,000 population, compared to 466.9 for the entire nation.
- Louisiana had one physician for every 337 people in 2007, compared to one physician for every 325 people nationwide.
- In the 2008 election, 62.1 percent of Louisiana's eligible voters voted, compared to 61.7 percent of eligible voters nationwide.
- Louisiana ranked 3rd among the states receiving federal aid in 2007, with $3,036 per capita.
- Louisiana's gross domestic product was $216 billion in 2007; it ranked 24th among the states.
- With $30.3 billion in exports in 2007, Louisiana ranked 10th in exports.
- Louisianans consumed 3.8 trillion Btu's of energy in 2006; the state ranked 8th in total consumption.
- In 2007, Louisiana exported $695 million worth of agricultural products, less than 1 percent of the U.S. total.

Table LA-1. Population by Sex, Age, Race, and Hispanic Origin

(Number, percent.)

Sex, age, race, and Hispanic origin	1990	2000	2008	Average annual percent change, 2000–2008
Total Population	4 219 973	4 468 976	4 410 796	-0.2
Percent of total U.S. population	1.7	1.6	1.5	X
Sex				
Male	2 031 386	2 162 903	2 140 798	-0.1
Female	2 188 587	2 306 073	2 269 998	-0.2
Age				
Under 5 years	334 650	317 392	310 716	-0.3
5 to 19 years	1 032 960	1 050 637	932 642	-1.5
20 to 64 years	2 383 372	2 584 018	2 627 124	0.2
65 years and over	468 991	516 929	540 314	0.6
Median age (years)	30.9	34.0	35.6	X
Race and Hispanic Origin[1]				
One race				
White	2 839 138	2 856 161	2 859 940	0.0
Black	1 299 281	1 451 944	1 410 457	-0.4
American Indian and Alaskan Native	18 541	25 477	28 230	1.3
Asian[2]	41 099	54 758	63 818	1.9
Native Hawaiian and Other Pacific Islander	X	1 240	1 846	5.1
Two or more races	X	48 265	46 505	-0.5
Hispanic (of any race)	93 044	107 738	148 463	4.1

[1]Data on race in 2000 and 2008 are not comparable to 1990. Individuals could only report one race in the 1990 census but could report one or more races on the 2000 census.
[2]Data in 1990 refer to Asian and Pacific Islanders.

Table LA-2. Marital Status

(Number, percent distribution.)

Sex and marital status	1990	2000	2007
Males, 15 Years and Over	1 503 716	1 648 133	1 632 653
Never married	30.9	31.2	35.1
Now married, except separated	56.3	54.5	49.7
Separated	3.0	2.2	2.1
Widowed	2.8	2.8	3.1
Divorced	7.0	9.2	10.0
Females, 15 Years and Over	1 680 787	1 818 247	1 772 926
Never married	24.4	26.3	29.5
Now married, except separated	50.0	48.2	44.7
Separated	3.9	2.9	3.0
Widowed	12.9	11.5	11.0
Divorced	8.9	11.1	11.8

Table LA-3. Households and Housing Characteristics

(Number, percent, and dollars.)

Item	1990	2000	2007	Average annual percent change, 2000–2007
Total Households	1 499 269	1 656 053	1 597 111	-0.5
Family households	1 089 882	1 156 438	1 080 025	-1.0
Married-couple family	803 282	809 498	745 988	-1.2
Other family	286 600	346 940	334 037	-0.5
Male householder, no wife present	52 471	71 865	77 196	1.0
Female householder, no husband present	234 129	275 075	256 841	-1.0
Nonfamily households	409 387	499 615	517 086	0.5
Householder living alone	356 060	419 200	436 640	0.6
Householder not living alone	53 327	80 415	80 446	0.0
Housing Characteristics				
Total housing units	1 716 241	1 847 181	1 858 586	0.1
Occupied housing units	1 499 269	1 656 053	1 597 111	-0.5
Owner-occupied	987 919	1 125 135	1 085 054	-0.5
Renter-occupied	511 350	530 918	512 057	-0.5
Average size	2.74	2.62	2.61	X
Financial Characteristics				
Median gross rent of renter-occupied housing units (dollars)	352	466	651	4.9
Median monthly owner costs for housing units with a mortgage (dollars)	595	816	1 074	4.0
Median value of owner-occupied housing units (dollars)	58 000	85 000	126 800	5.9

Table LA-4. Median Income and Poverty Status, 2007

(Number, percent.)

Characteristic	State		U.S.	
	Number	Percent	Number	Percent
Median Income				
Households (dollars)	40 926	X	50 740	X
Families (dollars)	50 727	X	61 173	X
Below Poverty Level				
Sex				
Male	317 133	15.8	16 576 071	11.5
Female	458 292	21.2	21 476 176	14.3
Age				
Under 18 years	283 350	26.8	13 097 100	18.0
Related children under 18 years	278 344	26.4	12 728 964	17.6
18 to 64 years	425 785	16.3	21 495 507	11.6
65 years and over	66 290	13.3	3 459 640	9.5

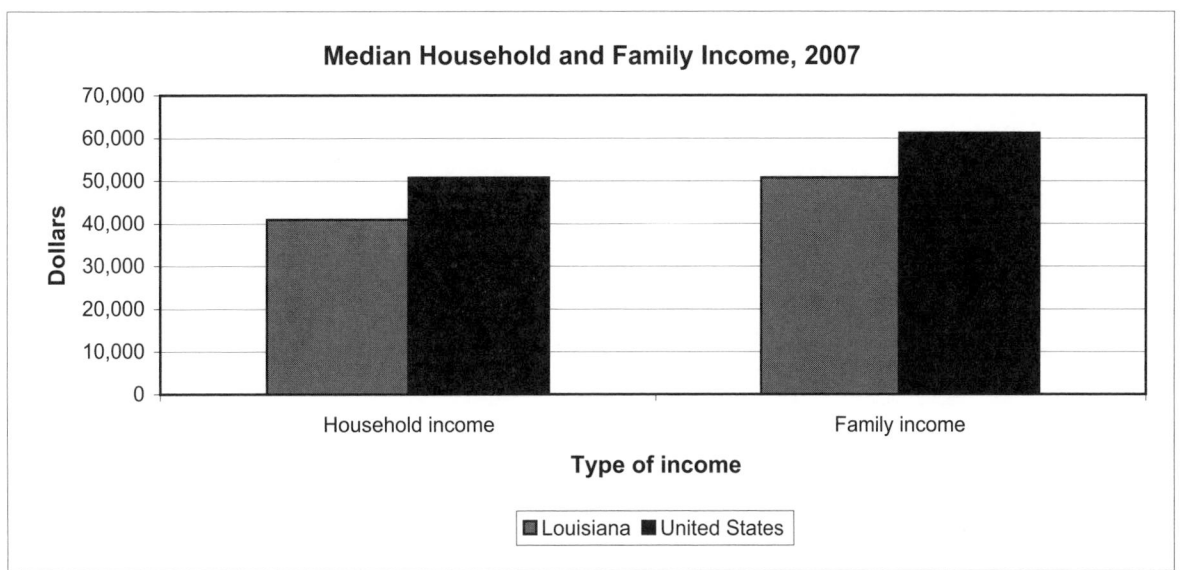

Median Household and Family Income, 2007

Table LA-5. Health Insurance Coverage Status for All Persons and Children Under 18 Years of Age

(Number, percent.)

Item	2000	2001	2002	2003	2004	2005	2006	2007
ALL PERSONS	4 366	4 390	4 447	4 429	4 421	4 088	4 212	4 197
Covered by Private or Government Health Insurance								
Number	3 611	3 591	3 654	3 563	3 715	3 363	3 291	3 421
Percent	82.7	81.8	82.2	80.5	84.0	82.3	78.1	81.5
Not Covered								
Number	755	799	793	866	707	725	921	776
Percent	17.3	18.2	17.8	19.5	16.0	17.7	21.9	18.5
Percent in the U.S. not covered	13.7	14.1	14.7	15.1	14.9	15.3	15.8	15.3
CHILDREN UNDER 18 YEARS OF AGE	1 233	1 235	1 173	1 197	1 149	1 064	1 067	1 097
Covered by Private or Government Health Insurance								
Number	1 051	1 088	1 038	1 024	1 067	974	897	960
Percent	85.2	88.1	88.5	85.5	92.9	91.6	84.1	87.5
Not Covered								
Number	182	147	135	173	81	89	170	137
Percent	14.8	11.9	11.5	14.5	7.1	8.4	15.9	12.5
Percent in the U.S. not covered	11.6	11.3	11.2	11.0	10.5	10.9	11.7	11.0

Table LA-6. Employment Status by Demographic Group, Preliminary 2008

(Number, percent.)

Characteristic	Civilian noninstitutional population	Civilian labor force		Employment		Unemployed	
		Number	Percent of population	Number	Percent of population	Number	Unemployment rate
TOTAL	3 272	2 045	62.5	1 943	59.4	102	5.0
Sex							
Men	1 541	1 077	70.0	1 019	66.2	58	5.4
Women	1 732	968	56.0	924	53.3	44	4.6
Race, Sex, and Hispanic Origin							
White	2 234	1 429	64.0	1 382	61.9	47	3.3
Men	1 082	793	73.2	768	70.9	25	3.2
Women	1 151	637	55.3	615	53.4	22	3.4
Black or African American	965	575	59.5	520	53.9	54	9.4
Men	424	260	61.4	228	53.7	32	12.5
Women	541	314	58.1	293	54.1	22	6.9
Hispanic	90	65	72.3	62	68.9	3	4.8
Men	60	51	85.2	49	82.2	2	3.6
Women	30	. . .	. . .	. . .	. . .	. . .	. . .
Age							
16 to 19 years	241	77	32.1	65	26.8	13	16.3
20 to 24 years	282	207	73.1	182	64.6	24	11.7
25 to 34 years	568	459	80.8	437	76.9	22	4.8
35 to 44 years	583	487	83.5	467	80.1	19	4.0
45 to 54 years	608	461	75.7	448	73.6	13	2.8
55 to 64 years	478	282	58.9	272	56.9	10	3.4
65 years and over	511	73	14.4	72	14.0	2	2.1

Note: Data in Table 6 are from the Current Population Survey (CPS) and do not match the estimates in Table 7. See notes and definitions for more details.

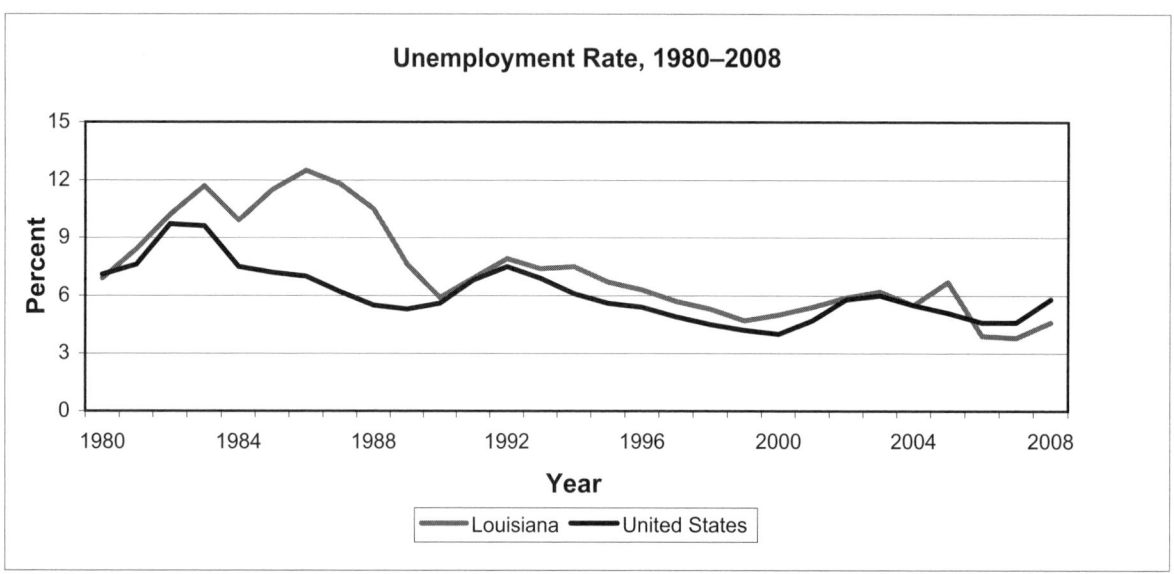

Table LA-7. Employment Status of the Civilian Noninstitutional Population Age 16 Years and Over

(Number, percent.)

Year	Civilian labor force	Civilian participation rate	Employed	Unemployed	Unemployment rate
1998	2 027 265	62.1	1 918 907	108 358	5.3
1999	2 022 162	61.6	1 926 732	95 430	4.7
2000	2 031 292	61.7	1 930 662	100 630	5.0
2001	2 030 887	61.6	1 922 110	108 777	5.4
2002	2 010 850	60.7	1 892 636	118 214	5.9
2003	2 024 274	60.8	1 898 829	125 445	6.2
2004	2 040 959	61.0	1 928 464	112 495	5.5
2005	2 076 498	63.0	1 937 009	139 489	6.7
2006	1 985 472	61.8	1 907 465	78 007	3.9
2007	2 025 777	61.5	1 949 401	76 376	3.8
2008	2 078 935	62.3	1 983 220	95 715	4.6

Table LA-8. Employment and Average Wages by Industry

(Estimates for 2001–2006 are based on the 2002 North American Industry Classification System [NAICS]. Estimates for 2007 are based on the 2007 NAICS.)

Industry	2001	2002	2003	2004	2005	2006	2007
	Number of jobs						
WAGE AND SALARY EMPLOYMENT BY INDUSTRY	2 033 800	2 019 981	2 025 043	2 032 757	2 002 947	1 968 780	2 031 158
Farm Wage and Salary Employment	9 389	9 148	6 977	7 508	7 202	8 844	7 750
Nonfarm Wage and Salary Employment	2 024 411	2 010 833	2 018 066	2 025 249	1 995 745	1 959 936	2 023 408
Private wage and salary employment	1 616 093	1 597 446	1 601 457	1 608 557	1 588 707	1 577 087	1 631 729
Forestry, fishing, hunting, and other	10 808	10 838	10 783	10 597	10 028	9 635	9 516
Mining	48 982	45 441	44 197	41 959	41 888	45 231	47 827
Utilities	10 008	10 122	9 911	9 747	9 693	9 533	9 341
Construction	129 929	124 295	123 717	121 260	123 751	135 553	138 780
Manufacturing	173 877	161 956	157 318	153 799	152 927	153 311	158 666
Durable goods manufacturing	88 295	81 411	79 412	78 487	79 165	83 027	87 601
Nondurable goods manufacturing	85 582	80 545	77 906	75 312	73 762	70 284	71 065
Wholesale trade	78 275	78 223	76 913	76 536	74 803	73 979	77 095
Retail trade	235 891	232 758	230 836	231 362	226 672	227 253	232 892
Transportation and warehousing	74 282	72 575	72 669	71 679	71 876	71 923	74 178
Information	30 380	29 171	29 203	29 867	29 359	27 164	27 880
Finance and insurance	63 817	64 950	66 508	65 965	63 010	61 515	61 116
Real estate and rental and leasing	35 328	34 401	34 481	35 044	34 230	33 323	34 777
Professional and technical services	73 417	74 100	75 492	78 792	79 418	83 138	87 042
Management of companies and enterprises	22 071	21 877	21 594	21 820	21 698	21 081	22 112
Administrative and waste services	92 049	90 111	89 133	90 487	92 783	96 023	98 774
Educational services	34 996	36 452	36 439	36 715	35 024	33 593	34 470
Health care and social assistance	200 965	206 799	214 727	219 511	218 309	211 015	221 680
Arts, entertainment, and recreation	41 708	40 578	39 256	39 938	37 480	32 690	34 822
Accommodation and food services	158 594	158 685	163 862	168 700	164 953	155 604	163 060
Other services, except public administration	100 716	104 114	104 418	104 779	100 805	95 523	97 701
Government and government enterprises	408 318	413 387	416 609	416 692	407 038	382 849	391 679
	Dollars						
AVERAGE WAGES AND SALARIES BY INDUSTRY	28 548	29 492	30 284	31 445	33 100	35 961	37 586
Average Farm Wages and Salaries	19 438	19 633	17 657	22 408	20 470	17 544	20 030
Average Nonfarm Wages and Salaries	28 590	29 537	30 327	31 479	33 146	36 044	37 653
Average private wages and salaries	28 879	29 619	30 254	31 365	33 054	36 381	37 888
Forestry, fishing, hunting, and other	25 013	25 283	26 291	26 071	28 160	29 772	31 495
Mining	55 071	55 367	57 761	60 084	64 493	71 779	74 574
Utilities	53 419	55 081	56 976	61 969	63 451	60 016	63 693
Construction	32 207	33 017	33 009	34 155	36 067	42 198	45 246
Manufacturing	41 718	43 992	45 429	47 802	49 178	52 110	53 943
Durable goods manufacturing	36 379	38 425	39 895	42 113	42 293	45 552	47 521
Nondurable goods manufacturing	47 226	49 619	51 070	53 730	56 567	59 857	61 859
Wholesale trade	37 780	38 536	39 831	41 839	44 819	49 451	50 885
Retail trade	18 772	19 487	20 146	20 525	21 489	23 628	23 813
Transportation and warehousing	37 218	37 971	38 647	40 440	42 566	47 098	50 923
Information	36 866	37 837	36 592	38 047	40 170	42 522	43 285
Finance and insurance	36 857	37 437	38 277	40 591	45 377	47 904	50 352
Real estate and rental and leasing	29 497	29 548	30 309	31 387	33 408	39 048	41 077
Professional and technical services	42 384	42 519	43 170	44 344	45 757	50 056	53 157
Management of companies and enterprises	46 180	47 401	47 736	50 575	58 006	57 492	61 687
Administrative and waste services	19 159	20 594	21 778	23 101	25 373	29 981	30 199
Educational services	22 820	23 822	23 450	24 271	24 790	25 584	26 589
Health care and social assistance	27 322	28 354	28 857	29 979	30 740	32 867	33 820
Arts, entertainment, and recreation	22 938	24 380	26 380	27 175	29 036	28 783	30 217
Accommodation and food services	12 534	12 937	13 206	13 620	14 211	15 699	16 313
Other services, except public administration	19 243	19 816	20 652	21 490	21 900	24 195	25 221
Government and government enterprises	27 447	29 221	30 606	31 916	33 503	34 658	36 675

Table LA-9. Employment Characteristics by Family Type

(Number, percent.)

Family type and labor force status	2005		2006		2007	
	Total	Families with own children under 18 years	Total	Families with own children under 18 years	Total	Families with own children under 18 years
TOTAL FAMILIES	1 137 005	533 956	1 072 568	487 520	1 080 025	489 360
FAMILY TYPE AND LABOR FORCE STATUS						
Married Coupled Families	768 751	324 420	748 396	308 348	745 988	302 177
Both husband and wife in labor force	48.9	62.0	49.5	63.6	48.5	62.4
Husband in labor force, wife not in labor force	24.7	29.0	24.6	28.3	26.4	30.4
Wife in labor force, husband not in labor force	8.0	4.8	8.0	4.7	7.7	4.5
Both husband and wife not in labor force	18.3	4.2	17.9	3.4	17.4	2.7
Other Families	368 254	209 536	324 172	179 172	334 037	187 183
Female householder, no husband present	79.5	83.0	77.6	81.6	76.9	81.3
In labor force	55.0	65.8	50.4	62.5	50.9	62.5
Not in labor force	24.6	17.2	27.3	19.1	26.0	18.8
Male householder, no wife present	20.5	17.0	22.4	18.4	23.1	18.7
In labor force	14.6	14.1	15.8	16.0	16.6	16.2
Not in labor force	5.8	2.8	6.6	2.4	6.5	2.4

Table LA-10. School Enrollment and Educational Attainment, 2007

(Number, percent.)

Item	State	U.S.
Enrollment		
Total population 3 years and over	4 117 874	289 295 761
Enrolled in school	1 131 956	79 329 527
Enrolled in preschool (percent)	6.9	6.2
Enrolled in grades K-12 (percent)	70.3	67.6
Enrolled in college or graduate school (percent)	22.9	26.2
Attainment		
Total population 25 years and over	2 742 822	197 892 369
Less than a high school diploma (percent)	20.1	15.5
High school diploma or more (percent)	79.9	84.5
Bachelor's degree or more (percent)	20.4	27.5
Graduate degree or more (percent)	6.6	10.1

Table LA-11. Educational Indicators

(Number, percent.)

Item	State	U.S.
Public Schools, 2006–2007 (except where noted)		
Number of school districts	99	17 742
Number of schools	1 527	99 639
Number of students	675 851	49 315 842
Student-teacher ratio	14.7	15.5
Expenditures per student (dollars)	$8 937	...
Averaged freshman graduation rate, 2005–2006	59.5	...
Dropout rate, grades 9–12, 2005–2006	8.3	3.7
Students eligible for free or reduced-price lunch (percent)	61.6	41.2
English-language learners (percent)	1.3	5.1
Students with IEP (percent)	13.2	12.7
Private Schools, 2007–2008 (except where noted)		
Number of schools	393	33 740
Number of students	123 476	5 072 451
High school graduates, 2006–2007	7 532	306 605
Student-teacher ratio	13.6	11.1

Table LA-12. Reported Voting and Registration of the Voting-Age Population, November 2008

(Number in thousands, percent.)

Item	Total population	Total citizen population	Registered			Voted		
			Total registered	Percent registered (total population)	Percent registered (total citizen population)	Total voted	Percent voted (total population)	Percent voted (total citizen population)
U.S. total	225 499	206 072	146 311	64.9	71.0	131 144	58.2	63.6
State total	3 161	3 056	2 393	75.7	78.3	2 149	68.0	70.3
Sex								
Male	1 478	1 427	1 101	74.5	77.1	984	66.6	68.9
Female	1 683	1 628	1 292	76.8	79.3	1 165	69.2	71.5
Race								
White alone	2 119	2 068	1 647	77.7	79.7	1 490	70.3	72.1
White non-Hispanic alone	2 023	2 014	1 612	79.7	80.0	1 458	72.1	72.4
Black alone	943	943	712	75.4	75.4	625	66.2	66.2
Asian alone	67	13	6	...	...	6	...	...
Hispanic (of any race)	100	58	39	39.2	...	32	32.0	...
White alone or in combination	2 141	2 090	1 665	77.8	79.7	1 508	70.5	72.2
Black alone or in combination	966	966	731	75.6	75.6	644	66.6	66.6
Asian alone or in combination	67	13	6	...	...	6	...	...

Table LA-13. Crime

(Number, rate per 100,000.)

Item	State			U.S.		
	2007	2008	Percent change	2007	2008	Percent change
Population	4 293 204	4 410 796	2.7	301 621 157	304 059 724	0.8
VIOLENT CRIME						
Number	31 317	28 944	-7.6	1 408 337	1 382 012	-1.9
Rate	729.5	656.2	-10.0	466.9	454.5	-2.7
Murder and Nonnegligent Manslaughter						
Number	608	527	-13.3	16 929	16 272	-3.9
Rate	14.2	11.9	-15.6	5.6	5.4	-4.7
Forcible Rape						
Number	1 393	1 232	-11.6	90 427	89 000	-1.6
Rate	32.4	27.9	-13.9	30.0	29.3	-2.4
Robbery						
Number	6 083	5 994	-1.5	445 125	441 855	-0.7
Rate	141.7	135.9	-4.1	147.6	145.3	-1.5
Aggravated Assault						
Number	23 233	21 191	-8.8	855 856	834 885	-2.5
Rate	541.2	480.4	-11.2	283.8	274.6	-3.2
PROPERTY CRIME						
Number	174 991	168 630	-3.6	9 843 481	9 767 915	-0.8
Rate	4 076.0	3 823.1	-6.2	3 263.5	3 212.5	-1.6
Burglary						
Number	44 602	43 320	-2.9	2 179 140	2 222 196	2.0
Rate	1 038.9	982.1	-5.5	722.5	730.8	1.2
Larceny-Theft						
Number	115 209	111 567	-3.2	6 568 572	6 588 873	0.3
Rate	2 683.5	2 529.4	-5.7	2 177.8	2 167.0	-0.5
Motor Vehicle Theft						
Number	15 180	13 743	-9.5	1 095 769	956 846	-12.7
Rate	353.6	311.6	-11.9	363.3	314.7	-13.4

Table LA-14. State Government Finances, 2007

(Dollars, percent distribution.)

Item	Thousands of dollars	Percent distribution
Total Revenue	33 286 017	X
General revenue	27 411 283	82.4
Intergovernmental revenue	12 417 474	37.3
Taxes	10 863 502	32.6
General sales	3 481 242	10.5
Selective sales	1 892 420	5.7
License taxes	568 849	1.7
Individual income tax	3 214 163	9.7
Corporate income tax	752 773	2.3
Other taxes	954 055	2.9
Current charges	1 840 690	5.5
Miscellaneous general revenue	2 289 617	6.9
Utility revenue	4 515	0.0
Liquor store revenue	0	0.0
Insurance trust revenue	5 870 219	17.6
Total Expenditure	27 855 931	100.0
Intergovernmental expenditure	6 262 247	22.5
Direct expenditure	21 593 684	77.5
Current operation	15 396 317	55.3
Capital outlay	1 947 983	7.0
Insurance benefits and repayments	2 835 232	10.2
Assistance and subsidies	561 968	2.0
Interest on debt	852 184	3.1
Exhibit: Salaries and wages	3 807 032	13.7
Total Expenditure	27 855 931	100.0
General expenditure	25 016 388	89.8
Intergovernmental expenditure	6 262 247	22.5
Direct expenditure	18 754 141	67.3
Education	7 708 209	27.7
Public welfare	4 918 292	17.7
Hospitals	843 838	3.0
Health	588 283	2.1
Highways	1 656 383	5.9
Police protection	316 352	1.1
Correction	651 468	2.3
Natural resources	483 495	1.7
Parks and recreation	318 698	1.1
Government administration	791 568	2.8
Interest on general debt	852 184	3.1
Other and unallocable	5 887 618	21.1
Utility expenditure	4 311	0.0
Liquor store expenditure	0	0.0
Insurance trust expenditure	2 835 232	10.2
Debt at End of Fiscal Year	14 251 968	X
Cash and Security Holdings	59 460 193	X

Table LA-15. State Government Tax Collections, 2008

(Dollars, percent distribution.)

Item	Thousands of dollars	Percent distribution
Total Taxes	11 003 870	X
Property taxes	46 643	0.4
Sales and gross receipts	5 538 890	50.3
General sales and gross receipts	3 459 383	31.4
Selective sales taxes	2 079 507	18.9
Alcoholic beverages	54 993	0.5
Amusements	742 831	6.8
Insurance premiums	478 288	4.3
Motor fuels	604 377	5.5
Pari-mutuels	4 474	0.0
Public utilities	13 965	0.1
Tobacco products	145 578	1.3
Other selective sales	35 001	0.3
Licenses	498 612	4.5
Corporation	252 900	2.3
Hunting and fishing	30 902	0.3
Motor vehicle	87 189	0.8
Motor vehicle operators	11 455	0.1
Public utility	5 453	0.0
Occupation and business, NEC	107 632	1.0
Other licenses	3 081	0.0
Income taxes	3 872 882	35.2
Individual income	3 169 686	28.8
Corporation net income	703 196	6.4
Other taxes	1 046 843	9.5
Death and gift	11 148	0.1
Severance	1 035 695	9.4

Table LA-16. Agriculture

(Number, acres, and dollars.)

Item	2002		2007		Percent change, 2002–2007
	Number	Percent of total	Number	Percent of total	
Number of farms	27 413		30 106		9.8
Farm Size					
Average size of farm (acres)	286		269		-5.9
Farms by size (number of farms)					
Fewer than 50 acres	11 292	41.2	13 676	45.4	21.1
50 to 499 acres	12 302	44.9	13 007	43.2	5.7
500 acres or more	3 819	13.9	3 423	11.4	-10.4
Land (Acres)					
Total land in farms	7 830 664		8 109 975		3.6
Total cropland	5 071 537	64.8	4 691 344	57.8	-7.5
Total harvested cropland	3 332 146	42.6	3 342 048	41.2	0.3
Irrigated land	938 841	12.0	954 353	11.8	1.7
Value of Sales (Dollars)					
Agricultural products sold ($1,000)	1 815 803		2 617 981		44.2
Average sales per farm	66 239		86 959		31.3
Sales of crops	1 065 611	58.7	1 604 647	61.3	50.6
Sales of livestock, poultry, and their products	750 192	41.3	1 013 334	38.7	35.1
Value of Sales (Number of Farms)					
Less than $10,000	18 235	66.5	20 855	69.3	14.4
$10,000 to $99,999	5 753	21.0	6 029	20.0	4.8
$100,000 to $999,999	3 125	11.4	2 536	8.4	-18.8
$1,000,000 or more	300	1.1	686	2.3	128.7
Farms by Type of Organization (Number of Farms)					
Family	24 915	90.9	25 716	85.4	3.2
Partnership	1 323	4.8	2 395	8.0	81.0
Corporation	1 041	3.8	1 775	5.9	70.5
Other: cooperative, estate or trust, institutional, etc	134	0.5	220	0.7	64.2
Value of Land and Buildings (Dollars)					
Estimated market value of land and buildings ($1,000)	16 686 859		12 163 119		-27.1
Land and buildings average value per farm	554 270		444 007		-19.9
Average value per acre	2 058		1 534		-25.5
Government Payments					
Number of farms receiving government payments	7 562	27.6	10 621	35.3	40.5
Payments (thousands of dollars)	123 599		169 333		37.0
Average payment per farm	16 345		15 943		-2.5
Farm Operator Characteristics					
Farm operators whose principal occupation is farming	14 805	54.0	12 591	41.8	-15.0
Farm operators whose principal occupation is other	12 608	46.0	17 515	58.2	38.9
Average age principal operator (years)	55.1		57.3		4.0

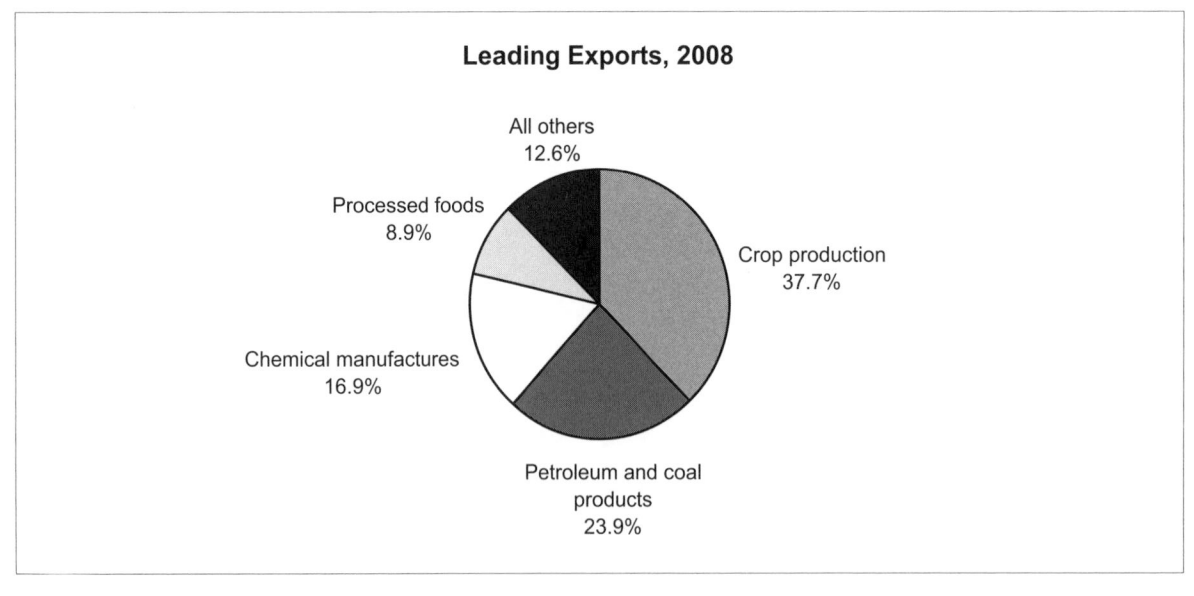

Leading Exports, 2008

All others 12.6%

Processed foods 8.9%

Crop production 37.7%

Chemical manufactures 16.9%

Petroleum and coal products 23.9%

MAINE

Facts and Figures

Location: Northeast corner of the United States; bordered on the N and E by New Brunswick, Canada; on the S by the Atlantic Ocean; on the W by New Hampshire; and on the NW by Quebec, Canada

Area: 35,385 sq. mi. (91,646 sq. km.); rank—39th

Population: 1,316,456 (2008 est.); rank—40th

Principal Cities: capital—Augusta; largest—Portland

Statehood: March 15, 1820; 23rd state

U.S. Congress: 2 senators, 2 representatives

State Motto: *Dirigo* ("I lead")

State Song: "State of Maine Song"

State Nickname: The Pine Tree State

Abbreviations: ME; Me.

State Symbols: flower—white pinecone and tassel; tree—Eastern white pine; bird—chickadee

At a Glance

- With an increase in population of 3.3 percent, Maine ranked 37th among the states in growth from 2000 to 2008.
- An estimated 9,348 marriages took place in Maine in 2008, compared to 4,709 divorces.
- The 2007 home ownership rate in Maine was 74.3 percent, giving it a ranking of 6th among the states.
- Maine's median household income in 2007 was $45,888, 35th among the states.
- In Maine, 12 percent of the population lived below the poverty level in 2007, ranking it 27th along with Colorado and Rhode Island.
- In 2006-07, 9.1 percent of Mainers did not have health insurance, compared to 15.5 percent of the total U.S. population.
- In 2007, 4.7 percent of Mainers were unemployed, compared to 4.6 percent nationwide.
- Maine ranked 22nd in the nation with 26.7 percent of its population 25 years old and over having a bachelor's degree in 2007.
- Maine's violent crime rate in 2007 was 118 per 100,000 population, compared to 466.9 for the entire nation.
- Maine had one physician for every 306 people in 2007, compared to one physician for every 325 people nationwide.
- In the 2008 election, 71.4 percent of Maine's eligible voters voted, compared to 61.7 percent of eligible voters nationwide.
- Maine ranked 11th among the states receiving federal aid in 2007, with $1,936 per capita.
- Maine's gross domestic product was $48 billion in 2007; it ranked 43rd among the states.
- With $2.8 billion in exports in 2007, Maine ranked 43rd in exports.
- Mainers consumed 457.8 billion Btu's of energy in 2006; the state ranked 42nd in total consumption.
- In 2007, Maine exported $97 million worth of agricultural products, less than 1 percent of the U.S. total.

Table ME-1. Population by Sex, Age, Race, and Hispanic Origin

(Number, percent.)

Sex, age, race, and Hispanic origin	1990	2000	2008	Average annual percent change, 2000–2008
Total Population	1 227 928	1 274 923	1 316 456	0.4
Percent of total U.S. population	0.5	0.5	0.4	X
Sex				
Male	597 850	620 309	642 369	0.4
Female	630 078	654 614	674 087	0.4
Age				
Under 5 years	85 722	70 726	71 459	0.1
5 to 19 years	261 012	264 759	237 707	-1.3
20 to 64 years	717 821	756 036	808 103	0.8
65 years and over	163 373	183 402	199 187	1.0
Median age (years)	33.8	38.6	42.0	X
Race and Hispanic Origin[1]				
One race				
White	1 208 360	1 236 014	1 268 930	0.3
Black	5 138	6 760	13 588	9.1
American Indian and Alaskan Native	5 998	7 098	7 889	1.3
Asian[2]	6 683	9 111	11 693	3.2
Native Hawaiian and Other Pacific Islander	X	382	484	3.0
Two or more races	X	12 647	13 872	1.2
Hispanic (of any race)	6 829	9 360	16 814	7.6

[1]Data on race in 2000 and 2008 are not comparable to 1990. Individuals could only report one race in the 1990 census but could report one or more races on the 2000 census.
[2]Data in 1990 refer to Asian and Pacific Islanders.

Table ME-2. Marital Status

(Number, percent distribution.)

Sex and marital status	1990	2000	2007
Males, 15 Years and Over	465 004	494 217	527 158
Never married	27.3	26.8	28.6
Now married, except separated	60.7	58.8	56.4
Separated	1.2	1.1	1.1
Widowed	2.6	2.8	2.8
Divorced	8.1	10.5	11.1
Females, 15 Years and Over	504 117	534 606	565 865
Never married	21.0	21.2	23.3
Now married, except separated	55.4	54.1	51.4
Separated	1.5	1.3	1.6
Widowed	12.1	11.0	10.1
Divorced	10.0	12.4	13.6

Table ME-3. Households and Housing Characteristics

(Number, percent, and dollars.)

Item	1990	2000	2007	Average annual percent change, 2000–2007
Total Households	465 312	518 200	543 952	0.7
Family households	328 685	340 685	355 547	0.6
Married-couple family	270 565	272 152	283 206	0.6
Other family	58 120	68 533	72 341	0.8
Male householder, no wife present	13 760	19 511	21 136	1.1
Female householder, no husband present	44 360	49 022	51 205	0.6
Nonfamily households	136 627	177 515	188 405	0.9
Householder living alone	108 474	139 969	148 311	0.8
Householder not living alone	28 153	37 546	40 094	0.9
Housing Characteristics				
Total housing units	587 045	651 901	696 681	1.0
Occupied housing units	465 312	518 200	543 952	0.7
Owner-occupied	327 888	370 905	402 257	1.2
Renter-occupied	137 424	147 295	141 695	-0.6
Average size	2.56	2.39	2.35	X
Financial Characteristics				
Median gross rent of renter-occupied housing units (dollars)	419	497	650	3.9
Median monthly owner costs for housing units with a mortgage (dollars)	664	923	1 249	4.4
Median value of owner-occupied housing units (dollars)	87 300	98 700	176 000	8.6

Table ME-4. Median Income and Poverty Status, 2007

(Number, percent.)

Characteristic	State		U.S.	
	Number	Percent	Number	Percent
Median Income				
Households (dollars)	45 888	X	50 740	X
Families (dollars)	56 266	X	61 173	X
Below Poverty Level				
Sex				
Male	65 880	10.5	16 576 071	11.5
Female	88 344	13.4	21 476 176	14.3
Age				
Under 18 years	41 973	15.4	13 097 100	18.0
Related children under 18 years	40 024	14.8	12 728 964	17.6
18 to 64 years	95 148	11.6	21 495 507	11.6
65 years and over	17 103	9.2	3 459 640	9.5

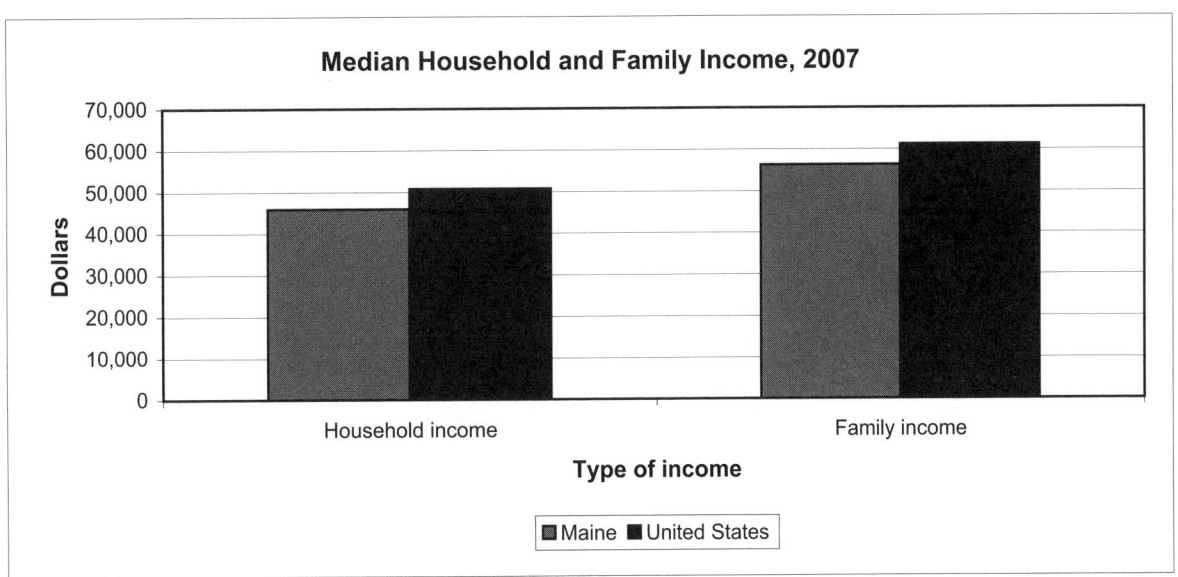

Table ME-5. Health Insurance Coverage Status for All Persons and Children Under 18 Years of Age

(Number, percent.)

Item	2000	2001	2002	2003	2004	2005	2006	2007
ALL PERSONS	1 269	1 279	1 269	1 283	1 294	1 320	1 315	1 313
Covered by Private or Government Health Insurance								
Number	1 135	1 150	1 129	1 154	1 179	1 185	1 192	1 197
Percent	89.4	89.9	89.0	90.0	91.1	89.7	90.7	91.2
Not Covered								
Number	135	129	140	128	115	136	122	115
Percent	10.6	10.1	11.0	10.0	8.9	10.3	9.3	8.8
Percent in the U.S. not covered	13.7	14.1	14.7	15.1	14.9	15.3	15.8	15.3
CHILDREN UNDER 18 YEARS OF AGE	287	265	273	287	286	279	286	281
Covered by Private or Government Health Insurance								
Number	262	249	252	270	272	258	268	267
Percent	91.4	93.8	92.2	94.0	95.3	92.3	93.6	94.9
Not Covered								
Number	25	16	21	17	13	21	18	14
Percent	8.6	6.2	7.8	6.0	4.7	7.7	6.4	5.1
Percent in the U.S. not covered	11.6	11.3	11.2	11.0	10.5	10.9	11.7	11.0

Table ME-6. Employment Status by Demographic Group, Preliminary 2008

(Number, percent.)

Characteristic	Civilian noninstitutional population	Civilian labor force		Employment		Unemployed	
		Number	Percent of population	Number	Percent of population	Number	Unemployment rate
TOTAL	1 065	707	66.3	669	62.8	38	5.4
Sex							
Men	512	371	72.0	349	68.1	22	5.9
Women	553	336	61.0	320	57.8	16	4.7
Race, Sex, and Hispanic Origin							
White	1 028	681	66.3	646	62.8	36	5.2
Men	494	357	72.3	337	68.2	20	5.7
Women	534	324	60.7	309	57.8	15	4.7
Black or African American	...	...	...	...	...	...	...
Men	...	...	...	...	...	...	...
Women	...	...	...	...	...	...	...
Hispanic	...	...	...	...	...	...	...
Men	...	...	...	...	...	...	...
Women	...	...	...	...	...	...	...
Age							
16 to 19 years	75	39	52.1	33	44.8	6	14.1
20 to 24 years	85	67	78.5	60	69.9	7	11.0
25 to 34 years	134	115	86.0	109	81.2	6	5.5
35 to 44 years	181	156	85.9	149	82.1	7	4.4
45 to 54 years	220	181	82.0	175	79.5	6	3.1
55 to 64 years	178	117	65.7	113	63.3	4	3.6
65 years and over	191	32	16.6	30	15.6	2	6.2

Note: Data in Table 6 are from the Current Population Survey (CPS) and do not match the estimates in Table 7. See notes and definitions for more details.

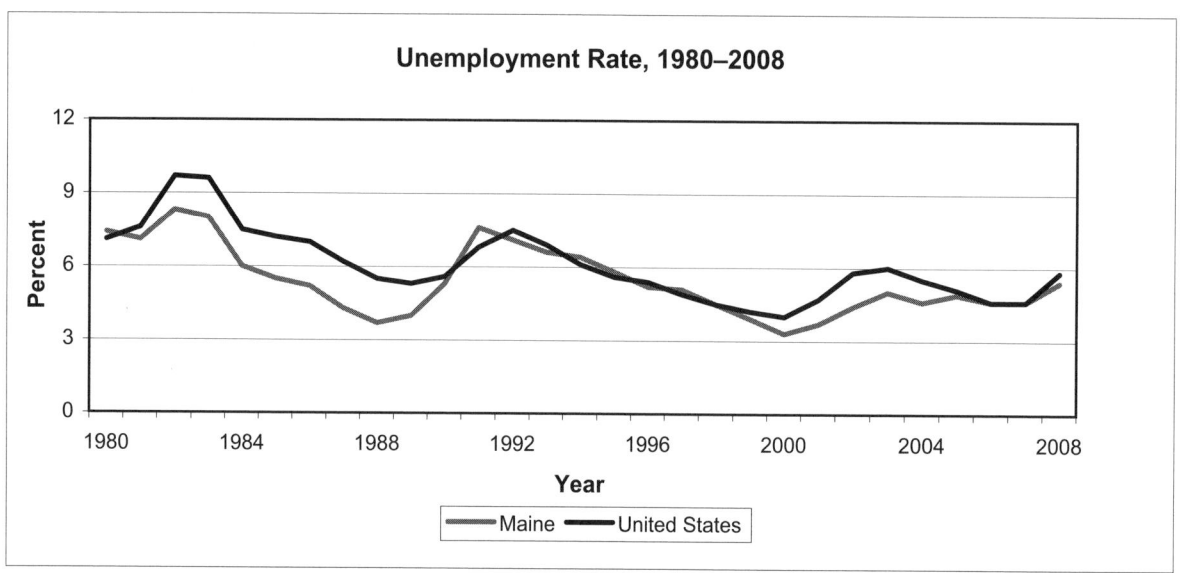

Table ME-7. Employment Status of the Civilian Noninstitutional Population Age 16 Years and Over

(Number, percent.)

Year	Civilian labor force	Civilian participation rate	Employed	Unemployed	Unemployment rate
1998	657 415	67.4	627 920	29 495	4.5
1999	667 673	67.8	641 351	26 322	3.9
2000	672 440	67.6	650 385	22 055	3.3
2001	675 981	67.3	650 699	25 282	3.7
2002	680 569	67.0	650 943	29 626	4.4
2003	684 689	66.7	650 458	34 231	5.0
2004	685 534	66.2	653 847	31 687	4.6
2005	694 285	66.5	660 557	33 728	4.9
2006	701 505	66.8	669 067	32 438	4.6
2007	702 549	66.5	669 948	32 601	4.6
2008	706 829	66.6	668 724	38 105	5.4

Table ME-8. Employment and Average Wages by Industry

(Estimates for 2001–2006 are based on the 2002 North American Industry Classification System [NAICS]. Estimates for 2007 are based on the 2007 NAICS.)

Industry	2001	2002	2003	2004	2005	2006	2007
	Number of jobs						
WAGE AND SALARY EMPLOYMENT BY INDUSTRY	635 298	633 637	635 209	640 563	637 164	641 360	644 036
Farm Wage and Salary Employment	4 070	3 984	4 140	3 455	3 399	3 108	3 064
Nonfarm Wage and Salary Employment	631 228	629 653	631 069	637 108	633 765	638 252	640 972
Private wage and salary employment	521 731	518 997	518 834	524 691	521 859	525 657	528 860
Forestry, fishing, hunting, and other	5 098	4 985	4 905	4 948	5 032	5 045	4 957
Mining	123	125	120	111	116	127	110
Utilities	2 247	2 236	2 002	1 911	1 910	1 856	1 949
Construction	30 941	30 607	31 794	32 217	31 808	32 403	31 945
Manufacturing	75 400	68 699	64 792	63 881	61 512	60 515	60 016
Durable goods manufacturing	39 425	36 042	34 061	33 926	32 604	31 973	31 795
Nondurable goods manufacturing	35 975	32 657	30 731	29 955	28 908	28 542	28 221
Wholesale trade	20 474	20 351	21 171	21 783	21 714	21 646	21 496
Retail trade	88 870	88 858	88 384	90 270	89 780	89 955	90 544
Transportation and warehousing	15 023	14 884	14 603	14 850	14 900	15 211	15 496
Information	12 159	11 584	11 330	11 056	11 338	11 307	11 362
Finance and insurance	28 025	27 979	27 838	27 399	26 662	26 346	25 789
Real estate and rental and leasing	6 724	6 927	7 051	7 349	7 395	7 312	7 366
Professional and technical services	24 644	24 219	23 784	24 234	24 357	24 894	25 037
Management of companies and enterprises	6 026	6 254	5 895	5 750	5 593	5 435	6 414
Administrative and waste services	22 768	22 586	22 518	21 421	21 858	22 777	23 819
Educational services	11 770	11 936	12 243	12 385	12 385	12 699	13 059
Health care and social assistance	88 652	91 971	93 998	97 894	98 907	100 879	101 671
Arts, entertainment, and recreation	8 091	8 390	8 768	8 574	8 520	8 446	8 682
Accommodation and food services	49 477	50 052	50 898	51 785	51 789	52 400	52 668
Other services, except public administration	25 219	26 354	26 740	26 873	26 283	26 404	26 480
Government and government enterprises	109 497	110 656	112 235	112 417	111 906	112 595	112 112
	Dollars						
AVERAGE WAGES AND SALARIES BY INDUSTRY	28 306	29 278	30 347	31 552	32 260	33 381	34 721
Average Farm Wages and Salaries	18 557	24 387	20 102	23 915	19 683	24 659	22 036
Average Nonfarm Wages and Salaries	28 369	29 309	30 414	31 593	32 328	33 424	34 782
Average private wages and salaries	28 136	28 948	29 963	31 124	31 749	32 864	34 189
Forestry, fishing, hunting, and other	27 304	27 783	28 770	31 077	32 800	35 291	37 353
Mining	27 114	29 696	29 283	29 477	31 466	32 591	38 627
Utilities	49 851	51 774	54 021	56 453	58 877	58 588	60 331
Construction	32 488	32 647	33 596	34 488	35 442	36 889	38 607
Manufacturing	36 322	38 064	40 143	40 890	41 358	42 813	44 409
Durable goods manufacturing	35 821	37 461	39 189	40 857	41 200	42 309	44 526
Nondurable goods manufacturing	36 871	38 730	41 200	40 927	41 537	43 377	44 278
Wholesale trade	39 929	41 110	42 550	43 947	45 239	47 402	49 610
Retail trade	19 841	20 584	21 325	21 884	22 087	22 520	23 148
Transportation and warehousing	29 769	30 101	31 319	32 732	33 660	34 459	34 990
Information	36 038	37 189	38 404	40 198	40 168	41 193	42 933
Finance and insurance	41 196	42 802	45 530	47 720	48 713	50 565	53 292
Real estate and rental and leasing	24 424	25 925	27 069	27 848	28 916	30 939	30 737
Professional and technical services	39 920	42 032	42 987	44 841	46 860	48 812	51 284
Management of companies and enterprises	51 210	52 065	52 428	66 383	59 222	60 265	66 461
Administrative and waste services	22 976	23 368	23 646	25 128	26 016	26 921	27 925
Educational services	23 666	25 271	26 300	26 738	27 604	28 417	29 873
Health care and social assistance	28 712	29 704	30 819	32 129	33 168	34 639	36 094
Arts, entertainment, and recreation	17 773	17 741	18 540	19 217	19 785	21 541	22 517
Accommodation and food services	13 165	13 698	14 105	14 781	15 207	15 850	16 254
Other services, except public administration	18 302	18 750	19 603	20 609	21 362	21 754	22 506
Government and government enterprises	29 479	31 002	32 501	33 783	35 025	36 038	37 576

Table ME-9. Employment Characteristics by Family Type

(Number, percent.)

Family type and labor force status	2005		2006		2007	
	Total	Families with own children under 18 years	Total	Families with own children under 18 years	Total	Families with own children under 18 years
TOTAL FAMILIES	355 469	150 548	358 314	155 398	355 547	152 951
FAMILY TYPE AND LABOR FORCE STATUS						
Married Coupled Families	278 075	100 195	276 972	104 149	283 206	106 019
Both husband and wife in labor force	55.7	69.2	56.1	70.4	57.4	73.0
Husband in labor force, wife not in labor force	17.8	22.6	18.5	24.3	17.3	22.0
Wife in labor force, husband not in labor force	8.3	6.0	7.7	3.4	7.3	2.9
Both husband and wife not in labor force	18.2	2.2	17.7	1.9	18.0	2.1
Other Families	77 394	50 353	81 342	51 249	72 341	46 932
Female householder, no husband present	66.9	68.5	71.0	71.9	70.8	73.0
In labor force	46.8	53.2	48.0	55.3	49.4	57.6
Not in labor force	20.1	15.3	23.0	16.6	21.4	15.4
Male householder, no wife present	33.1	31.5	29.0	28.1	29.2	27.0
In labor force	26.7	28.2	23.1	24.2	24.4	24.3
Not in labor force	6.4	3.3	5.9	3.9	4.9	2.7

Table ME-10. School Enrollment and Educational Attainment, 2007

(Number, percent.)

Item	State	U.S.
Enrollment		
Total population 3 years and over	1 274 921	289 295 761
Enrolled in school	307 355	79 329 527
Enrolled in preschool (percent)	4.7	6.2
Enrolled in grades K-12 (percent)	68.5	67.6
Enrolled in college or graduate school (percent)	26.8	26.2
Attainment		
Total population 25 years and over	922 232	197 892 369
Less than a high school diploma (percent)	10.6	15.5
High school diploma or more (percent)	89.4	84.5
Bachelor's degree or more (percent)	26.7	27.5
Graduate degree or more (percent)	9.2	10.1

Table ME-11. Educational Indicators

(Number, percent.)

Item	State	U.S.
Public Schools, 2006–2007 (except where noted)		
Number of school districts	303	17 742
Number of schools	672	99 639
Number of students	193 986	49 315 842
Student-teacher ratio	11.5	15.5
Expenditures per student (dollars)	$11 644	. . .
Averaged freshman graduation rate, 2005–2006	76.3	. . .
Dropout rate, grades 9–12, 2005–2006	5.4	3.7
Students eligible for free or reduced-price lunch (percent)	34.7	41.2
English-language learners (percent)	2.0	5.1
Students with IEP (percent)	17.7	12.7
Private Schools, 2007–2008 (except where noted)		
Number of schools	200	33 740
Number of students	19 553	5 072 451
High school graduates, 2006–2007	2 618	306 605
Student-teacher ratio	9.2	11.1

Table ME-12. Reported Voting and Registration of the Voting-Age Population, November 2008

(Number in thousands, percent.)

Item	Total population	Total citizen population	Registered — Total registered	Registered — Percent registered (total population)	Registered — Percent registered (total citizen population)	Voted — Total voted	Voted — Percent voted (total population)	Voted — Percent voted (total citizen population)
U.S. total	225 499	206 072	146 311	64.9	71.0	131 144	58.2	63.6
State total	1 020	1 005	801	78.5	79.7	716	70.2	71.2
Sex								
Male	492	484	380	77.3	78.6	336	68.3	69.4
Female	529	521	421	79.7	80.8	380	71.9	73.0
Race								
White alone	981	973	778	79.3	80.0	698	71.2	71.8
White non-Hispanic alone	967	959	770	79.7	80.3	691	71.5	72.0
Black alone	10	7	5	. . .	. . .	4	. . .	. . .
Asian alone	4	1	1	. . .	. . .	1	. . .	. . .
Hispanic (of any race)	17	15	9	. . .	. . .	8	. . .	. . .
White alone or in combination	1 004	993	794	79.1	79.9	709	70.7	71.4
Black alone or in combination	14	9	8	. . .	. . .	6	. . .	. . .
Asian alone or in combination	4	2	2	. . .	. . .	1	. . .	. . .

Table ME-13. Crime

(Number, rate per 100,000.)

Item	State 2007	State 2008	State Percent change	U.S. 2007	U.S. 2008	U.S. Percent change
Population	1 317 207	1 316 456	-0.1	301 621 157	304 059 724	0.8
VIOLENT CRIME						
Number	1 554	1 547	-0.5	1 408 337	1 382 012	-1.9
Rate	118.0	117.5	-0.4	466.9	454.5	-2.7
Murder and Nonnegligent Manslaughter						
Number	21	31	47.6	16 929	16 272	-3.9
Rate	1.6	2.4	47.7	5.6	5.4	-4.7
Forcible Rape						
Number	391	375	-4.1	90 427	89 000	-1.6
Rate	29.7	28.5	-4.0	30.0	29.3	-2.4
Robbery						
Number	349	333	-4.6	445 125	441 855	-0.7
Rate	26.5	25.3	-4.5	147.6	145.3	-1.5
Aggravated Assault						
Number	793	808	1.9	855 856	834 885	-2.5
Rate	60.2	61.4	1.9	283.8	274.6	-3.2
PROPERTY CRIME						
Number	31 992	32 285	0.9	9 843 481	9 767 915	-0.8
Rate	2 428.8	2 452.4	1.0	3 263.5	3 212.5	-1.6
Burglary						
Number	6 676	6 522	-2.3	2 179 140	2 222 196	2.0
Rate	506.8	495.4	-2.3	722.5	730.8	1.2
Larceny-Theft						
Number	24 057	24 587	2.2	6 568 572	6 588 873	0.3
Rate	1 826.4	1 867.7	2.3	2 177.8	2 167.0	-0.5
Motor Vehicle Theft						
Number	1 259	1 176	-6.6	1 095 769	956 846	-12.7
Rate	95.6	89.3	-6.5	363.3	314.7	-13.4

Table ME-14. State Government Finances, 2007

(Dollars, percent distribution.)

Item	Thousands of dollars	Percent distribution
Total Revenue	9 434 179	X
General revenue	7 428 346	78.7
Intergovernmental revenue	2 393 954	25.4
Taxes	3 581 680	38.0
General sales	1 054 812	11.2
Selective sales	635 893	6.7
License taxes	227 273	2.4
Individual income tax	1 358 301	14.4
Corporate income tax	183 852	1.9
Other taxes	121 549	1.3
Current charges	661 361	7.0
Miscellaneous general revenue	791 351	8.4
Utility revenue	0	0.0
Liquor store revenue	25	0.0
Insurance trust revenue	2 005 808	21.3
Total Expenditure	7 935 673	100.0
Intergovernmental expenditure	1 276 381	16.1
Direct expenditure	6 659 292	83.9
Current operation	5 141 624	64.8
Capital outlay	362 318	4.6
Insurance benefits and repayments	672 399	8.5
Assistance and subsidies	244 921	3.1
Interest on debt	238 030	3.0
Exhibit: Salaries and wages	741 360	9.3
Total Expenditure	7 935 673	100.0
General expenditure	7 263 274	91.5
Intergovernmental expenditure	1 276 381	16.1
Direct expenditure	5 986 893	75.4
Education	1 977 451	24.9
Public welfare	2 442 219	30.8
Hospitals	54 830	0.7
Health	476 005	6.0
Highways	497 630	6.3
Police protection	71 324	0.9
Correction	130 051	1.6
Natural resources	176 617	2.2
Parks and recreation	10 978	0.1
Government administration	292 306	3.7
Interest on general debt	238 030	3.0
Other and unallocable	895 833	11.3
Utility expenditure	0	0.0
Liquor store expenditure	0	0.0
Insurance trust expenditure	672 399	8.5
Debt at End of Fiscal Year	5 326 692	X
Cash and Security Holdings	20 427 835	X

Table ME-15. State Government Tax Collections, 2008

(Dollars, percent distribution.)

Item	Thousands of dollars	Percent distribution
Total Taxes	3 681 614	X
Property taxes	37 279	1.0
Sales and gross receipts	1 713 325	46.5
General sales and gross receipts	1 071 653	29.1
Selective sales taxes	641 672	17.4
Alcoholic beverages	20 673	0.6
Amusements	21 066	0.6
Insurance premiums	90 221	2.5
Motor fuels	229 849	6.2
Pari-mutuels	3 000	0.1
Public utilities	32 685	0.9
Tobacco products	150 499	4.1
Other selective sales	93 679	2.5
Licenses	233 711	6.3
Alcoholic beverages	4 148	0.1
Amusements	747	0.0
Corporation	7 969	0.2
Hunting and fishing	16 616	0.5
Motor vehicle	85 762	2.3
Motor vehicle operators	11 824	0.3
Occupation and business, NEC	98 076	2.7
Other licenses	8 569	0.2
Income taxes	1 632 788	44.3
Individual income	1 448 273	39.3
Corporation net income	184 515	5.0
Other taxes	64 511	1.8
Death and gift	39 891	1.1
Documentary and stock transfer	24 620	0.7

Table ME-16. Agriculture

(Number, acres, and dollars.)

Item	2002		2007		Percent change, 2002–2007
	Number	Percent of total	Number	Percent of total	
Number of farms	7 196		8 136		13.1
Farm Size					
Average size of farm (acres)	190		166		-12.6
Farms by size (number of farms)					
Fewer than 50 acres	2 779	38.6	3 429	42.1	23.4
50 to 499 acres	3 840	53.4	4 197	51.6	9.3
500 acres or more	577	8.0	510	6.3	-11.6
Land (Acres)					
Total land in farms	1 369 768		1 347 566		-1.6
Total cropland	536 839	39.2	529 253	39.3	-1.4
Total harvested cropland	394 121	28.8	393 738	29.2	-0.1
Irrigated land	19 703	1.4	20 994	1.6	6.6
Value of Sales (Dollars)					
Agricultural products sold ($1,000)	463 603		617 190		33.1
Average sales per farm	64 425		75 859		17.7
Sales of crops	222 356	48.0	326 573	52.9	46.9
Sales of livestock, poultry, and their products	241 247	52.0	290 617	47.1	20.5
Value of Sales (Number of Farms)					
Less than $10,000	5 093	70.8	5 608	68.9	10.1
$10,000 to $99,999	1 424	19.8	1 756	21.6	23.3
$100,000 to $999,999	617	8.6	685	8.4	11.0
$1,000,000 or more	62	0.9	87	1.1	40.3
Farms by Type of Organization (Number of Farms)					
Family	6 377	88.6	6 956	85.5	9.1
Partnership	321	4.5	544	6.7	69.5
Corporation	422	5.9	552	6.8	30.8
Other: cooperative, estate or trust, institutional, etc	76	1.1	84	1.0	10.5
Value of Land and Buildings (Dollars)					
Estimated market value of land and buildings ($1,000) ...	2 968 067		2 297 877		-22.6
Land and buildings average value per farm	364 807		322 690		-11.5
Average value per acre	2 203		1 637		-25.7
Government Payments					
Number of farms receiving government payments	1 244	17.3	1 459	17.9	17.3
Payments (thousands of dollars)	8 664		8 815		1.7
Average payment per farm	6 965		6 042		-13.3
Farm Operator Characteristics					
Farm operators whose principal occupation is farming ...	3 409	47.4	3 540	43.5	3.8
Farm operators whose principal occupation is other	3 787	52.6	4 596	56.5	21.4
Average age principal operator (years)	53.7		56.4		5.0

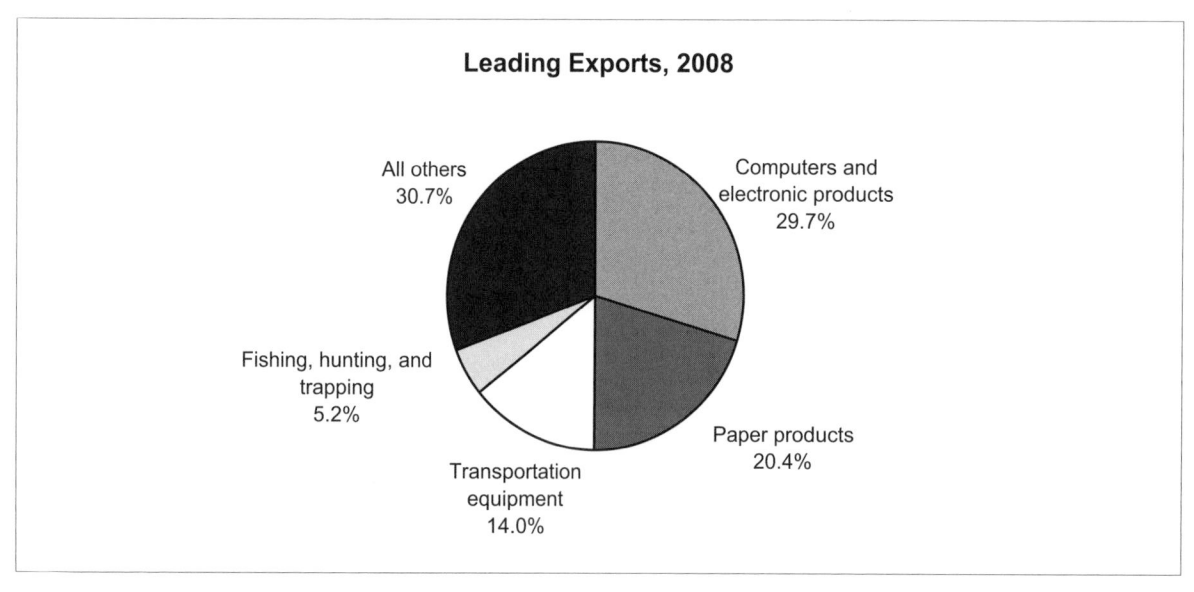

Leading Exports, 2008

All others 30.7%

Computers and electronic products 29.7%

Fishing, hunting, and trapping 5.2%

Transportation equipment 14.0%

Paper products 20.4%

MARYLAND

Facts and Figures

Location: Eastern United States; bordered on the N by Pennsylvania, on the E by Delaware and the Atlantic Ocean, and on the S and W by Virginia and West Virginia

Area: 12,407 sq. mi. (32,133 sq. km.); rank—42nd

Population: 5,633,597 (2008 est.); rank—19th

Principal Cities: capital—Annapolis; largest—Baltimore

Statehood: April 28, 1788; 7th state

U.S. Congress: 2 senators, 8 representatives

State Motto: *Fatti maschii parole femine* ("Manly deeds, womanly words")

State Song: "Maryland, My Maryland"

State Nicknames: The Old Line State; The Free State

Abbreviations: MD; Md.

State Symbols: flower—black-eyed susan; tree—white oak; bird—Baltimore oriole

At a Glance

- With an increase in population of 6.4 percent, Maryland ranked 24th among the states in growth from 2000 to 2008.
- An estimated 33,391 marriages took place in Maryland in 2008, compared to 16,210 divorces.
- The 2007 home ownership rate in Maryland was 71.7 percent, giving it a ranking of 19th among the states.
- Maryland's median household income in 2007 was $68,080, 1st among the states.
- In Maryland, 8.3 percent of the population lived below the poverty level in 2007, ranking it 47th.
- In 2006-07, 13.8 percent of Marylanders did not have health insurance, compared to 15.5 percent of the total U.S. population.
- In 2007, 3.6 percent of Marylanders were unemployed, compared to 4.6 percent nationwide.
- Maryland ranked 2nd in the nation with 35.2 percent of its population 25 years old and over having a bachelor's degree in 2007.
- Maryland's violent crime rate in 2007 was 641.9 per 100,000 population, compared to 466.9 for the entire nation.
- Maryland had one physician for every 213 people in 2007, compared to one physician for every 325 people nationwide.
- In the 2008 election, 67.7 percent of Maryland's eligible voters voted, compared to 61.7 percent of eligible voters nationwide.
- Maryland ranked 35th among the states receiving federal aid in 2007, with $1,312 per capita.
- Maryland's gross domestic product was $269 billion in 2007; it ranked 15th among the states.
- With $8.9 billion in exports in 2007, Maryland ranked 29th in exports.
- Marylanders consumed 1.45 trillion Btu's of energy in 2006; the state ranked 26th in total consumption.
- In 2007, Maryland exported $358 million worth of agricultural products, less than 1 percent of the U.S. total.

Table MD-1. Population by Sex, Age, Race, and Hispanic Origin

(Number, percent.)

Sex, age, race, and Hispanic origin	1990	2000	2008	Average annual percent change, 2000–2008
Total Population	4 781 468	5 296 486	5 633 597	0.8
Percent of total U.S. population	1.9	1.9	1.9	X
Sex				
Male	2 318 671	2 557 794	2 727 323	0.8
Female	2 462 797	2 738 692	2 906 274	0.7
Age				
Under 5 years	357 818	353 393	371 787	0.6
5 to 19 years	940 187	1 139 572	1 135 092	0.0
20 to 64 years	2 965 981	3 204 214	3 447 153	0.9
65 years and over	517 482	599 307	679 565	1.6
Median age (years)	32.9	36.0	37.7	X
Race and Hispanic Origin[1]				
One race				
White	3 393 964	3 391 308	3 571 589	0.6
Black	1 189 899	1 477 411	1 658 422	1.5
American Indian and Alaskan Native	12 972	15 423	20 321	3.5
Asian[2]	139 719	210 929	286 333	3.9
Native Hawaiian and Other Pacific Islander	X	2 303	4 234	7.9
Two or more races	X	103 587	92 698	-1.4
Hispanic (of any race)	125 102	227 916	375 830	6.5

[1]Data on race in 2000 and 2008 are not comparable to 1990. Individuals could only report one race in the 1990 census but could report one or more races on the 2000 census.
[2]Data in 1990 refer to Asian and Pacific Islanders.

Table MD-2. Marital Status

(Number, percent distribution.)

Sex and marital status	1990	2000	2007
Males, 15 Years and Over	1 814 522	1 972 921	2 149 920
Never married	32.4	31.0	35.5
Now married, except separated	55.4	56.3	51.4
Separated	3.3	2.8	2.4
Widowed	2.4	2.5	2.6
Divorced	6.4	7.4	8.1
Females, 15 Years and Over	1 979 591	2 186 715	2 357 560
Never married	26.1	26.8	31.3
Now married, except separated	50.3	49.7	45.8
Separated	4.1	3.4	3.0
Widowed	10.9	10.1	9.4
Divorced	8.6	10.1	10.6

Table MD-3. Households and Housing Characteristics

(Number, percent, and dollars.)

Item	1990	2000	2007	Average annual percent change, 2000–2007
Total Households	1 748 991	1 980 859	2 082 458	0.7
Family households	1 245 814	1 359 318	1 392 247	0.3
Married-couple family	948 563	994 549	1 008 897	0.2
Other family	297 251	364 769	383 350	0.7
Male householder, no wife present	65 362	84 893	100 443	2.4
Female householder, no husband present	231 889	279 876	282 907	0.2
Nonfamily households	503 177	621 541	690 211	1.5
Householder living alone	394 572	495 459	561 473	1.8
Householder not living alone	108 605	126 082	128 738	0.3
Housing Characteristics				
Total housing units	1 891 917	2 145 283	2 318 430	1.1
Occupied housing units	1 748 991	1 980 859	2 082 458	0.7
Owner-occupied	1 137 296	1 341 751	1 456 103	1.2
Renter-occupied	611 695	639 108	626 355	-0.3
Average size	2.67	2.61	2.63	X
Financial Characteristics				
Median gross rent of renter-occupied housing units (dollars)	548	689	1 000	5.5
Median monthly owner costs for housing units with a mortgage (dollars)	919	1 296	1 881	5.5
Median value of owner-occupied housing units (dollars)	115 500	146 000	347 000	13.2

Table MD-4. Median Income and Poverty Status, 2007

(Number, percent.)

Characteristic	State		U.S.	
	Number	Percent	Number	Percent
Median Income				
Households (dollars)	68 080	X	50 740	X
Families (dollars)	82 404	X	61 173	X
Below Poverty Level				
Sex				
Male	188 081	7.1	16 576 071	11.5
Female	265 618	9.4	21 476 176	14.3
Age				
Under 18 years	140 058	10.5	13 097 100	18.0
Related children under 18 years	132 127	10.0	12 728 964	17.6
18 to 64 years	261 245	7.5	21 495 507	11.6
65 years and over	52 396	8.2	3 459 640	9.5

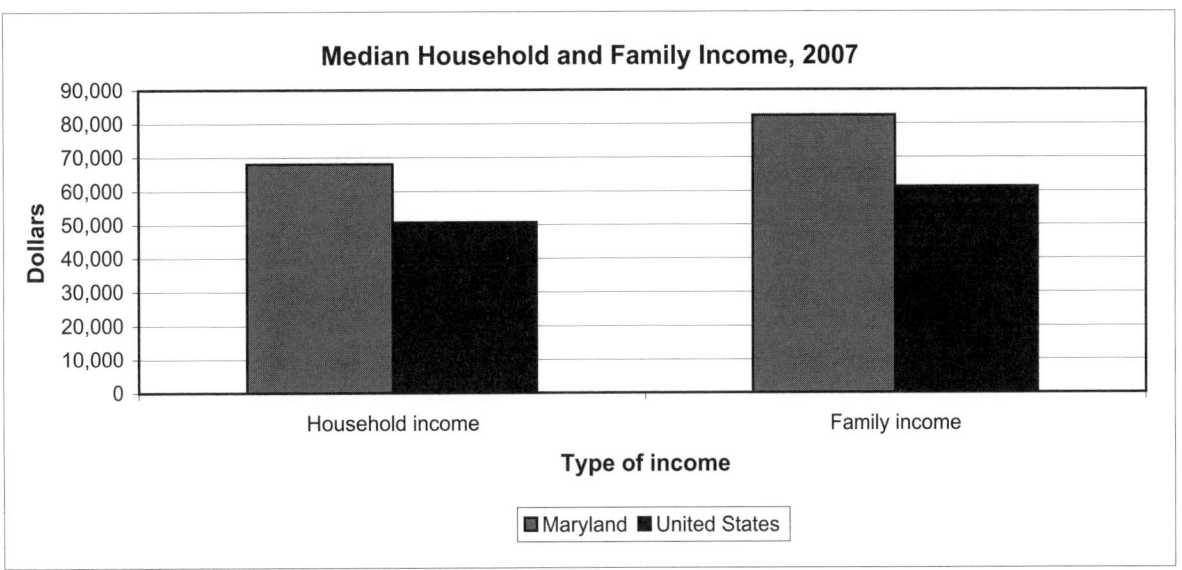

Median Household and Family Income, 2007

Table MD-5. Health Insurance Coverage Status for All Persons and Children Under 18 Years of Age

(Number, percent.)

Item	2000	2001	2002	2003	2004	2005	2006	2007
ALL PERSONS	5 261	5 326	5 458	5 493	5 550	5 569	5 613	5 565
Covered by Private or Government Health Insurance								
Number	4 750	4 703	4 784	4 759	4 809	4 823	4 836	4 804
Percent	90.3	88.3	87.7	86.7	86.6	86.6	86.2	86.3
Not Covered								
Number	511	623	674	733	742	746	776	762
Percent	9.7	11.7	12.3	13.3	13.4	13.4	13.8	13.7
Percent in the U.S. not covered	13.7	14.1	14.7	15.1	14.9	15.3	15.8	15.3
CHILDREN UNDER 18 YEARS OF AGE	1 387	1 422	1 403	1 411	1 389	1 383	1 384	1 382
Covered by Private or Government Health Insurance								
Number	1 259	1 295	1 278	1 303	1 259	1 268	1 247	1 237
Percent	90.7	91.0	91.1	92.4	90.6	91.7	90.1	89.5
Not Covered								
Number	128	127	125	108	130	115	137	146
Percent	9.3	9.0	8.9	7.6	9.4	8.3	9.9	10.5
Percent in the U.S. not covered	11.6	11.3	11.2	11.0	10.5	10.9	11.7	11.0

Table MD-6. Employment Status by Demographic Group, Preliminary 2008

(Number, percent.)

Characteristic	Civilian noninstitutional population	Civilian labor force		Employment		Unemployed	
		Number	Percent of population	Number	Percent of population	Number	Unemployment rate
TOTAL	4 360	3 004	68.9	2 877	66.0	128	4.2
Sex							
Men	2 059	1 532	74.0	1 460	70.9	72	4.7
Women	2 301	1 472	64.0	1 416	61.6	55	3.8
Race, Sex, and Hispanic Origin							
White	2 862	1 965	68.6	1 892	66.1	72	3.7
Men	1 387	1 050	75.7	1 007	72.6	43	4.1
Women	1 475	915	62.0	885	60.0	29	3.2
Black or African American	1 232	862	69.9	814	66.0	48	5.6
Men	545	387	71.0	361	66.3	26	6.6
Women	687	475	69.1	452	65.8	23	4.8
Hispanic	294	228	77.6	220	74.8	8	3.7
Men	153	133	87.2	128	83.6	6	4.1
Women	141	95	67.2	92	65.2	3	3.0
Age							
16 to 19 years	333	130	39.0	109	32.9	20	15.7
20 to 24 years	406	290	71.6	266	65.6	24	8.4
25 to 34 years	696	600	86.2	576	82.7	24	4.1
35 to 44 years	775	671	86.5	647	83.4	24	3.5
45 to 54 years	856	723	84.5	706	82.5	17	2.3
55 to 64 years	646	460	71.2	449	69.6	11	2.3
65 years and over	648	130	20.1	123	19.0	7	5.6

Note: Data in Table 6 are from the Current Population Survey (CPS) and do not match the estimates in Table 7. See notes and definitions for more details.

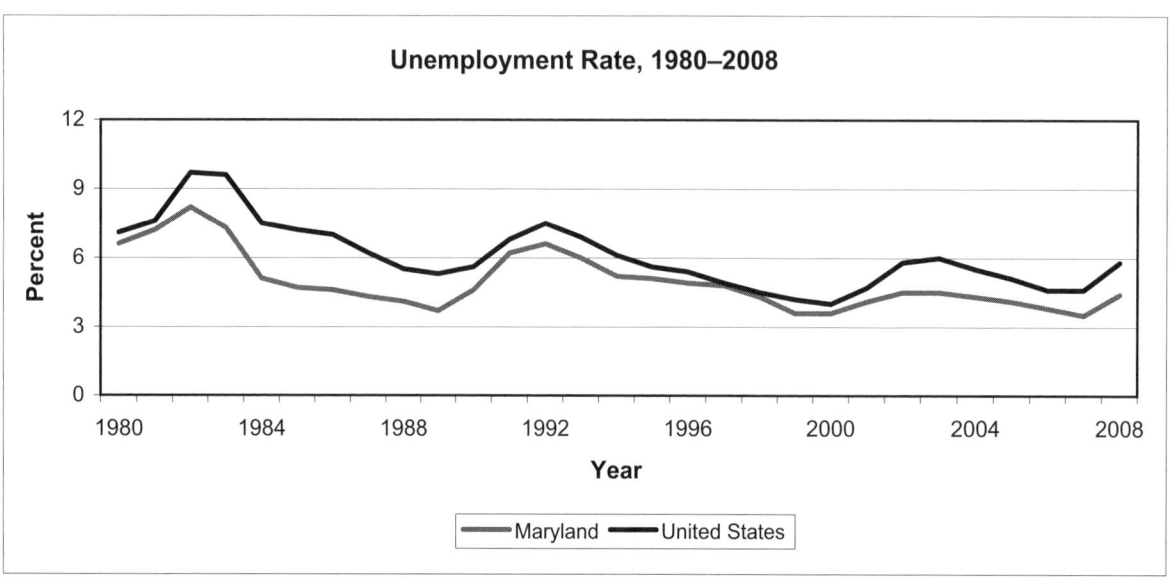

Table MD-7. Employment Status of the Civilian Noninstitutional Population Age 16 Years and Over

(Number, percent.)

Year	Civilian labor force	Civilian participation rate	Employed	Unemployed	Unemployment rate
1998	2 780 009	70.9	2 661 192	118 817	4.3
1999	2 787 870	70.5	2 687 843	100 027	3.6
2000	2 811 657	70.4	2 711 382	100 275	3.6
2001	2 827 047	69.7	2 712 268	114 779	4.1
2002	2 861 421	69.6	2 733 103	128 318	4.5
2003	2 870 027	68.9	2 741 325	128 702	4.5
2004	2 885 240	68.5	2 761 583	123 657	4.3
2005	2 931 946	68.8	2 810 748	121 198	4.1
2006	2 983 937	69.4	2 871 176	112 761	3.8
2007	2 987 698	69.0	2 882 447	105 251	3.5
2008	2 997 709	68.8	2 867 178	130 531	4.4

Table MD-8. Employment and Average Wages by Industry

(Estimates for 2001–2006 are based on the 2002 North American Industry Classification System [NAICS]. Estimates for 2007 are based on the 2007 NAICS.)

Industry	2001	2002	2003	2004	2005	2006	2007
	Number of jobs						
WAGE AND SALARY EMPLOYMENT BY INDUSTRY	2 620 715	2 635 632	2 645 754	2 668 061	2 702 019	2 737 646	2 752 963
Farm Wage and Salary Employment	6 526	6 649	5 741	5 622	5 485	5 754	5 539
Nonfarm Wage and Salary Employment	2 614 189	2 628 983	2 640 013	2 662 439	2 696 534	2 731 892	2 747 424
Private wage and salary employment	2 094 285	2 099 156	2 105 662	2 135 110	2 166 524	2 194 690	2 205 170
Forestry, fishing, hunting, and other	2 586	2 673	3 021	3 140	3 227	3 151	2 953
Mining	1 570	1 424	1 434	1 539	1 730	1 804	1 662
Utilities	10 859	10 045	9 968	9 784	9 740	9 755	9 957
Construction	171 933	172 605	174 475	183 077	189 868	194 963	194 348
Manufacturing	169 913	157 437	148 372	144 238	140 704	136 346	132 621
Durable goods manufacturing	91 849	84 000	78 291	76 491	74 355	71 910	71 204
Nondurable goods manufacturing	78 064	73 437	70 081	67 747	66 349	64 436	61 417
Wholesale trade	95 433	94 569	93 381	94 038	95 793	96 686	96 480
Retail trade	306 614	303 575	302 241	305 293	307 611	309 047	310 660
Transportation and warehousing	68 980	68 306	65 476	66 848	67 782	69 572	69 651
Information	58 958	54 841	51 687	50 351	50 633	50 979	50 815
Finance and insurance	106 565	108 850	113 078	112 694	113 114	113 440	110 648
Real estate and rental and leasing	48 028	48 012	48 709	48 810	50 181	49 737	49 174
Professional and technical services	209 354	209 318	212 637	217 462	224 424	229 633	231 340
Management of companies and enterprises	9 598	9 262	10 335	15 989	18 100	18 698	19 520
Administrative and waste services	151 386	150 229	150 294	153 794	155 327	156 807	156 133
Educational services	57 881	62 794	62 151	64 018	64 205	64 338	66 986
Health care and social assistance	272 498	282 196	290 010	294 151	299 838	308 882	316 051
Arts, entertainment, and recreation	34 121	35 226	35 746	37 594	37 758	38 599	38 744
Accommodation and food services	179 192	184 583	187 910	187 856	193 484	196 555	199 932
Other services, except public administration	138 816	143 211	144 737	144 434	143 005	145 698	147 495
Government and government enterprises	519 904	529 827	534 351	527 329	530 010	537 202	542 254
	Dollars						
AVERAGE WAGES AND SALARIES BY INDUSTRY	37 640	38 840	40 231	42 421	44 304	46 076	48 113
Average Farm Wages and Salaries	18 601	23 732	23 540	23 866	19 791	21 622	19 775
Average Nonfarm Wages and Salaries	37 687	38 878	40 267	42 460	44 354	46 127	48 170
Average private wages and salaries	36 675	37 466	38 831	40 651	42 432	44 167	46 029
Forestry, fishing, hunting, and other	21 651	21 951	23 118	24 231	25 532	25 967	26 257
Mining	50 836	47 835	47 965	48 576	50 775	49 980	51 431
Utilities	66 757	68 595	74 986	81 521	89 455	88 879	98 433
Construction	40 376	41 223	42 291	44 055	45 916	48 217	50 634
Manufacturing	47 099	48 399	50 113	53 264	54 016	55 931	60 251
Durable goods manufacturing	52 083	54 349	56 541	60 593	60 865	62 524	65 668
Nondurable goods manufacturing	41 235	41 593	42 931	44 988	46 340	48 572	53 971
Wholesale trade	51 987	52 675	54 495	56 919	59 219	61 716	64 589
Retail trade	24 021	24 659	25 251	26 052	26 570	27 139	27 480
Transportation and warehousing	35 837	36 564	37 375	38 913	40 421	41 426	42 748
Information	55 830	56 246	57 789	60 927	61 863	63 398	64 711
Finance and insurance	57 959	60 077	64 049	66 826	72 337	74 568	78 359
Real estate and rental and leasing	35 769	37 776	39 786	44 295	46 326	49 117	51 099
Professional and technical services	58 653	60 460	61 768	65 384	68 632	72 545	75 830
Management of companies and enterprises	52 829	54 357	64 473	73 086	86 364	89 953	94 703
Administrative and waste services	25 639	26 850	27 774	28 985	30 524	32 089	34 041
Educational services	30 354	31 157	33 941	35 166	36 764	38 154	39 289
Health care and social assistance	34 486	35 582	36 857	38 570	39 855	41 407	43 051
Arts, entertainment, and recreation	23 432	23 333	23 656	24 534	26 244	27 153	28 259
Accommodation and food services	16 598	16 481	17 248	16 155	16 636	17 704	18 418
Other services, except public administration	24 653	25 407	26 734	27 915	28 792	29 873	31 108
Government and government enterprises	41 764	44 476	45 926	49 782	52 210	54 134	56 878

Table MD-9. Employment Characteristics by Family Type

(Number, percent.)

Family type and labor force status	2005		2006		2007	
	Total	Families with own children under 18 years	Total	Families with own children under 18 years	Total	Families with own children under 18 years
TOTAL FAMILIES	1 397 971	666 636	1 405 655	670 052	1 392 247	653 008
FAMILY TYPE AND LABOR FORCE STATUS						
Married Coupled Families	1 021 849	459 655	1 018 096	456 367	1 008 897	443 740
Both husband and wife in labor force	57.6	68.1	59.5	70.9	59.3	70.0
Husband in labor force, wife not in labor force	21.2	26.1	20.3	24.6	20.9	24.9
Wife in labor force, husband not in labor force	6.8	3.2	6.7	3.2	6.8	3.6
Both husband and wife not in labor force	14.4	2.6	13.5	1.4	13.0	1.5
Other Families	376 122	206 981	387 559	213 685	383 350	209 268
Female householder, no husband present	76.1	79.8	74.9	77.9	73.8	76.1
In labor force	58.0	69.4	56.6	67.2	55.8	66.2
Not in labor force	18.1	10.4	18.3	10.8	18.0	9.9
Male householder, no wife present	23.9	20.2	25.1	22.1	26.2	23.9
In labor force	19.4	18.0	20.9	20.5	21.3	21.8
Not in labor force	4.6	2.2	4.2	1.5	4.9	2.1

Table MD-10. School Enrollment and Educational Attainment, 2007

(Number, percent.)

Item	State	U.S.
Enrollment		
Total population 3 years and over	5 395 841	289 295 761
Enrolled in school	1 524 249	79 329 527
Enrolled in preschool (percent)	6.2	6.2
Enrolled in grades K-12 (percent)	64.3	67.6
Enrolled in college or graduate school (percent)	29.5	26.2
Attainment		
Total population 25 years and over	3 713 487	197 892 369
Less than a high school diploma (percent)	12.6	15.5
High school diploma or more (percent)	87.4	84.5
Bachelor's degree or more (percent)	35.2	27.5
Graduate degree or more (percent)	15.7	10.1

Table MD-11. Educational Indicators

(Number, percent.)

Item	State	U.S.
Public Schools, 2006–2007 (except where noted)		
Number of school districts	25	17 742
Number of schools	1 446	99 639
Number of students	851 640	49 315 842
Student-teacher ratio	14.6	15.5
Expenditures per student (dollars)	$11 975	. . .
Averaged freshman graduation rate, 2005–2006	79.9	. . .
Dropout rate, grades 9–12, 2005–2006	3.9	3.7
Students eligible for free or reduced-price lunch (percent)	32.2	41.2
English-language learners (percent)	. . .	5.1
Students with IEP (percent)	12.4	12.7
Private Schools, 2007–2008 (except where noted)		
Number of schools	823	33 740
Number of students	143 661	5 072 451
High school graduates, 2006–2007	9 454	306 605
Student-teacher ratio	10.1	11.1

Table MD-12. Reported Voting and Registration of the Voting-Age Population, November 2008

(Number in thousands, percent.)

Item	Total population	Total citizen population	Registered — Total registered	Registered — Percent registered (total population)	Registered — Percent registered (total citizen population)	Voted — Total voted	Voted — Percent voted (total population)	Voted — Percent voted (total citizen population)
U.S. total	225 499	206 072	146 311	64.9	71.0	131 144	58.2	63.6
State total	4 218	3 824	2 828	67.0	73.9	2 611	61.9	68.3
Sex								
Male	1 984	1 783	1 254	63.2	70.3	1 153	58.1	64.6
Female	2 234	2 041	1 574	70.4	77.1	1 458	65.3	71.5
Race								
White alone	2 762	2 571	1 876	67.9	73.0	1 725	62.5	67.1
White non-Hispanic alone	2 521	2 449	1 793	71.1	73.2	1 644	65.2	67.1
Black alone	1 177	1 062	831	70.6	78.2	788	66.9	74.2
Asian alone	220	134	80	36.2	59.4	62	28.2	46.2
Hispanic (of any race)	269	145	93	34.5	63.9	91	34.0	62.9
White alone or in combination	2 793	2 600	1 897	67.9	73.0	1 745	62.5	67.1
Black alone or in combination	1 207	1 092	855	70.8	78.3	806	66.8	73.8
Asian alone or in combination	224	137	81	36.2	59.2	63	28.3	46.2

Table MD-13. Crime

(Number, rate per 100,000.)

Item	State 2007	State 2008	State Percent change	U.S. 2007	U.S. 2008	U.S. Percent change
Population	5 618 344	5 633 597	0.3	301 621 157	304 059 724	0.8
VIOLENT CRIME						
Number	36 062	35 393	-1.9	1 408 337	1 382 012	-1.9
Rate	641.9	628.2	-2.1	466.9	454.5	-2.7
Murder and Nonnegligent Manslaughter						
Number	553	493	-10.8	16 929	16 272	-3.9
Rate	9.8	8.8	-11.1	5.6	5.4	-4.7
Forcible Rape						
Number	1 179	1 127	-4.4	90 427	89 000	-1.6
Rate	21.0	20.0	-4.7	30.0	29.3	-2.4
Robbery						
Number	13 258	13 203	-0.4	445 125	441 855	-0.7
Rate	236.0	234.4	-0.7	147.6	145.3	-1.5
Aggravated Assault						
Number	21 072	20 570	-2.4	855 856	834 885	-2.5
Rate	375.1	365.1	-2.6	283.8	274.6	-3.2
PROPERTY CRIME						
Number	192 796	198 165	2.8	9 843 481	9 767 915	-0.8
Rate	3 431.5	3 517.6	2.5	3 263.5	3 212.5	-1.6
Burglary						
Number	37 095	38 849	4.7	2 179 140	2 222 196	2.0
Rate	660.2	689.6	4.4	722.5	730.8	1.2
Larceny-Theft						
Number	127 308	133 983	5.2	6 568 572	6 588 873	0.3
Rate	2 265.9	2 378.3	5.0	2 177.8	2 167.0	-0.5
Motor Vehicle Theft						
Number	28 393	25 333	-10.8	1 095 769	956 846	-12.7
Rate	505.4	449.7	-11.0	363.3	314.7	-13.4

Table MD-14. State Government Finances, 2007

(Dollars, percent distribution.)

Item	Thousands of dollars	Percent distribution
Total Revenue	34 848 081	X
General revenue	27 374 133	78.6
Intergovernmental revenue	7 199 413	20.7
Taxes	15 094 183	43.3
General sales	3 447 828	9.9
Selective sales	2 364 058	6.8
License taxes	722 214	2.1
Individual income tax	6 679 168	19.2
Corporate income tax	782 030	2.2
Other taxes	1 098 885	3.2
Current charges	2 836 999	8.1
Miscellaneous general revenue	2 243 538	6.4
Utility revenue	116 237	0.3
Liquor store revenue	0	0.0
Insurance trust revenue	7 357 711	21.1
Total Expenditure	31 610 548	100.0
Intergovernmental expenditure	7 568 283	23.9
Direct expenditure	24 042 265	76.1
Current operation	17 171 780	54.3
Capital outlay	2 104 467	6.7
Insurance benefits and repayments	2 792 465	8.8
Assistance and subsidies	1 091 802	3.5
Interest on debt	881 751	2.8
Exhibit: Salaries and wages	4 512 655	14.3
Total Expenditure	31 610 548	100.0
General expenditure	28 266 243	89.4
Intergovernmental expenditure	7 568 283	23.9
Direct expenditure	20 697 960	65.5
Education	9 705 518	30.7
Public welfare	6 847 770	21.7
Hospitals	494 736	1.6
Health	1 890 053	6.0
Highways	2 396 270	7.6
Police protection	419 201	1.3
Correction	1 376 322	4.4
Natural resources	519 805	1.6
Parks and recreation	269 792	0.9
Government administration	1 243 245	3.9
Interest on general debt	881 751	2.8
Other and unallocable	2 221 780	7.0
Utility expenditure	551 840	1.7
Liquor store expenditure	0	0.0
Insurance trust expenditure	2 792 465	8.8
Debt at End of Fiscal Year	19 017 465	X
Cash and Security Holdings	63 002 633	X

Table MD-15. State Government Tax Collections, 2008

(Dollars, percent distribution.)

Item	Thousands of dollars	Percent distribution
Total Taxes	16 605 830	X
Property taxes	630 809	3.8
Sales and gross receipts	6 248 816	37.6
General sales and gross receipts	3 748 933	22.6
Selective sales taxes	2 499 883	15.1
Alcoholic beverages	28 966	0.2
Amusements	14 783	0.1
Insurance premiums	414 233	2.5
Motor fuels	808 964	4.9
Pari-mutuels	1 806	0.0
Public utilities	133 513	0.8
Tobacco products	376 112	2.3
Other selective sales	721 506	4.3
Licenses	697 481	4.2
Alcoholic beverages	1 022	0.0
Amusements	30	0.0
Corporation	74 455	0.4
Hunting and fishing	15 247	0.1
Motor vehicle	442 018	2.7
Motor vehicle operators	29 373	0.2
Occupation and business, NEC	133 279	0.8
Other licenses	2 057	0.0
Income taxes	8 567 301	51.6
Individual income	7 831 977	47.2
Corporation net income	735 324	4.4
Other taxes	461 423	2.8
Death and gift	243 425	1.5
Documentary and stock transfer	154 491	0.9
Other	63 507	0.4

Table MD-16. Agriculture

(Number, acres, and dollars.)

Item	2002		2007		Percent change, 2002–2007
	Number	Percent of total	Number	Percent of total	
Number of farms	12 198		12 834		5.2
Farm Size					
Average size of farm (acres)	170		160		-5.9
Farms by size (number of farms)					
Fewer than 50 acres	5 830	47.8	6 143	47.9	5.4
50 to 499 acres	5 419	44.4	5 786	45.1	6.8
500 acres or more	949	7.8	905	7.1	-4.6
Land (Acres)					
Total land in farms	2 077 630		2 051 756		-1.2
Total cropland	1 487 218	71.6	1 405 442	68.5	-5.5
Total harvested cropland	1 282 004	61.7	1 246 603	60.8	-2.8
Irrigated land	80 828	3.9	92 805	4.5	14.8
Value of Sales (Dollars)					
Agricultural products sold ($1,000)	1 293 303		1 835 090		41.9
Average sales per farm	106 026		142 987		34.9
Sales of crops	450 202	34.8	629 303	34.3	39.8
Sales of livestock, poultry, and their products	843 101	65.2	1 205 787	65.7	43.0
Value of Sales (Number of Farms)					
Less than $10,000	7 382	60.5	7 505	58.5	1.7
$10,000 to $99,999	2 717	22.3	3 070	23.9	13.0
$100,000 to $999,999	1 874	15.4	1 820	14.2	-2.9
$1,000,000 or more	225	1.8	439	3.4	95.1
Farms by Type of Organization (Number of Farms)					
Family	10 577	86.7	10 609	82.7	0.3
Partnership	763	6.3	1 038	8.1	36.0
Corporation	726	6.0	977	7.6	34.6
Other: cooperative, estate or trust, institutional, etc	132	1.1	210	1.6	59.1
Value of Land and Buildings (Dollars)					
Estimated market value of land and buildings ($1,000)	14 432 211		8 452 963		-41.4
Land and buildings average value per farm	1 124 529		694 061		-38.3
Average value per acre	7 034		4 084		-41.9
Government Payments					
Number of farms receiving government payments	3 372	27.6	4 588	35.7	36.1
Payments (thousands of dollars)	33 131		33 386		0.8
Average payment per farm	9 825		7 277		-25.9
Farm Operator Characteristics					
Farm operators whose principal occupation is farming	6 977	57.2	6 269	48.8	-10.1
Farm operators whose principal occupation is other	5 221	42.8	6 565	51.2	25.7
Average age principal operator (years)	55.9		57.3		2.5

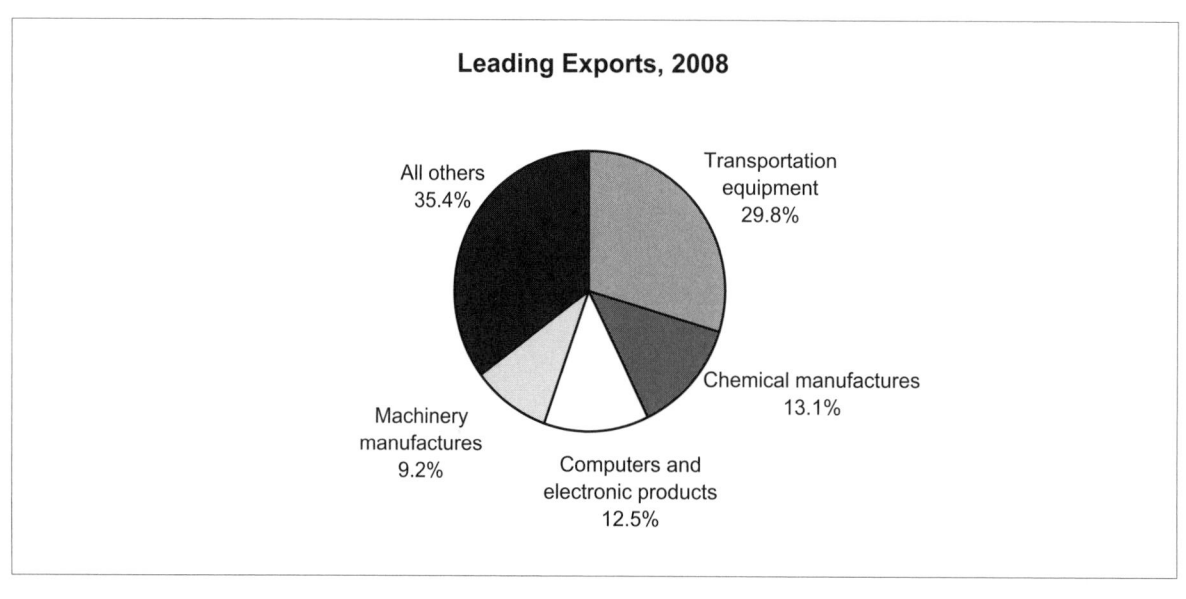

Leading Exports, 2008

All others 35.4%

Transportation equipment 29.8%

Chemical manufactures 13.1%

Computers and electronic products 12.5%

Machinery manufactures 9.2%

MASSACHUSETTS

Facts and Figures

Location: Northeastern United States; bordered on the N by Vermont and New Hampshire, on the E by the Atlantic Ocean, on the S by Connecticut and Rhode Island, and on the W by New York

Area: 10,555 sq. mi. (27,336 sq. km.); rank—44th

Population: 6,497,967 (2008 est.); rank—14th

Principal Cities: capital—Boston; largest—Boston

Statehood: February 6, 1788; 6th state

U.S. Congress: 2 senators, 10 representatives

State Motto: *Ense petit placidam sub libertate quietem* ("By the sword we seek peace, but peace only under liberty")

State Song: "All Hail to Massachusetts"

State Nickname: The Bay State

Abbreviations: MA; Mass.

State Symbols: flower—mayflower; tree—American elm; bird—chickadee

At a Glance

- With an increase in population of 2.3 percent, Massachusetts ranked 42nd among the states in growth from 2000 to 2008.
- An estimated 33,996 marriages took place in Massachusetts in 2008, compared to 12,992 divorces.
- The 2007 home ownership rate in Massachusetts was 64.3 percent, giving it a ranking of 46th among the states.
- Massachusetts's median household income in 2007 was $62,365, 7th among the states.
- In Massachusetts, 9.9 percent of the population lived below the poverty level in 2007, ranking it 40th along with Virginia.
- In 2006-07, 7.9 percent of Massachusettsans did not have health insurance, compared to 15.5 percent of the total U.S. population.
- In 2007, 4.6 percent of Massachusettsans were unemployed, compared to 4.6 percent nationwide.
- Massachusetts ranked 1st in the nation with 37.9 percent of its population 25 years old and over having a bachelor's degree in 2007.
- Massachusetts's violent crime rate in 2007 was 431.5 per 100,000 population, compared to 466.9 for the entire nation.
- Massachusetts had one physician for every 194 people in 2007, compared to one physician for every 325 people nationwide.
- In the 2008 election, 66.2 percent of Massachusetts's eligible voters voted, compared to 61.7 percent of eligible voters nationwide.
- Massachusetts ranked 13th among the states receiving federal aid in 2007, with $1,735 per capita.
- Massachusetts's gross domestic product was $352 billion in 2007; it ranked 13th among the states.
- With $25.4 billion in exports in 2007, Massachusetts ranked 13th in exports.
- Massachusettsans consumed 1.48 trillion Btu's of energy in 2006; the state ranked 25th in total consumption.
- In 2007, Massachusetts exported $201 million worth of agricultural products, less than 1 percent of the U.S. total.

Table MA-1. Population by Sex, Age, Race, and Hispanic Origin

(Number, percent.)

Sex, age, race, and Hispanic origin	1990	2000	2008	Average annual percent change, 2000–2008
Total Population	6 016 425	6 349 097	6 497 967	0.3
Percent of total U.S. population	2.4	2.3	2.1	X
Sex				
Male	2 888 745	3 058 816	3 153 176	0.4
Female	3 127 680	3 290 281	3 344 791	0.2
Age				
Under 5 years	412 473	397 268	383 568	-0.4
5 to 19 years	1 136 062	1 277 845	1 244 360	-0.3
20 to 64 years	3 648 606	3 813 822	3 998 941	0.6
65 years and over	819 284	860 162	871 098	0.2
Median age (years)	33.4	36.5	38.6	X
Race and Hispanic Origin[1]				
One race				
White	5 405 374	5 367 286	5 601 486	0.5
Black	300 130	343 454	455 880	3.6
American Indian and Alaskan Native	12 241	15 015	20 361	3.9
Asian[2]	143 392	238 124	321 130	3.8
Native Hawaiian and Other Pacific Islander	X	2 489	5 507	10.4
Two or more races	X	146 005	93 603	-5.4
Hispanic (of any race)	287 549	428 729	556 897	3.3

[1]Data on race in 2000 and 2008 are not comparable to 1990. Individuals could only report one race in the 1990 census but could report one or more races on the 2000 census.
[2]Data in 1990 refer to Asian and Pacific Islanders.

Table MA-2. Marital Status

(Number, percent distribution.)

Sex and marital status	1990	2000	2007
Males, 15 Years and Over	2 305 194	2 412 349	2 530 766
Never married	36.1	33.9	37.8
Now married, except separated	53.5	54.7	50.4
Separated	1.7	1.6	1.4
Widowed	2.8	2.7	2.6
Divorced	5.9	7.0	7.8
Females, 15 Years and Over	2 572 630	2 679 020	2 750 682
Never married	29.7	28.5	32.4
Now married, except separated	47.7	48.9	45.4
Separated	2.4	2.3	2.1
Widowed	12.1	10.8	9.6
Divorced	8.1	9.5	10.4

Table MA-3. Households and Housing Characteristics

(Number, percent, and dollars.)

Item	1990	2000	2007	Average annual percent change, 2000–2007
Total Households	2 247 110	2 443 580	2 449 133	0.0
Family households	1 514 746	1 576 696	1 561 198	-0.1
Married-couple family	1 170 275	1 197 917	1 166 023	-0.4
Other family	344 471	378 779	395 175	0.6
Male householder, no wife present	73 548	88 835	100 130	1.7
Female householder, no husband present	270 923	289 944	295 045	0.2
Nonfamily households	732 364	866 884	887 935	0.3
Householder living alone	580 774	684 345	712 927	0.6
Householder not living alone	151 590	182 539	175 008	-0.6
Housing Characteristics				
Total housing units	2 472 711	2 621 989	2 722 323	0.5
Occupied housing units	2 247 110	2 443 580	2 449 133	0.0
Owner-occupied	1 331 493	1 508 052	1 594 159	0.8
Renter-occupied	915 617	935 528	854 974	-1.3
Average size	2.58	2.51	2.55	X
Financial Characteristics				
Median gross rent of renter-occupied housing units (dollars)	580	684	946	4.7
Median monthly owner costs for housing units with a mortgage (dollars)	985	1 353	2 021	5.9
Median value of owner-occupied housing units (dollars)	162 200	185 700	366 400	10.2

Table MA-4. Median Income and Poverty Status, 2007

(Number, percent.)

Characteristic	State		U.S.	
	Number	Percent	Number	Percent
Median Income				
Households (dollars)	62 365	X	50 740	X
Families (dollars)	78 497	X	61 173	X
Below Poverty Level				
Sex				
Male	264 874	8.7	16 576 071	11.5
Female	356 412	11.1	21 476 176	14.3
Age				
Under 18 years	182 159	12.9	13 097 100	18.0
Related children under 18 years	176 091	12.6	12 728 964	17.6
18 to 64 years	363 943	9.0	21 495 507	11.6
65 years and over	75 184	9.3	3 459 640	9.5

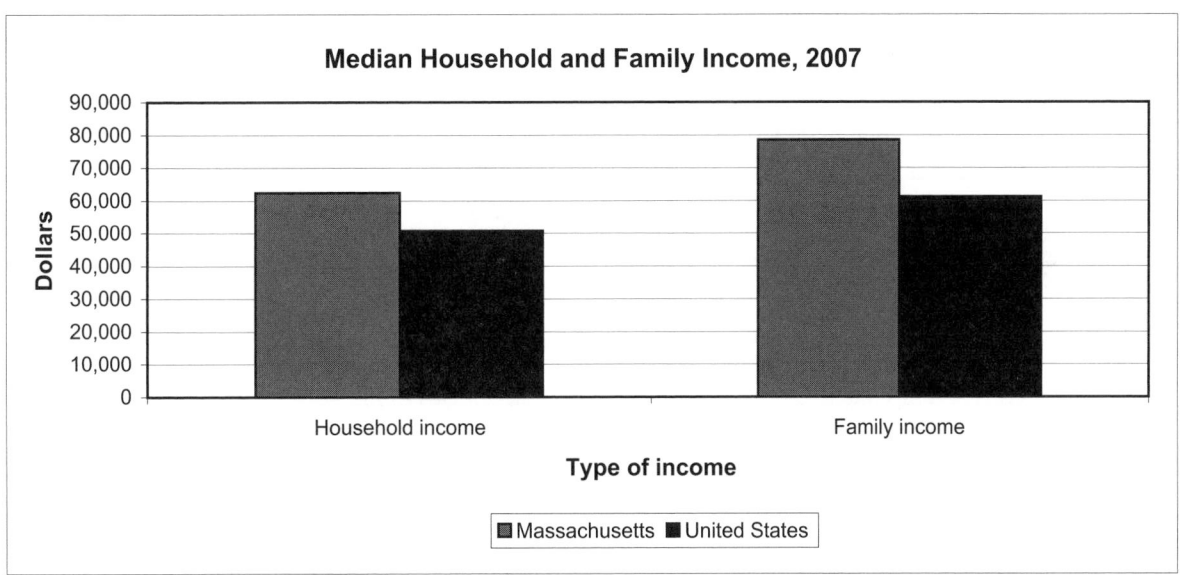

Median Household and Family Income, 2007

Table MA-5. Health Insurance Coverage Status for All Persons and Children Under 18 Years of Age

(Number, percent.)

Item	2000	2001	2002	2003	2004	2005	2006	2007
ALL PERSONS	6 293	6 322	6 470	6 367	6 370	6 328	6 335	6 340
Covered by Private or Government Health Insurance								
Number	5 765	5 844	5 857	5 720	5 650	5 745	5 678	6 000
Percent	91.6	92.4	90.5	89.8	88.7	90.8	89.6	94.6
Not Covered								
Number	527	479	614	647	720	583	657	340
Percent	8.4	7.6	9.5	10.2	11.3	9.2	10.4	5.4
Percent in the U.S. not covered	13.7	14.1	14.7	15.1	14.9	15.3	15.8	15.3
CHILDREN UNDER 18 YEARS OF AGE	1 431	1 382	1 490	1 501	1 488	1 499	1 470	1 435
Covered by Private or Government Health Insurance								
Number	1 345	1 321	1 408	1 387	1 401	1 436	1 367	1 392
Percent	94.0	95.6	94.5	92.5	94.2	95.8	93.0	97.0
Not Covered								
Number	86	61	82	113	87	63	103	43
Percent	6.0	4.4	5.5	7.5	5.8	4.2	7.0	3.0
Percent in the U.S. not covered	11.6	11.3	11.2	11.0	10.5	10.9	11.7	11.0

Table MA-6. Employment Status by Demographic Group, Preliminary 2008

(Number, percent.)

Characteristic	Civilian noninstitutional population	Civilian labor force		Employment		Unemployed	
		Number	Percent of population	Number	Percent of population	Number	Unemployment rate
TOTAL	5 135	3 421	66.6	3 238	63.1	183	5.3
Sex							
Men	2 458	1 777	72.0	1 673	68.1	104	5.9
Women	2 677	1 644	61.0	1 565	58.5	79	4.8
Race, Sex, and Hispanic Origin							
White	4 466	2 985	66.8	2 830	63.4	154	5.2
Men	2 140	1 558	72.8	1 466	68.5	92	5.9
Women	2 326	1 426	61.3	1 364	58.6	63	4.4
Black or African American	326	211	64.7	195	59.7	16	7.6
Men	152	101	66.7	95	62.7	6	6.1
Women	174	109	62.9	99	57.2	10	9.1
Hispanic	307	196	63.9	177	57.5	20	10.0
Men	137	99	72.3	86	63.0	13	12.8
Women	170	97	57.2	90	53.1	7	7.2
Age							
16 to 19 years	354	154	43.5	131	37.0	23	14.9
20 to 24 years	434	313	72.1	288	66.4	25	7.9
25 to 34 years	810	673	83.1	637	78.6	36	5.4
35 to 44 years	979	832	85.0	793	81.1	39	4.7
45 to 54 years	959	807	84.1	774	80.7	33	4.0
55 to 64 years	721	497	69.0	476	66.0	21	4.2
65 years and over	879	145	16.5	139	15.8	7	4.5

Note: Data in Table 6 are from the Current Population Survey (CPS) and do not match the estimates in Table 7. See notes and definitions for more details.

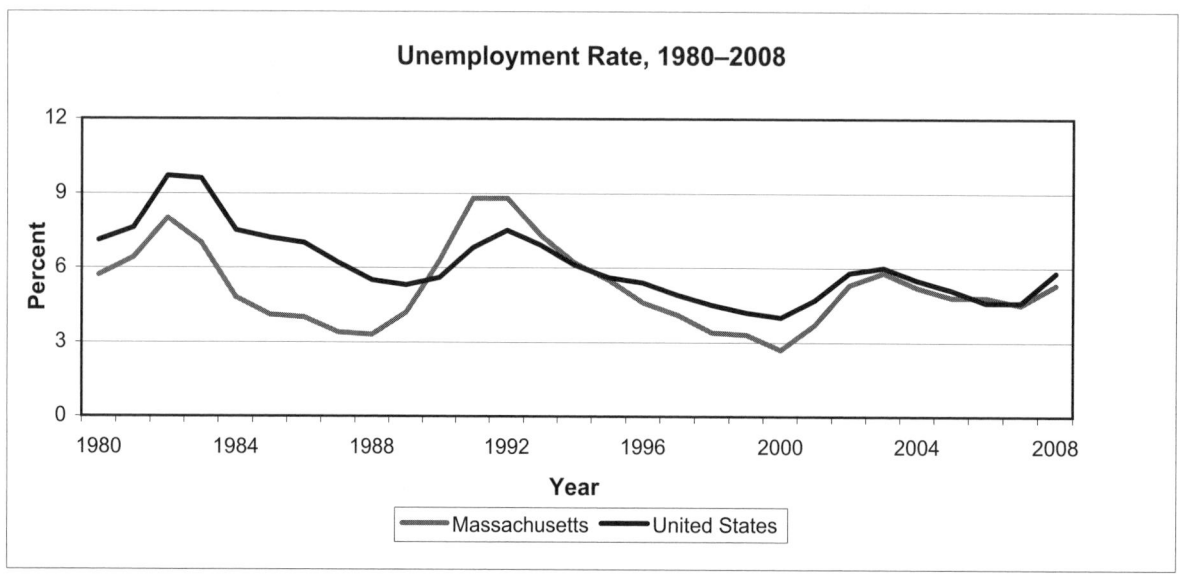

Table MA-7. Employment Status of the Civilian Noninstitutional Population Age 16 Years and Over

(Number, percent.)

Year	Civilian labor force	Civilian participation rate	Employed	Unemployed	Unemployment rate
1998	3 321 662	68.4	3 208 988	112 674	3.4
1999	3 355 324	68.6	3 245 761	109 563	3.3
2000	3 365 573	68.3	3 273 281	92 292	2.7
2001	3 401 336	68.4	3 275 343	125 993	3.7
2002	3 424 412	68.4	3 243 409	181 003	5.3
2003	3 406 710	67.8	3 209 062	197 648	5.8
2004	3 380 649	67.1	3 203 810	176 839	5.2
2005	3 376 590	66.8	3 213 051	163 539	4.8
2006	3 407 957	67.1	3 245 374	162 583	4.8
2007	3 415 613	66.8	3 262 646	152 967	4.5
2008	3 424 018	66.5	3 243 779	180 239	5.3

Table MA-8. Employment and Average Wages by Industry

(Estimates for 2001–2006 are based on the 2002 North American Industry Classification System [NAICS]. Estimates for 2007 are based on the 2007 NAICS.)

Industry	2001	2002	2003	2004	2005	2006	2007
	Number of jobs						
WAGE AND SALARY EMPLOYMENT BY INDUSTRY	3 492 806	3 420 242	3 363 033	3 351 104	3 367 045	3 394 815	3 431 297
Farm Wage and Salary Employment	5 138	5 012	5 203	4 342	4 265	3 903	3 844
Nonfarm Wage and Salary Employment	3 487 668	3 415 230	3 357 830	3 346 762	3 362 780	3 390 912	3 427 453
Private wage and salary employment	3 029 558	2 959 544	2 911 483	2 910 487	2 925 011	2 949 441	2 982 394
Forestry, fishing, hunting, and other	7 111	7 652	7 754	7 962	7 722	7 663	7 523
Mining	1 445	1 525	1 737	1 851	1 859	1 740	1 499
Utilities	11 999	11 114	10 606	10 096	9 644	9 683	9 896
Construction	144 142	146 208	142 303	143 689	144 563	145 761	142 284
Manufacturing	391 569	351 868	326 285	314 581	307 820	301 636	297 498
Durable goods manufacturing	263 837	232 836	212 070	205 867	201 422	197 872	196 538
Nondurable goods manufacturing	127 732	119 032	114 215	108 714	106 398	103 764	100 960
Wholesale trade	142 987	137 490	136 975	138 028	135 825	138 556	139 809
Retail trade	369 596	368 273	365 552	366 651	366 251	361 436	359 697
Transportation and warehousing	82 457	77 998	76 608	75 276	74 150	74 679	76 379
Information	111 814	100 304	91 507	87 249	87 584	87 478	88 041
Finance and insurance	189 718	187 227	182 529	177 671	181 661	185 604	186 914
Real estate and rental and leasing	46 577	45 929	46 095	46 369	46 639	46 136	45 204
Professional and technical services	257 099	239 887	232 110	236 046	244 179	253 633	259 298
Management of companies and enterprises	69 385	67 396	65 016	63 815	64 397	62 206	61 394
Administrative and waste services	168 936	157 381	156 590	161 576	164 219	169 437	173 705
Educational services	169 405	170 720	175 209	176 814	175 621	175 087	179 175
Health care and social assistance	429 315	440 260	444 172	450 241	457 599	469 673	487 744
Arts, entertainment, and recreation	43 848	46 254	47 976	48 563	48 773	49 304	50 657
Accommodation and food services	240 498	244 371	245 232	247 436	249 118	252 347	257 341
Other services, except public administration	151 657	157 687	157 227	156 573	157 387	157 382	158 336
Government and government enterprises	458 110	455 686	446 347	436 275	437 769	441 471	445 059
	Dollars						
AVERAGE WAGES AND SALARIES BY INDUSTRY	43 842	43 888	45 184	47 802	49 058	51 398	54 155
Average Farm Wages and Salaries	18 565	24 385	20 115	23 929	19 694	24 676	22 044
Average Nonfarm Wages and Salaries	43 879	43 917	45 223	47 833	49 095	51 429	54 191
Average private wages and salaries	44 730	44 533	45 719	48 321	49 574	52 013	54 939
Forestry, fishing, hunting, and other	37 462	38 888	41 656	45 781	53 656	50 538	53 934
Mining	46 902	47 790	48 697	49 671	50 439	53 704	55 123
Utilities	76 740	77 594	81 588	84 036	87 240	89 023	94 047
Construction	50 803	52 172	51 508	52 173	53 494	55 640	59 071
Manufacturing	54 363	55 366	58 259	60 804	62 382	64 966	69 465
Durable goods manufacturing	59 757	60 828	64 041	67 413	68 594	71 379	75 726
Nondurable goods manufacturing	43 222	44 680	47 522	48 288	50 622	52 736	57 277
Wholesale trade	61 789	60 981	64 259	67 012	67 193	72 775	74 697
Retail trade	24 801	25 197	26 116	27 051	27 492	27 330	27 598
Transportation and warehousing	35 932	36 893	37 511	38 834	39 960	41 082	42 538
Information	66 892	66 446	68 188	72 662	76 252	81 063	83 384
Finance and insurance	87 349	85 371	87 894	102 771	98 574	104 080	115 855
Real estate and rental and leasing	43 446	44 613	45 008	48 234	50 472	54 914	56 790
Professional and technical services	74 201	72 754	74 508	79 757	83 220	87 568	92 666
Management of companies and enterprises	67 494	64 101	67 978	75 062	81 308	88 661	99 754
Administrative and waste services	30 350	30 821	31 713	32 755	34 288	35 747	37 817
Educational services	31 329	33 347	33 419	34 718	35 842	37 334	39 286
Health care and social assistance	35 607	37 012	39 228	40 727	42 602	44 753	46 442
Arts, entertainment, and recreation	28 736	29 075	30 014	31 077	31 600	32 118	35 440
Accommodation and food services	17 244	17 362	17 907	18 736	19 149	19 882	20 462
Other services, except public administration	24 531	25 488	26 257	27 162	27 534	28 269	29 702
Government and government enterprises	38 251	39 910	41 986	44 574	45 895	47 528	49 181

Table MA-9. Employment Characteristics by Family Type

(Number, percent.)

Family type and labor force status	2005		2006		2007	
	Total	Families with own children under 18 years	Total	Families with own children under 18 years	Total	Families with own children under 18 years
TOTAL FAMILIES	1 569 672	749 771	1 565 973	735 720	1 561 198	736 985
FAMILY TYPE AND LABOR FORCE STATUS						
Married Coupled Families	1 166 209	529 330	1 175 784	528 590	1 166 023	515 818
Both husband and wife in labor force	57.3	66.7	59.2	69.4	58.7	70.4
Husband in labor force, wife not in labor force	20.4	26.5	19.7	25.6	19.9	24.7
Wife in labor force, husband not in labor force	6.9	3.8	6.7	3.2	7.1	3.2
Both husband and wife not in labor force	15.3	3.0	14.5	1.8	14.3	1.7
Other Families	403 463	220 441	390 189	207 130	395 175	221 167
Female householder, no husband present	74.7	79.7	74.3	80.4	74.7	78.4
In labor force	50.4	59.9	52.4	63.6	52.5	61.6
Not in labor force	24.3	19.8	21.9	16.8	22.1	16.8
Male householder, no wife present	25.3	20.3	25.7	19.6	25.3	21.6
In labor force	19.2	17.4	19.8	17.3	20.1	18.9
Not in labor force	6.1	2.9	5.9	2.2	5.2	2.6

Table MA-10. School Enrollment and Educational Attainment, 2007

(Number, percent.)

Item	State	U.S.
Enrollment		
Total population 3 years and over	6 227 590	289 295 761
Enrolled in school	1 707 545	79 329 527
Enrolled in preschool (percent)	6.8	6.2
Enrolled in grades K-12 (percent)	62.5	67.6
Enrolled in college or graduate school (percent)	30.7	26.2
Attainment		
Total population 25 years and over	4 369 419	197 892 369
Less than a high school diploma (percent)	11.6	15.5
High school diploma or more (percent)	88.4	84.5
Bachelor's degree or more (percent)	37.9	27.5
Graduate degree or more (percent)	16.0	10.1

Table MA-11. Educational Indicators

(Number, percent.)

Item	State	U.S.
Public Schools, 2006–2007 (except where noted)		
Number of school districts	498	17 742
Number of schools	1 879	99 639
Number of students	968 661	49 315 842
Student-teacher ratio	13.2	15.5
Expenditures per student (dollars)	$12 857	...
Averaged freshman graduation rate, 2005–2006	79.5	...
Dropout rate, grades 9–12, 2005–2006	3.4	3.7
Students eligible for free or reduced-price lunch (percent)	28.9	41.2
English-language learners (percent)	5.6	5.1
Students with IEP (percent)	16.5	12.7
Private Schools, 2007–2008 (except where noted)		
Number of schools	947	33 740
Number of students	127 967	5 072 451
High school graduates, 2006–2007	10 435	306 605
Student-teacher ratio	8.5	11.1

Table MA-12. Reported Voting and Registration of the Voting-Age Population, November 2008

(Number in thousands, percent.)

Item	Total population	Total citizen population	Registered			Voted		
			Total registered	Percent registered (total population)	Percent registered (total citizen population)	Total voted	Percent voted (total population)	Percent voted (total citizen population)
U.S. total	225 499	206 072	146 311	64.9	71.0	131 144	58.2	63.6
State total	4 962	4 533	3 293	66.4	72.6	3 044	61.3	67.1
Sex								
Male	2 385	2 168	1 583	66.4	73.0	1 458	61.1	67.2
Female	2 576	2 365	1 710	66.4	72.3	1 586	61.6	67.1
Race								
White alone	4 280	4 044	3 026	70.7	74.8	2 787	65.1	68.9
White non-Hispanic alone	4 021	3 867	2 928	72.8	75.7	2 715	67.5	70.2
Black alone	310	235	145	47.0	61.9	145	47.0	61.9
Asian alone	324	214	82	25.3	38.4	76	23.4	35.4
Hispanic (of any race)	286	193	103	36.2	53.6	77	26.9	39.9
White alone or in combination	4 310	4 075	3 056	70.9	75.0	2 813	65.3	69.0
Black alone or in combination	324	250	160	49.4	64.1	160	49.4	64.1
Asian alone or in combination	324	214	82	25.3	38.4	76	23.4	35.4

Table MA-13. Crime

(Number, rate per 100,000.)

Item	State			U.S.		
	2007	2008	Percent change	2007	2008	Percent change
Population	6 449 755	6 497 967	0.7	301 621 157	304 059 724	0.8
VIOLENT CRIME						
Number	27 832	29 174	4.8	1 408 337	1 382 012	-1.9
Rate	431.5	449.0	4.0	466.9	454.5	-2.7
Murder and Nonnegligent Manslaughter						
Number	184	167	-9.2	16 929	16 272	-3.9
Rate	2.9	2.6	-9.9	5.6	5.4	-4.7
Forcible Rape						
Number	1 634	1 736	6.2	90 427	89 000	-1.6
Rate	25.3	26.7	5.5	30.0	29.3	-2.4
Robbery						
Number	7 006	7 069	0.9	445 125	441 855	-0.7
Rate	108.6	108.8	0.2	147.6	145.3	-1.5
Aggravated Assault						
Number	19 008	20 202	6.3	855 856	834 885	-2.5
Rate	294.7	310.9	5.5	283.8	274.6	-3.2
PROPERTY CRIME						
Number	154 246	155 959	1.1	9 843 481	9 767 915	-0.8
Rate	2 391.5	2 400.1	0.4	3 263.5	3 212.5	-1.6
Burglary						
Number	35 662	36 094	1.2	2 179 140	2 222 196	2.0
Rate	552.9	555.5	0.5	722.5	730.8	1.2
Larceny-Theft						
Number	103 592	107 128	3.4	6 568 572	6 588 873	0.3
Rate	1 606.1	1 648.6	2.6	2 177.8	2 167.0	-0.5
Motor Vehicle Theft						
Number	14 992	12 737	-15.0	1 095 769	956 846	-12.7
Rate	232.4	196.0	-15.7	363.3	314.7	-13.4

Table MA-14. State Government Finances, 2007

(Dollars, percent distribution.)

Item	Thousands of dollars	Percent distribution
Total Revenue	49 425 934	X
General revenue	38 708 809	78.3
Intergovernmental revenue	9 617 501	19.5
Taxes	20 666 972	41.8
General sales	4 075 549	8.2
Selective sales	1 920 291	3.9
License taxes	675 925	1.4
Individual income tax	11 399 649	23.1
Corporate income tax	2 106 898	4.3
Other taxes	488 660	1.0
Current charges	3 552 093	7.2
Miscellaneous general revenue	4 872 243	9.9
Utility revenue	172 120	0.3
Liquor store revenue	0	0.0
Insurance trust revenue	10 545 005	21.3
Total Expenditure	44 048 424	100.0
Intergovernmental expenditure	9 364 680	21.3
Direct expenditure	34 683 744	78.7
Current operation	23 753 330	53.9
Capital outlay	2 447 945	5.6
Insurance benefits and repayments	4 368 821	9.9
Assistance and subsidies	662 936	1.5
Interest on debt	3 450 712	7.8
Exhibit: Salaries and wages	4 782 098	10.9
Total Expenditure	44 048 424	100.0
General expenditure	39 431 782	89.5
Intergovernmental expenditure	9 364 680	21.3
Direct expenditure	30 067 102	68.3
Education	10 657 235	24.2
Public welfare	12 195 223	27.7
Hospitals	512 551	1.2
Health	960 808	2.2
Highways	1 735 159	3.9
Police protection	567 989	1.3
Correction	1 209 443	2.7
Natural resources	336 316	0.8
Parks and recreation	231 553	0.5
Government administration	1 651 398	3.7
Interest on general debt	3 364 198	7.6
Other and unallocable	6 009 909	13.6
Utility expenditure	247 821	0.6
Liquor store expenditure	0	0.0
Insurance trust expenditure	4 368 821	9.9
Debt at End of Fiscal Year	67 938 742	X
Cash and Security Holdings	98 390 116	X

Table MA-15. State Government Tax Collections, 2008

(Dollars, percent distribution.)

Item	Thousands of dollars	Percent distribution
Total Taxes	21 836 357	X
Property taxes	96	0.0
Sales and gross receipts	6 032 982	27.6
General sales and gross receipts	4 098 089	18.8
Selective sales taxes	1 934 893	8.9
Alcoholic beverages	71 935	0.3
Amusements	3 494	0.0
Insurance premiums	396 196	1.8
Motor fuels	672 654	3.1
Pari-mutuels	3 496	0.0
Public utilities	24 148	0.1
Tobacco products	436 942	2.0
Other selective sales	326 028	1.5
Licenses	685 045	3.1
Alcoholic beverages	3 081	0.0
Amusements	439	0.0
Corporation	23 561	0.1
Hunting and fishing	5 289	0.0
Motor vehicle	287 738	1.3
Motor vehicle operators	92 881	0.4
Public utility	1 500	0.0
Occupation and business, NEC	167 563	0.8
Other licenses	102 993	0.5
Income taxes	14 676 098	67.2
Individual income	12 496 142	57.2
Corporation net income	2 179 956	10.0
Other taxes	442 136	2.0
Death and gift	253 966	1.2
Documentary and stock transfer	188 170	0.9

Table MA-16. Agriculture

(Number, acres, and dollars.)

Item	2002		2007		Percent change, 2002–2007
	Number	Percent of total	Number	Percent of total	
Number of farms	6 075		7 691		26.6
Farm Size					
Average size of farm (acres)	85		67		-21.2
Farms by size (number of farms)					
Fewer than 50 acres	3 646	60.0	5 084	66.1	39.4
50 to 499 acres	2 267	37.3	2 489	32.4	9.8
500 acres or more	162	2.7	118	1.5	-27.2
Land (Acres)					
Total land in farms	518 570		517 879		-0.1
Total cropland	207 734	40.1	187 406	36.2	-9.8
Total harvested cropland	159 253	30.7	153 993	29.7	-3.3
Irrigated land	23 720	4.6	23 133	4.5	-2.5
Value of Sales (Dollars)					
Agricultural products sold ($1,000)	384 314		489 820		27.5
Average sales per farm	63 262		63 687		0.7
Sales of crops	277 069	72.1	364 481	74.4	31.5
Sales of livestock, poultry, and their products	107 244	27.9	125 338	25.6	16.9
Value of Sales (Number of Farms)					
Less than $10,000	3 862	63.6	4 937	64.2	27.8
$10,000 to $99,999	1 522	25.1	1 951	25.4	28.2
$100,000 to $999,999	623	10.3	722	9.4	15.9
$1,000,000 or more	68	1.1	81	1.1	19.1
Farms by Type of Organization (Number of Farms)					
Family	5 020	82.6	6 318	82.1	25.9
Partnership	376	6.2	574	7.5	52.7
Corporation	559	9.2	641	8.3	14.7
Other: cooperative, estate or trust, institutional, etc	120	2.0	158	2.1	31.7
Value of Land and Buildings (Dollars)					
Estimated market value of land and buildings ($1,000)	6 376 531		4 589 677		-28.0
Land and buildings average value per farm	829 090		755 254		-8.9
Average value per acre	12 313		9 234		-25.0
Government Payments					
Number of farms receiving government payments	415	6.8	593	7.7	42.9
Payments (thousands of dollars)	4 268		4 603		7.8
Average payment per farm	10 284		7 763		-24.5
Farm Operator Characteristics					
Farm operators whose principal occupation is farming	3 283	54.0	3 688	48.0	12.3
Farm operators whose principal occupation is other	2 792	46.0	4 003	52.0	43.4
Average age principal operator (years)	54.9		56.3		2.6

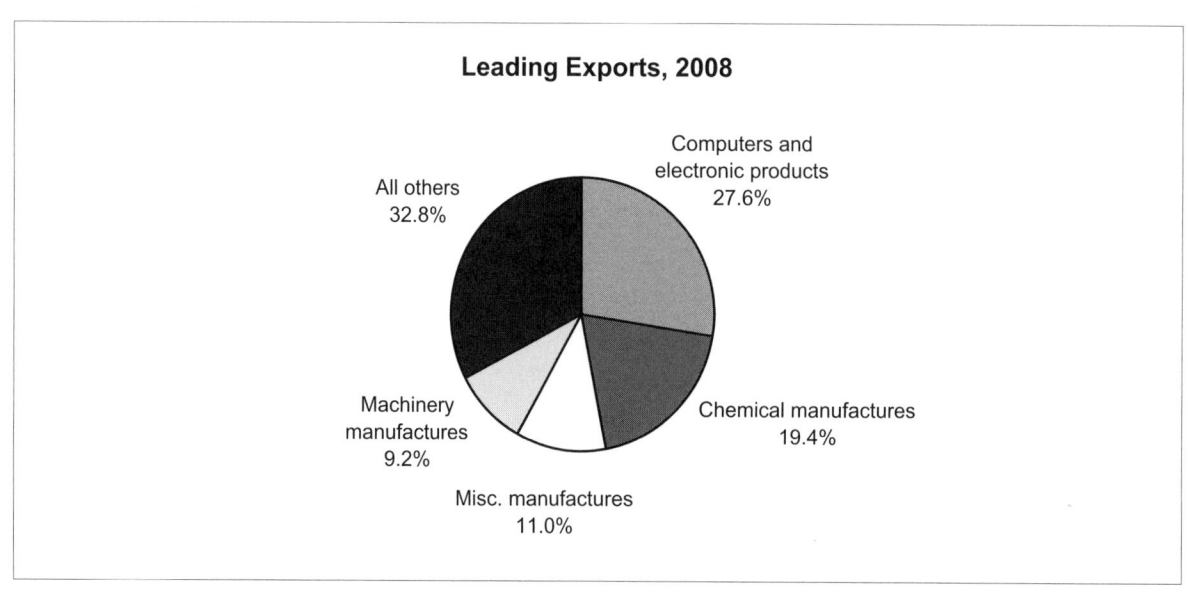

Leading Exports, 2008

Computers and electronic products 27.6%

All others 32.8%

Chemical manufactures 19.4%

Misc. manufactures 11.0%

Machinery manufactures 9.2%

MICHIGAN

Facts and Figures

Location: East north central United States; bordered on the N by Lake Superior, on the E by Ontario, Canada, and Lakes Huron and Erie, on the S by Indiana and Ohio, and on the W by Wisconsin and Lake Michigan

Area: 96,716 sq. mi. (250,494 sq. km.); rank—11th

Population: 10,003,422 (2008 est.); rank—8th

Principal Cities: capital—Lansing; largest—Detroit

Statehood: January 26, 1837; 26th state

U.S. Congress: 2 senators, 15 representatives

State Motto: *Si quaeris peninsulam amoenam, circumspice* ("If you seek a pleasant peninsula, look about you")

State Song: "Michigan, My Michigan"

State Nicknames: The Wolverine State; The Great Lakes State

Abbreviations: MI; Mich.

State Symbols: flower—apple blossom; tree—Eastern white pine; bird—robin

At a Glance

- With an increase in population of 0.7 percent, Michigan ranked 46th among the states in growth from 2000 to 2008.
- An estimated 55,726 marriages took place in Michigan in 2008, compared to 33,812 divorces.
- The 2007 home ownership rate in Michigan was 76.4 percent, giving it a ranking of 3rd among the states.
- Michigan's median household income in 2007 was $47,950, 26th among the states.
- In Michigan, 14 percent of the population lived below the poverty level in 2007, ranking it 16th.
- In 2006-07, 11 percent of Michiganites did not have health insurance, compared to 15.5 percent of the total U.S. population.
- In 2007, 7.1 percent of Michiganites were unemployed, compared to 4.6 percent nationwide.
- Michigan ranked 34th in the nation with 24.7 percent of its population 25 years old and over having a bachelor's degree in 2007.
- Michigan's violent crime rate in 2007 was 536 per 100,000 population, compared to 466.9 for the entire nation.
- Michigan had one physician for every 355 people in 2007, compared to one physician for every 325 people nationwide.
- In the 2008 election, 68.9 percent of Michigan's eligible voters voted, compared to 61.7 percent of eligible voters nationwide.
- Michigan ranked 36th among the states receiving federal aid in 2007, with $1,276 per capita.
- Michigan's gross domestic product was $382 billion in 2007; it ranked 12th among the states.
- With $44.6 billion in exports in 2007, Michigan ranked 7th in exports.
- Michiganites consumed 3 trillion Btu's of energy in 2006; the state ranked 10th in total consumption.
- In 2007, Michigan exported $1.2 billion worth of agricultural products, about 1.5 percent of the U.S. total.

Table MI-1. Population by Sex, Age, Race, and Hispanic Origin

(Number, percent.)

Sex, age, race, and Hispanic origin	1990	2000	2008	Average annual percent change, 2000–2008
Total Population	9 295 297	9 938 444	10 003 422	0.1
Percent of total U.S. population	3.7	3.5	3.3	X
Sex				
Male	4 512 781	4 873 095	4 923 929	0.1
Female	4 782 516	5 065 349	5 079 493	0.0
Age				
Under 5 years	702 554	672 005	625 526	-0.9
5 to 19 years	2 055 420	2 212 060	2 059 989	-0.9
20 to 64 years	5 428 862	5 835 361	6 013 585	0.4
65 years and over	1 108 461	1 219 018	1 304 322	0.8
Median age (years)	32.5	35.5	38.0	X
Race and Hispanic Origin[1]				
One race				
White	7 756 086	7 966 053	8 121 119	0.2
Black	1 291 706	1 412 742	1 424 595	0.1
American Indian and Alaskan Native	55 638	58 479	62 094	0.8
Asian[2]	104 983	176 510	236 559	3.7
Native Hawaiian and Other Pacific Islander	X	2 692	4 134	5.5
Two or more races	X	192 416	154 921	-2.7
Hispanic (of any race)	201 596	323 877	413 827	3.1

[1]Data on race in 2000 and 2008 are not comparable to 1990. Individuals could only report one race in the 1990 census but could report one or more races on the 2000 census.
[2]Data in 1990 refer to Asian and Pacific Islanders.

Table MI-2. Marital Status

(Number, percent distribution.)

Sex and marital status	1990	2000	2007
Males, 15 Years and Over	3 458 188	3 761 881	3 937 648
Never married	31.2	30.8	34.3
Now married, except separated	56.6	56.1	51.8
Separated	1.7	1.3	1.3
Widowed	2.6	2.5	2.6
Divorced	8.0	9.3	10.0
Females, 15 Years and Over	3 775 938	4 013 722	4 143 900
Never married	24.7	25.0	28.4
Now married, except separated	51.6	51.8	47.9
Separated	2.2	1.6	1.7
Widowed	11.5	10.4	9.9
Divorced	10.1	11.2	12.1

Table MI-3. Households and Housing Characteristics

(Number, percent, and dollars.)

Item	1990	2000	2007	Average annual percent change, 2000–2007
Total Households	3 419 331	3 785 661	3 849 007	0.2
Family households	2 439 171	2 575 699	2 560 681	-0.1
Married-couple family	1 883 143	1 947 710	1 913 467	-0.3
Other family	556 028	627 989	647 214	0.4
Male householder, no wife present	113 789	154 187	164 371	0.9
Female householder, no husband present	442 239	473 802	482 843	0.3
Nonfamily households	980 160	1 209 962	1 288 326	0.9
Householder living alone	809 449	993 607	1 085 626	1.3
Householder not living alone	170 711	216 355	202 700	-0.9
Housing Characteristics				
Total housing units	3 847 926	4 234 279	4 526 914	1.0
Occupied housing units	3 419 331	3 785 661	3 849 007	0.2
Owner-occupied	2 427 643	2 793 124	2 880 401	0.4
Renter-occupied	991 688	992 537	968 606	-0.3
Average size	2.66	2.56	2.55	X
Financial Characteristics				
Median gross rent of renter-occupied housing units (dollars)	423	546	683	3.2
Median monthly owner costs for housing units with a mortgage (dollars)	651	972	1 332	4.6
Median value of owner-occupied housing units (dollars)	60 100	115 600	153 100	4.1

Table MI-4. Median Income and Poverty Status, 2007

(Number, percent.)

Characteristic	State		U.S.	
	Number	Percent	Number	Percent
Median Income				
Households (dollars)	62 365	X	50 740	X
Families (dollars)	78 497	X	61 173	X
Below Poverty Level				
Sex				
Male	604 119	12.5	16 576 071	11.5
Female	772 539	15.4	21 476 176	14.3
Age				
Under 18 years	468 400	19.4	13 097 100	18.0
Related children under 18 years	454 418	19.0	12 728 964	17.6
18 to 64 years	809 995	13.1	21 495 507	11.6
65 years and over	98 263	8.0	3 459 640	9.5

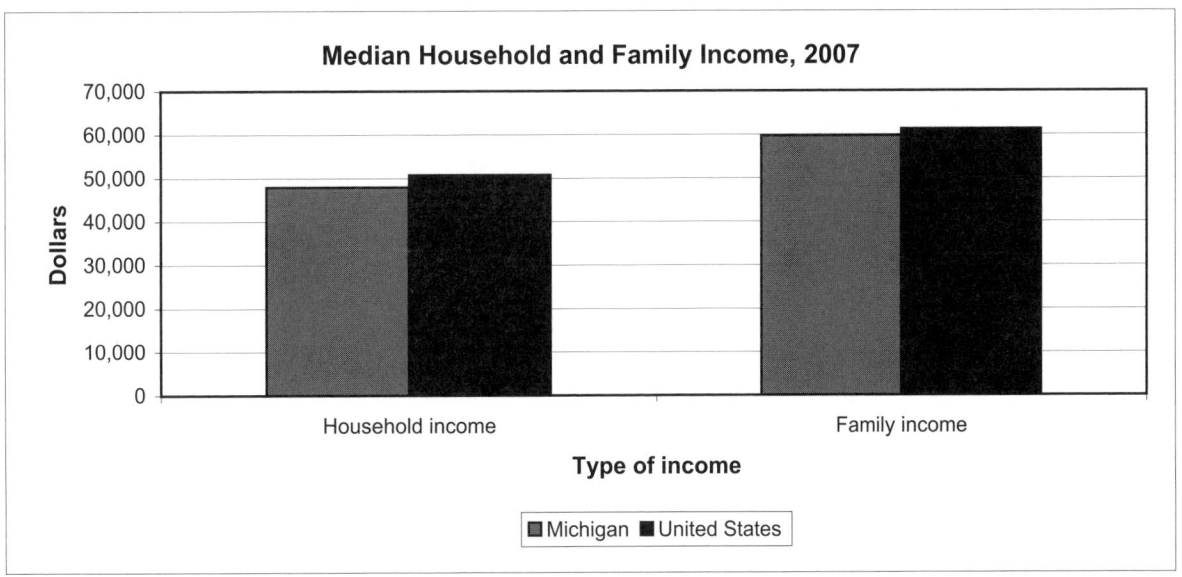

Table MI-5. Health Insurance Coverage Status for All Persons and Children Under 18 Years of Age

(Number, percent.)

Item	2000	2001	2002	2003	2004	2005	2006	2007
ALL PERSONS	9 836	9 892	9 910	9 918	9 974	9 982	9 970	9 927
Covered by Private or Government Health Insurance								
Number	8 998	8 926	8 831	8 905	8 865	8 949	8 928	8 776
Percent	91.5	90.2	89.1	89.8	88.9	89.7	89.5	88.4
Not Covered								
Number	838	966	1 079	1 013	1 109	1 033	1 043	1 151
Percent	8.5	9.8	10.9	10.2	11.1	10.3	10.5	11.6
Percent in the U.S. not covered	13.7	14.1	14.7	15.1	14.9	15.3	15.8	15.3
CHILDREN UNDER 18 YEARS OF AGE	2 484	2 427	2 542	2 522	2 545	2 554	2 446	2 419
Covered by Private or Government Health Insurance								
Number	2 359	2 247	2 388	2 388	2 393	2 427	2 330	2 270
Percent	95.0	92.6	93.9	94.7	94.0	95.0	95.3	93.8
Not Covered								
Number	125	180	154	134	152	128	116	149
Percent	5.0	7.4	6.1	5.3	6.0	5.0	4.7	6.2
Percent in the U.S. not covered	11.6	11.3	11.2	11.0	10.5	10.9	11.7	11.0

Table MI-6. Employment Status by Demographic Group, Preliminary 2008

(Number, percent.)

Characteristic	Civilian noninstitutional population	Civilian labor force		Employment		Unemployed	
		Number	Percent of population	Number	Percent of population	Number	Unemployment rate
TOTAL	7 818	4 952	63.3	4 542	58.1	410	8.3
Sex							
Men	3 784	2 622	69.0	2 383	63.0	239	9.1
Women	4 033	2 330	58.0	2 159	53.5	171	7.4
Race, Sex, and Hispanic Origin							
White	6 417	4 112	64.1	3 803	59.3	309	7.5
Men	3 145	2 221	70.6	2 033	64.6	188	8.4
Women	3 272	1 891	57.8	1 770	54.1	122	6.4
Black or African American	1 032	581	56.3	503	48.7	78	13.5
Men	459	267	58.2	227	49.4	41	15.2
Women	573	314	54.7	276	48.1	38	12.0
Hispanic	262	165	62.7	148	56.2	17	10.3
Men	135	101	74.8	92	67.7	10	9.5
Women	127	63	49.9	56	44.1	7	11.6
Age							
16 to 19 years	594	253	42.5	195	32.8	58	22.9
20 to 24 years	654	489	74.7	425	64.9	64	13.1
25 to 34 years	1 204	979	81.3	888	73.8	91	9.3
35 to 44 years	1 408	1 171	83.1	1 095	77.7	76	6.5
45 to 54 years	1 494	1 201	80.4	1 129	75.6	72	6.0
55 to 64 years	1 147	677	59.0	636	55.4	41	6.1
65 years and over	1 316	183	13.9	176	13.4	8	4.1

Note: Data in Table 6 are from the Current Population Survey (CPS) and do not match the estimates in Table 7. See notes and definitions for more details.

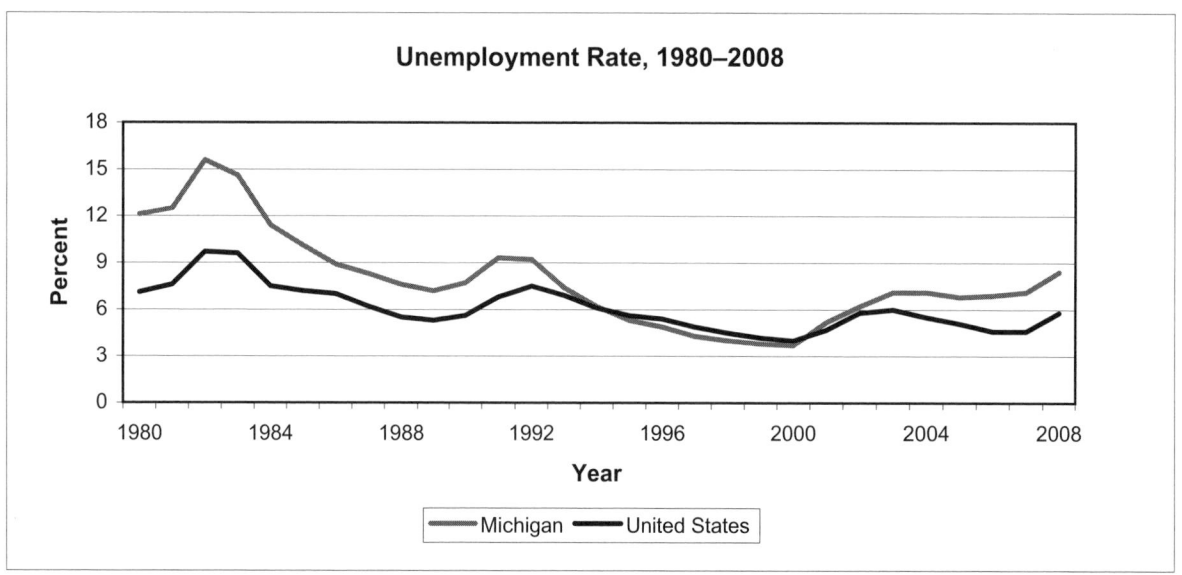

Unemployment Rate, 1980–2008

Table MI-7. Employment Status of the Civilian Noninstitutional Population Age 16 Years and Over

(Number, percent.)

Year	Civilian labor force	Civilian participation rate	Employed	Unemployed	Unemployment rate
1998	5 007 953	67.4	4 809 503	198 450	4.0
1999	5 089 421	68.1	4 897 144	192 277	3.8
2000	5 143 916	68.4	4 953 421	190 495	3.7
2001	5 143 869	67.9	4 876 338	267 531	5.2
2002	5 039 738	66.1	4 724 998	314 740	6.2
2003	5 033 308	65.6	4 675 567	357 741	7.1
2004	5 042 604	65.4	4 686 953	355 651	7.1
2005	5 064 944	65.4	4 718 084	346 860	6.8
2006	5 068 179	65.2	4 718 676	349 503	6.9
2007	5 023 910	64.5	4 666 650	357 260	7.1
2008	4 935 584	63.4	4 519 476	416 108	8.4

Table MI-8. Employment and Average Wages by Industry

(Estimates for 2001–2006 are based on the 2002 North American Industry Classification System [NAICS]. Estimates for 2007 are based on the 2007 NAICS.)

Industry	2001	2002	2003	2004	2005	2006	2007
	Number of jobs						
WAGE AND SALARY EMPLOYMENT BY INDUSTRY	4 709 546	4 623 143	4 556 178	4 535 259	4 524 489	4 461 127	4 402 734
Farm Wage and Salary Employment	18 977	17 634	18 791	19 118	17 297	16 069	18 629
Nonfarm Wage and Salary Employment	4 690 569	4 605 509	4 537 387	4 516 141	4 507 192	4 445 058	4 384 105
Private wage and salary employment	3 991 073	3 904 884	3 839 288	3 822 763	3 817 730	3 765 644	3 713 072
Forestry, fishing, hunting, and other	10 564	9 226	9 187	9 611	9 633	8 831	8 883
Mining	7 637	6 900	6 555	6 572	6 774	6 541	6 283
Utilities	21 254	20 643	20 628	20 567	20 899	20 741	20 422
Construction	213 954	207 348	197 241	197 765	194 611	182 259	168 998
Manufacturing	828 809	764 603	725 480	702 864	682 417	654 482	627 207
Durable goods manufacturing	660 411	606 176	569 588	550 202	531 716	506 228	482 083
Nondurable goods manufacturing	168 398	158 427	155 892	152 662	150 701	148 254	145 124
Wholesale trade	183 432	177 674	175 236	172 413	172 154	172 104	170 207
Retail trade	565 408	547 433	534 929	529 889	521 295	511 040	503 945
Transportation and warehousing	110 814	108 559	105 738	105 935	108 106	108 727	109 408
Information	75 682	73 879	70 476	68 499	66 354	64 996	64 151
Finance and insurance	155 210	158 244	162 900	161 390	161 854	161 652	157 079
Real estate and rental and leasing	57 773	57 810	58 277	58 913	59 597	58 188	57 459
Professional and technical services	282 318	273 763	264 609	259 394	261 028	258 232	257 402
Management of companies and enterprises	67 096	68 915	64 320	66 340	63 983	61 488	57 658
Administrative and waste services	268 964	265 348	268 702	273 431	282 586	279 720	276 984
Educational services	58 144	61 249	65 076	68 847	71 199	72 238	74 005
Health care and social assistance	472 382	484 448	494 307	500 706	515 372	525 485	537 897
Arts, entertainment, and recreation	65 282	65 326	65 719	65 164	65 403	64 505	65 147
Accommodation and food services	336 541	340 061	339 807	343 722	346 343	348 346	346 847
Other services, except public administration	209 809	213 455	210 101	210 741	208 122	206 069	203 090
Government and government enterprises	699 496	700 625	698 099	693 378	689 462	679 414	671 033
	Dollars						
AVERAGE WAGES AND SALARIES BY INDUSTRY	36 756	37 519	38 790	39 767	40 618	41 528	42 727
Average Farm Wages and Salaries	29 132	31 696	22 592	25 228	24 902	26 108	30 267
Average Nonfarm Wages and Salaries	36 786	37 542	38 857	39 829	40 678	41 584	42 780
Average private wages and salaries	37 244	37 857	39 187	40 150	40 878	41 693	42 886
Forestry, fishing, hunting, and other	18 452	19 055	19 851	20 879	21 194	21 958	22 626
Mining	44 359	44 160	47 348	50 519	53 063	57 105	62 622
Utilities	67 292	69 468	74 045	73 129	75 004	79 599	87 238
Construction	42 726	42 971	43 124	43 741	45 016	46 564	48 962
Manufacturing	49 656	51 928	55 672	56 272	56 706	57 948	59 694
Durable goods manufacturing	51 663	54 093	57 715	58 298	58 906	60 528	62 629
Nondurable goods manufacturing	41 788	43 644	48 207	48 970	48 945	49 140	49 946
Wholesale trade	50 950	51 496	53 430	55 730	57 557	59 101	61 521
Retail trade	21 669	22 473	22 950	23 561	23 790	24 183	24 590
Transportation and warehousing	40 866	42 016	43 800	45 515	45 168	44 381	46 080
Information	47 228	47 162	49 125	51 357	52 030	54 099	55 845
Finance and insurance	48 867	49 662	51 525	52 875	54 308	56 260	58 764
Real estate and rental and leasing	28 728	29 497	29 379	29 975	30 589	31 298	32 028
Professional and technical services	60 358	60 333	62 730	64 702	67 007	68 691	71 234
Management of companies and enterprises	84 414	77 463	81 429	90 652	94 215	92 453	99 606
Administrative and waste services	26 551	27 771	28 502	29 685	30 921	31 309	30 816
Educational services	22 646	23 044	24 063	24 491	25 509	26 132	27 542
Health care and social assistance	33 398	34 556	35 536	36 814	37 868	39 151	40 196
Arts, entertainment, and recreation	23 299	24 813	25 200	26 212	26 549	27 808	28 513
Accommodation and food services	12 237	12 498	12 778	13 195	13 399	13 804	14 329
Other services, except public administration	23 159	23 386	24 146	24 841	25 223	25 913	27 013
Government and government enterprises	34 177	35 781	37 043	38 060	39 571	40 975	42 196

Table MI-9. Employment Characteristics by Family Type

(Number, percent.)

Family type and labor force status	2005		2006		2007	
	Total	Families with own children under 18 years	Total	Families with own children under 18 years	Total	Families with own children under 18 years
TOTAL FAMILIES	2 594 228	1 214 787	2 579 201	1 194 613	2 560 681	1 177 239
FAMILY TYPE AND LABOR FORCE STATUS						
Married Coupled Families	1 946 772	835 163	1 938 688	819 240	1 913 467	797 079
Both husband and wife in labor force	52.0	64.4	52.8	66.8	52.5	66.8
Husband in labor force, wife not in labor force	21.4	27.9	21.2	27.5	21.0	26.5
Wife in labor force, husband not in labor force	7.5	4.6	7.5	3.7	7.7	4.2
Both husband and wife not in labor force	19.1	3.1	18.5	2.0	18.8	2.5
Other Families	647 456	379 624	640 513	375 373	647 214	380 160
Female householder, no husband present	73.9	76.7	74.2	77.2	74.6	77.6
In labor force	51.5	61.2	52.3	62.6	52.4	62.7
Not in labor force	22.4	15.4	21.9	14.6	22.2	14.9
Male householder, no wife present	26.1	23.3	25.8	22.8	25.4	22.4
In labor force	20.2	20.3	19.9	20.2	19.2	19.5
Not in labor force	5.9	3.0	6.0	2.7	6.2	2.9

Table MI-10. School Enrollment and Educational Attainment, 2007

(Number, percent.)

Item	State	U.S.
Enrollment		
Total population 3 years and over	9 695 571	289 295 761
Enrolled in school	2 755 790	79 329 527
Enrolled in preschool (percent)	5.4	6.2
Enrolled in grades K–12 (percent)	66.7	67.6
Enrolled in college or graduate school (percent)	27.9	26.2
Attainment		
Total population 25 years and over	6 647 129	197 892 369
Less than a high school diploma (percent)	12.6	15.5
High school diploma or more (percent)	87.4	84.5
Bachelor's degree or more (percent)	24.7	27.5
Graduate degree or more (percent)	9.5	10.1

Table MI-11. Educational Indicators

(Number, percent.)

Item	State	U.S.
Public Schools, 2006–2007 (except where noted)		
Number of school districts	842	17 742
Number of schools	4 136	99 639
Number of students	1 722 656	49 315 842
Student-teacher ratio	17.6	15.5
Expenditures per student (dollars)	$9 922	. . .
Averaged freshman graduation rate, 2005–2006	72.2	. . .
Dropout rate, grades 9–12, 2005–2006	3.5	3.7
Students eligible for free or reduced-price lunch (percent)	36.0	41.2
English-language learners (percent)	4.0	5.1
Students with IEP (percent)	14.0	12.7
Private Schools, 2007–2008 (except where noted)		
Number of schools	908	33 740
Number of students	139 314	5 072 451
High school graduates, 2006–2007	8 522	306 605
Student-teacher ratio	12.8	11.1

Table MI-12. Reported Voting and Registration of the Voting-Age Population, November 2008

(Number in thousands, percent.)

Item	Total population	Total citizen population	Registered — Total registered	Registered — Percent registered (total population)	Registered — Percent registered (total citizen population)	Voted — Total voted	Voted — Percent voted (total population)	Voted — Percent voted (total citizen population)
U.S. total	225 499	206 072	146 311	64.9	71.0	131 144	58.2	63.6
State total	7 487	7 176	5 531	73.9	77.1	4 865	65.0	67.8
Sex								
Male	3 609	3 474	2 590	71.8	74.6	2 249	62.3	64.7
Female	3 877	3 702	2 940	75.8	79.4	2 616	67.5	70.7
Race								
White alone	6 200	6 021	4 642	74.9	77.1	4 065	65.6	67.5
White non-Hispanic alone	6 005	5 874	4 557	75.9	77.6	3 995	66.5	68.0
Black alone	968	956	738	76.3	77.2	679	70.2	71.1
Asian alone	206	91	74	35.7	80.9	53	25.9	58.7
Hispanic (of any race)	198	147	85	43.2	58.2	70	35.5	47.8
White alone or in combination	6 258	6 079	4 680	74.8	77.0	4 099	65.5	67.4
Black alone or in combination	991	980	756	76.3	77.2	694	70.0	70.8
Asian alone or in combination	217	102	84	38.9	82.9	64	29.6	63.1

Table MI-13. Crime

(Number, rate per 100,000.)

Item	State 2007	State 2008	State Percent change	U.S. 2007	U.S. 2008	U.S. Percent change
Population	10 071 822	10 003 422	-0.7	301 621 157	304 059 724	0.8
VIOLENT CRIME						
Number	53 988	50 166	-7.1	1 408 337	1 382 012	-1.9
Rate	536.0	501.5	-6.4	466.9	454.5	-2.7
Murder and Nonnegligent Manslaughter						
Number	676	542	-19.8	16 929	16 272	-3.9
Rate	6.7	5.4	-19.3	5.6	5.4	-4.7
Forcible Rape						
Number	4 579	4 502	-1.7	90 427	89 000	-1.6
Rate	45.5	45.0	-1.0	30.0	29.3	-2.4
Robbery						
Number	13 414	12 964	-3.4	445 125	441 855	-0.7
Rate	133.2	129.6	-2.7	147.6	145.3	-1.5
Aggravated Assault						
Number	35 319	32 158	-8.9	855 856	834 885	-2.5
Rate	350.7	321.5	-8.3	283.8	274.6	-3.2
PROPERTY CRIME						
Number	308 775	293 585	-4.9	9 843 481	9 767 915	-0.8
Rate	3 065.7	2 934.8	-4.3	3 263.5	3 212.5	-1.6
Burglary						
Number	75 428	74 176	-1.7	2 179 140	2 222 196	2.0
Rate	748.9	741.5	-1.0	722.5	730.8	1.2
Larceny-Theft						
Number	191 196	183 168	-4.2	6 568 572	6 588 873	0.3
Rate	1 898.3	1 831.1	-3.5	2 177.8	2 167.0	-0.5
Motor Vehicle Theft						
Number	42 151	36 241	-14.0	1 095 769	956 846	-12.7
Rate	418.5	362.3	-13.4	363.3	314.7	-13.4

Table MI-14. State Government Finances, 2007

(Dollars, percent distribution.)

Item	Thousands of dollars	Percent distribution
Total Revenue	63 070 866	X
General revenue	48 784 813	77.3
Intergovernmental revenue	13 083 153	20.7
Taxes	23 848 753	37.8
General sales	7 983 098	12.7
Selective sales	3 618 995	5.7
License taxes	1 375 194	2.2
Individual income tax	6 442 678	10.2
Corporate income tax	1 786 213	2.8
Other taxes	2 642 575	4.2
Current charges	6 136 099	9.7
Miscellaneous general revenue	5 716 808	9.1
Utility revenue	0	0.0
Liquor store revenue	742 595	1.2
Insurance trust revenue	13 543 458	21.5
Total Expenditure	54 745 355	100.0
Intergovernmental expenditure	19 423 935	35.5
Direct expenditure	35 321 420	64.5
Current operation	24 902 318	45.5
Capital outlay	1 971 018	3.6
Insurance benefits and repayments	6 101 137	11.1
Assistance and subsidies	1 150 139	2.1
Interest on debt	1 196 808	2.2
Exhibit: Salaries and wages	5 594 998	10.2
Total Expenditure	54 745 355	100.0
General expenditure	48 040 183	87.8
Intergovernmental expenditure	19 423 935	35.5
Direct expenditure	28 616 248	52.3
Education	21 420 912	39.1
Public welfare	12 690 079	23.2
Hospitals	2 055 355	3.8
Health	1 090 937	2.0
Highways	2 808 637	5.1
Police protection	311 262	0.6
Correction	1 801 658	3.3
Natural resources	299 768	0.5
Parks and recreation	88 213	0.2
Government administration	1 086 384	2.0
Interest on general debt	1 196 808	2.2
Other and unallocable	3 190 170	5.8
Utility expenditure	1 800	0.0
Liquor store expenditure	602 235	1.1
Insurance trust expenditure	6 101 137	11.1
Debt at End of Fiscal Year	33 657 214	X
Cash and Security Holdings	111 745 432	X

Table MI-15. State Government Tax Collections, 2008

(Dollars, percent distribution.)

Item	Thousands of dollars	Percent distribution
Total Taxes	24 781 626	X
Property taxes	2 264 306	9.1
Sales and gross receipts	11 920 372	48.1
General sales and gross receipts	8 225 599	33.2
Selective sales taxes	3 694 773	14.9
Alcoholic beverages	138 779	0.6
Amusements	129 684	0.5
Insurance premiums	223 198	0.9
Motor fuels	994 937	4.0
Pari-mutuels	8 188	0.0
Public utilities	21 317	0.1
Tobacco products	1 076 087	4.3
Other selective sales	1 102 583	4.4
Licenses	1 354 001	5.5
Alcoholic beverages	14 124	0.1
Corporation	20 347	0.1
Hunting and fishing	47 073	0.2
Motor vehicle	892 817	3.6
Motor vehicle operators	51 928	0.2
Public utility	19 554	0.1
Occupation and business, NEC	151 006	0.6
Other licenses	157 152	0.6
Income taxes	8 959 372	36.2
Individual income	7 181 055	29.0
Corporation net income	1 778 317	7.2
Other taxes	283 575	1.1
Death and gift	234	0.0
Documentary and stock transfer	169 835	0.7
Severance	113 506	0.5

Table MI-16. Agriculture

(Number, acres, and dollars.)

Item	2002		2007		Percent change, 2002–2007
	Number	Percent of total	Number	Percent of total	
Number of farms	53 315		56 014		5.1
Farm Size					
Average size of farm (acres)	190		179		-5.8
Farms by size (number of farms)					
Fewer than 50 acres	21 898	41.1	24 945	44.5	13.9
50 to 499 acres	26 598	49.9	26 481	47.3	-0.4
500 acres or more	4 819	9.0	4 588	8.2	-4.8
Land (Acres)					
Total land in farms	10 142 958		10 031 807		-1.1
Total cropland	7 983 574	78.7	7 803 643	77.8	-2.3
Total harvested cropland	6 827 903	67.3	6 859 081	68.4	0.5
Irrigated land	456 278	4.5	500 428	5.0	9.7
Value of Sales (Dollars)					
Agricultural products sold ($1,000)	3 772 435		5 753 219		52.5
Average sales per farm	70 757		102 710		45.2
Sales of crops	2 362 628	62.6	3 329 928	57.9	40.9
Sales of livestock, poultry, and their products	1 409 807	37.4	2 423 291	42.1	71.9
Value of Sales (Number of Farms)					
Less than $10,000	33 147	62.2	34 671	61.9	4.6
$10,000 to $99,999	13 677	25.7	13 377	23.9	-2.2
$100,000 to $999,999	5 920	11.1	6 926	12.4	17.0
$1,000,000 or more	571	1.1	1 040	1.9	82.1
Farms by Type of Organization (Number of Farms)					
Family	48 070	90.2	48 687	86.9	1.3
Partnership	3 172	5.9	4 260	7.6	34.3
Corporation	1 817	3.4	2 494	4.5	37.3
Other: cooperative, estate or trust, institutional, etc	256	0.5	573	1.0	123.8
Value of Land and Buildings (Dollars)					
Estimated market value of land and buildings ($1,000)	34 199 659		27 143 604		-20.6
Land and buildings average value per farm	610 556		509 299		-16.6
Average value per acre	3 409		2 667		-21.8
Government Payments					
Number of farms receiving government payments	18 133	34.0	23 239	41.5	28.2
Payments (thousands of dollars)	144 771		118 871		-17.9
Average payment per farm	7 984		5 115		-35.9
Farm Operator Characteristics					
Farm operators whose principal occupation is farming	29 071	54.5	24 795	44.3	-14.7
Farm operators whose principal occupation is other	24 244	45.5	31 219	55.7	28.8
Average age principal operator (years)	54.2		56.3		3.9

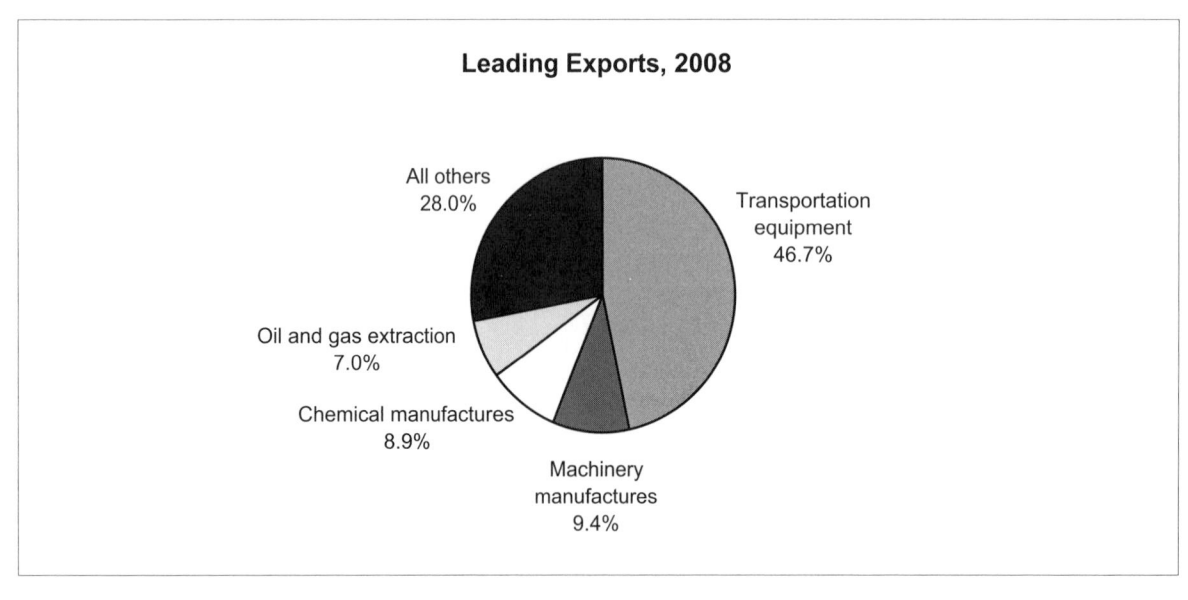

Leading Exports, 2008

All others 28.0%

Transportation equipment 46.7%

Oil and gas extraction 7.0%

Chemical manufactures 8.9%

Machinery manufactures 9.4%

MINNESOTA

Facts and Figures

Location: North central United States; bordered on the N by Canada (Manitoba and Ontario), on the E by Lake Superior and Wisconsin, on the S by Iowa, and on the W by North Dakota and South Dakota

Area: 86,939 sq. mi. (225,171 sq. km.); rank—12th

Population: 5,220,393 (2008 est.); rank—21st

Principal Cities: capital—St. Paul; largest—Minneapolis

Statehood: May 11, 1858; 32nd state

U.S. Congress: 2 senators, 8 representatives

State Motto: *L'Etoile du Nord* ("The Star of the North")

State Song: "Hail! Minnesota"

State Nicknames: The North Star State; The Land of 10,000 Lakes; The Gopher State

Abbreviations: MN; Minn.

State Symbols: flower—showy (pink and white) lady's slipper; tree—red (Norway) pine; bird—loon

At a Glance

- With an increase in population of 6.1 percent, Minnesota ranked 26th among the states in growth from 2000 to 2008.
- An estimated 28,820 marriages took place in Minnesota in 2008; Minnesota does not report its number of divorces.
- The 2007 home ownership rate in Minnesota was 73.5 percent, giving it a ranking of 13th among the states.
- Minnesota's median household income in 2007 was $55,802, 10th among the states.
- In Minnesota, 9.5 percent of the population lived below the poverty level in 2007, ranking it 43rd.
- In 2006-07, 8.8 percent of Minnesotans did not have health insurance, compared to 15.5 percent of the total U.S. population.
- In 2007, 4.6 percent of Minnesotans were unemployed, which was the same as the national average.
- Minnesota ranked 10th in the nation with 31 percent of its population 25 years old and over having a bachelor's degree in 2007.
- Minnesota's violent crime rate in 2007 was 288.7 per 100,000 population, compared to 466.9 for the entire nation.
- Minnesota had one physician for every 303 people in 2007, compared to one physician for every 325 people nationwide.
- In the 2008 election, 78.2 percent of Minnesota's eligible voters voted, compared to 61.7 percent of eligible voters nationwide.
- Minnesota ranked 31st among the states receiving federal aid in 2007, with $1,351 per capita.
- Minnesota's gross domestic product was $255 billion in 2007; it ranked 16th among the states.
- With $18.1 billion in exports in 2007, Minnesota ranked 20th in exports.
- Minnesotans consumed 1.82 trillion Btu's of energy in 2006; the state ranked 20th in total consumption.
- In 2007, Minnesota exported $3.6 billion worth of agricultural products, about 4.4 percent of the U.S. total.

Table MN-1. Population by Sex, Age, Race, and Hispanic Origin

(Number, percent.)

Sex, age, race, and Hispanic origin	1990	2000	2008	Average annual percent change, 2000–2008
Total Population	4 375 099	4 919 479	5 220 393	0.7
Percent of total U.S. population	1.8	1.7	1.7	X
Sex				
Male	2 145 183	2 435 631	2 599 899	0.8
Female	2 229 916	2 483 848	2 620 494	0.7
Age				
Under 5 years	336 800	329 594	358 471	1.1
5 to 19 years	956 746	1 105 251	1 043 935	-0.7
20 to 64 years	2 534 619	2 890 368	3 167 468	1.2
65 years and over	546 934	594 266	650 519	1.1
Median age (years)	32.4	35.4	37.3	X
Race and Hispanic Origin[1]				
One race				
White	4 130 395	4 400 282	4 648 528	0.7
Black	94 944	171 731	238 531	4.2
American Indian and Alaskan Native	49 909	54 967	64 503	2.0
Asian[2]	77 886	141 968	185 089	3.4
Native Hawaiian and Other Pacific Islander	X	1 979	3 251	6.4
Two or more races	X	82 742	80 491	-0.3
Hispanic (of any race)	53 884	143 382	216 574	5.3

[1]Data on race in 2000 and 2008 are not comparable to 1990. Individuals could only report one race in the 1990 census but could report one or more races on the 2000 census.
[2]Data in 1990 refer to Asian and Pacific Islanders.

Table MN-2. Marital Status

(Number, percent distribution.)

Sex and marital status	1990	2000	2007
Males, 15 Years and Over	1 635 377	1 889 936	2 059 605
Never married	30.8	31.3	33.3
Now married, except separated	59.2	57.7	55.1
Separated	1.1	0.9	1.0
Widowed	2.2	2.1	2.1
Divorced	6.6	8.0	8.6
Females, 15 Years and Over	1 743 785	1 967 819	2 104 140
Never married	24.1	25.0	26.9
Now married, except separated	55.4	55.0	52.4
Separated	1.3	1.2	1.3
Widowed	11.1	9.4	8.9
Divorced	8.1	9.5	10.4

Table MN-3. Households and Housing Characteristics

(Number, percent, and dollars.)

Item	1990	2000	2007	Average annual percent change, 2000–2007
Total Households	1 647 853	1 895 127	2 062 681	1.2
Family households	1 130 683	1 255 141	1 353 390	1.1
Married-couple family	942 524	1 018 245	1 074 338	0.8
Other family	188 159	236 896	279 052	2.4
Male householder, no wife present	46 605	68 114	84 832	3.2
Female householder, no husband present	141 554	168 782	194 220	2.0
Nonfamily households	517 170	639 986	709 291	1.5
Householder living alone	413 531	509 468	577 454	1.8
Householder not living alone	103 639	130 518	131 837	0.1
Housing Characteristics				
Total housing units	1 848 445	2 065 946	2 304 473	1.6
Occupied housing units	1 647 853	1 895 127	2 062 681	1.2
Owner-occupied	1 183 673	1 412 865	1 551 989	1.4
Renter-occupied	464 180	482 262	510 692	0.8
Average size	2.58	2.52	2.45	X
Financial Characteristics				
Median gross rent of renter-occupied housing units (dollars)	422	566	711	3.3
Median monthly owner costs for housing units with a mortgage (dollars)	724	1 044	1 500	5.3
Median value of owner-occupied housing units (dollars)	73 700	122 400	213 600	8.3

Table MN-4. Median Income and Poverty Status, 2007

(Number, percent.)

Characteristic	State		U.S.	
	Number	Percent	Number	Percent
Median Income				
Households (dollars)	55 802	X	50 740	X
Families (dollars)	69 172	X	61 173	X
Below Poverty Level				
Sex				
Male	213 059	8.4	16 576 071	11.5
Female	268 888	10.6	21 476 176	14.3
Age				
Under 18 years	148 649	12.0	13 097 100	18.0
Related children under 18 years	142 671	11.6	12 728 964	17.6
18 to 64 years	285 513	8.8	21 495 507	11.6
65 years and over	47 785	8.0	3 459 640	9.5

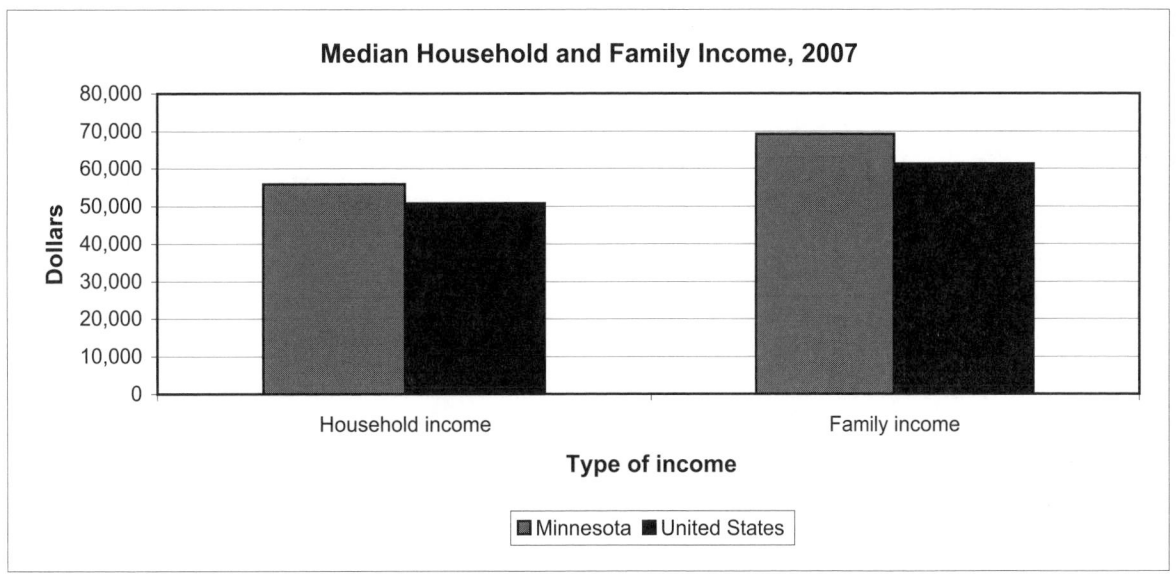

Median Household and Family Income, 2007

Minnesota ■ United States

Table MN-5. Health Insurance Coverage Status for All Persons and Children Under 18 Years of Age

(Number, percent.)

Item	2000	2001	2002	2003	2004	2005	2006	2007
ALL PERSONS	4 895	4 922	5 054	5 076	5 127	5 129	5 149	5 190
Covered by Private or Government Health Insurance								
Number	4 527	4 551	4 677	4 657	4 692	4 722	4 675	4 758
Percent	92.5	92.5	92.6	91.7	91.5	92.1	90.8	91.7
Not Covered								
Number	368	371	376	420	434	408	475	433
Percent	7.5	7.5	7.4	8.3	8.5	7.9	9.2	8.3
Percent in the U.S. not covered	13.7	14.1	14.7	15.1	14.9	15.3	15.8	15.3
CHILDREN UNDER 18 YEARS OF AGE	1 235	1 158	1 245	1 241	1 251	1 230	1 256	1 246
Covered by Private or Government Health Insurance								
Number	1 169	1 097	1 181	1 169	1 174	1 157	1 153	1 167
Percent	94.6	94.7	94.8	94.2	93.8	94.1	91.7	93.6
Not Covered								
Number	66	61	65	72	77	73	104	80
Percent	5.4	5.3	5.2	5.8	6.2	5.9	8.3	6.4
Percent in the U.S. not covered	11.6	11.3	11.2	11.0	10.5	10.9	11.7	11.0

Table MN-6. Employment Status by Demographic Group, Preliminary 2008

(Number, percent.)

Characteristic	Civilian noninstitutional population	Civilian labor force		Employment		Unemployed	
		Number	Percent of population	Number	Percent of population	Number	Unemployment rate
TOTAL	4 062	2 905	71.5	2 744	67.6	161	5.5
Sex							
Men	2 005	1 524	76.0	1 432	71.4	92	6.0
Women	2 057	1 381	67.0	1 312	63.8	69	5.0
Race, Sex, and Hispanic Origin							
White	3 684	2 621	71.2	2 491	67.6	131	5.0
Men	1 811	1 366	75.4	1 289	71.2	77	5.6
Women	1 873	1 256	67.0	1 201	64.2	54	4.3
Black or African American	157	120	76.6	100	63.6	20	16.9
Men	83	67	80.3	57	68.1	10	15.1
Women	74	54	72.4	43	58.5	10	19.2
Hispanic	132	108	82.0	100	75.9	8	7.5
Men	69	62	90.2	58	83.9	4	7.0
Women	63	46	72.9	42	67.0	4	8.0
Age							
16 to 19 years	280	152	54.2	131	46.8	21	13.7
20 to 24 years	368	311	84.5	282	76.6	29	9.4
25 to 34 years	736	648	88.1	613	83.2	36	5.5
35 to 44 years	671	595	88.5	567	84.5	27	4.6
45 to 54 years	792	698	88.1	669	84.4	29	4.2
55 to 64 years	554	397	71.6	380	68.5	17	4.2
65 years and over	660	105	15.9	103	15.5	2	2.3

Note: Data in Table 6 are from the Current Population Survey (CPS) and do not match the estimates in Table 7. See notes and definitions for more details.

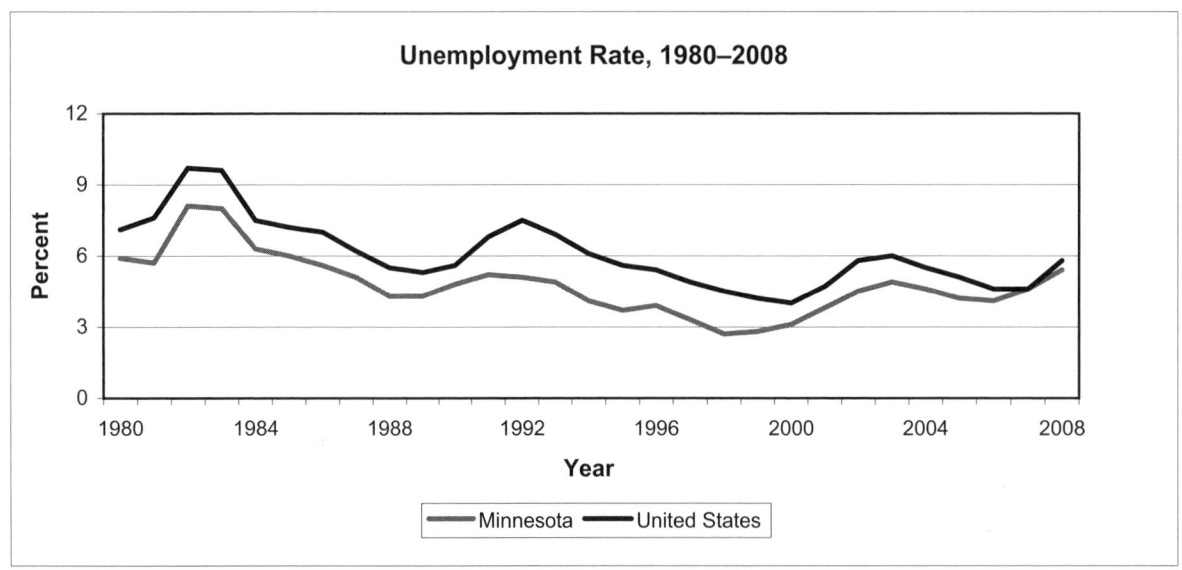

Table MN-7. Employment Status of the Civilian Noninstitutional Population Age 16 Years and Over

(Number, percent.)

Year	Civilian labor force	Civilian participation rate	Employed	Unemployed	Unemployment rate
1998	2 731 716	75.3	2 656 674	75 042	2.7
1999	2 763 825	75.1	2 686 942	76 883	2.8
2000	2 807 668	75.3	2 720 492	87 176	3.1
2001	2 866 024	75.8	2 755 808	110 216	3.8
2002	2 880 330	75.4	2 749 525	130 805	4.5
2003	2 891 661	75.0	2 750 938	140 723	4.9
2004	2 885 974	74.2	2 752 403	133 571	4.6
2005	2 879 707	73.3	2 759 488	120 219	4.2
2006	2 893 112	72.9	2 774 941	118 171	4.1
2007	2 910 811	72.6	2 776 290	134 521	4.6
2008	2 932 961	72.5	2 773 136	159 825	5.4

Table MN-8. Employment and Average Wages by Industry

(Estimates for 2001–2006 are based on the 2002 North American Industry Classification System [NAICS]. Estimates for 2007 are based on the 2007 NAICS.)

Industry	2001	2002	2003	2004	2005	2006	2007
	Number of jobs						
WAGE AND SALARY EMPLOYMENT BY INDUSTRY	2 783 816	2 763 914	2 759 379	2 781 833	2 822 533	2 853 267	2 870 254
Farm Wage and Salary Employment	17 576	16 722	18 487	18 049	18 289	16 240	16 585
Nonfarm Wage and Salary Employment	2 766 240	2 747 192	2 740 892	2 763 784	2 804 244	2 837 027	2 853 669
Private wage and salary employment	2 357 886	2 337 830	2 332 684	2 354 955	2 388 888	2 417 778	2 432 041
Forestry, fishing, hunting, and other	7 039	7 179	7 268	7 414	7 651	7 541	7 369
Mining	6 062	5 723	5 330	5 286	5 192	5 223	5 283
Utilities	12 605	12 276	11 975	11 929	11 919	11 956	12 100
Construction	127 790	129 221	129 780	133 176	134 232	130 849	124 330
Manufacturing	381 066	359 499	348 717	346 010	349 626	349 127	344 483
Durable goods manufacturing	243 865	227 529	218 790	221 121	225 477	226 067	221 706
Nondurable goods manufacturing	137 201	131 970	129 927	124 889	124 149	123 060	122 777
Wholesale trade	132 737	130 013	129 578	130 720	132 840	134 687	135 023
Retail trade	316 779	312 214	310 065	310 384	311 650	310 390	310 119
Transportation and warehousing	88 984	82 309	81 058	82 618	84 404	82 302	83 243
Information	70 072	67 418	61 084	59 493	59 232	57 874	58 244
Finance and insurance	135 604	137 418	141 325	141 102	143 252	144 780	142 659
Real estate and rental and leasing	38 117	38 148	38 632	39 635	39 777	39 818	40 604
Professional and technical services	132 030	126 637	124 834	125 547	128 307	132 774	137 125
Management of companies and enterprises	63 936	60 235	59 511	63 990	63 314	65 917	66 867
Administrative and waste services	121 111	116 958	116 926	120 205	123 394	129 846	131 840
Educational services	51 947	55 135	56 380	56 565	57 278	60 272	61 756
Health care and social assistance	303 890	321 101	332 670	341 140	351 032	366 222	380 160
Arts, entertainment, and recreation	36 173	37 899	38 679	37 975	38 829	40 166	40 573
Accommodation and food services	194 629	196 536	197 765	202 259	208 039	208 641	211 713
Other services, except public administration	137 315	141 911	141 107	139 507	138 920	139 393	138 550
Government and government enterprises	408 354	409 362	408 208	408 829	415 356	419 249	421 628
	Dollars						
AVERAGE WAGES AND SALARIES BY INDUSTRY	35 801	36 670	37 772	39 553	39 995	41 335	43 460
Average Farm Wages and Salaries	29 130	31 689	24 481	26 418	25 282	27 965	31 890
Average Nonfarm Wages and Salaries	35 843	36 700	37 862	39 639	40 091	41 412	43 527
Average private wages and salaries	36 351	37 046	38 196	40 077	40 501	41 826	44 074
Forestry, fishing, hunting, and other	17 929	19 241	19 547	20 595	20 448	21 885	23 463
Mining	49 222	49 325	54 290	56 612	60 895	65 021	65 783
Utilities	67 141	69 583	67 992	75 401	75 640	77 978	79 823
Construction	44 084	44 741	45 341	46 465	45 982	47 983	50 599
Manufacturing	42 437	44 337	46 536	49 007	48 813	50 238	52 258
Durable goods manufacturing	44 505	46 505	49 303	52 252	51 710	53 047	55 558
Nondurable goods manufacturing	38 762	40 599	41 876	43 262	43 553	45 078	46 299
Wholesale trade	51 390	52 646	54 471	57 276	59 637	62 201	64 649
Retail trade	21 084	21 732	22 145	23 060	22 784	23 107	23 556
Transportation and warehousing	41 619	42 179	43 088	44 088	43 354	41 389	45 291
Information	47 344	47 612	49 755	53 504	54 699	56 894	59 522
Finance and insurance	60 430	60 173	64 225	67 951	68 644	71 499	78 742
Real estate and rental and leasing	32 021	33 579	34 846	35 041	37 745	41 420	42 004
Professional and technical services	56 083	56 874	58 382	60 739	62 662	65 539	69 677
Management of companies and enterprises	77 691	79 569	79 156	88 343	91 710	91 044	103 546
Administrative and waste services	24 662	25 492	26 260	27 080	27 615	27 737	29 314
Educational services	22 233	22 542	23 293	24 117	24 956	25 594	27 167
Health care and social assistance	32 742	33 976	35 059	36 476	37 001	38 594	40 221
Arts, entertainment, and recreation	22 478	23 307	24 272	24 879	24 139	27 025	27 205
Accommodation and food services	12 530	12 750	13 172	13 582	13 688	14 453	14 868
Other services, except public administration	21 724	22 770	23 193	24 387	24 658	25 383	26 256
Government and government enterprises	32 914	34 729	35 952	37 118	37 733	39 023	40 375

Table MN-9. Employment Characteristics by Family Type

(Number, percent.)

Family type and labor force status	2005		2006		2007	
	Total	Families with own children under 18 years	Total	Families with own children under 18 years	Total	Families with own children under 18 years
TOTAL FAMILIES	1 329 046	643 222	1 330 451	638 704	1 353 390	649 336
FAMILY TYPE AND LABOR FORCE STATUS						
Married Coupled Families	1 064 228	473 255	1 064 699	467 638	1 074 338	469 908
Both husband and wife in labor force	61.6	73.1	62.8	74.1	62.7	74.7
Husband in labor force, wife not in labor force	16.5	21.0	16.6	21.2	16.7	21.3
Wife in labor force, husband not in labor force	6.7	3.5	6.3	3.4	6.4	2.8
Both husband and wife not in labor force	15.2	2.3	14.3	1.4	14.2	1.2
Other Families	264 818	169 967	265 752	171 066	279 052	179 428
Female householder, no husband present	69.4	72.1	69.8	72.6	69.6	71.5
In labor force	53.4	59.7	55.3	62.0	54.4	60.3
Not in labor force	16.0	12.4	14.5	10.5	15.2	11.2
Male householder, no wife present	30.6	27.9	30.2	27.4	30.4	28.5
In labor force	25.6	25.2	26.0	25.3	25.3	25.3
Not in labor force	5.1	2.7	4.2	2.2	5.1	3.1

Table MN-10. School Enrollment and Educational Attainment, 2007

(Number, percent.)

Item	State	U.S.
Enrollment		
Total population 3 years and over	4 986 504	289 295 761
Enrolled in school	1 350 308	79 329 527
Enrolled in preschool (percent)	6.4	6.2
Enrolled in grades K-12 (percent)	67.6	67.6
Enrolled in college or graduate school (percent)	25.9	26.2
Attainment		
Total population 25 years and over	3 429 364	197 892 369
Less than a high school diploma (percent)	9.0	15.5
High school diploma or more (percent)	91.0	84.5
Bachelor's degree or more (percent)	31.0	27.5
Graduate degree or more (percent)	10.0	10.1

Table MN-11. Educational Indicators

(Number, percent.)

Item	State	U.S.
Public Schools, 2006–2007 (except where noted)		
Number of school districts	566	17 742
Number of schools	2 691	99 639
Number of students	840 565	49 315 842
Student-teacher ratio	16.2	15.5
Expenditures per student (dollars)	$9 589	. . .
Averaged freshman graduation rate, 2005–2006	86.2	. . .
Dropout rate, grades 9–12, 2005–2006	3.1	3.7
Students eligible for free or reduced-price lunch (percent)	30.9	41.2
English-language learners (percent)	7.6	5.1
Students with IEP (percent)	14.0	12.7
Private Schools, 2007–2008 (except where noted)		
Number of schools	585	33 740
Number of students	90 973	5 072 451
High school graduates, 2006–2007	4 930	306 605
Student-teacher ratio	12.7	11.1

Table MN-12. Reported Voting and Registration of the Voting-Age Population, November 2008

(Number in thousands, percent.)

Item	Total population	Total citizen population	Registered			Voted		
			Total registered	Percent registered (total population)	Percent registered (total citizen population)	Total voted	Percent voted (total population)	Percent voted (total citizen population)
U.S. total	225 499	206 072	146 311	64.9	71.0	131 144	58.2	63.6
State total	3 898	3 678	2 931	75.2	79.7	2 759	70.8	75.0
Sex								
Male	1 927	1 810	1 394	72.4	77.0	1 295	67.2	71.6
Female	1 972	1 868	1 537	77.9	82.3	1 464	74.2	78.3
Race								
White alone	3 497	3 403	2 740	78.4	80.5	2 587	74.0	76.0
White non-Hispanic alone	3 387	3 343	2 707	79.9	81.0	2 558	75.5	76.5
Black alone	181	119	87	48.3	73.2	82	45.5	69.0
Asian alone	162	98	62	38.4	63.7	56	34.4	57.1
Hispanic (of any race)	128	68	39	30.4	. . .	35	27.6	. . .
White alone or in combination	3 543	3 448	2 770	78.2	80.3	2 612	73.7	75.7
Black alone or in combination	190	128	91	48.0	71.1	86	45.4	67.2
Asian alone or in combination	171	107	70	40.7	65.3	62	36.1	57.8

Table MN-13. Crime

(Number, rate per 100,000.)

Item	State			U.S.		
	2007	2008	Percent change	2007	2008	Percent change
Population	5 197 621	5 220 393	0.4	301 621 157	304 059 724	0.8
VIOLENT CRIME						
Number	15 003	13 717	-8.6	1 408 337	1 382 012	-1.9
Rate	288.7	262.8	-9.0	466.9	454.5	-2.7
Murder and Nonnegligent Manslaughter						
Number	116	109	-6.0	16 929	16 272	-3.9
Rate	2.2	2.1	-6.4	5.6	5.4	-4.7
Forcible Rape						
Number	1 873	1 805	-3.6	90 427	89 000	-1.6
Rate	36.0	34.6	-4.1	30.0	29.3	-2.4
Robbery						
Number	4 770	4 177	-12.4	445 125	441 855	-0.7
Rate	91.8	80.0	-12.8	147.6	145.3	-1.5
Aggravated Assault						
Number	8 244	7 626	-7.5	855 856	834 885	-2.5
Rate	158.6	146.1	-7.9	283.8	274.6	-3.2
PROPERTY CRIME						
Number	157 829	148 810	-5.7	9 843 481	9 767 915	-0.8
Rate	3 036.6	2 850.6	-6.1	3 263.5	3 212.5	-1.6
Burglary						
Number	29 670	26 410	-11.0	2 179 140	2 222 196	2.0
Rate	570.8	505.9	-11.4	722.5	730.8	1.2
Larceny-Theft						
Number	115 633	112 322	-2.9	6 568 572	6 588 873	0.3
Rate	2 224.7	2 151.6	-3.3	2 177.8	2 167.0	-0.5
Motor Vehicle Theft						
Number	12 526	10 078	-19.5	1 095 769	956 846	-12.7
Rate	241.0	193.1	-19.9	363.3	314.7	-13.4

Table MN-14. State Government Finances, 2007

(Dollars, percent distribution.)

Item	Thousands of dollars	Percent distribution
Total Revenue	38 745 022	X
General revenue	28 476 103	73.5
Intergovernmental revenue	6 680 661	17.2
Taxes	17 780 164	45.9
General sales	4 470 596	11.5
Selective sales	2 831 494	7.3
License taxes	973 363	2.5
Individual income tax	7 230 854	18.7
Corporate income tax	1 183 816	3.1
Other taxes	1 090 041	2.8
Current charges	2 228 370	5.8
Miscellaneous general revenue	1 786 908	4.6
Utility revenue	0	0.0
Liquor store revenue	0	0.0
Insurance trust revenue	10 268 919	26.5
Total Expenditure	31 880 478	100.0
Intergovernmental expenditure	10 686 237	33.5
Direct expenditure	21 194 241	66.5
Current operation	14 855 123	46.6
Capital outlay	1 449 984	4.5
Insurance benefits and repayments	3 612 997	11.3
Assistance and subsidies	784 705	2.5
Interest on debt	491 432	1.5
Exhibit: Salaries and wages	4 619 074	14.5
Total Expenditure	31 880 478	100.0
General expenditure	28 163 216	88.3
Intergovernmental expenditure	10 686 237	33.5
Direct expenditure	17 476 979	54.8
Education	11 654 016	36.6
Public welfare	8 415 365	26.4
Hospitals	327 807	1.0
Health	599 726	1.9
Highways	1 861 145	5.8
Police protection	327 884	1.0
Correction	535 237	1.7
Natural resources	482 422	1.5
Parks and recreation	180 162	0.6
Government administration	817 892	2.6
Interest on general debt	491 432	1.5
Other and unallocable	2 470 128	7.7
Utility expenditure	104 265	0.3
Liquor store expenditure	0	0.0
Insurance trust expenditure	3 612 997	11.3
Debt at End of Fiscal Year	8 866 611	X
Cash and Security Holdings	64 495 475	X

Table MN-15. State Government Tax Collections, 2008

(Dollars, percent distribution.)

Item	Thousands of dollars	Percent distribution
Total Taxes	18 320 891	X
Property taxes	712 463	3.9
Sales and gross receipts	7 433 063	40.6
General sales and gross receipts	4 550 838	24.8
Selective sales taxes	2 882 225	15.7
Alcoholic beverages	72 563	0.4
Amusements	43 219	0.2
Insurance premiums	347 045	1.9
Motor fuels	648 565	3.5
Pari-mutuels	967	0.0
Public utilities	47	0.0
Tobacco products	419 127	2.3
Other selective sales	1 350 692	7.4
Licenses	1 011 289	5.5
Alcoholic beverages	1 682	0.0
Amusements	1 137	0.0
Corporation	7 400	0.0
Hunting and fishing	57 947	0.3
Motor vehicle	511 513	2.8
Motor vehicle operators	50 168	0.3
Public utility	836	0.0
Occupation and business, NEC	330 155	1.8
Other licenses	50 451	0.3
Income taxes	8 817 738	48.1
Individual income	7 777 259	42.5
Corporation net income	1 040 479	5.7
Other taxes	346 338	1.9
Death and gift	115 523	0.6
Documentary and stock transfer	198 994	1.1
Severance	31 821	0.2

Table MN-16. Agriculture

(Number, acres, and dollars.)

Item	2002		2007		Percent change, 2002–2007
	Number	Percent of total	Number	Percent of total	
Number of farms	80 839		80 992		0.2
Farm Size					
Average size of farm (acres)	340		332		-2.4
Farms by size (number of farms)					
Fewer than 50 acres	20 137	24.9	20 614	25.5	2.4
50 to 499 acres	45 327	56.1	45 867	56.6	1.2
500 acres or more	15 375	19.0	14 511	17.9	-5.6
Land (Acres)					
Total land in farms	27 512 270		26 917 962		-2.2
Total cropland	22 729 158	82.6	21 948 603	81.5	-3.4
Total harvested cropland	19 398 309	70.5	19 267 018	71.6	-0.7
Irrigated land	454 850	1.7	506 357	1.9	11.3
Value of Sales (Dollars)					
Agricultural products sold ($1,000)	8 575 627		13 180 466		53.7
Average sales per farm	106 083		162 738		53.4
Sales of crops	4 562 882	53.2	7 048 913	53.5	54.5
Sales of livestock, poultry, and their products	4 012 745	46.8	6 131 554	46.5	52.8
Value of Sales (Number of Farms)					
Less than $10,000	38 932	48.2	39 924	49.3	2.5
$10,000 to $99,999	23 365	28.9	18 904	23.3	-19.1
$100,000 to $999,999	17 405	21.5	19 484	24.1	11.9
$1,000,000 or more	1 137	1.4	2 680	3.3	135.7
Farms by Type of Organization (Number of Farms)					
Family	73 018	90.3	70 055	86.5	-4.1
Partnership	5 056	6.3	6 227	7.7	23.2
Corporation	2 342	2.9	2 848	3.5	21.6
Other: cooperative, estate or trust, institutional, etc	423	0.5	1 862	2.3	340.2
Value of Land and Buildings (Dollars)					
Estimated market value of land and buildings ($1,000)	69 164 551		41 776 544		-39.6
Land and buildings average value per farm	853 968		517 132		-39.4
Average value per acre	2 569		1 513		-41.1
Government Payments					
Number of farms receiving government payments	43 927	54.3	56 657	70.0	29.0
Payments (thousands of dollars)	350 709		445 861		27.1
Average payment per farm	7 984		7 869		-1.4
Farm Operator Characteristics					
Farm operators whose principal occupation is farming	50 808	62.9	39 628	48.9	-22.0
Farm operators whose principal occupation is other	30 031	37.1	41 364	51.1	37.7
Average age principal operator (years)	52.9		55.3		4.5

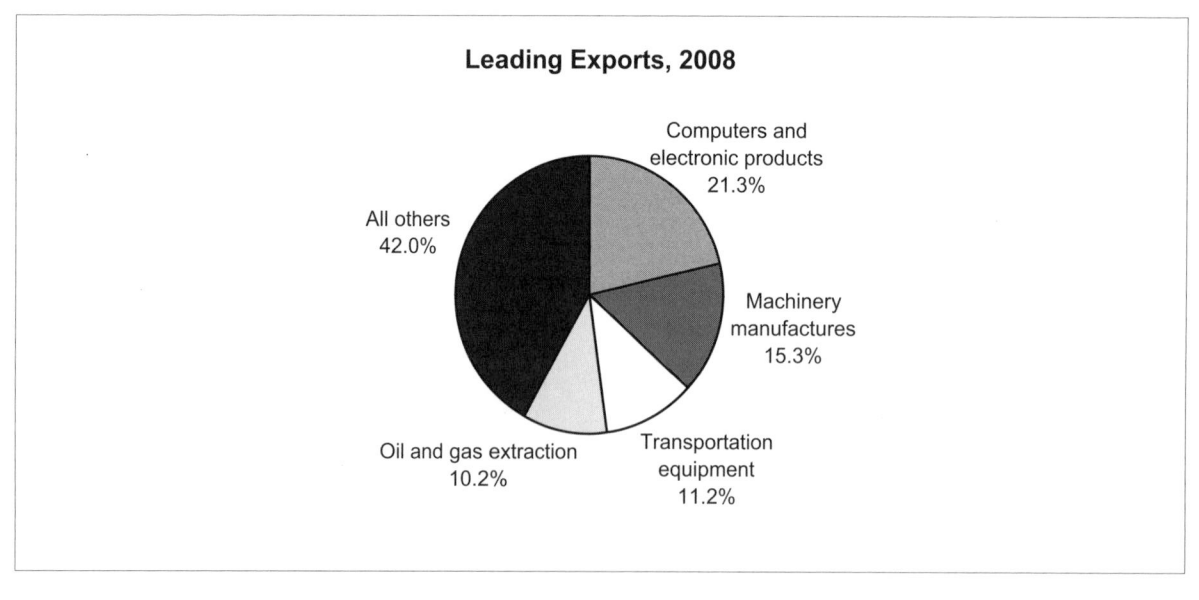

Leading Exports, 2008

Computers and electronic products 21.3%

Machinery manufactures 15.3%

Transportation equipment 11.2%

Oil and gas extraction 10.2%

All others 42.0%

MISSISSIPPI

Facts and Figures

Location: South central United States; bordered on the N by Tennessee, on the E by Alabama, on the S by Louisiana and the Gulf of Mexico, and on the W by Arkansas and Louisiana

Area: 48,430 sq. mi. (125,434 sq. km.); rank—32nd

Population: 2,938,618 (2008 est.); rank—31st

Principal Cities: capital—Jackson; largest—Jackson

Statehood: December 10, 1817; 20th state

U.S. Congress: 2 senators, 4 representatives

State Motto: *Virtute et armis* ("By valor and arms")

State Song: "Go, Mississippi"

State Nicknames: The Magnolia State; The Hospitality State

Abbreviations: MS; Miss.

State Symbols: flower—magnolia blossom; tree—Southern magnolia; bird—mockingbird

At a Glance

- With an increase in population of 3.3 percent, Mississippi ranked 36th among the states in growth from 2000 to 2008.
- An estimated 15,872 marriages took place in Mississippi in 2008, compared to 13,049 divorces.
- The 2007 home ownership rate in Mississippi was 74 percent, giving it a ranking of 8th among the states.
- Mississippi's median household income in 2007 was $36,338, 50th among the states.
- In Mississippi, 20.6 percent of the population lived below the poverty level in 2007, ranking it 1st.
- In 2006-07, 19.8 percent of Mississippians did not have health insurance, compared to 15.5 percent of the total U.S. population.
- In 2007, 6.1 percent of Mississippians were unemployed, compared to 4.6 percent nationwide.
- Mississippi ranked 49th in the nation with 18.9 percent of its population 25 years old and over having a bachelor's degree in 2007.
- Mississippi's violent crime rate in 2007 was 291.3 per 100,000 population, compared to 466.9 for the entire nation.
- Mississippi had one physician for every 490 people in 2007, compared to one physician for every 325 people nationwide.
- In the 2008 election, 61 percent of Mississippi's eligible voters voted, compared to 61.7 percent of eligible voters nationwide.
- Mississippi ranked 4th among the states receiving federal aid in 2007, with $2,821 per capita.
- Mississippi's gross domestic product was $89 billion in 2007; it ranked 35th among the states.
- With $5.2 billion in exports in 2007, Mississippi ranked 33rd in exports.
- Mississippians consumed 1.22 trillion Btu's of energy in 2006; the state ranked 28th in total consumption.
- In 2007, Mississippi exported $1.1 billion worth of agricultural products, about 1.4 percent of the U.S. total.

Table MS-1. Population by Sex, Age, Race, and Hispanic Origin

(Number, percent.)

Sex, age, race, and Hispanic origin	1990	2000	2008	Average annual percent change, 2000–2008
Total Population	2 573 216	2 844 658	2 938 618	0.4
Percent of total U.S. population	1.0	1.0	1.0	X
Sex				
Male	1 230 617	1 373 554	1 423 841	0.5
Female	1 342 599	1 471 104	1 514 777	0.4
Age				
Under 5 years	195 365	204 364	220 813	1.0
5 to 19 years	648 102	668 850	637 582	-0.6
20 to 64 years	1 408 465	1 627 921	1 708 625	0.6
65 years and over	321 284	343 523	371 598	1.0
Median age (years)	31.1	33.8	35.3	X
Race and Hispanic Origin[1]				
One race				
White	1 633 461	1 746 099	1 780 749	0.2
Black	915 057	1 033 809	1 092 588	0.7
American Indian and Alaskan Native	8 525	11 652	14 740	3.0
Asian[2]	13 016	18 626	23 699	3.1
Native Hawaiian and Other Pacific Islander	X	667	1 095	6.4
Two or more races	X	20 021	25 747	3.2
Hispanic (of any race)	15 931	39 569	65 798	6.6

[1]Data on race in 2000 and 2008 are not comparable to 1990. Individuals could only report one race in the 1990 census but could report one or more races on the 2000 census.
[2]Data in 1990 refer to Asian and Pacific Islanders.

Table MS-2. Marital Status

(Number, percent distribution.)

Sex and marital status	1990	2000	2007
Males, 15 Years and Over	913 815	1 046 252	1 089 885
Never married	30.1	30.6	34.6
Now married, except separated	57.3	54.6	50.3
Separated	2.5	2.4	2.2
Widowed	3.0	2.9	2.9
Divorced	7.1	9.5	9.9
Females, 15 Years and Over	1 038 813	1 157 363	1 197 080
Never married	23.6	25.1	28.2
Now married, except separated	50.1	48.6	44.8
Separated	3.3	3.2	3.6
Widowed	14.4	12.5	12.0
Divorced	8.6	10.6	11.4

Table MS-3. Households and Housing Characteristics

(Number, percent, and dollars.)

Item	1990	2000	2007	Average annual percent change, 2000–2007
Total Households	911 374	1 046 434	1 080 039	0.5
Family households	674 378	747 159	753 797	0.1
Married-couple family	498 240	520 844	511 683	-0.3
Other family	176 138	226 315	242 114	1.0
Male householder, no wife present	30 917	45 610	49 213	1.1
Female householder, no husband present	145 221	180 705	192 901	0.9
Nonfamily households	236 996	299 275	326 242	1.2
Householder living alone	212 949	257 708	282 811	1.3
Householder not living alone	24 047	41 567	43 431	0.6
Housing Characteristics				
Total housing units	1 010 423	1 161 953	1 254 936	1.1
Occupied housing units	911 374	1 046 434	1 080 039	0.5
Owner-occupied	651 587	756 967	769 923	0.2
Renter-occupied	259 787	289 467	310 116	1.0
Average size	2.75	2.63	2.61	X
Financial Characteristics				
Median gross rent of renter-occupied housing units (dollars)	309	439	609	4.8
Median monthly owner costs for housing units with a mortgage (dollars)	511	752	956	3.5
Median value of owner-occupied housing units (dollars)	45 100	71 400	96 000	4.3

Table MS-4. Median Income and Poverty Status, 2007

(Number, percent.)

Characteristic	State		U.S.	
	Number	Percent	Number	Percent
Median Income				
Households (dollars)	36 338	X	50 740	X
Families (dollars)	44 769	X	61 173	X
Below Poverty Level				
Sex				
Male	246 714	18.2	16 576 071	11.5
Female	334 820	22.9	21 476 176	14.3
Age				
Under 18 years	220 446	29.3	13 097 100	18.0
Related children under 18 years	215 644	28.9	12 728 964	17.6
18 to 64 years	309 855	18.0	21 495 507	11.6
65 years and over	51 233	14.9	3 459 640	9.5

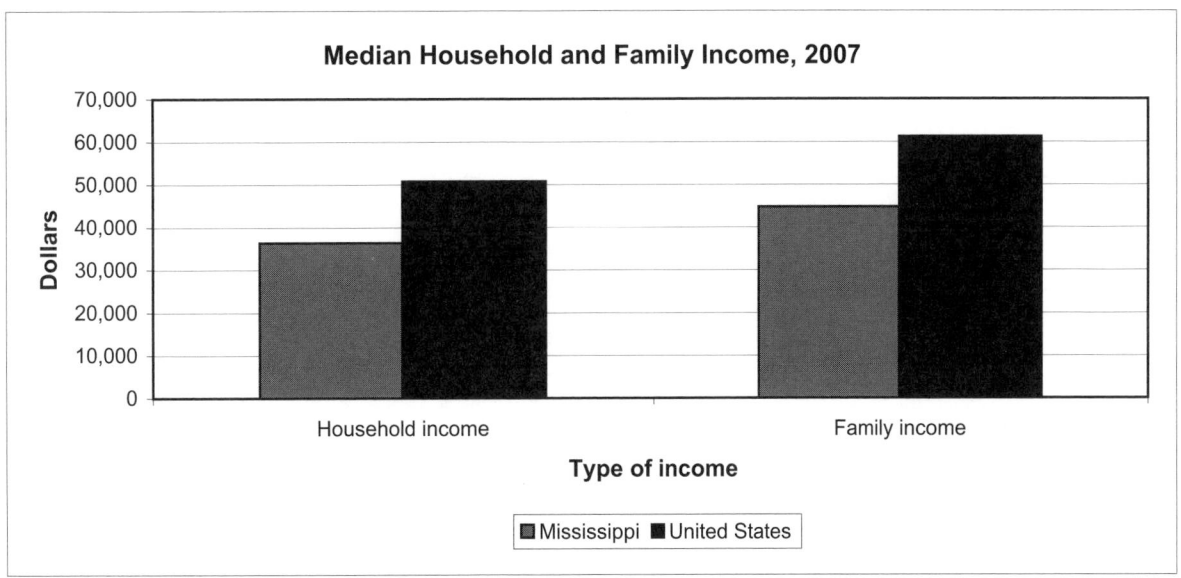

Table MS-5. Health Insurance Coverage Status for All Persons and Children Under 18 Years of Age

(Number, percent.)

Item	2000	2001	2002	2003	2004	2005	2006	2007
ALL PERSONS	2 800	2 799	2 787	2 854	2 868	2 854	2 892	2 903
Covered by Private or Government Health Insurance								
Number	2 439	2 351	2 338	2 353	2 391	2 370	2 292	2 358
Percent	87.1	84.0	83.9	82.4	83.3	83.1	79.2	81.2
Not Covered								
Number	361	448	450	501	478	483	600	545
Percent	12.9	16.0	16.1	17.6	16.7	16.9	20.8	18.8
Percent in the U.S. not covered	13.7	14.1	14.7	15.1	14.9	15.3	15.8	15.3
CHILDREN UNDER 18 YEARS OF AGE	780	787	764	760	768	754	774	778
Covered by Private or Government Health Insurance								
Number	712	708	681	669	665	669	628	684
Percent	91.3	89.9	89.1	88.0	86.6	88.7	81.1	87.9
Not Covered								
Number	68	79	83	91	103	85	146	94
Percent	8.7	10.1	10.9	12.0	13.4	11.3	18.9	12.1
Percent in the U.S. not covered	11.6	11.3	11.2	11.0	10.5	10.9	11.7	11.0

Table MS-6. Employment Status by Demographic Group, Preliminary 2008

(Number, percent.)

Characteristic	Civilian noninstitutional population	Civilian labor force		Employment		Unemployed	
		Number	Percent of population	Number	Percent of population	Number	Unemployment rate
TOTAL	2 188	1 314	60.1	1 229	56.1	86	6.5
Sex							
Men	1 027	688	67.0	639	62.2	49	7.2
Women	1 161	626	54.0	590	50.8	37	5.8
Race, Sex, and Hispanic Origin							
White	1 392	857	61.6	821	59.0	36	4.3
Men	677	461	68.1	443	65.4	18	3.9
Women	715	396	55.4	378	52.8	18	4.7
Black or African American	763	435	57.0	387	50.7	49	11.2
Men	337	218	64.6	187	55.4	31	14.2
Women	426	218	51.1	200	46.9	18	8.2
Hispanic	51	44	86.5	42	83.2	2	3.8
Men	34	31	91.6	30	89.4	1	2.4
Women	17	. . .	. . .	. . .	. . .	. . .	. . .
Age							
16 to 19 years	183	60	32.9	48	26.2	12	20.3
20 to 24 years	212	145	68.4	128	60.2	17	12.0
25 to 34 years	363	294	81.1	271	74.7	23	8.0
35 to 44 years	358	297	83.0	282	78.8	15	5.0
45 to 54 years	385	285	74.0	274	71.1	11	4.0
55 to 64 years	324	175	53.9	169	52.1	6	3.4
65 years and over	363	58	16.0	57	15.8	1	1.1

Note: Data in Table 6 are from the Current Population Survey (CPS) and do not match the estimates in Table 7. See notes and definitions for more details.

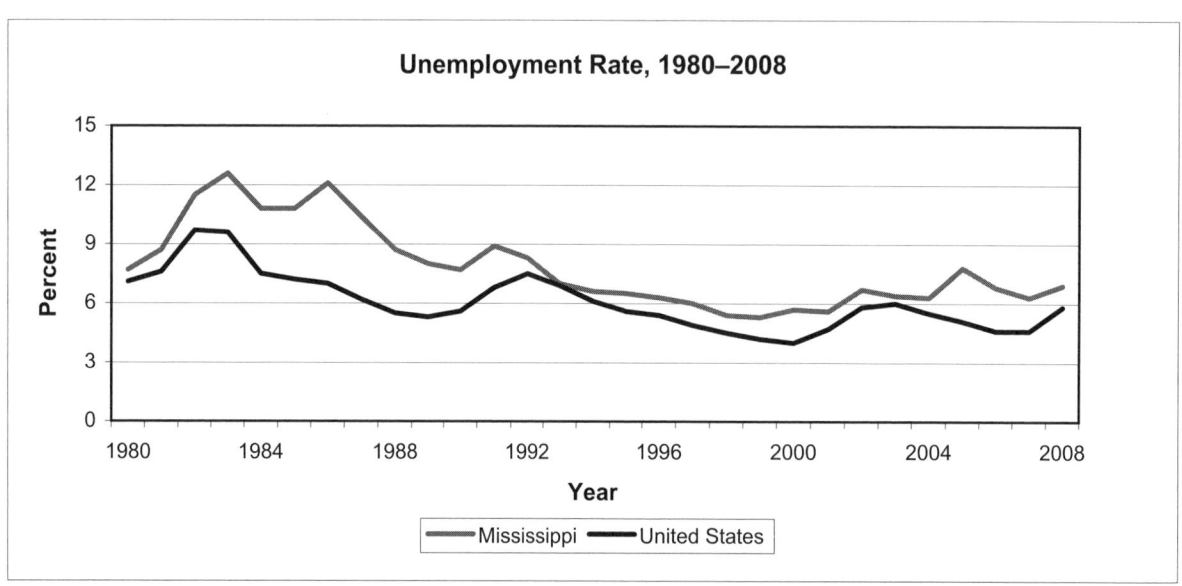

Table MS-7. Employment Status of the Civilian Noninstitutional Population Age 16 Years and Over

(Number, percent.)

Year	Civilian labor force	Civilian participation rate	Employed	Unemployed	Unemployment rate
1998	1 281 362	62.0	1 211 535	69 827	5.4
1999	1 291 684	62.0	1 223 725	67 959	5.3
2000	1 314 154	62.7	1 239 859	74 295	5.7
2001	1 302 564	61.9	1 229 884	72 680	5.6
2002	1 302 235	61.6	1 214 631	87 604	6.7
2003	1 310 099	61.7	1 226 293	83 806	6.4
2004	1 315 664	61.6	1 232 139	83 525	6.3
2005	1 325 646	61.8	1 222 682	102 964	7.8
2006	1 297 954	60.3	1 210 245	87 709	6.8
2007	1 306 633	60.1	1 224 774	81 859	6.3
2008	1 314 444	60.0	1 223 858	90 586	6.9

Table MS-8. Employment and Average Wages by Industry

(Estimates for 2001–2006 are based on the 2002 North American Industry Classification System [NAICS]. Estimates for 2007 are based on the 2007 NAICS.)

Industry	2001	2002	2003	2004	2005	2006	2007
	Number of jobs						
WAGE AND SALARY EMPLOYMENT BY INDUSTRY	1 222 997	1 217 358	1 208 447	1 216 606	1 216 971	1 231 291	1 242 841
Farm Wage and Salary Employment	9 693	9 398	7 197	7 714	7 413	9 085	8 163
Nonfarm Wage and Salary Employment	1 213 304	1 207 960	1 201 250	1 208 892	1 209 558	1 222 206	1 234 678
Private wage and salary employment	938 050	930 145	919 813	927 146	932 790	946 810	955 125
Forestry, fishing, hunting, and other	14 445	13 628	12 855	12 771	12 322	11 453	10 531
Mining	5 473	4 843	4 791	4 890	4 833	5 774	6 151
Utilities	7 983	8 104	7 950	7 958	7 876	7 849	7 589
Construction	53 978	56 048	52 525	51 150	54 170	59 573	61 068
Manufacturing	202 386	189 444	180 292	180 865	179 869	177 224	170 864
Durable goods manufacturing	125 969	119 126	114 046	117 318	117 782	117 597	113 913
Nondurable goods manufacturing	76 417	70 318	66 246	63 547	62 087	59 627	56 951
Wholesale trade	35 780	35 505	35 449	35 443	35 672	36 937	37 473
Retail trade	146 404	144 691	142 998	143 118	143 295	146 999	146 183
Transportation and warehousing	37 957	37 920	38 201	38 990	39 081	39 717	40 815
Information	16 981	16 049	15 062	14 544	14 357	13 737	13 404
Finance and insurance	34 595	34 284	34 411	34 209	34 493	34 887	35 272
Real estate and rental and leasing	11 947	12 087	12 200	12 322	12 393	12 401	12 705
Professional and technical services	30 011	30 190	31 055	32 145	34 518	36 386	36 776
Management of companies and enterprises	10 498	10 522	10 478	9 889	9 652	9 388	9 765
Administrative and waste services	38 638	39 527	39 668	42 952	45 988	50 481	51 542
Educational services	15 446	15 802	16 032	16 132	16 486	17 506	18 129
Health care and social assistance	99 422	102 741	105 582	107 756	109 234	111 602	115 388
Arts, entertainment, and recreation	21 927	15 227	14 243	14 135	13 233	11 936	14 081
Accommodation and food services	101 477	109 069	111 231	112 952	111 859	109 231	113 659
Other services, except public administration	52 702	54 464	54 790	54 925	53 459	53 729	53 730
Government and government enterprises	275 254	277 815	281 437	281 746	276 768	275 396	279 553
	Dollars						
AVERAGE WAGES AND SALARIES BY INDUSTRY	25 414	26 202	27 200	28 210	29 465	30 719	31 801
Average Farm Wages and Salaries	19 437	19 626	17 628	22 368	20 430	17 536	19 986
Average Nonfarm Wages and Salaries	25 462	26 254	27 257	28 247	29 520	30 817	31 879
Average private wages and salaries	25 414	26 098	26 930	27 833	28 987	30 417	31 425
Forestry, fishing, hunting, and other	21 642	22 117	23 297	23 941	25 183	27 034	28 166
Mining	41 597	43 397	44 637	45 769	50 268	55 517	60 364
Utilities	46 740	49 146	51 613	56 013	59 152	57 998	61 390
Construction	28 388	29 766	29 526	29 408	32 539	36 028	37 406
Manufacturing	29 353	30 343	31 940	33 205	34 491	35 740	37 245
Durable goods manufacturing	29 815	30 729	32 540	33 885	35 162	36 567	38 092
Nondurable goods manufacturing	28 591	29 691	30 908	31 950	33 218	34 110	35 552
Wholesale trade	35 517	36 560	37 818	40 086	42 144	44 968	46 453
Retail trade	18 008	18 458	19 154	19 636	20 436	21 568	21 604
Transportation and warehousing	31 627	32 118	33 263	34 526	35 823	36 997	37 844
Information	36 434	35 378	35 013	35 651	37 623	38 290	38 311
Finance and insurance	35 146	36 386	37 978	39 367	40 750	42 692	44 282
Real estate and rental and leasing	20 783	22 435	21 516	22 740	24 350	26 333	27 598
Professional and technical services	38 491	39 482	40 011	41 192	41 209	42 995	45 071
Management of companies and enterprises	46 523	49 203	51 639	54 942	55 597	62 329	66 996
Administrative and waste services	16 740	17 548	18 584	19 326	20 571	21 744	22 450
Educational services	17 383	17 934	18 402	19 071	19 804	20 762	21 249
Health care and social assistance	28 702	29 739	30 717	31 993	32 589	34 146	35 240
Arts, entertainment, and recreation	21 117	20 607	21 085	22 189	23 069	22 475	23 252
Accommodation and food services	14 165	14 788	15 042	15 469	15 955	15 914	16 667
Other services, except public administration	18 016	18 479	19 313	19 734	20 438	21 631	22 733
Government and government enterprises	25 626	26 775	28 326	29 610	31 316	32 192	33 427

Table MS-9. Employment Characteristics by Family Type

(Number, percent.)

Family type and labor force status	2005		2006		2007	
	Total	Families with own children under 18 years	Total	Families with own children under 18 years	Total	Families with own children under 18 years
TOTAL FAMILIES	759 999	353 863	1 330 451	638 704	753 797	333 345
FAMILY TYPE AND LABOR FORCE STATUS						
Married Coupled Families	503 632	204 895	1 064 699	467 638	511 683	202 081
Both husband and wife in labor force	50.9	66.5	62.8	74.1	49.7	63.7
Husband in labor force, wife not in labor force	21.7	24.7	16.6	21.2	22.9	27.4
Wife in labor force, husband not in labor force	8.8	5.7	6.3	3.4	8.6	5.5
Both husband and wife not in labor force	18.6	3.0	14.3	1.4	18.7	3.3
Other Families	256 367	148 968	265 752	171 066	242 114	131 264
Female householder, no husband present	79.8	82.4	69.8	72.6	79.7	82.8
In labor force	52.9	63.9	55.3	62.0	51.8	66.4
Not in labor force	26.9	18.5	14.5	10.5	27.9	16.5
Male householder, no wife present	20.2	17.6	30.2	27.4	20.3	17.2
In labor force	15.0	14.5	26.0	25.3	14.8	14.4
Not in labor force	5.2	3.1	4.2	2.2	5.6	2.7

Table MS-10. School Enrollment and Educational Attainment, 2007

(Number, percent.)

Item	State	U.S.
Enrollment		
Total population 3 years and over	2 792 307	289 295 761
Enrolled in school	794 170	79 329 527
Enrolled in preschool (percent)	6.8	6.2
Enrolled in grades K-12 (percent)	70.4	67.6
Enrolled in college or graduate school (percent)	22.8	26.2
Attainment		
Total population 25 years and over	1 838 878	197 892 369
Less than a high school diploma (percent)	21.5	15.5
High school diploma or more (percent)	78.5	84.5
Bachelor's degree or more (percent)	18.9	27.5
Graduate degree or more (percent)	6.4	10.1

Table MS-11. Educational Indicators

(Number, percent.)

Item	State	U.S.
Public Schools, 2006–2007 (except where noted)		
Number of school districts	163	17 742
Number of schools	1 062	99 639
Number of students	495 026	49 315 842
Student-teacher ratio	15.3	15.5
Expenditures per student (dollars)	$7 459	. . .
Averaged freshman graduation rate, 2005–2006	63.5	. . .
Dropout rate, grades 9–12, 2005–2006	3.1	3.7
Students eligible for free or reduced-price lunch (percent)	67.5	41.2
English-language learners (percent)	1.0	5.1
Students with IEP (percent)	13.5	12.7
Private Schools, 2007–2008 (except where noted)		
Number of schools	219	33 740
Number of students	47 955	5 072 451
High school graduates, 2006–2007	3 355	306 605
Student-teacher ratio	11.6	11.1

Table MS-12. Reported Voting and Registration of the Voting-Age Population, November 2008

(Number in thousands, percent.)

Item	Total population	Total citizen population	Registered			Voted		
			Total registered	Percent registered (total population)	Percent registered (total citizen population)	Total voted	Percent voted (total population)	Percent voted (total citizen population)
U.S. total	225 499	206 072	146 311	64.9	71.0	131 144	58.2	63.6
State total	2 109	2 064	1 589	75.3	77.0	1 439	68.2	69.7
Sex								
Male	1 000	969	741	74.1	76.4	648	64.8	66.9
Female	1 108	1 094	848	76.5	77.5	790	71.3	72.2
Race								
White alone	1 360	1 315	982	72.2	74.7	896	65.9	68.2
White non-Hispanic alone	1 313	1 308	980	74.6	75.0	895	68.1	68.4
Black alone	718	718	588	81.9	81.9	524	72.9	72.9
Asian alone	3	3	. . .	. . .	. . .	. . .	. . .	. . .
Hispanic (of any race)	54	15	10	. . .	. . .	10	. . .	. . .
White alone or in combination	1 372	1 327	992	72.3	74.8	907	66.1	68.3
Black alone or in combination	730	730	598	81.9	81.9	534	73.1	73.1
Asian alone or in combination	3	3	. . .	. . .	. . .	. . .	. . .	. . .

Table MS-13. Crime

(Number, rate per 100,000.)

Item	State			U.S.		
	2007	2008	Percent change	2007	2008	Percent change
Population	2 918 785	2 938 618	0.7	301 621 157	304 059 724	0.8
VIOLENT CRIME						
Number	8 502	8 373	-1.5	1 408 337	1 382 012	-1.9
Rate	291.3	284.9	-2.2	466.9	454.5	-2.7
Murder and Nonnegligent Manslaughter						
Number	208	237	13.9	16 929	16 272	-3.9
Rate	7.1	8.1	13.2	5.6	5.4	-4.7
Forcible Rape						
Number	1 040	890	-14.4	90 427	89 000	-1.6
Rate	35.6	30.3	-15.0	30.0	29.3	-2.4
Robbery						
Number	2 866	3 016	5.2	445 125	441 855	-0.7
Rate	98.2	102.6	4.5	147.6	145.3	-1.5
Aggravated Assault						
Number	4 388	4 230	-3.6	855 856	834 885	-2.5
Rate	150.3	143.9	-4.3	283.8	274.6	-3.2
PROPERTY CRIME						
Number	93 424	86 408	-7.5	9 843 481	9 767 915	-0.8
Rate	3 200.8	2 940.4	-8.1	3 263.5	3 212.5	-1.6
Burglary						
Number	27 959	26 024	-6.9	2 179 140	2 222 196	2.0
Rate	957.9	885.6	-7.5	722.5	730.8	1.2
Larceny-Theft						
Number	58 084	54 032	-7.0	6 568 572	6 588 873	0.3
Rate	1 990.0	1 838.7	-7.6	2 177.8	2 167.0	-0.5
Motor Vehicle Theft						
Number	7 381	6 352	-13.9	1 095 769	956 846	-12.7
Rate	252.9	216.2	-14.5	363.3	314.7	-13.4

Table MS-14. State Government Finances, 2007

(Dollars, percent distribution.)

Item	Thousands of dollars	Percent distribution
Total Revenue	22 398 649	X
General revenue	17 397 398	77.7
Intergovernmental revenue	9 103 302	40.6
Taxes	6 394 513	28.5
General sales	3 155 622	14.1
Selective sales	942 768	4.2
License taxes	395 529	1.8
Individual income tax	1 401 809	6.3
Corporate income tax	369 205	1.6
Other taxes	129 580	0.6
Current charges	1 246 016	5.6
Miscellaneous general revenue	653 567	2.9
Utility revenue	0	0.0
Liquor store revenue	234 990	1.0
Insurance trust revenue	4 766 261	21.3
Total Expenditure	18 628 639	100.0
Intergovernmental expenditure	5 086 220	27.3
Direct expenditure	13 542 419	72.7
Current operation	10 093 179	54.2
Capital outlay	1 500 204	8.1
Insurance benefits and repayments	1 538 611	8.3
Assistance and subsidies	183 551	1.0
Interest on debt	226 874	1.2
Exhibit: Salaries and wages	2 063 464	11.1
Total Expenditure	18 628 639	100.0
General expenditure	16 899 143	90.7
Intergovernmental expenditure	5 086 220	27.3
Direct expenditure	11 812 923	63.4
Education	5 116 749	27.5
Public welfare	4 175 865	22.4
Hospitals	860 626	4.6
Health	354 827	1.9
Highways	1 494 109	8.0
Police protection	115 294	0.6
Correction	326 751	1.8
Natural resources	277 718	1.5
Parks and recreation	41 056	0.2
Government administration	264 165	1.4
Interest on general debt	226 874	1.2
Other and unallocable	3 645 109	19.6
Utility expenditure	0	0.0
Liquor store expenditure	190 885	1.0
Insurance trust expenditure	1 538 611	8.3
Debt at End of Fiscal Year	5 858 340	X
Cash and Security Holdings	34 701 578	X

Table MS-15. State Government Tax Collections, 2008

(Dollars, percent distribution.)

Item	Thousands of dollars	Percent distribution
Total Taxes	6 618 349	X
Property taxes	50 481	0.8
Sales and gross receipts	4 076 912	61.6
General sales and gross receipts	3 135 390	47.4
Selective sales taxes	941 522	14.2
Alcoholic beverages	42 092	0.6
Amusements	194 037	2.9
Insurance premiums	193 872	2.9
Motor fuels	442 119	6.7
Public utilities	1 954	0.0
Tobacco products	58 327	0.9
Other selective sales	9 121	0.1
Licenses	418 771	6.3
Alcoholic beverages	2 929	0.0
Amusements	4 826	0.1
Corporation	129 770	2.0
Hunting and fishing	15 398	0.2
Motor vehicle	123 203	1.9
Motor vehicle operators	34 385	0.5
Public utility	7 897	0.1
Occupation and business, NEC	84 158	1.3
Other licenses	16 205	0.2
Income taxes	1 935 722	29.2
Individual income	1 551 079	23.4
Corporation net income	384 643	5.8
Other taxes	136 463	2.1
Death and gift	1 215	0.0
Severance	135 248	2.0

Table MS-16. Agriculture

(Number, acres, and dollars.)

Item	2002		2007		Percent change, 2002–2007
	Number	Percent of total	Number	Percent of total	
Number of farms	42 186		41 959		-0.5
Farm Size					
Average size of farm (acres)	263		273		3.8
Farms by size (number of farms)					
Fewer than 50 acres	12 641	30.0	12 290	29.3	-2.8
50 to 499 acres	25 348	60.1	25 142	59.9	-0.8
500 acres or more	4 197	9.9	4 527	10.8	7.9
Land (Acres)					
Total land in farms	11 097 543		11 456 241		3.2
Total cropland	5 822 786	52.5	5 530 825	48.3	-5.0
Total harvested cropland	4 139 341	37.3	4 223 708	36.9	2.0
Irrigated land	1 175 530	10.6	1 368 661	11.9	16.4
Value of Sales (Dollars)					
Agricultural products sold ($1,000)	3 116 295		4 876 781		56.5
Average sales per farm	73 870		116 227		57.3
Sales of crops	1 025 385	32.9	1 668 028	34.2	62.7
Sales of livestock, poultry, and their products	2 090 909	67.1	3 208 753	65.8	53.5
Value of Sales (Number of Farms)					
Less than $10,000	31 278	74.1	29 893	71.2	-4.4
$10,000 to $99,999	6 551	15.5	7 520	17.9	14.8
$100,000 to $999,999	3 686	8.7	2 896	6.9	-21.4
$1,000,000 or more	671	1.6	1 650	3.9	145.9
Farms by Type of Organization (Number of Farms)					
Family	39 035	92.5	36 353	86.6	-6.9
Partnership	2 166	5.1	3 769	9.0	74.0
Corporation	705	1.7	1 467	3.5	108.1
Other: cooperative, estate or trust, institutional, etc	280	0.7	370	0.9	32.1
Value of Land and Buildings (Dollars)					
Estimated market value of land and buildings ($1,000)	21 418 146		15 633 797		-27.0
Land and buildings average value per farm	510 454		370 689		-27.4
Average value per acre	1 870		1 381		-26.1
Government Payments					
Number of farms receiving government payments	12 383	29.4	17 187	41.0	38.8
Payments (thousands of dollars)	145 508		231 382		59.0
Average payment per farm	11 751		13 463		14.6
Farm Operator Characteristics					
Farm operators whose principal occupation is farming	20 582	48.8	15 935	38.0	-22.6
Farm operators whose principal occupation is other	21 604	51.2	26 024	62.0	20.5
Average age principal operator (years)	57.2		58.6		2.4

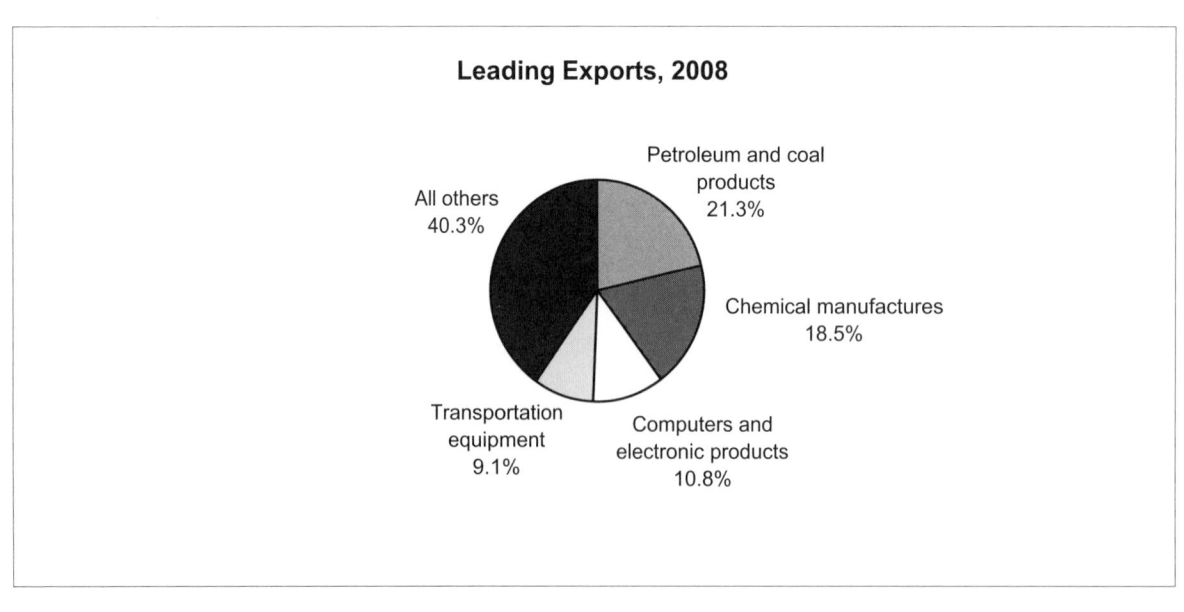

Leading Exports, 2008

Petroleum and coal products 21.3%

All others 40.3%

Chemical manufactures 18.5%

Computers and electronic products 10.8%

Transportation equipment 9.1%

MISSOURI

Facts and Figures

Location: Central United States; bordered on the N by Iowa, on the E by Illinois, Kentucky, and Tennessee, on the S by Arkansas, and on the W by Oklahoma, Kansas, and Nebraska

Area: 69,704 sq. mi. (180,533 sq. km.); rank—21st

Population: 5,911,605 (2008 est.); rank—18th

Principal Cities: capital—Jefferson City; largest—Kansas City

Statehood: August 10, 1821; 24th state

U.S. Congress: 2 senators, 9 representatives

State Motto: *Salus populi suprema lex esto* ("The welfare of the people shall be the supreme law")

State Song: "Missouri Waltz"

State Nickname: The Show Me State

Abbreviations: MO; Mo

State Symbols: flower—hawthorn; tree—flowering dogwood; bird—Eastern bluebird

At a Glance

- With an increase in population of 5.6 percent, Missouri ranked 27th among the states in growth from 2000 to 2008.
- An estimated 39,526 marriages took place in Missouri in 2008, compared to 22,495 divorces.
- The 2007 home ownership rate in Missouri was 70.4 percent; its ranking of 25th among the states was tied with that of Arizona and South Dakota.
- Missouri's median household income in 2007 was $45,114, 36th among the states.
- In Missouri, 13 percent of the population lived below the poverty level in 2007, ranking it 20th.
- In 2006-07, 12.9 percent of Missourians did not have health insurance, compared to 15.5 percent of the total U.S. population.
- In 2007, 5 percent of Missourians were unemployed, compared to 4.6 percent nationwide.
- Missouri ranked 35th in the nation with 24.5 percent of its population 25 years old and over having a bachelor's degree in 2007; its ranking was the same as Idaho's.
- Missouri's violent crime rate in 2007 was 504.9 per 100,000 population, compared to 466.9 for the entire nation.
- Missouri had one physician for every 368 people in 2007, compared to one physician for every 325 people nationwide.
- In the 2008 election, 68.1 percent of Missouri's eligible voters voted, compared to 61.7 percent of eligible voters nationwide.
- Missouri ranked 30th among the states receiving federal aid in 2007, with $1,353 per capita.
- Missouri's gross domestic product was $229 billion in 2007; it ranked 22nd among the states.
- With $13.5 billion in exports in 2007, Missouri ranked 26th in exports.
- Missourians consumed 1.91 trillion Btu's of energy in 2006; the state ranked 19th in total consumption.
- In 2007, Missouri exported $2.1 billion worth of agricultural products, about 2.5 percent of the U.S. total.

Table MO-1. Population by Sex, Age, Race, and Hispanic Origin

(Number, percent.)

Sex, age, race, and Hispanic origin	1990	2000	2008	Average annual percent change, 2000–2008
Total Population	5 117 073	5 595 211	5 911 605	0.7
Percent of total U.S. population	2.1	2.0	1.9	X
Sex				
Male	2 464 315	2 720 177	2 887 907	0.8
Female	2 652 758	2 875 034	3 023 698	0.6
Age				
Under 5 years	369 244	369 898	399 450	1.0
5 to 19 years	1 102 148	1 224 274	1 183 246	-0.4
20 to 64 years	2 928 000	3 245 660	3 523 674	1.0
65 years and over	717 681	755 379	805 235	0.8
Median age (years)	33.4	36.1	37.5	X
Race and Hispanic Origin[1]				
One race				
White	4 486 228	4 748 083	5 026 572	0.7
Black	548 208	629 391	679 223	1.0
American Indian and Alaskan Native	19 835	25 076	30 034	2.3
Asian[2]	41 277	61 595	85 898	4.2
Native Hawaiian and Other Pacific Islander	X	3 178	4 586	4.7
Two or more races	X	82 061	85 292	0.5
Hispanic (of any race)	61 702	118 592	189 700	6.0

[1]Data on race in 2000 and 2008 are not comparable to 1990. Individuals could only report one race in the 1990 census but could report one or more races on the 2000 census.
[2]Data in 1990 refer to Asian and Pacific Islanders.

Table MO-2. Marital Status

(Number, percent distribution.)

Sex and marital status	1990	2000	2007
Males, 15 Years and Over	1 896 107	2 114 280	2 270 770
Never married	27.2	27.8	31.1
Now married, except separated	60.4	58.0	53.9
Separated	1.7	1.6	2.0
Widowed	2.7	2.6	2.5
Divorced	7.9	10.0	10.5
Females, 15 Years and Over	2 112 391	2 300 111	2 438 076
Never married	20.9	22.1	24.9
Now married, except separated	54.0	53.1	49.6
Separated	2.2	2.0	2.3
Widowed	13.3	11.3	10.4
Divorced	9.7	11.5	12.8

Table MO-3. Households and Housing Characteristics

(Number, percent, and dollars.)

Item	1990	2000	2007	Average annual percent change, 2000–2007
Total Households	1 961 206	2 194 594	2 309 626	0.7
Family households	1 368 334	1 476 516	1 534 274	0.5
Married-couple family	1 104 723	1 140 866	1 156 746	0.2
Other family	263 611	335 650	377 528	1.7
Male householder, no wife present	55 436	81 890	100 571	3.0
Female householder, no husband present	208 175	253 760	276 957	1.3
Nonfamily households	592 872	718 078	775 352	1.1
Householder living alone	510 684	599 808	649 976	1.2
Householder not living alone	82 188	118 270	125 376	0.8
Housing Characteristics				
Total housing units	2 199 129	2 442 017	2 647 379	1.2
Occupied housing units	1 961 206	2 194 594	2 309 626	0.7
Owner-occupied	1 348 746	1 542 149	1 632 012	0.8
Renter-occupied	612 460	652 445	677 614	0.5
Average size	2.54	2.48	2.47	X
Financial Characteristics				
Median gross rent of renter-occupied housing units (dollars)	368	484	618	3.6
Median monthly owner costs for housing units with a mortgage (dollars)	600	861	1 152	4.2
Median value of owner-occupied housing units (dollars)	59 300	89 900	138 600	6.4

Table MO-4. Median Income and Poverty Status, 2007

(Number, percent.)

Characteristic	State		U.S.	
	Number	Percent	Number	Percent
Median Income				
Households (dollars)	45 114	X	50 740	X
Families (dollars)	55 947	X	61 173	X
Below Poverty Level				
Sex				
Male	246 714	18.2	16 576 071	11.5
Female	334 820	22.9	21 476 176	14.3
Age				
Under 18 years	220 446	29.3	13 097 100	18.0
Related children under 18 years	215 644	28.9	12 728 964	17.6
18 to 64 years	309 855	18.0	21 495 507	11.6
65 years and over	51 233	14.9	3 459 640	9.5

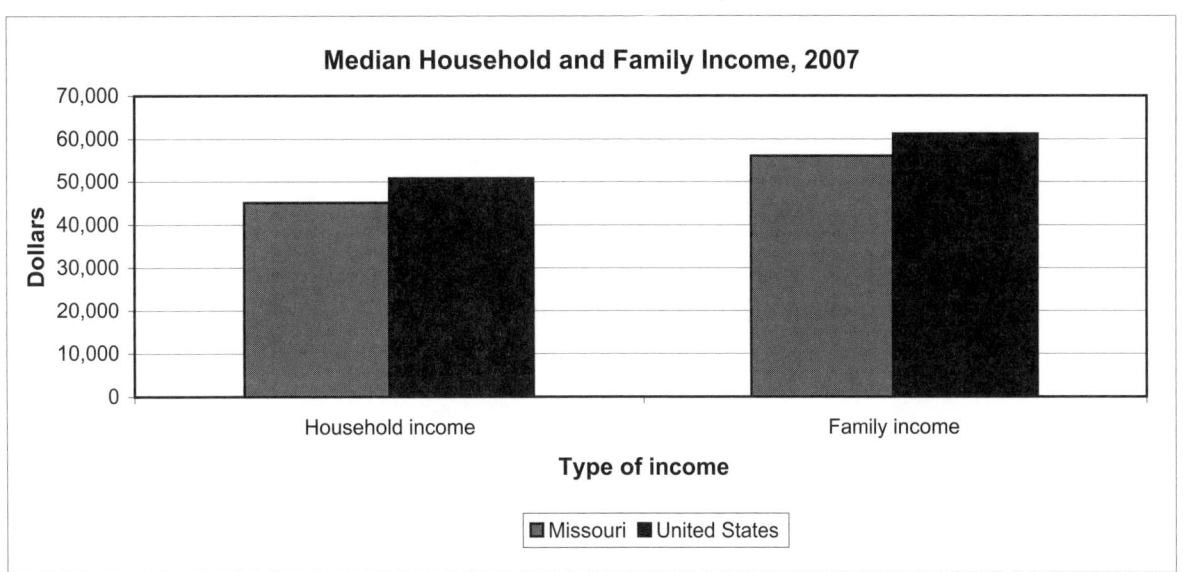

Table MO-5. Health Insurance Coverage Status for All Persons and Children Under 18 Years of Age

(Number, percent.)

Item	2000	2001	2002	2003	2004	2005	2006	2007
ALL PERSONS	5 523	5 525	5 585	5 623	5 614	5 710	5 800	5 791
Covered by Private or Government Health Insurance								
Number	5 012	5 000	4 963	5 018	4 944	5 041	5 028	5 062
Percent	90.7	90.5	88.9	89.2	88.1	88.3	86.7	87.4
Not Covered								
Number	511	525	622	605	670	668	772	729
Percent	9.3	9.5	11.1	10.8	11.9	11.7	13.3	12.6
Percent in the U.S. not covered	13.7	14.1	14.7	15.1	14.9	15.3	15.8	15.3
CHILDREN UNDER 18 YEARS OF AGE	1 425	1 403	1 374	1 406	1 411	1 384	1 398	1 442
Covered by Private or Government Health Insurance								
Number	1 325	1 342	1 309	1 303	1 308	1 281	1 271	1 291
Percent	93.0	95.6	95.3	92.7	92.7	92.5	90.9	89.6
Not Covered								
Number	99	61	64	103	103	104	127	150
Percent	7.0	4.4	4.7	7.3	7.3	7.5	9.1	10.4
Percent in the U.S. not covered	11.6	11.3	11.2	11.0	10.5	10.9	11.7	11.0

Table MO-6. Employment Status by Demographic Group, Preliminary 2008

(Number, percent.)

Characteristic	Civilian noninstitutional population	Civilian labor force		Employment		Unemployed	
		Number	Percent of population	Number	Percent of population	Number	Unemployment rate
TOTAL	4 555	3 023	66.4	2 840	62.3	183	6.1
Sex							
Men	2 184	1 583	73.0	1 484	68.0	99	6.3
Women	2 371	1 440	61.0	1 356	57.2	84	5.8
Race, Sex, and Hispanic Origin							
White	3 923	2 605	66.4	2 468	62.9	137	5.3
Men	1 900	1 390	73.2	1 311	69.0	79	5.7
Women	2 023	1 215	60.1	1 156	57.2	59	4.8
Black or African American	475	310	65.3	273	57.4	38	12.1
Men	209	142	68.0	125	59.7	17	12.2
Women	267	168	63.1	148	55.5	20	12.0
Hispanic	106	73	69.3	67	63.3	6	8.6
Men	61	48	78.2	44	72.5	3	7.3
Women	45	. . .	. . .	. . .	. . .	. . .	. . .
Age							
16 to 19 years	309	156	50.4	130	42.1	26	16.5
20 to 24 years	386	322	83.4	288	74.6	34	10.5
25 to 34 years	783	661	84.4	625	79.8	36	5.5
35 to 44 years	771	654	84.8	619	80.3	35	5.4
45 to 54 years	849	687	81.0	660	77.7	28	4.0
55 to 64 years	683	424	62.0	404	59.2	19	4.6
65 years and over	774	119	15.4	114	14.7	5	4.3

Note: Data in Table 6 are from the Current Population Survey (CPS) and do not match the estimates in Table 7. See notes and definitions for more details.

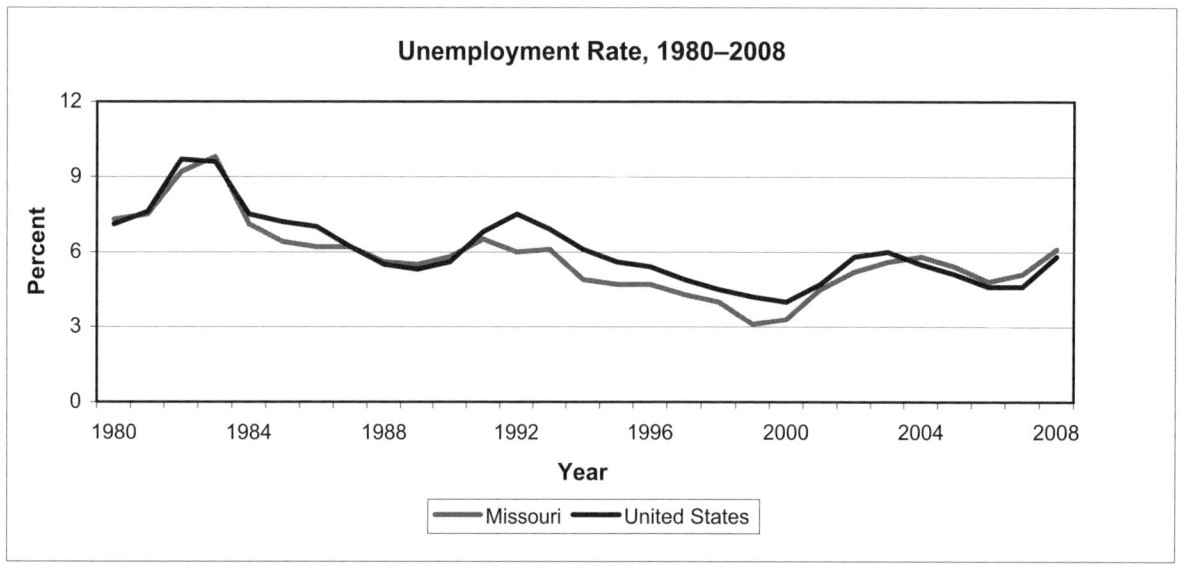

Table MO-7. Employment Status of the Civilian Noninstitutional Population Age 16 Years and Over

(Number, percent.)

Year	Civilian labor force	Civilian participation rate	Employed	Unemployed	Unemployment rate
1998	2 910 871	69.9	2 794 869	116 002	4.0
1999	2 911 190	69.3	2 819 853	91 337	3.1
2000	2 973 092	70.2	2 875 336	97 756	3.3
2001	3 002 714	70.3	2 867 853	134 861	4.5
2002	2 985 932	69.3	2 829 985	155 947	5.2
2003	2 979 187	68.6	2 813 571	165 616	5.6
2004	2 987 780	68.3	2 815 878	171 902	5.8
2005	2 997 744	67.8	2 836 963	160 781	5.4
2006	3 014 120	67.4	2 868 857	145 263	4.8
2007	3 023 106	67.0	2 870 262	152 844	5.1
2008	3 012 126	66.3	2 829 289	182 837	6.1

Table MO-8. Employment and Average Wages by Industry

(Estimates for 2001–2006 are based on the 2002 North American Industry Classification System [NAICS]. Estimates for 2007 are based on the 2007 NAICS.)

Industry	2001	2002	2003	2004	2005	2006	2007
				Number of jobs			
WAGE AND SALARY EMPLOYMENT BY INDUSTRY	2 857 176	2 832 324	2 826 017	2 836 526	2 868 171	2 904 497	2 924 316
Farm Wage and Salary Employment	11 426	11 234	10 098	8 270	9 243	8 721	8 263
Nonfarm Wage and Salary Employment	2 845 750	2 821 090	2 815 919	2 828 256	2 858 928	2 895 776	2 916 053
Private wage and salary employment	2 374 973	2 350 034	2 340 572	2 352 917	2 383 181	2 416 012	2 429 344
Forestry, fishing, hunting, and other	6 918	6 954	7 236	7 318	7 244	7 036	6 501
Mining	4 764	4 487	4 497	4 736	5 134	5 261	5 478
Utilities	12 780	12 795	12 063	11 926	11 925	12 022	12 309
Construction	146 309	143 909	143 799	146 179	149 142	152 957	152 457
Manufacturing	344 259	325 147	313 097	314 078	311 259	309 223	302 093
Durable goods manufacturing	212 170	199 647	192 931	195 984	194 587	191 895	184 654
Nondurable goods manufacturing	132 089	125 500	120 166	118 094	116 672	117 328	117 439
Wholesale trade	121 924	120 911	120 107	120 796	123 122	124 430	126 425
Retail trade	321 742	322 536	322 156	322 309	326 599	326 270	326 487
Transportation and warehousing	103 163	100 744	96 818	95 451	95 345	98 102	99 523
Information	74 988	71 044	68 013	65 700	63 861	63 282	63 639
Finance and insurance	118 749	119 245	121 299	120 207	120 449	123 608	123 666
Real estate and rental and leasing	41 741	41 126	41 612	41 296	41 728	41 035	41 376
Professional and technical services	123 460	120 833	120 687	122 157	127 040	131 929	134 378
Management of companies and enterprises	72 142	68 562	66 601	64 398	68 235	68 737	67 046
Administrative and waste services	129 296	124 642	124 388	127 491	132 512	138 632	143 720
Educational services	60 769	63 259	66 119	66 478	67 137	66 628	68 197
Health care and social assistance	293 564	300 125	304 107	307 565	314 330	321 620	327 727
Arts, entertainment, and recreation	45 078	45 649	45 281	46 484	46 830	47 307	47 538
Accommodation and food services	216 602	219 658	222 458	227 247	231 377	236 305	238 620
Other services, except public administration	136 725	138 408	140 234	141 101	139 912	141 628	142 164
Government and government enterprises	470 777	471 056	475 347	475 339	475 747	479 764	486 709
				Dollars			
AVERAGE WAGES AND SALARIES BY INDUSTRY	31 740	32 527	33 257	34 361	35 518	36 702	38 154
Average Farm Wages and Salaries	23 012	21 199	24 550	27 761	27 471	25 060	38 895
Average Nonfarm Wages and Salaries	31 775	32 572	33 288	34 381	35 544	36 737	38 152
Average private wages and salaries	32 255	32 957	33 636	34 748	35 931	37 147	38 622
Forestry, fishing, hunting, and other	19 781	21 361	28 397	25 321	24 136	24 726	26 546
Mining	46 001	47 044	52 574	57 678	72 878	76 486	77 251
Utilities	63 974	70 481	59 462	63 291	63 639	67 118	69 771
Construction	39 046	39 474	39 383	40 032	41 643	43 118	45 525
Manufacturing	38 521	39 994	41 338	42 622	43 848	45 553	46 788
Durable goods manufacturing	39 061	40 694	42 468	43 721	45 303	47 291	48 693
Nondurable goods manufacturing	37 655	38 881	39 523	40 798	41 421	42 711	43 791
Wholesale trade	44 096	44 504	45 810	48 077	50 103	52 210	54 631
Retail trade	20 369	20 880	21 415	21 781	22 054	22 606	23 223
Transportation and warehousing	35 627	37 731	38 068	38 061	39 253	40 251	41 120
Information	45 126	44 796	46 652	49 513	50 629	54 338	56 072
Finance and insurance	44 878	45 676	47 730	49 062	51 332	53 262	55 651
Real estate and rental and leasing	27 735	27 870	28 471	29 649	30 349	31 683	32 913
Professional and technical services	50 327	51 254	53 085	54 794	56 659	59 470	62 837
Management of companies and enterprises	62 346	64 056	64 401	70 399	76 220	76 269	80 468
Administrative and waste services	21 760	22 911	23 429	25 097	25 477	25 512	27 171
Educational services	27 060	27 631	27 257	28 496	29 780	31 662	33 202
Health care and social assistance	30 434	31 417	32 404	33 683	34 449	35 349	36 717
Arts, entertainment, and recreation	26 254	28 419	29 303	29 457	29 709	31 875	32 777
Accommodation and food services	12 547	12 824	13 075	13 442	13 911	14 143	14 889
Other services, except public administration	21 764	22 245	23 001	23 869	24 696	25 326	26 377
Government and government enterprises	29 353	30 652	31 578	32 561	33 601	34 671	35 810

Table MO-9. Employment Characteristics by Family Type

(Number, percent.)

Family type and labor force status	2005		2006		2007	
	Total	Families with own children under 18 years	Total	Families with own children under 18 years	Total	Families with own children under 18 years
TOTAL FAMILIES	1 520 559	700 215	1 518 860	702 249	1 534 274	698 787
FAMILY TYPE AND LABOR FORCE STATUS						
Married Coupled Families	1 150 439	475 959	1 154 259	482 044	1 156 746	474 403
Both husband and wife in labor force	54.1	68.0	54.5	68.6	55.4	70.8
Husband in labor force, wife not in labor force	20.3	25.2	21.1	25.6	19.7	23.6
Wife in labor force, husband not in labor force	7.5	4.1	7.3	3.9	7.6	3.8
Both husband and wife not in labor force	18.0	2.7	17.1	1.9	17.3	1.8
Other Families	370 120	224 256	364 601	220 205	377 528	224 384
Female householder, no husband present	74.1	75.7	75.1	78.2	73.4	77.9
In labor force	52.4	60.6	55.4	65.1	53.6	64.5
Not in labor force	21.7	15.0	19.7	13.1	19.7	13.3
Male householder, no wife present	25.9	24.3	24.9	21.8	26.6	22.1
In labor force	20.6	21.8	19.5	19.6	20.6	19.4
Not in labor force	5.3	2.6	5.4	2.2	6.0	2.8

Table MO-10. School Enrollment and Educational Attainment, 2007

(Number, percent.)

Item	State	U.S.
Enrollment		
Total population 3 years and over	5 644 226	289 295 761
Enrolled in school	1 509 780	79 329 527
Enrolled in preschool (percent)	6.2	6.2
Enrolled in grades K-12 (percent)	68.6	67.6
Enrolled in college or graduate school (percent)	25.2	26.2
Attainment		
Total population 25 years and over	3 882 538	197 892 369
Less than a high school diploma (percent)	14.4	15.5
High school diploma or more (percent)	85.6	84.5
Bachelor's degree or more (percent)	24.5	27.5
Graduate degree or more (percent)	8.9	10.1

Table MO-11. Educational Indicators

(Number, percent.)

Item	State	U.S.
Public Schools, 2006–2007 (except where noted)		
Number of school districts	550	17 742
Number of schools	2 384	99 639
Number of students	920 353	49 315 842
Student-teacher ratio	13.6	15.5
Expenditures per student (dollars)	$8 848	. . .
Averaged freshman graduation rate, 2005–2006	81.0	. . .
Dropout rate, grades 9–12, 2005–2006	4.1	3.7
Students eligible for free or reduced-price lunch (percent)	39.0	41.2
English-language learners (percent)	. . .	5.1
Students with IEP (percent)	15.4	12.7
Private Schools, 2007–2008 (except where noted)		
Number of schools	690	33 740
Number of students	112 368	5 072 451
High school graduates, 2006–2007	7 330	306 605
Student-teacher ratio	11.6	11.1

Table MO-12. Reported Voting and Registration of the Voting-Age Population, November 2008

(Number in thousands, percent.)

Item	Total population	Total citizen population	Registered — Total registered	Registered — Percent registered (total population)	Registered — Percent registered (total citizen population)	Voted — Total voted	Voted — Percent voted (total population)	Voted — Percent voted (total citizen population)
U.S. total	225 499	206 072	146 311	64.9	71.0	131 144	58.2	63.6
State total	4 430	4 326	3 224	72.8	74.5	2 846	64.2	65.8
Sex								
Male	2 120	2 063	1 510	71.2	73.2	1 318	62.2	63.9
Female	2 309	2 263	1 714	74.2	75.8	1 528	66.1	67.5
Race								
White alone	3 833	3 766	2 799	73.0	74.3	2 451	64.0	65.1
White non-Hispanic alone	3 745	3 722	2 779	74.2	74.7	2 432	64.9	65.3
Black alone	457	454	352	76.9	77.5	336	73.4	73.9
Asian alone	57	26	16	. . .	. . .	14	. . .	. . .
Hispanic (of any race)	98	50	25	25.2	. . .	20	20.2	. . .
White alone or in combination	3 903	3 833	2 849	73.0	74.3	2 490	63.8	65.0
Black alone or in combination	459	456	354	77.0	77.6	337	73.5	74.0
Asian alone or in combination	57	26	16	. . .	. . .	14	. . .	. . .

Table MO-13. Crime

(Number, rate per 100,000.)

Item	State 2007	State 2008	State Percent change	U.S. 2007	U.S. 2008	U.S. Percent change
Population	5 878 415	5 911 605	0.6	301 62?	304 059 724	0.8
VIOLENT CRIME						
Number	29 682	29 819	0.5	1 408 337	1 382 012	-1.9
Rate	504.9	504.4	-0.1	466.9	454.5	-2.7
Murder and Nonnegligent Manslaughter						
Number	385	455	18.2	16 929	16 272	-3.9
Rate	6.5	7.7	17.5	5.6	5.4	-4.7
Forcible Rape						
Number	1 714	1 615	-5.8	90 427	89 000	-1.6
Rate	29.2	27.3	-6.3	30.0	29.3	-2.4
Robbery						
Number	7 165	7 390	3.1	445 125	441 855	-0.7
Rate	121.9	125.0	2.6	147.6	145.3	-1.5
Aggravated Assault						
Number	20 418	20 359	-0.3	855 856	834 885	-2.5
Rate	347.3	344.4	-0.8	283.8	274.6	-3.2
PROPERTY CRIME						
Number	219 759	216 585	-1.4	9 843 481	9 767 915	-0.8
Rate	3 738.4	3 663.7	-2.0	3 263.5	3 212.5	-1.6
Burglary						
Number	43 446	45 788	5.4	2 179 140	2 222 196	2.0
Rate	739.1	774.5	4.8	722.5	730.8	1.2
Larceny-Theft						
Number	152 529	150 032	-1.6	6 568 572	6 588 873	0.3
Rate	2 594.7	2 537.9	-2.2	2 177.8	2 167.0	-0.5
Motor Vehicle Theft						
Number	23 784	20 765	-12.7	1 095 769	956 846	-12.7
Rate	404.6	351.3	-13.2	363.3	314.7	-13.4

Table MO-14. State Government Finances, 2007

(Dollars, percent distribution.)

Item	Thousands of dollars	Percent distribution
Total Revenue	32 728 288	X
General revenue	23 098 517	70.6
Intergovernmental revenue	8 005 044	24.5
Taxes	10 704 834	32.7
General sales	3 272 919	10.0
Selective sales	1 541 579	4.7
License taxes	630 431	1.9
Individual income tax	4 834 820	14.8
Corporate income tax	390 657	1.2
Other taxes	34 428	0.1
Current charges	2 299 457	7.0
Miscellaneous general revenue	2 089 182	6.4
Utility revenue	0	0.0
Liquor store revenue	0	0.0
Insurance trust revenue	9 629 771	29.4
Total Expenditure	25 318 686	100.0
Intergovernmental expenditure	5 626 071	22.2
Direct expenditure	19 692 615	77.8
Current operation	13 641 255	53.9
Capital outlay	1 689 175	6.7
Insurance benefits and repayments	2 877 254	11.4
Assistance and subsidies	435 697	1.7
Interest on debt	1 049 234	4.1
Exhibit: Salaries and wages	3 470 202	13.7
Total Expenditure	25 318 686	100.0
General expenditure	22 441 427	88.6
Intergovernmental expenditure	5 626 071	22.2
Direct expenditure	16 815 356	66.4
Education	7 964 401	31.5
Public welfare	5 804 854	22.9
Hospitals	1 210 980	4.8
Health	1 077 855	4.3
Highways	2 172 262	8.6
Police protection	198 852	0.8
Correction	669 121	2.6
Natural resources	339 545	1.3
Parks and recreation	38 340	0.2
Government administration	519 813	2.1
Interest on general debt	1 049 234	4.1
Other and unallocable	1 396 170	5.5
Utility expenditure	5	0.0
Liquor store expenditure	0	0.0
Insurance trust expenditure	2 877 254	11.4
Debt at End of Fiscal Year	18 715 821	X
Cash and Security Holdings	74 552 203	X

Table MO-15. State Government Tax Collections, 2008

(Dollars, percent distribution.)

Item	Thousands of dollars	Percent distribution
Total Taxes	10 965 171	X
Property taxes	28 970	0.3
Sales and gross receipts	4 770 631	43.5
General sales and gross receipts	3 228 274	29.4
Selective sales taxes	1 542 357	14.1
Alcoholic beverages	31 173	0.3
Amusements	345 771	3.2
Insurance premiums	283 960	2.6
Motor fuels	736 303	6.7
Tobacco products	109 365	1.0
Other selective sales	35 785	0.3
Licenses	650 763	5.9
Alcoholic beverages	4 771	0.0
Amusements	743	0.0
Corporation	88 705	0.8
Hunting and fishing	30 544	0.3
Motor vehicle	269 443	2.5
Motor vehicle operators	15 558	0.1
Public utility	20 930	0.2
Occupation and business, NEC	155 020	1.4
Other licenses	65 049	0.6
Income taxes	5 502 859	50.2
Individual income	5 118 849	46.7
Corporation net income	384 010	3.5
Other taxes	11 948	0.1
Death and gift	3 137	0.0
Documentary and stock transfer	8 728	0.1
Severance	21	0.0
Other	62	0.0

Table MO-16. Agriculture

(Number, acres, and dollars.)

Item	2002		2007		Percent change, 2002–2007
	Number	Percent of total	Number	Percent of total	
Number of farms	106 797		107 825		1.0
Farm Size					
Average size of farm (acres)	280		269		-3.9
Farms by size (number of farms)					
Fewer than 50 acres	24 696	23.1	29 054	26.9	17.6
50 to 499 acres	67 174	62.9	64 783	60.1	-3.6
500 acres or more	14 927	14.0	13 988	13.0	-6.3
Land (Acres)					
Total land in farms	29 946 035		29 026 573		-3.1
Total cropland	18 884 920	63.1	16 405 595	56.5	-13.1
Total harvested cropland	13 137 184	43.9	12 980 113	44.7	-1.2
Irrigated land	1 032 973	3.4	1 199 981	4.1	16.2
Value of Sales (Dollars)					
Agricultural products sold ($1,000)	4 983 255		7 512 926		50.8
Average sales per farm	46 661		69 677		49.3
Sales of crops	1 992 446	40.0	3 494 938	46.5	75.4
Sales of livestock, poultry, and their products	2 990 809	60.0	4 017 988	53.5	34.3
Value of Sales (Number of Farms)					
Less than $10,000	63 021	59.0	62 523	58.0	-0.8
$10,000 to $99,999	34 360	32.2	33 458	31.0	-2.6
$100,000 to $999,999	8 897	8.3	10 489	9.7	17.9
$1,000,000 or more	519	0.5	1 355	1.3	161.1
Farms by Type of Organization (Number of Farms)					
Family	98 435	92.2	94 818	87.9	-3.7
Partnership	5 563	5.2	8 202	7.6	47.4
Corporation	2 174	2.0	3 063	2.8	40.9
Other: cooperative, estate or trust, institutional, etc	625	0.6	1 742	1.6	178.7
Value of Land and Buildings (Dollars)					
Estimated market value of land and buildings ($1,000)	63 237 014		45 298 629		-28.4
Land and buildings average value per farm	586 478		424 347		-27.6
Average value per acre	2 179		1 508		-30.8
Government Payments					
Number of farms receiving government payments	43 379	40.6	45 102	41.8	4.0
Payments (thousands of dollars)	264 475		319 519		20.8
Average payment per farm	6 097		7 084		16.2
Farm Operator Characteristics					
Farm operators whose principal occupation is farming	61 035	57.2	45 031	41.8	-26.2
Farm operators whose principal occupation is other	45 762	42.8	62 794	58.2	37.2
Average age principal operator (years)	56.0		57.1		2.0

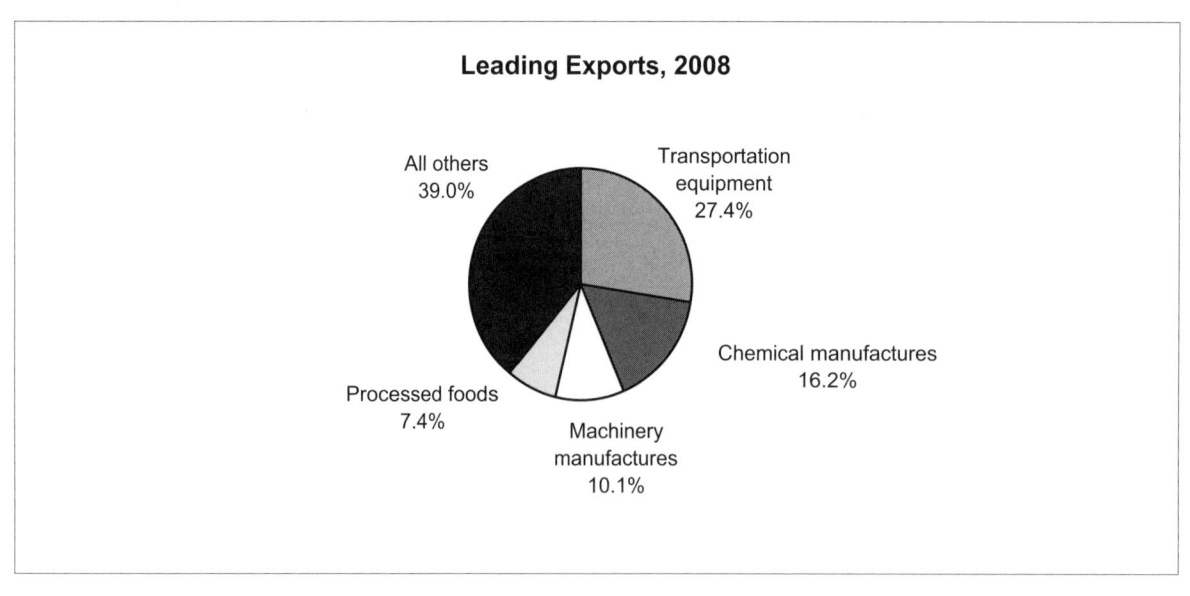

Leading Exports, 2008

All others 39.0%

Transportation equipment 27.4%

Chemical manufactures 16.2%

Machinery manufactures 10.1%

Processed foods 7.4%

MONTANA

Facts and Figures

Location: Northwestern United States; bordered on the N by Canada (British Columbia, Alberta, and Saskatchewan), on the E by North Dakota and South Dakota, on the S by Idaho and Wyoming, and on the W by Idaho

Area: 147,042 sq. mi. (380,838 sq. km.); rank—4th

Population: 967,440 (2008 est.); rank—44th

Principal Cities: capital—Helena; largest—Billings

Statehood: November 8, 1889; 41st state

U.S. Congress: 2 senators, 1 representative

State Motto: *Oro y plata* ("Gold and silver")

State Song: "Montana"

State Nicknames: The Treasure State; Big Sky Country

Abbreviations: MT; Mont.

State Symbols: flower—bitterroot; tree—ponderosa pine; bird—Western meadowlark

At a Glance

- With an increase in population of 7.2 percent, Montana ranked 20th among the states in growth from 2000 to 2008.
- An estimated 7,267 marriages took place in Montana in 2008, compared to 3,449 divorces.
- The 2007 home ownership rate in Montana was 67.3 percent, giving it a ranking of 39th among the states.
- Montana's median household income in 2007 was $43,531, 39th among the states.
- In Montana, 14.1 percent of the population lived below the poverty level in 2007, ranking it 15th.
- In 2006-07, 16.4 percent of Montanans did not have health insurance, compared to 15.5 percent of the total U.S. population.
- In 2007, 3.6 percent of Montanans were unemployed, compared to 4.6 percent nationwide.
- Montana ranked 21st in the nation with 27 percent of its population 25 years old and over having a bachelor's degree in 2007.
- Montana's violent crime rate in 2007 was 287.5 per 100,000 population, compared to 466.9 for the entire nation.
- Montana had one physician for every 371 people in 2007, compared to one physician for every 325 people nationwide.
- In the 2008 election, 66.3 percent of Montana's eligible voters voted, compared to 61.7 percent of eligible voters nationwide.
- Montana ranked 12th among the states receiving federal aid in 2007, with $1,918 per capita.
- Montana's gross domestic product was $34 billion in 2007; it ranked 46th among the states.
- With $1.1 billion in exports in 2007, Montana ranked 48th in exports.
- Montanans consumed 659 billion Btu's of energy in 2006; the state ranked 39th in total consumption.
- In 2007, Montana exported $723 million worth of agricultural products, less than 1 percent of the U.S. total.

Table MT-1. Population by Sex, Age, Race, and Hispanic Origin

(Number, percent.)

Sex, age, race, and Hispanic origin	1990	2000	2008	Average annual percent change, 2000–2008
Total Population	799 065	902 195	967 440	0.9
Percent of total U.S. population	0.3	0.3	0.3	X
Sex				
Male	395 769	449 480	484 485	0.9
Female	403 296	452 715	482 955	0.8
Age				
Under 5 years	59 257	54 869	61 114	1.4
5 to 19 years	185 089	202 571	185 327	-1.1
20 to 64 years	448 222	523 806	583 687	1.4
65 years and over	106 497	120 949	137 312	1.6
Median age (years)	33.8	37.5	39.3	X
Race and Hispanic Origin[1]				
One race				
White	741 111	817 229	875 221	0.9
Black	2 381	2 692	6 504	11.7
American Indian and Alaskan Native	47 679	56 068	62 303	1.3
Asian[2]	4 259	4 691	6 130	3.4
Native Hawaiian and Other Pacific Islander	X	470	690	4.9
Two or more races	X	15 730	16 592	0.7
Hispanic (of any race)	12 174	18 081	28 804	6.0

[1]Data on race in 2000 and 2008 are not comparable to 1990. Individuals could only report one race in the 1990 census but could report one or more races on the 2000 census.
[2]Data in 1990 refer to Asian and Pacific Islanders.

Table MT-2. Marital Status

(Number, percent distribution.)

Sex and marital status	1990	2000	2007
Males, 15 Years and Over	299 504	353 801	387 536
Never married	26.5	27.7	31.2
Now married, except separated	61.1	58.3	52.7
Separated	1.2	1.2	1.4
Widowed	2.5	2.6	2.4
Divorced	8.7	10.2	12.3
Females, 15 Years and Over	312 028	362 114	391 165
Never married	18.4	20.4	24.4
Now married, except separated	58.5	56.3	53.0
Separated	1.5	1.3	1.4
Widowed	11.8	10.4	9.2
Divorced	9.9	11.6	12.1

Table MT-3. Households and Housing Characteristics

(Number, percent, and dollars.)

Item	1990	2000	2007	Average annual percent change, 2000–2007
Total Households	306 163	358 667	371 954	0.5
Family households	211 666	237 407	240 727	0.2
Married-couple family	176 526	192 067	194 997	0.2
Other family	35 140	45 340	45 730	0.1
Male householder, no wife present	8 743	13 324	14 407	1.1
Female householder, no husband present	26 397	32 016	31 323	-0.3
Nonfamily households	94 497	121 260	131 227	1.1
Householder living alone	80 491	98 422	105 991	1.1
Householder not living alone	14 006	22 838	25 236	1.4
Housing Characteristics				
Total housing units	361 155	412 633	435 586	0.8
Occupied housing units	306 163	358 667	371 954	0.5
Owner-occupied	205 899	247 723	258 965	0.6
Renter-occupied	100 264	110 944	112 989	0.3
Average size	2.53	2.45	2.50	X
Financial Characteristics				
Median gross rent of renter-occupied housing units (dollars)	311	447	579	3.8
Median monthly owner costs for housing units with a mortgage (dollars)	575	863	1 141	4.1
Median value of owner-occupied housing units (dollars)	56 500	99 500	170 000	8.0

Table MT-4. Median Income and Poverty Status, 2007

(Number, percent.)

Characteristic	State		U.S.	
	Number	Percent	Number	Percent
Median Income				
Households (dollars)	43 531	X	50 740	X
Families (dollars)	53 497	X	61 173	X
Below Poverty Level				
Sex				
Male	59 551	12.8	16 576 071	11.5
Female	72 239	15.5	21 476 176	14.3
Age				
Under 18 years	39 660	18.3	13 097 100	18.0
Related children under 18 years	38 228	17.8	12 728 964	17.6
18 to 64 years	79 738	13.5	21 495 507	11.6
65 years and over	12 392	10.0	3 459 640	9.5

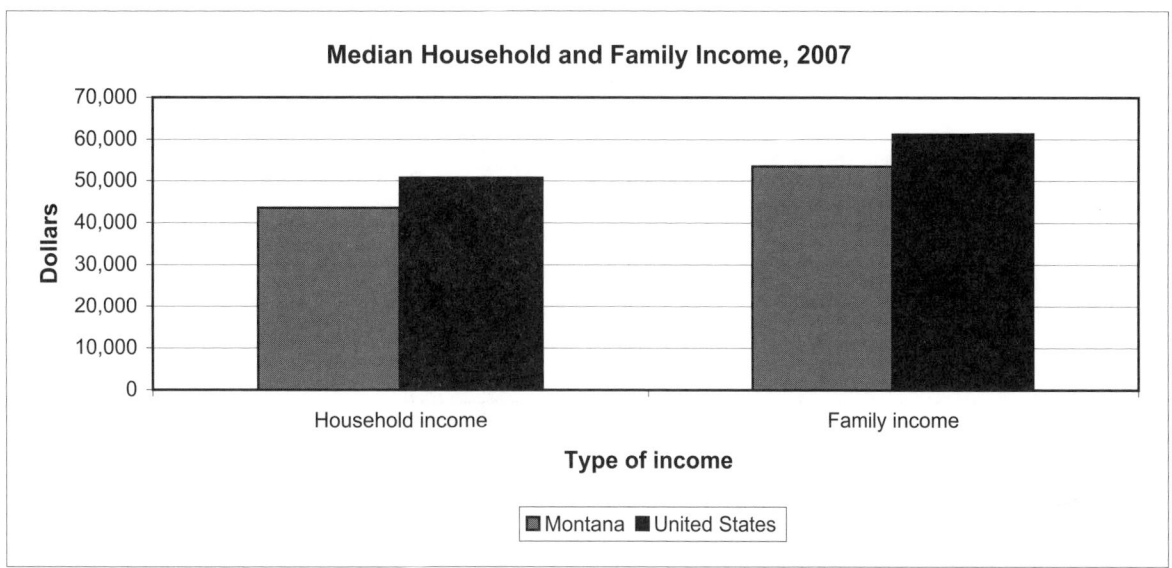

Table MT-5. Health Insurance Coverage Status for All Persons and Children Under 18 Years of Age

(Number, percent.)

Item	2000	2001	2002	2003	2004	2005	2006	2007
ALL PERSONS	892	892	906	917	912	928	931	939
Covered by Private or Government Health Insurance								
Number	746	773	773	743	746	783	772	793
Percent	83.6	86.7	85.4	81.1	81.8	84.4	82.9	84.4
Not Covered								
Number	146	119	133	173	166	145	160	146
Percent	16.4	13.3	14.6	18.9	18.2	15.6	17.1	15.6
Percent in the U.S. not covered	13.7	14.1	14.7	15.1	14.9	15.3	15.8	15.3
CHILDREN UNDER 18 YEARS OF AGE	226	221	217	216	215	215	212	219
Covered by Private or Government Health Insurance								
Number	192	194	186	178	185	184	181	191
Percent	84.9	87.8	85.8	82.3	86.1	85.8	85.5	87.4
Not Covered								
Number	34	27	31	38	30	30	31	28
Percent	15.1	12.2	14.2	17.7	13.9	14.2	14.5	12.6
Percent in the U.S. not covered	11.6	11.3	11.2	11.0	10.5	10.9	11.7	11.0

Table MT-6. Employment Status by Demographic Group, Preliminary 2008

(Number, percent.)

Characteristic	Civilian noninstitutional population	Civilian labor force		Employment		Unemployed	
		Number	Percent of population	Number	Percent of population	Number	Unemployment rate
TOTAL	760	509	66.9	483	63.5	26	5.2
Sex							
Men	377	267	71.0	253	67.1	15	5.5
Women	384	242	63.0	230	60.0	12	4.8
Race, Sex, and Hispanic Origin							
White	707	479	67.8	456	64.5	23	4.9
Men	351	251	71.6	239	68.0	13	5.0
Women	355	228	64.0	217	61.0	11	4.7
Black or African American	...	...	...	...	...	...	...
Men	...	...	...	...	...	...	...
Women	...	...	...	...	...	...	...
Hispanic	...	...	...	...	...	...	...
Men	...	...	...	...	...	...	...
Women	...	...	...	...	...	...	...
Age							
16 to 19 years	53	24	45.2	21	39.2	3	13.3
20 to 24 years	73	58	79.6	52	71.8	6	9.8
25 to 34 years	116	100	86.6	95	82.3	5	5.0
35 to 44 years	111	96	86.6	93	83.6	3	3.4
45 to 54 years	145	124	85.2	119	82.1	4	3.6
55 to 64 years	122	82	67.1	78	64.0	4	4.7
65 years and over	142	26	18.1	25	17.6	1	2.9

Note: Data in Table 6 are from the Current Population Survey (CPS) and do not match the estimates in Table 7. See notes and definitions for more details.

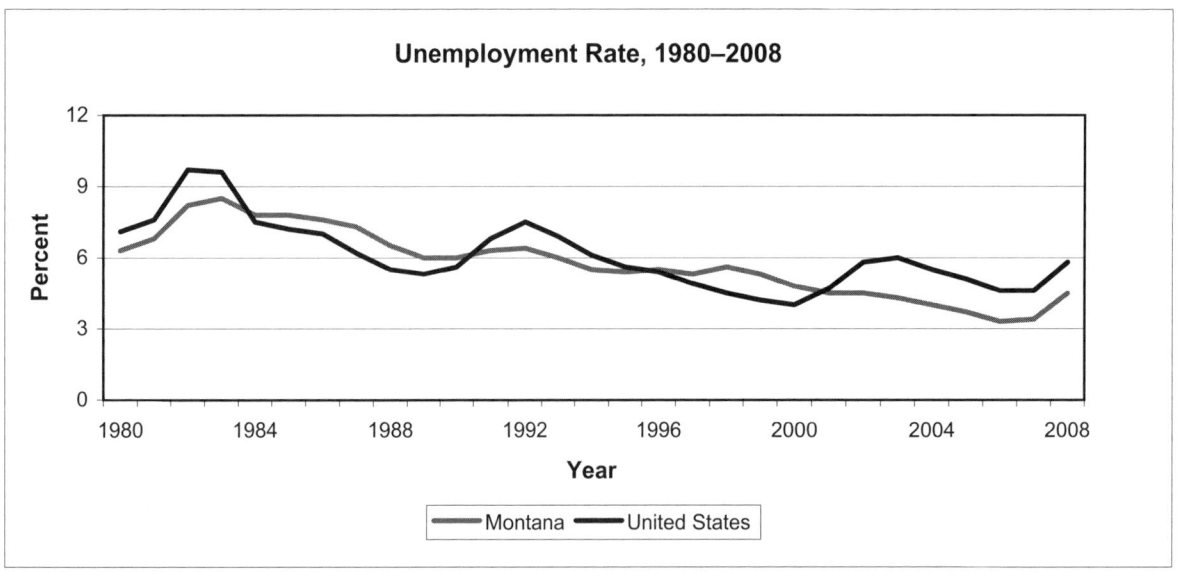

Table MT-7. Employment Status of the Civilian Noninstitutional Population Age 16 Years and Over

(Number, percent.)

Year	Civilian labor force	Civilian participation rate	Employed	Unemployed	Unemployment rate
1998	460 837	68.1	435 156	25 681	5.6
1999	465 256	68.3	440 646	24 610	5.3
2000	468 865	68.2	446 552	22 313	4.8
2001	468 963	67.7	447 827	21 136	4.5
2002	466 299	66.6	445 281	21 018	4.5
2003	470 472	66.5	450 190	20 282	4.3
2004	475 566	66.3	456 385	19 181	4.0
2005	482 255	66.3	464 625	17 630	3.7
2006	493 469	66.9	477 256	16 213	3.3
2007	502 031	67.1	484 737	17 294	3.4
2008	506 159	66.8	483 455	22 704	4.5

Table MT-8. Employment and Average Wages by Industry

(Estimates for 2001–2006 are based on the 2002 North American Industry Classification System [NAICS]. Estimates for 2007 are based on the 2007 NAICS.)

Industry	2001	2002	2003	2004	2005	2006	2007
	Number of jobs						
WAGE AND SALARY EMPLOYMENT BY INDUSTRY	419 015	422 329	428 584	439 296	449 412	462 437	473 271
Farm Wage and Salary Employment	6 325	6 309	5 934	6 056	5 697	5 696	5 382
Nonfarm Wage and Salary Employment	412 690	416 020	422 650	433 240	443 715	456 741	467 889
Private wage and salary employment	322 449	326 515	330 143	339 837	350 886	364 038	374 782
Forestry, fishing, hunting, and other	3 735	3 878	3 890	3 781	3 790	3 812	3 955
Mining	5 257	5 173	4 991	6 181	6 764	7 325	7 510
Utilities	3 169	2 928	2 825	2 900	2 925	2 983	3 058
Construction	22 052	22 434	24 177	25 848	28 664	31 277	33 446
Manufacturing	21 635	20 298	19 251	19 403	19 738	20 440	20 688
Durable goods manufacturing	14 590	13 388	12 348	12 186	12 480	12 911	13 138
Nondurable goods manufacturing	7 045	6 910	6 903	7 217	7 258	7 529	7 550
Wholesale trade	15 623	15 585	15 842	16 329	16 532	16 782	17 188
Retail trade	55 284	55 544	55 190	56 480	57 152	57 914	60 227
Transportation and warehousing	13 113	12 909	12 733	13 032	13 490	13 953	14 061
Information	7 973	7 823	7 698	7 808	7 824	7 768	7 647
Finance and insurance	14 285	14 772	15 416	15 839	16 029	16 620	16 145
Real estate and rental and leasing	5 153	5 166	5 429	5 764	5 944	6 243	6 218
Professional and technical services	16 587	17 167	17 297	17 627	18 667	19 705	20 101
Management of companies and enterprises	1 251	1 278	1 266	1 023	1 002	1 102	1 438
Administrative and waste services	15 009	14 712	15 305	15 789	16 582	18 293	20 348
Educational services	4 018	4 304	4 219	4 324	4 654	5 179	5 227
Health care and social assistance	48 435	50 818	51 263	52 759	54 576	55 864	57 070
Arts, entertainment, and recreation	8 490	8 999	9 930	10 262	10 737	11 503	12 194
Accommodation and food services	42 190	42 963	43 522	44 722	45 684	46 511	47 292
Other services, except public administration	19 190	19 764	19 899	19 966	20 132	20 764	20 969
Government and government enterprises	90 241	89 505	92 507	93 403	92 829	92 703	93 107
	Dollars						
AVERAGE WAGES AND SALARIES BY INDUSTRY	24 959	25 923	26 814	27 763	29 134	30 556	32 123
Average Farm Wages and Salaries	21 575	24 902	23 296	24 476	29 576	29 015	32 656
Average Nonfarm Wages and Salaries	25 010	25 938	26 863	27 809	29 128	30 575	32 117
Average private wages and salaries	24 317	24 991	25 855	26 870	28 161	29 619	31 172
Forestry, fishing, hunting, and other	19 370	21 413	21 377	22 202	23 071	25 725	26 964
Mining	52 592	52 597	53 033	53 787	58 141	64 832	67 750
Utilities	53 033	56 202	59 241	58 523	61 523	64 180	66 441
Construction	30 529	30 638	31 727	32 299	33 972	35 371	38 110
Manufacturing	32 433	33 380	34 567	35 298	36 837	37 641	39 758
Durable goods manufacturing	31 420	32 261	33 211	34 066	35 497	36 322	38 093
Nondurable goods manufacturing	34 530	35 548	36 992	37 377	39 141	39 904	42 656
Wholesale trade	32 262	33 535	34 141	35 996	38 103	40 472	43 244
Retail trade	18 480	19 314	20 045	20 667	21 174	22 175	23 124
Transportation and warehousing	33 592	33 919	34 696	36 614	38 132	39 605	40 653
Information	31 113	32 766	33 341	34 977	35 380	37 395	38 455
Finance and insurance	35 262	36 091	38 008	39 251	41 568	43 774	46 964
Real estate and rental and leasing	18 186	18 687	20 076	21 461	24 715	26 326	27 909
Professional and technical services	34 118	34 994	36 770	38 136	40 416	41 976	45 352
Management of companies and enterprises	35 575	36 316	37 180	41 084	47 697	51 166	53 186
Administrative and waste services	17 197	18 223	18 934	20 139	20 868	22 279	23 595
Educational services	16 312	16 533	17 130	18 248	17 921	18 407	19 456
Health care and social assistance	26 451	27 522	28 751	29 933	30 964	32 615	33 749
Arts, entertainment, and recreation	14 569	14 797	15 390	15 554	15 953	16 917	17 830
Accommodation and food services	10 878	11 159	11 473	11 852	12 252	12 956	13 796
Other services, except public administration	17 694	18 134	18 926	19 771	20 999	21 115	22 300
Government and government enterprises	27 489	29 394	30 460	31 226	32 784	34 329	35 921

Table MT-9. Employment Characteristics by Family Type

(Number, percent.)

Family type and labor force status	2005		2006		2007	
	Total	Families with own children under 18 years	Total	Families with own children under 18 years	Total	Families with own children under 18 years
TOTAL FAMILIES	236 793	101 959	240 412	103 613	240 727	99 809
FAMILY TYPE AND LABOR FORCE STATUS						
Married Coupled Families	191 961	72 594	197 345	77 371	194 997	70 936
Both husband and wife in labor force	54.4	66.3	55.6	68.0	53.1	66.5
Husband in labor force, wife not in labor force	19.0	25.8	19.2	25.5	19.9	26.7
Wife in labor force, husband not in labor force	7.9	4.8	7.8	3.7	8.4	4.4
Both husband and wife not in labor force	18.7	3.1	17.4	2.8	18.6	2.3
Other Families	44 832	29 365	43 067	26 242	45 730	28 873
Female householder, no husband present	70.6	74.8	69.9	71.7	68.5	70.6
In labor force	50.9	58.6	53.3	62.4	49.6	57.0
Not in labor force	19.7	16.2	16.6	9.3	18.9	13.6
Male householder, no wife present	29.4	25.2	30.1	28.3	31.5	29.4
In labor force	25.0	22.8	23.8	26.5	26.7	26.5
Not in labor force	4.4	2.4	6.3	1.7	4.8	2.9

Table MT-10. School Enrollment and Educational Attainment, 2007

(Number, percent.)

Item	State	U.S.
Enrollment		
Total population 3 years and over	921 868	289 295 761
Enrolled in school	230 258	79 329 527
Enrolled in preschool (percent)	5.2	6.2
Enrolled in grades K-12 (percent)	68.8	67.6
Enrolled in college or graduate school (percent)	26.0	26.2
Attainment		
Total population 25 years and over	641 019	197 892 369
Less than a high school diploma (percent)	10.0	15.5
High school diploma or more (percent)	90.0	84.5
Bachelor's degree or more (percent)	27.0	27.5
Graduate degree or more (percent)	8.6	10.1

Table MT-11. Educational Indicators

(Number, percent.)

Item	State	U.S.
Public Schools, 2006–2007 (except where noted)		
Number of school districts	515	17 742
Number of schools	836	99 639
Number of students	144 418	49 315 842
Student-teacher ratio	13.9	15.5
Expenditures per student (dollars)	$9 191	...
Averaged freshman graduation rate, 2005–2006	81.9	...
Dropout rate, grades 9–12, 2005–2006	3.7	3.7
Students eligible for free or reduced-price lunch (percent)	35.1	41.2
English-language learners (percent)	4.8	5.1
Students with IEP (percent)	12.8	12.7
Private Schools, 2007–2008 (except where noted)		
Number of schools	141	33 740
Number of students	13 778	5 072 451
High school graduates, 2006–2007	1 703	306 605
Student-teacher ratio	11.5	11.1

Table MT-12. Reported Voting and Registration of the Voting-Age Population, November 2008

(Number in thousands, percent.)

Item	Total population	Total citizen population	Registered — Total registered	Registered — Percent registered (total population)	Registered — Percent registered (total citizen population)	Voted — Total voted	Voted — Percent voted (total population)	Voted — Percent voted (total citizen population)
U.S. total	225 499	206 072	146 311	64.9	71.0	131 144	58.2	63.6
State total	731	724	516	70.6	71.3	473	64.7	65.4
Sex								
Male	358	355	247	69.0	69.6	227	63.2	63.8
Female	373	368	269	72.2	73.0	246	66.1	66.9
Race								
White alone	683	675	487	71.4	72.2	447	65.5	66.3
White non-Hispanic alone	668	665	479	71.7	72.1	440	65.9	66.2
Black alone	2	2	2	...	...	2	...	...
Asian alone	5	5	4	...	...	4	...	...
Hispanic (of any race)	15	11	9	...	...	8	...	...
White alone or in combination	693	686	495	71.3	72.1	453	65.3	66.0
Black alone or in combination	4	4	4	...	...	4	...	...
Asian alone or in combination	6	6	5	...	...	5	...	...

Table MT-13. Crime

(Number, rate per 100,000.)

Item	State 2007	State 2008	State Percent change	U.S. 2007	U.S. 2008	U.S. Percent change
Population	957 861	967 440	1.0	301 621 157	304 059 724	0.8
VIOLENT CRIME						
Number	2 754	2 497	-9.3	1 408 337	1 382 012	-1.9
Rate	287.5	258.1	-10.2	466.9	454.5	-2.7
Murder and Nonnegligent Manslaughter						
Number	14	23	64.3	16 929	16 272	-3.9
Rate	1.5	2.4	62.7	5.6	5.4	-4.7
Forcible Rape						
Number	290	294	1.4	90 427	89 000	-1.6
Rate	30.3	30.4	0.4	30.0	29.3	-2.4
Robbery						
Number	191	172	-9.9	445 125	441 855	-0.7
Rate	19.9	17.8	-10.8	147.6	145.3	-1.5
Aggravated Assault						
Number	2 259	2 008	-11.1	855 856	834 885	-2.5
Rate	235.8	207.6	-12.0	283.8	274.6	-3.2
PROPERTY CRIME						
Number	26 489	25 182	-4.9	9 843 481	9 767 915	-0.8
Rate	2 765.4	2 603.0	-5.9	3 263.5	3 212.5	-1.6
Burglary						
Number	3 027	3 332	10.1	2 179 140	2 222 196	2.0
Rate	316.0	344.4	9.0	722.5	730.8	1.2
Larceny-Theft						
Number	21 707	20 277	-6.6	6 568 572	6 588 873	0.3
Rate	2 266.2	2 095.9	-7.5	2 177.8	2 167.0	-0.5
Motor Vehicle Theft						
Number	1 755	1 573	-10.4	1 095 769	956 846	-12.7
Rate	183.2	162.6	-11.3	363.3	314.7	-13.4

Table MT-14. State Government Finances, 2007

(Dollars, percent distribution.)

Item	Thousands of dollars	Percent distribution
Total Revenue	7 129 303	X
General revenue	5 191 640	72.8
Intergovernmental revenue	1 813 956	25.4
Taxes	2 319 992	32.5
General sales	0	0.0
Selective sales	530 159	7.4
License taxes	308 304	4.3
Individual income tax	832 916	11.7
Corporate income tax	178 707	2.5
Other taxes	469 906	6.6
Current charges	497 189	7.0
Miscellaneous general revenue	560 503	7.9
Utility revenue	0	0.0
Liquor store revenue	63 960	0.9
Insurance trust revenue	1 873 703	26.3
Total Expenditure	5 554 244	100.0
Intergovernmental expenditure	1 175 674	21.2
Direct expenditure	4 378 570	78.8
Current operation	2 865 098	51.6
Capital outlay	622 143	11.2
Insurance benefits and repayments	602 110	10.8
Assistance and subsidies	99 584	1.8
Interest on debt	189 635	3.4
Exhibit: Salaries and wages	830 166	14.9
Total Expenditure	5 554 244	100.0
General expenditure	4 896 244	88.2
Intergovernmental expenditure	1 175 674	21.2
Direct expenditure	3 720 570	67.0
Education	1 688 003	30.4
Public welfare	837 857	15.1
Hospitals	42 590	0.8
Health	289 725	5.2
Highways	599 237	10.8
Police protection	40 448	0.7
Correction	146 574	2.6
Natural resources	234 061	4.2
Parks and recreation	13 094	0.2
Government administration	337 996	6.1
Interest on general debt	189 635	3.4
Other and unallocable	477 024	8.6
Utility expenditure	465	0.0
Liquor store expenditure	55 425	1.0
Insurance trust expenditure	602 110	10.8
Debt at End of Fiscal Year	4 649 819	X
Cash and Security Holdings	16 434 562	X

Table MT-15. State Government Tax Collections, 2008

(Dollars, percent distribution.)

Item	Thousands of dollars	Percent distribution
Total Taxes	2 457 929	X
Property taxes	220 327	9.0
Sales and gross receipts	544 402	22.1
Selective sales taxes	544 402	22.1
Alcoholic beverages	27 166	1.1
Amusements	63 150	2.6
Insurance premiums	65 419	2.7
Motor fuels	205 819	8.4
Pari-mutuels	73	0.0
Public utilities	48 843	2.0
Tobacco products	94 020	3.8
Other selective sales	39 912	1.6
Licenses	311 029	12.7
Alcoholic beverages	2 944	0.1
Amusements	8 220	0.3
Corporation	3 128	0.1
Hunting and fishing	46 797	1.9
Motor vehicle	143 972	5.9
Motor vehicle operators	7 916	0.3
Public utility	10	0.0
Occupation and business, NEC	90 416	3.7
Other licenses	7 626	0.3
Income taxes	1 031 777	42.0
Individual income	870 064	35.4
Corporation net income	161 713	6.6
Other taxes	350 394	14.3
Death and gift	18	0.0
Severance	347 221	14.1
Other	3 155	0.1

Table MT-16. Agriculture

(Number, acres, and dollars.)

Item	2002		2007		Percent change, 2002–2007
	Number	Percent of total	Number	Percent of total	
Number of farms	27 870		29 524		5.9
Farm Size					
Average size of farm (acres)	2 139		2 079		-2.8
Farms by size (number of farms)					
Fewer than 50 acres	6 489	23.3	7 379	25.0	13.7
50 to 499 acres	8 461	30.4	9 435	32.0	11.5
500 acres or more	12 920	46.4	12 710	43.0	-1.6
Land (Acres)					
Total land in farms	59 612 403		61 388 462		3.0
Total cropland	18 315 514	30.7	18 241 710	29.7	-0.4
Total harvested cropland	8 742 111	14.7	9 163 867	14.9	4.8
Irrigated land	1 976 111	3.3	2 013 167	3.3	1.9
Value of Sales (Dollars)					
Agricultural products sold ($1,000)	1 882 114		2 803 062		48.9
Average sales per farm	67 532		94 942		40.6
Sales of crops	733 324	39.0	1 273 721	45.4	73.7
Sales of livestock, poultry, and their products	1 148 791	61.0	1 529 340	54.6	33.1
Value of Sales (Number of Farms)					
Less than $10,000	14 055	50.4	15 695	53.2	11.7
$10,000 to $99,999	8 788	31.5	7 449	25.2	-15.2
$100,000 to $999,999	4 865	17.5	6 033	20.4	24.0
$1,000,000 or more	162	0.6	347	1.2	114.2
Farms by Type of Organization (Number of Farms)					
Family	22 448	80.5	22 625	76.6	0.8
Partnership	2 192	7.9	2 839	9.6	29.5
Corporation	2 730	9.8	3 509	11.9	28.5
Other: cooperative, estate or trust, institutional, etc	500	1.8	551	1.9	10.2
Value of Land and Buildings (Dollars)					
Estimated market value of land and buildings ($1,000)	47 567 755		23 280 911		-51.1
Land and buildings average value per farm	1 611 155		835 250		-48.2
Average value per acre	775		386		-50.2
Government Payments					
Number of farms receiving government payments	12 389	44.5	13 080	44.3	5.6
Payments (thousands of dollars)	210 749		221 977		5.3
Average payment per farm	17 011		16 971		-0.2
Farm Operator Characteristics					
Farm operators whose principal occupation is farming	17 710	63.5	14 957	50.7	-15.5
Farm operators whose principal occupation is other	10 160	36.5	14 567	49.3	43.4
Average age principal operator (years)	55.4		57.8		4.3

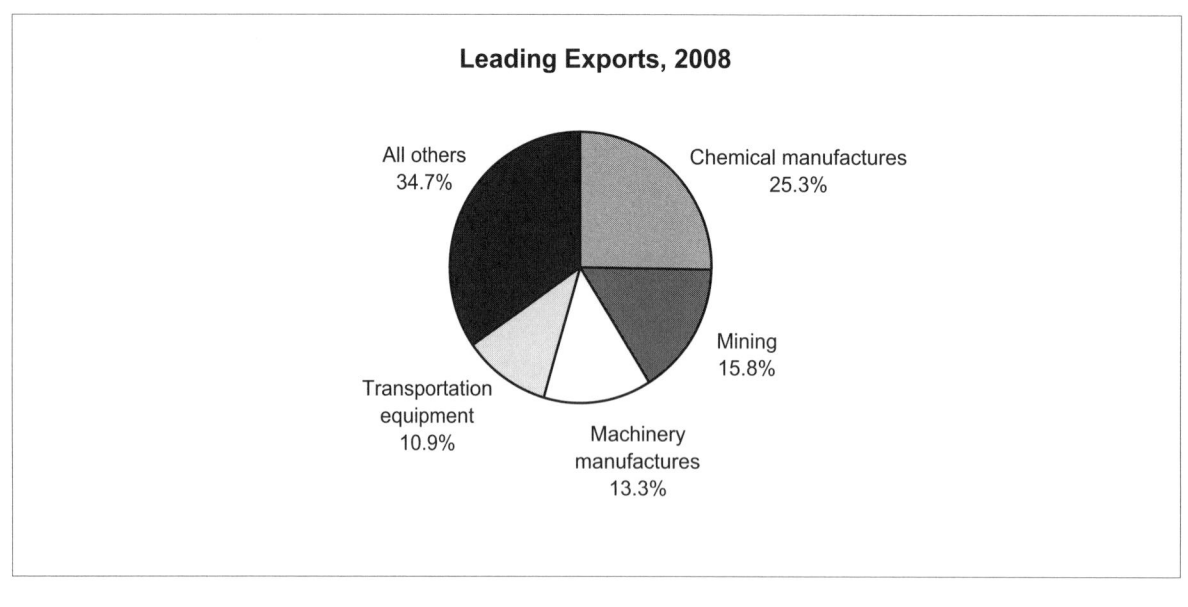

Leading Exports, 2008

All others 34.7%

Chemical manufactures 25.3%

Mining 15.8%

Machinery manufactures 13.3%

Transportation equipment 10.9%

NEBRASKA

Facts and Figures

Location: Central United States; bordered on the N by South Dakota, on the E by Iowa and Missouri, on the S by Kansas and Colorado, and on the W by Wyoming

Area: 77,354 sq. mi. (200,345 sq. km.); rank—16th

Population: 1,783,432 (2008 est.); rank—38th

Principal Cities: capital—Lincoln; largest—Omaha

Statehood: March 1, 1867; 37th state

U.S. Congress: 2 senators, 3 representatives

State Motto: Equality Before the Law

State Song: "Beautiful Nebraska"

State Nickname: The Cornhusker State

Abbreviations: NE; Nebr.; Neb.

State Symbols: flower—goldenrod; tree—cottonwood; bird—Western meadowlark

At a Glance

- With an increase in population of 4.2 percent, Nebraska ranked 33rd among the states in growth from 2000 to 2008.
- An estimated 12,559 marriages took place in Nebraska in 2008, compared to 6,129 divorces.
- The 2007 home ownership rate in Nebraska was 68.2 percent, giving it a ranking of 37th among the states.
- Nebraska's median household income in 2007 was $47,085, 32nd among the states.
- In Nebraska, 11.2 percent of the population lived below the poverty level in 2007, ranking it 33rd along with Kansas.
- In 2006-07, 12.8 percent of Nebraskans did not have health insurance, compared to 15.5 percent of the total U.S. population.
- In 2007, 3.1 percent of Nebraskans were unemployed, compared to 4.6 percent nationwide.
- Nebraska ranked 19th in the nation with 27.5 percent of its population 25 years old and over having a bachelor's degree in 2007.
- Nebraska's violent crime rate in 2007 was 302.4 per 100,000 population, compared to 466.9 for the entire nation.
- Nebraska had one physician for every 359 people in 2007, compared to one physician for every 325 people nationwide.
- In the 2008 election, 62.6 percent of Nebraska's eligible voters voted, compared to 61.7 percent of eligible voters nationwide.
- Nebraska ranked 34th among the states receiving federal aid in 2007, with $1,316 per capita.
- Nebraska's gross domestic product was $80 billion in 2007; it ranked 36th among the states.
- With $4.3 billion in exports in 2007, Nebraska ranked 37th in exports.
- Nebraskans consumed 2.14 trillion Btu's of energy in 2006; the state ranked 16th in total consumption.
- In 2007, Nebraska exported $4 billion worth of agricultural products, about 4.9 percent of the U.S. total.

Table NE-1. Population by Sex, Age, Race, and Hispanic Origin

(Number, percent.)

Sex, age, race, and Hispanic origin	1990	2000	2008	Average annual percent change, 2000–2008
Total Population	1 578 385	1 711 263	1 783 432	0.5
Percent of total U.S. population	0.6	0.6	0.6	X
Sex				
Male	769 439	843 351	884 280	0.6
Female	808 946	867 912	899 152	0.4
Age				
Under 5 years	119 606	117 048	132 092	1.5
5 to 19 years	356 644	387 288	368 255	-0.6
20 to 64 years	879 067	974 732	1 042 238	0.8
65 years and over	223 068	232 195	240 847	0.5
Median age (years)	32.9	35.3	36.2	X
Race and Hispanic Origin[1]				
One race				
White	1 480 558	1 533 261	1 629 566	0.8
Black	57 404	68 541	80 174	2.0
American Indian and Alaskan Native	12 410	14 896	18 949	3.1
Asian[2]	12 422	21 931	30 409	4.2
Native Hawaiian and Other Pacific Islander	X	836	1 377	6.4
Two or more races	X	23 953	22 957	-0.5
Hispanic (of any race)	36 969	94 425	140 498	5.1

[1]Data on race in 2000 and 2008 are not comparable to 1990. Individuals could only report one race in the 1990 census but could report one or more races on the 2000 census.
[2]Data in 1990 refer to Asian and Pacific Islanders.

Table NE-2. Marital Status

(Number, percent distribution.)

Sex and marital status	1990	2000	2007
Males, 15 Years and Over	583 134	654 559	689 329
Never married	27.9	29.2	32.0
Now married, except separated	61.8	59.1	55.7
Separated	1.0	1.0	1.0
Widowed	2.6	2.4	2.6
Divorced	6.7	8.3	8.7
Females, 15 Years and Over	631 861	687 863	716 193
Never married	21.0	22.5	24.9
Now married, except separated	56.8	55.7	52.7
Separated	1.2	1.3	1.5
Widowed	12.8	10.8	10.2
Divorced	8.1	9.7	10.7

Table NE-3. Households and Housing Characteristics

(Number, percent, and dollars.)

Item	1990	2000	2007	Average annual percent change, 2000–2007
Total Households	602 363	666 184	699 728	0.7
Family households	415 427	443 411	459 503	0.5
Married-couple family	350 514	360 996	364 528	0.1
Other family	64 913	82 415	94 975	2.0
Male householder, no wife present	14 738	22 072	26 602	2.7
Female householder, no husband present	50 175	60 343	68 373	1.8
Nonfamily households	186 936	222 773	240 225	1.1
Householder living alone	159 671	183 550	199 589	1.2
Householder not living alone	27 265	39 223	40 636	0.5
Housing Characteristics				
Total housing units	660 621	722 668	780 592	1.1
Occupied housing units	602 363	666 184	699 728	0.7
Owner-occupied	400 394	449 317	481 154	1.0
Renter-occupied	201 969	216 867	218 574	0.1
Average size	2.54	2.49	2.46	X
Financial Characteristics				
Median gross rent of renter-occupied housing units (dollars)	348	491	614	3.2
Median monthly owner costs for housing units with a mortgage (dollars)	610	895	1 199	4.3
Median value of owner-occupied housing units (dollars)	50 000	88 000	122 200	4.8

Table NE-4. Median Income and Poverty Status, 2007

(Number, percent.)

Characteristic	State		U.S.	
	Number	Percent	Number	Percent
Median Income				
Households (dollars)	47 085	X	50 740	X
Families (dollars)	58 587	X	61 173	X
Below Poverty Level				
Sex				
Male	83 454	9.8	16 576 071	11.5
Female	109 368	12.6	21 476 176	14.3
Age				
Under 18 years	65 309	14.9	13 097 100	18.0
Related children under 18 years	62 791	14.5	12 728 964	17.6
18 to 64 years	109 322	10.3	21 495 507	11.6
65 years and over	18 191	8.3	3 459 640	9.5

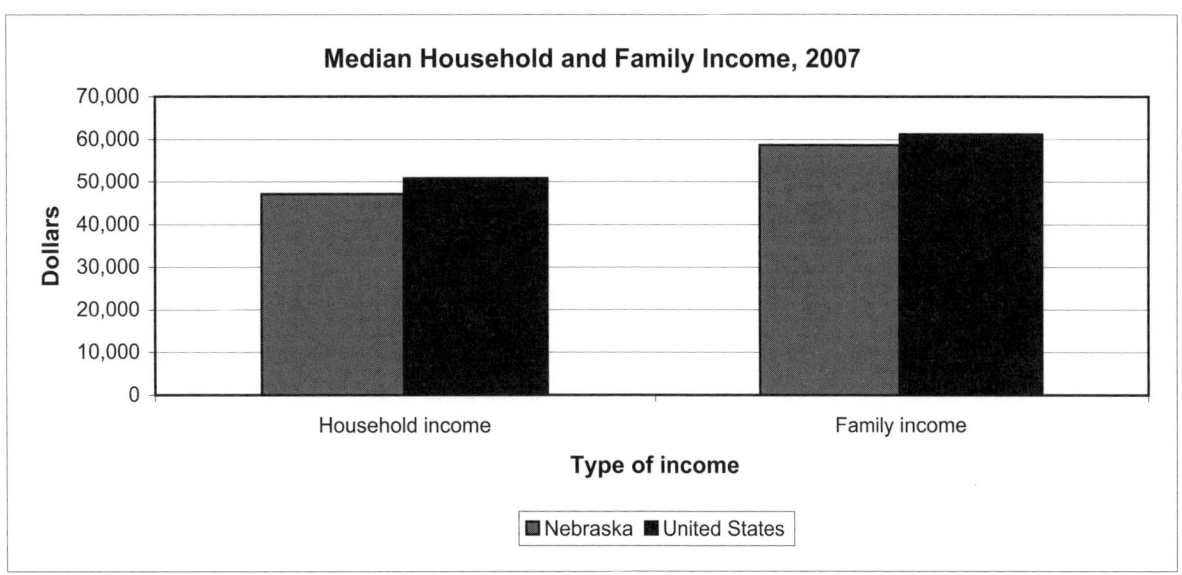

Table NE-5. Health Insurance Coverage Status for All Persons and Children Under 18 Years of Age

(Number, percent.)

Item	2000	2001	2002	2003	2004	2005	2006	2007
ALL PERSONS	1 686	1 683	1 704	1 727	1 729	1 766	1 767	1 753
Covered by Private or Government Health Insurance								
Number	1 546	1 537	1 542	1 546	1 549	1 581	1 549	1 522
Percent	91.7	91.3	90.5	89.5	89.6	89.5	87.7	86.8
Not Covered								
Number	140	146	161	181	180	185	217	232
Percent	8.3	8.7	9.5	10.5	10.4	10.5	12.3	13.2
Percent in the U.S. not covered	13.7	14.1	14.7	15.1	14.9	15.3	15.8	15.3
CHILDREN UNDER 18 YEARS OF AGE	441	437	439	448	439	439	444	452
Covered by Private or Government Health Insurance								
Number	412	408	416	417	413	416	399	407
Percent	93.4	93.2	94.7	93.2	94.1	94.7	89.9	90.0
Not Covered								
Number	29	30	23	30	26	23	45	45
Percent	6.6	6.8	5.3	6.8	5.9	5.3	10.1	10.0
Percent in the U.S. not covered	11.6	11.3	11.2	11.0	10.5	10.9	11.7	11.0

Table NE-6. Employment Status by Demographic Group, Preliminary 2008

(Number, percent.)

Characteristic	Civilian noninstitutional population	Civilian labor force		Employment		Unemployed	
		Number	Percent of population	Number	Percent of population	Number	Unemployment rate
TOTAL	1 358	1 001	73.7	969	71.3	33	3.3
Sex							
Men	666	530	80.0	511	76.7	19	3.5
Women	692	471	68.0	457	66.1	14	3.0
Race, Sex, and Hispanic Origin							
White	1 256	931	74.1	905	72.1	26	2.8
Men	618	495	80.1	480	77.7	15	3.0
Women	638	436	68.3	425	66.6	11	2.6
Black or African American	52	35	67.9	32	60.7	4	10.7
Men	. . .	. . .	. . .	. . .	. . .	. . .	. . .
Women	. . .	. . .	. . .	. . .	. . .	. . .	. . .
Hispanic	84	60	71.9	57	68.6	3	4.6
Men	43	37	86.5	35	82.4	2	4.7
Women	41	23	57.0	22	54.4	1	4.6
Age							
16 to 19 years	105	58	54.9	53	50.3	5	8.3
20 to 24 years	128	107	83.4	101	78.3	7	6.1
25 to 34 years	221	193	87.6	187	84.7	6	3.2
35 to 44 years	231	205	89.0	200	86.6	6	2.7
45 to 54 years	275	242	88.2	237	86.3	5	2.2
55 to 64 years	187	144	77.0	142	75.5	3	2.0
65 years and over	211	51	24.4	50	23.7	1	2.8

Note: Data in Table 6 are from the Current Population Survey (CPS) and do not match the estimates in Table 7. See notes and definitions for more details.

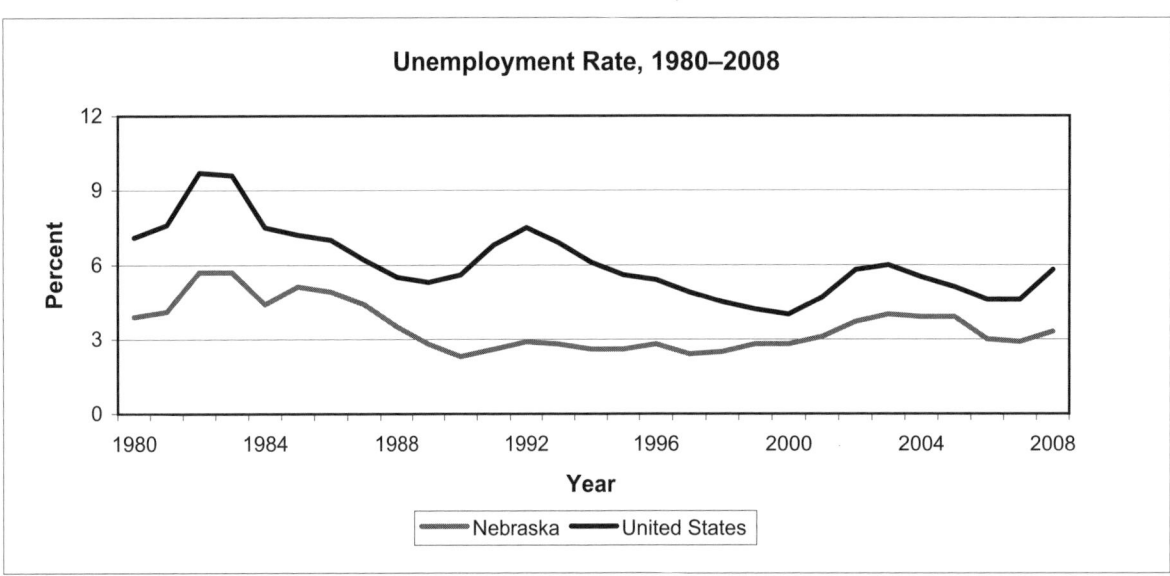

Table NE-7. Employment Status of the Civilian Noninstitutional Population Age 16 Years and Over

(Number, percent.)

Year	Civilian labor force	Civilian participation rate	Employed	Unemployed	Unemployment rate
1998	938 106	74.1	914 644	23 462	2.5
1999	942 189	73.9	916 270	25 919	2.8
2000	949 762	74.0	923 198	26 564	2.8
2001	955 820	74.0	925 783	30 037	3.1
2002	956 812	73.6	921 201	35 611	3.7
2003	970 303	74.2	931 622	38 681	4.0
2004	976 315	74.2	938 105	38 210	3.9
2005	975 693	73.6	937 964	37 729	3.9
2006	974 888	73.0	945 288	29 600	3.0
2007	984 665	73.3	955 678	28 987	2.9
2008	995 635	73.5	962 418	33 217	3.3

Table NE-8. Employment and Average Wages by Industry

(Estimates for 2001–2006 are based on the 2002 North American Industry Classification System [NAICS]. Estimates for 2007 are based on the 2007 NAICS.)

Industry	2001	2002	2003	2004	2005	2006	2007
	Number of jobs						
WAGE AND SALARY EMPLOYMENT BY INDUSTRY	959 958	953 235	956 844	963 675	974 410	983 989	998 672
Farm Wage and Salary Employment	13 408	12 503	13 082	12 122	13 081	11 155	11 761
Nonfarm Wage and Salary Employment	946 550	940 732	943 762	951 553	961 329	972 834	986 911
Private wage and salary employment	782 390	772 948	774 042	780 820	790 492	800 460	814 356
Forestry, fishing, hunting, and other	5 535	4 628	4 571	4 861	5 356	5 138	5 814
Mining	1 276	1 246	1 360	1 354	1 377	1 324	968
Utilities	1 500	1 732	1 949	1 923	1 700	1 636	1 692
Construction	45 969	46 394	47 834	49 158	48 145	48 856	51 093
Manufacturing	111 609	106 974	103 164	101 416	102 024	102 361	101 938
Durable goods manufacturing	54 007	50 355	47 505	47 082	48 610	49 837	50 280
Nondurable goods manufacturing	57 602	56 619	55 659	54 334	53 414	52 524	51 658
Wholesale trade	43 223	42 337	41 625	41 311	41 230	41 481	41 518
Retail trade	114 765	110 400	109 812	109 961	110 576	109 875	111 022
Transportation and warehousing	43 804	45 412	47 358	49 100	52 518	53 482	54 732
Information	23 434	22 044	21 024	20 539	20 482	19 636	19 701
Finance and insurance	51 235	50 932	52 193	52 767	53 432	55 011	55 972
Real estate and rental and leasing	9 979	9 890	9 813	10 117	9 977	9 918	9 920
Professional and technical services	36 144	35 729	36 298	37 796	39 122	42 087	43 015
Management of companies and enterprises	13 123	14 192	12 924	13 720	14 732	15 517	17 391
Administrative and waste services	51 233	47 465	45 363	44 559	45 213	46 008	46 272
Educational services	16 404	16 893	16 872	16 889	16 922	17 040	17 519
Health care and social assistance	93 042	96 201	99 447	101 313	103 381	105 208	107 857
Arts, entertainment, and recreation	10 963	11 092	11 308	11 753	11 942	12 112	12 846
Accommodation and food services	66 853	65 989	66 577	67 700	69 000	69 894	70 992
Other services, except public administration	42 299	43 398	44 550	44 583	43 363	43 876	44 094
Government and government enterprises	164 160	167 784	169 720	170 733	170 837	172 374	172 555
	Dollars						
AVERAGE WAGES AND SALARIES BY INDUSTRY	28 456	29 464	30 423	31 645	32 596	33 993	35 390
Average Farm Wages and Salaries	27 631	26 939	29 324	33 386	32 752	35 721	39 953
Average Nonfarm Wages and Salaries	28 468	29 498	30 438	31 622	32 594	33 974	35 336
Average private wages and salaries	28 212	29 170	30 041	31 237	32 207	33 662	35 078
Forestry, fishing, hunting, and other	12 796	14 309	15 596	14 451	15 801	16 617	17 716
Mining	34 749	35 331	37 863	40 691	41 033	41 481	41 173
Utilities	59 275	63 725	69 794	77 985	81 905	89 431	112 768
Construction	32 186	33 163	33 530	34 203	35 219	36 496	39 456
Manufacturing	32 464	33 442	34 677	35 758	36 544	38 329	39 410
Durable goods manufacturing	33 756	34 801	36 319	38 131	38 390	40 366	40 988
Nondurable goods manufacturing	31 252	32 233	33 276	33 701	34 864	36 397	37 875
Wholesale trade	36 502	37 627	38 614	41 077	42 410	44 136	46 452
Retail trade	18 293	19 076	19 541	20 266	20 350	20 986	21 587
Transportation and warehousing	41 933	41 256	40 883	42 458	43 599	45 448	45 470
Information	40 561	41 862	43 985	45 218	45 798	46 418	56 361
Finance and insurance	39 660	41 148	42 763	44 552	47 190	47 960	49 008
Real estate and rental and leasing	23 762	24 594	25 210	26 403	27 704	28 791	30 711
Professional and technical services	42 224	42 764	44 610	45 802	47 744	49 632	51 759
Management of companies and enterprises	51 928	53 932	57 968	59 993	64 274	70 773	74 042
Administrative and waste services	20 749	22 698	22 559	23 677	24 359	26 735	26 167
Educational services	22 304	22 487	22 970	24 119	24 860	26 491	27 426
Health care and social assistance	29 462	30 406	31 573	32 912	33 782	35 059	36 293
Arts, entertainment, and recreation	13 723	13 692	14 081	14 302	14 674	15 358	15 575
Accommodation and food services	10 614	10 735	10 982	11 440	11 641	12 031	12 387
Other services, except public administration	18 795	19 359	20 434	21 467	21 288	22 013	23 313
Government and government enterprises	29 684	31 007	32 246	33 386	34 385	35 419	36 553

Table NE-9. Employment Characteristics by Family Type

(Number, percent.)

Family type and labor force status	2005		2006		2007	
	Total	Families with own children under 18 years	Total	Families with own children under 18 years	Total	Families with own children under 18 years
TOTAL FAMILIES	455 129	221 168	462 408	220 854	459 503	218 837
FAMILY TYPE AND LABOR FORCE STATUS						
Married Coupled Families	364 290	162 703	371 052	163 752	364 528	156 711
Both husband and wife in labor force	61.6	72.8	63.1	74.1	62.1	74.7
Husband in labor force, wife not in labor force	18.9	21.9	18.3	21.9	18.1	21.4
Wife in labor force, husband not in labor force	6.1	3.3	6.1	2.8	6.1	2.6
Both husband and wife not in labor force	13.4	2.0	12.6	1.3	13.6	1.3
Other Families	90 839	58 465	91 356	57 102	94 975	62 126
Female householder, no husband present	73.1	77.6	71.6	75.4	72.0	74.4
In labor force	54.3	62.5	56.2	65.1	56.2	63.9
Not in labor force	18.8	15.2	15.4	10.3	15.8	10.6
Male householder, no wife present	26.9	22.4	28.4	24.6	28.0	25.6
In labor force	21.7	19.3	24.1	23.3	24.5	24.3
Not in labor force	5.2	3.0	4.3	1.3	3.5	1.3

Table NE-10. School Enrollment and Educational Attainment, 2007

(Number, percent.)

Item	State	U.S.
Enrollment		
Total population 3 years and over	1 696 811	289 295 761
Enrolled in school	480 588	79 329 527
Enrolled in preschool (percent)	6.1	6.2
Enrolled in grades K-12 (percent)	66.8	67.6
Enrolled in college or graduate school (percent)	27.1	26.2
Attainment		
Total population 25 years and over	1 139 229	197 892 369
Less than a high school diploma (percent)	10.4	15.5
High school diploma or more (percent)	89.6	84.5
Bachelor's degree or more (percent)	27.5	27.5
Graduate degree or more (percent)	8.8	10.1

Table NE-11. Educational Indicators

(Number, percent.)

Item	State	U.S.
Public Schools, 2006–2007 (except where noted)		
Number of school districts	312	17 742
Number of schools	1 198	99 639
Number of students	287 580	49 315 842
Student-teacher ratio	13.4	15.5
Expenditures per student (dollars)	$10 068	. . .
Averaged freshman graduation rate, 2005–2006	87.0	. . .
Dropout rate, grades 9–12, 2005–2006	2.7	3.7
Students eligible for free or reduced-price lunch (percent) ...	36.4	41.2
English-language learners (percent)	6.3	5.1
Students with IEP (percent)	15.6	12.7
Private Schools, 2007–2008 (except where noted)		
Number of schools	223	33 740
Number of students	35 872	5 072 451
High school graduates, 2006–2007	2 156	306 605
Student-teacher ratio	12.7	11.1

Table NE-12. Reported Voting and Registration of the Voting-Age Population, November 2008

(Number in thousands, percent.)

Item	Total population	Total citizen population	Registered — Total registered	Registered — Percent registered (total population)	Registered — Percent registered (total citizen population)	Voted — Total voted	Voted — Percent voted (total population)	Voted — Percent voted (total citizen population)
U.S. total	225 499	206 072	146 311	64.9	71.0	131 144	58.2	63.6
State total	1 308	1 253	939	71.8	74.9	844	64.5	67.3
Sex								
Male	640	611	443	69.3	72.5	391	61.1	63.9
Female	669	642	495	74.1	77.2	453	67.7	70.6
Race								
White alone	1 210	1 171	890	73.6	76.0	803	66.3	68.6
White non-Hispanic alone	1 139	1 128	864	75.9	76.7	781	68.5	69.2
Black alone	42	37	25	. . .	. . .	24	. . .	. . .
Asian alone	25	17	8	. . .	. . .	8	. . .	. . .
Hispanic (of any race)	76	47	28	36.8	. . .	24	31.6	. . .
White alone or in combination	1 221	1 182	898	73.5	76.0	809	66.2	68.4
Black alone or in combination	45	40	26	. . .	. . .	25	. . .	. . .
Asian alone or in combination	29	20	9	. . .	. . .	9	. . .	. . .

Table NE-13. Crime

(Number, rate per 100,000.)

Item	State 2007	State 2008	State Percent change	U.S. 2007	U.S. 2008	U.S. Percent change
Population	1 774 571	1 783 432	0.5	301 621 157	304 059 724	0.8
VIOLENT CRIME						
Number	5 367	5 416	0.9	1 408 337	1 382 012	-1.9
Rate	302.4	303.7	0.4	466.9	454.5	-2.7
Murder and Nonnegligent Manslaughter						
Number	68	68	0.0	16 929	16 272	-3.9
Rate	3.8	3.8	-0.5	5.6	5.4	-4.7
Forcible Rape						
Number	527	583	10.6	90 427	89 000	-1.6
Rate	29.7	32.7	10.1	30.0	29.3	-2.4
Robbery						
Number	1 108	1 299	17.2	445 125	441 855	-0.7
Rate	62.4	72.8	16.7	147.6	145.3	-1.5
Aggravated Assault						
Number	3 664	3 466	-5.4	855 856	834 885	-2.5
Rate	206.5	194.3	-5.9	283.8	274.6	-3.2
PROPERTY CRIME						
Number	56 102	51 338	-8.5	9 843 481	9 767 915	-0.8
Rate	3 161.4	2 878.6	-8.9	3 263.5	3 212.5	-1.6
Burglary						
Number	9 046	8 775	-3.0	2 179 140	2 222 196	2.0
Rate	509.8	492.0	-3.5	722.5	730.8	1.2
Larceny-Theft						
Number	41 855	38 375	-8.3	6 568 572	6 588 873	0.3
Rate	2 358.6	2 151.8	-8.8	2 177.8	2 167.0	-0.5
Motor Vehicle Theft						
Number	5 201	4 188	-19.5	1 095 769	956 846	-12.7
Rate	293.1	234.8	-19.9	363.3	314.7	-13.4

Table NE-14. State Government Finances, 2007

(Dollars, percent distribution.)

Item	Thousands of dollars	Percent distribution
Total Revenue	9 986 412	X
General revenue	8 380 410	83.9
Intergovernmental revenue	2 532 557	25.4
Taxes	4 071 032	40.8
General sales	1 484 170	14.9
Selective sales	468 433	4.7
License taxes	207 013	2.1
Individual income tax	1 650 895	16.5
Corporate income tax	213 027	2.1
Other taxes	47 494	0.5
Current charges	832 978	8.3
Miscellaneous general revenue	943 843	9.5
Utility revenue	0	0.0
Liquor store revenue	0	0.0
Insurance trust revenue	1 606 002	16.1
Total Expenditure	7 829 584	100.0
Intergovernmental expenditure	1 793 817	22.9
Direct expenditure	6 035 767	77.1
Current operation	4 687 774	59.9
Capital outlay	696 360	8.9
Insurance benefits and repayments	398 717	5.1
Assistance and subsidies	166 229	2.1
Interest on debt	86 687	1.1
Exhibit: Salaries and wages	1 978 616	25.3
Total Expenditure	7 829 584	100.0
General expenditure	7 430 867	94.9
Intergovernmental expenditure	1 793 817	22.9
Direct expenditure	5 637 050	72.0
Education	2 661 012	34.0
Public welfare	2 024 945	25.9
Hospitals	225 283	2.9
Health	426 557	5.4
Highways	557 579	7.1
Police protection	80 482	1.0
Correction	212 598	2.7
Natural resources	186 188	2.4
Parks and recreation	32 132	0.4
Government administration	187 943	2.4
Interest on general debt	86 687	1.1
Other and unallocable	749 461	9.6
Utility expenditure	0	0.0
Liquor store expenditure	0	0.0
Insurance trust expenditure	398 717	5.1
Debt at End of Fiscal Year	2 196 880	X
Cash and Security Holdings	14 349 936	X

Table NE-15. State Government Tax Collections, 2008

(Dollars, percent distribution.)

Item	Thousands of dollars	Percent distribution
Total Taxes	4 175 471	X
Property taxes	2 264	0.1
Sales and gross receipts	1 982 112	47.5
General sales and gross receipts	1 534 134	36.7
Selective sales taxes	447 978	10.7
Alcoholic beverages	26 254	0.6
Amusements	5 659	0.1
Insurance premiums	37 250	0.9
Motor fuels	294 149	7.0
Pari-mutuels	234	0.0
Public utilities	3 263	0.1
Tobacco products	75 479	1.8
Other selective sales	5 690	0.1
Licenses	206 783	5.0
Alcoholic beverages	453	0.0
Amusements	363	0.0
Corporation	7 157	0.2
Hunting and fishing	15 490	0.4
Motor vehicle	90 845	2.2
Motor vehicle operators	8 735	0.2
Occupation and business, NEC	62 755	1.5
Other licenses	20 985	0.5
Income taxes	1 958 997	46.9
Individual income	1 726 145	41.3
Corporation net income	232 852	5.6
Other taxes	25 315	0.6
Death and gift	6 844	0.2
Documentary and stock transfer	13 503	0.3
Severance	4 968	0.1

Table NE-16. Agriculture

(Number, acres, and dollars.)

Item	2002		2007		Percent change, 2002–2007
	Number	Percent of total	Number	Percent of total	
Number of farms	49 355		47 712		-3.3
Farm Size					
Average size of farm (acres)	930		953		2.5
Farms by size (number of farms)					
Fewer than 50 acres	7 320	14.8	8 851	18.6	20.9
50 to 499 acres	21 490	43.5	19 942	41.8	-7.2
500 acres or more	20 545	41.6	18 919	39.7	-7.9
Land (Acres)					
Total land in farms	45 903 116		45 480 358		-0.9
Total cropland	22 520 874	49.1	21 486 025	47.2	-4.6
Total harvested cropland	17 336 624	37.8	18 169 876	40.0	4.8
Irrigated land	7 625 170	16.6	8 558 559	18.8	12.2
Value of Sales (Dollars)					
Agricultural products sold ($1,000)	9 703 657		15 506 035		59.8
Average sales per farm	196 609		324 992		65.3
Sales of crops	3 388 265	34.9	6 843 325	44.1	102.0
Sales of livestock, poultry, and their products	6 315 392	65.1	8 662 710	55.9	37.2
Value of Sales (Number of Farms)					
Less than $10,000	15 069	30.5	15 020	31.5	-0.3
$10,000 to $99,999	18 502	37.5	13 116	27.5	-29.1
$100,000 to $999,999	14 764	29.9	17 016	35.7	15.3
$1,000,000 or more	1 020	2.1	2 560	5.4	151.0
Farms by Type of Organization (Number of Farms)					
Family	42 835	86.8	39 848	83.5	-7.0
Partnership	3 080	6.2	3 616	7.6	17.4
Corporation	3 065	6.2	3 571	7.5	16.5
Other: cooperative, estate or trust, institutional, etc	375	0.8	677	1.4	80.5
Value of Land and Buildings (Dollars)					
Estimated market value of land and buildings ($1,000)	52 692 729		35 726 993		-32.2
Land and buildings average value per farm	1 104 392		723 863		-34.5
Average value per acre	1 159		776		-33.0
Government Payments					
Number of farms receiving government payments	32 007	64.9	34 924	73.2	9.1
Payments (thousands of dollars)	347 517		387 340		11.5
Average payment per farm	10 858		11 091		2.1
Farm Operator Characteristics					
Farm operators whose principal occupation is farming	36 031	73.0	28 854	60.5	-19.9
Farm operators whose principal occupation is other	13 324	27.0	18 858	39.5	41.5
Average age principal operator (years)	53.9		55.9		3.7

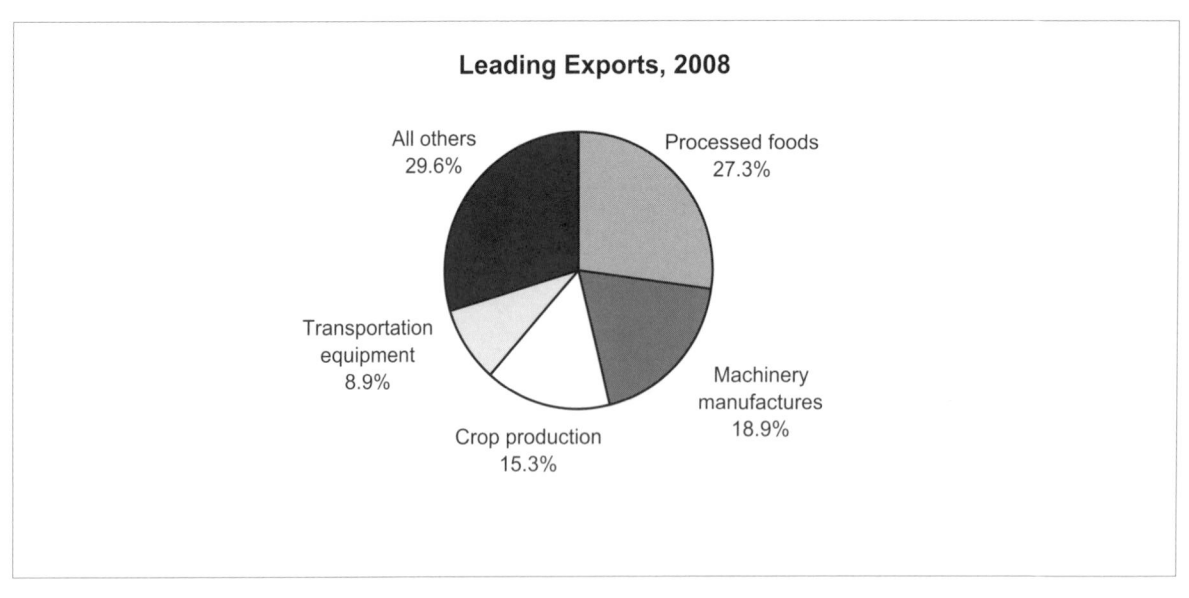

Leading Exports, 2008

All others 29.6%
Processed foods 27.3%
Transportation equipment 8.9%
Crop production 15.3%
Machinery manufactures 18.9%

NEVADA

Facts and Figures

Location: Western United States; bordered on the N by Oregon and Idaho, on the E by Utah and Arizona, on the S by Arizona and California, and on the W by California

Area: 110,561 sq. mi. (286,351 sq. km.); rank—7th

Population: 2,600,167 (2008 est.); rank—35th

Principal Cities: capital—Carson City; largest—Las Vegas

Statehood: October 31, 1864; 36th state

U.S. Congress: 2 senators, 3 representatives

State Motto: All for Our Country

State Song: "Home Means Nevada"

State Nicknames: The Silver State; The Sagebrush State

Abbreviations: NV; Nev.

State Symbols: flower—sagebrush; tree—single-leaf piñon and bristlecone pine; bird—mountain bluebird

At a Glance

- With an increase in population of 30.1 percent, Nevada ranked 1st among the states in growth from 2000 to 2008.
- An estimated 112,185 marriages took place in Nevada in 2008, compared to 16,909 divorces.
- The 2007 home ownership rate in Nevada was 63.3 percent, giving it a ranking of 47th among the states.
- Nevada's median household income in 2007 was $55,062, 14th among the states.
- In Nevada, 10.7 percent of the population lived below the poverty level in 2007, ranking it 37th.
- In 2006-07, 18.4 percent of Nevadans did not have health insurance, compared to 15.5 percent of the total U.S. population.
- In 2007, 4.6 percent of Nevadans were unemployed, compared to 4.6 percent nationwide.
- Nevada ranked 43rd in the nation with 21.8 percent of its population 25 years old and over having a bachelor's degree in 2007; its ranking was the same as Tennessee's.
- Nevada's violent crime rate in 2007 was 750.6 per 100,000 population, compared to 466.9 for the entire nation.
- Nevada had one physician for every 459 people in 2007, compared to one physician for every 325 people nationwide.
- In the 2008 election, 58.6 percent of Nevada's eligible voters voted, compared to 61.7 percent of eligible voters nationwide.
- Nevada ranked 50th among the states receiving federal aid in 2007, with $908 per capita.
- Nevada's gross domestic product was $127 billion in 2007; it ranked 31st among the states.
- With $5.7 billion in exports in 2007, Nevada ranked 32nd in exports.
- Nevadans consumed 766.6 billion Btu's of energy in 2006; the state ranked 36th in total consumption.
- In 2007, Nevada exported $43 million worth of agricultural products, less than 1 percent of the U.S. total.

Table NV-1. Population by Sex, Age, Race, and Hispanic Origin

(Number, percent.)

Sex, age, race, and Hispanic origin	1990	2000	2008	Average annual percent change, 2000–2008
Total Population	1 201 833	1 998 257	2 600 167	3.3
Percent of total U.S. population	0.5	0.7	0.9	X
Sex				
Male	611 880	1 018 051	1 324 590	3.3
Female	589 953	980 206	1 275 577	3.3
Age				
Under 5 years	92 217	145 817	199 175	4.0
5 to 19 years	235 730	415 684	526 308	3.0
20 to 64 years	746 255	1 217 827	1 577 967	3.3
65 years and over	127 631	218 929	296 717	3.9
Median age (years)	33.2	35.0	35.9	X
Race and Hispanic Origin[1]				
One race				
White	1 012 695	1 501 886	2 103 307	4.3
Black	78 771	135 477	210 677	5.7
American Indian and Alaskan Native	19 637	26 420	39 039	5.0
Asian[2]	38 127	90 266	161 366	7.5
Native Hawaiian and Other Pacific Islander	X	8 426	14 270	6.8
Two or more races	X	76 428	71 508	-0.8
Hispanic (of any race)	124 419	393 970	668 527	6.8

[1]Data on race in 2000 and 2008 are not comparable to 1990. Individuals could only report one race in the 1990 census but could report one or more races on the 2000 census.
[2]Data in 1990 refer to Asian and Pacific Islanders.

Table NV-2. Marital Status

(Number, percent distribution.)

Sex and marital status	1990	2000	2007
Males, 15 Years and Over	481 852	792 317	1 019 569
Never married	28.2	28.8	32.4
Now married, except separated	53.5	53.8	50.6
Separated	2.3	2.0	2.0
Widowed	2.3	2.5	2.5
Divorced	13.8	12.9	12.6
Females, 15 Years and Over	466 194	771 263	989 980
Never married	19.1	20.9	25.0
Now married, except separated	54.2	53.1	50.3
Separated	2.6	2.7	2.6
Widowed	9.0	8.6	7.7
Divorced	15.1	14.7	14.4

Table NV-3. Households and Housing Characteristics

(Number, percent, and dollars.)

Item	1990	2000	2007	Average annual percent change, 2000–2007
Total Households	466 297	751 165	954 067	3.5
Family households	307 400	498 333	631 720	3.4
Married-couple family	239 573	373 201	459 557	3.0
Other family	67 827	125 132	172 163	4.7
Male householder, no wife present	20 318	41 650	59 621	5.3
Female householder, no husband present	47 509	83 482	112 542	4.4
Nonfamily households	158 897	252 832	322 347	3.5
Householder living alone	119 627	186 745	250 235	4.3
Householder not living alone	39 270	66 087	72 112	1.3
Housing Characteristics				
Total housing units	518 858	827 457	1 102 409	4.2
Occupied housing units	466 297	751 165	954 067	3.5
Owner-occupied	255 388	457 247	576 376	3.4
Renter-occupied	210 909	293 918	377 691	3.6
Average size	2.53	2.62	2.65	X
Financial Characteristics				
Median gross rent of renter-occupied housing units (dollars)	509	699	980	4.9
Median monthly owner costs for housing units with a mortgage (dollars)	833	1 190	1 779	5.9
Median value of owner-occupied housing units (dollars)	95 300	142 000	311 300	11.9

Table NV-4. Median Income and Poverty Status, 2007

(Number, percent.)

Characteristic	State		U.S.	
	Number	Percent	Number	Percent
Median Income				
Households (dollars)	55 062	X	50 740	X
Families (dollars)	62 842	X	61 173	X
Below Poverty Level				
Sex				
Male	118 142	9.3	16 576 071	11.5
Female	151 811	12.1	21 476 176	14.3
Age				
Under 18 years	99 670	15.3	13 097 100	18.0
Related children under 18 years	95 227	14.7	12 728 964	17.6
18 to 64 years	151 147	9.5	21 495 507	11.6
65 years and over	19 136	6.8	3 459 640	9.5

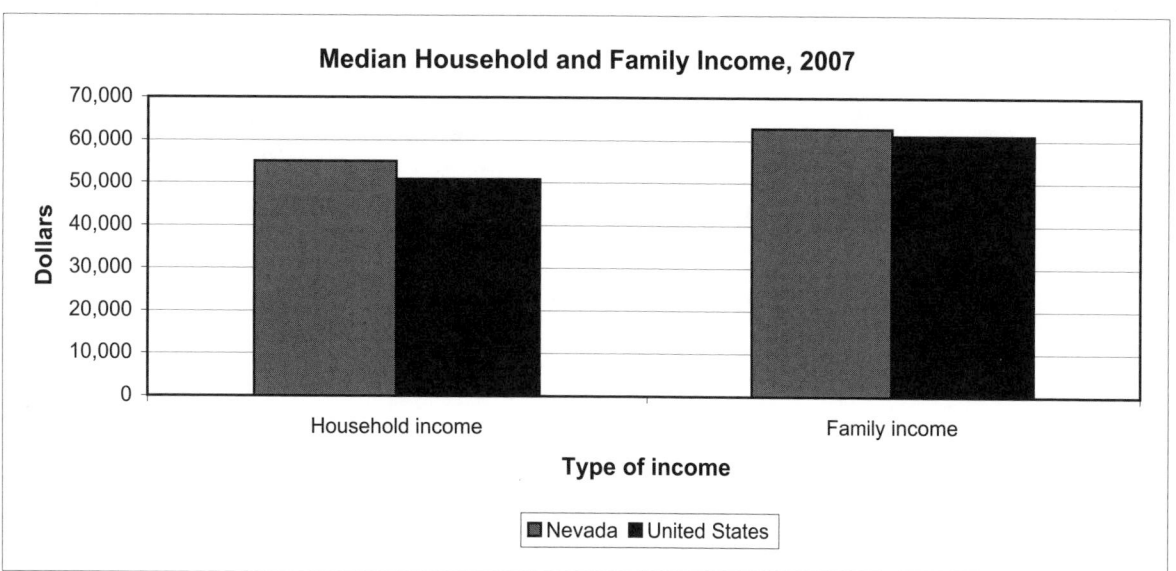

Median Household and Family Income, 2007

Nevada ■ United States

Table NV-5. Health Insurance Coverage Status for All Persons and Children Under 18 Years of Age

(Number, percent.)

Item	2000	2001	2002	2003	2004	2005	2006	2007
ALL PERSONS	2 048	2 135	2 121	2 250	2 392	2 448	2 535	2 568
Covered by Private or Government Health Insurance								
Number	1 712	1 807	1 709	1 840	1 952	2 030	2 039	2 126
Percent	83.6	84.6	80.6	81.8	81.6	82.9	80.4	82.8
Not Covered								
Number	336	328	412	410	440	418	496	441
Percent	16.4	15.4	19.4	18.2	18.4	17.1	19.6	17.2
Percent in the U.S. not covered	13.7	14.1	14.7	15.1	14.9	15.3	15.8	15.3
CHILDREN UNDER 18 YEARS OF AGE	555	583	578	594	620	648	649	660
Covered by Private or Government Health Insurance								
Number	467	505	467	494	521	555	527	566
Percent	84.2	86.6	80.8	83.1	84.1	85.7	81.2	85.7
Not Covered								
Number	88	78	111	100	99	93	122	94
Percent	15.8	13.4	19.2	16.9	15.9	14.3	18.8	14.3
Percent in the U.S. not covered	11.6	11.3	11.2	11.0	10.5	10.9	11.7	11.0

Table NV-6. Employment Status by Demographic Group, Preliminary 2008

(Number, percent.)

Characteristic	Civilian noninstitutional population	Civilian labor force		Employment		Unemployed	
		Number	Percent of population	Number	Percent of population	Number	Unemployment rate
TOTAL	1 998	1 390	69.6	1 305	65.3	85	6.1
Sex							
Men	1 010	776	77.0	728	72.1	48	6.2
Women	987	614	62.0	577	58.4	37	6.0
Race, Sex, and Hispanic Origin							
White	1 609	1 119	69.5	1 051	65.3	68	6.1
Men	820	632	77.1	592	72.1	40	6.4
Women	789	487	61.7	459	58.1	28	5.8
Black or African American	151	109	72.1	99	65.7	10	8.9
Men	75	57	76.6	54	72.4	3	5.6
Women	76	51	67.7	45	59.1	7	12.7
Hispanic	399	301	75.5	273	68.5	28	9.3
Men	216	189	87.5	170	78.8	19	10.0
Women	183	112	61.2	103	56.3	9	8.1
Age							
16 to 19 years	133	59	44.3	48	36.3	11	18.1
20 to 24 years	166	137	82.8	125	75.6	12	8.8
25 to 34 years	393	332	84.4	312	79.4	20	5.9
35 to 44 years	361	317	87.8	298	82.5	19	6.0
45 to 54 years	346	294	84.9	281	81.1	13	4.5
55 to 64 years	300	194	64.9	187	62.2	8	4.0
65 years and over	299	57	18.9	54	18.0	3	4.7

Note: Data in Table 6 are from the Current Population Survey (CPS) and do not match the estimates in Table 7. See notes and definitions for more details.

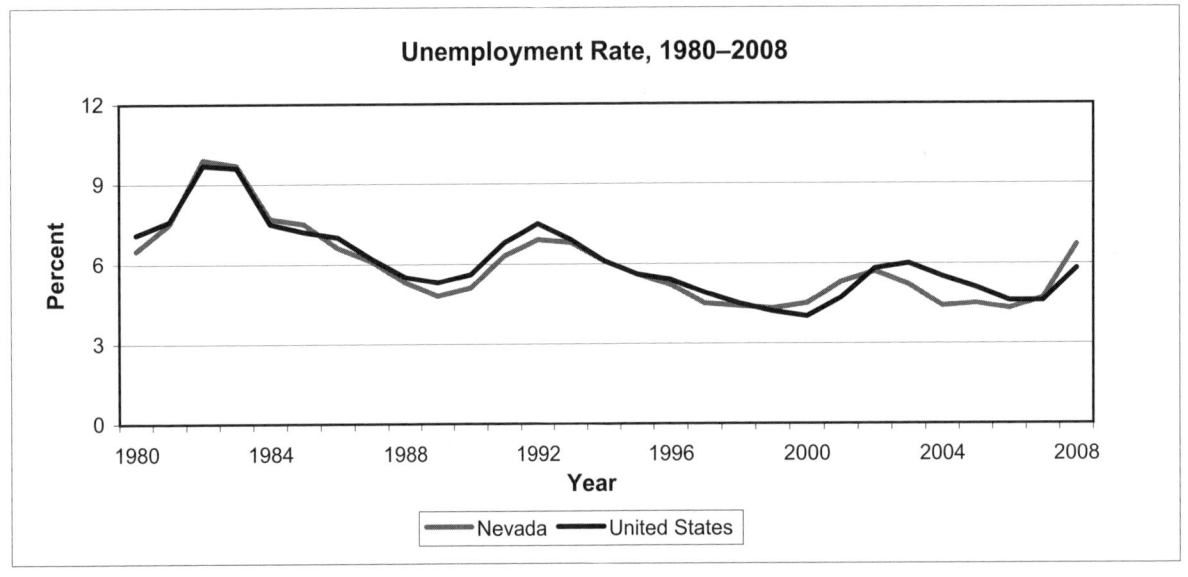

Table NV-7. Employment Status of the Civilian Noninstitutional Population Age 16 Years and Over

(Number, percent.)

Year	Civilian labor force	Civilian participation rate	Employed	Unemployed	Unemployment rate
1998	982 065	69.5	938 662	43 403	4.4
1999	1 022 584	69.6	978 969	43 615	4.3
2000	1 062 845	69.8	1 015 221	47 624	4.5
2001	1 101 020	69.7	1 042 182	58 838	5.3
2002	1 130 780	69.2	1 066 477	64 303	5.7
2003	1 153 910	68.3	1 093 507	60 403	5.2
2004	1 180 314	67.3	1 128 223	52 091	4.4
2005	1 225 144	67.5	1 170 367	54 777	4.5
2006	1 277 197	68.0	1 222 183	55 014	4.3
2007	1 322 643	68.5	1 260 276	62 367	4.7
2008	1 373 462	69.7	1 282 012	91 450	6.7

Table NV-8. Employment and Average Wages by Industry

(Estimates for 2001–2006 are based on the 2002 North American Industry Classification System [NAICS]. Estimates for 2007 are based on the 2007 NAICS.)

Industry	2001	2002	2003	2004	2005	2006	2007
	Number of jobs						
WAGE AND SALARY EMPLOYMENT BY INDUSTRY	1 092 292	1 095 078	1 134 441	1 201 965	1 273 415	1 330 763	1 343 336
Farm Wage and Salary Employment	2 558	2 034	2 477	2 326	2 268	2 267	1 953
Nonfarm Wage and Salary Employment	1 089 734	1 093 044	1 131 964	1 199 639	1 271 147	1 328 496	1 341 383
Private wage and salary employment	953 993	951 874	985 727	1 048 861	1 115 195	1 166 576	1 172 470
Forestry, fishing, hunting, and other	797	773	841	863	841	829	866
Mining	9 784	8 997	8 964	10 030	10 833	11 551	12 123
Utilities	4 514	5 088	5 070	5 133	4 659	4 643	4 533
Construction	95 210	96 309	104 565	122 557	139 709	147 840	138 418
Manufacturing	43 962	43 306	44 330	46 624	48 938	51 231	50 910
Durable goods manufacturing	29 563	29 466	30 478	32 338	33 893	35 314	34 818
Nondurable goods manufacturing	14 399	13 840	13 852	14 286	15 045	15 917	16 092
Wholesale trade	35 496	35 608	34 891	36 040	37 963	39 592	40 118
Retail trade	117 236	118 946	123 526	129 442	135 158	141 219	144 156
Transportation and warehousing	37 766	37 275	37 486	40 361	43 216	46 552	50 132
Information	18 923	17 031	15 900	14 979	14 767	15 243	15 935
Finance and insurance	35 222	35 323	37 425	37 583	39 184	40 315	38 555
Real estate and rental and leasing	21 739	22 674	23 112	24 609	25 971	27 530	28 405
Professional and technical services	41 455	42 901	45 959	50 871	53 682	57 471	58 300
Management of companies and enterprises	7 724	7 068	7 992	10 070	12 465	14 438	16 667
Administrative and waste services	68 915	66 767	70 464	78 457	85 804	90 792	88 122
Educational services	4 136	4 665	5 028	5 633	6 411	7 019	7 549
Health care and social assistance	67 512	71 124	74 480	78 723	82 540	85 433	89 618
Arts, entertainment, and recreation	28 905	28 904	30 117	30 467	31 129	31 871	32 579
Accommodation and food services	280 251	273 454	278 990	287 917	302 129	310 673	312 223
Other services, except public administration	34 446	35 661	36 587	38 502	39 796	42 334	43 261
Government and government enterprises	135 741	141 170	146 237	150 778	155 952	161 920	168 913
	Dollars						
AVERAGE WAGES AND SALARIES BY INDUSTRY	33 572	34 518	35 879	37 749	39 425	40 781	42 825
Average Farm Wages and Salaries	21 564	30 906	22 324	25 380	29 480	28 952	35 709
Average Nonfarm Wages and Salaries	33 600	34 525	35 908	37 773	39 443	40 801	42 836
Average private wages and salaries	32 869	33 709	35 043	36 927	38 688	39 959	42 026
Forestry, fishing, hunting, and other	18 366	22 294	22 000	22 513	23 603	24 814	26 687
Mining	58 696	62 144	62 733	63 448	62 911	69 367	75 190
Utilities	68 537	70 334	73 864	80 147	78 595	81 591	84 685
Construction	39 775	40 760	41 684	42 546	44 885	47 480	52 409
Manufacturing	39 522	39 222	41 547	42 597	43 590	45 138	47 860
Durable goods manufacturing	42 114	41 329	44 274	45 035	46 019	47 740	51 420
Nondurable goods manufacturing	34 200	34 735	35 547	37 078	38 118	39 365	40 157
Wholesale trade	45 927	46 219	47 693	50 731	53 356	55 694	58 009
Retail trade	25 211	25 634	26 048	27 196	28 042	28 437	28 395
Transportation and warehousing	31 370	32 507	34 277	35 588	37 020	37 630	38 420
Information	45 059	45 137	45 979	47 635	55 787	51 173	51 932
Finance and insurance	46 007	47 133	50 718	52 992	55 938	55 096	56 060
Real estate and rental and leasing	29 629	30 743	31 720	34 413	37 873	40 564	41 056
Professional and technical services	52 651	54 129	56 601	58 238	61 234	63 535	65 134
Management of companies and enterprises	98 753	105 811	123 518	147 529	147 909	127 253	148 581
Administrative and waste services	23 450	24 011	24 555	25 053	25 656	26 880	28 014
Educational services	26 610	28 030	28 209	29 507	31 749	31 859	33 183
Health care and social assistance	37 539	38 697	39 983	41 614	42 806	44 550	46 291
Arts, entertainment, and recreation	24 483	24 788	26 076	27 778	28 796	30 324	30 870
Accommodation and food services	26 151	26 958	27 761	29 276	30 502	31 788	33 191
Other services, except public administration	23 343	23 737	24 309	25 849	27 066	28 126	28 972
Government and government enterprises	38 734	40 026	41 741	43 659	44 843	46 870	48 452

Table NV-9. Employment Characteristics by Family Type

(Number, percent.)

Family type and labor force status	2005		2006		2007	
	Total	Families with own children under 18 years	Total	Families with own children under 18 years	Total	Families with own children under 18 years
TOTAL FAMILIES	589 291	277 842	612 349	295 566	631 720	299 596
FAMILY TYPE AND LABOR FORCE STATUS						
Married Coupled Families	430 798	184 995	443 841	195 919	459 557	202 557
Both husband and wife in labor force	51.2	59.7	51.8	60.2	52.5	62.5
Husband in labor force, wife not in labor force	25.6	33.4	25.4	32.6	24.5	31.4
Wife in labor force, husband not in labor force	7.1	3.7	7.1	3.8	7.2	3.9
Both husband and wife not in labor force	16.1	3.1	15.8	3.5	15.8	2.1
Other Families	158 493	92 847	168 508	99 647	172 163	97 039
Female householder, no husband present	67.6	72.4	64.5	67.3	65.4	69.3
In labor force	49.7	58.7	48.9	55.5	48.2	56.4
Not in labor force	18.0	13.7	15.6	11.8	17.2	12.9
Male householder, no wife present	32.4	27.6	35.5	32.7	34.6	30.7
In labor force	26.2	24.5	30.3	29.6	29.2	28.8
Not in labor force	6.2	3.1	5.2	3.2	5.4	1.8

Table NV-10. School Enrollment and Educational Attainment, 2007

(Number, percent.)

Item	State	U.S.
Enrollment		
Total population 3 years and over	2 449 264	289 295 761
Enrolled in school	613 526	79 329 527
Enrolled in preschool (percent)	4.3	6.2
Enrolled in grades K-12 (percent)	75.6	67.6
Enrolled in college or graduate school (percent)	20.1	26.2
Attainment		
Total population 25 years and over	1 686 098	197 892 369
Less than a high school diploma (percent)	16.3	15.5
High school diploma or more (percent)	83.7	84.5
Bachelor's degree or more (percent)	21.8	27.5
Graduate degree or more (percent)	7.5	10.1

Table NV-11. Educational Indicators

(Number, percent.)

Item	State	U.S.
Public Schools, 2006–2007 (except where noted)		
Number of school districts	19	17 742
Number of schools	591	99 639
Number of students	424 766	49 315 842
Student-teacher ratio	18.5	15.5
Expenditures per student (dollars)	$7 806	. . .
Averaged freshman graduation rate, 2005–2006	55.8	. . .
Dropout rate, grades 9–12, 2005–2006	7.7	3.7
Students eligible for free or reduced-price lunch (percent)	. . .	41.2
English-language learners (percent)	16.6	5.1
Students with IEP (percent)	11.4	12.7
Private Schools, 2007–2008 (except where noted)		
Number of schools	161	33 740
Number of students	22 310	5 072 451
High school graduates, 2006–2007	695	306 605
Student-teacher ratio	14.4	11.1

Table NV-12. Reported Voting and Registration of the Voting-Age Population, November 2008

(Number in thousands, percent.)

Item	Total population	Total citizen population	Registered			Voted		
			Total registered	Percent registered (total population)	Percent registered (total citizen population)	Total voted	Percent voted (total population)	Percent voted (total citizen population)
U.S. total	225 499	206 072	146 311	64.9	71.0	131 144	58.2	63.6
State total	1 946	1 714	1 147	59.0	66.9	1 027	52.8	59.9
Sex								
Male	982	863	581	59.1	67.3	519	52.8	60.1
Female	964	851	567	58.8	66.6	509	52.8	59.8
Race								
White alone	1 572	1 396	942	60.0	67.5	850	54.1	60.9
White non-Hispanic alone	1 212	1 194	830	68.5	69.5	746	61.5	62.5
Black alone	148	137	114	77.0	83.5	105	71.1	77.1
Asian alone	156	117	45	28.8	38.5	35	22.3	29.8
Hispanic (of any race)	392	228	131	33.3	57.2	119	30.4	52.1
White alone or in combination	1 604	1 424	958	59.7	67.3	863	53.8	60.6
Black alone or in combination	161	146	120	74.9	82.5	110	68.6	75.6
Asian alone or in combination	160	121	48	29.8	39.4	35	21.7	28.6

Table NV-13. Crime

(Number, rate per 100,000.)

Item	State			U.S.		
	2007	2008	Percent change	2007	2008	Percent change
Population	2 565 382	2 600 167	1.4	301 621 157	304 059 724	0.8
VIOLENT CRIME						
Number	19 257	18 837	-2.2	1 408 337	1 382 012	-1.9
Rate	750.6	724.5	-3.5	466.9	454.5	-2.7
Murder and Nonnegligent Manslaughter						
Number	192	163	-15.1	16 929	16 272	-3.9
Rate	7.5	6.3	-16.2	5.6	5.4	-4.7
Forcible Rape						
Number	1 096	1 102	0.5	90 427	89 000	-1.6
Rate	42.7	42.4	-0.8	30.0	29.3	-2.4
Robbery						
Number	6 932	6 473	-6.6	445 125	441 855	-0.7
Rate	270.2	248.9	-7.9	147.6	145.3	-1.5
Aggravated Assault						
Number	11 037	11 099	0.6	855 856	834 885	-2.5
Rate	430.2	426.9	-0.8	283.8	274.6	-3.2
PROPERTY CRIME						
Number	96 916	89 640	-7.5	9 843 481	9 767 915	-0.8
Rate	3 777.8	3 447.5	-8.7	3 263.5	3 212.5	-1.6
Burglary						
Number	24 840	24 156	-2.8	2 179 140	2 222 196	2.0
Rate	968.3	929.0	-4.1	722.5	730.8	1.2
Larceny-Theft						
Number	49 745	49 581	-0.3	6 568 572	6 588 873	0.3
Rate	1 939.1	1 906.8	-1.7	2 177.8	2 167.0	-0.5
Motor Vehicle Theft						
Number	22 331	15 903	-28.8	1 095 769	956 846	-12.7
Rate	870.5	611.6	-29.7	363.3	314.7	-13.4

Table NV-14. State Government Finances, 2007

(Dollars, percent distribution.)

Item	Thousands of dollars	Percent distribution
Total Revenue	14 183 611	X
General revenue	9 733 699	68.6
Intergovernmental revenue	2 091 256	14.7
Taxes	6 304 753	44.5
General sales	3 212 848	22.7
Selective sales	1 913 216	13.5
License taxes	801 560	5.7
Individual income tax	0	0.0
Corporate income tax	0	0.0
Other taxes	377 129	2.7
Current charges	662 572	4.7
Miscellaneous general revenue	675 118	4.8
Utility revenue	74 590	0.5
Liquor store revenue	0	0.0
Insurance trust revenue	4 375 322	30.8
Total Expenditure	10 755 326	100.0
Intergovernmental expenditure	3 826 539	35.6
Direct expenditure	6 928 787	64.4
Current operation	4 391 712	40.8
Capital outlay	965 809	9.0
Insurance benefits and repayments	1 220 038	11.3
Assistance and subsidies	157 558	1.5
Interest on debt	193 670	1.8
Exhibit: Salaries and wages	1 553 557	14.4
Total Expenditure	10 755 326	100.0
General expenditure	9 458 516	87.9
Intergovernmental expenditure	3 826 539	35.6
Direct expenditure	5 631 977	52.4
Education	3 924 517	36.5
Public welfare	1 641 032	15.3
Hospitals	240 770	2.2
Health	263 325	2.4
Highways	810 196	7.5
Police protection	96 649	0.9
Correction	294 380	2.7
Natural resources	140 048	1.3
Parks and recreation	23 480	0.2
Government administration	341 490	3.2
Interest on general debt	189 849	1.8
Other and unallocable	1 492 780	13.9
Utility expenditure	76 772	0.7
Liquor store expenditure	0	0.0
Insurance trust expenditure	1 220 038	11.3
Debt at End of Fiscal Year	4 140 910	X
Cash and Security Holdings	27 766 307	X

Table NV-15. State Government Tax Collections, 2008

(Dollars, percent distribution.)

Item	Thousands of dollars	Percent distribution
Total Taxes	6 115 584	X
Property taxes	192 050	3.1
Sales and gross receipts	4 930 452	80.6
General sales and gross receipts	3 077 433	50.3
Selective sales taxes	1 853 019	30.3
Alcoholic beverages	40 401	0.7
Amusements	1 047 800	17.1
Insurance premiums	256 814	4.2
Motor fuels	311 953	5.1
Public utilities	12 084	0.2
Tobacco products	134 617	2.2
Other selective sales	49 350	0.8
Licenses	826 397	13.5
Amusements	96 682	1.6
Corporation	72 249	1.2
Hunting and fishing	8 563	0.1
Motor vehicle	169 896	2.8
Motor vehicle operators	16 133	0.3
Occupation and business, NEC	457 382	7.5
Other licenses	5 492	0.1
Other taxes	166 685	2.7
Death and gift	0	0.0
Documentary and stock transfer	92 555	1.5
Severance	74 130	1.2

Table NV-16. Agriculture

(Number, acres, and dollars.)

Item	2002 Number	2002 Percent of total	2007 Number	2007 Percent of total	Percent change, 2002–2007
Number of farms	2 989		3 131		4.8
Farm Size					
Average size of farm (acres)	2 118		1 873		-11.6
Farms by size (number of farms)					
Fewer than 50 acres	1 396	46.7	1 529	48.8	9.5
50 to 499 acres	870	29.1	938	30.0	7.8
500 acres or more	723	24.2	664	21.2	-8.2
Land (Acres)					
Total land in farms	6 330 622		5 865 392		-7.3
Total cropland	940 295	14.9	753 718	12.9	-19.8
Total harvested cropland	549 076	8.7	504 311	8.6	-8.2
Irrigated land	746 653	11.8	691 030	11.8	-7.4
Value of Sales (Dollars)					
Agricultural products sold ($1,000)	446 989		513 269		14.8
Average sales per farm	149 545		163 931		9.6
Sales of crops	157 730	35.3	219 341	42.7	39.1
Sales of livestock, poultry, and their products	289 259	64.7	293 928	57.3	1.6
Value of Sales (Number of Farms)					
Less than $10,000	1 655	55.4	1 786	57.0	7.9
$10,000 to $99,999	753	25.2	730	23.3	-3.1
$100,000 to $999,999	512	17.1	524	16.7	2.3
$1,000,000 or more	69	2.3	91	2.9	31.9
Farms by Type of Organization (Number of Farms)					
Family	2 499	83.6	2 542	81.2	1.7
Partnership	205	6.9	284	9.1	38.5
Corporation	200	6.7	230	7.3	15.0
Other: cooperative, estate or trust, institutional, etc	85	2.8	75	2.4	-11.8
Value of Land and Buildings (Dollars)					
Estimated market value of land and buildings ($1,000)	3 596 558		2 849 414		-20.8
Land and buildings average value per farm	1 148 693		953 619		-17.0
Average value per acre	613		446		-27.2
Government Payments					
Number of farms receiving government payments	439	14.7	331	10.6	-24.6
Payments (thousands of dollars)	4 322		4 007		-7.3
Average payment per farm	9 845		12 105		23.0
Farm Operator Characteristics					
Farm operators whose principal occupation is farming	1 754	58.7	1 650	52.7	-5.9
Farm operators whose principal occupation is other	1 235	41.3	1 481	47.3	19.9
Average age principal operator (years)	55.9		57.5		2.9

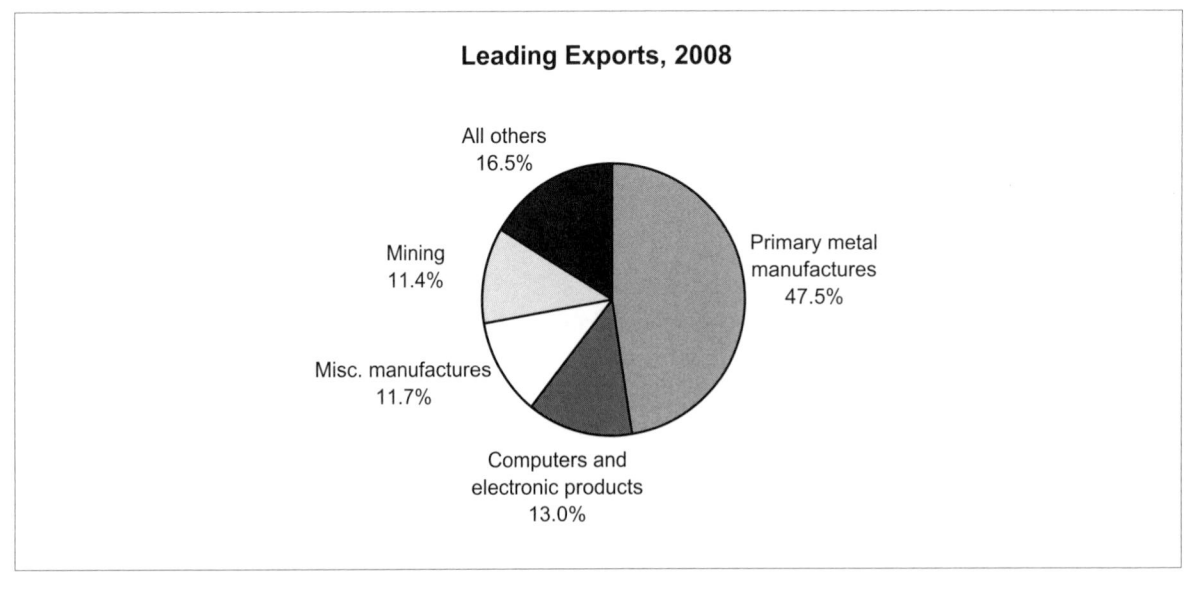

Leading Exports, 2008

All others 16.5%

Mining 11.4%

Misc. manufactures 11.7%

Computers and electronic products 13.0%

Primary metal manufactures 47.5%

NEW HAMPSHIRE

Facts and Figures

Location: Northeastern United States; bordered on the N by Canada (Quebec), on the E by Maine, on the SE by the Atlantic Ocean, on the S by Massachusetts, and on the W by Vermont

Area: 9,350 sq. mi. (24,216 sq. km.); rank—46th

Population: 1,315,809 (2008 est.); rank—41st

Principal Cities: capital—Concord; largest—Manchester

Statehood: June 21, 1788; 9th state

U.S. Congress: 2 senators, 2 representatives

State Motto: Live Free or Die

State Song: "Old New Hampshire"

State Nickname: The Granite State

Abbreviations: NH; N.H.

State Symbols: flower—purple lilac; tree—white birch; bird—purple finch

At a Glance

- With an increase in population of 6.5 percent, New Hampshire ranked 23rd among the states in growth from 2000 to 2008.
- An estimated 9,030 marriages took place in New Hampshire in 2008, compared to 4,909 divorces.
- The 2007 home ownership rate in New Hampshire was 73.3 percent; its ranking of 9th was tied with that of Indiana.
- New Hampshire's median household income in 2007 was $62,369, 6th among the states.
- In New Hampshire, 7.1 percent of the population lived below the poverty level in 2007, ranking it 50th.
- In 2006-07, 11 percent of New Hampshirites did not have health insurance, compared to 15.5 percent of the total U.S. population.
- In 2007, 3.6 percent of New Hampshirites were unemployed, compared to 4.6 percent nationwide.
- New Hampshire ranked 8th in the nation with 32.5 percent of its population 25 years old and over having a bachelor's degree in 2007.
- New Hampshire's violent crime rate in 2007 was 137.3 per 100,000 population, compared to 466.9 for the entire nation.
- New Hampshire had one physician for every 311 people in 2007, compared to one physician for every 325 people nationwide.
- In the 2008 election, 71.3 percent of New Hampshire's eligible voters voted, compared to 61.7 percent of eligible voters nationwide.
- New Hampshire ranked 39th among the states receiving federal aid in 2007, with $1,239 per capita.
- New Hampshire's gross domestic product was $57 billion in 2007; it ranked 41st among the states.
- With $2.9 billion in exports in 2007, New Hampshire ranked 42nd in exports.
- New Hampshirites consumed 313 billion Btu's of energy in 2006; the state ranked 46th in total consumption.
- In 2007, New Hampshire exported $19 million worth of agricultural products, less than 1 percent of the U.S. total.

Table NH-1. Population by Sex, Age, Race, and Hispanic Origin

(Number, percent.)

Sex, age, race, and Hispanic origin	1990	2000	2008	Average annual percent change, 2000–2008
Total Population	1 109 252	1 235 786	1 315 809	0.8
Percent of total U.S. population	0.4	0.4	0.4	X
Sex				
Male	543 544	607 687	649 087	0.8
Female	565 708	628 099	666 722	0.7
Age				
Under 5 years	84 565	75 685	75 297	-0.1
5 to 19 years	228 830	268 480	254 523	-0.7
20 to 64 years	670 828	743 651	816 011	1.2
65 years and over	125 029	147 970	169 978	1.7
Median age (years)	32.7	37.1	40.2	X
Race and Hispanic Origin[1]				
One race				
White	1 087 433	1 186 851	1 256 429	0.7
Black	7 198	9 035	16 015	7.4
American Indian and Alaskan Native	2 134	2 964	3 642	2.6
Asian[2]	9 343	15 931	25 147	5.9
Native Hawaiian and Other Pacific Islander	X	371	549	5.0
Two or more races	X	13 214	14 027	0.7
Hispanic (of any race)	11 333	20 489	34 676	6.8

[1]Data on race in 2000 and 2008 are not comparable to 1990. Individuals could only report one race in the 1990 census but could report one or more races on the 2000 census.
[2]Data in 1990 refer to Asian and Pacific Islanders.

Table NH-2. Marital Status

(Number, percent distribution.)

Sex and marital status	1990	2000	2007
Males, 15 Years and Over	422 521	476 409	523 636
Never married	28.6	27.7	31.2
Now married, except separated	60.2	59.1	55.6
Separated	1.4	1.2	1.0
Widowed	2.3	2.4	2.4
Divorced	7.5	9.6	9.8
Females, 15 Years and Over	449 800	502 232	551 837
Never married	22.6	22.3	25.2
Now married, except separated	56.4	55.7	51.9
Separated	1.7	1.5	1.6
Widowed	10.2	9.2	8.5
Divorced	9.1	11.3	12.9

Table NH-3. Households and Housing Characteristics

(Number, percent, and dollars.)

Item	1990	2000	2007	Average annual percent change, 2000–2007
Total Households	411 186	474 606	501 505	0.8
Family households	292 601	323 651	341 922	0.8
Married-couple family	245 307	262 438	275 674	0.7
Other family	47 294	61 213	66 248	1.1
Male householder, no wife present	12 517	18 261	19 592	1.0
Female householder, no husband present	34 777	42 952	46 656	1.2
Nonfamily households	118 585	150 955	159 583	0.8
Householder living alone	90 364	116 014	120 756	0.6
Householder not living alone	28 221	34 941	38 827	1.5
Housing Characteristics				
Total housing units	503 904	547 024	594 126	1.2
Occupied housing units	411 186	474 606	501 505	0.8
Owner-occupied	280 372	330 700	371 658	1.7
Renter-occupied	130 814	143 906	129 847	-1.5
Average size	2.62	2.53	2.54	X
Financial Characteristics				
Median gross rent of renter-occupied housing units (dollars)	549	646	892	4.7
Median monthly owner costs for housing units with a mortgage (dollars)	1 000	1 226	1 830	5.9
Median value of owner-occupied housing units (dollars)	129 300	133 300	261 800	10.1

Table NH-4. Median Income and Poverty Status, 2007

(Number, percent.)

Characteristic	State		U.S.	
	Number	Percent	Number	Percent
Median Income				
Households (dollars)	62 369	X	50 740	X
Families (dollars)	74 625	X	61 173	X
Below Poverty Level				
Sex				
Male	40 707	6.5	16 576 071	11.5
Female	49 497	7.6	21 476 176	14.3
Age				
Under 18 years	25 622	8.8	13 097 100	18.0
Related children under 18 years	24 216	8.3	12 728 964	17.6
18 to 64 years	54 445	6.6	21 495 507	11.6
65 years and over	10 137	6.5	3 459 640	9.5

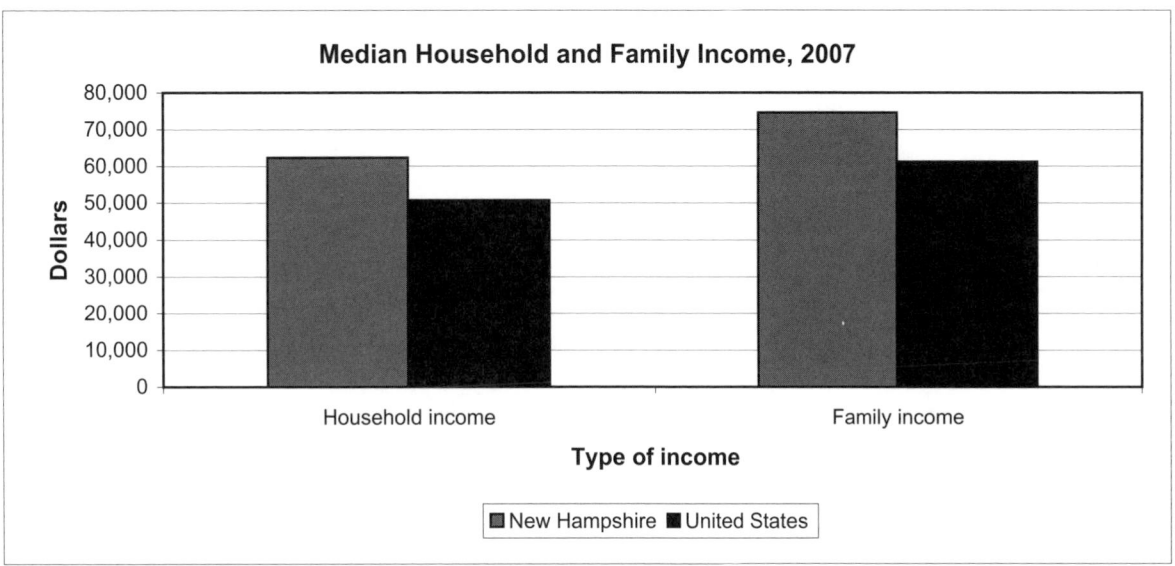

Table NH-5. Health Insurance Coverage Status for All Persons and Children Under 18 Years of Age

(Number, percent.)

Item	2000	2001	2002	2003	2004	2005	2006	2007
ALL PERSONS	1 233	1 258	1 266	1 264	1 293	1 301	1 309	1 314
Covered by Private or Government Health Insurance								
Number	1 133	1 145	1 146	1 142	1 163	1 175	1 159	1 177
Percent	92.0	91.0	90.5	90.3	89.9	90.3	88.5	89.5
Not Covered								
Number	99	113	120	122	131	126	150	137
Percent	8.0	9.0	9.5	9.7	10.1	9.7	11.5	10.5
Percent in the U.S. not covered	13.7	14.1	14.7	15.1	14.9	15.3	15.8	15.3
CHILDREN UNDER 18 YEARS OF AGE	295	289	304	309	305	298	301	296
Covered by Private or Government Health Insurance								
Number	274	269	290	294	286	282	278	277
Percent	92.7	93.0	95.4	95.2	93.8	94.7	92.5	93.5
Not Covered								
Number	21	20	14	15	19	16	22	19
Percent	7.3	7.0	4.6	4.8	6.2	5.3	7.5	6.5
Percent in the U.S. not covered	11.6	11.3	11.2	11.0	10.5	10.9	11.7	11.0

Table NH-6. Employment Status by Demographic Group, Preliminary 2008

(Number, percent.)

Characteristic	Civilian noninstitutional population	Civilian labor force		Employment		Unemployed	
		Number	Percent of population	Number	Percent of population	Number	Unemployment rate
TOTAL	1 049	743	70.8	715	68.1	28	3.8
Sex							
Men	513	392	76.0	376	73.2	16	4.0
Women	536	352	66.0	339	63.2	13	3.6
Race, Sex, and Hispanic Origin							
White	1 006	713	70.9	686	68.2	27	3.7
Men	491	374	76.2	359	73.1	15	4.0
Women	514	338	65.8	327	63.5	12	3.4
Black or African American	...	...	...	...	...	...	...
Men	...	...	...	...	...	...	...
Women	...	...	...	...	...	...	...
Hispanic	18	14	77.8	13	74.0	1	5.0
Men	...	...	...	...	...	...	...
Women	...	...	...	...	...	...	...
Age							
16 to 19 years	80	42	52.2	36	45.2	6	13.5
20 to 24 years	84	67	78.9	63	74.3	4	5.9
25 to 34 years	148	130	87.8	125	84.9	4	3.4
35 to 44 years	188	166	88.2	161	85.7	5	2.8
45 to 54 years	223	193	86.5	188	84.2	5	2.7
55 to 64 years	159	117	73.2	114	71.2	3	2.7
65 years and over	167	29	17.6	28	16.9	1	3.9

Note: Data in Table 6 are from the Current Population Survey (CPS) and do not match the estimates in Table 7. See notes and definitions for more details.

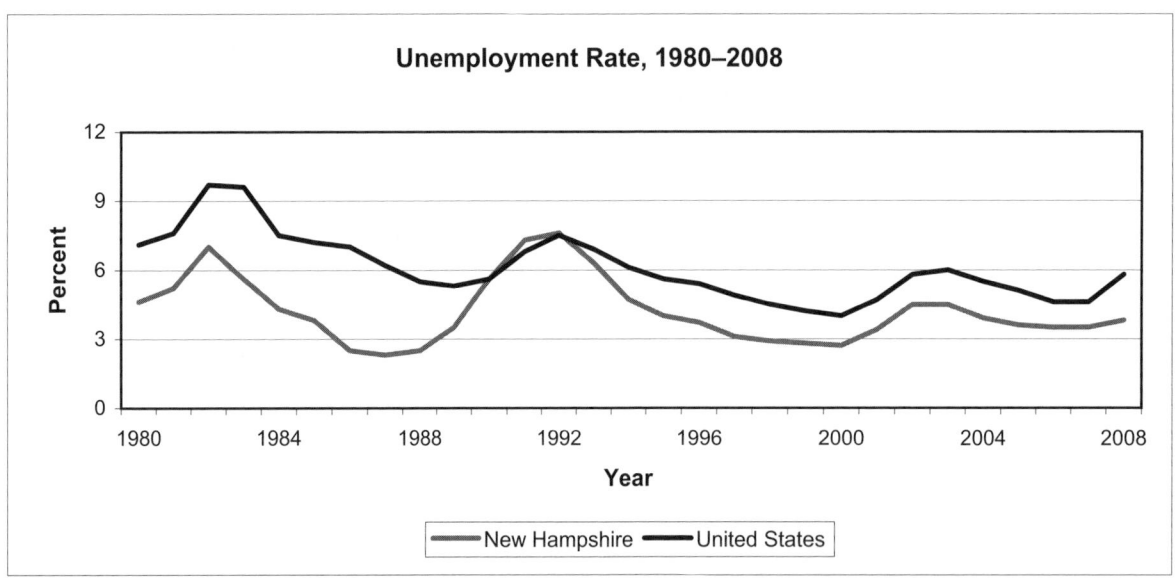

Unemployment Rate, 1980–2008

Table NH-7. Employment Status of the Civilian Noninstitutional Population Age 16 Years and Over

(Number, percent.)

Year	Civilian labor force	Civilian participation rate	Employed	Unemployed	Unemployment rate
1998	670 560	72.8	651 292	19 268	2.9
1999	684 904	73.2	666 066	18 838	2.8
2000	694 254	73.1	675 541	18 713	2.7
2001	704 908	73.0	680 706	24 202	3.4
2002	712 180	72.7	679 818	32 362	4.5
2003	711 065	71.6	679 420	31 645	4.5
2004	715 555	71.1	687 855	27 700	3.9
2005	723 402	71.1	697 120	26 282	3.6
2006	732 838	71.2	707 129	25 709	3.5
2007	738 212	71.1	712 231	25 981	3.5
2008	738 858	70.7	710 623	28 235	3.8

Table NH-8. Employment and Average Wages by Industry

(Estimates for 2001–2006 are based on the 2002 North American Industry Classification System [NAICS]. Estimates for 2007 are based on the 2007 NAICS.)

Industry	2001	2002	2003	2004	2005	2006	2007
	Number of jobs						
WAGE AND SALARY EMPLOYMENT BY INDUSTRY	647 747	642 652	644 672	651 088	657 077	663 915	667 162
Farm Wage and Salary Employment	1 895	1 767	1 856	1 551	1 554	1 401	1 402
Nonfarm Wage and Salary Employment	645 852	640 885	642 816	649 537	655 523	662 514	665 760
Private wage and salary employment	557 773	549 884	549 457	557 661	563 593	568 901	571 591
Forestry, fishing, hunting, and other	1 336	1 233	1 166	1 153	1 114	1 031	978
Mining	478	479	492	529	570	591	688
Utilities	2 800	2 939	2 853	2 795	2 772	2 790	2 791
Construction	28 324	29 082	29 952	30 531	30 553	30 499	28 462
Manufacturing	98 147	85 525	80 876	80 608	80 616	78 960	78 327
Durable goods manufacturing	74 256	63 589	59 941	60 722	61 435	59 962	59 957
Nondurable goods manufacturing	23 891	21 936	20 935	19 886	19 181	18 998	18 370
Wholesale trade	26 923	27 143	27 123	27 675	27 849	28 356	28 659
Retail trade	97 944	99 015	99 261	100 082	100 637	101 421	100 808
Transportation and warehousing	13 213	12 965	13 151	13 034	13 259	13 254	13 177
Information	13 575	12 882	12 236	12 525	12 757	12 584	12 372
Finance and insurance	27 457	28 248	28 571	28 684	29 127	29 588	29 346
Real estate and rental and leasing	8 198	8 065	8 098	8 336	8 543	8 356	8 177
Professional and technical services	28 153	26 794	26 424	27 427	29 533	30 745	31 584
Management of companies and enterprises	7 173	6 426	6 152	7 038	7 391	7 412	7 632
Administrative and waste services	23 686	22 861	23 552	24 517	25 116	26 221	28 094
Educational services	20 911	22 093	22 633	22 348	22 372	21 986	22 849
Health care and social assistance	70 858	73 234	75 150	76 301	77 957	80 562	82 869
Arts, entertainment, and recreation	11 212	11 523	11 886	12 483	11 532	11 724	11 441
Accommodation and food services	49 643	50 754	51 061	52 697	53 122	53 596	53 766
Other services, except public administration	27 742	28 623	28 820	28 898	28 773	29 225	29 571
Government and government enterprises	88 079	91 001	93 359	91 876	91 930	93 613	94 169
	Dollars						
AVERAGE WAGES AND SALARIES BY INDUSTRY	34 689	35 374	36 539	38 476	39 880	41 700	43 083
Average Farm Wages and Salaries	18 503	24 382	19 949	23 735	19 560	24 557	21 958
Average Nonfarm Wages and Salaries	34 736	35 404	36 587	38 512	39 928	41 737	43 127
Average private wages and salaries	35 485	36 096	37 212	39 085	40 535	42 513	43 834
Forestry, fishing, hunting, and other	27 513	27 985	30 281	32 239	33 291	36 406	41 303
Mining	43 916	46 927	43 439	47 204	49 549	49 878	50 541
Utilities	64 404	66 424	69 058	79 232	75 019	78 192	80 551
Construction	42 169	43 800	42 086	43 400	45 285	46 927	48 410
Manufacturing	44 670	46 077	48 187	50 626	51 867	55 441	57 772
Durable goods manufacturing	46 509	48 211	50 633	53 169	54 457	58 700	61 136
Nondurable goods manufacturing	38 954	39 889	41 185	42 860	43 570	45 154	46 795
Wholesale trade	59 829	59 168	60 248	62 832	66 316	68 540	71 316
Retail trade	23 163	23 901	25 067	25 584	26 044	26 253	26 460
Transportation and warehousing	30 561	30 978	31 459	33 477	33 724	35 079	35 718
Information	55 892	54 703	56 192	59 133	61 593	62 806	67 221
Finance and insurance	53 788	56 631	61 028	64 009	65 583	68 642	71 723
Real estate and rental and leasing	30 276	34 576	36 699	38 456	40 864	39 802	37 946
Professional and technical services	56 708	56 711	57 363	59 639	63 768	68 758	68 872
Management of companies and enterprises	69 027	67 327	73 448	91 696	93 353	116 449	104 996
Administrative and waste services	28 190	29 094	29 580	31 459	33 007	34 791	38 645
Educational services	26 328	28 138	30 051	32 195	33 198	35 177	36 665
Health care and social assistance	32 800	34 437	35 750	37 383	38 848	40 233	42 035
Arts, entertainment, and recreation	17 601	17 439	18 444	19 612	20 661	21 419	23 084
Accommodation and food services	14 994	15 328	15 875	16 413	16 635	17 247	17 688
Other services, except public administration	22 830	23 931	24 627	25 600	26 123	26 929	27 894
Government and government enterprises	29 990	31 221	32 909	35 031	36 206	37 020	38 838

Table NH-9. Employment Characteristics by Family Type

(Number, percent.)

Family type and labor force status	2005		2006		2007	
	Total	Families with own children under 18 years	Total	Families with own children under 18 years	Total	Families with own children under 18 years
TOTAL FAMILIES	337 615	162 496	335 509	152 073	341 922	155 423
FAMILY TYPE AND LABOR FORCE STATUS						
Married Coupled Families	269 992	120 247	267 935	110 669	275 674	114 242
Both husband and wife in labor force	59.1	69.7	60.7	71.4	59.7	69.5
Husband in labor force, wife not in labor force	19.5	24.2	19.7	23.7	20.3	26.8
Wife in labor force, husband not in labor force	6.6	3.3	6.2	3.6	7.2	3.1
Both husband and wife not in labor force	14.9	2.8	13.4	1.3	12.8	0.7
Other Families	67 623	42 249	67 574	41 404	66 248	41 181
Female householder, no husband present	70.5	72.1	68.0	71.3	70.4	72.2
In labor force	50.7	56.9	52.2	59.4	54.9	62.2
Not in labor force	19.8	15.3	15.9	11.9	15.5	10.0
Male householder, no wife present	29.5	27.9	32.0	28.7	29.6	27.8
In labor force	24.8	25.7	26.7	25.2	24.1	24.8
Not in labor force	4.7	2.2	5.2	3.5	5.4	3.0

Table NH-10. School Enrollment and Educational Attainment, 2007

(Number, percent.)

Item	State	U.S.
Enrollment		
Total population 3 years and over	1 272 745	289 295 761
Enrolled in school	335 383	79 329 527
Enrolled in preschool (percent)	5.8	6.2
Enrolled in grades K-12 (percent)	66.8	67.6
Enrolled in college or graduate school (percent)	27.3	26.2
Attainment		
Total population 25 years and over	895 981	197 892 369
Less than a high school diploma (percent)	9.5	15.5
High school diploma or more (percent)	90.5	84.5
Bachelor's degree or more (percent)	32.5	27.5
Graduate degree or more (percent)	11.5	10.1

Table NH-11. Educational Indicators

(Number, percent.)

Item	State	U.S.
Public Schools, 2006–2007 (except where noted)		
Number of school districts	274	17 742
Number of schools	483	99 639
Number of students	203 572	49 315 842
Student-teacher ratio	13.1	15.5
Expenditures per student (dollars)	$11 037	. . .
Averaged freshman graduation rate, 2005–2006	81.1	. . .
Dropout rate, grades 9–12, 2005–2006	3.2	3.7
Students eligible for free or reduced-price lunch (percent)	17.7	41.2
English-language learners (percent)	1.6	5.1
Students with IEP (percent)	15.4	12.7
Private Schools, 2007–2008 (except where noted)		
Number of schools	312	33 740
Number of students	23 200	5 072 451
High school graduates, 2006–2007	2 294	306 605
Student-teacher ratio	7.8	11.1

Table NH-12. Reported Voting and Registration of the Voting-Age Population, November 2008

(Number in thousands, percent.)

Item	Total population	Total citizen population	Registered			Voted		
			Total registered	Percent registered (total population)	Percent registered (total citizen population)	Total voted	Percent voted (total population)	Percent voted (total citizen population)
U.S. total	225 499	206 072	146 311	64.9	71.0	131 144	58.2	63.6
State total	1 015	994	756	74.5	76.0	708	69.8	71.2
Sex								
Male	493	485	360	73.0	74.2	337	68.3	69.5
Female	522	509	396	75.9	77.7	371	71.2	72.9
Race								
White alone	974	958	737	75.7	76.9	691	71.0	72.1
White non-Hispanic alone	957	945	727	76.0	77.0	683	71.4	72.3
Black alone	9	8	4	. . .	. . .	4	. . .	. . .
Asian alone	17	12	5	. . .	. . .	5	. . .	. . .
Hispanic (of any race)	18	14	11	. . .	. . .	8	. . .	. . .
White alone or in combination	986	971	744	75.4	76.6	697	70.7	71.8
Black alone or in combination	12	11	5	. . .	. . .	5	. . .	. . .
Asian alone or in combination	17	13	6	. . .	. . .	5	. . .	. . .

Table NH-13. Crime

(Number, rate per 100,000.)

Item	State			U.S.		
	2007	2008	Percent change	2007	2008	Percent change
Population	1 315 828	1 315 809	0.0	301 621 157	304 059 724	0.8
VIOLENT CRIME						
Number	1 807	2 069	14.5	1 408 337	1 382 012	-1.9
Rate	137.3	157.2	14.5	466.9	454.5	-2.7
Murder and Nonnegligent Manslaughter						
Number	15	13	-13.3	16 929	16 272	-3.9
Rate	1.1	1.0	-13.3	5.6	5.4	-4.7
Forcible Rape						
Number	333	391	17.4	90 427	89 000	-1.6
Rate	25.3	29.7	17.4	30.0	29.3	-2.4
Robbery						
Number	432	419	-3.0	445 125	441 855	-0.7
Rate	32.8	31.8	-3.0	147.6	145.3	-1.5
Aggravated Assault						
Number	1 027	1 246	21.3	855 856	834 885	-2.5
Rate	78.0	94.7	21.3	283.8	274.6	-3.2
PROPERTY CRIME						
Number	24 896	27 526	10.6	9 843 481	9 767 915	-0.8
Rate	1 892.0	2 091.9	10.6	3 263.5	3 212.5	-1.6
Burglary						
Number	4 986	4 286	-14.0	2 179 140	2 222 196	2.0
Rate	378.9	325.7	-14.0	722.5	730.8	1.2
Larceny-Theft						
Number	18 611	21 853	17.4	6 568 572	6 588 873	0.3
Rate	1 414.4	1 660.8	17.4	2 177.8	2 167.0	-0.5
Motor Vehicle Theft						
Number	1 299	1 387	6.8	1 095 769	956 846	-12.7
Rate	98.7	105.4	6.8	363.3	314.7	-13.4

Table NH-14. State Government Finances, 2007

(Dollars, percent distribution.)

Item	Thousands of dollars	Percent distribution
Total Revenue	7 171 927	X
General revenue	5 471 722	76.3
Intergovernmental revenue	1 775 088	24.8
Taxes	2 175 057	30.3
General sales	0	0.0
Selective sales	734 894	10.2
License taxes	209 662	2.9
Individual income tax	107 452	1.5
Corporate income tax	595 789	8.3
Other taxes	527 260	7.4
Current charges	736 814	10.3
Miscellaneous general revenue	784 763	10.9
Utility revenue	119	0.0
Liquor store revenue	438 700	6.1
Insurance trust revenue	1 261 386	17.6
Total Expenditure	6 226 121	100.0
Intergovernmental expenditure	1 408 445	22.6
Direct expenditure	4 817 676	77.4
Current operation	3 466 957	55.7
Capital outlay	405 815	6.5
Insurance benefits and repayments	456 494	7.3
Assistance and subsidies	123 974	2.0
Interest on debt	364 436	5.9
Exhibit: Salaries and wages	897 160	14.4
Total Expenditure	6 226 121	100.0
General expenditure	5 381 944	86.4
Intergovernmental expenditure	1 408 445	22.6
Direct expenditure	3 973 499	63.8
Education	1 942 448	31.2
Public welfare	1 445 654	23.2
Hospitals	56 244	0.9
Health	143 143	2.3
Highways	438 894	7.0
Police protection	49 463	0.8
Correction	110 297	1.8
Natural resources	63 123	1.0
Parks and recreation	12 873	0.2
Government administration	214 711	3.4
Interest on general debt	364 436	5.9
Other and unallocable	540 658	8.7
Utility expenditure	13 539	0.2
Liquor store expenditure	374 144	6.0
Insurance trust expenditure	456 494	7.3
Debt at End of Fiscal Year	7 690 409	X
Cash and Security Holdings	13 193 561	X

Table NH-15. State Government Tax Collections, 2008

(Dollars, percent distribution.)

Item	Thousands of dollars	Percent distribution
Total Taxes	2 251 179	X
Property taxes	387 623	17.2
Sales and gross receipts	792 947	35.2
Selective sales taxes	792 947	35.2
Alcoholic beverages	12 508	0.6
Amusements	236	0.0
Insurance premiums	85 820	3.8
Motor fuels	137 206	6.1
Pari-mutuels	2 916	0.1
Public utilities	78 723	3.5
Tobacco products	169 789	7.5
Other selective sales	305 749	13.6
Licenses	215 878	9.6
Alcoholic beverages	3 061	0.1
Amusements	322	0.0
Corporation	4 390	0.2
Hunting and fishing	9 720	0.4
Motor vehicle	93 679	4.2
Motor vehicle operators	13 226	0.6
Public utility	7 123	0.3
Occupation and business, NEC	81 536	3.6
Other licenses	2 821	0.1
Income taxes	732 730	32.5
Individual income	117 936	5.2
Corporation net income	614 794	27.3
Other taxes	122 001	5.4
Death and gift	132	0.0
Documentary and stock transfer	121 869	5.4

Table NH-16. Agriculture

(Number, acres, and dollars.)

Item	2002		2007		Percent change, 2002–2007
	Number	Percent of total	Number	Percent of total	
Number of farms	3 363		4 166		23.9
Farm Size					
Average size of farm (acres)	132		113		-14.4
Farms by size (number of farms)					
Fewer than 50 acres	1 542	45.9	2 159	51.8	40.0
50 to 499 acres	1 647	49.0	1 850	44.4	12.3
500 acres or more	174	5.2	157	3.8	-9.8
Land (Acres)					
Total land in farms	444 879		471 911		6.1
Total cropland	129 388	29.1	128 938	27.3	-0.3
Total harvested cropland	95 983	21.6	99 520	21.1	3.7
Irrigated land	2 292	0.5	2 482	0.5	8.3
Value of Sales (Dollars)					
Agricultural products sold ($1,000)	144 835		199 051		37.4
Average sales per farm	43 067		47 780		10.9
Sales of crops	83 149	57.4	106 467	53.5	28.0
Sales of livestock, poultry, and their products	61 686	42.6	92 584	46.5	50.1
Value of Sales (Number of Farms)					
Less than $10,000	2 483	73.8	3 003	72.1	20.9
$10,000 to $99,999	627	18.6	877	21.1	39.9
$100,000 to $999,999	233	6.9	257	6.2	10.3
$1,000,000 or more	20	0.6	29	0.7	45.0
Farms by Type of Organization (Number of Farms)					
Family	2 917	86.7	3 551	85.2	21.7
Partnership	206	6.1	299	7.2	45.1
Corporation	157	4.7	220	5.3	40.1
Other: cooperative, estate or trust, institutional, etc	83	2.5	96	2.3	15.7
Value of Land and Buildings (Dollars)					
Estimated market value of land and buildings ($1,000)	2 326 230		1 354 386		-41.8
Land and buildings average value per farm	558 385		400 943		-28.2
Average value per acre	4 929		3 131		-36.5
Government Payments					
Number of farms receiving government payments	359	10.7	423	10.2	17.8
Payments (thousands of dollars)	3 823		2 474		-35.3
Average payment per farm	10 648		5 848		-45.1
Farm Operator Characteristics					
Farm operators whose principal occupation is farming	1 636	48.6	1 930	46.3	18.0
Farm operators whose principal occupation is other	1 727	51.4	2 236	53.7	29.5
Average age principal operator (years)	54.1		56.2		3.9

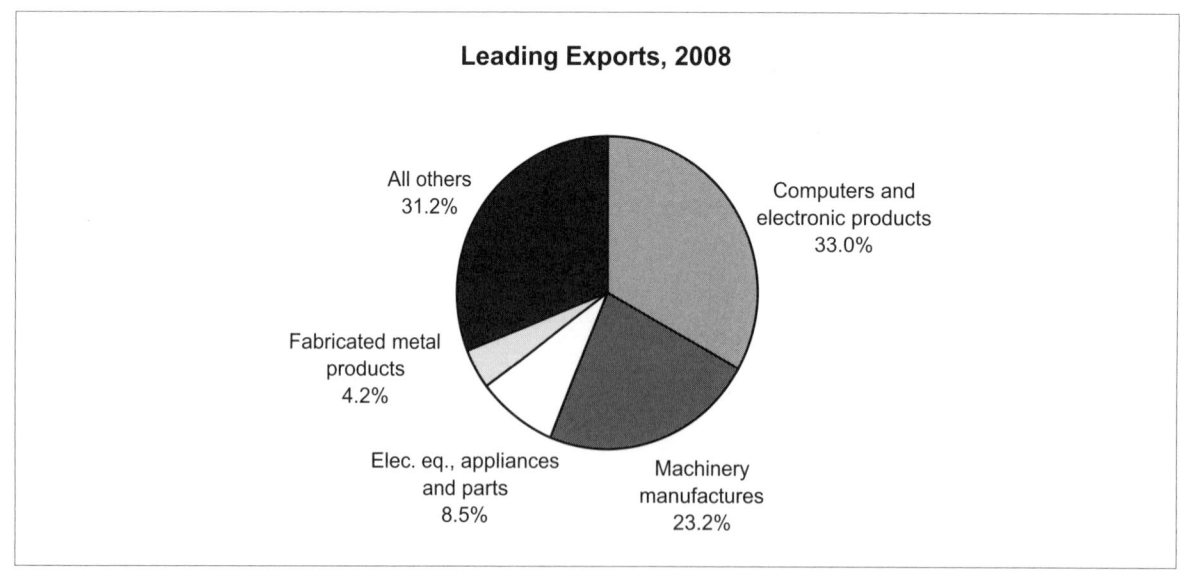

Leading Exports, 2008

All others 31.2%

Computers and electronic products 33.0%

Fabricated metal products 4.2%

Elec. eq., appliances and parts 8.5%

Machinery manufactures 23.2%

NEW JERSEY

Facts and Figures

Location: Middle Atlantic region of the United States; bordered on the N and NE by New York, on the E by the Atlantic Ocean, on the S by Delaware Bay, and on the W by Delaware and Pennsylvania

Area: 8,721 sq. mi. (22,588 sq. km.); rank—47th

Population: 8,682,661 (2008 est.); rank—11th

Principal Cities: capital—Trenton; largest—Newark

Statehood: December 18, 1787; 3rd state

U.S. Congress: 2 senators, 13 representatives

State Motto: Liberty and Prosperity

State Song: None

State Nickname: The Garden State

Abbreviations: NJ; N.J.

State Symbols: flower—common meadow violet; tree—red oak; bird—Eastern goldfinch

At a Glance

- With an increase in population of 3.2 percent, New Jersey ranked 38th among the states in growth from 2000 to 2008.
- An estimated 45,682 marriages took place in New Jersey in 2008, compared to 25,766 divorces.
- The 2007 home ownership rate in New Jersey was 68.3 percent; its ranking was 36th among the states.
- New Jersey's median household income in 2007 was $67,035, 2nd among the states.
- In New Jersey, 8.6 percent of the population lived below the poverty level in 2007, ranking it 46th.
- In 2006-07, 15.6 percent of New Jerseyites did not have health insurance, compared to 15.5 percent of the total U.S. population.
- In 2007, 4.2 percent of New Jerseyites were unemployed, compared to 4.6 percent nationwide.
- New Jersey ranked 5th in the nation with 33.9 percent of its population 25 years old and over having a bachelor's degree in 2007.
- New Jersey's violent crime rate in 2007 was 329.3 per 100,000 population, compared to 466.9 for the entire nation.
- New Jersey had one physician for every 284 people in 2007, compared to one physician for every 325 people nationwide.
- In the 2008 election, 66.2 percent of New Jersey's eligible voters voted, compared to 61.7 percent of eligible voters nationwide.
- New Jersey ranked 24th among the states receiving federal aid in 2007, with $1,379 per capita.
- New Jersey's gross domestic product was $465 billion in 2007; it ranked 8th among the states.
- With $30.1 billion in exports in 2007, New Jersey ranked 9th in exports.
- New Jerseyites consumed 2.6 trillion Btu's of energy in 2006; the state ranked 13th in total consumption.
- In 2007, New Jersey exported $245 million worth of agricultural products, less than 1 percent of the U.S. total.

Table NJ-1. Population by Sex, Age, Race, and Hispanic Origin

(Number, percent.)

Sex, age, race, and Hispanic origin	1990	2000	2008	Average annual percent change, 2000–2008
Total Population	7 730 188	8 414 350	8 682 661	0.4
Percent of total U.S. population	3.1	3.0	2.9	X
Sex				
Male	3 735 685	4 082 813	4 251 782	0.5
Female	3 994 503	4 331 537	4 430 879	0.3
Age				
Under 5 years	532 637	563 785	557 421	-0.1
5 to 19 years	1 479 415	1 720 322	1 719 338	0.0
20 to 64 years	4 686 111	5 017 107	5 254 961	0.6
65 years and over	1 032 025	1 113 136	1 150 941	0.4
Median age (years)	34.3	36.7	38.7	X
Race and Hispanic Origin[1]				
One race				
White	6 130 465	6 104 705	6 601 611	1.0
Black	1 036 825	1 141 821	1 255 868	1.2
American Indian and Alaskan Native	14 970	19 492	30 132	5.6
Asian[2]	272 521	480 276	664 251	4.1
Native Hawaiian and Other Pacific Islander	X	3 329	7 654	11.0
Two or more races	X	213 755	123 145	-6.7
Hispanic (of any race)	739 861	1 117 191	1 418 545	3.0

[1]Data on race in 2000 and 2008 are not comparable to 1990. Individuals could only report one race in the 1990 census but could report one or more races on the 2000 census.
[2]Data in 1990 refer to Asian and Pacific Islanders.

Table NJ-2. Marital Status

(Number, percent distribution.)

Sex and marital status	1990	2000	2007
Males, 15 Years and Over	2 964 562	3 176 413	3 383 409
Never married	32.8	31.1	34.9
Now married, except separated	56.8	57.7	54.0
Separated	2.2	2.0	1.8
Widowed	2.9	2.9	2.7
Divorced	5.4	6.2	6.6
Females, 15 Years and Over	3 258 962	3 478 920	3 608 655
Never married	25.9	25.3	28.9
Now married, except separated	51.1	51.8	48.2
Separated	2.9	2.7	2.6
Widowed	12.7	11.5	10.6
Divorced	7.5	8.7	9.6

Table NJ-3. Households and Housing Characteristics

(Number, percent, and dollars.)

Item	1990	2000	2007	Average annual percent change, 2000–2007
Total Households	2 794 711	3 064 645	3 149 910	0.4
Family households	2 021 346	2 154 539	2 185 324	0.2
Married-couple family	1 578 702	1 638 322	1 633 264	0.0
Other family	442 644	516 217	552 060	1.0
Male householder, no wife present	104 189	129 205	148 880	2.0
Female householder, no husband present	338 455	387 012	403 180	0.6
Nonfamily households	773 365	910 106	964 586	0.8
Householder living alone	646 171	751 287	816 464	1.2
Householder not living alone	127 194	158 819	148 122	-1.0
Housing Characteristics				
Total housing units	3 075 310	3 310 275	3 498 786	0.8
Occupied housing units	2 794 711	3 064 645	3 149 910	0.4
Owner-occupied	1 813 381	2 011 473	2 118 998	0.7
Renter-occupied	981 330	1 053 172	1 030 912	-0.3
Average size	2.70	2.68	2.70	X
Financial Characteristics				
Median gross rent of renter-occupied housing units (dollars)	592	751	1 026	4.6
Median monthly owner costs for housing units with a mortgage (dollars)	1 105	1 560	2 278	5.6
Median value of owner-occupied housing units (dollars)	161 200	170 800	372 300	11.8

Table NJ-4. Median Income and Poverty Status, 2007

(Number, percent.)

Characteristic	State		U.S.	
	Number	Percent	Number	Percent
Median Income				
Households (dollars)	67 035	X	50 740	X
Families (dollars)	81 823	X	61 173	X
Below Poverty Level				
Sex				
Male	304 939	7.3	16 576 071	11.5
Female	424 272	9.7	21 476 176	14.3
Age				
Under 18 years	236 098	11.6	13 097 100	18.0
Related children under 18 years	229 271	11.3	12 728 964	17.6
18 to 64 years	401 681	7.5	21 495 507	11.6
65 years and over	91 432	8.4	3 459 640	9.5

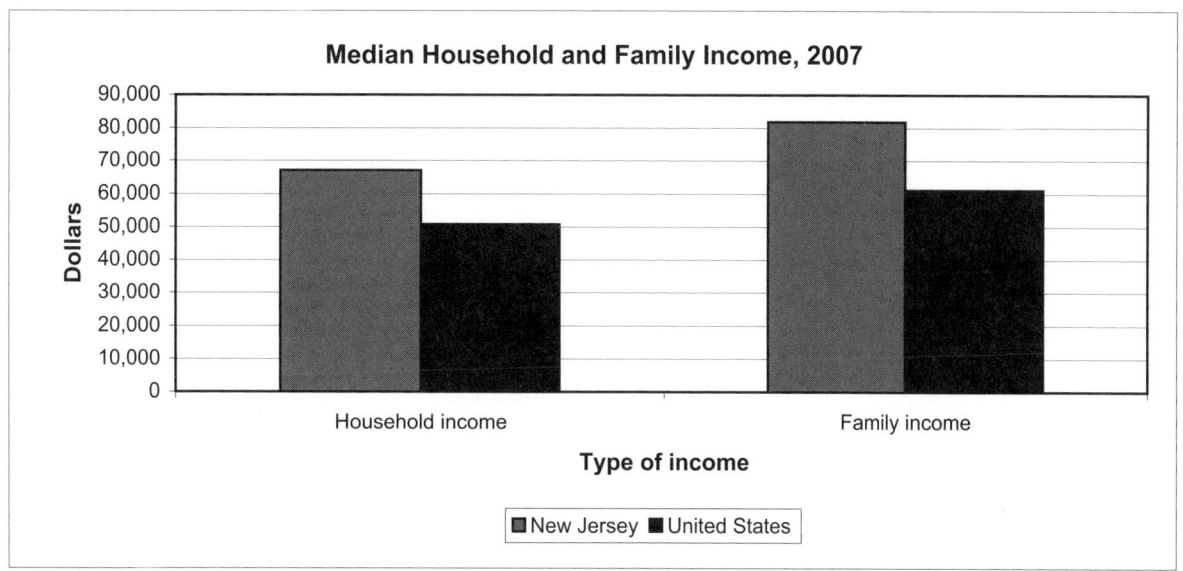

Table NJ-5. Health Insurance Coverage Status for All Persons and Children Under 18 Years of Age

(Number, percent.)

Item	2000	2001	2002	2003	2004	2005	2006	2007
ALL PERSONS	8 393	8 470	8 604	8 579	8 662	8 725	8 660	8 556
Covered by Private or Government Health Insurance								
Number	7 407	7 394	7 447	7 430	7 461	7 460	7 319	7 208
Percent	88.3	87.3	86.6	86.6	86.1	85.5	84.5	84.2
Not Covered								
Number	985	1 076	1 157	1 149	1 201	1 265	1 341	1 348
Percent	11.7	12.7	13.4	13.4	13.9	14.5	15.5	15.8
Percent in the U.S. not covered	13.7	14.1	14.7	15.1	14.9	15.3	15.8	15.3
CHILDREN UNDER 18 YEARS OF AGE	1 992	1 880	2 153	2 157	2 208	2 172	2 088	2 091
Covered by Private or Government Health Insurance								
Number	1 822	1 668	1 945	1 928	1 986	1 944	1 810	1 821
Percent	91.5	88.7	90.3	89.4	90.0	89.5	86.7	87.1
Not Covered								
Number	170	212	208	230	222	228	277	270
Percent	8.5	11.3	9.7	10.6	10.0	10.5	13.3	12.9
Percent in the U.S. not covered	11.6	11.3	11.2	11.0	10.5	10.9	11.7	11.0

Table NJ-6. Employment Status by Demographic Group, Preliminary 2008

(Number, percent.)

Characteristic	Civilian noninstitutional population	Civilian labor force		Employment		Unemployed	
		Number	Percent of population	Number	Percent of population	Number	Unemployment rate
TOTAL	6 794	4 529	66.7	4 285	63.1	244	5.4
Sex							
Men	3 268	2 407	74.0	2 268	69.4	139	5.8
Women	3 526	2 122	60.0	2 017	57.2	106	5.0
Race, Sex, and Hispanic Origin							
White	5 192	3 465	66.7	3 309	63.7	157	4.5
Men	2 509	1 860	74.1	1 772	70.6	87	4.7
Women	2 683	1 606	59.9	1 536	57.3	69	4.3
Black or African American	909	583	64.1	517	56.9	66	11.3
Men	407	274	67.4	234	57.5	40	14.7
Women	502	308	61.4	283	56.4	25	8.2
Hispanic	1 109	802	72.3	749	67.6	52	6.5
Men	568	465	81.9	434	76.5	31	6.6
Women	541	337	62.2	315	58.2	22	6.4
Age							
16 to 19 years	517	176	34.1	148	28.6	28	16.0
20 to 24 years	555	402	72.4	367	66.1	35	8.8
25 to 34 years	1 100	929	84.4	878	79.8	51	5.5
35 to 44 years	1 191	1 015	85.2	978	82.1	37	3.7
45 to 54 years	1 378	1 150	83.5	1 095	79.5	55	4.8
55 to 64 years	935	646	69.1	618	66.0	29	4.4
65 years and over	1 119	211	18.9	203	18.1	8	3.9

Note: Data in Table 6 are from the Current Population Survey (CPS) and do not match the estimates in Table 7. See notes and definitions for more details.

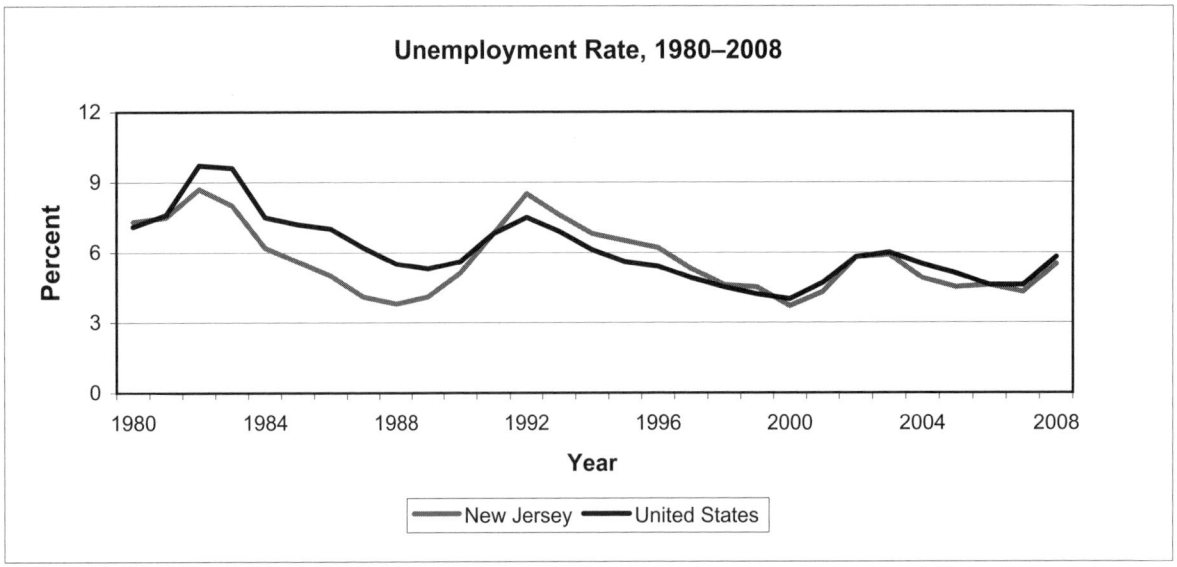

Table NJ-7. Employment Status of the Civilian Noninstitutional Population Age 16 Years and Over

(Number, percent.)

Year	Civilian labor force	Civilian participation rate	Employed	Unemployed	Unemployment rate
1998	4 242 366	66.8	4 047 062	195 304	4.6
1999	4 284 555	67.0	4 092 714	191 841	4.5
2000	4 287 783	66.6	4 130 310	157 473	3.7
2001	4 302 340	66.2	4 117 543	184 797	4.3
2002	4 370 809	66.8	4 117 265	253 544	5.8
2003	4 363 896	66.2	4 108 397	255 499	5.9
2004	4 358 908	65.8	4 144 223	214 685	4.9
2005	4 416 087	66.3	4 218 485	197 602	4.5
2006	4 477 496	66.9	4 269 645	207 851	4.6
2007	4 462 253	66.4	4 271 652	190 601	4.3
2008	4 496 727	66.6	4 251 195	245 532	5.5

Table NJ-8. Employment and Average Wages by Industry

(Estimates for 2001–2006 are based on the 2002 North American Industry Classification System [NAICS]. Estimates for 2007 are based on the 2007 NAICS.)

Industry	2001	2002	2003	2004	2005	2006	2007
	Number of jobs						
WAGE AND SALARY EMPLOYMENT BY INDUSTRY	4 099 979	4 088 023	4 081 639	4 106 994	4 143 334	4 176 064	4 184 945
Farm Wage and Salary Employment	9 162	9 487	8 166	7 992	7 753	8 170	7 826
Nonfarm Wage and Salary Employment	4 090 817	4 078 536	4 073 473	4 099 002	4 135 581	4 167 894	4 177 119
Private wage and salary employment	3 478 097	3 454 755	3 437 407	3 450 237	3 479 591	3 511 441	3 520 409
Forestry, fishing, hunting, and other	4 038	3 919	3 848	3 896	3 901	3 740	3 907
Mining	1 797	1 431	1 558	1 595	1 709	1 701	1 645
Utilities	16 145	15 808	15 168	15 015	14 143	13 972	13 403
Construction	164 720	168 488	166 242	172 287	174 853	180 607	177 884
Manufacturing	401 938	369 354	351 987	340 162	333 883	329 002	315 648
Durable goods manufacturing	182 864	163 661	155 933	151 009	147 984	146 141	140 182
Nondurable goods manufacturing	219 074	205 693	196 054	189 153	185 899	182 861	175 466
Wholesale trade	246 967	237 114	235 308	236 069	236 563	235 111	235 510
Retail trade	477 227	477 477	480 737	479 382	483 508	482 028	481 890
Transportation and warehousing	168 827	161 520	159 561	159 832	159 768	161 958	163 834
Information	124 156	111 875	102 947	99 579	98 142	98 247	97 732
Finance and insurance	207 573	210 746	211 744	211 065	213 839	216 286	212 081
Real estate and rental and leasing	55 016	57 267	59 596	60 409	61 177	62 092	61 672
Professional and technical services	295 091	281 393	274 275	275 784	283 705	292 781	301 559
Management of companies and enterprises	64 175	66 004	63 315	64 320	65 267	65 774	67 139
Administrative and waste services	254 557	260 900	253 385	259 363	258 885	256 665	258 129
Educational services	81 335	85 713	87 460	87 207	85 990	87 289	91 610
Health care and social assistance	426 893	442 749	452 850	460 123	473 118	484 328	493 480
Arts, entertainment, and recreation	46 179	48 536	50 568	51 891	52 684	52 842	54 913
Accommodation and food services	262 547	267 394	275 916	279 706	285 674	291 657	290 970
Other services, except public administration	178 916	187 067	190 942	192 552	192 782	195 361	197 403
Government and government enterprises	612 720	623 781	636 066	648 765	655 990	656 453	656 710
	Dollars						
AVERAGE WAGES AND SALARIES BY INDUSTRY	43 497	44 323	45 576	47 234	48 686	50 823	52 968
Average Farm Wages and Salaries	18 617	23 738	23 595	23 924	19 828	21 648	19 797
Average Nonfarm Wages and Salaries	43 552	44 371	45 620	47 280	48 740	50 880	53 030
Average private wages and salaries	43 549	44 218	45 417	47 039	48 550	50 781	52 942
Forestry, fishing, hunting, and other	19 994	21 158	21 080	21 742	21 745	22 432	23 985
Mining	52 606	53 252	52 056	56 273	58 003	57 384	60 542
Utilities	72 183	74 009	77 180	79 799	84 574	86 777	88 911
Construction	49 739	50 362	50 342	51 229	52 315	54 829	57 430
Manufacturing	51 075	53 012	56 038	59 006	61 185	65 412	69 478
Durable goods manufacturing	48 013	49 626	51 810	54 031	54 917	58 330	61 451
Nondurable goods manufacturing	53 631	55 705	59 400	62 978	66 174	71 073	75 891
Wholesale trade	60 196	60 588	64 217	64 526	65 934	68 908	71 997
Retail trade	26 784	27 522	28 048	28 172	28 389	29 259	29 920
Transportation and warehousing	37 995	39 005	40 130	42 156	43 948	44 606	46 421
Information	64 826	66 998	68 565	71 759	71 391	76 431	80 412
Finance and insurance	75 091	77 102	78 367	82 708	87 423	92 855	98 945
Real estate and rental and leasing	39 851	41 672	43 114	47 501	47 964	51 849	54 204
Professional and technical services	67 160	67 801	69 094	73 114	75 437	78 795	82 897
Management of companies and enterprises	85 642	88 404	95 459	99 086	110 028	112 540	121 404
Administrative and waste services	28 538	29 222	30 887	32 242	33 918	35 258	35 967
Educational services	30 712	31 393	33 020	30 856	31 731	32 935	34 153
Health care and social assistance	36 642	37 912	39 132	40 938	41 865	43 215	44 334
Arts, entertainment, and recreation	26 989	27 665	28 677	28 194	28 137	31 731	31 515
Accommodation and food services	19 124	19 582	19 823	20 629	20 943	21 794	22 344
Other services, except public administration	25 296	25 850	26 827	28 135	29 223	29 678	30 436
Government and government enterprises	43 574	45 219	46 717	48 559	49 749	51 407	53 500

Table NJ-9. Employment Characteristics by Family Type

(Number, percent.)

Family type and labor force status	2005 Total	2005 Families with own children under 18 years	2006 Total	2006 Families with own children under 18 years	2007 Total	2007 Families with own children under 18 years
TOTAL FAMILIES	2 172 279	1 046 196	2 180 404	1 051 687	2 185 324	1 051 006
FAMILY TYPE AND LABOR FORCE STATUS						
Married Coupled Families	1 628 661	768 063	1 631 340	772 130	1 633 264	770 704
Both husband and wife in labor force	53.3	62.0	55.7	64.4	55.3	64.3
Husband in labor force, wife not in labor force	24.6	31.4	23.4	30.2	23.8	30.1
Wife in labor force, husband not in labor force	6.6	4.0	6.8	3.5	6.8	3.7
Both husband and wife not in labor force	15.6	2.5	14.2	2.0	14.2	1.8
Other Families	543 618	278 133	549 064	279 557	552 060	280 302
Female householder, no husband present	72.7	76.7	73.6	78.0	73.0	76.9
In labor force	51.7	62.8	54.0	65.0	53.6	64.7
Not in labor force	21.1	14.0	19.7	13.1	19.4	12.2
Male householder, no wife present	27.3	23.3	26.4	22.0	27.0	23.1
In labor force	21.9	20.8	21.2	20.0	21.8	21.1
Not in labor force	5.3	2.5	5.1	1.9	5.2	2.0

Table NJ-10. School Enrollment and Educational Attainment, 2007

(Number, percent.)

Item	State	U.S.
Enrollment		
Total population 3 years and over	8 353 021	289 295 761
Enrolled in school	2 255 284	79 329 527
Enrolled in preschool (percent)	7.6	6.2
Enrolled in grades K-12 (percent)	67.4	67.6
Enrolled in college or graduate school (percent)	24.9	26.2
Attainment		
Total population 25 years and over	5 850 926	197 892 369
Less than a high school diploma (percent)	13.0	15.5
High school diploma or more (percent)	87.0	84.5
Bachelor's degree or more (percent)	33.9	27.5
Graduate degree or more (percent)	12.7	10.1

Table NJ-11. Educational Indicators

(Number, percent.)

Item	State	U.S.
Public Schools, 2006–2007 (except where noted)		
Number of school districts	673	17 742
Number of schools	2 579	99 639
Number of students	1 388 850	49 315 842
Student-teacher ratio	12.4	15.5
Expenditures per student (dollars)	$16 163	. . .
Averaged freshman graduation rate, 2005–2006	84.8	. . .
Dropout rate, grades 9–12, 2005–2006	1.6	3.7
Students eligible for free or reduced-price lunch (percent) ...	27.3	41.2
English-language learners (percent)	. . .	5.1
Students with IEP (percent)	. . .	12.7
Private Schools, 2007–2008 (except where noted)		
Number of schools	1 441	33 740
Number of students	204 486	5 072 451
High school graduates, 2006–2007	13 344	306 605
Student-teacher ratio	10.5	11.1

Table NJ-12. Reported Voting and Registration of the Voting-Age Population, November 2008

(Number in thousands, percent.)

Item	Total population	Total citizen population	Registered			Voted		
			Total registered	Percent registered (total population)	Percent registered (total citizen population)	Total voted	Percent voted (total population)	Percent voted (total citizen population)
U.S. total	225 499	206 072	146 311	64.9	71.0	131 144	58.2	63.6
State total	6 489	5 675	4 022	62.0	70.9	3 637	56.0	64.1
Sex								
Male	3 124	2 742	1 913	61.2	69.8	1 708	54.7	62.3
Female	3 365	2 933	2 109	62.7	71.9	1 929	57.3	65.8
Race								
White alone	4 991	4 492	3 233	64.8	72.0	2 912	58.3	64.8
White non-Hispanic alone	4 054	3 867	2 863	70.6	74.0	2 593	64.0	67.1
Black alone	846	769	513	60.6	66.7	475	56.2	61.8
Asian alone	567	370	238	41.9	64.2	215	38.0	58.2
Hispanic (of any race)	1 006	661	388	38.5	58.7	337	33.4	50.9
White alone or in combination	5 040	4 516	3 252	64.5	72.0	2 926	58.1	64.8
Black alone or in combination	862	784	526	61.0	67.1	489	56.7	62.3
Asian alone or in combination	581	381	246	42.3	64.5	218	37.6	57.4

Table NJ-13. Crime

(Number, rate per 100,000.)

Item	State			U.S.		
	2007	2008	Percent change	2007	2008	Percent change
Population	8 685 920	8 682 661	0.0	301 621 157	304 059 724	0.8
VIOLENT CRIME						
Number	28 601	28 351	-0.9	1 408 337	1 382 012	-1.9
Rate	329.3	326.5	-0.8	466.9	454.5	-2.7
Murder and Nonnegligent Manslaughter						
Number	380	376	-1.1	16 929	16 272	-3.9
Rate	4.4	4.3	-1.0	5.6	5.4	-4.7
Forcible Rape						
Number	1 050	1 122	6.9	90 427	89 000	-1.6
Rate	12.1	12.9	6.9	30.0	29.3	-2.4
Robbery						
Number	12 549	12 701	1.2	445 125	441 855	-0.7
Rate	144.5	146.3	1.2	147.6	145.3	-1.5
Aggravated Assault						
Number	14 622	14 152	-3.2	855 856	834 885	-2.5
Rate	168.3	163.0	-3.2	283.8	274.6	-3.2
PROPERTY CRIME						
Number	192 226	199 126	3.6	9 843 481	9 767 915	-0.8
Rate	2 213.1	2 293.4	3.6	3 263.5	3 212.5	-1.6
Burglary						
Number	37 482	40 401	7.8	2 179 140	2 222 196	2.0
Rate	431.5	465.3	7.8	722.5	730.8	1.2
Larceny-Theft						
Number	132 791	138 545	4.3	6 568 572	6 588 873	0.3
Rate	1 528.8	1 595.7	4.4	2 177.8	2 167.0	-0.5
Motor Vehicle Theft						
Number	21 953	20 180	-8.1	1 095 769	956 846	-12.7
Rate	252.7	232.4	-8.0	363.3	314.7	-13.4

Table NJ-14. State Government Finances, 2007

(Dollars, percent distribution.)

Item	Thousands of dollars	Percent distribution
Total Revenue	65 495 222	X
General revenue	49 746 594	76.0
Intergovernmental revenue	11 462 648	17.5
Taxes	29 106 788	44.4
General sales	8 345 601	12.7
Selective sales	3 596 641	5.5
License taxes	1 512 520	2.3
Individual income tax	11 539 894	17.6
Corporate income tax	2 876 591	4.4
Other taxes	1 235 541	1.9
Current charges	4 909 172	7.5
Miscellaneous general revenue	4 267 986	6.5
Utility revenue	773 920	1.2
Liquor store revenue	0	0.0
Insurance trust revenue	14 974 708	22.9
Total Expenditure	56 076 165	100.0
Intergovernmental expenditure	10 667 575	19.0
Direct expenditure	45 408 590	81.0
Current operation	29 361 123	52.4
Capital outlay	4 073 545	7.3
Insurance benefits and repayments	9 095 827	16.2
Assistance and subsidies	942 007	1.7
Interest on debt	1 936 088	3.5
Exhibit: Salaries and wages	8 784 646	15.7
Total Expenditure	56 076 165	100.0
General expenditure	44 920 677	80.1
Intergovernmental expenditure	10 667 575	19.0
Direct expenditure	34 253 102	61.1
Education	14 863 769	26.5
Public welfare	11 895 707	21.2
Hospitals	1 957 266	3.5
Health	1 311 145	2.3
Highways	2 615 630	4.7
Police protection	525 964	0.9
Correction	1 489 950	2.7
Natural resources	537 755	1.0
Parks and recreation	415 141	0.7
Government administration	1 774 230	3.2
Interest on general debt	1 931 092	3.4
Other and unallocable	5 603 028	10.0
Utility expenditure	2 059 661	3.7
Liquor store expenditure	0	0.0
Insurance trust expenditure	9 095 827	16.2
Debt at End of Fiscal Year	51 384 806	X
Cash and Security Holdings	111 844 139	X

Table NJ-15. State Government Tax Collections, 2008

(Dollars, percent distribution.)

Item	Thousands of dollars	Percent distribution
Total Taxes	30 616 510	X
Property taxes	2 998	0.0
Sales and gross receipts	12 519 601	40.9
General sales and gross receipts	8 915 515	29.1
Selective sales taxes	3 604 086	11.8
Alcoholic beverages	104 104	0.3
Amusements	412 986	1.3
Insurance premiums	542 920	1.8
Motor fuels	563 266	1.8
Public utilities	930 457	3.0
Tobacco products	789 351	2.6
Other selective sales	261 002	0.9
Licenses	1 452 361	4.7
Alcoholic beverages	7 804	0.0
Amusements	76 272	0.2
Corporation	313 322	1.0
Hunting and fishing	13 211	0.0
Motor vehicle	432 164	1.4
Motor vehicle operators	37 579	0.1
Public utility	1 475	0.0
Occupation and business, NEC	567 840	1.9
Other licenses	2 694	0.0
Income taxes	15 425 451	50.4
Individual income	12 605 545	41.2
Corporation net income	2 819 906	9.2
Other taxes	1 216 099	4.0
Death and gift	698 694	2.3
Documentary and stock transfer	517 405	1.7

Table NJ-16. Agriculture

(Number, acres, and dollars.)

Item	2002		2007		Percent change, 2002–2007
	Number	Percent of total	Number	Percent of total	
Number of farms	9 924		10 327		4.1
Farm Size					
Average size of farm (acres)	81		71		-12.3
Farms by size (number of farms)					
Fewer than 50 acres	6 992	70.5	7 764	75.2	11.0
50 to 499 acres	2 588	26.1	2 264	21.9	-12.5
500 acres or more	344	3.5	299	2.9	-13.1
Land (Acres)					
Total land in farms	805 682		733 450		-9.0
Total cropland	547 668	68.0	488 697	66.6	-10.8
Total harvested cropland	444 670	55.2	415 542	56.7	-6.6
Irrigated land	96 893	12.0	95 277	13.0	-1.7
Value of Sales (Dollars)					
Agricultural products sold ($1,000)	749 872		986 885		31.6
Average sales per farm	75 561		95 564		26.5
Sales of crops	657 494	87.7	851 653	86.3	29.5
Sales of livestock, poultry, and their products	92 378	12.3	135 233	13.7	46.4
Value of Sales (Number of Farms)					
Less than $10,000	7 044	71.0	6 954	67.3	-1.3
$10,000 to $99,999	1 821	18.3	2 226	21.6	22.2
$100,000 to $999,999	895	9.0	957	9.3	6.9
$1,000,000 or more	164	1.7	190	1.8	15.9
Farms by Type of Organization (Number of Farms)					
Family	8 578	86.4	8 679	84.0	1.2
Partnership	576	5.8	726	7.0	26.0
Corporation	701	7.1	829	8.0	18.3
Other: cooperative, estate or trust, institutional, etc	69	0.7	93	0.9	34.8
Value of Land and Buildings (Dollars)					
Estimated market value of land and buildings ($1,000)	11 255 226		7 358 731		-34.6
Land and buildings average value per farm	1 089 883		741 808		-31.9
Average value per acre	15 346		9 245		-39.8
Government Payments					
Number of farms receiving government payments	582	5.9	857	8.3	47.3
Payments (thousands of dollars)	4 441		6 988		57.4
Average payment per farm	7 630		8 154		6.9
Farm Operator Characteristics					
Farm operators whose principal occupation is farming	5 193	52.3	4 626	44.8	-10.9
Farm operators whose principal occupation is other	4 731	47.7	5 701	55.2	20.5
Average age principal operator (years)	55.1		57.1		3.6

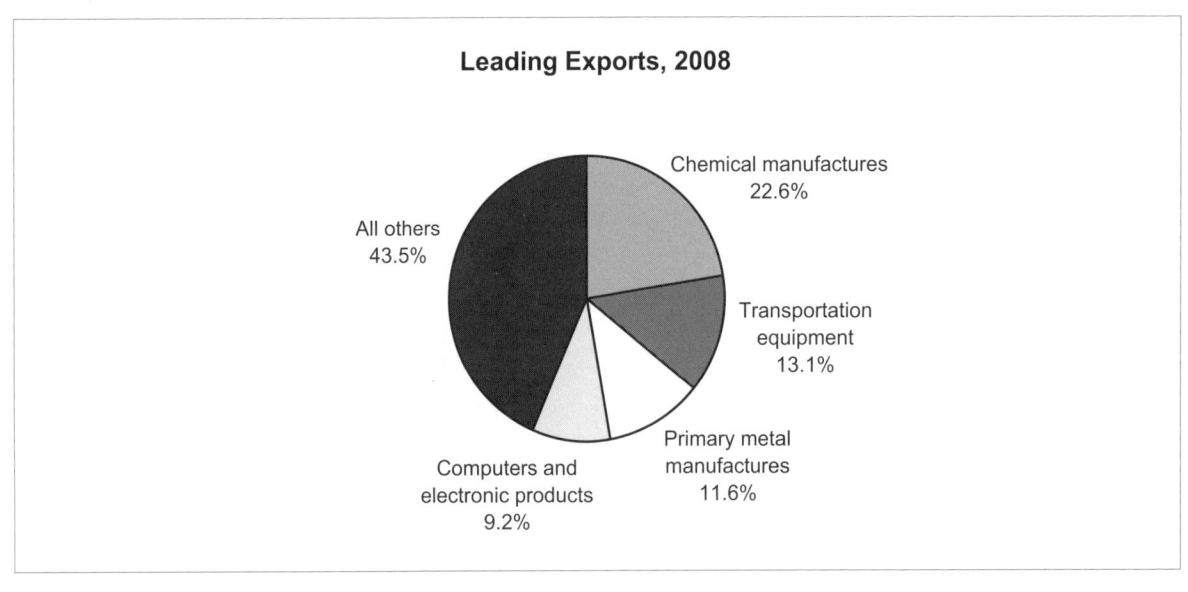

Leading Exports, 2008

- Chemical manufactures 22.6%
- All others 43.5%
- Transportation equipment 13.1%
- Primary metal manufactures 11.6%
- Computers and electronic products 9.2%

NEW MEXICO

Facts and Figures

Location: Southwestern United States; bordered on the N by Colorado, on the E by Oklahoma and Texas, on the S by Texas and Mexico, and on the W by Arizona; New Mexico is one of the Four Corner states—at its NW corner it touches Arizona, Colorado, and Utah

Area: 121,590 sq. mi. (314,915 sq. km.); rank—5th

Population: 1,984,356 (2008 est.); rank—36th

Principal Cities: capital—Santa Fe; largest—Albuquerque

Statehood: January 6, 1912; 47th state

U.S. Congress: 2 senators, 3 representatives

State Motto: *Crescit eundo* ("It grows as it goes")

State Song: "O, Fair New Mexico"

State Nickname: The Land of Enchantment

Abbreviations: NM; N. Mex.

State Symbols: flower—yucca; tree—piñon; bird—roadrunner

At a Glance

- With an increase in population of 9.1 percent, New Mexico ranked 17th among the states in growth from 2000 to 2008.
- An estimated 8,033 marriages took place in New Mexico in 2008, compared to 8,148 divorces.
- The 2007 home ownership rate in New Mexico was 71.5 percent; its ranking of 20th was tied with that of Louisiana and Virginia.
- New Mexico's median household income in 2007 was $41,452, 44th among the states.
- In New Mexico, 18.1 percent of the population lived below the poverty level in 2007, ranking it 3rd.
- In 2006-07, 22.7 percent of New Mexicans did not have health insurance, compared to 15.5 percent of the total U.S. population.
- In 2007, 3.7 percent of New Mexicans were unemployed, compared to 4.6 percent nationwide.
- New Mexico ranked 33rd in the nation with 24.8 percent of its population 25 years old and over having a bachelor's degree in 2007.
- New Mexico's violent crime rate in 2007 was 664.2 per 100,000 population, compared to 466.9 for the entire nation.
- New Mexico had one physician for every 356 people in 2007, compared to one physician for every 325 people nationwide.
- In the 2008 election, 60.3 percent of New Mexico's eligible voters voted, compared to 61.7 percent of eligible voters nationwide.
- New Mexico ranked 7th among the states receiving federal aid in 2007, with $2,213 per capita.
- New Mexico's gross domestic product was $76 billion in 2007; it ranked 37th among the states.
- With $2.6 billion in exports in 2007, New Mexico ranked 44th in exports.
- New Mexicans consumed 683.3 billion Btu's of energy in 2006; the state ranked 38th in total consumption.
- In 2007, New Mexico exported $269 million worth of agricultural products, less than 1 percent of the U.S. total.

Table NM-1. Population by Sex, Age, Race, and Hispanic Origin

(Number, percent.)

Sex, age, race, and Hispanic origin	1990	2000	2008	Average annual percent change, 2000–2008
Total Population	1 515 069	1 819 046	1 984 356	1.1
Percent of total U.S. population	0.6	0.6	0.7	X
Sex				
Male	745 253	894 317	978 326	1.1
Female	769 816	924 729	1 006 030	1.1
Age				
Under 5 years	125 878	130 628	148 323	1.6
5 to 19 years	366 629	434 231	412 995	-0.6
20 to 64 years	859 500	1 041 962	1 162 987	1.4
65 years and over	163 062	212 225	260 051	2.6
Median age (years)	31.1	34.6	35.8	X
Race and Hispanic Origin[1]				
One race				
White	1 146 028	1 214 253	1 666 790	4.0
Black	30 210	34 343	59 009	7.0
American Indian and Alaskan Native	134 355	173 483	192 235	1.3
Asian[2]	14 124	19 255	27 884	4.7
Native Hawaiian and Other Pacific Islander	X	1 503	2 854	8.3
Two or more races	X	66 327	35 584	-7.5
Hispanic (of any race)	579 224	765 386	891 013	1.9

[1]Data on race in 2000 and 2008 are not comparable to 1990. Individuals could only report one race in the 1990 census but could report one or more races on the 2000 census.
[2]Data in 1990 refer to Asian and Pacific Islanders.

Table NM-2. Marital Status

(Number, percent distribution.)

Sex and marital status	1990	2000	2007
Males, 15 Years and Over	552 408	677 967	767 194
Never married	29.3	30.5	36.0
Now married, except separated	57.8	55.0	48.6
Separated	1.6	1.6	1.7
Widowed	2.3	2.6	2.8
Divorced	9.0	10.4	10.9
Females, 15 Years and Over	584 092	720 529	793 610
Never married	22.5	24.7	28.2
Now married, except separated	54.2	51.2	45.9
Separated	2.0	2.0	2.2
Widowed	10.0	9.4	9.4
Divorced	11.3	12.8	14.4

Table NM-3. Households and Housing Characteristics

(Number, percent, and dollars.)

Item	1990	2000	2007	Average annual percent change, 2000–2007
Total Households	542 709	677 971	734 847	1.2
Family households	391 487	466 515	482 543	0.5
Married-couple family	303 789	341 818	338 847	-0.1
Other family	87 698	124 697	143 696	2.0
Male householder, no wife present	23 143	35 075	41 804	2.5
Female householder, no husband present	64 555	89 622	101 892	1.8
Nonfamily households	151 222	211 456	252 304	2.6
Householder living alone	124 883	172 181	206 644	2.6
Householder not living alone	26 339	39 275	45 660	2.2
Housing Characteristics				
Total housing units	632 058	780 579	862 095	1.4
Occupied housing units	542 709	677 971	734 847	1.2
Owner-occupied	365 965	474 445	514 491	1.2
Renter-occupied	176 744	203 526	220 356	1.1
Average size	2.74	2.63	2.62	X
Financial Characteristics				
Median gross rent of renter-occupied housing units (dollars)	372	503	637	3.4
Median monthly owner costs for housing units with a mortgage (dollars)	651	929	1 130	2.8
Median value of owner-occupied housing units (dollars)	69 800	108 100	155 400	5.3

Table NM-4. Median Income and Poverty Status, 2007

(Number, percent.)

Characteristic	State		U.S.	
	Number	Percent	Number	Percent
Median Income				
Households (dollars)	41 452	X	50 740	X
Families (dollars)	49 658	X	61 173	X
Below Poverty Level				
Sex				
Male	155 908	16.5	16 576 071	11.5
Female	193 251	19.7	21 476 176	14.3
Age				
Under 18 years	123 808	25.5	13 097 100	18.0
Related children under 18 years	120 999	25.0	12 728 964	17.6
18 to 64 years	192 692	16.2	21 495 507	11.6
65 years and over	32 659	13.3	3 459 640	9.5

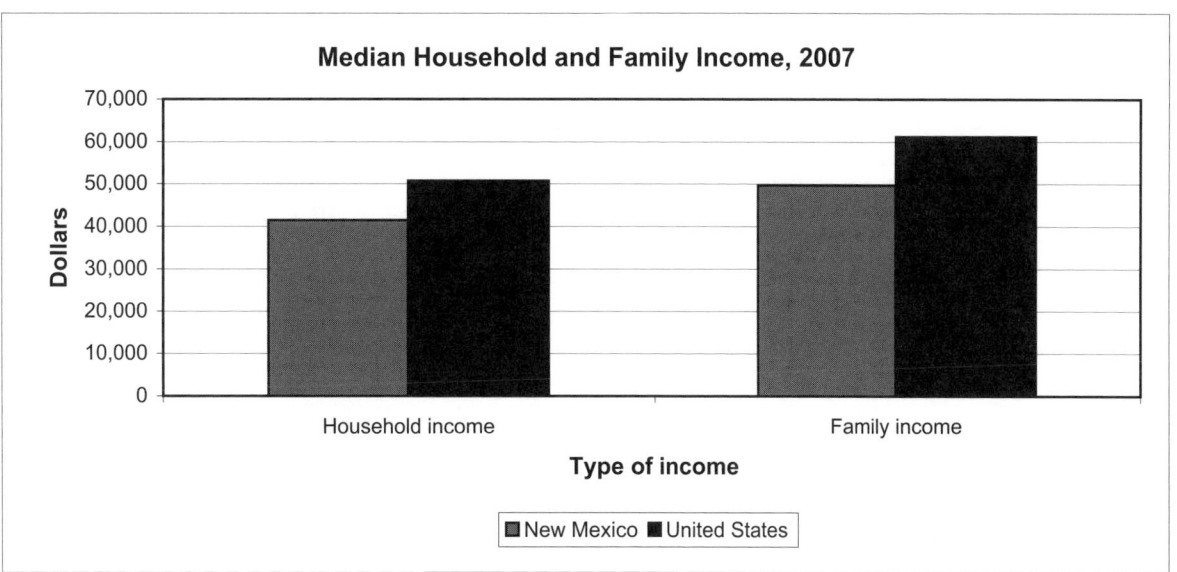

Table NM-5. Health Insurance Coverage Status for All Persons and Children Under 18 Years of Age

(Number, percent.)

Item	2000	2001	2002	2003	2004	2005	2006	2007
ALL PERSONS	1 799	1 804	1 840	1 871	1 902	1 938	1 943	1 946
Covered by Private or Government Health Insurance								
Number	1 373	1 440	1 461	1 461	1 525	1 545	1 498	1 509
Percent	76.3	79.8	79.4	78.1	80.2	79.7	77.1	77.5
Not Covered								
Number	426	364	379	410	377	393	445	437
Percent	23.7	20.2	20.6	21.9	19.8	20.3	22.9	22.5
Percent in the U.S. not covered	13.7	14.1	14.7	15.1	14.9	15.3	15.8	15.3
CHILDREN UNDER 18 YEARS OF AGE	504	497	502	495	495	493	520	495
Covered by Private or Government Health Insurance								
Number	415	427	430	429	423	394	428	419
Percent	82.3	86.0	85.6	86.8	85.4	80.0	82.1	84.5
Not Covered								
Number	89	70	72	65	72	99	93	77
Percent	17.7	14.0	14.4	13.2	14.6	20.0	17.9	15.5
Percent in the U.S. not covered	11.6	11.3	11.2	11.0	10.5	10.9	11.7	11.0

Table NM-6. Employment Status by Demographic Group, Preliminary 2008

(Number, percent.)

Characteristic	Civilian noninstitutional population	Civilian labor force		Employment		Unemployed	
		Number	Percent of population	Number	Percent of population	Number	Unemployment rate
TOTAL	1 522	971	63.8	928	61.0	43	4.4
Sex							
Men	736	515	70.0	494	67.1	21	4.2
Women	786	456	58.0	435	55.3	22	4.7
Race, Sex, and Hispanic Origin							
White	1 296	834	64.4	798	61.6	36	4.3
Men	637	454	71.2	435	68.2	19	4.2
Women	659	380	57.7	363	55.1	17	4.6
Black or African American	39	26	67.3	25	64.5	1	4.2
Men	...	...	...	...	...	...	...
Women	...	...	...	...	...	...	...
Hispanic	622	384	61.8	362	58.3	22	5.7
Men	316	220	69.7	208	65.9	12	5.4
Women	306	164	53.6	154	50.4	10	6.0
Age							
16 to 19 years	111	46	41.3	38	34.1	8	17.5
20 to 24 years	127	82	64.8	77	60.4	6	6.7
25 to 34 years	271	213	78.4	203	75.0	9	4.3
35 to 44 years	256	207	80.7	200	77.8	7	3.6
45 to 54 years	294	238	80.9	230	78.1	8	3.5
55 to 64 years	229	145	63.3	141	61.8	3	2.4
65 years and over	233	40	17.4	39	16.9	1	3.0

Note: Data in Table 6 are from the Current Population Survey (CPS) and do not match the estimates in Table 7. See notes and definitions for more details.

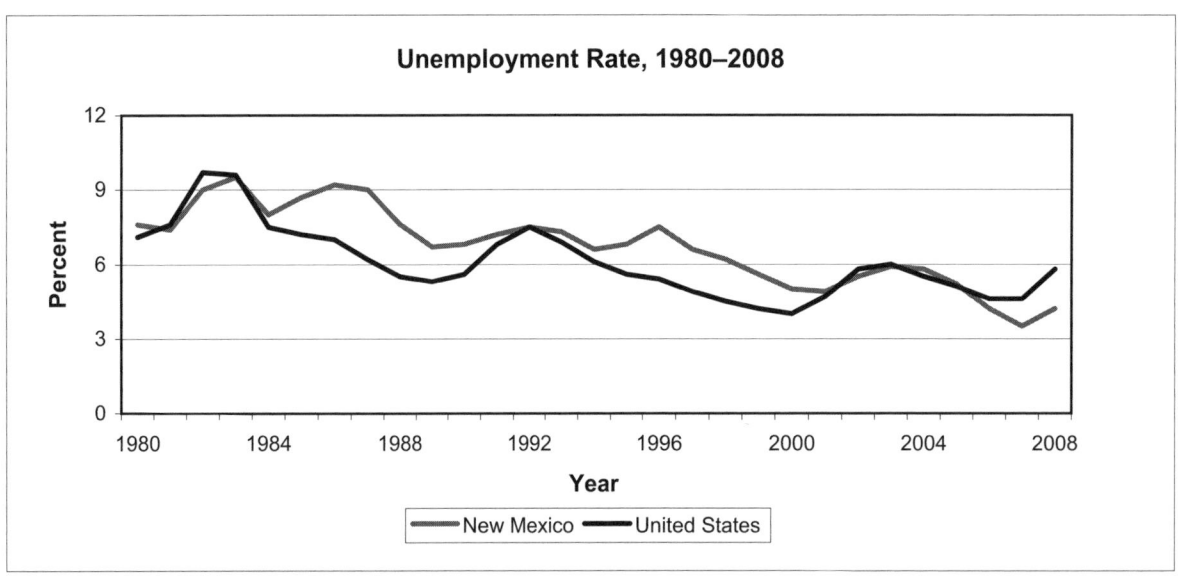

Table NM-7. Employment Status of the Civilian Noninstitutional Population Age 16 Years and Over

(Number, percent.)

Year	Civilian labor force	Civilian participation rate	Employed	Unemployed	Unemployment rate
1998	835 879	63.5	783 661	52 218	6.2
1999	839 988	63.1	793 052	46 936	5.6
2000	852 293	63.5	810 024	42 269	5.0
2001	863 682	63.7	821 003	42 679	4.9
2002	871 512	63.4	823 191	48 321	5.5
2003	888 468	63.7	835 835	52 633	5.9
2004	901 833	63.7	849 970	51 863	5.8
2005	917 569	63.8	870 288	47 281	5.2
2006	935 396	63.9	896 359	39 037	4.2
2007	945 700	63.6	912 167	33 533	3.5
2008	959 458	63.7	919 466	39 992	4.2

Table NM-8. Employment and Average Wages by Industry

(Estimates for 2001–2006 are based on the 2002 North American Industry Classification System [NAICS]. Estimates for 2007 are based on the 2007 NAICS.)

Industry	2001	2002	2003	2004	2005	2006	2007
	Number of jobs						
WAGE AND SALARY EMPLOYMENT BY INDUSTRY	801 610	809 872	822 438	838 544	855 049	877 954	887 936
Farm Wage and Salary Employment	6 621	6 389	6 820	6 785	7 391	7 223	6 989
Nonfarm Wage and Salary Employment	794 989	803 483	815 618	831 759	847 658	870 731	880 947
Private wage and salary employment	589 515	594 604	601 981	614 191	628 894	656 435	670 795
Forestry, fishing, hunting, and other	5 301	5 148	5 127	5 044	5 252	5 084	4 850
Mining	15 589	14 018	14 245	14 982	16 980	18 854	19 676
Utilities	4 198	4 045	4 023	3 953	3 964	4 010	4 271
Construction	49 164	47 652	49 160	52 354	56 424	61 293	61 151
Manufacturing	41 255	39 047	36 984	36 049	36 226	37 629	36 998
Durable goods manufacturing	29 370	27 548	25 569	24 822	24 976	26 118	25 659
Nondurable goods manufacturing	11 885	11 499	11 415	11 227	11 250	11 511	11 339
Wholesale trade	22 988	22 980	22 411	22 415	22 929	23 749	24 104
Retail trade	92 591	93 026	93 679	95 267	96 644	97 250	98 957
Transportation and warehousing	19 024	18 985	19 106	19 758	19 704	20 098	20 926
Information	17 154	16 796	15 820	14 881	14 735	15 946	16 054
Finance and insurance	22 933	23 075	23 385	23 495	23 590	23 674	23 377
Real estate and rental and leasing	9 955	10 162	10 336	10 651	11 026	11 375	11 623
Professional and technical services	42 127	42 176	44 017	45 252	46 326	53 537	58 952
Management of companies and enterprises	5 796	5 584	5 188	5 068	6 085	6 109	5 783
Administrative and waste services	43 489	43 748	42 232	42 693	43 648	45 980	46 994
Educational services	8 512	8 914	9 738	10 348	10 264	10 157	10 489
Health care and social assistance	74 429	80 932	86 097	90 107	92 233	94 956	98 333
Arts, entertainment, and recreation	7 576	7 804	8 142	8 385	8 627	8 711	8 997
Accommodation and food services	72 215	73 611	74 834	75 601	76 521	79 325	80 147
Other services, except public administration	35 219	36 901	37 457	37 888	37 716	38 698	39 113
Government and government enterprises	205 474	208 879	213 637	217 568	218 764	214 296	210 152
	Dollars						
AVERAGE WAGES AND SALARIES BY INDUSTRY	28 718	29 689	30 468	31 696	32 950	34 487	35 980
Average Farm Wages and Salaries	26 593	31 862	26 267	28 248	29 521	29 620	32 565
Average Nonfarm Wages and Salaries	28 736	29 671	30 503	31 724	32 980	34 528	36 008
Average private wages and salaries	27 621	28 126	28 872	30 028	31 278	33 287	35 043
Forestry, fishing, hunting, and other	13 584	14 544	14 994	15 937	16 205	17 580	18 200
Mining	46 615	47 482	48 728	51 438	54 660	60 264	61 909
Utilities	54 346	53 478	54 156	57 029	59 820	61 280	65 431
Construction	30 138	30 022	30 531	31 335	33 033	34 948	36 804
Manufacturing	38 079	37 868	39 587	40 507	41 677	43 959	47 288
Durable goods manufacturing	42 513	42 141	44 545	45 190	46 380	48 779	52 062
Nondurable goods manufacturing	27 123	27 632	28 482	30 153	31 237	33 023	36 486
Wholesale trade	36 316	37 464	38 286	40 032	41 286	44 100	46 253
Retail trade	20 744	21 164	21 688	22 593	22 967	23 926	24 618
Transportation and warehousing	33 577	34 212	34 852	37 132	39 016	40 941	42 234
Information	32 828	31 773	33 148	34 843	36 447	37 805	38 601
Finance and insurance	35 701	37 544	39 240	40 277	42 125	44 816	47 786
Real estate and rental and leasing	24 300	29 978	25 880	27 089	28 378	30 440	31 776
Professional and technical services	48 977	50 633	52 677	54 418	56 201	60 088	63 893
Management of companies and enterprises	41 264	43 094	42 080	46 951	48 433	48 216	52 989
Administrative and waste services	22 485	23 339	24 664	26 000	26 801	27 831	28 946
Educational services	21 725	21 749	21 637	23 143	25 056	25 884	27 121
Health care and social assistance	28 010	28 965	29 521	30 501	31 718	33 233	34 186
Arts, entertainment, and recreation	16 934	17 124	17 766	18 035	18 531	18 861	20 119
Accommodation and food services	11 888	12 281	12 625	13 241	13 718	14 348	14 977
Other services, except public administration	18 424	18 994	19 783	20 541	21 411	22 330	23 490
Government and government enterprises	31 935	34 071	35 097	36 512	37 872	38 327	39 087

Table NM-9. Employment Characteristics by Family Type

(Number, percent.)

Family type and labor force status	2005		2006		2007	
	Total	Families with own children under 18 years	Total	Families with own children under 18 years	Total	Families with own children under 18 years
TOTAL FAMILIES	482 759	225 137	477 430	224 763	482 543	224 302
FAMILY TYPE AND LABOR FORCE STATUS						
Married Coupled Families	348 421	141 812	345 376	144 158	338 847	138 034
Both husband and wife in labor force	47.7	59.0	48.5	60.6	47.5	59.5
Husband in labor force, wife not in labor force	24.0	30.7	24.3	31.3	24.5	33.5
Wife in labor force, husband not in labor force	8.6	5.4	7.6	4.4	7.9	3.4
Both husband and wife not in labor force	19.8	4.9	19.6	3.7	20.2	3.6
Other Families	134 338	83 325	132 054	80 605	143 696	86 268
Female householder, no husband present	72.6	74.0	69.7	72.8	70.9	72.9
In labor force	48.8	56.3	49.2	58.6	47.9	56.7
Not in labor force	23.8	17.7	20.6	14.1	23.0	16.2
Male householder, no wife present	27.4	26.0	30.3	27.2	29.1	27.1
In labor force	21.3	22.5	24.6	24.6	22.5	23.5
Not in labor force	6.0	3.4	5.6	2.6	6.6	3.6

Table NM-10. School Enrollment and Educational Attainment, 2007

(Number, percent.)

Item	State	U.S.
Enrollment		
Total population 3 years and over	1 888 527	289 295 761
Enrolled in school	532 906	79 329 527
Enrolled in preschool (percent)	5.1	6.2
Enrolled in grades K-12 (percent)	67.5	67.6
Enrolled in college or graduate school (percent)	27.3	26.2
Attainment		
Total population 25 years and over	1 267 808	197 892 369
Less than a high school diploma (percent)	17.7	15.5
High school diploma or more (percent)	82.3	84.5
Bachelor's degree or more (percent)	24.8	27.5
Graduate degree or more (percent)	10.2	10.1

Table NM-11. Educational Indicators

(Number, percent.)

Item	State	U.S.
Public Schools, 2006–2007 (except where noted)		
Number of school districts	95	17 742
Number of schools	839	99 639
Number of students	328 220	49 315 842
Student-teacher ratio	14.9	15.5
Expenditures per student (dollars)	$8 849	...
Averaged freshman graduation rate, 2005–2006	67.3	...
Dropout rate, grades 9–12, 2005–2006	5.5	3.7
Students eligible for free or reduced-price lunch (percent)	60.4	41.2
English-language learners (percent)	18.5	5.1
Students with IEP (percent)	14.6	12.7
Private Schools, 2007–2008 (except where noted)		
Number of schools	212	33 740
Number of students	23 582	5 072 451
High school graduates, 2006–2007	1 495	306 605
Student-teacher ratio	10.9	11.1

Table NM-12. Reported Voting and Registration of the Voting-Age Population, November 2008

(Number in thousands, percent.)

Item	Total population	Total citizen population	Registered			Voted		
			Total registered	Percent registered (total population)	Percent registered (total citizen population)	Total voted	Percent voted (total population)	Percent voted (total citizen population)
U.S. total	225 499	206 072	146 311	64.9	71.0	131 144	58.2	63.6
State total	1 473	1 352	937	63.6	69.3	846	57.4	62.6
Sex								
Male	720	653	445	61.8	68.2	395	54.8	60.5
Female	753	699	491	65.3	70.3	451	59.9	64.6
Race								
White alone	1 287	1 176	833	64.7	70.9	748	58.1	63.6
White non-Hispanic alone	666	654	496	74.5	75.8	468	70.3	71.5
Black alone	32	31	22	...	...	20	...	...
Asian alone	29	19	16	...	...	14	...	...
Hispanic (of any race)	640	539	346	54.1	64.2	289	45.2	53.7
White alone or in combination	1 293	1 181	838	64.9	71.0	753	58.3	63.8
Black alone or in combination	33	32	23	...	...	22	...	...
Asian alone or in combination	29	19	16	...	...	14	...	...

Table NM-13. Crime

(Number, rate per 100,000.)

Item	State			U.S.		
	2007	2008	Percent change	2007	2008	Percent change
Population	1 969 915	1 984 356	0.7	301 621 157	304 059 724	0.8
VIOLENT CRIME						
Number	13 085	12 896	-1.4	1 408 337	1 382 012	-1.9
Rate	664.2	649.9	-2.2	466.9	454.5	-2.7
Murder and Nonnegligent Manslaughter						
Number	162	142	-12.3	16 929	16 272	-3.9
Rate	8.2	7.2	-13.0	5.6	5.4	-4.7
Forcible Rape						
Number	1 032	1 139	10.4	90 427	89 000	-1.6
Rate	52.4	57.4	9.6	30.0	29.3	-2.4
Robbery						
Number	2 321	2 172	-6.4	445 125	441 855	-0.7
Rate	117.8	109.5	-7.1	147.6	145.3	-1.5
Aggravated Assault						
Number	9 570	9 443	-1.3	855 856	834 885	-2.5
Rate	485.8	475.9	-2.0	283.8	274.6	-3.2
PROPERTY CRIME						
Number	73 394	77 572	5.7	9 843 481	9 767 915	-0.8
Rate	3 725.7	3 909.2	4.9	3 263.5	3 212.5	-1.6
Burglary						
Number	18 992	21 713	14.3	2 179 140	2 222 196	2.0
Rate	964.1	1 094.2	13.5	722.5	730.8	1.2
Larceny-Theft						
Number	45 463	47 855	5.3	6 568 572	6 588 873	0.3
Rate	2 307.9	2 411.6	4.5	2 177.8	2 167.0	-0.5
Motor Vehicle Theft						
Number	8 939	8 004	-10.5	1 095 769	956 846	-12.7
Rate	453.8	403.4	-11.1	363.3	314.7	-13.4

Table NM-14. State Government Finances, 2007

(Dollars, percent distribution.)

Item	Thousands of dollars	Percent distribution
Total Revenue	16 781 588	X
General revenue	12 672 012	75.5
Intergovernmental revenue	4 219 834	25.1
Taxes	5 205 322	31.0
General sales	1 843 613	11.0
Selective sales	639 408	3.8
License taxes	237 561	1.4
Individual income tax	1 149 805	6.9
Corporate income tax	425 087	2.5
Other taxes	909 848	5.4
Current charges	991 898	5.9
Miscellaneous general revenue	2 254 958	13.4
Utility revenue	0	0.0
Liquor store revenue	0	0.0
Insurance trust revenue	4 109 576	24.5
Total Expenditure	14 907 060	100.0
Intergovernmental expenditure	4 144 807	27.8
Direct expenditure	10 762 253	72.2
Current operation	7 922 191	53.1
Capital outlay	1 016 784	6.8
Insurance benefits and repayments	1 250 392	8.4
Assistance and subsidies	237 591	1.6
Interest on debt	335 295	2.2
Exhibit: Salaries and wages	2 049 143	13.7
Total Expenditure	14 907 060	100.0
General expenditure	13 640 543	91.5
Intergovernmental expenditure	4 144 807	27.8
Direct expenditure	9 495 736	63.7
Education	4 844 691	32.5
Public welfare	3 115 453	20.9
Hospitals	734 720	4.9
Health	447 156	3.0
Highways	996 883	6.7
Police protection	168 929	1.1
Correction	341 179	2.3
Natural resources	213 460	1.4
Parks and recreation	71 399	0.5
Government administration	486 071	3.3
Interest on general debt	335 295	2.2
Other and unallocable	1 885 307	12.6
Utility expenditure	16 125	0.1
Liquor store expenditure	0	0.0
Insurance trust expenditure	1 250 392	8.4
Debt at End of Fiscal Year	7 323 101	X
Cash and Security Holdings	47 610 559	X

Table NM-15. State Government Tax Collections, 2008

(Dollars, percent distribution.)

Item	Thousands of dollars	Percent distribution
Total Taxes	5 674 530	X
Property taxes	57 665	1.0
Sales and gross receipts	2 663 292	46.9
General sales and gross receipts	1 949 768	34.4
Selective sales taxes	713 524	12.6
Alcoholic beverages	41 230	0.7
Amusements	56 149	1.0
Insurance premiums	144 256	2.5
Motor fuels	250 418	4.4
Pari-mutuels	660	0.0
Public utilities	35 777	0.6
Tobacco products	48 115	0.8
Other selective sales	136 919	2.4
Licenses	237 616	4.2
Amusements	609	0.0
Corporation	2 997	0.1
Hunting and fishing	23 104	0.4
Motor vehicle	179 367	3.2
Motor vehicle operators	4 780	0.1
Public utility	1 127	0.0
Occupation and business, NEC	25 438	0.4
Other licenses	194	0.0
Income taxes	1 616 918	28.5
Individual income	1 213 394	21.4
Corporation net income	403 524	7.1
Other taxes	1 099 039	19.4
Death and gift	39	0.0
Severance	1 089 836	19.2
Other	9 164	0.2

Table NM-16. Agriculture

(Number, acres, and dollars.)

Item	2002		2007		Percent change, 2002–2007
	Number	Percent of total	Number	Percent of total	
Number of farms	15 170		20 930		38.0
Farm Size					
Average size of farm (acres)	2 954		2 066		-30.1
Farms by size (number of farms)					
Fewer than 50 acres	6 781	44.7	10 876	52.0	60.4
50 to 499 acres	4 023	26.5	5 213	24.9	29.6
500 acres or more	4 366	28.8	4 841	23.1	10.9
Land (Acres)					
Total land in farms	44 810 083		43 238 049		-3.5
Total cropland	2 575 107	5.7	2 334 018	5.4	-9.4
Total harvested cropland	856 166	1.9	1 009 683	2.3	17.9
Irrigated land	844 799	1.9	830 048	1.9	-1.7
Value of Sales (Dollars)					
Agricultural products sold ($1,000)	1 700 030		2 175 080		27.9
Average sales per farm	112 065		103 922		-7.3
Sales of crops	397 257	23.4	553 140	25.4	39.2
Sales of livestock, poultry, and their products	1 302 773	76.6	1 621 940	74.6	24.5
Value of Sales (Number of Farms)					
Less than $10,000	10 363	68.3	15 268	72.9	47.3
$10,000 to $99,999	3 219	21.2	3 973	19.0	23.4
$100,000 to $999,999	1 326	8.7	1 381	6.6	4.1
$1,000,000 or more	262	1.7	308	1.5	17.6
Farms by Type of Organization (Number of Farms)					
Family	13 455	88.7	18 185	86.9	35.2
Partnership	885	5.8	1 456	7.0	64.5
Corporation	631	4.2	839	4.0	33.0
Other: cooperative, estate or trust, institutional, etc	199	1.3	450	2.2	126.1
Value of Land and Buildings (Dollars)					
Estimated market value of land and buildings ($1,000)	14 568 969		10 631 082		-27.0
Land and buildings average value per farm	696 081		698 908		0.4
Average value per acre	337		234		-30.6
Government Payments					
Number of farms receiving government payments	3 246	21.4	3 329	15.9	2.6
Payments (thousands of dollars)	50 201		43 377		-13.6
Average payment per farm	15 466		13 030		-15.8
Farm Operator Characteristics					
Farm operators whose principal occupation is farming	8 482	55.9	10 040	48.0	18.4
Farm operators whose principal occupation is other	6 688	44.1	10 890	52.0	62.8
Average age principal operator (years)	56.4		59.6		5.7

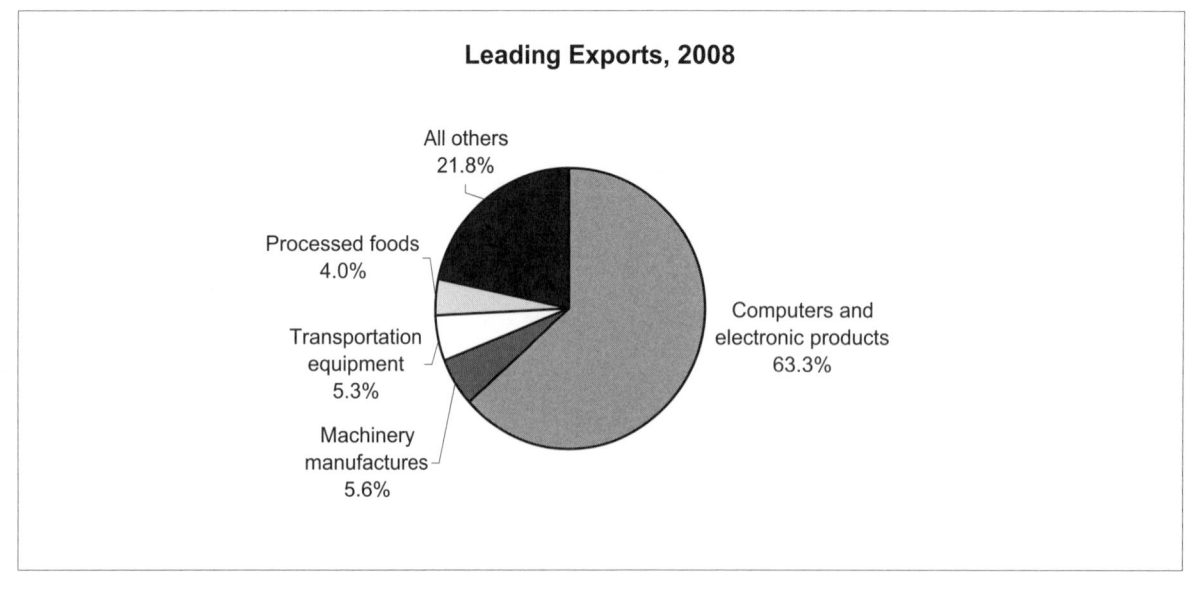

Leading Exports, 2008

All others 21.8%

Processed foods 4.0%

Transportation equipment 5.3%

Machinery manufactures 5.6%

Computers and electronic products 63.3%

NEW YORK

Facts and Figures

Location: Northeastern United States; bordered on the N by Canada (Ontario and Quebec) and Lake Ontario; on the E by Vermont, Massachusetts, and Connecticut; on the S by New Jersey and Pennsylvania; and on the W by Pennsylvania, Lake Erie, Canada (Ontario), and Lake Ontario

Area: 54,556 sq. mi. (141,299 sq. km.); rank—27th

Population: 19,490,297 (2008 est.); rank—3rd

Principal Cities: capital—Albany; largest—New York City

Statehood: July 26, 1788; 11th state

U.S. Congress: 2 senators, 29 representatives

State Motto: *Excelsior* ("Ever upward")

State Song: "I Love New York"

State Nickname: The Empire State

Abbreviations: NY; N.Y.

State Symbols: flower—rose; tree—sugar maple; bird—bluebird

At a Glance

- With an increase in population of 2.7 percent, New York ranked 40th among the states in growth from 2000 to 2008.
- An estimated 134,969 marriages took place in New York in 2008, compared to 52,251 divorces.
- The 2007 home ownership rate in New York was 55.9 percent, giving it a ranking of 50th among the states.
- New York's median household income in 2007 was $53,514, 18th among the states.
- In New York, 13.7 percent of the population lived below the poverty level in 2007, ranking it 17th.
- In 2006-07, 13.6 percent of New Yorkers did not have health insurance, compared to 15.5 percent of the total U.S. population.
- In 2007, 4.6 percent of New Yorkers were unemployed, which was the same as the national average.
- New York ranked 9th in the nation with 31.7 percent of its population 25 years old and over having a bachelor's degree in 2007.
- New York's violent crime rate in 2007 was 414.1 per 100,000 population, compared to 466.9 for the entire nation.
- New York had one physician for every 226 people in 2007, compared to one physician for every 325 people nationwide.
- In the 2008 election, 58 percent of New York's eligible voters voted, compared to 61.7 percent of eligible voters nationwide.
- New York ranked 6th among the states receiving federal aid in 2007, with $2,228 per capita.
- New York's gross domestic product was $1.1 trillion in 2007; it ranked 3rd among the states.
- With $71.1 billion in exports in 2007, New York ranked 3rd in exports.
- New Yorkers consumed 3.94 trillion Btu's of energy in 2006; the state ranked 5th in total consumption.
- In 2007, New York exported $2.1 billion worth of agricultural products, about 2.6 percent of the U.S. total.

Table NY-1. Population by Sex, Age, Race, and Hispanic Origin

(Number, percent.)

Sex, age, race, and Hispanic origin	1990	2000	2008	Average annual percent change, 2000–2008
Total Population	17 990 455	18 976 457	19 490 297	0.3
Percent of total U.S. population	7.2	6.7	6.4	X
Sex				
Male	8 625 673	9 146 748	9 462 063	0.4
Female	9 364 782	9 829 709	10 028 234	0.3
Age				
Under 5 years	1 255 764	1 239 417	1 208 495	-0.3
5 to 19 years	3 548 310	3 971 834	3 798 695	-0.6
20 to 64 years	10 822 659	11 316 854	11 875 435	0.6
65 years and over	2 363 722	2 448 352	2 607 672	0.8
Median age (years)	33.7	35.9	38.0	X
Race and Hispanic Origin[1]				
One race				
White	13 385 255	12 893 689	14 310 269	1.3
Black	2 859 055	3 014 385	3 362 736	1.4
American Indian and Alaskan Native	62 651	82 461	111 337	3.8
Asian[2]	693 760	1 044 976	1 368 585	3.4
Native Hawaiian and Other Pacific Islander	X	8 818	20 548	11.2
Two or more races	X	590 182	316 822	-7.5
Hispanic (of any race)	2 214 026	2 867 583	3 250 038	1.6

[1]Data on race in 2000 and 2008 are not comparable to 1990. Individuals could only report one race in the 1990 census but could report one or more races on the 2000 census.
[2]Data in 1990 refer to Asian and Pacific Islanders.

Table NY-2. Marital Status

(Number, percent distribution.)

Sex and marital status	1990	2000	2007
Males, 15 Years and Over	6 797 219	7 123 715	7 524 557
Never married	35.8	34.7	39.0
Now married, except separated	53.2	53.3	49.2
Separated	2.8	2.7	2.3
Widowed	2.9	2.8	2.7
Divorced	5.3	6.5	6.9
Females, 15 Years and Over	7 619 289	7 932 161	8 175 384
Never married	28.9	29.0	33.4
Now married, except separated	46.9	47.1	43.3
Separated	4.0	3.7	3.5
Widowed	12.7	11.2	10.3
Divorced	7.6	8.9	9.5

Table NY-3. Households and Housing Characteristics

(Number, percent, and dollars.)

Item	1990	2000	2007	Average annual percent change, 2000–2007
Total Households	6 639 322	7 056 860	7 099 940	0.1
Family households	4 489 312	4 639 387	4 594 823	-0.1
Married-couple family	3 315 845	3 289 514	3 222 112	-0.3
Other family	1 173 467	1 349 873	1 372 711	0.2
Male householder, no wife present	254 201	311 697	349 988	1.7
Female householder, no husband present	919 266	1 038 176	1 022 723	-0.2
Nonfamily households	2 150 010	2 417 473	2 505 117	0.5
Householder living alone	1 806 263	1 982 742	2 087 504	0.7
Householder not living alone	343 747	434 731	417 613	-0.6
Housing Characteristics				
Total housing units	7 226 891	7 679 307	7 940 072	0.5
Occupied housing units	6 639 322	7 056 860	7 099 940	0.1
Owner-occupied	3 464 436	3 739 166	3 941 790	0.8
Renter-occupied	3 174 886	3 317 694	3 158 150	-0.7
Average size	2.63	2.61	2.63	X
Financial Characteristics				
Median gross rent of renter-occupied housing units (dollars)	486	672	907	4.4
Median monthly owner costs for housing units with a mortgage (dollars)	894	1 357	1 865	4.6
Median value of owner-occupied housing units (dollars)	130 400	148 700	311 000	11.1

Table NY-4. Median Income and Poverty Status, 2007

(Number, percent.)

Characteristic	State		U.S.	
	Number	Percent	Number	Percent
Median Income				
Households (dollars)	53 514	X	50 740	X
Families (dollars)	64 602	X	61 173	X
Below Poverty Level				
Sex				
Male	1 106 435	12.2	16 576 071	11.5
Female	1 463 579	15.1	21 476 176	14.3
Age				
Under 18 years	844 424	19.4	13 097 100	18.0
Related children under 18 years	824 403	19.1	12 728 964	17.6
18 to 64 years	1 441 455	12.0	21 495 507	11.6
65 years and over	284 135	11.7	3 459 640	9.5

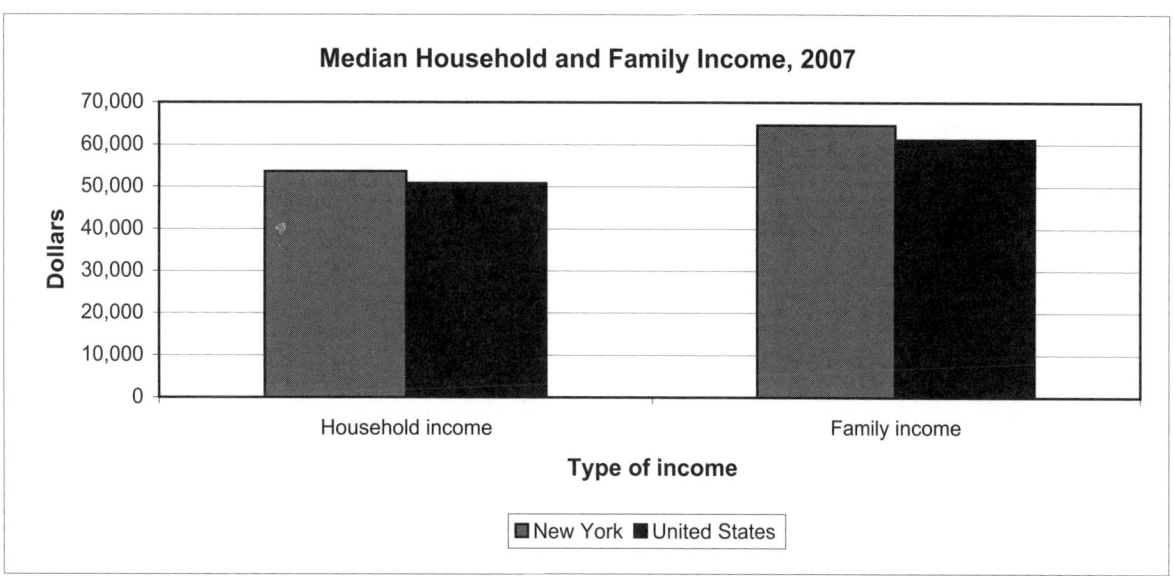

Median Household and Family Income, 2007

Dollars — Type of income

■ New York ■ United States

Table NY-5. Health Insurance Coverage Status for All Persons and Children Under 18 Years of Age

(Number, percent.)

Item	2000	2001	2002	2003	2004	2005	2006	2007
ALL PERSONS	18 788	18 827	19 283	18 970	19 054	19 022	19 040	19 062
Covered by Private or Government Health Insurance								
Number	15 787	15 996	16 336	16 187	16 652	16 548	16 378	16 543
Percent	84.0	85.0	84.7	85.3	87.4	87.0	86.0	86.8
Not Covered								
Number	3 001	2 831	2 947	2 784	2 402	2 474	2 662	2 519
Percent	16.0	15.0	15.3	14.7	12.6	13.0	14.0	13.2
Percent in the U.S. not covered	13.7	14.1	14.7	15.1	14.9	15.3	15.8	15.3
CHILDREN UNDER 18 YEARS OF AGE	4 606	4 565	4 663	4 572	4 599	4 534	4 547	4 437
Covered by Private or Government Health Insurance								
Number	4 120	4 148	4 224	4 154	4 289	4 187	4 167	4 042
Percent	89.4	90.9	90.6	90.9	93.3	92.3	91.6	91.1
Not Covered								
Number	487	417	438	418	310	347	380	395
Percent	10.6	9.1	9.4	9.1	6.7	7.7	8.4	8.9
Percent in the U.S. not covered	11.6	11.3	11.2	11.0	10.5	10.9	11.7	11.0

Table NY-6. Employment Status by Demographic Group, Preliminary 2008

(Number, percent.)

Characteristic	Civilian noninstitutional population	Civilian labor force		Employment		Unemployed	
		Number	Percent of population	Number	Percent of population	Number	Unemployment rate
TOTAL	15 231	9 604	63.1	9 074	59.6	530	5.5
Sex							
Men	7 256	5 066	70.0	4 763	65.6	303	6.0
Women	7 975	4 538	57.0	4 311	54.1	227	5.0
Race, Sex, and Hispanic Origin							
White	11 391	7 227	63.4	6 880	60.4	347	4.8
Men	5 517	3 886	70.4	3 688	66.8	197	5.1
Women	5 873	3 341	56.9	3 192	54.3	149	4.5
Black or African American	2 480	1 523	61.4	1 380	55.6	144	9.4
Men	1 091	712	65.3	630	57.7	82	11.6
Women	1 389	811	58.4	750	54.0	61	7.5
Hispanic	2 288	1 400	61.2	1 305	57.0	94	6.7
Men	1 114	799	71.7	746	67.0	53	6.6
Women	1 174	601	51.2	559	47.6	42	6.9
Age							
16 to 19 years	1 109	355	32.0	289	26.0	66	18.5
20 to 24 years	1 378	894	64.9	797	57.8	97	10.9
25 to 34 years	2 571	2 124	82.6	2 015	78.4	109	5.1
35 to 44 years	2 668	2 194	82.2	2 095	78.5	99	4.5
45 to 54 years	2 775	2 228	80.3	2 143	77.2	85	3.8
55 to 64 years	2 141	1 394	65.1	1 337	62.5	56	4.0
65 years and over	2 589	416	16.0	397	15.3	18	4.4

Note: Data in Table 6 are from the Current Population Survey (CPS) and do not match the estimates in Table 7. See notes and definitions for more details.

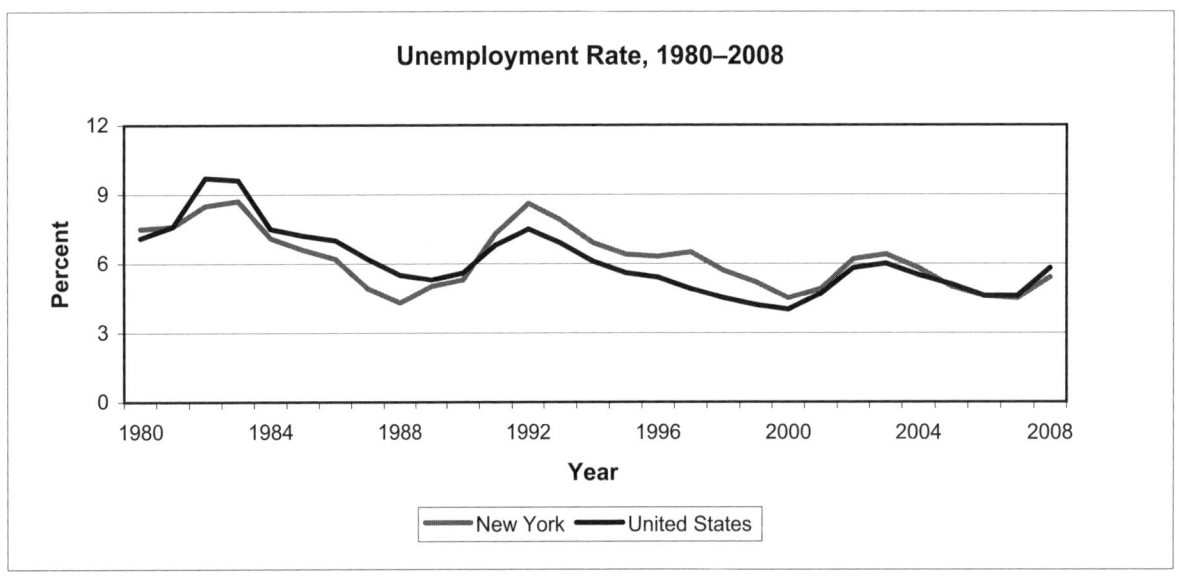

Table NY-7. Employment Status of the Civilian Noninstitutional Population Age 16 Years and Over

(Number, percent.)

Year	Civilian labor force	Civilian participation rate	Employed	Unemployed	Unemployment rate
1998	9 058 800	63.0	8 546 550	512 250	5.7
1999	9 134 079	63.1	8 657 431	476 648	5.2
2000	9 166 972	63.0	8 751 441	415 531	4.5
2001	9 193 266	62.7	8 743 924	449 342	4.9
2002	9 299 036	63.0	8 721 428	577 608	6.2
2003	9 299 000	62.6	8 703 889	595 111	6.4
2004	9 360 085	62.6	8 816 013	544 072	5.8
2005	9 442 870	62.7	8 967 792	475 078	5.0
2006	9 530 103	62.9	9 091 712	438 391	4.6
2007	9 574 776	62.7	9 140 869	433 907	4.5
2008	9 679 617	63.1	9 152 934	526 683	5.4

Table NY-8. Employment and Average Wages by Industry

(Estimates for 2001–2006 are based on the 2002 North American Industry Classification System [NAICS]. Estimates for 2007 are based on the 2007 NAICS.)

Industry	2001	2002	2003	2004	2005	2006	2007
	Number of jobs						
WAGE AND SALARY EMPLOYMENT BY INDUSTRY	8 906 825	8 769 557	8 727 501	8 775 838	8 840 630	8 924 994	9 047 065
Farm Wage and Salary Employment	21 271	21 367	22 008	18 346	17 768	16 440	16 002
Nonfarm Wage and Salary Employment	8 885 554	8 748 190	8 705 493	8 757 492	8 822 862	8 908 554	9 031 063
Private wage and salary employment	7 400 825	7 242 364	7 202 761	7 258 582	7 322 402	7 409 138	7 520 543
Forestry, fishing, hunting, and other	15 745	15 482	15 186	15 122	15 308	15 395	15 318
Mining	4 396	4 221	4 472	4 795	4 998	5 325	5 501
Utilities	43 030	42 719	41 340	39 592	39 561	39 237	38 829
Construction	343 293	334 192	332 083	334 347	336 859	349 187	365 620
Manufacturing	713 949	657 847	619 552	602 099	588 059	573 638	559 462
Durable goods manufacturing	411 713	376 582	351 219	343 530	337 751	333 329	328 839
Nondurable goods manufacturing	302 236	281 265	268 333	258 569	250 308	240 309	230 623
Wholesale trade	373 136	360 846	358 309	359 277	358 736	359 383	362 265
Retail trade	895 828	885 469	884 186	895 757	906 836	910 507	924 186
Transportation and warehousing	243 023	229 921	228 690	231 523	234 275	239 498	242 830
Information	326 372	298 265	277 672	270 926	271 818	269 974	265 938
Finance and insurance	575 847	545 006	535 471	536 602	545 051	560 050	562 559
Real estate and rental and leasing	190 346	186 140	187 923	190 146	192 244	192 390	193 749
Professional and technical services	574 190	547 566	544 819	552 579	567 211	588 033	609 765
Management of companies and enterprises	116 458	119 367	121 040	119 933	123 316	127 553	128 661
Administrative and waste services	440 213	420 937	414 750	421 601	430 037	429 144	438 737
Educational services	303 711	311 426	319 439	330 182	333 308	337 817	346 153
Health care and social assistance	1 164 801	1 192 246	1 215 892	1 231 538	1 249 166	1 273 117	1 294 019
Arts, entertainment, and recreation	128 226	129 850	130 845	137 107	136 431	139 076	143 149
Accommodation and food services	517 077	518 866	527 299	538 283	545 919	552 400	570 839
Other services, except public administration	431 184	441 998	443 793	447 173	443 269	447 414	452 963
Government and government enterprises	1 484 729	1 505 826	1 502 732	1 498 910	1 500 460	1 499 416	1 510 520
	Dollars						
AVERAGE WAGES AND SALARIES BY INDUSTRY	46 024	45 631	46 582	49 206	51 234	54 682	58 481
Average Farm Wages and Salaries	18 619	24 397	20 233	24 070	19 787	24 753	22 101
Average Nonfarm Wages and Salaries	46 090	45 682	46 649	49 259	51 297	54 737	58 546
Average private wages and salaries	47 104	46 449	47 345	50 133	52 314	56 145	60 436
Forestry, fishing, hunting, and other	69 260	70 026	67 679	67 584	67 487	66 121	67 769
Mining	43 674	44 410	47 062	47 319	48 783	50 458	54 332
Utilities	70 196	77 617	79 023	82 570	83 082	87 423	92 494
Construction	46 559	47 679	48 649	49 185	50 366	52 817	55 801
Manufacturing	44 856	46 167	48 168	50 076	51 764	53 582	55 847
Durable goods manufacturing	47 731	48 777	50 785	52 592	54 286	56 800	59 104
Nondurable goods manufacturing	40 940	42 674	44 743	46 734	48 360	49 118	51 202
Wholesale trade	54 672	55 779	57 610	60 234	62 302	65 411	69 071
Retail trade	24 228	24 962	25 666	26 486	27 219	28 136	29 163
Transportation and warehousing	36 719	37 328	38 028	38 965	39 831	41 197	43 137
Information	67 381	66 510	70 251	73 400	75 904	81 122	86 206
Finance and insurance	136 371	124 251	124 305	143 131	152 709	176 787	206 064
Real estate and rental and leasing	41 453	42 024	42 868	45 739	47 968	51 017	55 632
Professional and technical services	68 487	68 510	69 925	73 490	76 962	80 271	84 759
Management of companies and enterprises	106 178	112 635	107 336	115 018	120 312	125 907	140 911
Administrative and waste services	30 288	30 899	32 409	33 875	35 492	36 732	39 425
Educational services	29 963	31 167	32 184	32 931	34 408	35 890	37 443
Health care and social assistance	32 812	33 682	35 259	36 700	37 745	39 145	40 580
Arts, entertainment, and recreation	36 615	36 944	38 341	39 816	40 328	44 517	45 017
Accommodation and food services	18 276	18 543	19 068	20 011	20 748	22 077	22 911
Other services, except public administration	24 059	25 041	26 150	26 874	28 063	29 053	30 378
Government and government enterprises	41 032	41 997	43 311	45 027	46 335	47 782	49 132

Table NY-9. Employment Characteristics by Family Type

(Number, percent.)

Family type and labor force status	2005		2006		2007	
	Total	Families with own children under 18 years	Total	Families with own children under 18 years	Total	Families with own children under 18 years
TOTAL FAMILIES	4 615 803	2 169 861	4 573 941	2 128 535	4 594 823	2 117 702
FAMILY TYPE AND LABOR FORCE STATUS						
Married Coupled Families	3 194 969	1 429 289	3 200 366	1 422 947	3 222 112	1 413 595
Both husband and wife in labor force	50.7	60.5	52.1	62.3	52.4	62.7
Husband in labor force, wife not in labor force	23.6	31.1	23.5	31.1	23.1	30.5
Wife in labor force, husband not in labor force	8.1	5.0	7.7	4.3	7.7	4.4
Both husband and wife not in labor force	17.6	3.5	16.7	2.4	16.8	2.4
Other Families	1 420 834	740 572	1 373 575	705 588	1 372 711	704 107
Female householder, no husband present	75.0	79.9	75.4	80.2	74.5	79.0
In labor force	49.6	60.6	51.2	62.4	50.0	60.4
Not in labor force	25.5	19.3	24.2	17.8	24.5	18.6
Male householder, no wife present	25.0	20.1	24.6	19.8	25.5	21.0
In labor force	19.2	17.5	19.2	17.2	19.8	18.6
Not in labor force	5.8	2.5	5.4	2.6	5.7	2.5

Table NY-10. School Enrollment and Educational Attainment, 2007

(Number, percent.)

Item	State	U.S.
Enrollment		
Total population 3 years and over	18 584 644	289 295 761
Enrolled in school	5 071 883	79 329 527
Enrolled in preschool (percent)	6.1	6.2
Enrolled in grades K-12 (percent)	64.9	67.6
Enrolled in college or graduate school (percent)	29.0	26.2
Attainment		
Total population 25 years and over	12 900 108	197 892 369
Less than a high school diploma (percent)	15.9	15.5
High school diploma or more (percent)	84.1	84.5
Bachelor's degree or more (percent)	31.7	27.5
Graduate degree or more (percent)	13.5	10.1

Table NY-11. Educational Indicators

(Number, percent.)

Item	State	U.S.
Public Schools, 2006–2007 (except where noted)		
Number of school districts	866	17 742
Number of schools	4 710	99 639
Number of students	2 809 649	49 315 842
Student-teacher ratio	12.8	15.5
Expenditures per student (dollars)	$15 546	. . .
Averaged freshman graduation rate, 2005–2006	67.4	. . .
Dropout rate, grades 9–12, 2005–2006	4.6	3.7
Students eligible for free or reduced-price lunch (percent)	43.7	41.2
English-language learners (percent)	7.0	5.1
Students with IEP (percent)	16.0	12.7
Private Schools, 2007–2008 (except where noted)		
Number of schools	2 130	33 740
Number of students	458 231	5 072 451
High school graduates, 2006–2007	29 891	306 605
Student-teacher ratio	10.7	11.1

Table NY-12. Reported Voting and Registration of the Voting-Age Population, November 2008

(Number in thousands, percent.)

Item	Total population	Total citizen population	Registered			Voted		
			Total registered	Percent registered (total population)	Percent registered (total citizen population)	Total voted	Percent voted (total population)	Percent voted (total citizen population)
U.S. total	225 499	206 072	146 311	64.9	71.0	131 144	58.2	63.6
State total	14 665	12 849	8 458	57.7	65.8	7 559	51.5	58.8
Sex								
Male	6 999	6 044	3 912	55.9	64.7	3 471	49.6	57.4
Female	7 666	6 805	4 546	59.3	66.8	4 089	53.3	60.1
Race								
White alone	10 972	9 987	6 941	63.3	69.5	6 166	56.2	61.7
White non-Hispanic alone	9 259	8 857	6 211	67.1	70.1	5 519	59.6	62.3
Black alone	2 350	1 957	1 143	48.6	58.4	1 075	45.7	54.9
Asian alone	1 120	743	289	25.8	38.8	248	22.2	33.4
Hispanic (of any race)	2 042	1 348	836	40.9	62.0	743	36.4	55.1
White alone or in combination	11 143	10 107	7 018	63.0	69.4	6 229	55.9	61.6
Black alone or in combination	2 432	2 023	1 169	48.0	57.8	1 097	45.1	54.2
Asian alone or in combination	1 130	754	299	26.5	39.7	255	22.6	33.9

Table NY-13. Crime

(Number, rate per 100,000.)

Item	State			U.S.		
	2007	2008	Percent change	2007	2008	Percent change
Population	19 297 729	19 490 297	1.0	301 621 157	304 059 724	0.8
VIOLENT CRIME						
Number	79 915	77 585	-2.9	1 408 337	1 382 012	-1.9
Rate	414.1	398.1	-3.9	466.9	454.5	-2.7
Murder and Nonnegligent Manslaughter						
Number	801	836	4.4	16 929	16 272	-3.9
Rate	4.2	4.3	3.3	5.6	5.4	-4.7
Forcible Rape						
Number	2 926	2 801	-4.3	90 427	89 000	-1.6
Rate	15.2	14.4	-5.2	30.0	29.3	-2.4
Robbery						
Number	31 094	31 778	2.2	445 125	441 855	-0.7
Rate	161.1	163.0	1.2	147.6	145.3	-1.5
Aggravated Assault						
Number	45 094	42 170	-6.5	855 856	834 885	-2.5
Rate	233.7	216.4	-7.4	283.8	274.6	-3.2
PROPERTY CRIME						
Number	381 816	388 533	1.8	9 843 481	9 767 915	-0.8
Rate	1 978.6	1 993.5	0.8	3 263.5	3 212.5	-1.6
Burglary						
Number	64 857	65 735	1.4	2 179 140	2 222 196	2.0
Rate	336.1	337.3	0.4	722.5	730.8	1.2
Larceny-Theft						
Number	288 929	297 684	3.0	6 568 572	6 588 873	0.3
Rate	1 497.2	1 527.3	2.0	2 177.8	2 167.0	-0.5
Motor Vehicle Theft						
Number	28 030	25 114	-10.4	1 095 769	956 846	-12.7
Rate	145.3	128.9	-11.3	363.3	314.7	-13.4

Table NY-14. State Government Finances, 2007

(Dollars, percent distribution.)

Item	Thousands of dollars	Percent distribution
Total Revenue	178 908 359	X
General revenue	130 399 016	72.9
Intergovernmental revenue	47 324 109	26.5
Taxes	63 161 582	35.3
General sales	10 879 888	6.1
Selective sales	8 625 797	4.8
License taxes	1 327 930	0.7
Individual income tax	34 579 992	19.3
Corporate income tax	5 416 105	3.0
Other taxes	2 331 870	1.3
Current charges	8 033 534	4.5
Miscellaneous general revenue	11 879 791	6.6
Utility revenue	7 655 332	4.3
Liquor store revenue	0	0.0
Insurance trust revenue	40 854 011	22.8
Total Expenditure	151 338 991	100.0
Intergovernmental expenditure	50 525 675	33.4
Direct expenditure	100 813 316	66.6
Current operation	70 215 442	46.4
Capital outlay	10 269 777	6.8
Insurance benefits and repayments	14 115 445	9.3
Assistance and subsidies	1 427 044	0.9
Interest on debt	4 785 608	3.2
Exhibit: Salaries and wages	16 094 566	10.6
Total Expenditure	151 338 991	100.0
General expenditure	124 834 333	82.5
Intergovernmental expenditure	50 525 675	33.4
Direct expenditure	74 308 658	49.1
Education	37 086 748	24.5
Public welfare	46 614 760	30.8
Hospitals	4 599 507	3.0
Health	6 747 721	4.5
Highways	4 250 420	2.8
Police protection	906 359	0.6
Correction	3 126 699	2.1
Natural resources	499 438	0.3
Parks and recreation	577 578	0.4
Government administration	5 057 604	3.3
Interest on general debt	3 593 858	2.4
Other and unallocable	11 773 641	7.8
Utility expenditure	12 389 213	8.2
Liquor store expenditure	0	0.0
Insurance trust expenditure	14 115 445	9.3
Debt at End of Fiscal Year	110 084 829	X
Cash and Security Holdings	347 377 484	X

Table NY-15. State Government Tax Collections, 2008

(Dollars, percent distribution.)

Item	Thousands of dollars	Percent distribution
Total Taxes	65 400 355	X
Sales and gross receipts	20 179 747	30.9
General sales and gross receipts	11 294 737	17.3
Selective sales taxes	8 885 010	13.6
Alcoholic beverages	205 253	0.3
Amusements	951	0.0
Insurance premiums	1 137 058	1.7
Motor fuels	527 840	0.8
Pari-mutuels	30 875	0.0
Public utilities	793 359	1.2
Tobacco products	973 489	1.5
Other selective sales	5 216 185	8.0
Licenses	1 355 826	2.1
Alcoholic beverages	61 082	0.1
Amusements	79	0.0
Corporation	70 094	0.1
Hunting and fishing	43 277	0.1
Motor vehicle	860 519	1.3
Motor vehicle operators	145 084	0.2
Public utility	12 693	0.0
Occupation and business, NEC	147 920	0.2
Other licenses	15 078	0.0
Income taxes	41 601 778	63.6
Individual income	36 563 948	55.9
Corporation net income	5 037 830	7.7
Other taxes	2 263 004	3.5
Death and gift	1 037 531	1.6
Documentary and stock transfer	1 225 473	1.9

Table NY-16. Agriculture

(Number, acres, and dollars.)

Item	2002		2007		Percent change, 2002–2007
	Number	Percent of total	Number	Percent of total	
Number of farms	37 255		36 352		-2.4
Farm Size					
Average size of farm (acres)	206		197		-4.4
Farms by size (number of farms)					
Fewer than 50 acres	11 318	30.4	11 713	32.2	3.5
50 to 499 acres	22 451	60.3	21 586	59.4	-3.9
500 acres or more	3 486	9.4	3 053	8.4	-12.4
Land (Acres)					
Total land in farms	7 660 969		7 174 743		-6.3
Total cropland	4 841 367	63.2	4 314 954	60.1	-10.9
Total harvested cropland	3 846 368	50.2	3 651 278	50.9	-5.1
Irrigated land	74 663	1.0	68 010	0.9	-8.9
Value of Sales (Dollars)					
Agricultural products sold ($1,000)	3 117 834		4 418 634		41.7
Average sales per farm	83 689		121 551		45.2
Sales of crops	1 135 129	36.4	1 561 927	35.3	37.6
Sales of livestock, poultry, and their products	1 982 706	63.6	2 856 706	64.7	44.1
Value of Sales (Number of Farms)					
Less than $10,000	20 830	55.9	19 849	54.6	-4.7
$10,000 to $99,999	9 974	26.8	9 653	26.6	-3.2
$100,000 to $999,999	5 980	16.1	6 038	16.6	1.0
$1,000,000 or more	471	1.3	812	2.2	72.4
Farms by Type of Organization (Number of Farms)					
Family	32 654	87.6	30 621	84.2	-6.2
Partnership	2 846	7.6	3 347	9.2	17.6
Corporation	1 581	4.2	2 110	5.8	33.5
Other: cooperative, estate or trust, institutional, etc	174	0.5	274	0.8	57.5
Value of Land and Buildings (Dollars)					
Estimated market value of land and buildings ($1,000)	16 322 415		12 870 727		-21.1
Land and buildings average value per farm	449 010		345 504		-23.1
Average value per acre	2 275		1 708		-24.9
Government Payments					
Number of farms receiving government payments	9 896	26.6	10 596	29.1	7.1
Payments (thousands of dollars)	110 234		62 652		-43.2
Average payment per farm	11 139		5 913		-46.9
Farm Operator Characteristics					
Farm operators whose principal occupation is farming	22 664	60.8	19 624	54.0	-13.4
Farm operators whose principal occupation is other	14 591	39.2	16 728	46.0	14.6
Average age principal operator (years)	54.1		56.2		3.9

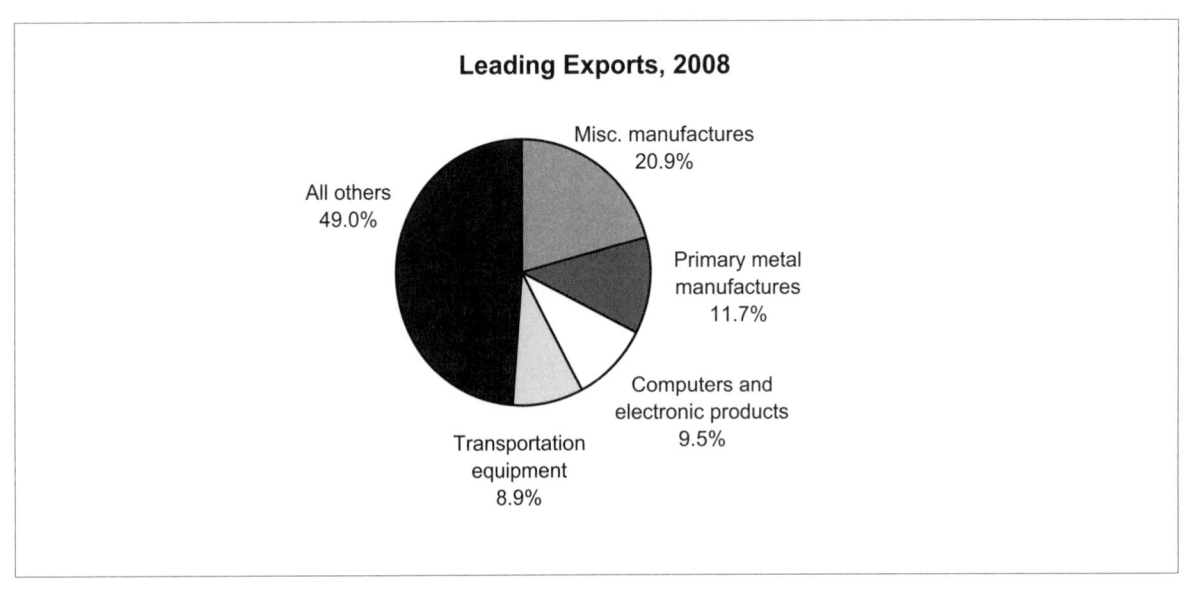

Leading Exports, 2008

Misc. manufactures 20.9%

All others 49.0%

Primary metal manufactures 11.7%

Computers and electronic products 9.5%

Transportation equipment 8.9%

NORTH CAROLINA

Facts and Figures

Location: Southeastern United States; bordered on the N by Virginia, on the E by the Atlantic Ocean, on the S by South Carolina and Georgia, and on the W by Tennessee

Area: 53,819 sq. mi. (139,389 sq. km.); rank—28th

Population: 9,222,414 (2008 est.); rank—10th

Principal Cities: capital—Raleigh; largest—Charlotte

Statehood: November 21, 1789; 12th state

U.S. Congress: 2 senators, 13 representatives

State Motto: *Esse quam videri* ("To be rather than to seem")

State Song: "The Old North State"

State Nicknames: The Tar Heel State; The Old North State

Abbreviations: NC; N.C.

State Symbols: flower—flowering dogwood; tree—pine; bird—cardinal

At a Glance

- With an increase in population of 14.6 percent, North Carolina ranked 9th among the states in growth from 2000 to 2008.
- An estimated 58,994 marriages took place in North Carolina in 2008, compared to 35,086 divorces.
- The 2007 home ownership rate in North Carolina was 70.3 percent; its ranking of 28th was tied with that of Connecticut and Oklahoma.
- North Carolina's median household income in 2007 was $44,670, 37th among the states.
- In North Carolina, 14.3 percent of the population lived below the poverty level in 2007, ranking it 12th along with Georgia.
- In 2006-07, 17.2 percent of North Carolinians did not have health insurance, compared to 15.5 percent of the total U.S. population.
- In 2007, 4.5 percent of North Carolinians were unemployed, compared to 4.6 percent nationwide.
- North Carolina ranked 28th in the nation with 25.6 percent of its population 25 years old and over having a bachelor's degree in 2007.
- North Carolina's violent crime rate in 2007 was 466.4 per 100,000 population, compared to 466.9 for the entire nation.
- North Carolina had one physician for every 348 people in 2007, compared to one physician for every 325 people nationwide.
- In the 2008 election, 65.8 percent of North Carolina's eligible voters voted, compared to 61.7 percent of eligible voters nationwide.
- North Carolina ranked 25th among the states receiving federal aid in 2007, with $1,377 per capita.
- North Carolina's gross domestic product was $399 billion in 2007; it ranked 9th among the states.
- With $23.4 billion in exports in 2007, North Carolina ranked 15th in exports.
- North Carolinians consumed 2.66 trillion Btu's of energy in 2006; the state ranked 12th in total consumption.
- In 2007, North Carolina exported $2.1 billion worth of agricultural products, about 2.6 percent of the U.S. total.

Table NC-1. Population by Sex, Age, Race, and Hispanic Origin

(Number, percent.)

Sex, age, race, and Hispanic origin	1990	2000	2008	Average annual percent change, 2000–2008
Total Population	6 628 637	8 049 313	9 222 414	1.7
Percent of total U.S. population	2.7	2.9	3.0	X
Sex				
Male	3 214 290	3 942 695	4 516 987	1.7
Female	3 414 347	4 106 618	4 705 427	1.7
Age				
Under 5 years	458 955	539 509	652 823	2.4
5 to 19 years	1 374 291	1 653 851	1 847 178	1.4
20 to 64 years	3 991 050	4 886 905	5 583 361	1.7
65 years and over	804 341	969 048	1 139 052	2.0
Median age (years)	33.0	35.3	36.9	X
Race and Hispanic Origin[1]				
One race				
White	5 008 491	5 804 656	6 818 808	2.0
Black	1 456 323	1 737 545	1 991 654	1.7
American Indian and Alaskan Native	80 155	99 551	115 635	1.9
Asian[2]	52 166	113 689	177 177	5.7
Native Hawaiian and Other Pacific Islander	X	3 983	6 776	6.9
Two or more races	X	103 260	112 364	1.1
Hispanic (of any race)	76 726	378 963	684 770	7.7

[1]Data on race in 2000 and 2008 are not comparable to 1990. Individuals could only report one race in the 1990 census but could report one or more races on the 2000 census.
[2]Data in 1990 refer to Asian and Pacific Islanders.

Table NC-2. Marital Status

(Number, percent distribution.)

Sex and marital status	1990	2000	2007
Males, 15 Years and Over	2 532 813	3 092 380	3 486 022
Never married	28.7	28.2	31.6
Now married, except separated	59.3	58.7	54.5
Separated	3.1	2.7	2.6
Widowed	2.4	2.4	2.5
Divorced	6.5	8.1	8.8
Females, 15 Years and Over	2 760 408	3 301 327	3 734 689
Never married	21.9	22.0	25.5
Now married, except separated	53.5	53.9	49.6
Separated	3.8	3.3	3.4
Widowed	12.8	10.9	10.1
Divorced	8.1	9.9	11.4

Table NC-3. Households and Housing Characteristics

(Number, percent, and dollars.)

Item	1990	2000	2007	Average annual percent change, 2000–2007
Total Households	2 517 026	3 132 013	3 540 875	1.8
Family households	1 812 053	2 158 869	2 366 894	1.3
Married-couple family	1 424 206	1 645 346	1 763 797	1.0
Other family	387 847	513 523	603 097	2.3
Male householder, no wife present	77 971	123 526	150 794	2.9
Female householder, no husband present	309 876	389 997	452 303	2.1
Nonfamily households	704 973	973 144	1 173 981	2.7
Householder living alone	596 959	795 271	980 821	3.0
Householder not living alone	108 014	177 873	193 160	1.2
Housing Characteristics				
Total housing units	2 818 193	3 523 944	4 124 066	2.3
Occupied housing units	2 517 026	3 132 013	3 540 875	1.8
Owner-occupied	1 711 817	2 172 355	2 418 252	1.5
Renter-occupied	805 209	959 658	1 122 623	2.3
Average size	2.54	2.49	2.48	X
Financial Characteristics				
Median gross rent of renter-occupied housing units (dollars)	382	548	678	3.1
Median monthly owner costs for housing units with a mortgage (dollars)	655	985	1 189	2.7
Median value of owner-occupied housing units (dollars)	65 300	108 300	145 700	4.3

Table NC-4. Median Income and Poverty Status, 2007

(Number, percent.)

Characteristic	State		U.S.	
	Number	Percent	Number	Percent
Median Income				
Households (dollars)	44 670	X	50 740	X
Families (dollars)	55 028	X	61 173	X
Below Poverty Level				
Sex				
Male	528 851	12.4	16 576 071	11.5
Female	730 137	16.1	21 476 176	14.3
Age				
Under 18 years	426 047	19.5	13 097 100	18.0
Related children under 18 years	415 531	19.2	12 728 964	17.6
18 to 64 years	716 747	12.9	21 495 507	11.6
65 years and over	116 194	11.0	3 459 640	9.5

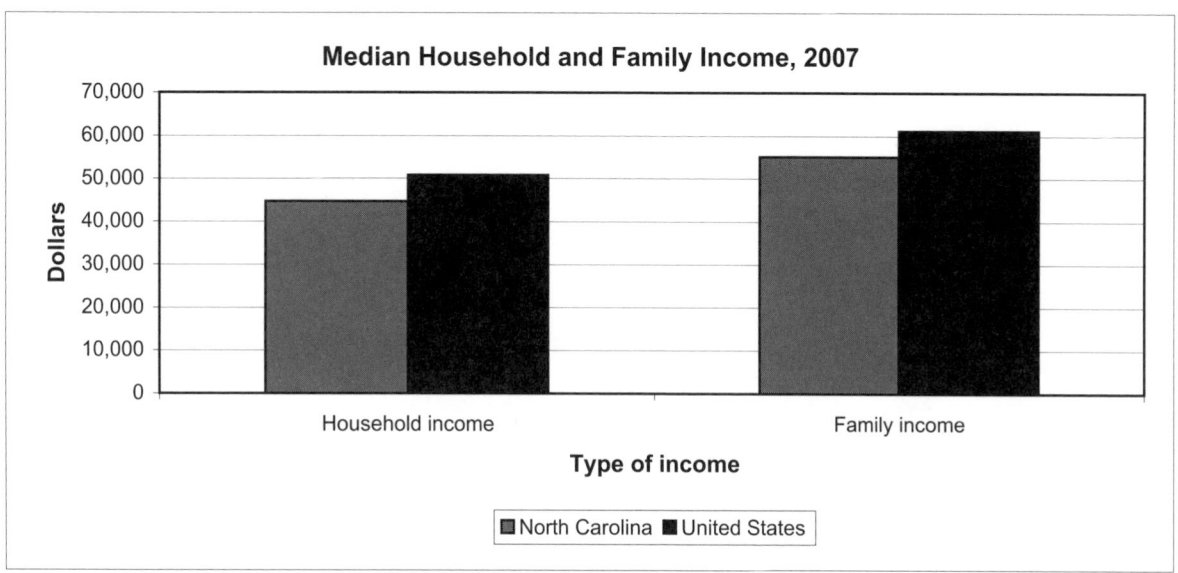

Median Household and Family Income, 2007

Table NC-5. Health Insurance Coverage Status for All Persons and Children Under 18 Years of Age

(Number, percent.)

Item	2000	2001	2002	2003	2004	2005	2006	2007
ALL PERSONS	7 997	8 098	8 162	8 253	8 435	8 561	8 851	9 183
Covered by Private or Government Health Insurance								
Number	6 951	6 987	6 825	6 855	7 182	7 249	7 266	7 673
Percent	86.9	86.3	83.6	83.1	85.2	84.7	82.1	83.6
Not Covered								
Number	1 046	1 111	1 337	1 398	1 252	1 312	1 585	1 510
Percent	13.1	13.7	16.4	16.9	14.8	15.3	17.9	16.4
Percent in the U.S. not covered	13.7	14.1	14.7	15.1	14.9	15.3	15.8	15.3
CHILDREN UNDER 18 YEARS OF AGE	2 010	2 115	2 049	2 082	2 145	2 205	2 198	2 247
Covered by Private or Government Health Insurance								
Number	1 810	1 888	1 795	1 839	1 931	1 946	1 891	1 975
Percent	90.1	89.3	87.6	88.3	90.0	88.3	86.0	87.9
Not Covered								
Number	200	227	254	243	214	259	307	272
Percent	9.9	10.7	12.4	11.7	10.0	11.7	14.0	12.1
Percent in the U.S. not covered	11.6	11.3	11.2	11.0	10.5	10.9	11.7	11.0

Table NC-6. Employment Status by Demographic Group, Preliminary 2008

(Number, percent.)

Characteristic	Civilian noninstitutional population	Civilian labor force		Employment		Unemployed	
		Number	Percent of population	Number	Percent of population	Number	Unemployment rate
TOTAL	7 033	4 548	64.7	4 258	60.5	290	6.4
Sex							
Men	3 344	2 402	72.0	2 242	67.0	160	6.7
Women	3 689	2 146	58.0	2 016	54.7	130	6.0
Race, Sex, and Hispanic Origin							
White	5 244	3 401	64.8	3 205	61.1	195	5.7
Men	2 557	1 867	73.0	1 759	68.8	109	5.8
Women	2 687	1 533	57.1	1 447	53.8	87	5.6
Black or African American	1 445	925	64.1	846	58.6	79	8.6
Men	636	426	67.0	384	60.3	43	10.0
Women	808	499	61.7	462	57.2	37	7.4
Hispanic	383	288	75.2	270	70.4	18	6.4
Men	214	195	91.1	186	86.8	9	4.7
Women	169	93	55.0	84	49.6	9	9.9
Age							
16 to 19 years	488	187	38.3	142	29.1	45	24.0
20 to 24 years	583	430	73.7	389	66.6	41	9.6
25 to 34 years	1 214	1 004	82.7	933	76.8	72	7.1
35 to 44 years	1 283	1 075	83.7	1 021	79.6	53	5.0
45 to 54 years	1 269	1 020	80.4	971	76.5	49	4.8
55 to 64 years	1 056	649	61.5	625	59.2	24	3.7
65 years and over	1 140	183	16.0	177	15.5	6	3.1

Note: Data in Table 6 are from the Current Population Survey (CPS) and do not match the estimates in Table 7. See notes and definitions for more details.

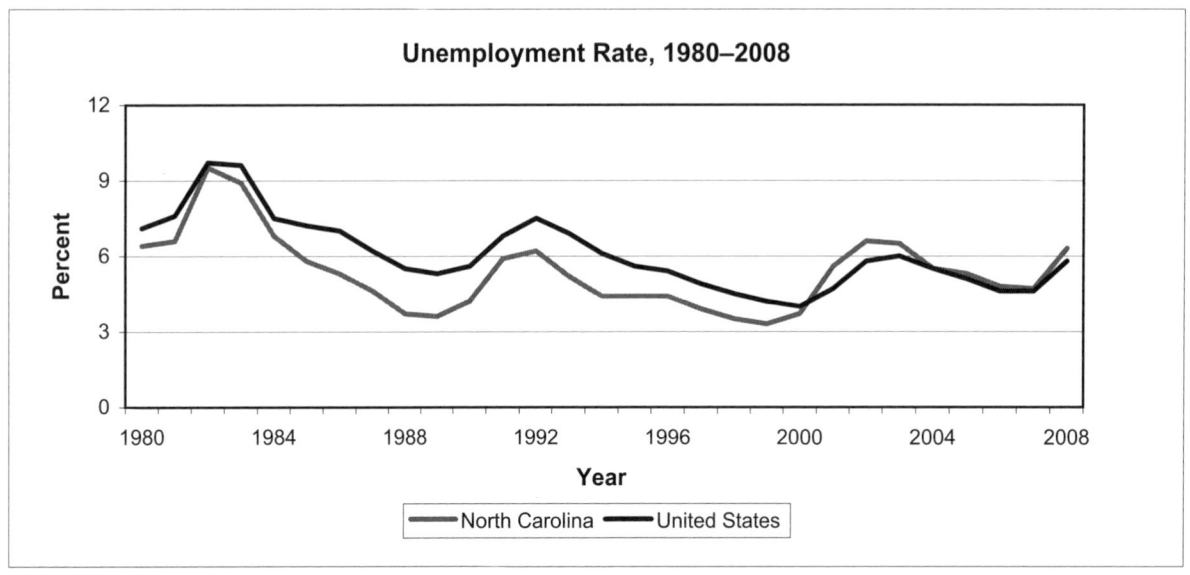

Table NC-7. Employment Status of the Civilian Noninstitutional Population Age 16 Years and Over

(Number, percent.)

Year	Civilian labor force	Civilian participation rate	Employed	Unemployed	Unemployment rate
1998	3 985 573	67.1	3 844 792	140 781	3.5
1999	4 053 949	67.1	3 921 244	132 705	3.3
2000	4 123 812	67.4	3 969 235	154 577	3.7
2001	4 164 911	67.1	3 929 977	234 934	5.6
2002	4 210 018	66.9	3 930 736	279 282	6.6
2003	4 247 830	66.6	3 973 635	274 195	6.5
2004	4 267 406	66.0	4 031 081	236 325	5.5
2005	4 337 060	65.9	4 108 306	228 754	5.3
2006	4 449 262	66.2	4 237 729	211 533	4.8
2007	4 506 144	65.5	4 292 816	213 328	4.7
2008	4 543 754	64.8	4 256 815	286 939	6.3

Table NC-8. Employment and Average Wages by Industry

(Estimates for 2001–2006 are based on the 2002 North American Industry Classification System [NAICS]. Estimates for 2007 are based on the 2007 NAICS.)

Industry	2001	2002	2003	2004	2005	2006	2007
	Number of jobs						
WAGE AND SALARY EMPLOYMENT BY INDUSTRY	4 117 025	4 082 005	4 062 357	4 122 797	4 203 740	4 319 731	4 423 523
Farm Wage and Salary Employment	26 834	28 799	27 143	24 456	22 633	23 364	24 664
Nonfarm Wage and Salary Employment	4 090 191	4 053 206	4 035 214	4 098 341	4 181 107	4 296 367	4 398 859
Private wage and salary employment	3 341 678	3 291 796	3 259 608	3 308 190	3 381 623	3 484 258	3 570 075
Forestry, fishing, hunting, and other	17 862	18 143	17 746	17 027	17 292	17 137	16 791
Mining	4 287	3 757	3 571	3 580	3 560	3 765	4 013
Utilities	D	14 408	14 181	13 610	13 322	13 311	12 635
Construction	237 840	228 564	220 471	229 068	241 853	255 056	264 604
Manufacturing	707 723	648 877	608 293	586 214	575 909	560 865	544 762
Durable goods manufacturing	359 253	321 533	301 150	299 163	301 208	299 125	292 982
Nondurable goods manufacturing	348 470	327 344	307 143	287 051	274 701	261 740	251 780
Wholesale trade	162 177	163 922	165 529	170 827	172 079	179 012	185 696
Retail trade	460 459	450 646	444 988	449 947	462 184	469 856	483 163
Transportation and warehousing	123 370	113 357	111 980	115 428	117 538	119 920	119 487
Information	D	79 304	75 381	72 563	72 602	73 335	73 337
Finance and insurance	140 099	141 397	142 193	145 218	148 611	156 364	157 903
Real estate and rental and leasing	48 654	49 169	49 022	50 017	52 117	54 356	56 151
Professional and technical services	159 806	156 768	156 136	161 167	170 264	182 899	194 588
Management of companies and enterprises	61 373	63 375	61 927	63 605	66 613	69 296	71 491
Administrative and waste services	208 054	208 523	212 619	218 347	225 721	238 619	246 457
Educational services	53 889	58 962	62 477	66 525	71 880	75 331	78 993
Health care and social assistance	352 927	369 424	382 704	399 181	417 216	437 331	460 833
Arts, entertainment, and recreation	47 884	48 227	47 959	48 490	48 484	51 722	54 492
Accommodation and food services	283 228	291 036	295 944	309 380	317 511	333 486	347 875
Other services, except public administration	175 567	183 937	186 487	187 996	186 867	192 597	196 804
Government and government enterprises	748 513	761 410	775 606	790 151	799 484	812 109	828 784
	Dollars						
AVERAGE WAGES AND SALARIES BY INDUSTRY	31 505	32 140	33 018	34 348	35 554	37 063	38 556
Average Farm Wages and Salaries	17 950	19 252	17 648	21 377	22 735	24 005	27 471
Average Nonfarm Wages and Salaries	31 594	32 232	33 121	34 425	35 624	37 135	38 618
Average private wages and salaries	31 628	32 174	32 987	34 322	35 396	36 880	38 216
Forestry, fishing, hunting, and other	18 864	20 418	21 144	22 474	23 012	23 859	24 965
Mining	45 282	43 015	45 343	49 809	58 879	62 187	63 762
Utilities	D	59 679	60 896	65 709	66 489	66 903	73 854
Construction	31 977	31 982	32 644	33 765	35 118	37 539	38 957
Manufacturing	37 056	38 282	39 512	41 612	42 610	44 776	47 078
Durable goods manufacturing	39 548	40 005	41 224	43 552	44 471	47 102	49 756
Nondurable goods manufacturing	34 486	36 590	37 834	39 590	40 570	42 118	43 962
Wholesale trade	43 350	44 578	46 511	48 872	51 317	53 412	55 696
Retail trade	21 171	21 557	21 950	22 512	23 118	23 637	24 325
Transportation and warehousing	35 241	35 819	36 158	37 042	37 009	37 787	38 962
Information	D	46 618	48 642	51 558	52 869	54 185	56 124
Finance and insurance	52 596	54 185	57 858	60 072	64 446	70 418	72 633
Real estate and rental and leasing	28 173	28 736	29 712	31 740	33 549	36 057	37 053
Professional and technical services	48 204	48 316	49 537	51 382	53 486	56 070	58 750
Management of companies and enterprises	61 564	65 371	67 998	74 205	78 635	79 568	82 069
Administrative and waste services	20 990	21 994	22 325	23 572	24 366	25 281	26 528
Educational services	28 225	28 201	28 059	28 737	28 575	29 645	30 961
Health care and social assistance	31 276	31 793	32 413	33 534	34 085	34 913	35 794
Arts, entertainment, and recreation	23 689	23 745	24 768	25 998	26 210	28 969	29 825
Accommodation and food services	12 717	12 812	13 068	13 441	13 862	14 263	14 791
Other services, except public administration	21 185	21 359	22 095	22 812	23 267	23 770	24 940
Government and government enterprises	31 438	32 480	33 686	34 859	36 587	38 225	40 350

Table NC-9. Employment Characteristics by Family Type

(Number, percent.)

Family type and labor force status	2005		2006		2007	
	Total	Families with own children under 18 years	Total	Families with own children under 18 years	Total	Families with own children under 18 years
TOTAL FAMILIES	2 290 199	1 068 489	2 310 456	1 051 848	2 366 894	1 081 696
FAMILY TYPE AND LABOR FORCE STATUS						
Married Coupled Families	1 680 709	706 941	1 706 840	702 992	1 763 797	729 188
Both husband and wife in labor force	53.0	64.2	54.1	66.3	53.5	66.1
Husband in labor force, wife not in labor force	22.3	29.1	21.5	27.6	22.5	27.7
Wife in labor force, husband not in labor force	7.7	3.9	7.4	3.8	7.7	4.1
Both husband and wife not in labor force	17.0	2.8	17.0	2.3	16.3	2.1
Other Families	609 490	361 548	603 616	348 856	603 097	352 508
Female householder, no husband present	74.5	79.1	75.3	78.8	75.0	78.4
In labor force	52.4	64.2	53.5	65.5	53.3	64.1
Not in labor force	22.1	14.9	21.9	13.3	21.7	14.3
Male householder, no wife present	25.5	20.9	24.7	21.2	25.0	21.6
In labor force	20.1	18.7	20.4	19.4	20.3	19.5
Not in labor force	5.4	2.2	4.3	1.8	4.7	2.2

Table NC-10. School Enrollment and Educational Attainment, 2007

(Number, percent.)

Item	State	U.S.
Enrollment		
Total population 3 years and over	8 681 137	289 295 761
Enrolled in school	2 332 078	79 329 527
Enrolled in preschool (percent)	6.0	6.2
Enrolled in grades K-12 (percent)	68.2	67.6
Enrolled in college or graduate school (percent)	25.8	26.2
Attainment		
Total population 25 years and over	5 959 907	197 892 369
Less than a high school diploma (percent)	17.0	15.5
High school diploma or more (percent)	83.0	84.5
Bachelor's degree or more (percent)	25.6	27.5
Graduate degree or more (percent)	8.6	10.1

Table NC-11. Educational Indicators

(Number, percent.)

Item	State	U.S.
Public Schools, 2006–2007 (except where noted)		
Number of school districts	249	17 742
Number of schools	2 520	99 639
Number of students	1 444 481	49 315 842
Student-teacher ratio	12.9	15.5
Expenditures per student (dollars)	$7 878	...
Averaged freshman graduation rate, 2005–2006	71.8	...
Dropout rate, grades 9–12, 2005–2006	...	3.7
Students eligible for free or reduced-price lunch (percent)	43.2	41.2
English-language learners (percent)	6.1	5.1
Students with IEP (percent)	13.3	12.7
Private Schools, 2007–2008 (except where noted)		
Number of schools	656	33 740
Number of students	108 810	5 072 451
High school graduates, 2006–2007	5 594	306 605
Student-teacher ratio	10.0	11.1

Table NC-12. Reported Voting and Registration of the Voting-Age Population, November 2008

(Number in thousands, percent.)

Item	Total population	Total citizen population	Registered			Voted		
			Total registered	Percent registered (total population)	Percent registered (total citizen population)	Total voted	Percent voted (total population)	Percent voted (total citizen population)
U.S. total	225 499	206 072	146 311	64.9	71.0	131 144	58.2	63.6
State total	6 845	6 477	4 902	71.6	75.7	4 370	63.8	67.5
Sex								
Male	3 249	3 052	2 231	68.7	73.1	2 006	61.7	65.7
Female	3 595	3 425	2 671	74.3	78.0	2 364	65.8	69.0
Race								
White alone	5 158	4 886	3 782	73.3	77.4	3 331	64.6	68.2
White non-Hispanic alone	4 811	4 791	3 715	77.2	77.5	3 270	68.0	68.3
Black alone	1 368	1 345	971	71.0	72.2	919	67.2	68.3
Asian alone	151	80	53	35.4	66.4	43	28.4	53.3
Hispanic (of any race)	374	118	83	22.2	70.3	77	20.7	65.4
White alone or in combination	5 193	4 922	3 815	73.5	77.5	3 358	64.7	68.2
Black alone or in combination	1 374	1 351	974	70.9	72.1	919	66.9	68.1
Asian alone or in combination	162	92	61	37.5	66.2	50	31.0	54.7

Table NC-13. Crime

(Number, rate per 100,000.)

Item	State			U.S.		
	2007	2008	Percent change	2007	2008	Percent change
Population	9 061 032	9 222 414	1.8	301 621 157	304 059 724	0.8
VIOLENT CRIME						
Number	42 262	43 099	2.0	1 408 337	1 382 012	-1.9
Rate	466.4	467.3	0.2	466.9	454.5	-2.7
Murder and Nonnegligent Manslaughter						
Number	585	604	3.2	16 929	16 272	-3.9
Rate	6.5	6.5	1.4	5.6	5.4	-4.7
Forcible Rape						
Number	2 385	2 284	-4.2	90 427	89 000	-1.6
Rate	26.3	24.8	-5.9	30.0	29.3	-2.4
Robbery						
Number	13 548	14 334	5.8	445 125	441 855	-0.7
Rate	149.5	155.4	4.0	147.6	145.3	-1.5
Aggravated Assault						
Number	25 744	25 877	0.5	855 856	834 885	-2.5
Rate	284.1	280.6	-1.2	283.8	274.6	-3.2
PROPERTY CRIME						
Number	370 354	372 961	0.7	9 843 481	9 767 915	-0.8
Rate	4 087.3	4 044.1	-1.1	3 263.5	3 212.5	-1.6
Burglary						
Number	108 800	111 602	2.6	2 179 140	2 222 196	2.0
Rate	1 200.7	1 210.1	0.8	722.5	730.8	1.2
Larceny-Theft						
Number	233 588	234 616	0.4	6 568 572	6 588 873	0.3
Rate	2 577.9	2 544.0	-1.3	2 177.8	2 167.0	-0.5
Motor Vehicle Theft						
Number	27 966	26 743	-4.4	1 095 769	956 846	-12.7
Rate	308.6	290.0	-6.0	363.3	314.7	-13.4

Table NC-14. State Government Finances, 2007

(Dollars, percent distribution.)

Item	Thousands of dollars	Percent distribution
Total Revenue	51 841 493	X
General revenue	42 340 472	81.7
Intergovernmental revenue	13 231 264	25.5
Taxes	22 612 798	43.6
General sales	5 202 423	10.0
Selective sales	3 663 582	7.1
License taxes	1 338 413	2.6
Individual income tax	10 588 951	20.4
Corporate income tax	1 565 544	3.0
Other taxes	253 885	0.5
Current charges	3 634 077	7.0
Miscellaneous general revenue	2 862 333	5.5
Utility revenue	103	0.0
Liquor store revenue	0	0.0
Insurance trust revenue	9 500 918	18.3
Total Expenditure	44 009 293	100.0
Intergovernmental expenditure	12 646 039	28.7
Direct expenditure	31 363 254	71.3
Current operation	23 101 400	52.5
Capital outlay	3 215 202	7.3
Insurance benefits and repayments	4 122 309	9.4
Assistance and subsidies	317 556	0.7
Interest on debt	606 787	1.4
Exhibit: Salaries and wages	7 549 959	17.2
Total Expenditure	44 009 293	100.0
General expenditure	39 735 713	90.3
Intergovernmental expenditure	12 646 039	28.7
Direct expenditure	27 089 674	61.6
Education	16 547 989	37.6
Public welfare	10 972 023	24.9
Hospitals	1 371 677	3.1
Health	1 536 226	3.5
Highways	2 998 418	6.8
Police protection	593 039	1.3
Correction	1 271 328	2.9
Natural resources	593 500	1.3
Parks and recreation	269 981	0.6
Government administration	1 052 968	2.4
Interest on general debt	606 787	1.4
Other and unallocable	1 921 777	4.4
Utility expenditure	151 271	0.3
Liquor store expenditure	0	0.0
Insurance trust expenditure	4 122 309	9.4
Debt at End of Fiscal Year	19 245 613	X
Cash and Security Holdings	95 292 038	X

Table NC-15. State Government Tax Collections, 2008

(Dollars, percent distribution.)

Item	Thousands of dollars	Percent distribution
Total Taxes	22 781 199	X
Sales and gross receipts	8 929 847	13.7
General sales and gross receipts	5 269 929	8.1
Selective sales taxes	3 659 918	5.6
Alcoholic beverages	260 382	0.4
Amusements	14 267	0.0
Insurance premiums	506 003	0.8
Motor fuels	1 582 400	2.4
Public utilities	388 780	0.6
Tobacco products	248 159	0.4
Other selective sales	659 927	1.0
Licenses	1 412 089	2.2
Alcoholic beverages	14 751	0.0
Corporation	447 501	0.7
Hunting and fishing	16 410	0.0
Motor vehicle	609 158	0.9
Motor vehicle operators	134 196	0.2
Occupation and business, NEC	184 940	0.3
Other licenses	5 133	0.0
Income taxes	12 200 339	18.7
Individual income	10 993 927	16.8
Corporation net income	1 206 412	1.8
Other taxes	238 924	0.4
Death and gift	176 254	0.3
Documentary and stock transfer	60 782	0.1
Severance	1 888	0.0

Table NC-16. Agriculture

(Number, acres, and dollars.)

Item	2002		2007		Percent change, 2002–2007
	Number	Percent of total	Number	Percent of total	
Number of farms	53 930		52 913		-1.9
Farm Size					
Average size of farm (acres)	168		160		-4.8
Farms by size (number of farms)					
Fewer than 50 acres	24 612	45.6	25 773	48.7	4.7
50 to 499 acres	25 409	47.1	23 616	44.6	-7.1
500 acres or more	3 909	7.2	3 524	6.7	-9.8
Land (Acres)					
Total land in farms	9 079 001		8 474 671		-6.7
Total cropland	5 472 128	60.3	4 895 204	57.8	-10.5
Total harvested cropland	4 308 209	47.5	4 188 658	49.4	-2.8
Irrigated land	264 057	2.9	232 075	2.7	-12.1
Value of Sales (Dollars)					
Agricultural products sold ($1,000)	6 961 686		10 313 628		48.1
Average sales per farm	129 087		194 917		51.0
Sales of crops	2 008 634	28.9	2 606 279	25.3	29.8
Sales of livestock, poultry, and their products	4 953 052	71.1	7 707 350	74.7	55.6
Value of Sales (Number of Farms)					
Less than $10,000	34 371	63.7	34 276	64.8	-0.3
$10,000 to $99,999	10 768	20.0	10 311	19.5	-4.2
$100,000 to $999,999	7 258	13.5	5 530	10.5	-23.8
$1,000,000 or more	1 533	2.8	2 796	5.3	82.4
Farms by Type of Organization (Number of Farms)					
Family	48 672	90.3	45 766	86.5	-6.0
Partnership	3 209	6.0	4 246	8.0	32.3
Corporation	1 823	3.4	2 625	5.0	44.0
Other: cooperative, estate or trust, institutional, etc	226	0.4	276	0.5	22.1
Value of Land and Buildings (Dollars)					
Estimated market value of land and buildings ($1,000)	34 715 171		27 977 090		-19.4
Land and buildings average value per farm	656 080		518 719		-20.9
Average value per acre	4 096		3 088		-24.6
Government Payments					
Number of farms receiving government payments	12 312	22.8	13 856	26.2	12.5
Payments (thousands of dollars)	97 696		147 334		50.8
Average payment per farm	7 935		10 633		34.0
Farm Operator Characteristics					
Farm operators whose principal occupation is farming	31 669	58.7	24 244	45.8	-23.4
Farm operators whose principal occupation is other	22 261	41.3	28 669	54.2	28.8
Average age principal operator (years)	56.1		57.3		2.1

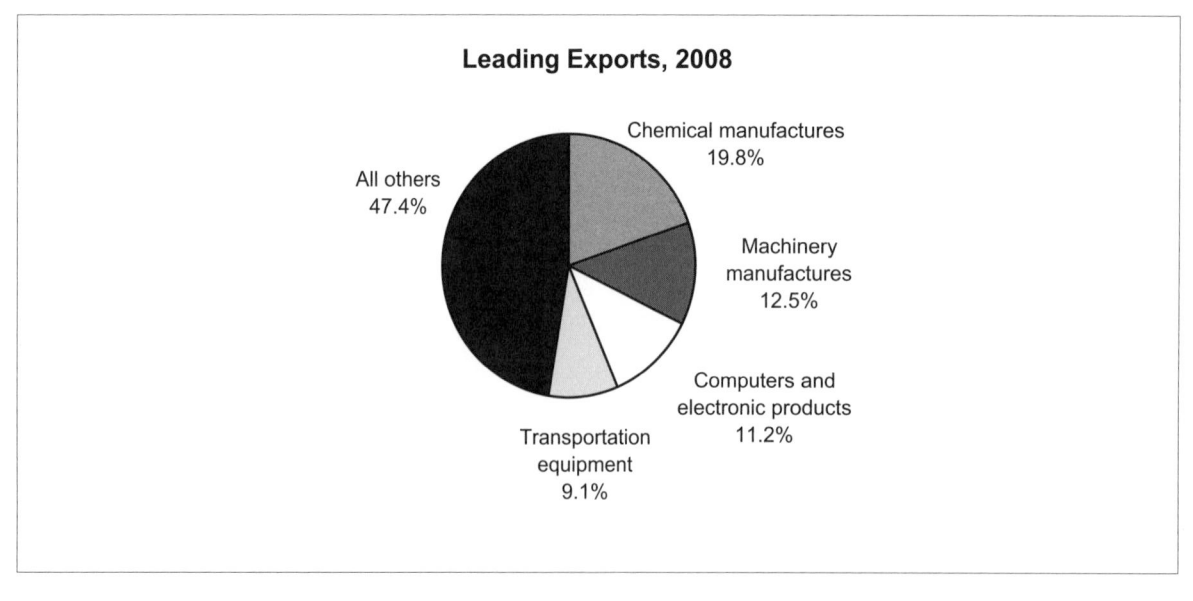

Leading Exports, 2008

- Chemical manufactures 19.8%
- Machinery manufactures 12.5%
- Computers and electronic products 11.2%
- Transportation equipment 9.1%
- All others 47.4%

NORTH DAKOTA

Facts and Figures

Location: North central United States; bordered on the N by Canada (Manitoba and Saskatchewan), on the E by Minnesota, on the S by South Dakota, and on the W by Montana

Area: 70,700 sq. mi. (183,112 sq. km.); rank—19th

Population: 641,481 (2008 est.); rank—48th

Principal Cities: capital—Bismarck; largest—Fargo

Statehood: November 2, 1889; 39th state

U.S. Congress: 2 senators, 1 representative

State Motto: Liberty and Union, Now and Forever, One and Inseparable

State Song: "North Dakota Hymn"

State Nicknames: The Peace Garden State; The Flickertail State; The Rough Rider State

Abbreviations: ND; N.D.; N. Dak.

State Symbols: flower—wild prairie rose; tree—American elm; bird—Western meadowlark

At a Glance

- With a decrease in population of 0.1 percent, North Dakota was one of only two states to lose population from 2000 to 2008; the other was Louisiana.
- An estimated 4,107 marriages took place in North Dakota in 2008, compared to 1,756 divorces.
- The 2007 home ownership rate in North Dakota was 66 percent; its ranking of 42nd was tied with that of Texas.
- North Dakota's median household income in 2007 was $43,753, 38th among the states.
- In North Dakota, 12.1 percent of the population lived below the poverty level in 2007, ranking it 24th along with Florida and Idaho.
- In 2006-07, 11.1 percent of North Dakotans did not have health insurance, compared to 15.5 percent of the total U.S. population.
- In 2007, 3.2 percent of North Dakotans were unemployed, compared to 4.6 percent nationwide.
- North Dakota ranked 27th in the nation with 25.7 percent of its population 25 years old and over having a bachelor's degree in 2007.
- North Dakota's violent crime rate in 2007 was 142.4 per 100,000 population, compared to 466.9 for the entire nation.
- North Dakota had one physician for every 362 people in 2007, compared to one physician for every 325 people nationwide.
- In the 2008 election, 65 percent of North Dakota's eligible voters voted, compared to 61.7 percent of eligible voters nationwide.
- North Dakota ranked 8th among the states receiving federal aid in 2007, with $2,008 per capita.
- North Dakota's gross domestic product was $28 billion in 2007; it ranked 49th among the states.
- With $2 billion in exports in 2007, North Dakota ranked 45th in exports.
- North Dakotans consumed 410.6 million Btu's of energy in 2006; the state ranked 44th in total consumption.
- In 2007, North Dakota exported $2.6 billion worth of agricultural products, about 3.1 percent of the U.S. total.

Table ND-1. Population by Sex, Age, Race, and Hispanic Origin

(Number, percent.)

Sex, age, race, and Hispanic origin	1990	2000	2008	Average annual percent change, 2000–2008
Total Population	638 800	642 200	641 481	0.0
Percent of total U.S. population	0.3	0.2	0.2	X
Sex				
Male	318 201	320 524	321 933	0.1
Female	320 599	321 676	319 548	-0.1
Age				
Under 5 years	47 845	39 400	41 896	0.8
5 to 19 years	147 520	144 064	123 697	-1.9
20 to 64 years	352 380	364 258	381 612	0.6
65 years and over	91 055	94 478	94 276	0.0
Median age (years)	32.3	36.2	37.1	X
Race and Hispanic Origin[1]				
One race				
White	604 142	593 181	586 272	-0.1
Black	3 524	3 916	6 956	7.4
American Indian and Alaskan Native	25 917	31 329	35 666	1.6
Asian[2]	3 462	3 606	4 759	3.5
Native Hawaiian and Other Pacific Islander	X	230	336	4.9
Two or more races	X	7 398	7 492	0.2
Hispanic (of any race)	4 665	7 786	13 227	6.8

[1]Data on race in 2000 and 2008 are not comparable to 1990. Individuals could only report one race in the 1990 census but could report one or more races on the 2000 census.
[2]Data in 1990 refer to Asian and Pacific Islanders.

Table ND-2. Marital Status

(Number, percent distribution.)

Sex and marital status	1990	2000	2007
Males, 15 Years and Over	241 899	253 900	261 920
Never married	30.7	32.0	34.2
Now married, except separated	60.7	57.5	53.9
Separated	0.7	0.6	1.0
Widowed	2.3	2.5	3.0
Divorced	5.6	7.3	7.9
Females, 15 Years and Over	248 204	258 381	260 416
Never married	21.2	23.2	25.4
Now married, except separated	58.8	56.0	54.1
Separated	0.9	0.8	1.3
Widowed	12.7	11.7	11.1
Divorced	6.4	8.2	8.1

Table ND-3. Households and Housing Characteristics

(Number, percent, and dollars.)

Item	1990	2000	2007	Average annual percent change, 2000–2007
Total Households	240 878	257 152	271 724	0.8
Family households	166 270	166 150	168 128	0.2
Married-couple family	142 374	137 433	137 132	0.0
Other family	23 896	28 717	30 996	1.1
Male householder, no wife present	6 373	8 569	10 585	3.1
Female householder, no husband present	17 523	20 148	20 411	0.2
Nonfamily households	74 608	91 002	103 596	1.9
Householder living alone	63 953	75 420	85 496	1.8
Householder not living alone	10 655	15 582	18 100	2.2
Housing Characteristics				
Total housing units	276 340	289 677	310 438	1.0
Occupied housing units	240 878	257 152	271 724	0.8
Owner-occupied	157 950	171 299	178 590	0.6
Renter-occupied	82 928	85 853	93 134	1.2
Average size	2.55	2.41	2.25	X
Financial Characteristics				
Median gross rent of renter-occupied housing units (dollars)	313	412	516	3.3
Median monthly owner costs for housing units with a mortgage (dollars)	608	818	1 093	4.2
Median value of owner-occupied housing units (dollars)	50 500	74 400	106 800	5.3

Table ND-4. Median Income and Poverty Status, 2007

(Number, percent.)

Characteristic	State		U.S.	
	Number	Percent	Number	Percent
Median Income				
Households (dollars)	43 753	X	50 740	X
Families (dollars)	58 827	X	61 173	X
Below Poverty Level				
Sex				
Male	32 165	10.4	16 576 071	11.5
Female	41 870	13.8	21 476 176	14.3
Age				
Under 18 years	18 937	13.4	13 097 100	18.0
Related children under 18 years	18 013	12.8	12 728 964	17.6
18 to 64 years	44 393	11.5	21 495 507	11.6
65 years and over	10 705	12.6	3 459 640	9.5

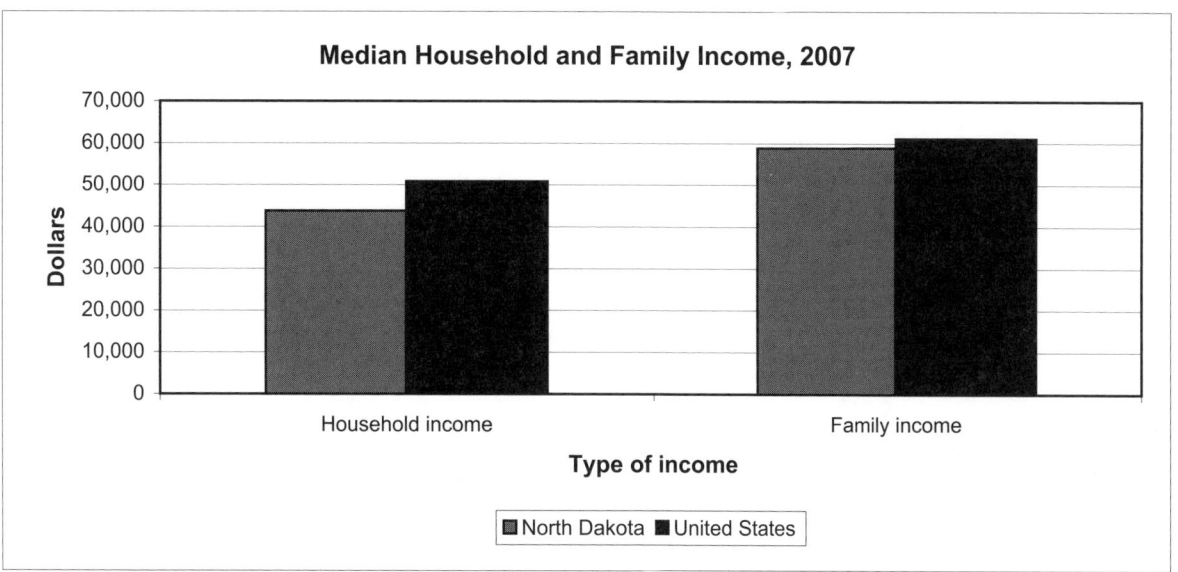

Median Household and Family Income, 2007

Table ND-5. Health Insurance Coverage Status for All Persons and Children Under 18 Years of Age

(Number, percent.)

Item	2000	2001	2002	2003	2004	2005	2006	2007
ALL PERSONS	623	621	633	631	627	626	617	615
Covered by Private or Government Health Insurance								
Number	557	566	570	570	564	558	541	553
Percent	89.3	91.2	90.0	90.3	89.9	89.0	87.8	90.0
Not Covered								
Number	66	55	63	61	63	69	75	61
Percent	10.7	8.8	10.0	9.7	10.1	11.0	12.2	10.0
Percent in the U.S. not covered	13.7	14.1	14.7	15.1	14.9	15.3	15.8	15.3
CHILDREN UNDER 18 YEARS OF AGE	145	130	147	146	144	142	144	146
Covered by Private or Government Health Insurance								
Number	131	120	136	136	131	129	130	135
Percent	90.0	92.7	92.8	92.9	90.9	91.1	89.7	92.1
Not Covered								
Number	15	9	11	10	13	13	15	11
Percent	10.0	7.3	7.2	7.1	9.1	8.9	10.3	7.9
Percent in the U.S. not covered	11.6	11.3	11.2	11.0	10.5	10.9	11.7	11.0

Table ND-6. Employment Status by Demographic Group, Preliminary 2008

(Number, percent.)

Characteristic	Civilian noninstitutional population	Civilian labor force		Employment		Unemployed	
		Number	Percent of population	Number	Percent of population	Number	Unemployment rate
TOTAL	500	374	74.8	363	72.5	12	3.2
Sex							
Men	248	198	80.0	191	76.9	7	3.5
Women	252	177	70.0	172	68.1	5	2.8
Race, Sex, and Hispanic Origin							
White	449	341	75.8	332	73.9	9	2.5
Men	223	179	80.5	174	78.3	5	2.8
Women	226	161	71.2	158	69.6	4	2.2
Black or African American	...	...	...	...	...	...	...
Men	...	...	...	...	...	...	...
Women	...	...	...	...	...	...	...
Hispanic	...	...	...	...	...	...	...
Men	...	...	...	...	...	...	...
Women	...	...	...	...	...	...	...
Age							
16 to 19 years	36	21	58.1	19	54.3	1	6.5
20 to 24 years	52	43	83.6	41	78.4	3	6.3
25 to 34 years	87	78	89.5	76	86.5	3	3.3
35 to 44 years	72	65	90.3	64	88.0	2	2.5
45 to 54 years	96	88	91.7	86	89.6	2	2.3
55 to 64 years	76	58	76.1	57	75.0	1	1.5
65 years and over	81	21	25.7	20	25.0	1	2.9

Note: Data in Table 6 are from the Current Population Survey (CPS) and do not match the estimates in Table 7. See notes and definitions for more details.

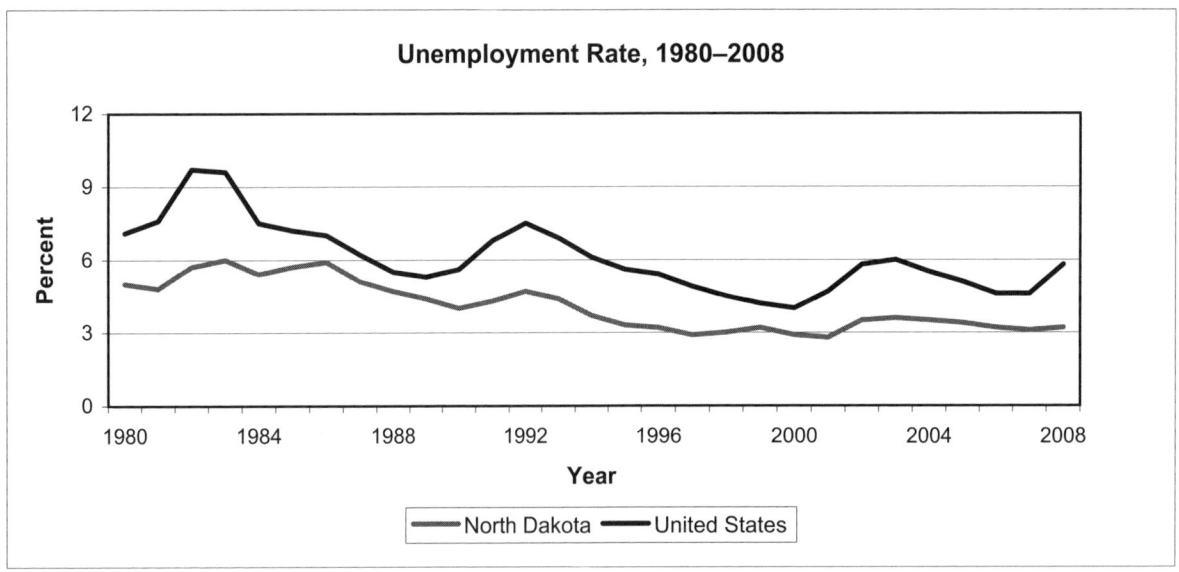

Unemployment Rate, 1980–2008

Table ND-7. Employment Status of the Civilian Noninstitutional Population Age 16 Years and Over

(Number, percent.)

Year	Civilian labor force	Civilian participation rate	Employed	Unemployed	Unemployment rate
1998	347 020	71.3	336 642	10 378	3.0
1999	347 634	71.6	336 481	11 153	3.2
2000	345 881	71.3	335 780	10 101	2.9
2001	345 820	71.4	336 228	9 592	2.8
2002	345 836	71.3	333 605	12 231	3.5
2003	348 929	71.8	336 353	12 576	3.6
2004	351 801	71.9	339 541	12 260	3.5
2005	356 039	72.5	343 784	12 255	3.4
2006	361 210	73.2	349 662	11 548	3.2
2007	366 042	73.9	354 659	11 383	3.1
2008	369 671	74.2	358 001	11 670	3.2

Table ND-8. Employment and Average Wages by Industry

(Estimates for 2001–2006 are based on the 2002 North American Industry Classification System [NAICS]. Estimates for 2007 are based on the 2007 NAICS.)

Industry	2001	2002	2003	2004	2005	2006	2007
	Number of jobs						
WAGE AND SALARY EMPLOYMENT BY INDUSTRY	348 245	349 050	350 984	359 253	365 350	373 401	378 719
Farm Wage and Salary Employment	5 360	4 938	3 639	4 881	4 683	4 601	4 414
Nonfarm Wage and Salary Employment	342 885	344 112	347 345	354 372	360 667	368 800	374 305
Private wage and salary employment	265 477	265 121	266 941	273 398	279 925	287 171	293 087
Forestry, fishing, hunting, and other	2 538	2 480	2 559	2 598	2 716	2 611	2 626
Mining	3 513	3 218	3 318	3 561	4 095	4 649	5 090
Utilities	3 380	3 382	3 346	3 228	3 218	3 235	3 298
Construction	16 032	15 538	16 408	17 700	17 911	18 954	19 733
Manufacturing	24 232	23 934	23 648	24 787	26 082	26 192	26 259
Durable goods manufacturing	16 009	15 757	15 396	16 358	17 591	17 820	17 799
Nondurable goods manufacturing	8 223	8 177	8 252	8 429	8 491	8 372	8 460
Wholesale trade	18 669	18 225	18 228	18 647	19 098	19 351	19 622
Retail trade	41 953	41 905	42 173	42 555	43 404	44 544	44 428
Transportation and warehousing	9 650	9 737	9 825	10 051	10 232	10 755	11 020
Information	8 499	7 955	7 698	7 423	7 381	7 516	7 618
Finance and insurance	14 629	14 852	15 231	15 384	15 518	15 911	16 402
Real estate and rental and leasing	3 331	3 323	3 314	3 321	3 377	3 462	3 504
Professional and technical services	9 648	9 588	10 075	10 895	11 656	12 399	12 741
Management of companies and enterprises	2 857	2 924	2 954	3 133	3 426	3 763	4 172
Administrative and waste services	12 482	12 177	11 221	11 526	12 328	12 794	13 164
Educational services	3 202	3 530	3 417	3 606	3 418	3 498	3 609
Health care and social assistance	44 361	44 966	46 028	46 533	47 227	48 245	48 995
Arts, entertainment, and recreation	3 260	3 506	3 604	3 734	3 635	3 677	3 770
Accommodation and food services	26 652	26 877	26 887	27 516	28 030	28 427	29 655
Other services, except public administration	16 589	17 004	17 007	17 200	17 173	17 188	17 381
Government and government enterprises	77 408	78 991	80 404	80 974	80 742	81 629	81 218
	Dollars						
AVERAGE WAGES AND SALARIES BY INDUSTRY	25 365	26 269	27 413	28 771	29 763	31 064	32 755
Average Farm Wages and Salaries	27 634	27 048	27 216	29 754	30 111	30 822	34 814
Average Nonfarm Wages and Salaries	25 329	26 258	27 415	28 758	29 758	31 067	32 731
Average private wages and salaries	25 237	25 967	27 077	28 486	29 459	30 911	32 660
Forestry, fishing, hunting, and other	16 227	16 821	16 998	18 117	19 559	20 383	21 740
Mining	48 304	48 953	50 777	52 729	56 937	64 461	69 639
Utilities	56 585	57 896	62 092	63 712	65 989	68 085	71 868
Construction	31 879	31 849	32 525	34 262	35 671	37 888	40 503
Manufacturing	31 561	32 448	34 036	35 964	36 334	38 231	40 128
Durable goods manufacturing	32 689	33 764	35 682	37 648	37 883	39 606	41 706
Nondurable goods manufacturing	29 365	29 911	30 963	32 695	33 127	35 304	36 807
Wholesale trade	33 204	34 449	36 081	38 330	40 104	41 904	44 391
Retail trade	18 202	18 779	19 275	19 805	20 208	20 675	21 702
Transportation and warehousing	33 957	33 958	35 118	37 286	38 897	40 448	41 980
Information	32 182	34 207	37 210	40 009	40 888	44 471	47 324
Finance and insurance	34 055	34 858	36 648	38 645	38 784	40 508	42 377
Real estate and rental and leasing	17 869	18 867	19 901	21 079	22 100	23 358	25 676
Professional and technical services	33 189	35 644	35 979	36 960	38 834	40 735	43 120
Management of companies and enterprises	44 834	44 798	46 912	55 354	53 736	54 188	59 579
Administrative and waste services	16 388	17 301	17 928	18 884	19 890	21 007	21 654
Educational services	18 837	18 772	19 469	19 230	19 226	19 940	20 853
Health care and social assistance	26 928	28 167	29 125	30 707	31 924	32 981	34 612
Arts, entertainment, and recreation	11 605	12 308	12 607	12 622	13 235	13 564	13 755
Accommodation and food services	9 624	9 959	10 335	10 600	10 956	11 486	12 015
Other services, except public administration	16 718	17 233	18 282	18 907	19 296	19 937	21 002
Government and government enterprises	25 646	27 234	28 537	29 674	30 793	31 613	32 985

Table ND-9. Employment Characteristics by Family Type

(Number, percent.)

Family type and labor force status	2005		2006		2007	
	Total	Families with own children under 18 years	Total	Families with own children under 18 years	Total	Families with own children under 18 years
TOTAL FAMILIES	165 806	74 747	169 022	75 140	168 128	75 814
FAMILY TYPE AND LABOR FORCE STATUS						
Married Coupled Families	137 932	57 670	138 355	56 302	137 132	55 777
Both husband and wife in labor force	61.6	77.0	62.8	76.3	64.2	78.4
Husband in labor force, wife not in labor force	16.5	17.6	16.6	19.5	15.4	17.4
Wife in labor force, husband not in labor force	6.6	3.2	5.8	2.8	6.7	3.2
Both husband and wife not in labor force	15.3	2.2	14.8	1.3	13.7	1.1
Other Families	27 874	17 077	30 667	18 838	30 996	20 037
Female householder, no husband present	69.3	74.5	69.6	75.5	65.9	73.2
In labor force	50.0	58.8	52.6	63.7	48.9	58.4
Not in labor force	19.3	15.7	17.0	11.8	17.0	14.8
Male householder, no wife present	30.7	25.5	30.4	24.5	34.1	26.8
In labor force	25.9	23.8	24.7	22.1	27.7	24.8
Not in labor force	4.8	1.7	5.7	2.5	6.5	1.9

Table ND-10. School Enrollment and Educational Attainment, 2007

(Number, percent.)

Item	State	U.S.
Enrollment		
Total population 3 years and over	613 185	289 295 761
Enrolled in school	165 522	79 329 527
Enrolled in preschool (percent)	4.6	6.2
Enrolled in grades K-12 (percent)	61.5	67.6
Enrolled in college or graduate school (percent)	33.9	26.2
Attainment		
Total population 25 years and over	413 331	197 892 369
Less than a high school diploma (percent)	11.0	15.5
High school diploma or more (percent)	89.0	84.5
Bachelor's degree or more (percent)	25.7	27.5
Graduate degree or more (percent)	6.4	10.1

Table ND-11. Educational Indicators

(Number, percent.)

Item	State	U.S.
Public Schools, 2006–2007 (except where noted)		
Number of school districts	238	17 742
Number of schools	534	99 639
Number of students	96 670	49 315 842
Student-teacher ratio	12.1	15.5
Expenditures per student (dollars)	$8 671	. . .
Averaged freshman graduation rate, 2005–2006	82.1	. . .
Dropout rate, grades 9–12, 2005–2006	2.1	3.7
Students eligible for free or reduced-price lunch (percent)	30.3	41.2
English-language learners (percent)	2.5	5.1
Students with IEP (percent)	. . .	12.7
Private Schools, 2007–2008 (except where noted)		
Number of schools	50	33 740
Number of students	6 345	5 072 451
High school graduates, 2006–2007	. . .	306 605
Student-teacher ratio	11.4	11.1

Table ND-12. Reported Voting and Registration of the Voting-Age Population, November 2008

(Number in thousands, percent.)

Item	Total population	Total citizen population	Registered			Voted		
			Total registered	Percent registered (total population)	Percent registered (total citizen population)	Total voted	Percent voted (total population)	Percent voted (total citizen population)
U.S. total	225 499	206 072	146 311	64.9	71.0	131 144	58.2	63.6
State total	484	476	399	82.3	83.7	321	66.3	67.5
Sex								
Male	238	232	189	79.5	81.4	147	61.9	63.4
Female	246	244	209	84.9	85.9	174	70.5	71.3
Race								
White alone	434	430	361	83.2	83.9	289	66.7	67.2
White non-Hispanic alone	428	426	358	83.7	84.0	288	67.3	67.6
Black alone	5	2	2	. . .	. . .	1	. . .	. . .
Asian alone	4	2	2	. . .	. . .	1	. . .	. . .
Hispanic (of any race)	6	5	3	. . .	. . .	1	. . .	. . .
White alone or in combination	439	436	366	83.3	84.0	294	66.9	67.5
Black alone or in combination	5	2	2	. . .	. . .	1	. . .	. . .
Asian alone or in combination	4	3	2	. . .	. . .	1	. . .	. . .

Table ND-13. Crime

(Number, rate per 100,000.)

Item	State			U.S.		
	2007	2008	Percent change	2007	2008	Percent change
Population	639 715	641 481	0.3	301 621 157	304 059 724	0.8
VIOLENT CRIME						
Number	911	1 068	17.2	1 408 337	1 382 012	-1.9
Rate	142.4	166.5	16.9	466.9	454.5	-2.7
Murder and Nonnegligent Manslaughter						
Number	12	3	-75.0	16 929	16 272	-3.9
Rate	1.9	0.5	-75.1	5.6	5.4	-4.7
Forcible Rape						
Number	207	232	12.1	90 427	89 000	-1.6
Rate	32.4	36.2	11.8	30.0	29.3	-2.4
Robbery						
Number	70	72	2.9	445 125	441 855	-0.7
Rate	10.9	11.2	2.6	147.6	145.3	-1.5
Aggravated Assault						
Number	622	761	22.3	855 856	834 885	-2.5
Rate	97.2	118.6	22.0	283.8	274.6	-3.2
PROPERTY CRIME						
Number	12 088	12 152	0.5	9 843 481	9 767 915	-0.8
Rate	1 889.6	1 894.4	0.3	3 263.5	3 212.5	-1.6
Burglary						
Number	2 164	2 106	-2.7	2 179 140	2 222 196	2.0
Rate	338.3	328.3	-2.9	722.5	730.8	1.2
Larceny-Theft						
Number	9 010	9 164	1.7	6 568 572	6 588 873	0.3
Rate	1 408.4	1 428.6	1.4	2 177.8	2 167.0	-0.5
Motor Vehicle Theft						
Number	914	882	-3.5	1 095 769	956 846	-12.7
Rate	142.9	137.5	-3.8	363.3	314.7	-13.4

Table ND-14. State Government Finances, 2007

(Dollars, percent distribution.)

Item	Thousands of dollars	Percent distribution
Total Revenue	4 786 348	X
General revenue	3 942 336	82.4
Intergovernmental revenue	1 227 870	25.7
Taxes	1 782 990	37.3
General sales	484 341	10.1
Selective sales	324 365	6.8
License taxes	127 842	2.7
Individual income tax	316 894	6.6
Corporate income tax	136 424	2.9
Other taxes	393 124	8.2
Current charges	577 370	12.1
Miscellaneous general revenue	354 106	7.4
Utility revenue	0	0.0
Liquor store revenue	0	0.0
Insurance trust revenue	844 012	17.6
Total Expenditure	3 777 523	100.0
Intergovernmental expenditure	741 535	19.6
Direct expenditure	3 035 988	80.4
Current operation	2 083 147	55.1
Capital outlay	414 737	11.0
Insurance benefits and repayments	336 348	8.9
Assistance and subsidies	60 205	1.6
Interest on debt	141 551	3.7
Exhibit: Salaries and wages	757 505	20.1
Total Expenditure	3 777 523	100.0
General expenditure	3 441 175	91.1
Intergovernmental expenditure	741 535	19.6
Direct expenditure	2 699 640	71.5
Education	1 245 407	33.0
Public welfare	706 358	18.7
Hospitals	15 044	0.4
Health	63 730	1.7
Highways	446 733	11.8
Police protection	23 737	0.6
Correction	54 283	1.4
Natural resources	152 590	4.0
Parks and recreation	22 198	0.6
Government administration	130 989	3.5
Interest on general debt	141 551	3.7
Other and unallocable	438 555	11.6
Utility expenditure	0	0.0
Liquor store expenditure	0	0.0
Insurance trust expenditure	336 348	8.9
Debt at End of Fiscal Year	1 792 485	X
Cash and Security Holdings	11 135 032	X

Table ND-15. State Government Tax Collections, 2008

(Dollars, percent distribution.)

Item	Thousands of dollars	Percent distribution
Total Taxes	2 312 056	X
Property taxes	1 901	X
Sales and gross receipts	873 406	37.8
General sales and gross receipts	530 078	22.9
Selective sales taxes	343 328	14.8
Alcoholic beverages	6 916	0.3
Amusements	9 196	0.4
Insurance premiums	37 426	1.6
Motor fuels	143 389	6.2
Pari-mutuels	548	0.0
Public utilities	34 438	1.5
Tobacco products	24 127	1.0
Other selective sales	87 288	3.8
Licenses	165 810	7.2
Alcoholic beverages	247	0.0
Amusements	285	0.0
Hunting and fishing	15 460	0.7
Motor vehicle	88 453	3.8
Motor vehicle operators	4 087	0.2
Public utility	6	0.0
Occupation and business, NEC	57 272	2.5
Income taxes	479 174	20.7
Individual income	317 249	13.7
Corporation net income	161 925	7.0
Other taxes	791 765	34.2
Death and gift	73	0.0
Severance	791 692	34.2

Table ND-16. Agriculture

(Number, acres, and dollars.)

Item	2002 Number	2002 Percent of total	2007 Number	2007 Percent of total	Percent change, 2002–2007
Number of farms	30 619		31 970		4.4
Farm Size					
Average size of farm (acres)	1 283		1 241		-3.3
Farms by size (number of farms)					
Fewer than 50 acres	2 040	6.7	2 655	8.3	30.1
50 to 499 acres	11 182	36.5	12 778	40.0	14.3
500 acres or more	17 397	56.8	16 537	51.7	-4.9
Land (Acres)					
Total land in farms	39 294 879		39 674 586		1.0
Total cropland	26 506 477	67.5	27 527 180	69.4	3.9
Total harvested cropland	19 908 697	50.7	22 035 717	55.5	10.7
Irrigated land	202 817	0.5	236 138	0.6	16.4
Value of Sales (Dollars)					
Agricultural products sold ($1,000)	3 233 366		6 084 218		88.2
Average sales per farm	105 600		190 310		80.2
Sales of crops	2 460 372	76.1	5 038 521	82.8	104.8
Sales of livestock, poultry, and their products	772 994	23.9	1 045 697	17.2	35.3
Value of Sales (Number of Farms)					
Less than $10,000	11 786	38.5	13 469	42.1	14.3
$10,000 to $99,999	10 004	32.7	7 021	22.0	-29.8
$100,000 to $999,999	8 544	27.9	10 307	32.2	20.6
$1,000,000 or more	285	0.9	1 173	3.7	311.6
Farms by Type of Organization (Number of Farms)					
Family	27 578	90.1	28 079	87.8	1.8
Partnership	2 289	7.5	2 834	8.9	23.8
Corporation	446	1.5	560	1.8	25.6
Other: cooperative, estate or trust, institutional, etc	306	1.0	497	1.6	62.4
Value of Land and Buildings (Dollars)					
Estimated market value of land and buildings ($1,000)	30 596 974		15 823 558		-48.3
Land and buildings average value per farm	957 053		517 448		-45.9
Average value per acre	771		404		-47.6
Government Payments					
Number of farms receiving government payments	23 892	78.0	26 708	83.5	11.8
Payments (thousands of dollars)	293 067		359 532		22.7
Average payment per farm	12 266		13 462		9.8
Farm Operator Characteristics					
Farm operators whose principal occupation is farming	21 644	70.7	18 525	57.9	-14.4
Farm operators whose principal occupation is other	8 975	29.3	13 445	42.1	49.8
Average age principal operator (years)	54.4		56.5		3.9

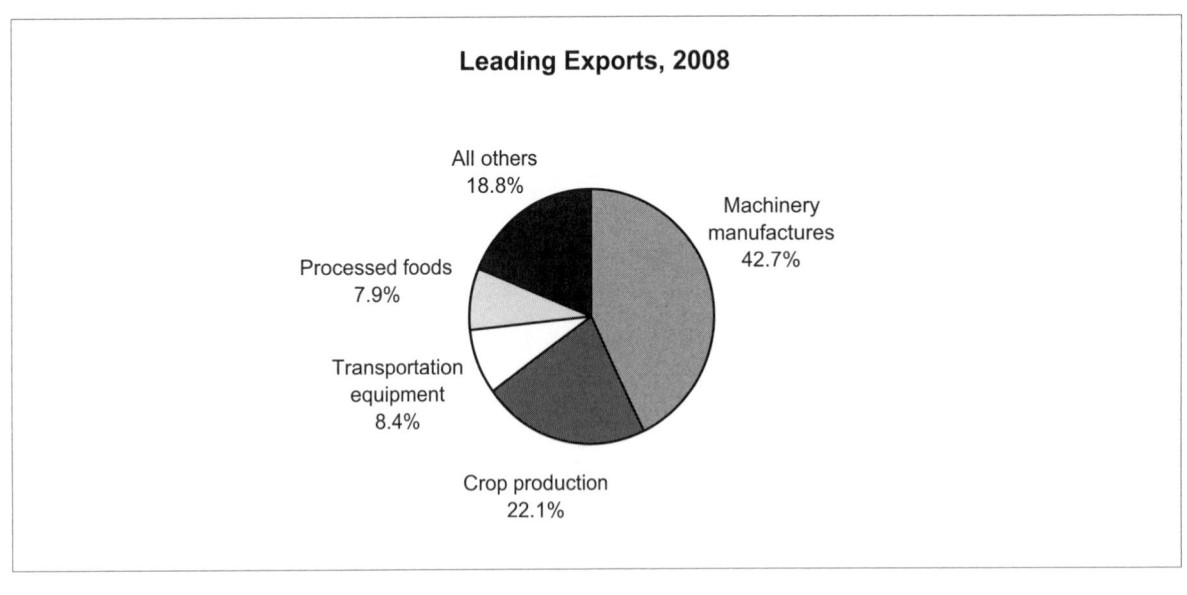

Leading Exports, 2008

All others 18.8%
Processed foods 7.9%
Transportation equipment 8.4%
Crop production 22.1%
Machinery manufactures 42.7%

OHIO

Facts and Figures

Location: East north central United States; bordered on the N by Michigan and Lake Erie, on the E by Pennsylvania and West Virginia, on the S by West Virginia and Kentucky, and on the W by Indiana

Area: 44,825 sq. mi. (116,096 sq. km.); rank—34th

Population: 11,485,910 (2008 est.); rank—7th

Principal Cities: capital—Columbus; largest—Columbus

Statehood: March 1, 1803; 17th state

U.S. Congress: 2 senators, 18 representatives

State Motto: With God, All Things Are Possible

State Song: "Beautiful Ohio"

State Nickname: The Buckeye State

Abbreviations: OH

State Symbols: flower—scarlet carnation; tree—Ohio buckeye; bird—cardinal

At a Glance

- With an increase in population of 1.2 percent, Ohio ranked 45th among the states in growth from 2000 to 2008.
- An estimated 70,574 marriages took place in Ohio in 2008, compared to 39,009 divorces.
- The 2007 home ownership rate in Ohio was 71.4 percent, giving it a ranking of 23rd among the states.
- Ohio's median household income in 2007 was $46,957, 33rd among the states.
- In Ohio, 13.1 percent of the population lived below the poverty level in 2007, ranking it 18th along with South Dakota.
- In 2006-07, 10.9 percent of Ohioans did not have health insurance, compared to 15.5 percent of the total U.S. population.
- In 2007, 5.6 percent of Ohioans were unemployed, compared to 4.6 percent nationwide.
- Ohio ranked 38th in the nation with 24.1 percent of its population 25 years old and over having a bachelor's degree in 2007.
- Ohio's violent crime rate in 2007 was 343.2 per 100,000 population, compared to 466.9 for the entire nation.
- Ohio had one physician for every 333 people in 2007, compared to one physician for every 325 people nationwide.
- In the 2008 election, 66.7 percent of Ohio's eligible voters voted, compared to 61.7 percent of eligible voters nationwide.
- Ohio ranked 27th among the states receiving federal aid in 2007, with $1,371 per capita.
- Ohio's gross domestic product was $466 billion in 2007; it ranked 7th among the states.
- With $42.6 billion in exports in 2007, Ohio ranked 8th in exports.
- Ohioans consumed 3.89 trillion Btu's of energy in 2006; the state ranked 7th in total consumption.
- In 2007, Ohio exported $2.2 billion worth of agricultural products, about 2.7 percent of the U.S. total.

Table OH-1. Population by Sex, Age, Race, and Hispanic Origin

(Number, percent.)

Sex, age, race, and Hispanic origin	1990	2000	2008	Average annual percent change, 2000–2008
Total Population	10 847 115	11 353 140	11 485 910	0.1
Percent of total U.S. population	4.4	4.0	3.8	X
Sex				
Male	5 226 340	5 512 262	5 603 768	0.2
Female	5 620 775	5 840 878	5 882 142	0.1
Age				
Under 5 years	785 149	754 930	743 750	-0.2
5 to 19 years	2 355 876	2 461 025	2 305 812	-0.8
20 to 64 years	6 299 129	6 629 428	6 865 511	0.4
65 years and over	1 406 961	1 507 757	1 570 837	0.5
Median age (years)	33.3	36.2	38.1	X
Race and Hispanic Origin[1]				
One race				
White	9 521 756	9 645 453	9 735 944	0.1
Black	1 154 826	1 301 307	1 382 358	0.8
American Indian and Alaskan Native	20 358	24 486	29 443	2.3
Asian[2]	91 179	132 633	181 362	4.0
Native Hawaiian and Other Pacific Islander	X	2 749	4 095	5.1
Two or more races	X	157 885	152 708	-0.4
Hispanic (of any race)	139 696	217 123	302 101	4.2

[1]Data on race in 2000 and 2008 are not comparable to 1990. Individuals could only report one race in the 1990 census but could report one or more races on the 2000 census.
[2]Data in 1990 refer to Asian and Pacific Islanders.

Table OH-2. Marital Status

(Number, percent distribution.)

Sex and marital status	1990	2000	2007
Males, 15 Years and Over	4 024 476	4 281 736	4 437 138
Never married	28.7	29.2	32.0
Now married, except separated	59.1	57.0	53.0
Separated	1.4	1.4	1.6
Widowed	2.7	2.7	2.8
Divorced	8.0	9.7	10.5
Females, 15 Years and Over	4 475 533	4 670 985	4 773 404
Never married	22.6	23.5	26.7
Now married, except separated	53.0	52.1	48.2
Separated	1.8	1.7	2.0
Widowed	12.4	11.1	10.5
Divorced	10.1	11.5	12.6

Table OH-3. Households and Housing Characteristics

(Number, percent, and dollars.)

Item	1990	2000	2007	Average annual percent change, 2000–2007
Total Households	4 087 546	4 445 773	4 505 995	0.2
Family households	2 895 223	2 993 023	2 962 303	-0.1
Married-couple family	2 294 111	2 285 798	2 209 685	-0.5
Other family	601 112	707 225	752 618	0.9
Male householder, no wife present	123 042	170 347	191 182	1.7
Female householder, no husband present	478 070	536 878	561 436	0.6
Nonfamily households	1 192 323	1 452 750	1 543 692	0.9
Householder living alone	1 020 450	1 215 614	1 304 363	1.0
Householder not living alone	171 873	237 136	239 329	0.1
Housing Characteristics				
Total housing units	4 371 945	4 783 051	5 065 254	0.8
Occupied housing units	4 087 546	4 445 773	4 505 995	0.2
Owner-occupied	2 758 149	3 072 522	3 139 659	0.3
Renter-occupied	1 329 397	1 373 251	1 366 336	-0.1
Average size	2.59	2.49	2.48	X
Financial Characteristics				
Median gross rent of renter-occupied housing units (dollars)	379	515	643	3.2
Median monthly owner costs for housing units with a mortgage (dollars)	625	963	1 242	3.7
Median value of owner-occupied housing units (dollars)	62 900	103 700	137 800	4.1

Table OH-4. Median Income and Poverty Status, 2007
(Number, percent.)

Characteristic	State		U.S.	
	Number	Percent	Number	Percent
Median Income				
Households (dollars)	46 597	X	50 740	X
Families (dollars)	58 374	X	61 173	X
Below Poverty Level				
Sex				
Male	622 803	11.5	16 576 071	11.5
Female	841 330	14.7	21 476 176	14.3
Age				
Under 18 years	500 745	18.5	13 097 100	18.0
Related children under 18 years	486 989	18.1	12 728 964	17.6
18 to 64 years	842 704	12.1	21 495 507	11.6
65 years and over	120 684	8.2	3 459 640	9.5

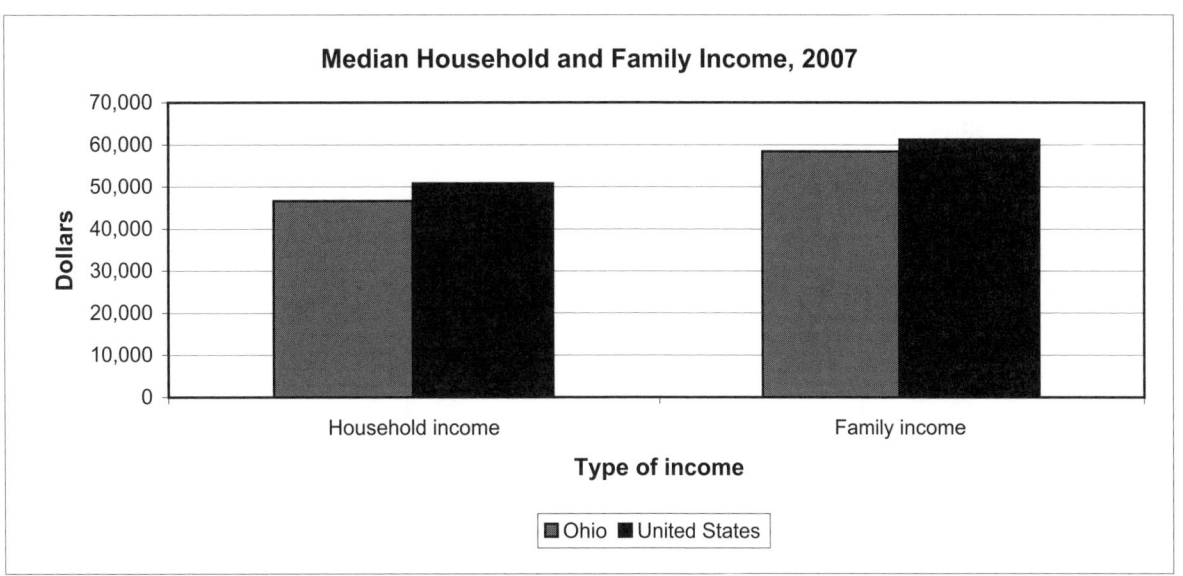

Table OH-5. Health Insurance Coverage Status for All Persons and Children Under 18 Years of Age
(Number, percent.)

Item	2000	2001	2002	2003	2004	2005	2006	2007
ALL PERSONS	11 178	11 191	11 282	11 247	11 270	11 334	11 319	11 300
Covered by Private or Government Health Insurance								
Number	9 987	9 993	10 031	9 957	10 077	10 046	10 181	9 979
Percent	89.3	89.3	88.9	88.5	89.4	88.6	89.9	88.3
Not Covered								
Number	1 191	1 198	1 252	1 290	1 193	1 288	1 138	1 322
Percent	10.7	10.7	11.1	11.5	10.6	11.4	10.1	11.7
Percent in the U.S. not covered	13.7	14.1	14.7	15.1	14.9	15.3	15.8	15.3
CHILDREN UNDER 18 YEARS OF AGE	2 771	2 667	2 908	2 860	2 806	2 724	2 784	2 790
Covered by Private or Government Health Insurance								
Number	2 491	2 476	2 690	2 633	2 584	2 517	2 626	2 551
Percent	89.9	92.8	92.5	92.1	92.1	92.4	94.3	91.4
Not Covered								
Number	280	192	218	227	222	207	157	239
Percent	10.1	7.2	7.5	7.9	7.9	7.6	5.7	8.6
Percent in the U.S. not covered	11.6	11.3	11.2	11.0	10.5	10.9	11.7	11.0

Table OH-6. Employment Status by Demographic Group, Preliminary 2008

(Number, percent.)

Characteristic	Civilian noninstitutional population	Civilian labor force		Employment		Unemployed	
		Number	Percent of population	Number	Percent of population	Number	Unemployment rate
TOTAL	8 906	5 981	67.2	5 595	62.8	386	6.5
Sex							
Men	4 277	3 094	72.0	2 883	67.4	211	6.8
Women	4 630	2 887	62.0	2 712	58.6	175	6.1
Race, Sex, and Hispanic Origin							
White	7 667	5 200	67.8	4 917	64.1	283	5.4
Men	3 716	2 719	73.2	2 559	68.9	160	5.9
Women	3 952	2 480	62.8	2 357	59.7	123	5.0
Black or African American	978	609	62.3	519	53.0	90	14.8
Men	439	281	64.1	237	54.0	44	15.7
Women	539	328	60.8	282	52.2	46	14.0
Hispanic	193	134	69.5	123	63.7	11	8.2
Men	103	82	80.2	76	74.3	6	7.4
Women	91	52	57.3	47	51.8	5	9.6
Age							
16 to 19 years	702	332	47.2	262	37.3	70	21.1
20 to 24 years	758	591	78.0	524	69.1	67	11.4
25 to 34 years	1 364	1 155	84.7	1 079	79.1	77	6.6
35 to 44 years	1 538	1 300	84.5	1 230	80.0	71	5.4
45 to 54 years	1 798	1 517	84.3	1 453	80.8	63	4.2
55 to 64 years	1 331	852	64.1	820	61.6	32	3.8
65 years and over	1 415	233	16.5	227	16.0	6	2.7

Note: Data in Table 6 are from the Current Population Survey (CPS) and do not match the estimates in Table 7. See notes and definitions for more details.

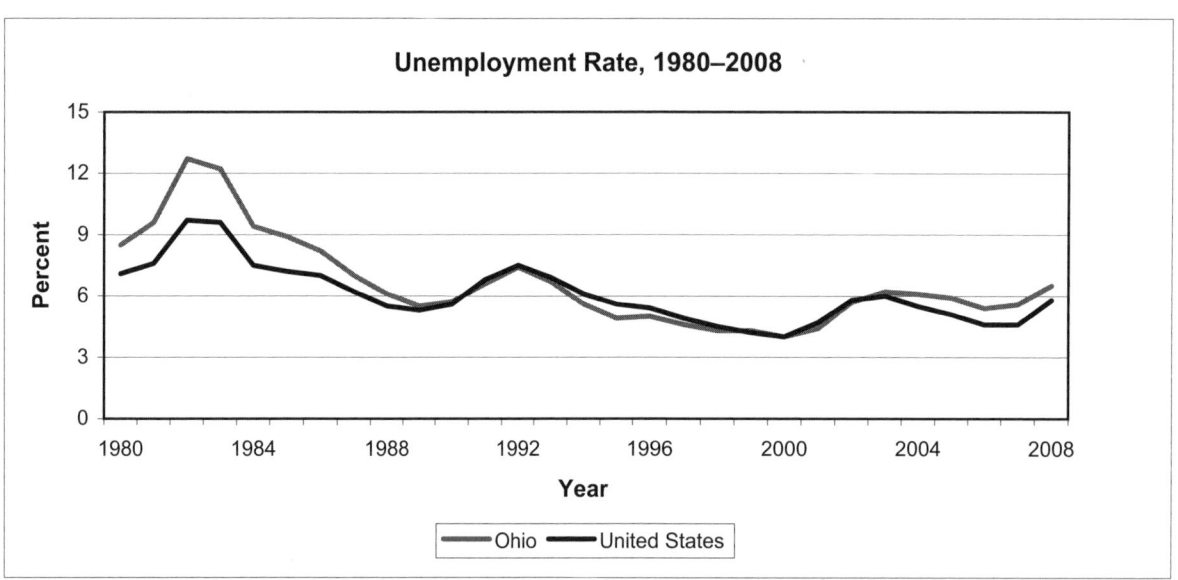

Table OH-7. Employment Status of the Civilian Noninstitutional Population Age 16 Years and Over

(Number, percent.)

Year	Civilian labor force	Civilian participation rate	Employed	Unemployed	Unemployment rate
1998	5 736 734	66.9	5 488 877	247 857	4.3
1999	5 780 725	67.2	5 534 376	246 349	4.3
2000	5 807 036	67.3	5 573 154	233 882	4.0
2001	5 825 649	67.2	5 566 735	258 914	4.4
2002	5 838 052	67.1	5 503 109	334 943	5.7
2003	5 860 021	67.0	5 498 936	361 085	6.2
2004	5 862 807	66.8	5 502 533	360 274	6.1
2005	5 889 451	66.9	5 544 569	344 882	5.9
2006	5 942 053	67.2	5 619 810	322 243	5.4
2007	5 976 724	67.3	5 640 938	335 786	5.6
2008	5 971 874	67.1	5 582 127	389 747	6.5

Table OH-8. Employment and Average Wages by Industry

(Estimates for 2001–2006 are based on the 2002 North American Industry Classification System [NAICS]. Estimates for 2007 are based on the 2007 NAICS.)

Industry	2001	2002	2003	2004	2005	2006	2007
	Number of jobs						
WAGE AND SALARY EMPLOYMENT BY INDUSTRY	5 753 257	5 659 347	5 614 191	5 619 910	5 631 114	5 641 863	5 632 102
Farm Wage and Salary Employment	18 062	14 171	15 748	14 772	14 420	15 560	17 187
Nonfarm Wage and Salary Employment	5 735 195	5 645 176	5 598 443	5 605 138	5 616 694	5 626 303	5 614 915
Private wage and salary employment	4 900 320	4 798 725	4 747 726	4 754 688	4 773 638	4 784 230	4 774 141
Forestry, fishing, hunting, and other	5 099	5 278	5 407	5 527	5 303	5 089	5 097
Mining	12 639	11 823	11 151	11 141	10 920	11 050	11 399
Utilities	24 371	22 163	21 433	20 530	20 470	20 741	21 051
Construction	249 753	247 040	241 476	243 999	241 163	238 478	232 398
Manufacturing	956 414	885 760	845 423	825 802	816 734	801 062	775 674
Durable goods manufacturing	673 226	611 363	578 951	566 812	561 776	552 658	533 049
Nondurable goods manufacturing	283 188	274 397	266 472	258 990	254 958	248 404	242 625
Wholesale trade	249 625	240 595	237 240	236 658	240 963	242 724	243 276
Retail trade	676 366	657 165	646 529	637 268	628 829	620 893	620 503
Transportation and warehousing	169 674	165 387	164 966	170 922	179 627	187 034	192 074
Information	106 160	100 866	96 516	92 716	90 302	88 913	87 815
Finance and insurance	232 646	234 625	236 507	236 762	232 646	235 203	232 929
Real estate and rental and leasing	75 445	73 970	72 620	72 177	71 993	70 441	68 882
Professional and technical services	252 707	241 039	240 428	241 035	246 407	252 742	259 488
Management of companies and enterprises	85 689	90 533	95 525	94 331	101 934	105 308	104 990
Administrative and waste services	311 918	302 764	296 462	308 173	313 834	315 797	316 666
Educational services	93 176	94 995	97 568	98 836	103 204	105 969	108 158
Health care and social assistance	631 477	647 778	662 166	675 788	690 539	705 488	717 625
Arts, entertainment, and recreation	72 592	72 814	72 255	72 420	71 932	69 632	69 406
Accommodation and food services	419 125	420 986	424 835	432 215	436 732	439 994	439 767
Other services, except public administration	275 444	283 144	279 219	278 388	270 106	267 672	266 943
Government and government enterprises	834 875	846 451	850 717	850 450	843 056	842 073	840 774
	Dollars						
AVERAGE WAGES AND SALARIES BY INDUSTRY	32 647	33 548	34 499	35 823	36 725	37 885	39 206
Average Farm Wages and Salaries	18 127	20 987	21 053	25 466	23 326	21 064	25 560
Average Nonfarm Wages and Salaries	32 693	33 579	34 537	35 850	36 760	37 932	39 247
Average private wages and salaries	32 595	33 376	34 291	35 627	36 516	37 766	39 077
Forestry, fishing, hunting, and other	18 236	19 104	19 326	20 241	21 101	21 777	23 477
Mining	47 139	46 979	48 257	51 315	55 297	58 099	58 784
Utilities	58 207	61 609	65 207	65 253	70 690	72 874	75 222
Construction	37 393	38 039	38 363	39 233	40 471	42 154	44 422
Manufacturing	42 546	43 993	45 701	47 429	48 058	49 884	51 360
Durable goods manufacturing	43 764	45 257	47 252	49 094	49 617	51 628	53 239
Nondurable goods manufacturing	39 652	41 177	42 329	43 785	44 622	46 005	47 232
Wholesale trade	45 265	46 171	47 379	49 913	51 376	53 309	55 677
Retail trade	21 164	21 873	22 388	22 680	22 749	22 887	23 348
Transportation and warehousing	35 039	36 032	37 017	38 235	39 620	41 042	41 797
Information	46 460	45 928	46 839	49 067	49 965	51 282	53 321
Finance and insurance	45 914	46 964	49 407	52 211	53 932	55 897	58 757
Real estate and rental and leasing	27 641	28 756	29 458	31 301	32 201	33 078	34 165
Professional and technical services	47 565	48 070	49 313	51 898	53 510	55 774	58 659
Management of companies and enterprises	63 994	69 905	69 468	79 591	84 218	85 638	89 660
Administrative and waste services	21 403	22 358	23 346	24 151	24 576	25 532	26 965
Educational services	22 589	23 207	23 716	24 598	24 908	25 742	26 367
Health care and social assistance	31 277	32 249	33 119	34 441	35 201	36 323	37 025
Arts, entertainment, and recreation	22 729	23 030	23 478	23 547	24 228	26 279	27 546
Accommodation and food services	11 829	12 079	12 302	12 624	12 804	13 179	13 928
Other services, except public administration	20 653	21 238	21 913	22 749	23 203	23 845	24 759
Government and government enterprises	33 264	34 734	35 908	37 098	38 137	38 872	40 214

Table OH-9. Employment Characteristics by Family Type

(Number, percent.)

Family type and labor force status	2005 Total	2005 Families with own children under 18 years	2006 Total	2006 Families with own children under 18 years	2007 Total	2007 Families with own children under 18 years
TOTAL FAMILIES	2 986 906	1 382 959	2 953 361	1 347 571	2 962 303	1 345 473
FAMILY TYPE AND LABOR FORCE STATUS						
Married Coupled Families	2 228 322	925 924	2 202 145	899 453	2 209 685	891 323
Both husband and wife in labor force	53.3	66.0	55.1	68.6	55.1	68.7
Husband in labor force, wife not in labor force	21.1	26.9	20.4	25.7	20.2	25.5
Wife in labor force, husband not in labor force	7.7	4.1	7.3	3.9	7.8	3.9
Both husband and wife not in labor force	17.9	3.0	17.2	1.9	16.9	1.8
Other Families	758 584	457 035	751 216	448 118	752 618	454 150
Female householder, no husband present	75.4	77.7	75.0	77.9	74.6	76.6
In labor force	52.3	61.1	54.0	63.6	52.2	61.2
Not in labor force	23.1	16.6	21.0	14.3	22.4	15.4
Male householder, no wife present	24.6	22.3	25.0	22.1	25.4	23.4
In labor force	18.8	19.5	19.7	19.6	20.0	20.9
Not in labor force	5.8	2.9	5.3	2.5	5.4	2.4

Table OH-10. School Enrollment and Educational Attainment, 2007

(Number, percent.)

Item	State	U.S.
Enrollment		
Total population 3 years and over	11 020 418	289 295 761
Enrolled in school	2 992 328	79 329 527
Enrolled in preschool (percent)	6.0	6.2
Enrolled in grades K-12 (percent)	67.8	67.6
Enrolled in college or graduate school (percent)	26.2	26.2
Attainment		
Total population 25 years and over	7 627 615	197 892 369
Less than a high school diploma (percent)	12.9	15.5
High school diploma or more (percent)	87.1	84.5
Bachelor's degree or more (percent)	24.1	27.5
Graduate degree or more (percent)	8.8	10.1

Table OH-11. Educational Indicators

(Number, percent.)

Item	State	U.S.
Public Schools, 2006–2007 (except where noted)		
Number of school districts	1 056	17 742
Number of schools	3 999	99 639
Number of students	1 836 722	49 315 842
Student-teacher ratio	16.6	15.5
Expenditures per student (dollars)	$9 940	...
Averaged freshman graduation rate, 2005–2006	79.2	...
Dropout rate, grades 9–12, 2005–2006	4.0	3.7
Students eligible for free or reduced-price lunch (percent)	33.7	41.2
English-language learners (percent)	1.6	5.1
Students with IEP (percent)	14.9	12.7
Private Schools, 2007–2008 (except where noted)		
Number of schools	1 189	33 740
Number of students	215 592	5 072 451
High school graduates, 2006–2007	13 056	306 605
Student-teacher ratio	13.2	11.1

Table OH-12. Reported Voting and Registration of the Voting-Age Population, November 2008

(Number in thousands, percent.)

Item	Total population	Total citizen population	Registered			Voted		
			Total registered	Percent registered (total population)	Percent registered (total citizen population)	Total voted	Percent voted (total population)	Percent voted (total citizen population)
U.S. total	225 499	206 072	146 311	64.9	71.0	131 144	58.2	63.6
State total	8 499	8 367	6 108	71.9	73.0	5 483	64.5	65.5
Sex								
Male	4 068	3 992	2 913	71.6	73.0	2 604	64.0	65.2
Female	4 431	4 375	3 196	72.1	73.0	2 879	65.0	65.8
Race								
White alone	7 330	7 240	5 285	72.1	73.0	4 722	64.4	65.2
White non-Hispanic alone	7 134	7 109	5 204	72.9	73.2	4 651	65.2	65.4
Black alone	915	896	680	74.4	75.9	630	68.9	70.3
Asian alone	130	108	56	43.2	52.2	51	38.8	46.9
Hispanic (of any race)	212	142	85	39.9	59.8	74	35.0	52.4
White alone or in combination	7 435	7 344	5 358	72.1	73.0	4 788	64.4	65.2
Black alone or in combination	968	950	720	74.3	75.8	665	68.7	70.0
Asian alone or in combination	146	124	67	46.2	54.7	62	42.3	50.0

Table OH-13. Crime

(Number, rate per 100,000.)

Item	State			U.S.		
	2007	2008	Percent change	2007	2008	Percent change
Population	11 466 917	11 485 910	0.2	301 621 157	304 059 724	0.8
VIOLENT CRIME						
Number	39 360	39 997	1.6	1 408 337	1 382 012	-1.9
Rate	343.2	348.2	1.5	466.9	454.5	-2.7
Murder and Nonnegligent Manslaughter						
Number	516	543	5.2	16 929	16 272	-3.9
Rate	4.5	4.7	5.1	5.6	5.4	-4.7
Forcible Rape						
Number	4 452	4 419	-0.7	90 427	89 000	-1.6
Rate	38.8	38.5	-0.9	30.0	29.3	-2.4
Robbery						
Number	18 260	18 719	2.5	445 125	441 855	-0.7
Rate	159.2	163.0	2.3	147.6	145.3	-1.5
Aggravated Assault						
Number	16 132	16 316	1.1	855 856	834 885	-2.5
Rate	140.7	142.1	1.0	283.8	274.6	-3.2
PROPERTY CRIME						
Number	396 209	391 862	-1.1	9 843 481	9 767 915	-0.8
Rate	3 455.2	3 411.7	-1.3	3 263.5	3 212.5	-1.6
Burglary						
Number	98 508	102 544	4.1	2 179 140	2 222 196	2.0
Rate	859.1	892.8	3.9	722.5	730.8	1.2
Larceny-Theft						
Number	263 922	260 786	-1.2	6 568 572	6 588 873	0.3
Rate	2 301.6	2 270.5	-1.4	2 177.8	2 167.0	-0.5
Motor Vehicle Theft						
Number	33 779	28 532	-15.5	1 095 769	956 846	-12.7
Rate	294.6	248.4	-15.7	363.3	314.7	-13.4

Table OH-14. State Government Finances, 2007

(Dollars, percent distribution.)

Item	Thousands of dollars	Percent distribution
Total Revenue	86 429 629	X
General revenue	52 147 780	60.3
Intergovernmental revenue	16 691 614	19.3
Taxes	24 810 567	28.7
General sales	7 781 270	9.0
Selective sales	3 442 052	4.0
License taxes	2 139 072	2.5
Individual income tax	10 031 665	11.6
Corporate income tax	1 302 582	1.5
Other taxes	113 926	0.1
Current charges	6 606 297	7.6
Miscellaneous general revenue	4 039 302	4.7
Utility revenue	0	0.0
Liquor store revenue	687 997	0.8
Insurance trust revenue	33 593 852	38.9
Total Expenditure	66 207 138	100.0
Intergovernmental expenditure	17 755 241	26.8
Direct expenditure	48 451 897	73.2
Current operation	29 490 697	44.5
Capital outlay	3 819 803	5.8
Insurance benefits and repayments	11 823 545	17.9
Assistance and subsidies	1 922 679	2.9
Interest on debt	1 395 173	2.1
Exhibit: Salaries and wages	7 502 351	11.3
Total Expenditure	66 207 138	100.0
General expenditure	53 953 051	81.5
Intergovernmental expenditure	17 755 241	26.8
Direct expenditure	36 197 810	54.7
Education	19 699 442	29.8
Public welfare	16 352 684	24.7
Hospitals	1 958 958	3.0
Health	2 537 498	3.8
Highways	3 479 916	5.3
Police protection	221 605	0.3
Correction	1 335 897	2.0
Natural resources	381 157	0.6
Parks and recreation	101 587	0.2
Government administration	1 826 756	2.8
Interest on general debt	1 395 173	2.1
Other and unallocable	4 662 378	7.0
Utility expenditure	0	0.0
Liquor store expenditure	430 542	0.7
Insurance trust expenditure	11 823 545	17.9
Debt at End of Fiscal Year	26 065 238	X
Cash and Security Holdings	199 957 033	X

Table OH-15. State Government Tax Collections, 2008

(Dollars, percent distribution.)

Item	Thousands of dollars	Percent distribution
Total Taxes	26 373 813	X
Property taxes	32 066	1.4
Sales and gross receipts	12 745 395	551.3
General sales and gross receipts	7 865 674	340.2
Selective sales taxes	4 879 721	211.1
Alcoholic beverages	92 696	4.0
Insurance premiums	443 861	19.2
Motor fuels	1 842 595	79.7
Pari-mutuels	10 714	0.5
Public utilities	1 141 926	49.4
Tobacco products	950 940	41.1
Other selective sales	396 989	17.2
Licenses	2 673 262	115.6
Alcoholic beverages	38 668	1.7
Amusements	17 775	0.8
Corporation	1 011 434	43.7
Hunting and fishing	37 535	1.6
Motor vehicle	811 167	35.1
Motor vehicle operators	79 622	3.4
Public utility	8 291	0.4
Occupation and business, NEC	647 128	28.0
Other licenses	21 642	0.9
Income taxes	10 602 139	458.6
Individual income	9 847 506	425.9
Corporation net income	754 633	32.6
Other taxes	320 951	13.9
Death and gift	306 795	13.3
Documentary and stock transfer	4 736	0.2
Severance	9 420	0.4

Table OH-16. Agriculture

(Number, acres, and dollars.)

Item	2002		2007		Percent change, 2002–2007
	Number	Percent of total	Number	Percent of total	
Number of farms	77 797		75 861		-2.5
Farm Size					
Average size of farm (acres)	187		184		-1.6
Farms by size (number of farms)					
Fewer than 50 acres	30 732	39.5	32 128	42.4	4.5
50 to 499 acres	40 042	51.5	36 999	48.8	-7.6
500 acres or more	7 023	9.0	6 734	8.9	-4.1
Land (Acres)					
Total land in farms	14 583 435		13 956 563		-4.3
Total cropland	11 424 499	78.3	10 832 772	77.6	-5.2
Total harvested cropland	10 041 416	68.9	9 991 007	71.6	-0.5
Irrigated land	40 685	0.3	37 959	0.3	-6.7
Value of Sales (Dollars)					
Agricultural products sold ($1,000)	4 263 549		7 070 212		65.8
Average sales per farm	54 804		93 200		70.1
Sales of crops	2 304 895	54.1	4 109 722	58.1	78.3
Sales of livestock, poultry, and their products	1 958 654	45.9	2 960 490	41.9	51.1
Value of Sales (Number of Farms)					
Less than $10,000	46 658	60.0	42 706	56.3	-8.5
$10,000 to $99,999	22 271	28.6	21 111	27.8	-5.2
$100,000 to $999,999	8 439	10.8	10 954	14.4	29.8
$1,000,000 or more	429	0.6	1 090	1.4	154.1
Farms by Type of Organization (Number of Farms)					
Family	70 890	91.1	66 382	87.5	-6.4
Partnership	4 549	5.8	5 737	7.6	26.1
Corporation	1 843	2.4	2 956	3.9	60.4
Other: cooperative, estate or trust, institutional, etc	515	0.7	786	1.0	52.6
Value of Land and Buildings (Dollars)					
Estimated market value of land and buildings ($1,000)	49 243 626		39 617 975		-19.5
Land and buildings average value per farm	649 130		509 307		-21.5
Average value per acre	3 528		2 732		-22.6
Government Payments					
Number of farms receiving government payments	28 851	37.1	38 069	50.2	32.0
Payments (thousands of dollars)	197 425		232 184		17.6
Average payment per farm	6 843		6 099		-10.9
Farm Operator Characteristics					
Farm operators whose principal occupation is farming	43 488	55.9	32 676	43.1	-24.9
Farm operators whose principal occupation is other	34 309	44.1	43 185	56.9	25.9
Average age principal operator (years)	53.8		55.7		3.5

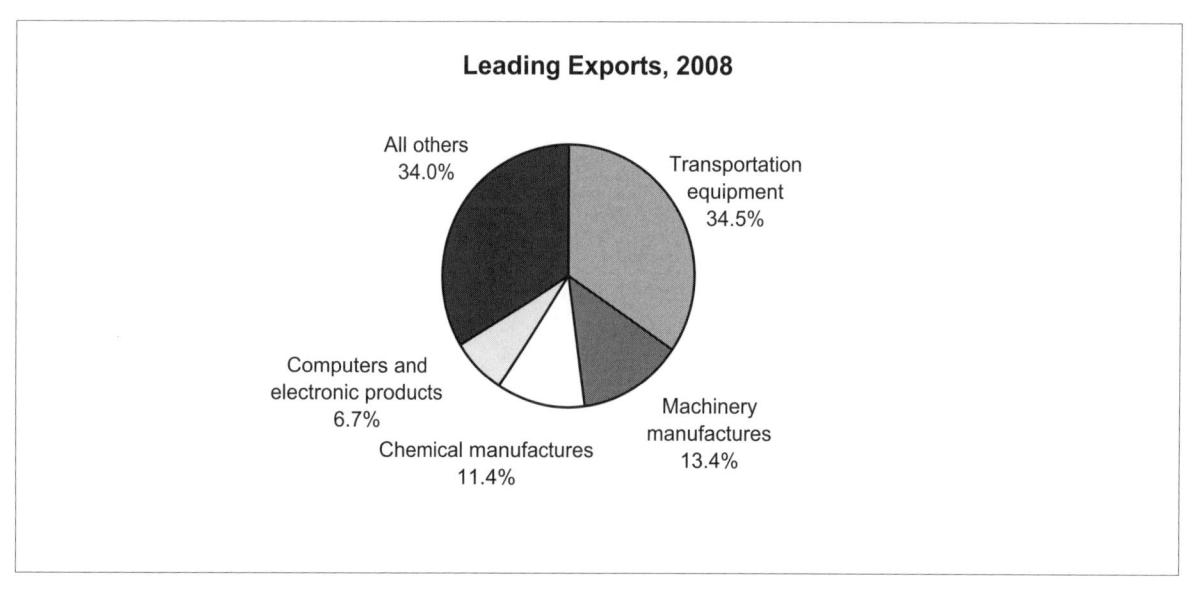

Leading Exports, 2008

All others 34.0%
Transportation equipment 34.5%
Computers and electronic products 6.7%
Chemical manufactures 11.4%
Machinery manufactures 13.4%

OKLAHOMA

Facts and Figures

Location: West south central United States; bordered on the N by Colorado and Kansas, on the E by Missouri and Arkansas, on the S by Texas, and on the W by Texas and New Mexico

Area: 69,898 sq. mi. (181,036 sq. km.); rank—20th

Population: 3,642,361 (2008 est.); rank—28th

Principal Cities: capital—Oklahoma City; largest—Oklahoma City

Statehood: November 16, 1907; 46th state

U.S. Congress: 2 senators, 5 representatives

State Motto: *Labor omnia vincit* ("Labor conquers all things")

State Song: "Oklahoma!"

State Nickname: The Sooner State

Abbreviations: OK; Okla.

State Symbols: flower—mistletoe; tree—redbud; bird—scissor-tailed flycatcher

At a Glance

- With an increase in population of 5.6 percent, Oklahoma ranked 29th among the states in growth from 2000 to 2008.
- An estimated 24,913 marriages took place in Oklahoma in 2008, compared to 18,088 divorces.
- The 2007 home ownership rate in Oklahoma was 70.3 percent; its ranking of 28th was tied with that of Connecticut and North Carolina.
- Oklahoma's median household income in 2007 was $41,567, 43rd among the states.
- In Oklahoma, 15.9 percent of the population lived below the poverty level in 2007, ranking it 9th along with Tennessee.
- In 2006-07, 18.4 percent of Oklahomans did not have health insurance, compared to 15.5 percent of the total U.S. population.
- In 2007, 4.4 percent of Oklahomans were unemployed, compared to 4.6 percent nationwide.
- Oklahoma ranked 41st in the nation with 22.8 percent of its population 25 years old and over having a bachelor's degree in 2007.
- Oklahoma's violent crime rate in 2007 was 499.6 per 100,000 population, compared to 466.9 for the entire nation.
- Oklahoma had one physician for every 499 people in 2007, compared to one physician for every 325 people nationwide.
- In the 2008 election, 56.7 percent of Oklahoma's eligible voters voted, compared to 61.7 percent of eligible voters nationwide.
- Oklahoma ranked 17th among the states receiving federal aid in 2007, with $1,529 per capita.
- Oklahoma's gross domestic product was $139 billion in 2007; it ranked 29th among the states.
- With $4.6 billion in exports in 2007, Oklahoma ranked 36th in exports.
- Oklahomans consumed 1.6 trillion Btu's of energy in 2006; the state ranked 23rd in total consumption.
- In 2007, Oklahoma exported $871 million worth of agricultural products, about 1 percent of the U.S. total.

Table OK-1. Population by Sex, Age, Race, and Hispanic Origin

(Number, percent.)

Sex, age, race, and Hispanic origin	1990	2000	2008	Average annual percent change, 2000–2008
Total Population	3 145 585	3 450 654	3 642 361	0.7
Percent of total U.S. population	1.3	1.2	1.2	X
Sex				
Male	1 530 819	1 695 895	1 798 841	0.7
Female	1 614 766	1 754 759	1 843 520	0.6
Age				
Under 5 years	226 523	236 353	266 547	1.5
5 to 19 years	709 107	765 927	739 203	-0.4
20 to 64 years	1 785 742	1 992 424	2 145 974	0.9
65 years and over	424 213	455 950	490 637	0.9
Median age (years)	33.1	35.5	36.1	X
Race and Hispanic Origin[1]				
One race				
White	2 583 512	2 628 434	2 846 186	1.0
Black	233 801	260 968	289 993	1.3
American Indian and Alaskan Native	252 420	273 230	291 390	0.8
Asian[2]	33 563	46 767	62 770	3.7
Native Hawaiian and Other Pacific Islander	X	2 372	3 863	6.3
Two or more races	X	155 985	148 159	-0.6
Hispanic (of any race)	86 160	179 304	278 620	5.7

[1]Data on race in 2000 and 2008 are not comparable to 1990. Individuals could only report one race in the 1990 census but could report one or more races on the 2000 census.
[2]Data in 1990 refer to Asian and Pacific Islanders.

Table OK-2. Marital Status

(Number, percent distribution.)

Sex and marital status	1990	2000	2007
Males, 15 Years and Over	1 170 478	1 318 729	1 405 701
Never married	24.9	25.8	29.3
Now married, except separated	62.1	59.5	54.4
Separated	1.5	1.6	1.8
Widowed	2.5	2.5	3.0
Divorced	9.0	10.6	11.5
Females, 15 Years and Over	1 272 570	1 398 823	1 462 594
Never married	17.3	19.1	21.9
Now married, except separated	56.6	55.3	50.8
Separated	1.9	1.9	2.5
Widowed	13.0	11.1	10.8
Divorced	11.2	12.5	14.0

Table OK-3. Households and Housing Characteristics

(Number, percent, and dollars.)

Item	1990	2000	2007	Average annual percent change, 2000–2007
Total Households	1 206 135	1 342 293	1 399 932	0.6
Family households	855 321	921 750	936 378	0.2
Married-couple family	695 961	717 611	707 497	-0.2
Other family	159 360	204 139	228 881	1.6
Male householder, no wife present	33 891	51 564	60 116	2.2
Female householder, no husband present	125 469	152 575	168 765	1.5
Nonfamily households	350 814	420 543	463 554	1.4
Householder living alone	309 369	358 560	389 604	1.2
Householder not living alone	41 445	61 983	73 950	2.6
Housing Characteristics				
Total housing units	1 406 499	1 514 400	1 623 100	1.0
Occupied housing units	1 206 135	1 342 293	1 399 932	0.6
Owner-occupied	821 188	918 259	955 146	0.6
Renter-occupied	384 947	424 034	444 786	0.7
Average size	2.53	2.49	2.50	X
Financial Characteristics				
Median gross rent of renter-occupied housing units (dollars)	340	456	588	3.7
Median monthly owner costs for housing units with a mortgage (dollars)	573	764	1 015	4.1
Median value of owner-occupied housing units (dollars)	47 600	70 700	103 000	5.5

Table OK-4. Median Income and Poverty Status, 2007

(Number, percent.)

Characteristic	State		U.S.	
	Number	Percent	Number	Percent
Median Income				
Households (dollars)	41 567	X	50 740	X
Families (dollars)	51 787	X	61 173	X
Below Poverty Level				
Sex				
Male	244 904	14.2	16 576 071	11.5
Female	312 126	17.5	21 476 176	14.3
Age				
Under 18 years	198 555	22.5	13 097 100	18.0
Related children under 18 years	193 822	22.1	12 728 964	17.6
18 to 64 years	312 366	14.5	21 495 507	11.6
65 years and over	46 109	10.1	3 459 640	9.5

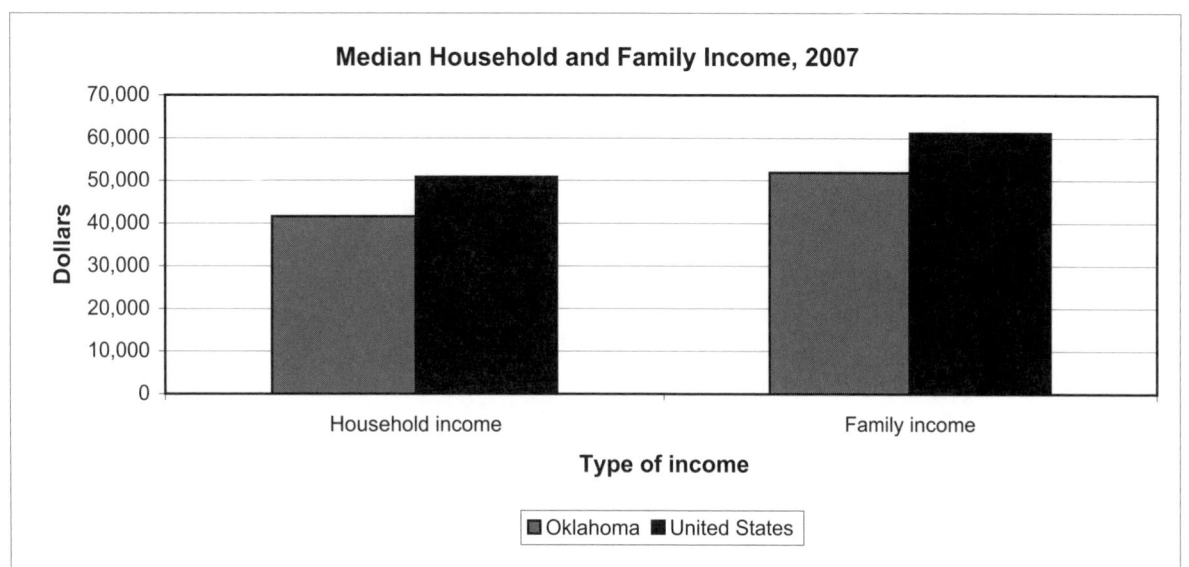

Median Household and Family Income, 2007

Table OK-5. Health Insurance Coverage Status for All Persons and Children Under 18 Years of Age

(Number, percent.)

Item	2000	2001	2002	2003	2004	2005	2006	2007
ALL PERSONS	3 384	3 382	3 477	3 438	3 444	3 505	3 492	3 551
Covered by Private or Government Health Insurance								
Number	2 761	2 786	2 885	2 752	2 783	2 878	2 831	2 920
Percent	81.6	82.4	83.0	80.0	80.8	82.1	81.1	82.2
Not Covered								
Number	624	597	592	686	661	627	661	631
Percent	18.4	17.6	17.0	20.0	19.2	17.9	18.9	17.8
Percent in the U.S. not covered	13.7	14.1	14.7	15.1	14.9	15.3	15.8	15.3
CHILDREN UNDER 18 YEARS OF AGE	873	871	880	861	852	867	913	920
Covered by Private or Government Health Insurance								
Number	728	744	778	707	714	772	799	804
Percent	83.4	85.3	88.4	82.1	83.8	89.0	87.5	87.4
Not Covered								
Number	145	128	102	154	138	95	114	116
Percent	16.6	14.7	11.6	17.9	16.2	11.0	12.5	12.6
Percent in the U.S. not covered	11.6	11.3	11.2	11.0	10.5	10.9	11.7	11.0

Table OK-6. Employment Status by Demographic Group, Preliminary 2008

(Number, percent.)

Characteristic	Civilian noninstitutional population	Civilian labor force		Employment		Unemployed	
		Number	Percent of population	Number	Percent of population	Number	Unemployment rate
TOTAL	2 762	1 761	63.8	1 696	61.4	66	3.7
Sex							
Men	1 332	960	72.0	923	69.3	37	3.9
Women	1 431	801	56.0	773	54.0	28	3.5
Race, Sex, and Hispanic Origin							
White	2 144	1 378	64.2	1 337	62.4	40	2.9
Men	1 033	759	73.4	737	71.3	22	2.9
Women	1 111	619	55.7	600	54.0	19	3.0
Black or African American	187	120	64.0	109	58.4	10	8.7
Men	88	56	64.1	51	57.7	6	10.0
Women	99	63	63.9	58	59.0	5	7.6
Hispanic	154	110	71.4	100	64.9	10	9.1
Men	78	66	84.7	59	74.9	8	11.6
Women	76	44	57.7	41	54.7	2	5.2
Age							
16 to 19 years	213	90	42.2	79	37.4	10	11.6
20 to 24 years	253	196	77.4	186	73.5	10	5.0
25 to 34 years	470	382	81.4	366	77.9	17	4.3
35 to 44 years	452	372	82.3	360	79.8	11	3.0
45 to 54 years	513	408	79.6	399	77.8	9	2.3
55 to 64 years	384	227	59.1	220	57.4	7	2.9
65 years and over	478	87	18.1	85	17.7	2	2.0

Note: Data in Table 6 are from the Current Population Survey (CPS) and do not match the estimates in Table 7. See notes and definitions for more details.

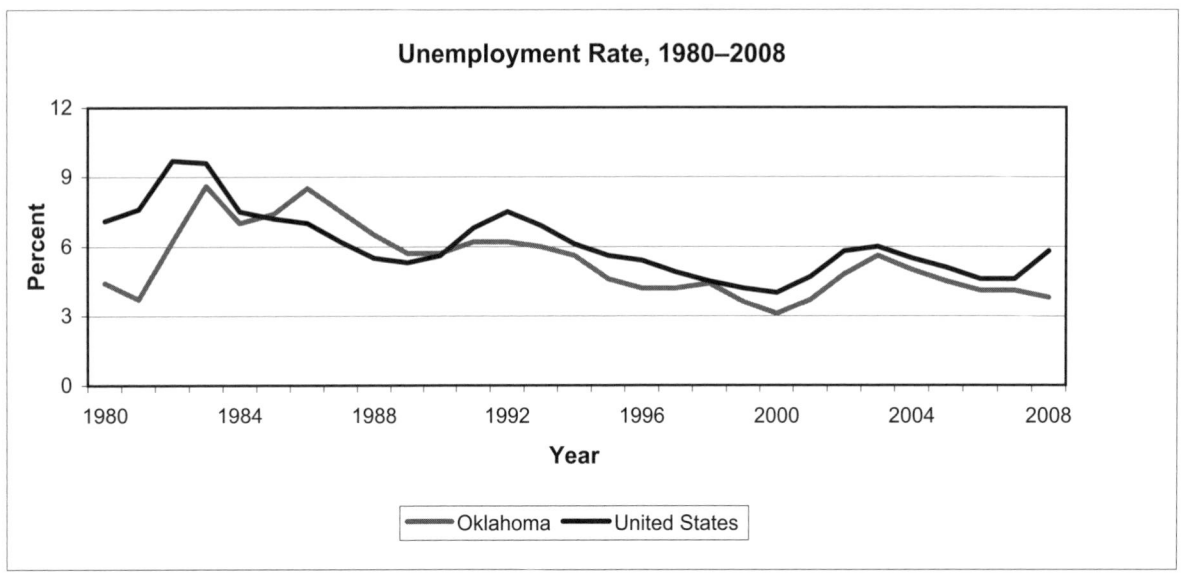

Table OK-7. Employment Status of the Civilian Noninstitutional Population Age 16 Years and Over

(Number, percent.)

Year	Civilian labor force	Civilian participation rate	Employed	Unemployed	Unemployment rate
1998	1 640 979	64.7	1 569 498	71 481	4.4
1999	1 650 302	64.4	1 590 838	59 464	3.6
2000	1 661 045	64.4	1 609 522	51 523	3.1
2001	1 676 254	64.6	1 614 627	61 627	3.7
2002	1 683 186	64.5	1 602 118	81 068	4.8
2003	1 694 085	64.5	1 598 614	95 471	5.6
2004	1 689 746	64.0	1 605 641	84 105	5.0
2005	1 701 703	64.0	1 625 062	76 641	4.5
2006	1 719 613	63.9	1 648 828	70 785	4.1
2007	1 738 010	63.9	1 667 493	70 517	4.1
2008	1 748 416	63.6	1 681 854	66 562	3.8

Table OK-8. Employment and Average Wages by Industry

(Estimates for 2001–2006 are based on the 2002 North American Industry Classification System [NAICS]. Estimates for 2007 are based on the 2007 NAICS.)

Industry	2001	2002	2003	2004	2005	2006	2007
	Number of jobs						
WAGE AND SALARY EMPLOYMENT BY INDUSTRY	1 590 962	1 567 359	1 537 603	1 557 205	1 589 915	1 633 443	1 661 528
Farm Wage and Salary Employment	14 018	11 841	9 137	11 856	11 545	11 173	12 061
Nonfarm Wage and Salary Employment	1 576 944	1 555 518	1 528 466	1 545 349	1 578 370	1 622 270	1 649 467
Private wage and salary employment	1 241 884	1 217 777	1 194 171	1 204 768	1 230 556	1 265 310	1 289 845
Forestry, fishing, hunting, and other	5 013	4 629	4 748	4 776	5 089	5 068	5 099
Mining	29 690	28 644	30 563	32 405	35 775	41 657	46 462
Utilities	11 042	10 858	9 470	9 511	9 719	10 042	10 544
Construction	69 175	67 317	65 904	64 893	68 638	72 990	74 081
Manufacturing	170 658	153 388	144 474	143 660	145 973	150 225	151 420
Durable goods manufacturing	113 950	100 561	93 976	94 074	96 278	100 872	103 408
Nondurable goods manufacturing	56 708	52 827	50 498	49 586	49 695	49 353	48 012
Wholesale trade	56 494	56 435	55 227	55 408	57 495	59 751	60 623
Retail trade	180 778	177 899	173 723	172 107	174 872	175 785	176 838
Transportation and warehousing	47 436	44 971	43 872	43 270	43 846	45 703	47 399
Information	36 744	35 116	30 758	30 385	30 264	29 826	28 568
Finance and insurance	55 909	56 547	57 393	58 012	56 357	57 516	58 494
Real estate and rental and leasing	23 895	23 975	23 199	23 870	24 584	25 020	24 688
Professional and technical services	60 448	60 918	60 630	61 427	63 809	65 488	67 336
Management of companies and enterprises	12 213	11 937	12 218	12 631	12 570	12 566	13 354
Administrative and waste services	99 365	93 704	91 125	97 471	98 749	102 090	104 724
Educational services	18 950	19 936	18 768	19 324	19 835	19 182	19 401
Health care and social assistance	156 482	161 492	163 929	165 384	169 626	173 491	177 945
Arts, entertainment, and recreation	13 909	14 043	13 869	14 469	15 182	16 388	17 760
Accommodation and food services	114 621	115 068	114 865	116 845	119 918	122 943	124 393
Other services, except public administration	79 062	80 900	79 436	78 920	78 255	79 579	80 716
Government and government enterprises	335 060	337 741	334 295	340 581	347 814	356 960	359 622
	Dollars						
AVERAGE WAGES AND SALARIES BY INDUSTRY	27 520	28 208	29 380	30 445	31 512	33 702	35 131
Average Farm Wages and Salaries	14 433	12 000	17 560	20 081	20 006	20 788	22 915
Average Nonfarm Wages and Salaries	27 636	28 331	29 450	30 525	31 596	33 791	35 221
Average private wages and salaries	27 304	27 802	28 899	30 078	31 162	33 663	34 980
Forestry, fishing, hunting, and other	16 376	16 498	17 936	19 839	20 305	20 852	21 813
Mining	53 626	53 557	56 259	59 747	65 346	86 810	78 501
Utilities	51 867	53 683	59 719	61 816	64 774	65 854	76 384
Construction	30 403	29 987	30 621	30 984	32 418	34 617	36 395
Manufacturing	34 141	35 746	37 588	38 574	39 401	41 305	42 602
Durable goods manufacturing	35 144	36 838	38 753	39 756	40 433	42 647	43 903
Nondurable goods manufacturing	32 124	33 665	35 421	36 330	37 401	38 562	39 800
Wholesale trade	37 955	39 099	38 931	41 482	42 982	45 770	47 992
Retail trade	19 061	19 529	20 105	20 629	21 157	22 002	22 817
Transportation and warehousing	36 470	36 380	37 714	40 061	41 085	42 858	44 657
Information	36 680	37 451	38 868	40 510	41 716	42 218	44 508
Finance and insurance	34 562	35 171	37 228	39 355	40 675	42 949	44 848
Real estate and rental and leasing	26 223	26 579	28 040	29 062	31 590	33 615	35 842
Professional and technical services	39 787	39 771	41 387	42 474	43 988	46 065	48 674
Management of companies and enterprises	48 568	47 401	52 422	57 877	58 251	69 643	69 406
Administrative and waste services	19 467	20 528	21 858	22 945	23 439	25 172	26 370
Educational services	19 888	20 156	21 739	22 273	22 928	24 715	26 266
Health care and social assistance	27 016	27 880	28 782	30 243	31 170	32 732	34 291
Arts, entertainment, and recreation	15 095	15 581	16 264	16 993	17 638	22 641	23 208
Accommodation and food services	11 076	11 337	11 483	11 741	12 183	12 867	13 419
Other services, except public administration	18 825	19 332	20 134	20 896	21 356	22 363	23 649
Government and government enterprises	28 869	30 240	31 420	32 107	33 132	34 247	36 081

Table OK-9. Employment Characteristics by Family Type

(Number, percent.)

Family type and labor force status	2005		2006		2007	
	Total	Families with own children under 18 years	Total	Families with own children under 18 years	Total	Families with own children under 18 years
TOTAL FAMILIES	934 124	429 096	927 086	421 781	936 378	419 415
FAMILY TYPE AND LABOR FORCE STATUS						
Married Coupled Families	704 462	289 606	699 421	283 138	707 497	286 581
Both husband and wife in labor force	50.0	61.7	50.4	62.2	51.8	62.9
Husband in labor force, wife not in labor force	24.4	30.6	24.7	30.8	24.2	30.9
Wife in labor force, husband not in labor force	7.6	4.3	7.5	4.4	6.8	3.7
Both husband and wife not in labor force	18.1	3.4	17.5	2.6	17.2	2.6
Other Families	229 662	139 490	227 665	138 643	228 881	132 834
Female householder, no husband present	73.2	77.7	72.3	75.5	73.7	77.7
In labor force	51.4	61.7	50.1	60.4	49.6	59.6
Not in labor force	21.7	16.0	22.2	15.0	24.1	18.2
Male householder, no wife present	26.8	22.3	27.7	24.5	26.3	22.3
In labor force	21.5	19.9	21.7	21.2	20.4	20.4
Not in labor force	5.3	2.4	6.0	3.3	5.8	1.9

Table OK-10. School Enrollment and Educational Attainment, 2007

(Number, percent.)

Item	State	U.S.
Enrollment		
Total population 3 years and over	3 464 447	289 295 761
Enrolled in school	927 808	79 329 527
Enrolled in preschool (percent)	6.3	6.2
Enrolled in grades K–12 (percent)	69.1	67.6
Enrolled in college or graduate school (percent) ...	24.6	26.2
Attainment		
Total population 25 years and over	2 340 504	197 892 369
Less than a high school diploma (percent)	15.2	15.5
High school diploma or more (percent)	84.8	84.5
Bachelor's degree or more (percent)	22.8	27.5
Graduate degree or more (percent)	7.6	10.1

Table OK-11. Educational Indicators

(Number, percent.)

Item	State	U.S.
Public Schools, 2006–2007 (except where noted)		
Number of school districts	600	17 742
Number of schools	1 796	99 639
Number of students	639 391	49 315 842
Student-teacher ratio	15.1	15.5
Expenditures per student (dollars)	$7 430	. . .
Averaged freshman graduation rate, 2005–2006 ...	77.8	. . .
Dropout rate, grades 9–12, 2005–2006	3.6	3.7
Students eligible for free or reduced-price lunch (percent) ...	55.2	41.2
English-language learners (percent)	6.0	5.1
Students with IEP (percent)	15.0	12.7
Private Schools, 2007–2008 (except where noted)		
Number of schools	300	33 740
Number of students	34 354	5 072 451
High school graduates, 2006–2007	2 033	306 605
Student-teacher ratio	8.8	11.1

Table OK-12. Reported Voting and Registration of the Voting-Age Population, November 2008

(Number in thousands, percent.)

Item	Total population	Total citizen population	Registered			Voted		
			Total registered	Percent registered (total population)	Percent registered (total citizen population)	Total voted	Percent voted (total population)	Percent voted (total citizen population)
U.S. total	225 499	206 072	146 311	64.9	71.0	131 144	58.2	63.6
State total	2 667	2 566	1 798	67.4	70.1	1 507	56.5	58.7
Sex								
Male	1 280	1 227	867	67.7	70.7	722	56.4	58.8
Female	1 386	1 339	931	67.1	69.5	785	56.6	58.6
Race								
White alone	2 080	2 022	1 436	69.1	71.0	1 210	58.2	59.8
White non-Hispanic alone	1 951	1 942	1 398	71.7	72.0	1 182	60.6	60.9
Black alone	194	185	142	73.1	76.6	119	61.6	64.5
Asian alone	30	24	10	. . .	. . .	7	. . .	. . .
Hispanic (of any race)	170	93	47	27.6	50.4	33	19.5	35.6
White alone or in combination	2 270	2 189	1 561	68.8	71.3	1 315	57.9	60.1
Black alone or in combination	212	203	150	70.6	73.7	128	60.1	62.7
Asian alone or in combination	31	25	10	. . .	. . .	7	. . .	. . .

Table OK-13. Crime

(Number, rate per 100,000.)

Item	State			U.S.		
	2007	2008	Percent change	2007	2008	Percent change
Population	3 617 316	3 642 361	0.7	301 621 157	304 059 724	0.8
VIOLENT CRIME						
Number	18 072	19 184	6.2	1 408 337	1 382 012	-1.9
Rate	499.6	526.7	5.4	466.9	454.5	-2.7
Murder and Nonnegligent Manslaughter						
Number	222	212	-4.5	16 929	16 272	-3.9
Rate	6.1	5.8	-5.2	5.6	5.4	-4.7
Forcible Rape						
Number	1 559	1 466	-6.0	90 427	89 000	-1.6
Rate	43.1	40.2	-6.6	30.0	29.3	-2.4
Robbery						
Number	3 373	3 683	9.2	445 125	441 855	-0.7
Rate	93.2	101.1	8.4	147.6	145.3	-1.5
Aggravated Assault						
Number	12 918	13 823	7.0	855 856	834 885	-2.5
Rate	357.1	379.5	6.3	283.8	274.6	-3.2
PROPERTY CRIME						
Number	127 562	125 384	-1.7	9 843 481	9 767 915	-0.8
Rate	3 526.4	3 442.4	-2.4	3 263.5	3 212.5	-1.6
Burglary						
Number	34 121	35 081	2.8	2 179 140	2 222 196	2.0
Rate	943.3	963.1	2.1	722.5	730.8	1.2
Larceny-Theft						
Number	79 982	79 422	-0.7	6 568 572	6 588 873	0.3
Rate	2 211.1	2 180.5	-1.4	2 177.8	2 167.0	-0.5
Motor Vehicle Theft						
Number	13 459	10 881	-19.2	1 095 769	956 846	-12.7
Rate	372.1	298.7	-19.7	363.3	314.7	-13.4

Table OK-14. State Government Finances, 2007

(Dollars, percent distribution.)

Item	Thousands of dollars	Percent distribution
Total Revenue	22 329 933	X
General revenue	17 234 417	77.2
Intergovernmental revenue	5 406 356	24.2
Taxes	8 267 606	37.0
General sales	1 964 098	8.8
Selective sales	975 897	4.4
License taxes	952 971	4.3
Individual income tax	2 774 851	12.4
Corporate income tax	561 375	2.5
Other taxes	1 038 414	4.7
Current charges	1 929 587	8.6
Miscellaneous general revenue	1 630 868	7.3
Utility revenue	476 320	2.1
Liquor store revenue	0	0.0
Insurance trust revenue	4 619 196	20.7
Total Expenditure	18 104 268	100.0
Intergovernmental expenditure	4 067 276	22.5
Direct expenditure	14 036 992	77.5
Current operation	10 042 003	55.5
Capital outlay	1 380 559	7.6
Insurance benefits and repayments	1 829 545	10.1
Assistance and subsidies	288 671	1.6
Interest on debt	496 214	2.7
Exhibit: Salaries and wages	2 939 901	16.2
Total Expenditure	18 104 268	100.0
General expenditure	15 846 257	87.5
Intergovernmental expenditure	4 067 276	22.5
Direct expenditure	11 778 981	65.1
Education	6 438 290	35.6
Public welfare	4 432 291	24.5
Hospitals	167 555	0.9
Health	704 210	3.9
Highways	1 285 952	7.1
Police protection	145 801	0.8
Correction	586 836	3.2
Natural resources	204 439	1.1
Parks and recreation	96 914	0.5
Government administration	532 516	2.9
Interest on general debt	434 980	2.4
Other and unallocable	816 473	4.5
Utility expenditure	428 466	2.4
Liquor store expenditure	0	0.0
Insurance trust expenditure	1 829 545	10.1
Debt at End of Fiscal Year	8 667 100	X
Cash and Security Holdings	38 542 690	X

Table OK-15. State Government Tax Collections, 2008

(Dollars, percent distribution.)

Item	Thousands of dollars	Percent distribution
Total Taxes	8 484 227	X
Sales and gross receipts	3 033 802	35.8
General sales and gross receipts	2 096 220	24.7
Selective sales taxes	937 582	11.1
Alcoholic beverages	86 433	1.0
Amusements	10 988	0.1
Insurance premiums	146 982	1.7
Motor fuels	384 814	4.5
Pari-mutuels	1 805	0.0
Public utilities	30 499	0.4
Tobacco products	252 374	3.0
Other selective sales	23 687	0.3
Licenses	1 034 864	12.2
Alcoholic beverages	5 030	0.1
Amusements	86 727	1.0
Corporation	52 713	0.6
Hunting and fishing	17 674	0.2
Motor vehicle	631 732	7.4
Motor vehicle operators	14 589	0.2
Public utility	5	0.0
Occupation and business, NEC	225 393	2.7
Other licenses	1 001	0.0
Income taxes	3 147 510	37.1
Individual income	2 787 445	32.9
Corporation net income	360 065	4.2
Other taxes	1 268 051	14.9
Death and gift	54 557	0.6
Documentary and stock transfer	16 138	0.2
Severance	1 184 765	14.0
Other	12 591	0.1

Table OK-16. Agriculture

(Number, acres, and dollars.)

Item	2002		2007		Percent change, 2002–2007
	Number	Percent of total	Number	Percent of total	
Number of farms	83 300		86 565		3.9
Farm Size					
Average size of farm (acres)	404		405		0.2
Farms by size (number of farms)					
Fewer than 50 acres	20 163	24.2	22 502	26.0	11.6
50 to 499 acres	48 133	57.8	48 859	56.4	1.5
500 acres or more	15 004	18.0	15 204	17.6	1.3
Land (Acres)					
Total land in farms	33 661 826		35 087 269		4.2
Total cropland	14 843 357	44.1	13 007 625	37.1	-12.4
Total harvested cropland	7 705 860	22.9	7 650 080	21.8	-0.7
Irrigated land	517 553	1.5	534 768	1.5	3.3
Value of Sales (Dollars)					
Agricultural products sold ($1,000)	4 456 404		5 806 061		30.3
Average sales per farm	53 498		67 072		25.4
Sales of crops	819 078	18.4	1 187 625	20.5	45.0
Sales of livestock, poultry, and their products	3 637 326	81.6	4 618 436	79.5	27.0
Value of Sales (Number of Farms)					
Less than $10,000	52 304	62.8	54 459	62.9	4.1
$10,000 to $99,999	24 546	29.5	24 943	28.8	1.6
$100,000 to $999,999	6 066	7.3	6 435	7.4	6.1
$1,000,000 or more	384	0.5	728	0.8	89.6
Farms by Type of Organization (Number of Farms)					
Family	78 197	93.9	77 412	89.4	-1.0
Partnership	3 392	4.1	5 905	6.8	74.1
Corporation	1 116	1.3	1 769	2.0	58.5
Other: cooperative, estate or trust, institutional, etc	595	0.7	1 479	1.7	148.6
Value of Land and Buildings (Dollars)					
Estimated market value of land and buildings ($1,000)	40 582 468		23 796 169		-41.4
Land and buildings average value per farm	468 809		285 730		-39.1
Average value per acre	1 157		699		-39.6
Government Payments					
Number of farms receiving government payments	24 316	29.2	27 015	31.2	11.1
Payments (thousands of dollars)	149 942		209 465		39.7
Average payment per farm	6 166		7 754		25.8
Farm Operator Characteristics					
Farm operators whose principal occupation is farming	46 053	55.3	36 052	41.6	-21.7
Farm operators whose principal occupation is other	37 247	44.7	50 513	58.4	35.6
Average age principal operator (years)	56.0		57.6		2.9

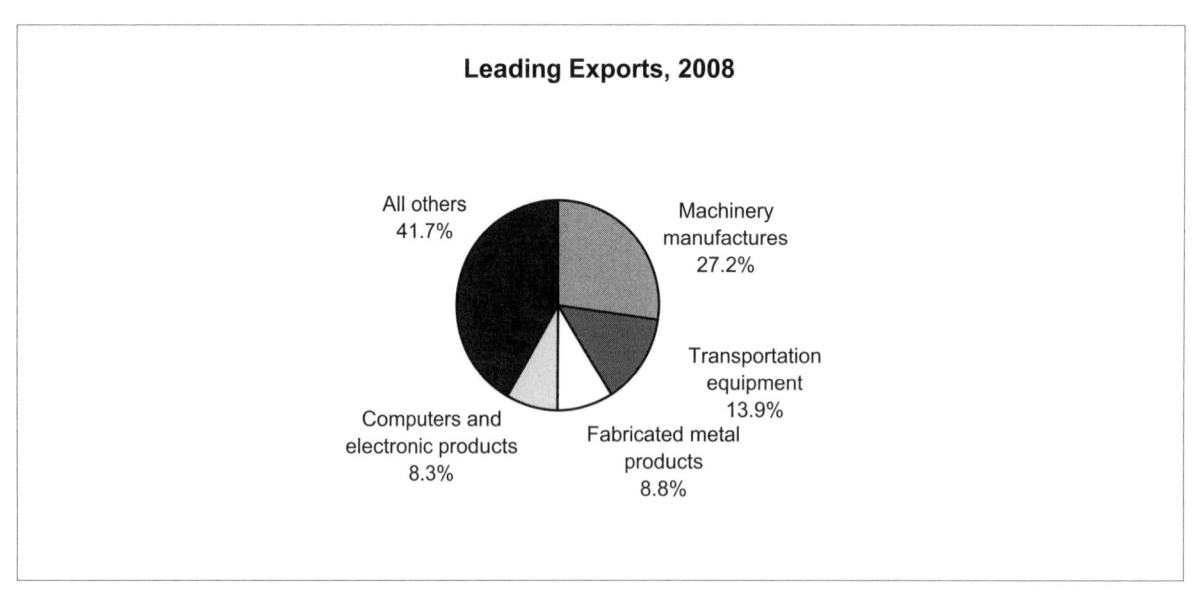

Leading Exports, 2008

All others 41.7%

Machinery manufactures 27.2%

Transportation equipment 13.9%

Fabricated metal products 8.8%

Computers and electronic products 8.3%

OREGON

Facts and Figures

Location: Northwestern United States; bordered on the N by Washington, on the E by Idaho, on the S by Nevada and California, and on the W by the Pacific Ocean

Area: 98,381 sq. mi. (254,805 sq. km.); rank—9th

Population: 3,790,060 (2008 est.); rank—27th

Principal Cities: capital—Salem; largest—Portland

Statehood: February 14, 1859; 33rd state

U.S. Congress: 2 senators, 5 representatives

State Motto: She Flies With Her Own Wings

State Song: "Oregon, My Oregon"

State Nickname: The Beaver State

Abbreviations: OR; Oreg.

State Symbols: flower—Oregon grape; tree—Douglas fir; bird—Western meadowlark

At a Glance

- With an increase in population of 10.8 percent, Oregon ranked 13th among the states in growth from 2000 to 2008.
- An estimated 27,172 marriages took place in Oregon in 2008, compared to 15,045 divorces.
- The 2007 home ownership rate in Oregon was 65.7 percent, giving it a ranking of 44th among the states.
- Oregon's median household income in 2007 was $48,730, 24th among the states.
- In Oregon, 12.9 percent of the population lived below the poverty level in 2007, ranking it 21st.
- In 2006-07, 17.3 percent of Oregonians did not have health insurance, compared to 15.5 percent of the total U.S. population.
- In 2007, 5.2 percent of Oregonians were unemployed, compared to 4.6 percent nationwide.
- Oregon ranked 18th in the nation with 28.3 percent of its population 25 years old and over having a bachelor's degree in 2007.
- Oregon's violent crime rate in 2007 was 287.6 per 100,000 population, compared to 466.9 for the entire nation.
- Oregon had one physician for every 311 people in 2007, compared to one physician for every 325 people nationwide.
- In the 2008 election, 67.8 percent of Oregon's eligible voters voted, compared to 61.7 percent of eligible voters nationwide.
- Oregon ranked 32nd among the states receiving federal aid in 2007, with $1,339 per capita.
- Oregon's gross domestic product was $158 billion in 2007; it ranked 26th among the states.
- With $16.5 billion in exports in 2007, Oregon ranked 23rd in exports.
- Oregonians consumed 1.1 trillion Btu's of energy in 2006; the state ranked 31st in total consumption.
- In 2007, Oregon exported $1.2 billion worth of agricultural products, about 1.5 percent of the U.S. total.

Table OR-1. Population by Sex, Age, Race, and Hispanic Origin

(Number, percent.)

Sex, age, race, and Hispanic origin	1990	2000	2008	Average annual percent change, 2000–2008
Total Population	2 842 321	3 421 399	3 790 060	1.3
Percent of total U.S. population	1.1	1.2	1.2	X
Sex				
Male	1 397 073	1 696 550	1 882 731	1.3
Female	1 445 248	1 724 849	1 907 329	1.3
Age				
Under 5 years	201 421	223 005	243 483	1.1
5 to 19 years	601 095	720 999	719 587	0.0
20 to 64 years	1 648 481	2 039 218	2 322 992	1.6
65 years and over	391 324	438 177	503 998	1.8
Median age (years)	34.5	36.3	38.0	X
Race and Hispanic Origin[1]				
One race				
White	2 636 787	2 961 623	3 416 377	1.8
Black	46 178	55 662	76 109	4.0
American Indian and Alaskan Native	38 496	45 211	54 405	2.3
Asian[2]	69 269	101 350	137 893	3.9
Native Hawaiian and Other Pacific Islander	X	7 976	11 034	4.1
Two or more races	X	104 745	94 242	-1.3
Hispanic (of any race)	112 707	275 314	416 044	5.3

[1]Data on race in 2000 and 2008 are not comparable to 1990. Individuals could only report one race in the 1990 census but could report one or more races on the 2000 census.
[2]Data in 1990 refer to Asian and Pacific Islanders.

Table OR-2. Marital Status

(Number, percent distribution.)

Sex and marital status	1990	2000	2007
Males, 15 Years and Over	1 083 101	1 336 805	1 496 140
Never married	27.0	28.5	32.1
Now married, except separated	59.3	57.1	52.6
Separated	1.7	1.5	1.6
Widowed	2.3	2.4	2.3
Divorced	9.7	10.6	11.3
Females, 15 Years and Over	1 146 659	1 385 329	1 542 799
Never married	19.4	21.9	24.7
Now married, except separated	55.5	53.9	50.4
Separated	2.1	1.9	2.1
Widowed	11.2	9.6	9.0
Divorced	11.8	12.7	13.8

Table OR-3. Households and Housing Characteristics

(Number, percent, and dollars.)

Item	1990	2000	2007	Average annual percent change, 2000–2007
Total Households	1 103 313	1 333 723	1 471 965	1.4
Family households	750 844	877 671	940 771	1.0
Married-couple family	613 297	692 532	734 363	0.8
Other family	137 547	185 139	206 408	1.6
Male householder, no wife present	35 785	54 357	58 458	1.0
Female householder, no husband present	101 762	130 782	147 950	1.8
Nonfamily households	352 469	456 052	531 194	2.2
Householder living alone	278 716	347 624	414 031	2.5
Householder not living alone	73 753	108 428	117 163	1.1
Housing Characteristics				
Total housing units	1 193 567	1 452 709	1 609 764	1.5
Occupied housing units	1 103 313	1 333 723	1 471 965	1.4
Owner-occupied	695 957	856 951	950 773	1.5
Renter-occupied	407 356	476 772	521 192	1.3
Average size	2.52	2.51	2.49	X
Financial Characteristics				
Median gross rent of renter-occupied housing units (dollars)	408	620	743	2.6
Median monthly owner costs for housing units with a mortgage (dollars)	650	1 125	1 508	4.3
Median value of owner-occupied housing units (dollars)	66 800	152 100	257 300	7.8

Table OR-4. Median Income and Poverty Status, 2007

(Number, percent.)

Characteristic	State		U.S.	
	Number	Percent	Number	Percent
Median Income				
Households (dollars)	48 730	X	50 740	X
Families (dollars)	59 152	X	61 173	X
Below Poverty Level				
Sex				
Male	211 609	11.7	16 576 071	11.5
Female	262 580	14.1	21 476 176	14.3
Age				
Under 18 years	143 391	16.9	13 097 100	18.0
Related children under 18 years	136 536	16.3	12 728 964	17.6
18 to 64 years	291 140	12.4	21 495 507	11.6
65 years and over	39 658	8.4	3 459 640	9.5

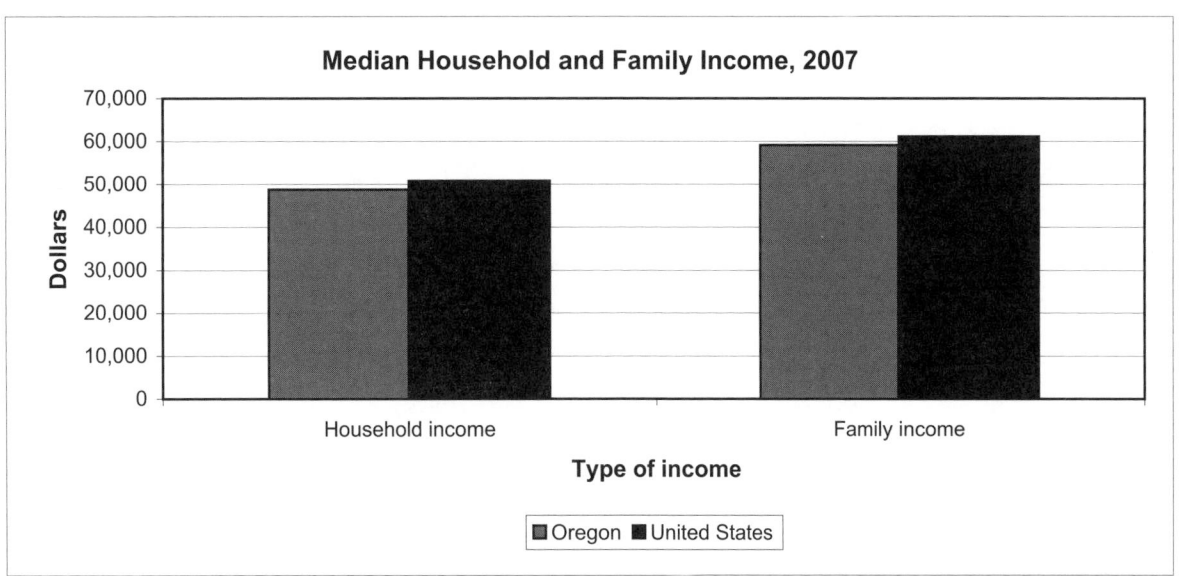

Median Household and Family Income, 2007

Table OR-5. Health Insurance Coverage Status for All Persons and Children Under 18 Years of Age

(Number, percent.)

Item	2000	2001	2002	2003	2004	2005	2006	2007
ALL PERSONS	3 420	3 462	3 510	3 569	3 582	3 627	3 715	3 762
Covered by Private or Government Health Insurance								
Number	3 003	3 030	3 016	2 979	2 999	3 062	3 051	3 130
Percent	87.8	87.5	85.9	83.5	83.7	84.4	82.1	83.2
Not Covered								
Number	417	432	494	590	583	566	665	632
Percent	12.2	12.5	14.1	16.5	16.3	15.6	17.9	16.8
Percent in the U.S. not covered	13.7	14.1	14.7	15.1	14.9	15.3	15.8	15.3
CHILDREN UNDER 18 YEARS OF AGE	863	876	836	836	859	881	870	864
Covered by Private or Government Health Insurance								
Number	767	783	742	727	769	790	755	772
Percent	88.8	89.4	88.7	87.0	89.5	89.6	86.9	89.4
Not Covered								
Number	97	93	95	109	90	91	114	92
Percent	11.2	10.6	11.3	13.0	10.5	10.4	13.1	10.6
Percent in the U.S. not covered	11.6	11.3	11.2	11.0	10.5	10.9	11.7	11.0

Table OR-6. Employment Status by Demographic Group, Preliminary 2008

(Number, percent.)

Characteristic	Civilian noninstitutional population	Civilian labor force		Employment		Unemployed	
		Number	Percent of population	Number	Percent of population	Number	Unemployment rate
TOTAL	2 986	1 973	66.1	1 845	61.8	127	6.4
Sex							
Men	1 464	1 054	72.0	976	66.7	78	7.4
Women	1 522	918	60.0	869	57.1	49	5.4
Race, Sex, and Hispanic Origin							
White	2 646	1 737	65.6	1 630	61.6	107	6.2
Men	1 283	918	71.6	852	66.4	66	7.2
Women	1 363	818	60.0	777	57.0	41	5.0
Black or African American	59	38	63.8	34	56.7	4	11.1
Men	...	...	...	...	...	...	...
Women	...	...	...	...	...	...	...
Hispanic	232	175	75.4	159	68.7	15	8.8
Men	136	116	85.4	105	77.7	10	8.9
Women	96	59	61.3	54	56.1	5	8.5
Age							
16 to 19 years	184	69	37.7	58	31.3	12	17.0
20 to 24 years	230	178	77.5	160	69.8	18	9.9
25 to 34 years	561	474	84.6	442	78.9	32	6.7
35 to 44 years	494	427	86.5	407	82.5	20	4.6
45 to 54 years	534	442	82.8	415	77.7	27	6.2
55 to 64 years	489	313	64.1	299	61.3	14	4.4
65 years and over	495	68	13.8	63	12.8	5	7.6

Note: Data in Table 6 are from the Current Population Survey (CPS) and do not match the estimates in Table 7. See notes and definitions for more details.

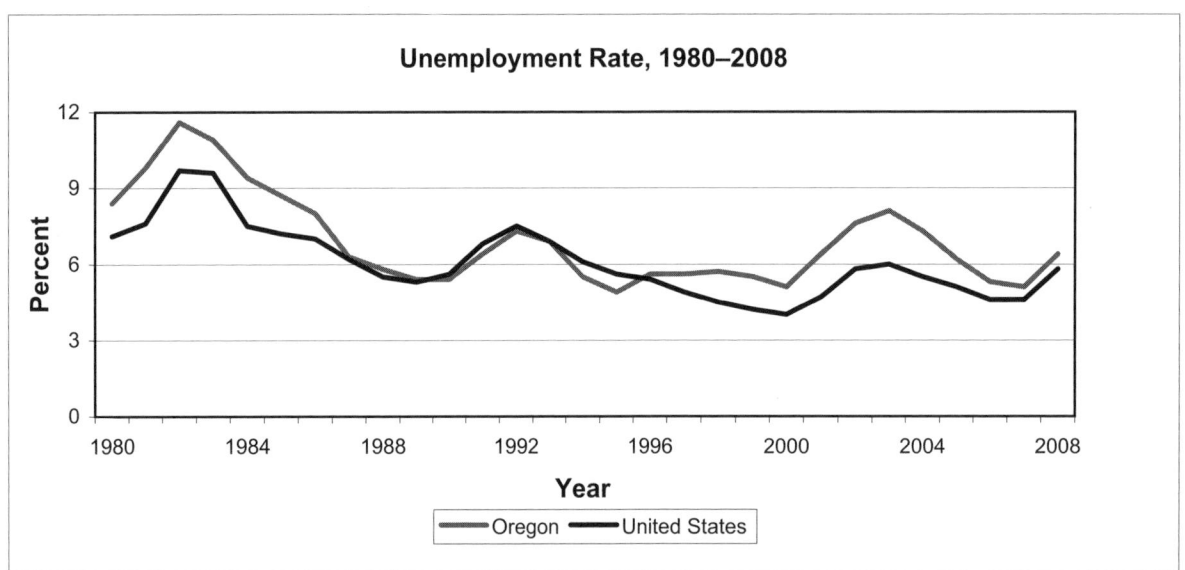

Table OR-7. Employment Status of the Civilian Noninstitutional Population Age 16 Years and Over

(Number, percent.)

Year	Civilian labor force	Civilian participation rate	Employed	Unemployed	Unemployment rate
1998	1 779 423	68.9	1 678 407	101 016	5.7
1999	1 795 724	68.7	1 697 288	98 436	5.5
2000	1 810 150	68.5	1 716 954	93 196	5.1
2001	1 828 497	68.2	1 711 041	117 456	6.4
2002	1 843 740	67.7	1 704 131	139 609	7.6
2003	1 850 024	67.1	1 699 679	150 345	8.1
2004	1 849 720	66.4	1 714 447	135 273	7.3
2005	1 862 642	65.8	1 747 420	115 222	6.2
2006	1 898 090	65.8	1 796 832	101 258	5.3
2007	1 924 576	65.6	1 825 661	98 915	5.1
2008	1 957 953	65.7	1 833 374	124 579	6.4

Table OR-8. Employment and Average Wages by Industry

(Estimates for 2001–2006 are based on the 2002 North American Industry Classification System [NAICS]. Estimates for 2007 are based on the 2007 NAICS.)

Industry	2001	2002	2003	2004	2005	2006	2007
	Number of jobs						
WAGE AND SALARY EMPLOYMENT BY INDUSTRY	1 694 999	1 677 018	1 692 056	1 727 902	1 774 090	1 821 057	1 848 280
Farm Wage and Salary Employment	27 740	27 698	28 413	29 716	29 174	29 785	30 429
Nonfarm Wage and Salary Employment	1 667 259	1 649 320	1 663 643	1 698 186	1 744 916	1 791 272	1 817 851
Private wage and salary employment	1 389 077	1 370 063	1 385 044	1 416 496	1 459 710	1 504 649	1 526 786
Forestry, fishing, hunting, and other	27 238	28 552	29 161	27 169	27 052	26 707	26 785
Mining	1 810	1 814	1 814	1 909	2 108	2 167	2 173
Utilities	5 374	5 246	5 217	5 306	4 841	4 810	4 689
Construction	83 105	81 072	79 791	85 171	93 340	103 441	106 629
Manufacturing	217 750	203 237	196 441	201 187	205 301	208 826	205 400
Durable goods manufacturing	162 734	150 026	144 078	148 594	153 223	155 961	151 947
Nondurable goods manufacturing	55 016	53 211	52 363	52 593	52 078	52 865	53 453
Wholesale trade	75 743	74 887	75 744	76 646	78 924	81 213	81 973
Retail trade	195 227	191 795	189 918	193 721	198 711	203 311	206 467
Transportation and warehousing	52 522	51 940	51 300	52 393	53 403	54 576	55 003
Information	39 971	36 367	33 836	32 998	33 728	34 984	36 289
Finance and insurance	59 137	59 540	61 563	60 264	61 587	63 684	63 111
Real estate and rental and leasing	29 483	28 019	28 461	28 471	28 768	28 865	28 817
Professional and technical services	69 466	66 673	65 341	66 714	69 194	72 282	74 616
Management of companies and enterprises	26 875	25 455	25 460	26 440	27 795	29 113	30 812
Administrative and waste services	84 724	85 172	83 849	87 769	93 925	97 334	96 319
Educational services	28 528	30 045	33 683	37 326	39 288	39 658	40 724
Health care and social assistance	161 050	167 597	187 082	190 312	194 276	198 098	203 004
Arts, entertainment, and recreation	20 634	20 502	21 148	21 699	21 821	22 995	24 283
Accommodation and food services	131 467	131 560	133 017	136 044	139 879	144 612	150 446
Other services, except public administration	78 973	80 590	82 218	84 957	85 769	87 973	89 246
Government and government enterprises	278 182	279 257	278 599	281 690	285 206	286 623	291 065
	Dollars						
AVERAGE WAGES AND SALARIES BY INDUSTRY	32 590	32 987	33 426	34 564	35 809	37 262	38 725
Average Farm Wages and Salaries	22 650	20 891	20 772	21 758	25 256	24 251	25 259
Average Nonfarm Wages and Salaries	32 755	33 190	33 642	34 788	35 986	37 478	38 951
Average private wages and salaries	32 660	32 935	33 333	34 527	35 747	37 287	38 752
Forestry, fishing, hunting, and other	25 755	27 742	27 277	27 560	29 087	30 215	31 686
Mining	36 376	38 445	40 047	40 946	42 889	45 659	48 127
Utilities	60 118	64 234	64 202	67 391	68 878	74 273	78 280
Construction	39 509	39 491	38 404	38 646	39 949	42 211	44 051
Manufacturing	43 959	43 507	44 965	46 820	48 125	49 617	51 632
Durable goods manufacturing	47 186	46 523	48 235	50 406	51 688	53 368	55 981
Nondurable goods manufacturing	34 414	35 004	35 966	36 690	37 641	38 549	39 268
Wholesale trade	47 017	48 362	50 000	53 841	56 079	58 325	61 343
Retail trade	22 393	23 034	23 329	24 043	24 490	25 193	25 677
Transportation and warehousing	34 041	34 400	34 924	36 531	38 098	39 880	40 529
Information	47 454	47 026	50 346	54 304	53 642	56 991	60 552
Finance and insurance	46 337	48 119	51 251	52 032	54 627	57 104	59 559
Real estate and rental and leasing	25 499	25 823	26 678	27 886	30 466	32 013	32 153
Professional and technical services	47 325	47 038	47 939	49 663	51 587	53 549	56 298
Management of companies and enterprises	59 506	59 693	61 664	64 813	69 115	71 517	75 051
Administrative and waste services	22 352	23 570	23 829	23 728	24 394	25 468	26 757
Educational services	19 259	19 566	18 464	18 312	18 461	19 458	20 190
Health care and social assistance	31 802	33 033	31 973	33 530	34 834	36 768	38 489
Arts, entertainment, and recreation	21 749	22 778	21 412	21 423	22 054	22 100	23 037
Accommodation and food services	13 315	13 699	14 225	14 787	15 448	16 105	16 507
Other services, except public administration	21 025	21 081	21 781	22 852	24 109	24 996	26 140
Government and government enterprises	33 230	34 439	35 179	36 099	37 206	38 482	39 991

Table OR-9. Employment Characteristics by Family Type

(Number, percent.)

Family type and labor force status	2005		2006		2007	
	Total	Families with own children under 18 years	Total	Families with own children under 18 years	Total	Families with own children under 18 years
TOTAL FAMILIES	908 835	416 965	927 071	418 035	940 771	419 947
FAMILY TYPE AND LABOR FORCE STATUS						
Married Coupled Families	703 761	289 771	719 045	289 408	734 363	292 913
Both husband and wife in labor force	51.3	61.9	52.3	63.3	52.3	64.2
Husband in labor force, wife not in labor force	22.8	31.3	22.8	31.7	21.9	29.7
Wife in labor force, husband not in labor force	7.3	4.4	6.9	3.2	7.2	4.0
Both husband and wife not in labor force	18.6	2.5	17.9	1.7	18.5	2.1
Other Families	205 074	127 194	208 026	128 627	206 408	127 034
Female householder, no husband present	70.0	73.8	71.1	71.8	71.7	75.9
In labor force	49.3	59.4	50.4	58.3	52.3	61.6
Not in labor force	20.7	14.4	20.7	13.5	19.4	14.3
Male householder, no wife present	30.0	26.2	28.9	28.2	28.3	24.1
In labor force	24.8	22.9	24.1	25.6	23.5	21.6
Not in labor force	5.2	3.2	4.8	2.6	4.8	2.5

Table OR-10. School Enrollment and Educational Attainment, 2007

(Number, percent.)

Item	State	U.S.
Enrollment		
Total population 3 years and over	3 606 878	289 295 761
Enrolled in school	913 405	79 329 527
Enrolled in preschool (percent)	5.3	6.2
Enrolled in grades K-12 (percent)	68.1	67.6
Enrolled in college or graduate school (percent)	26.6	26.2
Attainment		
Total population 25 years and over	2 547 452	197 892 369
Less than a high school diploma (percent)	12.0	15.5
High school diploma or more (percent)	88.0	84.5
Bachelor's degree or more (percent)	28.3	27.5
Graduate degree or more (percent)	10.3	10.1

Table OR-11. Educational Indicators

(Number, percent.)

Item	State	U.S.
Public Schools, 2006–2007 (except where noted)		
Number of school districts	223	17 742
Number of schools	1 285	99 639
Number of students	562 574	49 315 842
Student-teacher ratio	18.8	15.5
Expenditures per student (dollars)	$8 958	. . .
Averaged freshman graduation rate, 2005–2006	73.0	. . .
Dropout rate, grades 9–12, 2005–2006	4.2	3.7
Students eligible for free or reduced-price lunch (percent)	41.3	41.2
English-language learners (percent)	11.2	5.1
Students with IEP (percent)	13.8	12.7
Private Schools, 2007–2008 (except where noted)		
Number of schools	564	33 740
Number of students	53 243	5 072 451
High school graduates, 2006–2007	2 814	306 605
Student-teacher ratio	11.2	11.1

Table OR-12. Reported Voting and Registration of the Voting-Age Population, November 2008

(Number in thousands, percent.)

Item	Total population	Total citizen population	Registered			Voted		
			Total registered	Percent registered (total population)	Percent registered (total citizen population)	Total voted	Percent voted (total population)	Percent voted (total citizen population)
U.S. total	225 499	206 072	146 311	64.9	71.0	131 144	58.2	63.6
State total	2 904	2 687	1 961	67.5	73.0	1 818	62.6	67.6
Sex								
Male	1 416	1 302	913	64.5	70.1	835	59.0	64.1
Female	1 488	1 385	1 047	70.4	75.6	983	66.0	71.0
Race								
White alone	2 559	2 436	1 793	70.1	73.6	1 670	65.2	68.5
White non-Hispanic alone	2 383	2 349	1 759	73.8	74.9	1 640	68.8	69.8
Black alone	57	54	37	. . .	. . .	34	. . .	. . .
Asian alone	71	54	37	. . .	. . .	33	. . .	. . .
Hispanic (of any race)	261	100	43	16.4	42.7	39	14.9	38.6
White alone or in combination	2 637	2 514	1 848	70.1	73.5	1 716	65.1	68.3
Black alone or in combination	64	62	42	. . .	. . .	39	. . .	. . .
Asian alone or in combination	83	65	49	59.1	. . .	44	53.3	. . .

Table OR-13. Crime

(Number, rate per 100,000.)

Item	State			U.S.		
	2007	2008	Percent change	2007	2008	Percent change
Population	3 747 455	3 790 060	1.1	301 621 157	304 059 724	0.8
VIOLENT CRIME						
Number	10 777	9 747	-9.6	1 408 337	1 382 012	-1.9
Rate	287.6	257.2	-10.6	466.9	454.5	-2.7
Murder and Nonnegligent Manslaughter						
Number	73	82	12.3	16 929	16 272	-3.9
Rate	1.9	2.2	11.1	5.6	5.4	-4.7
Forcible Rape						
Number	1 255	1 156	-7.9	90 427	89 000	-1.6
Rate	33.5	30.5	-8.9	30.0	29.3	-2.4
Robbery						
Number	2 862	2 641	-7.7	445 125	441 855	-0.7
Rate	76.4	69.7	-8.8	147.6	145.3	-1.5
Aggravated Assault						
Number	6 587	5 868	-10.9	855 856	834 885	-2.5
Rate	175.8	154.8	-11.9	283.8	274.6	-3.2
PROPERTY CRIME						
Number	132 143	124 397	-5.9	9 843 481	9 767 915	-0.8
Rate	3 526.2	3 282.2	-6.9	3 263.5	3 212.5	-1.6
Burglary						
Number	22 821	20 879	-8.5	2 179 140	2 222 196	2.0
Rate	609.0	550.9	-9.5	722.5	730.8	1.2
Larceny-Theft						
Number	94 773	92 187	-2.7	6 568 572	6 588 873	0.3
Rate	2 529.0	2 432.3	-3.8	2 177.8	2 167.0	-0.5
Motor Vehicle Theft						
Number	14 549	11 331	-22.1	1 095 769	956 846	-12.7
Rate	388.2	299.0	-23.0	363.3	314.7	-13.4

Table OR-14. State Government Finances, 2007

(Dollars, percent distribution.)

Item	Thousands of dollars	Percent distribution
Total Revenue	30 587 369	X
General revenue	17 010 752	55.6
Intergovernmental revenue	4 653 941	15.2
Taxes	7 742 862	25.3
General sales	0	0.0
Selective sales	782 874	2.6
License taxes	832 937	2.7
Individual income tax	5 595 831	18.3
Corporate income tax	405 857	1.3
Other taxes	125 363	0.4
Current charges	2 209 940	7.2
Miscellaneous general revenue	2 404 009	7.9
Utility revenue	367	0.0
Liquor store revenue	375 753	1.2
Insurance trust revenue	13 200 497	43.2
Total Expenditure	20 605 597	100.0
Intergovernmental expenditure	5 047 346	24.5
Direct expenditure	15 558 251	75.5
Current operation	9 657 585	46.9
Capital outlay	1 305 315	6.3
Insurance benefits and repayments	3 699 819	18.0
Assistance and subsidies	386 890	1.9
Interest on debt	508 642	2.5
Exhibit: Salaries and wages	3 608 556	17.5
Total Expenditure	20 605 597	100.0
General expenditure	16 703 334	81.1
Intergovernmental expenditure	5 047 346	24.5
Direct expenditure	11 655 988	56.6
Education	6 076 628	29.5
Public welfare	3 854 060	18.7
Hospitals	1 002 426	4.9
Health	415 065	2.0
Highways	1 524 387	7.4
Police protection	228 593	1.1
Correction	697 622	3.4
Natural resources	392 433	1.9
Parks and recreation	87 041	0.4
Government administration	896 099	4.3
Interest on general debt	508 642	2.5
Other and unallocable	1 020 338	5.0
Utility expenditure	6 096	0.0
Liquor store expenditure	196 348	1.0
Insurance trust expenditure	3 699 819	18.0
Debt at End of Fiscal Year	11 303 477	X
Cash and Security Holdings	79 485 656	X

Table OR-15. State Government Tax Collections, 2008

(Dollars, percent distribution.)

Item	Thousands of dollars	Percent distribution
Total Taxes	7 250 033	X
Property taxes	21 569	0.3
Sales and gross receipts	760 579	10.5
Selective sales taxes	760 579	10.5
Alcoholic beverages	15 543	0.2
Amusements	50	0.0
Insurance premiums	50 034	0.7
Motor fuels	413 521	5.7
Pari-mutuels	3 673	0.1
Public utilities	22 803	0.3
Tobacco products	254 955	3.5
Licenses	888 615	12.3
Alcoholic beverages	2 999	0.0
Amusements	1 239	0.0
Corporation	13 494	0.2
Hunting and fishing	38 919	0.5
Motor vehicle	484 291	6.7
Motor vehicle operators	31 906	0.4
Public utility	1 011	0.0
Occupation and business, NEC	307 164	4.2
Other licenses	7 592	0.1
Income taxes	5 445 904	75.1
Individual income	4 968 791	68.5
Corporation net income	477 113	6.6
Other taxes	133 366	1.8
Death and gift	109 549	1.5
Documentary and stock transfer	12 002	0.2
Severance	11 815	0.2

Table OR-16. Agriculture

(Number, acres, and dollars.)

Item	2002 Number	2002 Percent of total	2007 Number	2007 Percent of total	Percent change, 2002–2007
Number of farms	40 033		38 553		-3.7
Farm Size					
Average size of farm (acres)	427		425		-0.5
Farms by size (number of farms)					
Fewer than 50 acres	25 005	62.5	23 688	61.4	-5.3
50 to 499 acres	10 928	27.3	10 770	27.9	-1.4
500 acres or more	4 100	10.2	4 095	10.6	-0.1
Land (Acres)					
Total land in farms	17 080 422		16 399 647		-4.0
Total cropland	5 417 387	31.7	5 010 408	30.6	-7.5
Total harvested cropland	3 119 384	18.3	3 037 261	18.5	-2.6
Irrigated land	1 907 627	11.2	1 845 194	11.3	-3.3
Value of Sales (Dollars)					
Agricultural products sold ($1,000)	3 195 497		4 386 143		37.3
Average sales per farm	79 822		113 769		42.5
Sales of crops	2 194 911	68.7	2 976 087	67.9	35.6
Sales of livestock, poultry, and their products	1 000 586	31.3	1 410 055	32.1	40.9
Value of Sales (Number of Farms)					
Less than $10,000	27 653	69.1	26 035	67.5	-5.9
$10,000 to $99,999	8 193	20.5	7 840	20.3	-4.3
$100,000 to $999,999	3 655	9.1	3 836	9.9	5.0
$1,000,000 or more	532	1.3	842	2.2	58.3
Farms by Type of Organization (Number of Farms)					
Family	35 375	88.4	32 793	85.1	-7.3
Partnership	2 284	5.7	2 907	7.5	27.3
Corporation	2 064	5.2	2 507	6.5	21.5
Other: cooperative, estate or trust, institutional, etc	310	0.8	346	0.9	11.6
Value of Land and Buildings (Dollars)					
Estimated market value of land and buildings ($1,000)	31 002 186		20 383 264		-34.3
Land and buildings average value per farm	804 145		508 882		-36.7
Average value per acre	1 890		1 202		-36.4
Government Payments					
Number of farms receiving government payments	4 430	11.1	5 115	13.3	15.5
Payments (thousands of dollars)	52 085		76 491		46.9
Average payment per farm	11 757		14 954		27.2
Farm Operator Characteristics					
Farm operators whose principal occupation is farming	21 580	53.9	17 825	46.2	-17.4
Farm operators whose principal occupation is other	18 453	46.1	20 728	53.8	12.3
Average age principal operator (years)	54.9		57.5		4.7

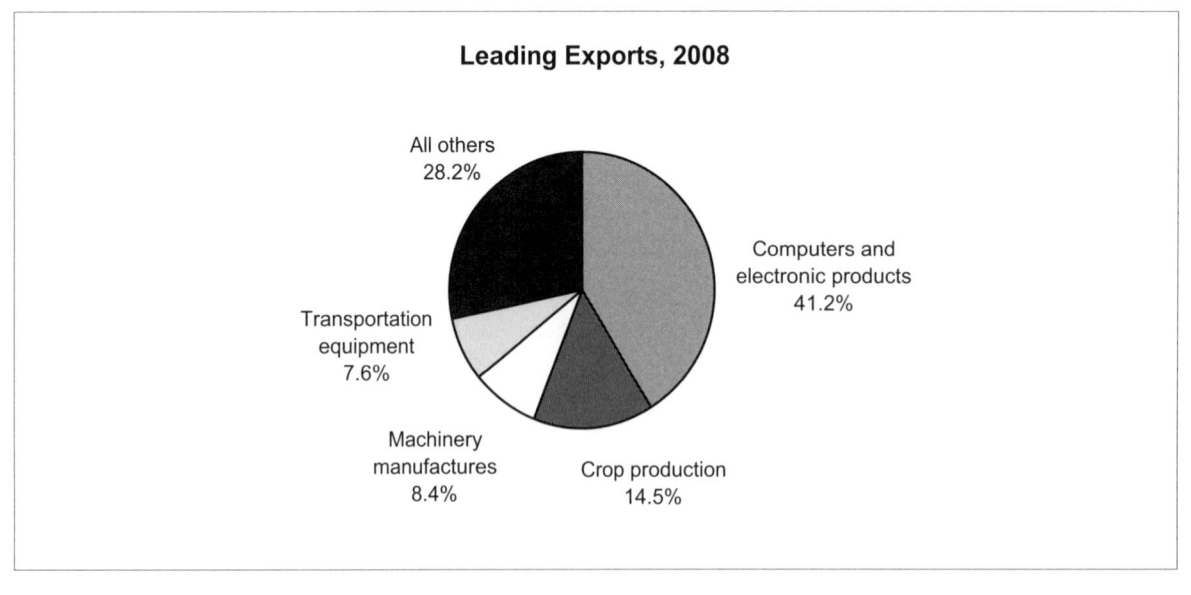

Leading Exports, 2008

All others 28.2%

Computers and electronic products 41.2%

Crop production 14.5%

Machinery manufactures 8.4%

Transportation equipment 7.6%

PENNSYLVANIA

Facts and Figures

Location: Northeastern United States; bordered on the N by Lake Erie and New York, on the E by New York and New Jersey, on the S by Delaware, Maryland, and West Virginia, and on the W by West Virginia and Ohio

Area: 46,055 sq. mi. (119,283 sq. km.); rank—33rd

Population: 12,488,279 (2008 est.); rank—6th

Principal Cities: capital—Harrisburg; largest—Philadelphia

Statehood: December 12, 1787; 2nd state

U.S. Congress: 2 senators, 19 representatives

State Motto: Virtue, Liberty, and Independence

State Song: "Pennsylvania"

State Nicknames: The Keystone State; The Quaker State

Abbreviations: PA; Penn.

State Symbols: flower—mountain laurel; tree—Eastern hemlock; bird—ruffed grouse

At a Glance

- With an increase in population of 1.4 percent, Pennsylvania ranked 44th among the states in growth from 2000 to 2008.
- An estimated 69,538 marriages took place in Pennsylvania in 2008, compared to 34,089 divorces.
- The 2007 home ownership rate in Pennsylvania was 72.9 percent, giving it a ranking of 16th among the states along with Kentucky.
- Pennsylvania's median household income in 2007 was $48,576, 25th among the states.
- In Pennsylvania, 11.6 percent of the population lived below the poverty level in 2007, ranking it 31st.
- In 2006-07, 9.8 percent of Pennsylvanians did not have health insurance, compared to 15.5 percent of the total U.S. population.
- In 2007, 4.3 percent of Pennsylvanians were unemployed, compared to 4.6 percent nationwide.
- Pennsylvania ranked 25th in the nation with 25.8 percent of its population 25 years old and over having a bachelor's degree in 2007; its ranking was the same as Florida's.
- Pennsylvania's violent crime rate in 2007 was 416.5 per 100,000 population, compared to 466.9 for the entire nation.
- Pennsylvania had one physician for every 287 people in 2007, compared to one physician for every 325 people nationwide.
- In the 2008 election, 64.2 percent of Pennsylvania's eligible voters voted, compared to 61.7 percent of eligible voters nationwide.
- Pennsylvania ranked 18th among the states receiving federal aid in 2007, with $1,528 per capita.
- Pennsylvania's gross domestic product was $531 billion in 2007; it ranked 6th among the states.
- With $29.2 billion in exports in 2007, Pennsylvania ranked 11th in exports.
- Pennsylvanians consumed 3.9 trillion Btu's of energy in 2006; the state ranked 6th in total consumption.
- In 2007, Pennsylvania exported $1.5 billion worth of agricultural products, about 1.8 percent of the U.S. total.

Table PA-1. Population by Sex, Age, Race, and Hispanic Origin

(Number, percent.)

Sex, age, race, and Hispanic origin	1990	2000	2008	Average annual percent change, 2000–2008
Total Population	11 881 643	12 281 054	12 448 279	0.2
Percent of total U.S. population	4.8	4.4	4.1	X
Sex				
Male	5 694 265	5 929 663	6 060 170	0.3
Female	6 187 378	6 351 391	6 388 109	0.1
Age				
Under 5 years	797 058	727 804	737 462	0.2
5 to 19 years	2 361 520	2 542 780	2 399 155	-0.7
20 to 64 years	6 893 959	7 091 305	7 401 091	0.5
65 years and over	1 829 106	1 919 165	1 910 571	-0.1
Median age (years)	34.9	38.0	39.9	X
Race and Hispanic Origin[1]				
One race				
White	10 520 201	10 484 203	10 633 888	0.2
Black	1 089 795	1 224 612	1 342 571	1.2
American Indian and Alaskan Native	14 733	18 348	27 181	5.0
Asian[2]	137 438	219 813	304 309	4.1
Native Hawaiian and Other Pacific Islander	X	3 417	6 096	7.5
Two or more races	X	142 224	134 234	-0.7
Hispanic (of any race)	232 262	394 088	593 986	5.3

[1]Data on race in 2000 and 2008 are not comparable to 1990. Individuals could only report one race in the 1990 census but could report one or more races on the 2000 census.
[2]Data in 1990 refer to Asian and Pacific Islanders.

Table PA-2. Marital Status

(Number, percent distribution.)

Sex and marital status	1990	2000	2007
Males, 15 Years and Over	4 494 327	4 686 277	4 892 737
Never married	30.6	30.1	33.8
Now married, except separated	58.0	57.4	52.8
Separated	2.2	1.9	1.9
Widowed	3.3	3.3	3.0
Divorced	5.9	7.3	8.4
Females, 15 Years and Over	5 046 796	5 175 436	5 278 603
Never married	24.4	24.6	28.1
Now married, except separated	51.4	51.5	47.9
Separated	2.7	2.4	2.4
Widowed	14.2	12.7	11.6
Divorced	7.3	8.8	9.9

Table PA-3. Households and Housing Characteristics

(Number, percent, and dollars.)

Item	1990	2000	2007	Average annual percent change, 2000–2007
Total Households	4 495 966	4 777 003	4 873 482	0.3
Family households	3 155 989	3 208 388	3 198 199	0.0
Married-couple family	2 502 072	2 467 673	2 421 180	-0.3
Other family	653 917	740 715	777 019	0.7
Male householder, no wife present	146 909	186 022	201 861	1.2
Female householder, no husband present	507 008	554 693	575 158	0.5
Nonfamily households	1 339 977	1 568 615	1 675 283	0.9
Householder living alone	1 150 694	1 320 941	1 410 516	0.9
Householder not living alone	189 283	247 674	264 767	1.0
Housing Characteristics				
Total housing units	4 938 140	5 249 750	5 478 158	0.6
Occupied housing units	4 495 966	4 777 003	4 873 482	0.3
Owner-occupied	3 176 121	3 406 337	3 491 156	0.4
Renter-occupied	1 319 845	1 370 666	1 382 326	0.1
Average size	2.57	2.48	2.46	X
Financial Characteristics				
Median gross rent of renter-occupied housing units (dollars)	404	531	685	3.7
Median monthly owner costs for housing units with a mortgage (dollars)	682	1 010	1 324	3.9
Median value of owner-occupied housing units (dollars)	69 100	97 000	155 000	6.9

Table PA-4. Median Income and Poverty Status, 2007

(Number, percent.)

Characteristic	State		U.S.	
	Number	Percent	Number	Percent
Median Income				
Households (dollars)	48 576	X	50 740	X
Families (dollars)	60 825	X	61 173	X
Below Poverty Level				
Sex				
Male	586 789	10.1	16 576 071	11.5
Female	806 237	13.1	21 476 176	14.3
Age				
Under 18 years	446 832	16.3	13 097 100	18.0
Related children under 18 years	433 643	15.9	12 728 964	17.6
18 to 64 years	791 876	10.6	21 495 507	11.6
65 years and over	154 318	8.7	3 459 640	9.5

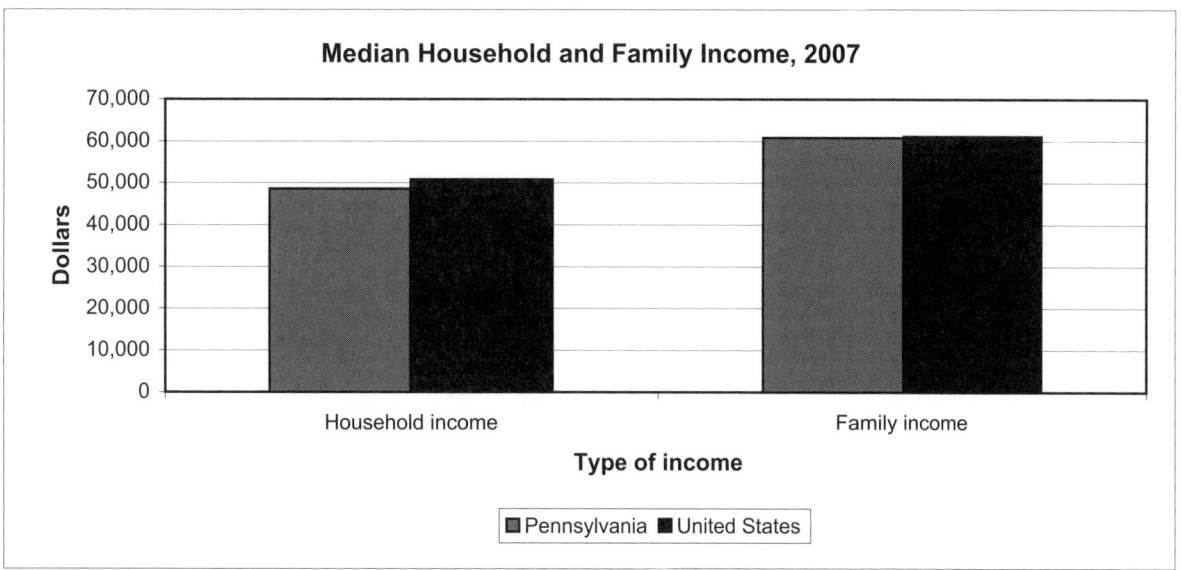

Table PA-5. Health Insurance Coverage Status for All Persons and Children Under 18 Years of Age

(Number, percent.)

Item	2000	2001	2002	2003	2004	2005	2006	2007
ALL PERSONS	12 064	12 102	12 190	12 155	12 175	12 281	12 345	12 313
Covered by Private or Government Health Insurance								
Number	11 101	11 052	10 905	10 856	10 844	11 085	11 108	11 138
Percent	92.0	91.3	89.5	89.3	89.1	90.3	90.0	90.5
Not Covered								
Number	963	1 050	1 285	1 298	1 331	1 196	1 237	1 176
Percent	8.0	8.7	10.5	10.7	10.9	9.7	10.0	9.5
Percent in the U.S. not covered	13.7	14.1	14.7	15.1	14.9	15.3	15.8	15.3
CHILDREN UNDER 18 YEARS OF AGE	2 827	2 747	2 843	2 852	2 844	2 830	2 778	2 775
Covered by Private or Government Health Insurance								
Number	2 641	2 534	2 561	2 624	2 573	2 621	2 575	2 568
Percent	93.4	92.2	90.1	92.0	90.5	92.6	92.7	92.6
Not Covered								
Number	186	213	282	228	271	209	203	207
Percent	6.6	7.8	9.9	8.0	9.5	7.4	7.3	7.4
Percent in the U.S. not covered	11.6	11.3	11.2	11.0	10.5	10.9	11.7	11.0

Table PA-6. Employment Status by Demographic Group, Preliminary 2008

(Number, percent.)

Characteristic	Civilian noninstitutional population	Civilian labor force		Employment		Unemployed	
		Number	Percent of population	Number	Percent of population	Number	Unemployment rate
TOTAL	9 823	6 416	65.3	6 075	61.8	341	5.3
Sex							
Men	4 700	3 368	72.0	3 170	67.5	197	5.9
Women	5 123	3 048	60.0	2 904	56.7	143	4.7
Race, Sex, and Hispanic Origin							
White	8 616	5 663	65.7	5 384	62.5	279	4.9
Men	4 160	3 002	72.2	2 838	68.2	164	5.5
Women	4 456	2 662	59.7	2 547	57.1	115	4.3
Black or African American	951	576	60.6	526	55.3	50	8.7
Men	421	268	63.8	242	57.4	27	10.0
Women	530	308	58.0	284	53.6	23	7.5
Hispanic	387	266	68.8	229	59.3	37	13.8
Men	198	151	76.4	126	63.9	25	16.3
Women	189	115	60.9	103	54.5	12	10.6
Age							
16 to 19 years	713	337	47.2	268	37.6	69	20.4
20 to 24 years	849	642	75.7	580	68.4	62	9.6
25 to 34 years	1 442	1 217	84.4	1 155	80.1	62	5.1
35 to 44 years	1 616	1 361	84.2	1 310	81.1	51	3.7
45 to 54 years	1 926	1 624	84.3	1 568	81.4	55	3.4
55 to 64 years	1 448	936	64.7	910	62.9	26	2.8
65 years and over	1 830	299	16.3	283	15.4	16	5.4

Note: Data in Table 6 are from the Current Population Survey (CPS) and do not match the estimates in Table 7. See notes and definitions for more details.

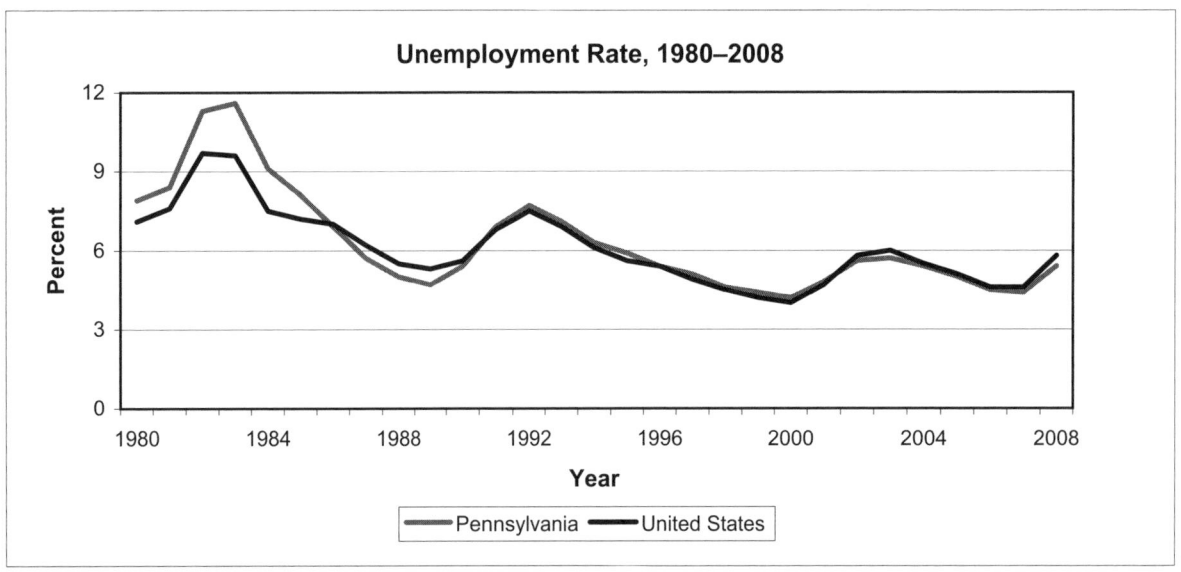

Table PA-7. Employment Status of the Civilian Noninstitutional Population Age 16 Years and Over

(Number, percent.)

Year	Civilian labor force	Civilian participation rate	Employed	Unemployed	Unemployment rate
1998	6 068 343	64.3	5 787 593	280 750	4.6
1999	6 077 826	64.2	5 809 824	268 002	4.4
2000	6 085 833	64.2	5 830 902	254 931	4.2
2001	6 167 570	64.9	5 874 153	293 417	4.8
2002	6 217 776	65.2	5 869 224	348 552	5.6
2003	6 144 967	64.2	5 795 701	349 266	5.7
2004	6 196 796	64.5	5 859 561	337 235	5.4
2005	6 247 696	64.7	5 937 007	310 689	5.0
2006	6 281 121	64.7	5 996 036	285 085	4.5
2007	6 297 105	64.5	6 022 924	274 181	4.4
2008	6 394 884	65.2	6 050 623	344 261	5.4

Table PA-8. Employment and Average Wages by Industry

(Estimates for 2001–2006 are based on the 2002 North American Industry Classification System [NAICS]. Estimates for 2007 are based on the 2007 NAICS.)

Industry	2001	2002	2003	2004	2005	2006	2007
	Number of jobs						
WAGE AND SALARY EMPLOYMENT BY INDUSTRY	5 933 267	5 891 385	5 853 072	5 882 291	5 945 756	6 010 011	6 053 306
Farm Wage and Salary Employment	22 558	22 604	19 469	19 055	18 508	19 483	18 683
Nonfarm Wage and Salary Employment	5 910 709	5 868 781	5 833 603	5 863 236	5 927 248	5 990 528	6 034 623
Private wage and salary employment	5 118 039	5 062 937	5 016 863	5 047 787	5 112 752	5 175 543	5 222 770
Forestry, fishing, hunting, and other	10 613	10 339	9 795	9 262	9 563	9 275	8 871
Mining	18 723	18 266	17 315	18 069	18 879	19 947	20 683
Utilities	32 989	31 478	27 669	25 591	22 548	21 042	21 111
Construction	259 539	257 519	256 204	259 384	264 374	270 734	271 611
Manufacturing	824 327	760 298	711 804	689 277	679 496	674 731	662 065
Durable goods manufacturing	494 219	452 524	422 190	414 023	414 481	416 030	409 308
Nondurable goods manufacturing	330 108	307 774	289 614	275 254	265 015	258 701	252 757
Wholesale trade	230 582	228 302	230 586	232 561	236 795	240 450	242 283
Retail trade	690 847	680 807	679 435	679 351	680 345	676 075	676 158
Transportation and warehousing	201 663	203 432	202 296	206 615	211 146	216 329	220 941
Information	133 440	124 054	119 092	112 894	110 383	109 500	108 019
Finance and insurance	276 357	276 264	278 785	277 437	275 690	276 637	272 955
Real estate and rental and leasing	71 681	71 879	70 217	69 680	69 725	69 379	68 752
Professional and technical services	306 109	301 828	302 370	305 945	313 295	323 176	329 317
Management of companies and enterprises	60 896	66 046	76 341	83 314	93 169	98 212	109 981
Administrative and waste services	273 516	266 466	257 784	272 681	276 923	278 095	286 757
Educational services	206 442	207 120	207 177	210 744	221 573	226 912	231 935
Health care and social assistance	764 224	783 540	795 565	810 907	835 348	864 945	881 590
Arts, entertainment, and recreation	76 234	78 848	80 248	82 231	84 109	85 970	88 620
Accommodation and food services	387 613	395 739	397 583	401 634	408 347	414 390	421 127
Other services, except public administration	292 244	300 712	296 597	300 210	301 044	299 744	299 994
Government and government enterprises	792 670	805 844	816 740	815 449	814 496	814 985	811 853
	Dollars						
AVERAGE WAGES AND SALARIES BY INDUSTRY	34 193	35 047	36 240	37 756	38 808	40 398	42 214
Average Farm Wages and Salaries	18 640	23 735	23 582	23 912	19 820	21 644	19 792
Average Nonfarm Wages and Salaries	34 252	35 091	36 282	37 801	38 867	40 459	42 284
Average private wages and salaries	34 134	34 894	36 105	37 650	38 772	40 457	42 321
Forestry, fishing, hunting, and other	21 873	22 400	23 162	24 674	24 835	25 791	26 358
Mining	46 738	47 103	48 075	50 399	53 508	54 753	56 719
Utilities	68 029	71 421	75 978	76 017	85 632	88 404	95 957
Construction	40 219	41 041	41 954	43 073	45 213	47 768	49 855
Manufacturing	41 089	42 533	43 665	45 335	46 730	48 607	50 145
Durable goods manufacturing	41 243	42 591	43 990	45 827	47 373	48 786	50 472
Nondurable goods manufacturing	40 858	42 447	43 191	44 596	45 725	48 318	49 616
Wholesale trade	46 676	47 815	49 948	53 480	55 557	58 152	61 256
Retail trade	21 081	21 577	22 302	22 637	23 013	23 580	24 093
Transportation and warehousing	35 135	35 497	35 876	37 175	37 180	37 903	38 960
Information	48 521	47 805	49 760	51 894	52 739	55 180	57 482
Finance and insurance	52 895	54 190	56 715	60 709	62 347	66 858	70 831
Real estate and rental and leasing	32 041	33 071	35 686	38 032	39 342	42 470	43 791
Professional and technical services	56 708	57 222	58 787	62 216	64 999	67 976	71 976
Management of companies and enterprises	64 568	64 588	72 266	78 749	84 084	87 948	97 273
Administrative and waste services	24 819	25 876	26 119	26 822	27 359	28 446	29 919
Educational services	28 781	30 583	31 957	32 920	32 985	33 976	34 959
Health care and social assistance	31 793	32 925	34 160	35 798	36 501	37 701	39 203
Arts, entertainment, and recreation	22 322	23 069	23 946	24 201	24 452	25 785	26 281
Accommodation and food services	13 104	13 368	13 683	14 212	14 563	15 078	15 908
Other services, except public administration	21 007	22 086	22 879	23 713	24 428	25 223	26 296
Government and government enterprises	35 014	36 323	37 372	38 740	39 466	40 472	42 042

Table PA-9. Employment Characteristics by Family Type

(Number, percent.)

Family type and labor force status	2005		2006		2007	
	Total	Families with own children under 18 years	Total	Families with own children under 18 years	Total	Families with own children under 18 years
TOTAL FAMILIES	908 835	416 965	3 174 335	1 376 539	3 198 199	1 380 193
FAMILY TYPE AND LABOR FORCE STATUS						
Married Coupled Families	703 761	289 771	2 402 123	956 783	2 421 180	962 900
Both husband and wife in labor force	51.3	61.9	53.5	67.1	54.3	67.7
Husband in labor force, wife not in labor force	22.8	31.3	21.5	27.4	20.6	26.6
Wife in labor force, husband not in labor force	7.3	4.4	7.0	3.5	7.1	3.4
Both husband and wife not in labor force	18.6	2.5	18.0	2.0	18.0	2.3
Other Families	205 074	127 194	772 212	419 756	777 019	417 293
Female householder, no husband present	70.0	73.8	73.4	76.1	74.0	76.4
In labor force	49.3	59.4	49.9	59.8	50.6	60.9
Not in labor force	20.7	14.4	23.6	16.4	23.4	15.5
Male householder, no wife present	30.0	26.2	26.6	23.9	26.0	23.6
In labor force	24.8	22.9	19.9	20.4	19.5	20.3
Not in labor force	5.2	3.2	6.6	3.5	6.5	3.3

Table PA-10. School Enrollment and Educational Attainment, 2007

(Number, percent.)

Item	State	U.S.
Enrollment		
Total population 3 years and over	11 995 478	289 295 761
Enrolled in school	3 090 671	79 329 527
Enrolled in preschool (percent)	6.0	6.2
Enrolled in grades K-12 (percent)	66.4	67.6
Enrolled in college or graduate school (percent)	27.6	26.2
Attainment		
Total population 25 years and over	8 436 765	197 892 369
Less than a high school diploma (percent)	13.2	15.5
High school diploma or more (percent)	86.8	84.5
Bachelor's degree or more (percent)	25.8	27.5
Graduate degree or more (percent)	9.9	10.1

Table PA-11. Educational Indicators

(Number, percent.)

Item	State	U.S.
Public Schools, 2006–2007 (except where noted)		
Number of school districts	739	17 742
Number of schools	3 288	99 639
Number of students	1 871 060	49 315 842
Student-teacher ratio	15.2	15.5
Expenditures per student (dollars)	$10 905	...
Averaged freshman graduation rate, 2005–2006	...	...
Dropout rate, grades 9–12, 2005–2006	2.7	3.7
Students eligible for free or reduced-price lunch (percent)	29.8	41.2
English-language learners (percent)	2.3	5.1
Students with IEP (percent)	15.6	12.7
Private Schools, 2007–2008 (except where noted)		
Number of schools	2 503	33 740
Number of students	281 958	5 072 451
High school graduates, 2006–2007	17 477	306 605
Student-teacher ratio	11.4	11.1

Table PA-12. Reported Voting and Registration of the Voting-Age Population, November 2008

(Number in thousands, percent.)

Item	Total population	Total citizen population	Registered			Voted		
			Total registered	Percent registered (total population)	Percent registered (total citizen population)	Total voted	Percent voted (total population)	Percent voted (total citizen population)
U.S. total	225 499	206 072	146 311	64.9	71.0	131 144	58.2	63.6
State total	9 449	9 206	6 451	68.3	70.1	5 747	60.8	62.4
Sex								
Male	4 493	4 384	3 014	67.1	68.8	2 664	59.3	60.8
Female	4 956	4 821	3 436	69.3	71.3	3 083	62.2	64.0
Race								
White alone	8 319	8 181	5 783	69.5	70.7	5 126	61.6	62.7
White non-Hispanic alone	7 997	7 901	5 619	70.3	71.1	4 981	62.3	63.0
Black alone	882	837	557	63.2	66.6	535	60.6	63.9
Asian alone	156	104	41	25.9	39.0	31	20.1	30.2
Hispanic (of any race)	361	319	189	52.4	59.3	161	44.6	50.5
White alone or in combination	8 375	8 236	5 829	69.6	70.8	5 165	61.7	62.7
Black alone or in combination	910	865	584	64.1	67.5	561	61.6	64.8
Asian alone or in combination	166	114	47	28.3	41.4	35	21.0	30.6

Table PA-13. Crime

(Number, rate per 100,000.)

Item	State			U.S.		
	2007	2008	Percent change	2007	2008	Percent change
Population	12 432 792	12 448 279	0.1	301 621 157	304 059 724	0.8
VIOLENT CRIME						
Number	51 782	51 036	-1.4	1 408 337	1 382 012	-1.9
Rate	416.5	410.0	-1.6	466.9	454.5	-2.7
Murder and Nonnegligent Manslaughter						
Number	723	701	-3.0	16 929	16 272	-3.9
Rate	5.8	5.6	-3.2	5.6	5.4	-4.7
Forcible Rape						
Number	3 450	3 478	0.8	90 427	89 000	-1.6
Rate	27.7	27.9	0.7	30.0	29.3	-2.4
Robbery						
Number	19 458	18 873	-3.0	445 125	441 855	-0.7
Rate	156.5	151.6	-3.1	147.6	145.3	-1.5
Aggravated Assault						
Number	28 151	27 984	-0.6	855 856	834 885	-2.5
Rate	226.4	224.8	-0.7	283.8	274.6	-3.2
PROPERTY CRIME						
Number	293 577	300 032	2.2	9 843 481	9 767 915	-0.8
Rate	2 361.3	2 410.2	2.1	3 263.5	3 212.5	-1.6
Burglary						
Number	56 020	58 620	4.6	2 179 140	2 222 196	2.0
Rate	450.6	470.9	4.5	722.5	730.8	1.2
Larceny-Theft						
Number	211 096	218 941	3.7	6 568 572	6 588 873	0.3
Rate	1 697.9	1 758.8	3.6	2 177.8	2 167.0	-0.5
Motor Vehicle Theft						
Number	26 461	22 471	-15.1	1 095 769	956 846	-12.7
Rate	212.8	180.5	-15.2	363.3	314.7	-13.4

Table PA-14. State Government Finances, 2007

(Dollars, percent distribution.)

Item	Thousands of dollars	Percent distribution
Total Revenue	83 384 773	X
General revenue	59 386 391	71.2
Intergovernmental revenue	16 323 614	19.6
Taxes	30 837 657	37.0
General sales	8 661 711	10.4
Selective sales	5 820 832	7.0
License taxes	2 847 005	3.4
Individual income tax	9 812 726	11.8
Corporate income tax	2 286 527	2.7
Other taxes	1 408 856	1.7
Current charges	6 646 149	8.0
Miscellaneous general revenue	5 578 971	6.7
Utility revenue	0	0.0
Liquor store revenue	1 349 124	1.6
Insurance trust revenue	22 649 258	27.2
Total Expenditure	68 292 746	100.0
Intergovernmental expenditure	15 189 027	22.2
Direct expenditure	53 103 719	77.8
Current operation	36 045 335	52.8
Capital outlay	5 035 059	7.4
Insurance benefits and repayments	8 464 813	12.4
Assistance and subsidies	1 785 701	2.6
Interest on debt	1 772 811	2.6
Exhibit: Salaries and wages	7 856 097	11.5
Total Expenditure	68 292 746	100.0
General expenditure	58 496 337	85.7
Intergovernmental expenditure	15 189 027	22.2
Direct expenditure	43 307 310	63.4
Education	18 257 623	26.7
Public welfare	19 146 526	28.0
Hospitals	2 523 454	3.7
Health	1 779 089	2.6
Highways	5 983 144	8.8
Police protection	719 268	1.1
Correction	1 720 374	2.5
Natural resources	622 515	0.9
Parks and recreation	259 693	0.4
Government administration	2 468 218	3.6
Interest on general debt	1 772 811	2.6
Other and unallocable	3 243 622	4.7
Utility expenditure	63 750	0.1
Liquor store expenditure	1 267 846	1.9
Insurance trust expenditure	8 464 813	12.4
Debt at End of Fiscal Year	37 125 118	X
Cash and Security Holdings	142 730 728	X

Table PA-15. State Government Tax Collections, 2008

(Dollars, percent distribution.)

Item	Thousands of dollars	Percent distribution
Total Taxes	32 123 740	X
Property taxes	58 681	0.8
Sales and gross receipts	15 306 013	211.1
General sales and gross receipts	8 873 309	122.4
Selective sales taxes	6 432 704	88.7
Alcoholic beverages	277 427	3.8
Amusements	791 573	10.9
Insurance premiums	698 200	9.6
Motor fuels	2 102 168	29.0
Pari-mutuels	23 230	0.3
Public utilities	1 354 940	18.7
Tobacco products	1 025 822	14.1
Other selective sales	159 344	2.2
Licenses	2 822 738	38.9
Alcoholic beverages	16 458	0.2
Amusements	261 229	3.6
Corporation	813 344	11.2
Hunting and fishing	71 095	1.0
Motor vehicle	814 486	11.2
Motor vehicle operators	61 881	0.9
Public utility	49 999	0.7
Occupation and business, NEC	717 456	9.9
Other licenses	16 790	0.2
Income taxes	12 599 859	173.8
Individual income	10 408 439	143.6
Corporation net income	2 191 420	30.2
Other taxes	1 336 449	18.4
Death and gift	803 367	11.1
Documentary and stock transfer	507 369	7.0
Other	25 713	0.4

Table PA-16. Agriculture

(Number, acres, and dollars.)

Item	2002		2007		Percent change, 2002–2007
	Number	Percent of total	Number	Percent of total	
Number of farms	58 105		63 163		8.7
Farm Size					
Average size of farm (acres)	133		124		-6.8
Farms by size (number of farms)					
Fewer than 50 acres	21 964	37.8	25 868	41.0	17.8
50 to 499 acres	33 728	58.0	34 848	55.2	3.3
500 acres or more	2 413	4.2	2 447	3.9	1.4
Land (Acres)					
Total land in farms	7 745 336		7 809 244		0.8
Total cropland	5 120 685	66.1	4 870 287	62.4	-4.9
Total harvested cropland	4 079 276	52.7	3 942 079	50.5	-3.4
Irrigated land	42 516	0.5	37 786	0.5	-11.1
Value of Sales (Dollars)					
Agricultural products sold ($1,000)	4 256 959		5 808 803		36.5
Average sales per farm	73 263		91 965		25.5
Sales of crops	1 320 914	31.0	1 869 706	32.2	41.5
Sales of livestock, poultry, and their products	2 936 045	69.0	3 939 097	67.8	34.2
Value of Sales (Number of Farms)					
Less than $10,000	35 409	60.9	38 850	61.5	9.7
$10,000 to $99,999	13 099	22.5	13 658	21.6	4.3
$100,000 to $999,999	9 091	15.6	9 713	15.4	6.8
$1,000,000 or more	506	0.9	942	1.5	86.2
Farms by Type of Organization (Number of Farms)					
Family	53 201	91.6	57 749	91.4	8.5
Partnership	3 428	5.9	3 265	5.2	-4.8
Corporation	1 249	2.1	1 719	2.7	37.6
Other: cooperative, estate or trust, institutional, etc	227	0.4	430	0.7	89.4
Value of Land and Buildings (Dollars)					
Estimated market value of land and buildings ($1,000)	37 289 908		26 331 894		-29.4
Land and buildings average value per farm	590 376		452 874		-23.3
Average value per acre	4 775		3 419		-28.4
Government Payments					
Number of farms receiving government payments	11 991	20.6	17 441	27.6	45.5
Payments (thousands of dollars)	85 794		75 975		-11.4
Average payment per farm	7 155		4 356		-39.1
Farm Operator Characteristics					
Farm operators whose principal occupation is farming	32 939	56.7	28 751	45.5	-12.7
Farm operators whose principal occupation is other	25 166	43.3	34 412	54.5	36.7
Average age principal operator (years)	53.1		55.2		4.0

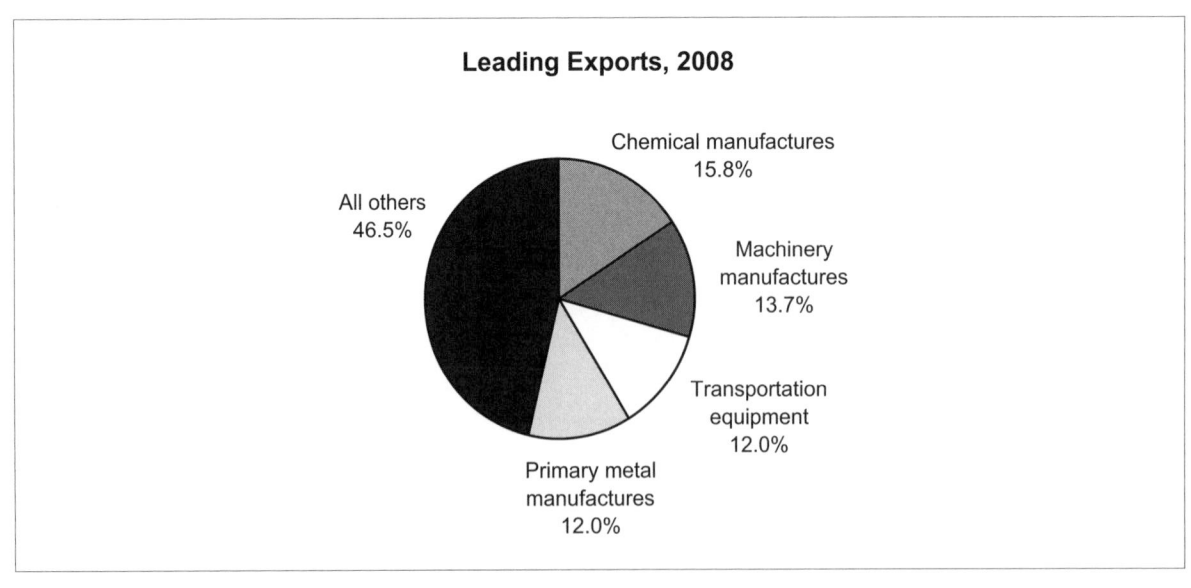

Leading Exports, 2008

Chemical manufactures 15.8%

Machinery manufactures 13.7%

Transportation equipment 12.0%

Primary metal manufactures 12.0%

All others 46.5%

RHODE ISLAND

Facts and Figures

Location: Eastern United States; bordered on the N by Massachusetts, on the E by Massachusetts and the Atlantic Ocean, on the S by Block Island Sound and the Atlantic Ocean, and on the W by Connecticut

Area: 1,545 sq. mi. (4,002 sq. km.); rank—50th

Population: 1,050,788 (2008 est.); rank—43rd

Principal Cities: capital—Providence; largest—Providence

Statehood: May 29, 1790; 13th state

U.S. Congress: 2 senators, 2 representatives

State Motto: Hope

State Song: "Rhode Island"

State Nickname: The Ocean State

Abbreviations: RI; R.I.

State Symbols: flower—violet; tree—red maple; bird—Rhode Island red

At a Glance

- With an increase in population of 0.2 percent, Rhode Island ranked 48th among the states in growth from 2000 to 2008.
- An estimated 6,487 marriages took place in Rhode Island in 2008, compared to 2,825 divorces.
- The 2007 home ownership rate in Rhode Island was 64.9 percent, giving it a ranking of 45th among the states.
- Rhode Island's median household income in 2007 was $53,568, 17th among the states.
- In Rhode Island, 12 percent of the population lived below the poverty level in 2007, ranking it 27th along with Colorado and Maine.
- In 2006-07, 9.7 percent of Rhode Islanders did not have health insurance, compared to 15.5 percent of the total U.S. population.
- In 2007, 4.9 percent of Rhode Islanders were unemployed, compared to 4.6 percent nationwide.
- Rhode Island ranked 12th in the nation with 29.8 percent of its population 25 years old and over having a bachelor's degree in 2007.
- Rhode Island's violent crime rate in 2007 was 227.3 per 100,000 population, compared to 466.9 for the entire nation.
- Rhode Island had one physician for every 239 people in 2007, compared to one physician for every 325 people nationwide.
- In the 2008 election, 62.5 percent of Rhode Island's eligible voters voted, compared to 61.7 percent of eligible voters nationwide.
- Rhode Island ranked 9th among the states receiving federal aid in 2007, with $1,999 per capita.
- Rhode Island's gross domestic product was $47 billion in 2007; it ranked 44th among the states.
- With $1.6 billion in exports in 2007, Rhode Island ranked 46th in exports.
- Rhode Islanders consumed 216 million Btu's of energy in 2006; the state ranked 49th in total consumption.
- In 2007, Rhode Island exported $11 million worth of agricultural products, less than 1 percent of the U.S. total.

Table RI-1. Population by Sex, Age, Race, and Hispanic Origin

(Number, percent.)

Sex, age, race, and Hispanic origin	1990	2000	2008	Average annual percent change, 2000–2008
Total Population	1 003 464	1 048 319	1 050 788	0.0
Percent of total U.S. population	0.4	0.4	0.3	X
Sex				
Male	481 496	503 635	508 705	0.1
Female	521 968	544 684	542 083	-0.1
Age				
Under 5 years	66 969	63 896	60 934	-0.6
5 to 19 years	193 999	218 720	204 660	-0.8
20 to 64 years	591 949	613 301	637 548	0.5
65 years and over	150 547	152 402	147 646	-0.4
Median age (years)	33.8	36.7	38.8	X
Race and Hispanic Origin[1]				
One race				
White	917 375	891 191	929 778	0.5
Black	38 861	46 908	66 847	4.5
American Indian and Alaskan Native	4 071	5 121	6 591	3.2
Asian[2]	18 325	23 665	29 099	2.6
Native Hawaiian and Other Pacific Islander	X	567	1 294	10.9
Two or more races	X	28 251	17 179	-6.0
Hispanic (of any race)	45 752	90 820	122 206	3.8

[1]Data on race in 2000 and 2008 are not comparable to 1990. Individuals could only report one race in the 1990 census but could report one or more races on the 2000 census.
[2]Data in 1990 refer to Asian and Pacific Islanders.

Table RI-2. Marital Status

(Number, percent distribution.)

Sex and marital status	1990	2000	2007
Males, 15 Years and Over	383 935	396 396	413 971
Never married	33.2	32.5	36.3
Now married, except separated	55.8	54.9	49.7
Separated	1.4	1.5	1.4
Widowed	3.1	3.0	3.0
Divorced	6.5	8.0	9.6
Females, 15 Years and Over	429 423	445 107	452 074
Never married	26.5	27.1	30.8
Now married, except separated	49.3	48.5	45.2
Separated	2.0	2.3	1.9
Widowed	13.3	11.5	10.7
Divorced	8.9	10.7	11.4

Table RI-3. Households and Housing Characteristics

(Number, percent, and dollars.)

Item	1990	2000	2007	Average annual percent change, 2000–2007
Total Households	377 977	408 424	402 538	-0.2
Family households	258 886	265 398	253 941	-0.6
Married-couple family	202 283	196 757	189 570	-0.5
Other family	56 603	68 641	64 371	-0.9
Male householder, no wife present	12 261	16 032	14 421	-1.5
Female householder, no husband present	44 342	52 609	49 950	-0.7
Nonfamily households	119 091	143 026	148 597	0.5
Householder living alone	99 111	116 678	123 506	0.8
Householder not living alone	19 980	26 348	25 091	-0.7
Housing Characteristics				
Total housing units	414 572	439 837	450 877	0.4
Occupied housing units	377 977	408 424	402 538	-0.2
Owner-occupied	224 792	245 156	256 033	0.6
Renter-occupied	153 185	163 268	146 505	-1.5
Average size	2.55	2.47	2.53	X
Financial Characteristics				
Median gross rent of renter-occupied housing units (dollars)	489	553	830	6.0
Median monthly owner costs for housing units with a mortgage (dollars)	891	1 205	1 788	5.8
Median value of owner-occupied housing units (dollars)	132 700	133 000	292 800	11.9

Table RI-4. Median Income and Poverty Status, 2007

(Number, percent.)

Characteristic	State		U.S.	
	Number	Percent	Number	Percent
Median Income				
Households (dollars)	53 568	X	50 740	X
Families (dollars)	70 187	X	61 173	X
Below Poverty Level				
Sex				
Male	53 086	10.8	16 576 071	11.5
Female	69 042	13.1	21 476 176	14.3
Age				
Under 18 years	40 468	17.5	13 097 100	18.0
Related children under 18 years	40 018	17.3	12 728 964	17.6
18 to 64 years	68 912	10.6	21 495 507	11.6
65 years and over	12 748	9.3	3 459 640	9.5

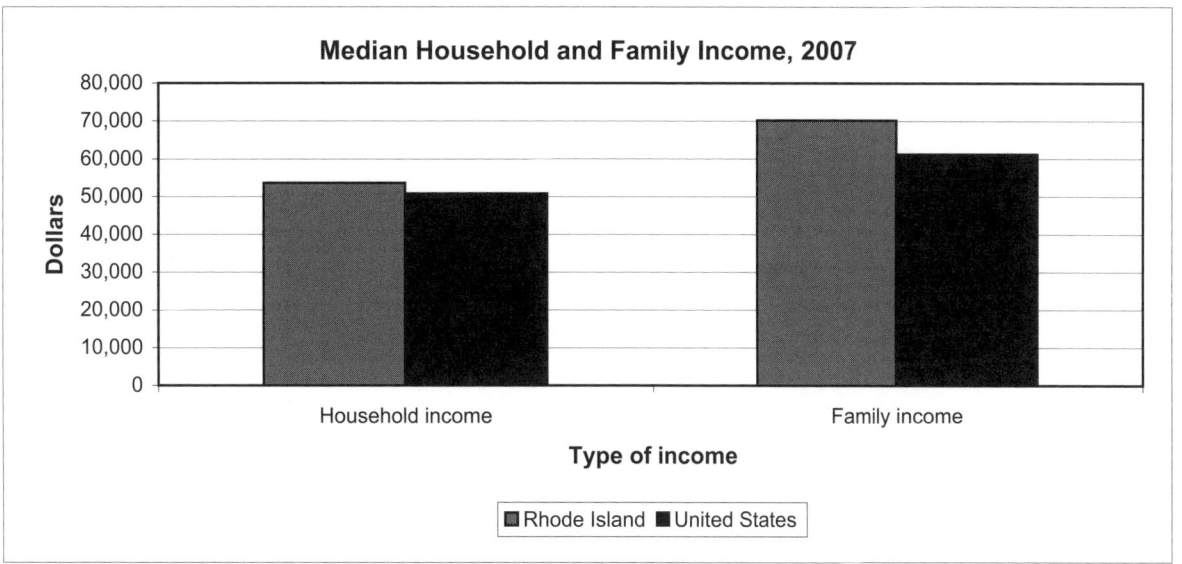

Table RI-5. Health Insurance Coverage Status for All Persons and Children Under 18 Years of Age

(Number, percent.)

Item	2000	2001	2002	2003	2004	2005	2006	2007
ALL PERSONS	1 036	1 043	1 056	1 053	1 056	1 054	1 054	1 044
Covered by Private or Government Health Insurance								
Number	962	966	957	949	947	932	963	931
Percent	92.9	92.6	90.6	90.1	89.7	88.5	91.4	89.2
Not Covered								
Number	74	77	99	104	109	122	91	113
Percent	7.1	7.4	9.4	9.9	10.3	11.5	8.6	10.8
Percent in the U.S. not covered	13.7	14.1	14.7	15.1	14.9	15.3	15.8	15.3
CHILDREN UNDER 18 YEARS OF AGE	246	245	238	251	252	251	237	238
Covered by Private or Government Health Insurance								
Number	237	234	227	239	234	232	227	217
Percent	96.3	95.6	95.3	95.2	92.9	92.4	95.9	91.2
Not Covered								
Number	9	11	11	12	18	19	10	21
Percent	3.7	4.4	4.7	4.8	7.1	7.6	4.1	8.8
Percent in the U.S. not covered	11.6	11.3	11.2	11.0	10.5	10.9	11.7	11.0

Table RI-6. Employment Status by Demographic Group, Preliminary 2008

(Number, percent.)

Characteristic	Civilian noninstitutional population	Civilian labor force		Employment		Unemployed	
		Number	Percent of population	Number	Percent of population	Number	Unemployment rate
TOTAL	837	567	67.8	522	62.4	45	7.9
Sex							
Men	399	295	74.0	268	67.3	27	9.1
Women	438	272	62.0	254	57.9	18	6.7
Race, Sex, and Hispanic Origin							
White	753	507	67.4	470	62.4	37	7.3
Men	360	265	73.8	243	67.6	22	8.4
Women	394	242	61.5	227	57.7	15	6.2
Black or African American	48	36	74.5	32	66.0	4	11.4
Men	23	18	79.9	16	69.0	2	13.6
Women	26	18	70.0	16	63.5	2	9.2
Hispanic	74	48	65.8	42	56.9	7	13.5
Men	32	24	74.7	21	64.8	3	13.2
Women	42	25	59.0	21	50.9	3	13.8
Age							
16 to 19 years	63	31	49.2	24	38.8	7	21.1
20 to 24 years	73	55	75.0	48	65.4	7	12.8
25 to 34 years	129	112	86.4	103	79.3	9	8.2
35 to 44 years	151	127	84.2	119	78.7	8	6.5
45 to 54 years	154	134	86.7	126	81.6	8	5.9
55 to 64 years	124	84	67.6	80	64.3	4	4.9
65 years and over	143	25	17.6	23	16.3	2	7.7

Note: Data in Table 6 are from the Current Population Survey (CPS) and do not match the estimates in Table 7. See notes and definitions for more details.

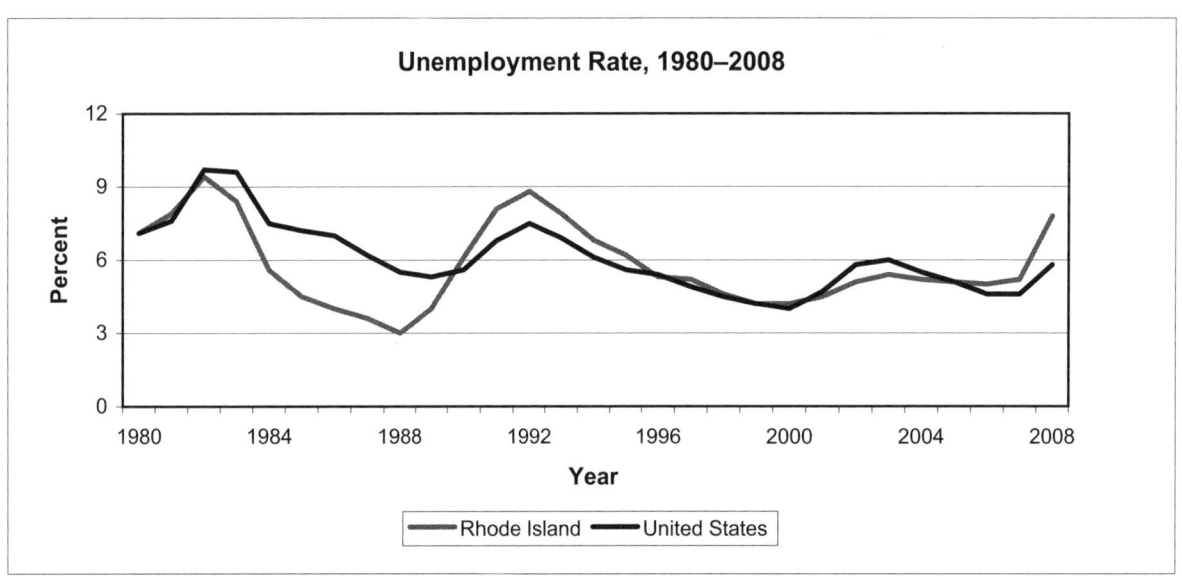

Table RI-7. Employment Status of the Civilian Noninstitutional Population Age 16 Years and Over

(Number, percent.)

Year	Civilian labor force	Civilian participation rate	Employed	Unemployed	Unemployment rate
1998	534 011	66.7	509 551	24 460	4.6
1999	541 407	67.1	518 848	22 559	4.2
2000	543 404	66.8	520 758	22 646	4.2
2001	545 461	66.5	520 677	24 784	4.5
2002	553 791	66.9	525 721	28 070	5.1
2003	563 580	67.5	533 265	30 315	5.4
2004	555 096	66.4	526 046	29 050	5.2
2005	562 382	67.3	533 924	28 458	5.1
2006	571 454	68.4	542 632	28 822	5.0
2007	572 483	68.6	542 571	29 912	5.2
2008	567 597	68.1	523 226	44 371	7.8

Table RI-8. Employment and Average Wages by Industry

(Estimates for 2001–2006 are based on the 2002 North American Industry Classification System [NAICS]. Estimates for 2007 are based on the 2007 NAICS.)

Industry	2001	2002	2003	2004	2005	2006	2007
	Number of jobs						
WAGE AND SALARY EMPLOYMENT BY INDUSTRY	503 871	503 653	507 537	511 181	511 765	513 993	513 562
Farm Wage and Salary Employment	686	679	704	588	577	528	520
Nonfarm Wage and Salary Employment	503 185	502 974	506 833	510 593	511 188	513 465	513 042
Private wage and salary employment	426 257	425 698	428 950	433 662	435 452	438 276	437 979
Forestry, fishing, hunting, and other	D	D	958	1 019	961	949	924
Mining	D	D	188	191	256	263	258
Utilities	D	D	1 174	1 095	1 149	1 149	1 116
Construction	19 741	D	21 739	21 883	22 533	23 596	22 872
Manufacturing	68 565	63 113	59 214	57 460	55 569	53 245	51 291
Durable goods manufacturing	45 820	41 681	38 698	D	36 519	34 539	33 273
Nondurable goods manufacturing	22 745	21 432	20 516	D	19 050	18 706	18 018
Wholesale trade	16 482	16 729	16 791	16 585	16 897	17 197	17 424
Retail trade	53 516	54 387	54 717	54 659	54 168	53 345	53 000
Transportation and warehousing	D	D	10 026	9 857	9 833	9 904	10 049
Information	10 998	11 231	11 082	10 945	10 839	11 046	10 501
Finance and insurance	25 426	25 855	26 366	26 188	26 406	27 254	27 175
Real estate and rental and leasing	6 510	6 400	6 570	6 879	6 972	7 115	6 984
Professional and technical services	20 350	20 194	20 529	21 316	22 135	22 708	23 003
Management of companies and enterprises	6 555	6 635	7 823	8 638	9 174	9 515	9 453
Administrative and waste services	24 579	23 565	22 999	25 158	25 421	25 481	25 020
Educational services	21 206	21 535	21 034	21 983	22 235	22 941	23 400
Health care and social assistance	69 779	71 538	73 565	74 729	75 788	77 512	79 243
Arts, entertainment, and recreation	7 497	7 539	7 756	7 800	7 862	8 129	8 613
Accommodation and food services	40 273	41 269	42 397	42 994	43 215	43 073	43 656
Other services, except public administration	22 516	23 415	24 022	24 283	24 039	23 854	23 997
Government and government enterprises	76 928	77 276	77 883	76 931	75 736	75 189	75 063
	Dollars						
AVERAGE WAGES AND SALARIES BY INDUSTRY	32 898	34 153	35 742	36 951	38 120	39 810	40 986
Average Farm Wages and Salaries	18 557	24 390	20 141	23 937	19 700	24 703	22 050
Average Nonfarm Wages and Salaries	32 917	34 166	35 764	36 966	38 141	39 826	41 005
Average private wages and salaries	31 813	32 902	34 552	35 648	36 785	38 448	39 558
Forestry, fishing, hunting, and other	D	D	34 710	33 642	34 858	38 383	37 540
Mining	D	D	45 293	44 586	43 441	47 053	46 167
Utilities	D	D	70 343	66 183	66 524	70 980	72 955
Construction	40 426	D	43 539	43 649	44 829	46 691	48 698
Manufacturing	36 701	38 056	39 151	40 799	41 700	43 575	46 077
Durable goods manufacturing	37 772	38 738	39 463	D	42 102	44 187	46 604
Nondurable goods manufacturing	34 543	36 728	38 563	D	40 931	42 445	45 105
Wholesale trade	47 185	47 868	49 680	51 595	54 376	55 509	59 020
Retail trade	21 985	22 931	23 806	24 502	24 932	25 261	26 662
Transportation and warehousing	D	D	31 844	32 585	33 075	35 007	34 999
Information	52 121	48 503	52 851	59 144	61 331	58 491	57 553
Finance and insurance	48 672	51 180	53 824	56 731	56 854	58 593	61 096
Real estate and rental and leasing	30 116	31 289	33 444	34 344	35 406	35 813	37 135
Professional and technical services	48 386	50 086	52 575	53 691	54 514	63 409	59 110
Management of companies and enterprises	62 443	63 379	83 075	77 524	82 326	89 316	96 504
Administrative and waste services	22 072	22 157	23 092	24 198	25 483	26 506	28 237
Educational services	27 971	29 400	31 456	32 040	33 733	34 593	36 319
Health care and social assistance	30 546	32 738	33 515	34 982	36 146	37 214	37 796
Arts, entertainment, and recreation	19 786	20 931	22 276	22 114	23 226	24 023	25 120
Accommodation and food services	14 221	14 776	15 128	15 623	15 974	16 548	16 846
Other services, except public administration	21 007	22 176	22 878	23 625	24 556	25 185	26 171
Government and government enterprises	39 039	41 132	42 440	44 396	45 934	47 857	49 448

Table RI-9. Employment Characteristics by Family Type

(Number, percent.)

Family type and labor force status	2005		2006		2007	
	Total	Families with own children under 18 years	Total	Families with own children under 18 years	Total	Families with own children under 18 years
TOTAL FAMILIES	259 048	119 016	262 352	119 247	253 941	117 132
FAMILY TYPE AND LABOR FORCE STATUS						
Married Coupled Families	190 076	79 854	190 694	78 038	189 570	79 596
Both husband and wife in labor force	58.0	71.5	57.3	70.1	57.3	71.7
Husband in labor force, wife not in labor force	18.3	20.6	19.2	23.8	19.5	22.2
Wife in labor force, husband not in labor force	7.2	5.4	7.6	4.1	7.2	3.9
Both husband and wife not in labor force	16.5	2.6	16.0	2.0	16.0	2.2
Other Families	68 972	39 162	71 658	41 209	64 371	37 536
Female householder, no husband present	73.8	80.7	76.1	81.3	77.6	85.0
In labor force	50.2	60.6	53.8	62.8	56.2	67.8
Not in labor force	23.6	20.1	22.2	18.4	21.4	17.2
Male householder, no wife present	26.2	19.3	23.9	18.7	22.4	15.0
In labor force	19.7	16.9	18.8	17.6	17.5	13.1
Not in labor force	6.5	2.4	5.1	1.1	4.9	1.9

Table RI-10. School Enrollment and Educational Attainment, 2007

(Number, percent.)

Item	State	U.S.
Enrollment		
Total population 3 years and over	1 021 687	289 295 761
Enrolled in school	284 749	79 329 527
Enrolled in preschool (percent)	5.9	6.2
Enrolled in grades K-12 (percent)	59.2	67.6
Enrolled in college or graduate school (percent)	34.9	26.2
Attainment		
Total population 25 years and over	710 152	197 892 369
Less than a high school diploma (percent)	17.0	15.5
High school diploma or more (percent)	83.0	84.5
Bachelor's degree or more (percent)	29.8	27.5
Graduate degree or more (percent)	11.8	10.1

Table RI-11. Educational Indicators

(Number, percent.)

Item	State	U.S.
Public Schools, 2006–2007 (except where noted)		
Number of school districts	52	17 742
Number of schools	336	99 639
Number of students	151 612	49 315 842
Student-teacher ratio	13.3	15.5
Expenditures per student (dollars)	$13 453	. . .
Averaged freshman graduation rate, 2005–2006	77.8	. . .
Dropout rate, grades 9–12, 2005–2006	4.0	3.7
Students eligible for free or reduced-price lunch (percent)	32.7	41.2
English-language learners (percent)	6.6	5.1
Students with IEP (percent)	20.0	12.7
Private Schools, 2007–2008 (except where noted)		
Number of schools	226	33 740
Number of students	23 951	5 072 451
High school graduates, 2006–2007	1 582	306 605
Student-teacher ratio	9.4	11.1

Table RI-12. Reported Voting and Registration of the Voting-Age Population, November 2008

(Number in thousands, percent.)

Item	Total population	Total citizen population	Registered			Voted		
			Total registered	Percent registered (total population)	Percent registered (total citizen population)	Total voted	Percent voted (total population)	Percent voted (total citizen population)
U.S. total	225 499	206 072	146 311	64.9	71.0	131 144	58.2	63.6
State total	804	752	568	70.6	75.5	507	63.0	67.4
Sex								
Male	380	354	258	67.8	72.8	228	59.9	64.4
Female	424	398	310	73.0	77.8	279	65.8	70.1
Race								
White alone	730	690	526	72.0	76.2	468	64.2	67.9
White non-Hispanic alone	669	655	507	75.7	77.3	451	67.4	68.9
Black alone	48	40	29	. . .	. . .	27	. . .	. . .
Asian alone	19	16	9	. . .	. . .	9	. . .	. . .
Hispanic (of any race)	71	42	22	. . .	. . .	20	. . .	. . .
White alone or in combination	732	692	527	72.0	76.2	469	64.1	67.8
Black alone or in combination	51	43	30	. . .	. . .	27	. . .	. . .
Asian alone or in combination	20	17	10	. . .	. . .	10	. . .	. . .

Table RI-13. Crime

(Number, rate per 100,000.)

Item	State			U.S.		
	2007	2008	Percent change	2007	2008	Percent change
Population	1 057 832	1 050 788	-0.7	301 621 157	304 059 724	0.8
VIOLENT CRIME						
Number	2 404	2 621	9.0	1 408 337	1 382 012	-1.9
Rate	227.3	249.4	9.8	466.9	454.5	-2.7
Murder and Nonnegligent Manslaughter						
Number	19	29	52.6	16 929	16 272	-3.9
Rate	1.8	2.8	53.7	5.6	5.4	-4.7
Forcible Rape						
Number	256	277	8.2	90 427	89 000	-1.6
Rate	24.2	26.4	8.9	30.0	29.3	-2.4
Robbery						
Number	751	879	17.0	445 125	441 855	-0.7
Rate	71.0	83.7	17.8	147.6	145.3	-1.5
Aggravated Assault						
Number	1 378	1 436	4.2	855 856	834 885	-2.5
Rate	130.3	136.7	4.9	283.8	274.6	-3.2
PROPERTY CRIME						
Number	27 743	29 849	7.6	9 843 481	9 767 915	-0.8
Rate	2 622.6	2 840.6	8.3	3 263.5	3 212.5	-1.6
Burglary						
Number	5 236	5 750	9.8	2 179 140	2 222 196	2.0
Rate	495.0	547.2	10.6	722.5	730.8	1.2
Larceny-Theft						
Number	19 281	20 899	8.4	6 568 572	6 588 873	0.3
Rate	1 822.7	1 988.9	9.1	2 177.8	2 167.0	-0.5
Motor Vehicle Theft						
Number	3 226	3 200	-0.8	1 095 769	956 846	-12.7
Rate	305.0	304.5	-0.1	363.3	314.7	-13.4

Table RI-14. State Government Finances, 2007

(Dollars, percent distribution.)

Item	Thousands of dollars	Percent distribution
Total Revenue	8 417 797	X
General revenue	6 279 168	74.6
Intergovernmental revenue	2 086 752	24.8
Taxes	2 766 046	32.9
General sales	875 619	10.4
Selective sales	480 968	5.7
License taxes	94 012	1.1
Individual income tax	1 085 600	12.9
Corporate income tax	179 168	2.1
Other taxes	50 679	0.6
Current charges	568 792	6.8
Miscellaneous general revenue	857 578	10.2
Utility revenue	31 646	0.4
Liquor store revenue	0	0.0
Insurance trust revenue	2 106 983	25.0
Total Expenditure	7 071 396	100.0
Intergovernmental expenditure	1 009 313	14.3
Direct expenditure	6 062 083	85.7
Current operation	4 131 213	58.4
Capital outlay	390 998	5.5
Insurance benefits and repayments	1 036 959	14.7
Assistance and subsidies	125 455	1.8
Interest on debt	377 458	5.3
Exhibit: Salaries and wages	1 083 955	15.3
Total Expenditure	7 071 396	100.0
General expenditure	5 909 356	83.6
Intergovernmental expenditure	1 009 313	14.3
Direct expenditure	4 900 043	69.3
Education	1 660 195	23.5
Public welfare	2 079 486	29.4
Hospitals	93 996	1.3
Health	162 119	2.3
Highways	263 915	3.7
Police protection	60 470	0.9
Correction	178 364	2.5
Natural resources	43 561	0.6
Parks and recreation	9 298	0.1
Government administration	380 956	5.4
Interest on general debt	377 458	5.3
Other and unallocable	599 538	8.5
Utility expenditure	125 081	1.8
Liquor store expenditure	0	0.0
Insurance trust expenditure	1 036 959	14.7
Debt at End of Fiscal Year	8 418 744	X
Cash and Security Holdings	16 967 285	X

Table RI-15. State Government Tax Collections, 2008

(Dollars, percent distribution.)

Item	Thousands of dollars	Percent distribution
Total Taxes	2 761 356	X
Property taxes	1 083	0.0
Sales and gross receipts	1 381 115	50.0
General sales and gross receipts	846 870	30.7
Selective sales taxes	534 245	19.3
Alcoholic beverages	11 495	0.4
Insurance premiums	52 553	1.9
Motor fuels	126 718	4.6
Pari-mutuels	2 806	0.1
Public utilities	100 332	3.6
Tobacco products	113 998	4.1
Other selective sales	126 343	4.6
Licenses	95 792	3.5
Alcoholic beverages	266	0.0
Amusements	710	0.0
Corporation	4 255	0.2
Hunting and fishing	1 986	0.1
Motor vehicle	52 248	1.9
Motor vehicle operators	660	0.0
Occupation and business, NEC	35 182	1.3
Other licenses	485	0.0
Income taxes	1 237 571	44.8
Individual income	1 091 705	39.5
Corporation net income	145 866	5.3
Other taxes	45 795	1.7
Death and gift	35 040	1.3
Documentary and stock transfer	10 461	0.4
Other	294	0.0

Table RI-16. Agriculture

(Number, acres, and dollars.)

Item	2002		2007		Percent change, 2002–2007
	Number	Percent of total	Number	Percent of total	
Number of farms	858		1 219		42.1
Farm Size					
Average size of farm (acres)	71		56		-21.1
Farms by size (number of farms)					
Fewer than 50 acres	513	59.8	837	68.7	63.2
50 to 499 acres	334	38.9	375	30.8	12.3
500 acres or more	11	1.3	7	0.6	-36.4
Land (Acres)					
Total land in farms	61 223		67 819		10.8
Total cropland	23 506	38.4	24 457	36.1	4.0
Total harvested cropland	17 820	29.1	19 325	28.5	8.4
Irrigated land	3 963	6.5	4 306	6.3	8.7
Value of Sales (Dollars)					
Agricultural products sold ($1,000)	55 546		65 908		18.7
Average sales per farm	64 740		54 067		-16.5
Sales of crops	47 138	84.9	55 602	84.4	18.0
Sales of livestock, poultry, and their products	8 408	15.1	10 306	15.6	22.6
Value of Sales (Number of Farms)					
Less than $10,000	495	57.7	774	63.5	56.4
$10,000 to $99,999	251	29.3	328	26.9	30.7
$100,000 to $999,999	104	12.1	104	8.5	0.0
$1,000,000 or more	8	0.9	13	1.1	62.5
Farms by Type of Organization (Number of Farms)					
Family	699	81.5	918	75.3	31.3
Partnership	52	6.1	110	9.0	111.5
Corporation	90	10.5	176	14.4	95.6
Other: cooperative, estate or trust, institutional, etc	17	2.0	15	1.2	-11.8
Value of Land and Buildings (Dollars)					
Estimated market value of land and buildings ($1,000)	1 141 263		564 812		-50.5
Land and buildings average value per farm	936 229		658 290		-29.7
Average value per acre	16 828		9 225		-45.2
Government Payments					
Number of farms receiving government payments	52	6.1	101	8.3	94.2
Payments (thousands of dollars)	528		743		40.7
Average payment per farm	10 145		7 353		-27.5
Farm Operator Characteristics					
Farm operators whose principal occupation is farming	442	51.5	621	50.9	40.5
Farm operators whose principal occupation is other	416	48.5	598	49.1	43.8
Average age principal operator (years)	54.3		56.3		3.7

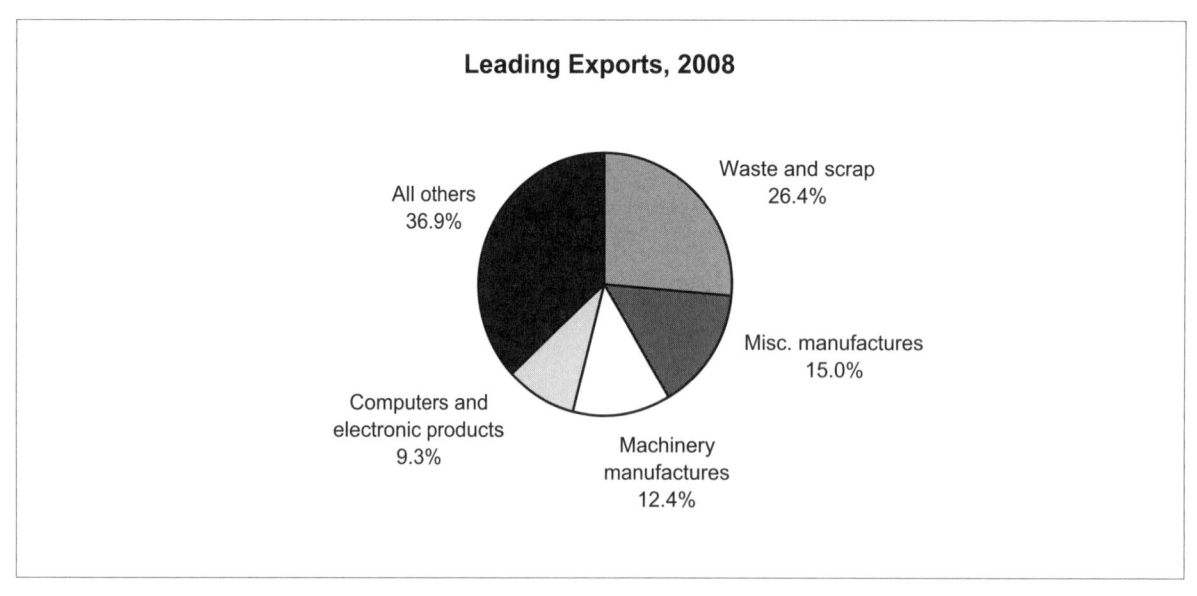

Leading Exports, 2008

- All others 36.9%
- Waste and scrap 26.4%
- Misc. manufactures 15.0%
- Machinery manufactures 12.4%
- Computers and electronic products 9.3%

SOUTH CAROLINA

Facts and Figures

Location: Southeastern United States; bordered on the N by North Carolina, on the E by the Atlantic Ocean, on the S by the Atlantic Ocean and Georgia, and on the W by Georgia

Area: 32,020 sq. mi. (82,932 sq. km.); rank—40th

Population: 4,479,800 (2008 est.); rank—24th

Principal Cities: capital—Columbia; largest—Columbia

Statehood: May 23, 1788; 8th state

U.S. Congress: 2 senators, 6 representatives

State Mottoes: *Animis opibusque parati* ("Prepared in mind and resources"); *Dum spiro, spero* ("While I breathe, I hope")

State Songs: "Carolina"; "South Carolina on My Mind"

State Nickname: The Palmetto State

Abbreviations: SC; S.C.

State Symbols: flower—yellow jessamine; tree—cabbage palmetto; bird—Carolina wren

At a Glance

- With an increase in population of 11.7 percent, South Carolina ranked 10th among the states in growth from 2000 to 2008.
- An estimated 28,578 marriages took place in South Carolina in 2008, compared to 11,382 divorces.
- The 2007 home ownership rate in South Carolina was 74.1 percent, giving it a ranking of 7th among the states.
- South Carolina's median household income in 2007 was $43,329, 41st among the states.
- In South Carolina, 15 percent of the population lived below the poverty level in 2007, ranking it 11th.
- In 2006-07, 16.2 percent of South Carolinians did not have health insurance, compared to 15.5 percent of the total U.S. population.
- In 2007, 5.6 percent of South Carolinians were unemployed, compared to 4.6 percent nationwide.
- South Carolina ranked 39th in the nation with 23.5 percent of its population 25 years old and over having a bachelor's degree in 2007.
- South Carolina's violent crime rate in 2007 was 788.3 per 100,000 population, compared to 466.9 for the entire nation.
- South Carolina had one physician for every 383 people in 2007, compared to one physician for every 325 people nationwide.
- In the 2008 election, 58.6 percent of South Carolina's eligible voters voted, compared to 61.7 percent of eligible voters nationwide.
- South Carolina ranked 33rd among the states receiving federal aid in 2007, with $1,331 per capita.
- South Carolina's gross domestic product was $153 billion in 2007; it ranked 28th among the states.
- With $16.6 billion in exports in 2007, South Carolina ranked 22nd in exports.
- South Carolinians consumed 1.7 trillion Btu's of energy in 2006; the state ranked 22nd in total consumption.
- In 2007, South Carolina exported $436 million worth of agricultural products, less than 1 percent of the U.S. total.

Table SC-1. Population by Sex, Age, Race, and Hispanic Origin

(Number, percent.)

Sex, age, race, and Hispanic origin	1990	2000	2008	Average annual percent change, 2000–2008
Total Population	3 486 703	4 012 012	4 479 800	1.4
Percent of total U.S. population	1.4	1.4	1.5	X
Sex				
Male	1 688 510	1 948 929	2 181 278	1.4
Female	1 798 193	2 063 083	2 298 522	1.4
Age				
Under 5 years	256 337	264 679	303 024	1.7
5 to 19 years	787 429	871 099	897 477	0.4
20 to 64 years	2 046 002	2 390 901	2 683 004	1.5
65 years and over	396 935	485 333	596 295	2.6
Median age (years)	31.9	35.4	37.6	X
Race and Hispanic Origin[1]				
One race				
White	2 406 974	2 695 560	3 079 779	1.7
Black	1 039 884	1 185 216	1 275 815	0.9
American Indian and Alaskan Native	8 246	13 718	19 091	4.2
Asian[2]	22 382	36 014	54 622	5.3
Native Hawaiian and Other Pacific Islander	X	1 628	2 744	6.7
Two or more races	X	39 950	47 749	2.3
Hispanic (of any race)	30 551	95 076	183 981	8.6

[1]Data on race in 2000 and 2008 are not comparable to 1990. Individuals could only report one race in the 1990 census but could report one or more races on the 2000 census.
[2]Data in 1990 refer to Asian and Pacific Islanders.

Table SC-2. Marital Status

(Number, percent distribution.)

Sex and marital status	1990	2000	2007
Males, 15 Years and Over	1 298 504	1 516 125	1 696 196
Never married	29.8	28.8	33.0
Now married, except separated	58.1	57.3	52.3
Separated	3.0	2.8	3.1
Widowed	2.5	2.7	2.9
Divorced	6.6	8.3	8.7
Females, 15 Years and Over	1 422 067	1 652 793	1 843 936
Never married	23.2	23.4	27.1
Now married, except separated	52.2	51.4	47.1
Separated	4.0	3.8	3.9
Widowed	12.8	11.5	10.7
Divorced	7.8	9.9	11.1

Table SC-3. Households and Housing Characteristics

(Number, percent, and dollars.)

Item	1990	2000	2007	Average annual percent change, 2000–2007
Total Households	1 258 044	1 533 854	1 702 564	1.5
Family households	928 206	1 072 822	1 152 062	1.0
Married-couple family	710 089	783 142	828 713	0.8
Other family	218 117	289 680	323 349	1.6
Male householder, no wife present	41 913	62 722	70 548	1.7
Female householder, no husband present	176 204	226 958	252 801	1.6
Nonfamily households	329 838	461 032	550 502	2.6
Householder living alone	281 347	383 142	469 895	3.0
Householder not living alone	48 491	77 890	80 607	0.5
Housing Characteristics				
Total housing units	1 424 155	1 753 670	2 022 033	2.1
Occupied housing units	1 258 044	1 533 854	1 702 564	1.5
Owner-occupied	878 704	1 107 617	1 192 466	1.1
Renter-occupied	379 340	426 237	510 098	2.6
Average size	2.68	2.53	2.50	X
Financial Characteristics				
Median gross rent of renter-occupied housing units (dollars)	376	510	645	3.4
Median monthly owner costs for housing units with a mortgage (dollars)	617	894	1 117	3.2
Median value of owner-occupied housing units (dollars)	60 700	94 900	133 900	5.0

Table SC-4. Median Income and Poverty Status, 2007

(Number, percent.)

Characteristic	State		U.S.	
	Number	Percent	Number	Percent
Median Income				
Households (dollars)	43 329	X	50 740	X
Families (dollars)	52 913	X	61 173	X
Below Poverty Level				
Sex				
Male	269 453	13.1	16 576 071	11.5
Female	372 305	16.8	21 476 176	14.3
Age				
Under 18 years	218 250	20.9	13 097 100	18.0
Related children under 18 years	213 858	20.6	12 728 964	17.6
18 to 64 years	357 435	13.4	21 495 507	11.6
65 years and over	66 073	12.0	3 459 640	9.5

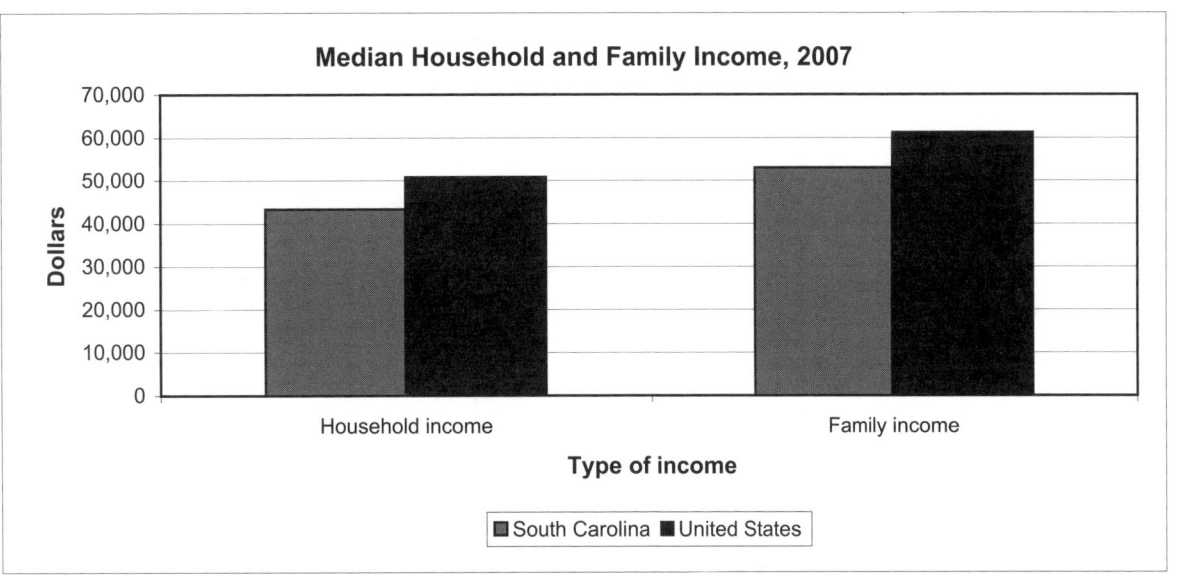

Table SC-5. Health Insurance Coverage Status for All Persons and Children Under 18 Years of Age

(Number, percent.)

Item	2000	2001	2002	2003	2004	2005	2006	2007
ALL PERSONS	3 973	4 009	3 997	4 064	4 124	4 181	4 226	4 384
Covered by Private or Government Health Insurance								
Number	3 500	3 537	3 514	3 509	3 515	3 459	3 553	3 664
Percent	88.1	88.2	87.9	86.3	85.2	82.7	84.1	83.6
Not Covered								
Number	473	473	483	555	608	721	672	721
Percent	11.9	11.8	12.1	13.7	14.8	17.3	15.9	16.4
Percent in the U.S. not covered	13.7	14.1	14.7	15.1	14.9	15.3	15.8	15.3
CHILDREN UNDER 18 YEARS OF AGE	1 014	1 016	998	1 027	1 031	1 016	1 042	1 070
Covered by Private or Government Health Insurance								
Number	928	921	931	938	951	912	930	918
Percent	91.5	90.7	93.3	91.3	92.3	89.8	89.3	85.8
Not Covered								
Number	86	95	67	89	80	104	112	152
Percent	8.5	9.3	6.7	8.7	7.7	10.2	10.7	14.2
Percent in the U.S. not covered	11.6	11.3	11.2	11.0	10.5	10.9	11.7	11.0

Table SC-6. Employment Status by Demographic Group, Preliminary 2008

(Number, percent.)

Characteristic	Civilian noninstitutional population	Civilian labor force		Employment		Unemployed	
		Number	Percent of population	Number	Percent of population	Number	Unemployment rate
TOTAL	3 431	2 134	62.2	1 992	58.1	142	6.7
Sex							
Men	1 621	1 103	68.0	1 032	63.7	71	6.4
Women	1 809	1 031	57.0	960	53.0	71	6.9
Race, Sex, and Hispanic Origin							
White	2 440	1 541	63.2	1 458	59.8	82	5.3
Men	1 186	832	70.2	791	66.7	41	5.0
Women	1 254	708	56.5	667	53.2	41	5.8
Black or African American	915	547	59.8	492	53.7	56	10.1
Men	404	249	61.7	221	54.7	29	11.5
Women	512	298	58.2	271	52.9	27	9.0
Hispanic	100	72	72.0	68	67.9	4	5.7
Men	59	51	86.1	49	82.7	2	3.9
Women	41	. . .	. . .	. . .	. . .	. . .	. . .
Age							
16 to 19 years	260	88	34.0	74	28.6	14	15.9
20 to 24 years	271	198	73.0	174	64.4	23	11.8
25 to 34 years	544	449	82.6	416	76.6	33	7.2
35 to 44 years	607	498	82.1	468	77.1	30	6.0
45 to 54 years	626	488	78.0	468	74.7	21	4.2
55 to 64 years	533	327	61.5	309	58.1	18	5.5
65 years and over	591	86	14.5	82	13.9	3	3.9

Note: Data in Table 6 are from the Current Population Survey (CPS) and do not match the estimates in Table 7. See notes and definitions for more details.

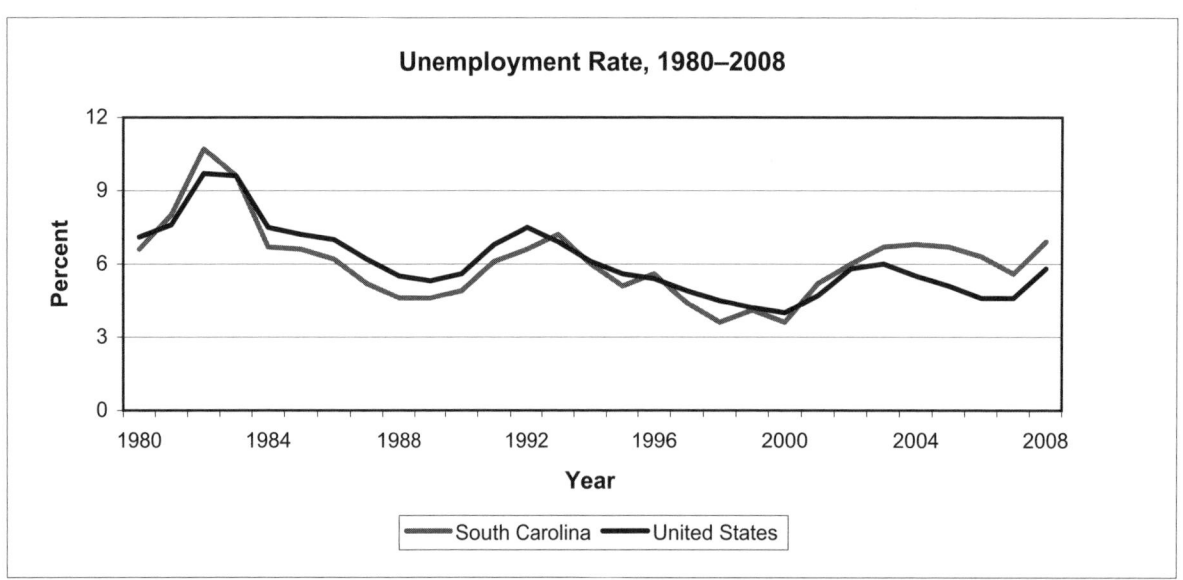

Unemployment Rate, 1980–2008

Table SC-7. Employment Status of the Civilian Noninstitutional Population Age 16 Years and Over

(Number, percent.)

Year	Civilian labor force	Civilian participation rate	Employed	Unemployed	Unemployment rate
1998	1 918 305	65.1	1 849 075	69 230	3.6
1999	1 956 674	65.5	1 876 895	79 779	4.1
2000	1 988 159	65.7	1 917 365	70 794	3.6
2001	1 935 614	63.2	1 834 871	100 743	5.2
2002	1 942 147	62.6	1 826 240	115 907	6.0
2003	1 987 676	63.4	1 854 419	133 257	6.7
2004	2 026 480	63.7	1 888 050	138 430	6.8
2005	2 067 160	63.9	1 927 671	139 489	6.7
2006	2 109 916	63.9	1 976 648	133 268	6.3
2007	2 125 073	63.1	2 006 178	118 895	5.6
2008	2 152 965	62.7	2 004 241	148 724	6.9

Table SC-8. Employment and Average Wages by Industry

(Estimates for 2001–2006 are based on the 2002 North American Industry Classification System [NAICS]. Estimates for 2007 are based on the 2007 NAICS.)

Industry	2001	2002	2003	2004	2005	2006	2007
	Number of jobs						
WAGE AND SALARY EMPLOYMENT BY INDUSTRY	1 943 667	1 924 136	1 927 428	1 947 847	1 974 675	2 017 654	2 052 720
Farm Wage and Salary Employment	7 430	7 962	7 442	8 324	7 149	7 673	6 858
Nonfarm Wage and Salary Employment	1 936 237	1 916 174	1 919 986	1 939 523	1 967 526	2 009 981	2 045 862
Private wage and salary employment	1 557 448	1 537 508	1 540 382	1 562 951	1 586 016	1 622 970	1 652 245
Forestry, fishing, hunting, and other	10 569	10 075	10 025	9 996	9 885	10 248	9 295
Mining	1 694	1 657	1 634	1 577	1 544	1 521	1 466
Utilities	12 350	12 168	11 955	11 795	11 668	12 085	11 984
Construction	117 794	117 100	117 263	119 048	122 396	131 027	129 363
Manufacturing	316 115	292 060	280 606	268 295	261 854	256 198	251 264
Durable goods manufacturing	150 360	140 521	137 396	136 530	137 890	137 946	139 492
Nondurable goods manufacturing	165 755	151 539	143 210	131 765	123 964	118 252	111 772
Wholesale trade	64 189	63 841	61 589	64 703	68 297	70 771	72 154
Retail trade	236 240	231 881	231 501	236 338	239 483	242 438	248 245
Transportation and warehousing	50 792	49 978	49 539	49 751	51 688	53 287	54 836
Information	29 167	28 458	27 620	27 527	27 177	27 607	27 857
Finance and insurance	62 353	64 362	67 616	67 879	68 160	71 449	72 332
Real estate and rental and leasing	27 084	26 962	26 798	26 818	29 455	30 583	31 581
Professional and technical services	65 430	65 549	66 102	69 537	71 146	74 265	77 833
Management of companies and enterprises	10 315	9 558	10 772	13 520	14 392	15 418	15 744
Administrative and waste services	116 275	113 509	116 290	122 971	128 425	131 636	137 701
Educational services	22 472	23 002	24 111	24 731	25 086	25 480	26 596
Health care and social assistance	137 171	142 632	145 800	148 883	153 452	159 485	165 491
Arts, entertainment, and recreation	25 549	25 513	26 407	26 860	26 747	27 483	28 505
Accommodation and food services	163 162	166 954	171 176	177 587	180 810	185 672	192 570
Other services, except public administration	88 727	92 249	93 578	95 135	94 351	96 317	97 428
Government and government enterprises	378 789	378 666	379 604	376 572	381 510	387 011	393 617
	Dollars						
AVERAGE WAGES AND SALARIES BY INDUSTRY	28 722	29 523	30 335	31 538	32 693	33 974	35 100
Average Farm Wages and Salaries	18 176	17 732	14 630	17 818	18 198	17 839	21 141
Average Nonfarm Wages and Salaries	28 762	29 572	30 396	31 597	32 746	34 036	35 147
Average private wages and salaries	28 560	29 219	29 979	31 054	32 186	33 514	34 506
Forestry, fishing, hunting, and other	23 583	23 232	24 198	24 727	25 751	26 250	28 740
Mining	38 700	39 509	39 764	42 640	44 554	45 629	46 887
Utilities	55 050	55 358	58 963	63 333	64 174	67 816	66 113
Construction	31 045	31 358	32 454	33 551	35 124	37 521	39 095
Manufacturing	35 847	37 592	39 008	40 383	41 864	43 609	44 935
Durable goods manufacturing	36 430	37 984	39 584	41 488	42 826	44 646	45 706
Nondurable goods manufacturing	35 318	37 229	38 455	39 239	40 794	42 399	43 974
Wholesale trade	39 973	41 493	42 759	45 025	47 219	49 869	52 894
Retail trade	20 772	21 208	21 680	22 287	22 789	23 421	23 754
Transportation and warehousing	31 584	32 270	33 548	34 628	35 680	36 563	37 144
Information	38 660	38 328	39 539	42 378	44 148	47 040	47 279
Finance and insurance	39 362	40 781	42 186	43 872	46 567	49 369	52 650
Real estate and rental and leasing	27 458	27 976	28 299	29 860	30 395	32 640	33 338
Professional and technical services	45 445	45 516	45 879	47 418	50 242	52 096	55 027
Management of companies and enterprises	44 811	48 030	53 063	61 149	57 342	58 620	60 254
Administrative and waste services	22 790	23 975	24 670	25 284	26 272	26 956	27 769
Educational services	20 177	20 889	21 112	21 595	22 717	23 938	24 652
Health care and social assistance	31 337	31 860	32 409	33 731	34 919	35 835	36 599
Arts, entertainment, and recreation	16 592	16 792	17 040	17 906	18 966	18 898	19 215
Accommodation and food services	12 741	12 976	13 326	13 808	14 238	14 879	15 222
Other services, except public administration	19 765	20 247	20 933	21 808	22 629	23 235	24 235
Government and government enterprises	29 595	31 005	32 088	33 849	35 071	36 223	37 838

Table SC-9. Employment Characteristics by Family Type

(Number, percent.)

Family type and labor force status	2005		2006		2007	
	Total	Families with own children under 18 years	Total	Families with own children under 18 years	Total	Families with own children under 18 years
TOTAL FAMILIES	1 103 327	490 768	1 122 724	494 898	1 152 062	497 769
FAMILY TYPE AND LABOR FORCE STATUS						
Married Coupled Families	787 694	314 154	798 196	312 487	828 713	318 961
Both husband and wife in labor force	50.7	65.3	51.7	66.7	51.5	66.6
Husband in labor force, wife not in labor force	22.3	26.7	21.9	26.7	22.7	27.6
Wife in labor force, husband not in labor force	8.5	4.8	8.0	4.0	7.1	4.0
Both husband and wife not in labor force	18.5	3.1	18.3	2.6	18.7	1.8
Other Families	315 633	176 614	324 528	182 411	323 349	178 808
Female householder, no husband present	78.6	80.5	78.0	82.2	78.2	82.2
In labor force	53.3	65.7	54.5	66.5	53.3	65.2
Not in labor force	25.3	14.8	23.4	15.7	24.8	17.0
Male householder, no wife present	21.4	19.5	22.0	17.8	21.8	17.8
In labor force	16.2	17.4	16.8	16.1	17.4	16.6
Not in labor force	5.2	2.0	5.2	1.7	4.4	1.3

Table SC-10. School Enrollment and Educational Attainment, 2007

(Number, percent.)

Item	State	U.S.
Enrollment		
Total population 3 years and over	4 231 703	289 295 761
Enrolled in school	1 096 305	79 329 527
Enrolled in preschool (percent)	5.9	6.2
Enrolled in grades K-12 (percent)	70.5	67.6
Enrolled in college or graduate school (percent)	23.6	26.2
Attainment		
Total population 25 years and over	2 909 779	197 892 369
Less than a high school diploma (percent)	17.9	15.5
High school diploma or more (percent)	82.1	84.5
Bachelor's degree or more (percent)	23.5	27.5
Graduate degree or more (percent)	8.2	10.1

Table SC-11. Educational Indicators

(Number, percent.)

Item	State	U.S.
Public Schools, 2006–2007 (except where noted)		
Number of school districts	102	17 742
Number of schools	1 195	99 639
Number of students	708 021	49 315 842
Student-teacher ratio	14.4	15.5
Expenditures per student (dollars)	$8 566	...
Averaged freshman graduation rate, 2005–2006	...	...
Dropout rate, grades 9–12, 2005–2006	...	3.7
Students eligible for free or reduced-price lunch (percent)	51.0	41.2
English-language learners (percent)	4.3	5.1
Students with IEP (percent)	8.7	12.7
Private Schools, 2007–2008 (except where noted)		
Number of schools	409	33 740
Number of students	56 492	5 072 451
High school graduates, 2006–2007	3 211	306 605
Student-teacher ratio	10.2	11.1

Table SC-12. Reported Voting and Registration of the Voting-Age Population, November 2008

(Number in thousands, percent.)

Item	Total population	Total citizen population	Registered			Voted		
			Total registered	Percent registered (total population)	Percent registered (total citizen population)	Total voted	Percent voted (total population)	Percent voted (total citizen population)
U.S. total	225 499	206 072	146 311	64.9	71.0	131 144	58.2	63.6
State total	3 313	3 202	2 385	72.0	74.5	2 100	63.4	65.6
Sex								
Male	1 564	1 498	1 052	67.2	70.2	926	59.2	61.8
Female	1 749	1 704	1 333	76.2	78.2	1 175	67.2	68.9
Race								
White alone	2 413	2 319	1 713	71.0	73.9	1 466	60.8	63.2
White non-Hispanic alone	2 307	2 282	1 692	73.4	74.2	1 448	62.8	63.5
Black alone	854	847	650	76.1	76.7	615	72.0	72.6
Asian alone	16	14	9	...	...	9	...	...
Hispanic (of any race)	111	37	21	18.6	...	18	16.4	...
White alone or in combination	2 424	2 327	1 715	70.8	73.7	1 466	60.5	63.0
Black alone or in combination	862	855	655	76.0	76.6	620	71.9	72.5
Asian alone or in combination	19	14	9	...	...	9	...	...

Table SC-13. Crime

(Number, rate per 100,000.)

Item	State			U.S.		
	2007	2008	Percent change	2007	2008	Percent change
Population	4 407 709	4 479 800	1.6	301 621 157	304 059 724	0.8
VIOLENT CRIME						
Number	34 746	32 691	-5.9	1 408 337	1 382 012	-1.9
Rate	788.3	729.7	-7.4	466.9	454.5	-2.7
Murder and Nonnegligent Manslaughter						
Number	352	305	-13.4	16 929	16 272	-3.9
Rate	8.0	6.8	-14.7	5.6	5.4	-4.7
Forcible Rape						
Number	1 739	1 638	-5.8	90 427	89 000	-1.6
Rate	39.5	36.6	-7.3	30.0	29.3	-2.4
Robbery						
Number	6 346	6 599	4.0	445 125	441 855	-0.7
Rate	144.0	147.3	2.3	147.6	145.3	-1.5
Aggravated Assault						
Number	26 309	24 149	-8.2	855 856	834 885	-2.5
Rate	596.9	539.1	-9.7	283.8	274.6	-3.2
PROPERTY CRIME						
Number	188 282	189 683	0.7	9 843 481	9 767 915	-0.8
Rate	4 271.7	4 234.2	-0.9	3 263.5	3 212.5	-1.6
Burglary						
Number	45 214	45 967	1.7	2 179 140	2 222 196	2.0
Rate	1 025.8	1 026.1	*	722.5	730.8	1.2
Larceny-Theft						
Number	126 042	126 064	*	6 568 572	6 588 873	0.3
Rate	2 859.6	2 814.1	-1.6	2 177.8	2 167.0	-0.5
Motor Vehicle Theft						
Number	17 026	17 652	3.7	1 095 769	956 846	-12.7
Rate	386.3	394.0	2.0	363.3	314.7	-13.4

Table SC-14. State Government Finances, 2007

(Dollars, percent distribution.)

Item	Thousands of dollars	Percent distribution
Total Revenue	27 530 567	X
General revenue	20 942 385	76.1
Intergovernmental revenue	7 097 636	25.8
Taxes	8 688 935	31.6
General sales	3 233 632	11.7
Selective sales	1 343 680	4.9
License taxes	471 080	1.7
Individual income tax	3 239 468	11.8
Corporate income tax	311 902	1.1
Other taxes	89 173	0.3
Current charges	3 573 831	13.0
Miscellaneous general revenue	1 581 983	5.7
Utility revenue	1 400 859	5.1
Liquor store revenue	0	0.0
Insurance trust revenue	5 187 323	18.8
Total Expenditure	24 824 628	100.0
Intergovernmental expenditure	4 870 680	19.6
Direct expenditure	19 953 948	80.4
Current operation	14 216 031	57.3
Capital outlay	1 829 973	7.4
Insurance benefits and repayments	2 310 807	9.3
Assistance and subsidies	861 432	3.5
Interest on debt	735 705	3.0
Exhibit: Salaries and wages	3 360 557	13.5
Total Expenditure	24 824 628	100.0
General expenditure	20 887 140	84.1
Intergovernmental expenditure	4 870 680	19.6
Direct expenditure	16 016 460	64.5
Education	7 462 708	30.1
Public welfare	5 404 269	21.8
Hospitals	1 309 736	5.3
Health	970 251	3.9
Highways	1 125 851	4.5
Police protection	196 501	0.8
Correction	470 894	1.9
Natural resources	259 490	1.0
Parks and recreation	117 228	0.5
Government administration	1 011 040	4.1
Interest on general debt	550 200	2.2
Other and unallocable	2 008 972	8.1
Utility expenditure	1 626 681	6.6
Liquor store expenditure	0	0.0
Insurance trust expenditure	2 310 807	9.3
Debt at End of Fiscal Year	14 981 290	X
Cash and Security Holdings	42 943 138	X

Table SC-15. State Government Tax Collections, 2008

(Dollars, percent distribution.)

Item	Thousands of dollars	Percent distribution
Total Taxes	8 455 463	X
Property taxes	9 935	0.4
Sales and gross receipts	4 279 163	155.0
General sales and gross receipts	3 051 608	110.5
Selective sales taxes	1 227 555	44.5
Alcoholic beverages	150 065	5.4
Amusements	37 957	1.4
Insurance premiums	125 696	4.6
Motor fuels	534 252	19.3
Public utilities	26 458	1.0
Tobacco products	31 073	1.1
Other selective sales	322 054	11.7
Licenses	433 877	15.7
Alcoholic beverages	7 377	0.3
Amusements	2 041	0.1
Corporation	77 908	2.8
Hunting and fishing	17 157	0.6
Motor vehicle	142 120	5.1
Motor vehicle operators	44 717	1.6
Occupation and business, NEC	131 930	4.8
Other licenses	10 627	0.4
Income taxes	3 660 313	132.6
Individual income	3 339 935	121.0
Corporation net income	320 378	11.6
Other taxes	72 175	2.6
Death and gift	344	0.0
Documentary and stock transfer	71 831	2.6

Table SC-16. Agriculture

(Number, acres, and dollars.)

Item	2002		2007		Percent change, 2002–2007
	Number	Percent of total	Number	Percent of total	
Number of farms	24 541		25 867		5.4
Farm Size					
Average size of farm (acres)	197		189		-4.1
Farms by size (number of farms)					
Fewer than 50 acres	10 242	41.7	10 929	42.3	6.7
50 to 499 acres	12 253	49.9	13 014	50.3	6.2
500 acres or more	2 046	8.3	1 924	7.4	-6.0
Land (Acres)					
Total land in farms	4 845 923		4 889 339		0.9
Total cropland	2 270 084	46.8	2 151 219	44.0	-5.2
Total harvested cropland	1 374 617	28.4	1 551 670	31.7	12.9
Irrigated land	95 642	2.0	132 439	2.7	38.5
Value of Sales (Dollars)					
Agricultural products sold ($1,000)	1 489 750		2 352 681		57.9
Average sales per farm	60 705		90 953		49.8
Sales of crops	593 245	39.8	798 490	33.9	34.6
Sales of livestock, poultry, and their products	896 505	60.2	1 554 190	66.1	73.4
Value of Sales (Number of Farms)					
Less than $10,000	19 243	78.4	19 820	76.6	3.0
$10,000 to $99,999	3 638	14.8	4 242	16.4	16.6
$100,000 to $999,999	1 334	5.4	1 174	4.5	-12.0
$1,000,000 or more	326	1.3	631	2.4	93.6
Farms by Type of Organization (Number of Farms)					
Family	22 755	92.7	22 989	88.9	1.0
Partnership	1 050	4.3	1 827	7.1	74.0
Corporation	556	2.3	845	3.3	52.0
Other: cooperative, estate or trust, institutional, etc	180	0.7	206	0.8	14.4
Value of Land and Buildings (Dollars)					
Estimated market value of land and buildings ($1,000)	13 973 359		10 081 357		-27.9
Land and buildings average value per farm	540 200		410 897		-23.9
Average value per acre	2 858		2 067		-27.7
Government Payments					
Number of farms receiving government payments	6 112	24.9	7 715	29.8	26.2
Payments (thousands of dollars)	38 384		67 253		75.2
Average payment per farm	6 280		8 717		38.8
Farm Operator Characteristics					
Farm operators whose principal occupation is farming	11 377	46.4	9 739	37.7	-14.4
Farm operators whose principal occupation is other	13 164	53.6	16 128	62.3	22.5
Average age principal operator (years)	56.9		58.5		2.8

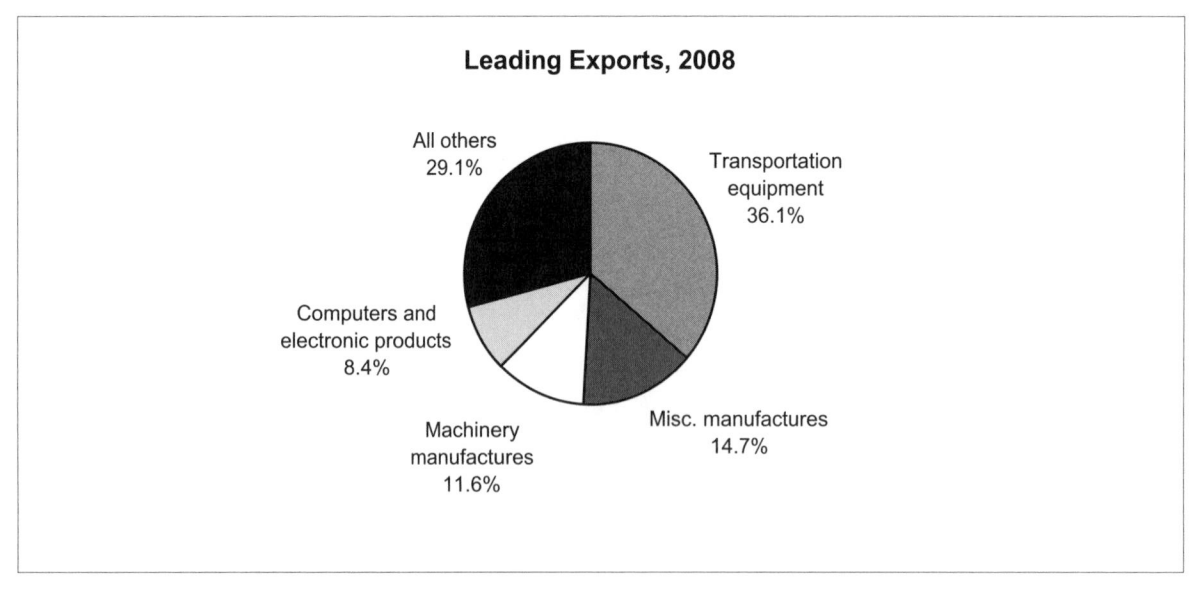

Leading Exports, 2008

All others 29.1%
Transportation equipment 36.1%
Computers and electronic products 8.4%
Machinery manufactures 11.6%
Misc. manufactures 14.7%

SOUTH DAKOTA

Facts and Figures

Location: North central United States; bordered on the N by North Dakota, on the E by Minnesota and Iowa, on the S by Nebraska, and on the W by Wyoming and Montana

Area: 77,117 sq. mi. (199,731 sq. km.); rank—17th

Population: 804,194 (2008 est.); rank—46th

Principal Cities: capital—Pierre; largest—Sioux Falls

Statehood: November 2, 1889; 40th state

U.S. Congress: 2 senators, 1 representative

State Motto: Under God the People Rule

State Song: "Hail, South Dakota"

State Nickname: The Mount Rushmore State

Abbreviations: SD; S.D.; S. Dak.

State Symbols: flower—pasqueflower; tree—Black Hills spruce; bird—ring-necked pheasant

At a Glance

- With an increase in population of 6.5 percent, South Dakota ranked 22nd among the states in growth from 2000 to 2008.
- An estimated 6,196 marriages took place in South Dakota in 2008, compared to 2,473 divorces.
- The 2007 home ownership rate in South Dakota was 70.4 percent, giving it a ranking of 25th along with Arizona and Missouri.
- South Dakota's median household income in 2007 was $43,424, 40th among the states.
- In South Dakota, 13.1 percent of the population lived below the poverty level in 2007, ranking it 18th along with Ohio.
- In 2006-07, 11 percent of South Dakotans did not have health insurance, compared to 15.5 percent of the total U.S. population.
- In 2007, 2.9 percent of South Dakotans were unemployed, compared to 4.6 percent nationwide.
- South Dakota ranked 32nd in the nation with 25 percent of its population 25 years old and over having at least a bachelor's degree in 2007.
- South Dakota's violent crime rate in 2007 was 169.2 per 100,000 population, compared to 466.9 for the entire nation.
- South Dakota had one physician for every 396 people in 2007, compared to one physician for every 325 people nationwide.
- In the 2008 election, 63.8 percent of South Dakota's eligible voters voted, compared to 61.7 percent of eligible voters nationwide.
- South Dakota ranked 14th among the states receiving federal aid in 2007, with $1,608 per capita.
- South Dakota's gross domestic product was $34 billion in 2007; it ranked 47th among the states.
- With $1.5 billion in exports in 2007, South Dakota ranked 47th in exports.
- South Dakotans consumed 271.9 million Btu's of energy in 2006; the state ranked 48th in total consumption.
- In 2007, South Dakota exported $1.9 billion worth of agricultural products, about 2.3 percent of the U.S. total.

Table SD-1. Population by Sex, Age, Race, and Hispanic Origin

(Number, percent.)

Sex, age, race, and Hispanic origin	1990	2000	2008	Average annual percent change, 2000–2008
Total Population	696 004	754 844	804 194	0.8
Percent of total U.S. population	0.3	0.3	0.3	X
Sex				
Male	342 498	374 558	400 861	0.9
Female	353 506	380 286	403 333	0.7
Age				
Under 5 years	54 504	51 069	58 566	1.7
5 to 19 years	164 803	176 412	162 895	-1.0
20 to 64 years	374 366	419 232	466 633	1.3
65 years and over	102 331	108 131	116 100	0.9
Median age (years)	32.4	35.6	37.3	X
Race and Hispanic Origin[1]				
One race				
White	637 515	669 404	709 217	0.7
Black	3 258	4 685	9 185	8.8
American Indian and Alaskan Native	50 575	62 283	68 000	1.1
Asian[2]	3 123	4 378	5 960	3.9
Native Hawaiian and Other Pacific Islander	X	261	415	6.0
Two or more races	X	10 156	11 417	1.5
Hispanic (of any race)	5 252	10 903	21 016	8.5

[1]Data on race in 2000 and 2008 are not comparable to 1990. Individuals could only report one race in the 1990 census but could report one or more races on the 2000 census.
[2]Data in 1990 refer to Asian and Pacific Islanders.

Table SD-2. Marital Status

(Number, percent distribution.)

Sex and marital status	1990	2000	2007
Males, 15 Years and Over	256 241	289 858	314 154
Never married	28.5	29.8	32.4
Now married, except separated	61.4	58.2	53.9
Separated	0.9	1.0	1.0
Widowed	2.6	2.4	2.7
Divorced	6.5	8.5	10.1
Females, 15 Years and Over	271 027	299 754	320 063
Never married	20.5	22.5	26.4
Now married, except separated	57.8	55.9	52.5
Separated	1.0	1.1	1.1
Widowed	13.4	11.4	10.3
Divorced	7.2	9.0	9.8

Table SD-3. Households and Housing Characteristics

(Number, percent, and dollars.)

Item	1990	2000	2007	Average annual percent change, 2000–2007
Total Households	259 034	290 245	312 912	1.1
Family households	180 306	194 330	205 206	0.8
Married-couple family	152 519	157 391	162 792	0.5
Other family	27 787	36 939	42 414	2.0
Male householder, no wife present	7 076	10 734	12 239	1.9
Female householder, no husband present	20 711	26 205	30 175	2.0
Nonfamily households	78 728	95 915	107 706	1.7
Householder living alone	68 308	80 040	90 284	1.7
Householder not living alone	10 420	15 875	17 422	1.3
Housing Characteristics				
Total housing units	292 436	323 208	356 264	1.4
Occupied housing units	259 034	290 245	312 912	1.1
Owner-occupied	171 161	197 940	213 029	1.1
Renter-occupied	87 873	92 305	99 883	1.1
Average size	2.59	2.50	2.45	X
Financial Characteristics				
Median gross rent of renter-occupied housing units (dollars)	306	426	526	3.1
Median monthly owner costs for housing units with a mortgage (dollars)	569	828	1 104	4.2
Median value of owner-occupied housing units (dollars)	45 000	79 600	118 700	5.9

Table SD-4. Median Income and Poverty Status, 2007

(Number, percent.)

Characteristic	State		U.S.	
	Number	Percent	Number	Percent
Median Income				
Households (dollars)	43 424	X	50 740	X
Families (dollars)	53 910	X	61 173	X
Below Poverty Level				
Sex				
Male	45 786	12.0	16 576 071	11.5
Female	54 913	14.2	21 476 176	14.3
Age				
Under 18 years	32 511	16.8	13 097 100	18.0
Related children under 18 years	31 618	16.4	12 728 964	17.6
18 to 64 years	56 048	11.9	21 495 507	11.6
65 years and over	12 140	11.5	3 459 640	9.5

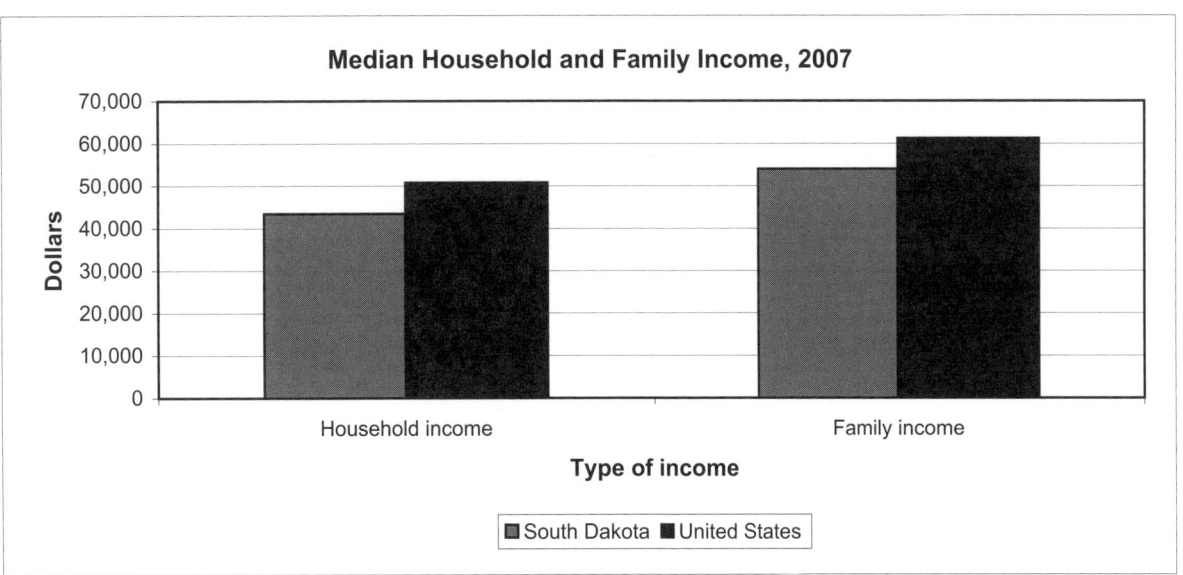

Median Household and Family Income, 2007

■ South Dakota ■ United States

Table SD-5. Health Insurance Coverage Status for All Persons and Children Under 18 Years of Age

(Number, percent.)

Item	2000	2001	2002	2003	2004	2005	2006	2007
ALL PERSONS	738	739	745	751	754	768	770	788
Covered by Private or Government Health Insurance								
Number	661	675	664	665	669	679	679	708
Percent	89.5	91.3	89.1	88.6	88.8	88.3	88.2	89.9
Not Covered								
Number	77	64	81	86	84	90	91	80
Percent	10.5	8.7	10.9	11.4	11.2	11.7	11.8	10.1
Percent in the U.S. not covered	13.7	14.1	14.7	15.1	14.9	15.3	15.8	15.3
CHILDREN UNDER 18 YEARS OF AGE	188	180	198	197	189	188	193	198
Covered by Private or Government Health Insurance								
Number	171	167	184	181	174	173	175	183
Percent	91.0	92.7	92.5	92.0	92.0	91.9	90.8	92.0
Not Covered								
Number	17	13	15	16	15	15	18	16
Percent	9.0	7.3	7.5	8.0	8.0	8.1	9.2	8.0
Percent in the U.S. not covered	11.6	11.3	11.2	11.0	10.5	10.9	11.7	11.0

Table SD-6. Employment Status by Demographic Group, Preliminary 2008

(Number, percent.)

Characteristic	Civilian noninstitutional population	Civilian labor force		Employment		Unemployed	
		Number	Percent of population	Number	Percent of population	Number	Unemployment rate
TOTAL	613	449	73.3	436	71.1	14	3.0
Sex							
Men	301	235	78.0	227	75.5	7	3.1
Women	312	215	69.0	209	66.9	6	2.9
Race, Sex, and Hispanic Origin							
White	563	420	74.6	409	72.7	11	2.5
Men	277	219	79.2	214	77.2	6	2.5
Women	286	201	70.2	196	68.4	5	2.5
Black or African American	...	...	...	...	...	...	...
Men	...	...	...	...	...	...	...
Women	...	...	...	...	...	...	...
Hispanic	11	9	81.3	8	75.6	1	6.9
Men	...	...	...	...	...	...	...
Women	...	...	...	...	...	...	...
Age							
16 to 19 years	43	24	56.1	21	50.1	3	10.7
20 to 24 years	59	48	81.2	45	76.7	3	5.6
25 to 34 years	98	87	88.2	84	85.9	2	2.6
35 to 44 years	95	87	91.5	85	89.4	2	2.3
45 to 54 years	120	106	88.5	103	86.2	3	2.6
55 to 64 years	87	69	79.0	68	78.1	1	1.1
65 years and over	111	29	26.2	28	25.7	1	1.8

Note: Data in Table 6 are from the Current Population Survey (CPS) and do not match the estimates in Table 7. See notes and definitions for more details.

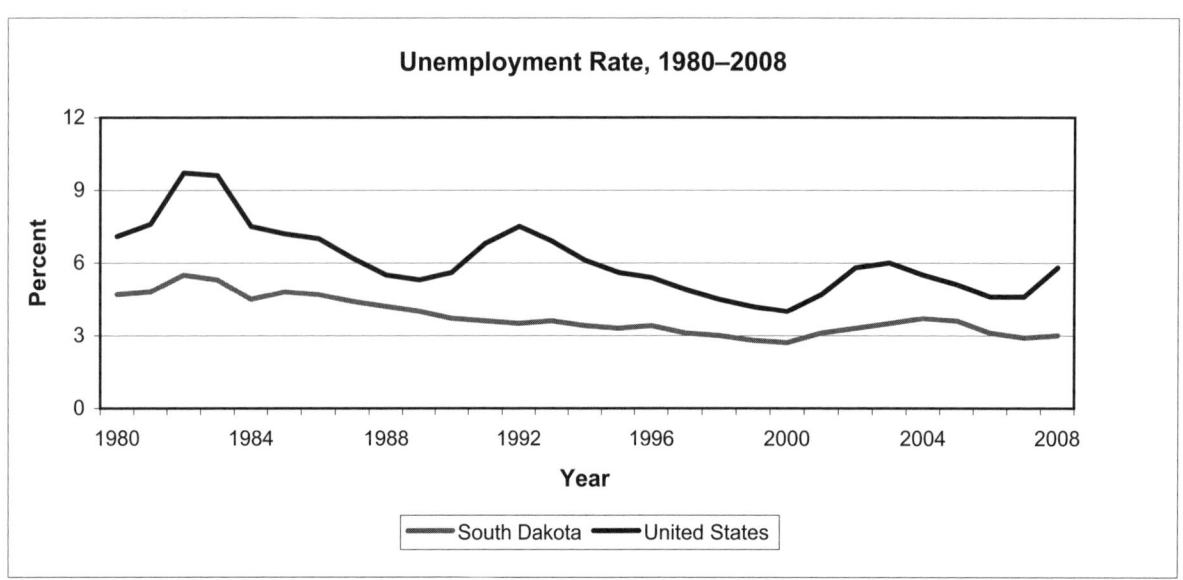

Table SD-7. Employment Status of the Civilian Noninstitutional Population Age 16 Years and Over

(Number, percent.)

Year	Civilian labor force	Civilian participation rate	Employed	Unemployed	Unemployment rate
1998	401 677	72.8	389 748	11 929	3.0
1999	406 328	73.0	394 898	11 430	2.8
2000	408 685	72.8	397 678	11 007	2.7
2001	413 264	73.0	400 352	12 912	3.1
2002	416 185	72.9	402 397	13 788	3.3
2003	423 045	73.5	408 089	14 956	3.5
2004	427 359	73.4	411 708	15 651	3.7
2005	430 444	73.1	414 784	15 660	3.6
2006	435 733	73.1	422 355	13 378	3.1
2007	442 085	73.2	429 445	12 640	2.9
2008	444 890	72.8	431 379	13 511	3.0

Table SD-8. Employment and Average Wages by Industry

(Estimates for 2001–2006 are based on the 2002 North American Industry Classification System [NAICS]. Estimates for 2007 are based on the 2007 NAICS.)

Industry	2001	2002	2003	2004	2005	2006	2007
	Number of jobs						
WAGE AND SALARY EMPLOYMENT BY INDUSTRY	399 554	398 576	399 590	405 833	411 387	419 731	427 818
Farm Wage and Salary Employment	4 883	4 535	3 290	4 495	4 308	4 249	4 102
Nonfarm Wage and Salary Employment	394 671	394 041	396 300	401 338	407 079	415 482	423 716
Private wage and salary employment	315 570	314 731	316 071	320 588	326 774	335 063	342 992
Forestry, fishing, hunting, and other	2 181	2 010	2 002	1 942	2 094	2 157	2 218
Mining	1 101	878	833	766	799	795	890
Utilities	2 035	2 071	2 040	2 046	2 141	2 241	2 235
Construction	19 230	19 353	20 119	20 752	21 796	22 610	22 966
Manufacturing	41 325	38 781	38 083	39 247	40 249	41 800	42 363
Durable goods manufacturing	28 007	26 068	25 459	26 430	27 360	28 575	29 089
Nondurable goods manufacturing	13 318	12 713	12 624	12 817	12 889	13 225	13 274
Wholesale trade	16 933	17 152	17 097	17 757	17 969	18 366	18 614
Retail trade	49 802	49 323	49 488	50 037	50 598	50 709	51 493
Transportation and warehousing	10 207	10 109	10 019	9 975	10 282	10 823	11 041
Information	6 832	6 854	6 791	6 733	6 776	6 975	7 178
Finance and insurance	24 787	24 796	24 468	24 401	24 901	26 192	27 517
Real estate and rental and leasing	3 627	3 510	3 554	3 764	3 891	3 862	3 821
Professional and technical services	9 085	8 906	8 891	9 270	10 237	10 606	11 074
Management of companies and enterprises	3 817	3 803	3 234	2 931	2 816	2 820	3 041
Administrative and waste services	13 510	12 657	12 580	12 507	12 402	13 132	14 149
Educational services	6 747	6 980	7 353	7 065	7 455	7 667	7 800
Health care and social assistance	47 641	48 950	50 579	51 158	51 883	52 723	54 167
Arts, entertainment, and recreation	6 301	6 215	6 361	6 551	6 889	6 852	7 161
Accommodation and food services	33 017	33 905	34 144	34 986	35 554	36 436	36 717
Other services, except public administration	17 392	18 478	18 435	18 700	18 042	18 297	18 547
Government and government enterprises	79 101	79 310	80 229	80 750	80 305	80 419	80 724
	Dollars						
AVERAGE WAGES AND SALARIES BY INDUSTRY	25 151	26 043	26 914	28 041	28 903	29 976	31 325
Average Farm Wages and Salaries	27 629	26 940	27 375	29 844	30 202	30 791	34 749
Average Nonfarm Wages and Salaries	25 120	26 033	26 910	28 021	28 890	29 968	31 292
Average private wages and salaries	24 922	25 751	26 568	27 645	28 480	29 635	31 050
Forestry, fishing, hunting, and other	14 596	16 283	17 072	18 503	19 034	19 668	22 885
Mining	40 234	40 940	39 303	40 260	42 257	44 706	47 291
Utilities	45 211	49 359	51 623	52 902	58 770	57 876	61 723
Construction	28 985	29 877	30 169	30 632	31 741	33 631	35 841
Manufacturing	29 818	30 791	32 074	33 514	34 370	35 494	37 083
Durable goods manufacturing	30 550	31 536	32 840	34 458	35 103	35 912	37 061
Nondurable goods manufacturing	28 280	29 266	30 530	31 569	32 816	34 591	37 131
Wholesale trade	33 651	34 536	35 525	38 423	40 010	41 146	43 170
Retail trade	18 118	18 694	19 344	19 872	20 151	20 807	21 479
Transportation and warehousing	29 611	30 311	31 253	33 165	34 460	36 536	37 150
Information	31 720	32 355	33 133	34 559	35 298	36 703	38 468
Finance and insurance	33 252	34 238	35 802	37 783	39 123	40 955	42 496
Real estate and rental and leasing	19 295	19 381	20 022	21 110	22 346	23 106	24 611
Professional and technical services	32 767	33 783	35 467	35 786	38 304	41 104	43 238
Management of companies and enterprises	60 775	57 385	59 679	65 906	71 777	65 747	72 074
Administrative and waste services	22 034	21 697	22 364	22 858	22 088	22 700	24 591
Educational services	18 805	20 081	20 155	20 514	20 533	20 885	21 818
Health care and social assistance	28 005	29 762	31 176	32 566	33 576	34 986	36 300
Arts, entertainment, and recreation	13 657	13 797	14 419	14 807	15 326	16 261	16 327
Accommodation and food services	10 087	10 619	10 904	11 240	11 363	11 881	12 415
Other services, except public administration	18 059	19 776	19 951	20 491	20 283	21 048	22 134
Government and government enterprises	25 910	27 150	28 261	29 511	30 555	31 354	32 321

Table SD-9. Employment Characteristics by Family Type

(Number, percent.)

Family type and labor force status	2005		2006		2007	
	Total	Families with own children under 18 years	Total	Families with own children under 18 years	Total	Families with own children under 18 years
TOTAL FAMILIES	203 891	95 989	205 964	89 991	205 206	91 000
FAMILY TYPE AND LABOR FORCE STATUS						
Married Coupled Families	161 051	67 818	166 211	66 467	162 792	61 980
Both husband and wife in labor force	60.7	76.9	63.9	79.5	64.1	79.9
Husband in labor force, wife not in labor force	14.8	15.3	16.0	16.1	15.6	16.2
Wife in labor force, husband not in labor force	7.5	4.2	5.7	2.6	5.8	2.5
Both husband and wife not in labor force	17.0	3.7	14.4	1.8	14.5	1.4
Other Families	42 840	28 171	39 753	23 524	42 414	29 020
Female householder, no husband present	69.9	72.4	69.9	74.2	71.1	73.3
In labor force	55.2	63.8	56.5	67.5	54.9	61.5
Not in labor force	14.7	8.6	13.4	6.7	16.2	11.9
Male householder, no wife present	30.1	27.6	30.1	25.8	28.9	26.7
In labor force	25.2	25.5	24.0	22.1	23.7	24.1
Not in labor force	4.9	2.2	6.1	3.7	5.2	2.6

Table SD-10. School Enrollment and Educational Attainment, 2007

(Number, percent.)

Item	State	U.S.
Enrollment		
Total population 3 years and over	762 516	289 295 761
Enrolled in school	204 394	79 329 527
Enrolled in preschool (percent)	6.4	6.2
Enrolled in grades K-12 (percent)	68.7	67.6
Enrolled in college or graduate school (percent)	24.9	26.2
Attainment		
Total population 25 years and over	512 902	197 892 369
Less than a high school diploma (percent)	11.8	15.5
High school diploma or more (percent)	88.2	84.5
Bachelor's degree or more (percent)	25.0	27.5
Graduate degree or more (percent)	7.0	10.1

Table SD-11. Educational Indicators

(Number, percent.)

Item	State	U.S.
Public Schools, 2006–2007 (except where noted)		
Number of school districts	188	17 742
Number of schools	736	99 639
Number of students	121 158	49 315 842
Student-teacher ratio	13.4	15.5
Expenditures per student (dollars)	$8 064	. . .
Averaged freshman graduation rate, 2005–2006	84.5	. . .
Dropout rate, grades 9–12, 2005–2006	4.4	3.7
Students eligible for free or reduced-price lunch (percent) ...	28.9	41.2
English-language learners (percent)	. . .	5.1
Students with IEP (percent)	14.6	12.7
Private Schools, 2007–2008 (except where noted)		
Number of schools	80	33 740
Number of students	10 692	5 072 451
High school graduates, 2006–2007	556	306 605
Student-teacher ratio	11.6	11.1

Table SD-12. Reported Voting and Registration of the Voting-Age Population, November 2008

(Number in thousands, percent.)

Item	Total population	Total citizen population	Registered			Voted		
			Total registered	Percent registered (total population)	Percent registered (total citizen population)	Total voted	Percent voted (total population)	Percent voted (total citizen population)
U.S. total	225 499	206 072	146 311	64.9	71.0	131 144	58.2	63.6
State total	590	575	442	74.9	76.9	390	66.1	67.8
Sex								
Male	291	282	207	71.2	73.4	178	61.2	63.1
Female	299	293	235	78.5	80.2	212	70.8	72.4
Race								
White alone	541	533	421	77.8	79.0	372	68.8	69.9
White non-Hispanic alone	533	527	419	78.6	79.4	370	69.6	70.3
Black alone	6	2	2	. . .	. . .	2	. . .	. . .
Asian alone	6	3	1	. . .	. . .	1	. . .	. . .
Hispanic (of any race)	11	8	3	. . .	. . .	3	. . .	. . .
White alone or in combination	547	538	423	77.4	423.0	374	68.4	69.5
Black alone or in combination	6	3	2	. . .	. . .	2	. . .	. . .
Asian alone or in combination	6	3	1	. . .	. . .	1	. . .	. . .

Table SD-13. Crime

(Number, rate per 100,000.)

Item	State			U.S.		
	2007	2008	Percent change	2007	2008	Percent change
Population	796 214	804 194	1.0	301 621 157	304 059 724	0.8
VIOLENT CRIME						
Number	1 347	1 620	20.3	1 408 337	1 382 012	-1.9
Rate	169.2	201.4	19.1	466.9	454.5	-2.7
Murder and Nonnegligent Manslaughter						
Number	17	26	52.9	16 929	16 272	-3.9
Rate	2.1	3.2	51.4	5.6	5.4	-4.7
Forcible Rape						
Number	308	432	40.3	90 427	89 000	-1.6
Rate	38.7	53.7	38.9	30.0	29.3	-2.4
Robbery						
Number	112	120	7.1	445 125	441 855	-0.7
Rate	14.1	14.9	6.1	147.6	145.3	-1.5
Aggravated Assault						
Number	910	1 042	14.5	855 856	834 885	-2.5
Rate	114.3	129.6	13.4	283.8	274.6	-3.2
PROPERTY CRIME						
Number	13 156	13 234	0.6	9 843 481	9 767 915	-0.8
Rate	1 652.3	1 645.6	-0.4	3 263.5	3 212.5	-1.6
Burglary						
Number	2 378	2 430	2.2	2 179 140	2 222 196	2.0
Rate	298.7	302.2	1.2	722.5	730.8	1.2
Larceny-Theft						
Number	10 043	10 004	-0.4	6 568 572	6 588 873	0.3
Rate	1 261.3	1 244.0	-1.4	2 177.8	2 167.0	-0.5
Motor Vehicle Theft						
Number	735	800	8.8	1 095 769	956 846	-12.7
Rate	92.3	99.5	7.8	363.3	314.7	-13.4

Table SD-14. State Government Finances, 2007

(Dollars, percent distribution.)

Item	Thousands of dollars	Percent distribution
Total Revenue	4 920 193	X
General revenue	3 293 293	66.9
Intergovernmental revenue	1 276 075	25.9
Taxes	1 257 084	25.5
General sales	711 321	14.5
Selective sales	307 282	6.2
License taxes	156 488	3.2
Individual income tax	0	0.0
Corporate income tax	76 665	1.6
Other taxes	5 328	0.1
Current charges	277 986	5.6
Miscellaneous general revenue	482 148	9.8
Utility revenue	0	0.0
Liquor store revenue	0	0.0
Insurance trust revenue	1 626 900	33.1
Total Expenditure	3 571 741	100.0
Intergovernmental expenditure	652 117	18.3
Direct expenditure	2 919 624	81.7
Current operation	1 959 292	54.9
Capital outlay	469 307	13.1
Insurance benefits and repayments	308 332	8.6
Assistance and subsidies	61 159	1.7
Interest on debt	121 534	3.4
Exhibit: Salaries and wages	789 124	22.1
Total Expenditure	3 571 741	100.0
General expenditure	3 263 409	91.4
Intergovernmental expenditure	652 117	18.3
Direct expenditure	2 611 292	73.1
Education	1 005 279	28.1
Public welfare	759 061	21.3
Hospitals	55 287	1.5
Health	116 675	3.3
Highways	521 948	14.6
Police protection	29 632	0.8
Correction	103 166	2.9
Natural resources	122 972	3.4
Parks and recreation	28 549	0.8
Government administration	152 045	4.3
Interest on general debt	121 534	3.4
Other and unallocable	247 261	6.9
Utility expenditure	0	0.0
Liquor store expenditure	0	0.0
Insurance trust expenditure	308 332	8.6
Debt at End of Fiscal Year	3 232 457	X
Cash and Security Holdings	12 947 662	X

Table SD-15. State Government Tax Collections, 2008

(Dollars, percent distribution.)

Item	Thousands of dollars	Percent distribution
Total Taxes	1 321 368	X
Sales and gross receipts	1 072 252	81.1
General sales and gross receipts	732 438	55.4
Selective sales taxes	339 814	25.7
Alcoholic beverages	13 808	1.0
Amusements	8 334	0.6
Insurance premiums	61 801	4.7
Motor fuels	129 619	9.8
Pari-mutuels	325	0.0
Public utilities	3 235	0.2
Tobacco products	63 903	4.8
Other selective sales	58 789	4.4
Licenses	172 165	13.0
Alcoholic beverages	319	0.0
Amusements	93	0.0
Corporation	3 210	0.2
Hunting and fishing	27 733	2.1
Motor vehicle	47 285	3.6
Motor vehicle operators	2 513	0.2
Occupation and business, NEC	78 529	5.9
Other licenses	12 483	0.9
Income taxes	69 879	5.3
Corporation net income	69 879	5.3
Other taxes	7 072	0.5
Death and gift	113	0.0
Documentary and stock transfer	121	0.0
Severance	6 838	0.5

Table SD-16. Agriculture

(Number, acres, and dollars.)

Item	2002		2007		Percent change, 2002–2007
	Number	Percent of total	Number	Percent of total	
Number of farms	31 736		31 169		-1.8
Farm Size					
Average size of farm (acres)	1 380		1 401		1.5
Farms by size (number of farms)					
Fewer than 50 acres	4 326	13.6	4 818	15.5	11.4
50 to 499 acres	11 846	37.3	11 783	37.8	-0.5
500 acres or more	15 564	49.0	14 568	46.7	-6.4
Land (Acres)					
Total land in farms	43 785 079		43 666 403		-0.3
Total cropland	20 318 036	46.4	19 094 311	43.7	-6.0
Total harvested cropland	13 492 286	30.8	15 278 709	35.0	13.2
Irrigated land	401 083	0.9	373 842	0.9	-6.8
Value of Sales (Dollars)					
Agricultural products sold ($1,000)	3 834 625		6 570 450		71.3
Average sales per farm	120 829		210 801		74.5
Sales of crops	1 575 910	41.1	3 383 497	51.5	114.7
Sales of livestock, poultry, and their products	2 258 715	58.9	3 186 953	48.5	41.1
Value of Sales (Number of Farms)					
Less than $10,000	10 138	31.9	10 787	34.6	6.4
$10,000 to $99,999	11 932	37.6	8 439	27.1	-29.3
$100,000 to $999,999	9 253	29.2	10 786	34.6	16.6
$1,000,000 or more	413	1.3	1 157	3.7	180.1
Farms by Type of Organization (Number of Farms)					
Family	28 189	88.8	26 633	85.4	-5.5
Partnership	2 163	6.8	2 658	8.5	22.9
Corporation	1 066	3.4	1 421	4.6	33.3
Other: cooperative, estate or trust, institutional, etc	318	1.0	457	1.5	43.7
Value of Land and Buildings (Dollars)					
Estimated market value of land and buildings ($1,000)	39 127 431		19 617 432		-49.9
Land and buildings average value per farm	1 255 332		618 651		-50.7
Average value per acre	896		442		-50.7
Government Payments					
Number of farms receiving government payments	20 259	63.8	22 911	73.5	13.1
Payments (thousands of dollars)	215 084		270 748		25.9
Average payment per farm	10 617		11 817		11.3
Farm Operator Characteristics					
Farm operators whose principal occupation is farming	23 049	72.6	18 775	60.2	-18.5
Farm operators whose principal occupation is other	8 687	27.4	12 394	39.8	42.7
Average age principal operator (years)	53.3		55.7		4.5

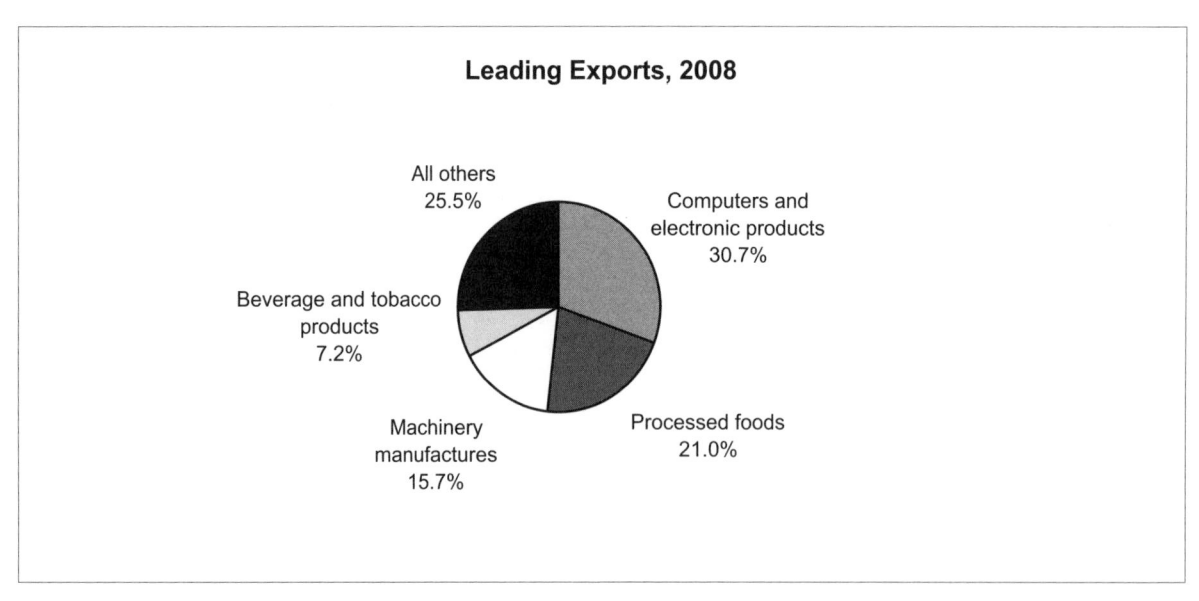

Leading Exports, 2008

All others 25.5%

Computers and electronic products 30.7%

Beverage and tobacco products 7.2%

Machinery manufactures 15.7%

Processed foods 21.0%

TENNESSEE

Facts and Figures

Location: South central United States; bordered on the N by Kentucky and Virginia, on the E by North Carolina, on the S by Georgia, Alabama, and Mississippi, and on the W by Arkansas and Missouri

Area: 42,143 sq. mi. (109,151 sq. km.); rank—36th

Population: 6,214,888 (2008 est.); rank—17th

Principal Cities: capital—Nashville; largest—Memphis

Statehood: June 1, 1796; 16th state

U.S. Congress: 2 senators, 9 representatives

State Motto: Agriculture and Commerce

State Song: "The Tennessee Waltz"

State Nickname: The Volunteer State

Abbreviations: TN; Tenn.

State Symbols: flower—iris; tree—yellow poplar (tulip poplar); bird—mockingbird

At a Glance

- With an increase in population of 9.2 percent, Tennessee ranked 16th among the states in growth from 2000 to 2008.
- An estimated 60,651 marriages took place in Tennessee in 2008, compared to 26,390 divorces.
- The 2007 home ownership rate in Tennessee was 70.2 percent, giving it a ranking of 31st along with Colorado.
- Tennessee's median household income in 2007 was $42,367, 42nd among the states.
- In Tennessee, 15.9 percent of the population lived below the poverty level in 2007, ranking it 9th along with Oklahoma.
- In 2006-07, 15 percent of Tennesseans did not have health insurance, compared to 15.5 percent of the total U.S. population.
- In 2007, 4.6 percent of Tennesseans were unemployed, which was the same as the national average.
- Tennessee ranked 43rd in the nation with 21.8 percent of its population 25 years old and over having a bachelor's degree in 2007; its ranking was the same as Nevada's.
- Tennessee's violent crime rate in 2007 was 753.3 per 100,000 population, compared to 466.9 for the entire nation.
- Tennessee had one physician for every 339 people in 2007, compared to one physician for every 325 people nationwide.
- In the 2008 election, 57.3 percent of Tennessee's eligible voters voted, compared to 61.7 percent of eligible voters nationwide.
- Tennessee ranked 21st among the states receiving federal aid in 2007, with $1,469 per capita.
- Tennessee's gross domestic product was $244 billion in 2007; it ranked 19th among the states.
- With $21.9 billion in exports in 2007, Tennessee ranked 16th in exports.
- Tennesseans consumed 2.31 trillion Btu's of energy in 2006; the state ranked 15th in total consumption.
- In 2007, Tennessee exported $770 million worth of agricultural products, almost 1 percent of the U.S. total.

Table TN-1. Population by Sex, Age, Race, and Hispanic Origin

(Number, percent.)

Sex, age, race, and Hispanic origin	1990	2000	2008	Average annual percent change, 2000–2008
Total Population	4 877 185	5 689 283	6 214 888	1.1
Percent of total U.S. population	2.0	2.0	2.0	X
Sex				
Male	2 348 928	2 770 275	3 029 115	1.1
Female	2 528 257	2 919 008	3 185 773	1.1
Age				
Under 5 years	333 415	374 880	416 334	1.3
5 to 19 years	1 043 032	1 186 152	1 220 384	0.4
20 to 64 years	2 881 920	3 424 940	3 758 544	1.2
65 years and over	618 818	703 311	819 626	1.9
Median age (years)	33.5	35.9	37.7	X
Race and Hispanic Origin[1]				
One race				
White	4 048 068	4 563 310	4 995 028	1.1
Black	778 035	932 809	1 042 811	1.4
American Indian and Alaskan Native	10 039	15 152	20 709	4.0
Asian[2]	31 839	56 662	82 539	4.8
Native Hawaiian and Other Pacific Islander	X	2 205	3 478	5.9
Two or more races	X	63 109	70 323	1.4
Hispanic (of any race)	32 741	123 838	231 272	8.1

[1]Data on race in 2000 and 2008 are not comparable to 1990. Individuals could only report one race in the 1990 census but could report one or more races on the 2000 census.
[2]Data in 1990 refer to Asian and Pacific Islanders.

Table TN-2. Marital Status

(Number, percent distribution.)

Sex and marital status	1990	2000	2007
Males, 15 Years and Over	1 831 058	2 169 327	2 385 599
Never married	26.7	26.6	30.5
Now married, except separated	60.5	58.9	53.2
Separated	1.8	1.7	2.0
Widowed	2.5	2.5	2.7
Divorced	8.5	10.4	11.6
Females, 15 Years and Over	2 036 246	2 353 303	2 558 888
Never married	20.1	20.7	24.1
Now married, except separated	54.0	53.6	48.6
Separated	2.4	2.3	2.6
Widowed	13.1	11.2	10.9
Divorced	10.4	12.2	13.7

Table TN-3. Households and Housing Characteristics

(Number, percent, and dollars.)

Item	1990	2000	2007	Average annual percent change, 2000–2007
Total Households	1 853 725	2 232 905	2 407 765	1.1
Family households	1 348 019	1 547 835	1 606 220	0.5
Married-couple family	1 059 569	1 173 960	1 185 380	0.1
Other family	288 450	373 875	420 840	1.7
Male householder, no wife present	55 751	85 976	109 543	3.5
Female householder, no husband present	232 699	287 899	311 297	1.1
Nonfamily households	505 706	685 070	801 545	2.3
Householder living alone	442 129	576 401	675 897	2.3
Householder not living alone	63 577	108 669	125 648	2.1
Housing Characteristics				
Total housing units	2 026 067	2 439 443	2 724 929	1.6
Occupied housing units	1 853 725	2 232 905	2 407 765	1.1
Owner-occupied	1 261 118	1 561 363	1 683 930	1.1
Renter-occupied	592 607	671 542	723 835	1.1
Average size	2.56	2.48	2.49	X
Financial Characteristics				
Median gross rent of renter-occupied housing units (dollars)	357	505	634	3.3
Median monthly owner costs for housing units with a mortgage (dollars)	594	882	1 105	3.3
Median value of owner-occupied housing units (dollars)	58 000	93 000	130 800	5.0

Table TN-4. Median Income and Poverty Status, 2007

(Number, percent.)

Characteristic	State		U.S.	
	Number	Percent	Number	Percent
Median Income				
Households (dollars)	42 367	X	50 740	X
Families (dollars)	51 945	X	61 173	X
Below Poverty Level				
Sex				
Male	406 659	13.9	16 576 071	11.5
Female	547 206	17.8	21 476 176	14.3
Age				
Under 18 years	331 269	23.0	13 097 100	18.0
Related children under 18 years	322 262	22.5	12 728 964	17.6
18 to 64 years	531 838	14.0	21 495 507	11.6
65 years and over	90 758	12.0	3 459 640	9.5

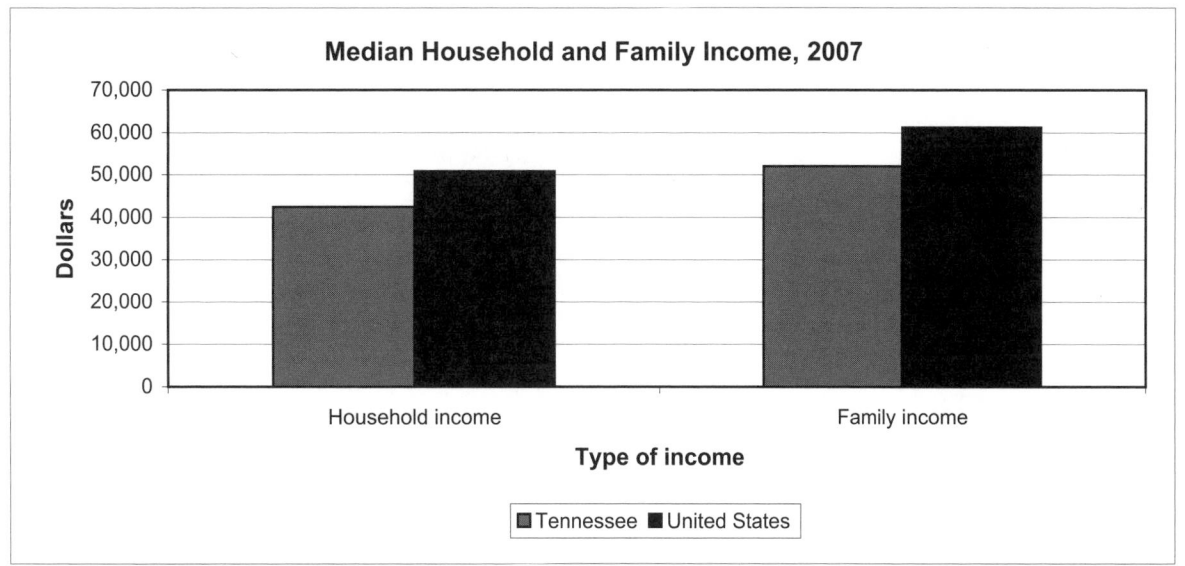

Table TN-5. Health Insurance Coverage Status for All Persons and Children Under 18 Years of Age

(Number, percent.)

Item	2000	2001	2002	2003	2004	2005	2006	2007
ALL PERSONS	5 645	5 682	5 672	5 909	5 857	5 867	5 920	6 150
Covered by Private or Government Health Insurance								
Number	5 060	5 084	5 081	5 161	5 091	5 069	5 111	5 268
Percent	89.6	89.5	89.6	87.3	86.9	86.4	86.3	85.6
Not Covered								
Number	585	598	590	748	766	798	809	883
Percent	10.4	10.5	10.4	12.7	13.1	13.6	13.7	14.4
Percent in the U.S. not covered	13.7	14.1	14.7	15.1	14.9	15.3	15.8	15.3
CHILDREN UNDER 18 YEARS OF AGE	1 400	1 415	1 381	1 391	1 409	1 403	1 469	1 479
Covered by Private or Government Health Insurance								
Number	1 314	1 330	1 296	1 254	1 276	1 276	1 376	1 344
Percent	93.9	94.0	93.8	90.1	90.6	90.9	93.6	90.9
Not Covered								
Number	86	85	85	137	133	127	94	135
Percent	6.1	6.0	6.2	9.9	9.4	9.1	6.4	9.1
Percent in the U.S. not covered	11.6	11.3	11.2	11.0	10.5	10.9	11.7	11.0

Table TN-6. Employment Status by Demographic Group, Preliminary 2008

(Number, percent.)

Characteristic	Civilian noninstitutional population	Civilian labor force		Employment		Unemployed	
		Number	Percent of population	Number	Percent of population	Number	Unemployment rate
TOTAL	4 820	3 047	63.2	2 847	59.1	200	6.6
Sex							
Men	2 307	1 624	70.0	1 521	65.9	103	6.3
Women	2 513	1 423	57.0	1 326	52.8	98	6.9
Race, Sex, and Hispanic Origin							
White	3 968	2 490	62.8	2 344	59.1	145	5.8
Men	1 926	1 369	71.1	1 294	67.2	76	5.5
Women	2 042	1 120	54.9	1 050	51.4	70	6.2
Black or African American	735	477	64.9	426	58.0	51	10.6
Men	327	217	66.4	192	58.9	25	11.3
Women	408	260	63.7	233	57.2	26	10.1
Hispanic	167	114	68.3	105	62.9	9	8.0
Men	91	81	88.9	76	83.2	5	6.4
Women	76	. . .	. . .	. . .	. . .	. . .	. . .
Age							
16 to 19 years	326	129	39.4	95	29.2	33	25.9
20 to 24 years	380	279	73.5	249	65.5	30	10.8
25 to 34 years	853	685	80.3	637	74.8	47	6.9
35 to 44 years	845	698	82.7	655	77.5	43	6.2
45 to 54 years	902	701	77.8	679	75.3	22	3.2
55 to 64 years	714	431	60.4	413	57.9	18	4.2
65 years and over	800	123	15.4	117	14.7	6	4.8

Note: Data in Table 6 are from the Current Population Survey (CPS) and do not match the estimates in Table 7. See notes and definitions for more details.

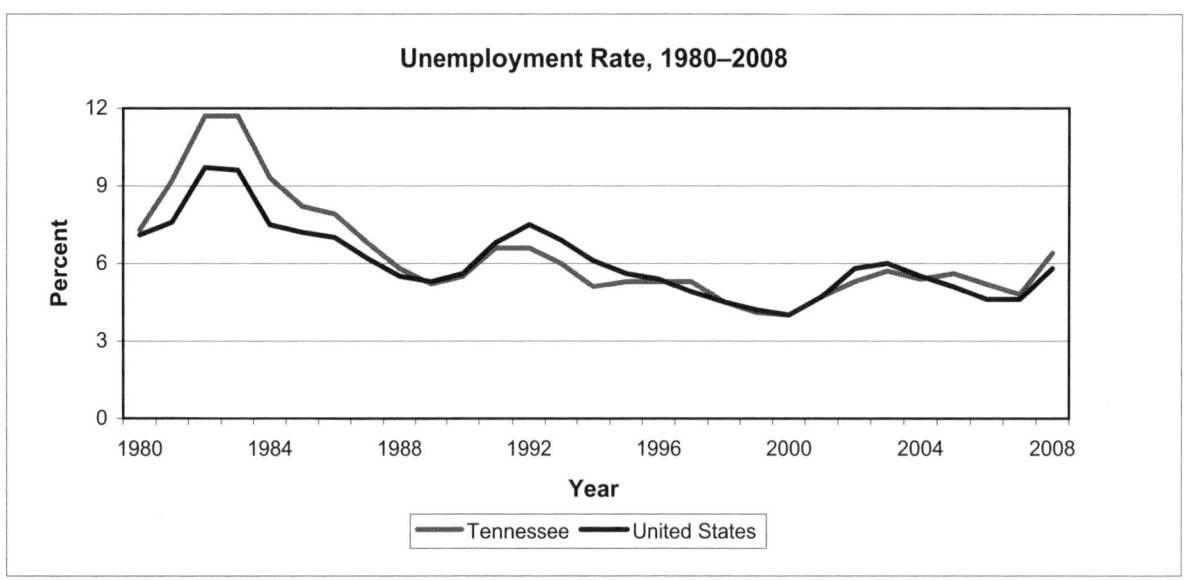

Unemployment Rate, 1980–2008

Table TN-7. Employment Status of the Civilian Noninstitutional Population Age 16 Years and Over

(Number, percent.)

Year	Civilian labor force	Civilian participation rate	Employed	Unemployed	Unemployment rate
1998	2 811 700	65.8	2 685 151	126 549	4.5
1999	2 838 738	65.7	2 722 124	116 614	4.1
2000	2 871 539	65.9	2 756 498	115 041	4.0
2001	2 863 516	65.1	2 728 523	134 993	4.7
2002	2 867 108	64.5	2 714 992	152 116	5.3
2003	2 896 135	64.5	2 731 371	164 764	5.7
2004	2 904 355	64.0	2 746 241	158 114	5.4
2005	2 934 586	63.8	2 771 206	163 380	5.6
2006	2 998 805	64.1	2 843 716	155 089	5.2
2007	3 013 380	63.5	2 867 579	145 801	4.8
2008	3 041 276	63.2	2 846 096	195 180	6.4

Table TN-8. Employment and Average Wages by Industry

(Estimates for 2001–2006 are based on the 2002 North American Industry Classification System [NAICS]. Estimates for 2007 are based on the 2007 NAICS.)

Industry	2001	2002	2003	2004	2005	2006	2007
	Number of jobs						
WAGE AND SALARY EMPLOYMENT BY INDUSTRY	2 804 467	2 782 126	2 788 024	2 834 846	2 869 267	2 913 817	2 930 859
Farm Wage and Salary Employment	11 759	10 564	13 185	12 761	10 099	9 935	9 748
Nonfarm Wage and Salary Employment	2 792 708	2 771 562	2 774 839	2 822 085	2 859 168	2 903 882	2 921 111
Private wage and salary employment	2 368 761	2 341 077	2 341 296	2 384 301	2 422 141	2 461 591	2 472 360
Forestry, fishing, hunting, and other	6 925	6 536	6 212	5 624	5 622	5 508	5 371
Mining	3 896	3 554	3 267	3 107	3 257	3 341	3 909
Utilities	3 555	3 557	3 572	3 521	3 551	3 525	3 586
Construction	124 879	118 453	120 078	121 447	125 925	134 978	137 891
Manufacturing	456 397	431 922	416 315	414 672	412 039	402 552	383 291
Durable goods manufacturing	278 550	262 608	253 094	256 024	258 653	254 520	239 658
Nondurable goods manufacturing	177 847	169 314	163 221	158 648	153 386	148 032	143 633
Wholesale trade	129 127	127 862	128 815	130 117	132 630	134 808	135 401
Retail trade	327 986	320 895	322 297	328 058	334 405	338 094	340 933
Transportation and warehousing	142 055	136 040	137 714	140 819	143 946	146 239	146 416
Information	53 884	51 913	50 561	49 184	49 635	49 867	49 861
Finance and insurance	105 637	103 938	105 678	107 540	107 646	109 818	110 577
Real estate and rental and leasing	35 860	35 404	36 094	36 503	36 875	37 195	37 243
Professional and technical services	103 579	103 443	105 590	106 971	110 082	113 686	115 061
Management of companies and enterprises	24 582	22 632	21 808	22 484	20 257	21 267	23 932
Administrative and waste services	179 491	183 096	167 231	181 480	186 230	189 418	191 051
Educational services	43 909	44 990	48 583	50 053	50 540	50 875	52 913
Health care and social assistance	253 306	264 361	275 396	282 553	293 553	303 036	310 962
Arts, entertainment, and recreation	27 247	27 633	29 010	29 605	30 715	31 600	31 860
Accommodation and food services	212 545	215 229	222 136	228 160	235 474	242 983	248 860
Other services, except public administration	133 901	139 619	140 939	142 403	139 759	142 801	143 242
Government and government enterprises	423 947	430 485	433 543	437 784	437 027	442 291	448 751
	Dollars						
AVERAGE WAGES AND SALARIES BY INDUSTRY	30 885	31 921	32 946	34 302	35 341	36 975	38 467
Average Farm Wages and Salaries	13 320	17 024	14 127	14 496	14 877	17 290	15 562
Average Nonfarm Wages and Salaries	30 959	31 977	33 035	34 392	35 414	37 043	38 544
Average private wages and salaries	31 141	32 122	33 127	34 517	35 550	37 266	38 807
Forestry, fishing, hunting, and other	17 400	17 460	18 011	19 858	20 333	21 112	21 721
Mining	45 093	44 880	44 796	48 172	51 225	56 939	54 403
Utilities	45 230	46 867	47 491	49 829	50 935	54 180	55 746
Construction	34 196	34 588	35 185	35 980	37 633	40 281	42 691
Manufacturing	36 852	38 599	40 055	41 973	42 740	44 653	46 310
Durable goods manufacturing	36 455	38 159	39 473	41 183	41 652	43 745	45 303
Nondurable goods manufacturing	37 474	39 281	40 958	43 247	44 573	46 215	47 992
Wholesale trade	41 913	43 294	44 789	47 755	49 705	52 772	55 051
Retail trade	21 883	22 621	23 103	23 574	24 262	25 005	26 033
Transportation and warehousing	37 361	39 074	39 852	41 232	42 904	44 495	46 005
Information	39 862	40 720	41 407	43 633	44 641	49 805	51 892
Finance and insurance	47 563	49 431	53 121	55 741	55 782	59 352	62 941
Real estate and rental and leasing	29 062	30 085	31 591	33 050	34 536	36 927	38 192
Professional and technical services	45 684	46 988	47 559	50 088	52 511	55 165	58 153
Management of companies and enterprises	45 452	48 320	53 874	57 734	66 019	74 183	75 575
Administrative and waste services	22 877	23 303	24 171	25 028	25 816	26 964	28 703
Educational services	27 802	29 864	30 709	32 283	34 915	37 000	38 835
Health care and social assistance	33 357	34 400	35 092	37 105	38 371	39 454	40 692
Arts, entertainment, and recreation	26 023	28 599	30 536	31 976	31 918	36 043	36 509
Accommodation and food services	13 886	14 279	14 496	14 885	15 387	15 932	16 732
Other services, except public administration	21 080	21 792	22 567	23 490	24 057	24 993	25 998
Government and government enterprises	29 942	31 190	32 537	33 712	34 658	35 798	37 093

Table TN-9. Employment Characteristics by Family Type

(Number, percent.)

Family type and labor force status	2005		2006		2007	
	Total	Families with own children under 18 years	Total	Families with own children under 18 years	Total	Families with own children under 18 years
TOTAL FAMILIES	1 604 310	726 328	1 597 016	719 044	1 606 220	703 385
FAMILY TYPE AND LABOR FORCE STATUS						
Married Coupled Families	1 178 184	481 597	1 178 105	476 625	1 185 380	460 290
Both husband and wife in labor force	50.4	62.8	51.6	63.9	51.4	64.5
Husband in labor force, wife not in labor force	23.6	29.4	23.3	29.0	23.0	28.6
Wife in labor force, husband not in labor force	7.7	4.1	7.7	4.1	8.0	4.3
Both husband and wife not in labor force	18.3	3.7	17.4	2.9	17.7	2.6
Other Families	426 126	244 731	418 911	242 419	420 840	243 095
Female householder, no husband present	75.0	79.4	74.4	78.4	74.0	77.4
In labor force	50.0	61.4	50.5	61.4	50.8	61.2
Not in labor force	25.0	17.9	23.9	17.1	23.1	16.2
Male householder, no wife present	25.0	20.6	25.6	21.6	26.0	22.6
In labor force	19.0	18.1	18.8	18.1	20.2	20.1
Not in labor force	5.9	2.5	6.8	3.4	5.9	2.5

Table TN-10. School Enrollment and Educational Attainment, 2007

(Number, percent.)

Item	State	U.S.
Enrollment		
Total population 3 years and over	5 915 117	289 295 761
Enrolled in school	1 487 774	79 329 527
Enrolled in preschool (percent)	5.4	6.2
Enrolled in grades K-12 (percent)	71.5	67.6
Enrolled in college or graduate school (percent)	23.1	26.2
Attainment		
Total population 25 years and over	4 122 693	197 892 369
Less than a high school diploma (percent)	18.6	15.5
High school diploma or more (percent)	81.4	84.5
Bachelor's degree or more (percent)	21.8	27.5
Graduate degree or more (percent)	7.6	10.1

Table TN-11. Educational Indicators

(Number, percent.)

Item	State	U.S.
Public Schools, 2006–2007 (except where noted)		
Number of school districts	136	17 742
Number of schools	1 710	99 639
Number of students	978 368	49 315 842
Student-teacher ratio	15.7	15.5
Expenditures per student (dollars)	$7 129	. . .
Averaged freshman graduation rate, 2005–2006	70.6	. . .
Dropout rate, grades 9–12, 2005–2006	2.8	3.7
Students eligible for free or reduced-price lunch (percent)	47.7	41.2
English-language learners (percent)	3.0	5.1
Students with IEP (percent)	10.1	12.7
Private Schools, 2007–2008 (except where noted)		
Number of schools	557	33 740
Number of students	106 098	5 072 451
High school graduates, 2006–2007	5 889	306 605
Student-teacher ratio	10.5	11.1

Table TN-12. Reported Voting and Registration of the Voting-Age Population, November 2008

(Number in thousands, percent.)

Item	Total population	Total citizen population	Registered — Total registered	Registered — Percent registered (total population)	Registered — Percent registered (total citizen population)	Voted — Total voted	Voted — Percent voted (total population)	Voted — Percent voted (total citizen population)
U.S. total	225 499	206 072	146 311	64.9	71.0	131 144	58.2	63.6
State total	4 692	4 529	2 921	62.3	64.5	2 516	53.6	55.5
Sex								
Male	2 220	2 141	1 295	58.3	60.5	1 119	50.4	52.2
Female	2 472	2 388	1 626	65.8	68.1	1 397	56.5	58.5
Race								
White alone	3 849	3 718	2 434	63.2	65.5	2 067	53.7	55.6
White non-Hispanic alone	3 685	3 654	2 402	65.2	65.7	2 038	55.3	55.8
Black alone	697	682	426	61.2	62.5	405	58.1	59.3
Asian alone	95	78	25	26.8	32.6	18	19.2	23.4
Hispanic (of any race)	178	73	37	20.9	. . .	34	19.2	. . .
White alone or in combination	3 875	3 744	2 454	63.3	65.5	2 081	53.7	55.6
Black alone or in combination	701	686	430	61.4	62.7	408	58.3	59.5
Asian alone or in combination	99	82	29	29.6	35.8	22	22.4	27.0

Table TN-13. Crime

(Number, rate per 100,000.)

Item	State 2007	State 2008	State Percent change	U.S. 2007	U.S. 2008	U.S. Percent change
Population	6 156 719	6 214 888	0.9	301 621 157	304 059 724	0.8
VIOLENT CRIME						
Number	46 380	44 897	-3.2	1 408 337	1 382 012	-1.9
Rate	753.3	722.4	-4.1	466.9	454.5	-2.7
Murder and Nonnegligent Manslaughter						
Number	397	408	2.8	16 929	16 272	-3.9
Rate	6.4	6.6	1.8	5.6	5.4	-4.7
Forcible Rape						
Number	2 174	2 062	-5.2	90 427	89 000	-1.6
Rate	35.3	33.2	-6.0	30.0	29.3	-2.4
Robbery						
Number	11 022	10 800	-2.0	445 125	441 855	-0.7
Rate	179.0	173.8	-2.9	147.6	145.3	-1.5
Aggravated Assault						
Number	32 787	31 627	-3.5	855 856	834 885	-2.5
Rate	532.5	508.9	-4.4	283.8	274.6	-3.2
PROPERTY CRIME						
Number	251 724	251 245	-0.2	9 843 481	9 767 915	-0.8
Rate	4 088.6	4 042.6	-1.1	3 263.5	3 212.5	-1.6
Burglary						
Number	61 715	65 006	5.3	2 179 140	2 222 196	2.0
Rate	1 002.4	1 046.0	4.3	722.5	730.8	1.2
Larceny-Theft						
Number	168 351	167 015	-0.8	6 568 572	6 588 873	0.3
Rate	2 734.4	2 687.3	-1.7	2 177.8	2 167.0	-0.5
Motor Vehicle Theft						
Number	21 658	19 224	-11.2	1 095 769	956 846	-12.7
Rate	351.8	309.3	-12.1	363.3	314.7	-13.4

Table TN-14. State Government Finances, 2007

(Dollars, percent distribution.)

Item	Thousands of dollars	Percent distribution
Total Revenue	29 469 615	X
General revenue	24 811 808	84.2
Intergovernmental revenue	8 341 938	28.3
Taxes	11 370 768	38.6
General sales	6 763 657	23.0
Selective sales	1 591 517	5.4
License taxes	1 259 679	4.3
Individual income tax	249 145	0.8
Corporate income tax	1 120 422	3.8
Other taxes	386 348	1.3
Current charges	1 870 313	6.3
Miscellaneous general revenue	3 228 789	11.0
Utility revenue	9	0.0
Liquor store revenue	0	0.0
Insurance trust revenue	4 657 798	15.8
Total Expenditure	24 992 628	100.0
Intergovernmental expenditure	6 161 614	24.7
Direct expenditure	18 831 014	75.3
Current operation	14 091 929	56.4
Capital outlay	1 727 797	6.9
Insurance benefits and repayments	1 657 069	6.6
Assistance and subsidies	1 147 708	4.6
Interest on debt	206 511	0.8
Exhibit: Salaries and wages	3 653 960	14.6
Total Expenditure	24 992 628	100.0
General expenditure	23 329 875	93.3
Intergovernmental expenditure	6 161 614	24.7
Direct expenditure	17 168 261	68.7
Education	7 860 649	31.5
Public welfare	8 067 623	32.3
Hospitals	393 670	1.6
Health	1 207 745	4.8
Highways	1 913 472	7.7
Police protection	140 725	0.6
Correction	769 362	3.1
Natural resources	282 659	1.1
Parks and recreation	148 692	0.6
Government administration	687 321	2.8
Interest on general debt	206 511	0.8
Other and unallocable	1 651 446	6.6
Utility expenditure	5 684	0.0
Liquor store expenditure	0	0.0
Insurance trust expenditure	1 657 069	6.6
Debt at End of Fiscal Year	4 141 541	X
Cash and Security Holdings	38 495 022	X

Table TN-15. State Government Tax Collections, 2008

(Dollars, percent distribution.)

Item	Thousands of dollars	Percent distribution
Total Taxes	11 538 430	X
Sales and gross receipts	8 612 382	74.6
General sales and gross receipts	6 832 948	59.2
Selective sales taxes	1 779 434	15.4
Alcoholic beverages	116 189	1.0
Insurance premiums	401 997	3.5
Motor fuels	872 892	7.6
Public utilities	9 627	0.1
Tobacco products	272 433	2.4
Other selective sales	106 296	0.9
Licenses	1 287 826	11.2
Alcoholic beverages	12 222	0.1
Amusements	252	0.0
Corporation	644 694	5.6
Hunting and fishing	32 401	0.3
Motor vehicle	270 176	2.3
Motor vehicle operators	43 827	0.4
Public utility	5 770	0.1
Occupation and business, NEC	271 065	2.3
Other licenses	7 419	0.1
Income taxes	1 296 866	11.2
Individual income	290 986	2.5
Corporation net income	1 005 880	8.7
Other taxes	341 356	3.0
Death and gift	103 464	0.9
Documentary and stock transfer	199 971	1.7
Severance	2 357	0.0
Other	35 564	0.3

Table TN-16. Agriculture

(Number, acres, and dollars.)

Item	2002		2007		Percent change, 2002–2007
	Number	Percent of total	Number	Percent of total	
Number of farms	87 595		79 280		-9.5
Farm Size					
Average size of farm (acres)	133		138		3.8
Farms by size (number of farms)					
Fewer than 50 acres	38 182	43.6	35 210	44.4	-7.8
50 to 499 acres	45 629	52.1	40 435	51.0	-11.4
500 acres or more	3 784	4.3	3 635	4.6	-3.9
Land (Acres)					
Total land in farms	11 681 533		10 969 798		-6.1
Total cropland	6 992 992	59.9	6 047 348	55.1	-13.5
Total harvested cropland	4 365 360	37.4	4 226 440	38.5	-3.2
Irrigated land	61 217	0.5	81 405	0.7	33.0
Value of Sales (Dollars)					
Agricultural products sold ($1,000)	2 199 814		2 617 394		19.0
Average sales per farm	25 113		33 015		31.5
Sales of crops	1 072 548	48.8	1 147 786	43.9	7.0
Sales of livestock, poultry, and their products	1 127 266	51.2	1 469 608	56.1	30.4
Value of Sales (Number of Farms)					
Less than $10,000	67 911	77.5	59 278	74.8	-12.7
$10,000 to $99,999	15 836	18.1	16 201	20.4	2.3
$100,000 to $999,999	3 595	4.1	3 410	4.3	-5.1
$1,000,000 or more	253	0.3	391	0.5	54.5
Farms by Type of Organization (Number of Farms)					
Family	82 866	94.6	72 675	91.7	-12.3
Partnership	3 996	4.6	5 568	7.0	39.3
Corporation	452	0.5	865	1.1	91.4
Other: cooperative, estate or trust, institutional, etc	281	0.3	172	0.2	-38.8
Value of Land and Buildings (Dollars)					
Estimated market value of land and buildings ($1,000)	37 057 079		28 534 393		-23.0
Land and buildings average value per farm	467 420		325 783		-30.3
Average value per acre	3 378		2 405		-28.8
Government Payments					
Number of farms receiving government payments	16 034	18.3	17 320	21.8	8.0
Payments (thousands of dollars)	59 231		95 744		61.6
Average payment per farm	3 694		5 528		49.6
Farm Operator Characteristics					
Farm operators whose principal occupation is farming	44 100	50.3	30 849	38.9	-30.0
Farm operators whose principal occupation is other	43 495	49.7	48 431	61.1	11.3
Average age principal operator (years)	56.0		57.8		3.2

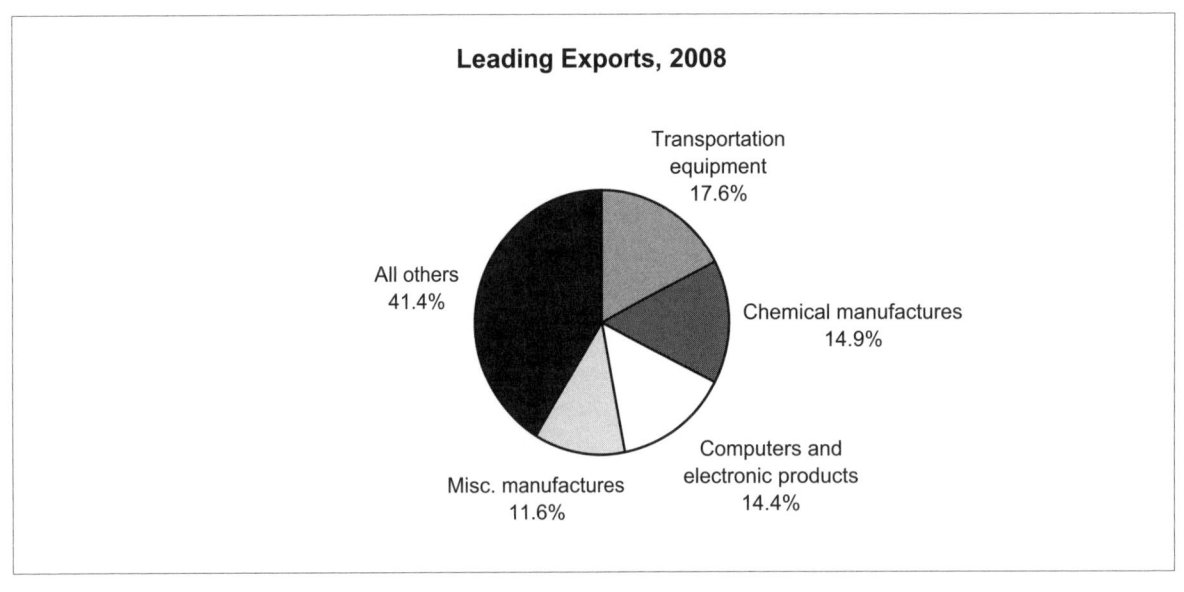

Leading Exports, 2008

Transportation equipment 17.6%

Chemical manufactures 14.9%

Computers and electronic products 14.4%

Misc. manufactures 11.6%

All others 41.4%

TEXAS

Facts and Figures

Location: West South Central United States; bordered on the N by Oklahoma, on the E by Arkansas and Louisiana, on the S by Mexico and the Gulf of Mexico, and on the W by Mexico and New Mexico

Area: 268,581 sq. mi. (695,621 sq. km.); rank—2nd

Population: 24,326,974 (2008 est.); rank—2nd

Principal Cities: capital—Austin; largest—Houston

Statehood: December 29, 1845; 28th state

U.S. Congress: 2 senators, 32 representatives

State Motto: Friendship

State Song: "Texas, Our Texas"

State Nickname: The Lone Star State

Abbreviations: TX; Tex.

State Symbols: flower—bluebonnet; tree—pecan; bird—mockingbird

At a Glance

- With an increase in population of 16.7 percent, Texas ranked 6th among the states in growth from 2000 to 2008.
- An estimated 179,451 marriages took place in Texas in 2008, compared to 77,649 divorces.
- The 2007 home ownership rate in Texas was 66 percent; its ranking of 42nd was tied with that of North Dakota.
- Texas's median household income in 2007 was $47,548, 28th among the states.
- In Texas, 16.3 percent of the population lived below the poverty level in 2007, ranking it 8th.
- In 2006-07, 24.8 percent of Texans did not have health insurance, compared to 15.5 percent of the total U.S. population.
- In 2007, 4.3 percent of Texans were unemployed, compared to 4.6 percent nationwide.
- Texas ranked 31st in the nation with 25.2 percent of its population 25 years old and over having at least a bachelor's degree in 2007.
- Texas's violent crime rate in 2007 was 510.6 per 100,000 population, compared to 466.9 for the entire nation.
- Texas had one physician for every 423 people in 2007, compared to one physician for every 325 people nationwide.
- In the 2008 election, 54.7 percent of Texas's eligible voters voted, compared to 61.7 percent of eligible voters nationwide.
- Texas ranked 43rd among the states receiving federal aid in 2007, with $1,179 per capita.
- Texas's gross domestic product was $1.14 trillion in 2007; it ranked 2nd among the states.
- With $168.2 billion in exports in 2007, Texas ranked 1st in exports.
- Texans consumed 11.74 trillion Btu's of energy in 2006; the state ranked 1st in total consumption.
- In 2007, Texas exported $5.2 billion worth of agricultural products, about 6.3 percent of the U.S. total.

Table TX-1. Population by Sex, Age, Race, and Hispanic Origin

(Number, percent.)

Sex, age, race, and Hispanic origin	1990	2000	2008	Average annual percent change, 2000–2008
Total Population	16 986 510	20 851 820	24 326 974	1.9
Percent of total U.S. population	6.8	7.4	8.0	X
Sex				
Male	8 365 963	10 352 910	12 143 558	2.0
Female	8 620 547	10 498 910	12 183 416	1.9
Age				
Under 5 years	1 390 054	1 624 628	2 027 307	2.8
5 to 19 years	4 002 217	4 921 608	5 394 639	1.2
20 to 64 years	9 877 663	12 233 052	14 432 805	2.1
65 years and over	1 716 576	2 072 532	2 472 223	2.2
Median age (years)	30.6	32.3	33.2	X
Race and Hispanic Origin[1]				
One race				
White	12 774 762	14 799 505	20 046 078	3.9
Black	2 021 632	2 404 566	2 898 143	2.4
American Indian and Alaskan Native	65 877	118 362	184 649	5.7
Asian[2]	319 459	562 319	841 016	5.2
Native Hawaiian and Other Pacific Islander	X	14 434	31 058	10.1
Two or more races	X	514 633	326 030	-5.5
Hispanic (of any race)	4 339 905	6 669 666	8 870 475	3.6

[1]Data on race in 2000 and 2008 are not comparable to 1990. Individuals could only report one race in the 1990 census but could report one or more races on the 2000 census.
[2]Data in 1990 refer to Asian and Pacific Islanders.

Table TX-2. Marital Status

(Number, percent distribution.)

Sex and marital status	1990	2000	2007
Males, 15 Years and Over	6 279 064	7 820 248	9 071 087
Never married	29.0	28.6	33.1
Now married, except separated	58.7	58.8	53.5
Separated	2.3	2.0	2.2
Widowed	2.1	2.1	2.2
Divorced	7.9	8.5	9.2
Females, 15 Years and Over	6 626 866	8 117 395	9 271 844
Never married	21.4	22.6	26.6
Now married, except separated	54.6	54.3	49.4
Separated	3.1	2.9	3.2
Widowed	10.6	9.1	8.8
Divorced	10.3	11.0	12.0

Table TX-3. Households and Housing Characteristics

(Number, percent, and dollars.)

Item	1990	2000	2007	Average annual percent change, 2000–2007
Total Households	6 070 937	7 393 354	8 244 022	1.6
Family households	4 343 878	5 247 794	5 790 823	1.4
Married-couple family	3 435 540	3 989 741	4 259 215	0.9
Other family	908 338	1 258 053	1 531 608	2.9
Male householder, no wife present	206 512	320 464	414 419	3.7
Female householder, no husband present	701 826	937 589	1 117 189	2.5
Nonfamily households	1 727 059	2 145 560	2 453 199	1.9
Householder living alone	1 452 936	1 752 141	2 034 905	2.2
Householder not living alone	274 123	393 419	418 294	0.9
Housing Characteristics				
Total housing units	7 008 999	8 157 575	9 433 119	2.1
Occupied housing units	6 070 937	7 393 354	8 244 022	1.6
Owner-occupied	3 695 115	4 716 959	5 373 524	1.9
Renter-occupied	2 375 822	2 676 395	2 870 498	1.0
Average size	2.73	2.74	2.83	X
Financial Characteristics				
Median gross rent of renter-occupied housing units (dollars)	395	574	734	3.6
Median monthly owner costs for housing units with a mortgage (dollars)	712	986	1 342	4.5
Median value of owner-occupied housing units (dollars)	58 900	82 500	120 900	5.6

Table TX-4. Median Income and Poverty Status, 2007

(Number, percent.)

Characteristic	State		U.S.	
	Number	Percent	Number	Percent
Median Income				
Households (dollars)	47 548	X	50 740	X
Families (dollars)	55 742	X	61 173	X
Below Poverty Level				
Sex				
Male	1 660 651	14.4	16 576 071	11.5
Female	2 130 532	18.1	21 476 176	14.3
Age				
Under 18 years	1 512 819	23.2	13 097 100	18.0
Related children under 18 years	1 485 493	22.9	12 728 964	17.6
18 to 64 years	2 003 381	13.8	21 495 507	11.6
65 years and over	274 983	12.0	3 459 640	9.5

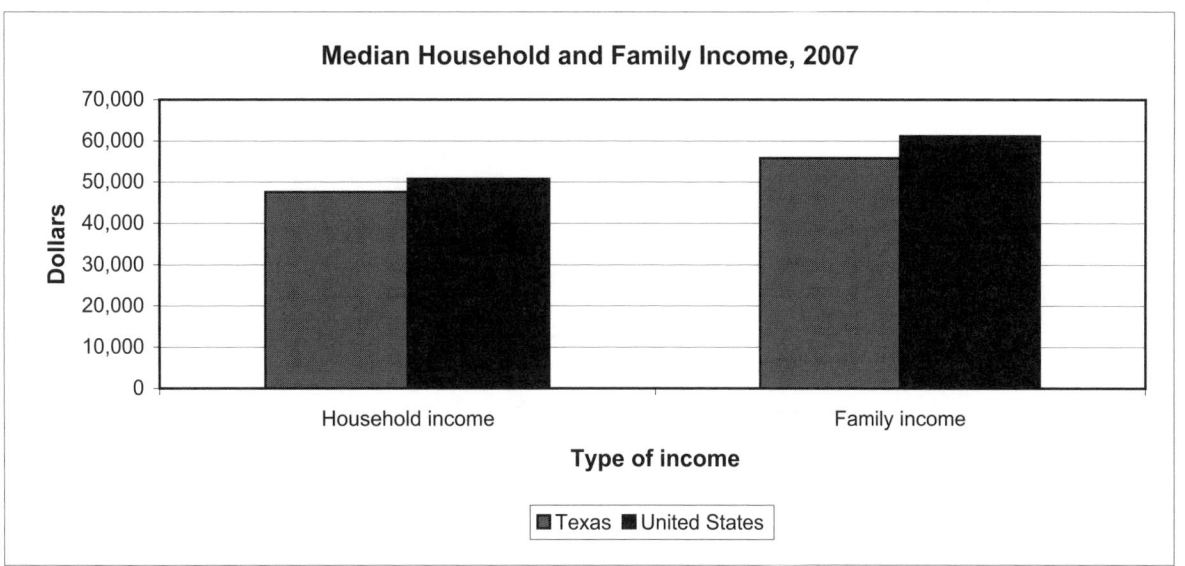

Table TX-5. Health Insurance Coverage Status for All Persons and Children Under 18 Years of Age

(Number, percent.)

Item	2000	2001	2002	2003	2004	2005	2006	2007
ALL PERSONS	20 720	21 065	21 529	21 858	22 331	22 819	23 236	23 704
Covered by Private or Government Health Insurance								
Number	16 070	16 169	16 053	16 609	16 926	17 426	17 533	17 742
Percent	77.6	76.8	74.6	76.0	75.8	76.4	75.5	74.8
Not Covered								
Number	4 650	4 896	5 476	5 249	5 405	5 394	5 704	5 962
Percent	22.4	23.2	25.4	24.0	24.2	23.6	24.5	25.2
Percent in the U.S. not covered	13.7	14.1	14.7	15.1	14.9	15.3	15.8	15.3
CHILDREN UNDER 18 YEARS OF AGE	6 075	6 208	6 049	6 330	6 306	6 477	6 556	6 720
Covered by Private or Government Health Insurance								
Number	4 701	4 899	4 718	5 088	5 000	5 253	5 164	5 285
Percent	77.4	78.9	78.0	80.4	79.3	81.1	78.8	78.6
Not Covered								
Number	1 375	1 309	1 330	1 243	1 307	1 224	1 392	1 435
Percent	22.6	21.1	22.0	19.6	20.7	18.9	21.2	21.4
Percent in the U.S. not covered	11.6	11.3	11.2	11.0	10.5	10.9	11.7	11.0

Table TX-6. Employment Status by Demographic Group, Preliminary 2008

(Number, percent.)

Characteristic	Civilian noninstitutional population	Civilian labor force		Employment		Unemployed	
		Number	Percent of population	Number	Percent of population	Number	Unemployment rate
TOTAL	17 876	11 733	65.6	11 166	62.5	567	4.8
Sex							
Men	8 739	6 542	75.0	6 234	71.3	309	4.7
Women	9 136	5 190	57.0	4 933	54.0	258	5.0
Race, Sex, and Hispanic Origin							
White	14 853	9 742	65.6	9 334	62.8	408	4.2
Men	7 335	5 534	75.4	5 310	72.4	224	4.0
Women	7 518	4 207	56.0	4 023	53.5	184	4.4
Black or African American	2 027	1 316	64.9	1 188	58.6	128	9.7
Men	918	624	67.9	555	60.4	69	11.1
Women	1 109	692	62.4	634	57.2	58	8.4
Hispanic	6 415	4 246	66.2	4 009	62.5	238	5.6
Men	3 248	2 558	78.8	2 420	74.5	138	5.4
Women	3 166	1 688	53.3	1 588	50.2	100	5.9
Age							
16 to 19 years	1 377	508	36.9	423	30.7	85	16.7
20 to 24 years	1 655	1 201	72.5	1 092	66.0	109	9.1
25 to 34 years	3 491	2 835	81.2	2 701	77.4	134	4.7
35 to 44 years	3 387	2 820	83.3	2 714	80.1	106	3.8
45 to 54 years	3 121	2 496	80.0	2 421	77.6	75	3.0
55 to 64 years	2 313	1 420	61.4	1 379	59.6	41	2.9
65 years and over	2 532	452	17.9	436	17.2	17	3.7

Note: Data in Table 6 are from the Current Population Survey (CPS) and do not match the estimates in Table 7. See notes and definitions for more details.

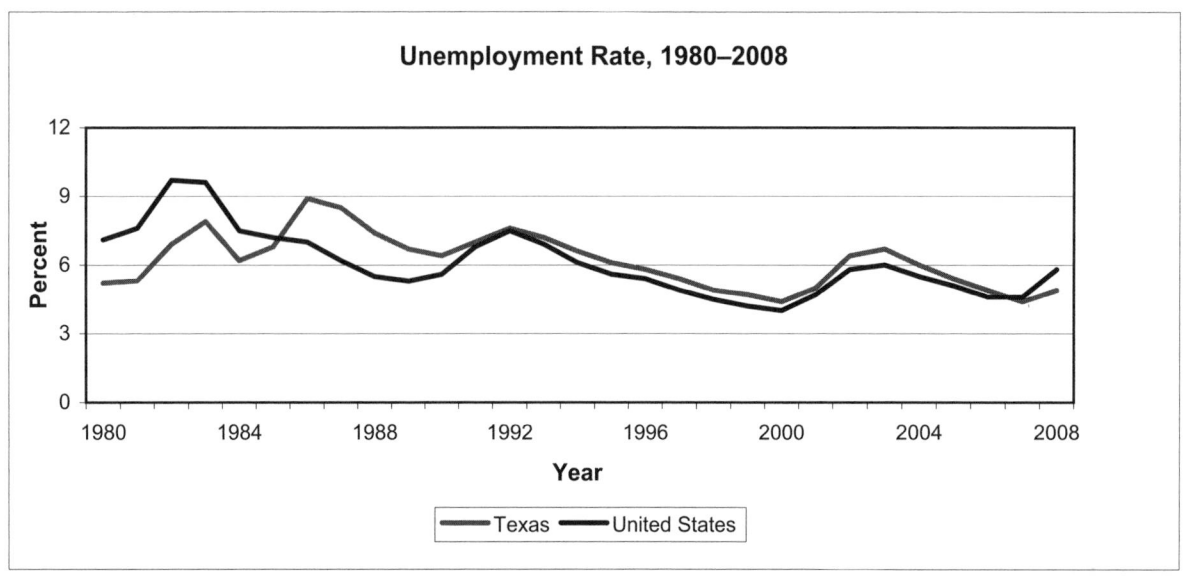

Unemployment Rate, 1980–2008

Table TX-7. Employment Status of the Civilian Noninstitutional Population Age 16 Years and Over

(Number, percent.)

Year	Civilian labor force	Civilian participation rate	Employed	Unemployed	Unemployment rate
1998	10 097 882	69.0	9 600 982	496 900	4.9
1999	10 250 025	68.7	9 766 299	483 726	4.7
2000	10 347 847	68.1	9 896 002	451 845	4.4
2001	10 519 335	67.8	9 991 920	527 415	5.0
2002	10 803 187	68.4	10 115 299	687 888	6.4
2003	10 964 756	68.2	10 228 640	736 116	6.7
2004	11 051 912	67.6	10 385 318	666 594	6.0
2005	11 170 574	67.0	10 568 414	602 160	5.4
2006	11 348 147	66.5	10 787 397	560 750	4.9
2007	11 474 987	65.8	10 972 152	502 835	4.4
2008	11 701 585	65.7	11 126 436	575 149	4.9

Table TX-8. Employment and Average Wages by Industry

(Estimates for 2001–2006 are based on the 2002 North American Industry Classification System [NAICS]. Estimates for 2007 are based on the 2007 NAICS.)

Industry	2001	2002	2003	2004	2005	2006	2007
	Number of jobs						
WAGE AND SALARY EMPLOYMENT BY INDUSTRY	10 028 925	9 955 099	9 911 731	10 016 467	10 269 460	10 622 471	10 946 777
Farm Wage and Salary Employment	59 461	50 351	47 526	42 664	46 425	38 821	43 234
Nonfarm Wage and Salary Employment	9 969 464	9 904 748	9 864 205	9 973 803	10 223 035	10 583 650	10 903 543
Private wage and salary employment	8 231 819	8 127 821	8 060 887	8 166 916	8 395 890	8 721 746	9 015 249
Forestry, fishing, hunting, and other	44 763	45 595	44 454	43 494	45 416	42 886	42 414
Mining	151 725	144 269	145 096	151 894	163 510	184 147	205 037
Utilities	51 055	51 941	48 527	47 420	46 010	44 713	45 735
Construction	604 851	592 164	575 044	567 435	589 133	628 733	670 367
Manufacturing	1 035 852	955 563	907 759	896 414	907 626	934 734	941 754
Durable goods manufacturing	652 758	595 235	564 817	564 218	577 637	606 739	617 286
Nondurable goods manufacturing	383 094	360 328	342 942	332 196	329 989	327 995	324 468
Wholesale trade	480 106	467 629	465 682	471 111	483 822	506 872	526 861
Retail trade	1 154 091	1 144 348	1 115 616	1 122 502	1 147 404	1 170 909	1 199 382
Transportation and warehousing	357 347	343 624	339 469	353 858	364 250	379 433	391 858
Information	270 023	250 186	236 791	226 930	223 977	224 060	222 178
Finance and insurance	404 114	410 345	421 001	428 168	440 093	459 603	467 566
Real estate and rental and leasing	178 566	177 275	175 259	176 561	179 131	182 698	188 047
Professional and technical services	502 235	486 528	481 478	496 959	523 239	555 439	587 922
Management of companies and enterprises	35 590	40 228	41 128	47 292	53 281	56 848	65 491
Administrative and waste services	582 435	562 961	555 897	578 777	612 113	653 049	674 510
Educational services	120 030	126 184	127 648	128 321	130 243	132 856	138 432
Health care and social assistance	898 722	937 801	974 303	998 661	1 028 975	1 062 572	1 098 651
Arts, entertainment, and recreation	98 428	101 900	101 972	105 718	106 831	109 592	112 775
Accommodation and food services	751 508	760 576	773 404	794 086	818 304	850 302	884 585
Other services, except public administration	510 378	528 704	530 359	531 315	532 532	542 300	551 684
Government and government enterprises	1 737 645	1 776 927	1 803 318	1 806 887	1 827 145	1 861 904	1 888 294
	Dollars						
AVERAGE WAGES AND SALARIES BY INDUSTRY	35 376	35 615	36 414	37 987	39 666	41 937	44 103
Average Farm Wages and Salaries	14 433	12 008	16 224	19 563	21 337	21 795	22 551
Average Nonfarm Wages and Salaries	35 501	35 735	36 511	38 066	39 750	42 011	44 189
Average private wages and salaries	36 291	36 231	36 925	38 571	40 329	42 693	44 902
Forestry, fishing, hunting, and other	18 525	19 008	19 482	20 523	21 986	22 887	23 706
Mining	77 808	79 490	81 390	87 556	98 420	102 628	107 581
Utilities	76 220	72 507	68 618	72 958	76 136	81 959	93 972
Construction	36 130	36 588	37 282	38 328	40 538	44 505	46 624
Manufacturing	46 103	46 774	48 641	51 181	54 230	57 303	59 948
Durable goods manufacturing	48 028	48 236	49 899	52 436	55 581	59 155	60 866
Nondurable goods manufacturing	42 822	44 357	46 569	49 050	51 864	53 878	58 200
Wholesale trade	53 136	51 806	53 081	55 841	58 504	61 351	64 592
Retail trade	23 482	23 894	24 458	24 856	25 551	26 188	26 625
Transportation and warehousing	44 499	42 763	43 189	44 332	45 447	47 920	50 294
Information	54 463	53 221	53 363	56 505	56 896	60 449	64 609
Finance and insurance	52 894	52 537	54 565	57 075	59 600	62 933	66 759
Real estate and rental and leasing	34 001	35 112	35 520	38 119	39 688	43 194	45 100
Professional and technical services	60 240	59 996	60 529	62 562	65 075	69 155	71 681
Management of companies and enterprises	61 371	60 291	64 084	74 952	87 344	91 189	101 036
Administrative and waste services	25 374	26 294	26 662	28 623	29 076	30 797	33 817
Educational services	26 313	26 801	27 549	29 009	30 045	31 016	32 108
Health care and social assistance	30 993	32 184	32 760	34 166	35 042	36 329	37 834
Arts, entertainment, and recreation	23 293	24 688	25 444	25 476	26 430	28 709	29 402
Accommodation and food services	14 492	14 602	14 860	15 408	15 928	16 664	16 956
Other services, except public administration	20 621	20 900	21 546	22 341	23 121	24 367	25 577
Government and government enterprises	31 758	33 469	34 662	35 784	37 087	38 819	40 783

Table TX-9. Employment Characteristics by Family Type

(Number, percent.)

Family type and labor force status	2005		2006		2007	
	Total	Families with own children under 18 years	Total	Families with own children under 18 years	Total	Families with own children under 18 years
TOTAL FAMILIES	5 597 885	2 854 739	5 686 517	2 887 476	5 790 823	2 929 071
FAMILY TYPE AND LABOR FORCE STATUS						
Married Coupled Families	4 122 975	1 989 726	4 173 567	2 005 164	4 259 215	2 038 863
Both husband and wife in labor force	50.7	57.9	52.0	59.5	51.1	58.6
Husband in labor force, wife not in labor force	28.0	34.8	28.1	34.8	28.9	35.8
Wife in labor force, husband not in labor force	6.3	3.8	5.9	3.2	6.1	3.2
Both husband and wife not in labor force	15.0	3.5	14.0	2.5	13.9	2.4
Other Families	1 474 910	865 013	1 512 950	882 312	1 531 608	890 208
Female householder, no husband present	73.7	78.1	73.6	77.9	72.9	77.5
In labor force	52.3	62.8	52.5	62.6	52.1	62.4
Not in labor force	21.3	15.4	21.1	15.3	20.8	15.1
Male householder, no wife present	26.3	21.9	26.4	22.1	27.1	22.5
In labor force	21.3	19.7	22.0	20.3	22.2	20.4
Not in labor force	5.0	2.2	4.4	1.9	4.9	2.1

Table TX-10. School Enrollment and Educational Attainment, 2007

(Number, percent.)

Item	State	U.S.
Enrollment		
Total population 3 years and over	22 734 069	289 295 761
Enrolled in school	6 615 812	79 329 527
Enrolled in preschool (percent)	6.7	6.2
Enrolled in grades K-12 (percent)	70.6	67.6
Enrolled in college or graduate school (percent)	22.7	26.2
Attainment		
Total population 25 years and over	14 836 320	197 892 369
Less than a high school diploma (percent)	20.9	15.5
High school diploma or more (percent)	79.1	84.5
Bachelor's degree or more (percent)	25.2	27.5
Graduate degree or more (percent)	8.2	10.1

Table TX-11. Educational Indicators

(Number, percent.)

Item	State	U.S.
Public Schools, 2006–2007 (except where noted)		
Number of school districts	1 274	17 742
Number of schools	8 867	99 639
Number of students	4 599 509	49 315 842
Student-teacher ratio	14.8	15.5
Expenditures per student (dollars)	$7 850	. . .
Averaged freshman graduation rate, 2005–2006	72.5	. . .
Dropout rate, grades 9–12, 2005–2006	4.3	3.7
Students eligible for free or reduced-price lunch (percent)	47.2	41.2
English-language learners (percent)	10.9	5.1
Students with IEP (percent)	10.7	12.7
Private Schools, 2007–2008 (except where noted)		
Number of schools	1 651	33 740
Number of students	235 241	5 072 451
High school graduates, 2006–2007	11 923	306 605
Student-teacher ratio	10.0	11.1

Table TX-12. Reported Voting and Registration of the Voting-Age Population, November 2008

(Number in thousands, percent.)

Item	Total population	Total citizen population	Registered — Total registered	Registered — Percent registered (total population)	Registered — Percent registered (total citizen population)	Voted — Total voted	Voted — Percent voted (total population)	Voted — Percent voted (total citizen population)
U.S. total	225 499	206 072	146 311	64.9	71.0	131 144	58.2	63.6
State total	17 295	15 040	10 123	58.5	67.3	8 435	48.8	56.1
Sex								
Male	8 434	7 212	4 693	55.6	65.1	3 862	45.8	53.6
Female	8 861	7 827	5 430	61.3	69.4	4 573	51.6	58.4
Race								
White alone	14 432	12 554	8 423	58.4	67.1	6 978	48.3	55.6
White non-Hispanic alone	8 388	8 213	6 048	72.1	73.6	5 311	63.3	64.7
Black alone	1 933	1 840	1 356	70.2	73.7	1 194	61.8	64.9
Asian alone	605	352	160	26.5	45.5	118	19.6	33.7
Hispanic (of any race)	6 241	4 493	2 441	39.1	54.3	1 697	27.2	37.8
White alone or in combination	14 614	12 721	8 519	58.3	67.0	7 053	48.3	55.4
Black alone or in combination	2 004	1 912	1 415	70.6	74.0	1 253	62.5	65.6
Asian alone or in combination	620	366	175	28.2	47.6	133	21.4	36.2

Table TX-13. Crime

(Number, rate per 100,000.)

Item	State 2007	State 2008	State Percent change	U.S. 2007	U.S. 2008	U.S. Percent change
Population	23 904 380	24 326 974	1.8	301 621 157	304 059 724	0.8
VIOLENT CRIME						
Number	122 054	123 564	1.2	1 408 337	1 382 012	-1.9
Rate	510.6	507.9	-0.5	466.9	454.5	-2.7
Murder and Nonnegligent Manslaughter						
Number	1 420	1 374	-3.2	16 929	16 272	-3.9
Rate	5.9	5.6	-4.9	5.6	5.4	-4.7
Forcible Rape						
Number	8 439	8 014	-5.0	90 427	89 000	-1.6
Rate	35.3	32.9	-6.7	30.0	29.3	-2.4
Robbery						
Number	38 769	37 753	-2.6	445 125	441 855	-0.7
Rate	162.2	155.2	-4.3	147.6	145.3	-1.5
Aggravated Assault						
Number	73 426	76 423	4.1	855 856	834 885	-2.5
Rate	307.2	314.1	2.3	283.8	274.6	-3.2
PROPERTY CRIME						
Number	985 142	969 570	-1.6	9 843 481	9 767 915	-0.8
Rate	4 121.2	3 985.6	-3.3	3 263.5	3 212.5	-1.6
Burglary						
Number	228 313	230 123	0.8	2 179 140	2 222 196	2.0
Rate	955.1	946.0	-1.0	722.5	730.8	1.2
Larceny-Theft						
Number	662 930	654 097	-1.3	6 568 572	6 588 873	0.3
Rate	2 773.3	2 688.8	-3.0	2 177.8	2 167.0	-0.5
Motor Vehicle Theft						
Number	93 899	85 350	-9.1	1 095 769	956 846	-12.7
Rate	392.8	350.8	-10.7	363.3	314.7	-13.4

Table TX-14. State Government Finances, 2007

(Dollars, percent distribution.)

Item	Thousands of dollars	Percent distribution
Total Revenue	114 728 001	X
General revenue	88 863 456	77.5
Intergovernmental revenue	28 277 613	24.6
Taxes	40 314 714	35.1
General sales	20 434 675	17.8
Selective sales	11 376 709	9.9
License taxes	5 735 796	5.0
Individual income tax	0	0.0
Corporate income tax	0	0.0
Other taxes	2 767 534	2.4
Current charges	9 683 702	8.4
Miscellaneous general revenue	10 587 427	9.2
Utility revenue	0	0.0
Liquor store revenue	0	0.0
Insurance trust revenue	25 864 545	22.5
Total Expenditure	90 623 748	100.0
Intergovernmental expenditure	21 915 924	24.2
Direct expenditure	68 707 824	75.8
Current operation	47 432 209	52.3
Capital outlay	8 631 940	9.5
Insurance benefits and repayments	9 855 992	10.9
Assistance and subsidies	1 743 694	1.9
Interest on debt	1 043 989	1.2
Exhibit: Salaries and wages	13 203 180	14.6
Total Expenditure	90 623 748	100.0
General expenditure	80 767 756	89.1
Intergovernmental expenditure	21 915 924	24.2
Direct expenditure	58 851 832	64.9
Education	34 408 665	38.0
Public welfare	20 646 360	22.8
Hospitals	3 288 025	3.6
Health	2 232 519	2.5
Highways	8 133 944	9.0
Police protection	611 716	0.7
Correction	3 302 304	3.6
Natural resources	941 465	1.0
Parks and recreation	107 938	0.1
Government administration	1 509 906	1.7
Interest on general debt	1 043 989	1.2
Other and unallocable	4 540 925	5.0
Utility expenditure	0	0.0
Liquor store expenditure	0	0.0
Insurance trust expenditure	9 855 992	10.9
Debt at End of Fiscal Year	23 909 021	X
Cash and Security Holdings	297 038 018	X

Table TX-15. State Government Tax Collections, 2008

(Dollars, percent distribution.)

Item	Thousands of dollars	Percent distribution
Total Taxes	44 675 953	X
Sales and gross receipts	33 365 192	74.7
General sales and gross receipts	21 668 972	48.5
Selective sales taxes	11 696 220	26.2
Alcoholic beverages	784 069	1.8
Amusements	26 529	0.1
Insurance premiums	1 405 057	3.1
Motor fuels	3 103 170	6.9
Pari-mutuels	9 956	0.0
Public utilities	1 015 882	2.3
Tobacco products	1 446 895	3.2
Other selective sales	3 904 662	8.7
Licenses	7 173 996	16.1
Alcoholic beverages	52 864	0.1
Amusements	8 210	0.0
Corporation	4 452 590	10.0
Hunting and fishing	92 462	0.2
Motor vehicle	1 518 188	3.4
Motor vehicle operators	115 935	0.3
Public utility	24 057	0.1
Occupation and business, NEC	872 045	2.0
Other licenses	37 645	0.1
Other taxes	4 136 765	9.3
Death and gift	5 580	0.0
Severance	4 131 185	9.2

Table TX-16. Agriculture

(Number, acres, and dollars.)

Item	2002		2007		Percent change, 2002–2007
	Number	Percent of total	Number	Percent of total	
Number of farms	228 926		247 437		8.1
Farm Size					
Average size of farm (acres)	567		527		-7.1
Farms by size (number of farms)					
Fewer than 50 acres	74 684	32.6	93 861	37.9	25.7
50 to 499 acres	113 055	49.4	113 395	45.8	0.3
500 acres or more	41 187	18.0	40 181	16.2	-2.4
Land (Acres)					
Total land in farms	129 877 666		130 398 753		0.4
Total cropland	38 657 710	29.8	33 667 177	25.8	-12.9
Total harvested cropland	17 750 938	13.7	19 174 301	14.7	8.0
Irrigated land	5 074 638	3.9	5 010 416	3.8	-1.3
Value of Sales (Dollars)					
Agricultural products sold ($1,000)	14 134 744		21 001 074		48.6
Average sales per farm	61 744		84 874		37.5
Sales of crops	3 731 751	26.4	6 565 576	31.3	75.9
Sales of livestock, poultry, and their products	10 402 993	73.6	14 435 499	68.7	38.8
Value of Sales (Number of Farms)					
Less than $10,000	163 674	71.5	175 773	71.0	7.4
$10,000 to $99,999	50 588	22.1	54 084	21.9	6.9
$100,000 to $999,999	13 182	5.8	14 701	5.9	11.5
$1,000,000 or more	1 482	0.6	2 879	1.2	94.3
Farms by Type of Organization (Number of Farms)					
Family	210 409	91.9	218 126	88.2	3.7
Partnership	12 720	5.6	20 657	8.3	62.4
Corporation	4 298	1.9	5 706	2.3	32.8
Other: cooperative, estate or trust, institutional, etc	1 499	0.7	2 948	1.2	96.7
Value of Land and Buildings (Dollars)					
Estimated market value of land and buildings ($1,000)	165 573 377		100 496 055		-39.3
Land and buildings average value per farm	669 154		439 066		-34.4
Average value per acre	1 270		768		-39.5
Government Payments					
Number of farms receiving government payments	42 217	18.4	48 027	19.4	13.8
Payments (thousands of dollars)	528 979		720 903		36.3
Average payment per farm	12 530		15 010		19.8
Farm Operator Characteristics					
Farm operators whose principal occupation is farming	122 719	53.6	98 692	39.9	-19.6
Farm operators whose principal occupation is other	106 207	46.4	148 745	60.1	40.1
Average age principal operator (years)	56.9		58.9		3.5

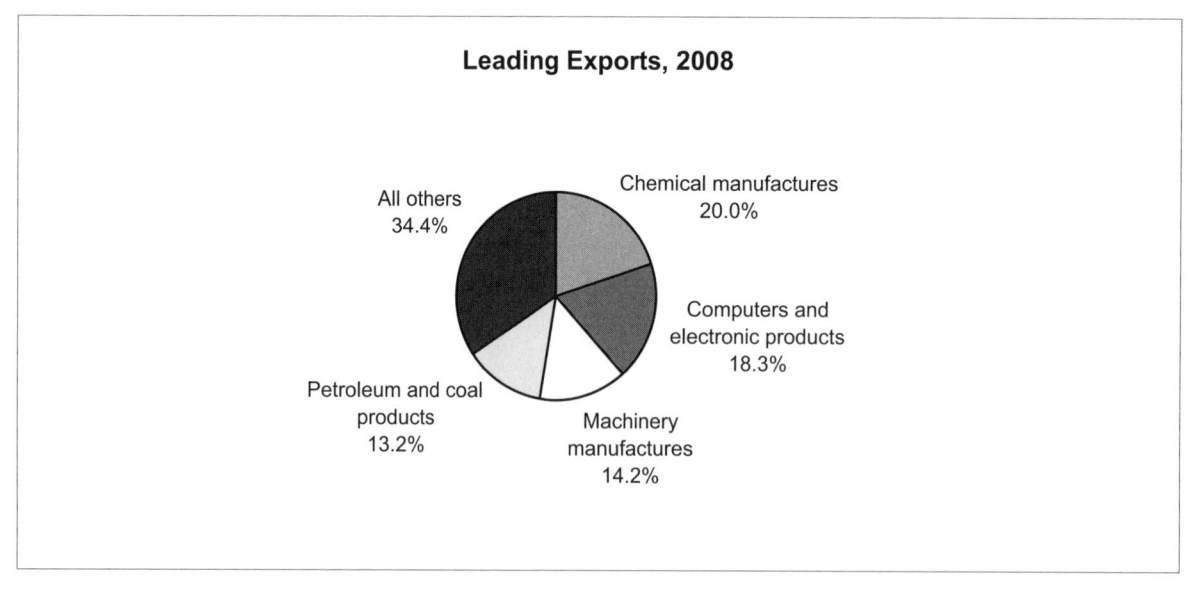

Leading Exports, 2008

All others 34.4%

Chemical manufactures 20.0%

Computers and electronic products 18.3%

Machinery manufactures 14.2%

Petroleum and coal products 13.2%

UTAH

Facts and Figures

Location: Western United States; bordered on the N by Idaho and Wyoming, on the E by Colorado, on the S by Arizona, and on the W by Nevada; Utah is one of the Four Corner states—at its SE corner it touches Arizona, Colorado, and New Mexico

Area: 84,899 sq. mi. (219,887 sq. km.); rank—13th

Population: 2,736,424 (2008 est.); rank—34th

Principal Cities: capital—Salt Lake City; largest—Salt Lake City

Statehood: January 4, 1896; 45th state

U.S. Congress: 2 senators, 3 representatives

State Motto: Industry

State Song: "Utah, We Love Thee"

State Nickname: The Beehive State

Abbreviations: UT

State Symbols: flower—sego lily; tree—blue spruce; bird—California seagull

At a Glance

- With an increase in population of 22.5 percent, Utah ranked 3rd among the states in growth from 2000 to 2008.
- An estimated 19,978 marriages took place in Utah in 2008, compared to 9,489 divorces.
- The 2007 home ownership rate in Utah was 74.9 percent, giving it a ranking of 4th among the states.
- Utah's median household income in 2007 was $55,109, 13th among the states.
- In Utah, 9.7 percent of the population lived below the poverty level in 2007, ranking it 42nd.
- In 2006-07, 15.1 percent of Utahns did not have health insurance, compared to 15.5 percent of the total U.S. population.
- In 2007, 2.6 percent of Utahns were unemployed, compared to 4.6 percent nationwide.
- Utah ranked 17th in the nation with 28.7 percent of its population 25 years old and over having a bachelor's degree in 2007.
- Utah's violent crime rate in 2007 was 234.8 per 100,000 population, compared to 466.9 for the entire nation.
- Utah had one physician for every 422 people in 2007, compared to one physician for every 325 people nationwide.
- In the 2008 election, 53.3 percent of Utah's eligible voters voted, compared to 61.7 percent of eligible voters nationwide.
- Utah ranked 47th among the states receiving federal aid in 2007, with $1,066 per capita.
- Utah's gross domestic product was $106 billion in 2007; it ranked 33rd among the states.
- With $7.8 billion in exports in 2007, Utah ranked 30th in exports.
- Utahns consumed 785.9 billion Btu's of energy in 2006; the state ranked 35th in total consumption.
- In 2007, Utah exported $344 million worth of agricultural products, less than 1 percent of the U.S. total.

Table UT-1. Population by Sex, Age, Race, and Hispanic Origin

(Number, percent.)

Sex, age, race, and Hispanic origin	1990	2000	2008	Average annual percent change, 2000–2008
Total Population	1 722 850	2 233 169	2 736 424	2.6
Percent of total U.S. population	0.7	0.8	0.9	X
Sex				
Male	855 759	1 119 031	1 381 261	2.7
Female	867 091	1 114 138	1 355 163	2.5
Age				
Under 5 years	169 633	209 378	268 916	3.2
5 to 19 years	519 975	601 599	667 359	1.3
20 to 64 years	883 284	1 231 970	1 553 947	2.9
65 years and over	149 958	190 222	246 202	3.3
Median age (years)	26.2	27.1	28.7	X
Race and Hispanic Origin[1]				
One race				
White	1 615 845	1 992 975	2 542 561	3.1
Black	11 576	17 657	34 880	8.9
American Indian and Alaskan Native	24 283	29 684	38 102	3.2
Asian[2]	33 371	37 108	53 996	4.8
Native Hawaiian and Other Pacific Islander	X	15 145	21 094	4.2
Two or more races	X	47 195	45 791	-0.4
Hispanic (of any race)	84 597	201 559	329 069	6.3

[1]Data on race in 2000 and 2008 are not comparable to 1990. Individuals could only report one race in the 1990 census but could report one or more races on the 2000 census.
[2]Data in 1990 refer to Asian and Pacific Islanders.

Table UT-2. Marital Status

(Number, percent distribution.)

Sex and marital status	1990	2000	2007
Males, 15 Years and Over	580 050	813 693	977 694
Never married	28.6	30.6	32.0
Now married, except separated	62.0	59.5	57.6
Separated	1.1	1.1	1.0
Widowed	1.6	1.6	1.5
Divorced	6.7	7.3	7.9
Females, 15 Years and Over	605 647	825 995	974 915
Never married	22.6	25.2	25.2
Now married, except separated	59.2	58.0	56.8
Separated	1.4	1.4	1.5
Widowed	8.1	6.6	6.3
Divorced	8.7	8.8	10.1

Table UT-3. Households and Housing Characteristics

(Number, percent, and dollars.)

Item	1990	2000	2007	Average annual percent change, 2000–2007
Total Households	537 273	701 281	835 320	2.5
Family households	410 862	535 294	629 901	2.4
Married-couple family	348 029	442 931	520 164	2.3
Other family	62 833	92 363	109 737	2.5
Male householder, no wife present	13 756	26 422	33 001	3.2
Female householder, no husband present	49 077	65 941	76 736	2.2
Nonfamily households	126 411	165 987	205 419	3.1
Householder living alone	101 640	124 756	162 012	3.8
Householder not living alone	24 771	41 231	43 407	0.7
Housing Characteristics				
Total housing units	598 388	768 594	925 295	2.7
Occupied housing units	537 273	701 281	835 320	2.5
Owner-occupied	365 979	501 547	599 201	2.6
Renter-occupied	171 294	199 734	236 119	2.4
Average size	3.15	3.13	3.11	X
Financial Characteristics				
Median gross rent of renter-occupied housing units (dollars)	369	597	733	3.0
Median monthly owner costs for housing units with a mortgage (dollars)	667	1 102	1 358	3.0
Median value of owner-occupied housing units (dollars)	68 700	146 100	218 700	5.9

Table UT-4. Median Income and Poverty Status, 2007

(Number, percent.)

Characteristic	State		U.S.	
	Number	Percent	Number	Percent
Median Income				
Households (dollars)	55 109	X	50 740	X
Families (dollars)	62 432	X	61 173	X
Below Poverty Level				
Sex				
Male	113 324	8.7	16 576 071	11.5
Female	137 760	10.7	21 476 176	14.3
Age				
Under 18 years	88 741	11.0	13 097 100	18.0
Related children under 18 years	86 285	10.7	12 728 964	17.6
18 to 64 years	147 091	9.4	21 495 507	11.6
65 years and over	15 252	6.8	3 459 640	9.5

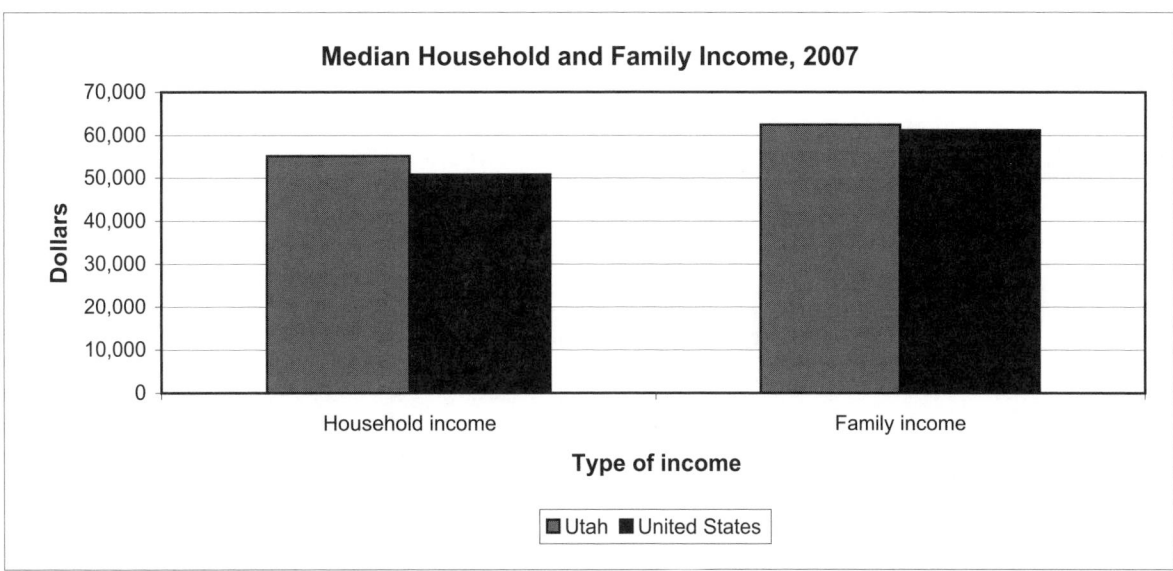

Table UT-5. Health Insurance Coverage Status for All Persons and Children Under 18 Years of Age

(Number, percent.)

Item	2000	2001	2002	2003	2004	2005	2006	2007
ALL PERSONS	2 242	2 262	2 310	2 352	2 393	2 524	2 537	2 657
Covered by Private or Government Health Insurance								
Number	1 983	1 940	2 015	2 062	2 075	2 110	2 094	2 317
Percent	88.5	85.8	87.3	87.7	86.7	83.6	82.6	87.2
Not Covered								
Number	259	322	294	290	318	414	442	340
Percent	11.5	14.2	12.7	12.3	13.3	16.4	17.4	12.8
Percent in the U.S. not covered	13.7	14.1	14.7	15.1	14.9	15.3	15.8	15.3
CHILDREN UNDER 18 YEARS OF AGE	729	724	756	766	773	762	801	832
Covered by Private or Government Health Insurance								
Number	669	642	686	698	693	668	681	746
Percent	91.8	88.6	90.7	91.1	89.7	87.7	85.0	89.6
Not Covered								
Number	60	82	70	68	79	94	120	87
Percent	8.2	11.4	9.3	8.9	10.3	12.3	15.0	10.4
Percent in the U.S. not covered	11.6	11.3	11.2	11.0	10.5	10.9	11.7	11.0

Table UT-6. Employment Status by Demographic Group, Preliminary 2008

(Number, percent.)

Characteristic	Civilian noninstitutional population	Civilian labor force		Employment		Unemployed	
		Number	Percent of population	Number	Percent of population	Number	Unemployment rate
TOTAL	1 933	1 374	71.1	1 326	68.6	49	3.5
Sex							
Men	966	787	82.0	754	78.1	32	4.1
Women	968	588	61.0	571	59.0	16	2.8
Race, Sex, and Hispanic Origin							
White	1 827	1 302	71.3	1 258	68.9	43	3.3
Men	913	745	81.5	717	78.5	28	3.8
Women	914	557	61.0	542	59.3	15	2.8
Black or African American	...	...	...	...	...	...	...
Men	...	...	...	...	...	...	...
Women	...	...	...	...	...	...	...
Hispanic	192	147	76.5	139	72.5	8	5.3
Men	105	94	89.2	89	84.8	5	4.9
Women	87	54	61.2	50	57.7	3	5.7
Age							
16 to 19 years	160	86	54.0	77	48.0	10	11.1
20 to 24 years	224	180	80.3	169	75.6	10	5.8
25 to 34 years	462	375	81.1	363	78.5	12	3.2
35 to 44 years	321	267	83.2	260	80.9	7	2.8
45 to 54 years	307	255	82.8	249	80.9	6	2.3
55 to 64 years	239	167	69.8	164	68.6	3	1.7
65 years and over	220	45	20.4	44	20.2	...	1.1

Note: Data in Table 6 are from the Current Population Survey (CPS) and do not match the estimates in Table 7. See notes and definitions for more details.

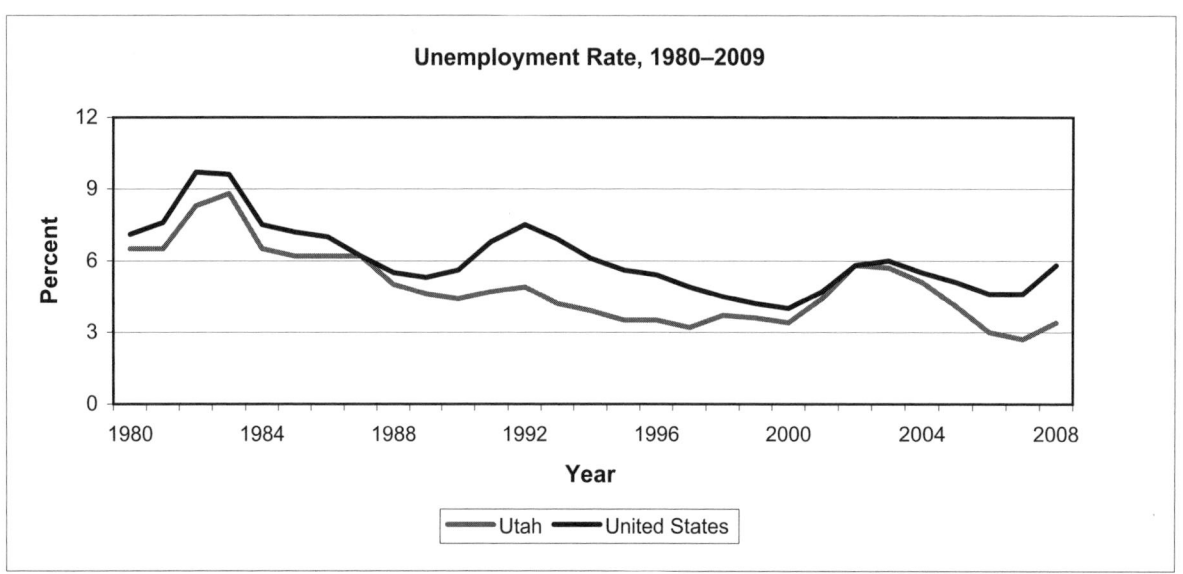

Table UT-7. Employment Status of the Civilian Noninstitutional Population Age 16 Years and Over

(Number, percent.)

Year	Civilian labor force	Civilian participation rate	Employed	Unemployed	Unemployment rate
1998	1 101 973	72.3	1 061 282	40 691	3.7
1999	1 120 591	72.1	1 080 441	40 150	3.6
2000	1 136 036	71.8	1 097 915	38 121	3.4
2001	1 159 433	71.6	1 108 547	50 886	4.4
2002	1 181 691	71.3	1 113 645	68 046	5.8
2003	1 207 436	71.4	1 139 129	68 307	5.7
2004	1 242 004	71.6	1 179 142	62 862	5.1
2005	1 280 038	71.8	1 226 922	53 116	4.1
2006	1 320 504	71.8	1 281 029	39 475	3.0
2007	1 356 550	71.5	1 319 784	36 766	2.7
2008	1 383 743	71.1	1 336 156	47 587	3.4

Table UT-8. Employment and Average Wages by Industry

(Estimates for 2001–2006 are based on the 2002 North American Industry Classification System [NAICS]. Estimates for 2007 are based on the 2007 NAICS.)

Industry	2001	2002	2003	2004	2005	2006	2007
	Number of jobs						
WAGE AND SALARY EMPLOYMENT BY INDUSTRY	1 139 861	1 133 831	1 136 048	1 167 465	1 211 202	1 269 528	1 316 887
Farm Wage and Salary Employment	4 739	3 955	4 757	4 431	4 473	4 476	3 855
Nonfarm Wage and Salary Employment	1 135 122	1 129 876	1 131 291	1 163 034	1 206 729	1 265 052	1 313 032
Private wage and salary employment	927 835	918 167	916 817	945 580	986 491	1 042 267	1 088 430
Forestry, fishing, hunting, and other	1 653	1 650	1 650	1 589	1 648	1 678	1 854
Mining	7 269	6 942	6 745	7 213	8 520	10 156	11 196
Utilities	4 240	4 064	3 897	3 920	3 955	4 056	4 128
Construction	74 402	70 530	70 335	75 499	84 738	98 502	107 065
Manufacturing	122 073	113 584	114 266	117 213	119 520	123 281	127 928
Durable goods manufacturing	84 365	76 524	76 634	78 437	81 035	83 700	87 778
Nondurable goods manufacturing	37 708	37 060	37 632	38 776	38 485	39 581	40 150
Wholesale trade	41 691	40 916	40 643	41 656	44 223	45 686	47 819
Retail trade	134 315	134 729	133 695	136 913	139 526	145 165	152 408
Transportation and warehousing	42 495	40 899	39 976	41 010	43 370	45 268	46 568
Information	32 527	29 980	29 267	29 479	31 103	31 116	29 175
Finance and insurance	49 320	49 868	50 928	50 966	52 364	55 470	57 793
Real estate and rental and leasing	14 670	15 197	15 612	15 983	17 111	18 239	19 116
Professional and technical services	53 000	52 048	53 124	54 150	58 063	64 040	67 838
Management of companies and enterprises	20 175	19 648	16 995	16 872	17 247	17 504	18 470
Administrative and waste services	64 673	61 913	61 418	66 384	70 409	74 579	78 162
Educational services	26 716	28 250	27 601	28 916	30 958	32 721	33 571
Health care and social assistance	85 473	89 406	93 471	97 425	101 420	105 779	110 283
Arts, entertainment, and recreation	17 409	17 697	16 390	16 696	17 240	18 291	19 026
Accommodation and food services	83 177	85 006	85 039	87 129	88 762	92 161	95 838
Other services, except public administration	52 557	55 840	55 765	56 567	56 314	58 575	60 192
Government and government enterprises	207 287	211 709	214 474	217 454	220 238	222 785	224 602
	Dollars						
AVERAGE WAGES AND SALARIES BY INDUSTRY	29 677	30 301	30 901	31 976	33 103	34 789	36 698
Average Farm Wages and Salaries	21 511	30 818	22 557	25 947	29 432	28 802	35 623
Average Nonfarm Wages and Salaries	29 711	30 299	30 936	31 999	33 116	34 810	36 701
Average private wages and salaries	29 758	30 112	30 722	31 799	32 931	34 752	36 674
Forestry, fishing, hunting, and other	20 145	17 615	18 165	18 598	19 721	22 602	25 577
Mining	50 962	49 277	50 779	54 833	57 159	62 446	67 380
Utilities	73 675	83 282	64 154	66 206	70 628	78 385	77 974
Construction	30 441	30 767	30 538	31 086	32 351	35 529	37 659
Manufacturing	36 250	36 613	37 589	38 390	39 574	41 692	44 034
Durable goods manufacturing	38 396	38 612	39 679	40 440	41 461	43 793	46 387
Nondurable goods manufacturing	31 448	32 485	33 332	34 242	35 601	37 250	38 891
Wholesale trade	41 744	42 143	42 720	44 927	46 637	49 831	52 925
Retail trade	20 215	20 603	21 336	22 393	23 008	24 352	25 969
Transportation and warehousing	35 689	36 883	37 785	39 209	39 163	39 251	43 833
Information	41 023	40 623	40 792	42 584	45 723	44 985	47 560
Finance and insurance	39 928	41 254	43 269	45 091	46 789	48 575	50 719
Real estate and rental and leasing	25 259	26 129	26 376	28 260	30 969	33 429	35 360
Professional and technical services	46 361	45 640	47 204	49 302	50 552	52 699	56 158
Management of companies and enterprises	48 914	47 337	51 137	53 595	57 491	62 116	64 237
Administrative and waste services	19 917	20 611	20 599	21 818	22 349	24 018	25 451
Educational services	20 840	21 163	22 038	22 589	23 437	24 202	24 988
Health care and social assistance	28 537	29 275	30 065	31 098	32 225	34 133	35 012
Arts, entertainment, and recreation	18 605	23 233	19 036	19 687	20 172	21 610	22 622
Accommodation and food services	11 897	12 242	12 397	12 789	13 430	14 422	15 106
Other services, except public administration	28 855	30 090	31 672	32 510	32 114	32 751	33 888
Government and government enterprises	29 500	31 109	31 847	32 868	33 949	35 085	36 835

Table UT-9. Employment Characteristics by Family Type

(Number, percent.)

Family type and labor force status	2005		2006		2007	
	Total	Families with own children under 18 years	Total	Families with own children under 18 years	Total	Families with own children under 18 years
TOTAL FAMILIES	593 103	319 338	614 705	326 556	629 901	332 089
FAMILY TYPE AND LABOR FORCE STATUS						
Married Coupled Families	487 182	256 873	503 636	262 538	520 164	270 610
Both husband and wife in labor force	52.6	56.1	52.2	56.0	53.4	57.7
Husband in labor force, wife not in labor force	28.7	38.7	30.0	39.8	29.1	39.0
Wife in labor force, husband not in labor force	5.4	3.4	5.2	2.7	4.6	2.0
Both husband and wife not in labor force	13.2	1.8	12.6	1.6	12.9	1.3
Other Families	105 921	62 465	111 069	64 018	109 737	61 479
Female householder, no husband present	69.3	70.5	69.4	73.0	69.9	74.3
In labor force	53.3	60.8	51.5	59.5	51.2	60.5
Not in labor force	16.0	9.6	18.0	13.5	18.7	13.8
Male householder, no wife present	30.7	29.5	30.6	27.0	30.1	25.7
In labor force	25.8	26.8	26.9	25.3	24.6	23.4
Not in labor force	4.9	2.7	3.7	1.7	5.4	2.2

Table UT-10. School Enrollment and Educational Attainment, 2007

(Number, percent.)

Item	State	U.S.
Enrollment		
Total population 3 years and over	2 492 269	289 295 761
Enrolled in school	839 582	79 329 527
Enrolled in preschool (percent)	6.1	6.2
Enrolled in grades K-12 (percent)	66.7	67.6
Enrolled in college or graduate school (percent)	27.2	26.2
Attainment		
Total population 25 years and over	1 495 759	197 892 369
Less than a high school diploma (percent)	9.8	15.5
High school diploma or more (percent)	90.2	84.5
Bachelor's degree or more (percent)	28.7	27.5
Graduate degree or more (percent)	9.1	10.1

Table UT-11. Educational Indicators

(Number, percent.)

Item	State	U.S.
Public Schools, 2006–2007 (except where noted)		
Number of school districts	103	17 742
Number of schools	1 012	99 639
Number of students	523 386	49 315 842
Student-teacher ratio	22.1	15.5
Expenditures per student (dollars)	$5 706	. . .
Averaged freshman graduation rate, 2005–2006	78.6	. . .
Dropout rate, grades 9–12, 2005–2006	3.3	3.7
Students eligible for free or reduced-price lunch (percent) ...	30.7	41.2
English-language learners (percent)	9.2	5.1
Students with IEP (percent)	11.7	12.7
Private Schools, 2007–2008 (except where noted)		
Number of schools	146	33 740
Number of students	17 551	5 072 451
High school graduates, 2006–2007	1 351	306 605
Student-teacher ratio	10.2	11.1

Table UT-12. Reported Voting and Registration of the Voting-Age Population, November 2008

(Number in thousands, percent.)

Item	Total population	Total citizen population	Registered — Total registered	Registered — Percent registered (total population)	Registered — Percent registered (total citizen population)	Voted — Total voted	Voted — Percent voted (total population)	Voted — Percent voted (total citizen population)
U.S. total	225 499	206 072	146 311	64.9	71.0	131 144	58.2	63.6
State total	1 859	1 768	1 056	56.8	59.7	939	50.5	53.1
Sex								
Male	938	890	495	52.8	55.6	431	45.9	48.4
Female	921	877	561	60.9	63.9	509	55.2	58.0
Race								
White alone	1 761	1 687	1 017	57.8	60.3	909	51.7	53.9
White non-Hispanic alone	1 624	1 597	993	61.1	62.2	888	54.7	55.6
Black alone	26	23	12	. . .	. . .	12	. . .	. . .
Asian alone	27	23	16	. . .	. . .	11	. . .	. . .
Hispanic (of any race)	138	92	24	17.4	26.3	21	15.4	23.3
White alone or in combination ..	1 768	1 694	1 021	57.7	60.3	913	51.7	53.9
Black alone or in combination ...	28	25	15	. . .	. . .	15	. . .	. . .
Asian alone or in combination ...	27	23	16	. . .	. . .	11	. . .	. . .

Table UT-13. Crime

(Number, rate per 100,000.)

Item	State 2007	State 2008	State Percent change	U.S. 2007	U.S. 2008	U.S. Percent change
Population	2 645 330	2 736 424	3.4	301 621 157	304 059 724	0.8
VIOLENT CRIME						
Number	6 210	6 070	-2.3	1 408 337	1 382 012	-1.9
Rate	234.8	221.8	-5.5	466.9	454.5	-2.7
Murder and Nonnegligent Manslaughter						
Number	58	39	-32.8	16 929	16 272	-3.9
Rate	2.2	1.4	-35.0	5.6	5.4	-4.7
Forcible Rape						
Number	908	893	-1.7	90 427	89 000	-1.6
Rate	34.3	32.6	-4.9	30.0	29.3	-2.4
Robbery						
Number	1 420	1 421	0.1	445 125	441 855	-0.7
Rate	53.7	51.9	-3.3	147.6	145.3	-1.5
Aggravated Assault						
Number	3 824	3 717	-2.8	855 856	834 885	-2.5
Rate	144.6	135.8	-6.0	283.8	274.6	-3.2
PROPERTY CRIME						
Number	92 594	91 873	-0.8	9 843 481	9 767 915	-0.8
Rate	3 500.3	3 357.4	-4.1	3 263.5	3 212.5	-1.6
Burglary						
Number	15 541	14 682	-5.5	2 179 140	2 222 196	2.0
Rate	587.5	536.5	-8.7	722.5	730.8	1.2
Larceny-Theft						
Number	68 241	69 996	2.6	6 568 572	6 588 873	0.3
Rate	2 579.7	2 557.9	-0.8	2 177.8	2 167.0	-0.5
Motor Vehicle Theft						
Number	8 812	7 195	-18.3	1 095 769	956 846	-12.7
Rate	333.1	262.9	-21.1	363.3	314.7	-13.4

Table UT-14. State Government Finances, 2007

(Dollars, percent distribution.)

Item	Thousands of dollars	Percent distribution
Total Revenue	15 863 997	X
General revenue	12 463 416	78.6
Intergovernmental revenue	3 076 320	19.4
Taxes	5 889 423	37.1
General sales	1 953 643	12.3
Selective sales	671 394	4.2
License taxes	202 454	1.3
Individual income tax	2 561 001	16.1
Corporate income tax	398 894	2.5
Other taxes	102 037	0.6
Current charges	2 359 410	14.9
Miscellaneous general revenue	1 138 263	7.2
Utility revenue	167	0.0
Liquor store revenue	193 362	1.2
Insurance trust revenue	3 207 052	20.2
Total Expenditure	12 774 196	100.0
Intergovernmental expenditure	2 601 367	20.4
Direct expenditure	10 172 829	79.6
Current operation	7 361 819	57.6
Capital outlay	1 140 723	8.9
Insurance benefits and repayments	1 022 488	8.0
Assistance and subsidies	373 507	2.9
Interest on debt	274 292	2.1
Exhibit: Salaries and wages	2 289 095	17.9
Total Expenditure	12 774 196	100.0
General expenditure	11 610 881	90.9
Intergovernmental expenditure	2 601 367	20.4
Direct expenditure	9 009 514	70.5
Education	5 230 850	40.9
Public welfare	2 113 615	16.5
Hospitals	767 175	6.0
Health	344 488	2.7
Highways	829 412	6.5
Police protection	116 946	0.9
Correction	310 334	2.4
Natural resources	176 761	1.4
Parks and recreation	55 482	0.4
Government administration	750 711	5.9
Interest on general debt	274 292	2.1
Other and unallocable	640 815	5.0
Utility expenditure	109	0.0
Liquor store expenditure	140 718	1.1
Insurance trust expenditure	1 022 488	8.0
Debt at End of Fiscal Year	5 926 589	X
Cash and Security Holdings	31 345 616	X

Table UT-15. State Government Tax Collections, 2008

(Dollars, percent distribution.)

Item	Thousands of dollars	Percent distribution
Total Taxes	5 944 879	X
Sales and gross receipts	2 644 034	44.5
General sales and gross receipts	1 964 119	33.0
Selective sales taxes	679 915	11.4
Alcoholic beverages	39 697	0.7
Insurance premiums	132 454	2.2
Motor fuels	377 261	6.3
Public utilities	30 619	0.5
Tobacco products	62 246	1.0
Other selective sales	37 638	0.6
Licenses	206 923	3.5
Alcoholic beverages	1 934	0.0
Corporation	3 633	0.1
Hunting and fishing	27 417	0.5
Motor vehicle	107 158	1.8
Motor vehicle operators	22 257	0.4
Occupation and business, NEC	38 417	0.6
Other licenses	6 107	0.1
Income taxes	2 987 767	50.3
Individual income	2 593 129	43.6
Corporation net income	394 638	6.6
Other taxes	106 155	1.8
Death and gift	95	0.0
Severance	106 060	1.8

Table UT-16. Agriculture

(Number, acres, and dollars.)

Item	2002		2007		Percent change, 2002–2007
	Number	Percent of total	Number	Percent of total	
Number of farms	15 282		16 700		9.3
Farm Size					
Average size of farm (acres)	768		664		-13.5
Farms by size (number of farms)					
Fewer than 50 acres	8 368	54.8	9 321	55.8	11.4
50 to 499 acres	4 769	31.2	5 178	31.0	8.6
500 acres or more	2 145	14.0	2 201	13.2	2.6
Land (Acres)					
Total land in farms	11 731 228		11 094 700		-5.4
Total cropland	2 067 437	17.6	1 837 904	16.6	-11.1
Total harvested cropland	961 037	8.2	964 702	8.7	0.4
Irrigated land	1 091 011	9.3	1 134 144	10.2	4.0
Value of Sales (Dollars)					
Agricultural products sold ($1,000)	1 115 898		1 415 678		26.9
Average sales per farm	73 020		84 771		16.1
Sales of crops	257 797	23.1	372 396	26.3	44.5
Sales of livestock, poultry, and their products	858 101	76.9	1 043 281	73.7	21.6
Value of Sales (Number of Farms)					
Less than $10,000	10 146	66.4	10 867	65.1	7.1
$10,000 to $99,999	3 549	23.2	4 217	25.3	18.8
$100,000 to $999,999	1 430	9.4	1 400	8.4	-2.1
$1,000,000 or more	157	1.0	216	1.3	37.6
Farms by Type of Organization (Number of Farms)					
Family	13 108	85.8	13 614	81.5	3.9
Partnership	1 315	8.6	1 645	9.9	25.1
Corporation	630	4.1	1 014	6.1	61.0
Other: cooperative, estate or trust, institutional, etc	229	1.5	427	2.6	86.5
Value of Land and Buildings (Dollars)					
Estimated market value of land and buildings ($1,000)	13 857 925		8 965 857		-35.3
Land and buildings average value per farm	829 816		586 310		-29.3
Average value per acre	1 249		756		-39.5
Government Payments					
Number of farms receiving government payments	2 987	19.5	2 960	17.7	-0.9
Payments (thousands of dollars)	26 669		22 759		-14.7
Average payment per farm	8 928		7 689		-13.9
Farm Operator Characteristics					
Farm operators whose principal occupation is farming	7 447	48.7	6 340	38.0	-14.9
Farm operators whose principal occupation is other	7 835	51.3	10 360	62.0	32.2
Average age principal operator (years)	55.2		57.4		4.0

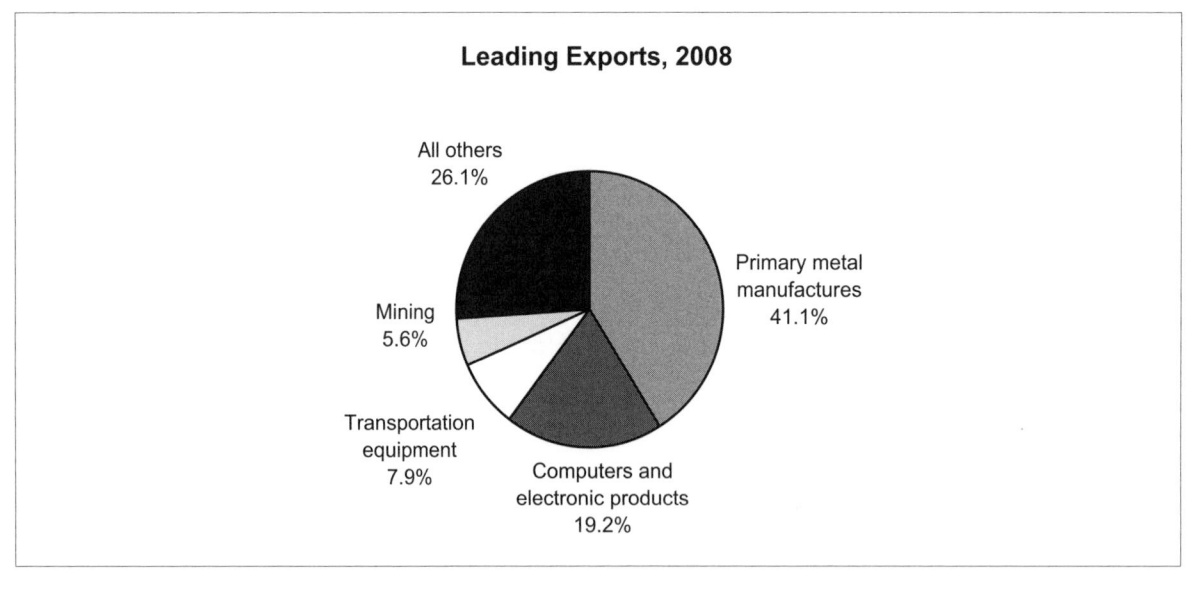

Leading Exports, 2008

All others 26.1%

Primary metal manufactures 41.1%

Mining 5.6%

Transportation equipment 7.9%

Computers and electronic products 19.2%

VERMONT

Facts and Figures

Location: Northeastern United States; bordered on the N by Canada (Quebec), on the E by New Hampshire, on the S by Massachusetts, and on the W by New York

Area: 9,614 sq. mi. (24,901 sq. km.); rank—45th

Population: 621,270 (2008 est.); rank—49th

Principal Cities: capital—Montpelier; largest—Burlington

Statehood: March 4, 1791; the 14th state

U.S. Congress: 2 senators, 1 representative

State Motto: Freedom and Unity

State Song: "These Green Mountains"

State Nickname: The Green Mountain State

Abbreviations: VT; Vt.

State Symbols: flower—red clover; tree—sugar maple; bird—hermit thrush

At a Glance

- With an increase in population of 2 percent, Vermont ranked 43rd among the states in growth from 2000 to 2008.
- An estimated 4,693 marriages took place in Vermont in 2008, compared to 2,225 divorces.
- The 2007 home ownership rate in Vermont was 73.7 percent, giving it a ranking of 11th along with Iowa.
- Vermont's median household income in 2007 was $49,907, 21st among the states.
- In Vermont, 10.1 percent of the population lived below the poverty level in 2007, ranking it 39th.
- In 2006-07, 10.7 percent of Vermonters did not have health insurance, compared to 15.5 percent of the total U.S. population.
- In 2007, 4 percent of Vermonters were unemployed, compared to 4.6 percent nationwide.
- Vermont ranked 6th in the nation with 33.6 percent of its population 25 years old and over having a bachelor's degree in 2007; its ranking was the same as Virginia's.
- Vermont's violent crime rate in 2007 was 124.3 per 100,000 population, compared to 466.9 for the entire nation.
- Vermont had one physician for every 227 people in 2007, compared to one physician for every 325 people nationwide.
- In the 2008 election, 66.7 percent of Vermont's eligible voters voted, compared to 61.7 percent of eligible voters nationwide.
- Vermont ranked 5th among the states receiving federal aid in 2007, with $2,491 per capita.
- Vermont's gross domestic product was $25 billion in 2007; it ranked 50th among the states.
- With $3.7 billion in exports in 2007, Vermont ranked 41st in exports.
- Vermonters consumed 163.7 billion Btu's of energy in 2006; the state ranked 50th in total consumption.
- In 2007, Vermont exported $47 million worth of agricultural products, less than 1 percent of the U.S. total.

Table VT-1. Population by Sex, Age, Race, and Hispanic Origin

(Number, percent.)

Sex, age, race, and Hispanic origin	1990	2000	2008	Average annual percent change, 2000–2008
Total Population	562 758	608 827	621 270	0.3
Percent of total U.S. population	0.2	0.2	0.2	X
Sex				
Male	275 492	298 337	305 723	0.3
Female	287 266	310 490	315 547	0.2
Age				
Under 5 years	41 261	33 989	32 635	-0.5
5 to 19 years	121 478	132 268	115 806	-1.6
20 to 64 years	333 856	365 060	386 180	0.7
65 years and over	66 163	77 510	86 649	1.4
Median age (years)	32.9	37.7	41.2	X
Race and Hispanic Origin[1]				
One race				
White	555 088	589 208	598 959	0.2
Black	1 951	3 063	5 378	7.3
American Indian and Alaskan Native	1 696	2 420	2 437	0.1
Asian[2]	3 215	5 217	7 055	3.8
Native Hawaiian and Other Pacific Islander	X	141	203	4.7
Two or more races	X	7 335	7 238	-0.2
Hispanic (of any race)	3 661	5 504	8 588	5.7

[1]Data on race in 2000 and 2008 are not comparable to 1990. Individuals could only report one race in the 1990 census but could report one or more races on the 2000 census.
[2]Data in 1990 refer to Asian and Pacific Islanders.

Table VT-2. Marital Status

(Number, percent distribution.)

Sex and marital status	1990	2000	2007
Males, 15 Years and Over	213 331	236 517	251 449
Never married	31.0	29.7	32.7
Now married, except separated	57.5	57.1	52.5
Separated	1.5	1.2	1.2
Widowed	2.4	2.4	2.5
Divorced	7.6	9.6	11.0
Females, 15 Years and Over	228 387	251 764	265 109
Never married	24.3	23.9	25.9
Now married, except separated	53.6	53.3	49.9
Separated	1.8	1.4	1.6
Widowed	11.0	10.0	9.3
Divorced	9.3	11.5	13.3

Table VT-3. Households and Housing Characteristics

(Number, percent, and dollars.)

Item	1990	2000	2007	Average annual percent change, 2000–2007
Total Households	210 650	240 634	252 580	0.7
Family households	144 895	157 763	163 979	0.6
Married-couple family	118 905	126 413	126 044	0.0
Other family	25 990	31 350	37 935	2.8
Male householder, no wife present	6 630	9 078	12 894	5.1
Female householder, no husband present	19 360	22 272	25 041	1.7
Nonfamily households	65 755	82 871	88 601	1.0
Householder living alone	49 366	63 112	69 702	1.4
Householder not living alone	16 389	19 759	18 899	-0.6
Housing Characteristics				
Total housing units	271 214	294 382	311 420	0.8
Occupied housing units	210 650	240 634	252 580	0.7
Owner-occupied	145 368	169 784	183 920	1.1
Renter-occupied	65 282	70 850	68 660	-0.4
Average size	2.57	2.44	2.38	X
Financial Characteristics				
Median gross rent of renter-occupied housing units (dollars)	446	553	756	4.6
Median monthly owner costs for housing units with a mortgage (dollars)	719	1 021	1 391	4.5
Median value of owner-occupied housing units (dollars)	95 600	111 500	205 400	9.1

Table VT-4. Median Income and Poverty Status, 2007

(Number, percent.)

Characteristic	State		U.S.	
	Number	Percent	Number	Percent
Median Income				
Households (dollars)	49 907	0.0	50 740	X
Families (dollars)	61 561	0.0	61 173	X
Below Poverty Level				
Sex				
Male	25 740	8.7	16 576 071	11.5
Female	34 849	11.4	21 476 176	14.3
Age				
Under 18 years	15 907	12.4	13 097 100	18.0
Related children under 18 years	14 871	11.7	12 728 964	17.6
18 to 64 years	38 621	9.9	21 495 507	11.6
65 years and over	6 061	7.5	3 459 640	9.5

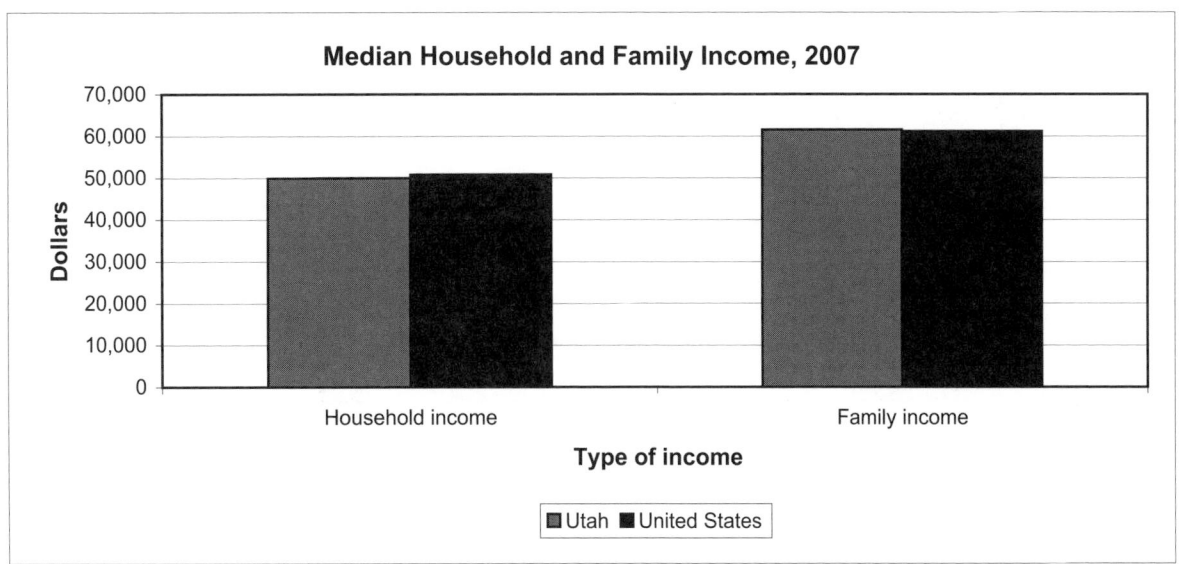

Table VT-5. Health Insurance Coverage Status for All Persons and Children Under 18 Years of Age

(Number, percent.)

Item	2000	2001	2002	2003	2004	2005	2006	2007
ALL PERSONS	601	607	619	611	617	622	620	614
Covered by Private or Government Health Insurance								
Number	552	551	555	555	552	550	557	545
Percent	91.7	90.9	89.7	90.8	89.5	88.5	89.8	88.8
Not Covered								
Number	50	55	64	56	65	72	63	69
Percent	8.3	9.1	10.3	9.2	10.5	11.5	10.2	11.2
Percent in the U.S. not covered	13.7	14.1	14.7	15.1	14.9	15.3	15.8	15.3
CHILDREN UNDER 18 YEARS OF AGE	140	127	138	138	134	133	133	129
Covered by Private or Government Health Insurance								
Number	134	123	130	133	128	126	122	117
Percent	96.0	96.9	94.3	96.1	95.3	94.7	92.0	90.6
Not Covered								
Number	6	4	8	5	6	7	11	12
Percent	4.0	3.1	5.7	3.9	4.7	5.3	8.0	9.4
Percent in the U.S. not covered	11.6	11.3	11.2	11.0	10.5	10.9	11.7	11.0

Table VT-6. Employment Status by Demographic Group, Preliminary 2008

(Number, percent.)

Characteristic	Civilian noninstitutional population	Civilian labor force		Employment		Unemployed	
		Number	Percent of population	Number	Percent of population	Number	Unemployment rate
TOTAL	505	354	70.1	336	66.6	17	4.9
Sex							
Men	246	183	74.0	174	70.7	9	5.0
Women	258	170	66.0	162	62.8	8	4.9
Race, Sex, and Hispanic Origin							
White	485	340	70.2	324	66.7	17	4.9
Men	236	176	74.3	167	70.7	9	4.9
Women	249	165	66.2	157	63.0	8	4.8
Black or African American	...	...	...	...	...	...	...
Men	...	...	...	...	...	...	...
Women	...	...	...	...	...	...	...
Hispanic	...	...	...	...	...	...	...
Men	...	...	...	...	...	...	...
Women	...	...	...	...	...	...	...
Age							
16 to 19 years	33	17	51.6	15	44.4	2	13.8
20 to 24 years	43	33	77.0	30	69.7	3	9.5
25 to 34 years	75	64	85.0	60	80.2	4	5.7
35 to 44 years	83	72	87.6	70	84.9	2	3.0
45 to 54 years	101	87	86.2	84	82.9	3	3.8
55 to 64 years	89	65	73.4	63	70.9	2	3.4
65 years and over	82	16	19.3	15	18.5	1	3.8

Note: Data in Table 6 are from the Current Population Survey (CPS) and do not match the estimates in Table 7. See notes and definitions for more details.

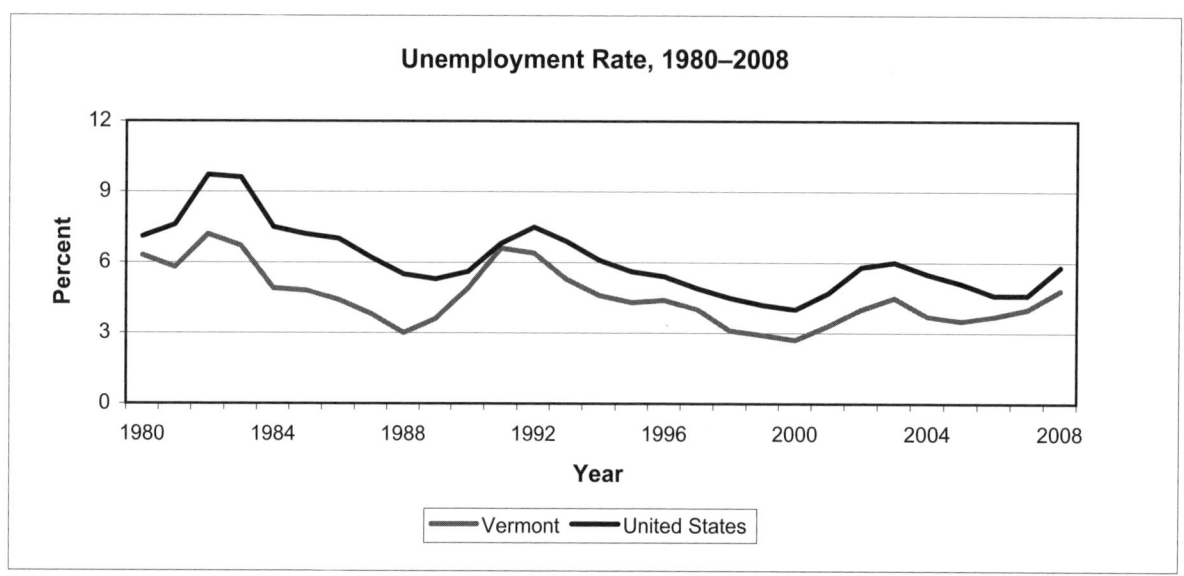

Table VT-7. Employment Status of the Civilian Noninstitutional Population Age 16 Years and Over

(Number, percent.)

Year	Civilian labor force	Civilian participation rate	Employed	Unemployed	Unemployment rate
1998	331 859	71.6	321 608	10 251	3.1
1999	335 415	71.6	325 581	9 834	2.9
2000	335 798	70.8	326 742	9 056	2.7
2001	341 234	71.3	330 099	11 135	3.3
2002	345 631	71.5	331 763	13 868	4.0
2003	346 770	71.1	331 292	15 478	4.5
2004	347 068	70.6	334 188	12 880	3.7
2005	349 093	70.5	336 849	12 244	3.5
2006	355 463	71.3	342 204	13 259	3.7
2007	353 992	70.6	339 945	14 047	4.0
2008	355 432	70.6	338 517	16 915	4.8

Table VT-8. Employment and Average Wages by Industry

(Estimates for 2001–2006 are based on the 2002 North American Industry Classification System [NAICS]. Estimates for 2007 are based on the 2007 NAICS.)

Industry	2001	2002	2003	2004	2005	2006	2007
	Number of jobs						
WAGE AND SALARY EMPLOYMENT BY INDUSTRY	319 611	319 400	318 386	321 867	323 744	326 118	326 442
Farm Wage and Salary Employment	2 829	2 948	3 031	2 526	2 439	2 263	2 196
Nonfarm Wage and Salary Employment	316 782	316 452	315 355	319 341	321 305	323 855	324 246
Private wage and salary employment	263 684	262 599	260 776	264 282	265 775	267 841	267 982
Forestry, fishing, hunting, and other	1 175	1 180	1 117	1 087	1 073	1 080	1 046
Mining	946	842	786	773	705	733	731
Utilities	1 660	1 718	1 732	1 719	1 709	1 731	1 743
Construction	15 823	15 476	16 007	17 309	17 487	18 001	17 430
Manufacturing	45 844	41 008	37 780	37 261	37 076	36 438	36 206
Durable goods manufacturing	33 668	29 592	26 927	26 588	26 619	26 375	26 308
Nondurable goods manufacturing	12 176	11 416	10 853	10 673	10 457	10 063	9 898
Wholesale trade	10 182	10 194	10 426	10 356	10 296	10 530	10 465
Retail trade	41 130	41 317	40 696	41 266	41 691	41 713	41 468
Transportation and warehousing	7 077	7 127	6 949	7 137	7 319	7 233	7 190
Information	6 798	D	6 509	6 382	6 258	6 080	5 949
Finance and insurance	10 256	10 186	10 273	10 110	9 981	10 075	9 947
Real estate and rental and leasing	3 155	3 178	3 204	3 363	3 368	3 378	3 419
Professional and technical services	13 255	13 114	13 057	13 375	13 563	14 002	14 005
Management of companies and enterprises	314	300	280	307	308	304	317
Administrative and waste services	8 002	7 758	7 913	8 406	8 765	8 708	8 749
Educational services	13 481	14 486	14 160	14 073	13 953	14 134	14 531
Health care and social assistance	37 105	40 052	42 020	43 104	44 274	45 359	46 968
Arts, entertainment, and recreation	3 630	3 859	3 910	3 927	4 067	4 118	4 141
Accommodation and food services	29 819	29 716	29 404	29 709	29 524	29 775	29 243
Other services, except public administration	14 032	D	14 553	14 618	14 358	14 449	14 434
Government and government enterprises	53 098	53 853	54 579	55 059	55 530	56 014	56 264
	Dollars						
AVERAGE WAGES AND SALARIES BY INDUSTRY	29 428	30 136	31 249	32 508	33 442	34 754	36 047
Average Farm Wages and Salaries	18 603	24 401	20 261	24 104	19 806	24 761	22 115
Average Nonfarm Wages and Salaries	29 524	30 190	31 355	32 575	33 545	34 824	36 141
Average private wages and salaries	29 451	29 942	30 947	32 122	33 038	34 319	35 613
Forestry, fishing, hunting, and other	23 706	24 308	25 733	26 361	26 798	27 730	28 809
Mining	34 997	38 929	41 141	39 762	41 651	46 868	48 286
Utilities	64 584	70 244	68 715	78 693	80 865	80 463	87 379
Construction	32 761	32 811	33 404	34 783	36 316	37 978	39 999
Manufacturing	41 378	42 771	44 169	45 274	46 299	47 715	49 164
Durable goods manufacturing	44 373	46 217	47 670	48 886	49 779	51 235	53 007
Nondurable goods manufacturing	33 094	33 838	35 484	36 276	37 441	38 491	38 948
Wholesale trade	41 071	42 499	44 193	44 662	45 854	47 165	48 042
Retail trade	20 899	21 611	22 438	23 350	23 753	24 293	24 938
Transportation and warehousing	30 772	31 169	31 919	33 207	33 427	34 639	35 756
Information	35 176	D	37 217	38 843	39 490	40 998	43 001
Finance and insurance	44 538	46 267	50 007	52 080	54 871	56 111	61 950
Real estate and rental and leasing	25 745	26 969	27 656	29 284	29 655	29 886	31 336
Professional and technical services	43 017	43 625	47 027	48 715	51 960	56 896	57 070
Management of companies and enterprises	47 003	50 673	55 996	57 844	63 068	64 395	66 741
Administrative and waste services	23 040	23 828	23 641	26 392	25 413	26 560	28 641
Educational services	21 774	21 872	23 067	24 977	26 146	27 163	27 898
Health care and social assistance	28 577	29 232	29 774	30 742	31 833	33 441	34 622
Arts, entertainment, and recreation	16 907	16 606	17 563	19 662	19 545	20 677	21 217
Accommodation and food services	15 040	15 643	16 277	17 063	17 436	17 910	18 793
Other services, except public administration	19 715	D	20 938	21 729	21 990	22 375	23 257
Government and government enterprises	29 888	31 396	33 303	34 748	35 971	37 240	38 657

Table VT-9. Employment Characteristics by Family Type

(Number, percent.)

Family type and labor force status	2005		2006		2007	
	Total	Families with own children under 18 years	Total	Families with own children under 18 years	Total	Families with own children under 18 years
TOTAL FAMILIES	156 832	70 287	162 721	74 020	163 979	75 340
FAMILY TYPE AND LABOR FORCE STATUS						
Married Coupled Families	120 684	46 838	127 054	51 220	126 044	49 804
Both husband and wife in labor force	60.6	74.2	60.2	75.4	62.9	79.3
Husband in labor force, wife not in labor force	16.8	20.6	16.8	20.2	14.9	15.7
Wife in labor force, husband not in labor force	7.4	3.5	7.8	3.0	6.7	2.6
Both husband and wife not in labor force	15.2	1.8	15.2	1.3	15.5	2.4
Other Families	36 148	23 449	35 667	22 800	37 935	25 536
Female householder, no husband present	68.1	67.1	71.9	76.2	66.0	69.2
In labor force	49.2	54.9	52.6	61.4	51.4	57.7
Not in labor force	19.0	12.2	19.3	14.8	14.6	11.5
Male householder, no wife present	31.9	32.9	28.1	23.8	34.0	30.8
In labor force	27.6	30.9	22.7	21.8	28.5	27.9
Not in labor force	4.2	2.0	5.4	2.0	5.5	2.9

Table VT-10. School Enrollment and Educational Attainment, 2007

(Number, percent.)

Item	State	U.S.
Enrollment		
Total population 3 years and over	603 450	289 295 761
Enrolled in school	154 373	79 329 527
Enrolled in preschool (percent)	6.2	6.2
Enrolled in grades K-12 (percent)	64.3	67.6
Enrolled in college or graduate school (percent)	29.5	26.2
Attainment		
Total population 25 years and over	427 339	197 892 369
Less than a high school diploma (percent)	9.7	15.5
High school diploma or more (percent)	90.3	84.5
Bachelor's degree or more (percent)	33.6	27.5
Graduate degree or more (percent)	12.9	10.1

Table VT-11. Educational Indicators

(Number, percent.)

Item	State	U.S.
Public Schools, 2006–2007 (except where noted)		
Number of school districts	358	17 742
Number of schools	330	99 639
Number of students	95 399	49 315 842
Student-teacher ratio	10.8	15.5
Expenditures per student (dollars)	$13 629	. . .
Averaged freshman graduation rate, 2005–2006	82.3	. . .
Dropout rate, grades 9–12, 2005–2006	. . .	3.7
Students eligible for free or reduced-price lunch (percent) ...	25.6	41.2
English-language learners (percent)	1.9	5.1
Students with IEP (percent)	12.4	12.7
Private Schools, 2007–2008 (except where noted)		
Number of schools	150	33 740
Number of students	11 712	5 072 451
High school graduates, 2006–2007	1 759	306 605
Student-teacher ratio	7.5	11.1

Table VT-12. Reported Voting and Registration of the Voting-Age Population, November 2008

(Number in thousands, percent.)

Item	Total population	Total citizen population	Registered — Total registered	Registered — Percent registered (total population)	Registered — Percent registered (total citizen population)	Voted — Total voted	Voted — Percent voted (total population)	Voted — Percent voted (total citizen population)
U.S. total	225 499	206 072	146 311	64.9	71.0	131 144	58.2	63.6
State total	487	476	345	70.9	72.5	308	63.2	64.7
Sex								
Male	238	234	164	68.8	70.2	146	61.1	62.3
Female	249	242	181	72.8	74.7	162	65.2	66.9
Race								
White alone	471	464	335	71.1	72.3	300	63.6	64.7
White non-Hispanic alone	467	460	333	71.4	72.4	298	63.9	64.7
Black alone	4	4	3	. . .	. . .	3	. . .	. . .
Asian alone	4	2	. . .	. . .	. . .	. . .	. . .	. . .
Hispanic (of any race)	5	3	2	. . .	. . .	2	. . .	. . .
White alone or in combination	478	470	341	71.3	72.5	304	63.6	64.6
Black alone or in combination	4	4	3	. . .	. . .	3	. . .	. . .
Asian alone or in combination	5	2	1	. . .	. . .	1	. . .	. . .

Table VT-13. Crime

(Number, rate per 100,000.)

Item	State 2007	State 2008	State Percent change	U.S. 2007	U.S. 2008	U.S. Percent change
Population	621 254	621 270	0.0	301 621 157	304 059 724	0.8
VIOLENT CRIME						
Number	772	844	9.3	1 408 337	1 382 012	-1.9
Rate	124.3	135.9	9.3	466.9	454.5	-2.7
Murder and Nonnegligent Manslaughter						
Number	12	17	41.7	16 929	16 272	-3.9
Rate	1.9	2.7	41.7	5.6	5.4	-4.7
Forcible Rape						
Number	123	127	3.3	90 427	89 000	-1.6
Rate	19.8	20.4	3.2	30.0	29.3	-2.4
Robbery						
Number	80	89	11.3	445 125	441 855	-0.7
Rate	12.9	14.3	11.2	147.6	145.3	-1.5
Aggravated Assault						
Number	557	611	9.7	855 856	834 885	-2.5
Rate	89.7	98.3	9.7	283.8	274.6	-3.2
PROPERTY CRIME						
Number	14 430	15 771	9.3	9 843 481	9 767 915	-0.8
Rate	2 322.7	2 538.5	9.3	3 263.5	3 212.5	-1.6
Burglary						
Number	3 106	3 462	11.5	2 179 140	2 222 196	2.0
Rate	500.0	557.2	11.5	722.5	730.8	1.2
Larceny-Theft						
Number	10 683	11 724	9.7	6 568 572	6 588 873	0.3
Rate	1 719.6	1 887.1	9.7	2 177.8	2 167.0	-0.5
Motor Vehicle Theft						
Number	641	585	-8.7	1 095 769	956 846	-12.7
Rate	103.2	94.2	-8.7	363.3	314.7	-13.4

Table VT-14. State Government Finances, 2007

(Dollars, percent distribution.)

Item	Thousands of dollars	Percent distribution
Total Revenue	5 437 494	X
General revenue	4 785 531	88.0
Intergovernmental revenue	1 379 970	25.4
Taxes	2 558 806	47.1
General sales	334 413	6.2
Selective sales	510 564	9.4
License taxes	116 683	2.1
Individual income tax	581 189	10.7
Corporate income tax	83 362	1.5
Other taxes	932 595	17.2
Current charges	457 732	8.4
Miscellaneous general revenue	389 023	7.2
Utility revenue	0	0.0
Liquor store revenue	41 123	0.8
Insurance trust revenue	610 840	11.2
Total Expenditure	4 993 860	100.0
Intergovernmental expenditure	1 415 922	28.4
Direct expenditure	3 577 938	71.6
Current operation	2 761 752	55.3
Capital outlay	294 121	5.9
Insurance benefits and repayments	240 923	4.8
Assistance and subsidies	121 286	2.4
Interest on debt	159 856	3.2
Exhibit: Salaries and wages	703 493	14.1
Total Expenditure	4 993 860	100.0
General expenditure	4 686 834	93.9
Intergovernmental expenditure	1 415 922	28.4
Direct expenditure	3 270 912	65.5
Education	2 153 209	43.1
Public welfare	1 202 700	24.1
Hospitals	18 162	0.4
Health	149 948	3.0
Highways	332 316	6.7
Police protection	77 135	1.5
Correction	114 748	2.3
Natural resources	70 337	1.4
Parks and recreation	13 796	0.3
Government administration	157 963	3.2
Interest on general debt	159 856	3.2
Other and unallocable	236 664	4.7
Utility expenditure	24 677	0.5
Liquor store expenditure	41 426	0.8
Insurance trust expenditure	240 923	4.8
Debt at End of Fiscal Year	3 052 469	X
Cash and Security Holdings	7 242 759	X

Table VT-15. State Government Tax Collections, 2008

(Dollars, percent distribution.)

Item	Thousands of dollars	Percent distribution
Total Taxes	2 544 163	X
Property taxes	810 051	31.8
Sales and gross receipts	855 261	33.6
General sales and gross receipts	338 941	13.3
Selective sales taxes	516 320	20.3
Alcoholic beverages	19 812	0.8
Insurance premiums	57 267	2.3
Motor fuels	91 535	3.6
Public utilities	10 532	0.4
Tobacco products	59 247	2.3
Other selective sales	277 927	10.9
Licenses	124 702	4.9
Alcoholic beverages	382	0.0
Corporation	4 887	0.2
Hunting and fishing	6 166	0.2
Motor vehicle	79 077	3.1
Motor vehicle operators	5 040	0.2
Occupation and business, NEC	27 221	1.1
Other licenses	1 929	0.1
Income taxes	707 802	27.8
Individual income	623 019	24.5
Corporation net income	84 783	3.3
Other taxes	46 347	1.8
Death and gift	15 688	0.6
Documentary and stock transfer	26 972	1.1
Other	3 687	0.1

Table VT-16. Agriculture

(Number, acres, and dollars.)

Item	2002 Number	2002 Percent of total	2007 Number	2007 Percent of total	Percent change, 2002–2007
Number of farms	6 571		6 984		6.3
Farm Size					
Average size of farm (acres)	189		177		-6.3
Farms by size (number of farms)					
Fewer than 50 acres	2 215	33.7	2 497	35.8	12.7
50 to 499 acres	3 802	57.9	3 953	56.6	4.0
500 acres or more	554	8.4	534	7.6	-3.6
Land (Acres)					
Total land in farms	1 244 909		1 233 313		-0.9
Total cropland	567 509	45.6	516 924	41.9	-8.9
Total harvested cropland	454 699	36.5	433 074	35.1	-4.8
Irrigated land	2 335	0.2	2 295	0.2	-1.7
Value of Sales (Dollars)					
Agricultural products sold ($1,000)	473 065		673 713		42.4
Average sales per farm	71 993		96 465		34.0
Sales of crops	71 583	15.1	99 262	14.7	38.7
Sales of livestock, poultry, and their products	401 482	84.9	574 451	85.3	43.1
Value of Sales (Number of Farms)					
Less than $10,000	3 982	60.6	4 117	58.9	3.4
$10,000 to $99,999	1 422	21.6	1 789	25.6	25.8
$100,000 to $999,999	1 090	16.6	950	13.6	-12.8
$1,000,000 or more	77	1.2	128	1.8	66.2
Farms by Type of Organization (Number of Farms)					
Family	5 716	87.0	5 848	83.7	2.3
Partnership	483	7.4	608	8.7	25.9
Corporation	281	4.3	400	5.7	42.3
Other: cooperative, estate or trust, institutional, etc	91	1.4	128	1.8	40.7
Value of Land and Buildings (Dollars)					
Estimated market value of land and buildings ($1,000)	3 580 584		2 542 909		-29.0
Land and buildings average value per farm	512 684		386 695		-24.6
Average value per acre	2 903		2 051		-29.3
Government Payments					
Number of farms receiving government payments	1 296	19.7	1 351	19.3	4.2
Payments (thousands of dollars)	24 377		6 773		-72.2
Average payment per farm	18 809		5 014		-73.3
Farm Operator Characteristics					
Farm operators whose principal occupation is farming	3 486	53.1	3 461	49.6	-0.7
Farm operators whose principal occupation is other	3 085	46.9	3 523	50.4	14.2
Average age principal operator (years)	53.9		56.5		4.8

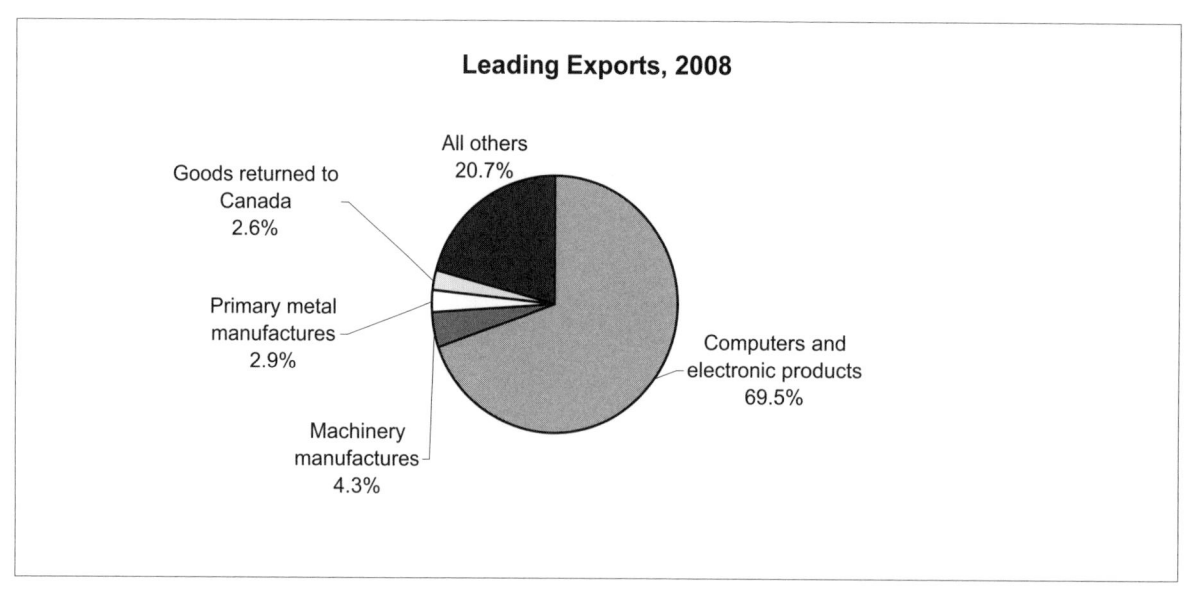

Leading Exports, 2008

- All others 20.7%
- Goods returned to Canada 2.6%
- Primary metal manufactures 2.9%
- Machinery manufactures 4.3%
- Computers and electronic products 69.5%

Facts and Figures

Location: Eastern United States; bordered on the N and NE by Maryland and the District of Columbia, on the E by the Atlantic Ocean, on the S by North Carolina and Tennessee, and on the W by Kentucky and West Virginia

Area: 42,774 sq. mi. (110,785 sq. km.); rank—35th

Population: 7,769,089 (2008 est.); rank—12th

Principal Cities: capital—Richmond; largest—Virginia Beach

Statehood: June 25, 1788; 10th state

U.S. Congress: 2 senators, 11 representatives

State Motto: *Sic semper tyrannis* ("Thus always to tyrants")

State Song: "Carry Me Back to Old Virginia"; the Virginia General Assembly (legislature) is in the process of selecting a new state song

State Nickname: The Old Dominion State

Abbreviations: VA; Va.

State Symbols: flower—flowering dogwood; tree—flowering dogwood; bird—cardinal

At a Glance

- With an increase in population of 9.7 percent, Virginia ranked 14th among the states in growth from 2000 to 2008.
- An estimated 56,882 marriages took place in Virginia in 2008, compared to 29,713 divorces.
- The 2007 home ownership rate in Virginia was 71.5 percent; its ranking of 20th was tied with that of Louisiana and New Mexico.
- Virginia's median household income in 2007 was $59,562, 9th among the states.
- In Virginia, 9.9 percent of the population lived below the poverty level in 2007, ranking it 40th along with Massachusetts.
- In 2006-07, 14.1 percent of Virginians did not have health insurance, compared to 15.5 percent of the total U.S. population.
- In 2007, 3.1 percent of Virginians were unemployed, compared to 4.6 percent nationwide.
- Virginia ranked 6th in the nation with 33.6 percent of its population 25 years old and over having a bachelor's degree in 2007; its ranking was the same as Vermont's.
- Virginia's violent crime rate in 2007 was 269.7 per 100,000 population, compared to 466.9 for the entire nation.
- Virginia had one physician for every 319 people in 2007, compared to one physician for every 325 people nationwide.
- In the 2008 election, 67.7 percent of Virginia's eligible voters voted, compared to 61.7 percent of eligible voters nationwide.
- Virginia ranked 49th among the states receiving federal aid in 2007, with $932 per capita.
- Virginia's gross domestic product was $383 billion in 2007; it ranked 11th among the states.
- With $16.9 billion in exports in 2007, Virginia ranked 41st in exports.
- Virginians consumed 2.54 trillion Btu's of energy in 2006; the state ranked 14th in total consumption.
- In 2007, Virginia exported $622 million worth of agricultural products, less than 1 percent of the U.S. total.

Table VA-1. Population by Sex, Age, Race, and Hispanic Origin

(Number, percent.)

Sex, age, race, and Hispanic origin	1990	2000	2008	Average annual percent change, 2000–2008
Total Population	6 187 358	7 078 515	7 769 089	1.2
Percent of total U.S. population	2.5	2.5	2.6	X
Sex				
Male	3 033 974	3 471 895	3 817 042	1.2
Female	3 153 384	3 606 620	3 952 047	1.1
Age				
Under 5 years	443 155	461 982	522 672	1.6
5 to 19 years	1 261 448	1 475 104	1 523 569	0.4
20 to 64 years	3 818 285	4 349 096	4 782 271	1.2
65 years and over	664 470	792 333	940 577	2.2
Median age (years)	32.5	35.7	37.1	X
Race and Hispanic Origin[1]				
One race				
White	4 791 739	5 120 110	5 673 913	1.3
Black	1 162 994	1 390 293	1 546 444	1.3
American Indian and Alaskan Native	15 282	21 172	28 595	3.8
Asian[2]	159 053	261 025	378 226	4.7
Native Hawaiian and Other Pacific Islander	X	3 946	6 823	7.1
Two or more races	X	143 069	135 088	-0.7
Hispanic (of any race)	160 288	329 540	531 396	6.2

[1]Data on race in 2000 and 2008 are not comparable to 1990. Individuals could only report one race in the 1990 census but could report one or more races on the 2000 census.
[2]Data in 1990 refer to Asian and Pacific Islanders.

Table VA-2. Marital Status

(Number, percent distribution.)

Sex and marital status	1990	2000	2007
Males, 15 Years and Over	2 386 768	2 724 334	3 018 129
Never married	30.7	29.1	33.2
Now married, except separated	57.8	58.2	54.1
Separated	2.8	2.6	2.3
Widowed	2.2	2.3	2.4
Divorced	6.5	7.9	8.1
Females, 15 Years and Over	2 534 543	2 899 294	3 190 916
Never married	23.6	23.5	27.2
Now married, except separated	53.6	53.4	49.5
Separated	3.4	3.2	2.9
Widowed	11.1	9.9	9.5
Divorced	8.3	10.0	10.9

Table VA-3. Households and Housing Characteristics

(Number, percent, and dollars.)

Item	1990	2000	2007	Average annual percent change, 2000–2007
Total Households	2 291 830	2 699 173	2 932 234	1.2
Family households	1 629 490	1 847 796	1 964 204	0.9
Married-couple family	1 302 219	1 426 044	1 483 385	0.6
Other family	327 271	421 752	480 819	1.9
Male householder, no wife present	72 165	101 462	121 474	2.6
Female householder, no husband present	255 106	320 290	359 345	1.7
Nonfamily households	662 340	851 377	968 030	1.9
Householder living alone	523 770	676 907	798 091	2.4
Householder not living alone	138 570	174 470	169 939	-0.4
Housing Characteristics				
Total housing units	2 496 334	2 904 192	3 273 206	1.7
Occupied housing units	2 291 830	2 699 173	2 932 234	1.2
Owner-occupied	1 519 521	1 837 939	2 038 098	1.5
Renter-occupied	772 309	861 234	894 136	0.5
Average size	2.61	2.54	2.55	X
Financial Characteristics				
Median gross rent of renter-occupied housing units (dollars)	495	650	892	4.6
Median monthly owner costs for housing units with a mortgage (dollars)	831	1 144	1 655	5.4
Median value of owner-occupied housing units (dollars)	90 400	125 400	262 100	11.1

Table VA-4. Median Income and Poverty Status, 2007

(Number, percent.)

Characteristic	State		U.S.	
	Number	Percent	Number	Percent
Median Income				
Households (dollars)	59 562	X	50 740	X
Families (dollars)	70 894	X	61 173	X
Below Poverty Level				
Sex				
Male	309 591	8.5	16 576 071	11.5
Female	433 089	11.3	21 476 176	14.3
Age				
Under 18 years	233 841	13.0	13 097 100	18.0
Related children under 18 years	226 656	12.7	12 728 964	17.6
18 to 64 years	428 831	8.9	21 495 507	11.6
65 years and over	80 008	9.2	3 459 640	9.5

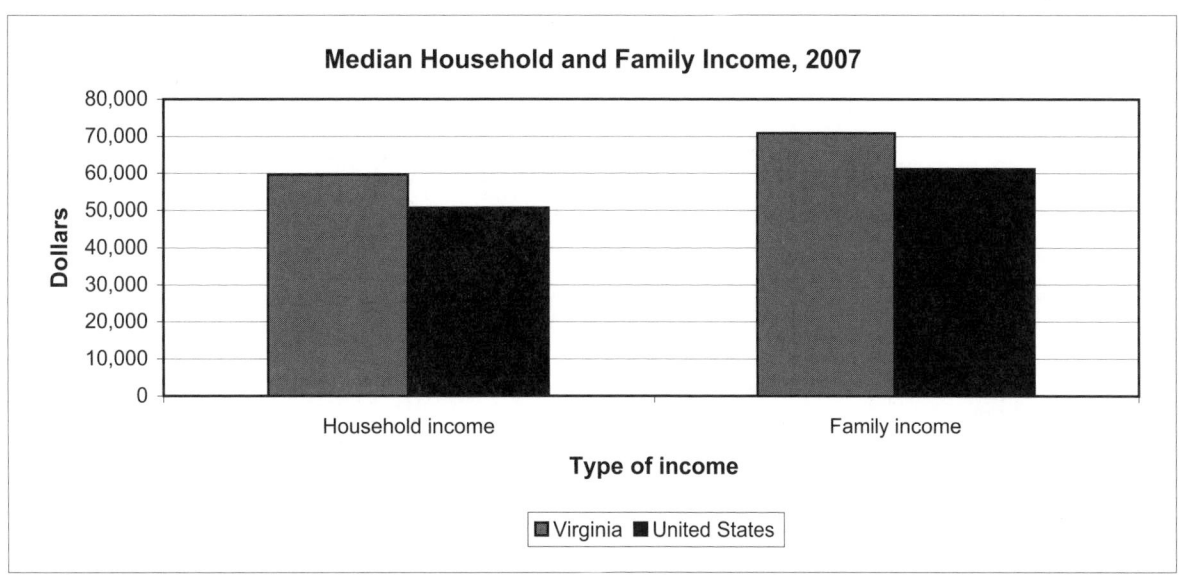

Median Household and Family Income, 2007

Table VA-5. Health Insurance Coverage Status for All Persons and Children Under 18 Years of Age

(Number, percent.)

Item	2000	2001	2002	2003	2004	2005	2006	2007
ALL PERSONS	6 992	7 105	7 118	7 383	7 386	7 454	7 538	7 684
Covered by Private or Government Health Insurance								
Number	6 245	6 401	6 216	6 396	6 465	6 503	6 532	6 548
Percent	89.3	90.1	87.3	86.6	87.5	87.2	86.7	85.2
Not Covered								
Number	747	704	902	986	922	951	1 006	1 135
Percent	10.7	9.9	12.7	13.4	12.5	12.8	13.3	14.8
Percent in the U.S. not covered	13.7	14.1	14.7	15.1	14.9	15.3	15.8	15.3
CHILDREN UNDER 18 YEARS OF AGE	1 781	1 856	1 792	1 813	1 837	1 828	1 827	1 833
Covered by Private or Government Health Insurance								
Number	1 599	1 740	1 579	1 658	1 705	1 672	1 643	1 646
Percent	89.8	93.7	88.1	91.4	92.8	91.5	89.9	89.8
Not Covered								
Number	182	116	213	155	132	156	185	187
Percent	10.2	6.3	11.9	8.6	7.2	8.5	10.1	10.2
Percent in the U.S. not covered	11.6	11.3	11.2	11.0	10.5	10.9	11.7	11.0

Table VA-6. Employment Status by Demographic Group, Preliminary 2008

(Number, percent.)

Characteristic	Civilian noninstitutional population	Civilian labor force		Employment		Unemployed	
		Number	Percent of population	Number	Percent of population	Number	Unemployment rate
TOTAL	5 943	4 160	70.0	3 994	67.2	166	4.0
Sex							
Men	2 835	2 165	76.0	2 073	73.1	92	4.2
Women	3 107	1 995	64.0	1 920	61.8	74	3.7
Race, Sex, and Hispanic Origin							
White	4 416	3 082	69.8	2 974	67.4	108	3.5
Men	2 137	1 645	77.0	1 583	74.1	62	3.8
Women	2 278	1 437	63.1	1 391	61.0	46	3.2
Black or African American	1 104	769	69.6	721	65.3	48	6.2
Men	492	353	71.7	329	66.9	24	6.7
Women	612	416	68.0	392	64.0	24	5.8
Hispanic	326	263	80.6	251	77.0	12	4.4
Men	186	170	91.7	162	87.4	8	4.7
Women	141	93	65.8	89	63.3	4	3.9
Age							
16 to 19 years	429	180	41.9	150	35.0	30	16.4
20 to 24 years	505	394	78.0	363	71.9	31	7.8
25 to 34 years	1 030	903	87.6	860	83.5	42	4.7
35 to 44 years	1 069	921	86.1	904	84.5	17	1.8
45 to 54 years	1 166	987	84.7	964	82.7	23	2.3
55 to 64 years	872	601	68.9	586	67.2	15	2.4
65 years and over	870	174	20.1	165	19.0	9	5.1

Note: Data in Table 6 are from the Current Population Survey (CPS) and do not match the estimates in Table 7. See notes and definitions for more details.

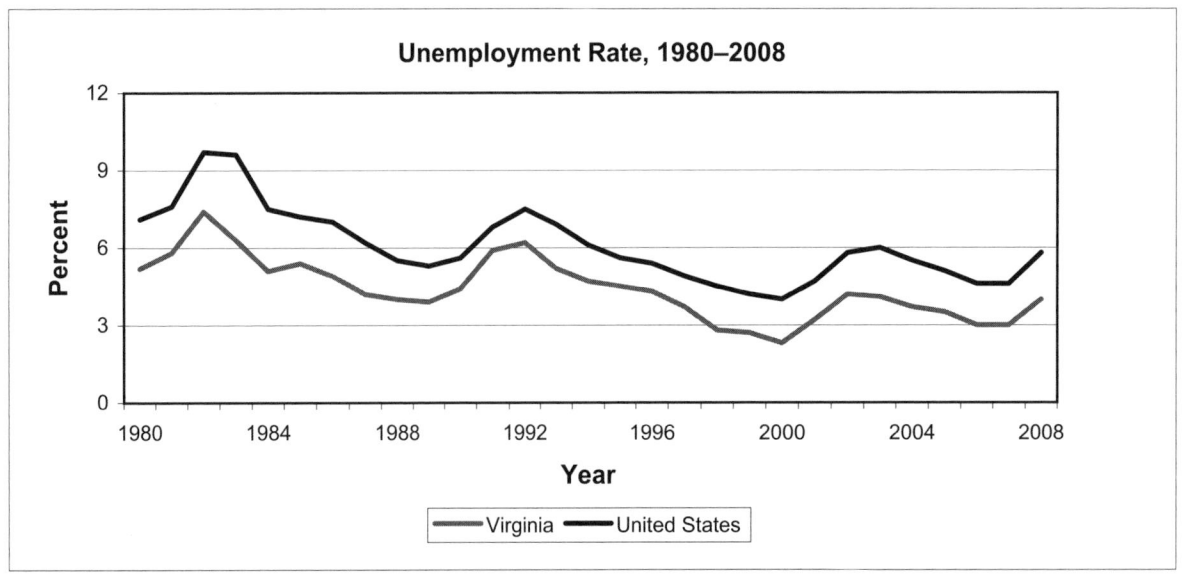

Table VA-7. Employment Status of the Civilian Noninstitutional Population Age 16 Years and Over

(Number, percent.)

Year	Civilian labor force	Civilian participation rate	Employed	Unemployed	Unemployment rate
1998	3 483 900	67.4	3 384 653	99 247	2.8
1999	3 536 409	67.5	3 441 589	94 820	2.7
2000	3 584 037	67.6	3 502 524	81 513	2.3
2001	3 655 371	67.9	3 537 719	117 652	3.2
2002	3 744 636	68.6	3 588 079	156 557	4.2
2003	3 802 819	68.8	3 647 095	155 724	4.1
2004	3 857 950	68.6	3 715 272	142 678	3.7
2005	3 935 250	68.9	3 797 488	137 762	3.5
2006	4 010 565	69.3	3 890 060	120 505	3.0
2007	4 067 520	69.4	3 945 479	122 041	3.0
2008	4 124 766	69.6	3 960 011	164 755	4.0

Table VA-8. Employment and Average Wages by Industry

(Estimates for 2001–2006 are based on the 2002 North American Industry Classification System [NAICS]. Estimates for 2007 are based on the 2007 NAICS.)

Industry	2001	2002	2003	2004	2005	2006	2007
	Number of jobs						
WAGE AND SALARY EMPLOYMENT BY INDUSTRY	3 793 657	3 771 719	3 788 131	3 871 609	3 953 120	4 010 422	4 042 849
Farm Wage and Salary Employment	11 001	12 236	13 633	11 257	9 150	9 632	7 121
Nonfarm Wage and Salary Employment	3 782 656	3 759 483	3 774 498	3 860 352	3 943 970	4 000 790	4 035 728
Private wage and salary employment	2 970 887	2 936 234	2 944 186	3 018 206	3 095 612	3 143 330	3 169 857
Forestry, fishing, hunting, and other	7 518	6 916	6 959	6 913	6 921	6 798	6 834
Mining	9 236	8 760	8 270	8 354	8 845	9 512	9 151
Utilities	11 906	11 964	11 098	10 935	11 039	10 977	11 206
Construction	225 164	222 746	226 885	240 890	253 462	258 402	248 910
Manufacturing	346 352	324 222	308 029	301 238	297 571	290 096	281 012
Durable goods manufacturing	192 978	178 883	169 030	168 427	170 379	170 437	164 760
Nondurable goods manufacturing	153 374	145 339	138 999	132 811	127 192	119 659	116 252
Wholesale trade	116 837	114 794	114 760	117 108	119 865	121 706	123 660
Retail trade	417 424	416 530	415 665	425 621	432 413	437 577	441 449
Transportation and warehousing	113 237	107 973	108 127	108 511	111 806	109 992	109 864
Information	119 913	107 651	99 312	97 080	93 876	92 248	91 261
Finance and insurance	127 094	130 308	133 836	133 565	135 693	138 433	135 795
Real estate and rental and leasing	56 815	56 274	57 810	59 538	61 102	60 497	60 599
Professional and technical services	302 405	298 498	307 296	326 624	345 329	360 673	372 230
Management of companies and enterprises	72 070	68 154	69 915	71 212	73 388	75 710	77 271
Administrative and waste services	201 198	197 173	192 684	200 190	205 681	208 950	213 546
Educational services	54 885	55 684	57 922	59 776	61 366	63 578	66 806
Health care and social assistance	292 792	303 779	311 142	319 369	335 493	346 223	358 361
Arts, entertainment, and recreation	44 945	46 225	45 053	46 137	47 013	48 033	49 207
Accommodation and food services	263 001	263 957	270 129	280 711	289 194	296 960	302 634
Other services, except public administration	188 095	194 626	199 294	204 434	205 555	206 965	210 061
Government and government enterprises	811 769	823 249	830 312	842 146	848 358	857 460	865 871
	Dollars						
AVERAGE WAGES AND SALARIES BY INDUSTRY	36 245	36 906	38 319	40 365	42 199	43 964	45 910
Average Farm Wages and Salaries	17 944	19 205	18 053	21 691	21 380	23 417	27 668
Average Nonfarm Wages and Salaries	36 298	36 964	38 392	40 419	42 247	44 013	45 942
Average private wages and salaries	36 164	36 400	37 777	39 717	41 538	43 255	45 073
Forestry, fishing, hunting, and other	20 174	20 989	21 796	22 982	23 518	24 845	25 892
Mining	44 670	44 720	45 862	49 747	52 277	53 918	55 011
Utilities	63 819	66 068	69 529	71 471	75 193	84 536	86 177
Construction	34 826	35 629	36 275	38 361	40 177	42 204	43 803
Manufacturing	37 950	38 904	40 462	41 909	43 577	45 321	47 744
Durable goods manufacturing	39 408	39 797	41 587	42 973	44 698	46 189	49 158
Nondurable goods manufacturing	36 115	37 806	39 095	40 561	42 074	44 085	45 741
Wholesale trade	51 394	51 130	52 991	56 171	57 755	60 923	63 597
Retail trade	21 262	21 970	22 580	23 325	23 926	24 425	24 673
Transportation and warehousing	36 013	37 292	37 207	38 682	39 543	41 445	42 020
Information	76 649	65 048	66 875	71 299	74 812	75 277	74 696
Finance and insurance	54 956	56 142	61 204	65 126	69 712	68 630	70 994
Real estate and rental and leasing	32 970	33 732	35 082	37 802	40 513	42 525	42 567
Professional and technical services	62 094	63 454	66 424	69 783	73 888	77 850	82 629
Management of companies and enterprises	64 663	69 441	72 819	80 792	86 297	90 610	97 355
Administrative and waste services	23 356	24 107	25 142	27 098	27 745	29 037	30 940
Educational services	25 411	27 072	27 717	29 496	30 309	31 820	34 023
Health care and social assistance	32 203	33 658	34 575	35 941	37 236	38 746	40 266
Arts, entertainment, and recreation	18 328	19 246	20 587	20 901	21 217	23 490	24 212
Accommodation and food services	13 720	14 048	14 583	15 276	15 583	16 441	17 004
Other services, except public administration	25 152	25 596	26 587	27 460	28 512	29 803	31 294
Government and government enterprises	36 788	38 975	40 573	42 936	44 835	46 795	49 121

Table VA-9. Employment Characteristics by Family Type

(Number, percent.)

Family type and labor force status	2005		2006		2007	
	Total	Families with own children under 18 years	Total	Families with own children under 18 years	Total	Families with own children under 18 years
TOTAL FAMILIES	1 938 966	891 668	1 939 891	903 624	1 964 204	906 249
FAMILY TYPE AND LABOR FORCE STATUS						
Married Coupled Families	1 478 636	635 231	1 466 223	637 004	1 483 385	637 131
Both husband and wife in labor force	54.7	65.1	56.3	66.2	56.2	67.1
Husband in labor force, wife not in labor force	22.8	28.4	22.5	28.1	22.4	27.8
Wife in labor force, husband not in labor force	7.1	3.4	6.8	3.5	6.8	3.1
Both husband and wife not in labor force	15.4	3.1	14.4	2.1	14.6	2.0
Other Families	460 330	256 437	473 668	266 620	480 819	269 118
Female householder, no husband present	74.5	79.0	74.8	77.7	74.7	78.0
In labor force	52.9	63.8	55.0	66.2	55.3	65.4
Not in labor force	21.6	15.2	19.7	11.5	19.5	12.5
Male householder, no wife present	25.5	21.0	25.2	22.3	25.3	22.0
In labor force	20.0	18.5	20.2	20.2	20.9	20.4
Not in labor force	5.4	2.5	5.0	2.0	4.3	1.6

Table VA-10. School Enrollment and Educational Attainment, 2007

(Number, percent.)

Item	State	U.S.
Enrollment		
Total population 3 years and over	7 409 419	289 295 761
Enrolled in school	2 027 205	79 329 527
Enrolled in preschool (percent)	6.2	6.2
Enrolled in grades K-12 (percent)	65.1	67.6
Enrolled in college or graduate school (percent)	28.7	26.2
Attainment		
Total population 25 years and over	5 104 681	197 892 369
Less than a high school diploma (percent)	14.1	15.5
High school diploma or more (percent)	85.9	84.5
Bachelor's degree or more (percent)	33.6	27.5
Graduate degree or more (percent)	13.7	10.1

Table VA-11. Educational Indicators

(Number, percent.)

Item	State	U.S.
Public Schools, 2006–2007 (except where noted)		
Number of school districts	231	17 742
Number of schools	2 203	99 639
Number of students	1 220 440	49 315 842
Student-teacher ratio	11.6	15.5
Expenditures per student (dollars)	$10 214	. . .
Averaged freshman graduation rate, 2005–2006	74.5	. . .
Dropout rate, grades 9–12, 2005–2006	2.7	3.7
Students eligible for free or reduced-price lunch (percent)	31.4	41.2
English-language learners (percent)	7.1	5.1
Students with IEP (percent)	14.1	12.7
Private Schools, 2007–2008 (except where noted)		
Number of schools	872	33 740
Number of students	116 934	5 072 451
High school graduates, 2006–2007	6 913	306 605
Student-teacher ratio	9.1	11.1

Table VA-12. Reported Voting and Registration of the Voting-Age Population, November 2008

(Number in thousands, percent.)

Item	Total population	Total citizen population	Registered			Voted		
			Total registered	Percent registered (total population)	Percent registered (total citizen population)	Total voted	Percent voted (total population)	Percent voted (total citizen population)
U.S. total	225 499	206 072	146 311	64.9	71.0	131 144	58.2	63.6
State total	5 720	5 316	3 950	69.1	74.3	3 650	63.8	68.7
Sex								
Male	2 725	2 495	1 789	65.6	71.7	1 641	60.2	65.8
Female	2 995	2 821	2 162	72.2	76.6	2 010	67.1	71.2
Race								
White alone	4 288	4 018	3 008	70.1	74.9	2 778	64.8	69.1
White non-Hispanic alone	3 983	3 912	2 945	73.9	75.3	2 716	68.2	69.4
Black alone	1 031	1 005	727	70.5	72.3	686	66.6	68.3
Asian alone	330	221	157	47.5	70.8	136	41.2	61.4
Hispanic (of any race)	330	132	74	22.5	56.5	74	22.5	56.5
White alone or in combination	4 321	4 051	3 032	70.2	74.8	2 798	64.8	69.1
Black alone or in combination	1 059	1 033	749	70.7	72.5	703	66.4	68.1
Asian alone or in combination	337	228	164	48.6	71.7	138	41.1	60.6

Table VA-13. Crime

(Number, rate per 100,000.)

Item	State			U.S.		
	2007	2008	Percent change	2007	2008	Percent change
Population	7 712 091	7 769 089	0.7	301 621 157	304 059 724	0.8
VIOLENT CRIME						
Number	20 798	19 882	-4.4	1 408 337	1 382 012	-1.9
Rate	269.7	255.9	-5.1	466.9	454.5	-2.7
Murder and Nonnegligent Manslaughter						
Number	406	368	-9.4	16 929	16 272	-3.9
Rate	5.3	4.7	-10.0	5.6	5.4	-4.7
Forcible Rape						
Number	1 745	1 758	0.7	90 427	89 000	-1.6
Rate	22.6	22.6	*	30.0	29.3	-2.4
Robbery						
Number	7 651	7 437	-2.8	445 125	441 855	-0.7
Rate	99.2	95.7	-3.5	147.6	145.3	-1.5
Aggravated Assault						
Number	10 996	10 319	-6.2	855 856	834 885	-2.5
Rate	142.6	132.8	-6.8	283.8	274.6	-3.2
PROPERTY CRIME						
Number	190 209	195 634	2.9	9 843 481	9 767 915	-0.8
Rate	2 466.4	2 518.1	2.1	3 263.5	3 212.5	-1.6
Burglary						
Number	31 688	31 993	1.0	2 179 140	2 222 196	2.0
Rate	410.9	411.8	0.2	722.5	730.8	1.2
Larceny-Theft						
Number	144 467	150 382	4.1	6 568 572	6 588 873	0.3
Rate	1 873.3	1 935.6	3.3	2 177.8	2 167.0	-0.5
Motor Vehicle Theft						
Number	14 054	13 259	-5.7	1 095 769	956 846	-12.7
Rate	182.2	170.7	-6.3	363.3	314.7	-13.4

Table VA-14. State Government Finances, 2007

(Dollars, percent distribution.)

Item	Thousands of dollars	Percent distribution
Total Revenue	47 155 581	X
General revenue	35 145 300	74.5
Intergovernmental revenue	6 883 654	14.6
Taxes	18 571 160	39.4
General sales	3 539 061	7.5
Selective sales	2 461 354	5.2
License taxes	673 592	1.4
Individual income tax	10 238 776	21.7
Corporate income tax	879 575	1.9
Other taxes	778 802	1.7
Current charges	5 887 307	12.5
Miscellaneous general revenue	3 803 179	8.1
Utility revenue	0	0.0
Liquor store revenue	502 403	1.1
Insurance trust revenue	11 507 878	24.4
Total Expenditure	36 774 042	100.0
Intergovernmental expenditure	10 438 607	28.4
Direct expenditure	26 335 435	71.6
Current operation	19 362 185	52.7
Capital outlay	2 315 170	6.3
Insurance benefits and repayments	2 651 593	7.2
Assistance and subsidies	1 184 514	3.2
Interest on debt	821 973	2.2
Exhibit: Salaries and wages	5 795 140	15.8
Total Expenditure	36 774 042	100.0
General expenditure	33 652 244	91.5
Intergovernmental expenditure	10 438 607	28.4
Direct expenditure	23 213 637	63.1
Education	13 185 813	35.9
Public welfare	6 982 641	19.0
Hospitals	2 541 320	6.9
Health	944 144	2.6
Highways	2 633 577	7.2
Police protection	661 221	1.8
Correction	1 425 372	3.9
Natural resources	225 791	0.6
Parks and recreation	166 471	0.5
Government administration	1 133 538	3.1
Interest on general debt	821 973	2.2
Other and unallocable	2 930 383	8.0
Utility expenditure	59 930	0.2
Liquor store expenditure	410 275	1.1
Insurance trust expenditure	2 651 593	7.2
Debt at End of Fiscal Year	19 683 529	X
Cash and Security Holdings	79 117 816	X

Table VA-15. State Government Tax Collections, 2008

(Dollars, percent distribution.)

Item	Thousands of dollars	Percent distribution
Total Taxes	18 408 276	X
Property taxes	22 153	0.1
Sales and gross receipts	6 093 335	33.1
General sales and gross receipts	3 656 789	19.9
Selective sales taxes	2 436 546	13.2
Alcoholic beverages	175 654	1.0
Amusements	72	0.0
Insurance premiums	396 858	2.2
Motor fuels	920 063	5.0
Public utilities	150 237	0.8
Tobacco products	168 118	0.9
Other selective sales	625 544	3.4
Licenses	653 176	3.5
Alcoholic beverages	11 335	0.1
Amusements	119	0.0
Corporation	54 591	0.3
Hunting and fishing	22 368	0.1
Motor vehicle	355 683	1.9
Motor vehicle operators	45 425	0.2
Occupation and business, NEC	159 171	0.9
Other licenses	4 484	0.0
Income taxes	10 902 062	59.2
Individual income	10 114 833	54.9
Corporation net income	787 229	4.3
Other taxes	737 550	4.0
Death and gift	153 377	0.8
Documentary and stock transfer	455 719	2.5
Severance	2 060	0.0
Other	126 394	0.7

Table VA-16. Agriculture

(Number, acres, and dollars.)

Item	2002		2007		Percent change, 2002–2007
	Number	Percent of total	Number	Percent of total	
Number of farms	47 606		47 383		-0.5
Farm Size					
Average size of farm (acres)	181		171		-5.5
Farms by size (number of farms)					
Fewer than 50 acres	17 109	35.9	18 707	39.5	9.3
50 to 499 acres	26 928	56.6	25 366	53.5	-5.8
500 acres or more	3 569	7.5	3 310	7.0	-7.3
Land (Acres)					
Total land in farms	8 624 829		8 103 925		-6.0
Total cropland	4 194 158	48.6	3 274 137	40.4	-21.9
Total harvested cropland	2 623 776	30.4	2 544 997	31.4	-3.0
Irrigated land	98 913	1.1	82 187	1.0	-16.9
Value of Sales (Dollars)					
Agricultural products sold ($1,000)	2 360 911		2 906 188		23.1
Average sales per farm	49 593		61 334		23.7
Sales of crops	718 219	30.4	858 301	29.5	19.5
Sales of livestock, poultry, and their products	1 642 692	69.6	2 047 887	70.5	24.7
Value of Sales (Number of Farms)					
Less than $10,000	32 039	67.3	31 773	67.1	-0.8
$10,000 to $99,999	11 646	24.5	11 882	25.1	2.0
$100,000 to $999,999	3 576	7.5	3 117	6.6	-12.8
$1,000,000 or more	345	0.7	611	1.3	77.1
Farms by Type of Organization (Number of Farms)					
Family	42 851	90.0	41 173	86.9	-3.9
Partnership	2 757	5.8	3 625	7.7	31.5
Corporation	1 723	3.6	2 269	4.8	31.7
Other: cooperative, estate or trust, institutional, etc	275	0.6	316	0.7	14.9
Value of Land and Buildings (Dollars)					
Estimated market value of land and buildings ($1,000)	34 141 249		23 329 488		-31.7
Land and buildings average value per farm	720 538		490 064		-32.0
Average value per acre	4 213		2 675		-36.5
Government Payments					
Number of farms receiving government payments	9 206	19.3	9 852	20.8	7.0
Payments (thousands of dollars)	54 677		54 940		0.5
Average payment per farm	5 939		5 577		-6.1
Farm Operator Characteristics					
Farm operators whose principal occupation is farming	25 500	53.6	20 294	42.8	-20.4
Farm operators whose principal occupation is other	22 106	46.4	27 089	57.2	22.5
Average age principal operator (years)	56.7		58.2		2.6

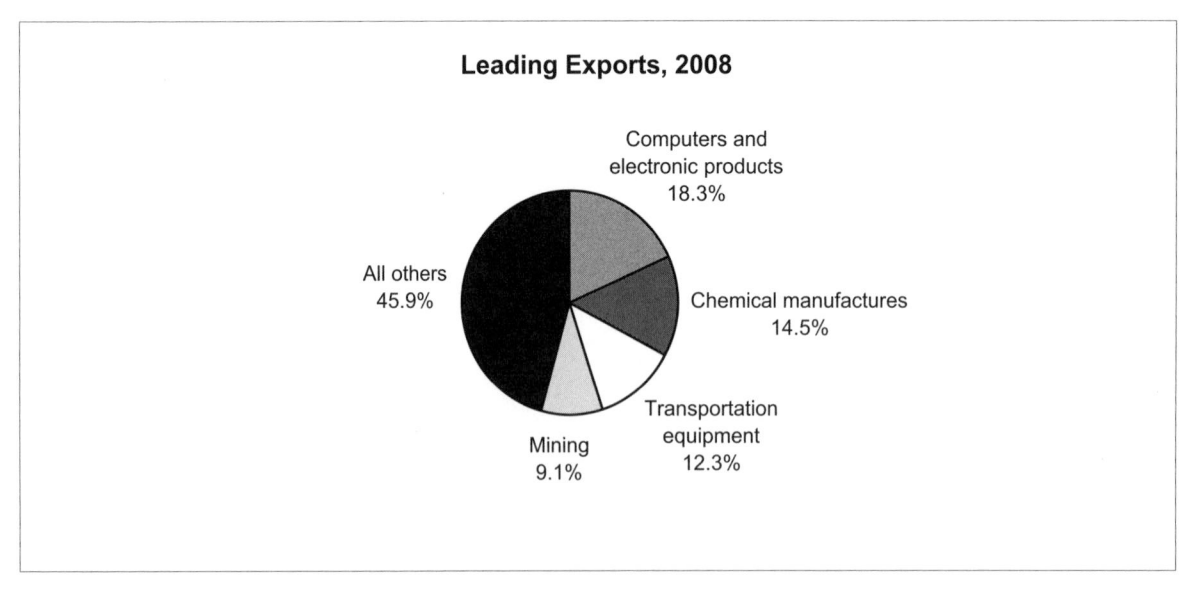

Leading Exports, 2008

Computers and electronic products 18.3%

Chemical manufactures 14.5%

Transportation equipment 12.3%

Mining 9.1%

All others 45.9%

WASHINGTON

Facts and Figures

Location: Northwestern United States; bordered on the N by Canada (British Columbia), on the E by Idaho, on the S by Oregon, and on the W by the Pacific Ocean

Area: 71,300 sq. mi. (184,665 sq. km.); rank—18th

Population: 6,549,224 (2008 est.); rank—13th

Principal Cities: capital—Olympia; largest—Seattle

Statehood: November 11, 1889; 42nd state

U.S. Congress: 2 senators, 9 representatives

State Motto: *Alki* ("By and by")

State Song: "Washington, My Home"

State Nickname: The Evergreen State

Abbreviations: WA; Wash.

State Symbols: flower—coast rhododendron; tree—Western hemlock; bird—willow goldfinch

At a Glance

- With an increase in population of 11.1 percent, Washington ranked 12th among the states in growth from 2000 to 2008.
- An estimated 42,133 marriages took place in Washington in 2008, compared to 24,558 divorces.
- The 2007 home ownership rate in Washington was 66.8 percent, giving it a ranking of 40th among the states.
- Washington's median household income in 2007 was $55,591, 11th among the states.
- In Washington, 11.4 percent of the population lived below the poverty level in 2007, ranking it 32nd.
- In 2006-07, 11.6 percent of Washingtonians did not have health insurance, compared to 15.5 percent of the total U.S. population.
- In 2007, 4.6 percent of Washingtonians were unemployed, which was the same as the national average.
- Washington ranked 11th in the nation with 30.3 percent of its population 25 years old and over having a bachelor's degree in 2007.
- Washington's violent crime rate in 2007 was 333.1 per 100,000 population, compared to 466.9 for the entire nation.
- Washington had one physician for every 318 people in 2007, compared to one physician for every 325 people nationwide.
- In the 2008 election, 67 percent of Washington's eligible voters voted, compared to 61.7 percent of eligible voters nationwide.
- Washington ranked 38th among the states receiving federal aid in 2007, with $1,248 per capita.
- Washington's gross domestic product was $311 billion in 2007; it ranked 14th among the states.
- With $66.4 billion in exports in 2007, Washington ranked 4th in exports.
- Washingtonians consumed 2.05 trillion Btu's of energy in 2006; the state ranked 17th in total consumption.
- In 2007, Washington exported $2.6 billion worth of agricultural products, about 3.2 percent of the U.S. total.

Table WA-1. Population by Sex, Age, Race, and Hispanic Origin

(Number, percent.)

Sex, age, race, and Hispanic origin	1990	2000	2008	Average annual percent change, 2000–2008
Total Population	4 866 692	5 894 121	6 549 224	1.3
Percent of total U.S. population	2.0	2.1	2.2	X
Sex				
Male	2 413 747	2 934 300	3 269 925	1.4
Female	2 452 945	2 959 821	3 279 299	1.3
Age				
Under 5 years	366 780	394 306	433 119	1.2
5 to 19 years	1 031 466	1 288 713	1 277 742	-0.1
20 to 64 years	2 893 158	3 548 954	4 054 486	1.7
65 years and over	575 288	662 148	783 877	2.1
Median age (years)	33.0	35.3	37.2	X
Race and Hispanic Origin[1]				
One race				
White	4 308 937	4 821 823	5 520 400	1.7
Black	149 801	190 267	245 000	3.2
American Indian and Alaskan Native	81 483	93 301	112 965	2.4
Asian[2]	210 958	322 335	437 783	3.9
Native Hawaiian and Other Pacific Islander	X	23 953	31 822	3.6
Two or more races	X	213 519	201 254	-0.7
Hispanic (of any race)	214 570	441 509	643 687	4.8

[1]Data on race in 2000 and 2008 are not comparable to 1990. Individuals could only report one race in the 1990 census but could report one or more races on the 2000 census.
[2]Data in 1990 refer to Asian and Pacific Islanders.

Table WA-2. Marital Status

(Number, percent distribution.)

Sex and marital status	1990	2000	2007
Males, 15 Years and Over	1 862 291	2 287 431	2 579 008
Never married	29.0	29.8	32.8
Now married, except separated	57.9	56.6	52.6
Separated	1.7	1.4	1.6
Widowed	2.1	2.1	2.2
Divorced	9.4	10.1	10.9
Females, 15 Years and Over	1 928 866	2 352 091	2 630 070
Never married	20.8	22.8	25.4
Now married, except separated	55.4	54.1	51.0
Separated	2.1	1.8	1.9
Widowed	9.9	8.6	8.4
Divorced	11.8	12.7	13.4

Table WA-3. Households and Housing Characteristics

(Number, percent, and dollars.)

Item	1990	2000	2007	Average annual percent change, 2000–2007
Total Households	1 872 431	2 271 398	2 501 509	1.4
Family households	1 264 934	1 499 127	1 619 537	1.1
Married-couple family	1 029 267	1 181 995	1 252 212	0.8
Other family	235 667	317 132	367 325	2.1
Male householder, no wife present	60 145	92 514	113 144	2.9
Female householder, no husband present	175 522	224 618	254 181	1.8
Nonfamily households	607 497	772 271	881 972	1.9
Householder living alone	476 320	594 325	696 182	2.3
Householder not living alone	131 177	177 946	185 790	0.6
Housing Characteristics				
Total housing units	2 032 378	2 451 075	2 744 324	1.6
Occupied housing units	1 872 431	2 271 398	2 501 509	1.4
Owner-occupied	1 171 580	1 467 009	1 652 733	1.7
Renter-occupied	700 851	804 389	848 776	0.8
Average size	2.53	2.53	2.53	X
Financial Characteristics				
Median gross rent of renter-occupied housing units (dollars)	445	663	816	3.0
Median monthly owner costs for housing units with a mortgage (dollars)	738	1 268	1 675	4.1
Median value of owner-occupied housing units (dollars)	93 200	168 300	300 800	8.6

Table WA-4. Median Income and Poverty Status, 2007

(Number, percent.)

Characteristic	State		U.S.	
	Number	Percent	Number	Percent
Median Income				
Households (dollars)	55 591	X	50 740	X
Families (dollars)	66 642	X	61 173	X
Below Poverty Level				
Sex				
Male	323 819	10.3	16 576 071	11.5
Female	401 353	12.6	21 476 176	14.3
Age				
Under 18 years	226 424	15.0	13 097 100	18.0
Related children under 18 years	215 350	14.4	12 728 964	17.6
18 to 64 years	440 291	10.8	21 495 507	11.6
65 years and over	58 457	7.9	3 459 640	9.5

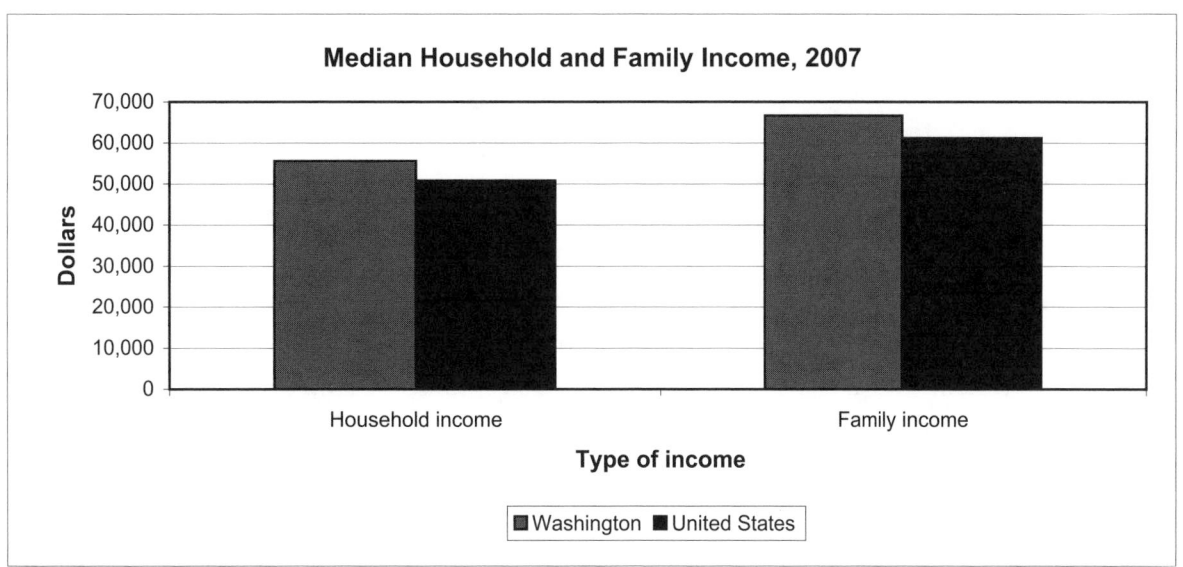

Median Household and Family Income, 2007

Table WA-5. Health Insurance Coverage Status for All Persons and Children Under 18 Years of Age

(Number, percent.)

Item	2000	2001	2002	2003	2004	2005	2006	2007
ALL PERSONS	5 872	5 930	6 001	6 091	6 118	6 250	6 318	6 509
Covered by Private or Government Health Insurance								
Number	5 099	5 160	5 164	5 157	5 359	5 422	5 572	5 773
Percent	86.8	87.0	86.1	84.7	87.6	86.7	88.2	88.7
Not Covered								
Number	772	771	837	934	759	828	746	737
Percent	13.2	13.0	13.9	15.3	12.4	13.3	11.8	11.3
Percent in the U.S. not covered	13.7	14.1	14.7	15.1	14.9	15.3	15.8	15.3
CHILDREN UNDER 18 YEARS OF AGE	1 532	1 506	1 525	1 484	1 512	1 525	1 518	1 558
Covered by Private or Government Health Insurance								
Number	1 392	1 338	1 388	1 360	1 412	1 391	1 413	1 452
Percent	90.8	88.9	91.0	91.6	93.4	91.3	93.1	93.2
Not Covered								
Number	140	168	137	125	100	133	105	106
Percent	9.2	11.1	9.0	8.4	6.6	8.7	6.9	6.8
Percent in the U.S. not covered	11.6	11.3	11.2	11.0	10.5	10.9	11.7	11.0

Table WA-6. Employment Status by Demographic Group, Preliminary 2008

(Number, percent.)

Characteristic	Civilian noninstitutional population	Civilian labor force		Employment		Unemployed	
		Number	Percent of population	Number	Percent of population	Number	Unemployment rate
TOTAL	5 103	3 483	68.3	3 297	64.6	186	5.3
Sex							
Men	2 508	1 878	75.0	1 768	70.5	110	5.8
Women	2 595	1 605	62.0	1 529	58.9	76	4.8
Race, Sex, and Hispanic Origin							
White	4 310	2 960	68.7	2 803	65.0	157	5.3
Men	2 118	1 591	75.1	1 497	70.7	93	5.9
Women	2 192	1 370	62.5	1 306	59.6	64	4.7
Black or African American	166	112	67.8	104	63.0	8	7.1
Men	90	66	73.8	61	67.9	5	8.1
Women	76	46	60.8	43	57.4	3	5.7
Hispanic	407	286	70.1	263	64.5	23	7.9
Men	207	163	78.4	151	73.0	11	6.9
Women	200	123	61.5	112	55.8	11	9.3
Age							
16 to 19 years	343	152	44.2	113	32.8	39	25.7
20 to 24 years	431	337	78.3	311	72.1	26	7.8
25 to 34 years	875	737	84.2	704	80.4	33	4.5
35 to 44 years	936	787	84.0	752	80.3	35	4.4
45 to 54 years	989	839	84.8	810	81.9	29	3.5
55 to 64 years	777	512	65.9	491	63.2	21	4.1
65 years and over	751	120	15.9	116	15.5	3	2.7

Note: Data in Table 6 are from the Current Population Survey (CPS) and do not match the estimates in Table 7. See notes and definitions for more details.

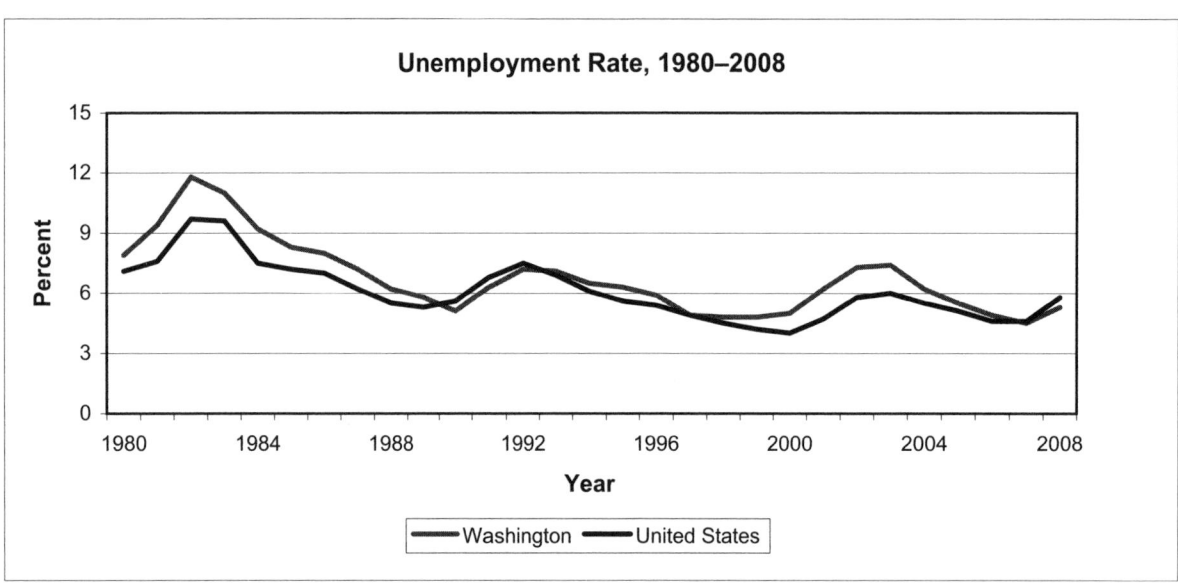

Table WA-7. Employment Status of the Civilian Noninstitutional Population Age 16 Years and Over

(Number, percent.)

Year	Civilian labor force	Civilian participation rate	Employed	Unemployed	Unemployment rate
1998	3 032 019	69.7	2 886 871	145 148	4.8
1999	3 066 165	69.5	2 917 577	148 588	4.8
2000	3 050 021	68.3	2 898 677	151 344	5.0
2001	3 052 714	67.3	2 863 705	189 009	6.2
2002	3 104 698	67.5	2 877 022	227 676	7.3
2003	3 146 154	67.4	2 913 230	232 924	7.4
2004	3 199 234	67.5	2 999 526	199 708	6.2
2005	3 258 844	67.6	3 079 482	179 362	5.5
2006	3 319 593	67.6	3 156 995	162 598	4.9
2007	3 391 248	67.8	3 237 358	153 890	4.5
2008	3 476 766	68.4	3 290 993	185 773	5.3

Table WA-8. Employment and Average Wages by Industry

(Estimates for 2001–2006 are based on the 2002 North American Industry Classification System [NAICS]. Estimates for 2007 are based on the 2007 NAICS.)

Industry	2001	2002	2003	2004	2005	2006	2007
	Number of jobs						
WAGE AND SALARY EMPLOYMENT BY INDUSTRY	2 942 687	2 902 830	2 915 249	2 954 619	3 029 519	3 121 441	3 194 420
Farm Wage and Salary Employment	44 445	44 138	47 314	41 510	42 589	43 705	40 707
Nonfarm Wage and Salary Employment	2 898 242	2 858 692	2 867 935	2 913 109	2 986 930	3 077 736	3 153 713
Private wage and salary employment	2 326 503	2 273 952	2 276 602	2 318 440	2 385 751	2 472 948	2 544 514
Forestry, fishing, hunting, and other	38 839	39 100	39 000	40 009	40 945	41 149	40 223
Mining	3 443	3 095	3 044	3 318	3 416	3 490	3 161
Utilities	4 826	4 553	4 434	4 437	4 477	4 599	4 733
Construction	165 784	160 502	162 614	170 769	184 564	203 015	216 336
Manufacturing	318 838	287 337	268 607	265 565	273 442	287 311	295 071
Durable goods manufacturing	226 618	200 733	184 925	183 777	192 169	204 855	212 926
Nondurable goods manufacturing	92 220	86 604	83 682	81 788	81 273	82 456	82 145
Wholesale trade	122 039	117 399	117 494	120 140	123 104	126 896	129 193
Retail trade	320 597	314 617	315 994	319 214	325 429	332 195	339 454
Transportation and warehousing	88 781	85 035	84 112	87 112	88 548	90 589	92 661
Information	99 058	93 692	91 646	91 906	94 491	98 658	102 880
Finance and insurance	102 460	102 156	106 303	106 096	107 216	109 156	107 117
Real estate and rental and leasing	48 964	48 608	50 625	51 276	51 528	53 190	53 543
Professional and technical services	150 589	146 247	144 563	145 662	151 408	157 064	166 201
Management of companies and enterprises	29 581	30 217	32 235	33 036	33 434	33 611	34 700
Administrative and waste services	124 435	121 979	123 909	133 494	141 940	148 795	153 534
Educational services	42 224	42 174	45 414	46 901	45 566	46 318	48 424
Health care and social assistance	272 232	280 730	286 547	292 258	300 626	309 682	318 791
Arts, entertainment, and recreation	42 318	43 826	44 912	47 181	47 240	47 639	48 859
Accommodation and food services	209 292	206 386	209 102	213 275	221 625	229 671	237 202
Other services, except public administration	142 203	146 299	146 047	146 791	146 752	149 920	152 431
Government and government enterprises	571 739	584 740	591 333	594 669	601 179	604 788	609 199
	Dollars						
AVERAGE WAGES AND SALARIES BY INDUSTRY	37 590	38 381	39 141	40 349	41 569	43 681	45 975
Average Farm Wages and Salaries	22 652	20 892	20 042	23 722	27 104	25 040	25 724
Average Nonfarm Wages and Salaries	37 819	38 651	39 456	40 586	41 775	43 946	46 236
Average private wages and salaries	38 369	38 969	39 611	40 687	41 802	44 090	46 433
Forestry, fishing, hunting, and other	26 576	27 726	28 981	29 569	30 192	32 480	34 023
Mining	47 034	48 190	49 683	51 653	53 193	55 858	58 719
Utilities	58 606	58 199	58 887	62 984	64 726	69 457	73 326
Construction	39 285	40 322	40 299	41 414	42 950	45 294	48 302
Manufacturing	47 802	51 021	50 638	52 351	55 436	58 678	60 150
Durable goods manufacturing	51 252	53 665	54 652	56 646	60 112	63 928	64 892
Nondurable goods manufacturing	39 325	44 891	41 767	42 703	44 382	45 636	47 858
Wholesale trade	47 774	48 784	50 012	53 717	54 660	57 921	60 795
Retail trade	25 176	26 121	26 650	27 567	28 664	29 423	31 024
Transportation and warehousing	39 360	40 609	41 649	43 717	44 769	46 020	47 010
Information	110 617	102 057	102 126	93 160	89 146	95 558	106 365
Finance and insurance	52 184	54 558	58 993	62 993	63 142	67 529	70 489
Real estate and rental and leasing	29 323	29 999	30 803	32 325	34 577	36 614	37 581
Professional and technical services	55 130	56 274	58 335	60 216	62 789	65 385	71 895
Management of companies and enterprises	65 408	67 773	69 937	76 201	75 629	86 543	90 104
Administrative and waste services	29 173	31 049	32 642	33 660	33 873	35 037	36 939
Educational services	21 368	22 293	21 391	22 101	23 521	24 241	25 254
Health care and social assistance	32 637	33 860	34 951	36 440	37 482	38 932	40 578
Arts, entertainment, and recreation	23 819	23 090	23 959	26 007	27 441	28 798	29 113
Accommodation and food services	14 574	15 091	15 602	16 260	16 858	18 331	17 929
Other services, except public administration	22 404	22 920	23 506	24 491	25 382	26 245	27 693
Government and government enterprises	35 582	37 413	38 859	40 191	41 667	43 357	45 415

Table WA-9. Employment Characteristics by Family Type

(Number, percent.)

Family type and labor force status	2005		2006		2007	
	Total	Families with own children under 18 years	Total	Families with own children under 18 years	Total	Families with own children under 18 years
TOTAL FAMILIES	1 574 432	750 848	1 595 147	758 568	1 619 537	764 019
FAMILY TYPE AND LABOR FORCE STATUS						
Married Coupled Families	1 219 685	522 405	1 235 060	533 876	1 252 212	534 345
Both husband and wife in labor force	52.3	61.1	53.9	62.9	53.3	62.5
Husband in labor force, wife not in labor force	23.0	30.9	23.2	31.5	23.5	31.5
Wife in labor force, husband not in labor force	6.8	4.4	6.8	3.7	6.8	3.9
Both husband and wife not in labor force	17.9	3.5	16.1	1.9	16.4	2.1
Other Families	354 747	228 443	360 087	224 692	367 325	229 674
Female householder, no husband present	70.6	73.8	69.5	72.7	69.2	73.0
In labor force	52.3	59.3	51.6	58.9	50.8	58.9
Not in labor force	18.3	14.5	18.0	13.8	18.4	14.1
Male householder, no wife present	29.4	26.2	30.5	27.3	30.8	27.0
In labor force	24.2	23.2	25.5	25.1	25.5	24.5
Not in labor force	5.2	3.0	5.0	2.2	5.3	2.5

Table WA-10. School Enrollment and Educational Attainment, 2007

(Number, percent.)

Item	State	U.S.
Enrollment		
Total population 3 years and over	6 210 115	289 295 761
Enrolled in school	1 602 027	79 329 527
Enrolled in preschool (percent)	5.8	6.2
Enrolled in grades K-12 (percent)	68.9	67.6
Enrolled in college or graduate school (percent)	25.3	26.2
Attainment		
Total population 25 years and over	4 327 936	197 892 369
Less than a high school diploma (percent)	10.7	15.5
High school diploma or more (percent)	89.3	84.5
Bachelor's degree or more (percent)	30.3	27.5
Graduate degree or more (percent)	10.8	10.1

Table WA-11. Educational Indicators

(Number, percent.)

Item	State	U.S.
Public Schools, 2006–2007 (except where noted)		
Number of school districts	308	17 742
Number of schools	2 326	99 639
Number of students	1 026 774	49 315 842
Student-teacher ratio	19.1	15.5
Expenditures per student (dollars)	$8 524	. . .
Averaged freshman graduation rate, 2005–2006	72.9	. . .
Dropout rate, grades 9–12, 2005–2006	5.5	3.7
Students eligible for free or reduced-price lunch (percent)	36.5	41.2
English-language learners (percent)	8.3	5.1
Students with IEP (percent)	12.0	12.7
Private Schools, 2007–2008 (except where noted)		
Number of schools	730	33 740
Number of students	86 811	5 072 451
High school graduates, 2006–2007	4 565	306 605
Student-teacher ratio	11.6	11.1

Table WA-12. Reported Voting and Registration of the Voting-Age Population, November 2008

(Number in thousands, percent.)

Item	Total population	Total citizen population	Registered — Total registered	Registered — Percent registered (total population)	Registered — Percent registered (total citizen population)	Voted — Total voted	Voted — Percent voted (total population)	Voted — Percent voted (total citizen population)
U.S. total	225 499	206 072	146 311	64.9	71.0	131 144	58.2	63.6
State total	4 912	4 600	3 299	67.2	71.7	3 073	62.6	66.8
Sex								
Male	2 418	2 265	1 553	64.3	68.6	1 439	59.5	63.5
Female	2 495	2 334	1 745	70.0	74.8	1 634	65.5	70.0
Race								
White alone	4 146	3 980	2 932	70.7	73.7	2 762	66.6	69.4
White non-Hispanic alone	3 801	3 729	2 788	73.4	74.8	2 631	69.2	70.6
Black alone	157	123	57	36.3	46.4	57	36.3	46.4
Asian alone	344	262	167	48.4	63.6	132	38.5	50.5
Hispanic (of any race)	404	280	160	39.6	57.0	148	36.6	52.7
White alone or in combination	4 295	4 124	3 033	70.6	73.5	2 855	66.5	69.2
Black alone or in combination	182	148	77	42.3	52.1	77	42.3	52.1
Asian alone or in combination	380	295	187	49.1	63.2	150	39.4	50.8

Table WA-13. Crime

(Number, rate per 100,000.)

Item	State 2007	State 2008	State Percent change	U.S. 2007	U.S. 2008	U.S. Percent change
Population	6 468 424	6 549 224	1.2	301 621 157	304 059 724	0.8
VIOLENT CRIME						
Number	21 546	21 691	0.7	1 408 337	1 382 012	-1.9
Rate	333.1	331.2	-0.6	466.9	454.5	-2.7
Murder and Nonnegligent Manslaughter						
Number	173	192	11.0	16 929	16 272	-3.9
Rate	2.7	2.9	9.6	5.6	5.4	-4.7
Forcible Rape						
Number	2 629	2 628	*	90 427	89 000	-1.6
Rate	40.6	40.1	-1.3	30.0	29.3	-2.4
Robbery						
Number	6 053	6 347	4.9	445 125	441 855	-0.7
Rate	93.6	96.9	3.6	147.6	145.3	-1.5
Aggravated Assault						
Number	12 691	12 524	-1.3	855 856	834 885	-2.5
Rate	196.2	191.2	-2.5	283.8	274.6	-3.2
PROPERTY CRIME						
Number	260 729	246 148	-5.6	9 843 481	9 767 915	-0.8
Rate	4 030.8	3 758.4	-6.8	3 263.5	3 212.5	-1.6
Burglary						
Number	52 704	52 478	-0.4	2 179 140	2 222 196	2.0
Rate	814.8	801.3	-1.7	722.5	730.8	1.2
Larceny-Theft						
Number	170 403	165 339	-3.0	6 568 572	6 588 873	0.3
Rate	2 634.4	2 524.6	-4.2	2 177.8	2 167.0	-0.5
Motor Vehicle Theft						
Number	37 622	28 331	-24.7	1 095 769	956 846	-12.7
Rate	581.6	432.6	-25.6	363.3	314.7	-13.4

Table WA-14. State Government Finances, 2007

(Dollars, percent distribution.)

Item	Thousands of dollars	Percent distribution
Total Revenue	47 030 140	X
General revenue	31 213 802	66.4
Intergovernmental revenue	7 892 810	16.8
Taxes	17 692 767	37.6
General sales	10 861 327	23.1
Selective sales	2 990 584	6.4
License taxes	882 114	1.9
Individual income tax	0	0.0
Corporate income tax	0	0.0
Other taxes	2 958 742	6.3
Current charges	3 488 845	7.4
Miscellaneous general revenue	2 139 380	4.5
Utility revenue	0	0.0
Liquor store revenue	503 747	1.1
Insurance trust revenue	15 312 591	32.6
Total Expenditure	37 116 177	100.0
Intergovernmental expenditure	8 644 100	23.3
Direct expenditure	28 472 077	76.7
Current operation	18 849 406	50.8
Capital outlay	3 044 145	8.2
Insurance benefits and repayments	4 657 200	12.5
Assistance and subsidies	980 953	2.6
Interest on debt	940 373	2.5
Exhibit: Salaries and wages	5 775 895	15.6
Total Expenditure	37 116 177	100.0
General expenditure	31 979 762	86.2
Intergovernmental expenditure	8 644 100	23.3
Direct expenditure	23 335 662	62.9
Education	13 027 431	35.1
Public welfare	6 982 213	18.8
Hospitals	1 598 218	4.3
Health	1 709 620	4.6
Highways	2 764 159	7.4
Police protection	311 756	0.8
Correction	1 090 342	2.9
Natural resources	799 327	2.2
Parks and recreation	133 020	0.4
Government administration	714 346	1.9
Interest on general debt	940 373	2.5
Other and unallocable	1 908 957	5.1
Utility expenditure	45 417	0.1
Liquor store expenditure	433 798	1.2
Insurance trust expenditure	4 657 200	12.5
Debt at End of Fiscal Year	21 058 558	X
Cash and Security Holdings	85 562 053	X

Table WA-15. State Government Tax Collections, 2008

(Dollars, percent distribution.)

Item	Thousands of dollars	Percent distribution
Total Taxes	17 944 925	X
Property taxes	1 741 691	9.7
Sales and gross receipts	14 400 668	80.2
General sales and gross receipts	11 344 622	63.2
Selective sales taxes	3 056 046	17.0
Alcoholic beverages	266 939	1.5
Amusements	43	0.0
Insurance premiums	415 028	2.3
Motor fuels	1 169 900	6.5
Pari-mutuels	3 221	0.0
Public utilities	468 017	2.6
Tobacco products	413 488	2.3
Other selective sales	319 410	1.8
Licenses	938 205	5.2
Alcoholic beverages	11 217	0.1
Amusements	15 457	0.1
Corporation	25 029	0.1
Hunting and fishing	31 944	0.2
Motor vehicle	487 422	2.7
Motor vehicle operators	61 978	0.3
Public utility	21 521	0.1
Occupation and business, NEC	231 363	1.3
Other licenses	52 274	0.3
Other taxes	864 361	4.8
Death and gift	110 602	0.6
Documentary and stock transfer	709 721	4.0
Severance	44 038	0.2

Table WA-16. Agriculture

(Number, acres, and dollars.)

Item	2002 Number	2002 Percent of total	2007 Number	2007 Percent of total	Percent change, 2002–2007
Number of farms	35 939		39 284		9.3
Farm Size					
Average size of farm (acres)	426		381		-10.6
Farms by size (number of farms)					
Fewer than 50 acres	20 669	57.5	24 001	61.1	16.1
50 to 499 acres	10 662	29.7	10 786	27.5	1.2
500 acres or more	4 608	12.8	4 497	11.4	-2.4
Land (Acres)					
Total land in farms	15 318 008		14 972 789		-2.3
Total cropland	8 038 469	52.5	7 609 210	50.8	-5.3
Total harvested cropland	4 894 634	32.0	4 387 169	29.3	-10.4
Irrigated land	1 823 155	11.9	1 735 917	11.6	-4.8
Value of Sales (Dollars)					
Agricultural products sold ($1,000)	5 330 740		6 792 856		27.4
Average sales per farm	148 327		172 917		16.6
Sales of crops	3 582 818	67.2	4 754 898	70.0	32.7
Sales of livestock, poultry, and their products	1 747 922	32.8	2 037 958	30.0	16.6
Value of Sales (Number of Farms)					
Less than $10,000	21 355	59.4	25 977	66.1	21.6
$10,000 to $99,999	7 989	22.2	7 342	18.7	-8.1
$100,000 to $999,999	5 662	15.8	4 717	12.0	-16.7
$1,000,000 or more	933	2.6	1 248	3.2	33.8
Farms by Type of Organization (Number of Farms)					
Family	30 525	84.9	32 547	82.9	6.6
Partnership	2 280	6.3	2 932	7.5	28.6
Corporation	2 748	7.6	3 266	8.3	18.9
Other: cooperative, estate or trust, institutional, etc	386	1.1	539	1.4	39.6
Value of Land and Buildings (Dollars)					
Estimated market value of land and buildings ($1,000)	29 822 309		22 414 438		-24.8
Land and buildings average value per farm	759 146		623 333		-17.9
Average value per acre	1 992		1 486		-25.4
Government Payments					
Number of farms receiving government payments	7 332	20.4	6 899	17.6	-5.9
Payments (thousands of dollars)	133 763		138 272		3.4
Average payment per farm	18 244		20 042		9.9
Farm Operator Characteristics					
Farm operators whose principal occupation is farming	21 013	58.5	18 021	45.9	-14.2
Farm operators whose principal occupation is other	14 926	41.5	21 263	54.1	42.5
Average age principal operator (years)	55.4		57.0		2.9

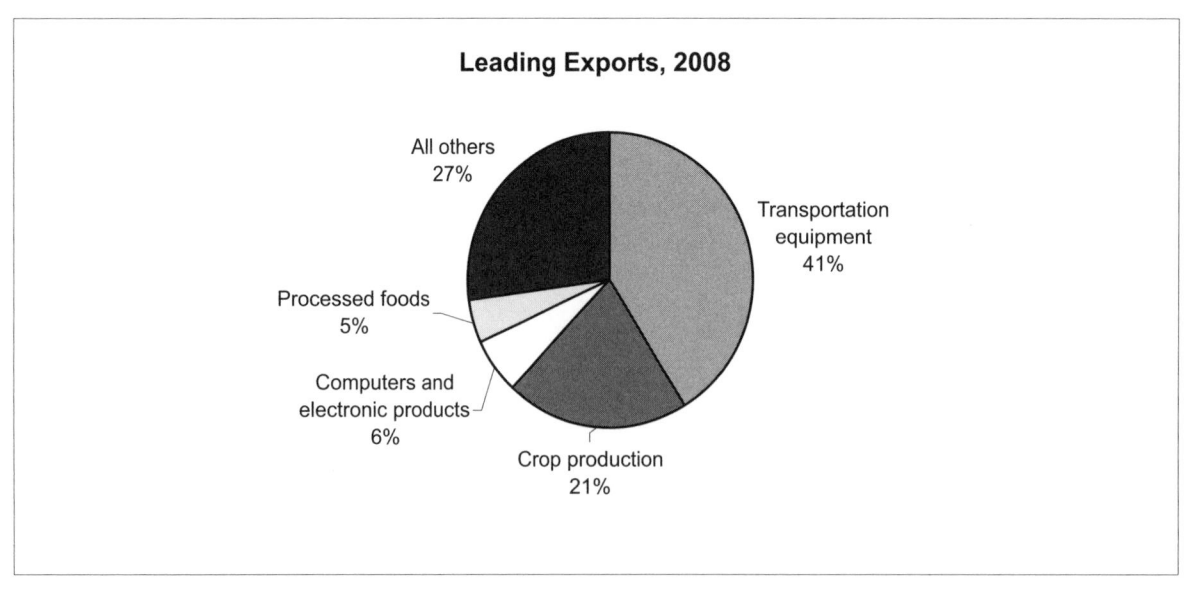

Leading Exports, 2008

All others 27%

Transportation equipment 41%

Processed foods 5%

Computers and electronic products 6%

Crop production 21%

WEST VIRGINIA

Facts and Figures

Location: East central United States; bordered on the N by Ohio and Pennsylvania, on the E by Pennsylvania, Maryland, and Virginia, on the S by Virginia and Kentucky, and on the W by Kentucky and Ohio

Area: 24,230 sq. mi. (62,755 sq. km.); rank—41st

Population: 1,814,468 (2008 est.); rank—37th

Principal Cities: capital—Charleston; largest—Charleston

Statehood: June 20, 1863; 35th state

U.S. Congress: 2 senators, 3 representatives

State Motto: *Montani semper liberi* (Mountaineers are always free)

State Songs: "West Virginia Hills"; "This Is My West Virginia"; "West Virginia, My Home Sweet Home"

State Nickname: The Mountain State

Abbreviations: WV; W. Va.

State Symbols: flower—rhododendron (great laurel); tree—sugar maple; bird—cardinal

At a Glance

- With an increase in population of 0.3 percent, West Virginia ranked 47th among the states in growth from 2000 to 2008.
- An estimated 12,299 marriages took place in West Virginia in 2008, compared to 8,641 divorces.
- The 2007 home ownership rate in West Virginia was 77.6 percent, giving it a ranking of 1st among the states.
- West Virginia's median household income in 2007 was $37,060, 49th among the states.
- In West Virginia, 16.9 percent of the population lived below the poverty level in 2007, ranking it 6th along with Alabama.
- In 2006-07, 13.8 percent of West Virginians did not have health insurance, compared to 15.5 percent of the total U.S. population.
- In 2007, 4.6 percent of West Virginians were unemployed, which was the same as the national average.
- West Virginia ranked 50th in the nation with 17.3 percent of its population 25 years old and over having a bachelor's degree in 2007.
- West Virginia's violent crime rate in 2007 was 275.2 per 100,000 population, compared to 466.9 for the entire nation.
- West Virginia had one physician for every 381 people in 2007, compared to one physician for every 325 people nationwide.
- In the 2008 election, 50.6 percent of West Virginia's eligible voters voted, compared to 61.7 percent of eligible voters nationwide.
- West Virginia ranked 10th among the states receiving federal aid in 2007, with $1,973 per capita.
- West Virginia's gross domestic product was $50 billion in 2007; it ranked 40th among the states.
- With $4 billion in exports in 2007, West Virginia ranked 40th in exports.
- West Virginians consumed 829.2 billion Btu's of energy in 2006; the state ranked 34th in total consumption.
- In 2007, West Virginia exported $46 million worth of agricultural products, less than 1 percent of the U.S. total.

Table WV-1. Population by Sex, Age, Race, and Hispanic Origin

(Number, percent.)

Sex, age, race, and Hispanic origin	1990	2000	2008	Average annual percent change, 2000–2008
Total Population	1 793 477	1 808 344	1 814 468	0.0
Percent of total U.S. population	1.0	0.6	0.6	X
Sex				
Male	861 536	879 170	888 696	0.1
Female	931 941	929 174	925 772	0.0
Age				
Under 5 years	106 659	101 805	105 435	0.4
5 to 19 years	396 742	352 910	328 296	-0.9
20 to 64 years	1 021 179	1 076 734	1 095 670	0.2
65 years and over	268 897	276 895	285 067	0.4
Median age (years)	35.3	38.9	40.6	X
Race and Hispanic Origin[1]				
One race				
White	1 725 523	1 718 777	1 715 122	0.0
Black	56 295	57 232	64 987	1.6
American Indian and Alaskan Native	2 458	3 606	4 203	1.9
Asian[2]	7 459	9 434	11 977	3.0
Native Hawaiian and Other Pacific Islander	X	400	536	3.7
Two or more races	X	15 788	17 643	1.4
Hispanic (of any race)	8 489	12 279	20 648	6.7

[1]Data on race in 2000 and 2008 are not comparable to 1990. Individuals could only report one race in the 1990 census but could report one or more races on the 2000 census.
[2]Data in 1990 refer to Asian and Pacific Islanders.

Table WV-2. Marital Status

(Number, percent distribution.)

Sex and marital status	1990	2000	2007
Males, 15 Years and Over	675 682	710 443	724 483
Never married	25.8	25.4	28.0
Now married, except separated	62.4	59.9	55.8
Separated	1.2	1.3	1.5
Widowed	3.1	3.2	3.6
Divorced	7.5	10.1	11.1
Females, 15 Years and Over	756 449	768 858	771 029
Never married	18.9	19.1	22.4
Now married, except separated	55.6	54.7	51.5
Separated	1.5	1.6	1.8
Widowed	15.3	13.9	12.3
Divorced	8.7	10.8	12.0

Table WV-3. Households and Housing Characteristics

(Number, percent, and dollars.)

Item	1990	2000	2007	Average annual percent change, 2000–2007
Total Households	688 557	736 481	733 849	-0.1
Family households	500 259	504 055	491 383	-0.4
Married-couple family	406 105	397 499	381 380	-0.6
Other family	94 154	106 556	110 003	0.5
Male householder, no wife present	20 627	27 436	30 012	1.3
Female householder, no husband present	73 527	79 120	79 991	0.2
Nonfamily households	188 298	232 426	242 466	0.6
Householder living alone	168 735	199 587	206 536	0.5
Householder not living alone	19 563	32 839	35 930	1.3
Housing Characteristics				
Total housing units	781 295	844 623	882 631	0.6
Occupied housing units	688 557	736 481	733 849	-0.1
Owner-occupied	510 058	553 699	549 401	-0.1
Renter-occupied	178 499	182 782	184 448	0.1
Average size	2.55	2.40	2.41	X
Financial Characteristics				
Median gross rent of renter-occupied housing units (dollars)	303	401	525	3.9
Median monthly owner costs for housing units with a mortgage (dollars)	498	713	881	3.1
Median value of owner-occupied housing units (dollars)	47 600	72 800	96 000	4.0

Table WV-4. Median Income and Poverty Status, 2007

(Number, percent.)

Characteristic	State		U.S.	
	Number	Percent	Number	Percent
Median Income				
Households (dollars)	37 060	X	50 740	X
Families (dollars)	46 338	X	61 173	X
Below Poverty Level				
Sex				
Male	133 599	15.5	16 576 071	11.5
Female	164 573	18.3	21 476 176	14.3
Age				
Under 18 years	86 277	22.8	13 097 100	18.0
Related children under 18 years	82 932	22.1	12 728 964	17.6
18 to 64 years	183 981	16.5	21 495 507	11.6
65 years and over	27 914	10.4	3 459 640	9.5

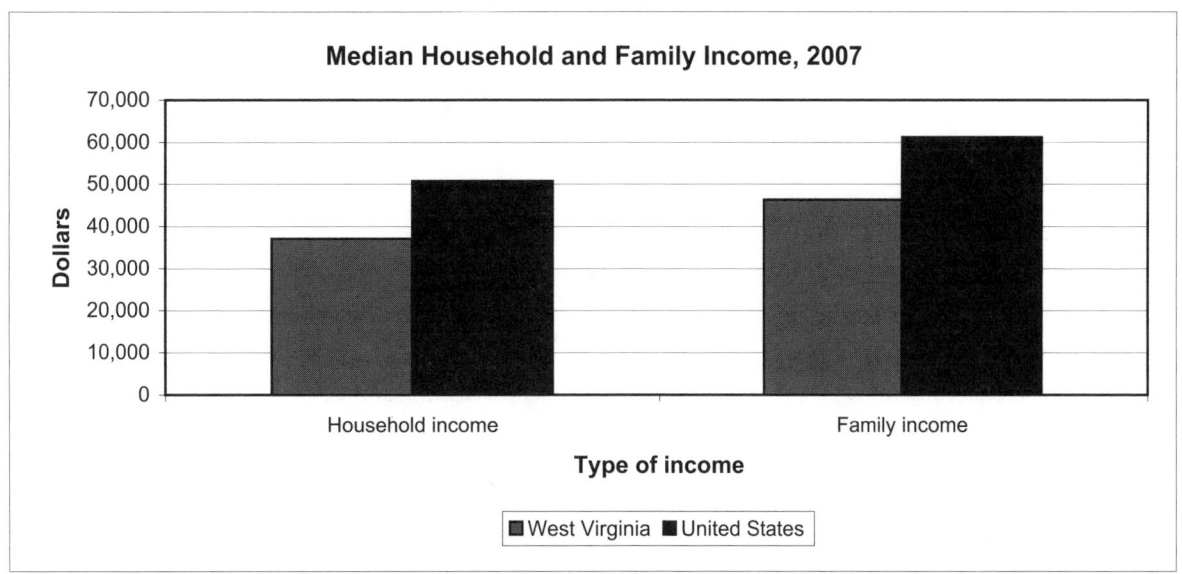

Median Household and Family Income, 2007

Table WV-5. Health Insurance Coverage Status for All Persons and Children Under 18 Years of Age

(Number, percent.)

Item	2000	2001	2002	2003	2004	2005	2006	2007
ALL PERSONS	1 775	1 772	1 751	1 787	1 792	1 799	1 814	1 795
Covered by Private or Government Health Insurance								
Number	1 528	1 546	1 501	1 495	1 503	1 495	1 570	1 541
Percent	86.1	87.2	85.7	83.6	83.9	83.1	86.5	85.9
Not Covered								
Number	247	226	251	292	289	304	245	254
Percent	13.9	12.8	14.3	16.4	16.1	16.9	13.5	14.1
Percent in the U.S. not covered	13.7	14.1	14.7	15.1	14.9	15.3	15.8	15.3
CHILDREN UNDER 18 YEARS OF AGE	394	388	386	400	388	387	395	394
Covered by Private or Government Health Insurance								
Number	352	360	347	366	354	361	361	376
Percent	89.3	92.9	90.1	91.6	91.3	93.4	91.5	95.4
Not Covered								
Number	42	28	38	34	34	26	34	18
Percent	10.7	7.1	9.9	8.4	8.7	6.6	8.5	4.6
Percent in the U.S. not covered	11.6	11.3	11.2	11.0	10.5	10.9	11.7	11.0

Table WV-6. Employment Status by Demographic Group, Preliminary 2008

(Number, percent.)

Characteristic	Civilian noninstitutional population	Civilian labor force		Employment		Unemployed	
		Number	Percent of population	Number	Percent of population	Number	Unemployment rate
TOTAL	1 450	822	56.7	786	54.2	36	4.4
Sex							
Men	701	445	63.0	423	60.3	22	4.9
Women	749	377	50.0	363	48.4	14	3.8
Race, Sex, and Hispanic Origin							
White	1 385	782	56.4	750	54.1	32	4.1
Men	669	424	63.4	404	60.4	20	4.7
Women	716	357	49.9	346	48.2	12	3.3
Black or African American	44	27	62.2	25	56.6	2	9.0
Men	21	. . .	. . .	. . .	. . .	. . .	. . .
Women	23	14	61.8	12	53.6	2	13.2
Hispanic	. . .	. . .	. . .	. . .	. . .	. . .	. . .
Men	. . .	. . .	. . .	. . .	. . .	. . .	. . .
Women	. . .	. . .	. . .	. . .	. . .	. . .	. . .
Age							
16 to 19 years	104	40	38.0	32	31.2	7	18.0
20 to 24 years	104	78	75.2	72	69.4	6	7.6
25 to 34 years	224	172	76.5	163	72.7	9	5.0
35 to 44 years	233	180	77.0	173	74.2	7	3.7
45 to 54 years	277	197	71.1	193	69.7	4	2.0
55 to 64 years	256	127	49.8	124	48.3	4	2.9
65 years and over	252	29	11.4	28	11.3	. . .	1.0

Note: Data in Table 6 are from the Current Population Survey (CPS) and do not match the estimates in Table 7. See notes and definitions for more details.

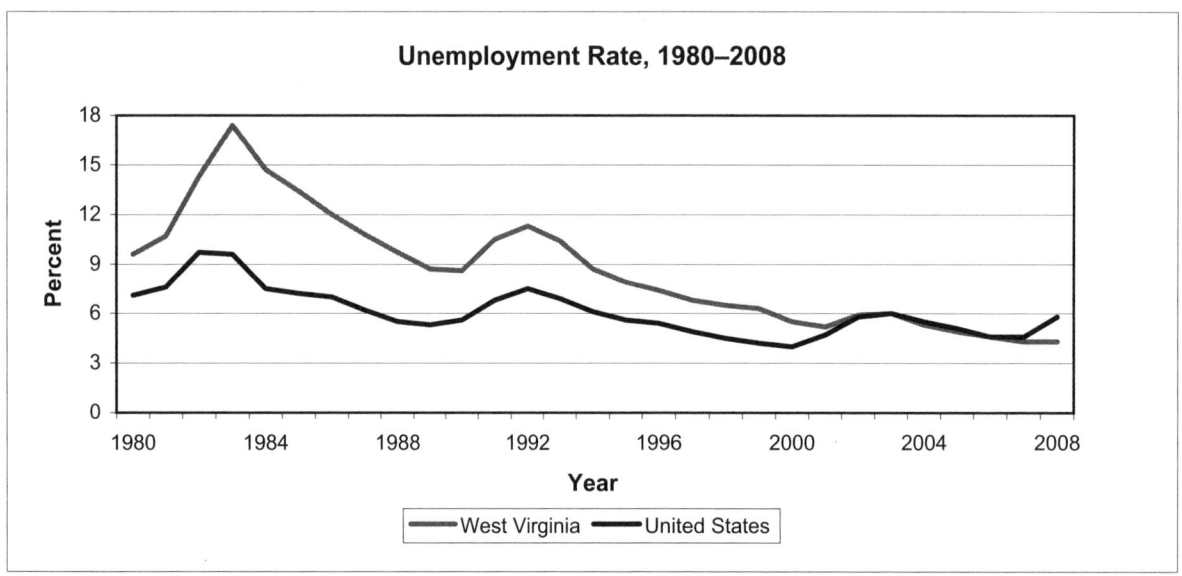

Table WV-7. Employment Status of the Civilian Noninstitutional Population Age 16 Years and Over

(Number, percent.)

Year	Civilian labor force	Civilian participation rate	Employed	Unemployed	Unemployment rate
1998	807 092	56.3	754 629	52 463	6.5
1999	813 380	56.8	762 395	50 985	6.3
2000	808 861	56.5	764 649	44 212	5.5
2001	800 623	56.1	758 904	41 719	5.2
2002	796 231	55.7	749 164	47 067	5.9
2003	789 578	55.1	742 424	47 154	6.0
2004	788 333	55.0	746 854	41 479	5.3
2005	797 844	55.5	758 525	39 319	4.9
2006	810 437	56.2	773 118	37 319	4.6
2007	813 195	56.3	777 961	35 234	4.3
2008	806 152	55.6	771 805	34 347	4.3

Table WV-8. Employment and Average Wages by Industry

(Estimates for 2001–2006 are based on the 2002 North American Industry Classification System [NAICS]. Estimates for 2007 are based on the 2007 NAICS.)

Industry	2001	2002	2003	2004	2005	2006	2007
	Number of jobs						
WAGE AND SALARY EMPLOYMENT BY INDUSTRY	733 604	732 605	728 107	736 661	744 053	753 642	756 401
Farm Wage and Salary Employment	1 888	1 791	2 242	2 168	1 687	1 682	1 628
Nonfarm Wage and Salary Employment	731 716	730 814	725 865	734 493	742 366	751 960	754 773
Private wage and salary employment	583 071	580 394	575 040	582 902	590 996	600 657	602 240
Forestry, fishing, hunting, and other	2 355	2 354	2 188	2 152	2 101	2 107	2 045
Mining	22 307	21 971	20 970	22 792	24 992	27 036	27 671
Utilities	6 886	6 718	6 315	6 226	6 145	6 205	6 259
Construction	36 226	35 004	34 239	36 214	38 287	40 969	40 389
Manufacturing	72 795	69 145	65 138	63 559	62 490	61 268	59 305
Durable goods manufacturing	44 915	42 706	40 057	39 617	39 374	38 535	37 341
Nondurable goods manufacturing	27 880	26 439	25 081	23 942	23 116	22 733	21 964
Wholesale trade	24 331	23 558	23 080	23 603	24 301	25 112	25 219
Retail trade	92 657	91 013	90 466	91 699	92 406	93 501	94 291
Transportation and warehousing	19 668	19 191	18 940	19 396	20 303	20 533	20 575
Information	13 823	12 891	12 793	11 928	11 667	11 494	11 454
Finance and insurance	22 461	23 178	22 647	21 867	21 518	22 271	21 875
Real estate and rental and leasing	7 289	7 301	7 353	7 495	7 620	7 785	7 869
Professional and technical services	23 982	24 587	24 747	25 258	25 871	26 245	26 031
Management of companies and enterprises	2 772	2 780	3 241	3 548	4 097	4 419	4 804
Administrative and waste services	32 345	30 807	30 106	30 995	30 921	31 271	32 090
Educational services	9 782	9 839	9 225	8 623	8 573	8 441	8 564
Health care and social assistance	94 787	98 358	99 598	101 245	102 603	103 069	104 381
Arts, entertainment, and recreation	8 613	9 696	10 074	10 928	9 811	9 723	9 945
Accommodation and food services	55 383	56 192	57 805	58 717	60 948	62 667	63 151
Other services, except public administration	34 609	35 811	36 115	36 657	36 342	36 541	36 322
Government and government enterprises	148 645	150 420	150 825	151 591	151 370	151 303	152 533
	Dollars						
AVERAGE WAGES AND SALARIES BY INDUSTRY	27 407	28 044	28 778	29 926	30 944	32 292	33 528
Average Farm Wages and Salaries	13 305	16 924	14 206	14 571	14 940	17 322	15 580
Average Nonfarm Wages and Salaries	27 443	28 071	28 823	29 971	30 981	32 326	33 567
Average private wages and salaries	27 046	27 517	28 090	29 333	30 298	31 751	33 044
Forestry, fishing, hunting, and other	18 657	18 724	19 142	20 002	21 158	23 215	24 665
Mining	49 670	50 324	51 476	54 437	57 196	59 974	63 454
Utilities	59 252	59 112	61 658	62 839	64 126	68 059	69 373
Construction	32 404	31 654	30 916	32 428	34 154	37 931	39 997
Manufacturing	38 992	39 629	40 834	42 713	43 007	44 126	45 654
Durable goods manufacturing	34 614	35 594	36 573	38 735	39 230	40 797	42 380
Nondurable goods manufacturing	46 046	46 146	47 639	49 296	49 441	49 769	51 220
Wholesale trade	36 423	37 958	38 823	40 870	42 110	44 466	45 979
Retail trade	17 736	18 427	18 921	19 501	19 842	20 405	21 070
Transportation and warehousing	35 989	36 257	37 316	38 875	39 836	41 079	42 507
Information	33 427	35 746	36 854	37 819	37 450	39 324	40 044
Finance and insurance	31 458	31 688	32 702	34 418	35 698	37 135	38 989
Real estate and rental and leasing	21 168	22 247	22 758	23 575	25 050	27 244	28 776
Professional and technical services	32 864	34 692	36 034	37 545	39 324	41 534	43 871
Management of companies and enterprises	45 921	44 726	46 113	49 621	56 258	58 344	63 890
Administrative and waste services	17 109	17 460	18 214	19 519	20 807	21 742	22 646
Educational services	16 396	16 268	16 094	17 730	18 133	19 550	20 518
Health care and social assistance	27 742	28 464	29 337	30 512	31 350	32 572	33 920
Arts, entertainment, and recreation	15 545	16 805	18 804	19 190	16 728	17 344	18 055
Accommodation and food services	11 519	11 879	12 180	12 540	13 233	13 682	14 206
Other services, except public administration	17 519	18 034	18 737	19 897	20 569	21 517	22 286
Government and government enterprises	29 001	30 207	31 618	32 426	33 645	34 607	35 633

Table WV-9. Employment Characteristics by Family Type

(Number, percent.)

Family type and labor force status	2005		2006		2007	
	Total	Families with own children under 18 years	Total	Families with own children under 18 years	Total	Families with own children under 18 years
TOTAL FAMILIES	500 147	199 478	502 381	201 073	491 383	195 852
FAMILY TYPE AND LABOR FORCE STATUS						
Married Coupled Families	388 743	141 543	390 066	141 234	381 380	138 439
Both husband and wife in labor force	42.6	56.6	43.4	58.3	43.4	57.5
Husband in labor force, wife not in labor force	22.6	30.4	23.6	32.2	23.2	32.6
Wife in labor force, husband not in labor force	9.4	6.4	8.8	4.3	9.5	5.6
Both husband and wife not in labor force	25.3	6.6	24.3	5.1	23.9	4.3
Other Families	111 404	57 935	112 315	59 839	110 003	57 413
Female householder, no husband present	72.8	73.6	72.1	73.2	72.7	76.6
In labor force	41.5	50.8	42.0	54.0	41.0	52.9
Not in labor force	31.3	22.9	30.1	19.2	31.7	23.7
Male householder, no wife present	27.2	26.4	27.9	26.8	27.3	23.4
In labor force	16.7	19.1	19.5	21.2	18.1	18.3
Not in labor force	10.5	7.3	8.4	5.6	9.2	5.1

Table WV-10. School Enrollment and Educational Attainment, 2007

(Number, percent.)

Item	State	U.S.
Enrollment		
Total population 3 years and over	1 754 732	289 295 761
Enrolled in school	414 852	79 329 527
Enrolled in preschool (percent)	6.0	6.2
Enrolled in grades K-12 (percent)	69.0	67.6
Enrolled in college or graduate school (percent)	25.0	26.2
Attainment		
Total population 25 years and over	1 261 455	197 892 369
Less than a high school diploma (percent)	18.8	15.5
High school diploma or more (percent)	81.2	84.5
Bachelor's degree or more (percent)	17.3	27.5
Graduate degree or more (percent)	6.6	10.1

Table WV-11. Educational Indicators

(Number, percent.)

Item	State	U.S.
Public Schools, 2006–2007 (except where noted)		
Number of school districts	57	17 742
Number of schools	771	99 639
Number of students	281 939	49 315 842
Student-teacher ratio	14.4	15.5
Expenditures per student (dollars)	$9 727	. . .
Averaged freshman graduation rate, 2005–2006	76.9	. . .
Dropout rate, grades 9–12, 2005–2006	3.9	3.7
Students eligible for free or reduced-price lunch (percent)	49.6	41.2
English-language learners (percent)	0.8	5.1
Students with IEP (percent)	17.2	12.7
Private Schools, 2007–2008 (except where noted)		
Number of schools	139	33 740
Number of students	13 400	5 072 451
High school graduates, 2006–2007	605	306 605
Student-teacher ratio	10.6	11.1

Table WV-12. Reported Voting and Registration of the Voting-Age Population, November 2008

(Number in thousands, percent.)

Item	Total population	Total citizen population	Registered			Voted		
			Total registered	Percent registered (total population)	Percent registered (total citizen population)	Total voted	Percent voted (total population)	Percent voted (total citizen population)
U.S. total	225 499	206 072	146 311	64.9	71.0	131 144	58.2	63.6
State total	1 395	1 387	917	65.7	66.1	741	53.1	53.4
Sex								
Male	673	669	438	65.1	65.4	350	51.9	52.2
Female	722	717	479	66.3	66.8	392	54.2	54.6
Race								
White alone	1 345	1 340	890	66.2	66.4	720	53.5	53.7
White non-Hispanic alone	1 336	1 333	885	66.2	66.3	715	53.5	53.6
Black alone	39	38	21	. . .	. . .	19	. . .	. . .
Asian alone	6	3	. . .	. . .	. . .	. . .	. . .	. . .
Hispanic (of any race)	9	6	5	. . .	. . .	5	. . .	. . .
White alone or in combination	1 350	1 345	894	66.2	66.5	722	53.5	53.7
Black alone or in combination	39	38	21	. . .	. . .	19	. . .	. . .
Asian alone or in combination	7	4	2	. . .	. . .	. . .	. . .	. . .

Table WV-13. Crime

(Number, rate per 100,000.)

Item	State			U.S.		
	2007	2008	Percent change	2007	2008	Percent change
Population	1 812 035	1 814 468	0.1	301 621 157	304 059 724	0.8
VIOLENT CRIME						
Number	4 987	4 968	-0.4	1 408 337	1 382 012	-1.9
Rate	275.2	273.8	-0.5	466.9	454.5	-2.7
Murder and Nonnegligent Manslaughter						
Number	64	60	-6.3	16 929	16 272	-3.9
Rate	3.5	3.3	-6.4	5.6	5.4	-4.7
Forcible Rape						
Number	369	362	-1.9	90 427	89 000	-1.6
Rate	20.4	20.0	-2.0	30.0	29.3	-2.4
Robbery						
Number	852	889	4.3	445 125	441 855	-0.7
Rate	47.0	49.0	4.2	147.6	145.3	-1.5
Aggravated Assault						
Number	3 702	3 657	-1.2	855 856	834 885	-2.5
Rate	204.3	201.5	-1.3	283.8	274.6	-3.2
PROPERTY CRIME						
Number	45 753	46 607	1.9	9 843 481	9 767 915	-0.8
Rate	2 525.0	2 568.6	1.7	3 263.5	3 212.5	-1.6
Burglary						
Number	10 814	11 066	2.3	2 179 140	2 222 196	2.0
Rate	596.8	609.9	2.2	722.5	730.8	1.2
Larceny-Theft						
Number	31 447	32 337	2.8	6 568 572	6 588 873	0.3
Rate	1 735.5	1 782.2	2.7	2 177.8	2 167.0	-0.5
Motor Vehicle Theft						
Number	3 492	3 204	-8.2	1 095 769	956 846	-12.7
Rate	192.7	176.6	-8.4	363.3	314.7	-13.4

Table WV-14. State Government Finances, 2007

(Dollars, percent distribution.)

Item	Thousands of dollars	Percent distribution
Total Revenue	11 945 313	X
General revenue	10 648 164	89.1
Intergovernmental revenue	3 256 627	27.3
Taxes	4 654 213	39.0
General sales	1 129 531	9.5
Selective sales	1 098 065	9.2
License taxes	182 098	1.5
Individual income tax	1 360 511	11.4
Corporate income tax	539 136	4.5
Other taxes	344 872	2.9
Current charges	1 232 116	10.3
Miscellaneous general revenue	1 505 208	12.6
Utility revenue	544	0.0
Liquor store revenue	69 729	0.6
Insurance trust revenue	1 226 876	10.3
Total Expenditure	9 766 972	100.0
Intergovernmental expenditure	2 074 429	21.2
Direct expenditure	7 692 543	78.8
Current operation	6 005 588	61.5
Capital outlay	943 538	9.7
Insurance benefits and repayments	405 947	4.2
Assistance and subsidies	161 837	1.7
Interest on debt	175 633	1.8
Exhibit: Salaries and wages	1 380 391	14.1
Total Expenditure	9 766 972	100.0
General expenditure	9 289 844	95.1
Intergovernmental expenditure	2 074 429	21.2
Direct expenditure	7 215 415	73.9
Education	3 572 629	36.6
Public welfare	2 405 778	24.6
Hospitals	88 713	0.9
Health	307 646	3.1
Highways	972 049	10.0
Police protection	61 691	0.6
Correction	233 639	2.4
Natural resources	178 911	1.8
Parks and recreation	51 015	0.5
Government administration	507 750	5.2
Interest on general debt	175 633	1.8
Other and unallocable	734 390	7.5
Utility expenditure	12 076	0.1
Liquor store expenditure	59 105	0.6
Insurance trust expenditure	405 947	4.2
Debt at End of Fiscal Year	5 628 065	X
Cash and Security Holdings	12 479 924	X

Table WV-15. State Government Tax Collections, 2008

(Dollars, percent distribution.)

Item	Thousands of dollars	Percent distribution
Total Taxes	4 879 151	X
Property taxes	4 627	0.1
Sales and gross receipts	2 266 891	46.5
General sales and gross receipts	1 109 822	22.7
Selective sales taxes	1 157 069	23.7
Alcoholic beverages	9 465	0.2
Insurance premiums	114 156	2.3
Motor fuels	404 221	8.3
Pari-mutuels	2 870	0.1
Public utilities	158 141	3.2
Tobacco products	114 669	2.4
Other selective sales	353 547	7.2
Licenses	190 711	3.9
Alcoholic beverages	16 327	0.3
Amusements	15	0.0
Corporation	6 750	0.1
Hunting and fishing	16 457	0.3
Motor vehicle	86 754	1.8
Motor vehicle operators	947	0.0
Public utility	20 811	0.4
Occupation and business, NEC	42 437	0.9
Other licenses	213	0.0
Income taxes	2 057 585	42.2
Individual income	1 518 746	31.1
Corporation net income	538 839	11.0
Other taxes	359 337	7.4
Death and gift	46	0.0
Documentary and stock transfer	11 699	0.2
Severance	347 592	7.1

Table WV-16. Agriculture

(Number, acres, and dollars.)

Item	2002		2007		Percent change, 2002–2007
	Number	Percent of total	Number	Percent of total	
Number of farms	20 812		23 618		13.5
Farm Size					
Average size of farm (acres)	172		157		-8.7
Farms by size (number of farms)					
Fewer than 50 acres	5 672	27.3	6 956	29.5	22.6
50 to 499 acres	13 829	66.4	15 420	65.3	11.5
500 acres or more	1 311	6.3	1 242	5.3	-5.3
Land (Acres)					
Total land in farms	3 584 668		3 697 606		3.2
Total cropland	1 173 032	32.7	942 132	25.5	-19.7
Total harvested cropland	648 635	18.1	692 003	18.7	6.7
Irrigated land	1 981	0.1	2 189	0.1	10.5
Value of Sales (Dollars)					
Agricultural products sold ($1,000)	482 814		591 665		22.5
Average sales per farm	23 199		25 051		8.0
Sales of crops	69 693	14.4	78 308	13.2	12.4
Sales of livestock, poultry, and their products	413 121	85.6	513 357	86.8	24.3
Value of Sales (Number of Farms)					
Less than $10,000	17 164	82.5	18 877	79.9	10.0
$10,000 to $99,999	2 953	14.2	3 992	16.9	35.2
$100,000 to $999,999	607	2.9	628	2.7	3.5
$1,000,000 or more	88	0.4	121	0.5	37.5
Farms by Type of Organization (Number of Farms)					
Family	19 862	95.4	22 488	95.2	13.2
Partnership	639	3.1	856	3.6	34.0
Corporation	220	1.1	209	0.9	-5.0
Other: cooperative, estate or trust, institutional, etc	91	0.4	65	0.3	-28.6
Value of Land and Buildings (Dollars)					
Estimated market value of land and buildings ($1,000)	8 819 799		4 817 217		-45.4
Land and buildings average value per farm	373 435		231 999		-37.9
Average value per acre	2 385		1 315		-44.9
Government Payments					
Number of farms receiving government payments	1 675	8.0	2 173	9.2	29.7
Payments (thousands of dollars)	5 180		2 929		-43.5
Average payment per farm	3 093		1 348		-56.4
Farm Operator Characteristics					
Farm operators whose principal occupation is farming	10 507	50.5	9 799	41.5	-6.7
Farm operators whose principal occupation is other	10 305	49.5	13 819	58.5	34.1
Average age principal operator (years)	56.3		58.1		3.2

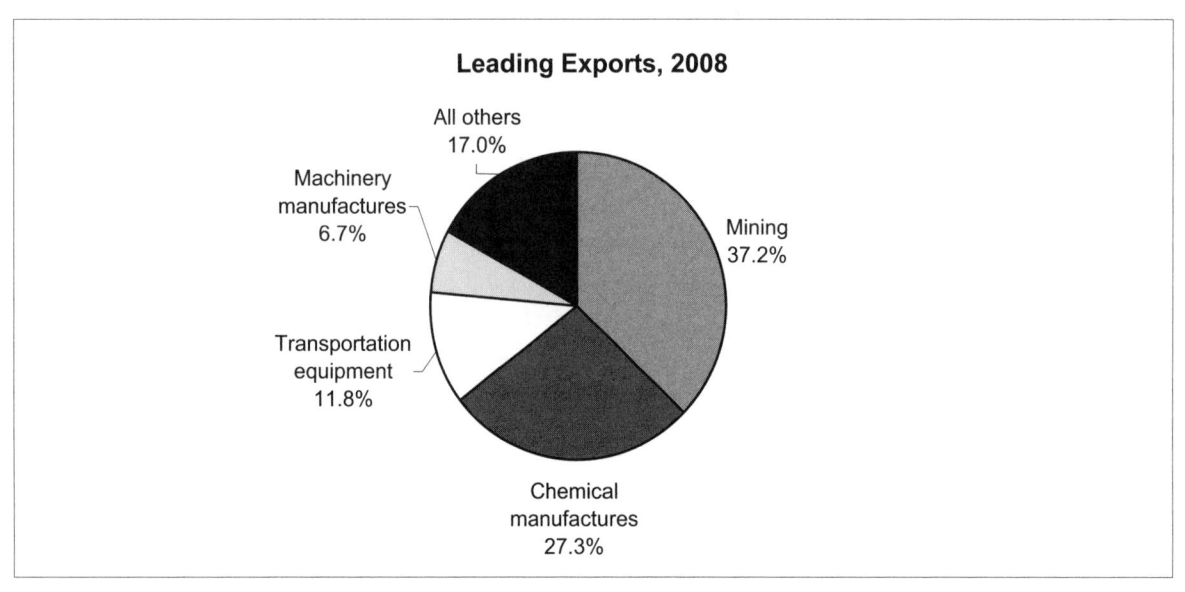

Leading Exports, 2008

All others 17.0%

Machinery manufactures 6.7%

Mining 37.2%

Transportation equipment 11.8%

Chemical manufactures 27.3%

WISCONSIN

Facts and Figures

Location: North central United States; bordered on the N by Michigan and Lake Superior, on the E by Lake Michigan, on the S by Illinois, and on the W by Iowa and Minnesota

Area: 65,498 sq. mi. (169,639 sq. km.); rank—23rd

Population: 5,627,967 (2008 est.); rank—20th

Principal Cities: capital—Madison; largest—Milwaukee

Statehood: May 29, 1848; 30th state

U.S. Congress: 2 senators, 8 representatives

State Motto: Forward

State Song: "On, Wisconsin!"

State Nickname: The Badger State

Abbreviations: WI; Wis.; Wisc.

State Symbols: flower—wood violet; tree—sugar maple; bird—robin

At a Glance

- With an increase in population of 4.9 percent, Wisconsin ranked 30th among the states in growth from 2000 to 2008.
- An estimated 31,586 marriages took place in Wisconsin in 2008, compared to 17,067 divorces.
- The 2007 home ownership rate in Wisconsin was 70.5 percent, giving it a ranking of 24th among the states.
- Wisconsin's median household income in 2007 was $50,578, 20th among the states.
- In Wisconsin, 10.8 percent of the population lived below the poverty level in 2007, ranking it 36th.
- In 2006-07, 8.5 percent of Wisconsinites did not have health insurance, compared to 15.5 percent of the total U.S. population.
- In 2007, 5 percent of Wisconsinites were unemployed, compared to 4.6 percent nationwide.
- Wisconsin ranked 29th in the nation with 25.4 percent of its population 25 years old and over having a bachelor's degree in 2007.
- Wisconsin's violent crime rate in 2007 was 290.9 per 100,000 population, compared to 466.9 for the entire nation.
- Wisconsin had one physician for every 340 people in 2007, compared to one physician for every 325 people nationwide.
- In the 2008 election, 72.5 percent of Wisconsin's eligible voters voted, compared to 61.7 percent of eligible voters nationwide.
- Wisconsin ranked 42nd among the states receiving federal aid in 2007, with $1,200 per capita.
- Wisconsin's gross domestic product was $232 billion in 2007; it ranked 21st among the states.
- With $18.8 billion in exports in 2007, Wisconsin ranked 19th in exports.
- Wisconsinites consumed 1.81 trillion Btu's of energy in 2006; the state ranked 21st in total consumption.
- In 2007, Wisconsin exported $2.1 billion worth of agricultural products, about 2.6 percent of the U.S. total.

Table WI-1. Population by Sex, Age, Race, and Hispanic Origin

(Number, percent.)

Sex, age, race, and Hispanic origin	1990	2000	2008	Average annual percent change, 2000–2008
Total Population	4 891 769	5 363 675	5 627 967	0.6
Percent of total U.S. population	2.0	1.9	1.9	X
Sex				
Male	2 392 935	2 649 041	2 797 649	0.7
Female	2 498 834	2 714 634	2 830 318	0.5
Age				
Under 5 years	360 730	342 340	362 277	0.7
5 to 19 years	1 077 179	1 189 753	1 113 171	-0.8
20 to 64 years	2 802 639	3 129 029	3 402 373	1.1
65 years and over	651 221	702 553	750 146	0.8
Median age (years)	32.8	36.0	38.2	X
Race and Hispanic Origin[1]				
One race				
White	4 512 523	4 769 857	5 046 806	0.7
Black	244 539	304 460	341 723	1.5
American Indian and Alaskan Native	39 387	47 228	55 844	2.1
Asian[2]	53 583	88 763	114 503	3.2
Native Hawaiian and Other Pacific Islander	X	1 630	2 478	5.4
Two or more races	X	66 895	66 613	-0.1
Hispanic (of any race)	93 194	192 921	285 827	5.0

[1]Data on race in 2000 and 2008 are not comparable to 1990. Individuals could only report one race in the 1990 census but could report one or more races on the 2000 census.
[2]Data in 1990 refer to Asian and Pacific Islanders.

Table WI-2. Marital Status

(Number, percent distribution.)

Sex and marital status	1990	2000	2007
Males, 15 Years and Over	1 833 873	2 072 397	2 234 086
Never married	30.5	30.2	33.5
Now married, except separated	58.9	57.9	54.1
Separated	1.2	1.1	1.0
Widowed	2.6	2.4	2.4
Divorced	6.8	8.4	9.1
Females, 15 Years and Over	1 967 276	2 167 164	2 290 362
Never married	23.8	24.3	26.7
Now married, except separated	54.7	54.6	51.4
Separated	1.5	1.3	1.4
Widowed	11.9	10.2	9.7
Divorced	8.1	9.7	10.8

Table WI-3. Households and Housing Characteristics

(Number, percent, and dollars.)

Item	1990	2000	2007	Average annual percent change, 2000–2007
Total Households	1 822 118	2 084 544	2 241 597	1.0
Family households	1 275 172	1 386 815	1 461 841	0.8
Married-couple family	1 048 010	1 108 597	1 149 189	0.5
Other family	227 162	278 218	312 652	1.7
Male householder, no wife present	52 632	77 918	92 791	2.5
Female householder, no husband present	174 530	200 300	219 861	1.3
Nonfamily households	546 946	697 729	779 756	1.6
Householder living alone	443 673	557 875	629 224	1.7
Householder not living alone	103 273	139 854	150 532	1.1
Housing Characteristics				
Total housing units	2 055 774	2 321 144	2 558 278	1.4
Occupied housing units	1 822 118	2 084 544	2 241 597	1.0
Owner-occupied	1 215 350	1 426 361	1 570 851	1.4
Renter-occupied	606 768	658 183	670 746	0.3
Average size	2.61	2.50	2.43	X
Financial Characteristics				
Median gross rent of renter-occupied housing units (dollars) .	399	540	673	3.2
Median monthly owner costs for housing units with a mortgage (dollars)	678	1 024	1 374	4.3
Median value of owner-occupied housing units (dollars)	62 100	112 200	168 800	6.0

Table WI-4. Median Income and Poverty Status, 2007

(Number, percent.)

Characteristic	State		U.S.	
	Number	Percent	Number	Percent
Median Income				
Households (dollars)	50 578	X	50 740	X
Families (dollars)	62 804	X	61 173	X
Below Poverty Level				
Sex				
Male	259 082	9.6	16 576 071	11.5
Female	329 205	12.0	21 476 176	14.3
Age				
Under 18 years	186 980	14.4	13 097 100	18.0
Related children under 18 years	178 440	13.9	12 728 964	17.6
18 to 64 years	343 273	10.0	21 495 507	11.6
65 years and over	58 034	8.3	3 459 640	9.5

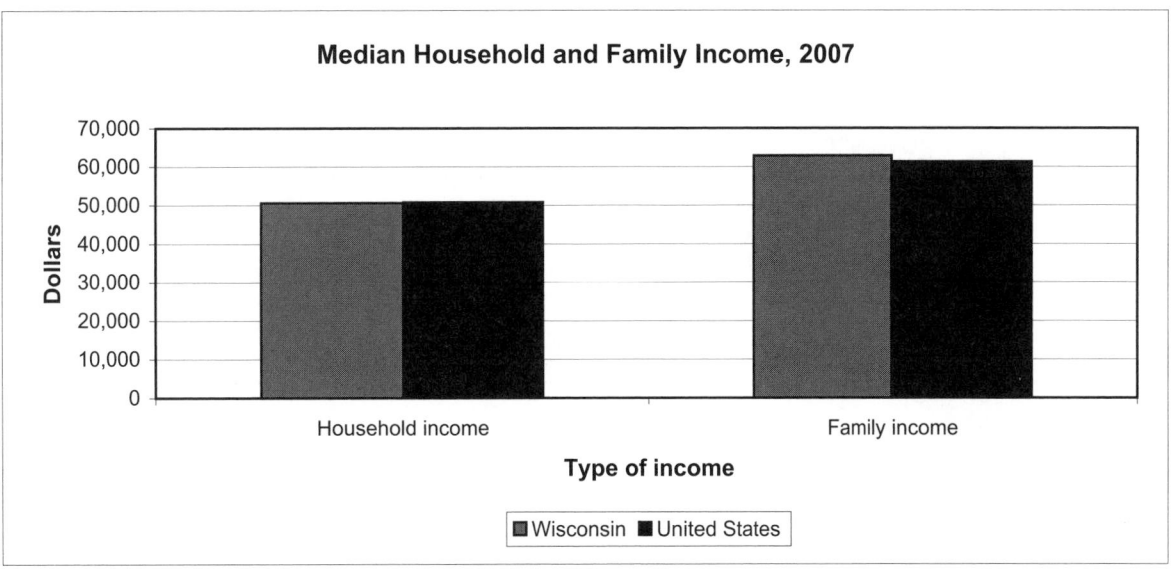

Median Household and Family Income, 2007

Table WI-5. Health Insurance Coverage Status for All Persons and Children Under 18 Years of Age

(Number, percent.)

Item	2000	2001	2002	2003	2004	2005	2006	2007
ALL PERSONS	5 320	5 336	5 475	5 429	5 463	5 447	5 476	5 473
Covered by Private or Government Health Insurance								
Number	4 922	4 944	4 958	4 860	4 912	4 938	4 995	5 023
Percent	92.5	92.7	90.6	89.5	89.9	90.7	91.2	91.8
Not Covered								
Number	398	392	517	569	551	509	481	451
Percent	7.5	7.3	9.4	10.5	10.1	9.3	8.8	8.2
Percent in the U.S. not covered	13.7	14.1	14.7	15.1	14.9	15.3	15.8	15.3
CHILDREN UNDER 18 YEARS OF AGE	1 334	1 281	1 358	1 348	1 308	1 303	1 290	1 329
Covered by Private or Government Health Insurance								
Number	1 277	1 229	1 299	1 248	1 246	1 212	1 227	1 252
Percent	95.8	95.9	95.6	92.5	95.3	93.1	95.1	94.2
Not Covered								
Number	56	52	59	101	62	90	63	77
Percent	4.2	4.1	4.4	7.5	4.7	6.9	4.9	5.8
Percent in the U.S. not covered	11.6	11.3	11.2	11.0	10.5	10.9	11.7	11.0

Table WI-6. Employment Status by Demographic Group, Preliminary 2008

(Number, percent.)

Characteristic	Civilian noninstitutional population	Civilian labor force		Employment		Unemployed	
		Number	Percent of population	Number	Percent of population	Number	Unemployment rate
TOTAL	4 395	3 098	70.5	2 953	67.2	145	4.7
Sex							
Men	2 159	1 610	75.0	1 527	70.7	84	5.2
Women	2 236	1 488	67.0	1 427	63.8	62	4.1
Race, Sex, and Hispanic Origin							
White	3 992	2 828	70.8	2 710	67.9	118	4.2
Men	1 974	1 484	75.2	1 414	71.6	70	4.7
Women	2 018	1 344	66.6	1 296	64.2	48	3.6
Black or African American	228	141	61.8	123	53.9	18	12.8
Men	100	61	61.0	53	53.1	8	13.0
Women	128	80	62.3	70	54.4	10	12.7
Hispanic	214	157	73.3	144	67.2	13	8.3
Men	121	104	85.8	96	79.6	8	7.3
Women	92	52	56.8	47	51.0	5	10.2
Age							
16 to 19 years	333	183	54.9	158	47.5	24	13.4
20 to 24 years	385	318	82.6	295	76.6	23	7.2
25 to 34 years	713	634	89.0	602	84.4	32	5.1
35 to 44 years	731	654	89.5	630	86.2	24	3.7
45 to 54 years	876	764	87.3	741	84.6	24	3.1
55 to 64 years	644	435	67.5	422	65.5	13	3.0
65 years and over	715	111	15.5	106	14.8	5	4.2

Note: Data in Table 6 are from the Current Population Survey (CPS) and do not match the estimates in Table 7. See notes and definitions for more details.

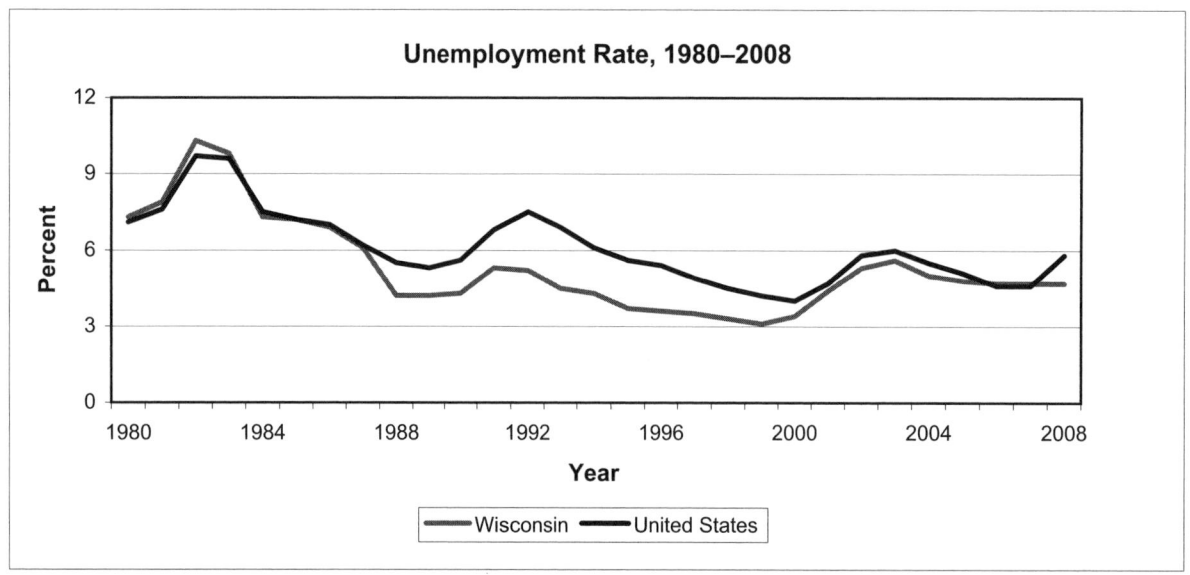

Table WI-7. Employment Status of the Civilian Noninstitutional Population Age 16 Years and Over

(Number, percent.)

Year	Civilian labor force	Civilian participation rate	Employed	Unemployed	Unemployment rate
1998	2 967 066	73.9	2 869 982	97 084	3.3
1999	2 970 026	73.4	2 879 024	91 002	3.1
2000	2 996 091	73.3	2 894 884	101 207	3.4
2001	3 030 998	73.4	2 897 937	133 061	4.4
2002	3 021 068	72.5	2 860 915	160 153	5.3
2003	3 033 674	72.1	2 862 587	171 087	5.6
2004	3 020 402	71.1	2 868 376	152 026	5.0
2005	3 031 825	70.8	2 886 560	145 265	4.8
2006	3 070 465	71.0	2 927 307	143 158	4.7
2007	3 093 763	71.0	2 948 131	145 632	4.7
2008	3 084 130	70.3	2 937 871	146 259	4.7

Table WI-8. Employment and Average Wages by Industry

(Estimates for 2001–2006 are based on the 2002 North American Industry Classification System [NAICS]. Estimates for 2007 are based on the 2007 NAICS.)

Industry	2001	2002	2003	2004	2005	2006	2007
	Number of jobs						
WAGE AND SALARY EMPLOYMENT BY INDUSTRY	2 898 594	2 874 373	2 880 828	2 909 275	2 931 773	2 954 379	2 966 255
Farm Wage and Salary Employment	20 995	19 471	24 892	24 856	25 683	23 984	25 127
Nonfarm Wage and Salary Employment	2 877 599	2 854 902	2 855 936	2 884 419	2 906 090	2 930 395	2 941 128
Private wage and salary employment	2 454 963	2 427 612	2 426 005	2 456 228	2 481 161	2 503 931	2 515 356
Forestry, fishing, hunting, and other	7 491	7 525	7 430	7 274	7 232	7 219	7 239
Mining	2 815	2 770	2 801	2 936	3 010	3 075	2 876
Utilities	12 309	11 886	11 638	11 669	11 542	11 369	11 177
Construction	130 702	129 753	129 892	132 671	133 025	132 447	130 600
Manufacturing	562 702	529 599	509 811	508 379	511 329	512 074	505 931
Durable goods manufacturing	349 769	325 906	313 198	314 985	320 959	323 268	318 768
Nondurable goods manufacturing	212 933	203 693	196 613	193 394	190 370	188 806	187 163
Wholesale trade	117 519	116 305	114 741	116 928	120 144	123 546	124 182
Retail trade	335 780	330 141	330 132	329 654	327 618	325 312	325 406
Transportation and warehousing	96 192	95 376	96 684	97 419	98 366	99 897	100 727
Information	53 973	51 425	50 160	50 734	50 413	49 736	50 446
Finance and insurance	126 380	127 943	130 695	131 935	132 793	134 148	134 871
Real estate and rental and leasing	27 814	28 046	28 275	28 875	29 154	29 228	29 039
Professional and technical services	95 707	95 679	95 814	96 723	99 224	102 357	104 188
Management of companies and enterprises	35 716	36 467	39 394	39 916	41 350	41 690	43 561
Administrative and waste services	119 426	119 274	118 152	124 401	130 914	134 210	137 709
Educational services	45 229	45 732	46 037	49 209	48 169	48 434	49 734
Health care and social assistance	311 327	320 570	328 457	335 013	341 220	348 740	354 505
Arts, entertainment, and recreation	34 489	35 308	36 635	36 781	36 627	37 370	38 292
Accommodation and food services	209 904	210 800	215 294	220 388	224 698	227 952	228 816
Other services, except public administration	129 488	133 013	133 963	135 323	134 333	135 127	136 057
Government and government enterprises	422 636	427 290	429 931	428 191	424 929	426 464	425 772
	Dollars						
AVERAGE WAGES AND SALARIES BY INDUSTRY	30 936	31 876	32 762	34 077	34 840	36 153	37 391
Average Farm Wages and Salaries	29 128	31 696	22 881	27 770	25 462	27 335	32 225
Average Nonfarm Wages and Salaries	30 949	31 878	32 848	34 132	34 923	36 225	37 435
Average private wages and salaries	30 911	31 857	32 745	34 109	34 869	36 229	37 468
Forestry, fishing, hunting, and other	22 964	23 475	24 137	25 488	25 821	26 999	28 300
Mining	42 727	43 502	43 370	45 769	46 380	47 328	49 050
Utilities	61 899	63 375	64 367	69 818	71 682	72 620	76 012
Construction	39 162	39 693	40 246	41 233	42 827	44 667	47 556
Manufacturing	39 033	40 377	41 952	44 009	44 311	45 921	47 068
Durable goods manufacturing	39 571	40 884	42 921	45 200	45 144	47 042	47 909
Nondurable goods manufacturing	38 149	39 567	40 408	42 069	42 908	44 000	45 635
Wholesale trade	41 731	43 283	44 578	46 481	48 301	50 003	51 165
Retail trade	19 236	20 165	20 281	20 791	21 039	21 556	21 916
Transportation and warehousing	32 301	32 855	33 496	34 801	36 269	37 056	37 932
Information	38 007	38 901	39 638	42 222	43 875	46 378	49 154
Finance and insurance	42 264	43 813	46 545	48 887	50 129	52 961	55 179
Real estate and rental and leasing	25 373	25 425	26 877	28 226	29 114	30 531	31 379
Professional and technical services	45 941	46 367	47 430	49 706	51 610	53 396	56 089
Management of companies and enterprises	63 254	65 977	68 347	73 513	74 397	81 354	82 171
Administrative and waste services	19 974	20 667	20 813	21 416	21 726	22 537	23 829
Educational services	23 127	24 319	25 469	25 196	26 273	27 691	29 358
Health care and social assistance	31 045	32 636	33 736	35 350	36 117	37 191	38 530
Arts, entertainment, and recreation	20 632	21 046	20 931	21 165	21 627	23 308	24 193
Accommodation and food services	10 386	10 653	10 946	11 327	11 518	12 036	12 455
Other services, except public administration	19 586	20 582	21 065	21 806	22 450	23 057	24 152
Government and government enterprises	31 168	31 993	33 426	34 265	35 235	36 200	37 245

Table WI-9. Employment Characteristics by Family Type

(Number, percent.)

Family type and labor force status	2005		2006		2007	
	Total	Families with own children under 18 years	Total	Families with own children under 18 years	Total	Families with own children under 18 years
TOTAL FAMILIES	1 440 637	667 284	1 456 314	677 418	1 461 841	666 856
FAMILY TYPE AND LABOR FORCE STATUS						
Married Coupled Families	1 127 844	469 325	1 147 656	478 000	1 149 189	468 951
Both husband and wife in labor force	58.8	72.3	60.7	74.2	60.5	75.4
Husband in labor force, wife not in labor force	17.2	21.0	17.1	21.1	16.7	19.8
Wife in labor force, husband not in labor force	7.2	3.8	7.0	3.3	6.8	3.1
Both husband and wife not in labor force	16.7	2.9	15.3	1.3	15.9	1.6
Other Families	312 793	197 959	308 658	199 418	312 652	197 905
Female householder, no husband present	70.0	73.1	70.0	73.7	70.3	73.0
In labor force	51.3	59.5	54.0	62.1	53.0	61.4
Not in labor force	18.6	13.5	16.0	11.7	17.3	11.6
Male householder, no wife present	30.0	26.9	30.0	26.3	29.7	27.0
In labor force	25.1	24.3	25.2	24.4	24.6	24.5
Not in labor force	5.0	2.7	4.8	1.9	5.1	2.5

Table WI-10. School Enrollment and Educational Attainment, 2007

(Number, percent.)

Item	State	U.S.
Enrollment		
Total population 3 years and over	5 391 121	289 295 761
Enrolled in school	1 439 037	79 329 527
Enrolled in preschool (percent)	5.3	6.2
Enrolled in grades K-12 (percent)	67.8	67.6
Enrolled in college or graduate school (percent)	26.9	26.2
Attainment		
Total population 25 years and over	3 727 260	197 892 369
Less than a high school diploma (percent)	11.0	15.5
High school diploma or more (percent)	89.0	84.5
Bachelor's degree or more (percent)	25.4	27.5
Graduate degree or more (percent)	8.5	10.1

Table WI-11. Educational Indicators

(Number, percent.)

Item	State	U.S.
Public Schools, 2006–2007 (except where noted)		
Number of school districts	460	17 742
Number of schools	2 242	99 639
Number of students	876 700	49 315 842
Student-teacher ratio	14.8	15.5
Expenditures per student (dollars)	$10 367	. . .
Averaged freshman graduation rate, 2005–2006	87.5	. . .
Dropout rate, grades 9–12, 2005–2006	2.2	3.7
Students eligible for free or reduced-price lunch (percent)	31.0	41.2
English-language learners (percent)	4.4	5.1
Students with IEP (percent)	14.7	12.7
Private Schools, 2007–2008 (except where noted)		
Number of schools	990	33 740
Number of students	123 174	5 072 451
High school graduates, 2006–2007	5 426	306 605
Student-teacher ratio	12.4	11.1

Table WI-12. Reported Voting and Registration of the Voting-Age Population, November 2008

(Number in thousands, percent.)

Item	Total population	Total citizen population	Registered			Voted		
			Total registered	Percent registered (total population)	Percent registered (total citizen population)	Total voted	Percent voted (total population)	Percent voted (total citizen population)
U.S. total	225 499	206 072	146 311	64.9	71.0	131 144	58.2	63.6
State total	4 212	4 053	3 095	73.5	76.4	2 887	68.5	71.2
Sex								
Male	2 084	1 993	1 501	72.0	75.3	1 403	67.3	70.4
Female	2 128	2 060	1 594	74.9	77.4	1 484	69.7	72.0
Race								
White alone	3 881	3 764	2 881	74.2	76.5	2 682	69.1	71.2
White non-Hispanic alone	3 639	3 620	2 806	77.1	77.5	2 617	71.9	72.3
Black alone	199	199	145	73.1	73.1	145	73.1	73.1
Asian alone	76	37	31	41.0	. . .	31	41.0	. . .
Hispanic (of any race)	247	150	77	31.3	51.6	66	26.9	44.4
White alone or in combination	3 903	3 786	2 892	74.1	76.4	2 692	69.0	71.1
Black alone or in combination	213	213	150	70.5	70.5	150	70.5	70.5
Asian alone or in combination	78	39	33	42.4	. . .	33	42.4	. . .

Table WI-13. Crime

(Number, rate per 100,000.)

Item	State			U.S.		
	2007	2008	Percent change	2007	2008	Percent change
Population	5 601 640	5 627 967	0.5	301 621 157	304 059 724	0.8
VIOLENT CRIME						
Number	16 296	15 421	-5.4	1 408 337	1 382 012	-1.9
Rate	290.9	274.0	-5.8	466.9	454.5	-2.7
Murder and Nonnegligent Manslaughter						
Number	183	146	-20.2	16 929	16 272	-3.9
Rate	3.3	2.6	-20.6	5.6	5.4	-4.7
Forcible Rape						
Number	1 223	1 120	-8.4	90 427	89 000	-1.6
Rate	21.8	19.9	-8.9	30.0	29.3	-2.4
Robbery						
Number	5 474	5 126	-6.4	445 125	441 855	-0.7
Rate	97.7	91.1	-6.8	147.6	145.3	-1.5
Aggravated Assault						
Number	9 416	9 029	-4.1	855 856	834 885	-2.5
Rate	168.1	160.4	-4.6	283.8	274.6	-3.2
PROPERTY CRIME						
Number	158 959	155 127	-2.4	9 843 481	9 767 915	-0.8
Rate	2 837.7	2 756.4	-2.9	3 263.5	3 212.5	-1.6
Burglary						
Number	27 839	27 479	-1.3	2 179 140	2 222 196	2.0
Rate	497.0	488.3	-1.8	722.5	730.8	1.2
Larceny-Theft						
Number	117 687	116 128	-1.3	6 568 572	6 588 873	0.3
Rate	2 100.9	2 063.4	-1.8	2 177.8	2 167.0	-0.5
Motor Vehicle Theft						
Number	13 433	11 520	-14.2	1 095 769	956 846	-12.7
Rate	239.8	204.7	-14.6	363.3	314.7	-13.4

Table WI-14. State Government Finances, 2007

(Dollars, percent distribution.)

Item	Thousands of dollars	Percent distribution
Total Revenue	40 164 298	X
General revenue	26 648 132	66.3
Intergovernmental revenue	6 769 288	16.9
Taxes	14 482 624	36.1
General sales	4 158 611	10.4
Selective sales	1 878 470	4.7
License taxes	860 536	2.1
Individual income tax	6 333 633	15.8
Corporate income tax	923 359	2.3
Other taxes	328 015	0.8
Current charges	3 146 243	7.8
Miscellaneous general revenue	2 249 977	5.6
Utility revenue	0	0.0
Liquor store revenue	0	0.0
Insurance trust revenue	13 516 166	33.7
Total Expenditure	30 895 963	100.0
Intergovernmental expenditure	9 744 914	31.5
Direct expenditure	21 151 049	68.5
Current operation	13 689 876	44.3
Capital outlay	1 891 883	6.1
Insurance benefits and repayments	4 089 087	13.2
Assistance and subsidies	508 765	1.6
Interest on debt	971 438	3.1
Exhibit: Salaries and wages	3 860 864	12.5
Total Expenditure	30 895 963	100.0
General expenditure	26 801 374	86.7
Intergovernmental expenditure	9 744 914	31.5
Direct expenditure	17 056 460	55.2
Education	10 176 419	32.9
Public welfare	6 393 090	20.7
Hospitals	951 128	3.1
Health	661 206	2.1
Highways	1 859 187	6.0
Police protection	125 814	0.4
Correction	1 027 163	3.3
Natural resources	595 231	1.9
Parks and recreation	35 527	0.1
Government administration	641 608	2.1
Interest on general debt	971 438	3.1
Other and unallocable	3 363 563	10.9
Utility expenditure	5 502	0.0
Liquor store expenditure	0	0.0
Insurance trust expenditure	4 089 087	13.2
Debt at End of Fiscal Year	21 461 270	X
Cash and Security Holdings	99 559 645	X

Table WI-15. State Government Tax Collections, 2008

(Dollars, percent distribution.)

Item	Thousands of dollars	Percent distribution
Total Taxes	15 088 662	X
Property taxes	124 513	0.8
Sales and gross receipts	6 317 062	41.9
General sales and gross receipts	4 268 068	28.3
Selective sales taxes	2 048 994	13.6
Alcoholic beverages	54 789	0.4
Amusements	388	0.0
Insurance premiums	172 073	1.1
Motor fuels	1 001 339	6.6
Pari-mutuels	908	0.0
Public utilities	327 060	2.2
Tobacco products	485 470	3.2
Other selective sales	6 967	0.0
Licenses	909 664	6.0
Alcoholic beverages	1 360	0.0
Amusements	549	0.0
Corporation	18 360	0.1
Hunting and fishing	69 615	0.5
Motor vehicle	406 806	2.7
Motor vehicle operators	36 391	0.2
Public utility	59 542	0.4
Occupation and business, NEC	312 167	2.1
Other licenses	4 874	0.0
Income taxes	7 503 616	49.7
Individual income	6 640 528	44.0
Corporation net income	863 088	5.7
Other taxes	233 807	1.5
Death and gift	158 790	1.1
Documentary and stock transfer	59 448	0.4
Severance	5 290	0.0
Other	10 279	0.1

Table WI-16. Agriculture

(Number, acres, and dollars.)

Item	2002 Number	2002 Percent of total	2007 Number	2007 Percent of total	Percent change, 2002–2007
Number of farms	77 131		78 463		1.7
Farm Size					
Average size of farm (acres)	204		194		-4.9
Farms by size (number of farms)					
Fewer than 50 acres	21 293	27.6	24 756	31.6	16.3
50 to 499 acres	49 479	64.1	47 602	60.7	-3.8
500 acres or more	6 359	8.2	6 105	7.8	-4.0
Land (Acres)					
Total land in farms	15 741 552		15 190 804		-3.5
Total cropland	10 728 655	68.2	10 116 279	66.6	-5.7
Total harvested cropland	8 928 083	56.7	8 884 628	58.5	-0.5
Irrigated land	385 902	2.5	377 291	2.5	-2.2
Value of Sales (Dollars)					
Agricultural products sold ($1,000)	5 623 275		8 967 358		59.5
Average sales per farm	72 906		114 288		56.8
Sales of crops	1 690 071	30.1	2 669 326	29.8	57.9
Sales of livestock, poultry, and their products	3 933 204	69.9	6 298 032	70.2	60.1
Value of Sales (Number of Farms)					
Less than $10,000	41 668	54.0	42 983	54.8	3.2
$10,000 to $99,999	21 533	27.9	18 833	24.0	-12.5
$100,000 to $999,999	13 256	17.2	15 154	19.3	14.3
$1,000,000 or more	674	0.9	1 493	1.9	121.5
Farms by Type of Organization (Number of Farms)					
Family	68 719	89.1	68 138	86.8	-0.8
Partnership	5 347	6.9	6 386	8.1	19.4
Corporation	2 726	3.5	3 333	4.2	22.3
Other: cooperative, estate or trust, institutional, etc	339	0.4	606	0.8	78.8
Value of Land and Buildings (Dollars)					
Estimated market value of land and buildings ($1,000)	48 994 488		35 799 490		-26.9
Land and buildings average value per farm	624 428		464 127		-25.7
Average value per acre	3 225		2 272		-29.6
Government Payments					
Number of farms receiving government payments	37 234	48.3	47 477	60.5	27.5
Payments (thousands of dollars)	247 942		195 787		-21.0
Average payment per farm	6 659		4 124		-38.1
Farm Operator Characteristics					
Farm operators whose principal occupation is farming	45 798	59.4	37 047	47.2	-19.1
Farm operators whose principal occupation is other	31 333	40.6	41 416	52.8	32.2
Average age principal operator (years)	53.0		55.0		3.8

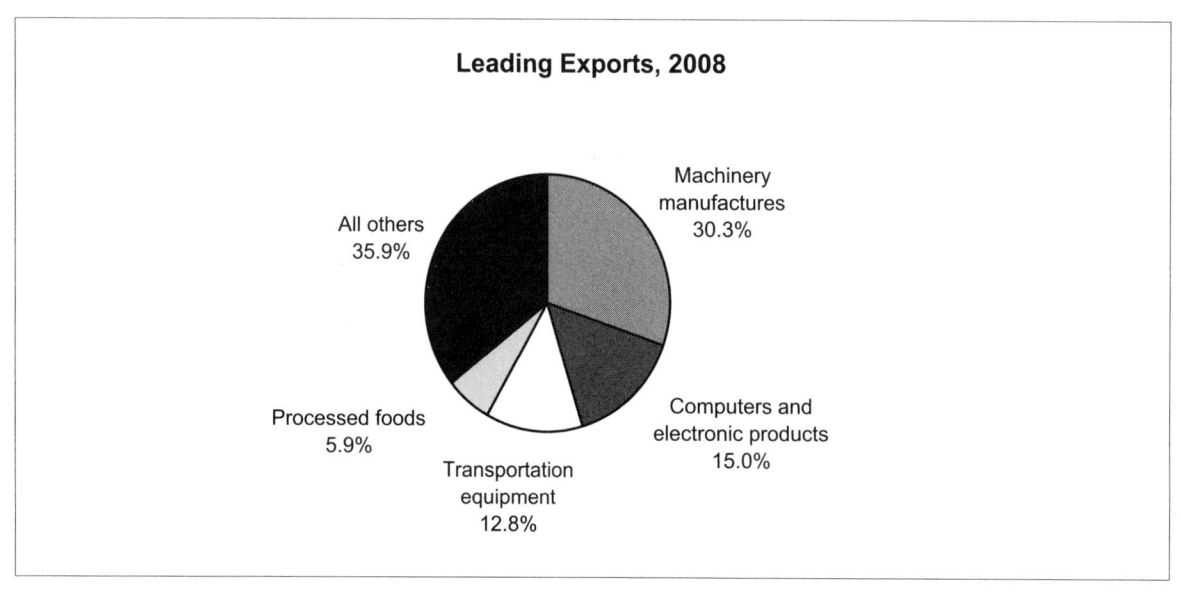

Leading Exports, 2008

Machinery manufactures 30.3%

All others 35.9%

Processed foods 5.9%

Transportation equipment 12.8%

Computers and electronic products 15.0%

WYOMING

Facts and Figures

Location: Western United States; bordered on the N by Montana, on the E by South Dakota and Nebraska, on the S by Colorado and Utah, and on the W by Utah and Idaho

Area: 97,814 sq. mi. (253,336 sq. km.); rank—10th

Population: 532,668 (2008 est.); rank—50th

Principal Cities: capital—Cheyenne; largest—Cheyenne

Statehood: July 10, 1890; 44th state

U.S. Congress: 2 senators, 1 representative

State Motto: Equal Rights

State Song: "Wyoming"

State Nicknames: The Equality State; The Cowboy State

Abbreviations: WY; Wyo.

State Symbols: flower—Indian paintbrush; tree—cottonwood; bird—Western meadowlark

At a Glance

- With an increase in population of 7.9 percent, Wyoming ranked 19th among the states in growth from 2000 to 2008.
- An estimated 4,722 marriages took place in Wyoming in 2008, compared to 2,727 divorces.
- The 2007 home ownership rate in Wyoming was 73.2 percent, giving it a ranking of 15th among the states.
- Wyoming's median household income in 2007 was $51,731, 19th among the states.
- In Wyoming, 8.7 percent of the population lived below the poverty level in 2007, ranking it 45th.
- In 2006-07, 14.1 percent of Wyomingites did not have health insurance, compared to 15.5 percent of the total U.S. population.
- In 2007, 2.9 percent of Wyomingites were unemployed, compared to 4.6 percent nationwide.
- Wyoming ranked 40th in the nation with 23.4 percent of its population 25 years old and over having a bachelor's degree in 2007.
- Wyoming's violent crime rate in 2007 was 239.3 per 100,000 population, compared to 466.9 for the entire nation.
- Wyoming had one physician for every 449 people in 2007, compared to one physician for every 325 people nationwide.
- In the 2008 election, 65.4 percent of Wyoming's eligible voters voted, compared to 61.7 percent of eligible voters nationwide.
- Wyoming ranked 1st among the states receiving federal aid in 2007, with $3,626 per capita.
- Wyoming's gross domestic product was $32 billion in 2007; it ranked 48th among the states.
- With $802 million in exports in 2007, Wyoming ranked 49th in exports.
- Wyomingites consumed 480.9 billion Btu's of energy in 2006; the state ranked 41st in total consumption.
- In 2007, Wyoming exported $61 million worth of agricultural products, less than 1 percent of the U.S. total.

Table WY-1. Population by Sex, Age, Race, and Hispanic Origin

(Number, percent.)

Sex, age, race, and Hispanic origin	1990	2000	2008	Average annual percent change, 2000–2008
Total Population	453 588	493 782	532 668	1.0
Percent of total U.S. population	0.2	0.2	0.2	X
Sex				
Male	227 007	248 374	270 190	1.1
Female	226 581	245 408	262 478	0.8
Age				
Under 5 years	34 780	30 940	38 253	2.7
5 to 19 years	114 341	114 406	105 340	-1.0
20 to 64 years	257 272	290 743	323 461	1.3
65 years and over	47 195	57 693	65 614	1.6
Median age (years)	32.0	36.2	36.8	X
Race and Hispanic Origin[1]				
One race				
White	427 061	454 670	500 001	1.2
Black	3 606	3 722	6 884	8.0
American Indian and Alaskan Native	9 479	11 133	13 555	2.5
Asian[2]	2 806	2 771	3 828	4.1
Native Hawaiian and Other Pacific Islander	X	302	512	6.8
Two or more races	X	8 883	7 888	-1.5
Hispanic (of any race)	25 751	31 669	41 162	3.3

[1]Data on race in 2000 and 2008 are not comparable to 1990. Individuals could only report one race in the 1990 census but could report one or more races on the 2000 census.
[2]Data in 1990 refer to Asian and Pacific Islanders.

Table WY-2. Marital Status

(Number, percent distribution.)

Sex and marital status	1990	2000	2007
Males, 15 Years and Over	168 395	195 412	212 622
Never married	25.6	26.6	30.5
Now married, except separated	61.9	58.8	52.6
Separated	1.0	1.0	1.5
Widowed	2.1	2.3	2.7
Divorced	9.4	11.3	12.7
Females, 15 Years and Over	170 879	195 433	207 054
Never married	17.8	20.0	22.1
Now married, except separated	60.6	57.5	54.0
Separated	1.2	1.3	1.6
Widowed	10.0	9.2	9.0
Divorced	10.4	12.0	13.4

Table WY-3. Households and Housing Characteristics

(Number, percent, and dollars.)

Item	1990	2000	2007	Average annual percent change, 2000–2007
Total Households	168 839	193 608	206 136	0.9
Family households	119 825	130 497	135 066	0.5
Married-couple family	100 800	106 179	106 431	0.0
Other family	19 025	24 318	28 635	2.4
Male householder, no wife present	5 035	7 481	11 240	6.0
Female householder, no husband present	13 990	16 837	17 395	0.5
Nonfamily households	49 014	63 111	71 070	1.7
Householder living alone	41 287	50 980	57 710	1.8
Householder not living alone	7 727	12 131	13 360	1.4
Housing Characteristics				
Total housing units	203 411	223 854	242 344	1.1
Occupied housing units	168 839	193 608	206 136	0.9
Owner-occupied	114 544	135 514	142 770	0.7
Renter-occupied	54 295	58 094	63 366	1.2
Average size	2.63	2.48	2.47	X
Financial Characteristics				
Median gross rent of renter-occupied housing units (dollars)	333	437	636	5.5
Median monthly owner costs for housing units with a mortgage (dollars)	612	825	1 162	5.0
Median value of owner-occupied housing units (dollars)	61 600	96 600	172 300	8.6

Table WY-4. Median Income and Poverty Status, 2007

(Number, percent.)

Characteristic	State		U.S.	
	Number	Percent	Number	Percent
Median Income				
Households (dollars)	51 731	X	50 740	X
Families (dollars)	63 947	X	61 173	X
Below Poverty Level				
Sex				
Male	19 051	7.3	16 576 071	11.5
Female	25 013	10.0	21 476 176	14.3
Age				
Under 18 years	14 318	11.6	13 097 100	18.0
Related children under 18 years	13 819	11.3	12 728 964	17.6
18 to 64 years	26 595	8.2	21 495 507	11.6
65 years and over	3 151	5.3	3 459 640	9.5

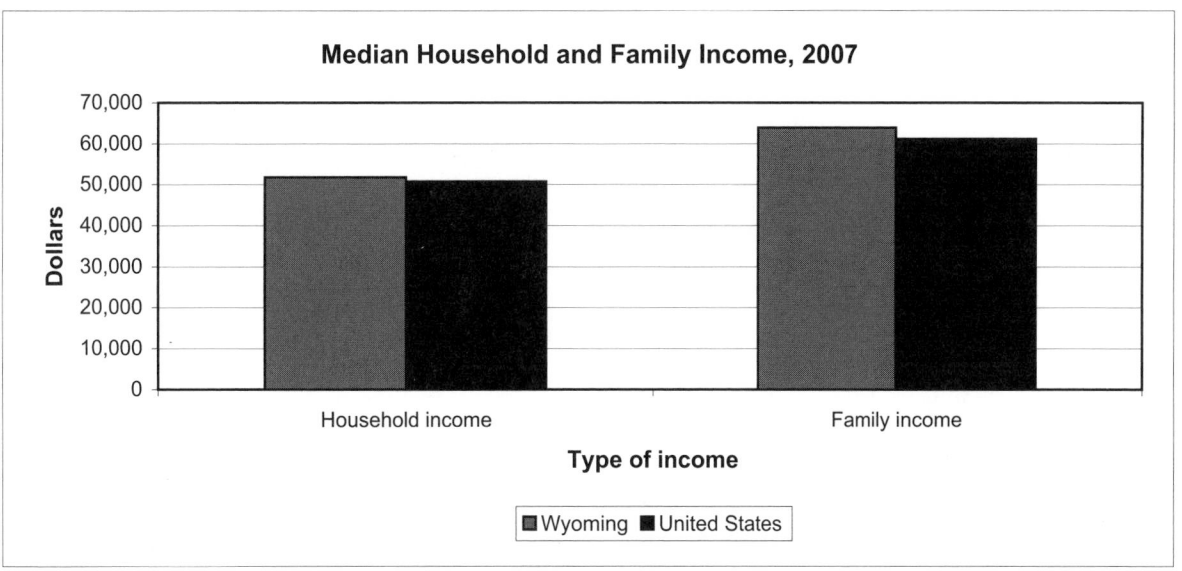

Table WY-5. Health Insurance Coverage Status for All Persons and Children Under 18 Years of Age

(Number, percent.)

Item	2000	2001	2002	2003	2004	2005	2006	2007
ALL PERSONS	486	488	488	488	498	511	516	518
Covered by Private or Government Health Insurance								
Number	412	416	406	414	435	436	441	447
Percent	84.7	85.1	83.2	84.9	87.2	85.4	85.4	86.4
Not Covered								
Number	74	73	82	74	64	75	75	70
Percent	15.3	14.9	16.8	15.1	12.8	14.6	14.6	13.6
Percent in the U.S. not covered	13.7	14.1	14.7	15.1	14.9	15.3	15.8	15.3
CHILDREN UNDER 18 YEARS OF AGE	126	122	121	119	117	118	123	127
Covered by Private or Government Health Insurance								
Number	110	109	105	105	107	105	113	115
Percent	87.4	89.5	86.7	88.1	91.2	89.2	91.8	90.4
Not Covered								
Number	16	13	16	14	10	13	10	12
Percent	12.6	10.5	13.3	11.9	8.8	10.8	8.2	9.6
Percent in the U.S. not covered	11.6	11.3	11.2	11.0	10.5	10.9	11.7	11.0

Table WY-6. Employment Status by Demographic Group, Preliminary 2008

(Number, percent.)

Characteristic	Civilian noninstitutional population	Civilian labor force		Employment		Unemployed	
		Number	Percent of population	Number	Percent of population	Number	Unemployment rate
TOTAL	411	294	71.5	285	69.4	9	3.0
Sex							
Men	206	163	79.0	158	76.7	5	2.8
Women	205	131	64.0	127	62.0	4	3.1
Race, Sex, and Hispanic Origin							
White	391	280	71.7	272	69.6	8	2.9
Men	196	155	78.9	150	76.7	4	2.7
Women	195	125	64.4	121	62.4	4	3.1
Black or African American	. . .	. . .	. . .	. . .	. . .	. . .	. . .
Men	. . .	. . .	. . .	. . .	. . .	. . .	. . .
Women	. . .	. . .	. . .	. . .	. . .	. . .	. . .
Hispanic	25	18	71.6	17	69.0	1	3.6
Men	15	12	81.1	11	78.5	. . .	3.2
Women	. . .	. . .	. . .	. . .	. . .	. . .	. . .
Age							
16 to 19 years	32	18	57.3	17	52.2	2	8.9
20 to 24 years	37	29	77.5	27	73.7	1	4.8
25 to 34 years	69	59	85.5	57	82.5	2	3.5
35 to 44 years	63	56	88.8	55	86.9	1	2.1
45 to 54 years	80	69	87.1	68	85.4	1	1.9
55 to 64 years	68	47	69.3	46	68.1	1	1.8
65 years and over	62	15	23.9	15	23.6	. . .	1.3

Note: Data in Table 6 are from the Current Population Survey (CPS) and do not match the estimates in Table 7. See notes and definitions for more details.

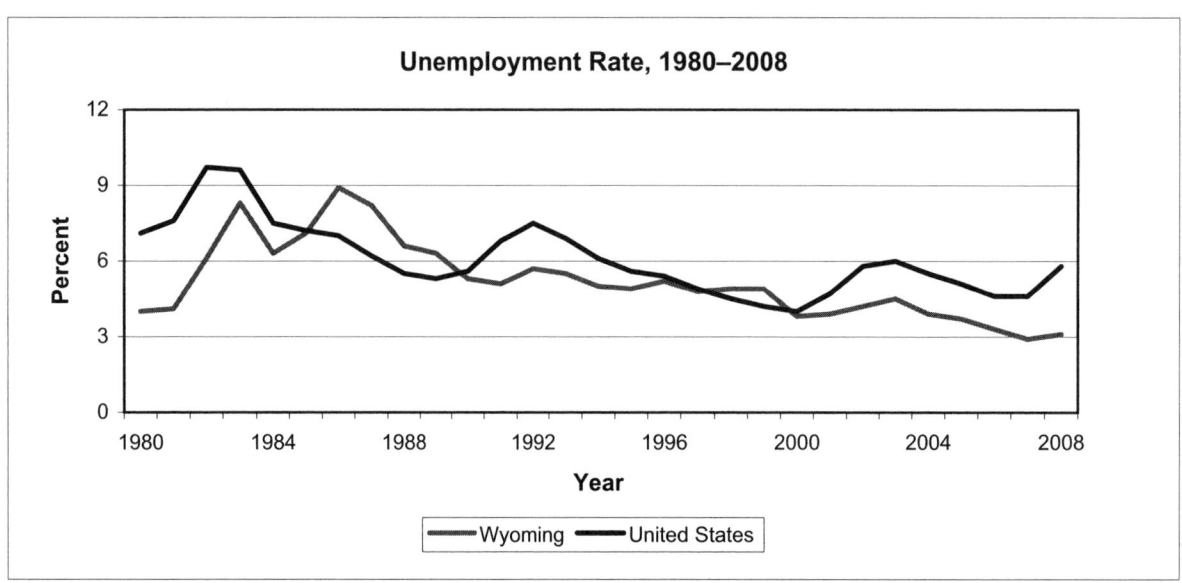

Table WY-7. Employment Status of the Civilian Noninstitutional Population Age 16 Years and Over

(Number, percent.)

Year	Civilian labor force	Civilian participation rate	Employed	Unemployed	Unemployment rate
1998	260 570	71.0	247 748	12 822	4.9
1999	264 676	71.5	251 828	12 848	4.9
2000	266 882	71.5	256 685	10 197	3.8
2001	269 985	72.0	259 508	10 477	3.9
2002	269 654	71.1	258 462	11 192	4.2
2003	271 607	71.0	259 489	12 118	4.5
2004	273 091	70.8	262 358	10 733	3.9
2005	277 238	71.2	266 986	10 252	3.7
2006	283 410	71.6	274 198	9 212	3.3
2007	288 433	71.6	280 087	8 346	2.9
2008	292 606	71.4	283 598	9 008	3.1

Table WY-8. Employment and Average Wages by Industry

(Estimates for 2001–2006 are based on the 2002 North American Industry Classification System [NAICS]. Estimates for 2007 are based on the 2007 NAICS.)

Industry	2001	2002	2003	2004	2005	2006	2007
	Number of jobs						
WAGE AND SALARY EMPLOYMENT BY INDUSTRY	259 827	262 455	264 771	269 754	277 758	290 441	301 277
Farm Wage and Salary Employment	3 448	3 548	3 347	3 367	3 207	3 210	3 032
Nonfarm Wage and Salary Employment	256 379	258 907	261 424	266 387	274 551	287 231	298 245
Private wage and salary employment	191 018	192 794	194 270	198 757	206 033	218 709	228 370
Forestry, fishing, hunting, and other	1 459	1 405	1 361	1 331	1 270	1 197	1 211
Mining	18 302	17 873	18 378	20 310	22 581	26 425	27 344
Utilities	D	D	2 142	2 206	2 282	2 317	2 473
Construction	20 326	D	20 347	20 043	21 559	24 813	27 496
Manufacturing	10 163	D	9 373	9 489	9 778	10 224	10 248
Durable goods manufacturing	5 080	D	D	D	5 188	5 486	5 499
Nondurable goods manufacturing	5 083	D	D	D	4 590	4 738	4 749
Wholesale trade	6 911	7 132	7 114	7 460	7 866	8 321	8 878
Retail trade	31 181	31 100	30 888	30 904	31 285	31 832	32 973
Transportation and warehousing	D	D	9 412	9 950	10 532	11 413	12 175
Information	D	D	4 187	4 320	4 315	4 190	4 032
Finance and insurance	6 354	6 794	7 018	7 035	7 012	7 219	7 195
Real estate and rental and leasing	3 388	3 544	3 499	3 727	4 066	4 279	4 551
Professional and technical services	7 988	8 069	8 074	8 422	8 936	9 603	10 080
Management of companies and enterprises	779	803	648	748	762	843	845
Administrative and waste services	7 620	7 440	7 531	6 865	6 858	7 256	8 084
Educational services	1 538	1 631	1 627	1 714	1 716	1 754	1 766
Health care and social assistance	18 609	19 210	20 046	20 786	21 233	21 618	22 435
Arts, entertainment, and recreation	3 490	2 665	2 752	2 832	2 856	2 941	3 036
Accommodation and food services	26 655	28 084	28 517	29 170	29 690	30 175	30 899
Other services, except public administration	D	D	11 356	11 445	11 436	12 289	12 649
Government and government enterprises	65 361	66 113	67 154	67 630	68 518	68 522	69 875
	Dollars						
AVERAGE WAGES AND SALARIES BY INDUSTRY	27 810	28 838	29 797	31 242	33 107	36 364	38 901
Average Farm Wages and Salaries	21 550	24 876	23 212	24 728	29 671	29 041	32 737
Average Nonfarm Wages and Salaries	27 894	28 892	29 881	31 324	33 147	36 446	38 964
Average private wages and salaries	27 892	28 512	29 390	30 903	32 832	36 504	38 953
Forestry, fishing, hunting, and other	21 256	21 853	20 646	20 602	18 091	18 165	19 140
Mining	53 088	54 466	55 884	58 617	61 778	67 560	71 809
Utilities	D	D	64 154	65 499	67 822	71 752	72 492
Construction	31 869	D	32 952	33 247	35 287	39 833	44 755
Manufacturing	36 505	D	37 292	38 672	40 349	42 291	45 561
Durable goods manufacturing	30 136	D	D	D	34 993	37 093	40 038
Nondurable goods manufacturing	42 870	D	D	D	46 403	48 311	51 957
Wholesale trade	36 706	36 934	38 679	41 671	43 445	48 143	50 389
Retail trade	18 718	19 302	19 870	20 732	21 486	22 913	24 088
Transportation and warehousing	D	D	41 569	42 887	45 303	48 976	50 550
Information	D	D	28 949	30 758	30 138	33 145	36 197
Finance and insurance	37 097	35 329	37 307	37 812	39 353	41 902	45 705
Real estate and rental and leasing	22 002	24 212	24 823	26 725	31 030	34 253	37 595
Professional and technical services	34 268	36 343	36 138	37 881	40 596	43 596	47 596
Management of companies and enterprises	41 397	58 588	80 451	80 430	86 030	91 639	90 639
Administrative and waste services	20 316	19 473	20 694	21 901	22 438	24 476	27 001
Educational services	17 895	22 074	20 383	20 986	22 156	23 475	24 466
Health care and social assistance	26 629	27 907	29 091	30 187	31 453	32 932	34 739
Arts, entertainment, and recreation	15 403	14 591	15 686	17 103	17 213	18 586	19 030
Accommodation and food services	11 656	12 395	12 868	13 784	14 677	17 793	17 266
Other services, except public administration	D	D	19 436	19 754	21 015	23 975	26 940
Government and government enterprises	27 898	30 002	31 302	32 564	34 094	36 263	39 002

Table WY-9. Employment Characteristics by Family Type

(Number, percent.)

Family type and labor force status	2005		2006		2007	
	Total	Families with own children under 18 years	Total	Families with own children under 18 years	Total	Families with own children under 18 years
TOTAL FAMILIES	133 902	57 493	136 835	60 264	135 066	57 666
FAMILY TYPE AND LABOR FORCE STATUS						
Married Coupled Families	109 498	41 761	110 284	42 658	106 431	39 784
Both husband and wife in labor force	58.5	67.5	57.9	69.2	61.3	73.1
Husband in labor force, wife not in labor force	20.4	26.0	20.2	26.8	18.9	22.0
Wife in labor force, husband not in labor force	7.1	4.5	6.1	2.2	5.8	3.6
Both husband and wife not in labor force	14.0	2.0	15.9	1.8	14.0	1.3
Other Families	24 404	15 732	26 551	17 606	28 635	17 882
Female householder, no husband present	63.0	66.4	65.2	67.8	60.7	66.5
In labor force	45.6	55.3	52.9	60.9	50.2	58.5
Not in labor force	17.4	11.1	12.2	7.0	10.5	8.0
Male householder, no wife present	37.0	33.6	34.8	32.2	39.3	33.5
In labor force	30.1	28.7	32.0	30.9	33.5	31.2
Not in labor force	7.0	4.9	2.8	1.3	5.8	2.3

Table WY-10. School Enrollment and Educational Attainment, 2007

(Number, percent.)

Item	State	U.S.
Enrollment		
Total population 3 years and over	501 219	289 295 761
Enrolled in school	127 145	79 329 527
Enrolled in preschool (percent)	7.1	6.2
Enrolled in grades K-12 (percent)	69.8	67.6
Enrolled in college or graduate school (percent)	23.2	26.2
Attainment		
Total population 25 years and over	342 256	197 892 369
Less than a high school diploma (percent)	8.8	15.5
High school diploma or more (percent)	91.2	84.5
Bachelor's degree or more (percent)	23.4	27.5
Graduate degree or more (percent)	7.7	10.1

Table WY-11. Educational Indicators

(Number, percent.)

Item	State	U.S.
Public Schools, 2006–2007 (except where noted)		
Number of school districts	62	17 742
Number of schools	383	99 639
Number of students	85 193	49 315 842
Student-teacher ratio	12.6	15.5
Expenditures per student (dollars)	$13 266	. . .
Averaged freshman graduation rate, 2005–2006	76.1	. . .
Dropout rate, grades 9–12, 2005–2006	5.7	3.7
Students eligible for free or reduced-price lunch (percent)	29.7	41.2
English-language learners (percent)	3.5	5.1
Students with IEP (percent)	16.4	12.7
Private Schools, 2007–2008 (except where noted)		
Number of schools	38	33 740
Number of students	2 112	5 072 451
High school graduates, 2006–2007	. . .	306 605
Student-teacher ratio	8.1	11.1

Table WY-12. Reported Voting and Registration of the Voting-Age Population, November 2008

(Number in thousands, percent.)

Item	Total population	Total citizen population	Registered Total registered	Registered Percent registered (total population)	Registered Percent registered (total citizen population)	Voted Total voted	Voted Percent voted (total population)	Voted Percent voted (total citizen population)
U.S. total	225 499	206 072	146 311	64.9	71.0	131 144	58.2	63.6
State total	397	389	270	67.9	69.3	250	62.9	64.3
Sex								
Male	199	195	127	64.0	65.2	118	59.2	60.4
Female	198	194	142	71.8	73.5	132	66.7	68.2
Race								
White alone	377	373	261	69.2	70.0	242	64.1	64.9
White non-Hispanic alone	361	359	252	70.0	70.3	235	65.1	65.4
Black alone	5	4	1	. . .	. . .	1	. . .	. . .
Asian alone	4	1	. . .	. . .	. . .	. . .	. . .	. . .
Hispanic (of any race)	18	15	8	. . .	. . .	7	. . .	. . .
White alone or in combination	382	378	265	69.4	70.2	246	64.3	65.0
Black alone or in combination	6	4	2	. . .	. . .	1	. . .	. . .
Asian alone or in combination	5	2	. . .	. . .	. . .	. . .	. . .	. . .

Table WY-13. Crime

(Number, rate per 100,000.)

Item	State 2007	State 2008	State Percent change	U.S. 2007	U.S. 2008	U.S. Percent change
Population	522 830	532 668	1.9	301 621 157	304 059 724	0.8
VIOLENT CRIME						
Number	1 251	1 236	-1.2	1 408 337	1 382 012	-1.9
Rate	239.3	232.0	-3.0	466.9	454.5	-2.7
Murder and Nonnegligent Manslaughter						
Number	16	10	-37.5	16 929	16 272	-3.9
Rate	3.1	1.9	-38.7	5.6	5.4	-4.7
Forcible Rape						
Number	160	180	12.5	90 427	89 000	-1.6
Rate	30.6	33.8	10.4	30.0	29.3	-2.4
Robbery						
Number	84	86	2.4	445 125	441 855	-0.7
Rate	16.1	16.1	0.5	147.6	145.3	-1.5
Aggravated Assault						
Number	991	960	-3.1	855 856	834 885	-2.5
Rate	189.5	180.2	-4.9	283.8	274.6	-3.2
PROPERTY CRIME						
Number	14 984	14 474	-3.4	9 843 481	9 767 915	-0.8
Rate	2 865.9	2 717.3	-5.2	3 263.5	3 212.5	-1.6
Burglary						
Number	2 348	2 184	-7.0	2 179 140	2 222 196	2.0
Rate	449.1	410.0	-8.7	722.5	730.8	1.2
Larceny-Theft						
Number	11 840	11 577	-2.2	6 568 572	6 588 873	0.3
Rate	2 264.6	2 173.4	-4.0	2 177.8	2 167.0	-0.5
Motor Vehicle Theft						
Number	796	713	-10.4	1 095 769	956 846	-12.7
Rate	152.2	133.9	-12.1	363.3	314.7	-13.4

Table WY-14. State Government Finances, 2007

(Dollars, percent distribution.)

Item	Thousands of dollars	Percent distribution
Total Revenue	5 844 703	X
General revenue	4 820 460	82.5
Intergovernmental revenue	1 947 258	33.3
Taxes	2 025 090	34.6
General sales	698 437	11.9
Selective sales	127 527	2.2
License taxes	126 316	2.2
Individual income tax	0	0.0
Corporate income tax	0	0.0
Other taxes	1 072 810	18.4
Current charges	149 646	2.6
Miscellaneous general revenue	698 466	12.0
Utility revenue	0	0.0
Liquor store revenue	73 518	1.3
Insurance trust revenue	950 725	16.3
Total Expenditure	4 536 373	100.0
Intergovernmental expenditure	1 570 347	34.6
Direct expenditure	2 966 026	65.4
Current operation	2 038 135	44.9
Capital outlay	402 925	8.9
Insurance benefits and repayments	415 498	9.2
Assistance and subsidies	49 669	1.1
Interest on debt	59 799	1.3
Exhibit: Salaries and wages	573 725	12.6
Total Expenditure	4 536 373	100.0
General expenditure	4 061 846	89.5
Intergovernmental expenditure	1 570 347	34.6
Direct expenditure	2 491 499	54.9
Education	1 352 159	29.8
Public welfare	610 218	13.5
Hospitals	1 697	0.0
Health	225 791	5.0
Highways	409 052	9.0
Police protection	38 315	0.8
Correction	117 171	2.6
Natural resources	269 861	5.9
Parks and recreation	32 814	0.7
Government administration	171 989	3.8
Interest on general debt	59 799	1.3
Other and unallocable	772 980	17.0
Utility expenditure	0	0.0
Liquor store expenditure	59 029	1.3
Insurance trust expenditure	415 498	9.2
Debt at End of Fiscal Year	1 205 067	X
Cash and Security Holdings	18 792 722	X

Table WY-15. State Government Tax Collections, 2008

(Dollars, percent distribution.)

Item	Thousands of dollars	Percent distribution
Total Taxes	2 168 016	X
Property taxes	278 812	12.9
Sales and gross receipts	879 034	40.5
General sales and gross receipts	744 371	34.3
Selective sales taxes	134 663	6.2
Alcoholic beverages	1 633	0.1
Insurance premiums	26 040	1.2
Motor fuels	75 013	3.5
Pari-mutuels	177	0.0
Public utilities	3 308	0.2
Tobacco products	27 362	1.3
Other selective sales	1 130	0.1
Licenses	120 773	5.6
Corporation	10 870	0.5
Hunting and fishing	32 691	1.5
Motor vehicle	55 722	2.6
Motor vehicle operators	2 215	0.1
Occupation and business, NEC	19 275	0.9
Other taxes	889 397	41.0
Death and gift	880	0.0
Severance	883 786	40.8
Other	4 731	0.2

Table WY-16. Agriculture

(Number, acres, and dollars.)

Item	2002		2007		Percent change, 2002–2007
	Number	Percent of total	Number	Percent of total	
Number of farms	9 422		11 069		17.5
Farm Size					
Average size of farm (acres)	3 651		2 726		-25.3
Farms by size (number of farms)					
Fewer than 50 acres	2 013	21.4	2 656	24.0	31.9
50 to 499 acres	3 213	34.1	4 173	37.7	29.9
500 acres or more	4 196	44.5	4 240	38.3	1.0
Land (Acres)					
Total land in farms	34 402 726		30 169 526		-12.3
Total cropland	2 989 804	8.7	2 576 017	8.5	-13.8
Total harvested cropland	1 298 709	3.8	1 536 240	5.1	18.3
Irrigated land	1 541 688	4.5	1 550 723	5.1	0.6
Value of Sales (Dollars)					
Agricultural products sold ($1,000)	863 887		1 157 535		34.0
Average sales per farm	91 688		104 575		14.1
Sales of crops	137 776	15.9	213 808	18.5	55.2
Sales of livestock, poultry, and their products	726 111	84.1	943 728	81.5	30.0
Value of Sales (Number of Farms)					
Less than $10,000	4 405	46.8	5 785	52.3	31.3
$10,000 to $99,999	3 210	34.1	3 158	28.5	-1.6
$100,000 to $999,999	1 712		1 962		14.6
$1,000,000 or more	95	1.0	164	1.5	72.6
Farms by Type of Organization (Number of Farms)					
Family	7 566	80.3	8 784	79.4	16.1
Partnership	928	9.8	1 024	9.3	10.3
Corporation	746	7.9	1 019	9.2	36.6
Other: cooperative, estate or trust, institutional, etc	182	1.9	242	2.2	33.0
Value of Land and Buildings (Dollars)					
Estimated market value of land and buildings ($1,000)	15 471 039		10 195 477		-34.1
Land and buildings average value per farm	1 397 691		1 080 945		-22.7
Average value per acre	513		290		-43.5
Government Payments					
Number of farms receiving government payments	3 163	33.6	2 790	25.2	-11.8
Payments (thousands of dollars)	37 913		28 157		-25.7
Average payment per farm	11 986		10 092		-15.8
Farm Operator Characteristics					
Farm operators whose principal occupation is farming	5 760	61.1	5 445	49.2	-5.5
Farm operators whose principal occupation is other	3 662	38.9	5 624	50.8	53.6
Average age principal operator (years)	54.1		57.1		5.5

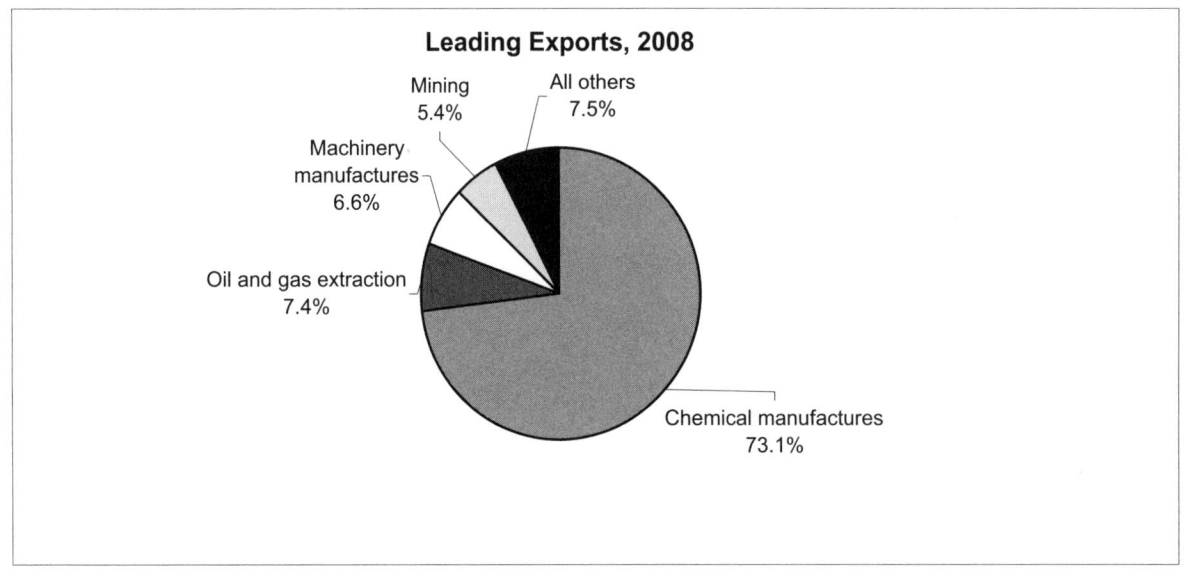

Leading Exports, 2008

Mining 5.4%

All others 7.5%

Machinery manufactures 6.6%

Oil and gas extraction 7.4%

Chemical manufactures 73.1%

NOTES AND DEFINITIONS

The state chapters in this book follow a standard plan of organization, and the same data sources are used for the tables and figures found in each chapter. These notes describe the standard data sources, which are presented by topic in the order in which they appear in each chapter. Definitions, brief descriptions of methodology, and sources of additional information are also provided. The text on the introductory page for each state is derived from many of the same data sources as the tables. In some instances, alternate government sources were used. Therefore, some data in the text may not match the data in the tables. In addition, references to rankings in the text only include the fifty states; the District of Columbia is excluded.

Symbols Used:

. . . = Not available.

* = Less than one-tenth of 1 percent.

D = Suppresses to avoid disclosure of data of individual companies.

L = Less than 10 jobs, but the estimates for this item are included in the total.

X = Not applicable.

Table 1. Population

Source: U.S. Department of Commerce. U.S Census Bureau. 1990 and 2000 Decennial Census. 2008 Population Estimates. <http://www.census.gov/acs/www/index.html>. Decennial census and 2008 Population Estimates data are accessed through American FactFinder. U.S. Census Bureau.

Population estimates and the decennial census. Population data for 2008 are estimates produced by the Census Bureau. The Bureau's Population Estimates Program (PEP) produces estimates of the population as of July 1 for each year following the most recently published decennial census (the actual physical count of the population made every ten years, which is described below). Existing data on births, deaths, and domestic and international immigration are used to update the decennial census base. PEP estimates are used to set federal funding allocations, update national surveys, and monitor recent demographic changes.

For the 2000 census, people (both civilian and military) were counted at their "usual residence," a principle followed in each census since 1790. Usual residence has been defined as the place in which a person lives and sleeps most frequently, as of April 1 of the census year. A person's usual residence may not be the same as his or her legal or voting residence. The geographic universe for the U.S. resident population is the 50 states and the District of Columbia. Residents of Puerto Rico and outlying areas (American Samoa, Guam, the Northern Mariana Islands,

and the U.S. Virgin Islands) under U.S. jurisdiction, U.S. citizens living abroad, and members of the U.S. armed forces serving overseas are excluded.

Noncitizens residing in the United States are included, regardless of their immigration status.

Persons temporarily away from their usual residence on Census Day (April 1), for reasons such as vacation or business trips, were counted as being at their usual residence. People who live at more than one residence during the week, month, or year were counted as being at the place in which they lived most of the year. However, people without a usual residence were counted as being where they were staying on Census Day.

Age, sex, race, and ethnicity. While estimates of the age and sex of the population are straightforward, estimates of race and ethnicity are not. Decennial census data on race and ethnicity are based on self-identification by the respondent, and the same respondent may answer differently on separate occasions. On the 2000 decennial census, respondents could report more than one race; in previous censuses, respondents had to identify themselves as belonging to only one race. For example, a respondent of partial American Indian descent may have self-identified as American Indian in 1990 and as both White and American Indian in 2000. As a result, race data from the 1990 census are not directly comparable with the 2000 census and subsequent estimates. The Office of Management and Budget (OMB) standards for collecting and presenting data on race, released in 1997, identified five race categories: White; Black or African American; American Indian and Alaska Native; Asian; and Native Hawaiian and Other Pacific Islander. For those not able to identify with these five categories, the classification "some other race" was an option. The OMB standards have been applied to all subsequent July 1 estimates of the population, making the 2000 and 2008 data directly comparable.

The Census Bureau treats Hispanic or Latino origin as a separate and distinct concept from race. Beginning with the 2000 census, a separate self-identification question was asked regarding Hispanic or Latino origin. Persons of Hispanic or Latino origin are those who classified themselves as belonging to one of the specific categories listed on the questionnaire—Mexican, Puerto Rican, Cuban, or Other Spanish/Hispanic origin (including those whose origins are from Spain, the Spanish-speaking countries of Central and South America, or the Dominican Republic). People who are Hispanic may be of any race and people in each race group may be Hispanic. The overlap of race and Hispanic origin is a major comparability issue, because Hispanics may be of any race. For a further discussion of this issue, see: U.S. Census Bureau. *U.S. Census Bureau Guidance on the Presentation and Comparison of Race and Hispanic Origin Data.* (June 12, 2003.) <http://www.census.gov/population/www/socdemo/compraceho.html>.

Table 2. Marital Status
Source: U.S. Department of Commerce. U.S Census Bureau. 1990 and 2000 Decennial Census. American Community Survey, 2007.
<http://www.census.gov/acs/www/index.html>.

Data on marital status was tabulated for persons 15 years and over. Marital status was reported for each person as either "now married," "widowed," "divorced," "separated," or "never married." Individuals who were living together (unmarried people, people in commonlaw marriages) reported the marital status which they considered most appropriate.

Now married, except separated. Includes people whose current marriage has not ended through widowhood, divorce, or separation (regardless of previous marital history). The category may also include couples who live together or people in common-law marriages if they consider this category the most appropriate. In certain tabulations, currently married people are further classified as "spouse present" or "spouse absent."

Separated. Refers to people who were not living with their spouse due to marital discord.

Divorced. Refers to people who reported being divorced and had not remarried.

Widowed. Refers to people whose last marriage ended with the death of their spouse and they had not remarried.

Never married. The term applies to those who had never been legally married or people whose only marriage ended in an annulment.

Table 3. Housing and Housing Characteristics
Source: U.S. Department of Commerce. U.S Census Bureau. 1990 and 2000 Decennial Census. American Community Survey, 2007. <http://www.census.gov/acs/www/index.html>.

The data for 1990, 2000, and 2007 were obtained from the Census Bureau. The data for average annual percent change, 2000–2007 were calculated by the editors.

Households. A household comprises one or more persons occupying a single housing unit, such as a house, apartment, or a room occupied as separate living quarters. A household may consist of a person living alone, a single family, two or more families living together, or any other group of unrelated individuals sharing a housing unit.

Householder. The person, or one of the people, in whose name the home is owned, being bought, or rented. If there is no such person present, any household member 15 years old and over can serve as the householder for the purposes of the census.

Two types of householders are distinguished: a family householder and a nonfamily householder. A family householder is a householder living with one or more people related to him or her by birth, marriage, or adoption. The householder and all people in the household related to him are family members. A nonfamily householder is a householder living alone or with nonrelatives only.

Housing unit. A house, an apartment, a mobile home or trailer, a group of rooms, or a single room occupied as separate living quarters, or if vacant, intended for occupancy as separate living quarters.

Median gross rent. The monthly amount of contract rent plus the estimated average monthly cost of utilities (electricity, gas, water and sewer) and fuels (oil, coal, kerosene, wood, etc.).

Median monthly owner-costs for housing units with a mortgage. The sum of payments for mortgages, deeds of trust, contracts to purchase, or similar debts on the property (including payments for the first mortgage, second mortgages, home equity loans, and other junior mortgages); real estate taxes; fire, hazard, and flood insurance on the property; utilities (electricity, gas, and water and sewer); and fuels (oil, coal, kerosene, wood, etc.). It also includes, where appropriate, the monthly condominium fee for condominiums and mobile home costs (installment loan payments, personal property taxes, site rent, registration fees, and license fees). Selected monthly owner costs were tabulated for all owner-occupied units, and usually are shown separately for units "with a mortgage" and for units "not mortgaged."

Median value of owner-occupied housing units. Data for the median value of owner-occupied housing units are respondents' estimates of how much their property would sell for if it was currently on the market.

Table 4. Median Income and Poverty Status.
Source: U.S. Department of Commerce. U.S. Census Bureau. American Community Survey, 2007.
<http://www.census.gov/acs/www/index.html>.

Median household income. Includes the income of the householder and all other individuals 15 years old and over in the household, whether they are related to the householder or not. Because many households consist of only one person, average household income is usually less than average family income. Total income is the sum of the amounts reported separately for wage or salary income; net self-employment income; interest, dividends, or net rental or royalty income or income from estates and trusts; Social Security or railroad retirement income; Supplemental Security Income (SSI); public assistance or welfare payments; retirement, survivor, or disability pensions; and all other income. Receipts from the following sources are not included as income: capital gains, money received from the sale of property (unless the recipient was engaged in the business of selling such property); the value of income "in kind" from food stamps, public housing subsidies, medical care, employer contributions for individuals, etc.; withdrawal of bank deposits; money borrowed; tax refunds; exchange of money between relatives living in the same household; gifts and lump-sum inheritances, insurance payments, and other types of lump-sum receipts.

Median family income. The incomes of all members 15 years old and over related to the householder are summed and treated as a single amount.

Poverty. Following OMB standards that have been in use since the late 1960s, the Census Bureau uses a set of money income thresholds that vary by family size and composition to determine the proportion of Americans in poverty. If a household's total income is less than the threshold for the applicable family size, age of householder, and number of children present in the family under 18 years of age, every individual in that household is considered to be living in poverty. In 2007, the poverty threshold for a family of four was $21,203.

Table 5. Health Insurance Coverage Status
Source: U.S. Department of Commerce. U.S. Census Bureau.
<http://www.census.gov/hhes/www/hlthins/hlthins.html>.

The Census Bureau collects health insurance data from two surveys. The data in Table 5 are from The Annual Social and Economic Supplement (ASEC) to the Current Population Survey (CPS). The CPS ASEC is a survey of about 78,000 households and includes detailed health insurance questions asked of the household respondent for every household resident. Respondents are asked about health insurance coverage in the previous calendar year. This survey is useful as a source of estimates of the insured and uninsured populations at the state level and is the most widely used source of data on health insurance coverage in the United States. In addition, it is the official source of estimates used to allocate federal funding to states for the State Children's Health Insurance Program (SCHIP). Numbers in Table 5 are shown in thousands.

Private health insurance. Coverage by a health plan provided through an employer or union or purchased by an individual from a private health insurance company.

Government health insurance includes plans funded by governments as the federal, state, or local level. The major categories of government health insurance are Medicare, Medicaid, the State Children's Health Insurance Program (SCHIP), military health care, state plans, and the Indian Health Service.

Table 6. Employment Status by Demographic Group.
Source: U.S. Department of Labor. Bureau of Labor Statistics. Current Population Survey.
<http://www.bls.gov/cps/>.

Annual data on the labor force, employment, and unemployment for state and local areas are available from two major sources: the Current Population Survey (CPS) and the Local Area Unemployment Statistics (LAUS) program. In Table 6, the data are obtained from the CPS. The CPS is a monthly survey of approximately 60,000 households conducted by the Census Bureau for the Bureau of Labor Statistics. It provides comprehensive data on topics such as the labor force, employment, unemployment, and persons not in the labor force. Numbers in Table 6 are shown in thousands.

Civilian noninstitutional population includes all persons 16 years of age and older residing in the 50 states and the District of Columbia who are not inmates of institutions (for example, penal and mental facilities, homes for the aged), and who are not on active duty in the Armed Forces.

Civilian labor force includes all persons classified as employed or unemployed who are not inmates of institutions (for example, penal and mental facilities, homes for the aged), and who are not on active duty in the Armed Forces. Civilians 16 years of age and over in the noninstitutional population who are not classified as employed or unemployed are defined as not in the labor force.

Employment includes persons 16 years and over in the civilian noninstitutional population who, during the reference week, (a) did any work at all (at least 1 hour) as paid employees; worked in their own business, profession, or on their own farm, or worked 15 hours or more as unpaid workers in an enterprise operated by a member of the family; and (b) all those who were not working but who had jobs or businesses from which they were temporarily absent because of vacation, illness, bad weather, childcare problems, maternity or paternity leave, labor-management dispute, job training, or other family or personal reasons, whether or not they were paid for the time off or were seeking other jobs.

Unemployed persons. All civilians who were not employed (according to the above definition) during the reference week, but who were available for work—except for temporary illness—and who had made specific efforts to find employment sometime during the previous four weeks. Persons who did not look for work because they were on layoff are also counted as unemployed.

Unemployment rate. The number of unemployed as a percentage of the civilian labor force.

Table 7. Employment Status of the Civilian Non-institutional Population.
Source: U.S. Department of Labor. Bureau of Labor Statistics. Local Area Unemployment Statistics. <http://www.bls.gov/lau/home.htm>.

The Local Area Unemployment Statistics (LAUS) program is a Federal-State cooperative effort in which monthly estimates of total employment and unemployment are prepared for approximately 7,300 areas.

The concepts and definitions underlying LAUS data come from the Current Population Survey (CPS), the household survey that is the official measure of the labor force for the nation. State monthly model estimates are controlled in "real time" to sum to national monthly labor force estimates from the CPS. These models combine current and historical data from the CPS, the Current Employment Statistics (CES) program, and State unemployment insurance (UI) systems. Estimates for seven large areas and their respective balances of State are also model-based. Estimates for the remainder of the substate labor market areas are produced through a building-block approach known as the "Handbook method." This procedure also uses data from several sources, including the CPS, the CES program, State UI systems, and the decennial census, to create estimates that are adjusted to the statewide measures of employment and unemployment. Below the labor market area level, estimates are prepared using disaggregation techniques based on inputs from the decennial census, annual population estimates, and current UI data.

Table 8. Employment and Average Wages by Industry.
Source: U.S. Department of Commerce. Bureau of Economic Analysis. <http://www.bea.gov/regional>.

In this table, the data by industry reflect the North American Industry Classification System (NAICS), a supply- or production-based system that replaced the Standard Industrial Classification (SIC) system in January 2003. Estimates of state employment and earnings by industry use NAICS from 2001 forward. NAICS was adopted to more fully reflect the current composition of U.S. businesses and to establish a standard measure of industry classification throughout the United States, Canada, and Mexico, in accordance with the North American Free Trade Agreement, to enhance cross-border comparisons among these trading partners.

Wage and salary employment, also referred to as wage and salary jobs, measures the average annual number of full-time and part-time jobs in each area by place-of-work. All jobs for which wages and salaries are paid are counted. Full-time and part-time jobs are counted with equal weight. Jury and witness service, as well as paid employment of prisoners, are not counted as wage and salary employment; the payments for these activities are classified as "other labor income" in the personal income measure. Corporate directorships are counted as self-employment. This concept of employment differs from that in the Current Population Survey (CPS), which is the source of the employment data in the table on population and labor force. The CPS is a household survey. It counts each individual only once, no matter how many jobs the person holds, and it includes only civilian employment.

Wages and salaries consist of the monetary remuneration of employees, including corporate officers salaries and bonuses, commissions, pay-in-kind, incentive payments, and tips. It reflects the amount of payments disbursed, but not necessarily earned during the year. Wage and salary disbursements are measured before deductions, such as social security contributions and union dues. In recent years, stock options have become a point of discussion. Wage and salary disbursements include stock options of nonqualified plans at the time that they have been exercised by the individual. Stock options are reported in wage and salary disbursements. The value that is included in wages is the difference between the exercise price and the price that the stock options were granted. Average annual wages and salaries were calculated by the editors by dividing total wages and salaries paid during the year in each sector by total wage and salary employment in that sector.

Table 9. Employment Characteristics by Family Type.
Source: U.S. Department of Commerce. U.S. Census Bureau. American Community Survey, 2005, 2006, and 2007. <http://www.census.gov/acs/www/index.html>

Civilian labor force. (See definition under Table 6.)

Employment. (See definition under Table 6.)

Family. A family consists of a householder and one or more other people living in the same household who are related to the householder by birth, marriage, or adoption. All people in a household who are related to the householder are regarded as members of his or her family. A family household may contain people not related to the householder, but those people are not included as part of the householder's family in tabulations. Thus, the number of family households is equal to the number of families, but family households may include more members than do families. A household can contain only one family for purposes of tabulations. Not all households contain families since a household may be comprised of a group of unrelated people or of one person living alone – these are called nonfamily households. Families are classified by type as either a "married-couple family" or "other family" according to the sex of the householder and the presence of relatives. The data on family type are based on answers to questions on sex and relationship that were asked of all people.

Married-couple family. A family in which the householder and his or her spouse are listed as members of the same household.

Other family:

Male householder, no wife present. A family with a male householder and no spouse of householder present.

Female householder, no husband present. A family with a female householder and no spouse of householder present.

Table 10. School Enrollment and Educational Attainment, 2007
Source: U.S. Department of Commerce. U.S. Census Bureau. American Community Survey, 2007.
<http://www.census.gov/acs/www/index.html>.

Data on school enrollment and educational attainment were derived from a sample of the population. Persons were classified as enrolled in school if they reported attending a "regular" public or private school (or college) during the year. The instructions were to "include only nursery school, kindergarten, elementary school, and schooling which would lead to a high school diploma or a college degree" as regular school. The Census Bureau defines a public school as "any school or college controlled and supported by a local, county, state, or federal government." Schools primarily supported and controlled by religious organizations or other private groups are defined as private schools.

Data on educational attainment are tabulated for the population 25 years old and over. The data were derived from a question that asked respondents for the highest level of school completed or the highest degree received. Persons who had passed a high school equivalency examination were considered high school graduates. Schooling received in foreign schools was to be reported as the equivalent grade or years in the regular American school system.

Vocational and technical training, such as barber school training; business, trade, technical, and vocational schools; or other training for a specific trade are specifically excluded.

High school graduate or more. This category includes persons whose highest degree was a high school diploma or its equivalent, and those who reported any level higher than a high school diploma.

Bachelor's degree or more. This category includes persons who have received bachelor's degrees, master's degrees, professional school degrees (such as law school or medical school degrees), and doctoral degrees.

Graduate degree or more. This category includes persons who have a master's degree, including the traditional MA and MS degrees and field-specific degrees, such as MSW, MEd, MBA, MLS, and MEng., or a professional school degree: medicine, dentistry, chiropractic, optometry, osteopathic medicine, pharmacy, podiatry, veterinary medicine, law, and theology.

Table 11. Education Indicators
Source: U.S. Department of Education, National Center for Education Statistics. *Common Core of Data.*
<http://nces.ed.gov/ccd/>.
Private School Universe Survey.
<http://nces.ed.gov/surveys/pss/>.

Public Schools

The data are from the Common Core of Data (CCD) state universe and include approximately 17,000 regular school districts with students in membership. Not included are special districts that typically offer research, administrative, or other support services to client agencies. The CCD data now include charter schools. Since charter schools are managed independently from the local school district, each one is considered a single district. Most of the CCD state data were compiled through the CCD "Build a Table" feature, which can be found on the Internet at <http://nces.ed.gov/ccd/bat>.

A **school district** or Local Education Agency (LEA) is a local-level education agency that exists primarily to operate public schools or to contract for public school services. A public school is controlled and operated by publicly elected or appointed officials, and it derives its primary support from public funds.

Regular schools do not focus primarily on special, vocational, or alternative education, though they may offer these programs in addition to the regular curriculum.

The primary grades include pre-kindergarten through grade 4. Middle school grades included grades 5 through 8. High school grades include grades 9 through 12. Ungraded students are included in the total but are not separately listed. Some states have no ungraded students.

The **student-teacher ratio** is calculated by dividing the number of students in all schools by the number of full-time equivalent teachers employed by all schools and agencies.

Current expenditures per student are derived by dividing total current expenditures by the fall student membership count from the CCD. Student membership consists of the count of students enrolled on or about October 1 and is comparable across all states.

The averaged freshman graduation rate provides an estimate of the percentage of high school students who graduate on time. The rate uses aggregate student enrollment data (to estimate the size of an incoming freshman class) and aggregate counts of the number of diplomas awarded 4 years later. The incoming freshman class size is estimated by summing the enrollment in 8th grade in one year, 9th grade in the next year, and 10th grade in the year after that, and then dividing by three. The averaging is intended to account for prior-year retentions in the 9th grade.

A **dropout** is a student who was enrolled in school at some time during the previous school year who was not enrolled at the beginning of the current school year and who had not graduated from high school or completed a state or district-approved educational program and who did not meet any of the following exclusionary conditions: transferal to another public school district, private school, or state- or district-approved educational program; temporary absence due to suspension or school-approved illness; or death.

Most of the states that reported on dropouts used an October through September cycle; however, the following states reported on a July through June cycle: Alabama, Arizona, Florida, Illinois, Maryland, New Jersey, New York, Tennessee, and Vermont.

The **Free and Reduced-Price Lunch** Program is a program under the National School Lunch Act that provides cash subsidies for free or reduced-price meals to students based on family size and income criteria. Participation in the Free and Reduced-Price Lunch Program depends on income, and eligibility is often used to estimate student needs.

Students who are English-language learners. This category includes the number of students who are served in appropriate programs of language assistance (e.g., English as a Second Language, High Intensity Language Training, and bilingual education). This designation changed from Limited-English Proficient (LEP) to English-Language Learners (ELL) in the 2001–2002 school year.

An **Individualized Education Program (IEP)** is a written instructional plan for students with disabilities who are designated as special education students under IDEA (Individuals with Disabilities Education Act). An IEP includes a statement of present levels of educational performance of a child; a statement of annual goals, including short-term instructional objectives; a statement of specific educational services to be provided and the extent to which the child will be able to participate in regular educational programs;

a projected date for initiation and the anticipated duration of services; appropriate objectives, criteria, and evaluation procedures; and schedules for determining, on at least an annual basis, whether instructional objectives are being achieved.

Private Schools

Since 1989, the Census Bureau has conducted the biennial Private School Universe Survey (PSS) for NCES. The PSS is designed to generate biennial data on the total number of private schools, students, and teachers and to build a universe of private schools in all of the states and the District of Columbia to serve as a sampling frame of private schools for NCES sample surveys. The target population for the PSS is every school in all of the states and the District of Columbia that are not primarily supported by public funds, provide instruction for one or more grades between kindergarten and grade 12 (or comparable ungraded levels), and have one or more teachers. Organizations or institutions that provide support for home schooling, but do not provide classroom instruction, are not included. Although the PSS has begun to collect limited data on the many private schools for which kindergarten is the highest grade, the data in this volume are for (traditional) schools that include at least one grade between grades 1 and 12.

A **private school** is controlled by an individual or agency other than a state, a subdivision of a state, or the federal government; is usually supported primarily by nonpublic funds; and the operation of its program does not rest with publicly elected or appointed officials. Private schools include both nonprofit and proprietary institutions.

The **student-teacher ratio** is calculated by dividing the number of students enrolled in all schools by the number of full-time equivalent teachers employed by all schools.

Table 12. Voting
Source: U.S. Department of Commerce. U.S. Census Bureau. November Supplement to the Current Population Survey (CPS). *Voting and Registration in the Election of November 2008.*
<http://www.census.gov/population/www/socdemo/voting.html>

Voter participation data are obtained from additional questions regarding voting and voter registration, which are added to the Current Population Survey each November. Because these data are from a sample of the noninstitutional population, they differ from the "official" tally of voter participation reported by the Clerk of the U.S. House of Representatives.

Voting, people eligible to register. The population of voting age includes a considerable number of people who meet the age requirement but cannot register and vote.

People who are not citizens are not eligible to vote. Among citizens of voting age, some people are not permitted to vote because they have been committed to penal institutions, mental hospitals, or other institutions, or because they fail to meet state and local resident requirements for various reasons. The eligibility to register is governed by state laws which differ in many respects.

Registration is the act of qualifying to vote by formally enrolling on a list of voters. People who have moved to another election district must take steps to have their names placed on the voting rolls in their new place of residence.

In a few states or parts of states, no formal registration is required. Voters merely present themselves at the polling place on election day with proof that they are of age and have met the appropriate residence requirements. Therefore, in these areas people who are citizens and of voting age, and who meet the residence requirement, would be considered as being registered.

Voter, reported participation. Voter participation data are derived from replies to the following question asked of people (excluding noncitizens) of voting age: "In any election some people are not able to vote because they are sick or busy, or have some other reason, and others do not want to vote. Did (this person) vote in the election held on November (date varies)?"

Those of voting age were classified as "voted" or "did not vote." In most tables, this "did not vote" class includes those reported as "did not vote," "do not know," noncitizens, and nonrespondents. Nonrespondents and people who reported that they did not know if they voted were included in the "did not vote" class because of the general over-reporting by respondents in the sample.

Voter, reported registration. The data on registration were obtained by tabulating replies to the following question for those people included in the category "did not vote." "Was (this person) registered to vote in the November (date varies) election?"

All people reported as having voted were assumed to have been registered. Therefore, the total registered population is obtained by combining the number of people who voted and people included in the category "did not vote," but who had registered.

Table 13. Crime
Source: U.S. Department of Justice. Federal Bureau of Investigation. Uniform Crime Reports. *Crime in the United States, 2008.*
< http://www.fbi.gov/ucr/cius2008/index.html>

The Uniform Crime Reports (UCR) Program, administered by the Federal Bureau of Investigation (FBI), was created in 1929 and collects information on the following crimes reported to law enforcement authorities: murder and nonnegligent manslaughter, forcible rape, robbery, aggravated assault, burglary, larceny-theft, motor vehicle theft, and arson. Law enforcement agencies also report arrest data for 21 additional crime categories.

The UCR Program compiles data from monthly law enforcement reports and from individual crime incident records transmitted directly to the FBI or to centralized state agencies that report to the FBI. The program thoroughly examines each report it receives for reasonableness, accuracy, and deviations that may indicate errors. Large variations in crime levels may indicate modified records procedures, incomplete reporting, or changes in a jurisdiction's boundaries. To identify any unusual fluctuations in an agency's crime counts, the program compares monthly reports to previous submissions of the agency and to those for similar agencies.

The FBI annually publishes its findings in a preliminary release in the spring of the following calendar year, followed by a detailed annual report, *Crime in the United States*, issued in the fall. (The printed copy of *Crime in the United States* is now published by Bernan Press.) In addition to crime counts and trends, this report includes data on crimes cleared, persons arrested (age, sex, and race), law enforcement personnel (including the number of sworn officers killed or assaulted), and the characteristics of homicides (including age, sex, and race of victims and offenders; victim-offender relationships; weapons used; and circumstances surrounding the homicides). Other periodic reports are also available from the UCR Program.

Note for Users
Since crime is a sociological phenomenon influenced by a variety of factors, the FBI discourages data users from ranking agencies and using the data as a measurement of the effectiveness of law enforcement. Until data users examine all the variables that affect crime in a town, city, county, state, region, or college or university, they can make no meaningful comparisons.

Violent crime is composed of four offenses: murder and nonnegligent manslaughter, forcible rape, robbery, and aggravated assault. According to the UCR Program's definition, violent crimes involve force or threat of force.

Criminal homicide. a.) Murder and nonnegligent manslaughter: the willful (nonnegligent) killing of one human being by another. Deaths caused by negligence, attempts to kill, assaults to kill, suicides, and accidental deaths are excluded. The program classifies justifiable homicides separately and limits the definition to (1) the killing of a felon by a law enforcement officer in the line of duty; or (2) the killing of a felon, during the commission of a felony, by a private citizen. b.) Manslaughter by negligence: the killing of another person through gross negligence. Traffic fatalities are excluded.

Forcible rape. The carnal knowledge of a female forcibly and against her will. Assaults and attempts to commit rape by force or threat of force are also included. Statutory rape (no force used—female victim is under the age of consent) and other sex offenses are excluded. Sexual attacks on males are counted as aggravated assaults or sex offenses, depending on the circumstances and the extent of any injuries.

Robbery. The taking or attempted taking of anything of value from the care, custody, or control of a person or persons by force or threat of force or violence and/or by putting the victim in fear.

Aggravated assault. An unlawful attack by one person upon another for the purpose of inflicting severe or aggravated bodily injury. This type of assault usually is accompanied by the use of a weapon or by means likely to produce death or great bodily harm. Attempted aggravated assaults that involve the display of—or threat to use—a gun, knife, or other weapon is included in this crime category because serious personal injury would likely result if the assault were completed. When aggravated assault and larceny-theft occur together, the offense falls under the category of robbery. Simple assaults are excluded.

Property crime includes the offenses of burglary, larceny-theft, motor vehicle theft, and arson. The object of the theft-type offenses is the taking of money or property, but there is no force or threat of force against the victims. The property crime category includes arson because the offense involves the destruction of property; however, arson victims may be subjected to force.

Burglary (breaking or entering). The unlawful entry of a structure to commit a felony or a theft. The use of force to gain entry need not have occurred. The Program has three subclassifications for burglary: forcible entry, unlawful entry where no force is used, and attempted forcible entry. The UCR definition of "structure" includes, for example, apartment, barn, house trailer or houseboat when used as a permanent dwelling, office, railroad car (but not automobile), stable, and vessel (i.e., ship).

Larceny-theft (except motor vehicle theft). The unlawful taking, carrying, leading, or riding away of property from the possession or constructive possession of another. Examples are thefts of bicycles or automobile accessories, shoplifting, pocket-picking, or the stealing of any property or article that is not taken by force and violence or by fraud. Attempted larcenies are included. Embezzlement, confidence games, forgery, worthless checks, and the like, are excluded.

Motor vehicle theft. The theft or attempted theft of a motor vehicle. It includes the stealing of automobiles, trucks, buses, motorcycles, snowmobiles, and the like. The taking of a motor vehicle for temporary use by persons having lawful access is excluded from this definition. A motor vehicle is self-propelled and runs on land surface and not on rails. Motorboats, construction equipment, airplanes, and farming equipment are specifically excluded from this category.

Table 14. State Government Finances
Source: U.S. Department of Commerce. U.S Census Bureau.
<http://www.census.gov/govs/index.html>.

The Census Bureau conducts an annual survey covering a range of government finance activities carried out by all state and local governments in the United States, including revenue, expenditures, debt, and assets. The data in this volume relate to state revenues and expenditures only, with the exception of the District of Columbia. Data reference state government fiscal years that ended on June 30, 2007. (Exceptions are Alabama and Michigan, whose fiscal years ended on September 30, 2007; New York, whose fiscal year ended on March 31, 2007; and Texas, whose fiscal year ended on August 31, 2007). Data for the District of Columbia are for the fiscal year 2006 which ended September 30. General revenue comprises all revenue except utilities, liquor store, and insurance trust revenue. Intergovernmental revenue is funds from other governments (mainly the federal government), including general support, grants, shared taxes, and loans or advances. Other data on government finance by state, not shown in this volume, include federal government expenditures, obligations, contract awards, and insurance programs.

Table 15. State Government Tax Collections
Source: U.S. Department of Commerce. U.S Census Bureau.
<http://www.census.gov/govs/www/statetax.html>.

State tax data include all required taxes taken by government for public purposes, except for employer and employee assessments for Social Security and unemployment compensation. These data are shown in this volume each state's fiscal year 2008. The data for the District of Columbia are from the fourth quarter of 2008. For more information, see the text under Table 14.

Table 16. Agriculture
Source: U.S. Department of Agriculture. National Agricultural Statistics Service.
<http/www.usda.gov/nass>.

The Census Bureau took a census of agriculture every 10 years from 1840 to 1920; since 1925, this census has been taken roughly once every 5 years. The 1997 Census of Agriculture was the first one conducted by the National Agricultural Statistics Service of the U.S. Department of Agriculture. Over time, the definition of a farm has varied. For recent censuses (including the 2007 census), a farm has been defined as any place from which $1,000 or more of agricultural products were produced and sold or normally would have been sold during the census year. Dollar figures are expressed in current dollars and have not been adjusted for inflation or deflation.

Farms by size. All farms were classified into size groups according to the total land area in the farm. The land area of a farm is an operating unit concept and includes land owned and operated as well as land rented from others. Land rented to or assigned to a tenant was considered part of the tenant's farm and not part of the owner's.

The acreage designated as **land in farms** consists primarily of agricultural land used for crops, pasture, or grazing. It also includes woodland and wasteland not actually under cultivation or used for pasture or grazing, provided that this land was part of the farm operator's total operation.

Land in farms is an operating-unit concept and includes all land owned and operated, as well as all land rented from others. Land used rent-free is classified as land rented from others. All land in Indian reservations used for growing crops or grazing livestock is classified as land in farms.

Total cropland includes cropland harvested, cropland used only for pasture or grazing, cropland on which all crops failed or were abandoned, cropland in cultivated summer fallow, and cropland idle or used for cover crops or soil improvement but not harvested and not pastured or grazed.

Harvested cropland. This category includes land from which crops were harvested and hay was cut, land used to grow short-rotation woody crops and land in orchards, citrus groves, Christmas trees, vineyards, nurseries, and greenhouses. Land from which two or more crops were harvested was counted only once. Land in tapped maple trees was included in woodland not pastured.

Irrigated land includes all land watered by any artificial or controlled means, such as sprinklers, flooding, furrows or ditches, sub-irrigation, and spreader dikes. Included are supplemental, partial, and preplant irrigation. Each acre was counted only once regardless of the number of times it was irrigated or harvested. Livestock lagoon waste water distributed by sprinkler or flood systems was also included.

Market **value of agricultural products sold** by farms represents the gross market value before taxes and the production expenses of all agricultural products sold or removed from the place in 2007, regardless of who received the pay-

ment. It is equivalent to total sales and it includes sales by the operator as well as the value of any share received by partners, landlords, contractors, and others associated with the operation. It includes value of direct sales and the value of commodities placed in the Commodity Credit Corporation (CCC) loan program. Market value of agricultural products sold does not include payments received for participation in other federal farm programs. Also, it does not include income from farm-related sources such as customwork and other agricultural services, or income from nonfarm sources. Sales figures are expressed in current dollars and have not been adjusted for inflation or deflation.

Farms by type of organization. All farms were classified by type of organization in the 2007 census. The classifications used were: 1. Family or individual (sole proprietorship), excluding partnership and corporation. 2. Partnership, including family partnership 3. Corporation, including family corporations. 4. Other, cooperative, estate or trust, institutional, etc.

Respondents were asked to report their estimate of the current market **value of land and buildings** owned, rented, or leased from others and rented and leased to others. Market value refers to the respondent's estimate of what the land and buildings would sell for under current market conditions.

Government payments. This category consists of direct payments as defined by the 2002 Farm Bill; payments from Conservation Reserve Program(CRP), Wetlands Reserve Program (WRP), Farmable Wetlands Program (FWP), and Conservation Reserve Enhancement Program (CREP); loan deficiency payments; disaster payments; other conservation programs; and all other federal farm programs under which payments were made directly to farm operators. Commodity Credit Corporation (CCC) proceeds, amount from State and local government agricultural program payments, and federal crop insurance payments were not tabulated in this category.

The term **operator** refers to a person who operates a farm by either doing the work or making day-to-day decisions about such activities as planting, harvesting, feeding, marketing, etc. The operator may be the owner, a member of the owner's household, a salaried manager, a tenant, a renter, or a sharecropper. If a person rents land to others or has land worked on shares by others, he/she is considered the operator only of the land that is retained for his/her own operation. The census collected information on the total number of operators, the total number of women operators, and demographic information for up to three operators per farm.

Farms by age and primary occupation of operator. Data on age and primary occupation were obtained from up to three operators per farm in 2007. When compared with 2002 results, the average age of farmers increased significantly. Older operators may be "retired" (with little if any sales) and still report farming as their primary occupation since they often have limited opportunity for off-farm jobs.

Primary occupation of operator. Data on age and primary occupation were obtained from up to three operators per farm. The primary occupation classifications used were:

1. *Farming or ranch work.* The operator spent 50 percent or more of his/her worktime during 2007 at farming or ranching.

2. *Other.* The operator spent less than 50 percent of his/her worktime during 2007 in farming or ranching operations.

Export Figure
Source: U.S. Department of Commerce. The International Trade Administration. Trade Stats Express.
<http://tse.export.gov/>.

State export data is reported by the exporter or agent, and denote the state from which the merchandise begins its journey to the port of export. This may not necessarily be the state in which the merchandise is actually grown or manufactured, or the actual location of the exporter. This method of calculating state exports is called "origin of movement." The origin of movement may not be the origin of transportation.

Whenever shipments are consolidated, the state of origin will reflect the consolidation point. This effect is particularly noticeable for non-manufactured goods, which are generally exported by intermediaries. For example, intermediaries located in inland states ship agricultural products down the Mississippi River for export from New Orleans. In these cases, Louisiana would be reported as the state of origin. The most visible result is a tendency to understate exports from some agricultural states and to overstate exports from states like Louisiana, which have ports that handle high-value shipments of farm products.

INDEX